AMIRA BADREIDIN'S

DICTION

COLLINS

Easy Learning

FRENCH
DICTIONARY

HarperCollins*Publishers*

first published 1996
© HarperCollins Publishers 1996
fifth reprint 1997
ISBN 0 00 470714-1 (Paperback)
ISBN 0 00 472107-1 (Vinyl)

project management
Ray Carrick, Michela Clari

general editor
Horst Kopleck

editorial coordination
Vivian Marr
Nicola Cooke

editors

Christine Penman	Daphne Day
Chantal Testa	Harry Campbell
Cécile Aubinière-Robb	Gavin Killip
Hélène Bernaërt	Elspeth Anderson
Sabine Citron	

computing staff
Ann Rautenbach

*our thanks to the following
for their help in researching the project*

Maree Airlie	Teresa Alvarez
Phyllis Gautier	Janet Gough
Sharon Hunter	Mary James
Cordelia Lilly	Carol MacLeod
Jill McNair	Janet Chalmers

maps
HarperCollins Cartographic

series editor
Lorna Sinclair

Corpus Acknowledgements
We would like to acknowledge the assistance of the many hundreds of individuals and companies who have kindly given permission for copyright material to be used in The Bank of English. The written sources include many national and regional newspapers in Britain and overseas; magazine and periodical publishers; and book publishers in Britain, the United States and Australia. Extensive spoken data has been provided by radio and television broadcasting companies; research workers at many universities and other institutions; and numerous individual contributors. We are grateful to them all.

A catalogue record for this book is available from the British Library

*Printed and bound in Great Britain by
Caledonian International Book Manufacturing Ltd, Glasgow, G64*

INTRODUCTION

Collins Easy Learning French Dictionary is an innovative new dictionary designed specifically for anyone starting to learn French. We are grateful to all those teachers who have contributed to its development by advising us on how to tailor it to the needs of their students. We also gratefully acknowledge the help of the Northern Examinations and Assessment Board, whom we have consulted throughout this project, and whose word lists and exam papers we carefully studied when compiling this dictionary.

HOW TO USE THE DICTIONARY

Using a dictionary is a skill you can improve with practice and by following some basic guidelines. This section gives you a detailed explanation of how to use the dictionary to ensure you get the most out of it.

The answers to all the questions in this section are on page 10.

MAKE SURE YOU LOOK IN THE RIGHT SIDE OF THE DICTIONARY

The French–English side comes first: you look there to find the meaning of a French word. The second part is English–French. That's what you need for translating into French. (To remind yourself which side is which, you could remember the phrase *French first*.) At the top of every page, you will see either **French → English** or **English → French**, so you can see immediately if you've got the side you want. The middle pages of the book have a grey border so that you can see where one side finishes and the other starts.

> **Check:** **1** Which side of the dictionary would you need to look up to translate *le fauteuil*?

FINDING THE WORD YOU WANT

When you are looking for a word, for example *nouveau*, look at the first letter – **n** – and find the **N** section in the French–English side. Look at page 170. At the top of the page, you'll find the words **néerlandais → n'importe**. These are the first and last words on that page. So **nouveau** is not going to be on page 170 because its second letter, **o**, comes after **i**, the second letter of **n'importe**. You have to go past all the words starting with **ne** and all the words starting with **ni** until you get to words starting with **no**. Scan down these until you find the word you want. Remember that even if a letter has an accent on it, it makes no difference to the alphabetical order.

MAKE SURE YOU LOOK AT THE RIGHT ENTRY

An entry is made up of a **word**, its *translations* and, often, example phrases to show you how to use the translations. If there is more than one entry for the same word, then there is a warning box to tell you so. Look at the following example entries:

flat ADJECTIVE
see also flat NOUN
1 *plat* ◇ *a flat roof* un toit plat
◇ *flat shoes* des chaussures plates
2 *crevé* (tyre) ◇ *I've got a flat tyre.* J'ai un pneu crevé.

flat NOUN
see also flat ADJECTIVE
l' *appartement* MASC ◇ *She lives in a flat.* Elle habite un appartement.

Check: 5 Which of the two entries above will help you translate the phrase *I live in a flat*?

Look for the two clues which are there to help you:
◇ an example similar to what you want to say
◇ the word NOUN

Always pay attention to information boxes – they tell you if there is more than one entry for the same word, give you guidance on grammatical points, and tell you about differences between French and British life.

NOUNS, PRONOUNS, ADJECTIVES, VERBS, ADVERBS, PREPOSITIONS

There are two entries for **flat** because this word can be a noun or an adjective. It helps to choose correctly between entries if you know how to recognize these different types of words.

Nouns and pronouns

Nouns often appear with words like *a, the, this, that, my, your* and *his*. They can be singular (abbreviated to SING in the dictionary):

a friend   the street   this year   my dog   your car

or plural (abbreviated to PL in the dictionary):

the facts   those people   his shoes   our holidays

They can be the subject of a verb:

Vegetables are good for you

or the object of a verb:

I play *tennis*

Words like *I, me, you, he, she, him, her* and *they* are pronouns. They can be used instead of nouns. You can refer to a person as *he* or *she* or to a thing as *it*.

> **Check:** *I bought my mother a box of chocolates.*
>
> **6** Which three words are nouns in this sentence?
> **7** Which of the nouns is plural?
> **8** Which word is a pronoun?

French nouns are either masculine or feminine (abbreviated to MASC and FEM). Masculine nouns are shown by **le**:

le bateau   *le* chien   *le* jardin

Feminine nouns are shown by **la**:

la porte   *la* robe   *la* souris

If a noun starts with a vowel or a vowel sound, then **le** or **la** becomes **l'**:

*l'*ami   *l'*eau   *l'*orage   *l'*histoire

The plural form of **le**, **la** and **l'** is **les**. As in English, the plural of most French nouns is made by adding **s**:

les chiens   *les* portes   *les* tables

If the singular form already ends in **s** or if it ends in **x**, then you don't have to add anything:

l'ananas   *les ananas*
la voix   *les voix*

Sometimes, however, the plural form is irregular and this is shown in the entry:

le **cheval**   NOUN
(PL les **chevaux**)
horse

horse   NOUN
le *cheval*
(les *chevaux*   PL)

> **Check:** *Je me brosse les dents tous les soirs.*
>
> **9** Two words in this sentence are nouns. Which ones?
> **10** Are they singular or plural?
> **11** What is the plural form of *le choix*?
> **12** Look in the dictionary to find the plural form of *le travail*.

Adjectives

Flat can be an adjective as well as a noun. Adjectives describe nouns: your tyre can be **flat**, you can have a pair of **flat** shoes.

> **Check:** **13** *dark* is an adjective in one of these sentences and a noun in the other. Which is which?
>
> *I'm not afraid of the dark.*
> *She's got dark hair.*

French adjectives can be masculine or feminine, singular or plural, depending on the noun they describe:

un **petit** garçon (MASC SING)
une **petite** fille (FEM SING = masculine singular + **e**)
trois **petits** garçons (MASC PL = masculine singular + **s**)
trois **petites** filles (FEM PL = masculine singular + **es**)

Only the masculine singular form of regular adjectives is shown in the dictionary. So if you want to find out what sort of shoes **des chaussures plates** are, look under **plat**.

If the feminine or the plural form of an adjective does *not* follow the above rules, then the irregular form is shown in the dictionary:

frais ADJECTIVE
(FEM SING **fraîche**)
fresh

fresh ADJECTIVE
frais MASC
fraîche FEM

bon ADJECTIVE
(FEM SING **bonne**)
good

good ADJECTIVE
bon MASC
bonne FEM

If the masculine form ends in **s** or **x**, then you don't need to add **s** to make the masculine plural. And if the masculine form ends in **e**, you don't add anything to form the feminine form. But remember – if the adjective ends in **é**, then it behaves like any regular adjective.

MASC SING	FEM SING	MASC PL	FEM PL
gris	grise	gris	grises
anxieux	anxieuse	anxieux	anxieuses
agréable	agréable	agréables	agréables
passé	passée	passés	passées

Some adjectives remain the same whether they're masculine, feminine or plural. This is also shown in the dictionary:

arrière ADJECTIVE (MASC, FEM, PL)
back

back ADJECTIVE
arrière MASC, FEM, PL

Check: 14 What is the feminine form of **vert**?
15 What is the masculine plural form of **aimable**?
16 What is the masculine singular form of **heureux**?
17 What is the masculine plural form of **gras**? And the feminine singular (look in the dictionary for this one)?

Verbs

His time in the race was a new world record.
She's going to record the programme for me.

Record in the first sentence is a noun. In the second, it is a verb.

One way to recognize a verb is that it frequently comes with a pronoun such as **I, you** or **she**, or with somebody's name. Verbs can relate to the present, the past or the future. They have a number of different forms to show this: **I'm going** (present), **he will go** (future), and **Nicola went by herself** (past). Often verbs appear with **to: they promised to go**. This basic form of the verb is called the infinitive.

In this dictionary, verbs are preceded by to, so you can identify them at a glance. No matter which of the four previous examples you want to translate, you should look up to **go**, not **going** or **went**. If you want to translate **I thought**, look up to **think**.

Check: 18 What would you look up to translate the verbs in these phrases?

| *I* **went** | *she's* **crying** | *he* **was lying** |
| *I* **did** *it* | *he's* **out** | *they've* **gone** |

Verbs have different endings, depending on whether you are talking about **je, tu, nous, ils** etc: **j'aime, tu aimes, nous aimons, ils aiment** etc. They also have different forms for the present, future, past etc. **Nous mangeons** (*we eat* = present), **nous avons mangé** (*we ate* = past). **Manger** is the infinitive and is the form that appears in the dictionary.

Sometimes the verb changes completely between the infinitive form and the **je, tu, il** etc form. For example, *I go* is **je vais** but *to go* is **aller** and **nous faisons** (*we do*) comes from **faire** (*to do*). **J'ai fait** (*I have done* or *I did*) also comes from **faire**.

On pages 284–297 of the dictionary, you will find tables of the most important forms of 14 French verbs. And on pages 298–299, you will find a list of the main forms of other French irregular verbs.

Adverbs

An adverb is a word that describes a verb or an adjective:

> *Write* **soon**.   *Check your work* **carefully**.
> *They arrived* **late**.   *The film was* **very** *good*.

In the sentence *The swimming pool is open daily*, **daily** is an adverb describing the adjective **open**. In the phrase *my daily routine*, **daily** is an adjective describing the noun **routine**. We use the same word in English but to get the right French translation, it is important to know if it's being used as an adjective or an adverb. When you look up **daily** you find:

> **daily** ADJECTIVE, ADVERB
> 1 *quotidien* MASC
> *quotidienne* FEM
> ◇ *It's part of my daily routine*. Ça fait partie de mon occupations quotidiennes.
> 2 *tous les jours*
> • **The pool is open daily from 9 a.m. to 6 p.m.** La piscine est ouverte tous les jours de neuf heures à dix-huit heures.

The examples show you **daily** being used as an adjective and as an adverb and will help you choose the right French translation.

Check:	Take the sentence *The menu changes daily*.
	19 Does **daily** go with the noun **menu** or the verb **changes**?
	20 Is it an adverb or an adjective?
	21 How would you translate **daily** in this sentence?

Prepositions

Prepositions are words like **for, with** and **across**, which are followed by nouns or pronouns:

> *I've got a present* **for** *David*.   *Come* **with** *me*.   *He ran* **across** *the road*.

Check:	*The party's over.*
	The shop's just over the road.
	22 In one of these sentences **over** is an adjective describing a noun, in the other it is a preposition followed by a noun. Which is which?

CHOOSING THE RIGHT TRANSLATION

The main translation of a word is shown on a new line in underlined italic to make it stand out from the rest of the entry. If there is more than one main translation for a word, each one is numbered. If an entry continues over the page, there is a signpost to indicate this.

Often you will see phrases in *italics*, preceded by a white diamond ◇. These show how the translation they follow can be used. They also help you choose the translation you want because they give examples of the context in which it can be used.

bouillant ADJECTIVE

1 *boiling* ◇ *Faites cuire les pâtes à l'eau bouillante.* Cook the pasta in boiling water.

2 *piping hot* ◇ *La soupe est servie bouillante.* The soup should be served piping hot.

to overlook VERB

1 *donner sur* (*have view of*) ◇ *The hotel overlooked the beach.* L'hôtel donnait sur la plage.

2 *négliger* (*forget about*) ◇ *He had overlooked one important problem.* Il avait négligé un problème important.

Check: 23 Use the dictionary to translate *That's a very hard question.*

Words often have more than one meaning and more than one translation: if you don't **get** to the station on time, you don't arrive on time, but if you say "I don't **get** it", you mean you don't understand. When you are translating from English, be careful to choose the French word that has the particular meaning you want. The dictionary offers you a lot of help with this. Look at the following entry:

pool NOUN

1 la *flaque* (*puddle*)

2 l' *étang* (*pond*)

3 la *piscine* (*for swimming*)

4 le *billard américain* (*game*)

A **pool** can be a puddle, a pond or a swimming pool; **pool** can also be a game. The underlined italic highlights all the main translations, the numbers tell you that there is more than one possible translation and the words in brackets in *italics* after the translations help you choose which translation you want.

Check: 24 How would you translate *I like playing pool*?

Never take the first translation you see without looking at the others. Always look to see if there is more than one translation in underlined italic.

Phrases in **bold type** preceded by a black diamond ◆ are phrases which are particularly common or important. Sometimes these phrases have a completely different translation from the main translation; sometimes the translation is the same. For example:

le dommage NOUN

damage ◇ *La tempête a causé d'importants dommages.* The storm caused a lot of damage.

◆ **C'est dommage.** It's a shame. ◇ *C'est dommage que tu ne puisses pas venir.* It's a shame you can't come.

to go out VERB

1 *sortir* (*person*) ◇ *Are you going out tonight?* Tu sors ce soir?

◆ **to go out with somebody** sortir avec quelqu'un ◇ *Are you going out with him?* Est-ce que tu sors avec lui?

2 *s'éteindre* (*light, fire, candle*) ◇ *Suddenly the lights went out.* Soudain, les lumières se sont éteintes.

When you look up a word, make sure you look beyond the main translations to see if the entry includes any **bold phrases**.

> **Check:** 25 In a job advert you read that applicants *doivent tous passer une visite médicale*. What must they all do?
>
> Look up **visite** and find the answer as quickly as possible by skimming down the **bold phrases**.

MAKING USE OF THE PHRASES IN THE DICTIONARY

Sometimes when you look up a word you will find not only the word, but the exact phrase you want. For example, you might want to say *What's the date today?* Look up **date** and you will find:

date NOUN
  la *date* ◦ *my date of birth* ma date de
  naissance
- **What's the date today?** Quel jour
  sommes-nous?

Sometimes you have to adapt what you find in the dictionary. If you want to say *I play darts* and look up **darts** you will find:

dart NOUN
  la *fléchette* ◦ *to play darts* jouer aux
  fléchettes

You have to substitute *je joue* for the infinitive form *jouer*. You will often have to adapt the infinitive in this way, adding the correct ending for **je, tu, il** etc and choosing the present, future or past form. For help with this, look at the verb tables. **Jouer** is a verb ending in *–er* so it follows the same pattern as **aimer**, which is set out on page 284.

> **Check:** 26 How would you say *We played football*?

Phrases containing nouns and adjectives also need to be adapted. You may need to make the noun plural, or the adjective feminine or plural. Remember that some nouns and adjectives have irregular feminine or plural forms and that this is shown in the entry.

> **Check:** 27 How would you say *The jewels are beautiful*?

DON'T OVERUSE THE DICTIONARY

It takes time to look up words so try to avoid using the dictionary unnecessarily, **especially in exams**. Think carefully about what you want to say and see if you can put it another way, using words you already know. To rephrase things you can:

- ◦ Use a word with a similar meaning. This is particularly easy with adjectives, as there are a lot of words which mean good, bad, big etc and you're sure to know at least one.

- ◦ Use negatives: if the cake you made was a total disaster, you could just say it wasn't very good.

- ◦ Use particular examples instead of general terms. If you are asked to describe the sports facilities in your area, and time is short, don't look up *facilities* – say something like "In our town there is a swimming pool and a football ground."

> **Check:** **28** You want to ask *Have you got any pets?* How could you avoid the word *pet* if you don't know it?
> **29** How could you say *The palace of Versailles is huge* without looking up the word *huge*?

You can also often guess the meaning of a French word by using others to give you a clue. If you see the sentence *j'écoute de la musique rap*, you may not know the meaning of the word **écoute**, but you do know it's a verb because it's preceded by **j'**. Therefore it must be something you can do to music: **listen**. So the translation is: *I listen to rap music* .

> **Check:** **30** In a description of a holiday centre you see a picture of bikes and read *On peut louer des vélos: 20F la journée*. You may not know the meaning of *louer*, but you can see that you have to pay 20 francs, which gives you a clue to what it could mean. What can you do – ride bikes, borrow bikes or hire bikes?

Answers

1 the French side
2 **nager**
3 **nouveau** comes after **Noël**
4 **chou-fleur** comes after **chocolat**
5 the second entry (the NOUN entry)
6 **mother**, **box** and **chocolates** are nouns
7 **chocolates** is plural
8 **I** is a pronoun
9 **dents** and **soirs** are nouns
10 they are both plural
11 **les choix**
12 **les travaux**
13 **dark** in the first sentence is a noun and in the second, it's an adjective
14 **verte**
15 **aimables**
16 **heureux**
17 the masculine plural form is **gras** and the feminine singular form is **grasse**
18 to **go**, to **cry**, to **lie**, to **do**, to **be**, to **go**
19 **daily** goes with the verb **changes**
20 it is an adverb
21 **tous les jours**
22 in the first sentence, **over** is an adjective and in the second, it's a preposition
23 **c'est une question très difficile**
24 **j'aime jouer au billard américain**
25 they must all have **a medical examination**
26 **nous avons joué au football**
27 **les bijoux sont beaux**
28 you could ask, "Have you got a cat or a dog?"
29 you could say, "Very big."
30 you can **hire** bikes

A

a VERB *see* **avoir**

> **a** *should not be confused with the preposition* **à**.

- **Il a beaucoup d'amis.** He has a lot of friends.
- **Il a mangé des frites.** He had some chips.
- **Il a neigé pendant la nuit.** It snowed during the night.
- **il y a (1)** there is ◇ *Il y a un bon film à la télé.* There's a good film on TV.
- **il y a (2)** there are ◇ *Il y a beaucoup de monde.* There are lots of people.

à PREPOSITION

> **à** *should not be confused with the verb form* **a**
> *See also* **au** (=à+le) *and* **aux** (=à+les).

[1] *at* ◇ *être à la maison* to be at home ◇ *à trois heures* at 3 o'clock

[2] *in* ◇ *être à Paris* to be in Paris ◇ *habiter au Portugal* to live in Portugal ◇ *habiter à la campagne* to live in the country ◇ *au printemps* in the spring ◇ *au mois de juin* in June

[3] *to* ◇ *aller à Paris* to go to Paris ◇ *aller au Portugal* to go to Portugal ◇ *aller à la campagne* to go to the country ◇ *donner quelque chose à quelqu'un* to give something to somebody ◇ *Cette veste appartient à Marie.* This jacket belongs to Marie. ◇ *Je n'ai rien à faire.* I've got nothing to do.

- **Ce livre est à Paul.** This book is Paul's.
- **Cette voiture est à nous.** This car is ours.

[4] *by* ◇ *à bicyclette* by bicycle ◇ *être payé à l'heure* to be paid by the hour

- **à pied** on foot
- **C'est à côté de chez moi.** It's near my house.
- **C'est à dix kilomètres d'ici.** It's 10 kilometres from here.
- **C'est à dix minutes d'ici.** It's 10 minutes from here.
- **cent kilomètres à l'heure** 100 kilometres an hour
- **À bientôt!** See you soon! ◇ *À demain!* See you tomorrow! ◇ *À samedi!* See you on Saturday! ◇ *À tout à l'heure!* See you later!

abandonner VERB

[1] *to abandon* ◇ *Avant les vacances, beaucoup de chiens sont abandonnés par leurs maîtres.* Before the holidays, a lot of dogs are abandoned by their owners.

[2] *to give up* ◇ *J'ai décidé*

d'abandonner la natation. I've decided to give up swimming.

l'**abeille** FEM NOUN
  bee

abîmer VERB
  to damage
- **s'abîmer** to get damaged

l'**abonnement** MASC NOUN
  [1] *season ticket*
  [2] *subscription* (to magazine)

s'**abonner** VERB
- **s'abonner à une revue** to take out a subscription to a magazine

l'**abord** MASC NOUN
- **d'abord** first ◇ *Je vais rentrer chez moi d'abord.* I'll go home first.

aboyer VERB
  to bark

l'**abri** MASC NOUN
  shelter
- **être à l'abri** to be under cover
- **se mettre à l'abri** to shelter

l'**abricot** MASC NOUN
  apricot

s'**abriter** VERB
  to shelter

l'**absence** FEM NOUN
  absence
- **Il est passé pendant ton absence.** He came while you were away.

absent ADJECTIVE
  absent

absolument ADVERB
  absolutely

l'**accélérateur** MASC NOUN
  accelerator

accélérer VERB
  to accelerate

l'**accent** MASC NOUN
  accent ◇ *Il a l'accent de Marseille.* He has a Marseilles accent.
- **un accent aigu** an acute accent
- **un accent grave** a grave accent
- **un accent circonflexe** a circumflex

accentuer VERB
  to stress

accepter VERB
  to accept
- **accepter de faire quelque chose** to agree to do something

l'**accessoire** MASC NOUN
  [1] *accessory* ◇ *les accessoires de mode* fashion accessories
  [2] *prop*

l'**accident** MASC NOUN
  accident ◇ *un accident de la route* a

road accident

accompagner VERB
to accompany

l'**accord** MASC NOUN
agreement
- **être d'accord** to agree ◇ *Tu es d'accord avec moi?* Do you agree with me?
- **se mettre d'accord** to come to an agreement
- **D'accord!** OK!

l'**accordéon** MASC NOUN
accordion ◇ *Ray joue de l'accordéon.* Ray plays the accordion.

l'**accoudoir** MASC NOUN
armrest

l'**accrochage** MASC NOUN
collision

accrocher VERB
- **accrocher quelque chose à (1)** to hang something on ◇ *Il a accroché sa veste au portemanteau.* He hung his jacket on the coat rack.
- **accrocher quelque chose à (2)** to hitch something up to ◇ *Ils ont accroché la remorque à leur voiture.* They hitched the trailer up to their car.
- **s'accrocher à quelque chose** to catch on something ◇ *Sa jupe s'est accrochée aux ronces.* Her skirt got caught on the brambles.

s'**accroupir** VERB
to squat down

l'**accueil** MASC NOUN
welcome ◇ *Il nous a remerciés de notre accueil.* He thanked us for our welcome.
- **Elle s'occupe de l'accueil des visiteurs.** She's in charge of looking after visitors.

accueillir VERB
to welcome

accumuler VERB
to accumulate
- **s'accumuler** to pile up

l'**accusé** MASC NOUN
accused ◇ *L'accusé a déclaré que...* The accused stated that...
- **un accusé de réception** an acknowledgement of receipt

l'**accusée** FEM NOUN
accused

accuser VERB
to accuse ◇ *accuser quelqu'un de quelque chose* to accuse somebody of something

l'**achat** MASC NOUN
purchase
- **faire des achats** to do some shopping

acheter VERB
to buy ◇ *J'ai acheté des gâteaux à la pâtisserie.* I bought some cakes at the cake shop.
- **acheter quelque chose à quelqu'un (1)** to buy something for somebody ◇ *Qu'est-ce que tu lui as acheté pour son anniversaire?* What did you buy him for his birthday?
- **acheter quelque chose à quelqu'un (2)** to buy something from somebody ◇ *J'ai acheté des œufs au fermier.* I bought some eggs from the farmer.

acide ADJECTIVE
see also **acide** NOUN
acid ◇ *Ce pamplemousse est trop acide.* This grapefruit is too acid.

l'**acide** MASC NOUN
see also **acide** ADJECTIVE
acid

l'**acier** MASC NOUN
steel

l'**acné** FEM NOUN
acne ◇ *Il a de l'acné.* He has acne.

acquérir VERB
to acquire

acquis VERB see **acquérir**

acquitter VERB
to acquit ◇ *L'accusé a été acquitté.* The accused was acquitted.

l'**acte** MASC NOUN
act
- **un acte de naissance** a birth certificate

l'**acteur** MASC NOUN
actor ◇ *Il est acteur.* He's an actor. ◇ *un acteur de cinéma* a film actor

actif ADJECTIVE
(FEM SING **active**)
active
- **la population active** the working population

l'**action** FEM NOUN
action
- **une bonne action** a good deed

s'**activer** VERB
  [1] *to bustle about* ◇ *Elle s'activait à préparer le repas.* She bustled about preparing the meal.
  [2] *to move oneself* ◇ *Allez! Active-toi!* Come on! Get moving!

l'**activité** FEM NOUN
activity

l'**actrice** FEM NOUN
actress ◇ *Elle est actrice.* She's an actress. ◇ *une actrice de cinéma* a film actress

l'**actualité** FEM NOUN
current events
- **un problème d'actualité** a topical issue

• **les actualités** the news
actuel ADJECTIVE
(FEM SING **actuelle**)
present ◇ _le système actuel_ the present system
• **à l'heure actuelle** at the present time
actuellement ADVERB
at present
l'**adaptateur** MASC NOUN
adaptor
l'**addition** FEM NOUN
1 _addition_ ◇ _Il a fait une erreur dans son addition._ He made a mistake in his addition.
2 _bill_ ◇ _L'addition, s'il vous plaît!_ Can we have the bill, please?
additionner VERB
to add up
adhésif ADJECTIVE
(FEM SING **adhésive**)
• **le ruban adhésif** sticky tape
l'**adjectif** MASC NOUN
adjective
admettre VERB
1 _to admit_ ◇ _Il refuse d'admettre qu'il s'est trompé._ He won't admit that he made a mistake.
2 _to allow_ ◇ _Les chiens ne sont pas admis dans le restaurant._ Dogs are not allowed in the restaurant.
l'**administration** FEM NOUN
administration
• **l'Administration** the Civil Service
admirable ADJECTIVE
wonderful
l'**admirateur** MASC NOUN
admirer
l'**admiratrice** FEM NOUN
admirer
admirer VERB
to admire
admis VERB _see_ **admettre**
l'**adolescence** FEM NOUN
adolescence
l'**adolescent** MASC NOUN
teenager
l'**adolescente** FEM NOUN
teenager
adopter VERB
to adopt
adorable ADJECTIVE
lovely
adorer VERB
to love ◇ _Elle adore le chocolat._ She loves chocolate. ◇ _J'adore jouer au tennis._ I love playing tennis.
l'**adresse** FEM NOUN
address
adresser VERB

• **adresser la parole à quelqu'un** to speak to someone
• **s'adresser à quelqu'un (1)** to speak to somebody ◇ _C'est à toi que je m'adresse._ It's you I'm speaking to.
• **s'adresser à quelqu'un (2)** to go and see somebody ◇ _Adressez-vous au patron._ Go and see the boss. ◇ _Adressez-vous aux renseignements._ Ask at the enquiry desk.
• **s'adresser à quelqu'un (3)** to be aimed at somebody ◇ _Ce film s'adresse surtout aux enfants._ This film is aimed mainly at children.
l'**adulte** MASC/FEM NOUN
adult
l'**adverbe** MASC NOUN
adverb
l'**adversaire** MASC/FEM NOUN
opponent
aérien ADJECTIVE
(FEM SING **aérienne**)
• **une compagnie aérienne** an airline
l'**aérobic** MASC NOUN
aerobics ◇ _Teresa fait de l'aérobic._ Teresa does aerobics.
l'**aérogare** FEM NOUN
terminal
l'**aéroglisseur** MASC NOUN
hovercraft
l'**aéroport** MASC NOUN
airport
l'**affaire** FEM NOUN
| _see also_ **les affaires** |
1 _case_ ◇ _une affaire de drogue_ a drugs case
2 _business_ ◇ _Son affaire marche bien._ His business is doing well.
• **une bonne affaire** a real bargain
• **Ça fera l'affaire.** This will do nicely.
• **avoir affaire à quelqu'un** to deal with somebody
les **affaires** FEM NOUN
| _see also_ **l'affaire** |
1 _things_ ◇ _Va chercher tes affaires!_ Go and get your things!
2 _business_ ◇ _Les affaires marchent bien en ce moment._ Business is good at the moment. ◇ _Mêle-toi de tes affaires._ (_informal_) Mind your own business.
• **un homme d'affaires** a businessman
• **le ministre des Affaires étrangères** the Foreign Secretary
l'**affection** FEM NOUN
affection
affectueux ADJECTIVE
(FEM SING **affectueuse**)
affectionate
l'**affiche** FEM NOUN

poster
afficher VERB
to put up ◇ *Ils ont affiché les résultats dehors.* They've put the results up outside.
- **"Défense d'afficher"** "Stick no bills"
affilée
- **d'affilée** ADVERB
at a stretch ◇ *Il a travaillé douze heures d'affilée.* He worked 12 hours at a stretch.
l'**affluence** FEM NOUN
- **les heures d'affluence** the rush hour
s'**affoler** VERB
to panic ◇ *Ne t'affole pas!* Don't panic!
affranchir VERB
to stamp
affreux ADJECTIVE
(FEM SING **affreuse**)
awful
affronter VERB
to face ◇ *L'Allemagne affronte l'Italie en finale.* Germany will face Italy in the final.
afin de CONJUNCTION
- **afin de faire quelque chose** so as to do something ◇ *Je me suis levé très tôt afin d'être prêt à temps.* I got up very early so as to be ready on time.
afin que CONJUNCTION
so that
afin que *is followed by a verb in the subjunctive.*
◇ *Il m'a téléphoné afin que je sois prêt à temps.* He phoned me so that I'd be ready on time.
africain ADJECTIVE, NOUN
(FEM SING **africaine**)
African
- **un Africain** an African (*man*)
- **une Africaine** an African (*woman*)
l'**Afrique** FEM NOUN
Africa
- **en Afrique (1)** in Africa
- **en Afrique (2)** to Africa
- **l'Afrique du Sud** South Africa
agacer VERB
to get on somebody's nerves ◇ *Tu m'agaces avec tes questions!* You're getting on my nerves with all your questions!
l'**âge** MASC NOUN
age
- **Quel âge as-tu?** How old are you?
âgé ADJECTIVE
old ◇ *Son père est âgé.* His father's old. ◇ *Il est âgé de dix ans.* He's 10 years old.
- **les personnes âgées** the elderly
l'**agence** FEM NOUN

[1] *agency*
- **une agence de voyages** a travel agency
[2] *office* ◇ *Nous avons plusieurs agences à Londres.* We have several offices in London.
- **une agence immobilière** an estate agent's
l'**agenda** MASC NOUN
diary (*for appointments*)
s'**agenouiller** VERB
to kneel down
l'**agent** MASC NOUN
- **un agent de police** a policeman
l'**agglomération** FEM NOUN
town
- **l'agglomération parisienne** Greater Paris
aggraver VERB
to make worse
- **s'aggraver** to worsen
agir VERB
to act ◇ *Il a agi par vengeance.* He acted out of vengeance.
- **Il s'agit de...** It's about... ◇ *Il s'agit du club de sport.* It's about the sports club. ◇ *De quoi s'agit-il?* What is it about?
- **Il s'agit de faire attention.** We must be careful.
agité ADJECTIVE
[1] *restless* ◇ *Les élèves sont agités.* The pupils are restless.
[2] *rough* ◇ *La mer est agitée.* The sea is rough.
- **un sommeil agité** broken sleep
agiter VERB
to shake ◇ *Agitez la bouteille.* Shake the bottle.
l'**agneau** MASC NOUN
(PL les **agneaux**)
lamb
l'**agrafe** FEM NOUN
staple (*for papers*)
l'**agrafeuse** FEM NOUN
stapler
agrandir VERB
[1] *to enlarge* ◇ *J'ai fait agrandir mes photos.* I've had my photos enlarged.
[2] *to extend* ◇ *Ils ont agrandi leur jardin.* They've extended their garden.
- **s'agrandir** to expand ◇ *Leur magasin s'est agrandi.* Their shop has expanded.
agréable ADJECTIVE
nice
agréer VERB
- **Veuillez agréer, Monsieur, l'expression de mes sentiments les meilleurs. Jean Ormal.** Yours sincerely, Jean Ormal.
agressif ADJECTIVE
(FEM SING **agressive**)

aggressive

agricole ADJECTIVE
agricultural ◇ *le matériel agricole* agricultural machinery
• **une exploitation agricole** a farm

l'**agriculteur** MASC NOUN
farmer
• **Il est agriculteur.** He's a farmer.

l'**agriculture** FEM NOUN
farming

ai VERB *see* **avoir**
• **J'ai deux chats.** I have two cats.
• **J'ai bien dormi.** I slept well.

l'**aide** FEM NOUN
[1] *help* ◇ *J'ai besoin de ton aide.* I need your help. ◇ *appeler quelqu'un à l'aide* to call to somebody for help
• **À l'aide!** Help!
[2] *aid* ◇ *une aide financière* financial aid
• **à l'aide de** using ◇ *J'ai réussi à ouvrir la boîte à l'aide d'un couteau.* I managed to open the tin using a knife.

aider VERB
to help

l'**aide-soignant** MASC NOUN
(PL les **aides-soignants**)
auxiliary nurse ◇ *Il est aide-soignant.* He's an auxiliary nurse.

l'**aide-soignante** FEM NOUN
(PL les **aides-soignantes**)
auxiliary nurse ◇ *Françoise est aide-soignante.* Françoise is an auxiliary nurse.

aie VERB *see* **avoir**

aïe EXCLAMATION
Ouch!

aigre ADJECTIVE
sour

l'**aiguille** FEM NOUN
needle ◇ *une aiguille à tricoter* a knitting needle
• **les aiguilles d'une montre** the hands of a watch

l'**ail** MASC NOUN
garlic

l'**aile** FEM NOUN
wing

aille VERB *see* **aller**

ailleurs ADVERB
somewhere else
• **partout ailleurs** everywhere else
• **nulle part ailleurs** nowhere else
• **d'ailleurs** besides

aimable ADJECTIVE
kind

l'**aimant** MASC NOUN
magnet

aimer VERB

[1] *to love* ◇ *Elle aime ses enfants.* She loves her children.
[2] *to like* ◇ *Tu aimes le chocolat?* Do you like chocolate? ◇ *J'aime bien ce garçon.* I like this boy. ◇ *J'aime bien jouer au tennis.* I like playing tennis. ◇ *J'aimerais aller en Grèce.* I'd like to go to Greece.
• **J'aimerais mieux ne pas y aller.** I'd rather not go.

aîné ADJECTIVE
see also **aîné** NOUN
elder ◇ *mon frère aîné* my big brother

l'**aîné** MASC NOUN
see also **aîné** ADJECTIVE
oldest child ◇ *Il est l'aîné.* He's the oldest child.

l'**aînée** FEM NOUN
oldest child ◇ *Elle est l'aînée.* She's the oldest child.

ainsi ADVERB
in this way ◇ *Il faut faire ainsi.* This is the way to do it.
• **C'est ainsi qu'il a réussi.** That's how he succeeded.
• **ainsi que** as well as
• **et ainsi de suite** and so on

l'**air** MASC NOUN
[1] *air* ◇ *l'air chaud* warm air
• **prendre l'air** to get some fresh air
[2] *tune* ◇ *Elle a joué un air au piano.* She played a tune on the piano.
• **Elle a l'air fatiguée.** She looks tired.
• **Il a l'air d'un clown.** He looks like a clown.

l'**aise** FEM NOUN
• **être à l'aise** to be at ease ◇ *Elle est à l'aise avec tout le monde.* She's at ease with everybody.
• **être mal à l'aise** to be ill at ease
• **se mettre à l'aise** to make oneself comfortable

ait VERB *see* **avoir**

ajouter VERB
to add

l'**alarme** FEM NOUN
alarm ◇ *donner l'alarme* to raise the alarm

l'**Albanie** FEM NOUN
Albania

l'**album** MASC NOUN
album

l'**alcool** MASC NOUN
alcohol ◇ *Je ne bois pas d'alcool.* I don't drink alcohol.
• **les alcools forts** spirits

alcoolisé ADJECTIVE
alcoholic

◆ **une boisson non alcoolisée** a soft drink

les **alentours** MASC NOUN
◆ **dans les alentours** in the area
◆ **aux alentours de Paris** in the Paris area
◆ **aux alentours de cinq heures** around 5 o'clock

l'**algèbre** FEM NOUN
algebra

Alger NOUN
Algiers

l'**Algérie** FEM NOUN
Algeria

algérien ADJECTIVE, NOUN
(FEM SING **algérienne**)
Algerian
◆ **un Algérien** an Algerian (*man*)
◆ **une Algérienne** an Algerian (*woman*)

l'**algue** FEM NOUN
seaweed

l'**aliment** MASC NOUN
food

l'**alimentation** FEM NOUN
☐ *groceries* ◇ *le rayon alimentation du supermarché* the grocery department in the supermarket
② *diet* ◇ *Elle a une alimentation saine.* She has a healthy diet.

l'**allée** FEM NOUN
☐ *path* ◇ *les allées du parc* the paths in the park
② *drive* (*in street names*)
◆ **les allées et venues** comings and goings

allégé ADJECTIVE
low-fat ◇ *un yaourt allégé* a low-fat yoghurt

l'**Allemagne** FEM NOUN
Germany
◆ **en Allemagne (1)** in Germany
◆ **en Allemagne (2)** to Germany

allemand ADJECTIVE, NOUN
German ◇ *Elle parle allemand.* She speaks German.
◆ **un Allemand** a German (*man*)
◆ **une Allemande** a German (*woman*)
◆ **les Allemands** the Germans

aller VERB
see also **aller** NOUN

Present tense:

je vais	nous allons
tu vas	vous allez
il/elle va	ils/elles vont

Past participle: *allé*

to go ◇ *Je suis allé à Londres.* I went to London. ◇ *Je dois y aller.* I've got to go. ◇ *Elle ira le voir.* She'll go and see him. ◇ *Je vais me fâcher.* I'm going to get angry.

◆ **s'en aller** to go away ◇ *Je m'en vais demain.* I'm going tomorrow.
◆ **aller bien à quelqu'un** to suit somebody ◇ *Cette robe te va bien.* This dress suits you.
◆ **Allez! Dépêche-toi!** Come on! Hurry up!
◆ **Comment allez-vous? – Je vais bien.** How are you? – I'm fine.
◆ **Comment ça va? – Ça va bien.** How are you? – I'm fine.
◆ **aller mieux** to be better

l'**aller** MASC NOUN
see also **aller** VERB
☐ *outward journey* ◇ *L'aller nous a pris trois heures.* The journey there took us three hours.
② *single* (*ticket*) ◇ *Je voudrais un aller pour Angers.* I'd like a single to Angers.
◆ **un aller simple** a single
◆ **un aller retour (1)** a return ticket ◇ *Je voudrais un aller retour pour Londres.* I'd like a return to London.
◆ **un aller retour (2)** a round trip ◇ *Il a fait l'aller retour en dix heures.* He did the round trip in ten hours.

allergique ADJECTIVE
◆ **allergique à** allergic to ◇ *Je suis allergique aux poils de chat.* I'm allergic to cat fur.

allô EXCLAMATION
Hello! ◇ *Allô! Je voudrais parler à Monsieur Simon.* Hello! I'd like to speak to Mr Simon.

l'**allocation** FEM NOUN
allowance
◆ **les allocations chômage** unemployment benefit

s'**allonger** VERB
to lie down ◇ *Il s'est allongé sur son lit.* He lay down on his bed.

allumer VERB
☐ *to put on* (*light*) ◇ *Tu peux allumer la lumière?* Can you put the light on?
② *to light* ◇ *Elle a allumé une cigarette.* She lit a cigarette.
◆ **s'allumer** (*light*) to come on ◇ *La lumière s'est allumée.* The light came on.

l'**allumette** FEM NOUN
match ◇ *une boîte d'allumettes* a box of matches

l'**allure** FEM NOUN
☐ *speed* ◇ *à toute allure* at top speed
② *look* ◇ *avoir une drôle d'allure* to look odd

l'**allusion** FEM NOUN
reference

alors ADVERB

1 *then* ◇ *Tu as fini? Alors je m'en vais.* Have you finished? I'm going then.

2 *so* ◇ *Alors je lui ai dit de partir.* So I told him to leave.

- **Et alors?** So what?

3 *at that time* ◇ *Il habitait alors à Paris.* He was living in Paris at that time.

- **alors que (1)** as ◇ *Il est arrivé alors que je partais.* He arrived just as I was leaving.

- **alors que (2)** while ◇ *Alors que je travaillais dur, lui se reposait.* While I was working hard, he was resting.

les Alpes FEM NOUN
Alps ◇ *dans les Alpes* in the Alps

l' **alphabet** MASC NOUN
alphabet

alphabétique ADJECTIVE
alphabetical ◇ *par ordre alphabétique* in alphabetical order

l' **alpinisme** MASC NOUN
mountaineering

l' **alpiniste** MASC/FEM NOUN
mountaineer

l' **Alsace** FEM NOUN
Alsace

l' **amande** FEM NOUN
almond

- **la pâte d'amandes** marzipan

l' **amant** MASC NOUN
lover

amateur ADJECTIVE
(FEM SING **amateur**)
see also **amateur** NOUN
amateur ◇ *Elle est pianiste amateur.* She's an amateur pianist.

l' **amateur** MASC NOUN
see also **amateur** ADJECTIVE
amateur

- **en amateur** as a hobby ◇ *Il fait de la photo en amateur.* He takes photos as a hobby.

- **C'est un amateur de musique.** He's a music lover.

l' **ambassade** FEM NOUN
embassy

l' **ambassadeur** MASC NOUN
ambassador

l' **ambiance** FEM NOUN
atmosphere ◇ *Je n'aime pas l'ambiance ici.* I don't like the atmosphere here. ◇ *Il y a de l'ambiance dans ce café.* This café has a lively atmosphere.

- **la musique d'ambiance** background music

l' **ambulance** FEM NOUN
ambulance

l' **âme** FEM NOUN
soul

améliorer VERB
to improve

- **s'améliorer** to improve ◇ *Le temps s'améliore.* The weather's improving.

l' **amende** FEM NOUN
fine ◇ *une amende de cinq cents francs* a 500 franc fine

amener VERB
to bring ◇ *Qu'est-ce qui t'amène?* What brings you here? ◇ *Est-ce que je peux amener un ami?* Can I bring a friend?

amer ADJECTIVE
(FEM SING **amère**)
bitter

américain ADJECTIVE, NOUN
(FEM SING **américaine**)
American

- **un Américain** an American (*man*)
- **une Américaine** an American (*woman*)

l' **Amérique** FEM NOUN
America

- **en Amérique (1)** in America
- **en Amérique (2)** to America
- **l'Amérique du Nord** North America
- **l'Amérique du Sud** South America

l' **ami** MASC NOUN
friend

- **C'est son petit ami.** He's her boyfriend.

amical ADJECTIVE
(MASC PL **amicaux**)
friendly

l' **amie** FEM NOUN
friend

- **C'est sa petite amie.** She's his girlfriend.

l' **amitié** FEM NOUN
friendship

- **Fais mes amitiés à Paul.** Give my regards to Paul.

- **Amitiés, Christèle.** (*in letter*) Best wishes, Christèle.

l' **amour** MASC NOUN
love

- **faire l'amour** to make love

amoureux ADJECTIVE
(FEM SING **amoureuse**)
in love ◇ *être amoureux de quelqu'un* to be in love with somebody

l' **amour-propre** MASC NOUN
self-esteem

l' **amphithéâtre** MASC NOUN
lecture theatre

amplement ADVERB

- **Nous avons amplement le temps.** We have plenty of time.

l' **ampoule** FEM NOUN

[1] *light bulb*
[2] *blister*   ◇ *J'ai une ampoule au pied.*
I've got a blister on my foot.
amusant   ADJECTIVE
amusing
les **amuse-gueule**   MASC NOUN
party nibbles
amuser   VERB
to amuse
◆ **s'amuser (1)** to play   ◇ *Les enfants s'amusent dehors.* The children are playing outside.
◆ **s'amuser (2)** to enjoy oneself   ◇ *On s'est bien amusés à cette soirée.* We really enjoyed ourselves at that party.
l' **an**   MASC NOUN
year
◆ **le premier de l'an** New Year's Day
◆ **le nouvel an** New Year
l' **analyse**   FEM NOUN
[1] *analysis*
[2] *test* (medical)   ◇ *une analyse d'urine* a urine test
l' **ananas**   MASC NOUN
pineapple
l' **ancêtre**   MASC / FEM NOUN
ancestor
l' **anchois**   MASC NOUN
anchovy
ancien   ADJECTIVE
(FEM SING **ancienne**)
[1] *former*   ◇ *C'est une ancienne élève.* She's a former pupil.
[2] *old*   ◇ *notre ancienne voiture* our old car
[3] *antique*   ◇ *un fauteuil ancien* an antique chair
l' **ancre**   FEM NOUN
anchor
Andorre   FEM NOUN
Andorra
l' **âne**   MASC NOUN
donkey
l' **ange**   MASC NOUN
angel
◆ **être aux anges** to be over the moon
l' **angine**   FEM NOUN
throat infection
anglais   ADJECTIVE, NOUN
(FEM SING **anglaise**)
English   ◇ *Est-ce que vous parlez anglais?* Do you speak English?
◆ **un Anglais** an Englishman
◆ **une Anglaise** an Englishwoman
◆ **les Anglais** the English
l' **angle**   MASC NOUN
[1] *angle*   ◇ *un angle droit* a right angle
[2] *corner*   ◇ *à l'angle de la rue* at the corner of the street

l' **Angleterre**   FEM NOUN
England
◆ **en Angleterre (1)** in England
◇ *J'habite en Angleterre.* I live in England.
◆ **en Angleterre (2)** to England   ◇ *Je suis allée en Angleterre le mois dernier.* I went to England last month.
anglo-   PREFIX
anglo-
◆ **les îles Anglo-Normandes** the Channel Islands
anglophone   ADJECTIVE
English-speaking
l' **animal**   MASC NOUN
(PL les **animaux**)
animal
l' **animateur**   MASC NOUN
[1] *host*   ◇ *Il est animateur à la télé.* He's a TV host.
[2] *youth leader*   ◇ *Pierre est animateur au centre sportif.* Pierre is a youth leader at the sports centre.
l' **animatrice**   FEM NOUN
[1] *host*   ◇ *Elle est animatrice à la télé.* She's a TV host.
[2] *youth leader*   ◇ *Cécile est animatrice au centre sportif.* Cécile is a youth leader at the sports centre.
animé   ADJECTIVE
lively   ◇ *Cette rue est très animée.* This is a very lively street.
◆ **un dessin animé** a cartoon
l' **anis**   MASC NOUN
aniseed
l' **anneau**   MASC NOUN
(PL les **anneaux**)
ring
l' **année**   FEM NOUN
year   ◇ *l'année dernière* last year
◇ *l'année prochaine* next year
l' **anniversaire**   MASC NOUN
[1] *birthday*   ◇ *C'est l'anniversaire de Janet.* It's Janet's birthday.
[2] *anniversary*   ◇ *un anniversaire de mariage* a wedding anniversary
l' **annonce**   FEM NOUN
advert   ◇ *J'ai lu votre annonce dans le journal.* I saw your advert in the newspaper.   ◇ *passer une annonce* to place an ad
◆ **les petites annonces** the small ads
annoncer   VERB
to announce   ◇ *Ils ont annoncé leurs fiançailles.* They've announced their engagement.
l' **annuaire**   MASC NOUN
phone book
annuel   ADJECTIVE
(FEM SING **annuelle**)

annual
annuler VERB
to cancel
anonyme ADJECTIVE
anonymous
l'**anorak** MASC NOUN
anorak
ANPE ABBREVIATION (= *Agence nationale pour l'emploi*)
national employment agency ◦ *Je suis allé à l'ANPE.* I went to the job centre.
l'**Antarctique** MASC NOUN
Antarctic
l'**antenne** FEM NOUN
[1] *aerial*
[2] *antenna*
• **être à l'antenne** to be on the air
l'**antibiotique** MASC NOUN
antibiotic
l'**antigel** MASC NOUN
antifreeze
les **Antilles** FEM NOUN
West Indies
• **aux Antilles (1)** in the West Indies
• **aux Antilles (2)** to the West Indies
antipathique ADJECTIVE
unpleasant ◦ *Je le trouve plutôt antipathique.* I find him rather unpleasant.
antipelliculaire ADJECTIVE
anti-dandruff
l'**antiquaire** MASC/FEM NOUN
antique dealer ◦ *Elle est antiquaire.* She's an antique dealer.
l'**antiquité** FEM NOUN
antique ◦ *un magasin d'antiquités* an antique shop
• **pendant l'antiquité** in classical times
antiseptique ADJECTIVE
see also antiseptique NOUN
antiseptic
l'**antiseptique** MASC NOUN
see also antiseptique ADJECTIVE
antiseptic
anxieux ADJECTIVE
(FEM SING **anxieuse**)
anxious ◦ *Il est anxieux de nature.* He's a born worrier.
août MASC NOUN
August
• **en août** in August
apercevoir VERB
to see ◦ *J'aperçois la côte.* I can see the shore.
• **s'apercevoir de quelque chose** to notice something
• **s'apercevoir que...** to notice that...

l'**apéritif** MASC NOUN
aperitif ◦ *Venez donc prendre l'apéritif ce soir!* Come round for drinks this evening!
apparaître VERB
to appear
l'**appareil** MASC NOUN
device
• **un appareil dentaire** a brace (*for teeth*)
• **les appareils ménagers** domestic appliances
• **un appareil photo** a camera
• **Qui est à l'appareil?** Who's speaking? (*on phone*)
apparemment ADVERB
apparently
l'**apparence** FEM NOUN
appearance
l'**apparition** FEM NOUN
appearance ◦ *Il n'a fait qu'une brève apparition.* He only appeared briefly.
l'**appartement** MASC NOUN
flat
appartenir VERB
• **appartenir à quelqu'un** to belong to somebody
apparu VERB *see* **apparaître**
l'**appel** MASC NOUN
[1] *cry* ◦ *un appel au secours* a cry for help
[2] *phone call*
• **faire appel à quelqu'un** to appeal to somebody
• **faire l'appel** to call the register (*in school*)
• **faire un appel de phares** to flash one's headlights
appeler VERB
to call ◦ *Elle a appelé le médecin.* She called the doctor. ◦ *J'ai appelé Richard à Londres.* I called Richard in London.
• **s'appeler** to be called ◦ *Comment ça s'appelle?* What is it called? ◦ *Elle s'appelle Muriel.* Her name's Muriel. ◦ *Comment tu t'appelles?* What's your name?
l'**appendicite** FEM NOUN
appendicitis
appétissant ADJECTIVE
appetizing
l'**appétit** MASC NOUN
appetite
• **Bon appétit!** Enjoy your meal!
applaudir VERB
to clap (*applaud*)
les **applaudissements** MASC NOUN
applause
appliquer VERB
[1] *to apply*

② *to enforce* ◇ *appliquer la loi* to enforce the law
• **s'appliquer** to apply oneself
apporter VERB
to bring
apprécier VERB
to appreciate
appréhender VERB
to dread ◇ *J'appréhende cette réunion.* I'm dreading this meeting.
apprendre VERB
① *to learn* ◇ *apprendre quelque chose par cœur* to learn something by heart
• **apprendre à faire quelque chose** to learn to do something ◇ *J'apprends à faire la cuisine.* I'm learning to cook.
② *to hear* ◇ *J'ai appris son départ.* I heard that she had left.
• **apprendre quelque chose à quelqu'un (1)** to teach somebody something ◇ *Ma mère m'a appris l'anglais.* My mother taught me English. ◇ *Elle lui a appris à conduire.* She taught him to drive.
• **apprendre quelque chose à quelqu'un (2)** to tell somebody something ◇ *Jean-Pierre m'a appris la nouvelle.* Jean-Pierre told me the news.
appris VERB *see* **apprendre**
approcher VERB
• **approcher de** to approach ◇ *Nous approchons de Paris.* We are approaching Paris.
• **s'approcher de** to come closer to ◇ *Ne t'approche pas, j'ai la grippe!* Don't get too close to me, I've got flu!
approuver VERB
to approve of ◇ *Je n'approuve pas ses méthodes.* I don't approve of his methods.
approximatif ADJECTIVE
(FEM SING **approximative**)
① *approximate* ◇ *un prix approximatif* an approximate price
② *rough* ◇ *un calcul approximatif* a rough calculation
l'**appui** MASC NOUN
support ◇ *J'ai besoin de votre appui.* I need your support.
appuyer VERB
① *to press* ◇ *appuyer sur un bouton* to press a button
② *to lean* ◇ *Elle a appuyé son vélo contre la porte.* She leaned her bike against the door.
• **s'appuyer** to lean ◇ *Elle s'est appuyée contre le mur.* She leaned against the wall. ◇ *Il s'est appuyé sur la table.* He leaned on the table.

après PREPOSITION, ADVERB
① *after* ◇ *après le déjeuner* after lunch ◇ *après son départ* after he had left ◇ *après qu'il est parti* after he had left ◇ *Nous viendrons après avoir fait la vaisselle.* We'll come after we've done the dishes.
② *afterwards* ◇ *aussitôt après* immediately afterwards
• **après coup** afterwards ◇ *J'y ai repensé après coup.* I thought about it again afterwards.
• **d'après** according to ◇ *D'après lui, c'est une erreur.* According to him, that's a mistake.
• **après tout** after all
après-demain ADVERB
the day after tomorrow
l'**après-midi** MASC OR FEM NOUN
afternoon
l'**aquarium** MASC NOUN
aquarium
arabe ADJECTIVE, NOUN
① *Arab* ◇ *les pays arabes* the Arab countries
② *Arabic* ◇ *la littérature arabe* Arabic literature ◇ *Il parle arabe.* He speaks Arabic.
• **un Arabe** an Arab (*man*)
• **une Arabe** an Arab (*woman*)
l'**Arabie Saoudite** FEM NOUN
Saudi Arabia
l'**araignée** FEM NOUN
spider
l'**arbitre** MASC NOUN
① *referee*
② *umpire*
l'**arbre** MASC NOUN
tree
• **un arbre généalogique** a family tree
l'**arbuste** MASC NOUN
shrub
l'**arc** MASC NOUN
bow ◇ *son arc et ses flèches* his bow and arrows
l'**arc-en-ciel** MASC NOUN
(PL les **arcs-en-ciel**)
rainbow
l'**archéologie** FEM NOUN
archaeology
l'**archéologue** MASC/FEM NOUN
archaeologist ◇ *Elle est archéologue.* She's an archaeologist.
l'**archipel** MASC NOUN
archipelago
l'**architecte** MASC NOUN
architect ◇ *Il est architecte.* He's an architect.
l'**architecture** FEM NOUN

architecture

l'**Arctique** MASC NOUN
Arctic

l'**ardoise** FEM NOUN
slate

l'**arène** FEM NOUN
bullring

+ **des arènes romaines** a Roman
amphitheatre

+ **l'arène politique** the political arena

l'**arête** FEM NOUN
fish bone

l'**argent** MASC NOUN
1 _silver_ ○ _une bague en argent_ a
silver ring
2 _money_ ○ _Je n'ai plus d'argent._ I
haven't got any more money.

+ **l'argent de poche** pocket money

+ **l'argent liquide** cash

argentin ADJECTIVE, NOUN
(FEM SING **argentine**)
Argentinian

+ **un Argentin** an Argentinian (_man_)

+ **une Argentine** an Argentinian (_woman_)

l'**Argentine** FEM NOUN
Argentina

l'**argile** FEM NOUN
clay

l'**argot** MASC NOUN
slang

l'**arme** FEM NOUN
weapon

+ **une arme à feu** a firearm

l'**armée** FEM NOUN
army

+ **l'armée de l'air** the Air Force

l'**armistice** MASC NOUN
armistice

l'**armoire** FEM NOUN
wardrobe

l'**armure** FEM NOUN
armour ○ _un chevalier en armure_ a
knight in armour

arnaquer (_informal_) VERB
to con

aromatisé ADJECTIVE
flavoured

l'**arôme** MASC NOUN
1 _aroma_
2 _flavouring_ (_added to food_)

arpenter VERB
to pace up and down ○ _Il arpentait le
couloir._ He was pacing up and down
the corridor.

arrache-pied

+ **d'arrache-pied** ADVERB
furiously ○ _travailler d'arrache-pied_ to
work furiously

arracher VERB

1 _to take out_ ○ _Le dentiste m'a
arraché une dent._ The dentist took one
of my teeth out.
2 _to tear out_ ○ _Arrachez la page._
Tear the page out.
3 _to pull up_ ○ _Elle a arraché les
mauvaises herbes._ She pulled up the
weeds.

+ **arracher quelque chose à quelqu'un**
to snatch something from somebody

arranger VERB
1 _to arrange_ ○ _arranger des fleurs
dans un vase_ to arrange flowers in a
vase
2 _to suit_ ○ _Ça m'arrange de partir plus
tôt._ It suits me to leave earlier.

+ **s'arranger** to come to an agreement
○ _Arrangez-vous avec le patron._ You'll
have to come to an agreement with the
boss.

+ **Je vais m'arranger pour venir.** I'll
organize things so that I can come.

+ **Ça va s'arranger.** Things will work
themselves out.

l'**arrestation** FEM NOUN
arrest ○ _en état d'arrestation_ under
arrest

l'**arrêt** MASC NOUN
stop ○ _un arrêt de bus_ a bus stop

+ **sans arrêt (1)** non-stop ○ _Elle travaille
sans arrêt._ She works non-stop.

+ **sans arrêt (2)** continually ○ _Ils se
disputent sans arrêt._ They quarrel
continually.

arrêter VERB
1 _to stop_

+ **Arrête!** Stop it!

+ **arrêter de faire quelque chose** to stop
doing something
2 _to switch off_ ○ _Il a arrêté le moteur._
He switched the engine off.
3 _to arrest_ ○ _Mon voisin a été arrêté._
My neighbour's been arrested.

+ **s'arrêter** to stop ○ _Elle s'est arrêtée
devant une vitrine._ She stopped in front
of a shop window.

+ **s'arrêter de faire quelque chose** to
stop doing something ○ _s'arrêter de
fumer_ to stop smoking

les **arrhes** FEM NOUN
deposit ○ _verser des arrhes_ to pay a
deposit

l'**arrière** MASC NOUN
see also **arrière** ADJECTIVE
back ○ _l'arrière de la maison_ the back
of the house

+ **à l'arrière** at the back

+ **en arrière** behind ○ _Ils sont restés en
arrière._ They stayed behind.

l'**arrière** ADJECTIVE (MASC, FEM, PL)

see also **arrière** NOUN

back ◇ *le siège arrière* the back seat ◇ *les roues arrière* the rear wheels

l'**arrière-grand-mère** FEM NOUN
(PL les **arrière-grands-mères**)
great-grandmother

l'**arrière-grand-père** MASC NOUN
(PL les **arrière-grands-pères**)
great-grandfather

l'**arrivée** FEM NOUN
arrival

arriver VERB
[1] *to arrive* ◇ *J'arrive à l'école à huit heures.* I arrive at school at 8 o'clock.
[2] *to happen* ◇ *Qu'est-ce qui est arrivé à Christian?* What happened to Christian?

• **arriver à faire quelque chose** to manage to do something ◇ *J'espère que je vais y arriver.* I hope I'll manage it.

• **Il m'arrive de dormir jusqu'à midi.** I sometimes sleep till midday.

arrogant ADJECTIVE
arrogant

l'**arrondissement** MASC NOUN
district

Paris, Lyons and Marseilles are divided into numbered districts called **arrondissements**.

arroser VERB
to water ◇ *Daphne arrose ses tomates.* Daphne is watering her tomatoes.

• **Ils ont arrosé leur victoire.** They had a drink to celebrate their victory.

l'**arrosoir** MASC NOUN
watering can

l'**art** MASC NOUN
art

l'**artère** FEM NOUN
[1] *artery*
[2] *thoroughfare* ◇ *les grandes artères de Paris* the main roads of Paris

l'**artichaut** MASC NOUN
artichoke

l'**article** MASC NOUN
[1] *article* ◇ *un article de journal* a newspaper article
[2] *item* ◇ *les articles en promotion* items on special offer

l'**articulation** FEM NOUN
joint ◇ *l'articulation du genou* the knee joint

articuler VERB
to pronounce clearly

artificiel ADJECTIVE
(FEM SING **artificielle**)
artificial

l'**artisan** MASC NOUN
self-employed craftsman

l'**artiste** MASC/FEM NOUN
[1] *artist*
[2] *performer*

artistique ADJECTIVE
artistic

as VERB see **avoir**

see also **as** NOUN

• **Tu as de beaux cheveux.** You've got nice hair.

l'**as** MASC NOUN

see also **as** VERB

ace ◇ *l'as de trèfle* the ace of clubs

l'**ascenseur** MASC NOUN
lift

l'**Ascension** FEM NOUN
Ascension

asiatique ADJECTIVE
Asiatic ◇ *la cuisine asiatique* Oriental cooking ◇ *le Sud-Est asiatique* South East Asia

l'**Asie** FEM NOUN
Asia

• **en Asie (1)** in Asia
• **en Asie (2)** to Asia

l'**aspect** MASC NOUN
appearance

l'**asperge** FEM NOUN
asparagus

l'**aspirateur** MASC NOUN
vacuum cleaner

• **passer l'aspirateur** to vacuum

l'**aspirine** FEM NOUN
aspirin

assaisonner VERB
to season

l'**assassin** MASC NOUN
murderer

assassiner VERB
to murder

assembler VERB
to assemble

• **s'assembler** to gather ◇ *Une foule énorme s'était assemblée.* A huge crowd had gathered.

s'**asseoir** VERB
to sit down ◇ *Asseyez-vous!* Sit down! ◇ *Assieds-toi!* Sit down!

assez ADVERB
[1] *enough* ◇ *Nous n'avons pas assez de temps.* We don't have enough time. ◇ *Est-ce qu'il y a assez de pain?* Is there enough bread?

• **J'en ai assez!** I've had enough!
[2] *quite* ◇ *Il faisait assez beau.* The weather was quite nice.

l'**assiette** FEM NOUN
plate ◇ *une assiette creuse* a soup

plate ◇ *une assiette à dessert* a dessert plate

• **une assiette anglaise** assorted cold meats

assis VERB *see* **asseoir**

assis ADJECTIVE
sitting ◇ *Il est assis par terre.* He's sitting on the floor.

l'**assistance** FEM NOUN
[1] *audience* ◇ *Y a-t-il un médecin dans l'assistance?* Is there a doctor in the audience?
[2] *aid* ◇ *l'assistance humanitaire* humanitarian aid
[3] *assistance* ◇ *avec l'assistance de quelqu'un* with the assistance of somebody

l'**assistant** MASC NOUN
assistant ◇ *Il était assistant d'anglais à Tourcoing.* He was an English assistant in Tourcoing.

• **un assistant social** a social worker

l'**assistante** FEM NOUN
assistant ◇ *Elle est assistante de français à Oxford.* She's a French assistant in Oxford.

• **une assistante sociale** a social worker

assister VERB
• **assister à un accident** to witness an accident
• **assister à un cours** to attend a class
• **assister à un concert** to be at a concert

l'**association** FEM NOUN
association

l'**associé** MASC NOUN
partner (*in business*)

l'**associée** FEM NOUN
partner (*in business*)

s'**associer** VERB
to go into partnership

assommer VERB
to knock out ◇ *Il l'a assommé avec une bouteille.* He knocked him out with a bottle.

l'**Assomption** FEM NOUN
Assumption

assorti ADJECTIVE
[1] *matching* ◇ *des couleurs assorties* matching colours
[2] *assorted* ◇ *des chocolats assortis* assorted chocolates

• **être assorti à quelque chose** to match something ◇ *Son sac est assorti à ses chaussures.* Her bag matches her shoes.

l'**assortiment** MASC NOUN
assortment

l'**assurance** FEM NOUN
[1] *insurance* ◇ *une assurance maladie* medical insurance

[2] *confidence* ◇ *parler avec assurance* to speak with confidence

assurer VERB
[1] *to insure* ◇ *La maison est assurée.* The house is insured. ◇ *être assuré contre quelque chose* to be insured against something
[2] *to assure* ◇ *Je t'assure que c'est vrai!* I assure you it's true!

• **s'assurer de quelque chose** to make sure of something ◇ *Il s'est assuré que la porte était fermée.* He made sure the door was shut.

l'**asthme** MASC NOUN
asthma ◇ *une crise d'asthme* an asthma attack

l'**astronaute** MASC/FEM NOUN
astronaut

l'**astronomie** FEM NOUN
astronomy

astucieux ADJECTIVE
(FEM SING **astucieuse**)
clever

l'**atelier** MASC NOUN
[1] *workshop*
[2] *studio* (*artist's*)

Athènes NOUN
Athens

l'**athlète** MASC/FEM NOUN
athlete

l'**athlétisme** MASC NOUN
athletics ◇ *un championnat d'athlétisme* an athletics championship

l'**Atlantique** MASC NOUN
Atlantic

l'**atlas** MASC NOUN
atlas

l'**atmosphère** FEM NOUN
atmosphere

atomique ADJECTIVE
atomic ◇ *la bombe atomique* the atomic bomb

atroce ADJECTIVE
terrible

attachant ADJECTIVE
lovable ◇ *un enfant attachant* a lovable child

attacher VERB
to tie up ◇ *Elle a attaché ses cheveux avec un élastique.* She tied her hair up with an elastic band.

• **s'attacher à quelqu'un** to become attached to somebody
• **une poêle qui n'attache pas** a non-stick frying pan

attaquer VERB
to attack

atteindre VERB
to reach

attendant

- **en attendant** ADVERB
  in the meantime

attendre VERB

to wait ◇ *attendre quelqu'un* to wait for someone ◇ *J'attends d'avoir un appartement à moi.* I'm waiting until I've got a flat of my own. ◇ *Attends qu'il ne pleuve plus.* Wait until it's stopped raining.

- **attendre un enfant** to be expecting a baby
- **s'attendre à** to expect ◇ *Je m'attends à ce qu'il soit en retard.* I expect he'll be late.

l' **attentat** MASC NOUN
- **un attentat à la bombe** a terrorist bombing

l' **attente** FEM NOUN
wait ◇ *deux heures d'attente* two hours' wait
- **la salle d'attente** the waiting room

attentif ADJECTIVE

(FEM SING **attentive**)
attentive

l' **attention** FEM NOUN
attention ◇ *à l'attention de* for the attention of
- **faire attention** to be careful
- **Attention!** Watch out! ◇ *Attention, tu vas te faire écraser!* Watch out, you'll get run over!

attentionné ADJECTIVE

thoughtful

atterrir VERB

to land

l' **atterrissage** MASC NOUN
landing (*of plane*)

attirant ADJECTIVE

attractive

attirer VERB

to attract ◇ *attirer l'attention de quelqu'un* to attract somebody's attention
- **s'attirer des ennuis** to get into trouble ◇ *Si tu continues, tu vas t'attirer des ennuis.* If you keep on like that, you'll get yourself into trouble.

l' **attitude** FEM NOUN
attitude

l' **attraction** FEM NOUN
- **un parc d'attractions** an amusement park

attraper VERB

to catch

attrayant ADJECTIVE

attractive

attrister VERB

to sadden

au PREPOSITION *see* **à**
au *is the contracted form of* à + le.
- **au printemps** in the spring

l' **aube** FEM NOUN
dawn ◇ *à l'aube* at dawn

l' **auberge de jeunesse** FEM NOUN
youth hostel

l' **aubergine** FEM NOUN
aubergine

aucun ADJECTIVE, PRONOUN
1. *no* ◇ *Il n'a aucun ami.* He's got no friends. ◇ *Aucun enfant ne pourrait le faire.* No child could do that.
2. *none* ◇ *Aucun d'entre eux n'est venu.* None of them came. ◇ *Aucune de mes amies n'aime le football.* None of my female friends like football. ◇ *Tu aimes ses films? – Je n'en ai vu aucun.* Do you like his films? – I haven't seen any of them.
- **sans aucun doute** without any doubt

au-delà ADVERB
- **au-delà de** beyond ◇ *Votre ticket n'est pas valable au-delà de cette limite.* Your ticket is not valid beyond this point.

au-dessous ADVERB
1. *downstairs* ◇ *Ils habitent au-dessous.* They live downstairs.
2. *underneath*
- **au-dessous de** under ◇ *au-dessous du pont* under the bridge ◇ *dix degrés au-dessous de zéro* ten degrees below zero

au-dessus ADVERB
1. *upstairs* ◇ *J'habite au-dessus.* I live upstairs.
2. *above*
- **au-dessus de** above ◇ *au-dessus de la table* above the table

audiovisuel ADJECTIVE
(FEM SING **audiovisuelle**)
audiovisual

l' **auditeur** MASC NOUN
listener (*to radio*)

l' **auditrice** FEM NOUN
listener (*to radio*)

l' **augmentation** FEM NOUN
rise

augmenter VERB

to increase

aujourd'hui ADVERB
today

auparavant ADVERB
first ◇ *Vous pouvez utiliser l'ordinateur mais auparavant vous devez taper le mot de passe.* You can use the computer but first you have to key in the password.

auquel PRONOUN
(MASC PL **auxquels**, FEM PL **auxquelles**)
auquel *is the contracted form of* **à + lequel**.
◊ *l'homme auquel j'ai parlé* the man I
spoke to

aura, aurai, auras, aurez, aurons, auront VERB *see* **avoir**

l'**aurore** FEM NOUN
daybreak

ausculter VERB
- **Le médecin l'a ausculté.** The doctor
listened to his chest.

aussi ADVERB
[1] *too* ◊ *Dors bien. – Toi aussi.* Sleep
well. – You too. ◊ *Lui aussi parle
espagnol.* He too speaks Spanish.
[2] *also* ◊ *J'aimerais aussi que tu
achètes le journal.* I'd also like you to
get the paper. ◊ *Je parle anglais et aussi
allemand.* I speak English and also
German.
- **aussi...que** as...as ◊ *aussi grand que
moi* as big as me

aussitôt ADVERB
straight away ◊ *aussitôt après son
retour* straight after his return
- **aussitôt que** as soon as ◊ *aussitôt que
tu auras fini* as soon as you've finished

l'**Australie** FEM NOUN
Australia
- **en Australie (1)** in Australia
- **en Australie (2)** to Australia

australien ADJECTIVE, NOUN
(FEM SING **australienne**)
Australian
- **un Australien** an Australian (*man*)
- **une Australienne** an Australian
(*woman*)

autant ADVERB
- **autant de (1)** so much ◊ *Je ne veux
pas autant de gâteau.* I don't want so
much cake.
- **autant de (2)** so many ◊ *Je n'ai jamais
vu autant de monde.* I've never seen so
many people.
- **autant...que (1)** as much...as ◊ *J'ai
autant d'argent que toi.* I've got as much
money as you have.
- **autant...que (2)** as many...as ◊ *J'ai
autant d'amis que lui.* I've got as many
friends as he has.
- **d'autant plus que** all the more since
◊ *Elle est d'autant plus déçue qu'il le lui
avait promis.* She's all the more
disappointed since he had promised
her.
- **d'autant moins que** even less since
◊ *C'est d'autant moins pratique pour lui
qu'il doit changer deux fois de train.* It's

even less convenient for him since he
has to change trains twice.

l'**auteur** MASC NOUN
author

l'**auto** FEM NOUN
car

l'**autobus** MASC NOUN
bus ◊ *en autobus* by bus

l'**autocar** MASC NOUN
coach ◊ *en autocar* by coach

autocollant ADJECTIVE
see also **autocollant** NOUN
self-adhesive ◊ *une étiquette
autocollante* a self-adhesive label
- **une enveloppe autocollante** a self-seal
envelope

l'**autocollant** MASC NOUN
see also **autocollant** ADJECTIVE
sticker

l'**auto-école** FEM NOUN
driving school

automatique ADJECTIVE
automatic

l'**automne** MASC NOUN
autumn
- **en automne** in autumn

automobile ADJECTIVE
see also **automobile** NOUN
- **une course automobile** a motor race

l'**automobile** FEM NOUN
see also **automobile** ADJECTIVE
car

l'**automobiliste** MASC/FEM NOUN
motorist

l'**autoradio** MASC NOUN
car radio

l'**autorisation** FEM NOUN
[1] *permission* ◊ *Il m'a donné
l'autorisation de sortir ce soir.* He's given
me permission to go out tonight.
[2] *permit* ◊ *Il faut une autorisation pour
camper ici.* You need a permit to camp
here.

autoriser VERB
to give permission for ◊ *Il m'a
autorisé à en parler.* He's given me
permission to talk about it.

autoritaire ADJECTIVE
authoritarian

l'**autorité** FEM NOUN
authority

l'**autoroute** FEM NOUN
motorway

l'**auto-stop** MASC NOUN
- **faire de l'auto-stop** to hitchhike

l'**auto-stoppeur** MASC NOUN
hitchhiker

l'**auto-stoppeuse** FEM NOUN
hitchhiker

autour ADVERB
around ◇ *autour de la maison* around the house

autre ADJECTIVE, PRONOUN
other ◇ *Je viendrai un autre jour.* I'll come some other day. ◇ *J'ai d'autres projets.* I've got other plans.
* **autre chose** something else
* **autre part** somewhere else
* **un autre** another ◇ *Tu veux un autre morceau de gâteau?* Would you like another piece of cake?
* **l'autre** the other ◇ *Non, pas celui-ci, l'autre.* No, not that one, the other one.
* **d'autres** others ◇ *Je t'en apporterai d'autres.* I'll bring you some others.
* **les autres** the others ◇ *Les autres sont arrivés plus tard.* The others arrived later.
* **ni l'un ni l'autre** neither of them
* **entre autres** among other things ◇ *Nous avons parlé, entre autres, de nos projets de vacances.* We talked about our holiday plans, among other things.

autrefois ADVERB
in the old days ◇ *Autrefois Saint-Tropez n'était qu'un village de pêcheurs.* In the old days Saint-Tropez was just a fishing village.

autrement ADVERB
[1] *differently* ◇ *Il l'a fait autrement.* He did it differently.
[2] *otherwise* ◇ *Je n'ai pas pu faire autrement.* I couldn't do otherwise.
* **autrement dit** in other words

l'Autriche FEM NOUN
Austria
* **en Autriche (1)** in Austria
* **en Autriche (2)** to Austria

autrichien ADJECTIVE, NOUN
(FEM SING **autrichienne**)
Austrian
* **un Autrichien** an Austrian (*man*)
* **une Autrichienne** an Austrian (*woman*)

l'autruche FEM NOUN
ostrich

aux PREPOSITION *see* **à**
| **aux** *is the contracted form of* **à + les**. |
◇ *J'ai dit aux enfants d'aller jouer.* I told the children to go and play.

auxquelles PRONOUN
| **auxquelles** *is the contracted form of* **à + lesquelles.** |
◇ *les revues auxquelles il est abonné* the magazines to which he subscribes

auxquels PRONOUN
| **auxquels** *is the contracted form of* **à + lesquels.** |
◇ *les enfants auxquels il a parlé* the

children he spoke to

l'avalanche FEM NOUN
avalanche

avaler VERB
to swallow

l'avance FEM NOUN
* **être en avance** to be early
* **à l'avance** beforehand ◇ *réserver longtemps à l'avance* to book well beforehand
* **d'avance** in advance ◇ *payer d'avance* to pay in advance

avancé ADJECTIVE
advanced ◇ *à un niveau avancé* at an advanced level
* **bien avancé** well under way ◇ *Les travaux sont déjà bien avancés.* The work is already well under way.

avancer VERB
[1] *to move forward* ◇ *Il avançait prudemment.* He was moving forward cautiously.
[2] *to bring forward* ◇ *La date de l'examen a été avancée.* The date of the exam has been brought forward.
[3] *to put forward* ◇ *Il a avancé sa montre d'une heure.* He put his watch forward an hour.
[4] *to be fast* (*watch*) ◇ *Ma montre avance d'une heure.* My watch is an hour fast.
[5] *to lend* ◇ *Peux-tu m'avancer cent francs?* Can you lend me 100 francs?

avant PREPOSITION, ADJECTIVE
| *see also* **avant** NOUN |
[1] *before* ◇ *avant qu'il ne pleuve* before it rains ◇ *avant de partir* before leaving
[2] *front* ◇ *la roue avant* the front wheel ◇ *le siège avant* the front seat

l'avant MASC NOUN
| *see also* **avant** PREPOSITION |
front ◇ *l'avant de la voiture* the front of the car
* **à l'avant** in front
* **en avant** forward ◇ *Il a fait un pas en avant.* He took a step forward.

l'avantage MASC NOUN
advantage

l'avant-bras MASC NOUN
(PL les **avant-bras**)
forearm

avant-dernier ADJECTIVE
(FEM **avant-dernière**, MASC PL **avant-derniers**)
last but one ◇ *l'avant-dernière page* the last page but one ◇ *Ils sont arrivés avant-derniers.* They arrived last but one.

avant-hier ADVERB

the day before yesterday ◇ *Il est arrivé avant-hier.* He arrived the day before yesterday.

avare ADJECTIVE
see also **avare** NOUN
miserly

l'**avare** MASC/FEM NOUN
see also **avare** ADJECTIVE
miser

avec PREPOSITION
with ◇ *avec mon père* with my father
◆ **Et avec ça?** Anything else? (*in shop*)

l'**avenir** MASC NOUN
future
◆ **à l'avenir** in future ◇ *À l'avenir, essayez d'être à l'heure.* Try to be on time in future.
◆ **dans un proche avenir** in the near future

l'**aventure** FEM NOUN
adventure

l'**avenue** FEM NOUN
avenue

l'**averse** FEM NOUN
shower (*of rain*)

avertir VERB
to warn
◆ **avertir quelqu'un de quelque chose** to warn somebody about something

l'**avertissement** MASC NOUN
warning

aveugle ADJECTIVE
blind

l'**avion** MASC NOUN
plane
◆ **aller en avion** to go by plane ◇ *Il est allé en Italie en avion.* He flew to Italy.
◆ **par avion** by airmail

l'**aviron** MASC NOUN
rowing

l'**avis** MASC NOUN
[1] *opinion* ◇ *J'aimerais avoir ton avis.* I'd like to have your opinion.
◆ **à mon avis** in my opinion
[2] *notice* ◇ *jusqu'à nouvel avis* until further notice
◆ **changer d'avis** to change one's mind

◇ *J'ai changé d'avis.* I've changed my mind.

l'**avocat** MASC NOUN
[1] *lawyer* ◇ *Il est avocat.* He's a lawyer.
[2] *avocado*

l'**avocate** FEM NOUN
lawyer ◇ *Elle est avocate.* She's a lawyer.

l'**avoine** FEM NOUN
oats ◇ *les flocons d'avoine* porridge oats

avoir VERB

Present tense:

j'ai	nous avons
tu as	vous avez
il/elle a	ils/elles ont

Past participle: *eu*

[1] *to have* ◇ *Ils ont deux enfants.* They have two children. ◇ *Il a les yeux bleus.* He's got blue eyes. ◇ *J'ai déjà mangé.* I've already eaten. ◇ *Est-ce que tu as vu ce film?* Have you seen this film? ◇ *Je lui ai parlé hier.* I spoke to him yesterday.
◆ **On t'a bien eu!** (*informal*) You've been had!
[2] *to be* ◇ *Il a trois ans.* He's three. ◇ *J'avais dix ans quand je l'ai rencontré.* I was ten when I met him.
◆ **il y a (1)** there is ◇ *Il y a quelqu'un à la porte.* There's somebody at the door.
◆ **il y a (2)** there are ◇ *Il y a des chocolats sur la table.* There are some chocolats on the table.
◆ **il y a (3)** ago ◇ *Je l'ai rencontré il y a deux ans.* I met him two years ago.
◆ **Qu'est-ce qu'il y a?** What's the matter?
◆ **Il n'y a qu'à partir plus tôt.** We'll just have to leave earlier.

l'**avortement** MASC NOUN
abortion

avril MASC NOUN
April
◆ **en avril** in April

ayez, ayons VERB *see* **avoir**

B

le **baby-foot** NOUN
table football ○ *jouer au baby-foot* to play table football

le **baby-sitting** NOUN
◆ **faire du baby-sitting** to babysit

le **bac** = baccalauréat

le **baccalauréat** NOUN
A levels ○ *Elle a passé son baccalauréat l'année dernière.* She did her A levels last year.

> The French baccalauréat, or bac for short, is taken at the age of 17 or 18. Students have to sit one of a variety of set subject combinations, rather than being able to choose any combination of subjects they want. If you pass you have the right to a place at university.

bâcler VERB
to botch up ○ *Je déteste le travail bâclé!* I hate work that's not done properly!

le **bagage** NOUN
luggage
◆ **faire ses bagages** to pack
◆ **les bagages à main** hand luggage ○ *un bagage à main* a piece of hand luggage

la **bagarre** NOUN
fight ○ *Une bagarre a éclaté à la fermeture du pub.* A fight broke out when the pub closed.

se **bagarrer** VERB
to fight ○ *Il s'est encore bagarré avec son frère.* He's been fighting with his brother again.

la **bagnole** NOUN (*informal*)
car

la **bague** NOUN
ring

la **baguette** NOUN
1. *stick of French bread*
2. *chopstick* ○ *manger avec des baguettes* to eat with chopsticks
◆ **une baguette magique** a magic wand

la **baie** NOUN
bay

se **baigner** VERB
to go swimming ○ *Si on allait se baigner?* Shall we go swimming?

la **baignoire** NOUN
bath (*bathtub*)

bâiller VERB
to yawn

le **bain** NOUN
bath ○ *prendre un bain* to take a bath ○ *prendre un bain de soleil* to sunbathe

le **baiser** NOUN
kiss

baisser VERB
1. *to turn down* ○ *Il fait moins froid, tu peux baisser le chauffage.* It's not so cold, you can turn down the heating.
2. *to fall* ○ *Le prix des CD a baissé.* The price of CDs has fallen.
◆ **se baisser** to bend down ○ *Il s'est baissé pour ramasser son mouchoir.* He bent down to pick up his handkerchief.

le **bal** NOUN
dance ○ *un bal populaire* a local dance
◆ **un bal costumé** a fancy dress ball

la **balade** NOUN (*informal*)
walk ○ *faire une balade* to go for a walk

se **balader** VERB (*informal*)
to wander around ○ *J'adore me balader dans les rues de Paris.* I love to wander around the streets of Paris.

le **baladeur** NOUN
personal stereo

le **balai** NOUN
broom ○ *Je vais donner un coup de balai dans la cuisine.* I'm going to sweep the kitchen.

la **balance** NOUN
scales PL (*for weighing*)
◆ **la Balance** Libra ○ *Todd est Balance.* Todd is Libra.

se **balancer** VERB
to swing

la **balançoire** NOUN
swing

balayer VERB
1. *to sweep* ○ *Jean-Pierre a balayé la cuisine.* Jean-Pierre swept the kitchen.
2. *to sweep up* ○ *Va balayer les feuilles sur la terrasse.* Go and sweep up the leaves on the terrace.

le **balayeur** NOUN
roadsweeper

balbutier VERB
to stammer

le **balcon** NOUN
balcony

la **baleine** NOUN
whale

la **balle** NOUN
1. *ball* ○ *une balle de tennis* a tennis ball
2. *bullet*

la **ballerine** NOUN
1. *ballet dancer*
2. *ballet shoe* ○ *une paire de ballerines rouges* a pair of red ballet

shoes

le **ballet** NOUN
ballet

le **ballon** NOUN
1 *ball* ◇ *lancer le ballon* to throw the ball
* **un ballon de football** a football
2 *balloon*

balnéaire ADJECTIVE
* **une station balnéaire** a seaside resort

banal ADJECTIVE
(MASC PL **banaux**)
1 *commonplace* ◇ *La violence est devenue banale à la télévision.* Violence has become commonplace on television.
2 *hackneyed* ◇ *L'intrigue du film est très banale.* The plot of the film is very hackneyed.

la **banane** NOUN
banana

le **banc** NOUN
bench

bancaire ADJECTIVE
* **une carte bancaire** a bank card

le **bandage** NOUN
bandage

la **bande** NOUN
1 *gang* ◇ *une bande de voyous* a gang of louts
2 *bunch* ◇ *C'est une bande d'idiots!* They are a bunch of idiots!
3 *bandage* ◇ *une bande Velpeau* ® a crepe bandage
* **une bande dessinée** a comic strip
  Comic strips are very popular in France with people of all ages.
* **une bande magnétique** a tape
* **la bande sonore** the sound track
* **Elle fait toujours bande à part.** She always keeps to herself.

le **bandeau** NOUN
(PL les **bandeaux**)
headband

bander VERB
to bandage ◇ *L'infirmière lui a bandé la jambe.* The nurse bandaged his leg.

le **bandit** NOUN
bandit

la **banlieue** NOUN
suburbs ◇ *Christèle habite en banlieue.* Christèle lives in the suburbs.
* **les lignes de banlieue** suburban lines
* **les trains de banlieue** commuter trains

la **banque** NOUN
bank

le **banquet** NOUN
dinner ◇ *le banquet annuel de l'association* the club's annual dinner

la **banquette** NOUN
seat ◇ *la banquette arrière de la voiture* the back seat of the car

le **banquier** NOUN
banker

le **baptême** NOUN
christening ◇ *le baptême de notre fille* our daughter's christening
* **C'était mon baptême de l'air.** It was the first time I had flown.

le **baquet** NOUN
tub

le **bar** NOUN
bar

la **baraque** NOUN (*informal*)
house ◇ *Elle habite dans une belle baraque.* She lives in a beautiful house.

barbare ADJECTIVE
barbaric

la **barbe** NOUN
beard ◇ *Il porte la barbe.* He's got a beard.
* **Quelle barbe!** (*informal*) What a drag!
* **la barbe à papa** candyfloss

barbouiller VERB
to daub ◇ *Les murs étaient barbouillés de graffitis.* The walls were daubed with graffiti.
* **J'ai l'estomac barbouillé.** (*informal*) I'm feeling queasy.

barbu ADJECTIVE
bearded ◇ *un grand barbu* a big, bearded man

barder VERB (*informal*)
* **Ça va barder!** There's going to be trouble!

le **baromètre** NOUN
barometer

la **barque** NOUN
rowing boat ◇ *Ils sont allés faire une promenade en barque.* They've gone for a row.

le **barrage** NOUN
dam
* **un barrage de police** a police roadblock

la **barre** NOUN
bar (*metal*) ◇ *une barre de fer* an iron bar

le **barreau** NOUN
(PL les **barreaux**)
bar (*on window*) ◇ *Il s'est retrouvé derrière les barreaux.* He ended up behind bars.

barrer VERB
to block ◇ *Il y a un tronc d'arbre qui barre la route.* There's a tree trunk blocking the road.
* **se barrer** (*informal*) to clear off

◦ *Barre-toi!* Clear off!

la **barrette** NOUN
hair slide

la **barrière** NOUN
fence

le **bar-tabac** NOUN
(PL les **bars-tabacs**)

A bar-tabac *is a bar which also sells cigarettes and stamps; you can tell a* bar-tabac *by the red diamond-shaped sign outside it.*

le **bas** NOUN
see also bas ADJECTIVE
1 *bottom* ◦ *en bas de la page* at the bottom of the page ◦ *en bas de l'escalier* at the bottom of the stairs
2 *stocking* ◦ *une paire de bas* a pair of stockings

bas ADJECTIVE, ADVERB
(FEM SING **basse**)
see also bas NOUN
low ◦ *parler à voix basse* to speak in a low voice

▪ **en bas (1)** down ◦ *Ça me donne le vertige de regarder en bas.* I get dizzy if I look down.

▪ **en bas (2)** (down) at the bottom ◦ *Son nom est tout en bas.* His name is down at the bottom. ◦ *Il y a un marchand de journaux en bas de la rue.* There's a newsagent's at the bottom of the street.

▪ **en bas (3)** downstairs ◦ *Elle habite en bas.* She lives downstairs.

le **bas-côté** NOUN
verge ◦ *Il s'est garé sur le bas-côté de la route.* He stopped his car on the verge.

la **bascule** NOUN
▪ **un fauteuil à bascule** a rocking chair

la **base** NOUN
base ◦ *la base de la pyramide* the base of the pyramid

▪ **de base** basic ◦ *Le pain et le lait sont des aliments de base.* Bread and milk are basic foods.

▪ **à base de** made from ◦ *des produits de beauté à base de plantes* cosmetics made from plants

▪ **une base de données** a database

le **basket** NOUN
basketball ◦ *jouer au basket* to play basketball

les **baskets** FEM NOUN
trainers ◦ *une paire de baskets* a pair of trainers

le/la **Basque** NOUN
Basque (person, language)

basque ADJECTIVE
Basque

basse ADJECTIVE see bas

la **basse-cour** NOUN
(PL les **basses-cours**)
farmyard

le **bassin** NOUN
1 *pond* ◦ *Il y a un bassin à poissons rouges dans le parc.* There's a goldfish pond in the park.
2 *pelvis* ◦ *une fracture du bassin* a fractured pelvis

la **bassine** NOUN
bowl (for washing)

le **bas-ventre** NOUN
stomach ◦ *Elle se plaint de douleurs dans le bas-ventre.* She is complaining of pains in her stomach.

la **bataille** NOUN
battle

le **bateau** NOUN
(PL les **bateaux**)
boat

le **bateau-mouche** NOUN
(PL les **bateaux-mouches**)
pleasure boat

bâti ADJECTIVE
▪ **bien bâti** well-built

le **bâtiment** NOUN
building

bâtir VERB
to build

le **bâton** NOUN
stick ◦ *un coup de bâton* a blow with a stick

le **battement** NOUN
▪ **J'ai dix minutes de battement.** I've got ten minutes free.

la **batterie** NOUN
1 *battery* ◦ *La batterie est à plat.* The battery is flat.
2 *drums* ◦ *jouer de la batterie* to play drums
▪ **la batterie de cuisine** the pots and pans

le **batteur** NOUN
drummer

battre VERB
to beat ◦ *Quand je le vois, mon cœur bat plus vite.* When I see him, my heart beats faster.

▪ **se battre** to fight ◦ *Je me bats souvent avec mon frère.* I fight a lot with my brother.

▪ **battre son plein** to in be full swing ◦ *A minuit, la fête battait son plein.* At midnight, the party was in full swing.

bavard ADJECTIVE
talkative

bavarder VERB
to chat

baver VERB
to dribble

baveux ADJECTIVE
(FEM SING **baveuse**)
runny   ◇ *une omelette baveuse* a
runny omelette

la **bavure** NOUN
blunder   ◇ *une bavure policière* a
police blunder

le **bazar** NOUN
general store
◆ **Quel bazar!** (*informal*) What a mess!

BCBG ADJECTIVE (= *bon chic bon genre*)
posh

la **BD** NOUN (= *bande dessinée*)
comic strip   ◇ *Marguerite adore les BD.*
Marguerite loves comic strips.

béant ADJECTIVE
gaping   ◇ *un trou béant* a gaping hole

beau ADJECTIVE, ADVERB
(MASC SING ALSO **bel**, FEM SING **belle**, MASC PL
beaux)
beau *changes to* **bel** *before a vowel and most
words beginning with "h".*
[1] *lovely*   ◇ *un bel été* a lovely
summer   ◇ *une belle journée* a fine day
[2] *beautiful*   ◇ *C'est une belle femme.*
She is a beautiful woman.
[3] *good-looking*   ◇ *C'est un beau
garçon.* He is a good-looking boy.
[4] *handsome*   ◇ *un bel homme* a
handsome man
◆ **Il fait beau aujourd'hui.** It's a nice day
today.
◆ **J'ai beau essayer, je n'y arrive pas.**
However hard I try, I just can't do it.

beaucoup ADVERB
[1] *a lot*   ◇ *Il boit beaucoup.* He drinks a
lot.
[2] *much*   ◇ *Elle n'a pas beaucoup
d'argent.* She hasn't got much money.
◇ *Janet est beaucoup plus grande que
moi.* Janet is much taller than me.
◆ **beaucoup de** a lot of   ◇ *Il y avait
beaucoup de monde au concert.* There
were a lot of people at the concert.
◇ *Elle fait beaucoup de fautes.* She
makes a lot of mistakes.
◆ **J'ai eu beaucoup de chance.** I was
very lucky.

le **beau-fils** NOUN
(PL les **beaux-fils**)
[1] *son-in-law*
[2] *stepson*

le **beau-frère** NOUN
(PL les **beaux-frères**)
brother-in-law

le **beau-père** NOUN
(PL les **beaux-pères**)

[1] *father-in-law*
[2] *stepfather*

la **beauté** NOUN
beauty

les **beaux-arts** MASC NOUN
fine arts

les **beaux-parents** MASC NOUN
in-laws

le **bébé** NOUN
baby

le **bec** NOUN
beak

la **bécane** NOUN (*informal*)
bike

la **bêche** NOUN
spade

bêcher VERB
to dig   ◇ *Il bêchait son jardin.* He was
digging the garden.

bégayer VERB
to stammer

beige ADJECTIVE
beige

le **beignet** NOUN
fritter   ◇ *les beignets aux pommes*
apple fritters

bel ADJECTIVE *see* **beau**

le/la **Belge** NOUN
Belgian

belge ADJECTIVE
Belgian

la **Belgique** NOUN
Belgium
◆ **en Belgique (1)** in Belgium
◆ **en Belgique (2)** to Belgium

le **bélier** MASC NOUN
ram
◆ **le Bélier** Aries   ◇ *Christine est Bélier.*
Christine's Aries.

belle ADJECTIVE *see* **beau**

la **belle-famille** NOUN
in-laws

la **belle-fille** NOUN
(PL les **belles-filles**)
[1] *daughter-in-law*
[2] *stepdaughter*

la **belle-mère** NOUN
(PL les **belles-mères**)
[1] *mother-in-law*
[2] *stepmother*

la **belle-sœur** NOUN
(PL les **belles-sœurs**)
sister-in-law

la **bénédiction** NOUN
blessing

le **bénéfice** NOUN
profit   ◇ *La société réalise de gros
bénéfices.* The company is making big
profits.

bénévole ADJECTIVE
　voluntary ◇ *du travail bénévole*
　voluntary work
bénir VERB
　to bless
bénit ADJECTIVE
　consecrated ◇ *l'eau bénite* holy water
la **béquille** NOUN
　crutch ◇ *Il marche avec des béquilles.*
　He walks on crutches.
le **berceau** NOUN
　(PL les **berceaux**)
　cradle
bercer VERB
　to rock
la **berceuse** NOUN
　lullaby
le **béret** NOUN
　beret
la **berge** NOUN
　bank (*of river*)
le **berger** NOUN
　shepherd
la **bergère** NOUN
　shepherdess
le **besoin** NOUN
　need
　● **avoir besoin de quelque chose** to
　need something ◇ *J'ai besoin d'argent.*
　I need some money. ◇ *J'ai besoin d'y*
　réfléchir. I need to think about it.
　● **une famille dans le besoin** a needy
　family
le **bétail** NOUN
　livestock
la **bête** NOUN
　see also **bête** ADJECTIVE
　animal
bête ADJECTIVE
　see also **bête** NOUN
　stupid
la **bêtise** NOUN
　● **faire une bêtise** to do something
　stupid ◇ *Je crois que j'ai fait une bêtise.*
　I think I've done something stupid.
　● **dire des bêtises** to talk nonsense
　◇ *Tu dis des bêtises!* You're talking
　nonsense!
le **béton** NOUN
　concrete
　● **un alibi en béton** a cast-iron alibi
la **betterave** NOUN
　beetroot ◇ *la salade de betterave*
　beetroot salad
le/la **beur** NOUN (*informal*)
　A **beur** *is a young person of North African origin*
　born in France.
le **beurre** NOUN
　butter ◇ *une sauce au beurre* a sauce

made with butter
beurrer VERB
　to butter
Beyrouth NOUN
　Beirut
le **bibelot** NOUN
　ornament
le **biberon** NOUN
　baby's bottle
la **Bible** NOUN
　Bible
le/la **bibliothécaire** NOUN
　librarian
la **bibliothèque** NOUN
　① *library* ◇ *emprunter un livre à la*
　bibliothèque to borrow a book from the
　library
　② *bookcase* ◇ *une bibliothèque en*
　chêne massif a bookcase made of solid
　oak
le **bic** ® NOUN
　Biro ®
la **biche** NOUN
　doe
la **bicyclette** NOUN
　bicycle
le **bidet** NOUN
　bidet
le **bidon** NOUN
　see also **bidon** ADJECTIVE
　can ◇ *un bidon d'essence* a can of
　petrol
bidon ADJECTIVE (*informal*)
　see also **bidon** NOUN
　phoney ◇ *Son histoire est*
　complètement bidon. His story is a
　complete load of rubbish.
le **bidonville** NOUN
　shanty town
la **Biélorussie** NOUN
　Belarus
le **bien** NOUN
　see also **bien** ADJECTIVE
　① *good* ◇ *le bien et le mal* good and
　evil ◇ *Jean m'a dit beaucoup de bien de*
　toi. Jean told me a lot of good things
　about you. ◇ *C'est pour son bien.* It's
　for his own good.
　● **faire du bien à quelqu'un** to do
　somebody good ◇ *Ses vacances lui ont*
　fait beaucoup de bien. His holiday has
　done him a lot of good.
　② *possession* ◇ *son bien le plus*
　précieux his most treasured possession
bien ADJECTIVE, ADVERB
　see also **bien** NOUN
　① *well* ◇ *Daphne travaille bien.*
　Daphne works well. ◇ *Je me sens bien.*
　I feel fine. ◇ *Je ne me sens pas bien.* I

don't feel well.

2 *good* ◇ *Ce restaurant est vraiment bien.* This restaurant is really good.

3 *quite* ◇ *bien assez* quite enough
- **Je veux bien le faire.** I'm quite willing to do it.
- **bien mieux** much better
- **J'espère bien y aller.** I very much hope to go.

4 *right* ◇ *Ce n'est pas bien de dire du mal des gens.* It's not right to say nasty things about people. ◇ *Il croyait bien faire.* He thought he was doing the right thing.
- **C'est bien fait pour lui!** It serves him right!

le **bien-être** NOUN
well-being ◇ *une sensation de bien-être* a feeling of well-being

la **bienfaisance** NOUN
charity
- **une œuvre de bienfaisance** a charity

bien que CONJUNCTION
although ◇ *Il fait assez chaud bien qu'il n'y ait pas de soleil.* It's quite warm although there's no sun.

bien sûr ADVERB
of course

bientôt ADVERB
soon ◇ *À bientôt!* See you soon!

le **bienvenu** NOUN
- **Vous êtes le bienvenu!** You're welcome! ◇ *Vous êtes tous les bienvenus!* You're all welcome!

la **bienvenue** NOUN
welcome ◇ *Bienvenue à Paris!* Welcome to Paris! ◇ *Vous êtes la bienvenue!* You're welcome!

la **bière** NOUN
beer
- **la bière blonde** lager
- **la bière brune** brown ale
- **la bière pression** draught beer

le **bifteck** NOUN
steak

le **bigoudi** NOUN
roller (*in hair*)

le **bijou** NOUN
(PL les **bijoux**)
jewel

la **bijouterie** NOUN
jeweller's

le **bijoutier** NOUN
jeweller

la **bijoutière** NOUN
jeweller ◇ *Elle est bijoutière.* She's a jeweller.

le **bilan** NOUN
- **faire le bilan de quelque chose** to

assess something ◇ *Il faut faire le bilan de la situation.* We need to assess the situation.

bilingue ADJECTIVE
bilingual

le **billard** NOUN
billiards
- **le billard américain** pool

la **bille** NOUN
marble (*toy*) ◇ *jouer aux billes* to play marbles

le **billet** NOUN
1 *ticket* ◇ *un billet d'avion* a plane ticket
2 *banknote* ◇ *un billet de cent francs* a 100 franc note

le **billion** NOUN
billion

la **biographie** NOUN
biography

la **biologie** NOUN
biology

biologique ADJECTIVE
1 *organic* ◇ *des légumes biologiques* organic vegetables
2 *biological* ◇ *des armes biologiques* biological weapons

la **Birmanie** NOUN
Burma

bis ADVERB
see also **bis** NOUN
◇ *Il habite au douze bis rue des Fleurs.* He lives at 12A rue des Fleurs.

le **bis** NOUN
see also **bis** ADVERB
encore

la **biscotte** NOUN
toasted bread (*sold in packets*)

le **biscuit** NOUN
biscuit
- **un biscuit de Savoie** a sponge cake

la **bise** NOUN
kiss ◇ *Grosses bises de Bretagne.* Love and kisses from Brittany.

bissextile ADJECTIVE
- **une année bissextile** a leap year

le **bistrot** NOUN (*informal*)
café

Cafés in France sell both alcoholic and non-alcoholic drinks.

bizarre ADJECTIVE
strange

la **blague** NOUN (*informal*)
1 *joke* ◇ *raconter une blague* to tell a joke
- **Sans blague!** No kidding!
2 *trick* ◇ *André nous a encore fait une blague!* André has played a trick on us again!

blaguer VERB (informal)
  to joke

le **blaireau** NOUN
  (PL les **blaireaux**)
  shaving brush

blâmer VERB
  to blame

blanc ADJECTIVE
  (FEM SING **blanche**)
  see also blanc NOUN
  1 *white* ◦ *un chemisier blanc* a white blouse
  2 *blank* ◦ *une page blanche* a blank page

le **blanc** NOUN
  see also blanc ADJECTIVE
  1 *white* ◦ *Colette est habillée tout en blanc.* Colette is dressed all in white.
  2 *white wine* ◦ *un verre de blanc* a glass of white wine
  ◆ **un blanc d'œuf** an egg white
  ◆ **un blanc de poulet** a chicken breast

le **Blanc** NOUN
  white man

la **Blanche** NOUN
  white woman

blanche ADJECTIVE see **blanc**

la **blanchisserie** NOUN
  laundry

le **blé** NOUN
  wheat

blessé ADJECTIVE
  see also blessé NOUN
  injured

le **blessé** NOUN
  see also blessé ADJECTIVE
  injured person ◦ *L'accident a fait trois blessés.* Three people were injured in the accident.

la **blessée** NOUN
  injured person

blesser VERB
  1 *to injure* ◦ *Il a été blessé dans un accident de voiture.* He was injured in a car accident.
  2 *to hurt* ◦ *Il a fait exprès de le blesser.* He hurt him on purpose.
  ◆ **se blesser** to hurt oneself ◦ *Je me suis blessé au pied.* I've hurt my foot.

la **blessure** NOUN
  injury

bleu ADJECTIVE
  see also bleu NOUN
  1 *blue* ◦ *une veste bleue* a blue jacket
  ◆ **bleu marine** navy blue
  2 *very rare* (steak)

le **bleu** NOUN
  see also bleu ADJECTIVE
  1 *blue* ◦ *Le bleu est ma couleur préférée.* Blue is my favourite colour.
  2 *bruise* ◦ *Il a un bleu au front.* He's got a bruise on his forehead.

le **bleuet** NOUN
  cornflower

le **bloc** NOUN
  pad ◦ *un bloc de papier à lettres* a pad of writing paper
  ◆ **le bloc opératoire** the operating theatre

le **bloc-notes** NOUN
  (PL les **blocs-notes**)
  note pad

blond ADJECTIVE
  blond
  ◆ **blond cendré** ash blond ◦ *Andrew a les cheveux blond cendré.* Andrew has ash blond hair.

bloquer VERB
  to block ◦ *bloquer le passage* to block the way
  ◆ **être bloqué dans un embouteillage** to be stuck in a traffic jam

se **blottir** VERB
  to huddle ◦ *Ils étaient blottis l'un contre l'autre.* They were huddled together.

la **blouse** NOUN
  overall

le **blouson** NOUN
  jacket ◦ *un blouson en cuir* a leather jacket

la **bobine** NOUN
  reel ◦ *une bobine de fil* a reel of thread

le **bocal** NOUN
  (PL les **bocaux**)
  jar

le **bœuf** NOUN
  1 *ox*
  2 *beef* ◦ *un rôti de bœuf* a joint of beef

bof EXCLAMATION (informal)
  ◆ **Le film t'a plu? – Bof! C'était pas terrible!** Did you like the film? – Well...it wasn't that great!
  ◆ **Comment ça va? – Bof! Pas terrible.** How is it going? – Oh...not too well actually.

le **bohémien** NOUN
  gipsy

la **bohémienne** NOUN
  gipsy

boire VERB
  to drink
  ◆ **boire un coup** (informal) to have a drink

le **bois** NOUN
  wood
  ◆ **en bois** wooden ◦ *une table en bois* a

wooden table
* **avoir la gueule de bois** (*informal*) to have a hangover

la **boisson** NOUN
drink

la **boîte** NOUN
1 *box* ◇ *une boîte d'allumettes* a box of matches
* **une boîte aux lettres** a letter box
* **une boîte postale** a PO Box
2 *tin* ◇ *une boîte de sardines* a tin of sardines
* **une boîte de conserve** a tin
* **en boîte** tinned ◇ *des petits pois en boîte* tinned peas
* **une boîte de nuit** a night club

boiter VERB
to limp

le **bol** NOUN
bowl
* **en avoir ras le bol** (*informal*) to be fed up ◇ *J'en ai ras le bol de ce boulot.* I'm fed up with this job.

bombarder VERB
to bomb

la **bombe** NOUN
1 *bomb* ◇ *une bombe atomique* an atomic bomb
2 *aerosol* ◇ *du déodorant en bombe* aérosol aerosol deodorant

bon ADJECTIVE, ADVERB
(FEM SING **bonne**)
see also bon NOUN
1 *good* ◇ *un bon restaurant* a good restaurant ◇ *Le tabac n'est pas bon pour la santé.* Smoking isn't good for you.
* **être bon en maths** to be good at maths
* **sentir bon** to smell nice
* **Bon voyage!** Have a good trip!
* **Bon weekend!** Have a nice weekend!
* **Bonne chance!** Good luck!
* **Bonne nuit!** Good night!
* **Bon anniversaire!** Happy birthday!
* **Bonne année!** Happy New Year!
2 *right* ◇ *Il est arrivé au bon moment.* He arrived at the right moment. ◇ *Ce n'est pas la bonne réponse.* That's not the right answer.
* **Il fait bon aujourd'hui.** It's nice today.
* **de bonne heure** early
* **bon marché** cheap ◇ *Les fraises ne sont pas bon marché en hiver.* Strawberries aren't cheap in winter.
* **Ah bon?** Really? ◇ *Je pars aux États-Unis la semaine prochaine. – Ah bon?* I'm going to the States next week. – Really?
* **J'aimerais vraiment que tu viennes! – Bon, d'accord.** I'd really like

you to come! – OK then, I will.

le **bon** NOUN
see also bon ADJECTIVE
voucher ◇ *un bon d'achat* a voucher
* **pour de bon** for good ◇ *Cette fois, c'est pour de bon.* This time it's for good.

le **bonbon** NOUN
sweet

bondé ADJECTIVE
crowded

bondir VERB
to leap

le **bonheur** NOUN
happiness
* **porter bonheur** to bring luck

le **bonhomme** NOUN
(PL les **bonshommes**)
* **un bonhomme de neige** a snowman

bonjour EXCLAMATION
1 *Hello!* ◇ *Donne le bonjour à tes parents de ma part.* Say hello to your parents for me.
2 *Good morning!*
3 *Good afternoon!*
bonjour is used in the morning and afternoon; in the evening **bonsoir** is used instead.
* **C'est simple comme bonjour!** It's easy as pie!

bonne ADJECTIVE see **bon**

le **bonnet** NOUN
hat ◇ *un bonnet de laine* a woolly hat
* **un bonnet de bain** a bathing cap

bonsoir EXCLAMATION
Good evening!

la **bonté** NOUN
kindness

le **bord** NOUN
1 *edge* ◇ *le bord de la table* the edge of the table
2 *side* ◇ *Jane a garé sa voiture au bord de la route.* Jane parked her car on the side of the road.
* **au bord de la mer** at the seaside
* **au bord de l'eau** by the water
* **monter à bord** to go on board
* **être au bord des larmes** to be on the verge of tears

le **bordeaux** NOUN
see also bordeaux ADJECTIVE
Bordeaux wine
* **du bordeaux rouge** claret

bordeaux ADJECTIVE
see also bordeaux NOUN
maroon ◇ *une jupe bordeaux* a maroon skirt

le **bordel** NOUN
brothel ◇ *Quel bordel!* (*informal*) What a bloody mess!

border VERB

1 *to line* ◇ *une route bordée d'arbres* a tree-lined street

2 *to trim* ◇ *un col bordé de dentelle* a collar trimmed with lace

3 *to tuck up* ◇ *Sa mère vient la border tous les soirs.* Her mother comes and tucks her up every night.

la **bordure** NOUN

border

* **une villa en bordure de mer** a villa right by the sea

la **Bosnie** NOUN

Bosnia

* **la Bosnie-Herzégovine** Bosnia-Herzegovina

la **bosse** NOUN

bump ◇ *Jacques a une grosse bosse au front.* Jacques has got a big bump on his forehead. ◇ *La route est pleine de bosses.* The road is very bumpy.

le **bossu** NOUN

hunchback

la **bossue** NOUN

hunchback

botanique ADJECTIVE

see also botanique NOUN

botanic ◇ *les jardins botaniques* the botanic gardens

la **botanique** NOUN

see also botanique ADJECTIVE

botany

la **botte** NOUN

1 *boot* ◇ *une paire de bottes* a pair of boots

* **les bottes de caoutchouc** wellington boots

2 *bunch* ◇ *une botte de radis* a bunch of radishes

le **bottin** ® NOUN

phone book

le **bouc** NOUN

1 *goatee beard*

2 *billy goat*

* **un bouc émissaire** a scapegoat

la **bouche** NOUN

mouth

* **le bouche à bouche** the kiss of life
* **une bouche d'égout** a manhole
* **une bouche de métro** an entrance to the underground

la **bouchée** NOUN

mouthful

* **une bouchée à la reine** a chicken vol-au-vent

boucher VERB

see also boucher NOUN

1 *to fill* ◇ *boucher un trou* to fill a hole

2 *to block* ◇ *L'évier est bouché.* The sink is blocked. ◇ *J'ai le nez bouché.* My nose is blocked.

le **boucher** NOUN

see also boucher VERB

butcher ◇ *Il est boucher.* He's a butcher.

la **bouchère** NOUN

butcher ◇ *Elle est bouchère.* She's a butcher.

la **boucherie** NOUN

butcher's

le **bouchon** NOUN

1 *top* (of plastic bottle)

2 *cork* (of wine bottle)

3 *hold-up* ◇ *Il y avait beaucoup de bouchons sur l'autoroute.* There were a lot of hold-ups on the motorway.

la **boucle** NOUN

curl (of hair)

* **une boucle d'oreille** an earring ◇ *une paire de boucles d'oreille* a pair of earrings

bouclé ADJECTIVE

curly

le **bouclier** NOUN

shield

le/la **bouddhiste** NOUN

Buddhist

bouder VERB

to sulk

le **boudin** NOUN

* **le boudin noir** black pudding
* **le boudin blanc** white pudding

la **boue** NOUN

mud

la **bouée** NOUN

buoy

* **une bouée de sauvetage** a life buoy

boueux ADJECTIVE

(FEM SING **boueuse**)

muddy

la **bouffe** NOUN (informal)

food ◇ *La bouffe est infecte à la cantine.* The food in the canteen is revolting.

la **bouffée** NOUN

* **une bouffée d'air frais** a breath of fresh air

bouffer VERB (informal)

to eat

le **bougeoir** NOUN

candlestick

bouger VERB

to move

la **bougie** NOUN

candle

la **bouillabaisse** NOUN

fish soup

bouillant ADJECTIVE

1. *boiling* ◦ *Faites cuire les pâtes à l'eau bouillante.* Cook the pasta in boiling water.

2. *piping hot* ◦ *La soupe est servie bouillante.* The soup should be served piping hot.

bouillir VERB

to boil ◦ *L'eau bout.* The water's boiling.

- **Je bous d'impatience.** I'm bursting with impatience.

la **bouilloire** NOUN

kettle

le **bouillon** NOUN

stock ◦ *du bouillon de légumes* vegetable stock

la **bouillotte** NOUN

hot-water bottle

le **boulanger** NOUN

baker ◦ *Il est boulanger.* He's a baker.

la **boulangère** NOUN

baker ◦ *Elle est boulangère.* She's a baker.

la **boulangerie** NOUN

baker's

la **boule** NOUN

ball ◦ *une boule de cristal* a crystal ball

- **une boule de neige** a snowball
- **jouer aux boules** to play bowls

le **boulevard** NOUN

boulevard

bouleverser VERB

1. *to move deeply* ◦ *Cette histoire déchirante m'a bouleversée.* This heartbreaking story moved me deeply.

2. *to shatter* ◦ *La mort de son ami l'a bouleversé.* He was shattered by the death of his friend.

3. *to turn upside down* ◦ *Cette rencontre a bouleversé sa vie.* This meeting turned his life upside down.

le **boulot** NOUN (informal)

1. *job* ◦ *Anita a trouvé du boulot.* Anita has found a job.

2. *work* ◦ *J'ai beaucoup de boulot en ce moment.* I've got a lot of work to do at the moment.

la **boum** NOUN (informal)

party

le **bouquet** NOUN

bunch of flowers ◦ *un bouquet de roses* a bunch of roses

le **bouquin** NOUN (informal)

book

bouquiner VERB (informal)

to read

bourdonner VERB

to buzz

le **bourg** NOUN

small market town

bourgeois ADJECTIVE

middle-class ◦ *un quartier bourgeois* a posh area

le **bourgeon** NOUN

bud

la **Bourgogne** NOUN

Burgundy

bourré ADJECTIVE

- **bourré de** stuffed with ◦ *un portefeuille bourré de billets* a wallet stuffed with banknotes
- **être bourré** (informal) to be plastered ◦ *Il était complètement bourré.* He was completely plastered.

le **bourreau** NOUN

(PL les **bourreaux**)

executioner

- **C'est un véritable bourreau de travail.** He's a real workaholic.

bourrer VERB

to stuff ◦ *bourrer une valise de vêtements* to stuff clothes into a case

la **bourse** NOUN

grant

- **la Bourse** the Stock Exchange

bous VERB *see* **bouillir**

la **bousculade** NOUN

crush ◦ *la bousculade dans les grands magasins au moment des soldes* the crush in the big stores at sale time

bousculer VERB

1. *to jostle* ◦ *être bousculé par la foule* to be jostled by the crowd

2. *to rush* ◦ *Je n'aime pas qu'on me bouscule.* I don't like to be rushed.

la **boussole** NOUN

compass

bout VERB *see* **bouillir**

le **bout** NOUN

1. *end* ◦ *Elle habite au bout de la rue.* She lives at the end of the street. ◦ *Jane est assise en bout de table.* Jane is sitting at the end of the table.

2. *tip* ◦ *le bout du nez* the tip of the nose

3. *bit* ◦ *un petit bout de fromage* a bit of cheese

- **un bout de papier** a scrap of paper
- **au bout de** after ◦ *Au bout d'un moment, il s'est endormi.* After a while he fell asleep.
- **Elle est à bout.** She's at the end of her tether.

la **bouteille** NOUN

bottle ◦ *une bouteille de vin rouge* a bottle of red wine

- **une bouteille de gaz** a gas cylinder

la **boutique** NOUN
shop
le **bouton** NOUN
[1] *button*
[2] *spot* (*on skin*) ◇ *J'ai un bouton sur le nez.* I've got a spot on my nose.
[3] *bud* ◇ *un bouton de rose* a rosebud
➤ **un bouton d'or** a buttercup
le **bowling** NOUN
[1] *tenpin bowling*
[2] *bowling alley*
la **boxe** NOUN
boxing
le **boxeur** NOUN
boxer
le **bracelet** NOUN
bracelet
le **bracelet-montre** NOUN
wristwatch
le **brancard** NOUN
stretcher
le **brancardier** NOUN
stretcher-bearer
la **branche** NOUN
branch
branché ADJECTIVE (*informal*)
trendy ◇ *avoir un look branché* to look trendy
brancher VERB
[1] *to connect* ◇ *Le téléphone est branché?* Is the phone connected?
[2] *to plug in* ◇ *L'aspirateur n'est pas branché.* The hoover isn't plugged in.
le **bras** NOUN
arm
la **brasse** NOUN
breaststroke ◇ *nager la brasse* to do the breaststroke
la **brasserie** NOUN
café-restaurant
brave ADJECTIVE
nice ◇ *C'est un brave type.* He's a nice enough fellow.
bravo EXCLAMATION
Bravo!
le **break** NOUN
estate car
la **brebis** NOUN
ewe
➤ **le fromage de brebis** sheep's cheese
bref ADJECTIVE, ADVERB
(FEM SING **brève**)
short ◇ *Sa lettre était brève.* His letter was short.
➤ **en bref** in brief ◇ *l'actualité en bref* the news in brief
➤ **...bref, ça s'est bien terminé.** ...to cut a long story short, it turned out all right in the end.

le **Brésil** NOUN
Brazil
la **Bretagne** NOUN
Brittany
la **bretelle** NOUN
strap ◇ *La bretelle de son soutien-gorge dépasse.* Her bra strap is showing.
➤ **les bretelles** braces ◇ *Il porte des bretelles.* He's wearing braces.
breton ADJECTIVE, NOUN
(FEM SING **bretonne**)
Breton ◇ *Ils parlent breton.* They speak Breton.
➤ **un Breton** a Breton (*man*)
➤ **une Bretonne** a Breton (*woman*)
➤ **les Bretons** the Bretons
brève ADJECTIVE *see* **bref**
le **brevet** NOUN
certificate
le **bricolage** NOUN
do-it-yourself ◇ *Elle aime le bricolage.* She likes doing DIY. ◇ *un magasin de bricolage* a DIY shop
la **bricole** NOUN (*informal*)
➤ **J'ai acheté une bricole pour le bébé de Sabine.** I've bought a little something for Sabine's baby.
➤ **J'ai encore quelques bricoles à faire avant de partir.** I've still got a few things to do before I go.
bricoler VERB
to do DIY ◇ *Pascal aime bricoler.* Pascal loves doing DIY.
le **bricoleur** NOUN
DIY enthusiast
la **bricoleuse** NOUN
DIY enthusiast
le **bridge** NOUN
bridge (*game*) ◇ *Horst adore jouer au bridge.* Horst loves playing bridge.
brièvement ADVERB
briefly ◇ *Expliquez-moi brièvement ce qui s'est passé.* Tell me briefly what happened.
la **brigade** NOUN
squad (*of police*) ◇ *la brigade des stups* (*informal*) the drugs squad
brillamment ADVERB
brilliantly ◇ *Il a réussi brillamment à son examen.* He did brilliantly in the exam.
brillant ADJECTIVE
[1] *brilliant* ◇ *une brillante carrière* a brilliant career ◇ *Ses notes ne sont pas brillantes.* His marks aren't brilliant.
[2] *shiny* ◇ *des cheveux brillants* shiny hair
briller VERB

to shine

le **brin** NOUN
- **un brin d'herbe** a blade of grass
- **un brin de muguet** a sprig of lily of the valley

la **brindille** NOUN
twig

la **brioche** NOUN
brioche bun

la **brique** NOUN
brick

le **briquet** NOUN
cigarette lighter

la **brise** NOUN
breeze

se **briser** VERB
to break ◇ *Le vase s'est brisé en mille morceaux.* The vase broke into a thousand pieces.

e/la **Britannique** NOUN
Briton
- **les Britanniques** the British

britannique ADJECTIVE
British

la **brocante** NOUN
junk ◇ *un magasin de brocante* a junk shop

le **brocanteur** NOUN
dealer in second-hand goods

la **brocanteuse** NOUN
dealer in second-hand goods

la **broche** NOUN
brooch ◇ *une broche en argent* a silver brooch
- **à la broche** spit-roasted ◇ *un poulet à la broche* a spit-roasted chicken

la **brochette** NOUN
skewer
- **les brochettes d'agneau** lamb kebabs

la **brochure** NOUN
brochure

broder VERB
to embroider

la **broderie** NOUN
embroidery

la **bronchite** NOUN
bronchitis ◇ *avoir une bronchite* to have bronchitis

le **bronze** NOUN
bronze ◇ *la médaille de bronze* the bronze medal

bronzer VERB
to get a tan ◇ *Il est bien bronzé.* He's got a good tan.
- **se bronzer** to sunbathe

la **brosse** NOUN
brush
- **une brosse à cheveux** a hairbrush
- **une brosse à dents** a toothbrush

- **Il est coiffé en brosse.** He's got a crew cut.

brosser VERB
to brush
- **se brosser les dents** to brush one's teeth ◇ *Je me brosse les dents tous les soirs.* I brush my teeth every night.

la **brouette** NOUN
wheelbarrow

le **brouillard** NOUN
fog ◇ *Il y a du brouillard.* It's foggy.

le **brouillon** NOUN
first draft ◇ *Ce n'est qu'un brouillon.* It's just a first draft.

les **broussailles** FEM NOUN
undergrowth

brouter VERB
to graze (animals)

broyer VERB
to crush
- **broyer du noir** to be down in the dumps

le **brugnon** NOUN
nectarine

le **bruit** NOUN
  [1] *noise* ◇ *J'ai entendu un bruit.* I heard a noise. ◇ *faire du bruit* to make a noise
- **sans bruit** without a sound
  [2] *rumour* ◇ *Des bruits circulent à son sujet.* There are rumours going round about him.

brûlant ADJECTIVE
  [1] *blazing* ◇ *un soleil brûlant* a blazing sun
  [2] *boiling hot* ◇ *Faith boit son café brûlant.* Faith drinks her coffee boiling hot.

le **brûlé** NOUN
smell of burning ◇ *Ça sent le brûlé.* There's a smell of burning.

brûler VERB
to burn
- **se brûler** to burn oneself

la **brûlure** NOUN
burn
- **des brûlures d'estomac** heartburn

la **brume** NOUN
mist

brun ADJECTIVE
brown
- **Catherine est brune.** Catherine's got dark hair.

le **brushing** NOUN
blow-dry ◇ *une coupe et un brushing* a cut and blow-dry

brusque ADJECTIVE
abrupt
- **d'un ton brusque** brusquely

brusquer VERB
 to rush ◇ *Il ne faut pas la brusquer.*
 You mustn't rush her.
brut ADJECTIVE
 • **le champagne brut** dry champagne
 • **le pétrole brut** crude oil
 • **son salaire brut** his gross salary
brutal ADJECTIVE
 (MASC PL **brutaux**)
 brutal
brutaliser VERB
 to knock about ◇ *Il a été brutalisé par
 la police.* He was treated roughly by the
 police.
Bruxelles NOUN
 Brussels
bruyamment ADVERB
 noisily
bruyant ADJECTIVE
 noisy
la **bruyère** NOUN
 heather
bu VERB *see* **boire**
la **bûche** NOUN
 log
 • **la bûche de Noël** the Yule log
 *This is what is usually eaten in France instead of
 Christmas pudding.*
le **bûcheron** NOUN
 woodcutter
le **budget** NOUN
 budget
le **buffet** NOUN
 1 *sideboard* ◇ *un buffet en chêne* an
 oak sideboard
 2 *buffet* ◇ *un buffet froid* a cold buffet
 ◇ *un buffet de gare* a station buffet
le **buisson** NOUN
 bush
la **Bulgarie** NOUN
 Bulgaria
la **bulle** NOUN
 bubble ◇ *une bulle de savon* a soap
 bubble
le **bulletin** NOUN
 1 *bulletin*

 • **le bulletin d'informations** the news
 bulletin
 2 *report* ◇ *Ton bulletin n'est pas
 fameux ce mois-ci.* Your school report
 isn't very good this month.
 • **le bulletin météorologique** the weather
 report
 • **le bulletin de salaire** pay slip
 • **le bulletin de vote** the ballot paper
le **bureau** NOUN
 (PL les **bureaux**)
 1 *desk* ◇ *Posez le dossier sur mon
 bureau.* Put the file on my desk.
 2 *office* ◇ *Il vous attend dans son
 bureau.* He's waiting for you in his
 office.
 • **un bureau de change** a bureau de
 change
 • **le bureau de poste** the post office
 • **le bureau de tabac** the tobacconist's
 • **le bureau de vote** the polling station
bus VERB *see* **boire**
le **bus** NOUN
 bus
le **buste** NOUN
 bust
but VERB *see* **boire**
le **but** NOUN
 1 *aim* ◇ *Ils n'ont pas de but dans la
 vie.* They have no aim in life.
 • **Quel est le but de votre visite?** What's
 the reason for your visit?
 • **dans le but de** with the intention of
 ◇ *Je suis venue dans le but de vous
 aider.* I came to help you.
 2 *goal* ◇ *marquer un but* to score a
 goal
le **butane** NOUN
 Calor gas ®
le **butin** NOUN
 loot ◇ *Les cambrioleurs se sont
 partagé le butin.* The burglars shared
 the stolen goods.
buvais, buvait VERB *see* **boire**
le **buvard** NOUN
 blotter

C

c' PRONOUN *see* **ce**

ça PRONOUN
  [1] *this* ◇ *Est-ce que vous pouvez me donner un peu de ça?* Can you give me a bit of this?
  [2] *that* ◇ *Est-ce que tu peux prendre ça, là-bas dans le coin?* Can you bring that from over there in the corner?
  [3] *it* ◇ *Ça ne fait rien.* It doesn't matter.
  ◆ **Comment ça va?** How are you?
  ◆ **Ça alors!** Well, well!
  ◆ **C'est ça.** That's right.
  ◆ **Ça y est!** That's it!

çà ADVERB
  ◆ **çà et là** here and there

la **cabane** NOUN
  hut

le **cabillaud** NOUN
  cod

la **cabine** NOUN
  cabin (*on a ship*)
  ◆ **une cabine d'essayage** a fitting room
  ◆ **une cabine téléphonique** a phone box

le **cabinet** NOUN
  surgery (*of doctor, of dentist*)
  ◆ **une chambre avec cabinet de toilette** a room with washing facilities

les **cabinets** MASC NOUN
  toilet

le **câble** NOUN
  cable

cabosser VERB
  to dent

la **cacahuète** NOUN
  peanut
  ◆ **le beurre de cacahuète** peanut butter

le **cacao** NOUN
  cocoa
  ◆ **le beurre de cacao** cocoa butter

cache-cache MASC NOUN
  ◆ **jouer à cache-cache** to play hide-and-seek

le **cachemire** NOUN
  cashmere ◇ *un pull en cachemire* a cashmere jumper

le **cache-nez** NOUN
  (PL les **cache-nez**)
  long woollen scarf

cacher VERB
  to hide ◇ *J'ai caché les cadeaux sous le lit.* I hid the presents under the bed.
  ◇ *Tu me caches quelque chose!* You're hiding something!
  ◆ **se cacher** to hide ◇ *Elle s'est cachée sous la table.* She's hiding under the

table.

le **cachet** NOUN
  [1] *tablet*
  ◆ **un cachet d'aspirine** an aspirin
  [2] *fee* (*for performer*) ◇ *Il a touché un gros cachet pour ce concert.* He got a big fee for the concert.
  ◆ **le cachet de la poste** the postmark

la **cachette** NOUN
  hiding place
  ◆ **en cachette** on the sly ◇ *Il est sorti en cachette sans réveiller ses parents.* He crept out on the sly without waking his parents.

le **cachot** NOUN
  dungeon

le **cactus** NOUN
  cactus

le **cadavre** NOUN
  corpse

le **Caddie** ® NOUN
  supermarket trolley

le **cadeau** NOUN
  (PL les **cadeaux**)
  present
  ◆ **faire un cadeau à quelqu'un** to give somebody a present

le **cadenas** NOUN
  padlock

cadet ADJECTIVE
  (FEM SING **cadette**)
  see also **cadet** NOUN
  [1] *younger* (*brother, sister*) ◇ *ma sœur cadette* my younger sister
  [2] *youngest* (*son, daughter*) ◇ *son fils cadet* his youngest son

le **cadet** NOUN
  see also **cadet** ADJECTIVE
  youngest ◇ *C'est le cadet de la famille.* He's the youngest of the family.

la **cadette** NOUN
  youngest ◇ *C'est la cadette de la famille.* She's the youngest of the family.

le **cadre** NOUN
  [1] *frame* ◇ *un cadre en bois* a wooden frame
  [2] *surroundings* ◇ *L'hôtel est situé dans un très beau cadre.* The hotel is set in beautiful surroundings.
  [3] *executive* ◇ *un cadre supérieur* a senior executive

le **cafard** NOUN
  cockroach
  ◆ **avoir le cafard** (*informal*) to be feeling down ◇ *J'ai le cafard.* I'm feeling

down.

le **café** NOUN

   ① *coffee* ◇ *un café au lait* a white coffee

   ② *café*

   Cafés in France sell both alcoholic and non-alcoholic drinks.

le **café-tabac** NOUN

   A café-tabac *is a bar which also sells cigarettes and stamps; you can tell a* café-tabac *by the red diamond-shaped sign outside it.*

la **cafetière** NOUN

   ① *coffee maker*

   ② *coffee pot*

la **cage** NOUN

   cage

   ✦ **la cage d'escalier** the stairwell

la **cagoule** NOUN

   balaclava

le **cahier** NOUN

   exercise book ◇ *mon cahier de brouillon* my rough book

la **caille** NOUN

   quail

le **caillou** NOUN

   (PL les **cailloux**)

   pebble

la **caisse** NOUN

   ① *box* ◇ *une caisse à outils* a tool box

   ② *till* ◇ *le ticket de caisse* the till receipt

   ③ *checkout* ◇ *J'ai dû faire la queue à la caisse.* I had to queue at the checkout.

le **caissier** NOUN

   cashier

la **caissière** NOUN

   cashier

le **cake** NOUN

   fruit cake

le **calcul** NOUN

   ① *calculation* ◇ *Je me suis trompé dans mes calculs.* I made a mistake in my calculations.

   ② *arithmetic* ◇ *Je ne suis pas très bon en calcul.* I'm not very good at arithmetic.

la **calculatrice** NOUN

   calculator

calculer VERB

   to work out ◇ *J'ai calculé combien ça allait coûter.* I worked out how much it was going to cost.

la **calculette** NOUN

   pocket calculator

la **cale** NOUN

   wedge

calé ADJECTIVE (*informal*)

   ✦ **Elle est calée en histoire.** She's really good at history.

le **caleçon** NOUN

   ① *boxer shorts*

   ② *leggings*

le **calendrier** NOUN

   calendar

le **calepin** NOUN

   notebook

caler VERB

   to stall ◇ *La voiture a calé dans une côte.* The car stalled on a hill.

câlin ADJECTIVE

   see also câlin NOUN

   cuddly

le **câlin** NOUN

   see also câlin ADJECTIVE

   cuddle ◇ *faire un câlin à quelqu'un* to give somebody a cuddle

le **calmant** NOUN

   tranquillizer

calme ADJECTIVE

   see also calme NOUN

   ① *quiet* ◇ *un endroit calme* a quiet place

   ② *calm* ◇ *Elle est restée très calme.* She stayed very calm.

le **calme** NOUN

   see also calme ADJECTIVE

   peace and quiet ◇ *J'ai besoin de calme pour travailler.* I need peace and quiet to work.

calmer VERB

   to soothe ◇ *Cette pommade calme les démangeaisons.* This ointment soothes itching.

   ✦ **se calmer** to calm down ◇ *Calme-toi!* Calm down!

la **calorie** NOUN

   calorie

le/la **camarade** NOUN

   friend

   ✦ **un camarade de classe** a school friend

le **cambriolage** NOUN

   burglary

cambrioler VERB

   to burgle

le **cambrioleur** NOUN

   burglar

la **cambrioleuse** NOUN

   burglar

la **camelote** NOUN (*informal*)

   junk ◇ *C'est vraiment de la camelote.* It's absolute junk.

la **caméra** NOUN

   camera (*cinema, TV*)

le **caméscope** ® NOUN

   camcorder

le **camion** NOUN

   lorry

la **camionnette** NOUN
van

le **camionneur** NOUN
lorry driver

la **camomille** NOUN
camomile tea

le **camp** NOUN
camp ◇ *un camp de prisonniers* a prison camp ◇ *un camp de vacances* a holiday camp

la **campagne** NOUN
1 *country*
• **à la campagne** in the country ◇ *Nous passons nos vacances à la campagne.* We spend our holidays in the country.
2 *campaign* ◇ *une campagne de marketing* a marketing campaign

camper VERB
to camp

le **campeur** NOUN
camper

la **campeuse** NOUN
camper

le **camping** NOUN
camping ◇ *faire du camping* to go camping
• **un terrain de camping** a campsite

le **Canada** NOUN
Canada
• **au Canada (1)** in Canada
• **au Canada (2)** to Canada

canadien ADJECTIVE, NOUN
(FEM SING **canadienne**)
Canadian
• **un Canadien** a Canadian (*man*)
• **une Canadienne** a Canadian (*woman*)

le **canal** NOUN
(PL les **canaux**)
canal

le **canapé** NOUN
1 *sofa*
2 *open sandwich*

le **canard** NOUN
duck

le **canari** NOUN
canary

le **cancer** NOUN
cancer ◇ *le cancer du poumon* lung cancer
• **le Cancer** Cancer ◇ *Sabine est Cancer.* Sabine's Cancer.

le **candidat** NOUN
1 *candidate* (*in exam, election*)
2 *applicant* (*for job*)

la **candidate** NOUN
1 *candidate* (*in exam, election*)
2 *applicant* (*for job*)

la **candidature** NOUN
• **poser sa candidature à un poste** to apply for a job ◇ *Il a posé sa candidature à des dizaines de postes.* He has applied for dozens of jobs.

le **caneton** NOUN
duckling

la **canette** NOUN
• **une canette de bière** a small bottle of beer

le **caniche** NOUN
poodle

la **canicule** NOUN
scorching heat

le **canif** NOUN
penknife

le **caniveau** NOUN
(PL les **caniveaux**)
gutter

la **canne** NOUN
walking stick
• **une canne à pêche** a fishing rod

la **cannelle** NOUN
cinnamon

le **canoë** NOUN
1 *canoe*
2 *canoeing* ◇ *faire du canoë* to go canoeing

le **canon** NOUN
1 *gun* ◇ *un canon antichar* an anti-tank gun
2 *cannon* ◇ *un boulet de canon* a cannon ball

le **canot** NOUN
dinghy ◇ *un canot pneumatique* a rubber dinghy
• **un canot de sauvetage** a lifeboat

la **cantatrice** NOUN
opera singer

la **cantine** NOUN
canteen

le **caoutchouc** NOUN
rubber
• **des bottes en caoutchouc** Wellington boots

le **cap** NOUN
cape ◇ *le cap Horn* Cape Horn

capable ADJECTIVE
• **Elle est capable de marcher pendant des heures.** She can walk for hours.
• **Il est capable de changer d'avis au dernier moment.** He's capable of changing his mind at the last minute.

la **cape** NOUN
cape

le **capitaine** NOUN
captain

la **capitale** NOUN
capital ◇ *la capitale de la France* the capital of France

le **capot** NOUN

bonnet (of car)
la **capote** NOUN (informal)
   condom
la **câpre** NOUN
   caper (food)
le **caprice** NOUN
   ◆ **faire des caprices** to make a fuss ◇ *Il n'aime pas les enfants qui font des caprices.* He doesn't like children who make a fuss.
  capricieux ADJECTIVE
   (FEM SING **capricieuse**)
   ◆ **un enfant capricieux** an awkward child
le **Capricorne** NOUN
   Capricorn ◇ *Helen est Capricorne.* Helen's Capricorn.
  captivant ADJECTIVE
   fascinating
la **captivité** NOUN
   captivity ◇ *en captivité* in captivity
  capturer VERB
   to capture
la **capuche** NOUN
   hood ◇ *un manteau à capuche* a coat with a hood
le **capuchon** NOUN
   cap (of pen)
la **capucine** NOUN
   nasturtium
le **car** NOUN
   ⸢ *see also* **car** CONJUNCTION ⸥
   coach ◇ *un car scolaire* a school bus
  car CONJUNCTION
   ⸢ *see also* **car** NOUN ⸥
   because ◇ *Nous sommes inquiets car il n'est pas encore rentré.* We're worried because he isn't back yet.
la **carabine** NOUN
   rifle
le **caractère** NOUN
   personality ◇ *Il a le même caractère que son père.* He's got the same personality as his father.
   ◆ **Il a bon caractère.** He's good-natured.
   ◆ **Elle a mauvais caractère.** She's bad-tempered.
   ◆ **Il n'a pas un caractère facile.** He isn't easy to get on with.
  caractéristique ADJECTIVE
   ⸢ *see also* **caractéristique** NOUN ⸥
   characteristic
la **caractéristique** NOUN
   ⸢ *see also* **caractéristique** ADJECTIVE ⸥
   characteristic
la **carafe** NOUN
   jug ◇ *une carafe d'eau* a jug of water
les **Caraïbes** FEM NOUN
   Caribbean Islands
le **caramel** NOUN

1 *caramel* ◇ *la crème caramel* crème caramel
2 *toffee*
la **caravane** NOUN
   caravan
  carbonique ADJECTIVE
   ◆ **le gaz carbonique** carbon dioxide
le **carburant** NOUN
   fuel
  cardiaque ADJECTIVE
   ◆ **une crise cardiaque** a heart attack
   ◆ **Ma tante est cardiaque.** My aunt has heart trouble.
le **cardigan** NOUN
   cardigan
le/la **cardiologue** NOUN
   heart specialist
le **carême** NOUN
   Lent
la **caresse** NOUN
   stroke ◇ *faire des caresses à un chat* to stroke a cat
  caresser VERB
   to stroke
la **carie** NOUN
   tooth decay ◇ *J'ai une carie.* I've got a hole in my tooth.
  caritatif ADJECTIVE
   (FEM SING **caritative**)
   ◆ **une organisation caritative** a charity
le **carnaval** NOUN
   carnival
le **carnet** NOUN
   1 *notebook*
   2 *book* ◇ *un carnet d'adresses* an address book ◇ *un carnet de chèques* a cheque book ◇ *un carnet de timbres* a book of stamps ◇ *un carnet de tickets* a book of tickets
   ⸢ *In the Paris metro it is cheaper to buy tickets in a book of ten, known as a* **carnet**. ⸥
   ◆ **mon carnet de notes** my school report
la **carotte** NOUN
   carrot ◇ *les carottes râpées* grated carrots
  carré ADJECTIVE
   ⸢ *see also* **carré** NOUN ⸥
   square
   ◆ **un mètre carré** a square metre
le **carré** NOUN
   ⸢ *see also* **carré** ADJECTIVE ⸥
   square
le **carreau** NOUN
   (PL les **carreaux**)
   1 *check* ◇ *une chemise à carreaux* a checked shirt
   2 *tile* (on floor, wall) ◇ *Je viens de laver les carreaux de la cuisine.* I've just washed the kitchen floor.

③ *pane* ◇ *Il a cassé un carreau.* He broke a windowpane.

④ *diamonds* (*cards*) ◇ *l'as de carreau* the ace of diamonds

le **carrefour** NOUN
junction

le **carrelage** NOUN
tiled floor

carrément ADVERB
① *completely* ◇ *C'est carrément impossible.* It's completely impossible.
② *straight out* ◇ *Dis-lui carrément ce que tu penses.* Tell him straight out what you think.

la **carrière** NOUN
career
● **un militaire de carrière** a professional soldier

la **carrure** NOUN
build ◇ *Il a une carrure d'athlète.* He has an athletic build.

le **cartable** NOUN
satchel

la **carte** NOUN
① *card*
● **une carte d'anniversaire** a birthday card
● **une carte postale** a postcard
● **une carte de vœux** a Christmas card
*The French send greetings cards (**les cartes de vœux**) in January rather than at Christmas, with best wishes for the New Year.*
● **une carte bancaire** a cash card
● **une carte de crédit** a credit card
● **une carte d'embarquement** a boarding card
● **une carte d'identité** an identity card
● **une carte de séjour** a residence permit
● **une carte téléphonique** a phonecard
● **un jeu de cartes** (1) a pack of cards
● **un jeu de cartes** (2) a card game
② *map* ◇ *une carte de France* a map of France ◇ *une carte routière* a road map
③ *menu* ◇ *la carte des vins* the wine list
● **manger à la carte** to eat à la carte ◇ *Nous avons décidé de manger à la carte.* We decided to choose from the à la carte menu.

le **carton** NOUN
① *cardboard* ◇ *un morceau de carton* a piece of cardboard
② *cardboard box* ◇ *un carton à chaussures* a shoe box

la **cartouche** NOUN
cartridge
● **une cartouche de cigarettes** a carton of cigarettes

le **cas** NOUN
(PL les **cas**)
case ◇ *plusieurs cas* several cases
● **ne faire aucun cas de** to take no notice of ◇ *Il ne fait aucun cas de ce qu'on lui dit.* He takes no notice of what people say to him.
● **en aucun cas** on no account
● **en tout cas** at any rate
● **au cas où** in case ◇ *Prends un sandwich au cas où la cantine serait fermée.* Take a sandwich in case the canteen's closed.
● **en cas de** in case of ◇ *En cas d'incendie, appelez ce numéro.* In case of fire, call this number.

la **cascade** NOUN
waterfall

le **cascadeur** NOUN
stuntman

la **caserne** NOUN
barracks

cash ADVERB
● **payer cash** to pay cash

le **casier** NOUN
locker

le **casque** NOUN
① *helmet*
② *headphones*

la **casquette** NOUN
cap

cassant ADJECTIVE
● **Il m'a parlé d'un ton cassant.** He spoke to me curtly.

le **casse-croûte** NOUN
(PL les **casse-croûte**)
snack

le **casse-noix** NOUN
(PL les **casse-noix**)
nutcrackers

casse-pieds ADJECTIVE (MASC, FEM, PL)
(*informal*)
● **Il est vraiment casse-pieds!** He's a real pain in the neck!

casser VERB
to break ◇ *J'ai cassé un verre.* I've broken a glass.
● **se casser** to break ◇ *Il s'est cassé la jambe au ski.* He broke his leg when he was skiing.
● **se casser la tête** (*informal*) to go to a lot of trouble ◇ *Je ne vais pas me casser la tête pour le dîner: je vais ouvrir une boîte de conserve.* I'm not going to go to a whole lot of trouble over dinner: I'll just open a tin.

la **casserole** NOUN
saucepan

le **casse-tête** NOUN
(PL les casse-tête)
- **C'est un vrai casse-tête!** It's a real headache!

la **cassette** NOUN
cassette

le **cassis** NOUN
blackcurrant

le **castor** NOUN
beaver

le **catalogue** NOUN
catalogue

la **catastrophe** NOUN
disaster

le **catch** NOUN
wrestling

le **catéchisme** NOUN
catechism

la **catégorie** NOUN
category

catégorique ADJECTIVE
firm ◇ *un refus catégorique* a flat refusal

la **cathédrale** NOUN
cathedral

catholique ADJECTIVE
see also catholique NOUN
Catholic

e/la **catholique** NOUN
see also catholique ADJECTIVE
Catholic

le **cauchemar** NOUN
nightmare ◇ *faire un cauchemar* to have a nightmare

la **cause** NOUN
cause
- **à cause de** because of ◇ *Nous n'avons pas pu sortir à cause du mauvais temps.* We couldn't go out because of the bad weather.

causer VERB
1 *to cause* ◇ *La tempête a causé beaucoup de dégâts.* The storm caused a lot of damage.
2 *to chat* ◇ *Nous n'avons pas beaucoup eu le temps de causer.* We didn't have much time to chat.

la **caution** NOUN
1 *bail*
2 *deposit*

le **cavalier** NOUN
1 *rider*
2 *partner* (at dance)

la **cavalière** NOUN
rider

la **cave** NOUN
cellar

la **caverne** NOUN
cave

le **CD** NOUN
(PL les CD)
CD

le **CD-ROM** NOUN
(PL les CD-ROM)
CD-ROM

la **CE** NOUN (= Communauté européenne)
EC

ce ADJECTIVE
(MASC SING **cet**, FEM SING **cette**, PL **ces**)
see also ce PRONOUN
ce changes to **cet** before a vowel and most words beginning with "h".
1 *this* ◇ *Tu peux prendre ce livre.* You can take this book. ◇ *cet après-midi* this afternoon ◇ *cet hiver* this winter
- **ce livre-ci** this book
- **cette voiture-ci** this car
2 *that* ◇ *Je n'aime pas du tout ce film.* I don't like that film at all.
- **ce livre-là** that book
- **cette voiture-là** that car

ce PRONOUN
see also ce ADJECTIVE
ce changes to **c'** before the vowel in **est**, **était** and **étaient**.
it ◇ *Ce n'est pas facile.* It's not easy.
- **c'est (1)** it is ◇ *C'est vraiment trop cher.* It's really too expensive. ◇ *Ouvre, c'est moi!* Open the door, it's me!
- **c'est (2)** he is ◇ *C'est un peintre du début du siècle.* He's a painter from the turn of the century.
- **c'est (3)** she is ◇ *C'est une romancière très célèbre.* She's a very famous novelist.
- **ce sont** they are ◇ *Ce sont des amis à mes parents.* They're friends of my parents'.
- **Qui est-ce?** Who is it?
- **Qu'est-ce que c'est?** What is it?
- **ce qui** what ◇ *C'est ce qui compte.* That's what matters.
- **tout ce qui** everything that ◇ *J'ai rangé tout ce qui traînait par terre.* I've tidied up everything that was on the floor.
- **ce que** what ◇ *Je vais lui dire ce que je pense.* I'm going to tell him what I think.
- **tout ce que** everything ◇ *Tu peux avoir tout ce que tu veux.* You can have everything you want.

ceci PRONOUN
this ◇ *Prends ceci, tu en auras besoin.* Take this, you'll need it.

céder VERB
to give in ◇ *Elle a tellement insisté qu'il a fini par céder.* She went on so much

that he eventually gave in.
+ **céder à** to give in to ◇ *Je ne veux pas céder à ses caprices.* I'm not going to give in to her whims.

la **cédille** NOUN
cedilla

la **ceinture** NOUN
belt ◇ *une ceinture en cuir* a leather belt
+ **votre ceinture de sécurité** your seatbelt

cela PRONOUN
1 *it* ◇ *Cela dépend.* It depends.
2 *that* ◇ *Je n'aime pas cela.* I don't like that.
+ **C'est cela.** That's right.
+ **à part cela** apart from that

célèbre ADJECTIVE
famous

célébrer VERB
to celebrate

le **céleri** NOUN
+ **le céleri-rave** celeriac
+ **le céleri en branche** celery

célibataire ADJECTIVE, NOUN
single
+ **un célibataire** a bachelor
+ **une célibataire** a single woman

celle PRONOUN *see* **celui**

celles PRONOUN *see* **ceux**

la **cellule** NOUN
cell

celui PRONOUN
(FEM **celle**, MASC PL **ceux**, FEM PL **celles**)
the one ◇ *Prends celui que tu préfères.* Take the one you like best. ◇ *Je n'ai pas d'appareil photo mais je peux emprunter celui de ma sœur.* I haven't got a camera but I can borrow my sister's.
◇ *Je n'ai pas de platine laser mais je peux emprunter celle de mon frère.* I haven't got a CD player but I can borrow my brother's.
+ **celui-ci** this one
+ **celle-ci** this one
+ **celui-là** that one
+ **celle-là** that one

la **cendre** NOUN
ash

le **cendrier** NOUN
ashtray

censé ADJECTIVE
+ **être censé faire quelque chose** to be supposed to do something ◇ *Vous êtes censé arriver à l'heure.* You're supposed to get here on time.

cent NUMBER
a hundred ◇ *cent francs* a hundred francs

cent *is spelt with an* **-s** *when there are two or more hundreds, but not when it is followed by another number, as in "a hundred and two".*
◇ *trois cents ans* three hundred years
◇ *cent deux kilomètres* a hundred and two kilometres ◇ *trois cent cinquante kilomètres* three hundred and fifty kilometres ◇ *trois cent mille kilomètres* three hundred thousand kilometres

la **centaine** NOUN
about a hundred ◇ *Il y avait une centaine de personnes dans la salle.* There were about a hundred people in the hall.
+ **des centaines de** hundreds of ◇ *Des centaines de réfugiés se sont présentés à l'ambassade.* Hundreds of refugees came to the embassy.

le **centenaire** NOUN
centenary

centième ADJECTIVE
hundredth

le **centilitre** NOUN
centilitre

le **centime** NOUN
centime
The franc is divided into 100 centimes.
◇ *une pièce de cinquante centimes* a 50-centime coin

le **centimètre** NOUN
centimetre

central ADJECTIVE
(MASC PL **centraux**)
central

la **centrale** NOUN
power station ◇ *une centrale nucléaire* a nuclear power station

le **centre** NOUN
centre
+ **un centre commercial** a shopping centre

le **centre-ville** NOUN
town centre

cependant ADVERB
however

le **cercle** NOUN
circle ◇ *Entourez d'un cercle la bonne réponse.* Put a circle round the right answer.
+ **un cercle vicieux** a vicious circle

le **cercueil** NOUN
coffin

la **céréale** NOUN
cereal ◇ *un bol de céréales* a bowl of cereal
+ **un pain aux cinq céréales** a multigrain loaf

la **cérémonie** NOUN
ceremony

le **cerf** NOUN
stag

le **cerf-volant** NOUN
(PL les **cerfs-volants**)
kite

la **cerise** NOUN
cherry

le **cerisier** NOUN
cherry tree

cerné ADJECTIVE
* **avoir les yeux cernés** to have shadows under one's eyes ◇ *Elle avait les yeux cernés.* She had shadows under her eyes.

cerner VERB
* **J'ai du mal à le cerner.** I can't figure him out.

certain ADJECTIVE
1 *certain* ◇ *Je suis certain que je l'ai remis en place.* I'm certain that I put it back. ◇ *Ce n'est pas certain.* It's not certain.
2 *some* ◇ *Certaines personnes n'aiment pas la crème.* Some people don't like cream.
* **un certain temps** quite some time ◇ *J'ai mis un certain temps à comprendre ce qu'elle disait.* It took me quite some time to understand what she was saying.

certainement ADVERB
1 *definitely* ◇ *C'est certainement le meilleur film que j'ai vu cette année.* It's definitely the best film I've seen this year.
2 *of course* ◇ *Est-ce que je peux t'emprunter ton stylo? – Mais certainement!* Can I borrow your pen? – Of course!

certains PRONOUN
1 *some* ◇ *certains de ses amis* some of his friends ◇ *certains d'entre vous* some of you
2 *some people* ◇ *Certains pensent que le film est meilleur que le roman.* Some people think that the film is better than the novel.

certes ADVERB
certainly ◇ *Nous nous connaissons, certes, mais nous ne sommes pas amis.* We know each other, certainly, but we are not friends.

le **certificat** NOUN
certificate

le **cerveau** NOUN
(PL les **cerveaux**)
brain

la **cervelle** NOUN
brain
* **se creuser la cervelle** (*informal*) to rack

one's brains

le **CES** NOUN (= *Collège d'enseignement secondaire*)
secondary school
In France pupils go to a CES between the ages of 11 and 15, and then to a lycée until the age of 18.

ces ADJECTIVE
1 *these* ◇ *Tu peux prendre ces photos si tu veux.* You can have these photos if you like.
* **ces photos-ci** these photos
2 *those* ◇ *Ces montagnes sont dangereuses en hiver.* Those mountains are dangerous in winter.
* **ces livres-là** those books

cesse
* **sans cesse** ADVERB *continually*
* **Elle me dérange sans cesse.** She keeps interrupting me.

cesser VERB
to stop ◇ *cesser de faire quelque chose* to stop doing something

le **cessez-le-feu** NOUN
(PL les **cessez-le-feu**)
ceasefire

c'est-à-dire ADVERB
that is ◇ *Est-ce que tu peux venir lundi prochain, c'est-à-dire le quinze?* Can you come next Monday, that's the 15th?

cet ADJECTIVE
(FEM SING **cette**)
ce changes to **cet** before a vowel and most words beginning with "h".
1 *this* ◇ *cet après-midi* this afternoon ◇ *cet hiver* this winter ◇ *cette année* this year
* **cette semaine-ci** this week
2 *that* ◇ *Est-ce que tu peux me passer cette assiette?* Could you pass me that plate?
* **cet après-midi-là** that afternoon
* **cette nuit (1)** tonight ◇ *On prévoit de l'orage pour cette nuit.* A storm is forecast for tonight.
* **cette nuit (2)** last night ◇ *J'ai très mal dormi cette nuit.* I slept very badly last night.

cette PRONOUN *see* **ce**

ceux PRONOUN
(FEM PL **celles**)
the ones ◇ *Prends ceux que tu préfères.* Take the ones you like best. ◇ *Je n'ai pas de skis mais je emprunter ceux de ma sœur.* I haven't got any skis but I can borrow my sister's. ◇ *Je n'ai pas de jumelles mais je*

peux emprunter celles de mon frère. I haven't got any binoculars but I can borrow my brother's.

* **ceux-ci** these ones
* **celles-ci** these ones
* **ceux-là** those ones
* **celles-là** those ones

chacun PRONOUN

① *each* ◇ *Il nous a donné un cadeau à chacun.* He gave us each a present. ◇ *Nous avons chacun donné dix francs.* We each gave 10 francs.

② *everyone* ◇ *Chacun fait ce qu'il veut.* Everyone does what they like.

le **chagrin** NOUN

* **avoir du chagrin** to be very upset ◇ *Elle a eu beaucoup de chagrin à la mort de sa tante.* She was terribly upset by the death of her aunt.

le **chahut** NOUN

bedlam ◇ *Il y avait du chahut dans la classe.* There was bedlam in the classroom.

la **chaîne** NOUN

① *chain* ◇ *une chaîne en or* a gold chain

② *channel* (*on TV*) ◇ *Le film passe sur quelque chaîne?* Which channel is the film on?

* **une chaîne hi-fi** a hi-fi system
* **une chaîne laser** a CD player
* **une chaîne stéréo** a music centre
* **travailler à la chaîne** to work on an assembly line

la **chair** NOUN

flesh

* **en chair et en os** in the flesh ◇ *J'ai vu Mel Gibson en chair et en os.* I saw Mel Gibson in the flesh.
* **avoir la chair de poule** to have goose pimples

la **chaise** NOUN

chair

* **une chaise longue** a deckchair

le **châle** NOUN

shawl

la **chaleur** NOUN

① *heat*

② *warmth*

chaleureux ADJECTIVE

(FEM SING **chaleureuse**)

warm ◇ *un accueil chaleureux* a warm welcome

se **chamailler** VERB (*informal*)

to squabble ◇ *Elle se chamaille sans cesse avec son frère.* She's always squabbling with her brother.

la **chambre** NOUN

room ◇ *C'est la chambre de Camille.*

This is Camille's room.

* **une chambre à coucher** a bedroom
* **une chambre d'amis** a spare room
* **une chambre à un lit** a single room
* **une chambre pour deux personnes** a double room

le **chameau** NOUN

(PL les **chameaux**)

camel

le **champ** NOUN

field

le **champagne** NOUN

champagne

le **champignon** NOUN

mushroom ◇ *une omelette aux champignons* a mushroom omelette

* **un champignon de Paris** a button mushroom

le **champion** NOUN

champion

le **championnat** NOUN

championship ◇ *le championnat du monde* the world championship

la **championne** NOUN

champion

la **chance** NOUN

① *luck*

* **Bonne chance!** Good luck!
* **avoir de la chance** to be lucky ◇ *Tu as de la chance de partir au soleil!* You're lucky, going off to the sun!

② *chance* ◇ *Il n'a aucune chance.* He's got no chance. ◇ *Il a des chances de réussir.* He's got a good chance of passing.

le **change** NOUN

exchange ◇ *le taux de change* the exchange rate

le **changement** NOUN

change ◇ *Il n'aime pas le changement.* He doesn't like changes.

changer VERB

to change ◇ *Il n'a pas beaucoup changé.* He hasn't changed much. ◇ *J'ai changé les draps ce matin.* I changed the sheets this morning. ◇ *J'ai changé trois cents francs.* I changed 300 francs.

* **se changer** to get changed ◇ *Je vais me changer avant de sortir.* I'm going to get changed before I go out.
* **changer de** to change ◇ *Je change de chaussures et j'arrive!* I'll change my shoes and then I'll be ready!
* **changer d'avis** to change one's mind ◇ *Appelle-moi si tu changes d'avis.* Give me a ring if you change your mind.

la **chanson** NOUN

song

le **chant** NOUN
  singing ◦ *des cours de chant* singing
  lessons
  ◦ **un chant de Noël** a Christmas carol
le **chantage** NOUN
  blackmail ◦ *faire du chantage à
  quelqu'un* to blackmail somebody
  chanter VERB
  to sing
le **chanteur** NOUN
  singer
la **chanteuse** NOUN
  singer
le **chantier** NOUN
  building site
la **Chantilly** NOUN
  whipped cream
  chantonner VERB
  to hum
le **chapeau** NOUN
  (PL les **chapeaux**)
  hat
la **chapelle** NOUN
  chapel
le **chapitre** NOUN
  chapter
  chaque ADJECTIVE
  ① *every* ◦ *chaque année* every year
  ② *each* ◦ *Ces verres coûtent cinquante
  francs chaque.* These glasses cost 50
  francs each.
le **char** NOUN
  tank (military)
le **charabia** NOUN (informal)
  gibberish ◦ *Je n'y comprends rien:
  c'est du charabia.* I don't understand
  any of it: it's gibberish.
la **charade** NOUN
  ① *riddle*
  ② *charade* ◦ *jouer aux charades* to
  play charades
le **charbon** NOUN
  coal
  ◦ **le charbon de bois** charcoal
la **charcuterie** NOUN
  ① *pork butcher's*
  ② *cold meats*
  > A charcuterie *sells cuts of pork and pork
  > products such as sausages, salami and pâté, as
  > well as various cooked dishes and salads;
  > charcuterie served at a meal is an assortment
  > of ham, sausage and pâtés.*
le **charcutier** NOUN
  pork butcher
la **charcutière** NOUN
  pork butcher
le **chardon** NOUN
  thistle
  charger VERB

  to load
  ◦ **charger quelqu'un de faire quelque
  chose** to tell somebody to do
  something ◦ *Paul m'a chargé de vous
  dire que la clé est sous le paillasson.*
  Paul told me to tell you that the key's
  under the mat.
le **chariot** NOUN
  trolley (at supermarket)
  charmant ADJECTIVE
  charming
le **charme** NOUN
  charm
  charmer VERB
  to charm
la **charrue** NOUN
  plough
la **chasse** NOUN
  ① *hunting* ◦ *un chien de chasse* a
  hunting dog
  ② *shooting* ◦ *la chasse au canard*
  duck shooting
  ◦ **tirer la chasse d'eau** to flush the toilet
le **chasse-neige** NOUN
  (PL les **chasse-neige**)
  snowplough
  chasser VERB
  ① *to hunt* ◦ *Mon père chasse le lapin.*
  My father hunts rabbits.
  ② *to chase away* ◦ *Ils ont chassé les
  cambrioleurs.* They chased away the
  robbers.
  ③ *to get rid of* ◦ *Ouvre donc la fenêtre
  pour chasser les odeurs de cuisine.*
  Open the window to get rid of the
  cooking smells.
le **chasseur** NOUN
  hunter
le **chat** NOUN
  cat
la **châtaigne** NOUN
  chestnut
le **châtaignier** NOUN
  chestnut tree
  châtain ADJECTIVE (MASC, FEM, PL)
  brown ◦ *J'ai les cheveux châtain.* I've
  got brown hair.
le **château** NOUN
  (PL les **châteaux**)
  ① *castle*
  ◦ **un château fort** a castle
  ② *palace* ◦ *le château de Versailles*
  the palace of Versailles
le **chaton** NOUN
  kitten
  chatouiller VERB
  to tickle
  chatouilleux ADJECTIVE
  (FEM SING **chatouilleuse**)

ticklish

la **chatte** NOUN
cat (female)

chaud ADJECTIVE
1 *warm* ◦ *des vêtements chauds* warm clothes
- **avoir chaud** to be warm ◦ *J'ai assez chaud.* I'm warm enough.
2 *hot* ◦ *Il fait chaud aujourd'hui.* It's hot today. ◦ *un plat chaud* a hot dish ◦ *Attention, c'est chaud!* Mind, it's hot! ◦ *J'ai trop chaud!* I'm too hot!

le **chauffage** NOUN
heating ◦ *Le chauffage est en panne.* The heating isn't working.
- **le chauffage central** central heating

le **chauffe-eau** NOUN
(PL les **chauffe-eau**)
water heater

chauffer VERB
to warm ◦ *Je vais mettre de l'eau à chauffer pour faire du thé.* I'm going to put some water on to make tea.

le **chauffeur** NOUN
driver

le **chaume** NOUN
- **un toit de chaume** a thatched roof

chausser VERB
- **Vous chaussez du combien?** What size shoe do you take?

la **chaussette** NOUN
sock

le **chausson** NOUN
slipper
- **un chausson aux pommes** an apple turnover

la **chaussure** NOUN
shoe
- **les chaussures de ski** ski boots

chauve ADJECTIVE
bald

la **chauve-souris** NOUN
(PL les **chauves-souris**)
bat (animal)

le **chef** NOUN
1 *head* ◦ *le chef de famille* the head of the family
- **le chef de l'État** the Head of State
2 *boss* ◦ *Je dois demander la permission à mon chef.* I have to get permission from my boss.
- **un chef d'entreprise** a company director
3 *chef* ◦ *la spécialité du chef* the chef's speciality
- **un chef d'orchestre** a conductor

le **chef-d'œuvre** NOUN
(PL les **chefs-d'œuvre**)
masterpiece

le **chemin** NOUN
1 *path* ◦ *Je suis descendu à la plage par un petit chemin.* I went down a little path to the beach.
2 *way* ◦ *Quel est le chemin le plus court pour aller à l'aéroport?* What's the quickest way to the airport?
- **en chemin** on the way ◦ *Je mangerai mon sandwich en chemin.* I'll eat my sandwich on the way.
- **les chemins de fer** the railways

la **cheminée** NOUN
1 *chimney*
2 *fireplace*

la **chemise** NOUN
1 *shirt* ◦ *une chemise à carreaux* a checked shirt
- **une chemise de nuit** a nightdress
2 *folder* ◦ *J'ai classé mes cours dans des chemises de couleurs différentes.* I've sorted my notes into different coloured folders.

le **chemisier** NOUN
blouse

le **chêne** NOUN
oak ◦ *une armoire en chêne* an oak wardrobe

le **chenil** NOUN
kennels

la **chenille** NOUN
caterpillar

le **chèque** NOUN
cheque
- **les chèques de voyage** traveller's cheques

le **chéquier** NOUN
cheque book

cher ADJECTIVE, ADVERB
(FEM SING **chère**)
1 *dear* ◦ *Chère Mélusine...* Dear Mélusine...
2 *expensive* ◦ *C'est trop cher.* It's too expensive. ◦ *coûter cher* to be expensive

chercher VERB
1 *to look for* ◦ *Je cherche mes clés.* I'm looking for my keys.
2 *to look up* ◦ *chercher un mot dans le dictionnaire* to look up a word in the dictionary
- **aller chercher (1)** to go to get ◦ *Elle est allée chercher du pain pour ce midi.* She's gone to get some bread for lunch.
- **aller chercher (2)** to pick up ◦ *J'irai te chercher à la gare.* I'll pick you up at the station.

le **chercheur** NOUN
scientist

la **chercheuse** NOUN

scientist

chère ADJECTIVE _see_ **cher**

chéri ADJECTIVE

see also **chéri** NOUN

darling ◇ _ma petite fille chérie_ my darling daughter

le **chéri** NOUN

see also **chéri** ADJECTIVE

darling

• **mon chéri** darling

la **chérie** NOUN

darling

• **ma chérie** darling

le **cheval** NOUN

(PL les **chevaux**)

horse ◇ _un cheval de course_ a racehorse

• **à cheval** on horseback

• **faire du cheval** to go riding

le **chevalier** NOUN

knight

la **chevalière** NOUN

signet ring

chevalin ADJECTIVE

• **une boucherie chevaline** a horsemeat butcher's

les **chevaux** MASC NOUN _see_ **cheval**

le **chevet** NOUN

• **une table de chevet** a bedside table

• **une lampe de chevet** a bedside lamp

les **cheveux** MASC NOUN

hair ◇ _Elle a les cheveux courts._ She's got short hair.

la **cheville** NOUN

ankle

la **chèvre** NOUN

goat

• **le fromage de chèvre** goat's cheese

le **chevreau** NOUN

(PL les **chevreaux**)

kid (animal, leather)

le **chèvrefeuille** NOUN

honeysuckle

le **chevreuil** NOUN

1 _roe deer_

2 _venison_ ◇ _un rôti de chevreuil_ roast venison

le **chewing-gum** NOUN

chewing gum

chez PREPOSITION

• **chez Pierre (1)** at Pierre's house

• **chez Pierre (2)** to Pierre's house

• **chez moi (1)** at my house ◇ _Je suis resté chez moi ce week-end._ I stayed at home this weekend.

• **chez moi (2)** to my house ◇ _Je vais rentrer chez moi._ I'm going home.

• **chez le dentiste (1)** at the dentist's ◇ _J'ai rendez-vous chez le dentiste_

demain matin. I've got an appointment at the dentist's tomorrow morning.

• **chez le dentiste (2)** to the dentist's ◇ _Je vais chez le dentiste._ I'm going to the dentist's.

chic ADJECTIVE

1 _smart_ ◇ _une tenue chic_ a smart outfit

2 _nice_ ◇ _C'est chic de ta part de m'avoir invité._ (informal) It was nice of you to invite me.

la **chicorée** NOUN

endive

le **chien** NOUN

dog

• **"Attention, chien méchant"** "Beware of the dog"

la **chienne** NOUN

bitch (dog)

le **chiffon** NOUN

cloth

chiffonner VERB

to crease ◇ _Ma robe est toute chiffonnée._ My dress is all creased.

le **chiffre** NOUN

figure ◇ _en chiffres ronds_ in round figures

• **les chiffres romains** Roman numerals

le **chignon** NOUN

bun (in hair) ◇ _Elle s'est fait un chignon._ She put her hair in a bun.

le **Chili** NOUN

Chile

la **chimie** NOUN

chemistry ◇ _un cours de chimie_ a chemistry lesson

chimique ADJECTIVE

chemical ◇ _une réaction chimique_ a chemical reaction

• **les produits chimiques** chemicals

la **Chine** NOUN

China

chinois ADJECTIVE, NOUN

Chinese ◇ _Il apprend le chinois._ He's learning Chinese.

• **un Chinois** a Chinese (man)

• **une Chinoise** a Chinese (woman)

• **les Chinois** the Chinese

le **chiot** NOUN

puppy

les **chips** FEM NOUN

crisps ◇ _un paquet de chips_ a packet of crisps

chirurgical ADJECTIVE

(MASC PL **chirurgicaux**)

• **une intervention chirurgicale** an operation

la **chirurgie** NOUN

surgery

• la chirurgie esthétique plastic surgery

le **chirurgien** NOUN
surgeon

le **choc** NOUN
shock ◇ *Ça m'a fait un sacré choc de le voir comme ça.* It gave me a hell of a shock to see him in that state.
• Elle est encore sous le choc. She's still in shock.

le **chocolat** NOUN
chocolate
• un chocolat chaud a hot chocolate
• le chocolat à croquer dark chocolate

le **chœur** NOUN
choir

choisir VERB
to choose

le **choix** NOUN
① *choice*
• avoir le choix to have the choice
② *selection* ◇ *Il n'y a pas beaucoup de choix dans ce magasin.* There's not a very wide selection of things in this shop.

le **chômage** NOUN
unemployment
• être au chômage to be unemployed

le **chômeur** NOUN
unemployed person ◇ *Il est chômeur.* He's unemployed.

la **chômeuse** NOUN
unemployed woman ◇ *Elle est chômeuse.* She's unemployed.

choquer VERB
to shock ◇ *Cette remarque m'a choqué.* I was shocked by that remark.

la **chose** NOUN
thing ◇ *J'ai fait des choses intéressantes pendant les vacances.* I did some interesting things during the holidays.
• C'est peu de chose. It's nothing really.

le **chou** NOUN
(PL les **choux**)
cabbage
• les choux de Bruxelles Brussels sprouts
• un chou à la crème a choux bun

le **chouchou** NOUN (*informal*)
teacher's pet

la **chouchoute** NOUN (*informal*)
teacher's pet

la **choucroute** NOUN
sauerkraut (*with sausages and ham*)

la **chouette** NOUN
see also **chouette** ADJECTIVE
owl

chouette ADJECTIVE
see also **chouette** NOUN (*informal*)
brilliant ◇ *Chouette alors!* Brilliant!

le **chou-fleur** NOUN
(PL les **choux-fleurs**)
cauliflower

chrétien ADJECTIVE
(FEM SING **chrétienne**)
Christian ◇ *Il est chrétien.* He's a Christian.

le **Christ** NOUN
Christ

chronologique ADJECTIVE
chronological

le **chronomètre** NOUN
stopwatch

chronométrer VERB
to time

le **chrysanthème** NOUN
chrysanthemum
Chrysanthemums are strongly associated with funerals in France.

chuchoter VERB
to whisper

chut EXCLAMATION
Shh!

la **chute** NOUN
fall
• faire une chute to fall
• une chute d'eau a waterfall
• la chute des cheveux hair loss
• les chutes de neige snowfalls

Chypre NOUN
Cyprus

-ci ADVERB
• ce livre-ci this book
• ces bottes-ci these boots

la **cible** NOUN
target

la **ciboulette** NOUN
chives

la **cicatrice** NOUN
scar

se **cicatriser** VERB
to heal up ◇ *Cette plaie s'est vite cicatrisée.* This wound has healed up quickly.

ci-contre ADVERB
opposite ◇ *la page ci-contre* the opposite page

ci-dessous ADVERB
below ◇ *la photo ci-dessous* the picture below

ci-dessus ADVERB
above

le **cidre** NOUN
cider

le **ciel** NOUN
① *sky* ◇ *un ciel nuageux* a cloudy sky
② *heaven* ◇ *être au ciel* to be in heaven

le **cierge** NOUN

candle (_in church_)

la **cigale** NOUN
cicada

le **cigare** NOUN
cigar ◇ _Il fume le cigare._ He smokes cigars.

la **cigarette** NOUN
cigarette

la **cigogne** NOUN
stork

ci-joint ADVERB
enclosed ◇ _Veuillez trouver ci-joint mon curriculum vitae._ Please find enclosed my CV.

le **cil** NOUN
eyelash

le **ciment** NOUN
cement

le **cimetière** NOUN
cemetery

le/la **cinéaste** NOUN
film-maker

le **cinéma** NOUN
cinema

cinq NUMBER
five ◇ _Il est cinq heures du matin._ It's five in the morning. ◇ _Il a cinq ans._ He's five.
✦ **le cinq février** the fifth of February

la **cinquantaine** NOUN
about fifty ◇ _Il y avait une cinquantaine de personnes._ There were about fifty people there.
✦ **Il a la cinquantaine.** He's in his fifties.

cinquante NUMBER
fifty ◇ _Il a cinquante ans._ He's fifty.
✦ **cinquante et un** fifty-one
✦ **cinquante-deux** fifty-two

cinquième ADJECTIVE
see also **cinquième** NOUN
fifth ◇ _au cinquième étage_ on the fifth floor

la **cinquième** NOUN
see also **cinquième** ADJECTIVE
second year
In French secondary schools, years are counted from the **sixième** (_youngest_) to **première** and **terminale** (_oldest_).
◇ _Mon frère est en cinquième._ My brother's in second year.

le **cintre** NOUN
coat hanger

le **cirage** NOUN
shoe polish

circonflexe ADJECTIVE
✦ **un accent circonflexe** a circumflex

la **circonstance** NOUN
circumstance ◇ _dans les circonstances actuelles_ in the present

circumstances

la **circulation** NOUN
1 _traffic_ ◇ _Il y avait beaucoup de circulation._ There was a lot of traffic.
2 _circulation_ ◇ _Elle a des problèmes de circulation._ She has bad circulation.

circuler VERB
to run ◇ _Il n'y a qu'un bus sur trois qui circule._ Only one bus in three is running.

la **cire** NOUN
wax

le **ciré** NOUN
oilskin jacket

cirer VERB
to polish (_shoes, floor_)

le **cirque** NOUN
circus

les **ciseaux** MASC NOUN
✦ **une paire de ciseaux** a pair of scissors

le **citadin** NOUN
city dweller

la **citation** NOUN
quotation

la **cité** NOUN
estate ◇ _J'habite dans une cité._ I live on an estate.
✦ **une cité universitaire** halls of residence
✦ **une cité-dortoir** a dormitory town

citer VERB
to quote

le **citoyen** NOUN
citizen

la **citoyenne** NOUN
citizen

le **citron** NOUN
lemon
✦ **un citron vert** a lime

la **citronnade** NOUN
still lemonade

la **citrouille** NOUN
pumpkin

le **civet** NOUN
stew ◇ _du civet de lapin_ rabbit stew

civil ADJECTIVE
civilian
✦ **en civil** in civilian clothes

la **civilisation** NOUN
civilization

clair ADJECTIVE, ADVERB
1 _light_ ◇ _vert clair_ light green ◇ _C'est une pièce très claire._ It's a very light room.
2 _clear_ (_water_)
✦ **voir clair** to see clearly
✦ **le clair de lune** moonlight

clairement ADVERB
clearly

la **clairière** NOUN

clearing

clandestin ADJECTIVE
• **un passager clandestin** a stowaway

la **claque** NOUN
slap ◇ *Elle m'a donné une claque.* She gave me a slap.

claquer VERB
1 *to bang* ◇ *On entend des volets qui claquent.* You can hear shutters banging.
2 *to slam* ◇ *Elle est partie en claquant la porte.* She left, slamming the door behind her.

les **claquettes** FEM NOUN
• **faire des claquettes** to tap-dance

la **clarinette** NOUN
clarinet ◇ *Gavin joue de la clarinette.* Gavin plays the clarinet.

la **classe** NOUN
1 *class* ◇ *C'est la meilleure élève de la classe.* She's the best pupil in the class.
◇ *voyager en première classe* to travel first class
2 *classroom*

classer VERB
to arrange ◇ *Les livres sont classés par ordre alphabétique.* The books are arranged in alphabetical order.

le **classeur** NOUN
ring binder

classique ADJECTIVE
1 *classical* ◇ *de la musique classique* classical music
2 *classic* ◇ *un style classique* a classic style

le **clavier** NOUN
keyboard (*of computer, typewriter*)

la **clé** NOUN
1 *key*
2 *clef* ◇ *la clé de sol* the treble clef
◇ *la clé de fa* the bass clef

la **clef** = **clé**

le **client** NOUN
customer

la **cliente** NOUN
customer

la **clientèle** NOUN
customers

cligner VERB
• **cligner des yeux** to blink

le **clignotant** NOUN
indicator ◇ *Il a mis son clignotant à gauche.* He's indicating left.

le **climat** NOUN
climate

la **climatisation** NOUN
air conditioning

climatisé ADJECTIVE
air-conditioned ◇ *L'hôtel est climatisé.* The hotel is air-conditioned.

le **clin d'œil** NOUN
(PL les **clins d'œil**)
wink
• **en un clin d'œil** in a flash

la **clinique** NOUN
private hospital

le **clochard** NOUN
tramp

la **cloche** NOUN
bell

le **clocher** NOUN
1 *church tower*
2 *steeple*

le **clou** NOUN
nail
• **un clou de girofle** a clove

le **clown** NOUN
clown

le **club** NOUN
club

le **cobaye** NOUN
guinea pig

le **coca** NOUN
Coke ®

la **cocaïne** NOUN
cocaine

la **coccinelle** NOUN
ladybird

cocher VERB
to tick ◇ *Cochez la bonne réponse.* Tick the right answer.

le **cochon** NOUN
see also cochon ADJECTIVE
pig
• **un cochon d'Inde** a guinea pig

cochon ADJECTIVE (*informal*)
see also cochon NOUN
dirty ◇ *une histoire cochonne* a dirty story

le **cocktail** NOUN
1 *cocktail*
2 *cocktail party*

le **coco** NOUN
• **une noix de coco** a coconut

cocorico EXCLAMATION
1 *Cock-a-doodle-doo!*
2 *Three cheers for France!*
The symbol of France is the cockerel and so cocorico! is sometimes used as an expression of French national pride.

la **cocotte** NOUN
casserole (*pan*)
• **une cocotte-minute** ® a pressure cooker

le **code** NOUN
code
• **le code de la route** the highway code
• **le code postal** the postcode

le **cœur** NOUN
heart
+ **avoir bon cœur** to be kind-hearted
+ **la dame de cœur** the queen of hearts
+ **avoir mal au cœur** to feel sick
+ **par cœur** by heart   ◦ *apprendre quelque chose par cœur* to learn something by heart

le **coffre** NOUN
[1] *boot* (of car)
[2] *chest* (furniture)

le **coffre-fort** NOUN
(PL les coffres-forts)
safe

le **coffret** NOUN
+ **un coffret à bijoux** a jewellery box

le **cognac** NOUN
brandy

se **cogner** VERB
+ **se cogner à quelque chose** to bang into something   ◦ *Je me suis cogné à la table.* I banged into the table. ◦ *Je me suis cogné la tête contre la porte du placard.* I banged my head on the cupboard door.

coiffé ADJECTIVE
+ **Tu es bien coiffée.** Your hair looks nice.

coiffer VERB
+ **se coiffer** to do one's hair

le **coiffeur** NOUN
hairdresser

la **coiffeuse** NOUN
hairdresser

la **coiffure** NOUN
hairstyle   ◦ *Cette coiffure te va bien.* That hairstyle suits you.
+ **un salon de coiffure** a hairdresser's

le **coin** NOUN
corner
+ **Tu habites dans le coin?** Do you live near here?
+ **Je ne suis pas du coin.** I'm not from here.
+ **le bistrot du coin** the local pub

coincé ADJECTIVE
[1] *stuck*   ◦ *La clé est coincée dans la serrure.* The key is stuck in the keyhole.
[2] *stuffy*   ◦ *Il est un peu coincé.* (informal) He's a bit stuffy.

coincer VERB
to jam   ◦ *La porte est coincée.* The door's jammed.

la **coïncidence** NOUN
coincidence

le **col** NOUN
[1] *collar*
[2] *pass* (of mountain)

la **colère** NOUN
anger
+ **Je suis en colère.** I'm angry.
+ **se mettre en colère** to get angry

le **colin** NOUN
hake

la **colique** NOUN
diarrhoea

le **colis** NOUN
parcel

collaborer VERB
to collaborate

collant ADJECTIVE
see also **collant** NOUN
[1] *sticky*
[2] *clingy*   ◦ *Je le trouve un peu collant.* (informal) He's always hanging around me.

le **collant** NOUN
see also **collant** ADJECTIVE
tights   ◦ *un collant en laine* woollen tights

la **colle** NOUN
[1] *glue*   ◦ *un tube de colle* a tube of glue
[2] *detention*   ◦ *J'ai une heure de colle samedi prochain.* (informal) I've got an hour's detention next Saturday.
+ **Je n'en sais rien: tu me poses une colle.** (informal) I really don't know: you've got me there.

la **collecte** NOUN
collection (of money)   ◦ *On a fait une collecte au profit des victimes.* There was a collection for the victims.

la **collection** NOUN
collection   ◦ *une collection de timbres* a stamp collection

collectionner VERB
to collect

le **collège** NOUN
secondary school

In France pupils go to a **collège** between the ages of 11 and 15, and then to a **lycée** until the age of 18.

le **collégien** NOUN
schoolboy

la **collégienne** NOUN
schoolgirl

le/la **collègue** NOUN
colleague

coller VERB
[1] *to stick*   ◦ *Il y a un chewing-gum collé sous la chaise.* There's a bit of chewing gum stuck under the chair.
[2] *to be sticky*   ◦ *Ce timbre ne colle plus.* This stamp won't stick on.
[3] *to press*   ◦ *J'ai collé mon oreille au mur.* I pressed my ear against the wall.

le **collier** NOUN

1 _necklace_ ◦ *un collier de perles* a pearl necklace
2 _collar_ (of dog, cat)

la **colline** NOUN
hill

la **colombe** NOUN
dove

la **colonie** NOUN
- **aller en colonie de vacances** to go to summer camp

la **colonne** NOUN
column
- **la colonne vertébrale** the spine

le **colorant** NOUN
colouring

le **coloris** NOUN
colour

le **coma** NOUN
coma ◦ *être dans le coma* to be in a coma

le **combat** NOUN
fighting ◦ *Les combats ont repris ce matin.* Fighting started again this morning.
- **un combat de boxe** a boxing match

le **combattant** NOUN
- **un ancien combattant** a war veteran

combattre VERB
to fight

combien ADVERB
1 _how much_ ◦ *Vous en voulez combien? Un kilo?* How much do you want? One kilo? ◦ *Combien est-ce que ça coûte?* How much does it cost? ◦ *Combien ça fait?* How much does it come to?
2 _how many_ ◦ *Tu en veux combien? Deux?* How many do you want? Two?
- **combien de (1)** how much ◦ *Combien de purée est-ce que je vous sers?* How much mashed potato shall I give you?
- **combien de (2)** how many ◦ *Combien de personnes as-tu invitées?* How many people have you invited?
- **combien de temps** how long ◦ *Combien de temps est-ce que tu seras absente?* How long will you be away?
- **On est le combien aujourd'hui? – On est le vingt.** What's the date today? – It's the 20th.

la **combinaison** NOUN
1 _combination_ ◦ *J'ai changé la combinaison de mon antivol.* I've changed the combination on my bike lock.
2 _slip_ (petticoat)
- **une combinaison de plongée** a wetsuit
- **une combinaison de ski** a ski suit

le **comble** NOUN

- **Alors ça, c'est le comble!** That's the last straw!

la **comédie** NOUN
comedy
- **une comédie musicale** a musical

le **comédien** NOUN
actor

la **comédienne** NOUN
actress

comestible ADJECTIVE
edible

comique ADJECTIVE
see also comique NOUN
comical

le **comique** NOUN
see also comique ADJECTIVE
comedian

le **commandant** NOUN
captain (of ship, plane)

la **commande** NOUN
order ◦ *un bon de commande* an order form
- **être aux commandes** to be at the controls

commander VERB
1 _to order_ ◦ *J'ai commandé une robe par catalogue.* I've ordered a dress from a catalogue.
2 _to give orders_ ◦ *C'est moi qui commande ici, pas vous!* I give the orders here, not you!

comme CONJUNCTION, ADVERB
1 _like_ ◦ *Il est comme son père.* He's like his father. ◦ *Je voudrais un manteau comme celui de la photo.* I'd like a coat like the one in the picture.
2 _for_ ◦ *Qu'est-ce que tu veux comme dessert?* What would you like for pudding?
3 _as_ ◦ *J'ai travaillé comme serveuse cet été.* I worked as a waitress this summer. ◦ *Faites comme vous voulez.* Do as you like.
- **comme ça** like this ◦ *Ça se plie comme ça.* You fold it like this. ◦ *C'était un poisson grand comme ça.* The fish was this big.
- **comme il faut** properly ◦ *Mets le couvert comme il faut!* Set the table properly!
- **Comme tu as grandi!** How you've grown!
- **Regarde comme c'est beau!** Look, isn't it lovely!
- **comme ci comme ça** so-so ◦ *Comment est-ce que tu as trouvé le film? – Comme ci comme ça.* What did you think of the film? – So-so.

le **commencement** NOUN

beginning
commencer VERB
to start ◇ *Les cours commencent à huit heures.* Lessons start at 8 o'clock. ◇ *Il a commencé à pleuvoir.* It started raining. ◇ *J'ai commencé de réviser pour les examens.* I've started revising for the exams.

comment ADVERB
how ◇ *Comment arrives-tu à travailler dans ce bruit?* How can you possibly work with this noise?
+ **Comment allez-vous?** How are you?
+ **Comment s'appelle-t-il?** What's his name?
+ **Comment?** What did you say?

le **commentaire** NOUN
comment

les **commérages** MASC NOUN
gossip

le **commerçant** NOUN
shopkeeper

le **commerce** NOUN
⓵ *trade* ◇ *le commerce extérieur* foreign trade
⓶ *business* ◇ *Il fait des études de commerce.* He's studying business.
⓷ *shop* ◇ *On trouve ça facilement dans le commerce.* You can easily find it in the shops.

commercial ADJECTIVE
(MASC PL **commerciaux**)
+ **un centre commercial** a shopping centre

le **commissaire** NOUN
police superintendent

le **commissariat** NOUN
police station

les **commissions** FEM NOUN
shopping ◇ *J'ai quelques commissions à faire.* I've got some shopping to do.

commode ADJECTIVE
see also **commode** NOUN
handy ◇ *Ce sac est très commode pour les voyages.* This bag is very handy for travelling.
+ **Son père n'est pas commode.** His father is a difficult character.

la **commode** NOUN
see also **commode** ADJECTIVE
chest of drawers

commun ADJECTIVE
shared ◇ *une salle de bain commune* a shared bathroom ◇ *Nous avons des intérêts communs.* We have interests in common.
+ **en commun** in common ◇ *Ils n'ont rien en commun.* They've got nothing in common.

+ **les transports en commun** public transport
+ **mettre quelque chose en commun** to share something ◇ *Nous mettons tous nos livres en commun.* We share all our books.

la **communauté** NOUN
community

la **communication** NOUN
communication
+ **une communication téléphonique** a telephone call

la **communion** NOUN
communion ◇ *faire sa première communion* to make one's first communion

communiquer VERB
to communicate

communiste ADJECTIVE
communist ◇ *le Parti communiste* the Communist Party

compact ADJECTIVE
compact
+ **un disque compact** a compact disc

la **compagne** NOUN
⓵ *companion*
⓶ *partner* (living together)

la **compagnie** NOUN
company ◇ *J'aime avoir de la compagnie.* I like to have company. ◇ *Je viendrai te tenir compagnie.* I'll come to keep you company.
+ **une compagnie d'assurances** an insurance company
+ **une compagnie aérienne** an airline

le **compagnon** NOUN
⓵ *companion*
⓶ *partner* (living together)

la **comparaison** NOUN
comparison ◇ *en comparaison de* in comparison with

comparer VERB
to compare

le **compartiment** NOUN
compartment (on train)

le **compas** NOUN
compass (for drawing circles)

compatible ADJECTIVE
compatible

la **compétence** NOUN
competence

compétent ADJECTIVE
competent

la **compétition** NOUN
competition

complet ADJECTIVE
(FEM SING **complète**)
see also **complet** NOUN
⓵ *complete* ◇ *les œuvres complètes*

de Shakespeare the complete works of
Shakespeare
[2] *full* ◇ *L'hôtel est complet.* The hotel
is full.
* **"complet"** "no vacancies"
* **le pain complet** wholemeal bread
le **complet** NOUN
see also complet ADJECTIVE
suit (for man)
complètement ADVERB
completely ◇ *J'avais complètement
oublié que tu viendrais.* I'd completely
forgotten that you were coming.
compléter VERB
to complete ◇ *Complétez les phrases
suivantes.* Complete the following
phrases.
complexe ADJECTIVE
complex
complexé ADJECTIVE
screwed up
la **complication** NOUN
complication
le/la **complice** NOUN
accomplice
les **compliments** MASC NOUN
compliment SING
* **faire des compliments** to compliment
◇ *Il m'a fait des compliments sur ma robe.*
He complimented me on my dress.
compliqué ADJECTIVE
complicated ◇ *C'est une histoire
compliquée.* It's a complicated story.
le **complot** NOUN
plot
le **comportement** NOUN
behaviour
comporter VERB
[1] *to consist of* ◇ *Le château comporte
trois parties.* The castle consists of three
parts.
[2] *to have* ◇ *Ce modèle comporte un
écran couleur.* This model has a colour
screen.
* **se comporter** to behave ◇ *Il s'est
comporté de façon odieuse.* He behaved
atrociously.
composer VERB
to compose (music, text)
* **composer un numéro** to dial a number
* **se composer de** to consist of
◇ *L'uniforme se compose d'une veste,
d'un pantalon et d'une cravate.* The
uniform consists of a jacket, trousers
and a tie.
le **compositeur** NOUN
composer
la **composition** NOUN
test ◇ *Nous avons une composition de*

français cet après-midi. We've got a
French test this afternoon.
la **compositrice** NOUN
composer
composter VERB
to punch ◇ *N'oublie pas de composter
ton billet avant de monter dans le train.*
Remember to punch your ticket before
you get on the train.
*In France you have to punch your ticket on the
platform to validate it before getting onto the
train.*
la **compote** NOUN
stewed fruit
* **la compote de prunes** stewed plums
compréhensible ADJECTIVE
understandable
compréhensif ADJECTIVE
(FEM SING **compréhensive**)
understanding
comprendre VERB
[1] *to understand* ◇ *Je ne comprends
pas ce que vous dites.* I don't
understand what you're saying.
[2] *to include* ◇ *Le forfait ne comprend
pas la location des skis.* The price
doesn't include ski hire.
le **comprimé** NOUN
tablet ◇ *un comprimé d'aspirine* an
aspirin
compris ADJECTIVE
included ◇ *Le service n'est pas
compris.* Service is not included.
* **y compris** including ◇ *Ils ont tout
vendu, y compris leur voiture.* They sold
everything, including their car.
* **non compris** excluding ◇ *un menu à
cent francs, vin non compris* a set menu
for 100 francs, excluding wine
* **cent francs tout compris** 100 francs
all-inclusive
la **comptabilité** NOUN
accounting ◇ *un cours de comptabilité*
a course in accounting
le/la **comptable** NOUN
accountant ◇ *Il est comptable.* He's
an accountant.
comptant ADVERB
* **payer comptant** to pay cash
le **compte** NOUN
account ◇ *J'ai déposé le chèque sur
mon compte.* I've paid the cheque into
my account.
* **Le compte est bon.** That's the right
amount.
* **tenir compte de (1)** to take into
account ◇ *Ils ont tenu compte de mon
expérience.* They took my experience
into account.

◆ **tenir compte de (2)** to take notice of
  ◦ *Il n'a pas tenu compte de mes conseils.*
  He took no notice of my advice.
◆ **travailler à son compte** to be
  self-employed
◆ **en fin de compte** all things considered
  ◦ *Le voyage ne s'est pas mal passé, en
  fin de compte.* The journey wasn't bad,
  all things considered.
compter VERB
  to count
le **compte rendu** NOUN
  (PL les **comptes rendus**)
  report
le **compteur** NOUN
  meter
le **comptoir** NOUN
  bar ◦ *au comptoir* at the bar
con ADJECTIVE (*rude*)
  (FEM SING **conne**)
  bloody stupid
se **concentrer** VERB
  to concentrate ◦ *J'ai du mal à me
  concentrer.* I find it hard to
  concentrate.
la **conception** NOUN
  design
concerner VERB
  to concern ◦ *en ce qui me concerne*
  as far as I'm concerned
◆ **Je ne me sens pas concerné.** I don't
  feel it's anything to do with me.
le **concert** NOUN
  concert
le/la **concierge** NOUN
  caretaker
conclure VERB
  to conclude
la **conclusion** NOUN
  conclusion
le **concombre** NOUN
  cucumber
concorder VERB
  to tally ◦ *Les dates concordent.* The
  dates tally.
le **concours** NOUN
  [1] *competition* ◦ *un concours de
  chant* a singing competition
  [2] *competitive exam*
concret ADJECTIVE
  (FEM SING **concrète**)
  concrete
conçu VERB
  designed ◦ *Ces appartements sont
  très mal conçus.* These flats are very
  badly designed.
la **concurrence** NOUN
  competition ◦ *La concurrence est vive
  sur ce marché.* There's a lot of

competition in this market.
le **concurrent** NOUN
  competitor
la **concurrente** NOUN
  competitor
condamner VERB
  to sentence ◦ *Il a été condamné à
  deux ans de prison.* He was sentenced
  to two years in prison. ◦ *condamner à
  mort* to sentence to death
la **condition** NOUN
  condition ◦ *Je le ferai à une
  condition...* I'll do it, on one condition...
◆ **à condition que** provided that ◦ *Je
  viendrai à condition qu'il me le demande.*
  I'll come provided he asks me to.
◆ **les conditions de travail** working
  conditions
le **conditionnel** NOUN
  conditional tense
le **conducteur** NOUN
  driver
la **conductrice** NOUN
  driver
conduire VERB
  to drive ◦ *Est-ce que tu sais conduire?*
  Can you drive? ◦ *Je te conduirai chez le
  docteur.* I'll drive you to the doctor's.
◆ **se conduire** to behave ◦ *Il s'est mal
  conduit.* He behaved badly.
la **conduite** NOUN
  behaviour
la **conférence** NOUN
  [1] *lecture* ◦ *donner une conférence* to
  give a lecture
  [2] *conference* ◦ *une conférence
  internationale* an international
  conference
se **confesser** VERB
  to go to confession
la **confiance** NOUN
  [1] *trust*
◆ **avoir confiance en quelqu'un** to trust
  somebody ◦ *Je n'ai pas confiance en
  lui.* I don't trust him.
  [2] *confidence*
◆ **Tu peux avoir confiance. Il sera à
  l'heure.** You don't need to worry. He'll
  be on time.
◆ **confiance en soi** self-confidence
  ◦ *Elle manque de confiance en elle.* She
  lacks self-confidence.
confiant ADJECTIVE
  confident
les **confidences** FEM NOUN
◆ **faire des confidences à quelqu'un** to
  confide in someone ◦ *Elle me fait
  quelquefois des confidences.* She
  sometimes confides in me.

confidentiel ADJECTIVE
(FEM SING **confidentielle**)
confidential

confier VERB
* **se confier à quelqu'un** to confide in somebody ◇ *Elle s'est confiée à sa meilleure amie.* She confided in her best friend.

confirmer VERB
to confirm

confiserie NOUN
sweet shop

confisquer VERB
to confiscate

confit ADJECTIVE
* **des fruits confits** crystallized fruits

confiture NOUN
jam ◇ *la confiture de fraises* strawberry jam
* **la confiture d'oranges** marmalade

conflit NOUN
conflict

confondre VERB
to mix up ◇ *On le confond souvent avec son frère.* People often mix him up with his brother.

confort NOUN
comfort
* **tout confort** with all mod cons ◇ *un appartement tout confort* a flat with all mod cons

confortable ADJECTIVE
comfortable ◇ *des chaussures confortables* comfortable shoes

confus ADJECTIVE
1 *unclear* ◇ *J'ai trouvé ses explications confuses.* I thought his explanation was unclear.
2 *embarrassed* ◇ *Il avait l'air confus.* He looked embarrassed.

confusion NOUN
1 *confusion*
2 *embarrassment* ◇ *rougir de confusion* to go red with embarrassment

congé NOUN
holiday ◇ *une semaine de congé* a week's holiday
* **en congé** on holiday ◇ *Je serai en congé la semaine prochaine.* I'll be on holiday next week.
* **un congé de maladie** sick leave ◇ *Il est en congé de maladie.* He's on sick leave.

congélateur NOUN
freezer

congeler VERB
to freeze

conjonctivite NOUN *conjunctivitis*

conjugaison NOUN
conjugation

connaissance NOUN
1 *knowledge* ◇ *...pour approfondir vos connaissances* ...to increase your knowledge
2 *acquaintance* ◇ *Ce n'est pas vraiment une amie, juste une connaissance.* She's not really a friend, just an acquaintance.
* **perdre connaissance** to lose consciousness

connaître VERB
to know ◇ *Je ne connais pas du tout cette région.* I don't know this area at all. ◇ *Je le connais de vue.* I know him by sight.
* **Ils se sont connus à Nantes.** They first met in Nantes.
* **s'y connaître en quelque chose** to know about something ◇ *Je ne m'y connais pas beaucoup en musique classique.* I don't know much about classical music.

connerie NOUN (*rude*)
bloody stupid thing ◇ *faire une connerie* to do something bloody stupid

connu ADJECTIVE
well-known ◇ *C'est un acteur connu.* He's a well-known actor.

conquérir VERB
to conquer

consacrer VERB
to devote ◇ *Il consacre beaucoup de temps à ses enfants.* He devotes a lot of time to his children. ◇ *Je suis désolé, je n'ai pas beaucoup de temps à vous consacrer.* I'm afraid I can't spare much time for you.

conscience NOUN
conscience ◇ *avoir mauvaise conscience* to have a guilty conscience
* **prendre conscience de** to become aware of ◇ *Ils ont fini par prendre conscience de la gravité de la situation.* They eventually became aware of the seriousness of the situation.

consciencieux ADJECTIVE
(FEM SING **consciencieuse**)
conscientious

conscient ADJECTIVE
conscious

consécutif ADJECTIVE
(FEM SING **consécutive**)
consecutive

conseil NOUN
advice ◇ *Est-ce que je peux te*

demander conseil? Can I ask you for some advice?

◆ **un conseil** a piece of advice

conseiller VERB

  [1] *to advise* ◇ Il a été mal conseillé. He has been badly advised.

  [2] *to recommend* ◇ Il m'a conseillé ce livre. He recommended this book to me.

le **consentement** NOUN

  consent ◇ le consentement des parents the parents' consent

consentir VERB

  to agree ◇ consentir à quelque chose to agree to something

la **conséquence** NOUN

  consequence

◆ **en conséquence** consequently

conséquent ADJECTIVE

◆ **par conséquent** consequently

le **conservatoire** NOUN

  school of music ◇ Elle fait du piano au conservatoire. She's learning the piano at the school of music.

la **conserve** NOUN

  tin ◇ Je vais ouvrir une conserve. I'll open a tin.

◆ **une boîte de conserve** a tin

◆ **les conserves** tinned food ◇ Il n'est pas bon de manger tous les jours des conserves. It's not healthy to eat tinned food every day.

◆ **en conserve** tinned ◇ des petits pois en conserve tinned peas

conserver VERB

  to keep ◇ J'ai conservé toutes ses lettres. I've kept all her letters.

◆ **se conserver** to keep ◇ Ce pain se conserve plus d'une semaine. This bread will keep for more than a week.

considérable ADJECTIVE

  considerable ◇ Il a fait des progrès considérables. He's made considerable progress.

la **considération** NOUN

◆ **prendre quelque chose en considération** to take something into consideration

considérer VERB

◆ **considérer que** to believe that ◇ Je considère que le gouvernement devrait investir davantage dans l'éducation. I believe that the government should invest more money in education.

la **consigne** NOUN

  left-luggage office

◆ **une consigne automatique** a left-luggage locker

consistant ADJECTIVE

  substantial ◇ un petit déjeuner consistant a substantial breakfast

consister VERB

◆ **consister à** to consist of ◇ Mon travail consiste à répondre au téléphone et à recevoir les clients. My job consists of answering the phone and welcoming the customers. ◇ En quoi consiste votre travail? What does your job involve?

consoler VERB

  to console

le **consommateur** NOUN

  [1] *consumer*

  [2] *customer* (in café)

la **consommation** NOUN

  [1] *consumption* ◇ la consommation d'électricité electricity consumption

  [2] *drink* ◇ Le billet d'entrée donne droit à une consommation gratuite. The ticket entitles you to one free drink.

la **consommatrice** NOUN

  [1] *consumer*

  [2] *customer* (in café)

consommer VERB

  [1] *to use* ◇ Ces grosses voitures consomment beaucoup d'essence. These big cars use a lot of petrol.

  [2] *to have a drink* ◇ Est-ce qu'on peut consommer à la terrasse? Can we have drinks outside?

la **consonne** NOUN

  consonant

constamment ADVERB

  constantly ◇ Elle se plaint constamment. She's constantly complaining.

constant ADJECTIVE

  constant

constater VERB

  to notice

constipé ADJECTIVE

  constipated

constitué ADJECTIVE

◆ **être constitué de** to consist of

constituer VERB

  to make up ◇ les États qui constituent la Fédération russe the states which make up the Russian Federation

la **construction** NOUN

  building ◇ des matériaux de construction building materials

◆ **une maison en construction** a house being built

construire VERB

  to build ◇ Ils font construire une maison neuve. They're having a new house built.

la **consultation** NOUN

◆ **les heures de consultation** surgery

hours
consulter VERB
[1] *to consult* ◇ *Tu devrais consulter un médecin.* You should see a doctor.
[2] *to see patients* ◇ *Le docteur ne consulte pas le samedi.* The doctor doesn't see patients on Saturdays.
le **contact** NOUN
contact ◇ *les contacts humains* human contact
• **Il a le contact facile.** He's very approachable.
▾ **garder le contact avec quelqu'un** to keep in touch with somebody
contacter VERB
to get in touch with ◇ *Je te contacterai dès que j'aurai des nouvelles.* I'll get in touch with you as soon as I have some news.
contagieux ADJECTIVE
(FEM SING **contagieuse**)
infectious ◇ *une maladie contagieuse* an infectious disease ◇ *Restez chez vous si vous êtes contagieux.* Stay at home if you've got something infectious.
contaminer VERB
to contaminate
conte de fées NOUN
(PL **les contes de fées**)
fairy tale
contempler VERB
to gaze at
contemporain ADJECTIVE
contemporary
• **un auteur contemporain** a modern writer
contenir VERB
to contain ◇ *un portefeuille contenant de l'argent* a wallet containing money
content ADJECTIVE
glad ◇ *Je suis content que tu sois venu.* I'm glad you've come.
• **content de** pleased with ◇ *Elle m'a dit qu'elle était contente de mon travail.* She told me she was pleased with my work.
contenter VERB
to please • *Il est difficile à contenter.* He's hard to please.
• **Je me contente de peu.** I can make do with very little.
contesté ADJECTIVE
controversial ◇ *Cette décision est très contestée.* This is a very controversial decision.
continent NOUN
continent
continu ADJECTIVE
continuous

• **faire la journée continue** to work without taking a full lunch break
continuellement ADVERB
constantly
continuer VERB
to carry on ◇ *Continuez sans moi!* Carry on without me! ◇ *Il ne veut pas continuer ses études.* He doesn't want to go on studying.
• **continuer à faire quelque chose** to go on doing something ◇ *Ils ont continué à regarder la télé sans me dire bonjour.* They went on watching TV without saying hello to me.
• **continuer de faire quelque chose** to go on doing something ◇ *Il continue de fumer malgré son asthme.* He keeps on smoking, despite his asthma.
contourner VERB
to go round ◇ *La route contourne la ville.* The road goes round the town.
le **contraceptif** NOUN
contraceptive
la **contraception** NOUN
contraception
le **contractuel** NOUN
traffic warden
la **contractuelle** NOUN
traffic warden
la **contradiction** NOUN
contradiction
▾ **par esprit de contradiction** just to be awkward ◇ *Il a refusé de venir par esprit de contradiction* He refused to come, just to be awkward.
le **contraire** NOUN
opposite ◇ *Il a fait le contraire de ce que je lui avais demandé.* He did the opposite of what I asked him.
• **au contraire** on the contrary
contrarier VERB
[1] *to annoy* ◇ *Il avait l'air contrarié.* He looked annoyed.
[2] *to upset* ◇ *Est-ce que tu serais contrariée si je ne venais pas?* Would you be upset if I didn't come?
le **contraste** NOUN
contrast
le **contrat** NOUN
contract ◇ *un contrat de travail* an employment contract
la **contravention** NOUN
parking ticket
contre PREPOSITION
[1] *against* ◇ *Ne mets pas ton vélo contre le mur.* Don't put your bike against the wall. ◇ *Tu es pour ou contre ce projet?* Are you for or against this plan?

PTO

2 *for* ◇ *échanger quelque chose contre quelque chose* to swap something for something

- **par contre** on the other hand

la **contrebande** NOUN
smuggling
- **des produits de contrebande** smuggled goods

la **contrebasse** NOUN
double bass

contrecœur
- **à contrecœur** ADVERB
reluctantly ◇ *Il est venu à contrecœur.* He came reluctantly.

contredire VERB
to contradict ◇ *Il ne supporte pas d'être contredit.* He can't stand being contradicted.

la **contre-indication** NOUN
- **"Contre-indication en cas d'eczéma"** "Should not be used by people with eczema"

le **contresens** NOUN
mistranslation

le **contretemps** NOUN
- **Désolé d'être en retard: j'ai eu un contretemps.** Sorry I'm late: I was held up.

contribuer VERB
- **contribuer à** to contribute to ◇ *Est-ce que tu veux contribuer au cadeau pour Marie?* Do you want to contribute to Marie's present?

le **contrôle** NOUN
1 *control* ◇ *le contrôle des passeports* passport control
2 *check*
- **un contrôle d'identité** an identity check
- **le contrôle des billets** ticket inspection
3 *test* ◇ *un contrôle antidopage* a drugs test
- **le contrôle continu** continuous assessment

contrôler VERB
to check ◇ *Personne n'a contrôlé mon billet.* Nobody checked my ticket.

le **contrôleur** NOUN
ticket inspector

la **contrôleuse** NOUN
ticket inspector

controversé ADJECTIVE
controversial

convaincre VERB
1 *to persuade* ◇ *Il a essayé de me convaincre de rester.* He tried to persuade me to stay.
2 *to convince* ◇ *Tu n'as pas l'air convaincu.* You don't look convinced.

la **convalescence** NOUN

convalescence

convenable ADJECTIVE
decent ◇ *un hôtel convenable* a decent hotel
- **Ce n'est pas convenable.** It's bad manners.

convenir VERB
- **convenir à** to suit ◇ *Est-ce que cette date te convient?* Does this date suit you? ◇ *J'espère que cela vous conviendra.* I hope this will suit you.
- **convenir de** to agree on ◇ *Nous avons convenu d'une date.* We've agreed on a date.

conventionné ADJECTIVE
- **un médecin conventionné** a Health Service doctor

All doctors in France charge for treatment, but patients of Health Service doctors get their money refunded by the government.

convenu ADJECTIVE
agreed ◇ *au moment convenu* at the agreed time

la **conversation** NOUN
conversation

la **convocation** NOUN
notification

convoquer VERB
- **convoquer quelqu'un à une réunion** to invite somebody to a meeting ◇ *Le directeur a convoqué tous les parents à la réunion.* The headmaster has invited all the parents to the meeting.

la **coopération** NOUN
co-operation

coopérer VERB
to co-operate

le **copain** NOUN (informal)
1 *friend* ◇ *C'est un bon copain.* He's a good friend.
2 *boyfriend* ◇ *Je l'ai vue avec son copain.* I saw her with her boyfriend.

la **copie** NOUN
1 *copy* ◇ *Ce tableau n'est qu'une copie.* This picture is only a copy.
2 *paper* ◇ *Il a des copies à corriger ce week-end.* He's got some papers to mark this weekend.

copier VERB
to copy

copieux ADJECTIVE
(FEM SING **copieuse**)
hearty ◇ *un repas copieux* a hearty meal

la **copine** NOUN (informal)
1 *friend* ◇ *Je sors avec une copine ce soir.* I'm going out with a friend tonight.
2 *girlfriend* ◇ *Je ne savais pas qu'il*

avait une copine. I didn't know he had a girlfriend.

le **coq** NOUN
cockerel

la **coque** NOUN
hull (of boat)

- **un œuf à la coque** a soft-boiled egg

le **coquelicot** NOUN
poppy

la **coqueluche** NOUN
whooping cough

le **coquillage** NOUN
1. _shellfish_
2. _shell_ ◇ Nous avons ramassé des coquillages sur la plage. We picked up some shells on the beach.

la **coquille** NOUN
shell
- **une coquille d'œuf** an eggshell
- **une coquille Saint-Jacques** a scallop

coquin ADJECTIVE
cheeky ◇ Il m'a regardé d'un air coquin. He gave me a cheeky look.

le **cor** NOUN
horn ◇ Je joue du cor. I play the horn.

le **corbeau** NOUN
(PL les corbeaux)
crow

la **corbeille** NOUN
basket ◇ une corbeille de fruits a basket of fruit
- **une corbeille à papier** a wastepaper basket

la **corde** NOUN
1. _rope_
2. _string_ (of violin, tennis racket)
- **une corde à linge** a clothes line

la **cordonnerie** NOUN
shoe repair shop

le **cordonnier** NOUN
cobbler

coriace ADJECTIVE
tough

la **corne** NOUN
horn

la **cornemuse** NOUN
bagpipes ◇ jouer de la cornemuse to play the bagpipes

le **cornet** NOUN
- **un cornet de frites** a bag of chips
- **un cornet de glace** an ice cream cone

le **cornichon** NOUN
gherkin

Cornouailles NOUN
Cornwall

le **corps** NOUN
body

correct ADJECTIVE

1. _correct_ ◇ Ce n'est pas tout à fait correct. That's not quite correct.
2. _reasonable_ ◇ un salaire correct a reasonable salary ◇ Le repas était tout à fait correct. The meal was quite reasonable.

la **correction** NOUN
correction

la **correspondance** NOUN
1. _correspondence_
- **un cours par correspondance** a correspondence course
2. _connection_ (train, plane) ◇ Il y a une correspondance pour Toulouse à dix heures. There's a connection for Toulouse at ten o'clock.

le **correspondant** NOUN
penfriend

la **correspondante** NOUN
penfriend

correspondre VERB
to correspond

le **corridor** NOUN
corridor

corriger VERB
to mark ◇ Le prof n'a pas encore corrigé nos copies. The teacher hasn't marked our papers yet.

corse ADJECTIVE, NOUN
Corsican
- **un Corse** a Corsican (man)
- **une Corse** a Corsican (woman)

la **Corse** NOUN
Corsica

la **corvée** NOUN
chore ◇ Quelle corvée! What a chore!

costaud ADJECTIVE
brawny

le **costume** NOUN
1. _suit_ (man's) ◇ Tu devrais mettre un costume et une cravate pour l'entretien. You should wear a suit and tie for the interview.
2. _costume_ (theatre) ◇ Nous avons fait nous-mêmes tous les costumes pour la pièce. We made all the costumes for the play ourselves.

la **côte** NOUN
1. _coastline_ ◇ La route longe la côte. The road follows the coastline.
- **la Côte d'Azur** the French Riviera
2. _hill_ ◇ J'ai grimpé la côte. I went up the hill.
3. _rib_ ◇ Il s'est cassé une côte en tombant. He broke a rib when he fell.
4. _chop_ ◇ une côte de porc a pork chop
- **une côte de bœuf** a rib of beef
- **côte à côte** side by side

le côté NOUN
side
- **à côté de (1)** next to ◇ *Le café est à côté du sucre.* The coffee's next to the sugar.
- **à côté de (2)** next door to ◇ *Il habite à côté de chez moi.* He lives next door to me.
- **de l'autre côté** on the other side ◇ *La pharmacie est de l'autre côté de la rue.* The chemist's is on the other side of the street.
- **De quel côté est-il parti?** Which way did he go?
- **mettre quelque chose de côté** to save something ◇ *J'ai mis de l'argent de côté.* I've saved some money.

la côtelette NOUN
chop ◇ *une côtelette d'agneau* a lamb chop

le coton NOUN
cotton ◇ *une chemise en coton* a cotton shirt
- **le coton hydrophile** cotton wool

le cou NOUN
neck

couchant ADJECTIVE
- **le soleil couchant** the setting sun

la couche NOUN
1 *layer* ◇ *la couche d'ozone* the ozone layer
2 *coat* (*of paint, varnish*)
3 *nappy*

couché ADJECTIVE
1 *lying down* ◇ *Il était couché sur le tapis.* He was lying on the carpet.
2 *in bed* ◇ *À huit heures, il était déjà couché.* He was already in bed at 8 o'clock.

le coucher NOUN
see also **coucher** VERB
- **un coucher de soleil** a sunset

se coucher VERB
see also **coucher** NOUN
1 *to go to bed* ◇ *Je me suis couché tard hier soir.* I went to bed late last night.
2 *to set* (*sun*)

la couchette NOUN
1 *couchette* (*on train*)
2 *bunk* (*on boat*)

le coude NOUN
elbow

coudre VERB
1 *to sew* ◇ *J'aime coudre.* I like sewing.
2 *to sew on* ◇ *Il ne sait même pas coudre un bouton.* He can't even sew a button on.

la couette NOUN
duvet

les couettes FEM NOUN
bunches ◇ *Quand j'étais petite, ma mère me faisait des couettes.* When I was little, my mother put my hair in bunches.

couler VERB
1 *to run* ◇ *Ne laissez pas couler les robinets.* Don't leave the taps running. ◇ *J'ai le nez qui coule.* My nose is running.
2 *to flow* ◇ *La rivière coulait lentement.* The river was flowing slowly.
3 *to leak* ◇ *Mon stylo coule.* My pen's leaking.
4 *to sink* ◇ *Un bateau a coulé pendant la tempête.* A boat sank during the storm.

la couleur NOUN
colour ◇ *une pellicule couleur* a colour film
- **Tu as pris des couleurs.** You've got a tan.

la couleuvre NOUN
grass snake

les coulisses FEM NOUN
wings (*in theatre*)
- **dans les coulisses** behind the scenes

le couloir NOUN
corridor

le coup NOUN
1 *knock* ◇ *donner un coup à quelque chose* to give something a knock
2 *blow* ◇ *Il m'a donné un coup!* He hit me!
- **un coup de pied** a kick
- **un coup de poing** a punch
3 *shock* ◇ *Ça m'a fait un coup de le voir comme ça!* (*informal*) It gave me a shock to see him like that!
- **un coup de feu** a shot
- **un coup de fil** (*informal*) a ring ◇ *Je te donnerai un coup de fil dans la soirée.* I'll give you a ring this evening.
- **donner un coup de main à quelqu'un** to give somebody a hand ◇ *Je viendrai te donner un coup de main.* I'll come and give you a hand.
- **un coup d'œil** a quick look ◇ *jeter un coup d'œil* to have a quick look
- **attraper un coup de soleil** to get sunburnt
- **un coup de téléphone** a phone call
- **un coup de tonnerre** a clap of thunder
- **boire un coup** (*informal*) to have a drink
- **après coup** afterwards ◇ *Après coup j'ai regretté de m'être mis en colère.* Afterwards I was sorry I'd got angry.

- **à tous les coups** (*informal*) every time ⋄ *Je me trompe de rue à tous les coups.* I get the street wrong every time.
- **du premier coup** first time ⋄ *Il a été reçu au permis du premier coup.* He passed his driving test first time.
- **sur le coup** at first ⋄ *Sur le coup je ne l'ai pas reconnu.* I didn't recognize him at first.

coupable ADJECTIVE
see also coupable NOUN
guilty

la **coupable** NOUN
see also coupable ADJECTIVE
culprit

la **coupe** NOUN
cup (sport) ⋄ *Ils ont remporté la coupe du monde.* They won the World Cup.
- **une coupe de cheveux** a haircut
- **une coupe de champagne** a glass of champagne

couper VERB
1 *to cut*
2 *to turn off* ⋄ *couper le courant* to turn off the electricity
3 *to take a short-cut* ⋄ *On peut couper par la forêt.* There's a short-cut through the woods.
- **couper l'appétit** to spoil one's appetite
- **se couper** to cut oneself ⋄ *Je me suis coupé le doigt avec une boîte de conserve.* I cut my finger on a tin.
- **couper la parole à quelqu'un** to interrupt somebody

le **couple** NOUN
couple

le **couplet** NOUN
verse ⋄ *le premier couplet* the first verse

la **coupure** NOUN
cut
- **une coupure de courant** a power cut

la **cour** NOUN
1 *yard* ⋄ *la cour de l'école* the school yard
2 *court* ⋄ *la cour de Louis XIV* the court of Louis XIV ⋄ *la cour d'assises* the criminal court

le **courage** NOUN
courage

courageux ADJECTIVE
(FEM SING **courageuse**)
brave

couramment ADVERB
1 *fluently* ⋄ *Elle parle couramment japonais.* She speaks Japanese fluently.
2 *commonly* ⋄ *C'est une expression que l'on emploie couramment.* It's a commonly used phrase.

courant ADJECTIVE
see also courant NOUN
1 *common* ⋄ *C'est une erreur courante.* It's a common mistake.
2 *standard* ⋄ *C'est un modèle courant.* It's a standard model.

le **courant** NOUN
see also courant ADJECTIVE
1 *current* (*of river*)
- **un courant d'air** a draught
2 *power* ⋄ *une panne de courant* a power cut
- **Je le ferai dans le courant de la semaine.** I'll do it some time during the week.
- **être au courant de quelque chose** to know about something ⋄ *Je ne suis pas au courant de ses projets pour l'été.* I don't know about her plans for the summer.
- **mettre quelqu'un au courant de quelque chose** to tell somebody about something
- **Tu es au courant?** Have you heard about it?
- **se tenir au courant de quelque chose** to keep up with something ⋄ *J'essaie de me tenir au courant de l'actualité.* I try to keep up with the news.

le **coureur** NOUN
runner
- **un coureur à pied** a runner
- **un coureur cycliste** a racing cyclist
- **un coureur automobile** a racing driver

la **coureuse** NOUN
runner

la **courgette** NOUN
courgette

courir VERB
to run ⋄ *Elle a traversé la rue en courant.* She ran across the street.
- **courir un risque** to run a risk

la **couronne** NOUN
crown

courons, courez VERB *see* courir

le **courrier** NOUN
post ⋄ *Est-ce qu'il y avait du courrier ce matin?* Was there any post this morning? ⋄ *N'oublie pas de poster le courrier.* Don't forget to post the letters.
- **le courrier électronique** E-mail

la **courroie** NOUN
- **la courroie du ventilateur** fan belt

le **cours** NOUN
1 *lesson* ⋄ *un cours d'espagnol* a Spanish lesson ⋄ *des cours particuliers* private lessons
2 *course* ⋄ *un cours intensif* a crash course

③ *rate* ◇ *le cours du change* the exchange rate
◆ **au cours de** during ◇ *Il a été réveillé trois fois au cours de la nuit.* He was woken up three times during the night.
la **course** NOUN
   ① *running* ◇ *la course de fond* long-distance running
   ② *race* ◇ *une course hippique* a horse race
   ③ *shopping* ◇ *J'ai juste une course à faire.* I've just got a bit of shopping to do.
◆ **faire les courses** to go shopping ◇ *Elle est partie faire les courses de la semaine.* She's gone to do her weekly shopping.
court ADJECTIVE
   see also **court** NOUN
   short
le **court** NOUN
   see also **court** ADJECTIVE
◆ **un court de tennis** a tennis court
couru VERB see **courir**
le **couscous** NOUN
   couscous
   couscous *is a spicy North African dish made with meat, vegetables and steamed semolina.*
le **cousin** NOUN
   cousin
la **cousine** NOUN
   cousin
le **coussin** NOUN
   cushion
le **coût** NOUN
   cost ◇ *le coût de la vie* the cost of living
le **couteau** NOUN
   (PL les **couteaux**)
   knife
coûter VERB
   to cost ◇ *Est-ce que ça coûte cher?* Does it cost a lot?
◆ **Combien ça coûte?** How much is it?
coûteux ADJECTIVE
   (FEM SING **coûteuse**)
   expensive
la **coutume** NOUN
   custom
la **couture** NOUN
   ① *sewing* ◇ *Je n'aime pas la couture.* I don't like sewing.
◆ **faire de la couture** to sew
   ② *seam* ◇ *La couture de mon pantalon s'est défaite.* The seam of my trousers has come undone.
le **couturier** NOUN
   fashion designer ◇ *un grand couturier* a top designer

la **couturière** NOUN
   dressmaker
le **couvercle** NOUN
   ① *lid* (*of pan*)
   ② *top* (*of tube, jar, spray can*)
couvert VERB see **couvrir**
couvert ADJECTIVE
   see also **couvert** NOUN
◆ **couvert de** covered with ◇ *Cet arbre est couvert de fleurs au printemps.* This tree is covered with blossom in spring.
   overcast (*sky*)
le **couvert** NOUN
   see also **couvert** ADJECTIVE
◆ **mettre le couvert** to lay the table
les **couverts** MASC NOUN
   cutlery ◇ *Les couverts sont dans le tiroir de gauche.* The cutlery is in the left-hand drawer.
la **couverture** NOUN
   blanket
le **couvre-lit** NOUN
   bedspread
couvrir VERB
   to cover ◇ *Le chien est revenu couvert de boue.* The dog came back covered with mud.
◆ **se couvrir (1)** to wrap up ◇ *Couvre-toi bien: il fait très froid dehors.* Wrap up well: it's very cold outside.
◆ **se couvrir (2)** to cloud over ◇ *Le ciel se couvre.* The sky's clouding over.
le **crabe** NOUN
   crab
cracher VERB
   to spit
le **crachin** NOUN
   drizzle
la **craie** NOUN
   chalk
craindre VERB
   to fear ◇ *Tu n'as rien à craindre.* You've got nothing to fear.
la **crainte** NOUN
   fear
◆ **de crainte de** for fear of ◇ *Il n'ose rien dire de crainte de la vexer.* He daren't say anything for fear of upsetting her.
craintif ADJECTIVE
   (FEM SING **craintive**)
   timid
la **crampe** NOUN
   cramp ◇ *J'ai une crampe au mollet.* I've got a cramp in my calf.
le **cran** NOUN
   hole (*in belt*)
◆ **avoir du cran** (*informal*) to have guts
le **crâne** NOUN
   skull

crâner VERB (*informal*)
  to show off
le **crapaud** NOUN
  toad
craquer VERB
  [1] *to creak* ◇ Le plancher craque. The floor creaks.
  [2] *to burst* ◇ Ma fermeture éclair a craqué. My zip's burst.
  [3] *to crack up* ◇ Je vais finir par craquer! (*informal*) I'm going to crack up at this rate!
  ◆ **Quand j'ai vu cette robe, j'ai craqué!** (*informal*) When I saw that dress, I couldn't resist it!
la **crasse** NOUN
  filth
la **cravate** NOUN
  tie
le **crawl** NOUN
  crawl ◇ nager le crawl to do the crawl
le **crayon** NOUN
  pencil ◇ un crayon de couleur a coloured pencil
  ◆ **un crayon feutre** a felt-tip pen
la **création** NOUN
  creation
la **crèche** NOUN
  [1] *nursery* ◇ Elle dépose ses enfants à la crèche à huit heures. She leaves her children at the nursery at 8 o'clock.
  [2] *nativity scene*
le **crédit** NOUN
  credit
créer VERB
  to create
la **crémaillère** NOUN
  ◆ **pendre la crémaillère** to have a house-warming party
la **crème** NOUN
  see also le crème
  cream
  ◆ **la crème Chantilly** whipped cream
  ◆ **la crème fouettée** whipped cream
  ◆ **une crème caramel** a crème caramel
  ◆ **une crème au chocolat** a chocolate dessert
le **crème** NOUN
  see also la crème
  white coffee ◇ un grand crème a large white coffee
crémeux ADJECTIVE
  (FEM SING **crémeuse**)
  creamy
la **crêpe** NOUN
  pancake
la **crêperie** NOUN
  pancake restaurant
le **crépuscule** NOUN
  dusk
le **cresson** NOUN
  watercress
la **Crète** NOUN
  Crete
creuser VERB
  to dig (*a hole*)
  ◆ **Ça creuse!** That gives you a real appetite!
  ◆ **se creuser la cervelle** (*informal*) to rack one's brains
creux ADJECTIVE
  (FEM SING **creuse**)
  hollow
la **crevaison** NOUN
  puncture
crevé ADJECTIVE
  [1] *punctured* ◇ un pneu crevé a puncture
  [2] *knackered* ◇ Je suis complètement crevé! (*informal*) I'm knackered!
crever VERB
  [1] *to burst* (*balloon*)
  [2] *to have a puncture* (*motorist*) ◇ J'ai crevé sur l'autoroute. I had a puncture on the motorway.
  ◆ **Je crève de faim!** (*informal*) I'm starving!
  ◆ **Je crève de froid!** (*informal*) I'm freezing!
la **crevette** NOUN
  prawn
  ◆ **une crevette rose** a prawn
  ◆ **une crevette grise** a shrimp
le **cri** NOUN
  [1] *scream* ◇ J'ai entendu un cri. I heard a scream. ◇ pousser des cris de douleur to scream with pain
  [2] *call* ◇ Il sait reconnaître les cris des oiseaux. He can identify the calls of birds.
  ◆ **C'est le dernier cri.** It's the latest fashion. ◇ Ces chaussures sont du dernier cri. These shoes are the latest fashion.
criard ADJECTIVE
  garish (*colours*)
le **cric** NOUN
  jack (*for car*)
crier VERB
  to shout
  ◆ **crier de douleur** to scream with pain
le **crime** NOUN
  [1] *crime* ◇ un crime de guerre a war crime
  [2] *murder* ◇ Un crime a été commis ici. There was a murder here.
le **criminel** NOUN
  [1] *criminal* ◇ un criminel de guerre a

war criminal

　　[2] *murderer*

la **criminelle** NOUN

　　[1] *criminal*

　　[2] *murderer*

le **crin** NOUN

　　horsehair

la **crinière** NOUN

　　mane

le **criquet** NOUN

　　grasshopper

la **crise** NOUN

　　[1] *crisis*

　◆ **la crise économique** the recession

　　[2] *attack*　◦ *une crise d'asthme* an asthma attack　◦ *une crise cardiaque* a heart attack

　◆ **une crise de foie** an upset stomach

　◆ **piquer une crise de nerfs** to go hysterical

　◆ **avoir une crise de fou rire** to have a fit of the giggles

le **cristal** NOUN

　　(PL les **cristaux**)

　　crystal　◦ *un verre en cristal* a crystal glass

le **critère** NOUN

　　criterion

critique ADJECTIVE

　　see also **critique** NOUN

　　critical

le **critique** NOUN

　　see also **la critique** and **critique** ADJECTIVE

　　critic　◦ *un critique de cinéma* a film critic

la **critique** NOUN

　　see also **le critique** and **critique** ADJECTIVE

　　[1] *criticism*　◦ *Elle ne supporte pas les critiques.* She can't stand being criticized.

　　[2] *review*　◦ *Le film a reçu de bonnes critiques.* The film's had good reviews.

critiquer VERB

　　to criticize

la **Croatie** NOUN

　　Croatia

le **crochet** NOUN

　　[1] *hook*

　　[2] *detour*　◦ *faire un crochet* to make a detour

　　[3] *crochet*　◦ *un pull au crochet* a crocheted sweater

le **crocodile** NOUN

　　crocodile

croire VERB

　　to believe　◦ *Il croit tout ce qu'on lui raconte.* He believes everything he's told.

　◆ **croire que** to think that　◦ *Tu crois*

qu'il fera meilleur demain? Do you think the weather will be better tomorrow?

　◆ **croire à quelque chose** to believe in something

　◆ **croire en Dieu** to believe in God

crois VERB *see* **croire**

croîs VERB *see* **croître**

le **croisement** NOUN

　　crossroads　◦ *Tournez à gauche au croisement.* Turn left at the crossroads.

croiser VERB

　◆ **J'ai croisé Anne-Laure dans la rue.** I bumped into Anne-Laure in the street.

　◆ **croiser les bras** to fold one's arms

　◆ **croiser les jambes** to cross one's legs

　◆ **se croiser** to pass each other　◦ *Nous nous croisons dans l'escalier tous les matins.* We pass each other on the stairs every morning.

la **croisière** NOUN

　　cruise

la **croissance** NOUN

　　growth

le **croissant** NOUN

　　croissant　◦ *un croissant au beurre* a butter croissant

croit VERB *see* **croire**

croître VERB

　　to grow

la **croix** NOUN

　　cross

　◆ **la Croix-Rouge** the Red Cross

le **croque-madame** NOUN

　　(PL les **croque-madame**)

　　toasted ham and cheese sandwich with fried egg on top

le **croque-monsieur** NOUN

　　(PL les **croque-monsieur**)

　　toasted ham and cheese sandwich

croquer VERB

　　to munch　◦ *croquer une pomme* to munch an apple

　◆ **le chocolat à croquer** plain chocolate

le **croquis** NOUN

　　sketch

la **crotte** NOUN

　◆ **une crotte de chien** dog dirt

le **crottin** NOUN

　　[1] *manure*　◦ *du crottin de cheval* horse manure

　　[2] *small goat's cheese*

croustillant ADJECTIVE

　　crusty

la **croûte** NOUN

　　[1] *crust* (of bread)

　◆ **en croûte** in pastry

　　[2] *rind* (of cheese)

　　[3] *scab* (on skin)

le **croûton** NOUN

1 *crust* (end of loaf)
2 *crouton* ◇ *des croûtons frottés d'ail* garlic croutons
croyons, croyez VERB *see* **croire**
les **CRS** MASC NOUN
French riot police
cru VERB *see* **croire**
cru ADJECTIVE
raw ◇ *la viande crue* raw meat
• **le jambon cru** Parma ham
crû VERB *see* **croître**
la **cruauté** NOUN
cruelty
la **cruche** NOUN
jug
les **crudités** FEM NOUN
assorted raw vegetables
cruel ADJECTIVE
(FEM SING **cruelle**)
cruel
les **crustacés** MASC NOUN
shellfish
le **cube** NOUN
cube
• **un mètre cube** a cubic metre
la **cueillette** NOUN
picking ◇ *la cueillette des champignons* mushroom picking
cueillir VERB
to pick (flowers, fruit)
la **cuiller** NOUN
spoon
• **une cuiller à café** a teaspoon
• **une cuiller à soupe** a soup spoon
la **cuillère** NOUN
spoon
• **une cuillère à café** a teaspoon
• **une cuillère à soupe** a soup spoon
la **cuillerée** NOUN
spoonful
le **cuir** NOUN
leather ◇ *un sac en cuir* a leather bag
• **le cuir chevelu** the scalp
cuire VERB
to cook ◇ *cuire quelque chose à feu vif* to cook something on a high heat
• **cuire quelque chose au four** to bake something
• **cuire quelque chose à la vapeur** to steam something
• **bien cuit** well done
• **trop cuit** overdone
la **cuisine** NOUN
1 *kitchen*
2 *cooking* ◇ *la cuisine française* French cooking
• **faire la cuisine** to cook
cuisiné ADJECTIVE
• **un plat cuisiné** a ready-made meal

cuisiner VERB
to cook ◇ *J'aime beaucoup cuisiner.* I love cooking.
le **cuisinier** NOUN
cook
la **cuisinière** NOUN
1 *cook*
2 *cooker* ◇ *une cuisinière à gaz* a gas cooker
la **cuisse** NOUN
thigh
• **une cuisse de poulet** a chicken leg
la **cuisson** NOUN
cooking ◇ *"une heure de cuisson"* "cooking time: one hour"
cuit VERB *see* **cuire**
le **cuivre** NOUN
copper
le **cul** NOUN (rude)
bum
le **culot** NOUN (informal)
cheek ◇ *Quel culot!* What a cheek!
◇ *Il a un sacré culot!* He's got a damn cheek!
la **culotte** NOUN
knickers
la **culpabilité** NOUN
guilt
le **cultivateur** NOUN
farmer
la **cultivatrice** NOUN
farmer
cultivé ADJECTIVE
cultured ◇ *Il est très cultivé.* He's very cultured.
cultiver VERB
to grow ◇ *Il cultive la vigne.* He grows grapes.
• **cultiver la terre** to farm the land
la **culture** NOUN
1 *farming* ◇ *les cultures intensives* intensive farming
2 *education* ◇ *Pour cet emploi, on demande une bonne culture générale.* For this job, a good general education is needed.
• **la culture physique** physical education
le **culturisme** NOUN
body-building
le **curé** NOUN
parish priest
le **cure-dent** NOUN
toothpick
curieux ADJECTIVE
(FEM SING **curieuse**)
curious
la **curiosité** NOUN
curiosity
la **cuvette** NOUN

bowl ◇ une cuvette en plastique a plastic bowl

cyclable ADJECTIVE

◆ **une piste cyclable** a cycle track

le **cycle** NOUN

cycle

le/la **cycliste** NOUN

cyclist

le **cyclomoteur** NOUN

moped

le **cyclone** NOUN

hurricane

le **cygne** NOUN

swan

D

d' PREPOSITION, ARTICLE *see* **de**

la **dactylo** NOUN

☐1 *typist* ◇ *Elle est dactylo.* She's a typist.

☐2 *typing* ◇ *Je prends des cours de dactylo.* I'm doing typing lessons.

le **daim** NOUN

suede ◇ *une veste en daim* a suede jacket

la **dame** NOUN

☐1 *lady*

☐2 *queen* (in cards, chess)

les **dames** FEM NOUN

draughts

le **Danemark** NOUN

Denmark

dangereux ADJECTIVE

(FEM SING **dangereuse**)

dangerous

danois ADJECTIVE, NOUN

(FEM SING **danoise**)

Danish ◇ *Il parle danois.* He speaks Danish.

- **un Danois** a Dane (*man*)
- **une Danoise** a Dane (*woman*)
- **les Danois** the Danish

dans PREPOSITION

☐1 *in* ◇ *Il est dans sa chambre.* He's in his bedroom. ◇ *dans deux mois* in two months' time

☐2 *into* ◇ *Il est entré dans mon bureau.* He came into my office.

☐3 *out of* ◇ *On a bu dans des verres en plastique.* We drank out of plastic glasses.

la **danse** NOUN

☐1 *dance* ◇ *la danse moderne* modern dance ◇ *des danses folkloriques* folk dances

- **la danse classique** ballet

☐2 *dancing* ◇ *des cours de danse* dancing lessons

danser VERB

to dance

le **danseur** NOUN

dancer

la **danseuse** NOUN

dancer

la **date** NOUN

date ◇ *votre date de naissance* your date of birth ◇ *la date limite de vente* the sell-by date

- **un ami de longue date** an old friend

dater VERB

- **dater de** to date from ◇ *Cette coutume date du moyen âge.* This

custom dates from the Middle Ages.

la **datte** NOUN

date (*fruit*)

le **dauphin** NOUN

dolphin

davantage ADVERB

- **davantage de** more ◇ *Il faudrait davantage de stages de formation.* There should be more training courses.

de PREPOSITION, ARTICLE

see also **du** (=de+le) *and* **des** (=de+les). *de changes to* **d'** *before a vowel and most words beginning with "h"*

☐1 *of* ◇ *le toit de la maison* the roof of the house ◇ *la voiture de Paul* Paul's car ◇ *la voiture de mes parents* my parents' car ◇ *la voiture d'Hélène* Hélène's car ◇ *deux bouteilles de vin* two bottles of wine ◇ *un litre d'essence* a litre of petrol

- **un bébé d'un an** a one-year-old baby
- **un billet de cinquante francs** a 50-franc note

☐2 *from* ◇ *de Londres à Paris* from London to Paris ◇ *Il vient de Londres.* He comes from London. ◇ *une lettre de Victor* a letter from Victor

☐3 *by* ◇ *augmenter de dix francs* to increase by ten francs

You use **de** *to form expressions with the meaning of* **some** *and* **any**.

- **Je voudrais de l'eau.** I'd like some water. ◇ *du pain et de la confiture* bread and jam
- **Il n'a pas de famille.** He hasn't got any family.
- **Il n'y a plus de biscuits.** There aren't any more biscuits.

le **dé** NOUN

☐1 *dice*

☐2 *thimble*

le **dealer** NOUN (*informal*)

drug-pusher

déballer VERB

to unpack

le **débardeur** NOUN

tank top

débarquer VERB

to disembark ◇ *Nous avons dû débarquer à Marseille.* We had to disembark at Marseilles.

- **débarquer chez quelqu'un** (*informal*) to descend on somebody ◇ *Ils ont débarqué chez nous à dix heures du soir.* They descended on us at ten o'clock at night.

le **débarras** NOUN
junk room
- **Bon débarras!** Good riddance!

débarrasser VERB
to clear ◇ *Tu peux débarrasser la table, s'il te plaît?* Can you clear the table please?
- **se débarrasser de quelque chose** to get rid of something ◇ *Je me suis débarrassé de mon vieux frigo.* I got rid of my old fridge.

le **débat** NOUN
debate

se **débattre** VERB
to struggle

débile ADJECTIVE
crazy ◇ *C'est complètement débile!* (*informal*) That's totally crazy!

débordé ADJECTIVE
- **être débordé** to be snowed under

déborder VERB
to overflow (*river*)
- **déborder d'énergie** to be full of energy

le **débouché** NOUN
job prospect ◇ *Quels débouchés y a-t-il après ces études?* What sort of job does this course qualify you for?

déboucher VERB
1 *to unblock* (*sink, pipe*)
2 *to open* (*bottle*)
- **déboucher sur** to lead into ◇ *La rue débouche sur une place.* The street leads into a square.

debout ADVERB
1 *standing up* ◇ *Il a mangé ses céréales debout.* He ate his cereal standing up.
2 *upright* ◇ *Mets les livres debout sur l'étagère.* Put the books upright on the shelf.
3 *up* ◇ *Tu es déjà debout?* Are you up already?
- **Debout!** Get up!

déboutonner VERB
to unbutton

débraillé ADJECTIVE
sloppily dressed

débrancher VERB
to unplug

le **débris** NOUN
- **des débris de verre** bits of glass

débrouillard ADJECTIVE
streetwise

se **débrouiller** VERB
to manage ◇ *C'était difficile, mais je ne me suis pas trop mal débrouillé.* It was difficult, but I managed OK.
- **Débrouille-toi tout seul.** Sort things out for yourself.

le **début** NOUN
beginning ◇ *au début* at the beginning
- **début mai** in early May

le **débutant** NOUN
beginner

la **débutante** NOUN
beginner

débuter VERB
to start

décaféiné ADJECTIVE
decaffeinated

le **décalage horaire** NOUN
time difference (*between time zones*) ◇ *Il y a une heure de décalage horaire entre la France et la Grande-Bretagne.* There's an hour's time difference between France and Britain.

décalquer VERB
to trace

décapiter VERB
to behead

décapotable ADJECTIVE
convertible

décapsuler VERB
- **décapsuler une bouteille** to take the top off a bottle

le **décapsuleur** NOUN
bottle-opener

décéder VERB
to die ◇ *Son père est décédé il y a trois ans.* His father died three years ago.

décembre MASC NOUN
December
- **en décembre** in December

décemment ADVERB
decently

décent ADJECTIVE
decent

la **déception** NOUN
disappointment

décerner VERB
to award

le **décès** NOUN
death

décevoir VERB
to disappoint

décharger VERB
to unload

se **déchausser** VERB
to take off one's shoes

les **déchets** MASC NOUN
waste ◇ *les déchets nucléaires* nuclear waste ◇ *les déchets toxiques* toxic waste

déchiffrer VERB
to decipher

déchirant ADJECTIVE
heart-rending

déchirer VERB
1 _to tear_ (clothes)
2 _to tear up_ ◇ déchirer une lettre to tear up a letter
3 _to tear out_ ◇ déchirer une page d'un livre to tear a page out of a book
- **se déchirer** to tear ◇ se déchirer un muscle to tear a muscle

la **déchirure** NOUN
tear (rip)
- **une déchirure musculaire** a torn muscle

décidé ADJECTIVE
determined
- **C'est décidé.** It's decided.

décidément ADVERB
certainly ◇ Décidément, je n'ai pas de chance aujourd'hui. I'm certainly not having much luck today.

décider VERB
to decide
- **décider de faire quelque chose** to decide to do something ◇ Ils ont décidé de passer leurs vacances en Normandie. They decided to go to Normandy for their holiday.
- **se décider** to make up one's mind ◇ Elle n'arrive pas à se décider. She can't make up her mind.

décisif ADJECTIVE
(FEM SING **décisive**)
decisive

la **décision** NOUN
decision

la **déclaration** NOUN
statement ◇ Je n'ai aucune déclaration à faire. I have no statement to make.
- **faire une déclaration de vol** to report something as stolen

déclarer VERB
to declare ◇ déclarer la guerre à un pays to declare war on a country
- **se déclarer** to break out ◇ Le feu s'est déclaré dans la cantine. The fire broke out in the canteen.

déclencher VERB
to set off (alarm, explosion)
- **se déclencher** to go off

le **déclic** NOUN
click

décoiffé ADJECTIVE
- **Elle était toute décoiffée.** Her hair was in a real mess.

le **décollage** NOUN
takeoff (of plane)

décollé ADJECTIVE
- **avoir les oreilles décollées** to have sticking-out ears

décoller VERB
1 _to unstick_ ◇ décoller une étiquette to unstick a label
- **se décoller** to come unstuck
2 _to take off_ ◇ L'avion a décollé avec dix minutes de retard. The plane took off ten minutes late.

décolleté ADJECTIVE
see also décolleté NOUN
low-cut

le **décolleté** NOUN
see also décolleté ADJECTIVE
- **un décolleté plongeant** a plunging neckline

se **décolorer** VERB
to fade ◇ Ce tee-shirt s'est décoloré au lavage. This T-shirt has faded in the wash.
- **se faire décolorer les cheveux** to have one's hair bleached

les **décombres** MASC NOUN
rubble

se **décommander** VERB
to cry off ◇ Elle devait venir mais elle s'est décommandée à la dernière minute. She was supposed to be coming, but she cried off at the last minute.

décongeler VERB
to thaw

déconner VERB (rude)
to talk rubbish ◇ Non mais, sans déconner, c'est vrai? No kidding, is that true?

déconseiller VERB
- **déconseiller à quelqu'un de faire quelque chose** to advise somebody not to do something ◇ Je lui ai déconseillé d'y aller. I advised him not to go.
- **C'est déconseillé.** It's not recommended.

décontracté ADJECTIVE
relaxed
- **s'habiller décontracté** to dress casually

se **décontracter** VERB
to relax ◇ Il est allé faire du footing pour se décontracter. He went jogging to relax.

le **décor** NOUN
décor

le **décorateur** NOUN
interior decorator

la **décoration** NOUN
decoration

la **décoratrice** NOUN
interior decorator

décorer VERB
to decorate

les **décors** MASC NOUN
1 _scenery_ (in play)

2 _set_ (_in film_)

décortiquer VERB
to shell
- **des crevettes décortiquées** peeled shrimps

découdre VERB
to unpick
- **se découdre** to come unstitched

découper VERB
1 _to cut out_ ◊ _J'ai découpé cet article dans le journal._ I cut this article out of the paper.
2 _to carve_ (_meat_)

décourageant ADJECTIVE
discouraging

décourager VERB
to discourage
- **se décourager** to get discouraged
◊ _Ne te décourage pas!_ Don't give up!

décousu ADJECTIVE
unstitched ◊ _L'ourlet est décousu._ The hem's come unstitched.

le **découvert** NOUN
overdraft

la **découverte** NOUN
discovery

découvrir VERB
to discover

décrire VERB
to describe

décrocher VERB
1 _to take down_ ◊ _Tu peux m'aider à décrocher les rideaux?_ Can you help me take down the curtains?
2 _to pick up the phone_ ◊ _Il a décroché et a composé le numéro._ He picked up the phone and dialled the number.
- **décrocher le téléphone** to take the phone off the hook

déçu VERB
disappointed

dédaigneux ADJECTIVE
(FEM SING **dédaigneuse**)
disdainful ◊ _d'un air dédaigneux_ disdainfully

le **dédain** NOUN
disdain ◊ _avec dédain_ with disdain

dedans ADVERB
inside ◊ _C'est une jolie boîte: qu'est-ce qu'il y a dedans?_ That's a nice box: what's in it?
- **là-dedans (1)** in there ◊ _J'ai trouvé les clés là-dedans._ I found the keys in there.
- **là-dedans (2)** in that ◊ _Il y a du vrai là-dedans._ There's some truth in that.

dédicacé ADJECTIVE
- **un exemplaire dédicacé** a signed copy

dédier VERB
to dedicate

déduire VERB
to take off ◊ _Tu as déduit les vingt francs que je te devais?_ Did you take off the twenty francs I owed you?
- **déduire que** to deduce that ◊ _J'en déduis qu'il m'a menti._ That means he must have been lying.

défaire VERB
to undo
- **se défaire** to come undone

la **défaite** NOUN
defeat

le **défaut** NOUN
fault

défavorable ADJECTIVE
unfavourable

défavorisé ADJECTIVE
underprivileged

défectueux ADJECTIVE
(FEM SING **défectueuse**)
faulty

défendu ADJECTIVE
forbidden ◊ _C'est défendu._ It's not allowed.

la **défense** NOUN
1 _defence_ ◊ _prendre la défense de quelqu'un_ to back somebody up
- **"défense de fumer"** "no smoking"
2 _tusk_ (_of elephant_)

le **défi** NOUN
challenge
- **d'un air de défi** defiantly
- **sur un ton de défi** defiantly

défier VERB
1 _to challenge_ ◊ _Je te défie de trouver un meilleur exemple._ I challenge you to find a better example.
2 _to dare_ ◊ _Il m'a défié d'aller à l'école en pyjama._ He dared me to go to school in my pyjamas.

défigurer VERB
to disfigure

le **défilé** NOUN
1 _parade_
- **un défilé de mode** a fashion show
2 _march_

défiler VERB
to march

définir VERB
to define

définitif ADJECTIVE
(FEM SING **définitive**)
final
- **en définitive** in the end ◊ _En définitive, ils ont décidé de rester._ In the end, they decided to stay.

définitivement ADVERB

for good ∘ _Elle s'est définitivement installée en Écosse en 1980._ She settled in Scotland for good in 1980.

déformer VERB
to stretch ∘ _Ne tire pas sur ton pull, tu vas le déformer._ Don't pull at your sweater, you'll stretch it.
• **se déformer** to stretch ∘ _Ce tee-shirt s'est déformé au lavage._ This T-shirt has stretched in the wash.

se **défouler** VERB
to unwind ∘ _Je fais du step pour me défouler._ I do step aerobics to unwind.

dégagé ADJECTIVE
• **d'un air dégagé** casually
• **sur un ton dégagé** casually

dégager VERB
[1] _to free_ ∘ _Ils ont mis une heure à dégager les victimes._ They took an hour to free the victims.
[2] _to clear_ ∘ _des gouttes qui dégagent le nez_ drops to clear your nose
• **Ça se dégage.** It's clearing up. (_weather_)

se **dégarnir** VERB
to go bald

les **dégâts** MASC NOUN
damage

le **dégel** NOUN
thaw

dégeler VERB
to thaw ∘ _faire dégeler un poulet congelé_ to thaw out a frozen chicken

dégivrer VERB
[1] _to defrost_
[2] _to de-ice_

dégonfler VERB
to let down ∘ _Quelqu'un a dégonflé mes pneus._ Somebody let down my tyres.
• **se dégonfler** (_informal_) to chicken out

dégouliner VERB
to trickle

dégourdi ADJECTIVE
smart ∘ _Il n'est pas très dégourdi._ He's pretty clueless.

dégourdir VERB
• **se dégourdir les jambes** to stretch one's legs

le **dégoût** NOUN
disgust ∘ _une expression de dégoût_ a disgusted expression
• **avec dégoût** disgustedly

dégoûtant ADJECTIVE
disgusting

dégoûté ADJECTIVE
disgusted
• **être dégoûté de tout** to be sick of everything

dégoûter VERB

to disgust ∘ _Ce genre de comportement me dégoûte._ That kind of behaviour makes me sick.
• **dégoûter quelqu'un de quelque chose** to put somebody off something ∘ _Ça m'a dégoûté de la viande._ That put me off meat.

se **dégrader** VERB
to deteriorate

le **degré** NOUN
degree
• **de l'alcool à 90 degrés** surgical spirit

dégringoler VERB
[1] _to rush down_ ∘ _Il a dégringolé l'escalier._ He rushed down the stairs.
[2] _to collapse_ ∘ _Elle a fait dégringoler la pile de livres._ She knocked over the stack of books.

dégueulasse ADJECTIVE (_rude_)
disgusting

le **déguisement** NOUN
disguise

déguiser VERB
• **se déguiser en quelque chose** to dress up as something ∘ _Elle s'était déguisée en vampire._ She was dressed up as a vampire.

déguster VERB
[1] _to taste_ (_food, wine_)
[2] _to enjoy_

dehors ADVERB
outside ∘ _Je t'attends dehors._ I'll wait for you outside.
• **jeter quelqu'un dehors** to throw somebody out
• **en dehors de** apart from ∘ _En dehors de lui, tout le monde était content._ Apart from him, everybody was happy.

déjà ADVERB
[1] _already_ ∘ _J'ai déjà fini._ I've already finished.
[2] _before_ ∘ _Tu es déjà venu en France?_ Have you been to France before?

déjeuner VERB
see also **déjeuner** NOUN
to have lunch

le **déjeuner** NOUN
see also **déjeuner** VERB
lunch

le **délai** NOUN
[1] _extension_ ∘ _J'ai demandé un délai d'une semaine._ I've asked for a week's extension.
[2] _time limit_ ∘ _être dans les délais_ to be within the time limit

délasser VERB
to relax ∘ _La lecture délasse._ Reading's relaxing.

D

* **se délasser** to relax　◇ *J'ai pris un bain pour me délasser.* I had a bath to relax.

délavé ADJECTIVE
　faded　◇ *un jean délavé* a pair of faded jeans

le **délégué** NOUN
　representative　◇ *les délégués de classe* the class representatives
　In French schools, each class elects two representatives or délégués de classe, *one boy and one girl.*

la **déléguée** NOUN
　representative

déléguer VERB
　to delegate

délibéré ADJECTIVE
　deliberate

délicat ADJECTIVE
　① *delicate*　◇ *avoir la peau délicate* to have delicate skin
　② *tricky*　◇ *une situation délicate* a tricky situation
　③ *tactful*　◇ *Il est toujours très délicat.* He's always very tactful.
　④ *thoughtful*　◇ *C'est une attention délicate de sa part.* That was a kind thought on his part.

délicatement ADVERB
　① *gently*
　② *tactfully*

le **délice** NOUN
　delight　◇ *Vivre ici est un vrai délice.* Living here is a real delight.　◇ *Ce gâteau est un vrai délice.* This cake's a real treat.

délicieux ADJECTIVE
　(FEM SING **délicieuse**)
　delicious

la **délinquance** NOUN
　crime　◇ *de nouvelles mesures pour combattre la délinquance juvénile* new measures to fight juvenile delinquency

le **délinquant** NOUN
　criminal

la **délinquante** NOUN
　criminal

délirer VERB
* **Mais tu délires!** (*informal*) You're crazy!

le **délit** NOUN
　criminal offence

délivrer VERB
　to set free (*prisoner*)

le **deltaplane** NOUN
　hang-glider
* **faire du deltaplane** to go hang-gliding

demain ADVERB
　tomorrow
* **À demain!** See you tomorrow!

la **demande** NOUN
request
* **une demande en mariage** an offer of marriage
* **"demandes d'emploi"** "situations wanted"

demandé ADJECTIVE
* **très demandé** very much in demand

demander VERB
　① *to ask for*　◇ *J'ai demandé la permission.* I've asked for permission.　◇ *Nous avons demandé notre chemin à un chauffeur de taxi.* We asked a taxi driver the way.　◇ *Je lui ai demandé de m'aider.* I asked him to help me.
　② *to require*　◇ *un travail qui demande beaucoup de concentration* a job that requires a lot of concentration
* **se demander** to wonder　◇ *Je me demande à quelle heure il va venir.* I wonder what time he'll come.

le **demandeur d'emploi** NOUN
　job-seeker

la **démangeaison** NOUN
　itching

démanger VERB
　to itch　◇ *Ça me démange.* It itches.

le **démaquillant** NOUN
　make-up remover

démaquiller VERB
* **se démaquiller** to remove one's make-up

la **démarche** NOUN
　① *walk*　◇ *Il a une drôle de démarche.* He's got a funny walk.
　② *step*　◇ *faire les démarches nécessaires pour obtenir quelque chose* to take the necessary steps to obtain something

démarrer VERB
　to start (*car*)

démêler VERB
　to untangle

le **déménagement** NOUN
　move　◇ *C'était le jour de notre déménagement.* It was the day we moved house.
* **un camion de déménagement** a removal van

déménager VERB
　to move house

le **déménageur** NOUN
　removal man

dément ADJECTIVE
　crazy

démentiel ADJECTIVE
　(FEM SING **démentielle**)
　insane　◇ *un projet démentiel* an insane scheme

se **démerder** VERB (*rude*)

to get by ◇ *Ne t'inquiète pas, il saura se démerder.* Don't worry, he'll get by.
- **Démerde-toi tout seul.** Sort things out for yourself.

demi ADJECTIVE, ADVERB
see also demi NOUN
half ◇ *Il a trois ans et demi.* He's three and a half.
- **Il est trois heures et demie.** It's half past three.
- **Il est midi et demi.** It's half past twelve.
- **à demi endormi** half asleep

le **demi** NOUN
see also demi ADJECTIVE
half pint of beer
- **Un demi, s'il vous plaît!** A beer please!

la **demi-baguette** NOUN
half a baguette

le **demi-cercle** NOUN
semicircle

la **demi-douzaine** NOUN
half-dozen ◇ *une demi-douzaine d'œufs* half a dozen eggs

la **demie** NOUN
half-hour ◇ *Le bus passe à la demie.* The bus comes by on the half-hour.

demi-écrémé ADJECTIVE
semi skimmed

la **demi-finale** NOUN
semifinal

le **demi-frère** NOUN
half-brother

la **demi-heure** NOUN
half an hour ◇ *dans une demi-heure* in half an hour ◇ *toutes les demi-heures* every half an hour

la **demi-journée** NOUN
half-day ◇ *On peut louer un parasol à la demi-journée.* You can hire a sun umbrella for a half-day.

le **demi-litre** NOUN
half litre ◇ *un demi-litre de lait* half a litre of milk

la **demi-livre** NOUN
half-pound ◇ *une demi-livre de tomates* half a pound of tomatoes

demi-sel ADJECTIVE
- **du beurre demi-sel** slightly salted butter

la **demi-sœur** NOUN
half-sister

la **démission** NOUN
resignation
- **donner sa démission** to resign

démissionner VERB
to resign

le **demi-tarif** NOUN
1 *half-price* ◇ *un billet à demi-tarif* a half-price season ticket

2 *half-fare* ◇ *voyager à demi-tarif* to travel half-fare

le **demi-tour** NOUN
- **faire demi-tour** to turn back ◇ *La nuit commence à tomber; il est temps de faire demi-tour.* It's getting dark; it's time we turned back.

la **démocratie** NOUN
democracy

démocratique ADJECTIVE
democratic

démodé ADJECTIVE
old-fashioned

la **demoiselle** NOUN
young lady
- **une demoiselle d'honneur** a bridesmaid

démolir VERB
to demolish

le **démon** NOUN
devil

démonter VERB
1 *to take down* (tent)
2 *to take apart* (machine)

démontrer VERB
to show

dénoncer VERB
to denounce
- **se dénoncer** to give oneself up ◇ *Il s'est dénoncé à la police.* He gave himself up to the police.

le **dénouement** NOUN
outcome

la **densité** NOUN
density

la **dent** NOUN
tooth ◇ *une dent de lait* a milk tooth ◇ *une dent de sagesse* a wisdom tooth

dentaire ADJECTIVE
dental

la **dentelle** NOUN
lace ◇ *un chemisier en dentelle* a lacy blouse

le **dentier** NOUN
denture

le **dentifrice** NOUN
toothpaste

le/la **dentiste** NOUN
dentist ◇ *Elle est dentiste.* She's a dentist.

le **déodorant** NOUN
deodorant

le **dépannage** NOUN
- **un service de dépannage** a breakdown service

dépanner VERB
1 *to fix* ◇ *Il a dépanné la voiture en cinq minutes.* He fixed the car in five minutes.

D

[2] *to help out* ◇ *Il m'a prêté cent francs pour me dépanner.* (informal) He lent me 100 francs to help me out.

la **dépanneuse** NOUN
breakdown lorry

le **départ** NOUN
departure ◇ *Le départ est à onze heures quinze.* The departure is at 11.15.
- **Je lui téléphonerai la veille de son départ.** I'll phone him the day before he leaves.

le **département** NOUN
[1] *department* ◇ *le département d'anglais à l'université* the English department at the university
[2] *administrative area*
France is divided into 96 départements, administrative areas rather like counties.
◇ *le département du Vaucluse* the Vaucluse region

dépasser VERB
[1] *to overtake* ◇ *Il y a une voiture qui essaie de nous dépasser.* There's a car trying to overtake us.
[2] *to pass* ◇ *Nous avons dépassé Dijon.* We've passed Dijon.
[3] *to exceed* (sum, limit)

dépaysé ADJECTIVE
- **se sentir un peu dépaysé** to feel a bit lost

se **dépêcher** VERB
to hurry ◇ *Dépêche-toi!* Hurry up!

dépendre VERB
- **dépendre de** to depend on ◇ *Ça dépend du temps.* It depends on the weather.
- **dépendre de quelqu'un** to be dependent on somebody
- **Ça dépend.** It depends.

dépenser VERB
to spend (money)

dépensier ADJECTIVE
(FEM SING **dépensière**)
- **Il est dépensier.** He's a big spender.
- **Elle n'est pas dépensière.** She's not exactly extravagant.

dépilatoire ADJECTIVE
- **une crème dépilatoire** a hair-removing cream

le **dépit** NOUN
- **en dépit de** in spite of ◇ *Il y est allé en dépit de mes conseils.* He went in spite of my advice.

déplacé ADJECTIVE
uncalled-for ◇ *C'était une remarque déplacée.* That remark was uncalled-for.

le **déplacement** NOUN

trip ◇ *Ça vaut le déplacement.* It's worth the trip.

déplacer VERB
[1] *to move* ◇ *Tu peux m'aider à déplacer la table?* Can you help me move the table?
[2] *to put off* ◇ *déplacer un rendez-vous* to put off an appointment
- **se déplacer (1)** to travel around ◇ *Il se déplace beaucoup pour son travail.* He travels around a lot for his work.
- **se déplacer (2)** to get around ◇ *Il a du mal à se déplacer.* He has difficulty getting around.
- **se déplacer une vertèbre** to slip a disc

déplaire VERB
- **Cela me déplaît.** I dislike this.

déplaisant ADJECTIVE
unpleasant

le **dépliant** NOUN
leaflet

déplier VERB
to unfold

déposer VERB
[1] *to leave* ◇ *J'ai déposé mon sac à la consigne.* I left my bag at the left luggage office.
[2] *to put down* ◇ *Déposez le paquet sur la table.* Put the parcel down on the table.
- **déposer quelqu'un** to drop somebody off

dépourvu ADJECTIVE
- **prendre quelqu'un au dépourvu** to take somebody by surprise ◇ *Sa question m'a pris au dépourvu.* His question took me by surprise.

la **dépression** NOUN
depression
- **faire de la dépression** to be suffering from depression
- **faire une dépression** to have a breakdown

déprimant ADJECTIVE
depressing

déprimer VERB
to get depressed ◇ *Il déprime tout le temps.* He gets depressed all the time.
- **Ce genre de temps me déprime.** This kind of weather makes me depressed.

depuis PREPOSITION, ADVERB
[1] *since* ◇ *Il habite Paris depuis 1983.* He's been living in Paris since 1983.
◇ *Je ne lui ai pas parlé depuis.* I haven't spoken to him since.
- **depuis que** since ◇ *Il a plu tous les jours depuis qu'elle est arrivée.* It's rained every day since she arrived.
[2] *for* ◇ *Il habite Paris depuis cinq ans.*

He's been living in Paris for five years.

- **Depuis combien de temps?** How long? ◇ *Depuis combien de temps est-ce que vous le connaissez?* How long have you known him?
- **Depuis quand?** How long? ◇ *Depuis quand est-ce que vous le connaissez?* How long have you known him?

le **député** NOUN
Member of Parliament

la **députée** NOUN
Member of Parliament

déraciner VERB
to uproot

le **dérangement** NOUN
- **en dérangement** out of order ◇ *Le téléphone est en dérangement.* The phone's out of order.

déranger VERB
[1] *to bother* ◇ *Excusez-moi de vous déranger.* I'm sorry to bother you.
- **Ne vous dérangez pas, je vais répondre au téléphone.** You stay there, I'll answer the phone.
[2] *to disorganize* ◇ *Ne dérange pas mes livres, s'il te plaît.* Don't disorganize my books, please.

déraper VERB
to skid

la **dermatologue** NOUN
dermatologist ◇ *Elle est dermatologue.* She's a dermatologist.

dernier ADJECTIVE
(FEM SING **dernière**)
[1] *last* ◇ *Il est arrivé dernier.* He arrived last. ◇ *la dernière fois* the last time
[2] *latest* ◇ *le dernier film de Spielberg* Spielberg's latest film
- **en dernier** last ◇ *Ajoutez le lait en dernier.* Put the milk in last.

dernièrement ADVERB
recently

dérouler VERB
[1] *to unroll*
[2] *to unwind*
- **se dérouler** to take place ◇ *L'action se déroule dans les années vingt.* The action takes place in the 1920s.
- **Tout s'est déroulé comme prévu.** Everything went as planned.

derrière ADVERB, PREPOSITION
see also **derrière** NOUN
behind

le **derrière** NOUN
see also **derrière** ADVERB
[1] *back* ◇ *la porte de derrière* the back door
[2] *backside* ◇ *un coup de pied dans le*

derrière a kick up the backside

des ARTICLE
des *is the contracted form of* **de + les.**
[1] *some* ◇ *Tu veux des chips?* Would you like some crisps?
des *is sometimes not translated.*
◇ *J'ai des cousins en France.* I have cousins in France. ◇ *pendant des mois* for months
[2] *any* ◇ *Tu as des frères?* Have you got any brothers? ◇ *la fin des vacances* the end of the holidays ◇ *la voiture des Durand* the Durands' car ◇ *Il arrive des États-Unis.* He's arriving from the United States.

dès PREPOSITION
as early as ◇ *dès le mois de novembre* from November
- **dès le début** right from the start
- **Il vous appellera dès son retour.** He'll call you as soon as he gets back.
- **dès que** as soon as ◇ *Il m'a reconnu dès qu'il m'a vu.* He recognized me as soon as he saw me.

désabusé ADJECTIVE
disillusioned

le **désaccord** NOUN
disagreement

désagréable ADJECTIVE
unpleasant

désaltérer VERB
- **L'eau gazeuse désaltère bien.** Sparkling water is very thirst-quenching.
- **se désaltérer** to quench one's thirst ◇ *Nous sommes allés dans un café pour nous désaltérer.* We went into a café to have a drink.

désapprobateur ADJECTIVE
(FEM SING **désapprobatrice**)
disapproving ◇ *un regard désapprobateur* a disapproving look

le **désastre** NOUN
disaster

le **désavantage** NOUN
disadvantage

désavantager VERB
- **désavantager quelqu'un** to put somebody at a disadvantage ◇ *Cette nouvelle loi va désavantager les femmes.* The new law will put women at a disadvantage.

descendre VERB
[1] *to go down* ◇ *Je suis tombé en descendant l'escalier.* I fell as I was going down the stairs.
[2] *to come down* ◇ *Attends en bas; je descends!* Wait downstairs; I'm coming down!

3 *to get down* ◇ *Vous pouvez descendre ma valise, s'il vous plaît?* Can you get my suitcase down, please?

4 *to get off* ◇ *Nous descendons à la prochaine station.* We're getting off at the next station.

la **descente** NOUN

way down ◇ *Je t'attendrai au bas de la descente.* I'll wait for you at the bottom of the hill.

- **une descente de police** a police raid

déséquilibré ADJECTIVE

unbalanced

déséquilibrer VERB

- **déséquilibrer quelqu'un** to throw somebody off balance ◇ *Le coup de poing l'a déséquilibré.* The punch threw him off balance.

désert ADJECTIVE

see also **désert** NOUN

deserted ◇ *Le dimanche, le centre commercial est désert.* On Sundays, the shopping centre is deserted.

- **une île déserte** a desert island

le **désert** NOUN

see also **désert** ADJECTIVE

desert

déserter VERB

to desert

désertique ADJECTIVE

desert ◇ *une région désertique* a desert region

désespéré ADJECTIVE

desperate

désespérer VERB

to despair ◇ *Il ne faut pas désespérer.* Don't despair.

le **désespoir** NOUN

despair

déshabiller VERB

to undress

- **se déshabiller** to get undressed

déshériter VERB

to disinherit

- **les déshérités** the underprivileged

déshydraté ADJECTIVE

dehydrated

désigner VERB

to choose ◇ *On l'a désignée pour remettre le prix.* She was chosen to present the prize.

- **désigner quelque chose du doigt** to point at something

le **désinfectant** NOUN

disinfectant

désinfecter VERB

to disinfect

désintéressé ADJECTIVE

1 *unselfish* ◇ *un acte désintéressé*

an unselfish action

2 *impartial* ◇ *un conseil désintéressé* impartial advice

désintéresser VERB

- **se désintéresser de quelque chose** to lose interest in something

le **désir** NOUN

1 *wish* ◇ *Vos désirs sont des ordres.* Your wish is my command.

2 *will* ◇ *le désir de réussir* the will to succeed

3 *desire* ◇ *Ses yeux brillaient de désir.* Her eyes were shining with desire.

désirer VERB

to want ◇ *Vous désirez?* (*in shop*) What would you like?

désobéir VERB

- **désobéir à quelqu'un** to disobey somebody

désobéissant ADJECTIVE

disobedient

désobligeant ADJECTIVE

unpleasant ◇ *faire une remarque désobligeante* to make an unpleasant remark

le **désodorisant** NOUN

air freshener

désolé ADJECTIVE

sorry ◇ *Je suis vraiment désolé.* I'm very sorry.

- **Désolé!** Sorry!

désopilant ADJECTIVE

hilarious

désordonné ADJECTIVE

untidy

le **désordre** NOUN

untidiness

- **Quel désordre!** What a mess!
- **en désordre** untidy ◇ *Sa chambre est toujours en désordre.* His bedroom is always untidy.

désormais ADVERB

from now on ◇ *Désormais, je boirai de l'eau.* From now on I'll drink water.

desquelles PRONOUN

desquelles *is the contracted form of* **de** + **lesquelles**.

◇ *des négociations au cours desquelles les patrons ont fait des concessions* negotiations during which the employers made concessions

desquels PRONOUN

desquels *is the contracted form of* **de** + **lesquels**.

◇ *les lacs au bord desquels nous avons campé* the lakes on the banks of which we camped

dessécher VERB

to dry out ◇ *Le soleil dessèche la*

peau. The sun dries your skin out.
desserrer VERB
  to loosen
le **dessert** NOUN
  pudding   ◇ *Qu'est-ce que vous désirez comme dessert?* What would you like for pudding?
le **dessin** NOUN
  drawing   ◇ *C'est un dessin de ma petite sœur.* It's a drawing my little sister did.
  ◆ **un dessin animé** a cartoon *(film)*
  ◆ **un dessin humoristique** a cartoon *(drawing)*
le **dessinateur** NOUN
  ◆ **un dessinateur industriel** a draughtsman
dessiner VERB
  to draw
dessous ADVERB
  see also **dessous** NOUN
  underneath
  ◆ **en dessous** underneath   ◇ *Soulève le pot de fleurs, la clé est en dessous.* Lift the flowerpot, the key's underneath.
  ◆ **par-dessous** underneath   ◇ *Le grillage ne sert à rien, les lapins passent par-dessous.* The fence is useless, the rabbits get in underneath.
  ◆ **là-dessous** under there   ◇ *Il s'est caché là-dessous.* He hid under there.
  ◆ **ci-dessous** below   ◇ *Complétez les phrases ci-dessous.* Complete the sentences below.
  ◆ **au-dessous de** below   ◇ *vingt degrés au-dessous de zéro* 20 degrees below zero
le **dessous** NOUN
  see also **dessous** ADVERB
  underneath
  ◆ **les voisins du dessous** the downstairs neighbours
  ◆ **les dessous** underwear   ◇ *des dessous en soie* silk underwear
le **dessous-de-plat** NOUN
  (PL les **dessous-de-plat**)
  tablemat
dessus ADVERB
  see also **dessus** NOUN
  on top   ◇ *un gâteau avec des bougies dessus* a cake with candles on top
  ◆ **par-dessus** over   ◇ *Nous avons sauté par-dessus la barrière.* We jumped over the gate.
  ◆ **au-dessus** above   ◇ *la taille au-dessus* the size above   ◇ *au-dessus du lit* above the bed
  ◆ **là-dessus (1)** on there   ◇ *Tu peux écrire là-dessus.* You can write on there.

  ◆ **là-dessus (2)** with that   ◇ *"Je démissionne!" Là-dessus, il est parti.* "I resign!" With that, he left.
  ◆ **ci-dessus** above   ◇ *l'exemple ci-dessus* the example above
le **dessus** NOUN
  see also **dessus** ADVERB
  top
  ◆ **les voisins du dessus** the upstairs neighbours
le/la **destinataire** NOUN
  addressee
la **destination** NOUN
  destination
  ◆ **les passagers à destination de Paris** passengers travelling to Paris
le **détachant** NOUN
  stain remover
détacher VERB
  to undo
le **détail** NOUN
  detail
  ◆ **en détail** in detail
le **détective** NOUN
  detective   ◇ *un détective privé* a private detective
déteindre VERB
  to fade *(in wash)*
détendre VERB
  to relax   ◇ *La lecture, ça me détend.* I find reading relaxing.
  ◆ **se détendre** to relax   ◇ *Il est allé prendre un bain pour se détendre.* He's gone to have a bath to relax.
la **détente** NOUN
  relaxation
le **détenu** NOUN
  prisoner
la **détenue** NOUN
  prisoner
se **détériorer** VERB
  to deteriorate
déterminé ADJECTIVE
  ① *determined*   ◇ *C'est un homme déterminé.* He's a determined man.
  ② *specific*   ◇ *un but déterminé* a specific aim
détestable ADJECTIVE
  horrible
détester VERB
  to hate
la **détonation** NOUN
  bang   ◇ *J'ai entendu une détonation.* I heard a bang.
le **détour** NOUN
  detour
  ◆ **Ça vaut le détour.** It's worth the trip.
le **détournement** NOUN
  ◆ **un détournement d'avion** a hijacking

détrempé ADJECTIVE
waterlogged

les **détritus** MASC NOUN
litter

détruire VERB
to destroy

la **dette** NOUN
debt

le **deuil** NOUN
- **être en deuil** to be in mourning

deux NUMBER
two ◇ *Il était deux heures.* It was two o'clock. ◇ *Elle a deux ans.* She's two.
- **deux fois** twice
- **tous les deux** both ◇ *Nous y sommes allées toutes les deux.* We both went.
- **le deux février** the second of February

deuxième ADJECTIVE
second ◇ *au deuxième étage* on the second floor

deuxièmement ADVERB
secondly

devais, devait, devaient VERB *see* devoir

dévaliser VERB
to rob

devant ADVERB, PREPOSITION
see also devant NOUN
1 *in front* ◇ *Il marchait devant.* He was walking in front.
2 *in front of* ◇ *Il était assis devant moi.* He was sitting in front of me.
- **passer devant** to go past ◇ *Nous sommes passés devant chez toi.* We went past your house.

le **devant** NOUN
see also devant ADVERB
front ◇ *le devant de la maison* the front of the house
- **les pattes de devant** the front legs

le **développement** NOUN
development
- **les pays en voie de développement** developing countries

développer VERB
to develop ◇ *donner une pellicule à développer* to take a film to be developed
- **se développer** to develop

devenir VERB
to become

devez VERB *see* devoir

la **déviation** NOUN
diversion

deviez VERB *see* devoir

deviner VERB
to guess

la **devinette** NOUN
riddle ◇ *poser une devinette à*

quelqu'un to ask somebody a riddle

devions VERB *see* devoir

dévisager VERB
- **dévisager quelqu'un** to stare at somebody

la **devise** NOUN
currency ◇ *les devises étrangères* foreign currency

dévisser VERB
to unscrew

dévoiler VERB
to unveil

devoir VERB
see also devoir NOUN

Present tense:	
je dois	nous devons
tu dois	vous devez
il/elle doit	ils/elles doivent

Past participle: *dû*
1 *to have to* ◇ *Je dois partir.* I've got to go.
2 *must* ◇ *Tu dois être fatigué.* You must be tired.
3 *to be due to* ◇ *Le nouveau centre commercial doit ouvrir en mai.* The new shopping centre is due to open in May.
- **devoir quelque chose à quelqu'un** to owe somebody something ◇ *Combien est-ce que je vous dois?* How much do I owe you?

le **devoir** NOUN
see also devoir VERB
1 *exercise*
- **les devoirs** homework
- **un devoir sur table** a written test
2 *duty* ◇ *Aller voter fait partie des devoirs du citoyen.* Voting is part of one's duty as a citizen.

devons VERB *see* devoir

dévorer VERB
to devour

dévoué ADJECTIVE
devoted

devra, devrai, devras, devrez, devrons, devront VERB *see* devoir

le **diabète** NOUN
diabetes

diabétique ADJECTIVE
diabetic ◇ *Je suis diabétique.* I'm diabetic.

le **diable** NOUN
devil

le **diabolo** NOUN
fruit cordial and lemonade
- **un diabolo menthe** a mint cordial and lemonade

diagonal ADJECTIVE
(MASC PL **diagonaux**)
diagonal

la **diagonale** NOUN
diagonal
* **en diagonale** diagonally

le **diagramme** NOUN
diagram

le **dialecte** NOUN
dialect

le **diamant** NOUN
diamond

le **diamètre** NOUN
diameter

la **diapo** NOUN (*informal*)
slide
* **une pellicule diapo** a slide film

la **diapositive** NOUN
slide ◇ *projeter des diapositives* to show some slides

la **diarrhée** NOUN
diarrhoea ◇ *avoir la diarrhée* to have diarrhoea

le **dictateur** NOUN
dictator

la **dictature** NOUN
dictatorship

la **dictée** NOUN
dictation

dicter VERB
to dictate

le **dictionnaire** NOUN
dictionary

diététique ADJECTIVE
* **un magasin diététique** a health food shop

le **dieu** NOUN
(PL les **dieux**)
god ◇ *Dieu* God ◇ *Mon Dieu!* Oh my God!

différent ADJECTIVE
1 *different* ◇ *pour des raisons différentes* for different reasons
2 *various* ◇ *pour différentes raisons* for various reasons
* **différent de** different to ◇ *Son point de vue est différent du mien.* His point of view is different to mine.

difficile ADJECTIVE
difficult ◇ *Son accent est difficile à comprendre.* His accent is difficult to understand.

difficilement ADVERB
* **faire quelque chose difficilement** to have trouble doing something ◇ *Ma grand-mère se déplace difficilement.* My grandmother has trouble getting around.
* **Je pouvais difficilement refuser.** It was difficult for me to refuse.

la **difficulté** NOUN
difficulty ◇ *avec difficulté* with difficulty
* **être en difficulté** to be in difficulties

digérer VERB
to digest

le **digestif** NOUN
after-dinner liqueur

digne ADJECTIVE
* **digne de** worthy of ◇ *digne de confiance* trustworthy

la **dignité** NOUN
dignity

le **dilemme** NOUN
dilemma ◇ *être devant un dilemme* to be faced with a dilemma

diluer VERB
to dilute

le **dimanche** NOUN
1 *Sunday* ◇ *Aujourd'hui, nous sommes dimanche.* It's Sunday today.
2 *on Sunday* ◇ *Dimanche, nous allons déjeuner chez mes grands-parents.* On Sunday we're having lunch at my grandparents'.
* **le dimanche** on Sundays ◇ *Le dimanche, je fais la grasse matinée.* I have a lie-in on Sundays.
* **tous les dimanches** every Sunday
* **dimanche dernier** last Sunday
* **dimanche prochain** next Sunday

diminuer VERB
to decrease * *Est-ce que tu peux diminuer le son?* Could you turn down the sound?

le **diminutif** NOUN
pet name

la **diminution** NOUN
1 *reduction*
2 *decrease*

la **dinde** NOUN
turkey ◇ *la dinde de Noël* the Christmas turkey

le **dindon** NOUN
turkey

> **le dindon** *refers to a live turkey, whereas* **la dinde** *refers to the meat.*

le **dîner** NOUN
see also **dîner** VERB
dinner (*evening meal*)

dîner VERB
see also **dîner** NOUN
to have dinner (*evening meal*)

dingue ADJECTIVE (*informal*)
crazy

diplomate ADJECTIVE
see also **diplomate** NOUN
diplomatic

le **diplomate** NOUN
see also **diplomate** ADJECTIVE
diplomat

la **diplomatie** NOUN
diplomacy

le **diplôme** NOUN
qualification

diplômé ADJECTIVE
qualified

dire VERB
1 *to say* ◇ *Il a dit qu'il ne viendrait pas.*
He said he wouldn't come.
- **on dit que...** they say that... ◇ *On dit que la nourriture est excellente là-bas.*
They say that the food is excellent there.
2 *to tell*
- **dire quelque chose à quelqu'un** to tell somebody something ◇ *Elle m'a dit la vérité.* She told me the truth. ◇ *Il nous a dit de regarder cette émission.* He told us to watch this programme.
- **On dirait qu'il va pleuvoir.** It looks as if it's going to rain.

direct ADJECTIVE
direct
- **en direct** live ◇ *une émission en direct* a live broadcast

directement ADVERB
straight ◇ *Il est rentré directement chez lui.* He went straight home.

le **directeur** NOUN
1 *headteacher* ◇ *Il est directeur.* He's a headteacher.
2 *manager* ◇ *Il est directeur du personnel.* He's a personnel manager.

la **direction** NOUN
1 *management* ◇ *la direction et les ouvriers* the management and the workers
2 *direction* ◇ *"toutes directions"* "all directions"

la **directrice** NOUN
1 *headteacher* ◇ *Elle est directrice.* She's a headteacher.
2 *manager* ◇ *Elle est directrice commerciale.* She's a sales manager.

dirent VERB *see* **dire**

le **dirigeant** NOUN
leader

la **dirigeante** NOUN
leader

diriger VERB
to manage ◇ *Il dirige une petite entreprise.* He manages a small company.
- **se diriger vers** to head for ◇ *Il se dirigeait vers la gare.* He was heading for the station.

dis VERB *see* **dire**
- **Dis-moi la vérité!** Tell me the truth!
- **dis donc** hey ◇ *Il a drôlement changé, dis donc!* Hey, he's really changed!

◇ *Dis donc, tu te souviens de Sam?* Hey, do you remember Sam?

disaient, disais, disait VERB *see* **dire**

la **discothèque** NOUN
disco (*club*)

le **discours** NOUN
speech

discret ADJECTIVE
(FEM SING **discrète**)
discreet

la **discrimination** NOUN
discrimination ◇ *la discrimination raciale* racial discrimination ◇ *la discrimination sexuelle* sex discrimination

la **discussion** NOUN
discussion

discutable ADJECTIVE
debatable

discuter VERB
1 *to talk* ◇ *Nous avons discuté pendant des heures.* We talked for hours.
2 *to argue* ◇ *C'est ce que j'ai décidé, alors ne discutez pas!* That's what I've decided, so don't argue!

disent, disiez, disions VERB *see* **dire**

disons VERB *see* **dire**
let's say ◇ *C'est à, disons, une demi-heure à pied.* It's half an hour's walk, say.

disparaître VERB
to disappear
- **faire disparaître quelque chose (1)** to make something disappear ◇ *Il a fait disparaître le lapin dans son chapeau.* He made the rabbit disappear in his hat.
- **faire disparaître quelque chose (2)** to get rid of something ◇ *Ils ont fait disparaître tous les documents compromettants.* They got rid of all the incriminating documents.

la **disparition** NOUN
disappearance
- **une espèce en voie de disparition** an endangered species

disparu ADJECTIVE
- **être porté disparu** to be reported missing

le **dispensaire** NOUN
community clinic

dispensé ADJECTIVE
- **être dispensé de quelque chose** to be excused something ◇ *Elle est dispensée de gymnastique.* She's excused gym.

disperser VERB
to break up ◇ *La police a dispersé les manifestants.* The police broke up the

demonstrators.

- **se disperser** to break up ◇ *Une fois l'ambulance partie, la foule s'est dispersée.* Once the ambulance had left, the crowd broke up.

disponible ADJECTIVE
available

disposé ADJECTIVE

- **être disposé à faire quelque chose** to be willing to do something ◇ *Il était disposé à m'aider.* He was willing to help me.

disposer VERB

- **disposer de quelque chose** to have access to something ◇ *Je dispose d'un ordinateur.* I have access to a computer.

la **disposition** NOUN

- **prendre ses dispositions** to make arrangements ◇ *Est-ce que vous avez pris vos dispositions pour partir en France?* Have you made arrangements to go to France?
- **avoir quelque chose à sa disposition** to have something at one's disposal ◇ *J'ai une voiture à ma disposition pour la semaine.* I have a car at my disposal for the week.
- **Je suis à votre disposition.** I am at your service.
- **Je tiens ces livres à votre disposition.** The books are at your disposal.

la **dispute** NOUN
argument

se **disputer** VERB
to argue

le **disquaire** NOUN
record dealer

le **disque** NOUN
record

- **un disque compact** a compact disc
- **le disque dur** hard disk

la **disquette** NOUN
diskette

disséminé ADJECTIVE
scattered

disséquer VERB
to dissect

la **dissertation** NOUN
essay

dissimuler VERB
to conceal

se **dissiper** VERB
to clear ◇ *Le brouillard va se dissiper dans l'après-midi.* The fog will clear during the afternoon.

le **dissolvant** NOUN
nail polish remover

dissoudre VERB
to dissolve

- **se dissoudre** to dissolve

dissuader VERB

- **dissuader quelqu'un de faire quelque chose** to dissuade somebody from doing something ◇ *Elle m'a dissuadé d'aller voir ce film.* She dissuaded me from going to see the film.

la **distance** NOUN
distance

la **distillerie** NOUN
distillery

distingué ADJECTIVE
distinguished

distinguer VERB
to distinguish

la **distraction** NOUN
entertainment ◇ *Il lit beaucoup: c'est sa seule distraction.* He reads a lot: it's his only form of entertainment.

distraire VERB

- **Va voir un film, ça te distraira.** Go and see a film, it'll take your mind off things.

distrait ADJECTIVE
absent-minded

distribuer VERB
[1] *to give out* ◇ *Distribue les livres, s'il te plaît.* Give out the books, please.
[2] *to deal* (cards)

le **distributeur** NOUN

- **un distributeur automatique** a vending machine
- **un distributeur de billets** a cash dispenser

dit VERB *see* **dire**

dit ADJECTIVE
known as ◇ *Pierre, dit Pierrot* Pierre, known as Pierrot

dites VERB *see* **dire**

- **Dites-moi ce que vous pensez.** Tell me what you think.
- **dites donc** hey ◇ *Dites-donc, vous, là-bas!* Hey, you there!

divers ADJECTIVE
diverse

- **pour diverses raisons** for various reasons

se **divertir** VERB
to enjoy oneself

divin ADJECTIVE
divine

diviser VERB
to divide ◇ *Quatre divisé par deux égalent deux.* 4 divided by 2 equals 2.

le **divorcé** NOUN
divorcee

la **divorcée** NOUN
divorcee

divorcer VERB

to get divorced
dix NUMBER
ten ◇ *Elle a dix ans.* She's ten. ◇ *à dix heures* at ten o'clock
- **le dix février** the tenth of February
dix-huit NUMBER ◇ *Elle a dix-huit ans.* She's eighteen. ◇ *à dix-huit heures* at 6 p.m.
dixième ADJECTIVE
tenth ◇ *au dixième étage* on the tenth floor
dix-neuf NUMBER ◇ *Elle a dix-neuf ans.* She's nineteen. ◇ *à dix-neuf heures* at 7 p.m.
dix-sept NUMBER ◇ *Elle a dix-sept ans.* She's seventeen. ◇ *à dix-sept heures* at 5 p.m.
la **dizaine** NOUN
about ten ◇ *une dizaine de jours* about ten days
le **do** NOUN
[1] *C* ◇ *en do majeur* in C major
[2] *do* ◇ *do, ré, mi...* do, re, mi...
le **docteur** NOUN
doctor ◇ *Elle est docteur.* She's a doctor.
le **documentaire** NOUN
documentary
le/la **documentaliste** NOUN
librarian
documenter VERB
- **se documenter sur quelque chose** to gather information on something
dodu ADJECTIVE
plump
le **doigt** NOUN
finger
- **les doigts de pied** the toes
dois, doit, doivent VERB see **devoir**
le **domaine** NOUN
[1] *estate* ◇ *Il possède un immense domaine en Normandie.* He owns a huge estate in Normandy.
[2] *field* ◇ *La chimie n'est pas mon domaine.* Chemistry's not my field.
domestique ADJECTIVE
see also domestique NOUN
domestic
- **les animaux domestiques** pets
le/la **domestique** NOUN
see also domestique ADJECTIVE
servant
le **domicile** NOUN
place of residence
- **à domicile** at home ◇ *Il travaille à domicile.* He works at home.
domicilié ADJECTIVE
- **"domicilié à:..."** "address:..."
dominer VERB

to dominate
- **se dominer** to control oneself
les **dominos** MASC NOUN
dominoes ◇ *jouer aux dominos* to play dominoes
le **dommage** NOUN
damage ◇ *La tempête a causé d'importants dommages.* The storm caused a lot of damage.
- **C'est dommage.** It's a shame. ◇ *C'est dommage que tu ne puisses pas venir.* It's a shame you can't come.
dompter VERB
to tame
le **dompteur** NOUN
animal tamer
la **dompteuse** NOUN
animal tamer
le **don** NOUN
[1] *donation*
[2] *gift* ◇ *avoir un don pour quelque chose* to have a gift for something
- **Elle a le don de m'énerver.** She's got a knack of getting on my nerves.
donc CONJUNCTION
so
le **donjon** NOUN
keep (*of castle*)
les **données** FEM NOUN
data
donner VERB
[1] *to give*
- **donner quelque chose à quelqu'un** to give somebody something ◇ *Elle m'a donné son adresse.* She gave me her address.
- **Ça m'a donné faim.** That made me feel hungry.
[2] *to give away* ◇ *Tu as toujours ta veste en daim?–Non, je l'ai donnée.* Have you still got your suede jacket?–No, I gave it away.
- **donner sur quelque chose** to overlook something ◇ *une fenêtre qui donne sur la mer* a window overlooking the sea
dont PRONOUN
[1] *of which* ◇ *deux livres, dont l'un est en anglais* two books, one of which is in English ◇ *le prix dont il est si fier* the prize he's so proud of
[2] *of whom* ◇ *dix blessés, dont deux grièvement* ten people injured, two of them seriously ◇ *la fille dont je t'ai parlé* the girl I told you about
doré ADJECTIVE
golden ◇ *une étoile dorée* a golden star
dorénavant ADVERB
from now on ◇ *Dorénavant, tu feras*

attention. From now on, you'll be careful.

dorloter VERB
to pamper

dormir VERB
[1] *to sleep* ◊ *Tu as bien dormi?* Did you sleep well?
[2] *to be asleep* ◊ *Ne faites pas de bruit, il dort.* Don't make any noise, he's asleep.

le **dortoir** NOUN
dormitory

le **dos** NOUN
back ◊ *dos à dos* back to back
- **faire quelque chose dans le dos de quelqu'un** to do something behind somebody's back ◊ *Elle me critique dans mon dos.* She criticizes me behind my back.
- **de dos** from behind
- **nager le dos crawlé** to swim backstroke
- **"voir au dos"** "see over"

la **dose** NOUN
dose ◊ *Ne pas dépasser la dose prescrite.* Do not exceed the stated dose.

le **dossier** NOUN
[1] *file* ◊ *une pile de dossiers* a stack of files
[2] *report* ◊ *un bon dossier scolaire* a good school report
[3] *feature* (*in magazine*)
[4] *back* (*of chair*)

la **douane** NOUN
customs

le **douanier** NOUN
customs officer

le **double** NOUN
- **le double** twice as much ◊ *Il gagne le double.* He earns twice as much. ◊ *le double du prix normal* twice the normal price
- **en double** in duplicate ◊ *Garde cette photo, je l'ai en double.* Keep this photo, I've got a copy of it.
- **le double messieurs** the men's doubles (*tennis*)

doubler VERB
[1] *to double* ◊ *Le prix a doublé en dix ans.* The price has doubled in 10 years.
[2] *to overtake* ◊ *Il est dangereux de doubler sur cette route.* It's dangerous to overtake on this road.
- **un film doublé** a dubbed film

douce ADJECTIVE *see* **doux**

doucement ADVERB
[1] *gently* ◊ *Il a frappé doucement à la porte.* He knocked gently at the door.
[2] *slowly* ◊ *Roulez doucement!* Drive

slowly! ◊ *Je ne comprends pas, parle plus doucement.* I don't understand, speak more slowly.

la **douceur** NOUN
[1] *softness* ◊ *Cette crème maintient la douceur de votre peau.* This cream keeps your skin soft.
[2] *gentleness* ◊ *parler avec douceur* to speak gently
- **L'avion a atterri en douceur.** The plane made a smooth landing.

la **douche** NOUN
shower
- **les douches** the shower room

se **doucher** VERB
to have a shower

doué ADJECTIVE
talented
- **être doué en quelque chose** to be good at something ◊ *Il est doué en maths.* He's good at maths.

douillet ADJECTIVE
(FEM SING **douillette**)
[1] *cosy* ◊ *un anorak douillet* a cosy anorak
[2] *soft* ◊ *Je ne supporte pas la douleur: je suis très douillette.* I can't stand pain: I'm a real softie.

la **douleur** NOUN
pain

douloureux ADJECTIVE
(FEM SING **douloureuse**)
painful

le **doute** NOUN
doubt
- **sans doute** probably

douter VERB
to doubt
- **douter de quelque chose** to doubt something ◊ *Je doute de sa sincérité.* I have my doubts about his sincerity.
- **se douter de quelque chose** to suspect something ◊ *Je ne me doutais de rien.* I didn't suspect anything.
- **Je m'en doutais.** I suspected as much.

douteux ADJECTIVE
(FEM SING **douteuse**)
[1] *dubious* ◊ *une plaisanterie d'un goût douteux* a joke in dubious taste
[2] *suspicious-looking* ◊ *un individu douteux* a suspicious-looking person

Douvres NOUN
Dover

doux ADJECTIVE
(FEM SING **douce**, MASC PL **doux**)
[1] *soft* ◊ *un tissu doux* soft material
◊ *les drogues douces* soft drugs
[2] *sweet* ◊ *du cidre doux* sweet cider
[3] *mild* ◊ *Il fait doux aujourd'hui.* It's

mild today.

[4] *gentle* ◇ *C'est quelqu'un de très doux.* He's a very gentle person.

* **en douce** on the quiet ◇ *Il m'a donné cinquante francs en douce.* He slipped me 50 francs on the quiet.

la **douzaine** NOUN
dozen ◇ *une douzaine d'œufs* a dozen eggs

* **une douzaine de personnes** about twelve people

douze NUMBER
twelve ◇ *Il a douze ans.* He's twelve.

* **le douze février** the twelfth of February

douzième ADJECTIVE
twelfth ◇ *au douzième étage* on the twelfth floor

la **dragée** NOUN
sugared almond

draguer VERB (*informal*)

* **draguer quelqu'un** to chat somebody up ◇ *Il est en train de la draguer.* He's chatting her up.

* **se faire draguer** to get chatted up ◇ *Elle aime se faire draguer.* She likes being chatted up.

le **dragueur** NOUN (*informal*)
flirt (*person*)

la **dragueuse** NOUN (*informal*)
flirt (*person*)

dramatique ADJECTIVE
tragic ◇ *une situation dramatique* a tragic situation

* **l'art dramatique** drama

le **drame** NOUN
drama (*incident*)

* **Ça n'est pas un drame si tu ne viens pas.** It's not the end of the world if you don't come.

le **drap** NOUN
sheet (*for bed*)

le **drapeau** NOUN
(PL les **drapeaux**)
flag ◇ *le drapeau français* the French flag

dressé ADJECTIVE
trained ◇ *un chien bien dressé* a well-trained dog

dresser VERB
[1] *to draw up* ◇ *dresser une liste* to draw up a list
[2] *to train* ◇ *dresser un chien* to train a dog

* **dresser l'oreille** to prick up one's ears ◇ *Quand elle a dit ça, il a dressé l'oreille.* When she said that, he pricked up his ears.

la **drogue** NOUN
drug ◇ *le problème de la drogue* the

drugs problem ◇ *la lutte contre la drogue* the war against drugs

* **les drogues douces** soft drugs
* **les drogues dures** hard drugs

le **drogué** NOUN
drug addict

la **droguée** NOUN
drug addict

droguer VERB

* **droguer quelqu'un** to drug somebody
* **se droguer** to take drugs

la **droguerie** NOUN
hardware shop

droit ADJECTIVE, ADVERB
see also **droit** NOUN
[1] *right* ◇ *le bras droit* the right arm ◇ *le côté droit* the right-hand side
[2] *straight* ◇ *une ligne droite* a straight line ◇ *Tiens-toi droite!* Stand up straight!

* **tout droit** straight on

le **droit** NOUN
see also **droit** ADJECTIVE
[1] *right* ◇ *les droits de l'homme* human rights

* **avoir le droit de faire quelque chose** to be allowed to do something ◇ *On n'a pas le droit de fumer à l'école.* We're not allowed to smoke at school.
[2] *law* ◇ *faire son droit* to study law ◇ *un étudiant en droit* a law student

la **droite** NOUN
see also **droit** ADJECTIVE
right ◇ *sur votre droite* on your right

* **à droite (1)** on the right ◇ *la troisième rue à droite* the third street on the right
* **à droite (2)** to the right ◇ *à droite de la fenêtre* to the right of the window ◇ *Tournez à droite.* Turn right.
* **la voie de droite** the right-hand lane
* **la droite** the right (*in politics*) ◇ *Elle est très à droite.* She's very right-wing.

droitier ADJECTIVE
(FEM SING **droitière**)
right-handed ◇ *Elle est droitière.* She's right-handed.

drôle ADJECTIVE
funny ◇ *Ça n'est pas drôle.* It's not funny.

* **un drôle de temps** funny weather

drôlement ADVERB (*informal*)
really ◇ *C'est drôlement bon.* It's really good.

du ARTICLE
du is the contracted form of *de* + *le*.
[1] *some* ◇ *Tu veux du fromage?* Would you like some cheese?
[2] *any* ◇ *Tu as du chocolat?* Have you got any chocolate? ◇ *la porte du garage*

the door of the garage ◇ *la femme du directeur* the headmaster's wife

dû VERB *see* **devoir**

see also **dû** ADJECTIVE

• **Nous avons dû nous arrêter.** We had to stop.

dû ADJECTIVE

(FEM **due**, MASC PL **dus**)

see also **dû** VERB

• **dû à** due to ◇ *un retard dû au mauvais temps* a delay due to bad weather

le **duc** NOUN

duke

la **duchesse** NOUN

duchess

dupe ADJECTIVE

• **Elle me ment mais je ne suis pas dupe.** She lies to me but I'm not taken in by that.

duquel PRONOUN

(MASC PL **desquels**, FEM PL **desquelles**)

duquel *is the contracted form of* **de** + **lequel**.

◇ *l'homme duquel il parle* the man he is talking about

dur ADJECTIVE, ADVERB

hard ◇ *travailler dur* to work hard

◇ *être dur avec quelqu'un* to be hard on somebody

durant PREPOSITION

1 *during* ◇ *durant la nuit* during the night

2 *for* ◇ *durant des années* for years

◇ *des mois durant* for months

la **durée** NOUN

length ◇ *Quelle est la durée des études d'ingénieur?* How long does it take to train as an engineer?

• **pour une durée de quinze jours** for a period of two weeks

• **de courte durée** short ◇ *un séjour de courte durée* a short stay

• **de longue durée** long ◇ *une absence de longue durée* a long absence

durement ADVERB

harshly

durer VERB

to last

la **dureté** NOUN

harshness ◇ *traiter quelqu'un avec dureté* to treat somebody harshly

dynamique ADJECTIVE

dynamic

dyslexique ADJECTIVE

dyslexic

D

E

l' **eau** FEM NOUN
(PL les **eaux**)
water
- **l'eau minérale** mineral water
- **l'eau plate** still water
- **tomber à l'eau** to fall through ◇ *Nos projets sont tombés à l'eau.* Our plans have fallen through.

éblouir VERB
to dazzle

l' **éboueur** MASC NOUN
dustman

ébouillanter VERB
to scald

l' **écaille** FEM NOUN
scale (*of fish*)

s' **écailler** VERB
to flake

l' **écart** MASC NOUN
gap
- **à l'écart de** away from ◇ *Ils se sont assis à l'écart des autres.* They sat down away from the others.

écarté ADJECTIVE
remote
- **les bras écartés** arms outstretched
- **les jambes écartées** legs apart

écarter VERB
to open wide (*arms, legs*)
- **s'écarter** to move ◇ *Ils se sont écartés pour le laisser passer.* They moved to let him pass.

l' **échafaudage** MASC NOUN
scaffolding

l' **échalote** FEM NOUN
shallot

l' **échange** MASC NOUN
exchange ◇ *en échange de* in exchange for

échanger VERB
to swap ◇ *Je t'échange ce timbre contre celui-là.* I'll swap you this stamp for that one.

l' **échantillon** MASC NOUN
sample

échapper VERB
- **échapper à** to escape from ◇ *Le prisonnier a réussi à échapper à la police.* The prisoner managed to escape from the police.
- **s'échapper** to escape ◇ *Il s'est échappé de prison.* He escaped from prison.
- **l'échapper belle** to have a narrow escape ◇ *Nous l'avons échappé belle.* We had a narrow escape.

l' **écharde** FEM NOUN
splinter of wood

l' **écharpe** FEM NOUN
scarf

s' **échauffer** VERB
to warm up (*before exercise*)

l' **échec** MASC NOUN
failure

les **échecs** MASC NOUN
chess ◇ *jouer aux échecs* to play chess

l' **échelle** FEM NOUN
1 *ladder*
2 *scale* (*of map*)

échevelé ADJECTIVE
dishevelled

l' **écho** MASC NOUN
echo

échouer VERB
- **échouer à un examen** to fail an exam

éclabousser VERB
to splash

l' **éclair** MASC NOUN
flash of lightning
- **un éclair au chocolat** a chocolate éclair

l' **éclairage** MASC NOUN
lighting

l' **éclaircie** FEM NOUN
bright interval

éclairer VERB
- **Cette lampe éclaire bien.** This lamp gives a good light.

l' **éclat** MASC NOUN
1 *fragment* (*of glass*) ◇ *La vase a volé en éclats.* The vase smashed into pieces.
2 *brightness* (*of sun, colour*)
- **des éclats de rire** roars of laughter

éclatant ADJECTIVE
brilliant ◇ *des dents d'une blancheur éclatante* brilliant white teeth

éclater VERB
1 *to burst* (*tyre, balloon*)
- **éclater de rire** to burst out laughing
- **éclater en sanglots** to burst into tears
2 *to break out* ◇ *La Seconde Guerre mondiale a éclaté en 1939.* The Second World War broke out in 1939.

écœurant ADJECTIVE
sickly

écœurer VERB
- **Tous ces mensonges m'écœurent.** All these lies make me sick.

l' **école** FEM NOUN
school ◇ *aller à l'école* to go to school ◇ *une école publique* a state school

◇ **une école maternelle** a nursery school *The* **école maternelle** *is a state school for 2-6 year-olds.*

l' **écolier** MASC NOUN
schoolboy

l' **écolière** FEM NOUN
schoolgirl

l' **écologie** FEM NOUN
ecology

écologique ADJECTIVE
ecological ◇ *une lessive écologique* an ecological washing powder

l' **économie** FEM NOUN
⊡ *economy* ◇ *l'économie de la France* the French economy
⊡ *economics* ◇ *un cours d'économie* an economics class

les **économies** FEM NOUN
savings
◆ **faire des économies** to save up ◇ *Je fais des économies pour partir en vacances.* I'm saving up for my holidays.

économique ADJECTIVE
⊡ *economic* ◇ *une crise économique* an economic crisis
⊡ *economical* ◇ *Il est plus économique d'acheter une grande boîte de lessive.* It's more economical to buy a big box of washing powder. ◇ *Cette petite voiture est économique.* This little car is cheap to run.

économiser VERB
to save

l' **écorce** FEM NOUN
⊡ *bark* (*of tree*)
⊡ *peel* (*of orange, lemon*)

s' **écorcher** VERB
◆ **Je me suis écorché le genou.** I've grazed my knee.

écossais ADJECTIVE, NOUN
(FEM SING **écossaise**)
⊡ *Scottish* ◇ *Elle est écossaise.* She's Scottish.
◆ **un Écossais** a Scot (*man*)
◆ **une Écossaise** a Scot (*woman*)
◆ **les Écossais** the Scots
⊡ *tartan* ◇ *une jupe écossaise* a tartan skirt

l' **Écosse** FEM NOUN
Scotland
◆ **en Écosse (1)** in Scotland ◇ *Il a passé une semaine en Écosse.* He spent a week in Scotland.
◆ **en Écosse (2)** to Scotland ◇ *Nous allons en Écosse l'été prochain.* We're going to Scotland next summer.

s' **écouler** VERB
⊡ *to flow out* (*water*)
⊡ *to pass* ◇ *Le temps s'écoule trop*

vite. Time passes too quickly.

écouter VERB
to listen to ◇ *J'aime écouter de la musique.* I like listening to music.
◆ **Écoute-moi!** Listen!

l' **écouteur** MASC NOUN
earpiece (*of phone*)

l' **écran** MASC NOUN
screen
◆ **le petit écran** television
◆ **l'écran total** sunblock

écraser VERB
⊡ *to crush* ◇ *Écrasez une gousse d'ail.* Crush a clove of garlic.
⊡ *to run over* ◇ *Regarde bien avant de traverser, sinon tu vas te faire écraser.* Look carefully before you cross or you'll get run over.
◆ **s'écraser** to crash ◇ *L'avion s'est écrasé dans le désert.* The plane crashed in the desert.

l' **écrevisse** FEM NOUN
crayfish

écrire VERB
to write ◇ *Nous nous écrivons régulièrement.* We write to each other regularly.
◆ **Ça s'écrit comment ?** How do you spell that?

l' **écrit** MASC NOUN
written paper ◇ *L'écrit d'anglais a lieu la semaine prochaine.* The written paper in English is next week.
◆ **par écrit** in writing

l' **écriteau** MASC NOUN
(PL les **écriteaux**)
notice

l' **écriture** FEM NOUN
writing ◇ *J'ai du mal à lire son écriture.* I can't read his writing.

l' **écrivain** MASC NOUN
writer ◇ *Elle est écrivain.* She's a writer.

l' **écrou** MASC NOUN
nut (*metal*)

s' **écrouler** VERB
to collapse

écru ADJECTIVE
off-white

l' **écureuil** MASC NOUN
squirrel

l' **écurie** FEM NOUN
stable

EDF ABBREVIATION (= Électricité de France)
French electricity company

Édimbourg NOUN
Edinburgh

éditer VERB
to publish ◇ *On vient d'éditer un*

nouveau dictionnaire. A new dictionary has just been published.

l'**éditeur** MASC NOUN
publisher

l'**édition** FEM NOUN
[1] *edition* ◦ *une édition de poche* a paperback edition
[2] *publishing* ◦ *Il travaille dans l'édition.* He works in publishing.

l'**édredon** MASC NOUN
eiderdown

l'**éducateur** MASC NOUN
teacher (*of people with special needs*)

éducatif ADJECTIVE
(FEM SING **éducative**)
educational ◦ *un jeu éducatif* an educational game

l'**éducation** FEM NOUN
[1] *education* ◦ *l'éducation physique* physical education ◦ *Il n'a pas beaucoup d'éducation.* He's not very well educated.
[2] *upbringing* ◦ *Il a reçu une éducation très stricte.* He had a very strict upbringing.

l'**éducatrice** FEM NOUN
teacher (*of people with special needs*)

éduquer VERB
to educate

effacer VERB
to rub out

effarant ADJECTIVE
amazing ◦ *Il a mangé une quantité effarante de pain.* He ate an amazing amount of bread.

effectivement ADVERB
indeed ◦ *Il est effectivement plus rapide de passer par là.* It is indeed quicker to go this way. ◦ *Oui, effectivement.* Yes, indeed.

effectuer VERB
[1] *to make* ◦ *Ils ont effectué de nombreux changements.* They have made a lot of changes.
[2] *to do* ◦ *On vient d'effectuer des travaux dans le bâtiment.* They have just done some work in the building.

effervescent ADJECTIVE
effervescent ◦ *un comprimé effervescent* an effervescent tablet

l'**effet** MASC NOUN
effect
◆ **faire de l'effet** to take effect ◦ *Ce médicament fait rapidement de l'effet.* This medicine takes effect quickly.
◆ **Ça m'a fait un drôle d'effet de le revoir.** It gave me a strange feeling to see him again.
◆ **en effet** yes indeed ◦ *Je ne me sens*

pas très bien. – En effet, tu as l'air pâle. I don't feel very well. – Yes, you do look pale.

efficace ADJECTIVE
[1] *efficient* ◦ *C'est une femme efficace.* She's an efficient woman.
[2] *effective* ◦ *un remède efficace* an effective remedy

s'**effondrer** VERB
to collapse

s'**efforcer** VERB
◆ **s'efforcer de faire quelque chose** to try hard to do something ◦ *Il s'efforce d'être aimable avec la clientèle.* He tries hard to be polite to the customers.

l'**effort** MASC NOUN
effort ◦ *faire un effort* to make an effort

effrayant ADJECTIVE
frightening

effrayer VERB
to frighten

effronté ADJECTIVE
cheeky ◦ *Ce gamin est vraiment effronté.* This kid's really cheeky.

effroyable ADJECTIVE
horrifying

égal ADJECTIVE
(MASC PL **égaux**)
equal ◦ *une quantité égale de farine et de sucre* an equal quantity of flour and sugar
◆ **Ça m'est égal. (1)** I don't mind. ◦ *Tu préfères du riz ou des pâtes? – Ça m'est égal.* Would you rather have rice or pasta? – I don't mind.
◆ **Ça m'est égal. (2)** I don't care. ◦ *Fais ce que tu veux, ça m'est égal.* Do what you like, I don't care.

également ADVERB
also ◦ *On appelle également la France l'Hexagone à cause de sa forme.* France is also called the Hexagon because of its shape.

égaler VERB
to equal

l'**égalité** FEM NOUN
equality
◆ **être à égalité** to be level ◦ *Maintenant les deux joueurs sont à égalité.* The two players are now level.

l'**égard** MASC NOUN
◆ **à cet égard** in this respect

égarer VERB
to mislay ◦ *J'ai égaré mes clés.* I've mislaid my keys.
◆ **s'égarer** to get lost ◦ *Ils se sont égarés dans la forêt.* They got lost in the forest.

l'**église** FEM NOUN
church ◇ _aller à l'église_ to go to
church

l'**égoïsme** MASC NOUN
selfishness

égoïste ADJECTIVE
selfish

l'**égratignure** FEM NOUN
scratch

l'**Égypte** FEM NOUN
Egypt

égyptien ADJECTIVE
(FEM SING **égyptienne**)
Egyptian

l'**élan** MASC NOUN
◆ **prendre de l'élan** to gather speed

s'**élancer** VERB
to hurl oneself

élargir VERB
to widen

l'**élastique** MASC NOUN
rubber band

l'**électeur** MASC NOUN
voter (man)

l'**élection** FEM NOUN
election ◇ _les élections présidentielles_
the presidential election

l'**électrice** FEM NOUN
voter (woman)

l'**électricien** MASC NOUN
electrician

l'**électricité** FEM NOUN
electricity ◇ _une facture d'électricité_
an electricity bill
◆ **allumer l'électricité** to turn on the light
◆ **éteindre l'électricité** to turn off the
light

électrique ADJECTIVE
electric ◇ _le courant électrique_ the
electric current

l'**électronique** FEM NOUN
electronics

élégant ADJECTIVE
smart

élémentaire ADJECTIVE
elementary

l'**éléphant** MASC NOUN
elephant

l'**élevage** MASC NOUN
cattle rearing ◇ _faire de l'élevage_ to
rear cattle
◆ **un élevage de porcs** a pig farm
◆ **un élevage de poulets** a chicken farm
◆ **les truites d'élevage** farmed trout

élevé ADJECTIVE
high ◇ _Le prix est trop élevé._ The
price is too high.
◆ **être bien élevé** to have good manners
◆ **être mal élevé** to have bad manners

l'**élève** MASC/FEM NOUN
pupil

élever VERB
1 _to bring up_ ◇ _Il a été élevé par sa
grand-mère._ He was brought up by his
grandmother.
2 _to breed_ ◇ _Son oncle élève des
chevaux._ His uncle breeds horses.
◆ **élever la voix** to raise one's voice
◆ **s'élever à** to come to ◇ _À combien
s'élèvent les dégâts?_ How much does
the damage come to?

l'**éleveur** MASC NOUN
breeder

éliminatoire ADJECTIVE
◆ **une note éliminatoire** a fail mark
◆ **une épreuve éliminatoire** a qualifying
round (sport)

éliminer VERB
to eliminate

élire VERB
to elect

elle PRONOUN
1 _she_ ◇ _Elle est institutrice._ She is a
primary school teacher.
2 _her_ ◇ _Vous pouvez avoir confiance
en elle._ You can trust her.
3 _it_ ◇ _Prends cette chaise: elle est plus
confortable._ Take this chair: it's more
comfortable.
elle _is also used for emphasis._
◇ _Elle, elle est toujours en retard!_ Oh,
SHE's always late!
◆ **elle-même** herself ◇ _Elle l'a choisi
elle-même._ She chose it herself.

elles PRONOUN
they ◇ _Où sont Anne et Rachel? – Elles
sont allées au cinéma._ Where are Anne
and Rachel? – They've gone to the
cinema.
◆ **elles-mêmes** themselves

éloigné ADJECTIVE
distant

s'**éloigner** VERB
to go far away ◇ _Ne vous éloignez
pas: le dîner est bientôt prêt!_ Don't go
far away: dinner will soon be ready!
◆ **Vous vous éloignez du sujet.** You are
getting off the point.

l'**Élysée** MASC NOUN
Élysée Palace
The Élysée is the residence of the French
president.

l'**emballage** MASC NOUN
◆ **le papier d'emballage** wrapping paper

emballer VERB
to wrap
◆ **s'emballer** (informal) to get excited
◇ _Il s'est emballé pour ce projet._ He got

really excited about this plan.

l'**embarquement** MASC NOUN
boarding ◇ *L'embarquement des passagers n'a pas encore été annoncé.* Passenger boarding has not been announced yet.

l'**embarras** MASC NOUN
embarrassment ◇ *Votre question me met dans l'embarras.* It's difficult for me to answer your question.
+ **Vous n'avez que l'embarras du choix.** The only problem is choosing.

embarrassant ADJECTIVE
embarrassing

embarrasser VERB
to embarrass ◇ *Cela m'embarrasse de vous demander encore un service.* I feel embarrassed to ask you to do something more for me.

embaucher VERB
to take on ◇ *L'entreprise vient d'embaucher cinquante ouvriers.* The firm has just taken on fifty workers.

les **embêtements** MASC NOUN
trouble

embêter VERB
to bother
+ **s'embêter** to be bored ◇ *Qu'est-ce qu'on s'embête ici!* Isn't it boring here!

l'**embouteillage** MASC NOUN
traffic jam

embrasser VERB
to kiss ◇ *Ils se sont embrassés.* They kissed each other.

s'**embrouiller** VERB
to get confused ◇ *Il s'embrouille dans ses explications.* He gets confused when he explains things.

émerveiller VERB
to dazzle

l'**émeute** FEM NOUN
riot

émigrer VERB
to emigrate

l'**émission** FEM NOUN
programme ◇ *une émission de télévision* a TV programme

s'**emmêler** VERB
to get tangled ◇ *Ma laine s'est emmêlée.* My wool has got tangled.

emménager VERB
to move in ◇ *Nous venons d'emménager dans une nouvelle maison.* We've just moved into a new house.

emmener VERB
to take ◇ *Ils m'ont emmené au cinéma pour mon anniversaire.* They took me to the cinema for my birthday.

emmerder VERB (*rude*)

+ **Ça m'emmerde!** It pisses me off!
+ **Je t'emmerde!** Piss off!
+ **s'emmerder** to be bored stiff

émotif ADJECTIVE
(FEM SING **émotive**)
emotional ◇ *Il est très émotif.* He's very emotional.

l'**émotion** FEM NOUN
emotion

émouvoir VERB
to move ◇ *Sa lettre l'a beaucoup émue.* She was deeply moved by his letter.

emparer VERB
+ **s'emparer de** to grab ◇ *Il s'est emparé de ma valise.* He grabbed my case.

l'**empêchement** MASC NOUN
+ **Nous avons eu un empêchement de dernière minute.** We were held up at the last minute.

empêcher VERB
to prevent ◇ *Le café le soir m'empêche de dormir.* Coffee at night keeps me awake.
+ **Il n'a pas pu s'empêcher de rire.** He couldn't help laughing.

l'**empereur** MASC NOUN
emperor

s'**empiffrer** VERB (*informal*)
to stuff one's face ◇ *Arrête de t'empiffrer!* Stop stuffing your face!

empiler VERB
to pile up

empirer VERB
to worsen ◇ *La situation a encore empiré.* The situation got even worse.

l'**emplacement** MASC NOUN
site ◇ *Un panneau indique l'emplacement de la vieille abbaye.* A sign shows the site of the old abbey.

l'**emploi** MASC NOUN
[1] *use* ◇ *prêt à l'emploi* ready for use
+ **le mode d'emploi** directions for use
[2] *job* ◇ *la création d'emplois* job creation
+ **un emploi du temps** a timetable

l'**employé** MASC NOUN
employee
+ **un employé de bureau** an office worker

l'**employée** FEM NOUN
employee
+ **une employée de banque** a bank clerk

employer VERB
[1] *to use* ◇ *Quelle méthode employez-vous?* What method do you use?
[2] *to employ* ◇ *L'entreprise emploie dix ingénieurs.* The firm employs ten

engineers.

l'**employeur** MASC NOUN
employer

empoisonner VERB
to poison

emporter VERB
to take ◇ *N'emportez que le strict nécessaire.* Only take the bare minimum.

• **plats à emporter** take-away meals
• **s'emporter** to lose one's temper ◇ *Je m'emporte facilement et finis souvent par le regretter.* I'm quick to lose my temper and I'm often sorry afterwards.

l'**empreinte** FEM NOUN
• **une empreinte digitale** a fingerprint

s'**empresser** VERB
• **s'empresser de faire quelque chose** to be quick to do something ◇ *Ils se sont empressés de nous annoncer la nouvelle.* They were quick to tell us the news.

emprisonner VERB
to imprison

l'**emprunt** MASC NOUN
loan

emprunter VERB
to borrow

• **emprunter quelque chose à quelqu'un** to borrow something from somebody ◇ *Est-ce que je peux t'emprunter dix francs?* Can I borrow ten francs from you?

ému ADJECTIVE
touched ◇ *J'ai été très ému par sa gentillesse.* I was very touched by her kindness.

en PREPOSITION, PRONOUN
1 *in* ◇ *Il habite en France.* He lives in France. ◇ *La mariée est en blanc.* The bride is in white. ◇ *Je le verrai en mai.* I'll see him in May.
2 *to* ◇ *Je vais en France cet été.* I'm going to France this summer.
3 *by* ◇ *C'est plus rapide en voiture.* It's quicker by car.
4 *made of* ◇ *C'est en verre.* It's made of glass. ◇ *un collier en argent* a silver necklace
5 *while* ◇ *Il s'est coupé le doigt en ouvrant une boîte de conserve.* He cut his finger while opening a tin.

• **Elle est sortie en courant.** She ran out.

> When en is used with **avoir** and **il y a**, it is not translated in English.

◇ *Est-ce que tu as un dictionnaire? – Oui, j'en ai un.* Have you got a dictionary? – Yes, I've got one.
◇ *Combien d'élèves y a-t-il dans ta classe? – Il y en a trente.* How many

pupils are there in your class? – There are 30.

> en is also used with verbs and expressions normally followed by **de** to avoid repeating the same word.

◇ *Si tu as un problème, tu peux m'en parler.* If you've got a problem, you can talk about it with me. ◇ *Est-ce que tu peux me rendre ce livre? J'en ai besoin.* Can you give me back that book? I need it. ◇ *Il a un beau jardin et il en est très fier.* He's got a beautiful garden and is very proud of it.

• **J'en ai assez.** I've had enough.

enceinte ADJECTIVE
pregnant ◇ *Elle est enceinte de six mois.* She's 6 months pregnant.

enchanté ADJECTIVE
delighted ◇ *Ma mère est enchantée de sa nouvelle voiture.* My mother's delighted with her new car.

• **Enchanté!** Pleased to meet you!

encombrant ADJECTIVE
bulky

encombrer VERB
to clutter

encore ADVERB
1 *still* ◇ *Il est encore au travail.* He's still at work. ◇ *Il reste encore deux morceaux de gâteau.* There are two bits of cake left.
2 *even* ◇ *C'est encore mieux.* That's even better.
3 *again* • *Il m'a encore demandé de l'argent.* He asked me for money again.

• **encore une fois** once again
• **pas encore** not yet ◇ *Je n'ai pas encore fini.* I haven't finished yet.

encourager VERB
to encourage

l'**encre** FEM NOUN
ink

l'**encyclopédie** FEM NOUN
encyclopaedia

l'**endive** FEM NOUN
chicory

endommager VERB
to damage

endormi ADJECTIVE
asleep

endormir VERB
to deaden ◇ *Cette piqûre sert à endormir le nerf.* This injection is to deaden the nerve.

• **s'endormir** to go to sleep

l'**endroit** MASC NOUN
place ◇ *C'est un endroit très tranquille.* It's a very quiet place.

E

- **à l'endroit (1)** the right way out
- **à l'endroit (2)** the right way up
endurant ADJECTIVE
  tough (person)
endurcir VERB
  to toughen up ◦ Ces exercices servent à endurcir les soldats. These exercises are to toughen up the soldiers.
- **s'endurcir** to become hardened
endurer VERB
  to endure
l'**énergie** FEM NOUN
  [1] _energy_ ◦ Je n'ai pas beaucoup d'énergie ce matin. I haven't got much energy this morning.
  [2] _power_ ◦ l'énergie nucléaire nuclear power
- **avec énergie** vigorously ◦ Il a protesté avec énergie. He protested vigorously.
énergique ADJECTIVE
  energetic ◦ C'est une femme très énergique. She's a very energetic woman.
- **des mesures énergiques** strong measures
énerver VERB
- **Il m'énerve!** He gets on my nerves!
- **Ce bruit m'énerve.** This noise gets on my nerves.
- **s'énerver** to get worked up
- **Ne t'énerve pas!** Take it easy!
l'**enfance** FEM NOUN
  childhood
- **Je le connais depuis l'enfance.** I've known him since I was a child.
l'**enfant** MASC/FEM NOUN
  child
l'**enfer** MASC NOUN
  hell
s'enfermer VERB
- **Il s'est enfermé dans sa chambre.** He shut himself up in his bedroom.
enfiler VERB
  [1] _to put on_ ◦ J'ai rapidement enfilé un pull avant de sortir. I quickly put on a sweater before going out.
  [2] _to thread_ ◦ J'ai du mal à enfiler cette aiguille. I am having difficulty threading this needle.
enfin ADVERB
  at last ◦ J'ai enfin réussi à le joindre. I have at last managed to contact him.
enflé ADJECTIVE
  swollen
enfler VERB
  to swell
enfoncer VERB
- **Il marchait, les mains enfoncées dans**

les poches. He was walking with his hands thrust into his pockets.
- **s'enfoncer** to sink ◦ Les roues de la voiture s'enfonçaient dans la boue. The wheels of the car were sinking into the mud.
s'**enfuir** VERB
  to run off
l'**engagement** MASC NOUN
  commitment
s'**engager** VERB
  to commit oneself ◦ Le Premier ministre s'est engagé à combattre le chômage. The Prime Minister has committed himself to fighting unemployment.
- **Il s'est engagé dans l'armée à dix-huit ans.** He joined the army when he was 18.
les **engelures** FEM NOUN
  chilblains
l'**engin** MASC NOUN
  machine
s'**engourdir** VERB
  to go numb ◦ Mes doigts se sont engourdis avec le froid. My fingers have gone numb with the cold.
engueuler VERB (informal)
- **engueuler quelqu'un** to tell somebody off ◦ Tu vas te faire engueuler! You're going to get a telling-off!
l'**énigme** FEM NOUN
  riddle
s'**enivrer** VERB
  to get drunk
enjamber VERB
  to stride over ◦ enjamber une barrière to stride over a fence
l'**enlèvement** MASC NOUN
  kidnapping
enlever VERB
  [1] _to take off_ ◦ Enlève donc ton manteau! Take off your coat!
  [2] _to kidnap_ ◦ Un groupe terroriste a enlevé la femme de l'ambassadeur. A terrorist group has kidnapped the ambassador's wife.
enneigé ADJECTIVE
  snowed up ◦ Les routes sont encore enneigées. The roads are still snowed up.
l'**ennemi** MASC NOUN
  enemy
l'**ennemie** FEM NOUN
  enemy
l'**ennui** MASC NOUN
  [1] _boredom_ ◦ C'est à mourir d'ennui. It's enough to bore you to death.
  [2] _problem_ ◦ avoir des ennuis to have problems

ennuyer VERB
to bother ◊ *J'espère que cela ne vous ennuie pas trop.* I hope it doesn't bother you too much.
→ **s'ennuyer** to be bored

ennuyeux ADJECTIVE
(FEM SING **ennuyeuse**)
1 *boring*
2 *awkward* ◊ *Tu ne peux pas venir plus tôt? C'est bien ennuyeux.* You can't come any earlier? That's rather awkward.

énorme ADJECTIVE
huge

énormément ADVERB
→ **Il a énormément grossi.** He's got terribly fat.
→ **Il y a énormément de neige.** There's an enormous amount of snow.

l'enquête FEM NOUN
1 *investigation* ◊ *La police a ouvert une enquête.* The police have begun an investigation.
2 *survey* ◊ *une enquête parmi les étudiants a montré que...* a survey of students has shown that...

enquêter VERB
to investigate ◊ *La police enquête actuellement sur le crime.* The police are currently investigating the crime.

enrageant ADJECTIVE
infuriating

enrager VERB
to be furious ◊ *J'enrage de n'avoir pas pu profiter de cette occasion.* I'm furious I wasn't able to take advantage of this opportunity.

l'enregistrement MASC NOUN
recording
→ **l'enregistrement des bagages** baggage check-in

enregistrer VERB
1 *to record* ◊ *Ils viennent d'enregistrer un nouvel album.* They've just recorded a new album.
2 *to check in* ◊ *Vous pouvez enregistrer plusieurs valises.* You can check in several cases.

s'enrhumer VERB
to catch a cold ◊ *Je suis enrhumé.* I've got a cold.

s'enrichir VERB
to get rich

enrouler VERB
to wind ◊ *Enroulez le fil autour de la bobine.* Wind the thread round the bobbin.

l'enseignant MASC NOUN
teacher

l'enseignante FEM NOUN
teacher

l'enseignement MASC NOUN
1 *education* ◊ *les réformes de l'enseignement* education reforms
2 *teaching* ◊ *l'enseignement des langues étrangères* the teaching of foreign languages

enseigner VERB
to teach ◊ *Mon père enseigne les maths dans un lycée.* My father teaches maths in a secondary school.

ensemble ADVERB
see also **ensemble** NOUN
together ◊ *tous ensemble* all together

l'ensemble NOUN
see also **ensemble** ADVERB
outfit ◊ *Elle portait un ensemble vert.* She was wearing a green outfit.
→ **l'ensemble de** the whole of ◊ *La grève a été suivie par l'ensemble du personnel.* The whole workforce went on strike.
→ **dans l'ensemble** on the whole

ensoleillé ADJECTIVE
sunny

ensuite ADVERB
then ◊ *Nous sommes allés au cinéma et ensuite au restaurant.* We went to the cinema and then to a restaurant.

entamer VERB
to start ◊ *Qui a entamé le gâteau?* Who's started the cake?

s'entasser VERB
to cram ◊ *Ils se sont tous entassés dans ma voiture.* They all crammed into my car.

entendre VERB
1 *to hear* ◊ *Je ne t'entends pas.* I can't hear you.
→ **J'ai entendu dire qu'il est dangereux de nager ici.** I've heard that it's dangerous to swim here.
2 *to mean* ◊ *Qu'est-ce que tu entends par là?* What do you mean by that?
→ **s'entendre** to get on ◊ *Il s'entend bien avec sa sœur.* He gets on well with his sister.

entendu ADJECTIVE
→ **C'est entendu!** Agreed! ◊ *Je passerai te prendre à sept heures, c'est entendu.* That's agreed then, I'll pick you up at 7 o'clock.
→ **bien entendu** of course ◊ *Il est bien entendu que je n'en parlerai à personne.* I won't tell anybody about it of course.

l'enterrement MASC NOUN
funeral (burial)

enterrer VERB

to bury

entêté ADJECTIVE
stubborn

s'**entêter** VERB
to persist ◇ *Il s'entête à refuser de voir le médecin.* He persists in refusing to go to the doctor.

l'**enthousiasme** MASC NOUN
enthusiasm

s'**enthousiasmer** VERB
to get enthusiastic ◇ *Il s'enthousiasme facilement.* He gets very enthusiastic about things.

entier ADJECTIVE
(FEM SING **entière**)
whole ◇ *Il a mangé une quiche entière.* He ate a whole quiche. ◇ *Je n'ai pas lu le livre en entier.* I haven't read the whole book.
◆ **le lait entier** full fat milk

entièrement ADVERB
completely

l'**entorse** FEM NOUN
sprain ◇ *Il s'est fait une entorse à la cheville.* He's sprained his ankle.

entourer VERB
to surround ◇ *Le jardin est entouré d'un mur de pierres.* The garden is surrounded by a stone wall.

l'**entracte** MASC NOUN
interval

l'**entraînement** MASC NOUN
training

entraîner VERB
1 *to lead* ◇ *Il se laisse facilement entraîner par les autres.* He's easily led.
2 *to train* ◇ *Il entraîne l'équipe de France depuis cinq ans.* He's been training the French team for five years.
3 *to involve* ◇ *Un mariage entraîne beaucoup de dépenses.* A wedding involves a lot of expense.
◆ **s'entraîner** to train ◇ *Il s'entraîne au foot tous les samedis matins.* He does football training every Saturday morning.

l'**entraîneur** MASC NOUN
trainer

entre PREPOSITION
between ◇ *Il est assis entre son père et son oncle.* He's sitting between his father and his uncle.
◆ **entre eux** among themselves
◆ **l'un d'entre eux** one of them

l'**entrecôte** FEM NOUN
rib steak

l'**entrée** FEM NOUN
1 *entrance*
2 *starter* (of meal) ◇ *Qu'est ce que*

vous prenez comme entrée? What would you like for the starter?

entreprendre VERB
to start on ◇ *Elle a entrepris des démarches pour essayer d'adopter un enfant.* She's started on the procedures for adopting a child.

l'**entrepreneur** MASC NOUN
contractor

l'**entreprise** FEM NOUN
firm

entrer VERB
1 *to come in* ◇ *Entrez donc!* Come on in!
2 *to go in* ◇ *Ils sont tous entrés dans la maison.* They all went into the house.
◆ **entrer à l'hôpital** to go into hospital

entre-temps ADVERB
meanwhile

l'**entretien** MASC NOUN
1 *maintenance* ◇ *un contrat d'entretien* a maintenance contract
2 *interview* ◇ *On m'a convoqué à un entretien pour un travail.* I've been called for a job interview.

l'**entrevue** FEM NOUN
interview ◇ *une entrevue avec le ministre* an interview with the minister

entrouvert ADJECTIVE
half-open ◇ *La porte était entrouverte.* The door was half open.

envahir VERB
to invade

l'**enveloppe** FEM NOUN
envelope

envelopper VERB
to wrap

envers PREPOSITION
see also **envers** NOUN
towards ◇ *Il est bien disposé envers elle.* He's well disposed towards her.
◇ *son attitude envers moi* his attitude to me

l'**envers** MASC NOUN
see also **envers** PREPOSITION
◆ **à l'envers** inside out ◇ *Je dois repasser ce chemisier à l'envers.* I have to iron this blouse inside out.

l'**envie** FEM NOUN
◆ **avoir envie de faire quelque chose** to feel like doing something ◇ *J'avais envie de pleurer.* I felt like crying. ◇ *J'ai envie d'aller aux toilettes.* I want to go to the toilet.
◆ **Cette glace me fait envie.** I fancy some of that ice cream.

envier VERB
to envy

environ ADVERB

about ◦ *C'est à soixante kilomètres environ.* It's about 60 kilometres.

l'**environnement** MASC NOUN
environment

les **environs** MASC NOUN
area ◦ *les environs de Nantes* the Nantes area ◦ *Il y a beaucoup de choses intéressantes à voir dans les environs.* There are a lot of interesting things to see in the area.
- **aux environs de dix-neuf heures** around 7 p.m.

envisager VERB
to consider ◦ *Est-ce que vous envisagez de travailler à l'étranger?* Are you considering working abroad?

s'**envoler** VERB
☐1 _to fly away_ ◦ *Le papillon s'est envolé.* The butterfly flew away.
☐2 _to blow away_ ◦ *Toutes mes feuilles de cours se sont envolées.* All my lecture notes blew away.

envoyer VERB
to send ◦ *Ma tante m'a envoyé une carte pour mon anniversaire.* My aunt sent me a card for my birthday.
- **envoyer quelqu'un chercher quelque chose** to send somebody to get something ◦ *Sa mère l'a envoyé chercher du pain.* His mother sent him to get some bread.

épais ADJECTIVE
(FEM SING **épaisse**)
thick

l'**épaisseur** FEM NOUN
thickness

épatant ADJECTIVE (*informal*)
great ◦ *C'est un type épatant.* He's a great guy.

l'**épaule** FEM NOUN
shoulder

l'**épée** FEM NOUN
sword

épeler VERB
to spell ◦ *Est-ce que vous pouvez épeler votre nom s'il vous plaît?* Can you spell your name please?

l'**épice** FEM NOUN
spice

épicé ADJECTIVE
spicy ◦ *Ce n'est pas assez épicé pour moi: je trouve ça trop fade.* It's not spicy enough for me: I think it's too bland.

l'**épicerie** FEM NOUN
grocer's shop

l'**épicier** MASC NOUN
grocer

l'**épicière** FEM NOUN
grocer

l'**épidémie** FEM NOUN
epidemic

épiler VERB
- **s'épiler les jambes** to shave one's legs
- **s'épiler les sourcils** to pluck one's eyebrows

les **épinards** MASC NOUN
spinach

l'**épine** FEM NOUN
thorn

l'**épingle** FEM NOUN
pin
- **une épingle de sûreté** a safety pin

l'**épisode** MASC NOUN
episode

éplucher VERB
to peel

l'**éponge** FEM NOUN
sponge

l'**époque** FEM NOUN
time ◦ *à cette époque de l'année* at this time of year
- **à l'époque** at that time ◦ *À l'époque, beaucoup de gens n'avaient pas l'eau courante.* At that time a lot of people didn't have running water.

l'**épouse** FEM NOUN
wife

épouser VERB
to marry

épouvantable ADJECTIVE
awful

l'**épouvante** FEM NOUN
terror
- **un film d'épouvante** a horror film

épouvanter VERB
to terrify

l'**époux** MASC NOUN
husband
- **les nouveaux époux** the newly-weds

l'**épreuve** FEM NOUN
☐1 _test_ ◦ *une épreuve orale* an oral test ◦ *une épreuve écrite* a written test
☐2 _event_ (*sport*)

éprouver VERB
to feel ◦ *Qu'est-ce que vous avez éprouvé à ce moment-là?* What did you feel at that moment?

épuisé ADJECTIVE
exhausted

épuiser VERB
to wear out ◦ *Ce travail m'a complètement épuisé.* This job has completely worn me out.
- **s'épuiser** to wear oneself out ◦ *Il s'épuise à garder un jardin impeccable.* He wears himself out keeping his garden immaculate.

l'**Équateur** MASC NOUN

Ecuador

l'**équateur** MASC NOUN
equator

l'**équation** FEM NOUN
equation

l'**équerre** FEM NOUN
set square

l'**équilibre** MASC NOUN
balance ◇ *J'ai failli perdre l'équilibre.* I nearly lost my balance.

équilibré ADJECTIVE
well-balanced

l'**équipage** MASC NOUN
crew

l'**équipe** FEM NOUN
team

équipé ADJECTIVE
◆ **bien équipé** well-equipped

l'**équipement** MASC NOUN
equipment

les **équipements** MASC NOUN
facilities ◇ *les équipements sportifs* sports facilities

l'**équitation** FEM NOUN
riding ◇ *faire de l'équitation* to go riding

l'**équivalent** MASC NOUN
equivalent

l'**erreur** FEM NOUN
mistake
◆ **faire erreur** to be mistaken

es VERB *see* **être**
◆ **Tu es très gentille.** You're very kind.

l'**escabeau** MASC NOUN
(PL les **escabeaux**)
stepladder

l'**escalade** FEM NOUN
climbing ◇ *faire de l'escalade* to go climbing

escalader VERB
to climb

l'**escale** FEM NOUN
◆ **faire escale** to stop off

l'**escalier** MASC NOUN
stairs

l'**escargot** MASC NOUN
snail

l'**esclavage** MASC NOUN
slavery

l'**esclave** MASC/FEM NOUN
slave

l'**escrime** FEM NOUN
fencing

l'**escroc** MASC NOUN
crook

l'**espace** MASC NOUN
space

s'**espacer** VERB
to become less frequent ◇ *Ses visites*

se sont peu à peu espacées. His visits became less and less frequent.

l'**espadrille** FEM NOUN
rope-soled sandal

l'**Espagne** FEM NOUN
Spain
◆ **en Espagne (1)** in Spain
◆ **en Espagne (2)** to Spain

espagnol ADJECTIVE, NOUN
Spanish ◇ *J'apprends l'espagnol.* I'm learning Spanish.
◆ **un Espagnol** a Spaniard (*man*)
◆ **une Espagnole** a Spaniard (*woman*)

l'**espèce** FEM NOUN
[1] *sort* ◇ *Elle portait une espèce de cape en velours.* She was wearing a sort of velvet cloak.
[2] *species* ◇ *une espèce en voie de disparition* an endangered species
◆ **Espèce d'idiot!** You idiot!

les **espèces** FEM NOUN
cash ◇ *payer en espèces* to pay cash

espérer VERB
to hope
◆ **J'espère bien.** I hope so. ◇ *Tu penses avoir réussi?–Oui, j'espère bien.* Do you think you've passed?–Yes, I hope so.

espiègle ADJECTIVE
mischievous

l'**espion** MASC NOUN
spy

l'**espionnage** MASC NOUN
spying
◆ **un roman d'espionnage** a spy novel

l'**espionne** FEM NOUN
spy

l'**espoir** MASC NOUN
hope

l'**esprit** MASC NOUN
mind ◇ *Ça ne m'est pas venu à l'esprit.* It didn't cross my mind.
◆ **avoir de l'esprit** to be witty ◇ *Il a beaucoup d'esprit.* He's very witty.

l'**esquimau** ®
(PL les **esquimaux**) MASC NOUN
ice lolly

l'**Esquimau** MASC NOUN
(PL les **Esquimaux**)
Eskimo

l'**Esquimaude** FEM NOUN
Eskimo

l'**essai** MASC NOUN
attempt ◇ *Ce n'est pas mal pour un coup d'essai.* It's not bad for a first attempt.
◆ **prendre quelqu'un à l'essai** to take somebody on for a trial period

essayer VERB
[1] *to try* ◇ *Essaie de rentrer de bonne*

heure. Try to come home early.

[2] *to try on* ◇ *Essaie donc ce pull: il devrait bien t'aller.* Try this sweater on: it ought to look good on you.

l'**essence** FEM NOUN
petrol

essentiel ADJECTIVE
(FEM SING **essentielle**)
essential

+ **Tu es là: c'est l'essentiel.** You're here: that's the main thing.

s'**essouffler** VERB
to get out of breath

l'**essuie-glace** MASC NOUN
windscreen wiper

essuyer VERB
to wipe

+ **essuyer la vaisselle** to dry the dishes

+ **s'essuyer** to dry oneself ◇ *Vous pouvez vous essuyer les mains avec cette serviette.* You can dry your hands on this towel.

est VERB *see* **être**
see also **est** ADJECTIVE, NOUN

+ **Elle est merveilleuse.** She's marvellous.

est ADJECTIVE
see also **est** VERB, NOUN

[1] *east* ◇ *la côte est des États-Unis* the east coast of the United States

[2] *eastern* • *dans la partie est du pays* in the eastern part of the country

l'**est** MASC NOUN
see also **est** VERB, ADJECTIVE
east ◇ *Je vis dans l'est de la France.* I live in the East of France.

+ **vers l'est** eastwards

+ **à l'est de Paris** east of Paris

+ **l'Europe de l'Est** Eastern Europe

+ **le vent d'est** the east wind

est-ce que ADVERB

+ **Est-ce que c'est cher?** Is it expensive?

+ **Quand est-ce qu'il part?** When is he leaving?

l'**esthéticienne** FEM NOUN
beautician

l'**estime** FEM NOUN

+ **J'ai beaucoup d'estime pour elle.** I think a lot of her.

estimer VERB

+ **estimer quelqu'un** to have great respect for somebody ◇ *Mon père l'estime beaucoup.* My father has a lot of respect for him.

+ **estimer que** to consider that ◇ *J'estime que c'est de sa faute.* I consider that it's his fault.

l'**estivant** MASC NOUN
holiday-maker

l'**estivante** FEM NOUN
holiday-maker

l'**estomac** MASC NOUN
stomach

l'**Estonie** FEM NOUN
Estonia

l'**estrade** FEM NOUN
platform

et CONJUNCTION
and

établir VERB
to establish

+ **s'établir à son compte** to set up in business

l'**établissement** MASC NOUN
establishment

+ **un établissement scolaire** a school

l'**étage** MASC NOUN
floor ◇ *au premier étage* on the first floor

+ **à l'étage** upstairs

l'**étagère** FEM NOUN
shelf

étaient VERB *see* **être**

l'**étain** MASC NOUN
tin

étais, était VERB *see* **être**

+ **Il était très jeune.** He was very young.

l'**étalage** MASC NOUN
display

étaler VERB
to spread ◇ *Il a étalé la carte sur la table.* He spread the map on the table.

étanche ADJECTIVE

[1] *watertight* ◇ *La toiture n'est pas étanche.* The roof isn't watertight.

[2] *waterproof* (watch)

l'**étang** MASC NOUN
pond

étant VERB *see* **être**

+ **Mes revenus étant limités...** My income being limited...

l'**étape** FEM NOUN
stage ◇ *une étape importante de la vie* an important stage in life

+ **faire étape** to stop off

l'**État** MASC NOUN
state (nation) ◇ *un chef d'État* a head of state

l'**état** MASC NOUN

[1] *state* (country)

[2] *condition* ◇ *en mauvais état* in poor condition

+ **remettre quelque chose en état** to repair something

+ **le bureau d'état civil** the registry office

les **États-Unis** MASC NOUN
United States

- **aux États-Unis (1)** in the United States
- **aux États-Unis (2)** to the United States

été VERB *see* **être**

see also été NOUN

- **Il a été promu.** He's been promoted.

l'**été** MASC NOUN

see also été VERB

summer

- **en été** in the summer

éteindre VERB

1 *to switch off* ◇ *N'oubliez pas d'éteindre la lumière en sortant.* Don't forget to switch off the light when you leave.

2 *to put out* (*cigarette*)

étendre VERB

to spread ◇ *Elle a étendu une nappe propre sur la table.* She spread a clean cloth on the table.

- **étendre le linge** to hang out the washing
- **s'étendre** to lie down ◇ *Je vais m'étendre cinq minutes.* I'm going to lie down for five minutes.

l'**éternité** FEM NOUN

- **J'ai attendu une éternité chez le médecin.** I waited for ages at the doctor's.

éternuer VERB

to sneeze

êtes VERB *see* **être**

- **Vous êtes en retard.** You're late.

étiez VERB *see* **être**

étinceler VERB

to sparkle

étions VERB *see* **être**

l'**étiquette** FEM NOUN

label ◇ *L'étiquette du pot de confiture s'est décollée.* The label has come off the jam pot.

s'**étirer** VERB

to stretch ◇ *Elle s'est étirée paresseusement.* She stretched lazily.

l'**étoile** FEM NOUN

star

- **une étoile de mer** a starfish
- **une étoile filante** a shooting star
- **dormir à la belle étoile** to sleep under the stars

étonnant ADJECTIVE

amazing

étonner VERB

to surprise ◇ *Cela m'étonnerait que le colis soit déjà arrivé.* I'd be surprised if the parcel had arrived yet.

étouffer VERB

- **On étouffe ici: ouvre donc les fenêtres.** It's stifling in here: open the windows.
- **s'étouffer** to choke ◇ *Ne mange pas si*

vite: tu vas t'étouffer! Don't eat so fast: you'll choke!

l'**étourderie** FEM NOUN

absent-mindedness

- **une erreur d'étourderie** a slip

étourdi ADJECTIVE

scatterbrained

l'**étourdissement** MASC NOUN

- **avoir des étourdissements** to feel dizzy

étrange ADJECTIVE

strange

étranger ADJECTIVE

(FEM SING **étrangère**)

see also étranger NOUN

foreign ◇ *un pays étranger* a foreign country

- **une personne étrangère** a stranger

l'**étranger** MASC NOUN

see also étranger ADJECTIVE

1 *foreigner*

2 *stranger*

- **à l'étranger** abroad

l'**étrangère** FEM NOUN

1 *foreigner*

2 *stranger*

étrangler VERB

to strangle

l'**être** MASC NOUN

see also être VERB

- **un être humain** a human being

être VERB

see also être NOUN

Present tense:	
je suis	nous sommes
tu es	vous êtes
il/elle est	ils/elles sont
Past participle: été	

1 *to be* ◇ *Je suis heureux.* I'm happy. ◇ *Mon père est instituteur.* My father's a primary school teacher. ◇ *Il est dix heures.* It's 10 o'clock.

2 *to have* ◇ *Il n'est pas encore arrivé.* He hasn't arrived yet.

les **étrennes** FEM NOUN

- **Nous avons donné des étrennes à la gardienne.** We gave the caretaker a New Year gift.

étroit ADJECTIVE

narrow

- **être à l'étroit** to be cramped ◇ *Nous sommes un peu à l'étroit dans cet appartement.* We're a bit cramped in this flat.

l'**étude** FEM NOUN

study ◇ *une étude de cas* a case study

- **faire des études** to be studying ◇ *Il fait des études de droit.* He's studying law.

l'**étudiant** MASC NOUN
student

l'**étudiante** FEM NOUN
student

étudier VERB
to study

l'**étui** MASC NOUN
case ◦ *un étui à lunettes* a glasses case

eu VERB *see* **avoir**
◆ **J'ai eu une bonne note.** I got a good mark.

euh EXCLAMATION
er ◦ *Euh...je ne m'en souviens pas.* Er...I can't remember.

l'**Europe** FEM NOUN
Europe
◆ **en Europe (1)** in Europe
◆ **en Europe (2)** to Europe

européen ADJECTIVE
(FEM SING **européenne**)
European

eux PRONOUN
them ◦ *Je pense souvent à eux.* I often think of them.
eux is also used for emphasis.
◦ *Elle a accepté l'invitation, mais eux ont refusé.* She accepted the invitation, but THEY refused.

évacuer VERB
to evacuate

s'**évader** VERB
to escape

l'**évangile** MASC NOUN
gospel

s'**évanouir** VERB
to faint

s'**évaporer** VERB
to evaporate

évasif ADJECTIVE
(FEM SING **évasive**)
evasive

l'**évasion** FEM NOUN
escape ◦ *Ils ont préparé leur évasion pendant des mois.* They spent months planning their escape.

éveillé ADJECTIVE
[1] *awake* ◦ *Il est resté éveillé toute la nuit.* He stayed awake all night.
[2] *bright* ◦ *C'est un enfant très éveillé pour son âge.* He's very bright for his age.

s'**éveiller** VERB
to awaken

l'**événement** MASC NOUN
event

l'**éventail** MASC NOUN
fan (hand-held)
◆ **un large éventail de prix** a wide range of prices

l'**éventualité** FEM NOUN

◆ **dans l'éventualité d'un retard** in the event of a delay

éventuel ADJECTIVE
(FEM SING **éventuelle**)
possible ◦ *une solution éventuelle* a possible solution ◦ *les conséquences éventuelles* the possible consequences

éventuellement ADVERB
possibly ◦ *Nous pourrions éventuellement avoir besoin de vous.* We may need you. ◦ *les difficultés que vous pourriez éventuellement rencontrer* the difficulties that you may have

l'**évêque** MASC NOUN
bishop

évidemment ADVERB
[1] *obviously* ◦ *Les tomates sont évidemment chères en cette saison.* Tomatoes are obviously dear at this time of year.
[2] *of course* ◦ *Est-ce que je peux utiliser ton téléphone?–Évidemment, tu n'as pas besoin de demander.* Can I use your phone?–Of course, you don't need to ask.

l'**évidence** FEM NOUN
◆ **C'est une évidence.** It's quite obvious.
◆ **de toute évidence** obviously ◦ *De toute évidence, il ne veut pas nous voir.* Obviously he doesn't want to see us.
◆ **être en évidence** to be clearly visible
◦ *La lettre était en évidence sur la table.* The letter was clearly visible on the table.
◆ **mettre en évidence** to reveal

évident ADJECTIVE
obvious

l'**évier** MASC NOUN
sink

éviter VERB
to avoid

évolué ADJECTIVE
advanced

évoluer VERB
to progress ◦ *La chirurgie esthétique a beaucoup évolué.* Plastic surgery has progressed a great deal.
◆ **Il a beaucoup évolué.** He has come on a great deal.

l'**évolution** FEM NOUN
[1] *development* ◦ *une évolution rapide* rapid development
[2] *evolution* ◦ *la théorie de l'évolution* the theory of evolution

évoquer VERB
to mention ◦ *Il a évoqué divers problèmes dans son discours.* He mentioned various problems in his speech.

E

exact ADJECTIVE

[1] *right* ◇ *Avez-vous l'heure exacte?* Have you got the right time? ◇ *Votre voiture est garée dehors, n'est-ce pas? – C'est exact.* Your car's parked outside, isn't it? – That's right.

[2] *exact* ◇ *Est-ce que vous pouvez m'indiquer le prix exact du billet?* Can you tell me the exact price of the ticket?

exactement ADVERB

exactly ◇ *C'est exactement ce que je cherchais.* That's exactly what I was looking for.

ex aequo ADJECTIVE

* **Ils sont arrivés ex aequo.** They finished neck and neck.

exagérer VERB

[1] *to exaggerate* ◇ *Vous exagérez!* You're exaggerating!

[2] *to go too far* ◇ *Ça fait trois fois que tu arrives en retard: tu exagères!* That's three times you've been late: you really go too far sometimes!

l'examen MASC NOUN

exam ◇ *Nous allons passer l'examen d'anglais vendredi matin.* We're doing our English exam on Friday morning. ◇ *un examen de français* a French exam

* **un examen médical** a medical

examiner VERB

to examine

exaspérant ADJECTIVE

infuriating

exaspérer VERB

to infuriate

l'excédent MASC NOUN

* **l' excédent de bagages** excess baggage

excéder VERB

to exceed ◇ *un contrat dont la durée n'excède pas deux ans* a contract for a period not exceeding two years

* **excéder quelqu'un** to drive somebody mad ◇ *Les cris des enfants l'excédaient.* The noise of the children was driving her mad.

excellent ADJECTIVE

excellent

excentrique ADJECTIVE

eccentric

excepté PREPOSITION

except ◇ *Toutes les chaussures excepté les sandales sont en solde.* All the shoes except sandals are reduced.

l'exception FEM NOUN

exception

exceptionnel ADJECTIVE

(FEM SING **exceptionnelle**)

exceptional

l'excès MASC NOUN

* **faire des excès** to overindulge ◇ *On fait souvent des excès aux environs de Noël.* People often overindulge around Christmas.

* **les excès de vitesse** speeding

excessif ADJECTIVE

(FEM SING **excessive**)

excessive

excitant ADJECTIVE

see also **excitant** NOUN

exciting

l'excitant MASC NOUN

see also **excitant** ADJECTIVE

stimulant ◇ *Le thé et le café sont des excitants.* Tea and coffee are stimulants.

l'excitation FEM NOUN

excitement

exciter VERB

to excite ◇ *Il était tout excité à l'idée de revoir ses cousins.* He was all excited about seeing his cousins again.

* **s'exciter** (*informal*) to get excited ◇ *Ne t'excite pas trop vite: ça ne va peut-être pas marcher!* Don't get excited too soon: it may not work!

l'exclamation FEM NOUN

exclamation

exclu ADJECTIVE

* **Il n'est pas exclu que...** It's not impossible that...

exclusif ADJECTIVE

(FEM SING **exclusive**)

exclusive

l'excursion FEM NOUN

[1] *trip* ◇ *faire une excursion* to go on a trip

[2] *walk* ◇ *une excursion dans la montagne* a walk in the hills

l'excuse FEM NOUN

[1] *excuse* ◇ *Il trouve toujours une bonne excuse pour ne pas faire la vaisselle.* He always finds a good excuse for not doing the washing-up.

[2] *apology* ◇ *présenter ses excuses* to offer one's apologies

* **un mot d'excuse** a note ◇ *Vous devez apporter un mot d'excuse signé par vos parents.* You have to bring a note signed by your parents.

excuser VERB

to excuse

* **Excusez-moi. (1)** Sorry! ◇ *Excusez-moi, je ne vous avais pas vu.* Sorry, I didn't see you.

* **Excusez-moi. (2)** Excuse me. ◇ *Excusez-moi, est-ce que vous avez l'heure?* Excuse me, have you got the time?

- **s'excuser** to apologize ⋄ *Il s'est excusé de son retard.* He apologized for being late.

exécuter VERB

[1] *to execute* ⋄ *Le prisonnier a été exécuté à l'aube.* The prisoner was executed at dawn.

[2] *to perform* ⋄ *Le pianiste va maintenant exécuter une valse de Chopin.* The pianist is now going to perform a waltz by Chopin.

l'**exemplaire** MASC NOUN
copy

l'**exemple** MASC NOUN
example ⋄ *donner l'exemple* to set an example

- **par exemple** for example

s'**exercer** VERB
to practise

l'**exercice** MASC NOUN
exercise

exhiber VERB
to show off ⋄ *Il aime bien exhiber ses décorations.* He likes showing off his medals.

- **s'exhiber** to expose oneself

l'**exhibitionniste** MASC NOUN
flasher

exigeant ADJECTIVE
hard to please ⋄ *Elle est vraiment exigeante.* She's really hard to please.

exiger VERB

[1] *to demand* ⋄ *Le propriétaire exige d'être payé immédiatement.* The landlord is demanding to be paid immediately.

[2] *to require* ⋄ *Ce travail exige beaucoup de patience.* This job requires a lot of patience.

l'**exil** MASC NOUN
exile

exister VERB
to exist ⋄ *Ça n'existe pas.* It doesn't exist. ⋄ *Ce manteau existe également en rose.* This coat's also available in pink.

exotique ADJECTIVE
exotic ⋄ *une plante exotique* an exotic plant ⋄ *un yaourt aux fruits exotiques* a tropical fruit yoghurt

expédier VERB
to send ⋄ *expédier un colis* to send a parcel

l'**expéditeur** MASC NOUN
sender

l'**expédition** FEM NOUN
expedition

- **l'expédition du courrier** the dispatch of the mail

l'**expéditrice** FEM NOUN
sender

l'**expérience** FEM NOUN

[1] *experience* ⋄ *Elle a plusieurs années d'expérience.* She's got several years' experience.

[2] *experiment* ⋄ *une expérience de chimie* a chemistry experiment

expérimenter VERB
to test ⋄ *Ces produits de beauté n'ont pas été expérimentés sur des animaux.* These cosmetics have not been tested on animals.

l'**expert** MASC NOUN
expert

l'**explication** FEM NOUN
explanation

- **une explication de texte** a critical analysis (*of a text*)

expliquer VERB
to explain ⋄ *Il m'a expliqué comment faire.* He explained to me how to do it.

- **ça s'explique** it's understandable

l'**exploit** MASC NOUN
achievement

l'**exploitation** FEM NOUN
exploitation ⋄ *Cet organisme lutte contre l'exploitation des femmes.* This organization fights against the exploitation of women.

- **une exploitation agricole** a farm

exploiter VERB
to exploit ⋄ *Il s'est fait exploiter par le patron du restaurant.* He was exploited by the owner of the restaurant.

explorer VERB
to explore

exploser VERB
to explode ⋄ *La bombe a explosé en pleine rue.* The bomb exploded in the middle of the street.

l'**explosif** MASC NOUN
explosive

l'**explosion** FEM NOUN
explosion

l'**exportateur** MASC NOUN
exporter

l'**exportation** FEM NOUN
export

l'**exportatrice** FEM NOUN
exporter

exporter VERB
to export

l'**exposé** MASC NOUN
talk ⋄ *On nous a demandé de faire un exposé sur l'environnement.* We were asked to give a talk on the environment.

exposer VERB

[1] *to show* ⋄ *Il expose ses peintures*

dans une galerie d'art. He shows his
paintings in a private art gallery.

[2] *to expose* ◇ *N'exposez pas la
pellicule à la lumière.* Do not expose the
film to light.

[3] *to set out* ◇ *Il nous a exposé les
raisons de son départ.* He set out the
reasons for his departure.

◆ **s'exposer au soleil** to stay out in the
sun ◇ *Ne vous exposez pas trop
longtemps au soleil.* Don't stay out too
long in the sun.

l'**exposition** FEM NOUN
exhibition ◇ *une exposition de
peinture* an exhibition of paintings

exprès ADVERB
[1] *on purpose* ◇ *Je suis sûr qu'il l'a fait
exprès.* I'm sure he did it on purpose.
[2] *specially* ◇ *Goûtes-y: j'ai fait ce
gâteau exprès pour toi.* Have a taste: I
made this cake specially for you.

l'**express** MASC NOUN
[1] *espresso* (coffee)
[2] *fast train* ◇ *Il a décidé de prendre
l'express de dix heures.* He decided to
catch the fast train at 10 o'clock.

l'**expression** FEM NOUN
[1] *expression*
[2] *phrase*

exprimer VERB
to express
◆ **s'exprimer** to express oneself ◇ *Il
s'exprime très bien pour un enfant de huit
ans.* For a child of 8, he expresses
himself very well.

exquis ADJECTIVE
exquisite

extérieur ADJECTIVE
see also **extérieur** NOUN

outside

l'**extérieur** MASC NOUN
see also **extérieur** ADJECTIVE

outside
◆ **à l'extérieur** outside ◇ *Les toilettes
sont à l'extérieur.* The toilet is outside.

l'**externat** MASC NOUN
day school

l'**externe** MASC/FEM NOUN
day pupil

l'**extincteur** MASC NOUN
fire extinguisher

extra ADJECTIVE (MASC, FEM, PL)
excellent ◇ *Ce fromage est extra!* This
cheese is excellent!

extraire VERB
to extract

l'**extrait** MASC NOUN
extract

extraordinaire ADJECTIVE
extraordinary

extravagant ADJECTIVE
extravagant

extrême ADJECTIVE
see also **extrême** NOUN

extreme ◇ *l'extrême droite et l'extrême
gauche* the far right and the far left

l'**extrême** MASC NOUN
see also **extrême** ADJECTIVE

extreme

extrêmement ADVERB
extremely

l'**Extrême-Orient** MASC NOUN
the Far East

l'**extrémité** FEM NOUN
end ◇ *La gare est à l'autre extrémité de
la ville.* The station is at the other end
of the town.

F

F. ABBREVIATION
franc

le **fa** NOUN
F

la **fabrication** NOUN
manufacture

fabriquer VERB
to make ◇ *fabriqué en France* made in France
* **Qu'est-ce qu'il fabrique?** (*informal*) What's he up to?

la **fac** NOUN (*informal*)
university

la **face** NOUN
* **face à face** face to face
* **en face de** opposite ◇ *Le bus s'arrête en face de chez moi.* The bus stops opposite my house.
* **faire face à quelque chose** to face something
* **Pile ou face? – Face.** Heads or tails? – Heads.

fâché ADJECTIVE
angry
* **être fâché contre quelqu'un** to be angry with somebody ◇ *Elle est fâchée contre moi.* She's angry with me.
* **être fâché avec quelqu'un** to be on bad terms with somebody ◇ *Elle est fâchée avec sa sœur.* She's on bad terms with her sister.

se **fâcher** VERB
* **se fâcher contre quelqu'un** to lose one's temper with somebody
* **se fâcher avec quelqu'un** to fall out with somebody ◇ *Il s'est fâché avec son frère.* He's fallen out with his brother.

facile ADJECTIVE
easy
* **facile à faire** easy to do

facilement ADVERB
easily

la **façon** NOUN
way ◇ *De quelle façon?* In what way?
* **de toute façon** anyway

le **facteur** NOUN
postman ◇ *Il est facteur.* He's a postman.

la **facture** NOUN
bill ◇ *une facture de gaz* a gas bill

facultatif ADJECTIVE
(FEM SING **facultative**)
optional

fade ADJECTIVE
tasteless ◇ *La soupe est un peu fade.*
The soup is a bit tasteless.

faible ADJECTIVE
weak ◇ *Je me sens encore faible.* I still feel a bit weak.
* **Il est faible en maths.** He's not very good at maths.

la **faiblesse** NOUN
weakness

la **faïence** NOUN
pottery

faillir VERB
* **J'ai failli tomber.** I nearly fell.

la **faim** NOUN
hunger
* **avoir faim** to be hungry

fainéant ADJECTIVE
lazy

faire VERB

Present tense:	
je fais	nous faisons
tu fais	vous faites
il/elle fait	ils/elles font
Past participle: fait	

1 *to make* ◇ *Je vais faire un gâteau pour ce soir.* I'm going to make a cake for tonight. ◇ *Ils font trop de bruit.* They're making too much noise. ◇ *Je voudrais me faire de nouveaux amis.* I'd like to make new friends.
2 *to do* ◇ *Qu'est-ce que tu fais?* What are you doing? ◇ *Il fait de l'italien.* He's doing Italian. ◇ *Qui veut bien faire la vaisselle?* Who'll do the dishes?
3 *to play* ◇ *Il fait du piano.* He plays the piano.
4 *to be* ◇ *Qu'est-ce qu'il fait chaud!* Isn't it hot! ◇ *Espérons qu'il fera beau demain.* Let's hope it'll be nice weather tomorrow.
* **faire tomber** to knock over ◇ *Le chat a fait tomber le vase.* The cat knocked over the vase.
* **faire faire quelque chose** to get something done ◇ *Je dois faire réparer ma voiture.* I've got to get my car repaired.
* **Je vais me faire couper les cheveux.** I'm going to get my hair cut.
* **Ne t'en fais pas!** Don't worry!

fais, faisaient, faisais, faisait VERB
see **faire**

le **faisan** NOUN
pheasant

faisiez, faisions, faisons, fait VERB
see **faire**

le **fait** NOUN

fact ◦ Le fait que... The fact that...
- **au fait** by the way ◦ Au fait, est-ce que tu as aimé le film d'hier? By the way, did you enjoy the film yesterday?
- **en fait** actually ◦ En fait je n'ai pas beaucoup de temps. I haven't got much time actually.

faites VERB see **faire**

la **falaise** NOUN
cliff

falloir VERB see **faut, faudra, faudrait**

famé ADJECTIVE
- **un quartier mal famé** a rough area

fameux ADJECTIVE
(FEM SING **fameuse**)
- **Ce n'est pas fameux.** It's not great.

familial ADJECTIVE
(MASC PL **familiaux**)
family ◦ une atmosphère familiale a family atmosphere
- **les allocations familiales** child benefit

familier ADJECTIVE
(FEM SING **familière**)
familiar ◦ C'est un nom qui m'est familier. The name's familiar.

la **famille** NOUN
[1] *family* ◦ une famille nombreuse a big family ◦ Nous passons Noël en famille. We have a family Christmas.
[2] *relatives* ◦ Il a de la famille à Paris. He's got relatives in Paris.

la **famine** NOUN
famine

la **fanfare** NOUN
band

fantaisie ADJECTIVE
- **des bijoux fantaisie** costume jewellery

fantastique ADJECTIVE
fantastic

le **fantôme** NOUN
ghost

la **farce** NOUN
[1] *stuffing* (for chicken, turkey)
[2] *practical joke* ◦ André aime faire des farces. André likes to play practical jokes.

farci ADJECTIVE
stuffed ◦ des tomates farcies stuffed tomatoes

la **farine** NOUN
flour

fasciner VERB
to fascinate

fasse, fassent, fasses, fassiez, fassions VERB see **faire**
- **Pourvu qu'il fasse beau demain!** Let's hope it'll be fine tomorrow!

fatal ADJECTIVE
fatal

- **C'était fatal.** It was bound to happen.

la **fatalité** NOUN
fate

fatigant ADJECTIVE
tiring

la **fatigue** NOUN
tiredness

fatigué ADJECTIVE
tired

se **fatiguer** VERB
to get tired

fauché ADJECTIVE (informal)
hard up

faudra VERB
faudra is the future tense of **falloir.**
- **Il faudra qu'on soit plus rapide demain.** We'll have to be quicker tomorrow.

faudrait VERB
faudrait is the conditional tense of **falloir.**
- **Il faudrait qu'on fasse attention.** We ought to be careful.

se **faufiler** VERB
- **Il s'est faufilé à travers la foule.** He made his way through the crowd.

la **faune** NOUN
wildlife

fausse ADJECTIVE see **faux**

faut VERB
faut is the present tense of **falloir.**
- **Il faut faire attention.** You've got to be careful.
- **Nous n'avons pas le choix, il faut y aller.** We've no choice, we've got to go.
- **Il faut que je parte.** I've got to go.
- **Il faut du courage pour faire ce métier.** It takes courage to do that job.

la **faute** NOUN
[1] *mistake* ◦ faire une faute to make a mistake
[2] *fault* ◦ Ce n'est pas de ma faute. It's not my fault.
- **sans faute** without fail ◦ Je t'appellerai sans faute. I'll phone you without fail.

le **fauteuil** NOUN
armchair
- **un fauteuil roulant** a wheelchair

faux ADJECTIVE, ADVERB
(FEM SING **fausse**)
see also **faux** NOUN
untrue ◦ C'est entièrement faux. It's totally untrue.
- **faire un faux pas** to trip
- **Il chante faux.** He sings out of tune.

le **faux** NOUN
see also **faux** ADJECTIVE
fake ◦ Ce tableau est un faux. This painting is a fake.

la **faveur** NOUN

favour
favori ADJECTIVE
(FEM SING **favorite**)
favourite
favoriser VERB
to favour ◇ *Ce système d'examen favorise ceux qui ont de la mémoire.* This exam system favours people with good memories.
le **fax** NOUN
fax
la **fée** NOUN
fairy
feignant ADJECTIVE (informal)
lazy
les **félicitations** FEM NOUN
congratulations
féliciter VERB
to congratulate
la **femelle** NOUN
female (animal)
féminin ADJECTIVE
1 *female* ◇ *les personnages féminins du roman* the female characters in the novel
2 *feminine* ◇ *Elle est très féminine.* She's very feminine.
3 *women's* ◇ *Elle joue dans l'équipe féminine de France.* She plays in the French women's team.
féministe ADJECTIVE
feminist
la **femme** NOUN
1 *woman*
2 *wife* ◇ *C'est la femme du directeur.* She's the headmaster's wife.
• **une femme au foyer** a housewife
• **une femme de ménage** a cleaning woman
le **fendre** VERB
to crack
la **fenêtre** NOUN
window
le **fenouil** NOUN
fennel
la **fente** NOUN
slot
le **fer** NOUN
iron
• **un fer à cheval** a horseshoe
• **un fer à repasser** an iron
fera, ferai, feras, ferez VERB see **faire**
férié ADJECTIVE
• **un jour férié** a public holiday
feriez, ferions VERB see **faire**
ferme ADJECTIVE
see also **ferme** NOUN
firm ◇ *Elle s'est montrée très ferme à*

mon égard. She was very firm with me.
la **ferme** NOUN
see also **ferme** ADJECTIVE
farm
fermé ADJECTIVE
1 *closed* ◇ *La pharmacie est fermée.* The chemist's is closed.
2 *off* ◇ *Est-ce que le gaz est fermé?* Is the gas off?
fermer VERB
1 *to close* ◇ *N'oublie pas de fermer la fenêtre.* Don't forget to close the window.
2 *to turn off* ◇ *As-tu bien fermé le robinet?* Have you turned the tap off?
la **fermeture** NOUN
• **les heures de fermeture** closing times
• **une fermeture éclair** ® a zip
le **fermier** NOUN
farmer
la **fermière** NOUN
1 *woman farmer*
2 *farmer's wife*
féroce ADJECTIVE
fierce ◇ *un animal féroce* a fierce animal
ferons, feront VERB see **faire**
les **fesses** FEM NOUN
buttocks
le **festival** NOUN
festival
la **fête** NOUN
1 *party* ◇ *Nous organisons une petite fête pour son anniversaire.* We're having a little party for his birthday.
• **faire la fête** to party
2 *name day* ◇ *C'est sa fête aujourd'hui.* It's his name day today.
• **une fête foraine** a funfair
• **la Fête Nationale** Bastille Day
• **les fêtes de fin d'année** the festive season
fêter VERB
to celebrate
le **feu** NOUN
(PL les **feux**)
1 *fire* ◇ *prendre feu* to catch fire
◇ *faire du feu* to make a fire
• **Au feu!** Fire!
2 *traffic light* ◇ *un feu rouge* a red light ◇ *Tournez à gauche aux feux.* Turn left at the lights.
• **Avez-vous du feu?** Have you got a light?
3 *heat* ◇ *...mijoter à feu doux* ...simmer over a gentle heat
• **un feu d'artifice** a firework display
le **feuillage** NOUN
leaves

la **feuille** NOUN
1 *leaf* ◇ *des feuilles mortes* fallen leaves
2 *sheet* ◇ *une feuille de papier* a sheet of paper
- **une feuille de maladie** a claim form for medical expenses

feuilleté ADJECTIVE
- **de la pâte feuilletée** flaky pastry

feuilleter VERB
to leaf through

le **feuilleton** NOUN
serial

le **feutre** NOUN
felt
- **un stylo-feutre** a felt-tip pen

la **fève** NOUN
broad bean

février MASC NOUN
February
- **en février** in February

fiable ADJECTIVE
reliable

les **fiançailles** FEM NOUN
engagement SING

fiancé ADJECTIVE
- **être fiancé à quelqu'un** to be engaged to somebody

se **fiancer** VERB
to get engaged

la **ficelle** NOUN
1 *string* ◇ *Passe-moi un bout de ficelle.* Give me a piece of string.
2 *thin baguette* (*bread*)

la **fiche** NOUN
form ◇ *Remplissez cette fiche s'il vous plaît.* Fill in this form please.

se **ficher** VERB (*informal*)
- **Je m'en fiche!** I don't care!
- **Fiche-moi la paix!** Leave me alone!
- **Quoi, tu n'as fait que ça? Tu te fiches de moi!** You've only done that much? You can't be serious!

fichu ADJECTIVE (*informal*)
- **Ce parapluie est fichu.** This umbrella's knackered.

fidèle ADJECTIVE
faithful

fier ADJECTIVE
(FEM SING **fière**)
proud

la **fierté** NOUN
pride

la **fièvre** NOUN
fever ◇ *J'ai de la fièvre.* I've got a temperature. ◇ *Il a trente-neuf de fièvre.* He's got a temperature of 39°C.

fiévreux ADJECTIVE
(FEM SING **fiévreuse**)
feverish

la **figue** NOUN
fig

la **figure** NOUN
1 *face* ◇ *Il a reçu le ballon en pleine figure.* The ball hit him smack in the face.
2 *figure* (*illustration*) ◇ *Voir figure 2.1, page 32.* See figure 2.1, page 32.

le **fil** NOUN
thread ◇ *le fil à coudre* sewing thread
- **le fil de fer** wire
- **un coup de fil** a phone call

la **file** NOUN
line (*of people, objects*)
- **une file d'attente** a queue ◇ *se mettre à la file* to join the queue
- **à la file** one after the other
- **en file indienne** in single file

filer VERB
to speed along ◇ *Les voitures filent sur l'autoroute.* The cars are speeding along the motorway.
- **File dans ta chambre!** Off to your room with you!

le **filet** NOUN
net

la **fille** NOUN
1 *girl* ◇ *C'est une école de filles.* It's a girls' school.
2 *daughter* ◇ *C'est leur fille aînée.* She's their oldest daughter.

la **fillette** NOUN
little girl

le **filleul** NOUN
godson

la **filleule** NOUN
goddaughter

le **film** NOUN
film
- **un film policier** a thriller
- **un film d'aventures** an adventure film
- **un film d'épouvante** a horror film

le **fils** NOUN
son

la **fin** NOUN
see also **fin** ADJECTIVE
end
- **sans fin** endless

fin ADJECTIVE
see also **fin** NOUN
fine
- **des fines herbes** mixed herbs

la **finale** NOUN
final ◇ *les quarts de finale* the quarter finals

finalement ADVERB
1 *at last* ◇ *Nous sommes finalement arrivés.* At last we arrived.

2 *after all* ◇ *Finalement, tu avais raison.* You were right after all.

fini ADJECTIVE
finished

finir VERB
to finish ◇ *Le cours finit à onze heures.* The lesson finishes at 11 o'clock. ◇ *Je viens de finir ce livre.* I've just finished this book.
* **Il a fini par se décider.** He made up his mind in the end.

finlandais ADJECTIVE, NOUN
Finnish ◇ *Ils parlent finlandais.* They speak Finnish.
* **un Finlandais** a Finn (*man*)
* **une Finlandaise** a Finn (*woman*)
* **les Finlandais** the Finnish

la **Finlande** NOUN
Finland

la **firme** NOUN
firm

fis VERB *see* **faire**

la **fissure** NOUN
crack

fit VERB *see* **faire**

fixe ADJECTIVE
1 *steady* ◇ *Il n'a pas d'emploi fixe.* He hasn't got a steady job.
2 *set* ◇ *Il mange toujours à heures fixes.* He always eats at set times.
* **un menu à prix fixe** a set menu

fixer VERB
1 *to fix* ◇ *Les volets sont fixés avec des crochets.* The shutters are fixed with hooks. ◇ *Nous avons fixé une heure pour nous retrouver.* We fixed a time to meet.
2 *to stare at* ◇ *Ne fixe pas les gens comme ça!* Don't stare at people like that!

le **flacon** NOUN
bottle ◇ *un flacon de parfum* a bottle of perfume

le **flageolet** NOUN
small haricot bean

flamand ADJECTIVE, NOUN
(FEM SING **flamande**)
1 *Flemish* ◇ *Il parle flamand chez lui.* He speaks Flemish at home.
2 *Fleming* (*Dutch-speaking Belgian*)
* **les Flamands** the Dutch-speaking Belgians

flambé ADJECTIVE
* **des bananes flambées** flambéed bananas

la **flamme** NOUN
flame
* **en flammes** on fire

flan NOUN

baked custard

flâner VERB
to stroll

la **flaque** NOUN
puddle (*of water*)

le **flash** NOUN
(PL **les flashes**)
flash (*of camera*)
* **un flash d'information** a newsflash

flatter VERB
to flatter

la **flèche** NOUN
arrow

les **fléchettes** FEM NOUN
darts ◇ *jouer aux fléchettes* to play darts

la **fleur** NOUN
flower

fleuri ADJECTIVE
1 *full of flowers* ◇ *Son jardin était très fleuri.* Her garden was full of flowers.
2 *flowery* ◇ *un papier peint fleuri* flowery wallpaper

fleurir VERB
to flower ◇ *Cette plante fleurit en automne.* This plant flowers in autumn.

le/la **fleuriste** NOUN
florist

le **fleuve** NOUN
river

le **flic** (*informal*) NOUN
cop

le **flipper** NOUN
pinball machine

flirter VERB
to flirt

le **flocon** NOUN
flake

flotter VERB
to float

flou ADJECTIVE
blurred

le **fluor** NOUN
* **le dentifrice au fluor** fluoride toothpaste

la **flûte** NOUN
flute ◇ *Je joue de la flûte.* I play the flute.
* **Flûte!** (*informal*) Heck!

la **foi** NOUN
faith

le **foie** NOUN
liver
* **une crise de foie** a stomach upset

le **foin** NOUN
hay
* **un rhume des foins** hay fever

la **foire** NOUN

fair
la **fois** NOUN
  time ◦ *la première fois* the first time
  ◦ *deux fois deux font quatre* 2 times 2 is
  4
  ◆ **une fois** once
  ◆ **deux fois** twice ◦ *deux fois plus de*
  gens twice as many people
  ◆ **une fois que** once ◦ *Tu te sentiras*
  mieux une fois que tu auras mangé.
  You'll feel better once you've had
  something to eat.
  ◆ **à la fois** at once ◦ *Je ne peux pas faire*
  deux choses à la fois. I can't do two
  things at once.
la **folie** NOUN
  madness ◦ *C'est de la folie pure!* It's
  absolute madness!
  ◆ **faire une folie** to be extravagant
folklorique ADJECTIVE
  folk ◦ *de la musique folklorique* folk
  music
folle ADJECTIVE
  (MASC SING **fou**)
  mad
foncé ADJECTIVE
  dark ◦ *bleu foncé* dark blue
foncer VERB (*informal*)
  ◆ **Je vais foncer à la boulangerie.** I'm
  just going to dash to the baker's.
la **fonction** NOUN
  function
  ◆ **une voiture de fonction** a company car
le/la **fonctionnaire** NOUN
  civil servant
fonctionner VERB
  to work
le **fond** NOUN
  ☐ *bottom* ◦ *Mon porte-monnaie est au*
  fond de mon sac. My purse is at the
  bottom of my bag.
  ☐ *end* ◦ *Les toilettes sont au fond du*
  couloir. The toilets are at the end of the
  corridor.
  ◆ **dans le fond** all things considered
  ◦ *Dans le fond, ce n'est pas si grave.* All
  things considered, it's not that bad.
fonder VERB
  to found
fondre VERB
  to melt ◦ *La tablette de chocolat a*
  fondu dans ma poche. The bar of
  chocolate melted in my pocket.
  ◆ **fondre en larmes** to burst into tears
fondu ADJECTIVE
  ◆ **du beurre fondu** melted butter
font VERB *see* **faire**
la **fontaine** NOUN
  fountain

le **foot** NOUN (*informal*)
  football
le **football** NOUN
  football ◦ *jouer au football* to play
  football
le **footballeur** NOUN
  footballer
le **footing** NOUN
  jogging ◦ *faire du footing* to go
  jogging
forain ADJECTIVE
  see also **forain** NOUN
  ◆ **une fête foraine** a funfair
le **forain** NOUN
  see also **forain** ADJECTIVE
  fairground worker
la **force** NOUN
  strength ◦ *Je n'ai pas beaucoup de*
  force dans les bras. I haven't got much
  strength in my arms.
  ◆ **à force de** by ◦ *Il a grossi à force de*
  manger autant. He got fat by eating so
  much.
  ◆ **de force** by force ◦ *Ils lui ont enlevé*
  son pistolet de force. They took the gun
  from him by force.
forcé ADJECTIVE
  forced ◦ *un sourire forcé* a forced
  smile
  ◆ **C'est forcé.** (*informal*) It's inevitable.
forcément ADVERB
  ◆ **Ça devait forcément arriver.** That was
  bound to happen.
  ◆ **pas forcément** not necessarily
la **forêt** NOUN
  forest
le **forfait** NOUN
  all-in price
  ◆ **C'est compris dans le forfait.** It's
  included in the price.
la **formalité** NOUN
  formality ◦ *Ce n'est qu'une simple*
  formalité. It's just a formality.
le **format** NOUN
  size
la **formation** NOUN
  training ◦ *la formation professionnelle*
  vocational training
  ◆ **Il a une formation d'ingénieur.** He is a
  trained engineer.
la **forme** NOUN
  shape
  ◆ **être en forme** to be in good shape
  ◆ **Je ne suis pas en forme aujourd'hui.**
  I'm not feeling too good today.
  ◆ **Tu as l'air en forme.** You're looking
  well.
formellement ADVERB
  strictly ◦ *Il est formellement interdit de*

fumer dans les couloirs. It is strictly forbidden to smoke in the corridors.

former VERB
to form

formidable ADJECTIVE
great

le **formulaire** NOUN
form

fort ADJECTIVE, ADVERB
[1] *strong* ◇ *Le café est trop fort.* The coffee's too strong.
[2] *good* ◇ *Il est très fort en espagnol.* He's very good at Spanish.
[3] *loud* ◇ *Est-ce vous pouvez parler plus fort?* Can you speak louder?
◆ **frapper fort** to hit hard

le **fortifiant** NOUN
tonic (*medicine*)

la **fortune** NOUN
fortune
◆ **de fortune** makeshift ◇ *Ils ont traversé la rivière sur un radeau de fortune.* They crossed the river on a makeshift raft.

le **fossé** NOUN
ditch

fou ADJECTIVE
(FEM SING **folle**)
mad
◆ **Il y a un monde fou sur la plage!** (*informal*) There are loads of people on the beach!
◆ **attraper le fou rire** to get the giggles

la **foudre** NOUN
lightning ◇ *L'arbre a été frappé par la foudre.* The tree was struck by lightning.

foudroyant ADJECTIVE
instant ◇ *un succès foudroyant* an instant hit

le **fouet** NOUN
whisk

la **fougère** NOUN
fern

fouiller VERB
to rummage

le **fouillis** NOUN
mess ◇ *Il y a du fouillis dans sa chambre.* His bedroom is a mess.

le **foulard** NOUN
scarf ◇ *un foulard en soie* a silk scarf

la **foule** NOUN
crowd
◆ **une foule de** masses of ◇ *J'ai une foule de choses à faire ce week-end.* I've got masses of things to do this weekend.

le **four** NOUN
oven ◇ *un four à micro-ondes* a microwave oven

la **fourchette** NOUN
fork

la **fourmi** NOUN
ant
◆ **avoir des fourmis dans les jambes** to have pins and needles

le **fourneau** NOUN
(PL les **fourneaux**)
stove

fourni ADJECTIVE
thick (*beard, hair*)

fournir VERB
to supply

les **fournitures** FEM NOUN
◆ **les fournitures scolaires** school stationery

fourré ADJECTIVE
filled ◇ *un gâteau fourré à la confiture d'abricot* a cake filled with apricot jam

fourrer (*informal*) VERB
to put ◇ *Où est-ce que tu as fourré mon passeport?* Where have you put my passport?

le **fourre-tout** NOUN
(PL les **fourre-tout**)
holdall

la **fourrure** NOUN
fur ◇ *un manteau de fourrure* a fur coat

foutre VERB (*rude*)
to do ◇ *Qu'est-ce qu'il fout?* What the hell is he doing?
◆ **Je n'en ai rien à foutre!** I don't give a damn!

foutu ADJECTIVE (*rude*)
[1] *knackered* ◇ *Mon stylo est foutu.* My pen's knackered.
[2] *bloody* ◇ *Qu'est-ce que j'ai fait de ce foutu stylo?* Where did I put that bloody pen?

le **foyer** NOUN
home ◇ *dans la plupart des foyers français* in most French homes
◆ **un foyer de jeunes** a youth club

la **fracture** NOUN
fracture

fragile ADJECTIVE
fragile ◇ *Attention, c'est fragile!* Be careful, it's fragile!

la **fragilité** NOUN
fragility

fraîche ADJECTIVE *see* **frais**

la **fraîcheur** NOUN
[1] *cool* ◇ *la fraîcheur du soir* the cool of the evening
[2] *freshness* ◇ *Je ne suis pas sûre de la fraîcheur du poisson.* I'm not sure about the freshness of the fish.

frais ADJECTIVE

(FEM SING **fraîche**)

see also **frais** NOUN

[1] *fresh* ◇ *des œufs frais* fresh eggs ◇ *Cette salade n'est pas très fraîche.* This lettuce isn't very fresh.

[2] *chilly* ◇ *Il fait un peu frais ce soir.* It's a bit chilly this evening.

[3] *cool* ◇ *des boissons fraîches* cool drinks

- **"servir frais"** "serve chilled"
- **mettre au frais** to put in a cool place

les **frais** MASC NOUN

see also **frais** ADJECTIVE

expenses

la **fraise** NOUN

strawberry ◇ *une fraise des bois* a wild strawberry

la **framboise** NOUN

raspberry

franc ADJECTIVE

(FEM SING **franche**)

see also **franc** NOUN

frank

le **franc** NOUN

see also **franc** ADJECTIVE

franc

The **franc** is the unit of currency in France, Belgium, Switzerland and many former French colonies; it is divided into 100 centimes.

français ADJECTIVE, NOUN

(FEM SING **française**)

French ◇ *Il parle français couramment.* He speaks French fluently.

- **un Français** a Frenchman
- **une Française** a Frenchwoman
- **les Français** the French

la **France** NOUN

France

- **en France (1)** in France ◇ *Je suis né en France.* I was born in France.
- **en France (2)** to France ◇ *Je pars en France pour Noël.* I'm going to France for Christmas.

franche ADJECTIVE *see* **franc**

franchement ADVERB

[1] *frankly* ◇ *Il m'a parlé franchement.* He spoke to me frankly.

[2] *really* ◇ *C'est franchement mauvais.* It's really bad.

franchir VERB

to get over

la **franchise** NOUN

frankness

francophone ADJECTIVE

French-speaking

la **frange** NOUN

fringe

la **frangipane** NOUN

almond cream

frapper VERB

to strike ◇ *Il l'a frappée au visage.* He struck her in the face. ◇ *Son air fatigué m'a frappé.* I was struck by how tired she looked.

fredonner VERB

to hum

le **freezer** NOUN

freezing compartment

le **frein** NOUN

brake

- **le frein à main** handbrake

freiner VERB

to brake

frêle ADJECTIVE

frail

le **frelon** NOUN

hornet

frémir VERB

shudder ◇ *Cette idée me fait frémir.* The idea makes me shudder.

fréquemment ADVERB

frequently

fréquent ADJECTIVE

frequent

fréquenté ADJECTIVE

busy ◇ *une rue très fréquentée* a very busy street

- **un bar mal fréquenté** a rough pub

fréquenter VERB

to see (person) ◇ *Je ne le fréquente pas beaucoup.* I don't see him often.

le **frère** NOUN

brother

le **friand** NOUN

- **un friand au fromage** a cheese puff

la **friandise** NOUN

sweet

le **fric** NOUN (informal)

cash

le **frigidaire** ® NOUN

refrigerator

le **frigo** NOUN (informal)

fridge

frileux ADJECTIVE

(FEM SING **frileuse**)

- **être frileux** to feel the cold ◇ *Je suis très frileuse.* I really feel the cold.

frimer VERB (informal)

to show off

les **fringues** FEM NOUN (informal)

clothes

fripé ADJECTIVE

crumpled

frire VERB

- **faire frire** to fry ◇ *Faites frire les boulettes dans de l'huile très chaude.* Fry the meatballs in very hot oil.

frisé ADJECTIVE
curly ◇ *Elle est très frisée.* She's got very curly hair.

le **frisson** NOUN
shiver

frissonner VERB
to shiver

frit ADJECTIVE
fried ◇ *du poisson frit* fried fish

les **frites** FEM NOUN
chips

la **friture** NOUN
[1] *fried food* ◇ *On lui a conseillé d'éviter les fritures.* He's been advised to avoid fried food.
[2] *fried fish* ◇ *Nous allons faire une friture ce soir.* We are going to have fried fish tonight.

froid ADJECTIVE
see also **froid** NOUN
cold ◇ *Ça me laisse froid.* It leaves me cold. ◇ *de la viande froide* cold meat

le **froid** NOUN
see also **froid** ADJECTIVE
cold
• **Il fait froid.** It's cold.
• **avoir froid** to be cold ◇ *Est-ce que tu as froid?* Are you cold?

se **froisser** VERB
[1] *to crease* ◇ *Ce tissu se froisse très facilement.* This material creases very easily.
[2] *to take offence* ◇ *Paul se froisse très facilement.* Paul's very quick to take offence.
• **se froisser un muscle** to strain a muscle

frôler VERB
[1] *to brush against* ◇ *Le chat m'a frôlé au passage.* The cat brushed against me as it went past.
[2] *to narrowly avoid* ◇ *Nous avons frôlé la catastrophe.* We narrowly avoided disaster.

le **fromage** NOUN
cheese
• **du fromage blanc** soft white cheese

le **froment** NOUN
wheat
• **une crêpe de froment** a pancake (*made with wheat flour*)

froncer VERB
• **froncer les sourcils** to frown

le **front** NOUN
forehead

la **frontière** NOUN
border

frotter VERB
to rub ◇ *se frotter les yeux* to rub one's eyes
• **frotter une allumette** to strike a match

le **fruit** NOUN
fruit
• **un fruit** a piece of fruit ◇ *Est-ce que vous voulez manger un fruit?* Would you like some fruit?
• **les fruits de mer** seafood

fruité ADJECTIVE
fruity

frustrer VERB
to frustrate

la **fugue** NOUN
• **faire une fugue** to run away

fuir VERB
[1] *to flee* ◇ *fuir devant un danger* to flee from danger
[2] *to drip* ◇ *Le robinet fuit.* The tap's dripping.

la **fuite** NOUN
[1] *leak* ◇ *Il y a une fuite de gaz.* There is a gas leak.
[2] *flight* (*escape*)
• **être en fuite** to be on the run

fumé ADJECTIVE
smoked ◇ *du saumon fumé* smoked salmon

la **fumée** NOUN
smoke

fumer VERB
to smoke

le **fumeur** NOUN
smoker

la **fumeuse** NOUN
smoker

fur NOUN
• **au fur et à mesure** ADVERB
as you go along ◇ *Je vérifie mon travail au fur et à mesure.* I check my work as I go along.
• **au fur et à mesure que** as ◇ *Je réponds à mon courrier au fur et à mesure que je le reçois.* I answer my mail as I receive it.

la **fureur** NOUN
fury
• **faire fureur** to be all the rage ◇ *Ce genre de sac fait fureur actuellement.* This sort of bag is all the rage at the moment.

furieux ADJECTIVE
(FEM SING **furieuse**)
furious

le **furoncle** NOUN
boil (*on skin*)

fus VERB see **être**

le **fuseau** NOUN
(PL les **fuseaux**)
ski pants

la **fusée** NOUN
　rocket
le **fusil** NOUN
　gun
fut VERB *see* **être**

futé ADJECTIVE
　crafty
le **futur** NOUN
　future

G

gâcher VERB
  to waste ◇ Je n'aime pas gâcher la
  nourriture. I don't like to waste food.
le **gâchis** NOUN
  waste
la **gaffe** NOUN
  • **faire une gaffe** to do something stupid
  • **Fais gaffe!** (_informal_) Watch out!
    ◇ Fais gaffe, la peinture est encore
    humide! Watch out: the paint's still
    wet!
le **gage** NOUN
  forfeit (_in a game_) ◇ recevoir un gage
  to pay a forfeit
le **gagnant** NOUN
  winner
la **gagnante** NOUN
  winner
  gagner VERB
  to win ◇ Qui a gagné? Who won?
  • **gagner du temps** to gain time
  • **Il gagne bien sa vie.** He makes a good
    living.
  gai ADJECTIVE
  cheerful ◇ Elle est très gaie. She's
  very cheerful.
la **gaieté** NOUN
  cheerfulness
la **galerie** NOUN
  gallery ◇ une galerie de peinture an
  art gallery
  • **une galerie marchande** a shopping
    arcade
le **galet** NOUN
  pebble
la **galette** NOUN
  1 _round flat cake_ ◇ une galette de
    blé noir a buckwheat pancake
  2 _biscuit_ ◇ des galettes pur beurre
    shortbread biscuits
  • **la galette des Rois**
    A galette des Rois is a cake eaten on Twelfth
    Night containing a figurine. The person who
    finds it is the king (or queen) and gets a paper
    crown. They then choose someone else to be their
    queen (or king).
  Galles FEM NOUN
  • **le pays de Galles** Wales
  • **le prince de Galles** the Prince of Wales
  gallois ADJECTIVE, NOUN
  Welsh ◇ un peintre gallois a Welsh
  painter
  • **un Gallois** a Welshman
  • **une Galloise** a Welshwoman
  • **les Gallois** the Welsh
le **galop** NOUN

  gallop
  galoper VERB
  to gallop
le **gamin** NOUN (_informal_)
  kid
la **gamine** NOUN (_informal_)
  kid
la **gamme** NOUN
  scale (_in music_) ◇ Je dois faire des
  gammes tous les soirs. I have to do my
  scales every night.
  • **une gamme de produits** a range of
    products
  gammée ADJECTIVE
  • **la croix gammée** the swastika
le **gant** NOUN
  glove ◇ des gants en laine woollen
  gloves
  • **un gant de toilette** a face cloth
le **garage** NOUN
  garage
le/la **garagiste** NOUN
  1 _garage owner_
  2 _mechanic_
la **garantie** NOUN
  guarantee
  garantir VERB
  to guarantee
le **garçon** NOUN
  1 _boy_
  2 _waiter_ (_in a café_)
  • **un vieux garçon** a bachelor
le **garde** NOUN
  see also la garde
  1 _warder_ (_in prison_)
  2 _security man_
  • **un garde du corps** a bodyguard
la **garde** NOUN
  see also le garde
  1 _guarding_ ◇ Il est chargé de la garde
    des prisonniers. He's responsible for
    guarding the prisoners.
  2 _guard_ ◇ la relève de la garde the
    changing of the guard
  • **être de garde** to be on duty ◇ Mon
    père est de garde ce soir. My father is
    on duty tonight. ◇ La pharmacie de
    garde ce week-end est... The duty
    chemist this weekend is...
  • **mettre en garde** to warn ◇ Elle m'a
    mis en garde contre les pickpockets. She
    warned me about pickpockets.
  garder VERB
  1 _to keep_ ◇ Est-ce que tu as gardé
    toutes ses lettres? Have you kept all his
    letters?

2 *to look after* ◇ *Je garde ma nièce samedi après-midi.* I'm looking after my niece on Saturday afternoon.

3 *to guard* ◇ *Ils ont pris un gros chien pour garder la maison.* They got a big dog to guard the house.

- **se garder** to keep ◇ *Ces crêpes se gardent bien.* These pancakes keep well.

la **garderie** NOUN
nursery

la **garde-robe** NOUN
wardrobe (*clothes*) ◇ *Elle a une garde-robe bien fournie.* She's got an extensive wardrobe.

le **gardien** NOUN
1 *caretaker*
2 *attendant* (*in a museum*)
- **un gardien de but** a goalkeeper
- **un gardien de la paix** a police officer

la **gardienne** NOUN
1 *caretaker*
2 *attendant* (*in a museum*)

la **gare** NOUN
see also **gare** EXCLAMATION
station ◇ *la gare routière* the bus station

gare EXCLAMATION
see also **gare** NOUN
- **Gare aux serpents!** Watch out for snakes!

garer VERB
to park
- **se garer** to park ◇ *Où t'es-tu garé?* Where are you parked?

garni ADJECTIVE
- **un plat garni** a dish served with accompaniments (*vegetables, chips, rice etc*)

le **gars** NOUN (*informal*)
guy

gaspiller VERB
to waste

le **gâteau** NOUN
(PL les **gâteaux**)
cake
- **les gâteaux secs** biscuits

gâter VERB
to spoil ◇ *Il aime gâter ses petits enfants.* He likes to spoil his grandchildren.
- **se gâter** to go bad ◇ *Le temps va se gâter.* The weather's going to break.

gauche ADJECTIVE
see also **gauche** NOUN
left ◇ *le bras gauche* the left arm ◇ *le côté gauche* the left-hand side

la **gauche** NOUN
see also **gauche** ADJECTIVE
left ◇ *sur votre gauche* on your left
- **à gauche (1)** on the left ◇ *la deuxième rue à gauche* the second street on the left
- **à gauche (2)** to the left ◇ *à gauche de l'armoire* to the left of the cupboard ◇ *Tournez à gauche.* Turn left.
- **la voie de gauche** the left-hand lane
- **la gauche** the left (*in politics*) ◇ *Il est de gauche.* He's left-wing.

gaucher ADJECTIVE
(FEM SING **gauchère**)
left-handed

la **gaufre** NOUN
waffle

la **gaufrette** NOUN
wafer

le **Gaulois** NOUN
Gaul ◇ *Astérix le Gaulois* Asterix the Gaul

gaulois ADJECTIVE
Gallic

le **gaz** NOUN
gas

gazeux ADJECTIVE
(FEM SING **gazeuse**)
- **une boisson gazeuse** a fizzy drink
- **de l'eau gazeuse** sparkling water

le **gazole** NOUN
diesel (*fuel*)

le **gazon** NOUN
lawn

le **géant** NOUN
giant

le **gel** NOUN
frost

la **gelée** NOUN
jelly

geler VERB
to freeze ◇ *Il a gelé cette nuit.* There was a frost last night.

la **gélule** NOUN
capsule (*containing medicine*)

les **Gémeaux** MASC NOUN
Gemini ◇ *Henry est Gémeaux.* Henry's Gemini.

gémir VERB
to moan

gênant ADJECTIVE
awkward ◇ *un silence gênant* an awkward silence

la **gencive** NOUN
gum (*in mouth*)

le **gendarme** NOUN
policeman

la **gendarmerie** NOUN
1 *police force*
2 *police station* ◇ *Vous devriez porter plainte à la gendarmerie.* You should go to the police station and report it.

le **gendre** NOUN

son-in-law

gêné ADJECTIVE
embarrassed

gêner VERB
[1] _to bother_ ◇ _Je ne voudrais pas vous gêner._ I don't want to bother you.
[2] _to feel awkward_ ◇ _Son regard la gênait._ The way he was looking at her made her feel awkward.

général ADJECTIVE
(MASC PL **généraux**)
see also **général** NOUN
general
• **en général** usually

le **général** NOUN
(PL les **généraux**)
see also **général** ADJECTIVE
general

généralement ADVERB
generally

la **généraliste** NOUN
family doctor

la **génération** NOUN
generation

généreux ADJECTIVE
(FEM SING **généreuse**)
generous

la **générosité** NOUN
generosity

le **genêt** NOUN
broom (bush)

la **génétique** NOUN
genetics

Genève NOUN
Geneva

génial ADJECTIVE (informal)
(MASC PL **géniaux**)
great ◇ _Le film d'hier soir était génial._ The film last night was great.

le **genou** NOUN
(PL les **genoux**)
knee ◇ _Elle est à genoux._ She's on her knees. ◇ _se mettre à genoux_ to kneel down

le **genre** NOUN
kind ◇ _C'est un genre de gâteau à la crème._ It's a kind of cream cake.

es **gens** MASC NOUN
people

gentil ADJECTIVE
(FEM SING **gentille**)
[1] _nice_ ◇ _Nos voisins sont très gentils._ Our neighbours are very nice.
[2] _kind_ ◇ _C'était très gentil de votre part._ It was very kind of you.

a **gentillesse** NOUN
kindness ◇ _Je l'ai remerciée de sa gentillesse._ I thanked her for her kindness. ◇ _C'est un homme d'une_

grande gentillesse. He is a very nice man.

gentiment ADVERB
[1] _nicely_ ◇ _Demande-le lui gentiment._ Ask him nicely.
[2] _kindly_ ◇ _Ils nous ont gentiment proposé de rester dîner._ They kindly invited us to stay for dinner.

la **géographie** NOUN
geography

la **géométrie** NOUN
geometry

gérer VERB
to manage

germain ADJECTIVE
• **un cousin germain** a first cousin

le **geste** NOUN
gesture ◇ _Il a voulu faire un geste._ He wanted to make a gesture.
• **Ne faites pas un geste!** Don't move!

la **gestion** NOUN
management

la **gifle** NOUN
slap across the face

gifler VERB
to slap across the face

gigantesque ADJECTIVE
gigantic

le **gigot** NOUN
leg of lamb

le **gilet** NOUN
[1] _waistcoat_ ◇ _un gilet en cuir_ a leather waistcoat
[2] _cardigan_ ◇ _un gilet tricoté main_ a hand-knitted cardigan
• **un gilet de sauvetage** a life jacket

le **gingembre** NOUN
ginger

la **girafe** NOUN
giraffe

le **gitan** NOUN
gipsy

la **gitane** NOUN
gipsy

le **gîte** NOUN
• **un gîte rural** a holiday house

la **glace** NOUN
[1] _ice_ ◇ _L'étang est recouvert de glace._ The pond is covered with ice.
[2] _ice cream_ ◇ _une glace à la fraise_ a strawberry ice cream
[3] _mirror_ ◇ _Il se regarde souvent dans la glace._ He often looks at himself in the mirror.

glacé ADJECTIVE
[1] _icy_ ◇ _Il soufflait un vent glacé._ An icy wind was blowing.
[2] _iced_ • _un thé glacé_ an iced tea

glacial ADJECTIVE
(MASC PL **glaciaux**)
icy

le **glaçon** NOUN
ice cube

glissant ADJECTIVE
slippery

glisser VERB
1 *to slip* ◇ *Il a glissé sur une peau de banane.* He slipped on a banana skin.
2 *to be slippery* ◇ *Attention, ça glisse!* Watch out, it's slippery!

global ADJECTIVE
(MASC PL **globaux**)
total ◇ *la somme globale* the total amount

la **gloire** NOUN
glory

la **godasse** NOUN (*informal*)
shoe

le **goéland** NOUN
seagull

le **golf** NOUN
1 *golf* ◇ *Il joue au golf.* He plays golf.
2 *golf course* ◇ *un golf dix-huit trous* an 18-hole golf course

le **golfe** NOUN
gulf
◆ **le golfe de Gascogne** the Bay of Biscay

la **gomme** NOUN
rubber

gommer VERB
to rub out

gonfler VERB
1 *to blow up* ◇ *gonfler un ballon* to blow up a balloon
2 *to pump up* ◇ *Tu devrais gonfler ton pneu arrière.* You should pump up your back tyre.

la **gorge** NOUN
1 *throat* ◇ *J'ai mal à la gorge.* I've got a sore throat.
2 *gorge* ◇ *les gorges du Tarn* the Tarn gorges

la **gorgée** NOUN
sip ◇ *une gorgée d'eau* a sip of water

le **gorille** NOUN
gorilla

le/la **gosse** NOUN (*informal*)
kid

le **goudron** NOUN
tar

le **gouffre** NOUN
chasm
◆ **Cette voiture est un vrai gouffre!** This car eats up money!

la **gourde** NOUN
water bottle

gourmand ADJECTIVE
greedy

la **gourmandise** NOUN
greed

la **gousse** NOUN
◆ **une gousse d'ail** a clove of garlic

le **goût** NOUN
taste ◇ *Ça n'a pas de goût.* It's got no taste. ◇ *Elle a très bon goût.* She's got very good taste.

goûter VERB
see also **goûter** NOUN
1 *to taste* ◇ *Goûte donc ce fromage: tu verras comme il est bon!* Have a taste of this cheese: you'll see how nice it is!
2 *to have a snack* (*in the afternoon*) ◇ *Les enfants goûtent généralement vers quatre heures.* The children usually have a snack around 4 o'clock.

le **goûter** NOUN
see also **goûter** VERB
afternoon snack

la **goutte** NOUN
drop

le **gouvernement** NOUN
government

gouverner VERB
to govern

la **grâce** NOUN
◆ **grâce à** thanks to ◇ *Je suis arrivé à l'heure grâce à toi.* I arrived on time thanks to you.

gracieux ADJECTIVE
(FEM SING **gracieuse**)
graceful

les **gradins** MASC NOUN
terraces (*in stadium*)

graduel ADJECTIVE
(FEM SING **graduelle**)
gradual

le **grain** NOUN
grain ◇ *un grain de sable* a grain of sand
◆ **un grain de beauté** a beauty spot
◆ **un grain de café** a coffee bean
◆ **un grain de raisin** a grape

la **graine** NOUN
seed

la **graisse** NOUN
fat

la **grammaire** NOUN
grammar

le **gramme** NOUN
gramme

grand ADJECTIVE, ADVERB
1 *tall* ◇ *Il est grand pour son âge.* He's tall for his age.
2 *big* ◇ *une grande valise* a big suitcase ◇ *C'est sa grande sœur.* She's his big sister.
◆ **une grande personne** a grown-up

3 *long* ◦ *un grand voyage* a long journey
- **les grandes vacances** the summer holidays
4 *great* ◦ *C'est un grand ami à moi.* He's a great friend of mine.
- **un grand magasin** a department store
- **une grande surface** a hypermarket
- **les grandes écoles** top ranking colleges (*at university level*)
- **au grand air** out in the open air ◦ *Ça te fera beaucoup de bien d'être au grand air.* It'll be very good for you to be out in the open air.
- **grand ouvert** wide open

grand-chose NOUN
- **pas grand-chose** not much ◦ *Je n'ai pas acheté grand-chose au marché.* I didn't buy much at the market. ◦ *Voici un petit cadeau: ce n'est pas grand-chose.* Here's a little present: it's nothing much.

la **Grande-Bretagne** NOUN
Britain

la **grandeur** NOUN
size

grandir VERB
to grow ◦ *Il a beaucoup grandi.* He's grown a lot.

la **grand-mère** NOUN
(PL les grands-mères)
grandmother

grand-peine NOUN
- **à grand-peine** ADVERB
with great difficulty

le **grand-père** NOUN
(PL les grands-pères)
grandfather

les **grands-parents** MASC NOUN
grandparents

la **grange** NOUN
barn

la **grappe** NOUN
- **une grappe de raisin** a bunch of grapes

gras ADJECTIVE
(FEM SING grasse)
1 *fatty* (*food*) ◦ *Évitez les aliments gras.* Avoid fatty foods.
2 *greasy* ◦ *des cheveux gras* greasy hair
3 *oily* ◦ *une peau grasse* oily skin
- **faire la grasse matinée** to have a lie-in

gratis ADJECTIVE, ADVERB
free ◦ *J'ai eu ce stylo gratis.* I got this pen free.

le **gratte-ciel** NOUN
(PL les gratte-ciel)
skyscraper

gratter VERB

1 *to scratch* ◦ *Ne gratte pas tes piqûres de moustiques!* Don't scratch your mosquito bites!
2 *to be itchy* ◦ *C'est épouvantable comme ça gratte!* It's terribly itchy!

gratuit ADJECTIVE
free ◦ *entrée gratuite* entrance free

grave ADJECTIVE
1 *serious* ◦ *une maladie grave* a serious illness ◦ *Il avait l'air grave.* He was looking serious.
2 *deep* ◦ *Il a une voix grave.* He's got a deep voice.
- **Ce n'est pas grave.** It doesn't matter. ◦ *J'ai oublié ma clé. – Ce n'est pas grave, j'ai la mienne.* I've forgotten my key. – It doesn't matter, I've got mine.

gravement ADVERB
seriously ◦ *Il a été gravement blessé.* He was seriously injured.

grec ADJECTIVE, NOUN
(FEM SING grecque)
Greek
- **J'apprends le grec.** I'm learning Greek.
- **un Grec** a Greek (*man*)
- **une Grecque** a Greek (*woman*)
- **les Grecs** the Greeks

la **Grèce** NOUN
Greece
- **en Grèce (1)** in Greece
- **en Grèce (2)** to Greece

la **grêle** NOUN
hail

grêler VERB
- **Il grêle.** It's hailing.

grelotter VERB
to shiver

la **grenade** NOUN
1 *pomegranate*
2 *grenade*

le **grenier** NOUN
attic

la **grenouille** NOUN
frog

la **grève** NOUN
1 *strike*
- **en grève** on strike ◦ *Les ouvriers sont en grève depuis dix jours.* The workers have been on strike for ten days.
- **faire grève** to be on strike
2 *shore* ◦ *Nous nous sommes promenés le long de la grève.* We went for a walk along the shore.

le/la **gréviste** NOUN
striker

grièvement ADVERB
- **grièvement blessé** seriously injured

la **griffe** NOUN
1 *claw* ◦ *Le chat m'a donné un coup*

de griffe. The cat scratched me.

2 *label* ◇ *la griffe d'un grand couturier* the label of a top designer

griffer VERB
to scratch ◇ *Le chat m'a griffé.* The cat scratched me.

grignoter VERB
to nibble

la **grillade** NOUN
grilled food ◇ *une grillade d'agneau* grilled lamb

la **grille** NOUN
1 *wire fence* ◇ *L'usine est entourée d'une haute grille.* The factory is surrounded by a high wire fence.
2 *metal gate* ◇ *Le facteur a sonné à la grille du jardin.* The postman rang at the garden gate.

le **grille-pain** NOUN
(PL les grille-pain)
toaster

griller VERB
1 *to toast*
◆ *du pain grillé* toast
2 *to grill* ◇ *des saucisses grillées* grilled sausages

la **grimace** NOUN
◆ **faire des grimaces** to make faces

grimper VERB
to climb

grincer VERB
to creak

grincheux ADJECTIVE
(FEM SING grincheuse)
grumpy

la **grippe** NOUN
flu
◆ **avoir la grippe** to have flu ◇ *J'ai eu une mauvaise grippe l'hiver dernier.* I had a bad attack of flu last winter.

grippé ADJECTIVE
◆ **être grippé** to have flu

gris ADJECTIVE
grey

le **Groenland** NOUN
Greenland

grogner VERB
1 *to growl* ◇ *Le chien a grogné quand je me suis approché de lui.* The dog growled when I went near it.
2 *to complain* ◇ *Arrête donc de grogner!* Stop complaining!

gronder VERB
◆ **se faire gronder** to get a telling off ◇ *Tu vas te faire gronder par ton père!* You're going to get a telling off from your father!

gros ADJECTIVE
(FEM SING grosse)

1 *big* ◇ *une grosse pomme* a big apple
2 *fat* ◇ *Je suis trop grosse pour porter ça!* I'm too fat to wear that!

la **groseille** NOUN
◆ **la groseille rouge** redcurrant
◆ **la groseille à maquereau** gooseberry

la **grossesse** NOUN
pregnancy

grossier ADJECTIVE
(FEM SING grossière)
rude ◇ *Ne sois pas si grossier!* Don't be so rude!
◆ **une erreur grossière** a bad mistake

grossir VERB
to put on weight ◇ *Il a beaucoup grossi.* He's put on a lot of weight.

grosso modo ADVERB
roughly ◇ *Dis-moi grosso modo ce que tu en penses.* Give me a rough idea what you think of it.

la **grotte** NOUN
cave

le **groupe** NOUN
group ◇ *votre groupe sanguin* your blood group

grouper VERB
to group ◇ *On nous a groupés dans différentes classes selon notre niveau.* We were grouped in different classes according to our level.
◆ **se grouper** to gather ◇ *Nous nous sommes groupés autour du feu.* We gathered round the fire.

le **guépard** NOUN
cheetah

la **guêpe** NOUN
wasp

guérir VERB
to recover ◇ *Il est maintenant complètement guéri.* He's now completely recovered.

la **guérison** NOUN
recovery

la **guerre** NOUN
war ◇ *en guerre* at war

guetter VERB
to look out for ◇ *Elle guette l'arrivée du facteur tous les matins.* She looks out for the postman every morning.

la **gueule** NOUN
mouth (*rude when used for people*) ◇ *Le chat a ramené une souris dans sa gueule.* The cat brought in a mouse in its mouth.
◆ **Ta gueule!** (*rude*) Shut your face!
◆ **avoir la gueule de bois** (*informal*) to have a hangover

gueuler (*informal*) VERB
to bawl

le **guichet** NOUN
counter (in bank, booking office)

le **guide** NOUN
guide

guider VERB
to guide

le **guidon** NOUN
handlebars

les **guillemets** MASC NOUN
inverted commas ◇ entre guillemets
in inverted commas

la **guirlande** NOUN
tinsel ◇ Nous avons décoré le sapin de
Noël avec des guirlandes. We decorated
the Christmas tree with tinsel.
◆ **des guirlandes en papier** paper chains

la **guitare** NOUN
guitar ◇ Sais-tu jouer de la guitare?
Can you play the guitar?

le **gymnase** NOUN
gym ◇ Le lycée a un nouveau
gymnase. The school's got a new gym.

la **gymnastique** NOUN
gymnastics ◇ faire de la gymnastique
to do one's exercises

G

H

habile ADJECTIVE
skilful ◇ *Il est très habile de ses mains.*
He is very clever with his hands.

habillé ADJECTIVE
1 *dressed* ◇ *Il n'est pas encore habillé.*
He's not dressed yet.
2 *smart* ◇ *Cette robe fait très habillé.*
This dress looks very smart.

s'**habiller** VERB
1 *to get dressed* ◇ *Je me suis
rapidement habillé.* I got dressed quickly.
2 *to dress up* ◇ *Est-ce qu'il faut
s'habiller pour la réception?* Do you
have to dress up to go to the party?

l'**habitant** MASC NOUN
inhabitant ◇ *Les habitants du quartier
sont contre ce projet.* The local people
are against this plan.

l'**habitante** FEM NOUN
inhabitant

habiter VERB
to live ◇ *Il habite à Montpellier.* He
lives in Montpellier.

les **habits** MASC NOUN
clothes

l'**habitude** FEM NOUN
habit ◇ *une mauvaise habitude* a bad
habit
◆ **avoir l'habitude de quelque chose** to
be used to something ◇ *Elle a
l'habitude des enfants.* She's used to
children. ◇ *Je n'ai pas l'habitude de
parler en public.* I'm not used to
speaking in public.
◆ **d'habitude** usually
◆ **comme d'habitude** as usual

habituel ADJECTIVE
(FEM SING **habituelle**)
usual

s'**habituer** VERB
◆ **s'habituer à quelque chose** to get used
to something ◇ *Il faudra que tu
t'habitues à te lever tôt.* You'll have to
get used to getting up early.

le **hachis** NOUN
mince
◆ **le hachis Parmentier** shepherd's pie

la **haie** NOUN
hedge

la **haine** NOUN
hatred

haïr VERB
to hate

l'**haleine** FEM NOUN
breath ◇ *avoir mauvaise haleine* to
have bad breath ◇ *être hors d'haleine*
to be out of breath

les **halles** FEM NOUN
covered market

la **halte** NOUN
stop ◇ *faire halte* to make a stop
◆ **Halte!** Stop!

l'**haltérophilie** FEM NOUN
weightlifting

l'**hameçon** MASC NOUN
fish hook

le **hamster** NOUN
hamster

la **hanche** NOUN
hip

le **handball** NOUN
handball ◇ *jouer au handball* to play
handball

le **handicapé** NOUN
handicapped man

la **handicapée** NOUN
handicapped woman

le **hareng** NOUN
herring
◆ **un hareng saur** a kipper

le **haricot** NOUN
bean
◆ **les haricots verts** runner beans
◆ **les haricots blancs** haricot beans

l'**harmonica** MASC NOUN
mouth organ

la **harpe** NOUN
harp

le **hasard** NOUN
coincidence ◇ *C'était un pur hasard.*
It was pure coincidence.
◆ **au hasard** at random ◇ *Choisis un
numéro au hasard.* Choose a number at
random.
◆ **par hasard** by chance ◇ *Je l'ai
rencontrée tout à fait par hasard au
supermarché.* I met her at the
supermarket quite by chance.
◆ **à tout hasard (1)** just in case ◇ *Prends
un parapluie à tout hasard.* Take an
umbrella just in case.
◆ **à tout hasard (2)** on the off chance
◇ *Je ne sais pas s'il est chez lui, mais je
vais l'appeler à tout hasard.* I don't
know if he's at home, but I'll phone on
the off chance.

la **hâte** NOUN
◆ **à la hâte** hurriedly ◇ *Elle s'est habillée
à la hâte.* She got dressed hurriedly.
◆ **J'ai hâte de te voir.** I can't wait to see
you.

la **hausse** NOUN

[1] *increase* ◦ *la hausse des prix* price increase
[2] *rise* ◦ *On annonce une légère hausse de température.* The forecast is for a slight rise in temperature.

hausser VERB
- **hausser les épaules** to shrug one's shoulders

haut ADJECTIVE, ADVERB
see also **haut** NOUN
[1] *high* ◦ *une haute montagne* a high mountain
[2] *aloud* ◦ *penser tout haut* to think aloud

le **haut** NOUN
see also **haut** ADJECTIVE
top
- **un mur de trois mètres de haut** a wall 3 metres high
- **en haut (1)** upstairs ◦ *La salle de bain est en haut.* The bathroom is upstairs.
- **en haut (2)** at the top ◦ *Le nid est tout en haut de l'arbre.* The nest is right at the top of the tree.

la **hauteur** NOUN
height

le **haut-parleur** NOUN
loudspeaker

l' **hebdomadaire** MASC NOUN
weekly (*magazine*)

héberger VERB
to put up ◦ *Mon cousin a dit qu'il nous hébergerait.* My cousin said he would put us up.

hélas ADVERB
unfortunately ◦ *Hélas, il ne restait plus de billets.* Unfortunately there were no tickets left.

l' **hélicoptère** MASC NOUN
helicopter

l' **hémorragie** FEM NOUN
haemorrhage

l' **herbe** FEM NOUN
grass
- **les herbes de Provence** mixed herbs

le **hérisson** NOUN
hedgehog

hériter VERB
to inherit

l' **héritier** MASC NOUN
heir

l' **héritière** FEM NOUN
heiress

hermétique ADJECTIVE
airtight

l' **héroïne** FEM NOUN
[1] *heroine* ◦ *l'héroïne du roman* the heroine of the novel
[2] *heroin* (*drug*)

le **héros** NOUN
hero

l' **hésitation** FEM NOUN
hesitation

hésiter VERB
to hesitate ◦ *Il n'a pas hésité à nous aider.* He didn't hesitate to help us. ◦ *J'ai hésité entre le pull vert et le cardigan jaune.* I couldn't decide between the green pullover and the yellow cardigan. ◦ *Est-ce que tu viens ce soir?–J'hésite...* Are you coming this evening?–I'm not sure...
- **sans hésiter** without hesitating

l' **heure** FEM NOUN
[1] *hour* ◦ *Le trajet dure six heures.* The journey lasts six hours.
[2] *time* ◦ *Vous avez l'heure?* Have you got the time?
- **Quelle heure est-il?** What time is it?
- **À quelle heure?** What time? ◦ *À quelle heure arrivons-nous?* What time do we arrive?
- **deux heures du matin** 2 o'clock in the morning
- **être à l'heure** to be on time
- **une heure de français** a period of French

heureusement ADVERB
luckily ◦ *Heureusement qu'il n'a pas été blessé.* Luckily he wasn't hurt.

heureux ADJECTIVE
(FEM SING **heureuse**)
happy

heurter VERB
to hit

l' **hexagone** MASC NOUN
hexagon
- **l'Hexagone** France
France is often referred to as l'Hexagone *because of its six-sided shape.*

le **hibou** NOUN
(PL les **hiboux**)
owl

hier ADVERB
yesterday
- **avant-hier** the day before yesterday

la **hi-fi** NOUN
stereo
- **une chaîne hi-fi** a stereo system

hippique ADJECTIVE
- **un club hippique** a riding centre
- **un concours hippique** a horse show

l' **hippopotame** MASC NOUN
hippopotamus

l' **hirondelle** FEM NOUN
swallow (*bird*)

l' **histoire** FEM NOUN
[1] *history* ◦ *un cours d'histoire* a

history lesson

[2] *story* ◇ *Ce roman raconte l'histoire de deux enfants.* This novel tells the story of two children.

- **Ne fais pas d'histoires!** Don't make a fuss!

historique ADJECTIVE

historic ◇ *un monument historique* a historic monument

l' **hiver** MASC NOUN

winter

- **en hiver** in winter

la **HLM** NOUN (= *habitation à loyer modéré*)

council flat

- **des HLM** council housing

le **hockey** NOUN

hockey

- **le hockey sur glace** ice hockey

hollandais ADJECTIVE, NOUN

Dutch

- **J'apprends le hollandais.** I'm learning Dutch.
- **un Hollandais** a Dutch man
- **une Hollandaise** a Dutch woman
- **les Hollandais** the Dutch

la **Hollande** NOUN

Holland

- **en Hollande (1)** in Holland
- **en Hollande (2)** to Holland

le **homard** NOUN

lobster

homéopathique ADJECTIVE

homeopathic

l' **hommage** MASC NOUN

tribute

l' **homme** MASC NOUN

man

- **un homme d'affaires** a businessman

homosexuel ADJECTIVE

(FEM SING **homosexuelle**)

homosexual

la **Hongrie** NOUN

Hungary

hongrois ADJECTIVE

Hungarian

honnête ADJECTIVE

honest

l' **honnêteté** FEM NOUN

honesty

l' **honneur** MASC NOUN

honour

la **honte** NOUN

shame ◇ *avoir honte de quelque chose* to be ashamed of something

l' **hôpital** MASC NOUN

(PL les **hôpitaux**)

hospital

le **hoquet** NOUN

- **avoir le hoquet** to have hiccups

l' **horaire** MASC NOUN

timetable

- **les horaires de train** the train timetable

l' **horizon** MASC NOUN

horizon

horizontal ADJECTIVE

(MASC PL **horizontaux**)

horizontal

l' **horloge** FEM NOUN

clock

l' **horreur** FEM NOUN

horror ◇ *un film d'horreur* a horror film

- **avoir horreur de** to hate ◇ *J'ai horreur du chou.* I hate cabbage.

horrible ADJECTIVE

horrible

hors PREPOSITION

- **hors de** out of ◇ *Elle est hors de danger maintenant.* She's out of danger now.
- **hors taxes** duty-free

le **hors-d'œuvre** NOUN

(PL les **hors-d'œuvre**)

starter (*food*)

hospitalier ADJECTIVE

(FEM SING **hospitalière**)

hospitable ◇ *Ils sont très hospitaliers.* They're very hospitable.

- **les services hospitaliers** hospital services

l' **hospitalité** FEM NOUN

hospitality

hostile ADJECTIVE

hostile

l' **hôte** MASC/FEM NOUN

[1] *host* ◇ *N'oubliez pas de remercier vos hôtes.* Don't forget to thank your hosts.

[2] *guest* ◇ *Cette ferme accueille des hôtes payants.* This farm takes paying guests.

l' **hôtel** MASC NOUN

hotel

- **l'hôtel de ville** the town hall

l' **hôtesse** FEM NOUN

hostess

- **une hôtesse de l'air** a stewardess

le **houx** NOUN

holly

l' **huile** FEM NOUN

oil

- **l'huile solaire** suntan oil

huit NUMBER

eight ◇ *Il est huit heures du matin.* It's eight in the morning. ◇ *Il a huit ans.* He's eight.

- **le huit février** the eighth of February

la **huitaine** NOUN
- **une huitaine de jours** about a week
  ◇ *Nous serons de retour dans une huitaine de jours.* We'll be back in about a week.

huitième ADJECTIVE
eighth ◇ *au huitième étage* on the eighth floor

l' **huître** FEM NOUN
oyster

humain ADJECTIVE
see also humain NOUN
human

l' **humain** MASC NOUN
see also humain ADJECTIVE
human being

l' **humeur** FEM NOUN
mood ◇ *Il est de bonne humeur.* He's in a good mood. ◇ *Elle était de mauvaise humeur.* She was in a bad mood.

humide ADJECTIVE
damp ◇ *L'herbe est humide.* The grass is damp. ◇ *un climat humide* a damp climate

humilier VERB
to humiliate

humoristique ADJECTIVE
humorous

- **des dessins humoristiques** cartoons

l' **humour** MASC NOUN
humour ◇ *Il n'a pas beaucoup d'humour.* He hasn't got much sense of humour.

hurler VERB
to howl

la **hutte** NOUN
hut

hydratant ADJECTIVE
- **une crème hydratante** a moisturizing cream

hygiénique ADJECTIVE
hygienic
- **une serviette hygiénique** a sanitary towel
- **le papier hygiénique** toilet paper

l' **hymne** MASC NOUN
- **l'hymne national** the national anthem

l' **hypermarché** MASC NOUN
hypermarket

hypermétrope ADJECTIVE
long-sighted

hypocrite ADJECTIVE
hypocritical ◇ *Il est hypocrite.* He's a hypocrite.

l' **hypothèse** FEM NOUN
hypothesis

H

l' iceberg MASC NOUN
iceberg

ici ADVERB
here ◇ *Les assiettes sont ici.* The plates are here.
- **La mer monte parfois jusqu'ici.** The sea sometimes comes in as far as this.
- **Jusqu'ici nous n'avons eu aucun problème avec la voiture.** So far we haven't had any problems with the car.

idéal ADJECTIVE
(MASC PL **idéaux**)
ideal ◇ *C'est l'endroit idéal pour faire un pique-nique.* It's an ideal place to have a picnic.

l' idée FEM NOUN
idea ◇ *C'est une bonne idée.* It's a good idea.

identifier VERB
to identify ◇ *La police a identifié le meurtrier.* The police have identified the murderer.

identique ADJECTIVE
identical ◇ *Ils ont obtenu des résultats identiques.* They obtained identical results.

l' identité FEM NOUN
identity
- **une pièce d'identité** a form of identification ◇ *Avez-vous une pièce d'identité?* Have you got any form of identification?

idiot ADJECTIVE
see also **idiot** NOUN
[1] *stupid* ◇ *une plaisanterie idiote* a stupid joke
[2] *silly* ◇ *Ne sois pas idiot!* Don't be silly!

l' idiot MASC NOUN
see also **idiot** ADJECTIVE
idiot

l' idiote FEM NOUN
idiot

ignorant ADJECTIVE
ignorant

ignorer VERB
[1] *not to know* ◇ *J'ignore son nom.* I don't know his name.
[2] *to ignore* ◇ *Il m'a complètement ignoré.* He completely ignored me.

il PRONOUN
[1] *he* ◇ *Il est parti ce matin de bonne heure.* He left early this morning.
[2] *it* ◇ *Méfie-toi de ce chien: il mord.* Be careful of that dog: it bites. ◇ *Il pleut.* It's raining.

l' île FEM NOUN
island
- **les îles Anglo-Normandes** the Channel Islands
- **les îles Britanniques** the British Isles
- **les îles Féroé** the Faroe Islands

illégal ADJECTIVE
(MASC PL **illégaux**)
illegal

illimité ADJECTIVE
unlimited

illisible ADJECTIVE
illegible ◇ *une écriture illisible* illegible handwriting

illuminer VERB
to floodlight ◇ *Le château est illuminé tous les soirs pendant l'été.* The castle is floodlit every night in the summer.

l' illusion FEM NOUN
illusion ◇ *Tu te fais des illusions!* You're deluding yourself!

l' illustration FEM NOUN
illustration

illustré ADJECTIVE
see also **illustré** NOUN
illustrated

l' illustré MASC NOUN
see also **illustré** ADJECTIVE
comic

illustrer VERB
to illustrate ◇ *Vous pouvez illustrer votre rédaction avec des exemples.* You may illustrate your essay with examples.

ils PRONOUN
they ◇ *Ils nous ont appelés hier soir.* They phoned us last night.

l' image FEM NOUN
picture ◇ *Les films donnent une fausse image de l'Amérique.* Films give a false picture of America.

l' imagination FEM NOUN
imagination ◇ *Elle a beaucoup d'imagination.* She's got a vivid imagination.

imaginer VERB
to imagine

l' imbécile MASC/FEM NOUN
idiot

l' imitation FEM NOUN
imitation

imiter VERB
to imitate

l' immatriculation FEM NOUN
- **une plaque d'immatriculation** a numberplate

l' **immédiat** MASC NOUN
- **dans l'immédiat** for the moment ◇ *Je n'ai pas besoin de ce livre dans l'immédiat.* I don't need this book for the moment.

immédiatement ADVERB
immediately

immense ADJECTIVE
1 *huge* ◇ *une immense fortune* a huge fortune
2 *tremendous* ◇ *un immense soulagement* a tremendous relief

l' **immeuble** MASC NOUN
block of flats

l' **immigration** FEM NOUN
immigration

l' **immigré** MASC NOUN
immigrant

l' **immigrée** FEM NOUN
immigrant

immobile ADJECTIVE
motionless

immobilier ADJECTIVE
(FEM SING **immobilière**)
- **une agence immobilière** an estate agent's

immobiliser VERB
to immobilize

immunisé ADJECTIVE
immunized

l' **impact** MASC NOUN
impact

impair ADJECTIVE
odd ◇ *un nombre impair* an odd number

impardonnable ADJECTIVE
unforgivable

l' **impasse** FEM NOUN
cul-de-sac

l' **impatience** FEM NOUN
impatience

impatient ADJECTIVE
impatient

impeccable ADJECTIVE
1 *immaculate* ◇ *Elle est toujours impeccable.* She's always immaculate.
2 *perfect* ◇ *Il a fait un travail impeccable.* He's done a perfect job.
◇ *C'est impeccable!* That's perfect!

l' **impératif** MASC NOUN
imperative

l' **impératrice** FEM NOUN
empress

l' **imperméable** MASC NOUN
raincoat

impertinent ADJECTIVE
cheeky ◇ *Ne sois pas impertinent!* Don't be cheeky!

impitoyable ADJECTIVE
merciless

impliquer VERB
to mean ◇ *Si tu vas à l'université, ça implique que tu vas devoir nous quitter.* If you go to university, it'll mean that you have to leave us.
- **être impliqué dans** to be involved in ◇ *Il est impliqué dans un scandale financier.* He's involved in a financial scandal.

impoli ADJECTIVE
rude

l' **importance** FEM NOUN
importance ◇ *C'est sans importance.* It doesn't matter.

important ADJECTIVE
1 *important* ◇ *un rôle important* an important role
2 *considerable* ◇ *une somme importante* a considerable sum

l' **importation** FEM NOUN
import ◇ *Les importations de pétrole ont baissé.* Oil imports have fallen.

importer VERB
see also n'importe
1 *to import* (goods)
2 *to matter* ◇ *Peu importe.* It doesn't matter.

imposant ADJECTIVE
imposing

imposer VERB
to impose
- **imposer quelque chose à quelqu'un** to make somebody do something

impossible ADJECTIVE
see also **impossible** NOUN
impossible

l' **impossible** MASC NOUN
see also **impossible** ADJECTIVE
- **Nous ferons l'impossible pour finir à temps.** We'll do our utmost to finish on time.

l' **impôt** MASC NOUN
tax

imprécis ADJECTIVE
imprecise

l' **impression** FEM NOUN
impression ◇ *Il a fait bonne impression à ma mère.* He made a good impression on my mother.

impressionnant ADJECTIVE
impressive

impressionner VERB
to impress

imprévisible ADJECTIVE
unpredictable

imprévu ADJECTIVE
unexpected

l' **imprimante** FEM NOUN

printer (*for computer*)

imprimé ADJECTIVE
printed ◦ *un tissu imprimé* a printed
fabric ◦ *C'est imprimé en grandes
lettres.* It's printed in large letters.

imprimer VERB
to print

impropre ADJECTIVE
• **impropre à la consommation** unfit for
human consumption

improviser VERB
to improvise

improviste ADVERB
• **arriver à l'improviste** to arrive
unexpectedly

l' **imprudence** FEM NOUN
carelessness
• **Ne fais pas d'imprudences!** Don't do
anything silly!

imprudent ADJECTIVE
[1] *unwise* ◦ *Il serait imprudent de
prendre la voiture aujourd'hui.* It would
be unwise to take the car today.
[2] *careless* ◦ *un conducteur imprudent*
a careless driver

impuissant ADJECTIVE
helpless ◦ *Elle se sentait
complètement impuissante.* She felt
completely helpless.

impulsif ADJECTIVE
(FEM SING **impulsive**)
impulsive

inabordable ADJECTIVE
prohibitive ◦ *des prix inabordables*
prohibitive prices

inaccessible ADJECTIVE
inaccessible ◦ *Cette plage est
inaccessible par la route.* This beach is
inaccessible by road.

inachevé ADJECTIVE
unfinished

inadmissible ADJECTIVE
intolerable ◦ *Ce type de
comportement est inadmissible!* This
sort of behaviour is intolerable!

inanimé ADJECTIVE
unconscious ◦ *On l'a retrouvé inanimé
sur la route.* He was found unconscious
on the road.

inaperçu ADJECTIVE
• **passer inaperçu** to go unnoticed

inattendu ADJECTIVE
unexpected

l' **inattention** FEM NOUN
• **une faute d'inattention** a careless
mistake

inaugurer VERB
to open (*an exhibition*)

incapable ADJECTIVE

incapable ◦ *être incapable de faire
quelque chose* to be incapable of doing
something

incassable ADJECTIVE
unbreakable

l' **incendie** MASC NOUN
fire ◦ *un incendie de forêt* a forest fire

incertain ADJECTIVE
[1] *uncertain* ◦ *Son avenir est encore
incertain.* His future is still uncertain.
[2] *unsettled* ◦ *Le temps est incertain.*
The weather is unsettled.

l' **incident** MASC NOUN
incident

inciter VERB
• **inciter quelqu'un à faire quelque chose**
to encourage somebody to do
something ◦ *J'ai incité mes parents à
partir en voyage.* I encouraged my
parents to go on a trip.

inclure VERB
to enclose ◦ *Veuillez inclure une
enveloppe timbrée libellée à votre
adresse.* Please enclose a stamped
addressed envelope.
• **jusqu'au dix mars inclus** until 10th
March inclusive

incohérent ADJECTIVE
incoherent

incollable ADJECTIVE
• **être incollable sur quelque chose**
(*informal*) to know everything there is to
know about something
• **le riz incollable** non-stick rice

incolore ADJECTIVE
colourless

incompétent ADJECTIVE
incompetent

incompris ADJECTIVE
misunderstood

l' **inconnu** MASC NOUN
stranger ◦ *Ne parle pas à des
inconnus.* Don't speak to strangers.
• **l'inconnu** the unknown ◦ *la peur de
l'inconnu* the fear of the unknown

l' **inconnue** FEM NOUN
stranger

inconsciemment ADVERB
unconsciously

inconscient ADJECTIVE
unconscious ◦ *Il est resté inconscient
quelques minutes.* He was unconscious
for several minutes.

incontestable ADJECTIVE
indisputable

incontournable ADJECTIVE
inevitable ◦ *l'incontournable petite
robe noire* the inevitable little black
dress

l'**inconvénient** MASC NOUN
disadvantage
- **si vous n'y voyez pas d'inconvénient**
if you have no objection

incorrect ADJECTIVE
1 *incorrect* ◇ *une réponse incorrecte*
an incorrect answer
2 *rude* ◇ *Il a été incorrect avec la
voisine.* He was rude to the woman
next door.

incroyable ADJECTIVE
incredible

inculper VERB
- **inculper de** to charge with ◇ *Il a été
inculpé de meurtre.* He was charged
with murder.

l'**Inde** FEM NOUN
India

indécis ADJECTIVE
1 *indecisive* ◇ *Il est constamment
indécis.* He's always indecisive.
2 *undecided* ◇ *Je suis encore indécis.*
I'm still undecided.

indéfiniment ADVERB
indefinitely

indélicat ADJECTIVE
tactless

indemne ADJECTIVE
unharmed ◇ *Il s'en est sorti indemne.*
He escaped unharmed.

indemniser VERB
to compensate ◇ *Les victimes
demandent maintenant à être
indemnisées.* The victims are now
demanding compensation.

indépendamment ADVERB
independently
- **indépendamment de** irrespective of
◇ *Les allocations familiales sont versées
indépendamment des revenus.* Child
benefit is given irrespective of income.

l'**indépendance** FEM NOUN
independence

indépendant ADJECTIVE
independent

l'**index** MASC NOUN
1 *index finger*
2 *index* (*in book*)

indicatif ADJECTIVE
(FEM SING **indicative**)
see also **indicatif** NOUN
- **à titre indicatif** for your information

l'**indicatif** MASC NOUN
see also **indicatif** ADJECTIVE
1 *dialling code*
2 *indicative* (*of verb*)
3 *theme tune* (*of TV programme*)

les **indications** FEM NOUN
instructions ◇ *Il suffit de suivre les*

indications. You just have to follow the
instructions.

l'**indice** MASC NOUN
clue ◇ *La police cherche des indices.*
The police are looking for clues.

indien ADJECTIVE, NOUN
(FEM SING **indienne**)
Indian
- **un Indien** an Indian (*man*)
- **une Indienne** an Indian (*woman*)

l'**indifférence** FEM NOUN
indifference

indifférent ADJECTIVE
indifferent

l'**indigène** MASC/FEM NOUN
native

indigeste ADJECTIVE
indigestible

l'**indigestion** FEM NOUN
indigestion

indigne ADJECTIVE
unworthy

indigner VERB
- **s'indigner de quelque chose** to get
indignant about something

indiqué ADJECTIVE
advisable ◇ *Ce n'est pas très indiqué.*
It's not really advisable.

indiquer VERB
to point out ◇ *Il m'a indiqué la mairie.*
He pointed out the town hall.

indirect ADJECTIVE
indirect

indiscipliné ADJECTIVE
unruly

indiscret ADJECTIVE
(FEM SING **indiscrète**)
indiscreet

indispensable ADJECTIVE
indispensable

indisposé ADJECTIVE
indisposed
- **être indisposée** to be having one's
period

l'**individu** MASC NOUN
individual

individuel ADJECTIVE
(FEM SING **individuelle**)
individual ◇ *servi en portions
individuelles* served in individual
portions
- **Vous aurez une chambre individuelle.**
You'll have a room of your own.

indolore ADJECTIVE
painless

l'**Indonésie** FEM NOUN
Indonesia

indulgent ADJECTIVE
indulgent

- **Elle est trop indulgente avec son fils.**
  She's not firm enough with her son.

l'**industrie** FEM NOUN
industry

industriel ADJECTIVE
(FEM SING **industrielle**)
see also industriel NOUN
industrial

l'**industriel** MASC NOUN
see also industriel ADJECTIVE
industrialist

inédit ADJECTIVE
unpublished

inefficace ADJECTIVE
1 *ineffective* (treatment)
2 *inefficient* ◇ *un service de transports publics inefficace* an inefficient public transport system

inégal ADJECTIVE
(MASC PL **inégaux**)
1 *unequal* ◇ *un combat inégal* an unequal struggle
2 *uneven* ◇ *la qualité est inégale* the quality varies

inévitable ADJECTIVE
unavoidable

- **C'était inévitable!** That was bound to happen!

inexact ADJECTIVE
inaccurate

in extremis ADVERB

- **Il a réussi à attraper son train in extremis.** He just managed to catch his train.
- **Ils ont évité un accident in extremis.** They avoided an accident by the skin of their teeth.

l'**infarctus** MASC NOUN
coronary

infatigable ADJECTIVE
indefatigable ◇ *Il est infatigable.* He's indefatigable.

infect ADJECTIVE
revolting (meal)

s'**infecter** VERB
to go septic ◇ *La plaie s'est infectée.* The wound has gone septic.

l'**infection** FEM NOUN
infection

inférieur ADJECTIVE
lower ◇ *les membres inférieurs* the lower limbs ◇ *C'est moins cher, mais de qualité inférieure.* It's cheaper but of lower quality.

infernal ADJECTIVE
(MASC PL **infernaux**)
terrible ◇ *Ils faisaient un bruit infernal.* They were making a terrible noise.

l'**infini** MASC NOUN

- **à l'infini** indefinitely ◇ *On pourrait en parler à l'infini.* We could discuss this indefinitely.

l'**infinitif** MASC NOUN
infinitive

l'**infirme** MASC/FEM NOUN
disabled person

l'**infirmerie** FEM NOUN
medical room ◇ *Elle est à l'infirmerie.* She's in the medical room.

l'**infirmier** MASC NOUN
nurse

l'**infirmière** FEM NOUN
nurse

inflammable ADJECTIVE
inflammable

l'**influence** FEM NOUN
influence

influencer VERB
to influence

l'**informaticien** MASC NOUN
computer scientist

l'**informaticienne** FEM NOUN
computer scientist

les **informations** FEM NOUN
1 *news* (on TV) ◇ *les informations de vingt heures* the 8 o'clock news
2 *information* ◇ *Je voudrais quelques informations, s'il vous plaît.* I'd like some information, please.

- **une information** a piece of information

l'**informatique** FEM NOUN
computing

informer VERB
to inform

- **s'informer** to find out ◇ *Je ne connais pas les heures de fermeture, mais je vais m'informer.* I don't know when they close, but I'm going to find out.

infuser VERB
1 *to brew* (tea)
2 *to infuse* (herbal tea)

l'**infusion** FEM NOUN
herbal tea

l'**ingénieur** MASC NOUN
engineer

ingrat ADJECTIVE
ungrateful

l'**ingrédient** MASC NOUN
ingredient

inhabituel ADJECTIVE
(FEM SING **inhabituelle**)
unusual

inhumain ADJECTIVE
inhuman

initial ADJECTIVE
(MASC PL **initiaux**)
initial

l'**initiale** FEM NOUN

initial

l'**initiation** FEM NOUN
introduction   ◇ *un stage d'initiation à la planche à voile* an introductory course in windsurfing

l'**initiative** FEM NOUN
initiative   ◇ *avoir de l'initiative* to have initiative

injecter VERB
to inject

l'**injection** FEM NOUN
injection

l'**injure** FEM NOUN
① *insult*   ◇ *Il a pris ça comme une injure.* He took this as an insult.
② *abuse*   ◇ *lancer des injures à quelqu'un* to hurl abuse at somebody

injurieux ADJECTIVE
(FEM SING **injurieuse**)
abusive (language)

injuste ADJECTIVE
unfair

innocent ADJECTIVE
innocent

innombrable ADJECTIVE
innumerable

innover VERB
to break new ground

inoccupé ADJECTIVE
empty   ◇ *un appartement inoccupé* an empty flat

inoffensif ADJECTIVE
(FEM SING **inoffensive**)
harmless

l'**inondation** FEM NOUN
flood

inoubliable ADJECTIVE
unforgettable

inoxydable ADJECTIVE
◆ *l'acier inoxydable* stainless steel

inquiet ADJECTIVE
(FEM SING **inquiète**)
worried

inquiétant ADJECTIVE
worrying

s'**inquiéter** VERB
to worry   ◇ *Ne t'inquiète pas!* Don't worry!

l'**inquiétude** FEM NOUN
anxiety

insatisfait ADJECTIVE
dissatisfied

l'**inscription** FEM NOUN
registration (for school, course)

s'**inscrire** VERB
◆ *s'inscrire à* (1) to join   ◇ *Je me suis inscrit au club de tennis.* I've joined the tennis club.
◆ *s'inscrire à* (2) to register   ◇ *N'attends*

pas trop pour t'inscrire à la fac. Don't leave it too long to register at the university.

l'**insecte** MASC NOUN
insect

insensible ADJECTIVE
insensitive   ◇ *Il la trouve insensible.* He thinks she's insensitive.

l'**insigne** MASC NOUN
badge

insignifiant ADJECTIVE
insignificant

insister VERB
to insist
◆ *N'insiste pas!* Don't keep on!

l'**insolation** FEM NOUN
sunstroke

insolent ADJECTIVE
cheeky

insouciant ADJECTIVE
carefree

insoutenable ADJECTIVE
unbearable   ◇ *une douleur insoutenable* an unbearable pain

inspecter VERB
to inspect

l'**inspecteur** MASC NOUN
inspector

l'**inspection** FEM NOUN
inspection

l'**inspectrice** FEM NOUN
inspector

inspirer VERB
to inspire
◆ *s'inspirer de* to take one's inspiration from   ◇ *Le peintre s'est inspiré d'un poème.* The painter took his inspiration from a poem.

instable ADJECTIVE
① *unsteady* (piece of furniture)
② *unstable* (person)

les **installations** FEM NOUN
facilities   ◇ *Cet appartement est pourvu de toutes les installations modernes.* This flat has all modern facilities.

installer VERB
① *to put up* (shelves)
② *to install* (gas, telephone)
◆ *s'installer* to settle in   ◇ *Nous nous sommes installés dans notre nouvel appartement.* We've settled into our new flat.
◆ *Installez-vous, je vous en prie.* Have a seat please.

l'**instant** MASC NOUN
moment   ◇ *dans un instant* in a moment   ◇ *Le dîner sera prêt dans un instant.* Dinner will be ready in a moment.   ◇ *pour l'instant* for the

moment

instantané ADJECTIVE

instant ◦ *du café instantané* instant coffee

l'**instinct** MASC NOUN
instinct

l'**institut** MASC NOUN
institute

l'**instituteur** MASC NOUN
primary school teacher

l'**institution** FEM NOUN
institution

l'**institutrice** FEM NOUN
primary school teacher

l'**instruction** FEM NOUN
1 *instruction* ◦ *J'ai suivi soigneusement ses instructions.* I followed his instructions carefully.
2 *education* ◦ *Il n'a pas beaucoup d'instruction.* He's not very well-educated.

s'**instruire** VERB
to educate oneself

instruit ADJECTIVE
educated

l'**instrument** MASC NOUN
instrument ◦ *un instrument de musique* a musical instrument

insuffisant ADJECTIVE
insufficient
➔ **"travail insuffisant"** (*on school report*) "must make more effort"

l'**insuline** FEM NOUN
insulin

l'**insulte** FEM NOUN
insult

insulter VERB
to insult

insupportable ADJECTIVE
unbearable

intact ADJECTIVE
intact

intégral ADJECTIVE
(MASC PL **intégraux**)
➔ **le texte intégral** unabridged version
➔ **un remboursement intégral** a full refund

l'**intégrisme** MASC NOUN
fundamentalism

l'**intelligence** FEM NOUN
intelligence

intelligent ADJECTIVE
intelligent

intense ADJECTIVE
intense

intensif ADJECTIVE
(FEM SING **intensive**)
intensive
➔ **un cours intensif** a crash course

l'**intention** FEM NOUN
intention
➔ **avoir l'intention de faire quelque chose** to intend to do something ◦ *J'ai l'intention de lui en parler.* I intend to speak to him about it.

l'**interdiction** FEM NOUN
➔ **"interdiction de stationner"** "no parking"
➔ **"interdiction de fumer"** "no smoking"

interdire VERB
to forbid ◦ *Ses parents lui ont interdit de sortir.* His parents have forbidden him to go out.

interdit ADJECTIVE
forbidden ◦ *Il est interdit de fumer dans les couloirs.* Smoking in the corridors is forbidden.

intéressant ADJECTIVE
interesting ◦ *un livre intéressant* an interesting book
➔ **On lui a fait une offre intéressante.** They made him an attractive offer.
➔ **On trouve des CD à des prix très intéressants dans ce magasin.** You can get very cheap CDs in this shop.

intéresser VERB
to interest
➔ **s'intéresser à** to be interested in ◦ *Est-ce que vous vous intéressez à la politique?* Are you interested in politics?

l'**intérêt** MASC NOUN
interest
➔ **avoir intérêt à faire quelque chose** to do well to do something ◦ *Tu as intérêt à te dépêcher si tu veux prendre le train de dix heures.* You'd better hurry up if you want to catch the 10 o'clock train.

l'**intérieur** MASC NOUN
inside ◦ *Il fait plus frais à l'intérieur de la maison.* It's cooler inside the house.

l'**interlocuteur** MASC NOUN
➔ **son interlocuteur** the man he's speaking to

l'**interlocutrice** FEM NOUN
➔ **son interlocutrice** the woman he's speaking to

l'**intermédiaire** MASC NOUN
intermediary
➔ **par l'intermédiaire de** through ◦ *Je l'ai rencontré par l'intermédiaire de sa sœur.* I met him through his sister.

l'**internat** MASC NOUN
boarding school

international ADJECTIVE
(MASC PL **internationaux**)
international

l'**interne** MASC/FEM NOUN
boarder

l'**Internet** MASC NOUN
Internet ◇ *sur Internet* on the
Internet

l'**interphone** MASC NOUN
intercom

l'**interprète** MASC/FEM NOUN
interpreter

interpréter VERB
to interpret

interrogatif ADJECTIVE
(FEM SING **interrogative**)
interrogative

l'**interrogation** FEM NOUN
1 *question*
2 *test* ◇ *une interrogation écrite* a
written test ◇ *une interrogation orale* an
oral test

l'**interrogatoire** MASC NOUN
questioning
◆ **C'est un interrogatoire ou quoi?** Am I
being cross-examined?

interroger VERB
to question

interrompre VERB
to interrupt

l'**interrupteur** MASC NOUN
switch

l'**interruption** FEM NOUN
interruption
◆ **sans interruption** without stopping
◇ *Il a parlé pendant deux heures sans
interruption.* He spoke for two hours
without stopping.

l'**intervalle** MASC NOUN
interval
◆ **dans l'intervalle** in the meantime

intervenir VERB
1 *to intervene*
2 *to take action* ◇ *La police est
intervenue.* The police took action.

l'**intervention** FEM NOUN
intervention ◇ *une intervention
militaire* a military intervention
◆ **une intervention chirurgicale** a
surgical operation

l'**interview** FEM NOUN
interview (on radio, TV)

l'**intestin** MASC NOUN
intestine

intime ADJECTIVE
intimate
◆ **un journal intime** a diary

intimider VERB
to intimidate

l'**intimité** FEM NOUN
◆ **dans l'intimité** in private ◇ *Ce que
vous faites dans l'intimité ne m'intéresse*

pas. What you do in private doesn't
interest me.
◆ **Le mariage a eu lieu dans l'intimité.**
The wedding ceremony was private.

intitulé ADJECTIVE
entitled

intolérable ADJECTIVE
intolerable

l'**intoxication** FEM NOUN
◆ **une intoxication alimentaire** food
poisoning

intransigeant ADJECTIVE
uncompromising

l'**intrigue** FEM NOUN
plot (of book, film)

l'**introduction** FEM NOUN
introduction

introduire VERB
to introduce

l'**intuition** FEM NOUN
intuition

inusable ADJECTIVE
hard-wearing

inutile ADJECTIVE
useless

l'**invalide** MASC/FEM NOUN
disabled person

l'**invasion** FEM NOUN
invasion

inventer VERB
1 *to invent*
2 *to make up* ◇ *inventer une excuse*
to make up an excuse

l'**inventeur** MASC NOUN
inventor

l'**invention** FEM NOUN
invention

inverse ADJECTIVE
see also **inverse** NOUN
◆ **dans l'ordre inverse** in reverse order
◆ **en sens inverse** in the opposite
direction

l'**inverse** MASC NOUN
see also **inverse** ADJECTIVE
reverse
◆ **Tu t'es trompé, c'est l'inverse.** You've
got it wrong, it's the other way round.

l'**investissement** MASC NOUN
investment

invisible ADJECTIVE
invisible

l'**invitation** FEM NOUN
invitation

l'**invité** MASC NOUN
guest

l'**invitée** FEM NOUN
guest

inviter VERB
to invite

involontaire ADJECTIVE
  unintentional ◇ *C'était tout à fait
  involontaire.* It was quite unintentional.
invraisemblable ADJECTIVE
  unlikely ◇ *une histoire invraisemblable*
  an implausible story
ira, irai, iraient, irais VERB *see* **aller**
◆ **J'irai demain au supermarché.** I'll go
  to the supermarket tomorrow.
l'**Irak** MASC NOUN
  Iraq
l'**Iran** MASC NOUN
  Iran
iras, irez VERB *see* **aller**
irlandais ADJECTIVE, NOUN
  (FEM SING **irlandaise**)
  Irish
◆ **un Irlandais** an Irishman
◆ **une Irlandaise** an Irishwoman
◆ **les Irlandais** the Irish
l'**Irlande** FEM NOUN
  Ireland
◆ **en Irlande (1)** in Ireland
◆ **en Irlande (2)** to Ireland
◆ **la République d'Irlande** the Irish
  Republic
◆ **l'Irlande du Nord** Northern Ireland
l'**ironie** FEM NOUN
  irony
ironique ADJECTIVE
  ironical
irons, iront VERB *see* **aller**
◆ **Nous irons à la plage cet après-midi.**
  We'll go to the beach this afternoon.
irrationnel ADJECTIVE
  (FEM SING **irrationnelle**)
  irrational
irréel ADJECTIVE
  (FEM SING **irréelle**)
  unreal
irrégulier ADJECTIVE
  (FEM SING **irrégulière**)
  irregular
irrésistible ADJECTIVE
  irresistible

irritable ADJECTIVE
  irritable
irriter VERB
  to irritate
islamique ADJECTIVE
  Islamic
l'**Islande** FEM NOUN
  Iceland
isolé ADJECTIVE
  isolated ◇ *une ferme isolée* an
  isolated farm
Israël MASC NOUN
  Israel
israélien ADJECTIVE, NOUN
  (FEM SING **israélienne**)
  Israeli
◆ **un Israélien** an Israeli (*man*)
◆ **une Israélienne** an Israeli (*woman*)
◆ **les Israéliens** the Israelis
israélite ADJECTIVE
  Jewish
l'**issue** FEM NOUN
◆ **une voie sans issue** a dead end
◆ **l'issue de secours** emergency exit
l'**Italie** FEM NOUN
  Italy
◆ **en Italie (1)** in Italy
◆ **en Italie (2)** to Italy
italien ADJECTIVE, NOUN
  (FEM SING **italienne**)
  Italian ◇ *J'apprends l'italien.* I'm
  learning Italian.
◆ **un Italien** an Italian (*man*)
◆ **une Italienne** (*woman*)
◆ **les Italiens** the Italians
l'**itinéraire** MASC NOUN
  route
l'**IUT** MASC NOUN (= *Institut universitaire de
  technologie*)
  institute of technology (*at university
  level*)
ivre ADJECTIVE
  drunk
l'**ivrogne** MASC / FEM NOUN
  drunkard

J

j' PRONOUN *see* **je**

la **jalousie** NOUN
> *jealousy*

jaloux ADJECTIVE
> (FEM SING **jalouse**)
> *jealous*

jamais ADVERB
> ⓵ *never* ◇ *Est-ce que tu vas souvent au cinéma?–Non, jamais.* Do you go to the cinema often?–No, never. ◇ *Il ne boit jamais d'alcool.* He never drinks alcohol.
> ⓶ *ever*
>
> *Phrases with* **jamais** *meaning* **ever** *are followed by a verb in the subjunctive.*
>
> ◇ *C'est la plus belle chose que j'aie jamais vue.* It's the most beautiful thing I've ever seen.

la **jambe** NOUN
> *leg*

le **jambon** NOUN
> *ham*
> • **le jambon cru** Parma ham

le **jambonneau** NOUN
> (PL les **jambonneaux**)
> *knuckle of ham*

janvier MASC NOUN
> *January*
> • **en janvier** in January

le **Japon** NOUN
> *Japan*
> • **au Japon (1)** in Japan
> • **au Japon (2)** to Japan

japonais ADJECTIVE, NOUN
> *Japanese* ◇ *Elle parle japonais.* She speaks Japanese.
> • **un Japonais** a Japanese (*man*)
> • **une Japonaise** a Japanese (*woman*)
> • **les Japonais** the Japanese

le **jardin** NOUN
> *garden*

le **jardinage** NOUN
> *gardening*

le **jardinier** NOUN
> *gardener*

la **jardinière** NOUN
> *gardener*

jaune ADJECTIVE
> *see also* **jaune** NOUN
> *yellow*

le **jaune** NOUN
> *see also* **jaune** ADJECTIVE
> *yellow*
> • **un jaune d'œuf** an egg yolk

jaunir VERB
> *to turn yellow*

la **jaunisse** NOUN
> *jaundice*

Javel NOUN
> • **l'eau de Javel** bleach

J.-C. ABBREVIATION (= *Jésus-Christ*)
> • **44 avant J.-C.** 44 BC
> • **115 après J.-C.** 115 AD

je PRONOUN
> **je** *changes to* **j'** *before a vowel and most words beginning with "h".*
> *I* ◇ *Je t'appellerai ce soir.* I'll phone you this evening. ◇ *J'arrive!* I'm coming! ◇ *J'hésite.* I'm not sure.

le **jean** NOUN
> *jeans*

Jésus-Christ MASC NOUN
> *Jesus Christ*

le **jet** NOUN
> ⓵ *jet* (*of water*)
> ⓶ *jet plane*

jetable ADJECTIVE
> *disposable*

la **jetée** NOUN
> *jetty*

jeter VERB
> ⓵ *to throw* ◇ *Il a jeté son manteau sur le lit.* He threw his coat onto the bed.
> ⓶ *to throw away* ◇ *Mes parents ne jettent jamais rien.* My parents never throw anything away.
> • **jeter un coup d'œil** to have a look ◇ *Jette un coup d'œil pour voir s'il y a des erreurs.* Have a look to see if there are any mistakes.

le **jeton** NOUN
> *counter* (*in board game*)

le **jeu** NOUN
> (PL les **jeux**)
> *game* ◇ *Je n'aime pas les jeux de société.* I don't like board games.
> • **un jeu de cartes (1)** a pack of cards
> • **un jeu de cartes (2)** a card game
> • **un jeu de mots** a pun
> • **les jeux vidéo** video games
> • **en jeu** at stake ◇ *Des vies humaines sont en jeu.* Human lives are at stake.

le **jeudi** NOUN
> ⓵ *Thursday* ◇ *Aujourd'hui, nous sommes jeudi.* It's Thursday today.
> ⓶ *on Thursday* ◇ *Il arrivera jeudi matin.* He's arriving on Thursday morning.
> • **le jeudi** on Thursdays ◇ *Le musée est fermé le jeudi.* The museum is closed on Thursdays.
> • **tous les jeudis** every Thursday

- **jeudi dernier** last Thursday
- **jeudi prochain** next Thursday

jeun
- **à jeun** ADVERB
  on an empty stomach ◇ *à prendre à jeun* to be taken on an empty stomach ◇ *Il faut être à jeun pour la prise de sang.* You mustn't have eaten anything before giving a blood sample.

jeune ADJECTIVE
young ◇ *un jeune homme* a young man ◇ *une jeune femme* a young woman
- **une jeune fille** a girl

la **jeunesse** NOUN
youth

la **joie** NOUN
joy

joindre VERB
1 *to put together* ◇ *On va joindre les deux tables.* We're going to put the two tables together.
2 *to contact* ◇ *Vous arriverez peut-être à le joindre chez lui.* Maybe you'll be able to contact him at home.

joint ADJECTIVE
- **une pièce jointe** an enclosure (*in letter*)

joli ADJECTIVE
pretty

le **jonc** NOUN
rush

la **jonquille** NOUN
daffodil

la **joue** NOUN
cheek

jouer VERB
1 *to play* ◇ *Elle est allée jouer avec les petits voisins.* She's gone to play with the children next door.
- **jouer de** to play (*instrument*) ◇ *Il joue de la guitare et du piano.* He plays the guitar and the piano.
- **jouer à** to play (*sport, game*) ◇ *Elle joue au tennis.* She plays tennis. ◇ *jouer aux dames* to play draughts
2 *to act* ◇ *Je trouve qu'il joue très bien dans ce film.* I think he acts very well in this film.
- **On joue Hamlet au Théâtre de la Ville.** Hamlet is on at the Théâtre de la Ville.

le **jouet** NOUN
toy

le **joueur** NOUN
player
- **être mauvais joueur** to be a bad loser

la **joueuse** NOUN
player

le **jour** NOUN
day ◇ *J'ai passé trois jours chez mes cousins.* I stayed with my cousins for three days.
- **Il fait jour.** It's daylight.
- **mettre quelque chose à jour** to update something
- **un jour férié** a public holiday

le **journal** NOUN
(PL les **journaux**)
1 *newspaper*
- **le journal télévisé** the television news
2 *diary* ◇ *Elle tient un journal depuis l'âge de douze ans.* She has been keeping a diary since she was 12.

journalier ADJECTIVE
(FEM SING **journalière**)
daily

le **journalisme** NOUN
journalism

le/la **journaliste** NOUN
journalist ◇ *Elle est journaliste.* She's a journalist.

la **journée** NOUN
day

joyeux ADJECTIVE
(FEM SING **joyeuse**)
happy
- **Joyeux anniversaire!** Happy birthday!
- **Joyeux Noël!** Merry Christmas!

le **judo** NOUN
judo

le **juge** NOUN
judge

juger VERB
to judge

juif ADJECTIVE
(FEM SING **juive**)
Jewish ◇ *la cuisine juive* Jewish cooking
- **un juif** a Jew (*man*)
- **une juive** a Jew (*woman*)

juillet MASC NOUN
July
- **en juillet** in July

juin MASC NOUN
June
- **en juin** in June

le **jumeau** NOUN
(PL les **jumeaux**)
twin

jumeler VERB
to twin ◇ *Saint-Brieuc est jumelée avec Aberystwyth.* Saint-Brieuc is twinned with Aberystwyth.

la **jumelle** NOUN
twin

les **jumelles** FEM NOUN
binoculars

la **jument** NOUN
mare

la **jungle** NOUN
   jungle

la **jupe** NOUN
   skirt

jurer VERB
   to swear   ◇ *Je jure que c'est vrai!* I
   swear it's true!

juridique ADJECTIVE
   legal

le **jury** NOUN
   jury

le **jus** NOUN
   juice
   • **un jus de fruit** a fruit juice

jusqu'à PREPOSITION
   [1] *as far as*   ◇ *Nous avons marché
   jusqu'au village.* We walked as far as the
   village.
   [2] *until*   ◇ *Il fait généralement chaud
   jusqu'à la mi-août.* It's usually hot until
   mid-August.
   • **jusqu'à ce que** until   ◇ *Tu peux rester
   ici jusqu'à ce qu'il cesse de pleuvoir.* You
   can stay here until it stops raining.
   • **jusqu'à présent** so far

juste ADJECTIVE, ADVERB
   [1] *fair*   ◇ *Il est sévère, mais juste.* He's
   strict but fair.
   [2] *tight*   ◇ *Cette veste est un peu juste.*
   This jacket is a bit tight.
   • **juste assez** just enough
   • **chanter juste** to sing in tune

justement ADVERB
   just   ◇ *C'est justement pour cela qu'il
   est parti!* That's just the reason why he
   left!

la **justesse** NOUN
   • **de justesse** only just   ◇ *Il a eu son
   permis de justesse.* He only just passed
   his driving test.

la **justice** NOUN
   justice

justifier VERB
   to justify

juteux ADJECTIVE
   (FEM SING **juteuse**)
   juicy

juvénile ADJECTIVE
   youthful

J

K

kaki ADJECTIVE
  khaki
le **kangourou** NOUN
  kangaroo
le **karaté** NOUN
  karate
la **kermesse** NOUN
  fair
  kidnapper VERB
  to kidnap
le **kilo** NOUN
  kilo
le **kilogramme** NOUN
  kilogramme
le **kilomètre** NOUN
  kilometre
le/la **kinésithérapeute** NOUN
  physiotherapist

le **kiosque** NOUN
  ◆ **un kiosque à journaux** a news stand
le **klaxon** NOUN
  horn (*of car*)
  klaxonner VERB
  to sound the horn
km ABBREVIATION (= *kilomètre*)
  ◆ **km/h** kph (= kilometres per hour)
K.-O. ADJECTIVE
  knocked out
  ◆ **mettre quelqu'un K.-O.** to knock
  somebody out ◇ *Il l'a mis K.-O. au*
  troisième round. He knocked him out in
  the third round.
  ◆ **Je suis complètement K.-O.** (*informal*)
  I'm knackered.
le **K-way** NOUN
  cagoule

L

l' ARTICLE, PRONOUN *see* **la, le**

la ARTICLE, PRONOUN

see also **la** NOUN

la *changes to* **l'** *before a vowel and most words beginning with "h".*

[1] *the* ◇ *la maison* the house ◇ *l'actrice* the actress ◇ *l'herbe* the grass

[2] *her* • *Je la connais depuis longtemps.* I've known her for a long time. ◇ *C'est une femme intelligente: je l'admire beaucoup.* She's an intelligent woman: I admire her very much.

[3] *it* ◇ *C'est une bonne émission: je la regarde toutes les semaines.* It's a good programme: I watch it every week.

[4] *one's*

• **se mordre la langue** to bite one's tongue ◇ *Je me suis mordu la langue.* I've bitten my tongue.

• **dix francs la douzaine** 10 francs a dozen

le la NOUN

see also **la** ARTICLE

[1] *A* ◇ *en la bémol* in A flat

[2] *la* ◇ *sol, la, si, do* so, la, ti, do

là ADVERB

[1] *there* ◇ *Ton livre est là, sur la table.* Your book's there, on the table.

[2] *here* ◇ *Elle n'est pas là.* She isn't here.

• **C'est là que... (1)** That's where... ◇ *C'est là que je suis né.* That's where I was born.

• **C'est là que... (2)** That's when... ◇ *C'est là que j'ai réalisé que je m'étais trompé.* That's when I realized that I had made a mistake.

là-bas ADVERB
over there

le labo NOUN (*informal*)
lab

le laboratoire NOUN
laboratory

labourer VERB
to plough

le labyrinthe NOUN
maze

le lac NOUN
lake

lacer VERB
to do up (*shoes*)

le lacet NOUN
lace

• **des chaussures à lacets** lace-up shoes

lâche ADJECTIVE
see also **lâche** NOUN

[1] *loose* ◇ *Le nœud est trop lâche.* The knot's too loose.

[2] *cowardly*

• **Il est lâche.** He's a coward.

le lâche NOUN
see also **lâche** ADJECTIVE
coward

lâcher VERB

[1] *to let go of* • *Il n'a pas lâché ma main de tout le film.* He didn't let go of my hand until the end of the film.

[2] *to drop* ◇ *Il a été tellement surpris qu'il a lâché son verre.* He was so surprised that he dropped his glass.

[3] *to fail* ◇ *Les freins ont lâché.* The brakes failed.

la lâcheté NOUN
cowardice

lacrymogène ADJECTIVE

• **le gaz lacrymogène** tear gas

la lacune NOUN
gap

là-dedans ADVERB
in there ◇ *Qu'est-ce qu'il y a là-dedans?* What's in there?

là-dessous ADVERB

[1] *under there* ◇ *Mon carnet d'adresses est quelque part là-dessous.* My address book is under there somewhere.

[2] *behind it* ◇ *Il y a quelque chose de louche là-dessous.* There's something fishy behind it.

là-dessus ADVERB
on there

là-haut ADVERB
up there

laid ADJECTIVE
ugly

la laideur NOUN
ugliness

le lainage NOUN
woollen garment

la laine NOUN
wool ◇ *un pull en laine* a wool jumper

laïque ADJECTIVE

• **une école laïque** a state school

la laisse NOUN
lead ◇ *Tenez votre chien en laisse.* Keep your dog on a lead.

laisser VERB

[1] *to leave* ◇ *J'ai laissé mon parapluie à la maison.* I've left my umbrella at home.

[2] *to let* ◇ *Laisse-le parler.* Let him speak.

◆ **Elle se laisse aller.** She's letting herself go.

le **laisser-aller** NOUN
carelessness

le **lait** NOUN
milk
◆ **un café au lait** a white coffee

la **laitue** NOUN
lettuce

les **lambeaux** MASC NOUN
◆ **en lambeaux** tattered

la **lame** NOUN
blade ◇ *une lame de rasoir* a razor blade

la **lamelle** NOUN
thin strip

lamentable ADJECTIVE
appalling

se **lamenter** VERB
to moan

le **lampadaire** NOUN
standard lamp

la **lampe** NOUN
lamp
◆ **une lampe de poche** a torch

la **lance** NOUN
spear

le **lancement** NOUN
launch

lancer VERB
| see also lancer NOUN |
[1] *to throw* ◇ *Lance-moi le ballon!* Throw me the ball!
[2] *to launch* ◇ *Ils viennent de lancer un nouveau modèle.* They've just launched a new model.
◆ **se lancer** to embark on ◇ *Il s'est lancé là-dedans sans bien réfléchir.* He embarked on it without thinking properly.

le **lancer** NOUN
| see also lancer VERB |
◆ **le lancer de poids** putting the shot

lancinant ADJECTIVE
◆ **une douleur lancinante** a shooting pain

le **landau** NOUN
pram

la **lande** NOUN
moor

le **langage** NOUN
language

la **langouste** NOUN
crayfish

la **langue** NOUN
[1] *tongue* ◇ *Un petit garçon m'a tiré la langue.* A little boy stuck out his tongue at me.
◆ **sa langue maternelle** his mother tongue
[2] *language* ◇ *une langue vivante* a modern language

la **lanière** NOUN
strap

le **lapin** NOUN
rabbit

le **laps** NOUN
◆ **un laps de temps** a space of time

la **laque** NOUN
hair spray

laquelle PRONOUN
(PL lesquelles)
[1] *which* ◇ *Laquelle de ces photos préfères-tu?* Which of these photos do you prefer? ◇ *À laquelle de tes sœurs ressembles-tu?* Which of your sisters do you look like?
[2] *whom* ◇ *la personne à laquelle vous faites référence* the person to whom you are referring
| laquelle *is often not translated in English.* |
◇ *la personne à laquelle je pense* the person I'm thinking of

le **lard** NOUN
streaky bacon

les **lardons** MASC NOUN
chunks of bacon

large ADJECTIVE, ADVERB
| see also large NOUN |
wide
◆ **voir large** to allow a bit extra ◇ *Achète un autre pain: il vaut mieux voir large.* Buy another loaf of bread: it's better to have a bit extra.

le **large** NOUN
| see also large ADJECTIVE |
◆ **cinq mètres de large** 5 m wide
◆ **le large** the open sea
◆ **au large de** off the coast of ◇ *Le bateau est actuellement au large du Portugal.* The boat is off the coast of Portugal at the moment.

largement ADVERB
◆ **Vous avez largement le temps.** You have plenty of time.
◆ **C'est largement suffisant.** That's ample.

la **largeur** NOUN
width

la **larme** NOUN
tear ◇ *être en larmes* to be in tears

la **laryngite** NOUN
laryngitis

le **laser** NOUN
laser
◆ **une chaîne laser** a compact disc player
◆ **un disque laser** a compact disc

lasser VERB

• **se lasser de** to get tired of ◇ *Il s'est lassé de la tapisserie à fleurs du salon.* He's got tired of the flowery wallpaper in the sitting room.

le **latin** NOUN
Latin

le **laurier** NOUN
laurel tree ◇ *une feuille de laurier* a bay leaf

lavable ADJECTIVE
washable

le **lavabo** NOUN
washbasin

le **lavage** NOUN
wash ◇ *Ce pull a rétréci au lavage.* This jumper has shrunk in the wash.

la **lavande** NOUN
lavender

le **lave-linge** NOUN
(PL les **lave-linge**)
washing machine

laver VERB
to wash
• **se laver** to wash ◇ *se laver les mains* to wash one's hands

la **laverie** NOUN
• **une laverie automatique** a launderette

le **lave-vaisselle** NOUN
(PL les **lave-vaisselle**)
dishwasher

le **ARTICLE, PRONOUN**
le *changes to l' before a vowel and most words beginning with "h".*
[1] *the* ◇ *le livre* the book • *l'arbre* the tree ◇ *l'hélicoptère* the helicopter
[2] *him* ◇ *Daniel est un vieil ami: je le connais depuis plus de vingt ans.* Daniel is an old friend: I've known him for over 20 years.
[3] *it* ◇ *Où est mon stylo? Je ne le trouve plus.* Where's my pen? I can't find it. ◇ *Où est le fromage?–Je l'ai mis au frigo.* Where's the cheese?–I've put it in the fridge.
[4] *one's*
• **se laver le visage** to wash one's face ◇ *Évitez de vous laver le visage avec du savon.* Avoid washing your face with soap.
• **dix francs le kilo** 10 francs a kilo
• **Il est arrivé le douze mai.** He arrived on 12 May.

lécher VERB
to lick

le **lèche-vitrine** NOUN
• **faire du lèche-vitrine** to go window-shopping

la **leçon** NOUN
lesson

le **lecteur** NOUN
[1] *reader*
[2] *foreign language assistant* (at a university)
• **un lecteur de cassettes** a cassette player
• **un lecteur de CD** a CD player

la **lectrice** NOUN
[1] *reader*
[2] *foreign language assistant* (at a university)

la **lecture** NOUN
reading

légal ADJECTIVE
(MASC PL **légaux**)
legal

la **légende** NOUN
[1] *legend*
[2] *key* (of map)

léger ADJECTIVE
(FEM SING **légère**)
[1] *light*
[2] *slight* ◇ *un léger retard* a slight delay
• **à la légère** thoughtlessly ◇ *Il a agi à la légère.* He acted thoughtlessly.

légèrement ADVERB
[1] *lightly* ◇ *Habille-toi légèrement. Il va faire chaud.* Wear light clothes: it's going to be hot.
[2] *slightly* ◇ *Il est légèrement plus grand que son frère.* He's slightly taller than his brother.

les **législatives** FEM NOUN
general election

le **légume** NOUN
vegetable

le **lendemain** NOUN
next day ◇ *le lendemain de son arrivée* the day after he arrived
• **le lendemain matin** the next morning

lent ADJECTIVE
slow

lentement ADVERB
slowly

la **lenteur** NOUN
slowness

la **lentille** NOUN
[1] *contact lens* ◇ *Est-ce que tu portes des lentilles?* Do you wear contact lenses?
[2] *lentil* ◇ *un rôti de porc aux lentilles* roast pork with lentils

le **léopard** NOUN
leopard

lequel PRONOUN
(FEM SING **laquelle**, MASC PL **lesquels**, FEM PL **lesquelles**)
[1] *which* ◇ *Lequel de ces films as-tu*

préféré? Which of the films did you prefer?

[2] *whom* ◇ *l'homme avec lequel elle a été vue pour la dernière fois* the man with whom she was last seen

lequel *is often not translated in English.*

◇ *le garçon avec lequel elle est sortie* the boy she went out with

les ARTICLE, PRONOUN
[1] *the* ◇ *les arbres* the trees
[2] *them* ◇ *Elle les a invités à dîner.* She invited them to dinner.
[3] *one's*
◆ **se brosser les dents** to brush one's teeth ◇ *Elle s'est brossé les dents.* She brushed her teeth.
◆ **dix francs les cinq** 10 francs for 5

la **lesbienne** NOUN
lesbian

lesquels PRONOUN
(FEM **lesquelles**)
[1] *which* ◇ *Lesquelles de ces photos as-tu choisies?* Which of the photos did you choose?
[2] *whom* ◇ *les personnes avec lesquelles il est associé* the people with whom he is in partnership

lesquels *is often not translated in English.*

◇ *les gens chez lesquels nous avons dîné* the people we had dinner with

la **lessive** NOUN
[1] *washing powder* ◇ *une marque de lessive* a brand of washing powder
[2] *wash* ◇ *Est-ce que vous avez quelque chose à mettre à la lessive?* Have you got anything to go in the wash?
◆ **faire la lessive** to do the washing

leste ADJECTIVE
nimble

la **Lettonie** NOUN
Latvia

la **lettre** NOUN
letter ◇ *écrire une lettre* to write a lettre

les **lettres** FEM NOUN
arts ◇ *la faculté de lettres* the Faculty of Arts

leur ADJECTIVE, PRONOUN
[1] *their* ◇ *leur ami* their friend
[2] *them* ◇ *Je leur ai dit la vérité.* I told them the truth.
◆ **le leur** theirs ◇ *mon camion et le leur* my truck and theirs ◇ *Ma voiture est rouge, la leur est bleue.* My car's red, theirs is blue.

leurs ADJECTIVE, PRONOUN
their ◇ *leurs amis* their friends
◆ **les leurs** theirs ◇ *tes livres et les leurs*

your books and theirs

levé ADJECTIVE
◆ **être levé** to be up ◇ *Est-ce qu'il est levé?* Is he up?

lever VERB
see also **lever** NOUN
to raise ◇ *Levez vos verres!* Raise your glasses! ◇ *Levez la main si vous connaissez la réponse.* Put your hand up if you know the answer.
◆ **lever les yeux** to look up
◆ **se lever (1)** to get up ◇ *Il se lève tous les jours à six heures.* He gets up at 6 o'clock every day. ◇ *Lève-toi!* Get up!
◆ **se lever (2)** to rise ◇ *Le soleil se lève actuellement à cinq heures.* At the moment the sun rises at 5 o'clock.

le **lever** NOUN
see also **lever** VERB
◆ **le lever du soleil** sunrise

le **levier** NOUN
lever

la **lèvre** NOUN
lip

le **lévrier** NOUN
greyhound

la **levure** NOUN
yeast
◆ **la levure chimique** baking powder

le **lexique** NOUN
word list

le **lézard** NOUN
lizard

la **liaison** NOUN
affair ◇ *Ils ont eu une liaison dans leur jeunesse.* They had an affair when they were younger.

la **libellule** NOUN
dragonfly

libérer VERB
to free ◇ *Les otages ont été libérés hier soir.* The hostages were freed last night.
◆ **se libérer** to find time ◇ *J'essaierai de me libérer cet après-midi.* I'll try to find time this afternoon.

la **liberté** NOUN
freedom
◆ **mettre en liberté** to release ◇ *Il a été mis en liberté au bout d'un an de prison.* He was released after a year in prison.

le/la **libraire** NOUN
bookseller

la **librairie** NOUN
bookshop

libre ADJECTIVE
[1] *free* ◇ *Tu es libre de faire ce que tu veux.* You are free to do as you wish. ◇ *Est-ce que cette place est libre?* Is this seat free?

2 *clear* ◇ *La route est libre: vous pouvez traverser.* The road is clear: you can cross.
- **une école libre** a private school

le **libre-service** NOUN
(PL les **libres-services**)
self-service store

la **Libye** NOUN
Libya

la **licence** NOUN
1 *degree* ◇ *une licence de droit* a law degree
2 *licence* ◇ *une licence d'exportation* an export licence

le **licencié** NOUN
graduate

la **licenciée** NOUN
graduate

licencier VERB
to make redundant ◇ *Ils viennent de licencier sept employés.* They've just made 7 employees redundant.

le **liège** NOUN
cork ◇ *des sets en liège* cork mats
- **un bouchon en liège** a cork (*for bottle*)

le **lien** NOUN
connection ◇ *Il n'y a aucun lien entre ces deux événements.* There's no connection between these two events.
- **un lien de parenté** a family tie

lier VERB
- **lier conversation avec quelqu'un** to get into conversation with somebody
- **se lier avec quelqu'un** to make friends with somebody ◇ *Je ne me lie pas facilement.* I don't make friends easily.

le **lierre** NOUN
ivy

le **lieu** NOUN
(PL les **lieux**)
place ◇ *votre lieu de travail* your place of work
- **avoir lieu** to take place ◇ *La cérémonie a eu lieu dans la salle des fêtes.* The ceremony took place in the village hall.
- **au lieu de** instead of ◇ *J'aimerais une pomme au lieu de la glace.* I'd like an apple instead of ice cream.

le **lièvre** NOUN
hare

la **ligne** NOUN
1 *line* (*phone, train*) ◇ *La ligne est mauvaise.* It's a bad line. ◇ *la ligne d'autobus numéro douze* the number 12 bus
2 *figure* ◇ *C'est mauvais pour la ligne.* It's bad for your figure.

ligoter VERB

to tie up

la **ligue** NOUN
league

le **lilas** NOUN
lilac

la **limace** NOUN
slug

la **lime** NOUN
- **une lime à ongles** a nail file

la **limitation** NOUN
- **la limitation de vitesse** the speed limit

la **limite** NOUN
1 *boundary* (of property, football pitch)
2 *limit* ◇ *Est-ce qu'il y a une limite d'âge?* Is there an age limit?
- **la date limite** the deadline
- **la date limite de vente** the sell-by-date

limiter VERB
to limit ◇ *Le nombre de billets est limité à deux par personne.* The number of tickets is limited to two per person.

la **limonade** NOUN
lemonade

le **lin** NOUN
linen ◇ *une veste en lin* a linen jacket

le **linge** NOUN
1 *linen* ◇ *le linge sale* dirty linen
2 *washing* ◇ *laver le linge* to do the washing
- **du linge de corps** underwear

la **lingerie** NOUN
underwear (women's)

le **lion** NOUN
lion
- **le Lion** Leo ◇ *Louise est Lion.* Louise is Leo.

la **lionne** NOUN
lioness

la **liqueur** NOUN
liqueur

liquide ADJECTIVE
see also **liquide** NOUN
liquid

le **liquide** NOUN
see also **liquide** ADJECTIVE
liquid
- **payer quelque chose en liquide** to pay cash for something

lire VERB
to read ◇ *Tu as lu "Madame Bovary"?* Have you read "Madame Bovary"?

lis, lisent, lisez VERB see **lire**
- **Je lis beaucoup.** I read a lot.

lisible ADJECTIVE
legible

lisse ADJECTIVE
smooth

la **liste** NOUN
list

- **faire la liste de** to make a list of ◇ *J'ai fait la liste de tout ce dont j'ai besoin.* I've made a list of all the things I need.

lit VERB *see* **lire**

le **lit** NOUN
 bed ◇ *aller au lit* to go to bed
- **faire son lit** to make one's bed ◇ *Je n'ai pas eu le temps de faire mon lit ce matin.* I haven't had time to make my bed this morning.
- **un lit de camp** a campbed

la **literie** NOUN
 bedding

la **litière** NOUN
 1 *litter* (for cat)
 2 *bedding* (of caged pet)

le **litre** NOUN
 litre

littéraire ADJECTIVE
- **une œuvre littéraire** a work of literature

la **littérature** NOUN
 literature

le **littoral** NOUN
 (PL les littoraux)
 coast

la **Lituanie** NOUN
 Lithuania

la **livraison** NOUN
 delivery
- **la livraison des bagages** baggage reclaim

le **livre** NOUN
 see also la livre
 book
- **un livre de poche** a paperback

la **livre** NOUN
 see also le livre
 pound
 The French livre is 500 grams.
 ◇ *une livre de beurre* a pound of butter
- **la livre sterling** the pound sterling
 ◇ *Le guide coûte trois livres.* The guide book costs £3.

livrer VERB
 to deliver

le **livret** NOUN
 booklet
- **le livret scolaire** the school report book

le **livreur** NOUN
 delivery man

local ADJECTIVE
 (MASC PL locaux)
 see also local NOUN
 local

le **local** NOUN
 (PL les locaux)
 see also local ADJECTIVE

 premises ◇ *Nous cherchons un local pour les répétitions.* We are looking for premises to rehearse in.

le/la **locataire** NOUN
 1 *tenant*
 2 *lodger* ◇ *Ils ont décidé de prendre un locataire.* They have decided to take a lodger.

la **location** NOUN
- **location de voitures** car rental
- **location de skis** ski hire

locaux ADJECTIVE, NOUN *see* **local**

la **locomotive** NOUN
 locomotive

la **loge** NOUN
 dressing room

le **logement** NOUN
 1 *housing*
 2 *accommodation*

loger VERB
 to stay ◇ *Elle loge chez sa cousine quand elle revient dans la région.* She stays with her cousin when she comes back to the area.
- **trouver à se loger** to find somewhere to live ◇ *J'ai eu du mal à trouver à me loger.* I had difficulty finding somewhere to live.

le **logiciel** NOUN
 software

logique ADJECTIVE
 see also logique NOUN
 logical

la **logique** NOUN
 see also logique ADJECTIVE
 logic

la **loi** NOUN
 law

loin ADVERB
 1 *far* ◇ *La gare n'est pas très loin d'ici.* The station is not very far from here.
 2 *far off* ◇ *Noël n'est plus tellement loin.* Christmas isn't far off now.
 3 *a long time ago* ◇ *Les vacances paraissent déjà tellement loin!* The holidays already seem such a long time ago!
- **au loin** in the distance ◇ *On aperçoit la mer au loin.* You can see the sea in the distance.
- **de loin (1)** from a long way away ◇ *On voit l'église de loin.* You can see the church from a long way away.
- **de loin (2)** by far ◇ *C'est de loin l'élève la plus brillante.* She is by far the brightest pupil.

lointain ADJECTIVE
 see also lointain NOUN
 distant ◇ *un pays lointain* a distant

country ◇ *C'est un parent lointain de ma mère.* He's a distant relation of my mother.

le **lointain** NOUN

see also lointain ADJECTIVE

- **dans le lointain** in the distance

le **loir** NOUN

dormouse

- **dormir comme un loir** to sleep like a log

les **loisirs** MASC NOUN

1 *free time* •• *Qu'est-ce que vous faites pendant vos loisirs?* What do you do in your free time?

2 *hobby* ◇ *Le ski et l'équitation sont des loisirs coûteux.* Skiing and riding are expensive hobbies.

le **Londonien** NOUN

Londoner

la **Londonienne** NOUN

Londoner

Londres NOUN

London ◇ *le métro de Londres* the London underground

- **à Londres (1)** in London
- **à Londres (2)** to London

long ADJECTIVE

(FEM SING **longue**)

see also long NOUN

long

le **long** NOUN

see also long ADJECTIVE

- **un bateau de trois mètres de long** a boat 3 m long
- **tout le long de** all along ◇ *Il y a des chemins de randonnée tout le long de la côte.* There are footpaths all along the coast.
- **marcher de long en large** to walk up and down

longtemps ADVERB

a long time ◇ *J'ai attendu longtemps chez le dentiste.* I waited a long time at the dentist's.

- **pendant longtemps** for a long time ◇ *On a cru pendant longtemps que la Terre était plate.* For a long time people thought the Earth was flat.
- **mettre longtemps à faire quelque chose** to take a long time to do something ◇ *Il a mis longtemps à répondre à ma lettre.* He took a long time to answer my letter.

longue ADJECTIVE *see* **long**

la **longue** NOUN

- **à la longue** in the end ◇ *Elle a fini par agacer tout le monde à la longue.* In the end she got on everybody's nerves.

longuement ADVERB

at length ◇ *Elle m'a longuement parlé de ses projets d'avenir.* She talked to me at length about her plans for the future.

la **longueur** NOUN

length

- **à longueur de journée** all day long ◇ *Elle mâche du chewing-gum à longueur de journée.* She chews gum all day long.

les **loques** FEM NOUN

- **être en loques** to be torn to bits ◇ *Sa chemise était en loques.* His shirt was torn to bits.

lors de PREPOSITION

during ◇ *Je l'ai rencontré lors de mon stage en entreprise.* I met him during my work placement.

lorsque CONJUNCTION

when ◇ *J'allais composer ton numéro lorsque tu as appelé.* I was about to dial your number when you called.

le **lot** NOUN

prize

- **le gros lot** the jackpot

la **loterie** NOUN

1 *lottery* ◇ *la loterie nationale* the National Lottery

2 *raffle* ◇ *J'ai gagné cet ours en peluche dans une loterie.* I won this teddy in a raffle.

la **lotion** NOUN

lotion ◇ *une bouteille de lotion solaire* a bottle of suntan lotion

- **une lotion après-rasage** an aftershave

le **lotissement** NOUN

housing estate

le **loto** NOUN

lottery

- **le loto sportif** the pools

le **loubard** NOUN (*informal*)

lout

louche ADJECTIVE

see also louche NOUN

fishy ◇ *une histoire louche* a fishy story

la **louche** NOUN

see also louche ADJECTIVE

ladle

loucher VERB

to squint

louer VERB

1 *to let* ◇ *Ils louent des chambres à des étudiants.* They let rooms to students.

- **"à louer"** "to let"

2 *to rent* ◇ *Je loue un petit appartement au centre-ville.* I rent a little flat in the centre of town.

3 *to hire* ◇ *Est-ce que vous louez des*

vélos? Do you hire bikes? ◦ *Nous allons louer une voiture pour le week-end.* We're going to hire a car for the weekend.

[4] *to praise* ◦ *Les journaux ont loué le courage des pompiers.* The newspapers praised the courage of the firefighters.

le **loup** NOUN
wolf

la **loupe** NOUN
magnifying glass

louper VERB (*informal*)
to miss ◦ *Dépêche-toi, tu vas louper ton train!* Hurry up, you'll miss your train!

lourd ADJECTIVE
heavy ◦ *Mon sac est très lourd.* My bag's very heavy.

la **loutre** NOUN
otter

la **loyauté** NOUN
loyalty

le **loyer** NOUN
rent

lu VERB *see* **lire**

la **lucarne** NOUN
skylight

la **luge** NOUN
sledge

lugubre ADJECTIVE
gloomy

lui PRONOUN
[1] *him* ◦ *Il a été très content du cadeau que je lui ai offert.* He was very pleased with the present I gave him. ◦ *C'est bien lui!* It's definitely him! ◦ *J'ai pensé à lui toute la journée.* I thought about him all day long.
[2] *to him* ◦ *Mon père est d'accord: je lui ai parlé ce matin.* My father said yes: I spoke to him this morning.
[3] *her* ◦ *Elle a été très contente du cadeau que je lui ai offert.* She was very pleased with the present I gave her.
[4] *to her* ◦ *Ma mère est d'accord: je lui ai parlé ce matin.* My mother said yes: I spoke to her this morning.
[5] *it* ◦ *Qu'est-ce que tu donnes à ton chat?—Je lui donne de la viande crue.* What do you give your cat?—I give it raw meat.

lui is also used for emphasis.
◦ *Lui, il est toujours en retard!* Oh him, he's always late!
 ◦ **lui-même** himself ◦ *Il a construit son bateau lui-même.* He built his boat himself.

la **lumière** NOUN
light
 ◦ **la lumière du jour** daylight

lumineux ADJECTIVE
(FEM SING **lumineuse**)
 ◦ **une enseigne lumineuse** a neon sign

lunatique ADJECTIVE
temperamental ◦ *Il est plutôt lunatique.* He's rather temperamental.

le **lundi** NOUN
[1] *Monday* ◦ *Aujourd'hui, nous sommes lundi.* It's Monday today.
[2] *on Monday* ◦ *Ils sont arrivés lundi.* They arrived on Monday.
 ◦ **le lundi** on Mondays ◦ *Le lundi, je vais à la piscine.* I go swimming on Mondays.
 ◦ **tous les lundis** every Monday
 ◦ **lundi dernier** last Monday
 ◦ **lundi prochain** next Monday
 ◦ **le lundi de Pâques** Easter Monday

la **lune** NOUN
moon
 ◦ **la lune de miel** honeymoon

les **lunettes** FEM NOUN
glasses
 ◦ **des lunettes de soleil** sunglasses
 ◦ **des lunettes de plongée** swimming goggles

la **lutte** NOUN
[1] *fight* ◦ *la lutte contre le racisme* the fight against racism
[2] *wrestling* ◦ *une épreuve de lutte* a wrestling bout

lutter VERB
to fight

le **luxe** NOUN
luxury
 ◦ **de luxe** luxury ◦ *un hôtel de luxe* a luxury hotel

luxueux ADJECTIVE
(FEM SING **luxueuse**)
luxurious

le **lycée** NOUN
secondary school

In France pupils go to a **collège** *between the ages of 11 and 15, and then to a* **lycée** *until the age of 18.*

le **lycéen** NOUN
secondary school pupil

la **lycéenne** NOUN
secondary school pupil

M

M. ABBREVIATION (= *Monsieur*)
_Mr_ ○ *M. Bernard* Mr Bernard
m' PRONOUN *see* **me**
ma ADJECTIVE
_my_ ○ *ma mère* my mother ○ *ma montre* my watch
les **macaronis** MASC NOUN
macaroni
la **Macédoine** NOUN
Macedonia
la **macédoine** NOUN
* **la macédoine de fruits** fruit salad
* **la macédoine de légumes** mixed vegetables
mâcher VERB
to chew
le **machin** NOUN (*informal*)
thingy ○ *Passe-moi le machin pour râper les carottes.* Pass me the thingy for grating carrots. ○ *Qu'est-ce que c'est que ce vieux machin?* What's this old thing?
la **machine** NOUN
machine
* **une machine à laver** a washing machine
* **une machine à écrire** a typewriter
* **une machine à coudre** a sewing machine
* **une machine à sous** a fruit machine
la **mâchoire** NOUN
jaw
mâchonner VERB
to chew
le **maçon** NOUN
bricklayer
Madame FEM NOUN
(PL **Mesdames**)
1 _Mrs_ ○ *Madame Legall* Mrs Legall
2 _lady_ ○ *Occupez-vous de Madame.* Could you look after this lady?
3 _Madam_ ○ *Madame,...* Dear Madam,... (*in letter*) ○ *Madame! Vous avez oublié votre parapluie!* Excuse me! You've forgotten your umbrella!
Mademoiselle FEM NOUN
(PL **Mesdemoiselles**)
1 _Miss_ ○ *Mademoiselle Martin* Miss Martin
2 _Madam_ ○ *Mademoiselle,...* Dear Madam,... (*in letter*)
le **magasin** NOUN
shop ○ *Les magasins ouvrent à huit heures.* The shops open at 8 o'clock.
le **magazine** NOUN
magazine

le **magicien** NOUN
magician
la **magicienne** NOUN
magician
la **magie** NOUN
magic ○ *un tour de magie* a magic trick
magique ADJECTIVE
magic ○ *une baguette magique* a magic wand
magistral ADJECTIVE
(MASC PL **magistraux**)
* **un cours magistral** a lecture (*at university*)
magnétique ADJECTIVE
magnetic
le **magnétophone** NOUN
tape recorder
* **un magnétophone à cassettes** a cassette recorder
le **magnétoscope** NOUN
video recorder
magnifique ADJECTIVE
superb
mai MASC NOUN
May
* **en mai** in May
maigre ADJECTIVE
1 _skinny_ ○ *Ma mère me trouve trop maigre.* My mother says I'm too skinny.
2 _lean_ (*meat*)
3 _low-fat_ (*cheese, yoghurt*)
maigrir VERB
to lose weight ○ *Il fait un régime pour essayer de maigrir.* He's on a diet, to try to lose weight. ○ *Elle a maigri de deux kilos en un mois.* She's lost two kilos in a month.
le **maillot de bain** NOUN
1 _swimsuit_
2 _swimming trunks_
la **main** NOUN
hand ○ *Donne-moi la main!* Give me your hand!
* **serrer la main à quelqu'un** to shake hands with somebody
* **se serrer la main** to shake hands ○ *Les deux présidents se sont serré la main.* The two presidents shook hands.
* **sous la main** to hand ○ *Est-ce que tu as son adresse sous la main?* Have you got his address to hand?
maintenant ADVERB
1 _now_ ○ *Qu'est-ce que tu veux faire maintenant?* What do you want to do now? * *C'est maintenant ou jamais* It's

now or never.

[2] *nowadays* ◦ *Maintenant la plupart des gens font leurs courses au supermarché.* Nowadays most people do their shopping at the supermarket.

maintenir VERB

to maintain ◦ *Il maintient qu'il n'était pas là le jour du crime.* He maintains he wasn't there on the day of the crime.

* **se maintenir** to hold ◦ *Espérons que le beau temps va se maintenir pour le week-end!* Let's hope the good weather will hold over the weekend!

le **maire** NOUN

mayor

la **mairie** NOUN

town hall

mais CONJUNCTION

but ◦ *C'est cher mais de très bonne qualité.* It's expensive, but very good quality.

le **maïs** NOUN

[1] *maize*

[2] *sweetcorn*

la **maison** NOUN

see also **maison** ADJECTIVE

house ◦ *Ils habitent dans la maison qui est au bout de la rue.* They live in the house at the end of the street.

* **à la maison (1)** at home ◦ *Je serai à la maison cet après-midi.* I'll be at home this afternoon.

* **à la maison (2)** home ◦ *Elle est rentrée à la maison.* She's gone home.

maison ADJECTIVE (MASC, FEM, PL)

see also **maison** NOUN

home-made ◦ *Je préfère les tartes maison à celles qui sont achetées.* I prefer home-made pies to bought ones.

le **maître** NOUN

[1] *teacher* (*in primary school*)

[2] *master* (*of dog*)

* **un maître d'hôtel** a head waiter (*in restaurant*)

* **un maître nageur** a lifeguard

la **maîtresse** NOUN

[1] *teacher* (*in primary school*)

[2] *mistress* ◦ *Il paraît qu'il a une maîtresse.* They say he's got a mistress.

la **maîtrise** NOUN

master's degree ◦ *Elle a une maîtrise d'anglais.* She's got a master's degree in English.

* **la maîtrise de soi** self-control

maîtriser VERB

* **se maîtriser** to control oneself ◦ *Il se met facilement en colère et a du mal à se maîtriser.* He loses his temper easily and finds it hard to control himself.

majestueux ADJECTIVE

(FEM SING **majestueuse**)

majestic

majeur ADJECTIVE

* **être majeur** to be 18 ◦ *Tu feras ce que tu voudras quand tu seras majeure.* You can do what you like once you're 18. ◦ *Elle sera majeure en août.* She comes of age in August.

* **la majeure partie** most ◦ *la majeure partie de mon salaire* most of my salary

la **majorité** NOUN

majority ◦ *dans la majorité des cas* in the majority of cases

* **la majorité et l'opposition** the government and the opposition

Majorque FEM NOUN

Majorca

la **majuscule** NOUN

capital letter ◦ *un M majuscule* a capital M

mal ADVERB, ADJECTIVE (MASC, FEM, PL)

see also **mal** NOUN

[1] *badly* ◦ *Ce travail a été mal fait.* The work was badly done. ◦ *Il a mal compris.* He misunderstood.

[2] *wrong* ◦ *C'est mal de mentir.* It's wrong to tell lies.

* **aller mal** to be ill ◦ *Son grand-père va très mal.* His grandfather is very ill.

* **pas mal** quite good ◦ *Je te trouve pas mal sur cette photo.* I think you look quite good in this photo.

le **mal** NOUN

(PL **les maux**)

see also **mal** ADVERB

[1] *ache* ◦ *J'ai mal à la tête.* I've got a headache. ◦ *J'ai mal aux dents.* I've got toothache. ◦ *J'ai mal au dos.* My back hurts. ◦ *Est-ce que vous avez mal à la gorge?* Have you got a sore throat?

* **Ça fait mal.** It hurts.

* **Où est-ce que tu as mal?** Where does it hurt?

* **faire mal à quelqu'un** to hurt somebody ◦ *Attention, tu me fais mal!* Be careful, you're hurting me!

* **se faire mal** to hurt oneself ◦ *Je me suis fait mal au bras.* I hurt my arm.

* **se donner du mal pour faire quelque chose** to go to a lot of trouble to do something ◦ *Il s'est donné beaucoup de mal pour que cette soirée soit réussie.* He went to a lot of trouble to make the party a success.

* **avoir le mal de mer** to be seasick

* **avoir le mal du pays** to be homesick

[2] *evil* ◦ *le bien et le mal* good and evil

* **dire du mal de quelqu'un** to speak ill of

somebody

malade ADJECTIVE

see also malade NOUN

ill

- **tomber malade** to fall ill

e/la **malade** NOUN

see also malade ADJECTIVE

patient

la **maladie** NOUN

illness

maladif ADJECTIVE

(FEM SING **maladive**)

sickly ◇ *C'est un enfant maladif.* He's a sickly child.

la **maladresse** NOUN

clumsiness

maladroit ADJECTIVE

clumsy

le **malaise** NOUN

- **avoir un malaise** to feel faint ◇ *Elle a eu un malaise après le déjeuner.* She felt faint after lunch.
- **Son arrivée a créé un malaise parmi les invités.** Her arrival made the guests feel uncomfortable.

la **malchance** NOUN

bad luck

mâle ADJECTIVE

male

la **malédiction** NOUN

curse

mal en point ADJECTIVE (MASC, FEM, PL)

- **Il avait l'air mal en point quand je l'ai vu hier soir.** He didn't look too good when I saw him last night.

le **malentendu** NOUN

misunderstanding

le **malfaiteur** NOUN

criminal

mal famé ADJECTIVE

(FEM SING **mal famée**, MASC PL **mal famés**)

- **un quartier mal famé** a seedy area

malgache ADJECTIVE

from Madagascar ◇ *Sa mère est malgache.* His mother's from Madagascar.

malgré PREPOSITION

in spite of ◇ *Il est toujours généreux malgré ses problèmes d'argent.* He's always generous in spite of his financial problems.

- **malgré tout** all the same ◇ *Il faisait mauvais mais nous sommes sortis malgré tout.* The weather was bad but we went out all the same.

le **malheur** NOUN

tragedy ◇ *Elle a eu beaucoup de malheurs dans sa vie.* She's had a lot of tragedy in her life.

- **faire un malheur** (*informal*) to be a smash hit ◇ *Leur dernier album a fait un malheur.* Their latest album was a smash hit.

malheureusement ADVERB

unfortunately

malheureux ADJECTIVE

(FEM SING **malheureuse**)

miserable ◇ *Qu'est-ce que tu as? Tu as l'air malheureux.* What's wrong with you? You look miserable.

malhonnête ADJECTIVE

dishonest

la **malice** NOUN

mischief ◇ *Son regard était plein de malice.* His eyes were full of mischief.

malicieux ADJECTIVE

(FEM SING **malicieuse**)

mischievous

malin ADJECTIVE

(FEM SING **maligne**)

crafty

- **C'est malin!** (*informal*) That's clever! ◇ *Ah c'est malin! Nous voilà enfermés à cause de toi!* That's clever! You've got us locked in!

la **malle** NOUN

trunk

malodorant ADJECTIVE

foul-smelling

malpropre ADJECTIVE

dirty

malsain ADJECTIVE

unhealthy

Malte MASC NOUN

Malta

maltraiter VERB

to ill-treat ◇ *Il maltraite son chien.* He ill-treats his dog.

- **des enfants maltraités** battered children

malveillant ADJECTIVE

malicious ◇ *des rumeurs malveillantes* malicious rumours

la **maman** NOUN

mum

la **mamie** NOUN

granny

le **mammifère** NOUN

mammal

la **manche** NOUN

see also le manche

1 *sleeve* (*of clothes*)

2 *leg* (*of game*) ◇ *Ils ont remporté la première manche du match.* They won the first leg of the match.

- **la Manche** the Channel

le **manche** NOUN

see also la manche

M

handle (of pan)

la **mandarine** NOUN
mandarin orange

le **manège** NOUN
merry-go-round

la **manette** NOUN
lever

mangeable ADJECTIVE
edible ◇ *C'est à peine mangeable!* It's practically inedible!

manger VERB
to eat

la **mangue** NOUN
mango

maniaque ADJECTIVE
fussy

la **manie** NOUN
1 *obsession*
- **avoir la manie de** to be obsessive about ◇ *Il a la manie du rangement.* He's obsessive about tidying up.
2 *habit* ◇ *J'essaie de respecter ses petites manies.* I try to go along with her little ways.

manier VERB
to handle

la **manière**
see also les manières NOUN
way
- **de manière à** so as to ◇ *Nous sommes partis tôt de manière à éviter la circulation.* We left early so as to avoid the traffic.
- **de toute manière** in any case ◇ *Je n'aurais pas pu venir de toute manière.* I couldn't have come in any case.

maniéré ADJECTIVE
affected

les **manières**
see also la manière FEM NOUN
1 *manners* ◇ *apprendre les bonnes manières* to learn good manners
2 *fuss* ◇ *Ne fais pas de manières: mange ta soupe!* Don't make a fuss: eat your soup!

le **manifestant** NOUN
demonstrator

la **manifestante** NOUN
demonstrator

la **manifestation** NOUN
demonstration ◇ *une manifestation pour la paix* a peace demonstration

manifester VERB
to demonstrate

manipuler VERB
1 *to handle* ◇ *Ce vase doit être manipulé avec soin.* This vase must be handled with care.
2 *to manipulate* ◇ *Tous les partis*

essaient de manipuler l'opinion publique. All the parties are trying to manipulate public opinion.

le **mannequin** NOUN
model ◇ *Elle est mannequin.* She's a model.

manœuvrer VERB
to manœuvre

le **manque** NOUN
- **le manque de** lack of ◇ *Le manque de sommeil peut provoquer toutes sortes de troubles.* Lack of sleep can cause all sorts of problems.
withdrawal ◇ *un drogué en état de manque* a drug addict suffering withdrawal symptoms

manqué ADJECTIVE
- **un garçon manqué** a tomboy

manquer VERB
to miss ◇ *Tu n'as rien manqué: le film n'était pas très bon.* You didn't miss anything: the film wasn't very good. ◇ *Il manque des pages à ce livre.* There are some pages missing from this book.
- **Mes parents me manquent.** I miss my parents.
- **Ma sœur me manque.** I miss my sister.
- **Il manque encore cent francs.** We are still 100 francs short.
- **manquer de** to lack ◇ *La quiche manque de sel.* The quiche hasn't got enough salt in it. ◇ *Je trouve qu'il a manqué de tact.* I don't think he was very tactful.
- **Il a manqué se tuer.** He nearly got killed.

le **manteau** NOUN
(PL les **manteaux**)
coat

manuel ADJECTIVE
(FEM SING **manuelle**)
see also manuel NOUN
manual

le **manuel** NOUN
see also manuel ADJECTIVE
1 *textbook*
2 *handbook*

le **maquereau** NOUN
(PL les **maquereaux**)
mackerel

la **maquette** NOUN
model ◇ *une maquette de bateau* a model boat

le **maquillage** NOUN
make-up

se **maquiller** VERB
to put on one's make-up ◇ *Je vais me maquiller en vitesse.* I'll just quickly put on my make-up.

le **marais** NOUN
marsh

le **marbre** NOUN
marble ◦ *une statue en marbre* a marble statue

le **marchand** NOUN
1 *shopkeeper*
- **un marchand de journaux** a newsagent
2 *stallholder* (in market)

la **marchande** NOUN
1 *shopkeeper*
- **une marchande de fruits et de légumes** a greengrocer
2 *stallholder* (in market)

marchander VERB
to haggle

la **marchandise** NOUN
goods

la **marche** NOUN
1 *step* ◦ *Fais attention à la marche!* Mind the step!
2 *walking* ◦ *La marche me fait du bien.* Walking does me good.
- **être en état de marche** to be in working order ◦ *Cette voiture est en parfait état de marche.* This car is in perfect running order.
- **Ne montez jamais dans un train en marche.** Never try to get into a moving train.
- **mettre en marche** to start ◦ *Comment est-ce qu'on met la machine à laver en marche?* How do you start the washing machine?
- **la marche arrière** reverse gear
- **faire marche arrière** to reverse
3 *march* ◦ *une marche militaire* a military march

le **marché** NOUN
market
- **un marché aux puces** a flea market

marcher VERB
1 *to walk* ◦ *Elle marche cinq kilomètres par jour.* She walks 5 kilometres every day.
2 *to run* ◦ *Le métro marche normalement aujourd'hui.* The underground is running normally today.
3 *to work* ◦ *Est-ce que l'ascenseur marche?* Is the lift working?
4 *to go well* ◦ *Est-ce que les affaires marchent actuellement?* Is business going well at the moment?
- **Alors les études, ça marche?** (informal) How are you getting on at school?
- **faire marcher quelqu'un** to pull somebody's leg ◦ *Il essaie de te faire marcher.* He's pulling your leg.

le **marcheur** NOUN
walker

la **marcheuse** NOUN
walker

le **mardi** NOUN
1 *Tuesday* ◦ *Aujourd'hui, nous sommes mardi.* It's Tuesday today.
2 *on Tuesday* ◦ *Ils reviennent mardi.* They're coming back on Tuesday.
- **le mardi** on Tuesdays ◦ *Le mardi, je vais à la gym.* I go to the gym on Tuesdays.
- **tous les mardis** every Tuesday
- **mardi dernier** last Tuesday
- **mardi prochain** next Tuesday
- **Mardi gras** Shrove Tuesday

la **mare** NOUN
pond

le **marécage** NOUN
marsh

la **marée** NOUN
tide ◦ *la marée haute* high tide ◦ *la marée basse* low tide ◦ *la marée montante* the rising tide ◦ *la marée descendante* the ebb tide

la **margarine** NOUN
margarine

la **marge** NOUN
margin

le **mari** NOUN
husband • *son mari* her husband

le **mariage** NOUN
1 *marriage*
2 *wedding* ◦ *un mariage civil* a registry office wedding ◦ *un mariage religieux* a church wedding

marié ADJECTIVE
see also marié NOUN
married

le **marié** NOUN
see also marié ADJECTIVE
bridegroom
- **les mariés** the bride and groom

la **mariée** NOUN
bride

se **marier** VERB
to marry ◦ *Elle s'est mariée avec un ami d'enfance.* She married a childhood friend.

marin ADJECTIVE
see also marin NOUN
sea ◦ *l'air marin* the sea air
- **un pull marin** a sailor's jersey

le **marin** NOUN
see also marin ADJECTIVE
sailor

marine ADJECTIVE (MASC, FEM, PL)
see also marine NOUN
- **bleu marine** navy-blue ◦ *un pull bleu*

M

marine a navy-blue sweater

la **marine** NOUN

see also marine ADJECTIVE

navy

- **la marine nationale** the French navy

la **marionnette** NOUN

puppet

la **marmelade** NOUN

stewed fruit

- **la marmelade de pommes** stewed apple
- **la marmelade d'oranges** marmalade

la **marmite** NOUN

cooking pot

marmonner VERB

to mumble

le **Maroc** NOUN

Morocco

marocain ADJECTIVE

Moroccan

la **maroquinerie** NOUN

leather goods shop

marquant ADJECTIVE

significant ◦ *un événement marquant*
a significant event

la **marque** NOUN

1 *mark* ◦ *des marques de doigts*
fingermarks

2 *make* ◦ *De quelle marque est ton
jean?* What make are your jeans?

3 *brand* ◦ *une grande marque de
cognac* a well-known brand of cognac

- **l'image de marque** the public image
  ◦ *Le ministre tient à son image de
  marque.* The minister cares about his
  public image.
- **une marque déposée** a registered
  trademark
- **A vos marques! prêts! partez!** Ready,
  steady, go!

marquer VERB

1 *to mark* ◦ *Peux-tu marquer sur la
carte où se trouve le village?* Can you
mark where the village is on the map?

2 *to score* ◦ *L'équipe adverse a
marqué dix points.* The opposing team
scored ten points.

3 *to celebrate* ◦ *On va sortir au
restaurant pour marquer ton anniversaire.*
We'll eat out to celebrate your birthday.

la **marraine** NOUN

godmother

marrant ADJECTIVE (informal)

funny

marre ADVERB (informal)

- **en avoir marre de quelque chose** to be
  fed up with something ◦ *J'en ai marre
  de faire la vaisselle.* I'm fed up with
  doing the dishes.

se **marrer** VERB (informal)

to have a good laugh ◦ *On s'est bien
marrés.* We had a good laugh.

le **marron** NOUN

see also marron ADJECTIVE

chestnut ◦ *la crème de marrons*
chestnut purée

marron ADJECTIVE (MASC, FEM, PL)

see also marron NOUN

brown ◦ *des chaussures marron*
brown shoes

le **marronnier** NOUN

chestnut tree

mars MASC NOUN

March

- **en mars** in March

le **marteau** NOUN

(PL les **marteaux**)

hammer

martyriser VERB

to batter ◦ *des enfants martyrisés*
battered children

masculin ADJECTIVE

1 *men's* ◦ *la mode masculine* men's
fashion

2 *masculine* ◦ *"chat" est un nom
masculin.* "chat" is a masculine noun.
◦ *Elle a une allure assez masculine.* She
looks rather masculine.

le **masque** NOUN

mask

le **massacre** NOUN

massacre

massacrer VERB

to massacre

le **massage** NOUN

massage

la **masse** NOUN

- **une masse de** (informal) masses of
  ◦ *J'ai une masse de choses à faire.* I've
  got masses of things to do.
- **produire en masse** to mass-produce
  ◦ *Ces jouets sont produits en masse en
  Chine.* These toys are mass-produced in
  China.
- **venir en masse** to come en masse
  ◦ *Les gens sont venus en masse pour
  accueillir Nelson Mandela.* People came
  en masse to welcome Nelson Mandela.

masser VERB

to massage

- **se masser** to gather ◦ *Les
  manifestants se sont massés devant
  l'ambassade.* The demonstrators
  gathered in front of the embassy.

massif ADJECTIVE

(FEM SING **massive**)

1 *solid* (gold, silver, wood) ◦ *un bracelet
en or massif* a solid gold bracelet

2 *massive* ◦ *une dose massive*

d'antibiotiques a massive dose of antibiotics

3 *mass*   ◦ *des départs massifs* a mass exodus

mat ADJECTIVE

matt   ◦ *blanc mat* matt white   ◦ *Je voudrais mes photos en mat.* I would like my photos matt.

◆ **être mat** to be checkmate *(chess)*

match NOUN

match   ◦ *un match de football* a football match

◆ **le match aller** the first leg

◆ **le match retour** the second leg

◆ **faire match nul** to draw

matelas NOUN

mattress

◆ **un matelas pneumatique** an air bed

matelassé ADJECTIVE

quilted   ◦ *une veste matelassée* a quilted jacket

matelot NOUN

sailor

matériaux MASC NOUN

materials

matériel NOUN

1 *equipment*   ◦ *du matériel de laboratoire* laboratory equipment

2 *gear*   ◦ *Il a pris tout son matériel de pêche avec lui.* He took all his fishing gear with him.

maternel ADJECTIVE

(FEM SING **maternelle**)

motherly   ◦ *Elle est très maternelle.* She's very motherly.

◆ **ma grand-mère maternelle** my mother's mother

◆ **mon oncle maternel** my mother's brother

maternelle NOUN

nursery school

The maternelle *is a state school for 2-6 year-olds.*

maternité NOUN

◆ **le congé de maternité** maternity leave   ◦ *Notre professeur de musique est en congé de maternité.* Our music teacher is on maternity leave.

mathématiques FEM NOUN

mathematics

maths FEM NOUN *(informal)*

maths

matière NOUN

subject   ◦ *Le latin est une matière facultative.* Latin is an optional subject.

◆ **sans matières grasses** fat-free

◆ **les matières premières** raw materials

matin NOUN

morning   ◦ *à trois heures du matin* at

3 o'clock in the morning   ◦ *du matin au soir* from morning till night

◆ **Je suis du matin.** I'm at my best in the morning.

◆ **de bon matin** early in the morning

matinal ADJECTIVE

(MASC PL **matinaux**)

morning   ◦ *Je fais ma gymnastique matinale avant de déjeuner.* I do my morning exercises before breakfast.

◆ **être matinal** to be up early   ◦ *Tu es bien matinal aujourd'hui!* You're up early today!

la matinée NOUN

morning   ◦ *Je t'appellerai demain dans la matinée.* I'll call you sometime tomorrow morning.   ◦ *en début de matinée* early in the morning

le matou NOUN

tomcat

matrimonial ADJECTIVE

(MASC PL **matrimoniaux**)

◆ **une agence matrimoniale** a marriage bureau

maudire VERB

to curse

maudit ADJECTIVE *(informal)*

blasted   ◦ *Où est passé ce maudit parapluie?* Where's that blasted umbrella got to?

maussade ADJECTIVE

sullen

mauvais ADJECTIVE, ADVERB

1 *bad*   ◦ *une mauvaise note* a bad mark   ◦ *Tu arrives au mauvais moment.* You've come at a bad time.

◆ **Il fait mauvais.** The weather's bad.

◆ **être mauvais en** to be bad at   ◦ *Je suis mauvais en allemand.* I'm bad at German.

2 *poor*   ◦ *J'ai trouvé que le film était mauvais.* I thought the film was poor.   ◦ *Il est en mauvaise santé.* His health is poor.

◆ **Tu as mauvaise mine.** You don't look well.

3 *wrong*   ◦ *Vous avez fait le mauvais numéro.* You've dialled the wrong number.

◆ **des mauvaises herbes** weeds

◆ **sentir mauvais** to smell

les maux MASC NOUN

◆ **des maux de ventre** stomachache

◆ **des maux de tête** headache

le maximum NOUN

maximum

◆ **au maximum (1)** as much as one can   ◦ *Remplis le seau au maximum.* Fill the bucket as full as you can.

* **au maximum (2)** at the very most
  ◇ *Ça va vous coûter deux cents francs au maximum.* It'll cost you 200 francs at the very most.

la **mayonnaise** NOUN
mayonnaise

le **mazout** NOUN
fuel oil

me PRONOUN

> **me** *changes to* **m'** *before a vowel and most words beginning with "h".*

☐ *me* ◇ *Elle me téléphone tous les jours.* She phones me every day. ◇ *Il m'attend depuis une heure.* He's been waiting for me for an hour.

② *to me* ◇ *Il me parle en allemand.* He talks to me in German. ◇ *Elle m'a expliqué la situation.* She explained the situation to me.

③ *myself* ◇ *Je vais me préparer quelque chose à manger.* I'm going to make myself something to eat.

> With reflexive verbs, **me** is often not translated.

◇ *Je me lève à sept heures tous les matins.* I get up at 7 every morning.

le **mec** NOUN (*informal*)
guy

le **mécanicien** NOUN
mechanic

la **mécanicienne** NOUN
mechanic

la **mécanique** NOUN
① *mechanics*
② *mechanism* (*of watch, clock*)

le **mécanisme** NOUN
mechanism

méchamment ADVERB
nastily ◇ *Il lui a répondu méchamment.* He answered him nastily.

la **méchanceté** NOUN
nastiness

méchant ADJECTIVE
nasty ◇ *C'est un homme méchant.* He's a nasty man. ◇ *Ne sois pas méchant avec ton petit frère.* Don't be nasty to your little brother.

* **"Attention, chien méchant"** "Beware of the dog"

la **mèche** NOUN
lock (*of hair*)

mécontent ADJECTIVE
* **mécontent de** unhappy with ◇ *Elle est mécontente de sa coupe de cheveux.* She's unhappy with her haircut.

le **mécontentement** NOUN
displeasure ◇ *Il a exprimé son mécontentement.* He expressed his displeasure.

la **médaille** NOUN
medal

le **médecin** NOUN
doctor ◇ *aller chez le médecin* to go to the doctor

la **médecine** NOUN
medicine (*subject*) ◇ *Il fait médecine.* He's studying medicine.

les **médias** MASC NOUN
media

médical ADJECTIVE
(MASC PL **médicaux**)
medical ◇ *la recherche médicale* medical research
* **passer une visite médicale** to have a medical

le **médicament** NOUN
medicine (*drug*)

médiéval ADJECTIVE
(MASC PL **médiévaux**)
medieval

médiocre ADJECTIVE
poor ◇ *des notes médiocres* poor marks

méditer VERB
to meditate

la **Méditerranée** NOUN
Mediterranean

méditerranéen ADJECTIVE
(FEM SING **méditerranéenne**)
Mediterranean

la **méduse** NOUN
jellyfish

la **méfiance** NOUN
mistrust

méfiant ADJECTIVE
mistrustful

se **méfier** VERB
* **se méfier de quelqu'un** to distrust somebody ◇ *Si j'étais toi, je me méfierais de lui.* If I were you, I wouldn't trust him.

la **mégarde** NOUN
* **par mégarde** by mistake ◇ *J'ai emporté son livre par mégarde.* I took his book by mistake.

le **mégot** NOUN
cigarette end

meilleur ADJECTIVE, ADVERB, NOUN
better ◇ *Ce serait meilleur avec du fromage râpé.* It would be better with grated cheese. ◇ *Il paraît que le film est meilleur que le livre.* They say that the film is better than the book.
* **le meilleur** the best ◇ *C'est elle qui est la meilleure en sport.* She's the best at sport. ◇ *Je préfère garder le meilleur pour la fin.* I like to keep the best for last.
* **le meilleur des deux** the better of the two

- **meilleur marché** cheaper ◇ *La bière est meilleur marché en France.* Beer's cheaper in France.

mélancolique ADJECTIVE
melancholy

le **mélange** NOUN
mixture

mélanger VERB
1 *to mix* ◇ *Mélangez le tout.* Mix everything together.
2 *to muddle up* ◇ *Tu mélanges tout!* You're muddling everything up!

la **mêlée** NOUN
scrum

mêler VERB
- **se mêler** to mix ◇ *Il ne cherche pas à se mêler aux autres.* He doesn't try to mix with the others.
- **Mêle-toi de ce qui te regarde!** (*informal*) Mind your own business!

la **mélodie** NOUN
melody

le **melon** NOUN
melon

le **membre** NOUN
1 *limb*
2 *member* ◇ *les pays membres de l'Union européenne* the member countries of the European Union

la **mémé** NOUN (*informal*)
granny

même ADJECTIVE, ADVERB, PRONOUN
1 *same* ◇ *J'ai le même manteau.* I've got the same coat. ◇ *Tiens, c'est curieux j'ai le même!* That's strange, I've got the same one!
- **en même temps** at the same time
- **moi-même** myself ◇ *Je l'ai fait moi-même.* I did it myself.
2 *even* ◇ *Il n'a même pas pleuré.* He didn't even cry.

la **mémoire** NOUN
memory

la **menace** NOUN
threat

menacer VERB
to threaten

le **ménage** NOUN
housework ◇ *faire le ménage* to do the housework
- **une femme de ménage** a cleaning woman

ménager ADJECTIVE
(FEM SING **ménagère**)
- **les travaux ménagers** housework

la **ménagère** NOUN
housewife

le **mendiant** NOUN
beggar

la **mendiante** NOUN
beggar

mendier VERB
to beg

mener VERB
to lead ◇ *Cette rue mène directement à la gare.* This street leads straight to the station.
- **Cela ne vous mènera à rien!** That will get you nowhere!

la **méningite** NOUN
meningitis

les **menottes** FEM NOUN
handcuffs

le **mensonge** NOUN
lie

la **mensualité** NOUN
monthly payment ◇ *en dix mensualités* in ten monthly payments

mensuel ADJECTIVE
(FEM SING **mensuelle**)
monthly

les **mensurations** FEM NOUN
measurements

la **mentalité** NOUN
mentality

le **menteur** NOUN
liar

la **menteuse** NOUN
liar

la **menthe** NOUN
mint

la **mention** NOUN
grade ◇ *Il a été reçu avec mention bien.* He got a grade B pass.

mentionner VERB
to mention

mentir VERB
to lie ◇ *Tu mens!* You're lying!

le **menton** NOUN
chin

menu ADJECTIVE, ADVERB
see also **menu** NOUN
1 *slim* ◇ *Elle est menue.* She's slim. ◇ *Elle est petite et menue.* She's petite.
2 *very fine* ◇ *Les oignons doivent être coupés menu.* The onions have to be cut up very fine.

le **menu** NOUN
see also **menu** ADJECTIVE
menu ◇ *le menu du jour* today's menu

la **menuiserie** NOUN
woodwork

le **menuisier** NOUN
joiner

le **mépris** NOUN
contempt ◇ *Il nous a traités avec mépris.* He treated us with contempt.

méprisant ADJECTIVE

M

contemptuous
mépriser VERB
to despise
la **mer** NOUN
  [1] *sea*   ◇ *en mer* at sea
  • **au bord de la mer** at the seaside
  • **la mer du Nord** the North Sea
  [2] *tide*   ◇ *La mer est basse.* The tide is
  out.   ◇ *La mer sera haute à sept heures.*
  It'll be high tide at 7 o'clock.
la **mercerie** NOUN
  [1] *haberdashery*
  [2] *haberdasher's shop*
merci EXCLAMATION
  thank you   ◇ *Merci de m'avoir*
  raccompagné. Thank you for taking me
  home.
  • **merci beaucoup** thank you very much
le **mercredi** NOUN
  [1] *Wednesday*   ◇ *Aujourd'hui, nous*
  sommes mercredi. It's Wednesday
  today.
  [2] *on Wednesday*   ◇ *Nous comptons*
  partir mercredi. We plan to leave on
  Wednesday.
  • **le mercredi** on Wednesdays   ◇ *Le*
  musée est fermé le mercredi. The
  museum is shut on Wednesdays.
  • **tous les mercredis** every Wednesday
  • **mercredi dernier** last Wednesday
  • **mercredi prochain** next Wednesday
la **merde** NOUN *(rude)*
  shit   ◇ *Merde!* Shit!
la **mère** NOUN
  mother
la **merguez** NOUN
  spicy sausage
méridional ADJECTIVE
  (MASC PL **méridionaux**)
  southern   ◇ *Il a un accent méridional.*
  He's got a southern accent.
la **meringue** NOUN
  meringue
mériter VERB
  to deserve
le **merlan** NOUN
  whiting
le **merle** NOUN
  blackbird
la **merveille** NOUN
  • **Cet ordinateur est une vraie merveille!**
  This computer's really wonderful!
  • **à merveille** wonderfully   ◇ *Elle se*
  porte à merveille depuis son opération.
  She's been wonderfully well since the
  operation.
merveilleux ADJECTIVE
  (FEM SING **merveilleuse**)
  marvellous

mes ADJECTIVE
  my   ◇ *mes parents* my parents
Mesdames FEM NOUN
  ladies   ◇ *Bonjour, Mesdames.* Good
  morning, ladies.
Mesdemoiselles FEM NOUN
  ladies   ◇ *Bonjour, Mesdemoiselles.*
  Good morning, ladies.
mesquin ADJECTIVE
  mean
le **message** NOUN
  message
la **messe** NOUN
  mass   ◇ *aller à la messe* to go to mass
  ◇ *la messe de minuit* midnight mass
messieurs MASC NOUN
  gentlemen   ◇ *Que puis-je faire pour*
  vous, Messieurs? What can I do for
  you, gentlemen?
  • **Messieurs,...** Dear Sirs,... *(in letter)*
la **mesure** NOUN
  [1] *measurement*   ◇ *J'ai pris les*
  mesures de la fenêtre. I took the
  measurements of the window.
  • **sur mesure** tailor-made   ◇ *un costume*
  sur mesure a tailor-made suit
  [2] *measure*   ◇ *L'établissement a pris*
  des mesures pour lutter contre le
  vandalisme. The school has taken
  measures to combat vandalism.
  • **au fur et à mesure** as one goes along
  ◇ *Quand je cuisine, je préfère faire la*
  vaisselle au fur et à mesure. When I'm
  cooking, I prefer to wash up as I go
  along.
  • **être en mesure de faire quelque chose**
  to be in a position to do something
  ◇ *Nous ne sommes pas en mesure de*
  vous renseigner. We are not in a
  position to give you any information.
mesurer VERB
  to measure   ◇ *Mesurez la longueur et*
  la largeur. Measure the length and the
  width.
  • **Il mesure un mètre quatre-vingts.** He's
  1 m 80 tall.
met VERB *see* **mettre**
le **métal** NOUN
  (PL les **métaux**)
  metal
métallique ADJECTIVE
  metallic
la **météo** NOUN
  weather forecast   ◇ *Qu'est-ce que dit*
  la météo pour cet après-midi? What's
  the weather forecast for this afternoon?
la **méthode** NOUN
  [1] *method*   ◇ *des méthodes*
  d'enseignement modernes modern

teaching methods
2 _tutor_ ◦ _une méthode de guitare_ a guitar tutor

le **métier** NOUN
job ◦ _Quel métier est-ce que tu aimerais faire plus tard?_ What job would you like to do when you're older?

le **mètre** NOUN
metre
* **un mètre ruban** a tape measure

le **métro** NOUN
underground ◦ _prendre le métro_ to go by underground

mets VERB _see_ **mettre**

le **metteur en scène** NOUN
(PL les metteurs en scène)
1 _producer_ (of play)
2 _director_ (of film)

mettre VERB

Present tense:	
je mets	nous mettons
tu mets	vous mettez
il/elle met	ils/elles mettent
Past participle: mis	

1 _to put_ ◦ _Où est-ce que tu as mis les clés?_ Where have you put the keys?
2 _to put on_ ◦ _Je mets mon manteau et j'arrive._ I'll put on my coat and then I'll be ready. ◦ _Il fait froid, je vais mettre le chauffage._ It's cold, I'm going to put the heating on
3 _to wear_ ◦ _Elle ne met pas souvent de jupe._ She doesn't often wear a skirt. ◦ _Je n'ai rien à me mettre!_ I've got nothing to wear!
4 _to take_ ◦ _Combien de temps as-tu mis pour aller à Lille?_ How long did it take you to get to Lille? ◦ _Elle met des heures à se préparer._ She takes hours getting ready.
* **mettre en marche** to start ◦ _Comment met-on la machine à laver en marche?_ How do you start the washing machine?
* **Vous pouvez vous mettre là.** You can sit there.
* **se mettre au lit** to get into bed
* **se mettre en maillot de bain** to put on one's swimsuit
* **se mettre à** to start ◦ _Il s'est mis à la peinture à cinquante ans._ He started painting when he was 50. ◦ _Il est temps de se mettre au travail._ It's time to start work. ◦ _Elle s'est mise à pleurer._ She started crying.

meuble NOUN
piece of furniture ◦ _Je me suis cogné contre un meuble._ I bumped into a piece of furniture. ◦ _Ce magasin vend_ _de beaux meubles._ This shop sells nice furniture.

le **meublé** NOUN
1 _furnished flat_
2 _furnished room_

meubler VERB
to furnish

le **meurtre** NOUN
murder

le **meurtrier** NOUN
murderer

la **meurtrière** NOUN
murderess

Mexico NOUN
Mexico City

le **Mexique** NOUN
Mexico

le **mi** NOUN
1 _E_ ◦ _mi bémol_ E flat
2 _mi_ ◦ _do, ré, mi..._ do, re, mi...

mi- PREFIX
1 _half-_ ◦ _mi-clos_ half-shut
2 _mid-_ ◦ _à la mi-janvier_ in mid-January

miauler VERB
to mew

la **miche** NOUN
loaf

mi-chemin
* **à mi-chemin** ADVERB
halfway

le **micro** NOUN
microphone

le **microbe** NOUN
germ

le **micro-ondes** NOUN
microwave oven

le **micro-ordinateur** NOUN
microcomputer

le **microscope** NOUN
microscope

le **midi** NOUN
1 _midday_ ◦ _à midi_ at midday
* **midi et demi** half past twelve
2 _lunchtime_ ◦ _On a bien mangé à midi._ We had a good meal at lunchtime.
* **le Midi** the South of France

la **mie** NOUN
breadcrumbs

le **miel** NOUN
honey

mien PRONOUN
* **le mien** mine ◦ _Ce vélo-là, c'est le mien._ That bike's mine.

mienne PRONOUN
* **la mienne** mine ◦ _Cette valise-là, c'est la mienne._ That case is mine.

miennes PRONOUN
* **les miennes** mine ◦ _Heureusement_

M

que tu as tes clés: j'ai oublié les miennes.
It's lucky you've got your keys: I forgot
mine.

miens PRONOUN
- **les miens** mine ◇ *Ces CD-là, ce sont
  les miens.* Those CDs are mine.

la **miette** NOUN
crumb (of bread, cake)

mieux ADVERB, ADJECTIVE, NOUN
better ◇ *Je la connais mieux que son
frère.* I know her better than her
brother. ◇ *Elle va mieux.* She's better.
◇ *Les cheveux courts lui vont mieux.* She
looks better with short hair.
- **Il vaut mieux que tu appelles ta mère.**
  You'd better phone your mother.
- **le mieux** the best ◇ *C'est la région que
  je connais le mieux.* It's the region I
  know best.
- **faire de son mieux** to do one's best
  ◇ *Essaie de faire de ton mieux.* Try to do
  your best.

mignon ADJECTIVE
(FEM SING **mignonne**)
sweet ◇ *Qu'est-ce qu'il est mignon!*
Isn't he sweet!

la **migraine** NOUN
migraine ◇ *J'ai la migraine.* I've got a
migraine.

mijoter VERB
to simmer

le **milieu** NOUN
(PL les **milieux**)
1 *middle*
- **au milieu de** in the middle of ◇ *Place
  le vase au milieu de la table.* Put the
  vase in the middle of the table.
- **au beau milieu de** in the middle of
  ◇ *Quelqu'un a sonné à la porte au beau
  milieu de la nuit.* Somebody rang the
  bell in the middle of the night.
  2 *background* ◇ *le milieu familial* the
  family background ◇ *Il vient d'un milieu
  modeste.* He comes from a modest
  background.
  3 *environment* ◇ *le milieu marin* the
  marine environment

militaire ADJECTIVE
see also **militaire** NOUN
military ◇ *faire son service militaire* to
do one's military service

le **militaire** NOUN
see also **militaire** ADJECTIVE
serviceman ◇ *Son père est militaire.*
His father is in the services.
- **un militaire de carrière** a professional
  soldier

mille NUMBER
a thousand ◇ *mille francs* a thousand

francs ◇ *deux mille personnes* two
thousand people

le **millefeuille** NOUN
vanilla slice

le **milliard** NOUN
thousand million ◇ *cinq milliards de
francs* five thousand million francs

le/la **milliardaire** NOUN
multimillionaire

le **millier** NOUN
thousand ◇ *des milliers de personnes*
thousands of people
- **par milliers** by the thousand

le **milligramme** NOUN
milligramme

le **millimètre** NOUN
millimetre

le **million** NOUN
million ◇ *deux millions de personnes*
two million people

le/la **millionnaire** NOUN
millionaire

le/la **mime** NOUN
mime artist

mimer VERB
to mimic

minable ADJECTIVE
1 *shabby* ◇ *un imperméable minable*
a shabby raincoat
2 *pathetic* ◇ *Mon moniteur de ski était
minable.* My skiing instructor was
pathetic.

mince ADJECTIVE
1 *thin* ◇ *une mince tranche de jambon*
a thin slice of ham
2 *slim* ◇ *Il est grand et mince.* He's
tall and slim.
- **Mince alors!** (*informal*) Oh bother!

la **minceur** NOUN
1 *thinness* ◇ *la minceur des murs* the
thinness of the walls
2 *slimness* ◇ *Elle enviait la minceur de
sa sœur.* She envied her sister's
slimness.

la **mine** NOUN
1 *expression*
2 *look* ◇ *Tu as bonne mine.* You look
well. ◇ *Il a mauvaise mine.* He doesn't
look well. ◇ *Elle avait une mine fatiguée.*
She was looking tired.
3 *appearance* ◇ *Il ne faut pas juger
les gens d'après leur mine.* You
shouldn't judge people by their
appearance.
4 *lead* (of pencil)
5 *mine* ◇ *une mine de charbon* a coal
mine
- **faire mine de faire quelque chose** to
  pretend to do something ◇ *Elle a fait*

mine de le croire. She pretended to believe him.
* **mine de rien** somehow or other ◇ *Elle a réussi mine de rien à le faire parler de lui.* Somehow or other she got him to talk about himself.

minéral ADJECTIVE
(MASC PL **minéraux**)
mineral ◇ *l'eau minérale* mineral water

minéralogique ADJECTIVE
* **une plaque minéralogique** a number plate

le **minet** NOUN
pussycat

la **minette** NOUN
pussycat (female)

mineur ADJECTIVE
see also **mineur** NOUN
minor

le **mineur** NOUN
see also **mineur** ADJECTIVE
1 *boy under 18*
* **les mineurs** the under-18s
2 *miner* ◇ *Mon grand-père était mineur.* My grandfather was a miner.

la **mineure** NOUN
girl under 18

a **minijupe** NOUN
miniskirt

e **minimum** NOUN
minimum ◇ *Il en fait le minimum.* He does the absolute minimum.
* **au minimum** at the very least

e **ministère** NOUN
ministry ◇ *le ministère des Affaires étrangères* the Foreign Office

e **ministre** NOUN
minister ◇ *le ministre des Affaires étrangères* the Foreign Secretary

e **Minitel** ® NOUN
Minitel *is France Telecom's online data service. You can use it instead of a phone directory, and to make bookings for transport, exhibitions etc.*

a **minorité** NOUN
minority

Minorque FEM NOUN
Minorca

e **minuit** NOUN
midnight ◇ *à minuit et quart* at a quarter past midnight

minuscule ADJECTIVE
see also **minuscule** NOUN
tiny

minuscule NOUN
see also **minuscule** ADJECTIVE
small letter

minute NOUN
minute

* **à la minute** just this minute ◇ *Je viens de l'appeler à la minute.* I've just this minute called him.

minutieux ADJECTIVE
(FEM SING **minutieuse**)
meticulous
* **C'est un travail minutieux.** It's a fiddly job.

la **mirabelle** NOUN
small yellow plum

le **miracle** NOUN
miracle

le **miroir** NOUN
mirror

mis VERB see **mettre**

mis ADJECTIVE
* **bien mis** well turned out ◇ *Elle est toujours bien mise.* She's always well turned out.

miser VERB (informal)
to bank on ◇ *On ne peut pas miser là-dessus.* We can't bank on it.

misérable ADJECTIVE
shabby-looking ◇ *une femme d'aspect misérable* a shabby-looking woman

la **misère** NOUN
extreme poverty
* **un salaire de misère** starvation wages

le/la **missionnaire** NOUN
missionary

mit VERB see **mettre**

la **mi-temps** NOUN
1 *half (of match)* ◇ *la première mi-temps* the first half ◇ *la deuxième mi-temps* the second half
2 *half-time* ◇ *Je lui parlerai à la mi-temps.* I'll speak to him at half-time.
* **travailler à mi-temps** to work part-time

la **mitraillette** NOUN
submachine gun

mixte ADJECTIVE
* **une école mixte** a mixed school

Mlle ABBREVIATION (= *Mademoiselle*)
(PL **Mlles**)
Miss ◇ *Mlle Renoir* Miss Renoir

Mme ABBREVIATION (= *Madame*)
(PL **Mmes**)
Mrs ◇ *Mme Leroy* Mrs Leroy

le **mobile** NOUN
motive ◇ *Quel était le mobile du crime?* What was the motive for the crime?

le **mobilier** NOUN
furniture

moche ADJECTIVE (informal)
1 *awful* ◇ *Cette couleur est vraiment moche.* That colour's really awful. ◇ *Je me trouve moche!* I think I look awful!
2 *rotten* ◇ *Il a la grippe, c'est moche*

M

pour lui. He's got flu, that's rotten for him.

la **mode** NOUN

see also le mode

fashion ◇ *être à la mode* to be fashionable

le **mode** NOUN

see also la mode

- **le mode d'emploi** directions for use
- **le mode de vie** the way of life

le **modèle** NOUN

[1] *model* ◇ *Le nouveau modèle sort en septembre.* The new model is coming out in September.

[2] *style* (*of clothes*) ◇ *Est-ce que vous avez le même modèle en plus grand?* Have you got the same style in a bigger size?

modéré ADJECTIVE

moderate

moderne ADJECTIVE

modern

moderniser VERB

to modernize

modeste ADJECTIVE

modest ◇ *Ne sois pas si modeste!* Don't be so modest!

la **modestie** NOUN

modesty

moelleux ADJECTIVE

(FEM SING **moelleuse**)

soft ◇ *un coussin moelleux* a soft cushion

moi PRONOUN

me ◇ *Coucou, c'est moi!* Hello, it's me!

- **Moi, je pense que tu as tort.** I personally think you're wrong.
- **à moi** mine ◇ *Ce livre n'est pas à moi.* This book isn't mine. ◇ *un ami à moi* a friend of mine

moi-même PRONOUN

myself ◇ *J'ai tricoté ce pull moi-même.* I knitted this jumper myself.

moindre ADJECTIVE

- **le moindre** the slightest ◇ *Il ne fait pas le moindre effort.* He doesn't make the slightest effort. ◇ *Je n'en ai pas la moindre idée.* I haven't the slightest idea.

le **moine** NOUN

monk

le **moineau** NOUN

(PL les **moineaux**)

sparrow

moins ADVERB, PREPOSITION

[1] *less* ◇ *Ça coûte moins de deux cents francs.* It costs less than 200 francs.

[2] *fewer* ◇ *Il y a moins de gens aujourd'hui.* There are fewer people

today.

- **Il est cinq heures moins dix.** It's 10 to 5.

[3] *minus* ◇ *quatre moins trois* 4 minus 3 ◇ *Il a fait moins cinq la nuit dernière.* It was minus five last night.

- **le moins** the least ◇ *C'est le modèle le moins cher.* It's the least expensive model. ◇ *Ce sont les plages qui sont les moins polluées.* These are the least polluted beaches. ◇ *C'est l'album que j'aime le moins.* This is the album I like the least.
- **de moins en moins** less and less ◇ *Il vient nous voir de moins en moins.* He comes to see us less and less often.
- **Il a trois ans de moins que moi.** He's three years younger than me.
- **au moins** at least ◇ *Ne te plains pas: au moins il ne pleut pas!* Don't complain: at least it's not raining!
- **à moins que** unless

à moins que *is followed by a verb in the subjunctive.*

◇ *Je te retrouverai à dix heures à moins que le train n'ait du retard.* I'll meet you at 10 o'clock unless the train's late.

le **mois** NOUN

month

le **moisi** NOUN

- **Ça sent le moisi.** It smells musty.

moisir VERB

to go mouldy ◇ *Le pain a moisi.* The bread's gone mouldy.

la **moisson** NOUN

harvest

moite ADJECTIVE

sweaty ◇ *J'ai toujours les mains moites.* My hands are always sweaty.

la **moitié** NOUN

half ◇ *Il a mangé la moitié du gâteau à lui seul.* He ate half the cake all by himself.

- **la moitié du temps** half the time
- **à la moitié de** halfway through ◇ *Elle est partie à la moitié du film.* She left halfway through the film.
- **à moitié** half ◇ *Ton verre est encore à moitié plein.* Your glass is still half-full. ◇ *Ce sac était à moitié prix.* This bag was half-price.
- **partager moitié moitié** to go halves ◇ *On partage moitié moitié, d'accord?* We'll go halves, OK?

la **molaire** NOUN

back tooth

la **Moldavie** NOUN

Moldova

molle ADJECTIVE

lethargic ◦ *Je la trouve un peu molle.* I find her a bit lethargic.

le **mollet** NOUN
see also mollet ADJECTIVE
calf (of leg)

mollet ADJECTIVE
see also mollet NOUN
• **un œuf mollet** a soft-boiled egg

e/la **môme** (informal) NOUN
kid

le **moment** NOUN
moment
• **en ce moment** at the moment ◦ *Nous avons beaucoup de travail en ce moment.* We have a lot of work at the moment.
• **pour le moment** for the moment ◦ *Nous ne pensons pas déménager pour le moment.* We're not thinking of moving for the moment.
• **au moment où** just as ◦ *Il est arrivé au moment où j'allais partir.* He turned up just as I was leaving.
• **à tout moment (1)** at any moment ◦ *Elle peut arriver à tout moment.* She could arrive at any moment.
• **à tout moment (2)** constantly ◦ *Il nous dérange à tout moment pour des riens.* He's constantly bothering us about silly little things.
• **sur le moment** at the time ◦ *Sur le moment je n'ai rien dit.* At the time I didn't say anything.
• **par moments** at times ◦ *Elle se sent seule par moments.* She feels lonely at times.

momentané ADJECTIVE
momentary

la **momie** NOUN
mummy (Egyptian)

mon ADJECTIVE
(FEM SING ma, PL mes)
my ◦ *mon frère* my brother ◦ *mon ami* my friend

la **monarchie** NOUN
monarchy

e **monastère** NOUN
monastery

e **monde** NOUN
world ◦ *faire le tour du monde* to go round the world
• **Il y a du monde.** There are a lot of people.
• **beaucoup de monde** a lot of people ◦ *Il y avait beaucoup de monde au concert.* There were a lot of people at the concert.
• **peu de monde** not many people

mondial ADJECTIVE
(MASC PL mondiaux)

[1] *world* ◦ *la population mondiale* the world population
[2] *world-wide* ◦ *une crise mondiale* a world-wide crisis

le **moniteur** NOUN
[1] *instructor* ◦ *un moniteur de voile* a sailing instructor
[2] *supervisor*

la **monitrice** NOUN
[1] *instructor* ◦ *une monitrice de ski* a ski instructor
[2] *supervisor*

la **monnaie** NOUN
• **une pièce de monnaie** a coin
• **avoir de la monnaie** to have change ◦ *Est-ce que tu as de la monnaie?* Have you got any change? ◦ *Est-ce que vous avez la monnaie de cent francs?* Do you have change for 100 francs?
• **rendre la monnaie à quelqu'un** to give somebody their change

monotone ADJECTIVE
monotonous

Monsieur MASC NOUN
(PL Messieurs)
[1] *Mr* ◦ *Monsieur Dupont* Mr Dupont
[2] *man* ◦ *Il y a un monsieur qui veut te voir.* There's a man to see you.
[3] *Sir* ◦ *Monsieur,...* Dear Sir,... (in letter) ◦ *Monsieur! Vous avez oublié votre parapluie!* Excuse me! You've forgotten your umbrella!

le **monstre** NOUN
see also monstre ADJECTIVE
monster

monstre ADJECTIVE
see also monstre NOUN
• **Nous avons un travail monstre.** We've got a terrific amount of work.

le **mont** NOUN
mount
• **le mont Everest** Mount Everest
• **le mont Blanc** Mont Blanc

la **montagne** NOUN
mountain ◦ *de hautes montagnes* high mountains ◦ *Nous passons tous les ans un mois à la montagne.* We spend a month in the mountains every year.
• **les montagnes russes** roller coaster

montagneux ADJECTIVE
(FEM SING montagneuse)
mountainous ◦ *une région montagneuse* a mountainous area

montant ADJECTIVE
[1] *rising* ◦ *la marée montante* the rising tide
[2] *high* ◦ *un pull à col montant* a high-necked jumper

M

monter VERB

　① *to go up* ◇ *Elle a du mal à monter les escaliers.* She has difficulty going upstairs. ◇ *Les prix ont encore monté.* Prices have gone up again.

　② *to assemble* ◇ *Est-ce que ces étagères sont difficiles à monter?* Are these shelves difficult to assemble?

　◆ **monter dans** to get on ◇ *Il est temps de monter dans l'avion.* It's time to get on the plane.

　◆ **monter sur** to stand on ◇ *Tu vas devoir monter sur une chaise pour changer l'ampoule.* You'll have to stand on a chair to change the light bulb.

　◆ **monter à cheval** to ride

la **montre** NOUN
　watch

montrer VERB
　to show ◇ *Est-ce que vous pouvez me montrer la gare sur le plan?* Can you show me the station on the map?

la **monture** NOUN
　frames (of glasses)

le **monument** NOUN
　monument

se **moquer** VERB

　◆ **se moquer de (1)** to make fun of ◇ *Ils se sont moqués de mes chaussures jaunes.* They made fun of my yellow shoes.

　◆ **se moquer de (2)** (*informal*) not to care about ◇ *Il se moque complètement de la mode.* He couldn't care less about fashion.

la **moquette** NOUN
　fitted carpet

moqueur ADJECTIVE
　(FEM SING **moqueuse**)
　mocking

le **moral** NOUN
　◆ **Elle a le moral.** She's in good spirits.
　◆ **J'ai le moral à zéro.** I'm feeling really down.

la **morale** NOUN
　moral ◇ *La morale de cette histoire est...* The moral of the story is...
　◆ **faire la morale à quelqu'un** to lecture somebody

le **morceau** NOUN
　(PL les **morceaux**)
　piece ◇ *un morceau de pain* a piece of bread

mordre VERB
　to bite

mordu ADJECTIVE
　◆ **Il est mordu de jazz.** (*informal*) He's crazy about jazz.

la **morgue** NOUN
　mortuary

le **morse** NOUN
　walrus

la **morsure** NOUN
　bite

la **mort** NOUN
　[see also **mort** ADJECTIVE]
　death

mort ADJECTIVE
　[see also **mort** NOUN]
　dead ◇ *Nous avons trouvé un oiseau mort.* We found a dead bird. ◇ *Napoléon est mort en 1821.* Napoleon died in 1821.
　◆ **Il était mort de peur.** He was scared to death.
　◆ **Je suis morte de fatigue.** I'm dead tired.

mortel ADJECTIVE
　(FEM SING **mortelle**)
　① *deadly* ◇ *un poison mortel* a deadly poison ◇ *Ces réunions de famille sont mortelles!* (*informal*) These family gatherings are deadly!
　② *fatal* ◇ *une chute mortelle* a fatal fall

la **morue** NOUN
　cod

Moscou NOUN
　Moscow

la **mosquée** NOUN
　mosque

le **mot** NOUN
　① *word* ◇ *mot à mot* word for word
　② *line* ◇ *Je vais lui écrire un mot pour lui dire qu'on arrive.* I'll drop her a line to say we're coming.
　◆ **des mots croisés** a crossword

le **motard** NOUN
　① *biker*
　② *motorcycle cop* (*informal*) ◇ *Il s'est fait arrêter par un motard pour excès de vitesse.* He was stopped for speeding by a motorcycle cop.

le **moteur** NOUN
　engine
　◆ **un bateau à moteur** a motor boat

le **motif** NOUN
　pattern ◇ *des rideaux avec un motif d'oiseaux* curtains with a bird pattern
　◆ **sans motif** for no reason ◇ *Il s'est fâché sans motif.* He got angry for no reason.

la **moto** NOUN
　motorbike

le/la **motocycliste** NOUN
　motorcyclist

mou ADJECTIVE
　(FEM SING **molle**)

1 _soft_ ◇ _Mon matelas est trop mou._
My mattress is too soft.
2 _lethargic_ ◇ _Je le trouve un peu mou._
I find him a bit lethargic.

la **mouche** NOUN
fly

se **moucher** VERB
to blow one's nose

le **moucheron** NOUN
midge

le **mouchoir** NOUN
handkerchief
* **un mouchoir en papier** a tissue

moudre VERB
to grind

la **moue** NOUN
pout
* **faire la moue** to pout

la **mouette** NOUN
seagull

la **moufle** NOUN
mitt

mouillé ADJECTIVE
wet

mouiller VERB
to get wet ◇ _J'ai mouillé les manches
de mon pull._ I got the sleeves of my
jumper wet.
* **se mouiller** to get wet ◇ _Attention, tu
vas te mouiller!_ Careful, you'll get wet!

moulant ADJECTIVE
figure-hugging ◇ _une robe moulante_
a figure-hugging dress

la **moule** NOUN
see also le moule
mussel

le **moule** NOUN
see also la moule
* **un moule à gâteaux** a cake tin

le **moulin** NOUN
mill

moulu VERB see **moudre**

mourir VERB
to die
* **mourir de faim** to starve ◇ _Des
centaines de personnes sont mortes de
faim._ Hundreds of people starved to
death.
* **Je meurs de faim!** I'm starving!
* **mourir de froid** to die of exposure
* **Je meurs de froid!** I'm freezing!
* **mourir d'envie de faire quelque chose**
to be dying to do something ◇ _Je
meurs d'envie d'aller me baigner._ I'm
dying to go for a swim.

a **mousse** NOUN
1 _moss_ ◇ _un rocher recouvert de
mousse_ a rock covered with moss
2 _froth_ (on beer)

3 _lather_ (of soap, shampoo)
4 _mousse_ ◇ _une mousse au chocolat_
a chocolate mousse ◇ _une mousse de
poisson_ a fish mousse
* **la mousse à raser** shaving foam

mousseux ADJECTIVE
(FEM SING **mousseuse**)
* **un vin mousseux** a sparkling wine

la **moustache** NOUN
moustache
* **les moustaches** whiskers

le **moustique** NOUN
mosquito

la **moutarde** NOUN
mustard

le **mouton** NOUN
1 _sheep_ ◇ _une peau de mouton_ a
sheepskin
2 _mutton_ ◇ _un gigot de mouton_ a leg
of mutton

le **mouvement** NOUN
movement

mouvementé ADJECTIVE
eventful ◇ _des vacances
mouvementées_ eventful holidays

moyen ADJECTIVE
(FEM SING **moyenne**)
see also moyen NOUN
1 _average_ ◇ _Je suis plutôt moyenne
en langues._ I'm just average at
languages.
2 _medium_ ◇ _Elle est de taille
moyenne._ She's of medium height.
* **le moyen âge** the Middle Ages

le **moyen** NOUN
see also moyen ADJECTIVE
way ◇ _Quel est le meilleur moyen de le
convaincre?_ What's the best way of
convincing him?
* **Je n'en ai pas les moyens.** I can't
afford it.
* **Ils n'ont pas les moyens de s'acheter
une voiture.** They can't afford to buy a
car.
* **un moyen de transport** a means of
transport
* **par tous les moyens** by every possible
means

la **moyenne** NOUN
* **avoir la moyenne** to get a pass mark
◇ _J'espère avoir la moyenne en maths._ I
hope to get a pass mark in maths.
* **en moyenne** on average
* **la moyenne d'âge** the average age

le **Moyen-Orient** NOUN
Middle East

muet ADJECTIVE
(FEM SING **muette**)
dumb

• **un film muet** a silent film

le **muguet** NOUN
lily of the valley

multiple ADJECTIVE
numerous ⋄ *en de multiples occasions*
on numerous occasions

multiplier VERB
to multiply

municipal ADJECTIVE
(MASC PL **municipaux**)
• **la bibliothèque municipale** the public
library

la **municipalité** NOUN
town council

les **munitions** FEM NOUN
ammunition

le **mur** NOUN
wall

mûr ADJECTIVE
1 *ripe* (*fruit*)
2 *mature* (*person*)

la **mûre** NOUN
bramble

mûrir VERB
1 *to ripen* ⋄ *Les fraises ont mis du
temps à mûrir.* The strawberries took a
while to ripen.
2 *to make mature* ⋄ *Cette
expérience l'a beaucoup mûrie.* That
experience has made her much more
mature.

murmurer VERB
to whisper ⋄ *Il m'a murmuré à l'oreille
qu'il allait partir.* He whispered in my ear
that he was going to go.

la **muscade** NOUN
nutmeg

le **muscat** NOUN
1 *muscat grape*
2 *muscatel* (*wine*) ⋄ *un verre de*

muscat a glass of muscatel

le **muscle** NOUN
muscle

musclé ADJECTIVE
muscular

le **museau** NOUN
(PL les **museaux**)
muzzle

le **musée** NOUN
museum

musical ADJECTIVE
(MASC PL **musicaux**)
musical
• **avoir l'oreille musicale** to be musical

le **music-hall** NOUN
variety ⋄ *une chanteuse de music-hall*
a variety singer

le **musicien** NOUN
musician

la **musicienne** NOUN
musician

la **musique** NOUN
music

musulman ADJECTIVE, NOUN
Muslim
• **un musulman** a Muslim (*man*)
• **une musulmane** a Muslim (*woman*)

la **mutation** NOUN
transfer ⋄ *Il a demandé sa mutation à
Paris.* He asked for a transfer to Paris.

myope ADJECTIVE
short-sighted

le **mystère** NOUN
mystery

mystérieux ADJECTIVE
(FEM SING **mystérieuse**)
mysterious

le **mythe** NOUN
myth

N

n' PRONOUN see **ne**

la **nage** NOUN
- **traverser une rivière à la nage** to swim across a river

la **nageoire** NOUN
fin

nager VERB
to swim

le **nageur** NOUN
swimmer

la **nageuse** NOUN
swimmer

naïf ADJECTIVE
(FEM SING **naïve**)
naïve

le **nain** NOUN
dwarf

la **naissance** NOUN
birth
- **votre date de naissance** your date of birth

naître VERB
to be born
- **Il est né en 1982.** He was born in 1982.

naïve ADJECTIVE see **naïf**

la **nana** NOUN (*informal*)
girl

la **nappe** NOUN
tablecloth

la **narine** NOUN
nostril

natal ADJECTIVE
native ◇ **mon pays natal** my native country

la **natation** NOUN
swimming ◇ **La natation est mon sport favori.** Swimming's my favourite sport.

national ADJECTIVE
(MASC PL **nationaux**)
national
- **la fête nationale espagnole** the national day of Spain

la **nationalité** NOUN
nationality

la **natte** NOUN
plait ◇ **Cécile avait des nattes.** Cécile had plaits.

la **nature** NOUN
see also **nature** ADJECTIVE
nature

nature ADJECTIVE
see also **nature** NOUN
plain ◇ **un yaourt nature** a plain yoghurt

naturel ADJECTIVE
(FEM SING **naturelle**)
natural

naturellement ADVERB
of course ◇ **Vous viendrez à notre fête? – Naturellement!** Are you coming to our party? – Of course!
◇ **Naturellement, il est encore en retard.** Of course, he's late again.

le **naufrage** NOUN
shipwreck

nautique ADJECTIVE
water
- **les sports nautiques** water sports
- **le ski nautique** water-skiing

le **navet** NOUN
turnip

la **navette** NOUN
shuttle ◇ **la navette entre la gare et l'aéroport** the shuttle between the station and the airport
- **faire la navette** to commute ◇ **Je fais la navette entre Paris et Ivry.** I commute between Paris and Ivry.

la **navigation** NOUN
- **La navigation est interdite ici.** Boats are not allowed here.

naviguer VERB
to sail

le **navire** NOUN
ship

ne ADVERB

> **ne** *is combined with words such as* **pas, personne, plus** *and* **jamais** *to form negative phrases.*

◇ **Je ne peux pas venir.** I can't come.
◇ **Ils ne vont jamais en boîte.** They never go to discos. ◇ **Je ne connais personne ici.** I don't know anyone here.

> **ne** *changes to* **n'** *before a vowel and most words beginning with "h".*

◇ **Je n'ai pas d'argent.** I haven't got any money. ◇ **Il n'habite plus à Paris.** He doesn't live in Paris any more.

> **ne** *is sometimes not translated.*

◇ **C'est plus loin que je ne le croyais.** It's further than I thought.

né VERB see **naître**
born ◇ **Elle est née en 1980.** She was born in 1980.

néanmoins ADVERB
nevertheless

nécessaire ADJECTIVE
necessary ◇ **Il est nécessaire de réserver.** It's necessary to book.

le **nectar** NOUN

• **le nectar d'abricot** apricot drink

néerlandais ADJECTIVE, NOUN
(FEM SING **néerlandaise**)
Dutch ◇ *Manon parle néerlandais.*
Manon speaks Dutch.

• **un Néerlandais** a Dutchman
• **une Néerlandaise** a Dutchwoman
• **les Néerlandais** the Dutch

négatif ADJECTIVE
(FEM SING **négative**)
see also **négatif** NOUN
negative

le **négatif** NOUN
see also **négatif** ADJECTIVE
negative (*of photo*)

négligé ADJECTIVE
scruffy ◇ *une tenue négligée* scruffy
clothes

la **neige** NOUN
snow

• **un bonhomme de neige** a snowman

neiger VERB
to snow

le **nénuphar** NOUN
water lily

le **néon** NOUN
neon ◇ *une lampe au néon* a neon
light ◇ *La cuisine est éclairée au néon.*
The kitchen has a neon light.

néo-zélandais ADJECTIVE, NOUN
(FEM SING **néo-zélandaise**)
New Zealand ◇ *Le champion
néo-zélandais a gagné la course.* The
New Zealand champion won the race.

• **un Néo-Zélandais** a New Zealander (*man*)
• **une Néo-Zélandaise** a New Zealander
(*woman*)

le **nerf** NOUN
nerve

• **taper sur les nerfs de quelqu'un** to get
on somebody's nerves ◇ *Il me tape sur
les nerfs.* He's getting on my nerves.

nerveux ADJECTIVE
(FEM SING **nerveuse**)
nervous

la **nervosité** NOUN
nervousness

n'est-ce pas ADVERB
n'est-ce pas *is used to check that something is
true.*
◇ *Nous sommes le douze aujourd'hui,
n'est-ce pas?* It's the 12th today, isn't
it? ◇ *Ils sont venus l'an dernier, n'est-ce
pas?* They came last year, didn't they?
◇ *Elle aura dix-huit ans en octobre,
n'est-ce pas?* She'll be 18 in October,
won't she?

net ADJECTIVE, ADVERB
(FEM SING **nette**)

[1] *clear* ◇ *L'image n'est pas nette.* The
picture isn't very clear.
[2] *net* ◇ *Poids net: 500 g.* Net weight:
500 g.
[3] *flatly* ◇ *Il a refusé net de nous aider.*
He flatly refused to help us.

• **s'arrêter net** to stop dead

nettement ADVERB
much ◇ *Ce magasin est nettement plus
cher.* This shop is much more
expensive.

le **nettoyage** NOUN
cleaning

• **le nettoyage à sec** dry cleaning

nettoyer VERB
to clean

neuf NUMBER
see also **neuf** ADJECTIVE
nine ◇ *Claire a neuf ans.* Claire's
nine. ◇ *Il est neuf heures du matin.* It's
nine in the morning.

• **le neuf février** the ninth of February

neuf ADJECTIVE
(FEM SING **neuve**)
see also **neuf** NUMBER
new ◇ *des chaussures neuves* new
shoes

neutre ADJECTIVE
neutral

neuve ADJECTIVE *see* **neuf**

neuvième ADJECTIVE
ninth ◇ *au neuvième étage* on the
ninth floor

le **neveu** NOUN
(PL les **neveux**)
nephew

le **nez** NOUN
nose

• **se trouver nez à nez avec quelqu'un** to
come face to face with somebody

ni CONJUNCTION

• **ni...ni...** neither...nor... ◇ *Je n'aime ni
les lentilles ni les épinards.* I like neither
lentils nor spinach. ◇ *Elles ne sont
venues ni l'une ni l'autre.* Neither of
them came.

la **niche** NOUN
kennel

le **nid** NOUN
nest

la **nièce** NOUN
niece

nier VERB
to deny

n'importe ADVERB

• **n'importe qui** anybody ◇ *N'ouvre pas
la porte à n'importe qui.* Don't open the
door to just anybody.
• **n'importe quoi** anything ◇ *Je ferais*

n'importe quoi pour elle. I'd do anything for her.
- **Tu dis n'importe quoi.** You're talking rubbish.
- **n'importe où** anywhere ◇ *On trouve ces fleurs n'importe où.* You can find these flowers anywhere.
- **Ne laisse pas tes affaires n'importe où.** Don't leave your things lying everywhere.
- **n'importe quand** any time ◇ *Tu peux venir n'importe quand.* You can come any time.
- **n'importe comment** any old how ◇ *Ces livres sont rangés n'importe comment.* These books have been put away any old how.

le **niveau** NOUN
(PL les **niveaux**)
[1] *level* ◇ *le niveau de l'eau* the water level
[2] *standard* ◇ *Ces deux enfants n'ont pas le même niveau.* These two children aren't at the same level.
- **le niveau de vie** the standard of living

noble ADJECTIVE
noble

la **noblesse** NOUN
nobility

la **noce** NOUN
wedding
- **un repas de noce** a wedding reception

nocif ADJECTIVE
(FEM SING **nocive**)
harmful ◇ *une substance nocive* a harmful substance

nocturne ADJECTIVE
see also **nocturne** NOUN
[1] *nocturnal* ◇ *un oiseau nocturne* a nocturnal bird
[2] *by night* ◇ *Découvrez le Paris nocturne!* Discover Paris by night!

la **nocturne** NOUN
see also **nocturne** ADJECTIVE
late-night opening ◇ *Nocturne le vendredi jusqu'à vingt-trois heures.* Late-night opening until 11 p.m. on Fridays.

le **Noël** NOUN
Christmas ◇ *Qu'est-ce que tu as eu pour Noël?* What did you get for Christmas?
- **Joyeux Noël!** Merry Christmas!

e **nœud** NOUN
[1] *knot* ◇ *Il a fait un nœud à la corde.* He tied a knot in the rope.
[2] *bow* ◇ *Janet avait un nœud dans les cheveux.* Janet had a bow in her hair.
- **un nœud papillon** a bow tie

noir ADJECTIVE
see also **noir** NOUN
[1] *black* ◇ *Elle porte une robe noire.* She's wearing a black dress. ◇ *Elle est noire.* She's black.
[2] *dark* ◇ *Il fait noir dehors.* It's dark outside.

le **noir** NOUN
see also **noir** ADJECTIVE
dark ◇ *J'ai peur du noir.* I'm afraid of the dark.
- **le travail au noir** moonlighting

le **Noir** NOUN
black man
- **les Noirs** black people

la **Noire** NOUN
black woman

la **noisette** NOUN
hazelnut

la **noix** NOUN
(PL les **noix**)
walnut
- **une noix de coco** a coconut
- **les noix de cajou** cashew nuts
- **une noix de beurre** a knob of butter

le **nom** NOUN
[1] *name* ◇ *votre nom* your name
- **mon nom de famille** my surname
- **son nom de jeune fille** her maiden name
[2] *noun* (in grammar)

le **nombre** NOUN
number ◇ *Treize est un nombre impair.* Thirteen is an odd number. ◇ *un grand nombre d'amis* a large number of friends

nombreux ADJECTIVE
(FEM SING **nombreuse**)
[1] *many* ◇ *Il a gagné de nombreux matchs.* He's won many matches.
[2] *large* ◇ *une famille nombreuse* a large family
- **peu nombreux** few ◇ *Nous étions peu nombreux à la réunion.* There were few of us at the meeting.

le **nombril** NOUN
navel

nommer VERB
[1] *to name* ◇ *Il n'a voulu nommer personne.* He didn't want to name anybody.
[2] *to appoint* ◇ *Il a été nommé directeur.* He was appointed director.

non ADVERB
no ◇ *Tu as vu Jean-Pierre? – Non.* Have you seen Jean-Pierre? – No.
- **non seulement** not only ◇ *Il est non seulement intelligent, mais aussi très gentil.* Not only is he intelligent, he's

also very nice.
- **moi non plus** Neither do I. ◇ *Je n'aime pas les hamburgers. –Moi non plus.* I don't like hamburgers. –Neither do I. ◇ *Il n'y est pas allé et moi non plus.* He didn't go and neither did I.

non alcoolisé ADJECTIVE
non-alcoholic ◇ *les boissons non alcoolisées* non-alcoholic drinks

le **non-fumeur** NOUN
non-smoker ◇ *Gavin est un non-fumeur.* Gavin's a non-smoker.
- **une voiture non-fumeurs** a no-smoking carriage

le **nord** NOUN
see also nord ADJECTIVE
north ◇ *Ils vivent dans le nord de l'île.* They live in the north of the island.
- **vers le nord** northwards
- **au nord de Paris** north of Paris
- **l'Afrique du Nord** North Africa
- **le vent du nord** the north wind

nord ADJECTIVE
see also nord NOUN
1 *north* ◇ *la face nord du Mont-Blanc* the north face of Mont-Blanc
- **le pôle Nord** the North Pole
2 *northern* ◇ *Nous avons visité la partie nord de l'île.* We visited the northern part of the island.

le **nord-est** NOUN
north-east ◇ *les régions du nord-est* north-eastern regions

le **nord-ouest** NOUN
north-west
- **l'Europe du nord-ouest** north-west Europe

normal ADJECTIVE
(MASC PL **normaux**)
1 *normal* ◇ *un bébé normal* a normal baby
2 *natural* ◇ *C'est tout à fait normal.* It's perfectly natural.
- **Vous trouvez que c'est normal?** Does that seem right to you?

normalement ADVERB
normally ◇ *Les aéroports fonctionnent tous normalement.* The airports are all working normally.
- **Normalement, elle doit arriver à huit heures.** She's supposed to arrive at 8 o'clock.
- **Tu es libre ce week-end? –Oui, normalement.** Are you free this weekend? –Yes, I should be.

normand ADJECTIVE
- **un village normand** a village in Normandy
- **la côte normande** the coast of Normandy

la **Normandie** NOUN
Normandy

la **Norvège** NOUN
Norway

norvégien ADJECTIVE, NOUN
(FEM SING **norvégienne**)
Norwegian
- **Elle parle norvégien.** She speaks Norwegian.
- **un Norvégien** a Norwegian (*man*)
- **une Norvégienne** a Norwegian (*woman*)

nos ADJECTIVE
our ◇ *Où sont nos affaires?* Where are our things?

le **notaire** NOUN
solicitor ◇ *Son père est notaire.* His father's a solicitor.

la **note** NOUN
1 *note* ◇ *J'ai pris des notes pendant la conférence.* I took notes at the lecture. ◇ *Il a joué quelques notes au piano.* He played a few notes on the piano.
2 *mark* ◇ *Vincent a de bonnes notes en maths.* Vincent's got good marks in maths.
3 *bill* ◇ *Il n'a pas payé sa note.* He didn't pay his bill.

noter VERB
to make a note of ◇ *Tu as noté leur adresse?* Did you make a note of their address?

les **notions** FEM NOUN
basics ◇ *Il faut avoir des notions d'anglais.* You have to have some basic English. ◇ *Elle a des notions de comptabilité.* She knows the basics of accounting.

notre ADJECTIVE
(PL **nos**)
our ◇ *Voici notre maison.* Here's our house.

nôtre PRONOUN
- **le nôtre** ours ◇ *À qui est ce chien? –C'est le nôtre.* Whose dog is it? –It's ours. ◇ *Leur voiture est rouge, la nôtre est bleue.* Their car is red, ours is blue.

nôtres PRONOUN
- **les nôtres** ours ◇ *Ces places-là sont les nôtres.* Those seats are ours.

nouer VERB
to tie

les **nouilles** FEM NOUN
noodles

nourrir VERB
to feed

la **nourriture** NOUN
food

nous PRONOUN
1 _we_ ◇ _Nous avons deux enfants._ We have two children.
2 _us_ ◇ _Viens avec nous._ Come with us.
- **nous-mêmes** ourselves

nouveau ADJECTIVE
(MASC SING ALSO **nouvel**, FEM SING **nouvelle**, MASC PL **nouveaux**)
see also nouveau NOUN
new ◇ _Il me faut un nouveau pantalon._ I need some new trousers. ◇ _Elle a une nouvelle voiture._ She's got a new car.
nouveau _changes to_ nouvel _before a vowel and most words beginning with "h"._
◇ _Il y a un nouvel élève dans ma classe._ There's a new boy in my class.
- **le nouvel an** New Year

le **nouveau** NOUN
(PL les **nouveaux**)
see also nouveau ADJECTIVE
new pupil ◇ _Il y a plusieurs nouveaux dans la classe._ There are several new pupils in the class.
- **de nouveau** again ◇ _Il pleut de nouveau._ It's raining again.

la **nouveauté** NOUN
novelty

nouvel, nouvelle ADJECTIVE _see_ **nouveau**

la **nouvelle** NOUN
1 _news_ ◇ _Tu connais la nouvelle? Teresa a gagné au loto._ Have you heard the news? Teresa won the lottery.
◇ _C'est une bonne nouvelle._ That's good news.
2 _short story_ ◇ _une nouvelle de Maupassant_ a short story by Maupassant
- **les nouvelles** the news ◇ _J'ai écouté les nouvelles à la radio._ I listened to the news on the radio.
- **avoir des nouvelles de quelqu'un** to hear from somebody ◇ _Je n'ai pas eu de nouvelles de lui._ I haven't heard from him.

la **Nouvelle-Zélande** NOUN
New Zealand

novembre MASC NOUN
November
- **en novembre** in November

e **noyau** NOUN
(PL les **noyaux**)
stone (of fruit) ◇ _un noyau d'abricot_ an apricot stone

le **noyer** NOUN
see also noyer VERB
walnut tree

se **noyer** VERB
see also noyer NOUN
to drown ◇ _Il s'est noyé dans la rivière._ He drowned in the river.

nu ADJECTIVE
1 _naked_ ◇ _Ils se sont baignés nus._ They went for a swim naked. ◇ _tout nus_ stark naked
2 _bare_ ◇ _Elle avait les bras nus._ Her arms were bare. ◇ _Les murs étaient nus._ The walls were bare.

le **nuage** NOUN
cloud
- **un nuage de lait** a drop of milk

nuageux ADJECTIVE
(FEM SING **nuageuse**)
cloudy

nucléaire ADJECTIVE
nuclear ◇ _l'énergie nucléaire_ nuclear power

le/la **nudiste** NOUN
nudist

la **nuit** NOUN
night ◇ _Ils ont fait du bruit toute la nuit._ They were noisy all night.
- **Il fait nuit.** It's dark.
- **cette nuit** tonight • _Il va rentrer cette nuit._ He'll be back tonight.
- **Bonne nuit!** Good night!

nul ADJECTIVE
(FEM SING **nulle**)
rubbish
- **Ce film est nul.** (_informal_) This film's rubbish.
- **un match nul** a draw (_in sport_) ◇ _Ils ont fait match nul._ It was a draw.
- **nulle part** nowhere ◇ _Je ne le vois nulle part._ I can't see it anywhere.

le **numéro** NOUN
number ◇ _J'habite au numéro trois._ I live at number 3.
- **mon numéro de téléphone** my phone number

nu-pieds ADJECTIVE, ADVERB
barefoot ◇ _Il se promenait nu-pieds._ He was walking barefoot.

la **nuque** NOUN
nape of the neck

le **nylon** NOUN
nylon

N

O

obéir VERB
to obey
* **obéir à quelqu'un** to obey somebody ◇ _Elle refuse d'obéir à ses parents._ She refuses to obey her parents.

obéissant ADJECTIVE
obedient

l'**objet** MASC NOUN
object
* **les objets de valeur** valuables
* **les objets trouvés** the lost property office

obligatoire ADJECTIVE
compulsory

obliger VERB
* **obliger quelqu'un à faire quelque chose** to force somebody to do something
* **Je suis bien obligé d'accepter.** I can't really refuse.

obscur ADJECTIVE
dark

l'**obscurité** FEM NOUN
darkness ◇ _dans l'obscurité_ in the dark

l'**obsédé** MASC NOUN
sex maniac
* **un obsédé sexuel** a sex maniac

obséder VERB
to obsess ◇ _Il est obsédé par le travail._ He's obsessed by work.

l'**observation** FEM NOUN
comment ◇ _J'ai une ou deux observations à faire._ I've got one or two comments to make.

observer VERB
1. _to watch_ ◇ _Il observait les canards sur le lac._ He watched the ducks on the lake.
2. _to observe_ ◇ _Ils observent le règlement._ They observe the rules.

l'**obstacle** MASC NOUN
1. _obstacle_ ◇ _surmonter un obstacle_ to overcome an obstacle
2. _fence_ (_in show jumping_)
* **une course d'obstacles** an obstacle race

obtenir VERB
1. _to get_ ◇ _Ils ont obtenu cinquante pour cent des voix._ They got 50% of the votes.
2. _to achieve_ ◇ _Nous avons obtenu de bons résultats._ We achieved good results.

l'**occasion** FEM NOUN
1. _opportunity_ ◇ _C'est une occasion à_ ne pas manquer. It's an opportunity not to be missed.
2. _occasion_ ◇ _à l'occasion de son anniversaire_ on the occasion of his birthday ◇ _à plusieurs occasions_ on several occasions
3. _bargain_ ◇ _Cet ordinateur est une bonne occasion._ This computer's a real bargain.
* **d'occasion** second-hand ◇ _une voiture d'occasion_ a second-hand car

l'**Occident** MASC NOUN
West
* **en Occident** in the West

occidental ADJECTIVE
(MASC PL **occidentaux**)
western
* **les pays occidentaux** the West

l'**occupation** FEM NOUN
occupation ◇ _la France sous l'Occupation_ France during the Occupation

occupé ADJECTIVE
1. _busy_ ◇ _Le directeur est très occupé._ The director's very busy.
2. _taken_ ◇ _Est-ce que cette place est occupée?_ Is this seat taken?
3. _engaged_ ◇ _Les toilettes sont occupées._ The toilet's engaged. ◇ _La ligne est occupée._ The line's engaged.

occuper VERB
to occupy ◇ _Les enfants ne sont pas faciles à occuper quand il pleut._ Children aren't easy to keep occupied when it rains.
* **s'occuper de quelque chose (1)** to be in charge of something ◇ _Elle s'occupe d'un club de sport._ She's in charge of a sports club.
* **s'occuper de quelque chose (2)** to deal with something ◇ _Je vais m'occuper de ce dossier._ I'm going to deal with this file.
* **On s'occupe de vous?** (_in a shop_) Are you being attended to?

l'**océan** MASC NOUN
ocean ◇ _l'océan Indien_ the Indian Ocean

octobre MASC NOUN
October
* **en octobre** in October

l'**odeur** FEM NOUN
smell ◇ _Il y a une drôle d'odeur ici._ There's a funny smell round here.

l'**œil** MASC NOUN
(PL **les yeux**)

eye ◇ *J'ai quelque chose dans l'œil.* I've got something in my eye.
- **à l'œil** *(informal)* for free ◇ *Il est entré à l'œil.* He got in for free.

l'**œillet** MASC NOUN
carnation

l'**œuf** MASC NOUN
egg
- **un œuf à la coque** a soft-boiled egg
- **un œuf dur** a hard-boiled egg
- **un œuf au plat** a fried egg
- **les œufs brouillés** scrambled eggs
- **un œuf de Pâques** an Easter egg

l'**œuvre** FEM NOUN
work ◇ *J'étudie une œuvre de Molière.* I'm studying one of Molière's works.
- **une œuvre d'art** a work of art

offert VERB *see* **offrir**

l'**office** MASC NOUN
- **un office du tourisme** a tourist office

officiel ADJECTIVE
(FEM SING **officielle**)
official

l'**officier** MASC NOUN
officer ◇ *Il est officier de marine.* He's a naval officer.

l'**offre** FEM NOUN
offer ◇ *une offre spéciale* a special offer
- **"offres d'emploi"** "situations vacant"

offrir VERB
- **offrir quelque chose (1)** to offer something ◇ *On lui a offert un poste de secrétaire.* They offered her a secretarial post. ◇ *Elle lui a offert à boire.* She offered him a drink.
- **offrir quelque chose (2)** to give something ◇ *Il lui a offert des roses.* He gave her roses.
- **s'offrir quelque chose** to treat oneself to something ◇ *Je me suis offert une nouvelle paire de chaussures.* I treated myself to a new pair of shoes.

l'**oie** FEM NOUN
goose

l'**oignon** MASC NOUN
onion

l'**oiseau** MASC NOUN
(PL les **oiseaux**)
bird

l'**olive** FEM NOUN
olive ◇ *l'huile d'olive* olive oil

olympique ADJECTIVE
- **les Jeux Olympiques** the Olympic Games

l'**ombre** FEM NOUN
1 *shade* ◇ *Je vais me mettre à l'ombre* I'm going to sit in the shade.

2 *shadow*
- **l'ombre à paupières** eye shadow

l'**omelette** FEM NOUN
omelette

on PRONOUN
1 *we* ◇ *On va à la plage demain.* We're going to the beach tomorrow. ◇ *On a pensé que ça te ferait plaisir.* We thought you'd be pleased.
2 *someone* ◇ *On m'a volé mon porte-monnaie.* Someone has stolen my purse.
- **On m'a dit d'attendre.** I was told to wait.
- **On vous demande au téléphone.** There's a phone call for you.
3 *you* ◇ *On peut visiter le château en été.* You can visit the castle in the summer. ◇ *D'ici on peut voir la côte française.* From here you can see the French coast.

l'**oncle** MASC NOUN
uncle

l'**onde** FEM NOUN
wave (on radio) ◇ *sur les grandes ondes* on long wave

l'**ongle** MASC NOUN
nail
- **se couper les ongles** to cut one's nails ◇ *Elle s'est coupé les ongles.* She cut her nails.

ont VERB *see* **avoir**
- **Ils ont beaucoup d'argent.** They've got lots of money.
- **Elles ont passé de bonnes vacances.** They had a good holiday.

l'**ONU** FEM NOUN (= *Organisation des Nations unies*)
UN (= United Nations)

onze NUMBER
eleven ◇ *Elle a onze ans.* She's eleven. ◇ *à onze heures* at eleven o'clock
- **le onze février** the eleventh of February

onzième ADJECTIVE
eleventh ◇ *au onzième étage* on the eleventh floor

l'**opéra** MASC NOUN
opera

l'**opération** FEM NOUN
operation

opérer VERB
to operate on ◇ *Elle a été opérée de l'appendicite.* She was operated on for appendicitis.
- **se faire opérer** to have an operation ◇ *Elle s'est fait opérer.* She's had an operation.

l'**opinion** FEM NOUN
opinion

opposé ADJECTIVE

see also opposé NOUN

opposite ◇ *Elle est partie dans la direction opposée.* She went off in the opposite direction.

◆ **être opposé à quelque chose** to be opposed to something

l'**opposé** MASC NOUN

see also opposé ADJECTIVE

the opposite

opposer VERB

◆ **opposer quelqu'un à quelqu'un** to pit somebody against somebody ◇ *Ce match oppose les Français aux Allemands.* This match pits the French against the Germans.

◆ **s'opposer** to conflict ◇ *Ces deux points de vue s'opposent.* These two points of view conflict.

◆ **s'opposer à quelque chose** to oppose something ◇ *Son père s'oppose à son mariage.* Her father's against her marriage.

l'**opposition** FEM NOUN
opposition

◆ **par opposition à** as opposed to ◇ *la littérature contemporaine par opposition à la littérature classique* modern literature, as opposed to classics

◆ **faire opposition à un chèque** to stop a cheque

l'**opticien** MASC NOUN
optician ◇ *Il est opticien.* He's an optician.

l'**opticienne** FEM NOUN
optician ◇ *Elle est opticienne.* She's an optician.

optimiste ADJECTIVE
optimistic

l'**option** FEM NOUN
option

◆ **une matière à option** an optional subject

l'**or** MASC NOUN

see also or CONJUNCTION

gold ◇ *un bracelet en or* a gold bracelet

or CONJUNCTION

see also or NOUN

and yet ◇ *Il était sûr de gagner, or il a perdu.* He was sure he would win, and yet he lost.

l'**orage** MASC NOUN
thunderstorm

orageux ADJECTIVE
(FEM SING **orageuse**)
stormy

oral ADJECTIVE
(MASC PL **oraux**)

see also oral NOUN

◆ **une épreuve orale** an oral exam

◆ **à prendre par voie orale** to be taken orally

l'**oral** MASC NOUN
(PL les **oraux**)

see also oral ADJECTIVE

oral (*exam*) ◇ *un oral de français* a French oral

l'**orange** FEM NOUN

see also orange ADJECTIVE

orange (*fruit*)

orange ADJECTIVE (MASC, FEM, PL)

see also orange NOUN

orange (*in colour*) ◇ *des fleurs orange* orange flowers

l'**orchestre** MASC NOUN

[1] *orchestra* ◇ *un orchestre symphonique* a symphony orchestra

[2] *band* ◇ *un orchestre de jazz* a jazz band

ordinaire ADJECTIVE

see also ordinaire NOUN

[1] *ordinary* ◇ *des gens ordinaires* ordinary people

[2] *standard* ◇ *un format ordinaire* a standard size

l'**ordinaire** MASC NOUN

see also ordinaire ADJECTIVE

two-star (petrol)

◆ **sortir de l'ordinaire** to be out of the ordinary

l'**ordinateur** MASC NOUN
computer

l'**ordonnance** FEM NOUN
prescription

ordonné ADJECTIVE
tidy

ordonner VERB

◆ **ordonner à quelqu'un de faire quelque chose** to order somebody to do something ◇ *Il m'a ordonné de sortir.* He ordered me to leave.

l'**ordre** MASC NOUN

order ◇ *par ordre alphabétique* in alphabetical order

◆ **mettre en ordre** to tidy up

◆ **jusqu'à nouvel ordre** until further notice

les **ordures** FEM NOUN
rubbish

◆ **jeter quelque chose aux ordures** to throw something in the bin

l'**oreille** FEM NOUN
ear

l'**oreiller** MASC NOUN
pillow

les **oreillons** MASC NOUN
  mumps
l'**organe** MASC NOUN
  organ (in body)
l'**organisateur** MASC NOUN
  organizer
l'**organisation** FEM NOUN
  organization
l'**organisatrice** FEM NOUN
  organizer
  organiser VERB
  to organize
  • **s'organiser** to get organized ◇ *Il ne sait pas s'organiser.* He can't get himself organized.
l'**organisme** MASC NOUN
  body (organization)
l'**orgue** MASC NOUN
  organ ◇ *Carl joue de l'orgue.* Carl plays the organ.
  orgueilleux ADJECTIVE
  (FEM SING **orgueilleuse**)
  proud
l'**Orient** MASC NOUN
  East
  • **en Orient** in the East
  oriental ADJECTIVE
  (MASC PL **orientaux**)
  1 *oriental* ◇ *un palais oriental* an oriental palace
  2 *eastern* ◇ *la frontière orientale de la Pologne* Poland's eastern border
l'**orientation** FEM NOUN
  orientation
  • **avoir le sens de l'orientation** to have a good sense of direction
  • **l'orientation professionnelle** careers advice
  originaire ADJECTIVE
  • **Elle est originaire de Paris.** She's from Paris.
  original ADJECTIVE
  (MASC PL **originaux**)
  see also original NOUN
  original ◇ *un film en version originale* a film in the original language
l'**original** MASC NOUN
  (PL les **originaux**)
  see also original ADJECTIVE
  original ◇ *L'original est au Louvre.* The original is in the Louvre.
  • **un vieil original** an old eccentric
l'**origine** FEM NOUN
  origin
  • **à l'origine** originally
l'**orphelin** MASC NOUN
  orphan
l'**orpheline** FEM NOUN
  orphan

l'**orteil** MASC NOUN
  toe
l'**orthographe** FEM NOUN
  spelling
l'**os** MASC NOUN
  bone
  oser VERB
  to dare
  • **oser faire quelque chose** to dare to do something
l'**otage** MASC NOUN
  hostage
  ôter VERB
  1 *to take off* ◇ *Elle a ôté son manteau.* She took off her coat.
  2 *to take away*
  ou CONJUNCTION
  or
  • **ou...ou...** either...or...
  • **ou bien** or else ◇ *On pourrait aller au cinéma ou bien rentrer directement.* We could go to the cinema or else go straight home.
  où PRONOUN, ADVERB
  1 *where* ◇ *Où est Nick?* Where's Nick? ◇ *Où allez-vous?* Where are you going? ◇ *Je sais où il est.* I know where he is. ◇ *C'est la maison où je suis né.* That's the house where I was born. ◇ *la ville d'où je viens* the town I come from
  2 *that* ◇ *Le jour où il est parti, tout le monde a pleuré.* The day that he left, everyone cried.
  • **Par où allons-nous passer?** Which way are we going to go?
l'**ouate** FEM NOUN
  cotton wool
  oublier VERB
  1 *to forget* ◇ *N'oublie pas de fermer la porte.* Don't forget to shut the door.
  2 *to leave* ◇ *J'ai oublié mon sac chez Sabine.* I left my bag at Sabine's.
l'**ouest** MASC NOUN
  see also ouest ADJECTIVE
  west ◇ *Elle vit dans l'ouest de l'Angleterre.* She lives in the West of England.
  • **à l'ouest de Paris** west of Paris
  • **vers l'ouest** westwards
  • **l'Europe de l'Ouest** Western Europe
  • **le vent d'ouest** the west wind
  ouest ADJECTIVE (MASC, FEM, PL)
  see also ouest NOUN
  1 *west* ◇ *la côte ouest de l'Écosse* the west coast of Scotland
  2 *western* ◇ *la partie ouest du pays* the western part of the country
  ouf EXCLAMATION
  phew!

oui   ADVERB
yes

l' **ouragan**   MASC NOUN
hurricane

l' **ourlet**   MASC NOUN
seam

l' **ours**   MASC NOUN
bear

* **un ours en peluche** a teddy bear

l' **outil**   MASC NOUN
tool

ouvert   VERB   *see* **ouvrir**

ouvert   ADJECTIVE
1 *open* ◇ *Le magasin est ouvert.* The shop's open.
2 *on* ◇ *Il a laissé le robinet ouvert.* He left the tap on.

* **avoir l'esprit ouvert** to be open-minded

l' **ouverture**   FEM NOUN *opening* ◇ *les heures d'ouverture* opening hours

l' **ouvre-boîte**   MASC NOUN
tin opener

l' **ouvre-bouteille**   MASC NOUN
bottle-opener

l' **ouvrier**   NOUN
worker ◇ *Son père est ouvrier dans une usine.* His father's a factory worker.

l' **ouvrière**   NOUN
worker

ouvrir   VERB
to open ◇ *Ouvrez!* Open up! ◇ *Elle a ouvert la porte.* She opened the door.

* **s'ouvrir** to open ◇ *La porte s'est ouverte.* The door opened.

l' **ovni**   MASC NOUN (= *objet volant non identifié*)
UFO

l' **oxygène**   MASC NOUN
oxygen

P

le **Pacifique** NOUN
Pacific ◇ *l'océan Pacifique* the Pacific Ocean

la **pagaille** NOUN
mess SING ◇ *Quelle pagaille!* What a mess!

la **page** NOUN
page ◇ *Tournez la page.* Turn the page.

la **paie** NOUN
wages

le **paiement** NOUN
payment

le **paillasson** NOUN
doormat

la **paille** NOUN
straw

le **pain** NOUN
1 *bread* ◇ *un morceau de pain* a piece of bread ◇ *une tranche de pain* a slice of bread
2 *loaf* ◇ *J'ai acheté un pain.* I bought a loaf of bread.
* **le pain complet** wholemeal bread
* **le pain d'épice** gingerbread
* **le pain de mie** sandwich loaf
* **le pain grillé** toast

pair ADJECTIVE
even ◇ *un nombre pair* an even number
* **une jeune fille au pair** an au pair

la **paire** NOUN
pair ◇ *une paire de chaussures* a pair of shoes

paisible ADJECTIVE
peaceful ◇ *un village paisible* a peaceful village

la **paix** NOUN
peace
* **faire la paix (1)** to make peace ◇ *Les deux pays ont fait la paix.* The two countries have made peace with each other.
* **faire la paix (2)** to make it up ◇ *Laure a fait la paix avec son frère.* Laure made it up with her brother.
* **avoir la paix** to have peace and quiet ◇ *J'aimerais bien avoir la paix.* I'd like to have a bit of peace and quiet.
* **Fiche-lui la paix!** (*informal*) Leave him alone!

le **palais** NOUN
1 *palace* ◇ *le palais de Buckingham* Buckingham Palace
2 *palate* (*in mouth*)

pâle ADJECTIVE

pale ◇ *bleu pâle* pale blue

la **Palestine** NOUN
Palestine

la **pâleur** NOUN
paleness

le **palier** NOUN
landing ◇ *Il m'attendait sur le palier.* He was waiting for me on the landing.

pâlir VERB
to go pale

la **palme** NOUN
flipper (*for swimming*)

palmé ADJECTIVE
webbed ◇ *Les canards ont les pieds palmés.* Ducks have webbed feet.

le **palmier** NOUN
palm tree

palpitant ADJECTIVE
thrilling ◇ *un roman palpitant* a thrilling novel

le **pamplemousse** NOUN
grapefruit

le **panaché** NOUN
shandy

la **pancarte** NOUN
sign ◇ *Il y a une pancarte dans la vitrine.* There's a sign in the window.

pané ADJECTIVE
fried in breadcrumbs ◇ *du poisson pané* fish in breadcrumbs

le **panier** NOUN
basket

la **panique** NOUN
panic

paniquer VERB
to panic

la **panne** NOUN
breakdown
* **être en panne** to have broken down ◇ *L'ascenseur est en panne.* The lift's not working.
* **tomber en panne** to break down ◇ *Nous sommes tombés en panne sur l'autoroute.* We broke down on the motorway. ◇ *Nous sommes tombés en panne d'essence.* We've run out of petrol.
* **une panne de courant** a power cut

le **panneau** NOUN
(PL les **panneaux**)
sign ◇ *Ce panneau dit que la maison est à vendre.* This sign says that the house is for sale.
* **panneau d'affichage (1)** advertising hoarding
* **panneau d'affichage (2)** arrivals and

departures board (*in station*)

le **panorama** NOUN
panorama

le **pansement** NOUN
1 *dressing* (*bandage*)
2 *sticking plaster*

le **pantalon** NOUN
trousers PL ◇ *Son pantalon est trop court.* His trousers are too short.
* **un pantalon de ski** a pair of ski pants

la **panthère** NOUN
panther

la **pantoufle** NOUN
slipper

le **paon** NOUN
peacock

le **papa** NOUN
dad

le **pape** NOUN
pope

la **papeterie** NOUN
stationer's

le **papi** NOUN (*informal*)
granddad

le **papier** NOUN
paper ◇ *une feuille de papier* a sheet of paper
* **Vos papiers, s'il vous plaît.** Your identity papers, please.
* **les papiers d'identité** identity papers
* **le papier à lettres** writing paper
* **le papier hygiénique** toilet paper
* **le papier peint** wallpaper

le **papillon** NOUN
butterfly

le **paquebot** NOUN
liner

la **pâquerette** NOUN
daisy

Pâques MASC NOUN
Easter ◇ *Je viendrai te voir à Pâques.* I'll come and see you at Easter.
* **les œufs de Pâques** Easter eggs

In France, Easter eggs are said to be brought by the Easter bells or **cloches de Pâques** which fly from Rome and drop them in people's gardens.

le **paquet** NOUN
1 *packet* ◇ *Je voudrais un paquet de cigarettes.* I'd like a packet of cigarettes.
2 *parcel* ◇ *Sa mère lui a envoyé un paquet.* His mother sent him a parcel.

le **paquet-cadeau** NOUN
(PL les **paquets-cadeaux**)
gift-wrapped parcel ◇ *La vendeuse m'a fait un paquet-cadeau.* The shop assistant gift-wrapped it for me.

par PREPOSITION
1 *by* ◇ *Le Tour de France a été*
remporté par un Écossais. The Tour de France was won by a Scotsman.
* **deux par deux** two by two ◇ *Les élèves sont entrés deux par deux.* The pupils went in two by two.
2 *with* ◇ *Son nom commence par un H.* His name begins with H.
3 *out of* ◇ *Elle regardait par la fenêtre.* She was looking out of the window.
◇ *par habitude* out of habit
4 *via* ◇ *Nous sommes passés par Lyon pour aller à Grenoble.* We went via Lyons to Grenoble.
5 *through* ◇ *Il faut passer par la douane avant de prendre l'avion.* You have to go through customs before boarding the plane.
6 *per* ◇ *Prenez trois cachets par jour.* Take three tablets per day. ◇ *Le voyage coûte deux mille francs par personne.* The trip costs two thousand francs per person.
* **par ici (1)** this way ◇ *Il faut passer par ici pour y arriver.* You have to go this way to get there.
* **par ici (2)** round here ◇ *Il y a beaucoup de touristes par ici.* There are lots of tourists round here.
* **par-ci, par-là** here and there

le **parachute** NOUN
parachute

le/la **parachutiste** NOUN
parachutist

le **paradis** NOUN
heaven

les **parages** MASC NOUN
* **dans les parages** in the area ◇ *Il n'y a pas d'hôtel dans les parages.* There are no hotels in the area.

le **paragraphe** NOUN
paragraph

paraître VERB
1 *to seem* ◇ *Ça paraît incroyable.* It seems unbelievable.
2 *to look* ◇ *Elle paraît plus jeune que son frère.* She looks younger than her brother.
* **il paraît que** it seems that ◇ *Il paraît que c'est la faute de la direction.* It seems that it's the management's fault.

le **parallèle** NOUN
see also la **parallèle**
parallel ◇ *Il a fait un parallèle entre ces deux événements.* He drew a parallel between the two events.

la **parallèle** NOUN
see also le **parallèle**
parallel line

paralysé ADJECTIVE

paralysed

le **parapluie** NOUN
umbrella

le **parasol** NOUN
parasol

le **parc** NOUN
[1] *park* ◇ *Le dimanche, Chantal va se promener au parc.* On Sundays Chantal goes for a walk in the park.
- **un parc d'attractions** an amusement park
[2] *grounds* ◇ *Le château est situé au milieu d'un grand parc.* The castle is surrounded by extensive grounds.

parce que CONJUNCTION
because ◇ *Il n'est pas venu parce qu'il n'avait pas de voiture.* He didn't come because he didn't have a car.

le **parcmètre** NOUN
parking meter

parcourir VERB
[1] *to cover* ◇ *Gavin a parcouru cinquante kilomètres à vélo.* Gavin covered 50 kilometres on his bike.
[2] *to glance through* ◇ *J'ai parcouru le journal d'aujourd'hui.* I glanced through today's newspaper.

le **parcours** NOUN
journey

par-dessous ADVERB
underneath ◇ *Il portait un pull et une chemise par-dessous.* He was wearing a jumper with a shirt underneath.

le **pardessus** NOUN
overcoat

par-dessus ADVERB, PREPOSITION
[1] *on top* ◇ *Elle porte un chemisier et un pull rouge par-dessus.* She's wearing a blouse with a red jumper on top.
[2] *over* ◇ *Elle a sauté par-dessus le mur.* She jumped over the wall.
- **en avoir par-dessus la tête** to have had enough ◇ *J'en ai par-dessus la tête de tous ces problèmes.* I've had enough of all these problems.

pardon NOUN
see also pardon EXCLAMATION
forgiveness

pardon EXCLAMATION
see also pardon NOUN
[1] *sorry!* ◇ *Oh, pardon! J'espère que je ne vous ai pas fait mal.* Oh, sorry! I hope I didn't hurt you.
- **demander pardon à quelqu'un** to apologize to somebody ◇ *Il leur a demandé pardon.* He apologized to them.
- **Je vous demande pardon.** I'm sorry.
[2] *excuse me!* ◇ *Pardon, madame!*

Pouvez-vous me dire où se trouve la poste? Excuse me! Could you tell me where the post office is?
[3] *pardon?* ◇ *Pardon? Je n'ai pas compris ce que vous avez dit.* Pardon? I didn't understand what you said.

pardonner VERB
to forgive ◇ *Nous lui avons pardonné de nous avoir menti.* We forgave him for lying to us.

le **pare-brise** NOUN
(PL. les **pare-brise**)
windscreen

le **pare-chocs** NOUN
bumper

pareil ADJECTIVE
(FEM SING **pareille**)
[1] *the same* ◇ *Ces deux maisons ne sont pas pareilles.* These two houses aren't the same.
[2] *like that* ◇ *J'aime bien sa voiture. J'en voudrais une pareille.* I like his car. I'd like one like that.
[3] *such* ◇ *Je refuse d'écouter des bêtises pareilles.* I won't listen to such nonsense.
- **sans pareil** unequalled ◇ *Il a joué cette symphonie avec un talent sans pareil.* He played this symphony with unequalled talent.

la **parenthèse** NOUN
bracket ◇ *entre parenthèses* in brackets

les **parents** MASC NOUN
parents

la **paresse** NOUN
laziness

paresseux ADJECTIVE
(FEM SING **paresseuse**)
lazy

parfait ADJECTIVE
perfect

parfaitement ADVERB
perfectly ◇ *Il parle parfaitement l'arabe.* He speaks perfect Arabic.

parfois ADVERB
sometimes

le **parfum** NOUN
[1] *perfume*
[2] *flavour* ◇ *Je voudrais une glace.—Quel parfum veux-tu?* I'd like an ice cream.—What flavour would you like?

parfumé ADJECTIVE
[1] *fragrant* ◇ *une rose très parfumée* a very fragrant rose
[2] *flavoured* ◇ *des biscuits parfumés au café* coffee-flavoured biscuits

la **parfumerie** NOUN

P

perfume shop

le **pari** NOUN
bet

parier VERB
to bet

Paris NOUN
Paris

- **à Paris (1)** in Paris
- **à Paris (2)** to Paris

parisien ADJECTIVE, NOUN
(FEM SING **parisienne**)
[1] *Parisian* ⋄ *un célèbre couturier parisien* a famous Parisian designer
[2] *Paris* ⋄ *le métro parisien* the Paris metro
- **un Parisien** a Parisian (*man*)
- **une Parisienne** a Parisian (*woman*)

le **parking** NOUN
car park

le **parlement** NOUN
parliament

parler VERB
[1] *to speak* ⋄ *Vous parlez français?* Do you speak French?
[2] *to talk* ⋄ *Nous étions en train de parler quand le directeur est entré.* We were talking when the headmaster came in.
- **parler de quelque chose à quelqu'un** to tell somebody about something ⋄ *Il m'a parlé de sa nouvelle voiture.* He told me about his new car.

parmi PREPOSITION
among ⋄ *Ils étaient parmi les meilleurs de la classe.* They were among the best pupils in the class.

la **paroi** NOUN
wall

la **paroisse** NOUN
parish

la **parole** NOUN
[1] *speech* ⋄ *l'usage de la parole* the power of speech
[2] *word* ⋄ *Il m'a donné sa parole.* He gave me his word. ⋄ *Elle a tenu parole.* She kept her word.
- **les paroles** lyrics ⋄ *J'aime les paroles de cette chanson.* I like the lyrics of this song.

le **parquet** NOUN
floor (*wooden*)

le **parrain** NOUN
godfather

parrainer VERB
to sponsor ⋄ *Cette entreprise parraine notre équipe de rugby.* This firm is sponsoring our rugby team.

pars VERB *see* **partir**

la **part** NOUN

[1] *share* ⋄ *Vous n'avez pas eu votre part.* You haven't had your share.
[2] *piece* ⋄ *une part de gâteau* a piece of cake
- **prendre part à quelque chose** to take part in something ⋄ *Il va prendre part à la réunion.* He's going to take part in the meeting.
- **de la part de (1)** on behalf of ⋄ *Je dois vous remercier de la part de mon frère.* I must thank you on behalf of my brother.
- **de la part de (2)** from ⋄ *C'est un cadeau pour toi, de la part de Françoise.* It's a present for you, from Françoise.
- **à part** except ⋄ *Ils sont tous venus, à part Christian.* They all came, except Christian.

partager VERB
[1] *to share* ⋄ *Ils partagent un appartement.* They share a flat.
[2] *to divide* ⋄ *Janet a partagé le gâteau en quatre.* Janet divided the cake into four.

le/la **partenaire** NOUN
partner

le **parti** NOUN
party ⋄ *le Parti socialiste* the Socialist Party

le **participant** NOUN
participant

la **participante** NOUN
participant

la **participation** NOUN
participation

le **participe** NOUN
participle
- **le participe passé** the past participle
- **le participe présent** the present participle

participer VERB
- **participer à quelque chose (1)** to take part in something ⋄ *André va participer à la course.* André is going to take part in the race.
- **participer à quelque chose (2)** to contribute to something ⋄ *Je voudrais participer aux frais.* I would like to contribute to the cost.

la **particularité** NOUN
characteristic

particulier ADJECTIVE
(FEM SING **particulière**)
[1] *private* ⋄ *une maison particulière* a private house
[2] *distinctive* ⋄ *Ce vin a un arôme particulier.* This wine has a distinctive flavour.
[3] *particular* ⋄ *Dans ce cas particulier,*

je ne peux rien faire. In this particular case, I can't do anything.
- **en particulier (1)** particularly ◊ *J'aime les fruits, en particulier les fraises.* I like fruit, particularly strawberries.
- **en particulier (2)** in private ◊ *Est-ce que je peux vous parler en particulier?* Can I speak to you in private?

particulièrement ADVERB
particularly

la **partie** NOUN
1 *part* ◊ *Une partie du groupe partira en Italie.* Part of the group will go to Italy.
2 *game* ◊ *Nous avons fait une partie de tennis.* We played a game of tennis. ◊ *une partie de cartes* a game of cards
- **en partie** partly ◊ *Cela explique en partie le problème.* That partly explains the problem.
- **en grande partie** largely ◊ *Son histoire est en grande partie vraie.* His story is largely true.
- **faire partie de** to be part of ◊ *Ce tableau fait partie d'une très belle collection.* This picture is part of a very beautiful collection.

partiel ADJECTIVE
(FEM SING **partielle**)
partial

partir VERB
to go ◊ *Je lui ai téléphoné mais il était déjà parti.* I phoned him but he'd already gone.
- **partir en vacances** to go on holiday
- **partir de** to leave ◊ *Il est parti de Nice à sept heures.* He left Nice at 7.
- **à partir de** from ◊ *Je serai chez moi à partir de huit heures.* I'll be at home from eight o'clock onwards.

la **partition** NOUN
score (*in music*) ◊ *une partition de piano* a piano score

partout ADVERB
everywhere

paru VERB *see* **paraître**

a **parution** NOUN
publication ◊ *Ce roman a eu beaucoup de succès dès sa parution.* This novel was very successful from the moment it came out.

parvenir VERB
- **parvenir à faire quelque chose** to manage to do something ◊ *Elle est finalement parvenue à ouvrir la porte.* She finally managed to open the door.
- **faire parvenir quelque chose à quelqu'un** to send something to

somebody ◊ *Je vous ferai parvenir le colis avant lundi.* I'll send you the parcel before Monday.

pas ADVERB
[see also **pas** NOUN]
- **ne...pas** not ◊ *Il ne pleut pas.* It's not raining. ◊ *Elle n'est pas venue.* She didn't come. ◊ *Ils n'ont pas de voiture.* They haven't got a car.
- **Vous viendrez à notre soirée, n'est-ce pas?** You're coming to our party, aren't you?
- **C'est Harry qui a gagné, n'est-ce pas?** Harry won, didn't he?
- **pas moi** not me ◊ *Elle veut aller au cinéma, pas moi.* She wants to go to the cinema, but I don't.
- **pas du tout** not at all ◊ *Je n'aime pas du tout ça.* I don't like that at all.
- **pas mal** not bad ◊ *Ce n'est pas mal pour un début.* That's not bad for a first attempt. ◊ *Comment allez-vous? – Pas mal.* How are you? – Not bad.
- **pas mal de** quite a lot of ◊ *Il y avait pas mal de monde au concert.* There were quite a lot of people at the concert.

le **pas** NOUN
[see also **pas** ADVERB]
1 *pace* ◊ *Il marchait d'un pas rapide.* He walked at a fast pace.
2 *step* ◊ *Faites trois pas en avant.* Take three steps forward.
3 *footstep* ◊ *J'entends des pas dans l'escalier.* I can hear footsteps on the stairs.
- **au pas** at walking pace ◊ *Le cheval est parti au pas.* The horse set off at walking pace.
- **faire les cent pas** to pace up and down ◊ *Il faisait les cent pas dans le corridor.* He was pacing up and down the corridor.

le **passage** NOUN
passage ◊ *J'ai traduit un passage de ce livre.* I translated a passage from this book.
- **Il a été éclaboussé au passage de la voiture.** He was soaked by a passing car.
- **de passage** passing through ◊ *Nous sommes de passage à Toulouse.* We're just passing through Toulouse.
- **un passage clouté** a pedestrian crossing
- **un passage souterrain** a subway

passager ADJECTIVE
(FEM SING **passagère**)
[see also **passager** NOUN]
temporary

le **passager** NOUN
> see also passager ADJECTIVE

passenger
* **un passager clandestin** a stowaway

la **passagère** NOUN
passenger

le **passant** NOUN
passer-by

la **passante** NOUN
passer-by

passé ADJECTIVE
> see also passé NOUN

[1] _last_ ◇ _Je l'ai vu la semaine passée._ I saw him last week.

[2] _past_ ◇ _Il est minuit passé._ It's past midnight.

le **passé** NOUN
> see also passé ADJECTIVE

[1] _past_ ◇ _dans le passé_ in the past

[2] _past tense_ ◇ _Mettez ce verbe au passé._ Put this verb into the past tense.
* **le passé composé** the perfect tense
* **le passé simple** the past historic

le **passeport** NOUN
passport

passer VERB

[1] _to cross_ ◇ _Nous avons passé la frontière belge._ We crossed the Belgian border.

[2] _to go through_ ◇ _Il faut passer la douane en sortant._ You have to go through customs on the way out.

[3] _to take_ ◇ _Gordon a passé ses examens la semaine dernière._ Gordon took his exams last week.

[4] _to spend_ ◇ _Elle a passé la journée à ne rien faire._ She spent the day doing nothing. ◇ _Ils passent toujours leurs vacances au Danemark._ They always spend their holidays in Denmark.

[5] _to pass_ ◇ _Passe-moi le sel, s'il te plaît._ Pass me the salt, please.

[6] _to show_ ◇ _On passe "Le Kid" au cinéma cette semaine._ They're showing "The Kid" at the cinema this week.

[7] _to call in_ ◇ _Je passerai chez vous ce soir._ I'll call in this evening.
* **Ne quittez pas, je vous passe Madame Chevalier.** Hold on please, I'm putting you through to Mrs Chevalier.
* **passer par** to go through ◇ _Ils sont passés par Paris pour aller à Tours._ They went through Paris to get to Tours.
* **en passant** in passing ◇ _Je lui ai dit en passant que j'allais me marier._ I told him in passing that I was getting married.
* **laisser passer** to let through ◇ _Il m'a laissé passer._ He let me through.
* **se passer (1)** to take place ◇ _Cette_

histoire se passe au moyen âge. This story takes place in the Middle Ages.
* **se passer (2)** to go ◇ _Comment se sont passés tes examens?_ How did your exams go?
* **se passer (3)** to happen ◇ _Que s'est-il passé? Un accident?_ What happened? Was there an accident?
* **Qu'est-ce qui se passe? Pourquoi est-ce qu'elle pleure?** What's the matter? Why is she crying?
* **se passer de** to do without ◇ _Je me passerai de café ce matin._ I'll do without coffee this morning.

la **passerelle** NOUN

[1] _footbridge_ (over river)

[2] _gangway_ (onto plane, boat)

le **passe-temps** NOUN
pastime

passif ADJECTIVE
(FEM SING **passive**)
> see also passif NOUN

passive

le **passif** NOUN
> see also passif ADJECTIVE

passive ◇ _Mettez ce verbe au passif._ Put this verb into the passive.

la **passion** NOUN
passion

passionnant ADJECTIVE
fascinating

passionné ADJECTIVE
keen ◇ _Donald est un lecteur passionné._ Donald is a keen reader.
* **Il est passionné de voile.** He's a sailing fanatic.

passionner VERB
* **Son travail le passionne.** He's passionate about his work.
* **se passionner pour quelque chose** to have a passion for something ◇ _Harry se passionne pour les perroquets._ Harry has a passion for parrots.

la **passoire** NOUN
sieve

la **pastèque** NOUN
watermelon

le **pasteur** NOUN
minister (priest)

la **patate** NOUN (informal)
potato
* **une patate douce** a sweet potato

la **pâte** NOUN

[1] _pastry_

[2] _dough_

[3] _cake mixture_
* **la pâte à crêpes** pancake batter
* **la pâte à modeler** Plasticine ®
* **la pâte d'amandes** marzipan

le pâté NOUN
pâté ◇ *Nous avons mangé du pâté en entrée.* We had pâté as a starter.
* **un pâté de maisons** a block (*of houses*)

paternel ADJECTIVE
(FEM SING **paternelle**)
* **ma grand-mère paternelle** my father's mother
* **mon oncle paternel** my father's brother

les pâtes FEM NOUN
pasta

la patience NOUN
patience

patient ADJECTIVE
see also patient NOUN
patient

le patient NOUN
see also patient ADJECTIVE
patient

la patiente NOUN
patient

patienter VERB
to wait ◇ *Veuillez patienter un instant, s'il vous plaît.* Please wait a moment.

le patin NOUN
1 *skate* ◇ *Nic a enfilé ses patins.* Nic put her skates on.
2 *skating* ◇ *Ils font du patin tous les mercredis.* They go skating every Wednesday.
* **les patins à glace** ice skates
* **les patins à roulettes** roller skates

le patinage NOUN
skating
* **le patinage artistique** figure skating

patiner VERB
to skate

le patineur NOUN
skater

la patineuse NOUN
skater

la patinoire NOUN
ice rink

la pâtisserie NOUN
cake shop
* **faire de la pâtisserie** to bake
◇ *J'adore faire de la pâtisserie.* I love baking.
* **les pâtisseries** cakes

le pâtissier NOUN
confectioner

la pâtissière NOUN
confectioner

la patrie NOUN
homeland

le patron NOUN
1 *boss*
2 *pattern* (for dressmaking)

la patronne NOUN
boss
* **Elle est patronne de café.** She runs a café.

patronner VERB
to sponsor ◇ *Le festival est patronné par des entreprises locales.* The festival is sponsored by local businesses.

la patrouille NOUN
patrol

la patte NOUN
1 *paw* (of dog, cat)
2 *leg* (of bird, animal)

paumer VERB (informal)
to lose ◇ *J'ai paumé mes clefs.* I've lost my keys.

la paupière NOUN
eyelid

la pause NOUN
1 *break* ◇ *Ils font une pause.* They're having a break.
2 *pause* ◇ *Il y a eu une pause dans la conversation.* There was a pause in the conversation.

pauvre ADJECTIVE
poor ◇ *Sa famille est pauvre.* His family is poor. ◇ *Pauvre Jean-Pierre! Il n'a pas eu de chance!* Poor Jean-Pierre! He was unlucky!

la pauvreté NOUN
poverty

pavé ADJECTIVE
cobbled ◇ *Les rues étaient pavées.* The streets were cobbled.

le pavillon NOUN
house ◇ *Ils habitent un pavillon de banlieue.* They've got a house in the suburbs.

payant ADJECTIVE
paying ◇ *Ce sont des hôtes payants.* They're paying guests.
* **C'est payant.** You have to pay.
◇ *L'entrée de la boîte est payante.* You have to pay to get into the nightclub.

la paye NOUN
wages

payer VERB
1 *to pay for* ◇ *Combien as-tu payé ta voiture?* How much did you pay for your car?
* **J'ai payé ce T-shirt vingt francs.** I paid 20 francs for this T-shirt.
2 *to pay* ◇ *Elle a été payée aujourd'hui.* She got paid today. ◇ *Son métier paye bien.* His job pays good money.
* **faire payer quelque chose à quelqu'un** to charge somebody for something
◇ *Il me l'a fait payer dix francs.* He

P

charged me 10 francs for it.

- **payer quelque chose à quelqu'un** to buy somebody something ◇ *Allez, je vous paye un verre.* Come on, I'll buy you a drink.

le **pays** NOUN
country
- **du pays** local ◇ *le vin du pays* the local wine

le **paysage** NOUN
landscape

le **paysan** NOUN
farmer

la **paysanne** NOUN
farmer

les **Pays-Bas** MASC NOUN
Netherlands
- **aux Pays-Bas (1)** in the Netherlands
- **aux Pays-Bas (2)** to the Netherlands

le **Pays de Galles** NOUN
Wales
- **au Pays de Galles (1)** in Wales ◇ *Daphne habite au Pays de Galles.* Daphne lives in Wales.
- **au Pays de Galles (2)** to Wales ◇ *Elle part au Pays de Galles la semaine prochaine.* She is going to Wales next week.

le **PC** NOUN
see also PC ABBREVIATION
PC (= personal computer) ◇ *Il a tapé le rapport sur son PC.* He typed the report on his PC.
PC ABBREVIATION (= *Parti communiste*)
see also PC NOUN
Communist Party

le **PDG** ABBREVIATION (= *président-directeur général*)
MD (= managing director)

le **péage** NOUN
1 *toll* ◇ *Nous avons payé cinquante francs de péage.* We paid a toll of 50 francs.
2 *tollbooth* ◇ *Sabine s'est arrêtée au péage de l'autoroute.* Sabine stopped at the motorway tollbooth.
French motorways charge a toll.

la **peau** NOUN
(PL les **peaux**)
skin ◇ *Elle a la peau douce.* She's got soft skin.

le/la **Peau-Rouge** NOUN
(PL les **Peaux-Rouges**)
Red Indian

la **pêche** NOUN
1 *peach*
2 *fishing*
- **aller à la pêche** to go fishing
- **la pêche à la ligne** angling

le **péché** NOUN
sin

pêcher VERB
1 *to fish for* ◇ *Ils sont partis pêcher la truite.* They've gone fishing for trout.
2 *to catch* ◇ *Jacques a pêché deux saumons.* Jacques caught two salmon.

le **pêcheur** NOUN
fisherman ◇ *Son père est pêcheur.* His father's a fisherman.
- **un pêcheur à la ligne** an angler

pédagogique ADJECTIVE
educational

la **pédale** NOUN
pedal

pédestre ADJECTIVE
- **une randonnée pédestre** a ramble

le **peigne** NOUN
comb

peigner VERB
to comb ◇ *Elle peigne sa poupée.* She's combing her doll's hair.
- **se peigner** to comb one's hair ◇ *Il faut que je me peigne.* I must comb my hair.

le **peignoir** NOUN
dressing gown
- **un peignoir de bain** a bathrobe

peindre VERB
to paint

la **peine** NOUN
trouble
- **avoir de la peine à faire quelque chose** to have trouble doing something ◇ *J'ai eu beaucoup de peine à la convaincre.* I had a lot of trouble convincing her.
- **se donner de la peine** to make a real effort ◇ *Il s'est donné beaucoup de peine pour obtenir ces renseignements.* He made a real effort to get this information.
- **prendre la peine de faire quelque chose** to go to the trouble of doing something ◇ *Il a pris la peine de me rapporter ma valise.* He went to the trouble of returning my case to me.
- **faire de la peine à quelqu'un** to upset somebody ◇ *Ça me fait de la peine de la voir pleurer.* It upsets me to see her crying.
- **ce n'est pas la peine** there's no point ◇ *Ce n'est pas la peine de téléphoner.* There's no point in phoning.
- **à peine (1)** hardly ◇ *J'ai à peine eu le temps de me changer.* I hardly had time to get changed.
- **à peine (2)** only just ◇ *Elle vient à peine de se lever.* She's only just got

up.

le **peintre** NOUN
painter

la **peinture** NOUN

1 *painting* ◇ On expose des peintures de Gautier au musée. There's an exhibition of Gautier's paintings at the museum.

2 *paint* ◇ J'ai acheté de la peinture verte. I bought some green paint.

• "peinture fraîche" "wet paint"

pêle-mêle ADVERB
higgledy-piggledy

la **pelle** NOUN

1 *shovel*
2 *spade*

la **pellicule** NOUN
film ◇ une pellicule couleur a colour film

es **pellicules** FEM NOUN
dandruff SING

la **pelote** NOUN
ball ◇ une pelote de laine a ball of wool

la **pelouse** NOUN
lawn

la **peluche** NOUN

• un animal en peluche a soft toy

pencher VERB
to tilt ◇ Ce tableau penche vers la droite. The picture's tilting to the right.

• se pencher (1) to lean over ◇ Françoise s'est penchée sur son cahier. Françoise leant over her exercise book.

• se pencher (2) to bend down ◇ Il s'est penché pour ramasser sa casquette. He bent down to pick his cap up.

• se pencher (3) to lean out ◇ Annick s'est penchée par la fenêtre. Annick leant out of the window.

pendant PREPOSITION
during ◇ Ça s'est passé pendant l'été. It happened during the summer.

• pendant que while ◇ Christian a téléphoné pendant que Chantal prenait son bain. Christian phoned while Chantal was having a bath.

pendentif NOUN
pendant

penderie NOUN
wardrobe (for hanging clothes)

pendre VERB
to hang ◇ Il a pendu sa veste dans l'armoire. He hung his jacket in the wardrobe.

• pendre quelqu'un to hang somebody ◇ L'assassin a été pendu. The murderer was hanged.

pendule NOUN *clock*

pénétrer VERB

1 *to enter* ◇ Ils ont pénétré dans la maison en passant par le jardin. They entered the house through the garden.

2 *to penetrate* ◇ L'armée a pénétré sur le territoire ennemi. The army penetrated enemy territory.

pénible ADJECTIVE
hard ◇ Travailler sur un chantier est pénible. Working on a building site is hard.

• Il est vraiment pénible. He's a real nuisance.

péniblement ADVERB
with difficulty

la **péniche** NOUN
barge

le **pénis** NOUN
penis

la **pénombre** NOUN
half-light

la **pensée** NOUN
thought ◇ Il était perdu dans ses pensées. He was lost in thought.

penser VERB
to think ◇ Je pense que Yann a eu raison de partir. I think Yann was right to leave.

• penser à quelque chose to think about something • Je pense à mes vacances. I'm thinking about my holidays. ◇ C'est une bonne occasion, pensez-y. It's a good opportunity, think about it.

• faire penser quelqu'un à quelque chose to remind someone of something ◇ Cette photo me fait penser à la Grèce. This photo reminds me of Greece.

• faire penser quelqu'un à faire quelque chose to remind someone to do something ◇ Fais-moi penser à téléphoner à Claire. Remind me to phone Claire.

• penser faire quelque chose to be planning to do something ◇ Ils pensent partir en Espagne en juillet. They're planning to go to Spain in July.

la **pension** NOUN

1 *boarding school* ◇ Leur fille est en pension. Their daughter is at boarding school.

2 *pension* ◇ Ma grand-mère reçoit sa pension tous les mois. My grandma gets her pension every month.

3 *boarding house*

• la pension complète full board

le/la **pensionnaire** NOUN

boarder
le **pensionnat** NOUN
   boarding school
la **pente** NOUN
   slope ◇ *une pente raide* a steep slop
  ◆ **en pente** sloping ◇ *Le toit de cette
   maison est en pente.* This house has a
   sloping roof.
la **Pentecôte** NOUN
   Whitsun
le **pépin** NOUN
   ① *pip* ◇ *Cette orange est pleine de
   pépins.* This orange is full of pips.
   ② *problem* ◇ *avoir un pépin* (informal)
   to have a slight problem
perçant ADJECTIVE
   ① *sharp* ◇ *Il a une vue perçante.* He
   has very sharp eyes.
   ② *piercing* ◇ *un cri perçant* a piercing
   cry
percer VERB
   to pierce ◇ *Christèle s'est fait percer
   les oreilles.* Christèle has had her ears
   pierced.
le **perdant** NOUN
   loser
la **perdante** NOUN
   loser
perdre VERB
   to lose ◇ *Cécile a perdu ses clés.*
   Cécile's lost her keys.
  ◆ **J'ai perdu mon chemin.** I've lost my
   way.
  ◆ **perdre du temps** to waste time ◇ *J'ai
   perdu beaucoup de temps ce matin.* I've
   wasted a lot of time this morning.
   ◇ *Nous avons perdu notre temps à cette
   réunion.* That meeting was a waste of
   time.
  ◆ **se perdre** to get lost ◇ *Je me suis
   perdu en route.* I got lost on the way
   here.
perdu VERB *see* **perdre**
le **père** NOUN
   father
  ◆ **le père Noël** Father Christmas
perfectionné ADJECTIVE
   sophisticated
perfectionner VERB
   to improve ◇ *Elle a besoin de
   perfectionner son anglais.* She needs to
   improve her English.
périmé ADJECTIVE
   out-of-date ◇ *Mon passeport est
   périmé.* My passport's out of date.
  ◆ **Ces yaourts sont périmés.** These
   yoghurts are past their use-by date.
la **période** NOUN
   period

périodique ADJECTIVE
   periodic
périphérique ADJECTIVE
   see also périphérique NOUN
   outlying ◇ *un quartier périphérique* an
   outlying district
le **périphérique** NOUN
   see also périphérique ADJECTIVE
   ring road
la **perle** NOUN
   pearl
la **permanence** NOUN
  ◆ **assurer une permanence** to operate a
   basic service ◇ *Ma banque assure une
   permanence le samedi matin.* My bank
   operates a basic service on Saturday
   mornings.
  ◆ **être de permanence** to be on duty
   ◇ *Sophie ne peut pas venir, elle est de
   permanence ce soir.* Sophie can't come,
   she's on duty tonight.
  ◆ **en permanence** permanently ◇ *Elle
   se plaint en permanence.* She's always
   complaining.
permanent ADJECTIVE
   ① *permanent* ◇ *Il a un poste
   permanent.* He has a permanent job.
   ② *continuous* ◇ *J'en ai assez de tes
   critiques permanentes.* I've had enough
   of your constant criticism.
la **permanente** NOUN
   perm
permettre VERB
   to allow
  ◆ **permettre à quelqu'un de faire quelque
   chose** to allow somebody to do
   something ◇ *Sa mère lui permet de
   sortir le soir.* His mother allows him to
   go out at night.
le **permis** NOUN
   permit ◇ *Il vous faut un permis pour
   camper ici.* You need a permit to camp
   here.
  ◆ **le permis de conduire** driving licence
  ◆ **un permis de séjour** a residence permit
  ◆ **un permis de travail** a work permit
la **permission** NOUN
   permission ◇ *Qui t'a donné la
   permission d'entrer?* Who gave you
   permission to come in?
  ◆ **avoir la permission de faire quelque
   chose** to have permission to do
   something ◇ *J'ai la permission d'utiliser
   sa chaîne hi-fi.* I've got his permission
   to use his hi-fi.
  ◆ **être en permission** to be on leave (*from
   the army*)
le **Pérou** NOUN
   Peru

perpétuel ADJECTIVE
(FEM SING **perpétuelle**)
perpetual

le **perroquet** NOUN
parrot

la **perruche** NOUN
budgie

la **perruque** NOUN
wig

le **persil** NOUN
parsley

le **personnage** NOUN
[1] _figure_ ◇ _les grands personnages de l'histoire de France_ the important figures in French history
[2] _character_ ◇ _le personnage principal du film_ the main character in the film

la **personnalité** NOUN
[1] _personality_ ◇ _Ray a une personnalité forte._ Ray has a strong personality.
[2] _prominent figure_ ◇ _Il y avait beaucoup de personnalités politiques à ce dîner._ There were lots of prominent political figures at the dinner.

la **personne** NOUN
see also **personne** PRONOUN
person ◇ _Il y avait une trentaine de personnes dans la pièce._ There were about 30 people in the room. ◇ _une personne âgée_ an elderly person
+ **en personne** in person

personne PRONOUN
see also **personne** NOUN
[1] _nobody_ ◇ _Il n'y a personne à la maison._ There's nobody at home. ◇ _Personne n'est venu le chercher._ Nobody came to fetch him.
[2] _anybody_ ◇ _Elle ne veut voir personne._ She doesn't want to see anybody.

personnel ADJECTIVE
(FEM SING **personnelle**)
see also **personnel** NOUN
personal

le **personnel** NOUN
see also **personnel** ADJECTIVE
staff ◇ _Il nous faut plus de personnel._ We need more staff.
+ **le service du personnel** the personnel department

personnellement ADVERB
personally ◇ _Personnellement, je ne suis pas d'accord._ Personally, I don't agree.

la **perspective** NOUN
prospect ◇ _Les perspectives sont encourageantes._ The prospects are encouraging.

+ **perspectives d'avenir** prospects ◇ _Il y a des perspectives d'avenir dans ce métier._ This job has good prospects.
+ **en perspective (1)** in prospect ◇ _Il y a des changements en perspective._ Changes are in prospect.
+ **en perspective (2)** in perspective ◇ _Il a dessiné la maison en perspective._ He drew the house in perspective.

persuader VERB
to persuade
+ **persuader quelqu'un de faire quelque chose** to persuade somebody to do something ◇ _Elle m'a persuadé de l'accompagner au cinéma._ She persuaded me to go to the cinema with her.

la **perte** NOUN
[1] _loss_ ◇ _des pertes d'emploi_ job losses
[2] _waste_ ◇ _Cette réunion a été une perte de temps._ The meeting was a waste of time.

perturber VERB
to disrupt ◇ _Un camion en panne perturbait la circulation._ A lorry had broken down and was disrupting the traffic.

le **pèse-personne** NOUN
bathroom scales PL

peser VERB
to weigh ◇ _Elle pèse cent kilos._ She weighs 100 kilos.

pessimiste ADJECTIVE
pessimistic

le **pétale** NOUN
petal

la **pétanque** NOUN
pétanque _is a type of bowls played in France, especially in the south._

le **pétard** NOUN
firecracker

péter VERB (rude)
to fart

petit ADJECTIVE
[1] _small_ ◇ _Sonia habite une petite ville._ Sonia lives in a small town.
[2] _little_ ◇ _Phyllis a une jolie petite maison._ Phyllis has a nice little house.
+ **petit à petit** bit by bit
+ **un petit ami** a boyfriend
+ **une petite amie** a girlfriend
+ **le petit déjeuner** breakfast
+ **un petit pain** a bread roll
+ **les petites annonces** the small ads
+ **des petits pois** garden peas
+ **les petits** young (of animal) ◇ _la lionne et ses petits_ the lioness and her young

la **petite-fille** NOUN
(PL les **petites-filles**)

P

granddaughter

le **petit-fils** NOUN
(PL les **petits-fils**)
grandson

les **petits-enfants** MASC NOUN
grandchildren

le **pétrole** NOUN
oil ◇ *une lampe à pétrole* an oil lamp

peu ADVERB, NOUN
not much ◇ *J'ai peu mangé à midi.* I
didn't eat much for lunch. ◇ *Il voyage
peu.* He doesn't travel much.

* **un peu** a bit ◇ *Elle est un peu timide.*
She's a bit shy. ◇ *un peu de gâteau* a
bit of cake

* **un petit peu** a little bit ◇ *un petit peu
de crème* a little bit of cream

* **peu de (1)** not many ◇ *Il y a peu de
bons films au cinéma.* There aren't very
many good films on at the cinema.
◇ *Elle a peu d'amis.* She hasn't got
many friends.

* **peu de (2)** not much ◇ *Il a peu
d'espoir de réussir.* He doesn't have
much hope of succeeding. ◇ *Il lui reste
peu d'argent.* He hasn't got much
money left.

* **à peu près (1)** more or less ◇ *J'ai à
peu près fini.* I've more or less finished.

* **à peu près (2)** about ◇ *Le voyage
prend à peu près deux heures.* The
journey takes about two hours.

* **peu à peu** little by little

* **peu avant** shortly before

* **peu après** shortly afterwards

* **de peu** only just ◇ *Chantal a manqué
son train de peu.* Chantal only just
missed her train.

le **peuple** NOUN
people ◇ *le peuple français* the
French people

la **peur** NOUN
fear

* **avoir peur de** to be afraid of ◇ *Il a
peur du noir.* He's afraid of the dark.

* **avoir peur de faire quelque chose** to
be frightened of doing something
◇ *Elle a peur d'y aller toute seule.* She's
frightened of going on her own.

* **faire peur à quelqu'un** to frighten
somebody ◇ *Cet homme-là me fait
peur.* That man frightens me.

peureux ADJECTIVE
(FEM SING **peureuse**)
fearful

peut VERB *see* **pouvoir**

* **Il ne peut pas venir.** He can't come.

peut-être ADVERB
perhaps ◇ *Je l'ai peut-être oublié à la*

maison. Perhaps I've left it at home.

* **peut-être que** perhaps ◇ *Peut-être
qu'elles n'ont pas pu téléphoner.* Perhaps
they weren't able to phone.

peuvent, peux VERB *see* **pouvoir**

* **Je ne peux pas le faire.** I can't do it.

p. ex. ABBREVIATION (= *par exemple*)
e.g.

le **phare** NOUN
[1] *lighthouse* ◇ *On voit le phare
depuis le pont du bateau.* You can see
the lighthouse from the ship's deck.
[2] *headlight* ◇ *Il a laissé les phares de
sa voiture allumés.* He left his
headlights on.

la **pharmacie** NOUN
chemist's
Chemist's shops in France are identified by a
special green cross outside the shop.

le **pharmacien** NOUN
pharmacist

la **pharmacienne** NOUN
pharmacist

le **phénomène** NOUN
phenomenon

la **philosophie** NOUN
philosophy

le **phoque** NOUN
seal (*animal*)

la **photo** NOUN
photograph ◇ *Elle a fait développer
ses photos.* She's had her photographs
developed.

* **en photo** in photographs ◇ *Je n'ai vu
Venise qu'en photo.* I've only seen
Venice in photographs.

* **prendre quelqu'un en photo** to take a
photo of somebody ◇ *Claire nous a
pris en photo.* Claire took a photo of us.

* **une photo d'identité** a passport
photograph

la **photocopie** NOUN
photocopy

photocopier VERB
to photocopy

la **photocopieuse** NOUN
photocopier

le/la **photographe** NOUN
photographer

la **photographie** NOUN
[1] *photography*
[2] *photograph*

photographier VERB
to photograph

la **phrase** NOUN
sentence

physique ADJECTIVE
see also **physique** NOUN
physical

le **physique** NOUN
> see also la physique and physique ADJECTIVE

+ **Il a un physique agréable.** He's quite good-looking.

la **physique** NOUN
> see also le physique and physique ADJECTIVE

physics ⋄ *Il est professeur de physique.* He's a physics teacher.

e/la **pianiste** NOUN
pianist ⋄ *Elle est pianiste.* She's a pianist.

le **piano** NOUN
piano

le **pic** NOUN
peak ⋄ *les pics enneigés des Pyrénées* the snowy peaks of the Pyrenees

+ **à pic (1)** vertically ⋄ *La falaise tombe à pic dans la mer.* The cliff drops vertically into the sea.

+ **à pic (1)** just at the right time ⋄ *Tu es arrivé à pic.* You arrived just at the right time.

la **pièce** NOUN
[1] _room_ ⋄ *Mon lit est au centre de la pièce.* My bed is in the middle of the room.

+ **un cinq-pièces** a five-roomed flat
[2] _play_ ⋄ *On joue une pièce d'Anouilh au théâtre.* There's a play by Anouilh on at the theatre.

[3] _part_ ⋄ *Il faut changer une pièce du moteur.* There's an engine part which needs changing.

[4] _coin_ ⋄ *des pièces d'un franc* some one-franc coins

+ **cinquante francs pièce** 50 francs each ⋄ *J'ai acheté ces T-shirts dix francs pièce.* I bought these T-shirts for ten francs each.

+ **un maillot une pièce** a one-piece swimsuit

+ **un maillot deux-pièces** a bikini

+ **Avez-vous une pièce d'identité?** Have you got any identification?

le **pied** NOUN
foot ⋄ *J'ai mal aux pieds.* My feet are hurting.

+ **à pied** on foot

+ **avoir pied** to be able to touch the bottom ⋄ *Justine n'aime pas nager là où elle n'a pas pied.* Justine doesn't like swimming where she can't touch the bottom.

e **pied-noir** NOUN
(PL les **pieds-noirs**)

> A pied-noir is a French person born in Algeria; most of them moved to France during the Algerian war in the 1950s.

⋄ *Sa grand-mère est pied-noir.* His grandmother was born in Algeria.

le **piège** NOUN
trap

+ **prendre quelqu'un au piège** to trap somebody

piéger VERB
to trap

+ **un colis piégé** a parcel bomb

+ **une voiture piégée** a car bomb

la **pierre** NOUN
stone

+ **une pierre précieuse** a precious stone

le **piéton** NOUN
pedestrian

la **piétonne** NOUN
pedestrian

piétonnier ADJECTIVE
(FEM SING **piétonnière**)

+ **une rue piétonnière** a pedestrianized street

+ **un quartier piétonnier** a pedestrianized area

la **pieuvre** NOUN
octopus

le **pigeon** NOUN
pigeon

piger VERB (*informal*)
to understand

la **pile** NOUN
> see also pile ADVERB

[1] _pile_ ⋄ *Il y a une pile de disques sur la table.* There's a pile of records on the table.

[2] _battery_ ⋄ *Les piles de mon magnétophone sont usées.* The batteries in my tape recorder have run out.

pile ADVERB
> see also pile NOUN

+ **à deux heures pile** at two on the dot

+ **jouer à pile ou face** to toss up

+ **Pile ou face?** Heads or tails?

le **pilote** NOUN
pilot

+ **un pilote de course** a racing driver

+ **un pilote de ligne** an airline pilot

piloter VERB
to fly (*a plane*)

la **pilule** NOUN
pill

+ **prendre la pilule** to be on the pill

le **piment** NOUN
chilli

le **pin** NOUN
pine

le **pinard** NOUN (*informal*)
wine

la **pince** NOUN
[1] _pliers_ PL (*tool*)
[2] _pincer_ (*of crab*)

P

+ **une pince à épiler** tweezers
+ **une pince à linge** a clothes peg

le **pinceau** NOUN
(PL les **pinceaux**)
paintbrush

la **pincée** NOUN
+ **une pincée de sel** a pinch of salt

pincer VERB
to pinch ◇ *Elle m'a pincé le bras.* She pinched my arm.

le **pingouin** NOUN
penguin

le **ping-pong** NOUN
table tennis ◇ *jouer au ping-pong* to play table tennis

la **pintade** NOUN
guinea fowl

le **pion** NOUN
[1] *pawn* (in chess)
[2] *piece* (in draughts)
[3] *supervisor* (man)
In French secondary schools, the teachers are not responsible for supervising the pupils outside class. This job is done by people called pions *or* surveillants.

la **pionne** NOUN
supervisor (woman)

la **pipe** NOUN
pipe ◇ *Mon grand-père fume la pipe.* My granddad smokes a pipe.

piquant ADJECTIVE
[1] *prickly*
[2] *spicy*

le **pique** NOUN
see also la pique
spades PL ◇ *l'as de pique* the ace of spades

la **pique** NOUN
see also le pique
cutting remark ◇ *envoyer des piques à quelqu'un* to make cutting remarks to somebody

le **pique-nique** NOUN
picnic

piquer VERB
[1] *to bite* ◇ *Nous avons été piqués par les moustiques.* We were bitten by mosquitoes.
[2] *to burn* ◇ *Cette sauce me pique la langue.* This sauce is burning my tongue.
[3] *to steal* ◇ *On m'a piqué mon porte-monnaie.* (informal) I've had my purse stolen.
+ **se piquer** to prick oneself ◇ *Il s'est piqué avec une aiguille.* He pricked himself with a needle.

le **piquet** NOUN
[1] *post* ◇ *Le chien est attaché à un*

piquet. The dog is tied to a post.
[2] *peg* ◇ *Il nous manque un des piquets de la tente.* One of our tent pegs is missing.

la **piqûre** NOUN
[1] *injection* ◇ *Le médecin lui a fait une piqûre.* The doctor gave him an injection.
[2] *bite* ◇ *une piqûre de moustique* a mosquito bite
[3] *sting* ◇ *une piqûre d'abeille* a bee sting

le **pirate** NOUN
pirate

pire ADJECTIVE, NOUN
worse ◇ *C'est encore pire qu'avant.* It's even worse than before.
+ **le pire** the worst ◇ *C'est la pire journée que j'aie jamais passée.* That's the worst day I've ever had. ◇ *Ce gamin est le pire de la bande.* That boy is the worst in the group.
+ **le pire de** the worst of ◇ *Le pire de tout, c'est qu'on s'ennuie tout le temps.* The worst of it is that we're always bored.

la **piscine** NOUN
swimming pool

la **pistache** NOUN
pistachio ◇ *une glace à la pistache* a pistachio ice cream

la **piste** NOUN
[1] *lead* ◇ *La police est sur une piste.* The police are following a lead.
[2] *runway* ◇ *L'avion s'est posé sur la piste.* The plane landed on the runway.
[3] *ski run* ◇ *Le skieur a descendu la piste.* The skier came down the ski run.
+ **une piste artificielle** a dry ski slope
+ **la piste de danse** the dance floor
+ **une piste cyclable** a cycle track

le **pistolet** NOUN
pistol

pistonner VERB
+ **Il a été pistonné pour avoir ce travail.** They pulled some strings to get him this job.

la **pitié** NOUN
pity
+ **Il me fait pitié.** I feel sorry for him.
+ **avoir pitié de quelqu'un** to feel sorry for somebody

pittoresque ADJECTIVE
picturesque

le **placard** NOUN
cupboard

la **place** NOUN
[1] *place* ◇ *Vincent a eu la troisième place au concours.* Vincent got third

place in the competition.

[2] *square* ◇ *la place du village* the village square

[3] *space* ◇ *Il ne reste plus de place pour se garer.* There's no more space to park. ◇ *Ça prend de la place.* It takes up a lot of room.

[4] *seat* ◇ *Toutes les places ont été vendues.* All the seats have been sold. ◇ *Il y a vingt places assises.* There are 20 seats. ◇ *remettre quelque chose en place* to put something back in its place

- **sur place** on the spot
- **à la place** instead ◇ *Il ne reste plus de tarte; désirez-vous quelque chose d'autre à la place?* There's no pie left; would you like something else instead?
- **à la place de** instead of

placer VERB

[1] *to seat* ◇ *Nous étions placés à côté du directeur.* We were seated next to the manager.

[2] *to invest* ◇ *Il a placé ses économies en Bourse.* He invested his money on the Stock Exchange.

le **plafond** NOUN
ceiling

la **plage** NOUN
beach

la **plaie** NOUN
wound

plaindre VERB

- **plaindre quelqu'un** to feel sorry for somebody ◇ *Je te plains.* I feel sorry for you.
- **se plaindre** to complain ◇ *Il n'arrête pas de se plaindre.* He never stops complaining.
- **se plaindre à quelqu'un** to complain to somebody ◇ *Ils se sont plaints au directeur.* They complained to the manager.
- **se plaindre de quelque chose** to complain about something ◇ *Elle s'est plainte du bruit.* She complained about the noise.

la **plaine** NOUN
plain (*level area*)

la **plainte** NOUN
complaint

- **porter plainte** to lodge a complaint

plaire VERB

- **Ce cadeau me plaît beaucoup.** I like this present a lot.
- **Ce film plaît beaucoup aux jeunes.** The film is very popular with young people.
- **Elle lui plaît.** He fancies her.
- **s'il te plaît** please

- **s'il vous plaît** please

plaisanter VERB
to joke

la **plaisanterie** NOUN
joke

le **plaisir** NOUN
pleasure

- **faire plaisir à quelqu'un** to please somebody ◇ *J'y suis allé pour lui faire plaisir.* I went there to please him. ◇ *Ce cadeau me fait très plaisir.* I'm very pleased with this present.

plaît VERB *see* **plaire**

le **plan** NOUN
plan

- **au premier plan** in the foreground

la **planche** NOUN
plank

- **une planche à repasser** an ironing board
- **une planche à roulettes** a skateboard

le **plancher** NOUN
floor

planer VERB

[1] *to glide* ◇ *L'avion planait dans le ciel.* The plane was gliding in the sky.

[2] *to have one's head in the clouds* ◇ *Ce garçon plane complètement.* (*informal*) He's not with us at all.

la **planète** NOUN
planet

la **plante** NOUN
plant

planter VERB

[1] *to plant* ◇ *Daphné a planté des tomates.* Daphne planted some tomatoes.

[2] *to hammer in* ◇ *Jean-Pierre a planté un clou dans le mur.* Jean-Pierre hammered a nail into the wall.

[3] *to pitch* ◇ *André a planté sa tente au bord du lac.* André pitched his tent next to the lake.

- **Ne reste pas planté là!** Don't just stand there!
- **se planter** (*informal*) to fail ◇ *Je me suis planté en maths.* I failed maths.

la **plaque** NOUN
(metal) plate

- **une plaque de verglas** a patch of ice
- **une plaque de chocolat** a bar of chocolate
- **une plaque d'immatriculation** a number plate (*of car*)

plaqué ADJECTIVE

- **plaqué or** gold-plated
- **plaqué argent** silver-plated

plaquer VERB (*informal*)

[1] *to ditch* ◇ *Elle a plaqué son copain.*

She ditched her boyfriend.
  ② *to pack in* ◇ *Il a plaqué son boulot.*
  He packed in his job.
la **plaquette** NOUN
  • **une plaquette de chocolat** a bar of
    chocolate
  • **une plaquette de beurre** a pack of
    butter
le **plastique** NOUN
  plastic
  plat ADJECTIVE
  | see also **plat** NOUN |
  flat
  • **être à plat ventre** to be lying face down
  • **l'eau plate** still water
le **plat** NOUN
  | see also **plat** ADJECTIVE |
  ① *dish* ◇ *un plat en inox* a stainless
    steel dish
  ② *course* ◇ *le plat principal* the main
    course
  • **un plat cuisiné** a pre-cooked meal
  • **le plat de résistance** the main course
  • **le plat du jour** the dish of the day
le **platane** NOUN
  plane tree
le **plateau** NOUN
  (PL les **plateaux**)
  ① *tray*
  • **un plateau de fromages** a selection of
    cheeses
  ② *plateau*
le **platine** NOUN
  | see also **la platine** |
  platinum
la **platine** NOUN
  | see also **le platine** |
  turntable (*of record player*)
  • **une platine laser** a CD player
le **plâtre** NOUN
  plaster ◇ *une statue en plâtre* a statue
    made of plaster ◇ *avoir un bras dans le
    plâtre* to have an arm in plaster
  plein ADJECTIVE
  | see also **plein** NOUN |
  full
  • **à plein temps** full-time – *Elle travaille
    à plein temps.* She works full-time.
  • **en plein air** in the open air
  • **en pleine nuit** in the middle of the
    night
  • **en plein jour** in broad daylight
le **plein** NOUN
  | see also **plein** ADJECTIVE |
  • **faire le plein** to fill up (*petrol tank*)
    ◇ *Faites le plein, s'il vous plaît.* Fill it up,
    please.
  pleurer VERB
  to cry

pleut VERB *see* **pleuvoir**
pleuvoir VERB
  to rain ◇ *Il pleut.* It's raining.
le **pli** NOUN
  ① *fold*
  ② *pleat* ◇ *Elle a repassé les plis de sa
    jupe.* She ironed the pleats of her skirt.
  ③ *crease* ◇ *Il y a un pli sur la manche
    de ta chemise.* There's a crease in the
    sleeve of your shirt.
  pliant ADJECTIVE
  folding ◇ *un lit pliant* a folding bed
  plier VERB
  ① *to fold* ◇ *Elle a plié sa serviette.* She
    folded her towel.
  ② *to bend* ◇ *Elle a plié le bras.* She
    bent her arm.
le **plomb** NOUN
  ① *lead* ◇ *Ces jouets sont en plomb.*
    These toys are made of lead.
  ② *fuse* ◇ *Les plombs ont sauté.* The
    fuses have blown.
  • **l'essence sans plomb** unleaded petrol
le **plombier** NOUN
  plumber
  • **Il est plombier.** He's a plumber.
la **plongée** NOUN
  diving ◇ *faire de la plongée* to go
    diving
le **plongeoir** NOUN
  diving board
le **plongeon** NOUN
  dive
  plonger VERB
  to dive ◇ *Jean a plongé dans la
    piscine.* Jean dived into the swimming
    pool.
  • **J'ai plongé ma main dans l'eau.** I
    plunged my hand into the water.
  plu VERB *see* **plaire, pleuvoir**
la **pluie** NOUN
  rain ◇ *sous la pluie* in the rain
la **plume** NOUN
  feather ◇ *une plume d'oiseau* a bird's
    feather
  • **un stylo à plume** a fountain pen
  plupart
  • **la plupart** PRONOUN
    most (of them) ◇ *La plupart ont moins
    de quinze ans.* Most of them are under
    15.
  • **la plupart des** most ◇ *La plupart des
    gens ont vu ce film.* Most people have
    seen this film.
  • **la plupart du temps** most of the time
le **pluriel** NOUN
  plural
  plus ADVERB, PREPOSITION
  • **ne...plus (1)** not...any more ◇ *Je ne*

veux plus le voir. I don't want to see
him any more.

* **ne...plus (2)** no longer   ◇ *Il ne travaille
plus ici.* He's no longer working here.
* **Je n'ai plus de pain.** I've got no bread
left.
* **plus...que** more...than   ◇ *Il est plus
intelligent que son frère.* He's more
intelligent than his brother.   ◇ *Il
travaille plus que moi.* He works more
than me.   ◇ *Elle est plus grande que moi.*
She's bigger than me.
* **C'est le plus grand de la famille.** He's
the tallest in his family.
* **plus...plus...** the more...the more...
◇ *Plus il gagne d'argent, plus il en veut.*
The more money he earns, the more he
wants.
* **plus de (1)** more   ◇ *Il nous faut plus de
pain.* We need more bread.
* **plus de (2)** more than   ◇ *Il y avait plus
de dix personnes.* There were more
than 10 people.
* **de plus** more   ◇ *Il nous faut un joueur
de plus.* We need one more player.
◇ *Le voyage a pris trois heures de plus
que prévu.* The journey took 3 hours
more than planned.
* **en plus** more   ◇ *J'ai apporté quelques
gâteaux en plus.* I brought a few more
cakes.
* **de plus en plus** more and more   ◇ *Il y
a de plus en plus de touristes par ici.*
There are more and more tourists round
here.   ◇ *Il fait de plus en plus chaud.* It's
getting hotter and hotter.
* **plus ou moins** more or less
* **Quatre plus deux égalent six.** 4 plus 2
is 6.

plusieurs PRONOUN
several   ◇ *Elle a acheté plusieurs
chemises.* She bought several shirts.
◇ *Il y en a plusieurs.* There are several of
them.

le **plus-que-parfait** NOUN
pluperfect

plutôt ADVERB
1 *quite*   ◇ *Elle est plutôt jolie.* She's
quite pretty.
2 *rather*   ◇ *L'eau est plutôt froide.* The
water's rather cold.
3 *instead*   ◇ *Demande-leur plutôt de
venir avec toi.* Ask them to come with
you instead.
* **plutôt que** rather than   ◇ *Invite Marie
plutôt que Nathalie.* Invite Marie rather
than Nathalie.

pluvieux ADJECTIVE
(FEM SING **pluvieuse**)

rainy

le **pneu** NOUN
tyre

la **pneumonie** NOUN
pneumonia

la **poche** NOUN
pocket
* **l'argent de poche** pocket money
* **un livre de poche** a paperback

la **poêle** NOUN
frying pan
* **une poêle à frire** a frying pan

le **poème** NOUN
poem

la **poésie** NOUN
1 *poetry*
2 *poem*

le **poète** NOUN
poet

le **poids** NOUN
weight   ◇ *vendre quelque chose au
poids* to sell something by weight
* **prendre du poids** to put on weight
◇ *Il a pris du poids.* He's put on weight.
* **perdre du poids** to lose weight   ◇ *Elle
a perdu du poids.* She's lost weight.
* **un poids lourd** a lorry

la **poignée** NOUN
1 *handful*   ◇ *une poignée de sel* a
handful of salt
2 *handle*   ◇ *la poignée de la porte* the
door handle
* **une poignée de main** a handshake

le **poignet** NOUN
1 *wrist*   ◇ *Je me suis fait mal au
poignet.* I've hurt my wrist.
2 *cuff* (of shirt)

le **poil** NOUN
1 *hair*   ◇ *Il y a des poils de chat partout
sur la moquette.* There are cat hairs all
over the carpet.
2 *fur*   ◇ *Ton chien a un beau poil.* Your
dog's got lovely fur.
ADJECTIVE
hairy

poinçonner VERB
to punch   ◇ *Le contrôleur a poinçonné
les billets.* The conductor punched the
tickets.

le **poing** NOUN
fist
* **un coup de poing** a punch

le **point** NOUN
1 *point*   ◇ *Je ne suis pas d'accord sur
ce point.* I don't agree with this point.
◇ *Son point faible, c'est qu'elle est trop
gentille.* Her weak point is she's too
nice.
* **point de vue** point of view

2 *full stop*

* **être sur le point de faire quelque chose** to be just about to do something ◇ *J'étais sur le point de te téléphoner.* I was just about to phone you.
* **mettre au point** to finalize
* **Ce n'est pas encore au point.** It's not finalized yet.
* **à point** medium ◇ *Comment voulez-vous votre steak? – À point.* How would you like your steak? – Medium.
* **un point d'exclamation** an exclamation mark
* **un point d'interrogation** a question mark

la **pointe** NOUN
point ◇ *la pointe d'un couteau* the point of a knife

* **être à la pointe du progrès** to be in the forefront of progress
* **sur la pointe des pieds** on tiptoe
* **les heures de pointe** peak hours

le **pointillé** NOUN
dotted line

pointu ADJECTIVE
pointed ◇ *un chapeau pointu* a pointed hat

la **pointure** NOUN
size (of shoes) ◇ *Quelle est votre pointure?* What size shoes do you take?

le **point-virgule** NOUN
semicolon

la **poire** NOUN
pear

le **poireau** NOUN
(PL les **poireaux**)
leek ◇ *la soupe aux poireaux* leek soup

le **pois** NOUN
pea

* **les petits pois** peas
* **les pois chiches** chickpeas
* **à pois** spotted ◇ *une robe à pois* a spotted dress

le **poison** NOUN
poison

le **poisson** NOUN
fish ◇ *Je n'aime pas le poisson.* I don't like fish. ◇ *André a pêché deux poissons.* André caught two fish.

* **les Poissons** Pisces ◇ *Monique est Poissons.* Monique is Pisces.
* **Poisson d'avril!** April fool!

Pinning a paper fish to somebody's back is a traditional April fool joke in France.

* **un poisson rouge** a goldfish

la **poissonnerie** NOUN
fish shop

le **poissonnier** NOUN

fishmonger

la **poitrine** NOUN
1 *chest* ◇ *J'ai mal à la poitrine.* My chest hurts.
2 *bust* ◇ *Quel est votre tour de poitrine?* What's your bust size?

le **poivre** NOUN
pepper (spice)

le **poivron** NOUN
pepper (vegetable)

le **pôle** NOUN
pole

* **le pôle Nord** the North Pole
* **le pôle Sud** the South Pole

poli ADJECTIVE
polite

la **police** NOUN
police ◇ *La police recherche le voleur.* The police are looking for the thief.

* **police secours** emergency services ◇ *Ils ont appelé police secours.* They phoned the emergency services.
* **une police d'assurance** an insurance policy

policier ADJECTIVE
(FEM SING **policière**)
see also **policier** NOUN

* **un roman policier** a detective novel

le **policier** NOUN
see also **policier** ADJECTIVE
policeman ◇ *Il est policier.* He's a policeman.

la **politesse** NOUN
politeness

la **politique** NOUN
politics ◇ *La politique ne l'intéresse pas du tout.* He's not at all interested in politics.

* **un homme politique** a politician

la **pollution** NOUN
pollution

le **polo** NOUN
polo shirt

la **Pologne** NOUN
Poland

polonais ADJECTIVE, NOUN
(FEM SING **polonaise**)
Polish ◇ *Elle parle polonais.* She speaks Polish.

* **un Polonais** a Pole (man)
* **une Polonaise** a Pole (woman)
* **les Polonais** the Polish

la **Polynésie** NOUN
Polynesia

la **pommade** NOUN
ointment

la **pomme** NOUN
apple

* **les pommes de terre** potatoes

◆ **les pommes frites** chips

la **pompe** NOUN
pump
◆ **une pompe à essence** a petrol pump
◆ **les pompes funèbres** undertakers

le **pompier** NOUN
fireman

pondre VERB
to lay (*eggs*)

le **poney** NOUN
pony

le **pont** NOUN
[1] *bridge*
[2] *deck* (*of ship*)
◆ **faire le pont** to take a long weekend
 ◇ *Nous faisons le pont pour la Pentecôte.*
We're taking a long weekend for
Whitsun.

populaire ADJECTIVE
[1] *popular* ◇ *Ce chanteur est très
populaire en France.* This singer's very
popular in France.
[2] *working-class* ◇ *un quartier
populaire de la ville* a working-class area
of town

la **population** NOUN
population

le **porc** NOUN
[1] *pig* ◇ *Ils élèvent des porcs.* They
breed pigs.
[2] *pork* ◇ *du rôti de porc* roast pork

la **porcelaine** NOUN
china ◇ *une tasse en porcelaine* a
china cup

le **port** NOUN
[1] *harbour*
[2] *port*

le **portail** NOUN
gate

portatif ADJECTIVE
(FEM SING **portative**)
portable

la **porte** NOUN
[1] *door* ◇ *Ferme la porte, s'il te plaît.*
Close the door, please.
◆ **la porte d'entrée** the front door
[2] *gate* ◇ *Vol 432 à destination de
Paris: porte numéro trois.* Flight 432 to
Paris: gate 3.
◆ **mettre quelqu'un à la porte** to sack
somebody

le **porte-bagages** NOUN
luggage rack

le **porte-clés** NOUN
key ring

la **portée** NOUN
◆ **à portée de la main** within arm's reach
◆ **hors de portée** out of reach

le **portefeuille** NOUN
wallet

le **portemanteau** NOUN
(PL les **portemanteaux**)
[1] *coat hanger*
[2] *coat rack*

le **porte-monnaie** NOUN
(PL les **porte-monnaie**)
purse

porter VERB
[1] *to carry* ◇ *Il portait une valise.* He
was carrying a suitcase.
[2] *to wear* ◇ *Elle porte une jolie robe
bleue.* She's wearing a lovely blue dress.
◆ **se porter bien** to be well
◆ **se porter mal** to be unwell

la **portière** NOUN
door (*of car*)

la **portion** NOUN
portion

le **porto** NOUN
port (*wine*)

le **portrait** NOUN
portrait

portugais ADJECTIVE, NOUN
(FEM SING **portugaise**)
Portuguese ◇ *Il parle portugais.* He
speaks Portuguese.
◆ **un Portugais** a Portuguese (*man*)
◆ **une Portugaise** a Portuguese (*woman*)
◆ **les Portugais** the Portuguese

le **Portugal** NOUN
Portugal
◆ **au Portugal (1)** in Portugal
◆ **au Portugal (2)** to Portugal

poser VERB
[1] *to put down* ◇ *J'ai posé la cafetière
sur la table.* I put the coffee pot down
on the table.
[2] *to pose* ◇ *Cela pose un problème.*
That poses a problem.
◆ **poser une question à quelqu'un** to ask
somebody a question
◆ **se poser** to land ◇ *L'avion s'est posé
à huit heures.* The plane landed at 8
o'clock.

positif ADJECTIVE
(FEM SING **positive**)
positive

la **position** NOUN
position

posséder VERB
to own ◇ *Ils possèdent une jolie
maison.* They own a lovely house.

la **possibilité** NOUN
possibility

possible ADJECTIVE
possible ◇ *Alain leur a dit que ce n'était
pas possible.* Alain told them it wasn't
possible.

P

- **le plus de gens possible** as many people as possible
- **le plus tôt possible** as early as possible
- **le moins d'argent possible** as little money as possible
- **Il travaille le moins possible.** He works as little as possible.
- **dès que possible** as soon as possible
- **faire son possible** to do all one can ◇ *Je ferai tout mon possible.* I'll do all I can.

la **poste** NOUN

> see also le poste

[1] *post* ◇ *Je vais l'envoyer par la poste.* I'm going to send it by post.

[2] *post office* ◇ *Je vais à la poste pour acheter des timbres.* I'm going to the post office to buy some stamps.

- **mettre une lettre à la poste** to post a letter

le **poste** NOUN

> see also la poste

[1] *post* ◇ *Jean-Pierre a trouvé un poste de professeur.* Jean-Pierre has found a teaching post.

[2] *extension* (phone) ◇ *Pouvez-vous me passer le poste de M. Salzedo?* Can you put me through to Mr Salzedo's extension?

[3] *set* ◇ *un poste de radio* a radio set

- **un poste de police** a police station

poster VERB

> see also poster NOUN

to post ◇ *Je vais poster ce colis.* I'm going to post this parcel.

le **poster** NOUN

> see also poster VERB

poster ◇ *un poster de la Grèce* a poster of Greece

postérieur ADJECTIVE

[1] *later* ◇ *Ce document est postérieur à mille trois cent quatorze.* This document is from later than 1314.

[2] *back* ◇ *la partie postérieure de ma jambe* the back of my leg

le **pot** NOUN

jar ◇ *J'ai fait trois pots de confiture.* I've made three jars of jam.

- **prendre un pot** (informal) to have a drink ◇ *On va prendre un pot ce soir.* We're going for a drink tonight.
- **un pot de fleurs** a plant pot

potable ADJECTIVE

- **eau potable** drinking water
- **"eau non potable"** "not drinking water"

le **potage** NOUN

soup

le **potager** NOUN

vegetable garden

le **pot-au-feu** NOUN

(PL les pot-au-feu)

beef stew

le **pote** NOUN (*informal*)

mate ◇ *Je sors avec mes potes ce soir.* I'm going out with my mates tonight.

le **poteau** NOUN

(PL les poteaux)

post ◇ *Il s'est appuyé contre un poteau.* He leant against a post.

- **un poteau indicateur** a signpost

potentiel ADJECTIVE

(FEM SING potentielle)

potential

la **poterie** NOUN

[1] *pottery* ◇ *Elle fait de la poterie à l'école.* She does pottery at school.

[2] *piece of pottery* ◇ *J'ai acheté deux poteries.* I bought two pieces of pottery.

le **potier** NOUN

potter

le **pou** NOUN

(PL les poux)

louse

la **poubelle** NOUN

dustbin

le **pouce** NOUN

[1] *thumb* ◇ *Je me suis coincé le pouce dans la porte.* I trapped my thumb in the door.

[2] *inch* ◇ *Un pouce fait à peu près deux virgule cinq centimètres.* 1 inch equals roughly 2.5 centimetres.

- **manger sur le pouce** to have a quick snack

la **poudre** NOUN

[1] *powder*

[2] *face powder*

- **la poudre à laver** washing powder
- **le lait en poudre** powdered milk
- **le café en poudre** instant coffee

le **poulain** NOUN

foal

la **poule** NOUN

hen

le **poulet** NOUN

[1] *chicken* ◇ *J'adore le poulet.* I love chicken.

[2] *cop* ◇ *Il s'est fait attraper par les poulets.* (informal) He got caught by the cops.

le **pouls** NOUN

pulse ◇ *Il m'a pris le pouls.* He took my pulse.

le **poumon** NOUN

lung

la **poupée** NOUN

doll

pour PREPOSITION

for   ◊ _C'est un cadeau pour toi._ It's a
present for you.   ◊ _Qu'est-ce que tu veux
pour ton petit déjeuner?_ What would
you like for breakfast?

• **pour faire quelque chose** to do
something   ◊ _Je lui ai téléphoné pour
l'inviter._ I phoned him to invite him.

• **pour que** so that

> **pour que** is followed by a verb in the
> subjunctive.

◊ _Je lui ai prêté mon pull pour qu'elle n'ait
pas froid._ I lent her my jumper so that
she wouldn't be cold.

• **pour cent** per cent

le **pourboire** NOUN

tip   ◊ _Il a donné un pourboire au garçon._
He gave the waiter a tip.

le **pourcentage** NOUN

percentage

pourquoi ADVERB, CONJUNCTION

why   ◊ _Pourquoi est-ce qu'il ne vient
pas avec nous?_ Why isn't he coming
with us?   ◊ _Elle ne m'a pas dit pourquoi._
She didn't tell me why.

pourra, pourrai, pourras, pourrez
VERB see **pouvoir**

pourri ADJECTIVE

rotten

pourrir VERB

to go bad   ◊ _Ces poires ont pourri._
These pears have gone bad.

pourrons, pourront VERB see
pouvoir

la **poursuite** NOUN

chase

• **se lancer à la poursuite de quelqu'un**
to chase after somebody

poursuivre VERB

to carry on with   ◊ _Ils ont poursuivi
leur travail._ They carried on with their
work.

• **se poursuivre** to go on   ◊ _Le concert
s'est poursuivi très tard._ The concert
went on very late.

pourtant ADVERB

yet   ◊ _Il a raté son examen. Pourtant, il
n'est pas bête._ He failed his exam, yet
he's not stupid.

• **C'est pourtant facile!** But it's easy!

pourvu ADJECTIVE

• **pourvu que...** let's hope that...

> **pourvu que** is followed by a verb in the
> subjunctive.

◊ _Pourvu qu'il ne pleuve pas!_ Let's hope
it doesn't rain!

pousser VERB

1 _to push_   ◊ _Ils ont dû pousser la_

voiture. They had to push the car.

2 _to grow_   ◊ _Mes cheveux poussent
vite._ My hair grows quickly.

• **pousser un cri** to give a cry

• **se pousser** to move over
◊ _Pousse-toi, je ne vois rien._ Move over,
I can't see a thing.

la **poussette** NOUN

pushchair

la **poussière** NOUN

1 _dust_   ◊ _La table est couverte de
poussière._ The table's covered in dust.

2 _speck of dust_   ◊ _J'ai une poussière
dans l'œil._ I've got a speck of dust in
my eye.

poussiéreux ADJECTIVE

(FEM SING **poussiéreuse**)

dusty

le **poussin** NOUN

chick

le **pouvoir** NOUN

> see also **pouvoir** VERB

power   ◊ _Le Premier ministre a
beaucoup de pouvoir._ The prime
minister has a lot of power.

pouvoir VERB

> see also **pouvoir** NOUN

Present tense:

je peux	nous pouvons
tu peux	vous pouvez
il/elle peut	ils/elles peuvent

Past participle: _pu_

can   ◊ _Je peux lui téléphoner si tu veux._
I can phone her if you want.   ◊ _Puis-je
venir vous voir samedi?_ May I come and
see you on Saturday?   ◊ _Je ne pourrai
pas venir samedi._ I can't come on
Saturday.   ◊ _J'ai fait tout ce que j'ai pu._ I
did all I could.

• **Je n'en peux plus.** I'm exhausted.

• **Il se peut que...** It's possible that...

> **il se peut que** is followed by a verb in the
> subjunctive.

◊ _Il se peut qu'elle ait déménagé._ It's
possible that she's moved house.   ◊ _Il se
peut que j'y aille._ I might go.

la **prairie** NOUN

meadow

la **pratique** NOUN

> see also **pratique** ADJECTIVE

practice   ◊ _Je manque de pratique._ I'm
out of practice.

pratique ADJECTIVE

> see also **pratique** NOUN

practical   ◊ _Ce sac est très pratique._
This bag's very practical.

pratiquement ADVERB

virtually   ◊ _J'ai pratiquement fini._ I've
virtually finished.

pratiquer VERB
  to practise ◇ *Je dois pratiquer mon espagnol.* I need to practise my Spanish.
+ **Pratiquez-vous un sport?** Do you do any sport?

le **pré** NOUN
  meadow

la **précaution** NOUN
  precaution ◇ *prendre ses précautions* to take precautions
+ **par précaution** as a precaution ◇ *Il a pris une assurance par précaution.* He took out insurance as a precaution.
+ **"à manipuler avec précaution"** "handle with care"

précédemment ADVERB
  previously

précédent ADJECTIVE
  previous

précieux ADJECTIVE
  (FEM SING **précieuse**)
  precious
+ **une pierre précieuse** a precious stone
+ **de précieux conseils** invaluable advice

le **précipice** NOUN
  ravine ◇ *Leur voiture est tombée dans un précipice.* Their car fell into a ravine.

précipitamment ADVERB
  hurriedly ◇ *Chantal est partie précipitamment.* Chantal left hurriedly.

la **précipitation** NOUN
  haste ◇ *Il a agi avec précipitation.* He acted hastily.

se **précipiter** VERB
  to rush

précis ADJECTIVE
  precise

précisément ADVERB
  precisely

préciser VERB
  ⒈ *to be more specific about*
  ◇ *Pouvez-vous préciser ce que vous voulez dire?* Can you be more specific about what you want to say?
  ⒉ *to specify* ◇ *Pouvez-vous préciser les raisons de ce changement?* Can you specify the reasons for this change?

la **précision** NOUN
  ⒈ *precision*
  ⒉ *detail* ◇ *Je vais vous donner quelques précisions.* I'm going to give you some details.

la **préfecture** NOUN
  A préfecture is the headquarters of a département, one of the 96 administrative areas of France.
+ **la préfecture de police** the police headquarters

préférable ADJECTIVE
  preferable

préféré ADJECTIVE
  favourite

la **préférence** NOUN
  preference ◇ *Je n'ai pas de préférence.* I've no preference.
+ **de préférence** preferably

préférer VERB
  to prefer ◇ *Je préfère la cuisine de Teresa.* I prefer Teresa's cooking. ◇ *Je préfère manger à la cantine.* I prefer to eat in the canteen.
+ **Je préférerais du thé.** I'd rather have tea.
+ **préférer quelqu'un à quelqu'un** to prefer somebody to somebody ◇ *Je le préfère à son frère.* I prefer him to his brother.

préhistorique ADJECTIVE
  prehistoric

le **préjugé** NOUN
  prejudice ◇ *avoir des préjugés contre quelqu'un* to be prejudiced against somebody

premier ADJECTIVE
  (FEM SING **première**)
  see also **première** NOUN
  first ◇ *au premier étage* on the first floor ◇ *C'est notre premier jour de vacances.* It's the first day of our holiday. ◇ *C'est la première fois que je viens ici.* It's the first time I've been here. ◇ *le premier mai* the first of May ◇ *Il est arrivé premier.* He came first.
+ **le Premier ministre** the Prime Minister

la **première** NOUN
  see also **premier** ADJECTIVE
  ⒈ *first class* ◇ *Nous avons voyagé en première.* We travelled first class.
  ⒉ *first gear* ◇ *Passe en première pour prendre ce virage.* Change into first to go round this bend.
  ⒊ *lower sixth form*
  In French secondary schools, years are counted from the sixième (youngest) to première and terminale (oldest).
  ◇ *Ma sœur est en première.* My sister's in the lower sixth.

premièrement ADVERB
  firstly

prendre VERB
  to take ◇ *Prends tes affaires et viens avec moi.* Take your things and come with me.
+ **prendre quelque chose à quelqu'un** to take something from somebody ◇ *Il m'a pris mon stylo!* He's taken my pen!
+ **passer prendre** to pick up ◇ *Je dois passer prendre Richard.* I have to pick

up Richard.
* **prendre à gauche** to turn left
  ◦ *Prenez à gauche en arrivant au rond-point.* Turn left at the roundabout.
* **Il se prend pour Napoléon.** He thinks he's Napoleon.
* **s'en prendre à quelqu'un** to lay into somebody (*verbally*) ◦ *Il s'en est pris à moi.* He laid into me.
* **s'y prendre** to set about it ◦ *Tu t'y prends mal!* You're setting about it the wrong way!

le **prénom** NOUN
  first name ◦ *Quel est votre prénom?* What's your first name?

la **préparation** NOUN
  preparation

préparer VERB
  1 *to prepare* ◦ *Elle prépare le dîner.* She's preparing dinner.
  2 *to make* ◦ *Je vais préparer le café.* I'm going to make the coffee.
  3 *to prepare for* ◦ *Laure prépare son examen d'économie.* Laure's preparing for her economics exam.
* **se préparer** to get ready ◦ *Ils se préparent à partir.* They're getting ready to go.

la **préposition** NOUN
  preposition

près ADVERB
* **tout près** nearby ◦ *J'habite tout près.* I live nearby.
* **près de (1)** near (to) ◦ *Est-ce que c'est près d'ici?* Is it near here?
* **près de (2)** next to ◦ *Assieds-toi près de moi.* Sit down next to me.
* **près de (3)** nearly ◦ *Il y avait près de cinq cents spectateurs.* There were nearly 500 spectators.
* **de près** closely ◦ *Il a regardé la photo de près.* He looked closely at the photo.
* **à peu de chose près** more or less

la **présence** NOUN
  1 *presence* ◦ *Sa présence est rassurante.* His presence is reassuring.
  2 *attendance* ◦ *La présence aux cours est obligatoire.* Attendance at lessons is compulsory.

présent ADJECTIVE
  see also **présent** NOUN
  present

le **présent** NOUN
  see also **présent** ADJECTIVE
  present tense
* **à présent** now

la **présentation** NOUN
  presentation
* **faire les présentations** to do the

introductions

présenter VERB
  to present ◦ *Il présentait le spectacle.* He presented the show.
* **présenter quelqu'un à quelqu'un** to introduce somebody to somebody ◦ *Il m'a présenté à sa sœur.* He introduced me to his sister.
* **Marc, je te présente Anaïs.** Marc, this is Anaïs.
* **se présenter (1)** to introduce oneself ◦ *Elle s'est présentée à ses collègues.* She introduced herself to her colleagues.
* **se présenter (2)** to arise ◦ *Si l'occasion se présente, nous irons en Écosse.* If the chance arises, we'll go to Scotland.
* **se présenter (3)** to stand ◦ *Monsieur Legros se présente encore aux élections.* Mr Legros is standing for election again.

le **préservatif** NOUN
  condom

préserver VERB
  to protect
* **préserver de** to protect from ◦ *Nous avons ramassé les chaises du jardin pour les préserver de l'humidité.* We brought the garden chairs in to protect them from the damp.

le **président** NOUN
  1 *president* ◦ *le président des États-Unis* the president of the United States
  2 *chairman* ◦ *le président du conseil d'administration* the chairman of the board of directors
* **le président directeur général** the chairman and managing director

présider VERB
  1 *to chair* ◦ *Duncan a présidé la réunion.* Duncan chaired the meeting.
  2 *to be the guest of honour* ◦ *Il présidait à table.* He was the guest of honour at the table.

presque ADVERB
  nearly ◦ *Il est presque six heures.* It's nearly 6 o'clock. ◦ *Nous sommes presque arrivés.* We're nearly there.
* **presque rien** hardly anything ◦ *Elle n'a presque rien mangé.* She's hardly eaten anything.
* **presque pas** hardly at all ◦ *Il ne dort presque pas.* He hardly sleeps at all.
* **presque pas de** hardly any ◦ *Il n'y a presque pas de place.* There's hardly any space.

la **presqu'île** NOUN
  peninsula

la **presse** NOUN
　press ◇ *les représentants de la presse*
　representatives of the press
pressé ADJECTIVE
　1 *in a hurry* ◇ *Je ne peux pas rester,*
　je suis pressé. I can't stay, I'm in a
　hurry.
　2 *urgent* ◇ *Ce n'est pas très pressé.*
　It's not very urgent.
◆ **une orange pressée** a fresh orange
　juice
presser VERB
　1 *to squeeze* ◇ *Tu peux me presser*
　un citron? Can you squeeze me a
　lemon?
　2 *to be urgent* ◇ *Est-ce que ça*
　presse? Is it urgent?
◆ **se presser** to hurry up ◇ *Allez,*
　presse-toi, on va être en retard! Come
　on, hurry up, we're going to be late!
◆ **Rien ne presse.** There's no hurry.
le **pressing** NOUN
　dry-cleaner's
la **pression** NOUN
　1 *pressure*
◆ **faire pression sur quelqu'un** to put
　pressure on somebody
　2 *draught beer* (*informal*)
prêt ADJECTIVE
　see also **prêt** NOUN
　ready ◇ *Le déjeuner est prêt.* Lunch is
　ready. ◇ *Tu es prête?* Are you ready?
le **prêt** NOUN
　see also **prêt** ADJECTIVE
　loan
le **prêt-à-porter** NOUN
　ready-to-wear clothes
prétendre VERB
◆ **prétendre que** to claim that ◇ *Il*
　prétend qu'il ne la connaît pas. He
　claims he doesn't know her.
prétendu ADJECTIVE
　so-called ◇ *un prétendu expert* a
　so-called expert
prétentieux ADJECTIVE
　(FEM SING **prétentieuse**)
　pretentious
prêter VERB
◆ **prêter quelque chose à quelqu'un** to
　lend something to someone ◇ *Il m'a*
　prêté sa voiture. He lent me his car.
◆ **prêter attention à quelque chose** to
　pay attention to something
le **prétexte** NOUN
　excuse ◇ *Il avait un prétexte pour ne*
　pas venir. He had an excuse for not
　coming.
◆ **sous aucun prétexte** on no account
　◇ *Ne le dérangez sous aucun prétexte.*

On no account must you disturb him.
prétexter VERB
　to give as an excuse ◇ *Elle a prétexté*
　une réunion. She gave a meeting as her
　excuse. ◇ *Il a prétexté qu'il avait un*
　rendez-vous. He gave the excuse that
　he had an appointment.
le **prêtre** NOUN
　priest
la **preuve** NOUN
　1 *evidence* ◇ *Il y a des preuves contre*
　lui. There's evidence against him.
　2 *proof* ◇ *Vous n'avez aucune preuve.*
　You haven't got any proof.
◆ **faire preuve de courage** to show
　courage
◆ **faire ses preuves** to prove oneself
　◇ *Pour être embauché ici, il faut faire ses*
　preuves. To be employed here, you
　need to prove yourself.
prévenir VERB
◆ **prévenir quelqu'un** to warn somebody
　◇ *Je te préviens, il est de mauvaise*
　humeur. I'm warning you, he's in a bad
　mood.
la **prévention** NOUN
　prevention
◆ **des mesures de prévention**
　preventative measures
◆ **la prévention routière** road safety
la **prévision** NOUN
◆ **les prévisions météorologiques** the
　weather forecast
◆ **en prévision de quelque chose** in
　anticipation of something
prévoir VERB
　1 *to plan* ◇ *Nous prévoyons un*
　pique-nique pour dimanche. We're
　planning to have a picnic on Sunday.
◆ **Le départ est prévu pour dix heures.**
　The departure's scheduled for 10
　o'clock.
　2 *to allow* ◇ *J'ai prévu assez à*
　manger pour quatre. I allowed enough
　food for four.
　3 *to foresee* ◇ *J'avais prévu qu'il*
　serait en retard. I'd foreseen that he'd
　be late.
◆ **Je prévois qu'il me faudra une heure**
　de plus. I reckon on it taking me
　another hour.
prier VERB
　to pray to ◇ *Les Grecs priaient*
　Dionysos. The Greeks prayed to
　Dionysos.
◆ **prier quelqu'un de faire quelque chose**
　to ask somebody to do something
　◇ *Elle l'a prié de sortir.* She asked him to
　leave.

* **je vous en prie (1)** please do ◇ *Je peux m'asseoir? – Je vous en prie.* May I sit down? – Please do.
* **je vous en prie (2)** please ◇ *Je vous en prie, ne me laissez pas seule.* Please, don't leave me alone.
* **je vous en prie (3)** don't mention it ◇ *Merci pour votre aide. – Je vous en prie.* Thanks for your help. – Don't mention it.

la **prière** NOUN
  prayer ◇ *faire ses prières* to say one's prayers
* **"prière de ne pas fumer"** "no smoking please"

le **primaire** NOUN
  primary education ◇ *Ses enfants sont encore en primaire.* His children are still in primary education.
* **l'école primaire** primary school

la **prime** NOUN
  [1] *bonus* ◇ *Il a eu une prime en récompense de son travail.* He received a bonus for his work.
  [2] *free gift* ◇ *J'ai eu ce stylo en prime avec l'agenda.* I got this pen as a free gift with the diary.
  [3] *premium* ◇ *une prime d'assurance* an insurance premium

la **primevère** NOUN
  primrose

le **prince** NOUN
  prince ◇ *le prince Charles* Prince Charles

la **princesse** NOUN
  princess ◇ *la princesse Diana* Princess Diana

principal ADJECTIVE
  (MASC PL **principaux**)
  see also **principal** NOUN
  main ◇ *le rôle principal* the main role

le **principal** NOUN
  (PL les **principaux**)
  see also **principal** ADJECTIVE
  [1] *headmaster* ◇ *le principal du collège* the headmaster of the school
  [2] *main thing* ◇ *Personne n'a été blessé; c'est le principal.* Nobody was injured; that's the main thing.

le **principe** NOUN
  principle
* **pour le principe** on principle
* **en principe (1)** as a rule ◇ *Il déjeune en principe à midi et demi.* As a rule he has lunch at 12.30.
* **en principe (2)** in theory ◇ *En principe Anne doit arriver lundi.* In theory, Anne should arrive on Monday.

le **printemps** NOUN
  spring
* **au printemps** in spring

la **priorité** NOUN
  [1] *priority* ◇ *C'est à faire en priorité.* It needs to be done as a priority.
  [2] *right of way* ◇ *Tu n'as pas la priorité.* You haven't got right of way.

pris VERB see **prendre**

pris ADJECTIVE
  [1] *taken* ◇ *Est-ce que cette place est prise?* Is this seat taken?
  [2] *busy* ◇ *Je serai très pris la semaine prochaine.* I'll be very busy next week.
* **avoir le nez pris** to have a stuffy nose
* **être pris de panique** to be panic-stricken

la **prise** NOUN
  [1] *plug*
  [2] *socket*
* **une prise de courant** a power point
* **une prise multiple** an adaptor
* **une prise de sang** a blood test

la **prison** NOUN
  prison ◇ *aller en prison* to go to prison ◇ *être en prison* to be in prison

prisonnier ADJECTIVE
  see also **prisonnier** NOUN
  captive

le **prisonnier** NOUN
  see also **prisonnier** ADJECTIVE
  prisoner

la **prisonnière** NOUN
  prisoner

prit VERB see **prendre**

privé ADJECTIVE
  private ◇ *la propriété privée* private property ◇ *ma vie privée* my private life
* **en privé** in private

priver VERB
* **priver quelqu'un de quelque chose** to deprive somebody of something ◇ *Le prisonnier a été privé de nourriture.* The prisoner was deprived of food.
* **Tu seras privé de dessert!** You won't get any pudding!

le **prix** NOUN
  [1] *price* ◇ *Je n'arrive pas à lire le prix de ce livre.* I can't see the price of this book.
  [2] *prize* ◇ *Cécile a eu le prix de la meilleure actrice.* Cécile got the prize for best actress.
* **hors de prix** exorbitantly priced ◇ *Les repas sont hors de prix ici!* The price of meals here is exorbitant!
* **à aucun prix** not at any price ◇ *Je n'irai là-bas à aucun prix.* I'm not going there, not at any price.
* **à tout prix** at all costs ◇ *Je veux à tout*

prix voir ce film. I want to see this film at all costs.

probable ADJECTIVE
 likely ◦ *Il est probable qu'elle viendra.* It's likely she'll come.
- **C'est peu probable.** That's unlikely.

probablement ADVERB
 probably

le **problème** NOUN
 problem

le **procédé** NOUN
 process

le **procès** NOUN
 trial ◦ *Le procès du meurtrier commence mardi.* The murder trial starts on Tuesday.
- **Il est en procès avec son employeur.** He's involved in a lawsuit with his employer.

prochain ADJECTIVE
 next ◦ *Nous descendons au prochain arrêt.* We're getting off at the next stop.
- **la prochaine fois** next time
- **la semaine prochaine** next week
- **À la prochaine!** See you!

prochainement ADVERB
 soon

proche ADJECTIVE
 1 *near* ◦ *Les magasins les plus proches étaient à trois kilomètres.* The nearest shops were 3 kilometres away.
 ◦ *dans un proche avenir* in the near future
 2 *close* ◦ *un ami proche* a close friend
- **proche de** near to ◦ *La cathédrale est proche du château.* The cathedral is near the castle.
- **le Proche-Orient** the Middle East

les **proches** MASC NOUN
 close relatives

proclamer VERB
 to proclaim

procurer VERB
- **procurer quelque chose à quelqu'un** to get something for somebody ◦ *C'est lui qui m'a procuré ce travail.* He got me this job.
- **se procurer quelque chose** to get something ◦ *Je me suis procuré leur dernier catalogue.* I got their latest catalogue.

le **producteur** NOUN
 producer

la **production** NOUN
 production

la **productrice** NOUN
 producer

produire VERB
 to produce

- **se produire** to take place ◦ *Ces changements se sont produits l'an dernier.* The changes took place last year.

le **produit** NOUN
 product ◦ *les produits de beauté* beauty products

le **prof** NOUN (*informal*)
 teacher ◦ *Elle est prof de maths.* She's a maths teacher.

le **professeur** NOUN
 1 *teacher* ◦ *Philippe est professeur d'histoire.* Philippe's a history teacher.
 2 *professor* ◦ *le professeur Dupont* Professor Dupont
- **un professeur de faculté** a university lecturer

la **profession** NOUN
 profession ◦ *Quelle est votre profession?* What's your profession?
- **"sans profession"** "unemployed"

professionnel ADJECTIVE
 (FEM SING **professionnelle**)
 professional

le **profil** NOUN
 1 *profile* (*of person*) ◦ *de profil* in profile
 2 *contours* (*of object*)

le **profit** NOUN
 profit ◦ *La société a fait des profits importants.* The company made significant profits.
- **tirer profit de quelque chose** to profit from something
- **au profit de** in aid of ◦ *un spectacle au profit de l'UNICEF* a show in aid of UNICEF

profiter VERB
- **profiter de quelque chose** to take advantage of something ◦ *Profitez du beau temps pour aller faire du vélo.* Take advantage of the good weather and go cycling.
- **Profitez-en bien!** Make the most of it!

profond ADJECTIVE
 deep

la **profondeur** NOUN
 depth

le **programme** NOUN
 1 *programme* ◦ *le programme du festival* the festival programme
 2 *syllabus* ◦ *le programme de maths* the maths syllabus
 3 *program* ◦ *un programme informatique* a computer program

programmer VERB
 1 *to show* ◦ *Ce film est programmé dimanche soir.* The film is scheduled for Sunday evening.

2 *to program* ◇ *Mon ordinateur n'est pas programmé pour ça.* My computer isn't programmed to do that.

e**progrès** NOUN
progress ◇ *faire des progrès* to make progress

progresser VERB
to progress

progressif ADJECTIVE
(FEM SING **progressive**)
progressive

e**projecteur** NOUN
1 *projector* ◇ *Le projecteur de diapositives est en panne.* The slide projector is broken.
2 *spotlight* ◇ *Elle était sous les projecteurs.* She was under the spotlight.

e**projet** NOUN
1 *plan* ◇ *des projets de vacances* holiday plans
2 *draft* ◇ *le projet de construction d'un musée* the draft for the construction of a museum
• **un projet de loi** a bill (*in parliament*)

projeter VERB
1 *to plan* ◇ *Ils projettent d'acheter une maison.* They're planning to buy a house.
2 *to cast* ◇ *une ombre projetée sur le mur* a shadow cast onto the wall
• **Elle a été projetée hors de la voiture.** She was thrown out of the car.

prolonger VERB
1 *to prolong* ◇ *Je vais prolonger mes vacances en Espagne.* I'm going to prolong my holidays in Spain.
2 *to extend* ◇ *Je vais prolonger mon abonnement.* I'm going to extend my subscription.
• **se prolonger** to go on ◇ *La réunion s'est prolongée tard.* The meeting went on late.

promenade NOUN
walk ◇ *Il y a de belles promenades par ici.* There are some nice walks round here.
• **faire une promenade** to go for a walk
• **faire une promenade en voiture** to go for a drive
• **faire une promenade à vélo** to go for a bike ride

promener VERB
to take for a walk ◇ *Cordelia promène son chien tous les jours.* Cordelia takes her dog for a walk every day.
• **se promener** to go for a walk
◇ *Chantal est partie se promener.*

Chantal has gone for a walk.

la**promesse** NOUN
promise ◇ *faire une promesse* to make a promise ◇ *tenir sa promesse* to keep one's promise

promettre VERB
to promise ◇ *On m'a promis une augmentation.* They promised me a pay rise. ◇ *Elle m'a promis de me téléphoner.* She promised to phone me.

la**promotion** NOUN
promotion ◇ *Il espère avoir bientôt une promotion.* He's hoping to get promotion soon.
• **être en promotion** to be on special offer ◇ *Les côtes de porc sont en promotion.* Pork chops are on special offer.

le**pronom** NOUN
pronoun

prononcer VERB
1 *to pronounce* ◇ *Le russe est difficile à prononcer.* Russian is difficult to pronounce.
2 *to deliver* ◇ *prononcer un discours* to deliver a speech
• **se prononcer** to be pronounced ◇ *Le "e" final ne se prononce pas.* The final "e" isn't pronounced.

la**prononciation** NOUN
pronunciation

la**propagande** NOUN
propaganda

se**propager** VERB
to spread ◇ *Le feu s'est propagé rapidement.* The fire spread quickly.

la**proportion** NOUN
proportion

le**propos** NOUN
• **à propos** by the way ◇ *À propos, quand est-ce que tu viens?* By the way, when are you coming?
• **à propos de quelque chose** about something ◇ *C'est à propos de la soirée de vendredi.* It's about the party on Friday.

proposer VERB
• **proposer quelque chose à quelqu'un (1)** to suggest something to somebody ◇ *Nous lui avons proposé une promenade en bateau.* We suggested going on a boat ride to him.
• **proposer quelque chose à quelqu'un (2)** to offer somebody something ◇ *Ils m'ont proposé des chocolats.* They offered me some chocolates.

la**proposition** NOUN
offer ◇ *J'accepte ta proposition avec plaisir.* I'll be pleased to accept your

offer.

propre ADJECTIVE

see also **propre** NOUN

[1] *clean* ◇ *Ce mouchoir n'est pas propre.* This handkerchief isn't clean.

[2] *own* ◇ *Gordon l'a fabriqué de ses propres mains.* Gordon made it with his own hands.

◆ **propre à** characteristic of ◇ *C'est une coutume propre au Berry.* It's a custom you find in the Berry region.

le **propre** NOUN

see also **propre** ADJECTIVE

◆ **recopier quelque chose au propre** to make a fair copy of something

proprement ADVERB

properly ◇ *Mange proprement!* Eat properly!

◆ **le village proprement dit** the village itself

◆ **à proprement parler** strictly speaking

la **propreté** NOUN

cleanliness

le **propriétaire** NOUN

see also la **propriétaire**

[1] *owner*

[2] *landlord*

la **propriétaire** NOUN

see also le **propriétaire**

[1] *owner*

[2] *landlady*

la **propriété** NOUN

property ◇ *la propriété privée* private property

le **prospectus** NOUN

leaflet

prospère ADJECTIVE

prosperous

la **prostituée** NOUN

prostitute

protecteur ADJECTIVE

(FEM SING **protectrice**)

[1] *protective* ◇ *un vernis protecteur* a protective varnish

[2] *patronizing* ◇ *un ton protecteur* a patronizing tone

la **protection** NOUN

protection

protéger VERB

to protect

la **protéine** NOUN

protein

protestant ADJECTIVE

(FEM SING **protestante**)

Protestant ◇ *une église protestante* a Protestant church

◆ **Il est protestant.** He's a Protestant.

la **protestation** NOUN

protest

protester VERB

to protest ◇ *Ils protestent contre leurs conditions de travail.* They're protesting about their working conditions.

prouver VERB

to prove

la **provenance** NOUN

origin

◆ **un avion en provenance de Berlin** a plane arriving from Berlin

provenir VERB

◆ **provenir de (1)** to come from ◇ *Ces tomates proviennent d'Espagne.* These tomatoes come from Spain.

◆ **provenir de (2)** to be the result of ◇ *Cela provient d'un manque d'organisation.* This is the result of a lack of organization.

le **proverbe** NOUN

proverb

la **province** NOUN

province

◆ **en province** in the provinces ◇ *Ils habitent en province.* They live in the provinces.

le **proviseur** NOUN

headteacher (of state secondary school) ◇ *Elle est proviseur.* She's a headteacher.

la **provision** NOUN

supply ◇ *une provision de pommes de terre* a supply of potatoes

les **provisions** FEM NOUN

food ◇ *Nous n'avons plus beaucoup de provisions.* We haven't got much food left.

provisoire ADJECTIVE

temporary ◇ *un emploi provisoire* a temporary job

provoquer VERB

[1] *to provoke* ◇ *Il l'a provoquée en la traitant d'imbécile.* He provoked her by calling her stupid.

[2] *to cause* ◇ *Cet accident a provoqué la mort de quarante personnes.* The accident caused the death of 40 people.

la **proximité** NOUN

proximity

◆ **à proximité** nearby ◇ *Sabine habite à proximité.* Sabine lives nearby.

prudemment ADVERB

[1] *carefully* ◇ *Conduisez prudemment.* Drive carefully.

[2] *wisely* ◇ *Prudemment, il a fait des économies.* Wisely, he saved some money.

la **prudence** NOUN

caution

◆ **avec prudence** carefully ◇ *Ils ont*

conduit avec prudence. They drove carefully.

prudent ADJECTIVE
[1] _careful_ ◇ Soyez prudents! Be careful!
[2] _wise_ ◇ Laisse ton passeport à la maison, c'est plus prudent. It would be wiser to leave your passport at home.

la **prune** NOUN
plum

le **pruneau** NOUN
(PL les **pruneaux**)
prune

la **psychiatre** NOUN
psychiatrist

la **psychologie** NOUN
psychology

psychologique ADJECTIVE
psychological

la **psychologue** NOUN
psychologist

les **PTT** FEM NOUN (= Postes et Télécommunications)
Post Office

pu VERB see **pouvoir**
◆ Je n'ai pas pu venir. I couldn't come.

la **pub** NOUN (informal)
[1] _advertising_ ◇ Il y a trop de pub à la télé. There's too much advertising on TV.
[2] _adverts_ ◇ Le film a été coupé par la pub. The film was interrupted by adverts.

public ADJECTIVE
(FEM SING **publique**)
see also **public** NOUN
public ◇ un jardin public a public park
◆ une école publique a state school

public NOUN
see also **public** ADJECTIVE
[1] _public_ ◇ Ce parc est ouvert au public. The park's open to the public.
[2] _audience_ ◇ Le public a applaudi le chanteur. The audience applauded the singer.
◆ en public in public ◇ Je déteste parler en public. I hate speaking in public.

publicitaire ADJECTIVE
◆ une agence publicitaire an advertising agency
◆ un film publicitaire a publicity film

publicité NOUN
[1] _advertising_ ◇ Muriel travaille dans la publicité. Muriel works in advertising.
[2] _advert_ ◇ Il y a trop de publicités dans ce journal. There are too many adverts in this newspaper.

publier VERB
to publish ◇ Bob vient de publier son

nouveau roman. Bob has just published his new novel.

publique ADJECTIVE see **public**

la **puce** NOUN
[1] _flea_ ◇ Ce chien a des puces. This dog has fleas.
[2] _chip_ ◇ une puce électronique a microchip
◆ une carte à puce a smart card

les **puces** FEM NOUN
flea market

puer VERB
to stink ◇ Ça pue le tabac ici! It stinks of tobacco round here!

puéril ADJECTIVE
childish

puis VERB
see also **puis** ADVERB see **pouvoir**
◆ Puis-je venir vous voir samedi? May I come and see you on Saturday?

puis ADVERB
see also **puis** VERB
then ◇ Faites dorer le poulet, puis ajoutez le vin blanc. Fry the chicken till golden, then add white wine.

puisque CONJUNCTION
since ◇ Puisque c'est si cher, nous irons manger ailleurs. Since it's so expensive, we'll eat elsewhere.

la **puissance** NOUN
power

puissant ADJECTIVE
powerful

le **puits** NOUN
well ◇ Il a un puits dans son jardin. He's got a well in his garden.

le **pull** NOUN
jumper

le **pull-over** NOUN
jumper

le **pulvérisateur** NOUN
spray ◇ un pulvérisateur de parfum a perfume spray

pulvériser VERB
[1] _to pulverize_ ◇ L'explosion a pulvérisé le bâtiment. The explosion pulverized the building.
[2] _to spray_ ◇ Il a pulvérisé de l'insecticide sur ses plantes. He sprayed insecticide on his plants.

la **punaise** NOUN
drawing pin

punir VERB
to punish ◇ Il a été puni pour avoir menti. He was punished for lying.

la **punition** NOUN
punishment

le **pupitre** NOUN
desk (for pupil)

P

pur   ADJECTIVE
    ☐1 *pure*   ◇ *L'eau de cette source est très pure.* The water from this spring is very pure.
    ☐2 *neat* (*undiluted*)   ◇ *du whisky pur* neat whisky   ◇ *de l'eau de Javel pure* concentrated bleach
   ➤ **c'est de la folie pure** it's sheer madness
la **purée**   NOUN
    mashed potatoes
   ➤ **la purée de marrons** chestnut purée
la **putain**   NOUN (*rude*)
    whore
le **puzzle**   NOUN
    jigsaw puzzle
le **p.-v.**   NOUN   (= *procès-verbal*)
    parking ticket
le **pyjama**   NOUN
    pyjamas PL
la **pyramide**   NOUN
    pyramid
les **Pyrénées**   FEM NOUN
    Pyrenees
   ➤ **dans les Pyrénées** in the Pyrenees

Q

le **QI** NOUN (= *quotient intellectuel*)
IQ

le **quai** NOUN
[1] *quay* ◇ *être à quai* to be alongside the quay
[2] *platform* ◇ *Le train partira du quai numéro quatre.* The train will leave from platform 4.

qualifier VERB
• **se qualifier** to qualify ◇ *Bob s'est qualifié pour la demi-finale.* Bob has qualified for the semifinal.

la **qualité** NOUN
quality ◇ *Ces outils sont de très bonne qualité.* These are very good quality tools.

quand CONJUNCTION, ADVERB
when ◇ *Quand est-ce que tu pars en vacances?* When are you going on holiday? ◇ *Quand je serai riche, j'achèterai une belle maison.* When I'm rich, I'll buy a nice house.
• **quand même** all the same ◇ *Je ne voulais pas de dessert, mais j'en ai mangé quand même.* I didn't want any dessert, but I had some all the same.

quant à PREPOSITION
regarding ◇ *Quant au problème de chauffage...* Regarding the problem with the heating... ◇ *Quant à moi, je n'arriverai qu'à dix heures.* As for me, I won't be arriving till 10 o'clock.

a **quantité** NOUN
amount
• **des quantités de** a great deal of ◇ *Ils ont invité des quantités de gens.* They invited a lot of people.

a **quarantaine** NOUN
about forty ◇ *une quarantaine de personnes* about forty people
• **Elle a la quarantaine.** She's in her forties.

quarante NUMBER
forty ◇ *Elle a quarante ans.* She's forty.
• **quarante et un** forty-one
• **quarante-deux** forty-two

e **quart** NOUN
quarter
• **le quart de** a quarter of ◇ *Elle a mangé le quart du gâteau.* She ate a quarter of the cake.
• **trois quarts** three quarters
• **un quart d'heure** a quarter of an hour
• **deux heures et quart** a quarter past two
• **dix heures moins le quart** a quarter to ten
• **Un quart d'eau minérale, s'il vous plaît.** A small bottle of mineral water, please.

le **quartier** NOUN
[1] *area* (of town) ◇ *un quartier tranquille* a quiet area
• **un cinéma de quartier** a local cinema
[2] *piece* ◇ *un quartier d'orange* a piece of orange

le **quartz** NOUN
• **une montre à quartz** a quartz watch

quasi ADVERB
nearly ◇ *La quasi-totalité des récoltes a été détruite.* Nearly all of the crop was destroyed.

quasiment ADVERB
nearly ◇ *Le film est quasiment fini.* The film's nearly finished.
• **quasiment jamais** hardly ever ◇ *Ils ne vont quasiment jamais en boîte.* They hardly ever go clubbing.

quatorze NUMBER
fourteen ◇ *Mon frère a quatorze ans.* My brother's fourteen. ◇ *à quatorze heures* at 2 p.m.
• **le quatorze février** the fourteenth of February

quatre NUMBER
four ◇ *Il est quatre heures du matin.* It's four in the morning. ◇ *Il a quatre ans.* He's four.
• **le quatre février** the fourth of February
• **faire les quatre cents coups** to be a bit wild ◇ *Todd a fait les quatre cents coups dans sa jeunesse.* Todd was a bit wild in his youth.

quatre-vingts NUMBER
eighty

quatre-vingts is spelt with an -s when it is followed by a noun, but not when it is followed by another number.

◇ *quatre-vingts francs* eighty francs
◇ *Elle a quatre-vingt-deux ans.* She's eighty-two.
• **quatre-vingt-dix** ninety
• **quatre-vingt-onze** ninety-one
• **quatre-vingt-quinze** ninety-five
• **quatre-vingt-dix-huit** ninety-eight

quatrième ADJECTIVE
see also **quatrième** NOUN
fourth ◇ *au quatrième étage* on the fourth floor

la **quatrième** NOUN
see also **quatrième** ADJECTIVE
third year

In French secondary schools, years are counted from the **sixième** (youngest) to **première** and **terminale** (oldest).

◇ *Mon frère est en quatrième.* My brother's in third year.

que CONJUNCTION, PRONOUN, ADVERB

⚊1 *that* ◇ *Il sait que tu es là.* He knows that you're here. ◇ *la dame que j'ai rencontrée hier* the lady that I met yesterday ◇ *Le gâteau qu'elle a fait est délicieux.* The cake she's made is delicious.

● **Je veux que tu viennes.** I want you to come.

⚊2 *what* ◇ *Que fais-tu?* What are you doing? ◇ *Que vas-tu lui dire?* What are you going to tell him?

● **Qu'est-ce que...?** What...? ◇ *Qu'est-ce que tu fais?* What are you doing? ◇ *Qu'est-ce que c'est?* What's that?

● **plus...que** more...than ◇ *C'est plus difficile que je ne le pensais.* It's more difficult than I thought. ◇ *Il est plus grand que moi.* He's bigger than me.

● **aussi...que** as...as ◇ *Elle est aussi jolie que sa sœur.* She's as pretty as her sister. ◇ *Le train est aussi cher que l'avion.* The train is as expensive as the plane.

● **ne...que** only ◇ *Il ne boit que de l'eau.* He only drinks water. ◇ *Je ne l'ai vu qu'une fois.* I've only seen him once.

● **Qu'il est bête!** He's so silly!

quel ADJECTIVE

(FEM SING **quelle**)

⚊1 *who* ◇ *Quel est ton chanteur préféré?* Who's your favourite singer?

⚊2 *what* ◇ *Quelle est ta couleur préférée?* What's your favourite colour? ◇ *Quelle heure est-il?* What time is it? ◇ *Quelle bonne surprise!* What a surprise!

⚊3 *which* ◇ *Quel groupe préfères-tu?* Which band do you like best?

● **quel que soit (1)** whoever ◇ *quel que soit le coupable* whoever is guilty

● **quel que soit (2)** whatever ◇ *quel que soit votre avis* whatever your opinion

quelle ADJECTIVE *see* **quel**

quelque ADJECTIVE, ADVERB

⚊1 *some* ◇ *Il a quelques amis à Paris.* He has some friends in Paris. ◇ *J'ai acheté quelques disques.* I bought some records.

⚊2 *a few* ◇ *Il reste quelques bouteilles.* There are a few bottles left.

⚊3 *few* ◇ *Ils ont fini les quelques bouteilles qui restaient.* They finished the few bottles that were left.

● **quelque chose (1)** something ◇ *J'ai quelque chose pour toi.* I've got

something for you. ◇ *Je voudrais quelque chose de moins cher.* I'd like something cheaper.

● **quelque chose (2)** anything ◇ *Avez-vous quelque chose à déclarer?* Have you got anything to declare? ◇ *Tu as pensé à quelque chose d'autre?* Did you think of anything else?

● **quelque part (1)** somewhere ◇ *J'ai oublié mon sac quelque part.* I've left my bag somewhere.

● **quelque part (2)** anywhere ◇ *Vous allez quelque part ce week-end?* Are you going anywhere this weekend?

quelquefois ADVERB

sometimes

quelques-uns PRONOUN

(FEM **quelques-unes**)

some ◇ *As-tu vu ses films? J'en ai vu quelques-uns.* Have you seen his films? I've seen some of them.

quelqu'un PRONOUN

⚊1 *somebody* ◇ *Quelqu'un t'a appelé.* Somebody phoned you. ◇ *Il y a quelqu'un à la porte.* There's somebody at the door.

⚊2 *anybody* ◇ *Est-ce que quelqu'un a vu mon parapluie?* Has anybody seen my umbrella? ◇ *Il y a quelqu'un?* Is there anybody there?

la **querelle** NOUN

quarrel

qu'est-ce que *see* **que**

qu'est-ce qui *see* **qui**

la **question** NOUN

⚊1 *question* ◇ *Je t'ai posé une question.* I asked you a question.

⚊2 *matter* ◇ *Ils se sont disputés pour des questions d'argent.* They argued over money matters.

● **Il n'en est pas question.** There's no question of it. ◇ *Il n'est pas question que je paye.* There's no question of me paying.

● **De quoi est-il question?** What's it about?

● **Il est question de l'organisation du concert.** It's about the organization of the concert.

● **hors de question** out of the question ◇ *Il est hors de question que nous restions ici.* It's out of the question that we stay here.

le **questionnaire** NOUN

questionnaire

questionner VERB

to question

la **queue** NOUN

⚊1 *tail* ◇ *Le chien a agité la queue.* The

dog wagged its tail.
- **faire la queue** to queue
- **une queue de cheval** a ponytail
- 2 *rear* ◦ *en queue du train* at the rear of the train
- 3 *bottom* ◦ *en queue de liste* at the bottom of the list
- 4 *stalk* (of fruit, leaf) ◦ *la queue d'une cerise* a cherry stalk

qui PRONOUN
- 1 *who* ◦ *Qui a téléphoné?* Who phoned? ◦ *Le peintre qui a peint ce tableau est un génie.* The artist who painted this picture is a genius.
- 2 *whom* ◦ *C'est la personne à qui j'ai parlé hier.* It's the person whom I spoke to yesterday.
- 3 *that* ◦ *Donne-moi la veste qui est sur la chaise.* Give me the jacket that's on the chair.
- **Qui est-ce qui...?** Who...? ◦ *Qui est-ce qui t'emmène au spectacle?* Who's taking you to the show?
- **Qui est-ce que...?** Who...? ◦ *Qui est-ce que tu as vu à cette soirée?* Who did you see at the party?
- **Qu'est-ce qui...?** What...? ◦ *Qu'est-ce qui est sur la table?* What's on the table? ◦ *Qu'est-ce qui te prend?* What's the matter with you?
- **À qui est ce sac?** Whose bag is this?
- **À qui parlais-tu?** Who were you talking to?

la**quille** NOUN
- **un jeu de quilles** skittles

la**quincaillerie** NOUN
ironmonger's (shop)

la**quinzaine** NOUN
about fifteen ◦ *Il y avait une quinzaine de personnes.* There were about fifteen people there.
- **une quinzaine de jours** a fortnight

quinze NUMBER
fifteen ◦ *Anaïs a quinze ans.* Anaïs is

fifteen. ◦ *à quinze heures* at 3 p.m.
- **le quinze février** the fifteenth of February
- **dans quinze jours** in a fortnight's time

quitter VERB
to leave ◦ *J'ai quitté la maison à huit heures.* I left the house at 8 o'clock.
- **se quitter** to part ◦ *Les deux amis se sont quittés devant le café.* The two friends parted in front of the café.
- **Ne quittez pas.** (on telephone) Hold the line. ◦ *Ne quittez pas, je vous passe Monsieur Divan.* Hold the line, I'll put you through to Monsieur Divan.

quoi PRONOUN
what? ◦ *À quoi penses-tu?* What are you thinking about? ◦ *C'est quoi, ce truc?* What's this thing?
- **Quoi de neuf?** What's new?
- **As-tu de quoi écrire?** Have you got anything to write with?
- **Je n'ai pas de quoi acheter une voiture.** I can't afford to buy a car.
- **Quoi qu'il arrive.** Whatever happens.
- **Il n'y a pas de quoi.** Don't mention it.
- **Il n'y a pas de quoi s'énerver.** There's no reason for getting worked up.
- **En quoi puis-je vous aider?** How may I help you?

quoique CONJUNCTION
even though ◦ *Il va l'acheter quoique ce soit cher.* He's going to buy it even though it's expensive.

quotidien ADJECTIVE
(FEM SING **quotidienne**)
see also quotidien NOUN
daily ◦ *Il est parti faire sa promenade quotidienne.* He's gone for his daily walk.

le**quotidien** NOUN
see also quotidien ADJECTIVE
daily paper ◦ *Le Monde est un quotidien.* Le Monde is a daily paper.

q

R

le **rab** NOUN (*informal*)
    seconds (*of meal*) ◇ *Il y a du rab?* Are there any seconds?

le **rabais** NOUN
    reduction (*in price*)
    ✦ **au rabais** at a discount

raccompagner VERB
    to take home ◇ *Tu peux me raccompagner?* Can you take me home?

le **raccourci** NOUN
    shortcut

raccrocher VERB
    to hang up (*telephone*)

la **race** NOUN
    1 *race* ◇ *la race humaine* the human race
    2 *breed* ◇ *De quelle race est ton chat?* What breed is your cat?
    ✦ **de race** pedigree ◇ *un chien de race* a pedigree dog

racheter VERB
    1 *to buy another* ◇ *J'ai racheté un portefeuille.* I've bought another wallet. ◇ *racheter du lait* to buy more milk
    2 *to buy* ◇ *Il m'a racheté ma moto.* He bought my bike from me.

la **racine** NOUN
    root

raciste ADJECTIVE
    racist

raconter VERB
    ✦ **raconter quelque chose à quelqu'un** to tell somebody about something ◇ *Raconte-moi ce qui s'est passé.* Tell me what happened. ◇ *Raconte-moi une histoire.* Tell me a story.
    ✦ **Qu'est-ce que tu racontes?** What are you talking about?

le **radar** NOUN
    radar

le **radiateur** NOUN
    radiator
    ✦ **un radiateur électrique** an electric heater

radin ADJECTIVE (*informal*)
    stingy

la **radio** NOUN
    1 *radio* ◇ *à la radio* on the radio
    2 *X-ray*
    ✦ **passer une radio** to have an X-ray ◇ *Elle a passé une radio des poumons.* She had a chest X-ray.

le **radio-réveil** NOUN
    (PL les **radios-réveils**)
    clock radio

le **radis** NOUN
    radish

raffoler VERB
    ✦ **raffoler de** to be crazy about ◇ *Elle raffole de la tarte aux pommes.* She really loves apple tart.

rafraîchir VERB
    to cool down
    ✦ **se rafraîchir (1)** to get cooler ◇ *Le temps se rafraîchit.* The weather's getting cooler.
    ✦ **se rafraîchir (2)** to freshen up ◇ *Il a pris une douche pour se rafraîchir.* He had a shower to freshen up.

rafraîchissant ADJECTIVE
    refreshing

la **rage** NOUN
    rabies
    ✦ **une rage de dents** raging toothache

le **ragoût** NOUN
    stew

raide ADJECTIVE
    1 *steep* ◇ *Cette pente est raide.* This is a steep slope.
    2 *straight* ◇ *Laure a les cheveux raides.* Laure has straight hair.
    3 *stiff* ◇ *Son bras est encore raide.* His arm's still stiff.
    4 *flat broke* ◇ *Je suis raide ce mois-ci.* (*informal*) I'm flat broke this month.

la **raie** NOUN
    1 *skate* (*fish*)
    2 *parting* (*in hair*)

le **rail** NOUN
    rail ◇ *par rail* by rail

le **raisin** NOUN
    grapes ◇ *le raisin blanc* green grapes
    ✦ **des raisins secs** raisins

la **raison** NOUN
    reason ◇ *sans raison* for no reason ◇ *Raison de plus pour y aller.* All the more reason for going.
    ✦ **Ce n'est pas une raison.** That's no excuse.
    ✦ **avoir raison** to be right ◇ *Tu as raison.* You're right.
    ✦ **en raison de** because of ◇ *en raison d'une grève* because of a strike

raisonnable ADJECTIVE
    sensible ◇ *Elle est très raisonnable pour son âge.* She's very sensible for her age.

le **raisonnement** NOUN
    reasoning ◇ *J'ai du mal à suivre son raisonnement.* I have difficulty

following his reasoning.
rajouter VERB
to add
ralentir VERB
to slow down
râler VERB (*informal*)
to moan
le **ramassage** NOUN
* **le ramassage scolaire** the school bus service
ramasser VERB
[1] *to pick up* ◇ *Il a ramassé son crayon.* He picked up his pencil.
[2] *to take in* ◇ *Il a ramassé les copies.* He took in the exam papers.
la **rame** NOUN
[1] *oar* (*of boat*)
[2] *train* (*on the underground*)
le **rameau** NOUN
(PL les **rameaux**)
branch
* **le dimanche des Rameaux** Palm Sunday
ramener VERB
[1] *to bring back* ◇ *Je t'ai ramené un souvenir de Grèce.* I've brought you back a present from Greece.
[2] *to take home* ◇ *Tu me ramènes?* Will you take me home?
ramer VERB
to row ◇ *C'est Jean-Pierre qui ramait.* Jean-Pierre was rowing.
la **rampe** NOUN
banister
la **rancune** NOUN
* **garder rancune à quelqu'un** to bear somebody a grudge
* **Sans rancune!** No hard feelings!
rancunier ADJECTIVE
(FEM SING **rancunière**)
vindictive
la **randonnée** NOUN
* **une randonnée à vélo** a bike ride
* **une randonnée pédestre** a ramble
le **rang** NOUN
row (*line*) ◇ *au premier rang* in the front row ◇ *se mettre en rangs* to get into rows
la **rangée** NOUN
row (*line*) ◇ *une rangée de chaises* a row of chairs
ranger VERB
[1] *to put away* ◇ *J'ai rangé tes affaires.* I've put your things away.
[2] *to tidy up* ◇ *Va ranger ta chambre.* Go and tidy up your room.
le **rap** NOUN
rap ◇ *Robert est chanteur de rap.* Robert's a rap singer.

râper VERB
to grate ◇ *le fromage râpé* grated cheese
rapide ADJECTIVE
[1] *fast* ◇ *Cette voiture est très rapide.* This is a very fast car.
[2] *quick* ◇ *J'ai jeté un coup d'œil rapide sur ton travail.* I had a quick glance at your work.
rapidement ADVERB
quickly
le **rappel** NOUN
[1] *booster* (*vaccination*)
[2] *curtain call*
rappeler VERB
to call back ◇ *Je te rappelle dans cinq minutes.* I'll call you back in 5 minutes.
* **rappeler quelque chose à quelqu'un** to remind somebody of something ◇ *Cette odeur me rappelle mon enfance.* This smell reminds me of my childhood.
* **rappeler à quelqu'un de faire quelque chose** to remind somebody to do something ◇ *Rappelle-moi d'acheter des billets.* Remind me to get tickets.
* **se rappeler** to remember ◇ *Il s'est rappelé qu'il avait une course à faire.* He remembered he had some shopping to do.
le **rapport** NOUN
see also **les rapports**
[1] *report* ◇ *Il a écrit un rapport.* He wrote a report.
[2] *connection* ◇ *Je ne vois pas le rapport.* I can't see the connection.
* **par rapport à** in comparison with
rapporter VERB
to bring back ◇ *Je leur ai rapporté un cadeau.* I brought them back a present.
le **rapporteur** NOUN
telltale
la **rapporteuse** NOUN
telltale
les **rapports** MASC NOUN
see also **le rapport**
relations ◇ *Leurs rapports avec leurs voisins se sont améliorés.* Their relations with their neighbours have improved.
* **les rapports sexuels** sexual intercourse
rapprocher VERB
[1] *to bring together* ◇ *Cet accident a rapproché les deux frères.* The accident brought the two brothers together.
[2] *to bring closer* ◇ *Il a rapproché le fauteuil de la télé.* He brought the armchair closer to the TV.
* **se rapprocher** to come closer

R

◇ *Rapproche-toi, tu verras mieux.* Come closer, you'll see better.

la **raquette** NOUN
1 *racket* (tennis)
2 *bat* (table tennis)

rare ADJECTIVE
rare ◇ *une plante rare* a rare plant

rarement ADVERB
rarely

ras ADJECTIVE, ADVERB
short ◇ *un chien à poil ras* a short-haired dog
* **à ras bords** to the brim ◇ *Il a rempli son verre à ras bords.* He filled his glass to the brim.
* **en avoir ras le bol de quelque chose** (*informal*) to be fed up with something
* **un pull ras du cou** a crew-neck jumper

raser VERB
to shave off ◇ *Ray a rasé sa barbe.* Ray has shaved off his beard.
* **se raser** to shave

le **rasoir** NOUN
  see also rasoir ADJECTIVE
razor

rasoir ADJECTIVE (MASC, FEM, PL) (*informal*)
  see also rasoir NOUN
dead boring

rassembler VERB
to assemble ◇ *Il a rassemblé les enfants dans la cour.* He assembled the children in the playground.
* **se rassembler** to gather together ◇ *Les passagers se sont rassemblés près du car.* The passengers gathered near the coach.

rassurer VERB
to reassure
* **Je suis rassuré.** I don't need to worry any more.
* **se rassurer** to be reassured ◇ *Rassure-toi!* Don't worry!

le **rat** NOUN
rat

raté ADJECTIVE
unsuccessful ◇ *Le gâteau est raté.* The cake's a failure.

le **râteau** NOUN
(PL les **râteaux**)
rake

rater VERB
1 *to miss* ◇ *Chantal a raté son train.* Chantal missed her train.
2 *to fail* ◇ *J'ai raté mon examen de maths.* I failed my maths exam. ◇ *Elle a raté sa quiche.* Her quiche didn't turn out right.

RATP ABBREVIATION
Paris transport authority

rattacher VERB
to tie up again ◇ *rattacher ses lacets* to tie up one's laces

rattraper VERB
1 *to recapture* ◇ *La police a rattrapé le voleur.* The police recaptured the thief.
2 *to catch up with* ◇ *Je vais rattraper Cécile.* I'll catch up with Cécile.
3 *to make up for* ◇ *Il faut rattraper le temps perdu.* We must make up for lost time.
* **se rattraper** to make up for it ◇ *Je n'ai pas le temps de sortir mais je me rattraperai après les examens.* I haven't got time to go out, but I'll make up for it after the exams.

la **rature** NOUN
correction ◇ *un texte sans ratures* a text with no corrections

ravi ADJECTIVE
* **être ravi** to be delighted ◇ *Ils étaient ravis de nous voir.* They were delighted to see us. ◇ *Je suis ravi que vous puissiez venir.* I'm delighted that you can come.

rayé ADJECTIVE
striped ◇ *une chemise rayée* a striped shirt

rayer VERB
1 *to scratch* ◇ *Il a rayé la peinture de sa voiture.* He scratched the paintwork of his car.
2 *to cross off* ◇ *Son nom a été rayé de la liste.* His name has been crossed off the list.

le **rayon** NOUN
1 *ray* ◇ *un rayon de soleil* a ray of sunshine
2 *radius* ◇ *le rayon d'un cercle* the radius of a circle
3 *shelf* ◇ *les rayons d'une bibliothèque* the shelves of a bookcase
4 *department* ◇ *le rayon hi-fi vidéo* the hi-fi and video department
* **les rayons X** X-rays

la **rayure** NOUN
stripe

le **ré** NOUN
1 *D* ◇ *en ré majeur* in D major
2 *re* ◇ *do, ré, mi...* do, re, mi...

la **réaction** NOUN
reaction

réagir VERB
to react

le **réalisateur** NOUN
director (*of film*) ◇ *Il est réalisateur.* He's a film director.

la **réalisatrice** NOUN

director (of film) ◇ *Elle est réalisatrice.* She's a film director.

réaliser VERB
1 *to carry out* ◇ *Ils ont réalisé leur projet.* They carried out their plan.
2 *to fulfil* ◇ *Il a réalisé son rêve.* He has fulfilled his dream.
3 *to realize* ◇ *Tu réalises ce que tu dis?* Do you realize what you're saying?
4 *to make* ◇ *réaliser un film* to make a film
• **se réaliser** to come true ◇ *Mon rêve s'est réalisé.* My dream has come true.

réaliste ADJECTIVE
realistic

la **réalité** NOUN
reality
• **en réalité** in fact

rebondir VERB
to bounce

le **rebord** NOUN
edge ◇ *le rebord du lavabo* the edge of the washbasin
• **le rebord de la fenêtre** the window ledge

recaler VERB (informal)
• **J'ai été recalé en maths.** I failed maths.

récemment ADVERB
recently

récent ADJECTIVE
recent

la **réception** NOUN
reception desk

/la **réceptionniste** NOUN
receptionist ◇ *Elle est réceptionniste.* She's a receptionist.

la **recette** NOUN
recipe

recevoir VERB
1 *to receive* ◇ *J'ai reçu une lettre.* I received a letter.
2 *to see* ◇ *Il a reçu trois clients ce matin.* He has seen three clients this morning.
3 *to have round* ◇ *Je reçois des amis à dîner.* I'm having friends for dinner.
• **être reçu à un examen** to pass an exam

le **rechange** NOUN
• **de rechange** spare (battery, bulb) ◇ *des vêtements de rechange* a change of clothes

la **recharge** NOUN
refill

le **réchaud** NOUN
stove

réchauffer VERB
1 *to reheat* ◇ *Je vais réchauffer les légumes.* I'll reheat the vegetables.
2 *to warm up* ◇ *Un bon café va te réchauffer.* A nice cup of coffee will warm you up.
• **se réchauffer** to warm oneself ◇ *Je vais me réchauffer près du feu.* I'll go and warm myself by the fire.

la **recherche** NOUN
research ◇ *Je voudrais faire de la recherche.* I'd like to do research.
• **être à la recherche de quelque chose** to be looking for something ◇ *Je suis à la recherche d'un emploi.* I'm looking for a job.
• **les recherches** search ◇ *La police a interrompu les recherches.* The police called off the search.

rechercher VERB
to look for ◇ *La police recherche l'assassin.* The police are looking for the killer.

la **rechute** NOUN
relapse

le **récipient** NOUN
container

le **récit** NOUN
story

réciter VERB
to recite

la **réclamation** NOUN
complaint ◇ *J'ai une réclamation à faire.* I want to make a complaint
• **les réclamations** the complaints department

la **réclame** NOUN
advert ◇ *une réclame de lessive* an advert for washing powder
• **en réclame** on special offer ◇ *Le saumon était en réclame au supermarché.* Salmon was on special offer at the supermarket.

réclamer VERB
1 *to demand* ◇ *Nous réclamons la semaine de trente heures.* We demand a 30-hour week.
2 *to complain* ◇ *Elles sont toujours en train de réclamer.* They're always complaining about something.

reçois VERB see **recevoir**

la **récolte** NOUN
harvest

récolter VERB
1 *to harvest* ◇ *Ils ont récolté le blé.* They harvested the wheat.
2 *to collect* ◇ *Ils ont récolté deux mille francs.* They collected 2000 francs.
3 *to get* ◇ *Il a récolté une amende.* (informal) He got a fine.

le **recommandé** NOUN
• **en recommandé** by registered mail

R

◇ *Je voudrais envoyer ce paquet en recommandé.* I'd like to send this parcel registered.

recommander VERB
to recommend ◇ *Je vous recommande ce restaurant.* I recommend this restaurant.

recommencer VERB
[1] *to start again* ◇ *Il a recommencé à pleuvoir.* It's started raining again.
[2] *to do again* ◇ *S'il n'est pas puni, il va recommencer.* If he's not punished he'll do it again.

la **récompense** NOUN
reward

récompenser VERB
to reward ◇ *Il m'a récompensée de mes efforts.* He rewarded me for my efforts.

réconcilier VERB
◆ **se réconcilier avec quelqu'un** to be make it up with somebody ◇ *Il s'est réconcilié avec sa sœur.* He has made it up with his sister.

reconnaissant ADJECTIVE
grateful

reconnaître VERB
[1] *to recognize* ◇ *Je ne l'ai pas reconnu.* I didn't recognize him.
[2] *to admit* ◇ *Je reconnais que j'ai eu tort.* I admit I was wrong.

reconstruire VERB
to rebuild

le **record** NOUN
record ◇ *battre un record* to break a record

recouvrir VERB
to cover ◇ *La neige recouvre le sol.* The ground is covered in snow.

la **récréation** NOUN
break ◇ *Les élèves sont en récréation.* The pupils are having their break.
◆ **la cour de récréation** the playground (*of school*)

le **rectangle** NOUN
rectangle

rectangulaire ADJECTIVE
rectangular

rectifier VERB
to correct

le **reçu** NOUN
see also reçu VERB
receipt

reçu VERB see **recevoir**
see also reçu NOUN
◆ **J'ai reçu un colis ce matin.** I received a parcel this morning.
◆ **être reçu à un examen** to pass an exam

reculer VERB

[1] *to step back* ◇ *Il a reculé pour la laisser entrer.* He stepped back to let her in.
[2] *to reverse* ◇ *J'ai reculé pour laisser passer le camion.* I reversed to let the lorry past.
[3] *to postpone* ◇ *Ils ont reculé la date du spectacle.* They postponed the show.

reculons
◆ **à reculons** ADVERB
backwards ◇ *Elle est entrée à reculons.* She came in backwards.

récupérer VERB
[1] *to get back* ◇ *Je vais récupérer ma voiture au garage.* I'm going to get my car back from the garage.
[2] *to make up* ◇ *J'ai des heures à récupérer.* I've got time to make up.
[3] *to recover* ◇ *J'ai besoin de récupérer.* I need to recover.

recycler VERB
to recycle
◆ **se recycler** to retrain ◇ *Il a décidé de se recycler en informatique.* He decided to retrain as a computer programmer.

la **rédaction** NOUN
essay

redemander VERB
[1] *to ask again for* ◇ *Je vais lui redemander son adresse.* I'll ask him for his address again.
[2] *to ask for more* ◇ *Je vais redemander des carottes.* I'm going to ask for more carrots.

redescendre VERB
to go back down ◇ *Il est redescendu au premier étage.* He went back down to the first floor. ◇ *Elle a redescendu l'escalier.* She went back down the stairs.

rédiger VERB
to write (*an essay*)

redoubler VERB
to repeat a year ◇ *Il a raté son examen et doit redoubler.* He's failed his exam and will have to repeat the year.

la **réduction** NOUN
[1] *reduction* ◇ *une réduction du nombre des touristes* a reduction in the number of tourists
[2] *discount* ◇ *une réduction de cent francs* a 100 franc discount

réduire VERB
to cut ◇ *Ils ont réduit leurs prix.* They've cut their prices. ◇ *Il a réduit de moitié ses dépenses.* He has cut his spending by half.

réel ADJECTIVE
(FEM SING **réelle**)

real

réellement ADVERB
really

refaire VERB
1 *to do again* ◇ *Je dois refaire ce rapport.* I've got to do this report again.
2 *to take up again* ◇ *Je voudrais refaire de la gym.* I'd like to take up gymnastics again.

le **réfectoire** NOUN
refectory

la **référence** NOUN
reference
* **faire référence à quelque chose** to refer to something
* **Ce n'est pas une référence!** That's no recommendation!

réfléchi ADJECTIVE
reflexive (verb)
* **C'est tout réfléchi.** My mind's made up.

réfléchir VERB
to think ◇ *Il est en train de réfléchir.* He's thinking.
* **réfléchir à quelque chose** to think about something ◇ *Je vais réfléchir à ta proposition.* I'll think about your suggestion.

le **reflet** NOUN
reflection ◇ *les reflets du soleil sur la mer* the reflection of the sun on the sea

refléter VERB
to reflect

le **réflexe** NOUN
reflex ◇ *avoir de bons réflexes* to have good reflexes

la **réflexion** NOUN
1 *thought* ◇ *Elle est en pleine réflexion.* She's deep in thought.
2 *remark* ◇ *faire des réflexions désagréables* to make nasty remarks
* **réflexion faite** on reflection

le **refrain** NOUN
chorus (of song)

le **réfrigérateur** NOUN
refrigerator

refroidir VERB
to cool ◇ *Laissez le gâteau refroidir.* Leave the cake to cool.
* **se refroidir** to get colder ◇ *Le temps se refroidit.* It's getting colder.

réfugier VERB
to take shelter ◇ *Je me suis réfugié sous un arbre.* I took shelter under a tree.

refus NOUN
refusal
* **Ce n'est pas de refus.** I wouldn't say

no. ◇ *Voulez-vous une bière? – Ce n'est pas de refus.* Would you like a beer? – I wouldn't say no.

refuser VERB
to refuse ◇ *Il a refusé de payer sa part.* He refused to pay his share. ◇ *On lui a refusé une augmentation.* He was refused a pay rise.
* **Je refuse qu'on me parle ainsi!** I won't let anybody talk to me like that!

se **régaler** VERB
* **Merci beaucoup: je me suis régalé!** Thank you very much: it was absolutely delicious!

le **regard** NOUN
look ◇ *Il lui a jeté un regard interrogateur.* He gave him an enquiring look. ◇ *On voyait à son regard qu'elle était contrariée.* You could tell from the look in her eyes that she was upset.
* **Tous les regards se sont tournés vers lui.** All eyes turned towards him.

regarder VERB
1 *to look at* ◇ *Il regardait ses photos de vacances.* He was looking at his holiday photos. ◇ *Regarde! J'ai presque fini.* Look! I've nearly finished.
2 *to watch* ◇ *Je regarde la télévision.* I'm watching television. ◇ *Regarde où tu mets les pieds!* Watch where you put your feet!
3 *to concern* ◇ *Ça ne nous regarde pas.* It doesn't concern us.
* **ne pas regarder à la dépense** to spare no expense

le **régime** NOUN
1 *régime* (of a country)
2 *diet* ◇ *un régime sans sel* a salt-free diet ◇ *se mettre au régime* to go on a diet ◇ *suivre un régime* to be on a diet
* **un régime de bananes** a bunch of bananas

la **région** NOUN
region

régional ADJECTIVE
(MASC PL **régionaux**)
regional

le **registre** NOUN
register

la **règle** NOUN
1 *ruler* ◇ *Il a souligné son nom avec une règle.* He underlined his name with a ruler.
2 *rule* ◇ *C'est la règle.* That's the rule. ◇ *en règle générale* as a general rule
* **être en règle** to be in order ◇ *Mes papiers sont en règle.* My papers are in

R

order.
* **les règles** period (*menstruation*)

le **règlement** NOUN

rules ◇ *Le règlement est affiché à l'entrée.* The rules are up on the wall by the entrance.

régler VERB

1 *to adjust* ◇ *Il faut que je règle mon rétroviseur.* I'll have to adjust my rear-view mirror.

2 *to tune* ◇ *J'ai réglé ma radio sur 476 FM.* I tuned my radio to 476 FM.

3 *to set* ◇ *J'ai réglé le thermostat à vingt degrés.* I've set the thermostat to 20 degrees.

4 *to solve* ◇ *Le problème est réglé.* The problem's solved.

5 *to settle* ◇ *Elle a réglé sa facture.* She's settled her bill. ◇ *J'ai réglé Jean-Pierre pour l'essence.* I've settled up with Jean-Pierre for the petrol.

la **réglisse** NOUN

liquorice

le **règne** NOUN

reign ◇ *sous le règne de Henri IV* in the reign of Henry IV

régner VERB

to reign

le **regret** NOUN

regret
* **à regret** reluctantly

regretter VERB

1 *to regret* ◇ *Elle regrette ce qu'elle a dit.* She regrets saying what she did.
* **Je regrette.** I'm sorry. ◇ *Je regrette, je ne peux pas vous aider.* I'm sorry, I can't help you.

2 *to miss* ◇ *Je regrette mon ancien travail.* I miss my old job.

regrouper VERB

to group together ◇ *Nous avons regroupé les enfants suivant leur âge.* We grouped the children together according to age.
* **se regrouper** to gather together ◇ *Les agriculteurs se sont regroupés pour constituer un syndicat.* The farmers joined together to form a union.

régulier ADJECTIVE

(FEM SING **régulière**)

1 *regular* ◇ *des livraisons régulières* regular deliveries ◇ *des bus réguliers* a regular bus service

2 *steady* ◇ *à un rythme régulier* at a steady rate

3 *scheduled* ◇ *des vols réguliers pour Marseille* scheduled flights to Marseilles

régulièrement ADVERB

regularly

le **rein** NOUN

kidney
* **les reins** back (*of body*) ◇ *J'ai mal aux reins.* My back hurts.

la **reine** NOUN

queen

rejoindre VERB

to go back to ◇ *J'ai rejoint mes amis.* I went back to my friends.
* **Je te rejoins au café.** I'll see you at the café.
* **se rejoindre** to meet up ◇ *Elles se sont rejointes une heure après.* They met up an hour later.

relâcher VERB

to release (*prisoner, animal*)
* **se relâcher** to get slack ◇ *Il se relâche dans son travail.* His work is getting careless.

le **relais** NOUN

relay race ◇ *le relais quatre fois cent mètres* the 4 x 100 metre relay
* **prendre le relais** to take over

la **relation** NOUN

relationship
* **les relations franco-britanniques** Anglo-French relations

se **relaxer** VERB

to relax

se **relayer** VERB

* **se relayer pour faire quelque chose** to take it in turns to do something

le **relevé** NOUN

* **un relevé de compte** a bank statement

relever VERB

1 *to collect* ◇ *Je relève les copies dans cinq minutes.* I'll collect the papers in five minutes.

2 *to react to* ◇ *Je n'ai pas relevé sa réflexion.* I didn't react to his remark.
* **relever la tête** to look up
* **se relever** to get up ◇ *Il est tombé mais s'est relevé aussitôt.* He fell, but got up immediately.

la **religieuse** NOUN

1 *nun* ◇ *Marie est religieuse.* Marie is a nun.

2 *choux cream bun* ◇ *des religieuses au chocolat* choux buns with chocolate cream and icing

religieux ADJECTIVE

(FEM **religieuse**)

religious

la **religion** NOUN

religion

relire VERB

1 *to read over* ◇ *Il a relu sa copie avant de la rendre.* He read his exam paper over before handing it in.

2 *to read again* ◦ *Je voudrais relire ce roman.* I'd like to read this novel again.

remarquable ADJECTIVE
remarkable

la **remarque** NOUN
1 *remark* ◦ *Il a fait une remarque désagréable.* He made a nasty remark.
2 *comment* ◦ *Avez-vous des remarques à faire?* Have you any comments to make?

remarquer VERB
to notice ◦ *J'ai remarqué qu'elle avait l'air triste.* I noticed she was looking sad.
◆ **faire remarquer quelque chose à quelqu'un** to point something out to somebody ◦ *Je lui ai fait remarquer que c'était un peu cher.* I pointed out to him that it was rather expensive.
◆ **Remarquez, il n'est pas si bête que ça.** Mind you, he's not as stupid as all that.
◆ **se remarquer** to be noticeable ◦ *David ne s'est pas rasé ce matin. Ça se remarque.* It's obvious David didn't shave this morning.
◆ **se faire remarquer** to call attention to oneself

le **remboursement** NOUN
refund

rembourser VERB
to pay back ◦ *Il m'a remboursé l'argent qu'il me devait.* He paid me back the money he owed me.
◆ **"satisfait ou remboursé"** "satisfaction or your money back"

remercier VERB
to thank ◦ *Je te remercie pour ton cadeau.* Thank you for your present.
◆ **remercier quelqu'un d'avoir fait quelque chose** to thank somebody for doing something ◦ *Je vous remercie de m'avoir invité.* Thank you for inviting me.

remettre VERB
1 *to put back on* ◦ *Elle a remis son pull.* She put her sweater back on.
2 *to put back* ◦ *Il a remis sa veste dans l'armoire.* He put his jacket back in the wardrobe.
3 *to put off* ◦ *J'ai dû remettre mon rendez-vous.* I've had to put my appointment off.
◆ **se remettre** to recover (*from illness*) ◦ *Mélusine s'est bien remise de son opération.* Mélusine has fully recovered from her operation.

remonte-pente NOUN
ski-lift

remonter VERB

1 *to go back up* ◦ *Il est remonté au premier étage.* He has gone back up to the first floor.
2 *to go up* ◦ *Ils ont remonté la pente.* They went up the hill.
3 *to buck up* ◦ *Cette nouvelle m'a un peu remontée.* The news bucked me up a bit.
◆ **remonter le moral à quelqu'un** to cheer somebody up

le **remords** NOUN
◆ **avoir des remords** to feel remorse

la **remorque** NOUN
trailer (*of car*)

le **remplaçant** NOUN
supply teacher

la **remplaçante** NOUN
supply teacher

remplacer VERB
to replace ◦ *Il faut remplacer cette ampoule.* We need to replace this bulb. ◦ *Il remplace le prof de maths.* He's replacing the maths teacher.
◆ **remplacer par** to replace with

rempli ADJECTIVE
busy ◦ *une journée bien remplie* a very busy day
◆ **rempli de** full of ◦ *La salle était remplie de monde.* The room was full of people.

remplir VERB
1 *to fill up* ◦ *Elle a rempli son verre de vin.* She filled her glass with wine.
2 *to fill in* ◦ *Tu as rempli ton formulaire?* Have you filled in your form?
◆ **se remplir** to fill up ◦ *La salle s'est remplie de monde.* The room filled up with people.

remuer VERB
1 *to move* ◦ *Elle a remué le bras.* She moved her arm.
2 *to stir* ◦ *Remuez la sauce pendant deux minutes.* Stir the sauce for two minutes.
◆ **se remuer** (*informal*) to go to a lot of trouble ◦ *Ils se sont beaucoup remués pour organiser cette soirée.* They went to a lot of trouble organizing this party.

le **renard** NOUN
fox

la **rencontre** NOUN
◆ **faire la rencontre de quelqu'un** to meet somebody ◦ *J'ai fait la rencontre de personnes intéressantes ce soir.* I met some interesting people this evening.
◆ **aller à la rencontre de quelqu'un** to go and meet somebody ◦ *Je viendrai à ta*

R

rencontre. I'll come and meet you.

rencontrer VERB
to meet

- **se rencontrer** to meet ◇ *Ils se sont rencontrés il y a deux ans.* They met two years ago.

le **rendez-vous** NOUN
[1] *appointment* ◇ *J'ai rendez-vous chez le coiffeur.* I've got an appointment at the hairdresser's.
◇ *prendre rendez-vous avec quelqu'un* to make an appointment with somebody
[2] *date* ◇ *Tu sors ce soir? – Oui, j'ai un rendez-vous.* Are you going out tonight? – Yes, I've got a date.

- **donner rendez-vous à quelqu'un** to arrange to meet somebody

rendre VERB
[1] *to give back* ◇ *J'ai rendu ses disques à Christine.* I've given Christine her records back.
[2] *to take back* ◇ *J'ai rendu mes livres à la bibliothèque.* I've taken my books back to the library.

- **rendre quelqu'un célèbre** to make somebody famous
- **se rendre** to give oneself up ◇ *Le meurtrier s'est rendu à la police.* The murderer gave himself up to the police.
- **se rendre compte de quelque chose** to realize something

le **renfermé** NOUN
- **sentir le renfermé** to smell stuffy

renifler VERB
to sniff

le **renne** NOUN
reindeer

renommé ADJECTIVE
renowned ◇ *La Bretagne est renommée pour ses plages.* Brittany is renowned for its beaches.

renoncer VERB
- **renoncer à** to give up ◇ *Ils ont renoncé à leur projet.* They've given up their plan.
- **renoncer à faire quelque chose** to give up the idea of doing something

renouveler VERB
to renew (passport, contract)
- **se renouveler** to happen again ◇ *J'espère que ça ne se renouvellera pas.* I hope that won't happen again.

le **renseignement** NOUN
piece of information ◇ *Il me manque un renseignement.* There's one piece of information I still need.

- **les renseignements (1)** information ◇ *Il m'a donné des renseignements.* He

gave me some information.
- **les renseignements (2)** information desk
- **les renseignements (3)** directory inquiries

renseigner VERB
- **renseigner quelqu'un sur quelque chose** to give somebody information about something
- **Est-ce que je peux vous renseigner?** Can I help you?
- **se renseigner** to find out ◇ *Je vais me renseigner pour voir s'il n'y a pas un vol direct.* I'm going to find out if there's a direct flight.

rentable ADJECTIVE
profitable

la **rentrée** NOUN
- **la rentrée (des classes)** the start of the new school year

rentrer VERB
[1] *to come in* ◇ *Rentre, tu vas prendre froid.* Come in, you'll catch cold.
[2] *to go in* ◇ *Elle est rentrée dans le magasin.* She went into the shop.
[3] *to get home* ◇ *Je suis rentré à sept heures hier soir.* I got home at 7 o'clock last night.
[4] *to put away* ◇ *Tu as rentré la voiture?* Have you put the car away?
- **rentrer dans** to crash into ◇ *Sa voiture est rentrée dans un arbre.* He crashed into a tree.
- **rentrer dans l'ordre** to get back to normal

la **renverse** NOUN
- **tomber à la renverse** to fall backwards

renverser VERB
[1] *to knock over* ◇ *J'ai renversé mon verre.* I knocked my glass over.
[2] *to knock down* ◇ *Elle a été renversée par une voiture.* She was knocked down by a car.
[3] *to spill* ◇ *Il a renversé de l'eau partout.* He has spilt water everywhere.
- **se renverser** to fall over (glass, vase)

renvoyer VERB
[1] *to send back* ◇ *Je t'ai renvoyé ton courrier.* I've sent your mail back to you.
[2] *to dismiss* ◇ *On a renvoyé deux employés.* Two employees have been dismissed.

la **réparation** NOUN
repair

réparer VERB
to repair

repartir VERB
to set off again ◇ *Il s'est arrêté pour déjeuner avant de repartir.* He stopped

for lunch before setting off again.
◇ *Maree était là tout à l'heure, mais elle est repartie.* Maree was here a moment ago, but she's gone again.
* **repartir à zéro** to start again from scratch

le **repas** NOUN
meal
* **le repas de midi** lunch
* **le repas du soir** dinner

repasser VERB
1 *to come back* ◇ *Je repasserai demain.* I'll come back tomorrow.
2 *to go back* ◇ *Je dois repasser au magasin.* I've got to go back to the shop.
3 *to iron* ◇ *J'ai repassé ma chemise.* I've ironed my shirt.
4 *to resit* ◇ *Elle doit repasser son examen de maths.* She's got to resit her maths exam.

repérer VERB
to spot ◇ *J'ai repéré deux fautes.* I spotted two mistakes.
* **se repérer** to find one's way around ◇ *J'ai du mal à me repérer de nuit.* I have difficulty finding my way around when it's dark.

répéter VERB
1 *to repeat* ◇ *Elle répète toujours la même chose.* She keeps repeating the same thing.
2 *to rehearse* ◇ *Les acteurs répètent une scène.* The actors are rehearsing a scene.
* **se répéter** to happen again ◇ *J'espère que cela ne se répétera pas!* I hope this won't happen again!

la **répétition** NOUN
1 *repetition* ◇ *Il y a beaucoup de répétitions ce texte.* There's a lot of repetition in this text.
* **des grèves à répétition** repeated strikes
2 *rehearsal* ◇ *Ils ont une répétition cet après-midi.* They've got a rehearsal this afternoon.
* **la répétition générale** the dress rehearsal

le **répondeur** NOUN
answering machine

répondre VERB
to answer ◇ *répondre à quelqu'un* to answer somebody

réponse NOUN
answer ◇ *C'est la bonne réponse.* That's the right answer.

reportage NOUN
1 *report* ◇ *J'ai vu ce reportage aux informations.* I saw that report on the news.
2 *story* ◇ *J'ai lu ce reportage dans "La Gazette".* I read that story in "La Gazette".

le **reporter** NOUN
reporter ◇ *Christian est reporter.* Christian is a reporter.

le **repos** NOUN
rest

reposer VERB
to put back down ◇ *Elle a reposé son verre sur la table.* She put her glass back down on the table.
* **se reposer** to have a rest ◇ *Tu pourras te reposer demain.* You'll be able to have a rest tomorrow.
* **se reposer sur quelqu'un** to rely on somebody

repousser VERB
1 *to grow again* ◇ *Ses cheveux ont repoussé.* Her hair has grown again.
2 *to postpone* ◇ *Le voyage est repoussé.* The trip's been postponed.

reprendre VERB
1 *to take back* ◇ *Il a repris son livre.* He's taken his book back.
2 *to go back to* ◇ *Elle a repris le travail.* She went back to work.
3 *to start again* ◇ *La réunion reprendra à deux heures.* The meeting will start again at 2 o'clock.
* **reprendre du pain** to take more bread
* **reprendre la route** to set off again
* **reprendre son souffle** to get one's breath back

le **représentant** NOUN
rep ◇ *Il est représentant chez Harper Collins.* He's a rep for Harper Collins.

la **représentante** NOUN
rep ◇ *Elle est représentante.* She'a a sales rep.

la **représentation** NOUN
performance ◇ *la dernière représentation d'une pièce* the final performance of a play

représenter VERB
to show ◇ *Le tableau représente un enfant et un chat.* The picture shows a child with a cat.
* **se représenter** to arise again ◇ *Cette occasion ne se représentera pas.* This opportunity won't arise again.

le **reproche** NOUN
* **faire des reproches à quelqu'un** to reproach somebody

reprocher VERB
* **reprocher quelque chose à quelqu'un** to reproach somebody for something ◇ *Il m'a reproché mon retard.* He

reproached me for being late.
- **Qu'est-ce que tu lui reproches?** What have you got against him?

la **reproduction** NOUN
reproduction

reproduire VERB
to reproduce
- **se reproduire** to happen again ◦ *Je te promets que ça ne se reproduira pas!* I promise it won't happen again!

républicain ADJECTIVE
republican

la **république** NOUN
republic ◦ *la République française* the French Republic

répugnant ADJECTIVE
repulsive

la **réputation** NOUN
reputation

le **requin** NOUN
shark

le **RER** NOUN
Greater Paris high-speed train service

le **réseau** NOUN
(PL les **réseaux**)
network

la **réservation** NOUN
reservation

la **réserve** NOUN
stock ◦ *avoir quelque chose en réserve* to have a stock of something
- **mettre quelque chose en réserve** to put something aside

réserver VERB
1. *to reserve* ◦ *Cette table est réservée.* This table is reserved.
2. *to book* ◦ *Nous avons réservé une chambre.* We've booked a room.
3. *to save* ◦ *Je t'ai réservé une part de gâteau.* I've saved you a piece of cake.

le **réservoir** NOUN
petrol tank

la **résidence** NOUN
block of flats
- **une résidence secondaire** a second home

résistant ADJECTIVE
1. *hard-wearing* ◦ *Ce tissu est résistant.* This fabric is hard-wearing.
2. *robust* ◦ *Il est très résistant.* He's very robust.

résister VERB
to resist

résolu ADJECTIVE
- **Le problème est résolu.** The problem's solved.

résoudre VERB
to solve

le **respect** NOUN
respect

respecter VERB
to respect

la **respiration** NOUN
breathing

respirer VERB
to breathe

la **responsabilité** NOUN
responsibility

responsable ADJECTIVE
see also responsable NOUN
responsible ◦ *être responsable de quelque chose* to be responsible for something

le/la **responsable** NOUN
see also responsable ADJECTIVE
1. *person in charge* ◦ *Je voudrais parler au responsable.* I'd like to speak to the person in charge.
2. *person responsible* ◦ *Il faut punir les responsables.* Those responsible must be punished.

ressembler VERB
- **ressembler à (1)** to look like ◦ *Elle ne ressemble pas à sa sœur.* She doesn't look like her sister.
- **ressembler à (2)** to be like ◦ *Ça ressemble à un conte de fées.* It's like a fairy tale.
- **se ressembler (1)** to look alike ◦ *Les deux frères ne se ressemblent pas.* The two brothers don't look alike.
- **se rassembler (2)** to be alike ◦ *Ces deux pays ne se ressemblent pas.* These two countries aren't alike.

le **ressort** NOUN
spring (metal) ◦ *Le ressort est cassé.* The spring is broken.

ressortir VERB
to go out again

le **restaurant** NOUN
restaurant

le **reste** NOUN
rest
- **un reste de poulet** some left-over chicken
- **les restes** the left-overs

rester VERB
1. *to stay* ◦ *Je reste à la maison ce week-end.* I'm staying at home this weekend.
2. *to be left* ◦ *Il reste du pain.* There's some bread left. ◦ *Il me reste assez de temps.* I still have enough time.
- **Il ne me reste plus qu'à...** I've just got to... ◦ *Il ne me reste plus qu'à ranger mes affaires.* I've just got to put my things away.

- **Restons-en là.** Let's leave it at that.

le **résultat** NOUN
  result   ◇ _le résultat des examens_ the exam results

le **résumé** NOUN
  summary

résumer VERB
  to summarize

le **retard** NOUN
  delay   ◇ _un retard de livraison_ a delay in delivery
- **avoir du retard** to be late
- **être en retard de deux heures** to be two hours late
- **prendre du retard** to be delayed

retarder VERB
  ☐ _to be slow_   ◇ _Ma montre retarde._ My watch is slow.
  ☐ _to put back_   ◇ _Je dois retarder la pendule d'une heure._ I've got to put the clock back an hour.
- **être retardé** to be delayed   ◇ _J'ai été retardé par un coup de téléphone._ I was held up by a phone call.

retenir VERB
  ☐ _to remember_   ◇ _Tu as retenu leur adresse?_ Do you remember their address?
  ☐ _to book_   ◇ _J'ai retenu une chambre à l'hôtel._ I've booked a room at the hotel.
- **retenir son souffle** to hold one's breath

retenu ADJECTIVE
  ☐ _reserved_   ◇ _Cette place est retenue._ This seat is reserved.
  ☐ _held up_   ◇ _J'ai été retenu par un coup de téléphone._ I was held up by a phone call.

la **retenue** NOUN
  detention   ◇ _Gerry est en retenue._ Gerry's in detention.

retirer VERB
  ☐ _to withdraw_   ◇ _Elle a retiré de l'argent._ She withdrew some money.
  ☐ _to take off_   ◇ _Il a retiré son pull._ He took off his sweater.

le **retour** NOUN
  return
- **être de retour** to be back   ◇ _Je serai de retour la semaine prochaine._ I'll be back next week.

retourner VERB
  ☐ _to go back_   ◇ _Est-ce que tu es retourné à Londres?_ Have you been back to London?
  ☐ _to turn over_   ◇ _Elle a retourné la crêpe._ She turned the pancake over.
  ◇ _Il a retourné la poubelle._ He turned the bin upside down.

- **se retourner (1)** to turn round   ◇ _Janet s'est retournée._ Janet turned round.
- **se retourner (2)** to turn over   ◇ _La voiture s'est retournée._ The car turned over.

la **retraite** NOUN
- **être à la retraite** to be retired
- **prendre sa retraite** to retire

retraité ADJECTIVE
  see also retraité NOUN
  retired   ◇ _Mon oncle est maintenant retraité._ My uncle's now retired.

le **retraité** NOUN
  see also retraité ADJECTIVE
  pensioner

la **retraitée** NOUN
  pensioner

rétrécir VERB
  to shrink   ◇ _Son pull a rétréci au lavage._ Her sweater shrank in the wash.
- **se rétrécir** to get narrower   ◇ _La rue se rétrécit._ The street gets narrower.

retrouver VERB
  ☐ _to find_   ◇ _J'ai retrouvé mon portefeuille._ I've found my wallet.
  ☐ _to meet up with_   ◇ _Je te retrouve au café à trois heures._ I'll meet you at the café at 3 o'clock.
- **se retrouver (1)** to meet up   ◇ _Ils se sont retrouvés devant le cinéma._ They met up in front of the cinema.
- **se retrouver (2)** to find one's way around   ◇ _Je n'arrive pas à me retrouver._ I can't find my way around.

le **rétroviseur** NOUN
  rear-view mirror

la **réunion** NOUN
  meeting

se **réunir** VERB
  to meet   ◇ _Ils se sont réunis à cinq heures._ They met at 5 o'clock.

réussi ADJECTIVE
  successful   ◇ _une soirée très réussie_ a very successful party
- **être réussi** to be a success   ◇ _Le repas était très réussi._ The meal was delicious.

réussir VERB
  to be successful   ◇ _Tous ses enfants ont très bien réussi._ All her children are very successful.
- **réussir à faire quelque chose** to succeed in doing something
- **réussir à un examen** to pass an exam

la **réussite** NOUN
  success

la **revanche** NOUN
  return match
- **prendre sa revanche** to get one's own

back ◇ *Il a pris sa revanche en refusant de lui prêter son vélo.* He got his own back by refusing to lend him his bike.

◆ **en revanche** on the other hand ◇ *C'est cher mais en revanche c'est de la bonne qualité.* It is dear but on the other hand it's good quality.

le **rêve** NOUN
  dream
◆ **de rêve** fantastic ◇ *des vacances de rêve* fantastic holidays

le **réveil** NOUN
  alarm clock

le **réveille-matin** NOUN
  (PL les **réveille-matin**)
  alarm clock

réveiller VERB
  to wake up ◇ *réveiller quelqu'un* to wake somebody up
◆ **se réveiller** to wake up

le **réveillon** NOUN
◆ **le réveillon du premier de l'an** New Year's Eve celebrations
◆ **le réveillon de Noël** Christmas Eve celebrations

réveillonner VERB
  ☐1 *to celebrate New Year's Eve*
  ☐2 *to celebrate Christmas Eve*

revenir VERB
  to come back ◇ *Reviens vite!* Come back soon! ◇ *Son nom m'est revenu cinq minutes après.* His name came back to me five minutes later.
◆ **Ça revient au même.** It comes to the same thing.
◆ **Ça revient cher.** It costs a lot.
◆ **Je n'en reviens pas!** I can't get over it!
◆ **revenir sur ses pas** to retrace one's steps

le **revenu** NOUN
  income

rêver VERB
  to dream
◆ **rêver de quelque chose** to dream of something ◇ *J'ai rêvé de mes vacances cette nuit.* I dreamt about my holidays last night.

le **réverbère** NOUN
  street lamp

le **revers** NOUN
  ☐1 *backhand* ◇ *Becker a un excellent revers.* Becker has an excellent backhand.
  ☐2 *lapel* (of jacket)
◆ **le revers de la médaille** the other side of the coin

revient VERB see **revenir**

réviser VERB
  ☐1 *to revise* ◇ *Je dois réviser mon*

anglais. I've got to revise my English.
  ☐2 *to service* ◇ *Je dois faire réviser ma voiture.* I must get my car serviced.

la **révision** NOUN
  revision

revoir VERB
  ☐1 *to see again* ◇ *J'ai revu Sophie hier soir.* I saw Sophie again last night.
  ☐2 *to revise* ◇ *Il est en train de revoir sa géographie.* He's revising his geography.
◆ **au revoir** goodbye

la **révolution** NOUN
  revolution ◇ *la Révolution française* the French Revolution

le **revolver** NOUN
  revolver

la **revue** NOUN
  magazine

le **rez-de-chaussée** NOUN
  ground floor ◇ *au rez-de-chaussée* on the ground floor

le **Rhin** NOUN
  Rhine

le **rhinocéros** NOUN
  rhinoceros

le **Rhône** NOUN
  Rhone

la **rhubarbe** NOUN
  rhubarb

le **rhum** NOUN
  rum

le **rhume** NOUN
  cold ◇ *J'ai attrapé un rhume.* I've caught a cold.
◆ **un rhume de cerveau** a head cold
◆ **le rhume des foins** hay fever

ri VERB see **rire**
◆ **Nous avons bien ri.** We had a good laugh.

riche ADJECTIVE
  ☐1 *well-off* ◇ *Sa famille est très riche.* His family's very well-off.
  ☐2 *rich* ◇ *riche en vitamines* rich in vitamins

le **rideau** NOUN
  (PL les **rideaux**)
  curtain ◇ *tirer les rideaux* to draw the curtains

ridicule ADJECTIVE
  ridiculous ◇ *Je trouve ça complètement ridicule.* I think that's absolutely ridiculous.

rien PRONOUN
  see also **rien** NOUN
  ☐1 *nothing* ◇ *Qu'est-ce que tu as acheté? – Rien.* What have you bought? – Nothing. ◇ *Ça n'a rien à voir.* It has nothing to do with it.
◆ **rien d'intéressant** nothing interesting

* **rien d'autre** nothing else
* **rien du tout** nothing at all
  2 *anything* ◦ *Il n'a rien dit.* He didn't say anything.
* **rien que (1)** just ◦ *rien que pour lui faire plaisir* just to please him ◦ *Rien que la voiture coûte un million.* The car alone costs a million.
* **rien que (2)** nothing but ◦ *rien que la vérité* nothing but the truth
* **De rien!** Not at all! ◦ *Merci beaucoup!–De rien!* Thank you very much!–Not at all!

le **rien** NOUN
> see also **rien** PRONOUN
* **pour un rien** at the slightest thing ◦ *Il se met en colère pour un rien.* He loses his temper over the slightest thing.
* **en un rien de temps** in no time at all

rigoler VERB (informal)
  1 *to laugh* ◦ *Elle a rigolé en le voyant tomber.* She laughed when she saw him fall.
  2 *to have fun* ◦ *On a bien rigolé hier soir.* We had good fun last night.
  3 *to be joking* ◦ *Ne te fâche pas, je rigolais.* Don't get upset, I was only joking.
* **pour rigoler** for a laugh

rigolo ADJECTIVE (informal)
  (FEM SING **rigolote**)
  funny

rincer VERB
  to rinse

rire VERB
> see also **rire** NOUN
  to laugh ◦ *Ce film m'a vraiment fait rire.* That film really made me laugh. ◦ *Nous avons bien ri.* We had a good laugh.
* **pour rire** for a laugh

le **rire** NOUN
> see also **rire** VERB
  laughter ◦ *Il a un rire communicatif.* He has an infectious laugh.

le **risque** NOUN
  1 *risk* ◦ *prendre des risques* to take risks ◦ *à tes risques et périls* at your own risk
  2 *danger* ◦ *Il n'y a pas de risque qu'il le sache.* There's no danger of him finding out.

risqué ADJECTIVE
  risky

risquer VERB
  to risk
* **Ça ne risque rien.** It's quite safe.
* **Il risque de se tuer.** He could get himself killed.

* **C'est ce qui risque de se passer.** That's what might well happen.

le **rivage** NOUN
  shore

la **rivière** NOUN
  river

le **riz** NOUN
  rice

le **RMI** NOUN
  Income Support ◦ *Il touche le RMI.* He's on Income Support.

RN ABBREVIATION (= route nationale)
  A road

la **robe** NOUN
  dress
* **une robe de soirée** an evening dress
* **une robe de mariée** a wedding dress
* **une robe de chambre** a dressing gown

le **robinet** NOUN
  tap

le **robot** NOUN
  robot

la **roche** NOUN
  rock (stone)

le **rocher** NOUN
  rock

le **rock** NOUN
  rock (music) ◦ *un chanteur de rock* a rock singer

les **rognons** MASC NOUN
  kidneys (in cooking)

le **roi** NOUN
  king
* **le jour des Rois** Twelfth Night

le **rôle** NOUN
  role

romain ADJECTIVE
  Roman ◦ *des ruines romaines* Roman remains

le **roman** NOUN
  novel
* **un roman policier** a detective story
* **un roman d'espionnage** a spy story

le **romancier** NOUN
  novelist

rompre VERB
  1 *to split up* ◦ *Paul et Justine ont rompu.* Paul and Justine have split up.
  2 *to break off* ◦ *Ils ont rompu leurs fiançailles.* They've broken off their engagement.

les **ronces** FEM NOUN
  brambles

ronchonner VERB (informal)
  to grouse

rond ADJECTIVE
> see also **rond** NOUN
  1 *round* ◦ *La Terre est ronde.* The earth is round.

R

◆ **ouvrir des yeux ronds** to stare in
amazement
　② _chubby_　◇ _Il a les joues rondes._ He
has chubby cheeks.
　③ _drunk_　◇ _Il est complètement rond._
(_informal_) He's completely drunk.
le **rond** NOUN
　see also rond ADJECTIVE
　circle　◇ _Elle a dessiné un rond sur le_
sable. She drew a circle in the sand.
◆ **en rond** in a circle　◇ _Ils se sont assis_
en rond. They sat down in a circle.
◆ **tourner en rond** to go round in circles
◆ **Je n'ai plus un rond.** (_informal_) I
haven't a penny left.
la **rondelle** NOUN
　slice　◇ _une rondelle de citron_ a slice of
lemon
le **rond-point** NOUN
　(PL les ronds-points)
　roundabout　◇ _La voiture s'est arrêtée_
au rond-point. The car stopped at the
roundabout.
　ronfler VERB
　to snore
le **rosbif** NOUN
　roast beef
la **rose** NOUN
　see also rose ADJECTIVE
　rose
　rose ADJECTIVE
　see also rose NOUN
　pink
le **rosé** NOUN
　rosé (wine)　◇ _Je prendrai un verre de_
rosé. I'll have a glass of rosé.
le **rosier** NOUN
　rosebush
le **rôti** NOUN
　roast meat
◆ **un rôti de bœuf** a joint of beef
　rôtir VERB
　to roast　◇ _faire rôtir quelque chose_ to
roast something
la **roue** NOUN
　wheel　◇ _une roue de secours_ a spare
wheel
　rouge ADJECTIVE
　see also rouge NOUN
　red
le **rouge** NOUN
　see also rouge ADJECTIVE
　① _red_　◇ _Le rouge est ma couleur_
préférée. Red is my favourite colour.
　② _red wine_　◇ _un verre de rouge_ a
glass of red wine
◆ **passer au rouge (1)** to change to red
　◇ _Le feu est passé au rouge._ The light
changed to red.

◆ **passer au rouge (2)** to go through a
red light　◇ _Jean-Pierre est passé au_
rouge. Jean-Pierre went through a red
light.
◆ **un rouge à lèvres** a lipstick
la **rougeole** NOUN
　measles
　rougir VERB
　① _to blush_　◇ _Il a rougi en me voyant._
He blushed when he saw me.
　② _to flush_　◇ _Il a rougi de colère._ He
flushed with anger.
la **rouille** NOUN
　rust
　rouillé ADJECTIVE
　rusty
　rouiller VERB
　to go rusty
　roulant ADJECTIVE
◆ **un fauteuil roulant** a wheelchair
◆ **une table roulante** a trolley
le **rouleau** NOUN
　(PL les rouleaux)
　roll　◇ _un rouleau de papier peint_ a roll
of wallpaper
◆ **un rouleau à pâtisserie** a rolling pin
　rouler VERB
　① _to go_　◇ _Le train roulait à 250 km/h._
The train was going at 250 km an hour.
　② _to drive_　◇ _Il a roulé sans s'arrêter._
He drove without stopping.
　③ _to roll_　◇ _Gilles a roulé une cigarette._
Gilles rolled a cigarette.
　④ _to roll up_　◇ _Il a roulé le tapis._ He
rolled the carpet up.
　⑤ _to con_　◇ _Ils se sont fait rouler._
(_informal_) They were conned.
◆ **Alors, ça roule?** (_informal_) How's it
going?
la **Roumanie** NOUN
　Romania
le **rouquin** NOUN (_informal_)
　redhead
la **rouquine** NOUN (_informal_)
　redhead
　rousse ADJECTIVE _see_ **roux**
la **rousse** NOUN
　redhead
la **route** NOUN
　① _road_　◇ _au bord de la route_ at the
roadside
◆ **une route nationale** an A road
　② _way_　◇ _Je ne connais pas la route._ I
don't know the way.
◆ **Il y a trois heures de route.** It's a
3-hour journey.
◆ **en route** on the way　◇ _Ils se sont_
arrêtés en route pour pique-niquer. They
stopped on the way for a picnic.

* **mettre en route** to start up ◇ *Il a mis le moteur en route.* He started the engine up.
* **se mettre en route** to set off ◇ *Il s'est mis en route à cinq heures.* He set off at 5 o'clock.

le **routier** NOUN
1. *lorry driver* ◇ *Son père est routier.* His father's a lorry driver.
2. *transport café* ◇ *Nous avons mangé dans un routier.* We ate in a transport café.

la **routine** NOUN
routine

roux ADJECTIVE
(FEM SING **rousse**)
see also **roux** NOUN
1. *red* ◇ *Harry a les cheveux roux.* Harry has red hair.
2. *red-haired* ◇ *Isobel est rousse.* Isobel's red-haired.

le **roux** NOUN
see also **roux** ADJECTIVE
redhead

royal ADJECTIVE
(MASC PL **royaux**)
royal

le **royaume** NOUN
kingdom
* **le Royaume-Uni** the United Kingdom

le **ruban** NOUN
ribbon
* **le ruban adhésif** adhesive tape

la **rubéole** NOUN
German measles

la **ruche** NOUN
hive

rudement ADVERB (*informal*)

terribly ◇ *C'était rudement bon.* It was terribly good.

la **rue** NOUN
street

la **ruelle** NOUN
alley

le **rugby** NOUN
rugby ◇ *Yann joue au rugby.* Yann plays rugby.

la **ruine** NOUN
ruin ◇ *les ruines de la cathédrale* the ruins of the cathedral

ruiner VERB
to ruin

le **ruisseau** NOUN
(PL les **ruisseaux**)
stream

la **rumeur** NOUN
rumour

la **rupture** NOUN
break-up

la **ruse** NOUN
trickery ◇ *une ruse* a trick

rusé ADJECTIVE
cunning

russe ADJECTIVE, NOUN
Russian ◇ *Il parle russe.* He speaks Russian.
* **un Russe** a Russian (*man*)
* **une Russe** a Russian (*woman*)
* **les Russes** the Russians

la **Russie** NOUN
Russia

le **rythme** NOUN
1. *rhythm* ◇ *J'aime le rythme de cette musique.* I like the beat of this music.
2. *pace* ◇ *Il marche à un bon rythme.* He walks at a good pace.

R

S

s' PRONOUN *see* se

sa ADJECTIVE

[1] *his* ◇ Paul est allé voir sa grand-mère. Paul's gone to see his grandmother.

[2] *her* ◇ Elle a embrassé sa mère. She kissed her mother.

le sable NOUN
sand
+ des sables mouvants quicksand

le sablé NOUN
shortbread biscuit

le sabot NOUN
[1] *clog*
[2] *hoof* (of horse)

le sac NOUN
bag
+ un sac de voyage a travel bag
+ un sac de couchage a sleeping bag
+ un sac à main a handbag
+ un sac à dos a rucksack

le sachet NOUN
sachet (of sugar, coffee)
+ du potage en sachet packet soup
+ un sachet de thé a tea bag

la sacoche NOUN
bag
+ une sacoche de bicyclette a saddlebag

sacré ADJECTIVE
sacred

sage ADJECTIVE
[1] *good* (well-behaved) ◇ Sois sage. Be good.
[2] *wise* (sensible) ◇ Il serait plus sage d'attendre. It would be wiser to wait.

la sagesse NOUN
wisdom ◇ Il a eu la sagesse de ne pas y aller. He wisely didn't go.
+ une dent de sagesse a wisdom tooth

le Sagittaire NOUN
Sagittarius ◇ Michèle est Sagittaire. Michèle is Sagittarius.

saignant ADJECTIVE
rare (meat)

saigner VERB
to bleed
+ saigner du nez to have a nosebleed

sain ADJECTIVE
healthy
+ sain et sauf safe and sound

saint ADJECTIVE

see also saint NOUN

holy ◇ la semaine sainte Holy Week ◇ le Saint-Esprit the Holy Spirit
+ la Sainte Vierge the Blessed Virgin
+ le vendredi saint Good Friday

le saint NOUN

see also saint ADJECTIVE

saint

la sainte NOUN
saint

sais VERB *see* savoir
+ Je ne sais pas. I don't know.

saisir VERB
to take hold of
+ saisir l'occasion de faire quelque chose to seize the opportunity to do something

la saison NOUN
season ◇ Ce n'est pas la saison des fraises. Strawberries are out of season. ◇ un temps de saison seasonable weather
+ la saison des vendanges harvest time

sait VERB *see* savoir
+ Il sait que... He knows that...

la salade NOUN
[1] *lettuce*
[2] *salad* ◇ une salade composée a mixed salad ◇ une salade de fruits a fruit salad

le saladier NOUN
salad bowl

le salaire NOUN
salary

le salarié NOUN
salaried employee

la salariée NOUN
salaried employee

le salaud NOUN (rude)
bastard

sale ADJECTIVE
dirty

salé ADJECTIVE
[1] *salty* ◇ La soupe est trop salée. The soup's too salty.
[2] *salted* ◇ du beurre salé salted butter
[3] *savoury* ◇ des biscuits salés savoury biscuits

saler VERB
to put salt in ◇ J'ai oublié de saler la soupe. I forgot to put salt in the soup.

la saleté NOUN
dirt ◇ J'ai horreur de la saleté. I hate dirt. ◇ Il y a une saleté sur ta chemise. There's some dirt on your shirt.
+ faire des saletés to make a mess

salir VERB
+ salir quelque chose to get something dirty
+ se salir to get oneself dirty ◇ Mets un tablier, sinon tu vas te salir. Put on an

apron or you'll get yourself dirty.

la **salle** NOUN
  ☐ 1 _room_
  ☐ 2 _audience_ ◦ *Toute la salle l'a applaudi.* The whole audience applauded him.
  ☐ 3 _ward_ (*in hospital*) ◦ *Il est à la salle douze.* He's in Ward 12.

* **la salle à manger** the dining room
* **la salle de séjour** the living room
* **la salle de bains** the bathroom
* **la salle d'attente** the waiting room
* **une salle de classe** a classroom
* **une salle de concert** a concert hall
* **la salle d'embarquement** the departure lounge

le **salon** NOUN
  lounge

* **un salon de thé** a tearoom
* **un salon de coiffure** a hair salon
* **un salon de beauté** a beauty salon

la **salope** NOUN (*rude*)
  bitch

la **salopette** NOUN
  ☐ 1 _dungarees_
  ☐ 2 _overalls_

saluer VERB

* **saluer quelqu'un (1)** to say hello to somebody ◦ *Je l'ai croisé dans la rue et il m'a salué.* I met him in the street and he said hello.
* **saluer quelqu'un (2)** to say goodbye to somebody ◦ *Il nous a salués et il est parti.* He said goodbye and left.

salut EXCLAMATION (*informal*)
  _Hi!_

e **samedi** NOUN
  ☐ 1 _Saturday_ ◦ *Aujourd'hui, nous sommes samedi.* It's Saturday today.
  ☐ 2 _on Saturday_ ◦ *Nous sommes allés au cinéma samedi.* We went to the cinema on Saturday.

* **le samedi** on Saturdays ◦ *Le magasin ferme à dix-huit heures le samedi.* The shop closes at 6 p.m. on Saturdays.
* **tous les samedis** every Saturday
* **samedi dernier** last Saturday
* **samedi prochain** next Saturday

SAMU NOUN
  ambulance service

sandale NOUN
  sandal

sang NOUN
  blood

* **en sang** covered in blood

sang-froid NOUN

* **garder son sang-froid** to keep calm
* **perdre son sang-froid** to lose one's cool
* **faire quelque chose de sang-froid** to

do something in cold blood

le **sanglier** NOUN
  wild boar

le **sanglot** NOUN

* **éclater en sanglots** to burst into tears

la **Sanisette** ® NOUN
  Superloo ®

sans PREPOSITION
  without ◦ *Elle est venue sans son frère.* She came without her brother.

* **un pull sans manches** a sleeveless sweater

le/la **sans-abri** NOUN
  (PL les **sans-abri**)
  homeless person ◦ *les sans-abri* the homeless

sans-gêne ADJECTIVE
  inconsiderate

la **santé** NOUN
  health ◦ *en bonne santé* in good health

* **Santé!** Cheers!

saoudien ADJECTIVE, NOUN
  (FEM SING **saoudienne**)
  Saudi Arabian

* **un Saoudien** a Saudi Arabian (*man*)
* **une Saoudienne** a Saudi Arabian (*woman*)

le **sapeur-pompier** NOUN
  (PL les **sapeurs-pompiers**)
  fireman

* **les sapeurs-pompiers** the fire brigade

le **sapin** NOUN
  fir tree

* **un sapin de Noël** a Christmas tree

la **Sardaigne** NOUN
  Sardinia

satisfaire VERB
  to satisfy

satisfaisant ADJECTIVE
  satisfactory

satisfait ADJECTIVE
  satisfied ◦ *être satisfait de quelque chose* to be satisfied with something

la **sauce** NOUN
  ☐ 1 _sauce_
  ☐ 2 _gravy_

la **saucisse** NOUN
  sausage

le **saucisson** NOUN
  salami

sauf PREPOSITION
  except ◦ *Tout le monde est venu sauf lui.* Everyone came except him.

* **sauf si** unless ◦ *Nous irons pique-niquer, sauf s'il fait mauvais.* We'll go for a picnic, unless the weather's bad.
* **sauf que** except that ◦ *Tout s'est bien passé, sauf que nous sommes arrivés en*

S

retard. Everything went OK, except that we arrived late.

le **saumon** NOUN
  salmon

saur ADJECTIVE
- **un hareng saur** a kipper

le **saut** NOUN
  jump
- **le saut en longueur** the long jump
- **le saut en hauteur** the high jump
- **le saut à la perche** the pole vault
- **le saut à l'élastique** bungee jumping
- **un saut périlleux** a somersault

sauter VERB
  to jump ◇ *Nous avons sauté par-dessus la barrière.* We jumped over the gate.
- **sauter à la corde** to skip (*with a rope*)
- **faire sauter quelque chose** to blow something up ◇ *On a fait sauter le commissariat de police la nuit dernière.* The police station was blown up last night.

la **sauterelle** NOUN
  grasshopper

sauvage ADJECTIVE
  [1] *wild* ◇ *les animaux sauvages* wild animals ◇ *faire du camping sauvage* to camp in the wild
- **une région sauvage** an unspoiled area
  [2] *shy* ◇ *Il est un peu sauvage.* He's a bit shy.

sauver VERB
  to save
- **se sauver (1)** to run away ◇ *Il s'est sauvé à toutes jambes.* He ran away as fast as he could.
- **se sauver (2)** (*informal*) to be off ◇ *Allez, je me sauve!* Right, I'm off.

le **sauvetage** NOUN
  rescue

le **sauveur** NOUN
  saviour

savais, savait VERB *see* **savoir**
- **Je ne savais pas qu'il devait venir.** I didn't know he was going to come.

le **savant** NOUN
  scientist

savent VERB *see* **savoir**
- **Ils ne savent pas ce qu'ils veulent.** They don't know what they want.

la **saveur** NOUN
  flavour

savez VERB *see* **savoir**
- **Est-ce que vous savez où elle habite?** Do you know where she lives?

savoir VERB
  to know ◇ *Je ne sais pas où il est allé.* I don't know where he's gone. ◇ *Nous*

ne savons pas s'il est bien arrivé. We don't know if he's arrived safely. ◇ *Tu savais que Canberra était la capitale de l'Australie?* Did you know that Canberra was the capital of Australia? ◇ *Il ne sait pas ce qu'il va faire ce week-end.* He doesn't know what he's going to do this weekend.
- **Tu sais nager?** Can you swim?

le **savon** NOUN
  soap

la **savonnette** NOUN
  bar of soap

savons VERB *see* **savoir**

savoureux ADJECTIVE
  (FEM SING **savoureuse**)
  tasty

le **saxo** NOUN (*informal*)
  see also la saxo
  [1] *sax*
  [2] *sax player*

la **saxo** NOUN (*informal*)
  see also le saxo
  sax player

le **scandale** NOUN
  scandal
- **faire scandale** to cause a scandal ◇ *Ce film a fait scandale.* The film caused a scandal.

scandaleux ADJECTIVE
  (FEM SING **scandaleuse**)
  outrageous

le/la **Scandinave** NOUN
  Scandinavian

scandinave ADJECTIVE
  Scandinavian

la **Scandinavie** NOUN
  Scandinavia

le **scarabée** NOUN
  beetle

la **scène** NOUN
  scene ◇ *une scène d'amour* a love scene ◇ *la scène du crime* the scene of the crime ◇ *Il m'a fait une scène.* He made a scene.
- **une scène de ménage** a domestic row

sceptique ADJECTIVE
  sceptical

le **schéma** NOUN
  diagram

schématique ADJECTIVE
- **l'explication schématique d'une théorie** the broad outline of a theory
- **Cette interprétation est un peu trop schématique.** This interpretation is a bit oversimplified.

la **scie** NOUN
  saw
- **une scie à métaux** a hacksaw

la **science** NOUN
science
- **les sciences physiques** physics
- **les sciences naturelles** biology
- **sciences po** (*informal*) politics ◇ *Mon frère fait sciences po à Paris.* My brother is studying politics in Paris.

scientifique ADJECTIVE
see also scientifique NOUN
scientific

/la **scientifique** NOUN
see also scientifique ADJECTIVE
1 *scientist*
2 *science student*

scier VERB
to saw

scolaire ADJECTIVE
school ◇ *l'année scolaire* the school year ◇ *les vacances scolaires* the school holidays ◇ *mon livret scolaire* my school report

le **Scorpion** NOUN
Scorpio ◇ *Catherine est Scorpion.* Catherine is Scorpio.

le **Scotch** ® NOUN
adhesive tape

le **scrupule** NOUN
scruple

sculpter VERB
to sculpt

le **sculpteur** NOUN
sculptor

la **sculpture** NOUN
sculpture

a **SDF** NOUN (= *sans domicile fixe*)
homeless person
- **les SDF** the homeless

se PRONOUN
se *forms part of reflexive constructions.*
1 *himself* ◇ *Il se regarde dans la glace.* He's looking at himself in the mirror.
2 *herself* ◇ *Elle se regarde dans la glace.* She's looking at herself in the mirror.
3 *itself* ◇ *Le chien s'est fait mal.* The dog hurt itself.
4 *oneself* ◇ *se regarder dans une glace* to look at oneself in a mirror
5 *themselves* ◇ *Ils se sont regardés dans la glace.* They looked at themselves in the mirror.
se *changes to* **s'** *before a vowel and most words beginning with "h".*
◇ *Elle s'admire dans sa nouvelle robe.* She's admiring herself in her new dress.
6 *each other* ◇ *Ils s'aiment.* They love each other.

séance NOUN

1 *session* ◇ *une séance de rééducation* a physiotherapy session
2 *showing* (*at the cinema*) ◇ *La prochaine séance est à dix-neuf heures.* The next showing is at 7 p.m.

le **seau** NOUN
(PL les **seaux**)
bucket

sec ADJECTIVE
(FEM SING **sèche**)
1 *dry* ◇ *Mon jean n'est pas encore sec.* My jeans aren't dry yet.
2 *dried* ◇ *des figues sèches* dried figs

le **sèche-cheveux** NOUN
(PL les **sèche-cheveux**)
hair dryer

le **sèche-linge** NOUN
(PL les **sèche-linge**)
tumble dryer

sécher VERB
1 *to dry*
2 *to be stumped* ◇ *J'ai complètement séché à l'interro de maths.* (*informal*) I was completely stumped in the maths test.
- **se sécher** to dry oneself ◇ *Sèche-toi avec cette serviette.* Dry yourself with this towel.

la **sécheresse** NOUN
drought ◇ *une terrible sécheresse* a terrible drought

second ADJECTIVE
see also second NOUN
second ◇ *Il est arrivé second.* He came second.

le **second** NOUN
see also second ADJECTIVE
second floor ◇ *Elle habite au second.* She lives on the second floor.

secondaire ADJECTIVE
secondary ◇ *l'enseignement secondaire* secondary education
- **des effets secondaires** side effects

la **seconde** NOUN
1 *second* ◇ *Attends une seconde!* Wait a second!
2 *fifth year*
In French secondary schools, years are counted from the **sixième** (*youngest*) *to* **première** *and* **terminale** (*oldest*).
◇ *Ma sœur est en seconde.* My sister's in fifth year.
3 *second class* ◇ *voyager en seconde* to travel second-class

secouer VERB
to shake ◇ *secouer la tête* to shake one's head

secourir VERB
to rescue

le **secourisme** NOUN
first aid ◇ *J'ai un brevet de secourisme.* I've got a first aid qualification.

le **secours** NOUN
help ◇ *Il est allé chercher du secours.* He went to get help. ◇ *Au secours!* Help!
- **les premiers secours** first aid
- **une sortie de secours** an emergency exit
- **la roue de secours** the spare wheel

le **secret** NOUN
> see also **secret** ADJECTIVE
secret

secret ADJECTIVE
(FEM SING **secrète**)
> see also **secret** NOUN
secret

le **secrétaire** NOUN
> see also **la secrétaire**
> [1] *secretary*
> [2] *writing desk*

la **secrétaire** NOUN
> see also **le secrétaire**
secretary

le **secrétariat** NOUN
secretary's office

le **secteur** NOUN
sector ◇ *le secteur public* the public sector ◇ *le secteur privé* the private sector

la **sécu** NOUN (*informal*)
Social Security

la **sécurité** NOUN
[1] *safety*
- **être en sécurité** to be safe ◇ *On ne se sent pas en sécurité dans ce quartier.* You don't feel safe in this neighbourhood.
- **la sécurité routière** road safety
- **une ceinture de sécurité** a seatbelt
[2] *security* ◇ *par mesure de sécurité* as a security measure
- **la sécurité sociale** Social Security
- **la sécurité de l'emploi** job security

séduisant ADJECTIVE
attractive

le **seigle** NOUN
rye ◇ *un pain de seigle* a loaf of rye bread

le **seigneur** NOUN
lord
- **le Seigneur** the Lord

le **sein** NOUN
breast
- **au sein de** within ◇ *Chaque pays est autonome au sein de l'Europe.* Each country is independent within Europe.

seize NUMBER
sixteen ◇ *Elle a seize ans.* She's sixteen. ◇ *à seize heures* at 4 p.m.
- **le seize février** the sixteenth of February

seizième ADJECTIVE
sixteenth

le **séjour** NOUN
stay ◇ *J'ai fait un séjour d'une semaine en Italie.* I stayed in Italy for a week.

le **sel** NOUN
salt

sélectionner VERB
to select

le **self** NOUN (*informal*)
self-service restaurant

le **self-service** NOUN
self-service restaurant

la **selle** NOUN
saddle

selon PREPOSITION
according to ◇ *selon lui* according to him ◇ *selon mon humeur* according to what mood I'm in ◇ *Ils sont répartis selon leur âge.* They're divided up according to age.

la **semaine** NOUN
week
- **en semaine** on weekdays

semblable ADJECTIVE
similar

le **semblant** NOUN
- **faire semblant de faire quelque chose** to pretend to do something ◇ *Il fait semblant de dormir.* He's pretending to be asleep.

sembler VERB
to seem ◇ *Le temps semble s'améliorer.* The weather seems to be improving. ◇ *Il me semble inutile de s'en inquiéter.* It seems pointless to me to worry about it.

la **semelle** NOUN
[1] *sole*
[2] *insole*

la **semoule** NOUN
semolina

le **sens** NOUN
[1] *sense* ◇ *avoir le sens de l'humour* to have a sense of humour ◇ *Je n'ai pas le sens de l'orientation.* I've got no sense of direction. ◇ *Ça n'a pas de sens.* It doesn't make sense.
- **le bon sens** common sense
[2] *direction* ◇ *Tu tournes la poignée dans le mauvais sens.* You're turning the handle in the wrong direction.
- **sens dessus dessous** upside down
- **un sens interdit** a one-way street

◇ *J'ai failli prendre un sens interdit.* I nearly went the wrong way down a one-way street.

◆ **un sens unique** a one-way street

sensé ADJECTIVE
sensible

sensible ADJECTIVE
[1] *sensitive* ◇ *Elle est très sensible.* She's very sensitive. ◇ *Ce film est déconseillé aux personnes sensibles.* This film contains scenes which some viewers may find disturbing.
[2] *visible* ◇ *une amélioration sensible* a visible improvement

sensiblement ADVERB
[1] *visibly* ◇ *Elle a sensiblement progressé.* She's made visible progress.
[2] *approximately* ◇ *Nous sommes sensiblement de la même taille.* We're approximately the same height.

la **sentence** NOUN
sentence (judgement)

le **sentier** NOUN
path

le **sentiment** NOUN
feeling

sentimental ADJECTIVE
(MASC PL **sentimentaux**)
sentimental

sentir VERB
[1] *to smell* ◇ *Ça sent bon.* That smells good. ◇ *Ça sent mauvais.* It smells bad.
[2] *to smell of* ◇ *Ça sent les frites ici.* It smells of chips in here.
[3] *to taste* ◇ *Est-ce que tu sens l'ail dans le rôti?* Can you taste the garlic in the roast?
[4] *to feel* ◇ *Ça t'a fait mal?—Non, je n'ai rien senti.* Did it hurt?—No, I didn't feel a thing. ◇ *Je ne me sens pas bien.* I don't feel well.

◆ **Il ne peut pas la sentir.** (*informal*) He can't stand her.

séparé ADJECTIVE
separated ◇ *Mes parents sont séparés.* My parents are separated.

séparément ADVERB
separately

séparer VERB
to separate ◇ *Séparez le blanc du jaune.* Separate the yolk from the white.

◆ **se séparer** to separate ◇ *Mes parents se sont séparés l'année dernière.* My parents separated last year.

sept NUMBER
seven ◇ *Il est arrivé à sept heures.* He arrived at seven o'clock. ◇ *Elle a sept ans.* She's seven.

◆ **le sept février** the seventh of February

septembre MASC NOUN
September

◆ **en septembre** in September

le **septennat** NOUN

le septennat *is the seven-year term of office of the French President.*

septième ADJECTIVE
seventh ◇ *au septième étage* on the seventh floor

sera, serai, seras, serez VERB *see* **être**

◆ **Je serai de retour à dix heures.** I'll be back at 10 o'clock.

la **série** NOUN
series

sérieusement ADVERB
seriously

sérieux ADJECTIVE
(FEM SING **sérieuse**)
see also **sérieux** NOUN
[1] *serious* ◇ *Il plaisantait?—Non, il était sérieux.* Was he joking?—No, he was serious.
[2] *responsible* ◇ *C'est un employé très sérieux.* He's a very responsible employee.

le **sérieux** NOUN
see also **sérieux** ADJECTIVE

◆ **garder son sérieux** to keep a straight face ◇ *J'ai eu du mal à garder mon sérieux.* I had trouble keeping a straight face.

◆ **prendre quelque chose au sérieux** to take something seriously

◆ **prendre quelqu'un au sérieux** to take somebody seriously

◆ **Il manque un peu de sérieux.** He's not very responsible.

la **seringue** NOUN
syringe

séronégatif ADJECTIVE
(FEM SING **séronégative**)
HIV-negative

serons, seront VERB *see* **être**

séropositif ADJECTIVE
(FEM SING **séropositive**)
HIV-positive

le **serpent** NOUN
snake

la **serre** NOUN
greenhouse

◆ **l'effet de serre** the greenhouse effect

serré ADJECTIVE
[1] *tight* ◇ *Mon pantalon est trop serré.* My trousers are too tight.
[2] *close-fought* ◇ *Ça a été un match serré.* It was a close-fought game.

serrer VERB

+ **Ce pantalon me serre trop.** These trousers are too tight for me.
+ **serrer la main à quelqu'un** to shake hands with somebody
+ **se serrer** to squeeze up ◇ *Serrez-vous un peu pour que je puisse m'asseoir.* Squeeze up a bit so I càn sit down.
+ **serrer quelqu'un dans ses bras** to hug somebody

la **serrure** NOUN
lock

sers, sert VERB *see* **servir**

le **serveur** NOUN
waiter

la **serveuse** NOUN
waitress

serviable ADJECTIVE
helpful

le **service** NOUN
1 *service* (*in restaurant*) ◇ *Le service est compris.* Service is included.
+ **être de service** to be on duty
+ **hors service** out of order
+ **faire le service** to serve (*at table*) ◇ *Tu peux faire le service s'il te plaît?* Could you serve please?
2 *favour* ◇ *rendre service à quelqu'un* to do somebody a favour ◇ *Est-ce que je peux te demander un service?* Can I ask you a favour?
3 *serve* (*sport*) ◇ *Il a un bon service.* He's got a good serve.
+ **le service militaire** military service
+ **les services sociaux** the social services
+ **les services secrets** the secret service

la **serviette** NOUN
1 *towel* ◇ *une serviette de bain* a bath towel
+ **une serviette hygiénique** a sanitary towel
2 *serviette* (*napkin*)
3 *briefcase*

servir VERB
to serve ◇ *On vous sert?* Are you being served?
+ **À toi de servir.** (*tennis*) It's your serve.
+ **se servir** to help oneself ◇ *Servez-vous.* Help yourself.
+ **se servir de** to use ◇ *Tu te sers souvent de ton vélo?* Do you use your bike a lot?
+ **servir à quelqu'un** to be of use to somebody ◇ *Ça m'a beaucoup servi.* It was very useful.
+ **À quoi ça sert?** What's it for?
+ **Ça ne sert à rien.** It's no use. ◇ *Ça ne sert à rien d'insister.* It's no use insisting.

ses ADJECTIVE

1 *his* ◇ *Il est parti voir ses grands-parents.* He's gone to see his grandparents.
2 *her* ◇ *Delphine a oublié ses baskets.* Delphine's forgotten her trainers.
3 *its* ◇ *la ville et ses alentours* the town and its surroundings

seul ADJECTIVE, ADVERB
1 *alone* ◇ *vivre seul* to live alone
2 *by oneself* ◇ *Elle est venue seule.* She came by herself.
+ **faire quelque chose tout seul** to do something by oneself ◇ *Elle a fait ça toute seule?* Did she do it by herself?
+ **se sentir seul** to feel lonely
+ **un seul livre** one book only ◇ *Vous avez droit à un seul livre.* You're entitled to one book only.
+ **Il reste une seule nectarine.** There's only one nectarine left.
+ **le seul livre que...** the only book that... ◇ *C'est le seul Agatha Christie que je n'aie pas lu.* That's the only Agatha Christie I haven't read.
+ **le seul** the only one ◇ *C'est la seule que je ne connaisse pas.* She's the only one I don't know.

seulement ADVERB
only
+ **non seulement...mais** not only...but ◇ *Non seulement il a plu, mais en plus il a fait froid.* Not only did it rain, but it was cold as well.

sévère ADJECTIVE
strict ◇ *Mon prof de maths est très sévère.* My maths teacher is very strict.

sexuel ADJECTIVE
(FEM SING **sexuelle**)
sexual ◇ *la discrimination sexuelle* sexual discrimination ◇ *l'éducation sexuelle* sex education

le **shampooing** NOUN
shampoo
+ **se faire un shampooing** to wash one's hair

le **short** NOUN
shorts ◇ *Il était en short.* He was wearing shorts.

le **si** NOUN
see also **si** CONJUNCTION
1 *B* ◇ *en si bémol* in B flat
2 *ti* ◇ *la, si, do* la, ti, do

si CONJUNCTION, ADVERB
see also **si** NOUN
1 *if* ◇ *si tu veux* if you like ◇ *Je me demande si elle va venir.* I wonder if she'll come. ◇ *si seulement* if only
2 *so* ◇ *Elle est si gentille.* She's so kind. ◇ *Tout s'est passé si vite.*

Everything happened so fast.

3 _yes_ ◇ _Tu n'es pas allé à l'école habillé comme ça? – Si._ You didn't go to school dressed like that? – Yes I did.

la **Sicile** NOUN
Sicily

le **sida** NOUN
AIDS ◇ _Il a le sida._ He's got AIDS.

le **siècle** NOUN
century ◇ _le vingtième siècle_ the twentieth century

le **siège** NOUN
1 _seat_ (in vehicle)
2 _head office_

sien PRONOUN
◆ **le sien (1)** his ◇ _C'est le vélo de Paul? – Oui, c'est le sien._ Is this Paul's bike? – Yes, it's his.
◆ **le sien (2)** hers ◇ _C'est le vélo d'Isabelle? – Oui, c'est le sien._ Is this Isabelle's bike? – Yes, it's hers.

sienne PRONOUN
◆ **la sienne (1)** his ◇ _C'est la montre de Paul? – Oui, c'est la sienne._ Is this Paul's watch? – Yes, it's his.
◆ **la sienne (2)** hers ◇ _C'est la montre d'Isabelle? – Oui, c'est la sienne._ Is this Isabelle's watch? – Yes, it's hers.

siennes PRONOUN
◆ **les siennes (1)** his ◇ _Ce sont les cassettes de Christian? – Oui, ce sont les siennes._ Are these Christian's cassettes? – Yes, they're his.
◆ **les siennes (2)** hers ◇ _Ce sont les lunettes de Daphne? – Oui, ce sont les siennes._ Are these Daphne's glasses? – Yes, they're hers.

siens PRONOUN
◆ **les siens (1)** his ◇ _Ce sont les sandwichs de Pierre? – Oui, ce sont les siens._ Are these Pierre's sandwiches? – Yes, they're his.
◆ **les siens (2)** hers ◇ _Ce sont les sandwichs de Justine? – Oui, ce sont les siens._ Are these Justine's sandwiches? – Yes, they're hers.

sieste NOUN
nap ◇ _faire la sieste_ to have a nap

siffler VERB
to whistle

sifflet NOUN
whistle

sigle NOUN
acronym

signal NOUN
(PL les **signaux**)
signal

signe NOUN
sign

◆ **faire un signe de la main** to wave
◆ **faire signe à quelqu'un d'entrer** to beckon to somebody to come in

signer VERB
to sign

la **signification** NOUN
meaning

signifier VERB
to mean ◇ _Que signifie ce mot?_ What does this word mean?

le **silence** NOUN
silence
◆ **Silence!** Be quiet!

silencieux ADJECTIVE
(FEM SING **silencieuse**)
1 _silent_ ◇ _Elle est restée silencieuse._ She remained silent.
2 _quiet_ ◇ _C'est très silencieux ici._ It's very quiet here.

la **silhouette** NOUN
figure ◇ _J'ai vu une silhouette dans le brouillard._ I saw a figure in the mist.

similaire ADJECTIVE
similar

le **simple** NOUN
singles (tennis) ◇ _le simple messieurs_ the men's singles ◇ _le simple dames_ the ladies' singles

simuler VERB
to simulate

simultané ADJECTIVE
simultaneous

sincère ADJECTIVE
sincere

la **sincérité** NOUN
sincerity

le **singe** NOUN
monkey

le **singulier** NOUN
singular ◇ _au féminin singulier_ in the feminine singular

sinistre ADJECTIVE
sinister

sinon CONJUNCTION
otherwise ◇ _Dépêche-toi, sinon je pars sans toi._ Hurry up, otherwise I'll leave without you.

la **sinusite** NOUN
sinusitis ◇ _avoir de la sinusite_ to have sinusitis

la **sirène** NOUN
mermaid
◆ **la sirène d'alarme** the fire alarm

le **sirop** NOUN
syrup
◆ **le sirop contre la toux** cough mixture

le **site** NOUN
setting ◇ _un site très sauvage_ a totally unspoiled setting

- **un site pittoresque** a beauty spot
- **un site touristique** a tourist attraction
- **un site archéologique** an archaeological site

sitôt ADVERB
- **sitôt dit, sitôt fait** no sooner said than done
- **pas de sitôt** not for a long time ⋄ *On ne le reverra pas de sitôt.* We won't see him again for a long time.

la **situation** NOUN
1 *situation*
- **la situation de famille** marital status
2 *job* ⋄ *Il a une belle situation.* He's got a good job.

se **situer** VERB
to be situated ⋄ *Versailles se situe à l'ouest de Paris.* Versailles is situated to the west of Paris.
- **bien situé** well situated

six NUMBER
six ⋄ *Il est rentré à six heures.* He got back at six o'clock. ⋄ *Il a six ans.* He's six.
- **le six février** the sixth of February

sixième ADJECTIVE
see also **sixième** NOUN
sixth ⋄ *au sixième étage* on the sixth floor

la **sixième** NOUN
see also **sixième** ADJECTIVE
first year
In French secondary schools, years are counted from the sixième (youngest) to première and terminale (oldest).
⋄ *Mon frère est en sixième.* My brother's in first year.

le **ski** NOUN
1 *ski* ⋄ *J'ai loué des skis.* I hired skis.
2 *skiing* ⋄ *J'adore le ski.* I love skiing. ⋄ *faire du ski* to go skiing
- **le ski de fond** cross-country skiing
- **le ski nautique** water-skiing
- **le ski de piste** downhill skiing
- **le ski de randonnée** cross-country skiing

skier VERB
to ski

le **skieur** NOUN
skier

la **skieuse** NOUN
skier

le **slip** NOUN
pants
- **un slip de bain** swimming trunks

la **Slovaquie** NOUN
Slovakia

la **Slovénie** NOUN
Slovenia

le **SMIC** NOUN
guaranteed minimum wage ⋄ *Il touche le SMIC.* He's on the legal minimum wage.

le **smoking** NOUN
dinner suit

la **SNCF** NOUN (= Société nationale des chemins de fer français)
French railways

snob ADJECTIVE
(FEM SING **snob**)
snobbish

sobre ADJECTIVE
1 *sober*
2 *plain* ⋄ *C'est une veste très sobre.* It's a very plain jacket.

social ADJECTIVE
(MASC PL **sociaux**)
social

le/la **socialiste** NOUN
socialist

la **société** NOUN
1 *society*
2 *company* ⋄ *une société d'ingénierie* an engineering company

la **sociologie** NOUN
sociology

la **socquette** NOUN
ankle sock

la **sœur** NOUN
sister
- **une bonne sœur** (*informal*) a nun

soi PRONOUN
oneself ⋄ *avoir confiance en soi* to have confidence in oneself
- **rester chez soi** to stay at home
- **Ça va de soi.** It goes without saying.

soi-disant ADVERB, ADJECTIVE
supposedly ⋄ *Il était soi-disant parti à Paris.* He had supposedly left for Paris.
- **un soi-disant poète** a so-called poet

la **soie** NOUN
silk

la **soif** NOUN
thirst
- **avoir soif** to be thirsty

soigner VERB
to look after (*ill person, animal*)
⋄ *Soigne-toi bien ce week-end!* Take good care of yourself this weekend!

soigneux ADJECTIVE
(FEM SING **soigneuse**)
careful ⋄ *Tu devrais être plus soigneux avec tes livres.* You should be more careful with your books.

soi-même PRONOUN
oneself ⋄ *Il vaut mieux le faire soi-même.* It's better to do it oneself.

le **soin** NOUN

care
* **prendre soin de quelque chose** to take care of something ◇ *Prends bien soin de ce livre.* Take good care of this book.

les **soins** MASC NOUN
treatment
* **les premiers soins** first aid
* **"aux bons soins de Madame Martin"** (*on letter*) "c/o Mrs Martin"

le **soir** NOUN
evening ◇ *ce soir* this evening
* **demain soir** tomorrow night
* **hier soir** last night

la **soirée** NOUN
evening ◇ *en tenue de soirée* in evening dress

sois VERB *see* **être**
* **Sois tranquille!** Be quiet!

soit CONJUNCTION
* **soit..., soit...** either...or... ◇ *soit lundi, soit mardi* either Monday or Tuesday

la **soixantaine** NOUN
about sixty ◇ *une soixantaine de personnes* about sixty people
* **Elle a la soixantaine.** She's in her sixties.

soixante NUMBER
sixty ◇ *Il a soixante ans.* He's sixty.
◇ *soixante et un* sixty-one
◇ *soixante-deux* sixty-two
* **soixante et onze** seventy-one
* **soixante-quinze** seventy-five

soixante-dix NUMBER
seventy ◇ *Il a soixante dix ans.* He's seventy.

le **soja** NOUN
soya
* **des germes de soja** beansprouts

le **sol** NOUN
1 _floor_ ◇ *un sol carrelé* a tiled floor
* **à même le sol** on the floor
2 _soil_ ◇ *sur le sol français* on French soil
3 _G_ ◇ *sol dièse* G sharp
4 _so_ ◇ *do, ré, mi, fa, sol...* do, re, mi, fa, so...

solaire ADJECTIVE
solar ◇ *le système solaire* the solar system
* **la crème solaire** sun cream

le **soldat** NOUN
soldier

le **solde** NOUN
* **être en solde** to be reduced ◇ *Les chemisiers sont en solde.* The blouses are reduced.
* **les soldes** the sales ◇ *faire les soldes* to go round the sales ◇ *les soldes de janvier* the January sales

soldé ADJECTIVE
* **être soldé** to be reduced ◇ *un article soldé à dix francs* an item reduced to 10 francs

la **sole** NOUN
sole (*fish*)

le **soleil** NOUN
sun ◇ *au soleil* in the sun
* **Il y a du soleil.** It's sunny.

le **solfège** NOUN
musical theory ◇ *Il joue du violon sans connaître le solfège.* He plays the violin but he can't read music.

solidaire ADJECTIVE
* **être solidaire de quelqu'un** to back somebody up

solide ADJECTIVE
1 _strong_ (*person*)
2 _solid_ (*object*)

solitaire ADJECTIVE
see also **solitaire** NOUN
solitary

le/la **solitaire** NOUN
see also **solitaire** ADJECTIVE
loner

la **solitude** NOUN
loneliness

la **solution** NOUN
solution
* **une solution de facilité** an easy way out

sombre ADJECTIVE
dark

la **somme** NOUN
see also **le somme**
sum

le **somme** NOUN
see also **la somme**
nap ◇ *faire un somme* to take a nap

le **sommeil** NOUN
sleep
* **avoir sommeil** to be sleepy

sommes VERB *see* **être**
* **Nous sommes en vacances.** We're on holiday.

le **sommet** NOUN
summit

le **somnifère** NOUN
sleeping pill

somptueux ADJECTIVE
(FEM SING **somptueuse**)
sumptuous

son ADJECTIVE
(FEM SING **sa**, PL **ses**)
see also **son** NOUN
1 _his_ ◇ *son père* his father ◇ *Il a perdu son portefeuille.* He's lost his wallet.
2 _her_ ◇ *son père* her father ◇ *Elle a*

perdu son sac. She's lost her bag.

le **son** NOUN

see also son ADJECTIVE

[1] *sound* ◇ *Le son n'est pas très bon.* The sound's not very good. ◇ *baisser le son* to turn the sound down

[2] *bran*

◆ **le pain de son** brown bread

le **sondage** NOUN

survey

◆ **un sondage d'opinion** an opinion poll

sonner VERB

to ring ◇ *On a sonné.* Somebody rang the doorbell. ◇ *Le téléphone a sonné.* The phone rang.

la **sonnerie** NOUN

bell (*electric*) ◇ *La sonnerie du téléphone l'a réveillé.* He was woken by the phone ringing.

la **sonnette** NOUN

bell ◇ *la sonnette d'alarme* the alarm bell

la **sono** NOUN (*informal*)

sound system

sont VERB *see* être

◆ **Ils sont en vacances.** They're on holiday.

sophistiqué ADJECTIVE

sophisticated

le **sort** NOUN

[1] *spell* ◇ *jeter un sort à quelqu'un* to cast a spell on somebody

◆ **un mauvais sort** a curse

[2] *fate* ◇ *abandonner quelqu'un à son triste sort* to leave somebody to their fate

◆ **tirer au sort** to draw lots

la **sorte** NOUN

sort ◇ *C'est une sorte de gâteau.* It's a sort of cake. ◇ *toutes sortes de choses* all sorts of things

la **sortie** NOUN

way out ◇ *Où est la sortie?* Where's the way out?

◆ **la sortie de secours** the emergency exit

◆ **Attends-moi à la sortie de l'école.** Meet me after school.

sortir VERB

[1] *to go out* ◇ *Il est sorti sans rien dire.* He went out without saying a word. ◇ *Il est sorti acheter un journal.* He's gone out to buy a newspaper. ◇ *J'aime sortir.* I like going out.

[2] *to come out* ◇ *Elle sort de l'hôpital demain.* She's coming out of hospital tomorrow. ◇ *Je l'ai rencontré en sortant de la pharmacie.* I met him coming out of the chemist's. ◇ *Ce modèle vient juste de sortir.* This model has just

come out.

[3] *to take out* ◇ *Elle a sorti son porte-monnaie de son sac.* She took her purse out of her handbag. ◇ *Je vais sortir la voiture du garage.* I'll get the car out of the garage.

◆ **sortir avec quelqu'un** to be going out with somebody ◇ *Tu sors avec lui?* Are you going out with him?

◆ **s'en sortir** to manage ◇ *Ne t'en fais pas, tu t'en sortiras.* Don't worry, you'll manage OK.

la **sottise** NOUN

◆ **Ne fais pas de sottises.** Don't do anything silly.

◆ **Ne dis pas de sottises.** Don't talk nonsense.

le **sou** NOUN

◆ **une machine à sous** a fruit machine

◆ **Je n'ai pas un sou sur moi.** I haven't got a penny on me.

◆ **être près de ses sous** (*informal*) to be tight-fisted

le **souci** NOUN

worry

◆ **se faire du souci** to worry

soucieux ADJECTIVE

(FEM SING **soucieuse**)

worried ◇ *Tu as l'air soucieux.* You look worried.

la **soucoupe** NOUN

saucer

◆ **une soucoupe volante** a flying saucer

soudain ADJECTIVE, ADVERB

[1] *sudden* ◇ *une douleur soudaine* a sudden pain

[2] *suddenly* ◇ *Soudain, il s'est fâché.* Suddenly, he got angry.

le **souffle** NOUN

breath

◆ **à bout de souffle** out of breath

le **soufflé** NOUN

soufflé ◇ *un soufflé au fromage* a cheese soufflé

souffler VERB

[1] *to blow* ◇ *Le vent soufflait fort.* The wind was blowing hard.

[2] *to blow out* ◇ *Souffle les bougies!* Blow out the candles!

la **souffrance** NOUN

suffering

souffrir VERB

to be in pain ◇ *Il souffre beaucoup.* He's in a lot of pain.

◆ **Il ne peux pas la souffrir.** (*informal*) He can't stand her.

le **souhait** NOUN

wish ◇ *faire un souhait* to make a wish ◇ *Tous nos souhaits de réussite.*

All our best wishes for your success.
◇ *les souhaits de bonne année* New
Year's wishes
* **Atchoum! – À tes souhaits!**
Atchoo! – Bless you!

souhaiter VERB
to wish ◇ *Il souhaite aller à l'université.*
He wishes to go to university. ◇ *Nous
vous souhaitons une bonne année.* We
wish you a happy New Year.

soûl ADJECTIVE (*informal*)
drunk

soulager VERB
to relieve

soulever VERB
1 *to lift* ◇ *Je n'arrive pas à soulever
cette valise.* I can't lift this suitcase.
2 *to raise* ◇ *Il faudra soulever la
question lors de la réunion.* We'll have
to raise the matter at the meeting.

le **soulier** NOUN
shoe

souligner VERB
to underline

le **soupçon** NOUN
suspicion
* **un soupçon de** a dash of ◇ *Ajoutez un
soupçon de rhum.* Add a dash of rum.

soupçonner VERB
to suspect

la **soupe** NOUN
soup

le **soupir** NOUN
sigh

soupirer VERB
to sigh

souple ADJECTIVE
1 *supple* (*person*)
2 *flexible* (*system*)

la **source** NOUN
spring ◇ *l'eau de source* spring water

le **sourcil** NOUN
eyebrow

sourd ADJECTIVE
deaf

souriant ADJECTIVE
cheerful

le **sourire** NOUN
see also **sourire** VERB
smile

sourire VERB
see also **sourire** NOUN
to smile ◇ *sourire à quelqu'un* to
smile at somebody

la **souris** NOUN
mouse

sournois ADJECTIVE
sly

sous PREPOSITION

under
* **sous terre** underground
* **sous la pluie** in the rain

sous-entendu ADJECTIVE
see also **sous-entendu** NOUN
implied

le **sous-entendu** NOUN
see also **sous-entendu** ADJECTIVE
insinuation

sous-marin ADJECTIVE
see also **sous-marin** NOUN
underwater

le **sous-marin** NOUN
see also **sous-marin** ADJECTIVE
submarine

le **sous-sol** NOUN
basement

le **sous-titre** NOUN
subtitle

sous-titré ADJECTIVE
with subtitles

la **soustraction** NOUN
subtraction

les **sous-vêtements** MASC NOUN
underwear SING

soutenir VERB
to support ◇ *Il m'a toujours soutenu
contre elle.* He's always supported me
against her.
* **soutenir que** to maintain that ◇ *Elle
soutenait que c'était impossible.* She
maintained that it was impossible.
* **soutenir l'allure** to keep up ◇ *Il
marchait trop vite et je n'arrivais pas à
soutenir l'allure.* He was walking too fast
and I couldn't keep up.

souterrain ADJECTIVE
see also **souterrain** NOUN
underground

le **souterrain** NOUN
see also **souterrain** ADJECTIVE
underground passage

le **soutien** NOUN
support

le **soutien-gorge** NOUN
(PL les **soutiens-gorge**)
bra

le **souvenir** NOUN
see also **se souvenir** VERB
1 *memory* ◇ *garder un bon souvenir
de quelque chose* to have happy
memories of something
2 *souvenir* ◇ *un souvenir de Lourdes*
a souvenir of Lourdes
* **Garde ce livre en souvenir de moi.**
Keep the book: it'll remind you of me.

se **souvenir** VERB
see also **souvenir** NOUN
* **se souvenir de quelque chose** to

remember something   ◇ *Je ne me souviens pas de son adresse.* I can't remember his address.
- **se souvenir que** to remember that
  ◇ *Je me souviens qu'il neigeait ce jour-là.* I remember it was snowing that day.

souvent ADVERB
often

soyez, soyons VERB *see* **être**
- **Soyons clairs!** Let's be clear about this!

spacieux ADJECTIVE
(FEM SING **spacieuse**)
spacious

les **spaghettis** MASC NOUN
spaghetti

le **sparadrap** NOUN
sticking plaster

le **speaker** NOUN
announcer

la **speakerine** NOUN
announcer

spécial ADJECTIVE
(MASC PL **spéciaux**)
1. *special*   ◇ *Qu'est-ce que tu fais ce week-end? – Rien de spécial.* What are you doing this weekend? – Nothing special.
- **les effets spéciaux** special effects
  2. *peculiar*   ◇ *Elle a des goûts un peu spéciaux.* She has rather peculiar tastes.

spécialement ADVERB
1. *specially*   ◇ *Il est venu spécialement pour te parler.* He came specially to speak to you.
2. *particularly*   ◇ *Ce n'est pas spécialement difficile.* It's not particularly difficult.

se **spécialiser** VERB
- **se spécialiser dans quelque chose** to specialize in something   ◇ *Je me suis spécialisé en histoire contemporaine.* I specialized in modern history.

le/la **spécialiste** NOUN
specialist

la **spécialité** NOUN
speciality

spécifier VERB
to specify

le **spectacle** NOUN
show

spectaculaire ADJECTIVE
spectacular

le **spectateur** NOUN
1. *member of the audience*
2. *spectator*

la **spectatrice** NOUN
1. *member of the audience*
2. *spectator*

la **spéléologie** NOUN

potholing

spirituel ADJECTIVE
1. *spiritual*
2. *witty*

splendide ADJECTIVE
magnificent

spontané ADJECTIVE
spontaneous

le **sport** NOUN
see also **sport** ADJECTIVE
sport   ◇ *faire du sport* to do sport
- **les sports d'hiver** winter sports

sport ADJECTIVE (MASC, FEM, PL)
see also **sport** NOUN
casual   ◇ *une veste sport* a casual jacket

sportif ADJECTIVE
(FEM SING **sportive**)
see also **sportif** NOUN
1. *sporty*   ◇ *Elle est très sportive.* She's very sporty.
2. *sports*   ◇ *un club sportif* a sports club

le **sportif** NOUN
see also **sportif** ADJECTIVE
sportsman

la **sportive** NOUN
sportswoman

le **spot** NOUN
spotlight
- **un spot publicitaire** a commercial break

le **square** NOUN
public gardens

le **squelette** NOUN
skeleton

stable ADJECTIVE
stable
- **un emploi stable** a steady job

le **stade** NOUN
stadium

le **stage** NOUN
training course

le/la **stagiaire** NOUN
see also **stagiaire** ADJECTIVE
trainee

stagiaire ADJECTIVE
see also **stagiaire** NOUN
trainee   ◇ *un professeur stagiaire* a trainee teacher

le **stand** NOUN
1. *stand* (at exhibition)
2. *stall* (at fair)

le/la **standardiste** NOUN
operator

la **station** NOUN
- **une station de métro** an underground station
- **une station de taxis** a taxi rank

+ **une station de ski** a ski resort

le **stationnement** NOUN
  parking
+ **"stationnement interdit"** "no parking"

stationner VERB
  to park

la **station-service** NOUN
  (PL les **stations-service**)
  service station

la **statistique** NOUN
  statistic

le **steak** NOUN
  steak
+ **un steak frites** steak and chips
+ **un steak haché** a hamburger

la **sténo** NOUN
  shorthand   ◇ *un cours de sténo* a
  shorthand course

la **sténodactylo** NOUN
  shorthand typist

stérile ADJECTIVE
  sterile

stimulant ADJECTIVE
  stimulating

stimuler VERB
  to stimulate

le **stop** NOUN
  stop sign
+ **faire du stop** to hitchhike

stopper VERB
  to stop

le **store** NOUN
  ① *blind* (on window)
  ② *awning*

le **strapontin** NOUN
  foldaway seat

la **stratégie** NOUN
  strategy

stratégique ADJECTIVE
  strategic

stressant ADJECTIVE
  stressful

strict ADJECTIVE
  ① *strict* (person)   ◇ *Ma prof de français
  est très stricte.* My French teacher's
  very strict.
  ② *severe* (clothes)   ◇ *une tenue très
  stricte* a very severe outfit
+ **le strict minimum** the bare minimum

la **strophe** NOUN
  stanza

studieux ADJECTIVE
  (FEM SING **studieuse**)
  studious

le **studio** NOUN
  ① *studio flat*
  ② *studio*   ◇ *un studio de télévision* a
  television studio

stupéfait ADJECTIVE
  astonished

les **stupéfiants** MASC NOUN
  narcotics

stupéfier VERB
  to astonish   ◇ *Sa réponse m'a stupéfié.*
  I was astonished by his answer.

la **stupidité** NOUN
  stupidity

le/la **styliste** NOUN
  designer

le **stylo** NOUN
  pen
+ **un stylo plume** a fountain pen
+ **un stylo bille** a ballpoint pen
+ **un stylo-feutre** a felt-tip pen

su VERB *see* **savoir**
+ **Si j'avais su...** If I'd known...

subir VERB
  to suffer (defeat)
+ **subir une opération** to have an
  operation

subit ADJECTIVE
  sudden

subitement ADVERB
  suddenly

subjectif ADJECTIVE
  (FEM SING **subjective**)
  subjective

le **subjonctif** NOUN
  subjunctive

substituer VERB
  to substitute   ◇ *substituer un mot à un
  autre* to substitute one word for
  another

subtil ADJECTIVE
  subtle

la **subvention** NOUN
  subsidy

subventionner VERB
  to subsidize

le **succès** NOUN
  success   ◇ *avoir du succès* to be
  successful

le **successeur** NOUN
  successor

la **succursale** NOUN
  branch (of company)

sucer VERB
  to suck

la **sucette** NOUN
  lollipop

le **sucre** NOUN
  sugar
+ **un sucre** a sugar-lump   ◇ *Je prends
  deux sucres dans mon café.* I take two
  lumps of sugar in my coffee.
+ **du sucre en morceaux** lump sugar
+ **un sucre d'orge** a barley sugar
+ **du sucre en poudre** caster sugar

- **du sucre glace** icing sugar
sucré ADJECTIVE
  ☐1 *sweet* ◦ *Ce gâteau est un peu trop sucré.* This cake is a bit too sweet.
  ☐2 *sweetened* ◦ *du lait concentré sucré* sweetened condensed milk
les **sucreries** FEM NOUN
  sweet things
le **sucrier** NOUN
  sugar bowl
le **sud** NOUN
  see also sud ADJECTIVE
  south ◦ *Ils vivent dans le sud de la France.* They live in the South of France.
- **vers le sud** southwards
- **au sud de Paris** south of Paris
- **l'Amérique du Sud** South America
- **le vent du sud** the south wind
sud ADJECTIVE
  see also sud NOUN
  ☐1 *south* ◦ *la côte sud de l'Espagne* the south coast of Spain
- **le pôle sud** the South Pole
  ☐2 *southern* ◦ *Nous avons visité la partie sud du pays.* We visited the southern part of the country.
sud-africain ADJECTIVE
  South African
sud-américain ADJECTIVE
  South American
le **sud-est** NOUN
  south-east ◦ *au sud-est* in the south-east
le **sud-ouest** NOUN
  south-west ◦ *au sud-ouest* in the south-west
la **Suède** NOUN
  Sweden
suédois ADJECTIVE, NOUN
  (FEM SING **suédoise**)
  Swedish ◦ *Ils parlent suédois.* They speak Swedish.
- **un Suédois** a Swede (*man*)
- **une Suédoise** a Swede (*woman*)
- **les Suédois** the Swedes
suer VERB
  to sweat
la **sueur** NOUN
  sweat
- **en sueur** sweating
suffire VERB
  to be enough ◦ *Tiens, voilà dix francs. Ça te suffit?* Here's 10 francs. Is that enough for you?
- **Ça suffit!** That's enough!
suffisamment ADVERB
  enough ◦ *Ça n'est pas suffisamment grand.* It's not big enough. ◦ *Il n'y a*

pas suffisamment de chaises. There aren't enough chairs.
suffisant ADJECTIVE
  ☐1 *sufficient* ◦ *Ça n'est pas une raison suffisante.* That's not sufficient reason.
  ☐2 *smug* ◦ *Il est un peu trop suffisant.* He's rather smug.
suffoquer VERB
  to suffocate
suggérer VERB
  to suggest
se **suicider** VERB
  to commit suicide
suis VERB see **être**, see **suivre**
- **Je suis écossais.** I'm Scottish.
- **Suis-moi.** Follow me.
suisse ADJECTIVE, NOUN
  see also la Suisse
  Swiss ◦ *le franc suisse* the Swiss franc
- **un Suisse** a Swiss man
- **une Suisse** a Swiss woman
- **les Suisses** the Swiss
la **Suisse** NOUN
  see also suisse ADJECTIVE
  Switzerland ◦ *la Suisse allemande* German-speaking Switzerland ◦ *la Suisse romande* French-speaking Switzerland
la **suite** NOUN
  ☐1 *rest* ◦ *Je vous raconterai la suite de l'histoire demain.* I'll tell you the rest of the story tomorrow.
  ☐2 *sequel* (*to book, film*)
- **tout de suite** straightaway ◦ *J'y vais tout de suite.* I'll go straightaway.
- **de suite** in succession ◦ *Il a commis la même erreur trois fois de suite.* He made the same mistake three times in succession.
- **par la suite** subsequently ◦ *Il s'est avéré par la suite qu'il était coupable.* He subsequently turned out to be guilty.
suivant ADJECTIVE
  following ◦ *le jour suivant* the following day ◦ *l'exercice suivant* the following exercise
- **Au suivant!** Next!
suivre VERB
  ☐1 *to follow* ◦ *Il m'a suivie jusque chez moi.* He followed me home. ◦ *Vous me suivez ou est-ce que je parle trop vite?* Are you following me or am I speaking too fast?
  ☐2 *to do* ◦ *Je suis un cours d'anglais à la fac.* I'm doing an English course at college.
  ☐3 *to keep up* ◦ *Il n'arrive pas à suivre en maths.* He can't keep up in maths. ◦ *J'aime suivre l'actualité.* I like to keep

up with the news.
- ◆ **"à suivre"** "to be continued"
- ◆ **suivre un régime** to be on a diet

sujet ADJECTIVE

(FEM SING **sujette**)

see also sujet NOUN

- ◆ **être sujet à** to be prone to ◇ *Il est sujet au vertige.* He suffers from vertigo.

le **sujet** NOUN

see also sujet ADJECTIVE

subject

- ◆ **au sujet de** about ◇ *C'est à quel sujet?–C'est au sujet de l'annonce parue dans "Le Monde" d'aujourd'hui.* What's it about?–It's about the advertisement in today's "Le Monde".
- ◆ **un sujet de conversation** a topic of conversation
- ◆ **un sujet d'examen** an examination question
- ◆ **un sujet de plaisanterie** something to joke about

le **super** NOUN

4-star petrol

superficiel ADJECTIVE

(FEM SING **superficielle**)

superficial

superflu ADJECTIVE

superfluous

supérieur ADJECTIVE

see also supérieur NOUN

1. *upper* ◇ *la lèvre supérieure* the upper lip
2. *superior* ◆ *qualité supérieure* superior quality ◇ *Il a toujours l'air tellement supérieur!* He always looks so superior!
- ◆ **supérieur à** greater than ◇ *Choisissez un nombre supérieur à cent.* Choose a number greater than 100.

le **supérieur** NOUN

see also supérieur ADJECTIVE

superior ◇ *mon supérieur hiérarchique* my immediate superior

le **superlatif** NOUN

superlative

le **supermarché** NOUN

supermarket

superposé ADJECTIVE

- ◆ **des lits superposés** bunk beds

superstitieux ADJECTIVE

(FEM SING **superstitieuse**)

superstitious

le **suppléant** NOUN

supply teacher

la **suppléante** NOUN

supply teacher

le **supplément** NOUN

- ◆ **payer un supplément** to pay an

additional charge
- ◆ **Le vin est en supplément.** Wine is extra.
- ◆ **un supplément de travail** extra work

supplémentaire ADJECTIVE

additional ◇ *Voici quelques exercices supplémentaires.* Here are some additional exercises.

- ◆ **faire des heures supplémentaires** to do overtime

le **supplice** NOUN

torture ◇ *C'était un supplice.* It was torture.

supplier VERB

- ◆ **supplier quelqu'un de faire quelque chose** to beg somebody to do something ◇ *Je t'en supplie!* I'm begging you!

supportable ADJECTIVE

bearable

supporter VERB

to stand (tolerate) ◇ *Je ne supporte pas l'hypocrisie.* I can't stand hypocrisy. ◇ *Elle ne supporte pas qu'on la critique.* She can't stand being criticized. ◇ *Je ne peux pas la supporter.* I can't stand her. ◇ *Je supporte mal la chaleur.* I can't stand hot weather.

supposer VERB

to suppose

supprimer VERB

1. *to cut* ◇ *Deux mille emplois ont été supprimés dans le secteur public.* Two thousand jobs have been cut in the public sector.
2. *to cancel* ◇ *Le train de Londres a été supprimé.* The train to London has been cancelled.
3. *to get rid of* ◇ *Ils ont supprimé les témoins gênants.* They got rid of the awkward witnesses.

sur PREPOSITION

1. *on* ◇ *Pose-le sur la table.* Put it down on the table. ◇ *Vous verrez l'hôpital sur votre droite.* You'll see the hospital on your right. ◇ *une conférence sur Balzac* a lecture on Balzac
2. *in* ◇ *une personne sur dix* 1 person in 10
3. *out of* ◇ *J'ai eu quatorze sur vingt en maths.* I got 14 out of 20 in maths.
4. *by* ◇ *quatre mètres sur deux* 4 metres by 2

sûr ADJECTIVE

1. *sure* ◇ *Tu es sûr?* Are you sure?
- ◆ **sûr et certain** absolutely certain
2. *reliable* ◇ *C'est quelqu'un de très sûr.* He's a very reliable person.

3 *safe* ◇ *Ce quartier n'est pas très sûr la nuit.* This neighbourhood isn't very safe at night.
- **sûr de soi** self-confident ◇ *Elle est très sûre d'elle.* She's very self-confident.

sûrement ADVERB
certainly ◇ *Sûrement pas!* Certainly not! ◇ *Il est sûrement déjà parti.* He's sure to have already left.

la **sûreté** NOUN
- **mettre quelque chose en sûreté** to put something in a safe place

le **surf** NOUN
surfing

la **surface** NOUN
surface
- **les grandes surfaces** the supermarkets

surgelé ADJECTIVE
frozen ◇ *des frites surgelées* frozen chips

les **surgelés** MASC NOUN
frozen food

surhumain ADJECTIVE
superhuman

sur-le-champ ADVERB
immediately

le **surlendemain** NOUN
- **le surlendemain de son arrivée** two days after he arrived
- **le surlendemain dans la matinée** two days later, in the morning

se **surmener** VERB
to work too hard ◇ *Ne te surmène pas trop pendant le week-end.* Don't work too hard over the weekend.

surmonter VERB
to overcome ◇ *Il nous reste de nombreux obstacles à surmonter.* We still have many obstacles to overcome.

surnaturel ADJECTIVE
(FEM SING **surnaturelle**)
supernatural

le **surnom** NOUN
nickname

surnommer NOUN
to nickname ◇ *On l'a surnommé "Kiki".* We nicknamed him "Kiki".

surpeuplé ADJECTIVE
overpopulated

surprenant ADJECTIVE
surprising

surprendre VERB
to surprise ◇ *Ça me surprendrait beaucoup qu'il arrive à l'heure.* I'd be very surprised if he arrived on time.
- **surprendre quelqu'un en train de faire quelque chose** to catch somebody doing something ◇ *Je l'ai surpris en*

train de fouiller dans mon placard. I caught him rummaging in my cupboard.

surpris ADJECTIVE
surprised ◇ *Il était surpris de me voir.* He was surprised to see me.

la **surprise** NOUN
surprise ◇ *faire une surprise à quelqu'un* to give somebody a surprise

sursauter VERB
to jump ◇ *J'ai sursauté en entendant mon nom.* I jumped when I heard my name.

surtout ADVERB
1 *especially* ◇ *Il est assez timide, surtout avec les filles.* He's rather shy, especially with girls.
2 *above all* ◇ *Ce canapé est joli et surtout, il n'est pas salissant.* This sofa is pretty, and even more important, it doesn't show the dirt. ◇ *Surtout, ne répète pas ce que je t'ai dit!* Whatever you do, don't repeat what I told you!

le **surveillant** NOUN
supervisor (man)
> In French secondary schools, the teachers are not responsible for supervising the pupils outside class. This job is done by people called surveillants or pions.

la **surveillante** NOUN
supervisor (woman)

surveiller VERB
1 *to keep an eye on* ◇ *Tu peux surveiller mes bagages?* Can you keep an eye on my luggage?
2 *to keep a watch on* ◇ *La police a surveillé la maison pendant une semaine.* The police kept the house under surveillance for a week.
3 *to supervise* ◇ *Nous sommes toujours surveillés pendant la récréation.* We're always supervised during break.
- **surveiller un examen** to invigilate an exam
- **surveiller sa ligne** to watch one's figure

le **survêtement** NOUN
tracksuit ◇ *un haut de survêtement* a tracksuit top ◇ *un pantalon de survêtement* tracksuit bottoms

la **survie** NOUN
survival

le **survivant** NOUN
survivor

la **survivante** NOUN
survivor

survivre VERB
to survive ◇ *survivre à un accident* to survive an accident

survoler VERB
  to fly over
susceptible ADJECTIVE
  touchy
suspect ADJECTIVE
  suspicious ◇ *dans des circonstances suspectes* under suspicious circumstances
suspecter VERB
  to suspect
le **suspense** NOUN
  suspense
  ◆ **un film à suspense** a thriller
la **suture** NOUN
  ◆ **un point de suture** a stitch
svelte ADJECTIVE
  slender
SVP ABBREVIATION (= *s'il vous plaît*)
  please
la **syllabe** NOUN
  syllable
symbolique ADJECTIVE
  symbolic
symboliser VERB
  to symbolize
symétrique ADJECTIVE
  symmetrical
sympa ADJECTIVE (*informal*)
  nice ◇ *Elle est très sympa.* She's a really nice person.
la **sympathie** NOUN
  ◆ **J'ai beaucoup de sympathie pour lui.** I like him a lot.

sympathique ADJECTIVE
  nice ◇ *Ce sont des gens très sympathiques.* They're very nice people.
sympathiser VERB
  to get on well ◇ *Nous avons immédiatement sympathisé avec nos voisins.* We got on well with our neighbours straight away.
le **symptôme** NOUN
  symptom
le **syndicat** NOUN
  trade union
  ◆ **le syndicat d'initiative** the tourist information office
synonyme ADJECTIVE
  see also **synonyme** NOUN
  synonymous ◇ *être synonyme de* to be synonymous with
le **synonyme** NOUN
  see also **synonyme** ADJECTIVE
  synonym
synthétique ADJECTIVE
  synthetic
la **Syrie** NOUN
  Syria
syrien ADJECTIVE
  (FEM SING **syrienne**)
  Syrian
systématique ADJECTIVE
  systematic
le **système** NOUN
  system

S

T

t' PRONOUN see **te**

ta ADJECTIVE
your ◇ *J'ai vu ta sœur hier.* I saw your sister yesterday.

le **tabac** NOUN
1. *tobacco* ◇ *le tabac blond* light tobacco ◇ *le tabac brun* dark tobacco
2. *smoking* ◇ *Le tabac est mauvais pour la santé.* Smoking is bad for you.

la **table** NOUN
table
- **mettre la table** to lay the table
- **se mettre à table** to sit down to eat
- **À table!** Dinner's ready!
- **une table de nuit** a bedside table
- **"table des matières"** "contents"

le **tableau** NOUN
(PL les **tableaux**)
painting ◇ *un tableau de Monet* a painting by Monet
- **le tableau d'affichage** the notice board
- **le tableau noir** the blackboard

la **tablette** NOUN
- **une tablette de chocolat** a bar of chocolate

le **tablier** NOUN
apron

le **tabouret** NOUN
stool

la **tache** NOUN
mark (*stain*)
- **des taches de rousseur** freckles

la **tâche** NOUN
task

tacher VERB
to leave a stain

le **tact** NOUN
tact ◇ *avoir du tact* to be tactful

la **tactique** NOUN
tactics
- **changer de tactique** to try something different

la **taie** NOUN
- **une taie d'oreiller** a pillowcase

la **taille** NOUN
1. *waist* ◇ *Elle a la taille fine.* She has a slim waist.
2. *height* ◇ *un homme de taille moyenne* a man of average height
3. *size* ◇ *Avez-vous ma taille?* Have you got my size?

le **taille-crayon** NOUN
pencil sharpener

le **tailleur** NOUN
1. *tailor*
2. *suit* (*lady's*)

- **Il est assis en tailleur.** He's sitting cross-legged.

se **taire** VERB
to stop talking
- **Taisez-vous!** Be quiet!

le **talon** NOUN
heel

le **tambour** NOUN
drum

la **Tamise** NOUN
Thames

le **tampon** NOUN
pad ◇ *un tampon à récurer* a scouring pad
- **un tampon hygiénique** a tampon

tamponneuse ADJECTIVE
- **les autos tamponneuses** dodgems

tandis que CONJUNCTION
while ◇ *Il a toujours de bonnes notes, tandis que les miennes sont mauvaises.* He always gets good marks, while mine are poor.

tant ADVERB
so much ◇ *Je l'aime tant!* I love him so much!
- **tant de (1)** so much ◇ *tant de nourriture* so much food
- **tant de (2)** so many ◇ *tant de livres* so many books
- **tant que (1)** until ◇ *Tu ne sortiras pas tant que tu n'auras pas fini tes devoirs.* You're not going out until you've finished your homework.
- **tant que (2)** while ◇ *Profites-en tant que tu peux.* Make the most of it while you can.
- **tant mieux** so much the better
- **tant pis** never mind

la **tante** NOUN
aunt

tantôt ADVERB
sometimes ◇ *Nous venons tantôt à pied, tantôt en bus.* Sometimes we walk, sometimes we come by bus.

le **tapage** NOUN
1. *racket* ◇ *Ils ont fait du tapage toute la nuit.* They made a racket all night long.
2. *fuss* ◇ *On a fait beaucoup de tapage autour de cette affaire.* There was a lot of fuss about that business.

taper VERB
to beat down ◇ *Le soleil tape.* The sun's really beating down.
- **taper quelqu'un** to hit somebody ◇ *Maman, il m'a tapé!* Mum, he hit me!

- **taper sur quelque chose** to bang on something
- **taper des pieds** to stamp one's feet
- **taper des mains** to clap one's hands
- **taper à la machine** to type ◇ *Tu sais taper à la machine?* Can you type? ◇ *Je vais taper cette lettre.* I'm going to type this letter.

le **tapis** NOUN
carpet

tapisser VERB
to paper

la **tapisserie** NOUN
1 *wallpaper* ◇ *Tu aimes la tapisserie de ma chambre?* Do you like the wallpaper in my bedroom?
2 *tapestry*

taquiner VERB
to tease

tard ADVERB
late
- **plus tard** later on
- **au plus tard** at the latest

tardif ADJECTIVE
(FEM SING **tardive**)
late ◇ *un petit déjeuner tardif* a late breakfast

le **tarif** NOUN
- **le tarif des consommations** the price list (*in café*)
- **une communication à tarif réduit** an off-peak phone call
- **un billet de train à tarif réduit** a concessionary train ticket
- **un billet de train à plein tarif** a full-price train ticket
- **Est-ce que vous faites un tarif de groupe?** Is there a reduction for groups?

la **tarte** NOUN
tart

la **tartine** NOUN
slice of bread ◇ *une tartine de confiture* a slice of bread and jam

tartiner VERB
to spread
- **le fromage à tartiner** cheese spread

le **tas** NOUN
heap ◇ *un tas de charbon* a heap of coal
- **un tas de** (*informal*) loads of ◇ *J'ai lu un tas de livres pendant les vacances.* I read loads of books in the holidays.

la **tasse** NOUN
cup

le **taureau** NOUN
(PL les **taureaux**)
bull
- **le Taureau** Taurus ◇ *Ils sont tous les deux Taureau.* They're both Taurus.

le **taux** NOUN
rate ◇ *le taux de change* the exchange rate

la **taxe** NOUN
tax
- **la boutique hors taxes** the duty-free shop

le **taxi** NOUN
taxi

tchèque ADJECTIVE
Czech
- **la République tchèque** the Czech Republic

te PRONOUN

te *changes to* **t'** *before a vowel and most words beginning with "h"*

1 *you* ◇ *Je te vois.* I can see you. ◇ *Il t'a vu?* Did he see you?
2 *to you* ◇ *Est-ce qu'il te parle en français?* Does he talk to you in French? ◇ *Elle t'a parlé?* Did she speak to you?
3 *yourself* ◇ *Tu vas te rendre malade.* You'll make yourself sick.

With reflexive verbs, **te** *is often not translated.*
◇ *Comment tu t'appelles?* What's your name?

le **technicien** NOUN
technician

la **technicienne** NOUN
technician

technique ADJECTIVE
see also **technique** NOUN
technical

la **technique** NOUN
see also **technique** ADJECTIVE
technique

la **technologie** NOUN
technology

le **teint** NOUN
complexion ◇ *Elle a le teint clair.* She's got a fair complexion.

la **teinte** NOUN
shade (*colour*)

le **teinturier** NOUN
dry cleaner's ◇ *Je vais porter ce manteau chez le teinturier.* I'm going to take this coat to the dry cleaner's.

tel ADJECTIVE
(FEM SING **telle**)
- **Il a un tel enthousiasme!** He's got such enthusiasm!
- **rien de tel** nothing like ◇ *Il n'y a rien de tel qu'une bonne nuit de sommeil.* There's nothing like a good night's sleep.
- **J'ai tout laissé tel quel.** I left everything as it was

PTO⟩

◆ **tel que** such as

la **télé** NOUN
telly ◇ *à la télé* on telly

la **télécarte** NOUN
phonecard

la **télécommande** NOUN
remote control

la **télécopie** NOUN
fax

le **télégramme** NOUN
telegram

le **téléphérique** NOUN
cable car

le **téléphone** NOUN
telephone ◇ *Elle est au téléphone.*
She's on the phone.

téléphoner VERB
to phone ◇ *Je vais téléphoner à Claire.*
I'll phone Claire. ◇ *Je peux téléphoner?*
Can I make a phone call?

le **télésiège** NOUN
chairlift

le **téléski** NOUN
ski-tow

le **téléspectateur** NOUN
viewer (TV)

la **téléspectatrice** NOUN
viewer (TV)

le **téléviseur** NOUN
television set

la **télévision** NOUN
television ◇ *à la télévision* on
television

telle ADJECTIVE
◆ **Je n'ai jamais eu une telle peur.** I've
never had such a fright.
◆ **telle que** such as

tellement ADVERB
1 *so* ◇ *Andrew est tellement gentil.*
Andrew's so nice. ◇ *Il travaille tellement.*
He works so hard.
2 *so much* ◇ *Il a tellement mangé
que...* He ate so much that...
3 *so many* ◇ *Il y avait tellement de
monde.* There were so many people.

telles ADJECTIVE
such ◇ *Je n'ai jamais entendu de telles
âneries!* I've never heard such
nonsense!

tels ADJECTIVE
such ◇ *Nous n'avons pas de tels
orages chez nous.* We don't have such
storms back home.

le **témoignage** NOUN
testimony

témoigner VERB
to testify

le **témoin** NOUN
witness

la **température** NOUN
temperature ◇ *avoir de la température*
to have a temperature

la **tempête** NOUN
storm

temporaire ADJECTIVE
temporary

le **temps** NOUN
1 *weather* ◇ *Quel temps fait-il?*
What's the weather like?
2 *time* ◇ *Je n'ai pas le temps.* I
haven't got time. ◇ *Prends ton temps.*
Take your time. ◇ *Il est temps de partir.*
It's time to go.
◆ **juste à temps** just in time
◆ **de temps en temps** from time to time
◆ **en même temps** at the same time
◆ **à temps** in time ◇ *Il est arrivé à temps
pour le match.* He arrived in time for
the match.
◆ **à plein temps** full time ◇ *Elle travaille
à plein temps.* She works full time.
◆ **à temps partiel** part time ◇ *le travail à
temps partiel* part-time work
◆ **dans le temps** at one time ◇ *Dans le
temps, on pouvait circuler en vélo sans
danger.* At one time, it was safe to go
around by bike.
3 *tense* (of verb)

tenais, tenait VERB see **tenir**

la **tendance** NOUN
◆ **avoir tendance à faire quelque chose**
to tend to do something ◇ *Il a
tendance à exagérer.* He tends to
exaggerate.

tendre ADJECTIVE
see also **tendre** VERB
tender

tendre VERB
see also **tendre** ADJECTIVE
to stretch out ◇ *Ils ont tendu une
corde entre deux arbres.* They stretched
out a rope between two trees.
◆ **tendre quelque chose à quelqu'un** to
hold something out to somebody ◇ *Il
lui a tendu les clés.* He held out the keys
to her.
◆ **tendre la main** to hold out one's hand
◆ **tendre le bras** to reach out
◆ **tendre un piège à quelqu'un** to set a
trap for someone

tendrement ADVERB
tenderly

la **tendresse** NOUN
tenderness

tendu ADJECTIVE
tense ◇ *Il était très tendu aujourd'hui.*
He was very tense today.

tenir VERB

to hold ◇ *Tu peux tenir la lampe, s'il te plaît?* Can you hold the torch, please? ◇ *Il tenait un enfant par la main.* He was holding a child by the hand.
- **Tenez votre chien en laisse.** Keep your dog on the lead.
- **tenir à quelqu'un** to be attached to somebody ◇ *Il tient beaucoup à elle.* He's very attached to her.
- **tenir à faire quelque chose** to be determined to do something ◇ *Elle tient à y aller.* She's determined to go.
- **tenir de quelqu'un** to take after somebody ◇ *Il tient de son père.* He takes after his father.
- **Tiens, voilà un stylo.** Here's a pen.
- **Tiens, c'est Alain là-bas!** Look, that's Alain over there!
- **Tiens?** Really?
- **se tenir (1)** to stand ◇ *Il se tenait près de la porte.* He was standing by the door.
- **se tenir (2)** to be held ◇ *La foire va se tenir place du marché.* The fair will be held in the market place.
- **se tenir droit (1)** to stand up straight ◇ *Tiens-toi droit pour que je puisse te mesurer.* Stand up straight so I can measure you.
- **se tenir droit (2)** to sit up straight ◇ *Arrête de manger le nez dans ton assiette, tiens-toi droit.* Don't slouch while you're eating, sit up straight.
- **Tiens-toi bien!** Behave yourself!

le **tennis** NOUN
  [1] *tennis* ◇ *Elle joue au tennis.* She plays tennis.
  [2] *tennis court* ◇ *Il est au tennis.* He's at the tennis court.
- **les tennis** trainers

tentant ADJECTIVE
  tempting

la **tentation** NOUN
  temptation

la **tentative** NOUN
  attempt

la **tente** NOUN
  tent

tenter VERB
  to tempt ◇ *J'ai été tenté de tout abandonner.* I was tempted to give up. ◇ *Ça ne me tente vraiment pas d'aller à la piscine.* I don't really fancy going to the swimming pool.
- **tenter de faire quelque chose** to try to do something ◇ *Il a tenté plusieurs fois de s'évader.* He tried several times to escape.

tenu VERB *see* **tenir**

la **tenue** NOUN
  clothes
- **en tenue de soirée** in evening dress

le **terme** NOUN
- **à court terme** short-term
- **à long terme** long-term

la **terminale** NOUN
  final year

  In French secondary schools, years are counted from the sixième (youngest) to première and terminale (oldest).

terminer VERB
  to finish
- **se terminer** to end ◇ *Les vacances se terminent demain.* The holidays end tomorrow.

le **terminus** NOUN
  terminus

le **terrain** NOUN
  land ◇ *Il veut acheter un terrain en Normandie.* He wants to buy some land in Normandy.
- **un terrain de camping** a campsite
- **un terrain de football** a football pitch
- **un terrain de golf** a golf course
- **un terrain de jeu** a playground
- **un terrain de sport** a sports ground
- **un terrain vague** a piece of waste ground

la **terrasse** NOUN
  terrace
- **Si on s'asseyait en terrasse?** Shall we sit outside? *(at café)*

la **terre** NOUN
  earth
- **la Terre** the Earth
- **Elle s'est assise par terre.** She sat on the floor.
- **Il est tombé par terre.** He fell down.
- **la terre cuite** terracotta ◇ *un pot en terre cuite* a terracotta pot
- **la terre glaise** clay

terrible ADJECTIVE
  terrible ◇ *Quelque chose de terrible est arrivé.* Something terrible has happened.
- **pas terrible** *(informal)* nothing special ◇ *Ce film n'est pas terrible.* The film's nothing special.

la **terrine** NOUN
  pâté

le **territoire** NOUN
  territory

le/la **terroriste** NOUN
  terrorist

tes ADJECTIVE
  your ◇ *J'aime bien tes baskets.* I like your trainers.

le **test** NOUN

test

le **testament** NOUN
will ◦ *Il est mort sans testament.* He died without leaving a will.

tester VERB
to test

le **tétanos** NOUN
tetanus

le **têtard** NOUN
tadpole

la **tête** NOUN
head ◦ *de la tête aux pieds* from head to foot
* **se laver la tête** to wash one's hair
* **la tête la première** headfirst
* **tenir tête à quelqu'un** to stand up to somebody
* **faire la tête** to sulk
* **en avoir par-dessus la tête** to be fed up

têtu ADJECTIVE
stubborn

le **texte** NOUN
text

le **TGV** NOUN (= *train à grande vitesse*)
high-speed train

le **thé** NOUN
tea ◦ *Je vous offre un thé?* Would you like a cup of tea?

le **théâtre** NOUN
theatre
* **faire du théâtre** to act ◦ *Est-ce que tu as déjà fait du théâtre?* Have you ever acted?

la **théière** NOUN
teapot

le **thème** NOUN
[1] *subject* ◦ *Quel est le thème de l'émission?* What's the programme about?
[2] *prose* (*translation into the foreign language*)

la **théorie** NOUN
theory

le **thermomètre** NOUN
thermometer

le **thon** NOUN
tuna

le **tibia** NOUN
[1] *shinbone* ◦ *une fracture du tibia* a broken shinbone
[2] *shin* ◦ *Il m'a donné un coup de pied dans le tibia.* He kicked me in the shin.

le **tic** NOUN
nervous twitch

le **ticket** NOUN
ticket ◦ *un ticket de métro* an underground ticket
* **le ticket de caisse** the till receipt

tiède ADJECTIVE
[1] *warm* (*water, air*)
[2] *lukewarm* (*food, drink*)

tien PRONOUN
* **le tien** yours ◦ *J'ai oublié mon stylo. Tu peux me prêter le tien?* I've forgotten my pen. Can you lend me yours?

tienne PRONOUN
* **la tienne** yours ◦ *Ce n'est pas ma raquette, c'est la tienne.* It's not my racket, it's yours.
* **À la tienne!** Cheers!

tiennes PRONOUN
* **les tiennes** yours ◦ *J'ai pris mes baskets, mais j'ai oublié les tiennes.* I've brought my trainers, but I've forgotten yours.

tiens PRONOUN
* **les tiens** yours ◦ *Je ne trouve pas mes feutres. Je peux utiliser les tiens?* I can't find my felt pens. Can I use yours?

tiens, tient VERB *see* **tenir**

le **tiers** NOUN
third ◦ *Un tiers de la classe était pour.* A third of the class were in favour.
* **le tiers monde** the Third World

la **tige** NOUN
stem

le **tigre** NOUN
tiger

le **tilleul** NOUN
lime tea

le **timbre** NOUN
stamp

timide ADJECTIVE
shy

timidement ADVERB
shyly

la **timidité** NOUN
shyness

le **tir** NOUN
shooting
* **le tir à l'arc** archery

le **tirage** NOUN
* **par tirage au sort** by drawing lots ◦ *Les prix seront attribués par tirage au sort.* The prizes will be awarded by drawing lots.

le **tire-bouchon** NOUN
corkscrew

la **tirelire** NOUN
money box

tirer VERB
[1] *to pull* ◦ *Elle a tiré un mouchoir de son sac.* She pulled a handkerchief out of her bag. ◦ *Il m'a tiré les cheveux.* He pulled my hair. ◦ *"Tirer"* "Pull"
[2] *to draw* ◦ *tirer les rideaux* to draw

the curtains ◇ *tirer un trait* to draw a line ◇ *tirer des conclusions* to draw conclusions
* **tirer au sort** to draw lots
 ③ *to fire* ◇ *Il a tiré plusieurs coups de feu.* He fired several shots. ◇ *Il a tiré sur les policiers.* He fired at the police.

le **tiret** NOUN
 dash (hyphen)

le **tiroir** NOUN
 drawer

la **tisane** NOUN
 herbal tea

tisser VERB
 to weave

le **tissu** NOUN
 material
* **un sac en tissu** a cloth bag

le **titre** NOUN
 title
* **les gros titres** the headlines
* **un titre de transport** a travel ticket

tituber VERB
 to stagger

e **toast** NOUN
 ① *piece of toast*
 ② *toast* ◇ *porter un toast à quelqu'un* to drink a toast to somebody

e **toboggan** NOUN
 slide

toi PRONOUN
 you ◇ *Ça va?–Oui, et toi?* How are you?–Fine, and you? ◇ *J'ai faim, pas toi?* I'm hungry, aren't you?
* **Assieds-toi.** Sit down.
* **C'est à toi de jouer.** It's your turn to play.
* **Est-ce que ce stylo est à toi?** Is this pen yours?

toile NOUN
* **un pantalon de toile** cotton trousers
* **un sac de toile** a canvas bag
* **une toile cirée** an oilcloth
* **une toile d'araignée** a cobweb

toilette NOUN
 ① *wash* ◇ *faire sa toilette* to have a wash
 ② *outfit* ◇ *une toilette élégante* an elegant outfit

toilettes FEM NOUN
 toilet

toi-même PRONOUN
 yourself ◇ *Tu as fait ça toi-même?* Did you do it yourself?

toit NOUN
 roof
* **un toit ouvrant** a sunroof

tolérant ADJECTIVE
 tolerant

tolérer VERB
 to tolerate

la **tomate** NOUN
 tomato

la **tombe** NOUN
 grave

le **tombeau** NOUN
 (PL les **tombeaux**)
 tomb

la **tombée** NOUN
* **à la tombée de la nuit** at nightfall

tomber VERB
 to fall ◇ *Attention, tu vas tomber!* Be careful, you'll fall!
* **laisser tomber (1)** to drop ◇ *Elle a laissé tomber son stylo.* She dropped her pen.
* **laisser tomber (2)** to give up ◇ *Il a laissé tomber le piano.* He gave up the piano.
* **laisser tomber (3)** to let down ◇ *Il ne laisse jamais tomber ses amis.* He never lets his friends down.
* **tomber sur quelqu'un** to bump into someone ◇ *Je suis tombé sur lui en sortant de chez Pierre.* I bumped into him coming out of Pierre's place.
* **Ça tombe bien.** That's lucky.
* **Il tombe de sommeil.** He's asleep on his feet.

ton ADJECTIVE
 (FEM SING **ta**, PL **tes**)
 see also **ton** NOUN
 your ◇ *C'est ton stylo?* Is this your pen?

le **ton** NOUN
 see also **ton** ADJECTIVE
 ① *tone of voice* ◇ *Ne me parle pas sur ce ton.* Don't speak to me in that tone of voice.
 ② *colour* ◇ *J'adore les tons pastel.* I love pastel colours.

la **tonalité** NOUN
 dialling tone

la **tondeuse** NOUN
 lawnmower

tondre VERB
 to mow

tonique ADJECTIVE
 fortifying

la **tonne** NOUN
 tonne

le **tonneau** NOUN
 (PL les **tonneaux**)
 barrel

le **tonnerre** NOUN
 thunder

le **tonus** NOUN
* **avoir du tonus** to be energetic

T

le **torchon** NOUN
tea towel

tordre VERB
◆ **se tordre la cheville** to twist one's ankle

tordu ADJECTIVE
[1] *bent* ◇ *Ce clou est un peu tordu.* This nail's a bit bent.
[2] *crazy* ◇ *une histoire complètement tordue* a crazy story

le **torrent** NOUN
mountain stream

le **torse** NOUN
chest ◇ *Il était torse nu.* He was bare-chested.

le **tort** NOUN
◆ **avoir tort** to be wrong
◆ **donner tort à quelqu'un** to lay the blame on somebody

le **torticolis** NOUN
stiff neck ◇ *J'ai le torticolis.* I've got a stiff neck.

la **tortue** NOUN
tortoise

la **torture** NOUN
torture

torturer VERB
to torture

tôt ADVERB
early
◆ **au plus tôt** at the earliest
◆ **tôt ou tard** sooner or later

total ADJECTIVE
(MASC PL **totaux**)
see also **total** NOUN
total

le **total** NOUN
(PL **les totaux**)
see also **total** ADJECTIVE
total ◇ *faire le total* to work out the total
◆ **au total** in total

totalement ADVERB
totally

la **totalité** NOUN
◆ **la totalité des profs** all the teachers
◆ **la totalité du personnel** the entire staff

touchant ADJECTIVE
touching

toucher VERB
[1] *to touch* ◇ *Ne touche pas à mes livres!* Don't touch my books!
◆ **Nos deux jardins se touchent.** Our gardens are next to each other.
[2] *to feel* ◇ *Ce pull a l'air doux. Je peux toucher?* That sweater looks soft. Can I feel it?
[3] *to hit* ◇ *La balle l'a touché en pleine poitrine.* The bullet hit him right in the

chest.
[4] *to affect* ◇ *Ces nouvelles réformes ne nous touchent pas.* The new reforms don't affect us.
[5] *to receive* ◇ *Il a touché une grosse somme d'argent.* He received a large sum of money.

toujours ADVERB
[1] *always* ◇ *Il est toujours très gentil.* He's always very nice.
◆ **pour toujours** forever
[2] *still* ◇ *Quand nous sommes revenus, il était toujours là.* When we got back he was still there.

le **toupet** NOUN (*informal*)
◆ **avoir du toupet** to have a nerve

la **tour** NOUN
see also le **tour**
[1] *tower* ◇ *la Tour Eiffel* the Eiffel Tower
[2] *tower block* ◇ *Il y a beaucoup de tours dans ce quartier.* There are a lot of tower blocks in this area.

le **tour** NOUN
see also la **tour**
turn ◇ *C'est ton tour de jouer.* It's your turn to play.
◆ **faire un tour** to go for a walk ◇ *Allons faire un tour dans le parc.* Let's go for a walk in the park.
◆ **faire un tour en voiture** to go for a drive
◆ **faire un tour à vélo** to go for a ride ◇ *Tu veux aller faire un tour à vélo?* Do you want to go for a bike ride?
◆ **faire le tour du monde** to travel round the world

le **tourbillon** NOUN
whirlpool

le/la **touriste** NOUN
tourist

se **tourmenter** VERB
to fret ◇ *Ne te tourmente pas, ça s'arrangera.* Don't fret about it, it'll be all right.

le **tournant** NOUN
[1] *bend* ◇ *Il y a beaucoup de tournants dangereux sur cette route.* There are a lot of dangerous bends on this road.
[2] *turning point* ◇ *Ça a été un tournant dans sa vie.* It was a turning point in his life.

la **tournée** NOUN
[1] *round* ◇ *Le facteur commence sa tournée à sept heures du matin.* The postman starts his round at 7 o'clock in the morning. ◇ *Allez, qu'est-ce que vous voulez boire? C'est ma tournée.* Right, what are you drinking? It's my round.

tour [2] *tour* ◦ *Il est en tournée aux États-Unis.* He's on tour in the United States.

tourner VERB
[1] *to turn* ◦ *Tournez à droite au prochain feu.* Turn right at the lights. ◦ *Tourne-toi un peu plus vers moi, et souris!* Turn towards me a bit more, and smile!
[2] *to go sour* ◦ *Le lait a tourné.* The milk's gone sour.
◦ **mal tourner** to go wrong ◦ *Ça a mal tourné.* It all went wrong.
◦ **tourner le dos à quelqu'un** to have one's back to somebody

le **tournesol** NOUN
sunflower

le **tournevis** NOUN
screwdriver

le **tournoi** NOUN
tournament

la **tourte** NOUN
pie ◦ *une tourte aux poireaux* a leek pie

tous ADJECTIVE, PRONOUN *see* **tout**

la **Toussaint** NOUN
All Saints' Day

tousser VERB
to cough

tout ADJECTIVE, ADVERB, PRONOUN
(MASC PL **tous**, FEM PL **toutes**)
[1] *all* ◦ *tout le lait* all the milk ◦ *toute la nuit* all night ◦ *tous les livres* all the books ◦ *toutes les filles* all the girls ◦ *tout le temps* all the time ◦ *C'est tout.* That's all. ◦ *Je les connais tous.* I know them all. ◦ *Nous y sommes toutes allées.* We all went. ◦ *Ça fait combien en tout?* How much is that all together?
◦ **Il est tout seul.** He's all alone.
◦ **pas du tout** not at all
[2] *every* ◦ *tous les jours* every day ◦ *tous les deux jours* every two days
◦ **tout le monde** everybody
◦ **tous les deux** both ◦ *Nous y sommes allés tous les deux.* We both went.
◦ **tous les trois** all three ◦ *Je les ai invités tous les trois.* I invited all three of them.
[3] *everything* ◦ *Il a tout organisé.* He organized everything.
[4] *very* ◦ *Elle habite tout près.* She lives very close.
◦ **tout en haut** right at the top
◦ **tout droit** straight ahead
◦ **tout d'abord** first of all
◦ **tout à coup** suddenly
◦ **tout à fait** absolutely
◦ **tout à l'heure (1)** just now ◦ *Je l'ai vu tout à l'heure.* I saw him just now.
◦ **tout à l'heure (2)** in a moment ◦ *Je finirai ça tout à l'heure.* I'll finish it in a moment.
◦ **À tout à l'heure!** See you later!
◦ **tout de suite** straight away

toutefois ADVERB
however

toutes ADJECTIVE, PRONOUN *see* **tout**

la **toux** NOUN
cough

le/la **toxicomane** NOUN
drug addict

le **trac** NOUN
◦ **avoir le trac** to be feeling nervous

la **trace** NOUN
[1] *trace* ◦ *Le voleur n'a pas laissé de traces.* The thief left no traces.
[2] *mark* ◦ *des traces de doigts* finger marks
◦ **des traces de pas** footprints

tracer VERB
to draw ◦ *tracer un trait* to draw a line

le **tracteur** NOUN
tractor

la **tradition** NOUN
tradition

traditionnel ADJECTIVE
(FEM SING **traditionnelle**)
traditional

le **traducteur** NOUN
translator

la **traduction** NOUN
translation

la **traductrice** NOUN
translator

traduire VERB
to translate

le **trafic** NOUN
traffic
◦ **le trafic de drogue** drug trafficking

le **trafiquant** NOUN
◦ **un trafiquant de drogue** a drug trafficker

tragique ADJECTIVE
tragic

trahir VERB
to betray

la **trahison** NOUN
betrayal

le **train** NOUN
train
◦ **un train électrique** a train set
◦ **Il est en train de manger.** He's eating.

le **traîneau** NOUN
(PL **les traîneaux**)
sledge

traîner VERB

[1] *to wander around* ◇ *J'ai vu des jeunes qui traînaient en ville.* I saw some young people wandering around town.
[2] *to hang about* ◇ *Dépêche-toi, ne traîne pas!* Hurry up, don't hang about!
[3] *to drag on* ◇ *La réunion a traîné jusqu'à midi.* The meeting dragged on till 12 o'clock.
- **traîner des pieds** to drag one's feet

le **train-train** NOUN
humdrum routine

traire VERB
to milk

le **trait** NOUN
[1] *line* ◇ *Tracez un trait.* Draw a line.
[2] *feature* ◇ *Elle a les traits fins.* She has delicate features.
- **boire quelque chose d'un trait** to drink something down in one gulp
- **un trait d'union** a hyphen

le **traitement** NOUN
treatment
- **le traitement de texte** word processing

traiter VERB
to treat ◇ *Elle le traite comme un chien.* She treats him like a dog.
- **Il m'a traité d'imbécile.** He called me an idiot.
- **traiter de** to be about ◇ *Cet article traite des sans-abri.* This article is about the homeless.

le **traiteur** NOUN
caterer

le **trajet** NOUN
[1] *journey* ◇ *Il n'a pas arrêté de parler pendant tout le trajet.* He talked for the whole journey. ◇ *J'ai une heure de trajet pour aller au travail.* My journey to work takes an hour.
[2] *route* ◇ *C'est le trajet le plus court.* It's the shortest route.

le **tramway** NOUN
tram

tranchant ADJECTIVE
sharp (knife)

la **tranche** NOUN
slice

tranquille ADJECTIVE
quiet ◇ *Cette rue est très tranquille.* This is a very quiet street.
- **Sois tranquille, il ne va rien lui arriver.** Don't worry, nothing will happen to him.
- **Tiens-toi tranquille!** Be quiet!
- **Laisse-moi tranquille.** Leave me alone.
- **Laisse ça tranquille.** Leave it alone.

la **tranquillité** NOUN
peace and quiet

transférer VERB

to transfer

transformer VERB
[1] *to transform* ◇ *Son séjour en France l'a transformé.* His stay in France has transformed him.
[2] *to convert* ◇ *Ils ont transformé la grange en garage.* They've converted the barn into a garage.
- **se transformer en** to turn into ◇ *La chenille se transforme en papillon.* The caterpillar turns into a butterfly.

la **transfusion** NOUN
- **une transfusion sanguine** a blood transfusion

transiger VERB
to compromise

transmettre VERB
- **transmettre quelque chose à quelqu'un** to pass something on to somebody

transpercer VERB
to go through ◇ *La pluie a transpercé mes vêtements.* The rain went through my clothes.

la **transpiration** NOUN
perspiration

transpirer VERB
to perspire

le **transport** NOUN
transport
- **les transports en commun** public transport

transporter VERB
[1] *to carry* ◇ *Le train transportait des marchandises.* The train was carrying freight.
[2] *to move* ◇ *Je ne sais pas comment je vais transporter mes affaires.* I don't know how I'm going to move my stuff.

traumatiser VERB
to traumatize

le **travail** NOUN
(PL les **travaux**)
[1] *work* ◇ *J'ai beaucoup de travail.* I've got a lot of work.
[2] *job* ◇ *Il a un travail intéressant.* He's got an interesting job.
- **le travail au noir** moonlighting

travailler VERB
to work

travailleur ADJECTIVE
(FEM SING **travailleuse**)
see also **travailleur** NOUN
hard-working

le **travailleur** NOUN
see also **travailleur** ADJECTIVE
worker

la **travailleuse** NOUN
worker

travaillistes MASC NOUN
the Labour Party

travaux MASC NOUN
1 *work* ◇ *des travaux de construction* building work
2 *roadworks* ◇ *Il y a beaucoup de bruit à cause des travaux dans la rue.* There's a lot of noise from the roadworks.
- **être en travaux** to be undergoing alterations
- **les travaux dirigés** supervised practical work
- **les travaux manuels** handicrafts
- **les travaux ménagers** housework

travers NOUN
- **en travers de** across ◇ *Il y avait un arbre en travers de la route.* There was a tree lying across the road.
- **de travers** crooked ◇ *Son chapeau était de travers.* His hat was crooked.
- **comprendre de travers** to misunderstand ◇ *Elle comprend toujours tout de travers.* She always gets the wrong idea.
- **J'ai avalé de travers.** Something went down the wrong way.
- **à travers** through ◇ *Cette vitre est tellement sale qu'on ne voit rien à travers.* This window is so dirty you can't see anything through it.

traversée NOUN
crossing

traverser VERB
1 *to cross* ◇ *Traversez la rue.* Cross the street.
2 *to go through* ◇ *Nous avons traversé la France pour aller en Espagne.* We went through France on the way to Spain. ◇ *La pluie a traversé mon manteau.* The rain went through my coat.

traversin NOUN
bolster

trébucher VERB
to trip up

trèfle NOUN
1 *clover*
2 *clubs* (at cards) ◇ *le roi de trèfle* the king of clubs

treize NUMBER
thirteen ◇ *Il a treize ans.* He's thirteen. ◇ *à treize heures* at 1 p.m.
le treize février the thirteenth of February

treizième ADJECTIVE
thirteenth

tréma NOUN
diaeresis

le tremblement de terre NOUN
earthquake

trembler VERB
to shake ◇ *trembler de peur* to shake with fear
- **trembler de froid** to shiver

trempé ADJECTIVE
soaking wet

tremper VERB
to soak
- **tremper sa main dans l'eau** to dip one's hand in the water

le tremplin NOUN
springboard

la trentaine NOUN
about thirty ◇ *une trentaine de personnes* about thirty people
- **Il a la trentaine.** He's in his thirties.

trente NUMBER
thirty ◇ *Elle a trente ans.* She's thirty.
- **le trente janvier** the thirtieth of January
- **trente et un** thirty-one
- **trente-deux** thirty-two

trentième ADJECTIVE
thirtieth

très ADVERB
very

le trésor NOUN
treasure

la tresse NOUN
plait

la tribu NOUN
tribe

le tribunal NOUN
(PL les **tribunaux**)
court

tricher VERB
to cheat

tricolore ADJECTIVE
three-coloured
- **le drapeau tricolore** the French tricolour

le drapeau tricolore *is the French flag which is blue, white and red.*

le tricot NOUN
1 *knitting* ◇ *On fait du tricot à l'école.* We do knitting at school.
2 *sweater* ◇ *Mets un tricot, il fait froid.* Put a sweater on, it's cold.

tricoter VERB
to knit

trier VERB
to sort out ◇ *Je vais trier mes papiers avant de partir en vacances.* I'm going to sort out my papers before I go on holiday.

le trimestre NOUN
term

trinquer VERB

T

to clink glasses

le **triomphe** NOUN
triumph

triompher VERB
to triumph

les **tripes** FEM NOUN
tripe

le **triple** NOUN
+ **Ça m'a coûté le triple.** It cost me three times as much.
+ **Il gagne le triple de mon salaire.** He earns three times my salary.

tripler VERB
to treble

les **triplés** MASC NOUN
triplets

triste ADJECTIVE
sad

la **tristesse** NOUN
sadness

le **trognon** NOUN
core ◇ *un trognon de pomme* an apple core

trois NUMBER
three ◇ *à trois heures du matin* at three in the morning ◇ *Elle a trois ans.* She's three. ◇ *trois fois* three times
+ **le trois février** the third of February

troisième ADJECTIVE
see also **troisième** NOUN
third ◇ *au troisième étage* on the third floor

la **troisième** NOUN
see also **troisième** ADJECTIVE
fourth year
In French secondary schools, years are counted from the **sixième** (youngest) to **première** and **terminale** (oldest).
◇ *Mon frère est en troisième.* My brother's in fourth year.

les **trois-quarts** MASC NOUN
three-quarters ◇ *les trois-quarts de la classe* three-quarters of the class

le **trombone** NOUN
1 *trombone* ◇ *Il joue du trombone.* He plays the trombone.
2 *paper clip*

la **trompe** NOUN
trunk ◇ *la trompe d'un éléphant* an elephant's trunk

tromper VERB
to deceive
+ **se tromper** to make a mistake ◇ *Tout le monde peut se tromper.* Anyone can make a mistake.
+ **se tromper de jour** to get the wrong day
+ **Vous vous êtes trompé de numéro.** You've got the wrong number.

la **trompette** NOUN
trumpet ◇ *Il joue de la trompette.* He plays the trumpet.
+ **Il a le nez en trompette.** He's got a turned-up nose.

le **tronc** NOUN
trunk ◇ *un tronc d'arbre* a tree trunk

trop ADVERB
1 *too* ◇ *Il conduit trop vite.* He drives too fast.
2 *too much* ◇ *J'ai trop mangé.* I've eaten too much.
+ **trop de (1)** too much ◇ *J'ai acheté trop de pain.* I bought too much bread. ◇ *trois francs de trop* 3 francs too much
+ **trop de (2)** too many ◇ *J'ai apporté trop de vêtements.* I've brought too many clothes.
+ **trois personnes de trop** 3 people too many

le **tropique** NOUN
tropic

le **trottoir** NOUN
pavement

le **trou** NOUN
hole
+ **J'ai eu un trou de mémoire.** My mind went blank.

trouble ADJECTIVE, ADVERB
cloudy ◇ *L'eau est trouble.* The water's cloudy.
+ **Sans mes lunettes je vois trouble.** Without my glasses I can't see properly.

les **troubles** MASC NOUN
+ **une période de troubles politiques** a period of political instability

trouer VERB
to make a hole in ◇ *Il a troué la moquette avec sa cigarette.* He made a hole in the carpet with his cigarette.

la **trouille** NOUN
+ **avoir la trouille** (informal) to be scared to death

la **troupe** NOUN
troop
+ **une troupe de théâtre** a theatre company

le **troupeau** NOUN
(PL les **troupeaux**)
+ **un troupeau de moutons** a flock of sheep
+ **un troupeau de vaches** a herd of cows

la **trousse** NOUN
pencil case
+ **une trousse de toilette** a toilet bag

trouver VERB
1 *to find* ◇ *Je ne trouve pas mes lunettes.* I can't find my glasses.
2 *to think* ◇ *Je trouve que c'est bête.*

I think it's stupid.

- **se trouver** to be ◇ *Où se trouve la poste?* Where is the post office? ◇ *Marseille se trouve dans le sud de la France.* Marseilles is in the South of France.
- **se trouver mal** to pass out

truc NOUN (*informal*)
[1] *thing* ◇ *un truc en plastique* a thing made of plastic ◇ *J'ai plein de trucs à faire ce week-end.* I've got loads of things to do this weekend.
[2] *trick* ◇ *Je vais te montrer un truc qui réussit à tous les coups.* I'll show you a trick that never fails.

truite NOUN
trout

TSVP ABBREVIATION (= *tournez s'il vous plaît*)
PTO (= please turn over)

tu PRONOUN
you ◇ *Est-ce que tu as un animal familier?* Have you got a pet?

tuba NOUN
[1] *tuba* ◇ *Je joue du tuba.* I play the tuba.
[2] *snorkel*

tube NOUN
[1] *tube* ◇ *un tube de dentifrice* a tube of toothpaste
- **un tube de rouge à lèvres** a lipstick
[2] *hit* ◇ *Ça va être le tube de l'été.* It's going to be this summer's hit.

tuer VERB
to kill
- **se tuer** to get killed ◇ *Il s'est tué dans un accident de voiture.* He got killed in a car accident.

tue-tête
- **à tue-tête** ADVERB
at the top of one's voice ◇ *crier à tue-tête* to shout at the top of one's voice ◇ *Il chantait à tue-tête.* He was singing at the top of his voice.

tuile NOUN
tile ◇ *un toit en tuiles* a tiled roof

tunique NOUN
tunic

Tunisie NOUN
Tunisia

tunisien ADJECTIVE
(FEM SING **tunisienne**)
Tunisian

le **tunnel** NOUN
tunnel
- **le tunnel sous la Manche** the Channel Tunnel

turbulent ADJECTIVE
boisterous

turc ADJECTIVE, NOUN
(FEM SING **turque**)
Turkish ◇ *Il parle turc.* He speaks Turkish.
- **un Turc** a Turk (*man*)
- **une Turque** a Turk (*woman*)

la **Turquie** NOUN
Turkey

tutoyer VERB
- **tutoyer quelqu'un** to address somebody as "tu"

> **tutoyer quelqu'un** means to use **tu** when speaking to someone, rather than **vous**. Use **tu** only when talking to one person and when that person is someone of your own age or whom you know well; use **vous** to everyone else. If in doubt use **vous**.

- **On se tutoie?** Shall we use "tu" to each other?

le **tuyau** NOUN
(PL les **tuyaux**)
[1] *pipe*
- **un tuyau d'arrosage** a hosepipe
[2] *tip* ◇ *Il m'a donné un bon tuyau.* (*informal*) He gave me a handy tip.

la **TVA** NOUN (= *taxe sur la valeur ajoutée*)
VAT

le **tympan** NOUN
eardrum

le **type** NOUN (*informal*)
guy ◇ *C'est un type formidable.* He's a great guy.

typique ADJECTIVE
typical

le **tyran** NOUN
tyrant ◇ *C'est un vrai tyran.* He's a real tyrant.

le/la **tzigane** NOUN
gipsy

T

U

un ARTICLE, PRONOUN, ADJECTIVE

1 *a* ◇ *un garçon* a boy
an ◇ *un œuf* an egg
2 *one* ◇ *l'un des meilleurs* one of the best ◇ *un citron et deux oranges* one lemon and two oranges ◇ *Combien de timbres? – Un.* How many stamps? – One. ◇ *Elle a un an.* She's one year old.

➔ **l'un..., l'autre...** one..., the other...
◇ *L'un est grand, l'autre est petit.* One is tall, the other is short.

➔ **les uns..., les autres...** some..., others...
◇ *Les uns marchaient, les autres couraient.* Some were walking, others were running.

➔ **l'un ou l'autre** either of them
◇ *Prends l'un ou l'autre, ça m'est égal.* Take either of them, I don't mind.

➔ **un par un** one by one ◇ *Ils entraient un par un.* They went in one by one.

unanime ADJECTIVE
unanimous

l'**unanimité** FEM NOUN
➔ **à l'unanimité** unanimously

une ARTICLE, PRONOUN, ADJECTIVE

1 *a* ◇ *une fille* a girl
an ◇ *une pomme* an apple
2 *one* ◇ *une pomme et deux bananes* one apple and two bananas ◇ *Combien de cartes postales? – Une.* How many postcards? – One. ◇ *à une heure du matin* at one in the morning ◇ *l'une des meilleures* one of the best

➔ **l'une..., l'autre...** one..., the other...
◇ *L'une est grande, l'autre est petite.* One is tall, the other is short.

➔ **les unes..., les autres...** some..., others... ◇ *Les unes marchaient, les autres couraient.* Some were walking, others were running.

➔ **l'une ou l'autre** either of them
◇ *Prends l'une ou l'autre, ça m'est égal.* Take either of them, I don't mind.

➔ **une par une** one by one ◇ *Elles entraient une par une.* They went in one by one.

uni ADJECTIVE
1 *plain* ◇ *un tissu uni* a plain fabric
2 *close-knit* ◇ *une famille unie* a close-knit family

l'**uniforme** MASC NOUN
uniform

l'**union** FEM NOUN
union

➔ **l'ex-Union soviétique** the former Soviet Union

unique ADJECTIVE
unique ◇ *Tout individu a des empreintes uniques.* Everyone's fingerprints are unique. ◇ *C'est une occasion unique.* It's a unique opportunity.

➔ **Il est fils unique.** He's an only child.

➔ **Elle est fille unique.** She's an only child.

uniquement ADVERB
only

l'**unité** FEM NOUN
1 *unity* ◇ *l'unité européenne* European unity
2 *unit* ◇ *une unité de mesure* a unit of measurement

l'**univers** MASC NOUN
universe

universitaire ADJECTIVE
university ◇ *un diplôme universitaire* a university degree

➔ **faire des études universitaires** to study at university

l'**université** FEM NOUN
university ◇ *aller à l'université* to go to university

l'**urgence** FEM NOUN
➔ **C'est une urgence.** It's urgent.

➔ **Il n'y a pas urgence.** It's not urgent.

➔ **le service des urgences** the accident and emergency department

➔ **Il a été transporté d'urgence à l'hôpital.** He was rushed to hospital.

➔ **Téléphonez d'urgence.** Phone as soon as possible.

urgent ADJECTIVE
urgent

l'**urine** FEM NOUN
urine

les **USA** MASC NOUN
USA

➔ **aux USA (1)** in the USA

➔ **aux USA (2)** to the USA

l'**usage** MASC NOUN
use ◇ *à usage interne* for internal use ◇ *à usage externe* for external use only

➔ **hors d'usage** out of action ◇ *Cet appareil est hors d'usage.* That machine's out of action.

usagé ADJECTIVE
1 *old* ◇ *un manteau usagé* an old coat
2 *used* ◇ *une seringue usagée* a used syringe

l'**usager** MASC NOUN
user ◇ *les usagers de la route* road
users

usé ADJECTIVE
worn ◇ *Mon jean est un peu usé.* My
jeans are a bit worn.

s'**user** VERB
to wear out ◇ *Mes baskets se sont
usées en quinze jours.* My trainers wore
out in two weeks.

l'**usine** FEM NOUN
factory ◇ *une usine de sardines* a
sardine factory

l'**ustensile** MASC NOUN
• **un ustensile de cuisine** a kitchen
utensil

usuel ADJECTIVE
(FEM SING **usuelle**)
everyday ◇ *la langue usuelle*
everyday language

utile ADJECTIVE
useful

l'**utilisation** FEM NOUN
use ◇ *L'utilisation des calculatrices est
interdite.* It is forbidden to use
calculators.

utiliser VERB
to use

l'**utilité** FEM NOUN
use ◇ *Ce gadget n'est pas d'une
grande utilité.* This gadget isn't much
use.

V

va VERB _see_ **aller**

les **vacances** FEM NOUN
holidays ◇ _aller en vacances_ to go on
holiday ◇ _être en vacances_ to be on
holiday
- **les grandes vacances** the summer
holidays

le **vacancier** NOUN
holiday-maker

la **vacancière** NOUN
holiday-maker

le **vacarme** NOUN
racket ◇ _Qu'est-ce que c'est que ce
vacarme?_ What's all this racket?

le **vaccin** NOUN
vaccination

la **vaccination** NOUN
vaccination ◇ _La vaccination est
obligatoire._ Vaccination is compulsory.

vacciner VERB
to vaccinate ◇ _se faire vacciner contre
la rubéole_ to be vaccinated against
German measles

la **vache** NOUN
see also **vache** ADJECTIVE
cow

vache ADJECTIVE (_informal_)
see also **vache** NOUN
mean ◇ _C'est vraiment vache, ce qu'il
a dit._ What he said was really mean.
◇ _Il est vache._ He's a mean sod.

vachement ADVERB (_informal_)
really ◇ _Viens te baigner, l'eau est
vachement chaude._ Come in the water,
it's really warm.

le **vagabond** NOUN
tramp

le **vagin** NOUN
vagina

la **vague** NOUN
see also **vague** ADJECTIVE
wave (_in sea_)

vague ADJECTIVE
see also **vague** NOUN
vague ◇ _J'ai un vague souvenir de lui._
I vaguely remember him.

vain ADJECTIVE
- **en vain** in vain

vaincre VERB
1 _to defeat_ ◇ _L'armée a été vaincue._
The army was defeated.
2 _to overcome_ ◇ _Il a réussi à vaincre
sa timidité._ He managed to overcome
his shyness.

le **vainqueur** NOUN
winner

vais VERB _see_ **aller**
- **Je vais écrire à mes cousins.** I'm
going to write to my cousins.

le **vaisseau** NOUN
(PL les **vaisseaux**)
- **un vaisseau spatial** a spaceship
- **un vaisseau sanguin** a blood vessel

la **vaisselle** NOUN
1 _washing-up_ ◇ _Je vais faire la
vaisselle._ I'll do the washing-up.
2 _dishes_ ◇ _Tu peux ranger la vaisselle
s'il te plaît?_ Can you put the dishes
away please?

valable ADJECTIVE
valid ◇ _Ce billet d'avion est valable un
an._ This plane ticket is valid for one
year.

le **valet** NOUN
jack (_in card games_) ◇ _le valet de
carreau_ the jack of diamonds

la **valeur** NOUN
value ◇ _sans valeur_ of no value
- **des objets de valeur** valuables ◇ _Ne
laissez pas d'objets de valeur dans votre
chambre._ Don't leave any valuables in
your room.

valider VERB
to stamp ◇ _Vous devez faire valider
votre billet avant votre départ._ You must
get your ticket stamped before you leave.

la **valise** NOUN
suitcase

la **vallée** NOUN
valley

valoir VERB
to be worth ◇ _Ça vaut combien?_ How
much is it worth? ◇ _Cette voiture vaut
très cher._ This car's worth a lot of
money.
- **Ça vaut mieux.** That would be better.
◇ _Il vaut mieux ne rien dire._ It would be
better to say nothing.
- **valoir la peine** to be worth it ◇ _Ça
vaudrait la peine d'essayer._ It would be
worth a try.

le **vampire** NOUN
vampire

le **vandalisme** NOUN
vandalism

la **vanille** NOUN
vanilla ◇ _une glace à la vanille_ a
vanilla ice cream

la **vanité** NOUN
vanity

vaniteux ADJECTIVE
(FEM SING **vaniteuse**)

se **vanter** VERB
to boast

la **vapeur** NOUN
steam ◇ *des légumes cuits à la vapeur* steamed vegetables

la **varappe** NOUN
rock climbing ◇ *faire de la varappe* to go rock climbing

variable ADJECTIVE
changeable (weather)

la **varicelle** NOUN
chickenpox ◇ *Elle a la varicelle.* She's got chickenpox.

varié ADJECTIVE
varied ◇ *Son travail est très varié.* His job is very varied.

varier VERB
to vary
* **Le menu varie tous les jours.** The menu changes every day.

la **variété** NOUN
variety ◇ *Il n'y a pas beaucoup de variété.* There isn't much variety.
* **une émission de variétés** a television variety show

vas VERB *see* **aller**

le **vase** NOUN
see also la vase
vase

la **vase** NOUN
see also le vase
mud

vaste ADJECTIVE
vast

vaudrait, vaut VERB *see* **valoir**

le **vautour** NOUN
vulture

le **veau** NOUN
(PL les veaux)
[1] *calf* (animal)
[2] *veal* (meat)

vécu VERB *see* **vivre**
* **Il a vécu à Paris pendant dix ans.** He lived in Paris for ten years.

la **vedette** NOUN
[1] *star* ◇ *une vedette de cinéma* a film star
[2] *motor boat*
* **une vedette de police** a police launch

végétal ADJECTIVE
(MASC PL **végétaux**)
vegetable ◇ *l'huile végétale* vegetable oil

végétarien ADJECTIVE
(FEM SING **végétarienne**)
vegetarian ◇ *Je suis végétarien.* I'm a vegetarian.

végétation NOUN
vegetation

le **véhicule** NOUN
vehicle

la **veille** NOUN
the day before ◇ *la veille de son départ* the day before he left ◇ *la veille au soir* the previous evening
* **la veille de Noël** Christmas Eve
* **la veille du jour de l'An** New Year's Eve

veinard ADJECTIVE (informal)
* **Qu'est-ce qu'il est veinard!** He's such a lucky devil!

la **veine** NOUN
vein
* **avoir de la veine** (informal) to be lucky

le/la **véliplanchiste** NOUN
windsurfer

le **vélo** NOUN
bike ◇ *faire du vélo* to go cycling
* **un vélo tout-terrain** a mountain bike

le **vélomoteur** NOUN
moped

le **velours** NOUN
velvet ◇ *une robe en velours* a velvet dress
* **le velours côtelé** corduroy ◇ *un pantalon en velours côtelé* corduroy trousers

les **vendanges** FEM NOUN
grape harvest ◇ *On fait les vendanges en septembre.* The grape harvest is in September.

le **vendeur** NOUN
shop assistant

la **vendeuse** NOUN
shop assistant

vendre VERB
to sell
* **vendre quelque chose à quelqu'un** to sell somebody something ◇ *Il m'a vendu son vélo.* He sold me his bike.
* **"à vendre"** "for sale"

le **vendredi** NOUN
[1] *Friday* ◇ *Aujourd'hui, nous sommes vendredi.* It's Friday today.
[2] *on Friday* ◇ *Il est venu vendredi.* He came on Friday.
* **le vendredi** on Fridays ◇ *Je joue au foot le vendredi.* I play football on Fridays.
* **tous les vendredis** every Friday
* **vendredi dernier** last Friday
* **vendredi prochain** next Friday
* **le Vendredi saint** Good Friday

vénéneux ADJECTIVE
(FEM SING **vénéneuse**)
poisonous (plant) ◇ *un champignon vénéneux* a poisonous mushroom

la **vengeance** NOUN
revenge

se **venger** VERB
to get revenge

venimeux ADJECTIVE
(FEM SING **venimeuse**)
poisonous (animal) ◇ *un serpent venimeux* a poisonous snake

le **venin** NOUN
poison

venir VERB
to come ◇ *Il viendra demain.* He'll come tomorrow. ◇ *Il est venu nous voir.* He came to see us.
◆ **venir de** to have just ◇ *Je viens de le voir.* I've just seen him. ◇ *Je viens de lui téléphoner.* I've just phoned him.
◆ **faire venir quelqu'un** to call somebody out ◇ *faire venir le médecin* to call the doctor out

le **vent** NOUN
wind ◇ *Il y a du vent.* It's windy.

la **vente** NOUN
sale ◇ *une vente de charité* a jumble sale
◆ **une vente aux enchères** an auction

le **ventilateur** NOUN
fan (for cooling)

le **ventre** NOUN
stomach ◇ *avoir mal au ventre* to have stomachache

venu VERB see **venir**

le **ver** NOUN
worm
◆ **un ver de terre** an earthworm

le **verbe** NOUN
verb

le **verdict** NOUN
verdict

le **verger** NOUN
orchard

verglacé ADJECTIVE
icy ◇ *La route était verglacée.* The road was icy.

le **verglas** NOUN
black ice

véridique ADJECTIVE
truthful

la **vérification** NOUN
check ◇ *une vérification d'identité* an identity check

vérifier VERB
to check

véritable ADJECTIVE
real ◇ *C'était un véritable cauchemar.* It was a real nightmare.
◆ **en cuir véritable** made of real leather

la **vérité** NOUN
truth ◇ *dire la vérité* to tell the truth

verni ADJECTIVE
varnished
◆ **des chaussures vernies** patent leather shoes

vernir VERB
to varnish

le **vernis** NOUN
varnish ◇ *le vernis à ongles* nail varnish

verra, verrai, verras VERB see **voir**
◆ **on verra...** we'll see...

le **verre** NOUN
1 *glass* ◇ *une table en verre* a glass table ◇ *un verre d'eau* a glass of water
◆ **boire un verre** to have a drink
2 *lens* (of spectacles) ◇ *des verres de contact* contact lenses

verrez, verrons, verront VERB see **voir**

le **verrou** NOUN
bolt (on door)

verrouiller VERB
to bolt ◇ *N'oublie pas de verrouiller la porte du garage.* Don't forget to bolt the garage door.

la **verrue** NOUN
wart

le **vers** NOUN
see also **vers** PREPOSITION
line (of poetry) ◇ *au troisième vers* in the third line

vers PREPOSITION
see also **vers** NOUN
1 *towards* ◇ *Il allait vers la gare.* He was going towards the station.
2 *at about* ◇ *Il est rentré chez lui vers cinq heures.* He went home at about 5 o'clock.

verse
◆ **à verse** ADVERB ◇ *Il pleut à verse.* It's pouring with rain.

le **Verseau** NOUN
Aquarius ◇ *Georges est Verseau.* Georges is Aquarius.

le **versement** NOUN
instalment ◇ *en cinq versements* in 5 instalments

verser VERB
to pour ◇ *Est-ce que tu peux me verser un verre d'eau?* Could you pour me a glass of water?

la **version** NOUN
1 *version*
2 *translation* (from the foreign language)
◆ **un film en version originale** a film in the original language

le **verso** NOUN
back (of sheet of paper)
◆ **voir au verso** see overleaf

vert ADJECTIVE
green

la **vertèbre** NOUN
vertebra

vertical ADJECTIVE
(MASC PL **verticaux**)
vertical

le **vertige** NOUN
vertigo ◇ *avoir le vertige* to have vertigo

la **verveine** NOUN
verbena tea

la **vessie** NOUN
bladder

la **veste** NOUN
jacket

le **vestiaire** NOUN
1 *cloakroom* (in theatre, museum)
2 *changing room* (at sports ground)

le **vestibule** NOUN
hall

le **vêtement** NOUN
garment
- **les vêtements** clothes

la **vétérinaire** NOUN
vet ◇ *Elle est vétérinaire.* She's a vet.

le **veuf** NOUN
widower ◇ *Il est veuf.* He's a widower.

veuille, veuillez, veuillons, veulent, veut VERB *see* **vouloir**
- **Veuillez fermer la porte en sortant.** Please shut the door when you go out.

la **veuve** NOUN
widow ◇ *Elle est veuve.* She's a widow.

veux VERB *see* **vouloir**

vexer VERB
- **vexer quelqu'un** to hurt somebody's feelings
- **se vexer** to be offended

la **viande** NOUN
meat
- **la viande hachée** mince

vibrer VERB
to vibrate

le **vice** NOUN
vice

vicieux ADJECTIVE
(FEM SING **vicieuse**)
lecherous ◇ *Il est un peu vicieux.* He's a bit of a lecher.

la **victime** NOUN
victim

la **victoire** NOUN
victory

vide ADJECTIVE
see also **vide** NOUN
empty

le **vide** NOUN
see also **vide** ADJECTIVE
vacuum ◇ *emballé sous vide* vacuum-packed
- **avoir peur du vide** to be afraid of heights

la **vidéo** NOUN
see also **vidéo** ADJECTIVE
video

vidéo ADJECTIVE (MASC, FEM, PL)
see also **vidéo** NOUN
video ◇ *une cassette vidéo* a video cassette ◇ *un jeu vidéo* a video game ◇ *une caméra vidéo* a video camera

le **vidéoclip** NOUN
music video

le **vidéoclub** NOUN
video shop

vider VERB
to empty

la **vie** NOUN
life
- **être en vie** to be alive

vieil ADJECTIVE
vieil is used with a masculine singular noun in place of **vieux** when the noun begins with a vowel sound.
old ◇ *un vieil arbre* an old tree ◇ *un vieil homme* an old man

le **vieillard** NOUN
old man

vieille ADJECTIVE
(MASC SING **vieux**)
see also **vieille** NOUN
old ◇ *une vieille dame* an old lady
- **une vieille fille** an old maid

la **vieille** NOUN
see also **vieille** ADJECTIVE
old woman
- **Eh bien, ma vieille...** (informal) Well, my dear...

la **vieillesse** NOUN
old age

vieillir VERB
to age ◇ *Il a beaucoup vieilli depuis la dernière fois que je l'ai vu.* He's aged a lot since I last saw him.

viendrai, vienne, viens VERB *see* **venir**
- **Je viendrai dès que possible.** I'll come as soon as possible.
- **Je voudrais que tu viennes.** I'd like you to come.
- **Viens ici!** Come here!

la **Vierge** NOUN
see also **vierge** ADJECTIVE
Virgo ◇ *Pascal est Vierge.* Pascal is Virgo.
- **la Vierge** the Virgin Mary

V

vierge ADJECTIVE
see also vierge NOUN
1 *virgin* ◇ *Il est vierge.* He's a virgin.
2 *blank* ◇ *une cassette vierge* a blank cassette
le **Viêt-Nam** NOUN
Vietnam
vietnamien ADJECTIVE, NOUN
(FEM SING **vietnamienne**)
Vietnamese
+ **un Vietnamien** a Vietnamese *(man)*
+ **une Vietnamienne** a Vietnamese *(woman)*
+ **les Vietnamiens** the Vietnamese
vieux ADJECTIVE
(FEM SING **vieille**)
see also vieux NOUN
old ◇ *Il fait plus vieux que son âge.* He looks older than he is.
+ **un vieux garçon** a bachelor
le **vieux** NOUN
see also vieux ADJECTIVE
old man ◇ *Eh bien, mon vieux...* *(informal)* Well, my old mate...
+ **les vieux** old people
vieux jeu ADJECTIVE (MASC, FEM, PL)
old-fashioned ◇ *Il est un peu vieux jeu.* He's a bit old-fashioned.
vif ADJECTIVE
(FEM SING **vive**)
1 *sharp* *(mentally)* ◇ *Il est très vif.* He's very sharp.
+ **avoir l'esprit vif** to be quick-witted
2 *crisp* ◇ *L'air est plus vif à la campagne qu'en ville.* The air is crisper in the country than in the town.
3 *bright* *(colour)* ◇ *un bleu vif* a bright blue
la **vigne** NOUN
vine
+ **des champs de vigne** vineyards
le **vigneron** NOUN
wine grower
la **vignette** NOUN
tax disc
le **vignoble** NOUN
vineyard
vilain ADJECTIVE
1 *naughty* ◇ *C'est très vilain de dire des mensonges.* It's very naughty to tell lies.
2 *ugly* ◇ *Il n'est pas vilain.* He's not bad-looking.
la **villa** NOUN
villa ◇ *une villa en multipropriété* a time-share villa
le **village** NOUN
village
le **villageois** NOUN

villager
la **villageoise** NOUN
villager
la **ville** NOUN
town ◇ *Je vais en ville.* I'm going into town.
+ **une grande ville** a city
le **vin** NOUN
wine ◇ *le vin de pays* the local wine
◇ *le vin ordinaire* the table wine
le **vinaigre** NOUN
vinegar
la **vinaigrette** NOUN
French dressing
vingt NUMBER
twenty ◇ *Elle a vingt ans.* She's twenty. ◇ *à vingt heures* at 8 p.m.
+ **le vingt février** the twentieth of February
+ **vingt et un** twenty-one
+ **vingt-deux** twenty-two
la **vingtaine** NOUN
about twenty ◇ *une vingtaine de personnes* about twenty people
+ **Il a une vingtaine d'années.** He's about twenty.
vingtième ADJECTIVE
twentieth
le **viol** NOUN
rape
violemment ADVERB
violently
la **violence** NOUN
violence
violent ADJECTIVE
violent
violer VERB
to rape
violet ADJECTIVE
(FEM SING **violette**)
purple
la **violette** NOUN
violet *(flower)*
le **violon** NOUN
violin ◇ *Je joue du violon.* I play the violin.
le **violoncelle** NOUN
cello ◇ *Elle joue du violoncelle.* She plays the cello.
le/la **violoniste** NOUN
violinist
la **vipère** NOUN
viper
le **virage** NOUN
bend ◇ *une route pleine de virages dangereux* a road full of dangerous bends
la **virgule** NOUN
1 *comma*

2 *decimal point* ◇ *trois virgule cinq* three point five

le **virus** NOUN
virus

vis VERB *see* **vivre**
see also **vis** NOUN
◆ *Je vis en Écosse.* I live in Scotland.

la **vis** NOUN
see also **vis** VERB
screw

le **visa** NOUN
visa

le **visage** NOUN
face ◇ *Elle a le visage rond.* She's got a round face.

vis-à-vis de PREPOSITION
with regard to ◇ *Ce n'est pas très juste vis-à-vis de lui.* It's not very fair to him.

viser VERB
to aim at ◇ *Il faut viser la cible.* You have to aim at the target.

la **visibilité** NOUN
visibility

visible ADJECTIVE
visible

la **visière** NOUN
peak (of cap)

la **visite** NOUN
visit
◆ *rendre visite à quelqu'un* to visit somebody ◇ *Je vais rendre visite à mon grand-père.* I'm going to visit my grandfather.
◆ *avoir de la visite* to have visitors ◇ *Nous avons de la visite aujourd'hui.* We've got visitors today.
◆ *une visite médicale* a medical examination

visiter VERB
to visit

le **visiteur** NOUN
visitor

la **visiteuse** NOUN
visitor

le **vison** NOUN
mink (fur) ◇ *un manteau en vison* a mink coat

vit VERB *see* **vivre**
◆ *Il vit chez ses parents.* He lives with his parents.

vital ADJECTIVE
(MASC PL **vitaux**)
vital ◇ *C'est une question vitale.* It's of vital importance.

la **vitamine** NOUN
vitamin

vite ADVERB
1 *quick* ◇ *Vite, ils arrivent!* Quick,

they're coming! ◇ *Je peux aller dire au revoir à Claire? – Oui, mais fais vite!* Can I go and say goodbye to Claire? – Yes, but be quick! ◇ *Prenons la voiture, ça ira plus vite.* Let's take the car, it'll be quicker.
◆ *Le temps passe vite.* Time flies.
2 *fast* ◇ *Il roule trop vite.* He drives too fast.
3 *soon* ◇ *Il va vite oublier.* He'll soon forget.
◆ *Il a vite compris.* He understood immediately.

la **vitesse** NOUN
1 *speed* ◇ *à toute vitesse* at top speed ◇ *Nous sommes rentrés à toute vitesse.* We rushed back home.
2 *gear* ◇ *en première vitesse* in first gear

le **vitrail** NOUN
(PL les **vitraux**)
stained-glass window

la **vitre** NOUN
window ◇ *Il a cassé une vitre.* He broke a window.

la **vitrine** NOUN
shop window

vivant ADJECTIVE
1 *living* ◇ *les êtres vivants* living creatures ◇ *les expériences sur les animaux vivants* experiments on live animals
2 *lively* ◇ *Elle est très vivante.* She's very lively.

vive ADJECTIVE
(MASC SING **vif**)
see also **vive** EXCLAMATION
1 *sharp* (mentally) ◇ *Elle est très vive.* She's very sharp.
2 *bright* (colour)
◆ *à vive allure* at a brisk pace
◆ *de vive voix* in person ◇ *Je te le dirai de vive voix.* I'll tell you about it when I see you.

vive EXCLAMATION
see also **vive** ADJECTIVE
◆ *Vive le roi!* Long live the king!

vivement EXCLAMATION
◆ *Vivement les vacances!* Roll on the holidays!

vivre VERB
to live ◇ *J'aimerais vivre à l'étranger.* I'd like to live abroad. ◇ *Et ton grand-père? Il vit encore?* What about your grandfather? Is he still alive?

vlan EXCLAMATION
wham!

la **VO** NOUN
◆ *un film en VO* a film in the original

V

language

le **vocabulaire** NOUN
vocabulary

la **vocation** NOUN
vocation

le **vœu** NOUN
(PL les **vœux**)
wish ◇ *faire un vœu* to make a wish
◇ *Meilleurs vœux de bonne année!* Best
wishes for the New Year!

la **vogue** NOUN
fashion ◇ *C'est très en vogue en ce
moment.* It's very fashionable at the
moment.

voici PREPOSITION
1 *this is* ◇ *Voici mon frère et voilà ma
sœur.* This is my brother and that's my
sister.
2 *here is* ◇ *Tu as perdu ton stylo?
Tiens, en voici un autre.* Have you lost
your pen? Here's another one.
◆ **Le voici!** Here he is! ◇ *Tu veux tes
clés? Tiens, les voici!* You want your
keys? Here you are!

la **voie** NOUN
lane ◇ *une route à trois voies* a 3-lane
road
◆ **par voie buccale** orally ◇ *à prendre
par voie buccale* to be taken orally
◆ **la voie ferrée** the railway track

voilà PREPOSITION
1 *there is* ◇ *Tiens! Voilà Paul.* Look!
There's Paul. ◇ *Tu as perdu ton stylo?
Tiens, en voilà un autre.* Have you lost
your pen? There's another one.
◆ **Les voilà!** There they are!
2 *that is* ◇ *Voilà ma sœur.* That's my
sister.

le **voile** NOUN
see also la **voile**
veil ◇ *un voile de mariée* a wedding
veil

la **voile** NOUN
see also le **voile**
1 *sail*
2 *sailing* ◇ *faire de la voile* to go
sailing
◆ **un bateau à voiles** a sailing boat

le **voilier** NOUN
sailing boat

voir VERB

Present tense:
je vois	nous voyons
tu vois	vous voyez
il/elle voit	ils/elles voient
Past participle: *vu*

to see ◇ *Venez me voir quand vous
serez à Paris.* Come and see me when
you're in Paris. ◇ *Je ne vois pas*

pourquoi il a fait ça. I can't see why he
did that.
◆ **faire voir quelque chose à quelqu'un**
to show somebody something ◇ *Il m'a
fait voir sa collection de timbres.* He
showed me his stamp collection.
◆ **se voir** to be obvious ◇ *Est-ce que
cette tache se voit?* Does that stain
show? ◇ *Ça fait des années qu'elle n'a
pas joué au tennis – Oui, ça se voit!* She
hasn't played tennis for years – Yes, you
can tell!
◆ **avoir quelque chose à voir avec** to
have something to do with ◇ *Ça n'a
rien à voir avec lui, c'est entre toi et moi.*
It's nothing to do with him, it's
between you and me.
◆ **Je ne peux vraiment pas la voir.**
(*informal*) I really can't stand her.

le **voisin** NOUN
neighbour

le **voisinage** NOUN
◆ **dans le voisinage** in the vicinity

la **voisine** NOUN
neighbour

la **voiture** NOUN
car ◇ *une voiture de sport* a sports car

la **voix** NOUN
(PL les **voix**)
1 *voice* ◇ *à voix basse* in a low voice
◆ **à haute voix** aloud
2 *vote* ◇ *Il a obtenu cinquante pour
cent des voix.* He got 50% of the votes.

le **vol** NOUN
1 *flight*
◆ **à vol d'oiseau** as the crow flies
◆ **le vol à voile** gliding
2 *theft* ◇ *un vol à main armée* an
armed robbery

la **volaille** NOUN
poultry

le **volant** NOUN
1 *steering wheel* ◇ *Est-ce que tu
veux que je prenne le volant?* Do you
want me to take the wheel?
2 *shuttlecock*

le **volcan** NOUN
volcano

la **volée** NOUN
volley (*in tennis*)
◆ **rattraper une balle à la volée** to catch a
ball in mid-air

voler VERB
1 *to fly* ◇ *J'aimerais savoir voler.* I'd
like to be able to fly.
2 *to steal* ◇ *On a volé mon appareil
photo.* My camera's been stolen.
◆ **voler quelque chose à quelqu'un** to
steal something from somebody ◇ *Ça*

n'est pas son stylo, il me l'a volé. That's not his pen, he stole it from me.
- **voler quelqu'un** to rob somebody

le **volet** NOUN
  shutter

le **voleur** NOUN
  thief

la **voleuse** NOUN
  thief

le **volley** NOUN
  volleyball ◇ *jouer au volley* to play volleyball

le/la **volontaire** NOUN
  volunteer

la **volonté** NOUN
  willpower ◇ *Il a beaucoup de volonté.* He's got a lot of willpower.
- **la bonne volonté** goodwill
- **la mauvaise volonté** lack of goodwill

volontiers ADVERB
  ① *gladly* ◇ *Je l'aiderais volontiers s'il me le demandais.* I'd gladly help him if he asked me.
  ② *please* ◇ *Voulez-vous boire quelque chose? – Volontiers!* Would you like something to drink? – Yes, please!

le **volume** NOUN
  volume ◇ *un dictionnaire en deux volumes* a two-volume dictionary

volumineux ADJECTIVE
  (FEM SING **volumineuse**)
  bulky

vomir VERB
  to vomit ◇ *Il a vomi toute la nuit.* He was vomiting all night.

vont VERB *see* **aller**

vos ADJECTIVE
  your ◇ *Rangez vos jouets, les enfants!* Children, put your toys away! ◇ *Merci pour vos fleurs, M. Durand.* Thanks for your flowers, Mr Durand.

le **vote** NOUN
  vote

voter VERB
  to vote

votre ADJECTIVE
  (PL **vos**)
  your ◇ *C'est votre manteau?* Is this your coat?

vôtre PRONOUN
- **le vôtre** yours ◇ *J'aime bien notre prof de maths, mais le vôtre est plus patient.* I like our maths teacher, but yours is more patient. ◇ *À qui est cette écharpe? C'est la vôtre?* Whose is this scarf? Is it yours?
- **À la vôtre!** Cheers!

vôtres PRONOUN
- **les vôtres** yours ◇ *J'ai oublié mes*

lunettes de soleil. Vous avez apporté les vôtres? I've forgotten my sunglasses. Have you brought yours?

voudra, voudrai, voudrais, voudras, voudrez, voudrons, voudront VERB *see* **vouloir**
- **Je voudrais...** I'd like... ◇ *Je voudrais deux litres de lait, s'il vous plaît.* I'd like two litres of milk, please.

vouloir VERB

Present tense:	
je veux	nous voulons
tu veux	vous voulez
il/elle veut	ils/elles veulent
Past participle: *voulu*	

  to want ◇ *Elle veut un vélo pour Noël.* She wants a bike for Christmas. ◇ *Je ne veux pas de dessert.* I don't want any pudding. ◇ *Il ne veut pas venir.* He doesn't want to come. ◇ *On va au cinéma? – Si tu veux.* Shall we go to the cinema? – If you like.
- **Je veux bien.** I'll be happy to. ◇ *Je veux bien le faire à ta place si ça t'arrange.* I don't mind doing it for you if you prefer.
- **Voulez-vous une tasse de thé? – Je veux bien.** Would you like a cup of tea? – Yes please.
- **sans le vouloir** without meaning to ◇ *Je l'ai vexé sans le vouloir.* I upset him without meaning to.
- **en vouloir à quelqu'un** to be angry at somebody ◇ *Il m'en veut de ne pas l'avoir invité à mon anniversaire.* He's angry at me for not inviting him to my birthday party.
- **vouloir dire** to mean ◇ *Qu'est-ce que ça veut dire?* What does that mean?

voulu VERB *see* **vouloir**

vous PRONOUN
  ① *you* ◇ *Vous aimez la pizza?* Do you like pizza?
  ② *to you* ◇ *Je vous écrirai bientôt.* I'll write to you soon.
  ③ *yourself* ◇ *Vous vous êtes fait mal?* Have you hurt yourself?
- **vous-même** yourself ◇ *Vous l'avez fait vous-même?* Did you do it yourself?

vouvoyer VERB
- **vouvoyer quelqu'un** to address somebody as "vous"

  vouvoyer quelqu'un *means to use* **vous** *when speaking to someone, rather than* **tu**. *Use* **tu** *only when talking to one person and when that person is someone of your own age or whom you know well; use* **vous** *to everyone else. If in doubt use* **vous**.
- **Est-ce que je dois vouvoyer ta sœur?**

Should I use "vous" to your sister?

le **voyage** NOUN
journey ◇ *Avez-vous fait bon voyage?*
Did you have a good journey?
+ **Bon voyage!** Have a good trip!

voyager VERB
to travel

le **voyageur** NOUN
passenger

la **voyageuse** NOUN
passenger

voyaient, voyais, voyait VERB *see*
voir

la **voyelle** NOUN
vowel

voyez, voyiez, voyions VERB *see*
voir

voyons VERB *see* **voir**
[1] *let's see* ◇ *Voyons ce qu'on peut faire.* Let's see what we can do.
[2] *come on* ◇ *Voyons, sois raisonnable!* Come on, be reasonable!

le **voyou** NOUN
hooligan

vrac
+ **en vrac** ADVERB
loose ◇ *du thé en vrac* loose tea

vrai ADJECTIVE
true ◇ *une histoire vraie* a true story

◇ *C'est vrai?* Is that true?
+ **à vrai dire** to tell the truth

vraiment ADVERB
really

vraisemblable ADJECTIVE
likely ◇ *C'est peu vraisemblable.*
That's not very likely. ◇ *Il va falloir trouver une excuse vraisemblable.* We'll have to find a convincing excuse.

le **VTT** NOUN (= *vélo tout-terrain*)
mountain bike

vu VERB *see* **voir**
+ **être bien vu** to be popular (*person*)
◇ *Est-ce qu'il est bien vu à l'école?* Is he popular at school?
+ **être mal vu** to be disapproved of
◇ *C'est mal vu de fumer ici.* They don't like people smoking here.

la **vue** NOUN
[1] *eyesight* ◇ *J'ai une mauvaise vue.*
I've got bad eyesight.
[2] *view* ◇ *Il y a une belle vue d'ici.*
There's a lovely view from here.
+ **à vue d'œil** visibly ◇ *Elle grandit à vue d'œil.* Every time you see her, she's got taller.

vulgaire ADJECTIVE
vulgar ◇ *Ne dit pas ça, c'est très vulgaire.* Don't say that, it's very vulgar.

W

le **wagon** NOUN
railway carriage

le **wagon-lit** NOUN
(PL les **wagons-lits**)
sleeper (*on train*)

le **wagon-restaurant** NOUN
(PL les **wagons-restaurants**)
restaurant car

le **walkman** ® NOUN
Walkman ®

wallon ADJECTIVE, NOUN
(FEM SING **wallonne**)
Walloon (*French-speaking Belgian*)

◆ **les Wallons** the French-speaking Belgians

la **Wallonie** NOUN
French-speaking Belgium

les **W.-C.** MASC NOUN
toilet

le **week-end** NOUN
weekend

le **western** NOUN
western (*film*)

le **whisky** NOUN
(PL les **whiskies**)
whisky

X

le **xylophone** NOUN
xylophone ◇ *Elle joue du xylophone.* She plays the xylophone.

Y

y PRONOUN
there ◇ *Nous y sommes allés l'été dernier.* We went there last summer.
◇ *Regarde dans le tiroir: je pense que les clés y sont.* Look in the drawer: I think the keys are in there.

> **y** *replaces phrases with* **à** *in constructions like the ones below.*

◆ **Je pensais à l'examen. – Mais arrête d'y penser!** I was thinking about the exam. – Well, stop thinking about it!

◆ **Je ne m'attendais pas à ça. – Eh bien moi, je m'y attendais.** I wasn't expecting that. – Well, I was expecting it.

le **yaourt** NOUN
yoghurt ◇ *un yaourt nature* a plain yoghurt ◇ *un yaourt aux fruits* a fruit yoghurt

les **yeux** MASC NOUN
(SING **œil**)
eyes ◇ *Elle a les yeux bleus.* She's got blue eyes.

le **yoga** NOUN
yoga

le **yoghourt** NOUN
yoghurt

la **Yougoslavie** NOUN
Yugoslavia

◆ **l'ex-Yougoslavie** the former Yugoslavia

youpi EXCLAMATION
Yippee!

le **yoyo** NOUN
yo-yo

Z

zapper VERB
to channel hop

le **zèbre** NOUN
zebra

le **zéro** NOUN
zero
- **Ils ont gagné trois à zéro.** They won three-nil.

zézayer VERB
to lisp ◇ *Il zézaie.* He's got a lisp.

le **zigzag** NOUN
- **faire des zigzags** to zigzag

la **zone** NOUN
zone
- **une zone industrielle** an industrial estate

le **zoo** NOUN
zoo

zut EXCLAMATION
Oh heck!

PUZZLES AND WORDGAMES

Introduction

The puzzles and wordgames on the following pages have been designed to give you practice in using your dictionary. Make sure you read the "How to use the dictionary" section at the front of this book before you start. Don't worry, there are answers at the end of the wordgames in case you get really stuck!

WORDGAME 1

CHOOSING THE RIGHT TRANSLATION

Complete the crossword below by looking up the English words in the list and finding the correct French translations. There is a slight catch, however! All the English words have more than one French translation, but only one will fit correctly into each part of the crossword.

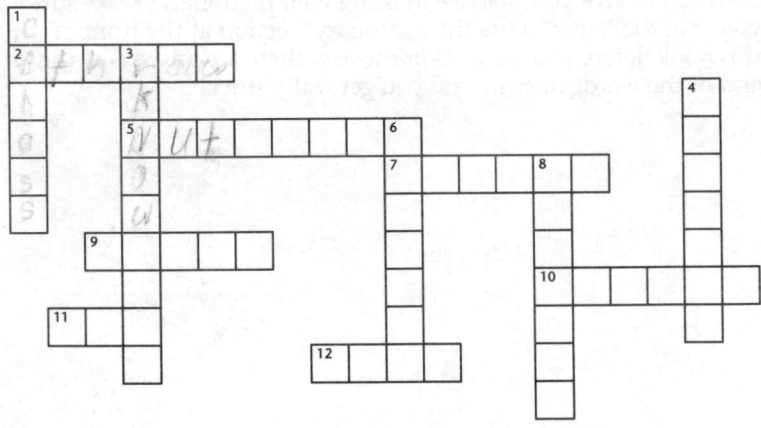

1. CLASS
2. THROW
3. KNOW
4. FIND

5. NUT
6. TAKE
7. CALF
8. PLACE

9. DINNER
10. STAY
11. HARD
12. LATE

WORDGAME 2

NOUNS, ADJECTIVES, ADVERBS & VERBS

In each sentence below a word has been shaded. Put a tick in the
appropriate box to show whether it's a **noun**, **adjective**, adverb or
verb each time. Look in the section "How to use the dictionary" at
the front of the book to remind you what nouns, adjectives,
adverbs and verbs are. Remember, there may be more than one
entry for each word.

SENTENCE	Noun	Adj	Adv	Verb
1. La ferme de mes parents est en Alsace.				
2. Il n'est pas franc.				
3. Le magasin ferme dans deux minutes.				
4. Le dîner est à 20 heures.				
5. Tu veux goûter ma mousse au chocolat?				
6. Je n'aime pas la bière.				
7. C'est un faux passeport.				
8. J'entends des pas dans l'escalier.				
9. Ce film nous a fait rire.				
10. Cette voiture est mal garée.				

WORDGAME 3

NOUNS

This list contains the feminine form of some French nouns. Use your dictionary to find the **masculine** form. Remember, the masculine form usually appears in a separate entry.

Use your dictionary to find the **plural** of the following nouns. Remember, the plural form appears in brackets and in bold on the line below the singular form.

MASCULINE	FEMININE	SINGULAR	PLURAL
	danseuse	chou	
	boulangère	canal	
	Américaine	bateau	
	animatrice	sapeur–pompier	
	avocate	neveu	
	Parisienne	travail	
	libraire	vœu	
	téléspectatrice	voix	
	pionne	œil	
	veuve	croque-monsieur	

WORDGAME 4

ADJECTIVES

Use the French–English side of your dictionary to find the **feminine singular** form of these adjectives. Remember, the feminine singular form appears in brackets and in bold on the line below the masculine form.

MASCULINE	FEMININE
1. naturel	
2. beau	
3. heureux	
4. américain	
5. gros	
6. blanc	
7. faux	
8. sec	
9. favori	
10. frais	
11. bon	
12. fou	
13. public	
14. naïf	

VERB TENSES

Use the verb tables on pages 284 to 297 to help you fill in the blanks in the table below.

INFINITIVE	PRESENT	IMPERFECT	FUTURE
faire		je	
se laver	il		
voir			nous
finir			elle
avoir		il	
aller	vous		
être	elles		
vouloir		ils	
devoir	tu		
mettre			je
dire		il	
pouvoir			nous

WORDGAME 6

«MOTS CODÉS»

In the boxes below, the letters of eight French words have been replaced by numbers. A number represents the same letter each time.

Try to crack the code and find the eight words. If you need help, use your dictionary.

Here is a clue: all the words you are looking for have something to do with CLOTHES.

1 P[1] [2] [3] [4] [2] [5] [6] [3]

2 [7] [8] P[1] E[9]

3 [10] [11] [3] [11] [7] [8] P[1] [9]

4 [10] [2] [3] [4] [9] [2] [8]

5 P[1] [8] [3] [3]

6 [12] [13] [2] P[1] [9] [2] [8]

7 [12] [13] [2] [8] [14] [14] [9] [4] [4] [9]

8 [12] [13] [2] [8] [14] [14] [8] [15] [9]

«MOTS CUISINÉS»

Here is a list of French words for things you will find in the kitchen.
Unfortunately, they have all been jumbled up. Try to work out what
each word is and put the word in the boxes on the right. You will
see there are five shaded boxes below. The five letters in the shaded
boxes make up *another* French word for an object you can find in
the kitchen.

1 féac   Tu prends du sucre
dans ton _____ ?

2 rever   Encore un _____
de vin ?

3 lesvisale   Je déteste faire
la _____.

4 rascosele   Elle a fait cuire les pâtes
dans une grande ____.

5 grifo   Le fromage est
dans le _____ .

The word you are looking for is:

ANSWERS

WORDGAME 1
1. classe
2. lancer
3. connaître
4. trouver
5. noisette
6. emmener
7. mollet
8. endroit
9. dîner
10. rester
11. dur
12. tard

WORDGAME 2
1. noun
2. adjective
3. verb
4. noun
5. verb
6. adverb
7. adjective
8. noun
9. verb
10. adverb

WORDGAME 3
Masculine forms
1. danseur
2. boulanger
3. Américain
4. animateur
5. avocat
6. Parisien
7. libraire
8. téléspectateur
9. pion
10. veuf

WORDGAME 3
Plural forms
1. choux
2. canaux
3. bateaux
4. sapeurs–pompiers
5. neveux
6. travaux
7. vœux
8. voix
9. yeux
10. croque–monsieur

WORDGAME 4
1. naturelle
2. belle
3. heureuse
4. américaine
5. grosse
6. blanche
7. fausse
8. sèche
9. favorite
10. fraîche
11. bonne
12. folle
13. publique
14. naïve

WORDGAME 5
1. je faisais
2. il se lave
3. nous verrons
4. elle finira
5. il avait
6. vous allez
7. elles sont
8. ils voulaient
9. tu dois
10. je mettrai
11. il disait
12. nous pourrons

WORDGAME 6
1. pantalon
2. jupe
3. minijupe
4. manteau
5. pull
6. chapeau
7. chaussette
8. chaussure

WORDGAME 7
1. café
2. verre
3. vaisselle
4. casserole
5. frigo
missing word – évier

FRENCH VERB TABLES

CONTENTS

FRENCH VERB TABLES

This section contains fourteen important French verbs that you need to learn. All French verbs fall into two main categories – **regular** and **irregular** – and it is important to learn which verbs fall into which category.

The tables are arranged in the following order:

1. Regular verbs – **aimer, finir, attendre** and **se laver**
2. Very important irregular verbs – **avoir** and **être**
3. Other common irregular verbs – **aller, devoir, dire, faire, mettre, pouvoir, voir** and **vouloir**

At the top of each table you will find the infinitive, the imperative and the past participle. The lower section of the table shows you how to form six tenses of the verb:

PRESENT	e.g. je fais = I **do** *or* I **am doing**
*PRESENT SUBJUNCTIVE**	e.g. je fasse = I **do**
IMPERFECT	e.g. je faisais = I **was doing** *or* I **did**
PERFECT	e.g. j'ai fait = I **did** *or* I **have done**
FUTURE	e.g. je ferai = I **will do**
CONDITIONAL	e.g. je ferais = I **would do**

> * The French side of your dictionary will tell you which words must be followed by the subjunctive.

1. REGULAR VERBS

There are three groups of regular verbs:

1. "–ER" verbs = verbs that end in –er like **aimer** on p284 and **se laver** on p287
2. "–IR" verbs = verbs that end in –ir like **finir** on p285
3. "–RE" verbs = verbs that end in –re like **attendre** on p286

They are called regular verbs because they follow one of three set patterns. When you have learnt these patterns, you will be able to form *any* regular verb.

HOW TO FORM A REGULAR VERB

i. a) To form the present, imperfect or present subjunctive tense, take the infinitive minus the last two letters. This is called the **stem** e.g. *aimer* → **aim–** , *finir* → **fin–** , and *attendre* → **attend–**

   b) To form the future or conditional tense, the stem is the whole infinitive for "–ER" and "–IR" verbs and the infinitive minus its final "e" for "–RE" verbs e.g. *aimer* → **aimer**, *finir* → **finir** and *attendre* → **attendr–**

ii) Next add the appropriate **ending**. You need to ask yourself three questions:

   a) **What sort of verb** am I using (–ER, –IR or –RE)?
   b) **Who** is doing the verb (je, tu, il *etc*)?
   c) **When** are they doing it (in the present, the past or the future)?

Look at the verb tables for **aimer, finir** and **attendre**. The verb endings are in bold and underlined. These endings can be tagged onto the stem of *any* regular verb.

2. AVOIR AND ÊTRE

Avoir (to have) and être (to be) are very important verbs which **must** be learnt. You use them when you want to say "I have" *etc* or "I am" *etc*. The present tense of avoir or être is also used to form the **perfect tense**. In most cases, avoir is used to form the perfect, but verbs of movement like aller (to go) and venir (to come) use être – e.g. the French for both "he's gone" and "he went" is il *est* allé, not il *a* allé. You will have to learn which verbs use être.

HOW TO FORM THE PERFECT TENSE
   a) Take the infinitive of a French verb e.g. **donner**
   b) Does it use **avoir** or **être** to form the perfect tense? e.g. **donner** uses **avoir**
   c) Take the present tense form of **avoir** or **être** that goes with the person who **did** the action e.g. he gave – the French for "he" is **il**, so to form the perfect tense of **donner** we use **il a**
   d) Add the **past participle** – this is shown near the top of each verb table. If you want to form the past participle of *any* regular verb, simply take the infinitive of the verb, knock off the last two letters and add the following endings:

   "–ER" verbs add é – e.g. aimer → aim<u>é</u>
   "–IR" verbs add i – e.g. finir → fin<u>i</u>
   "–RE" verbs add u – e.g. attendre → attend<u>u</u>

   In our example, **donner** is a regular "–ER" verb, so the past participle is donn + é → **donné**
   e) The French for "he gave" is "**il a donné**"

3. IRREGULAR VERBS

Many French verbs are irregular and this means you have to learn them individually. There are tables of the most important irregular verbs such as **avoir** (to have), **être** (to be) and **faire** (to do) in this section. When you are translating from French and meet an unfamiliar verb form, you may be able to guess from the context that it comes from one of these verbs, and you can use the verb table to check. The most common irregular verb parts are listed on the French side of the dictionary, so you could also look there.

HOW TO USE THE VERB TABLES
You will find some useful example phrases at the top of each verb table, but if you can't find what you need to say or write in French there, use the verb table itself to help you. Imagine that you want to find the French for "he wants". Here's how to do it:

   a) Look up **want** on the English–French side of the dictionary to find the French translation
   b) French translation = **vouloir**
   c) Turn to the verb tables section of your dictionary and find **vouloir**
   d) When does he want it? He wants it **now**, so look for the heading *PRESENT*
   e) Who wants it? **He** does. The French for "he" is **il** so look for **il** under the *PRESENT* heading
   f) The French for "he wants" is "**il veut**"

aimer

to like *or* to love

IMPERATIVE
aim**e**
aim**ons**
aim**ez**

PAST PARTICIPLE
aim**é**

EXAMPLE PHRASES

*Tu **aimes** le chocolat?* Do you like chocolate?

*Je t'**aime**.* I love you.

*J'**aimerais** aller en Grèce.* I'd like to go to Greece.

PRESENT

j' aim**e**
tu aim**es**
il aim**e**
nous aim**ons**
vous aim**ez**
ils aim**ent**

PERFECT

j' ai aim**é**
tu as aim**é**
il a aim**é**
nous avons aim**é**
vous avez aim**é**
ils ont aim**é**

FUTURE

j' aimer**ai**
tu aimer**as**
il aimer**a**
nous aimer**ons**
vous aimer**ez**
ils aimer**ont**

PRESENT SUBJUNCTIVE

j' aim**e**
tu aim**es**
il aim**e**
nous aim**ions**
vous aim**iez**
ils aim**ent**

IMPERFECT

j' aim**ais**
tu aim**ais**
il aim**ait**
nous aim**ions**
vous aim**iez**
ils aim**aient**

CONDITIONAL

j' aimer**ais**
tu aimer**ais**
il aimer**ait**
nous aimer**ions**
vous aimer**iez**
ils aimer**aient**

finir

to finish

EXAMPLE PHRASES

Finis ta soupe! Finish your soup!

J'**ai fini**! I've finished!

Je **finirai** mes devoirs demain. I'll finish my homework tomorrow.

IMPERATIVE
finis
finissons
finissez

PAST PARTICIPLE
fini

PRESENT

je	finis
tu	finis
il	finit
nous	finissons
vous	finissez
ils	finissent

PERFECT

j'	ai fini
tu	as fini
il	a fini
nous	avons fini
vous	avez fini
ils	ont fini

FUTURE

je	finirai
tu	finiras
il	finira
nous	finirons
vous	finirez
ils	finiront

PRESENT SUBJUNCTIVE

je	finisse
tu	finisses
il	finisse
nous	finissions
vous	finissiez
ils	finissent

IMPERFECT

je	finissais
tu	finissais
il	finissait
nous	finissions
vous	finissiez
ils	finissaient

CONDITIONAL

je	finirais
tu	finirais
il	finirait
nous	finirions
vous	finiriez
ils	finiraient

attendre

to wait

attend**s**
attend**ons**
attend**ez**

PAST PARTICIPLE
attend**u**

EXAMPLE PHRASES

Attends–moi! Wait for me!

*Tu **attends** depuis longtemps?* Have you been waiting long?

*Je l'**ai attendu** à la poste.* I waited for him at the post office.

PRESENT

j' attend**s**
tu attend**s**
il attend
nous attend**ons**
vous attend**ez**
ils attend**ent**

PRESENT SUBJUNCTIVE

j' attend**e**
tu attend**es**
il attend**e**
nous attend**ions**
vous attend**iez**
ils attend**ent**

PERFECT

j' ai attend**u**
tu as attend**u**
il a attend**u**
nous avons attend**u**
vous avez attend**u**
ils ont attend**u**

IMPERFECT

j' attend**ais**
tu attend**ais**
il attend**ait**
nous attend**ions**
vous attend**iez**
ils attend**aient**

FUTURE

j' attendr**ai**
tu attendr**as**
il attendr**a**
nous attendr**ons**
vous attendr**ez**
ils attendr**ont**

CONDITIONAL

j' attendr**ais**
tu attendr**ais**
il attendr**ait**
nous attendr**ions**
vous attendr**iez**
ils attendr**aient**

se laver

to wash (oneself)

EXAMPLE PHRASES

*Je **me lave** chaque matin.* I have a wash every morning.

*Il **s'est lavé** les mains.* He washed his hands.

*Elle va **se laver** les cheveux.* She's going to wash her hair.

IMPERATIVE
lave–toi
lavons–nous
lavez–vous

PAST PARTICIPLE
lavé

PRESENT
je me lave
tu te laves
il se lave
nous nous lavons
vous vous lavez
ils se lavent

PRESENT SUBJUNCTIVE
je me lave
tu te laves
il se lave
nous nous lavions
vous vous laviez
ils se lavent

PERFECT
je me suis lavé
tu t'es lavé
il s'est lavé
nous nous sommes lavés
vous vous êtes lavé(s)
ils se sont lavés

IMPERFECT
je me lavais
tu te lavais
il se lavait
nous nous lavions
vous vous laviez
ils se lavaient

FUTURE
je me laverai
tu te laveras
il se lavera
nous nous laverons
vous vous laverez
ils se laveront

CONDITIONAL
je me laverais
tu te laverais
il se laverait
nous nous laverions
vous vous laveriez
ils se laveraient

avoir

to have

IMPERATIVE

aie
ayons
ayez

PAST PARTICIPLE

eu

EXAMPLE PHRASES

*Il **a** les yeux bleus.* He's got blue eyes.

*Quel âge **as**–tu?* How old are you?

*Il **a eu** un accident.* He's had an accident.

*J'**avais** faim.* I was hungry.

PRESENT

j' **ai**
tu **as**
il **a**
nous av**ons**
vous av**ez**
ils **ont**

PRESENT SUBJUNCTIVE

j' **aie**
tu **aies**
il **ait**
nous **ayons**
vous **ayez**
ils **aient**

PERFECT

j' ai **eu**
tu as **eu**
il a **eu**
nous avons **eu**
vous avez **eu**
ils ont **eu**

IMPERFECT

j' av**ais**
tu av**ais**
il av**ait**
nous av**ions**
vous av**iez**
ils av**aient**

FUTURE

j' **aurai**
tu **auras**
il **aura**
nous **aurons**
vous **aurez**
ils **auront**

CONDITIONAL

j' **aurais**
tu **aurais**
il **aurait**
nous **aurions**
vous **auriez**
ils **auraient**

être

to be

EXAMPLE PHRASES

Mon père est professeur. My father's a teacher.

Quelle heure est-il? – Il est 10 heures. What time is it? – It's 10 o'clock.

Ils ne sont pas encore arrivés. They haven't arrived yet.

IMPERATIVE
sois
soyons
soyez

PAST PARTICIPLE
été

PRESENT

je	**suis**
tu	**es**
il	**est**
nous	**sommes**
vous	**êtes**
ils	**sont**

PRESENT SUBJUNCTIVE

je	**sois**
tu	**sois**
il	**soit**
nous	**soyons**
vous	**soyez**
ils	**soient**

PERFECT

j'	ai	**été**
tu	as	**été**
il	a	**été**
nous	avons	**été**
vous	avez	**été**
ils	ont	**été**

IMPERFECT

j'	**étais**
tu	**étais**
il	**était**
nous	**étions**
vous	**étiez**
ils	**étaient**

FUTURE

je	**serai**
tu	**seras**
il	**sera**
nous	**serons**
vous	**serez**
ils	**seront**

CONDITIONAL

je	**serais**
tu	**serais**
il	**serait**
nous	**serions**
vous	**seriez**
ils	**seraient**

aller

to go

IMPERATIVE
va
all**ons**
all**ez**

PAST PARTICIPLE
all**é**

EXAMPLE PHRASES

*Vous **allez** au cinéma?* Are you going to the cinema?

*Je **suis allé** à Londres.* I went to London.

*Est–ce que tu **es** déjà **allé** en Allemagne?* Have you ever been to Germany?

PRESENT
je **vais**
tu **vas**
il **va**
nous all**ons**
vous all**ez**
ils **vont**

PERFECT
je suis all**é**
tu es all**é**
il est all**é**
nous sommes all**és**
vous êtes all**é(s)**
ils sont all**és**

FUTURE
j' **irai**
tu **iras**
il **ira**
nous **irons**
vous **irez**
ils **iront**

PRESENT SUBJUNCTIVE
j' **aille**
tu **ailles**
il **aille**
nous all**ions**
vous all**iez**
ils **aillent**

IMPERFECT
j' all**ais**
tu all**ais**
il all**ait**
nous all**ions**
vous all**iez**
ils all**aient**

CONDITIONAL
j' **irais**
tu **irais**
il **irait**
nous **irions**
vous **iriez**
ils **iraient**

devoir

to have to

*Je **dois** aller faire les courses ce matin.*
I have to do the shopping this morning.

*Il **a dû** faire ses devoirs hier soir.* He had to
do his homework last night.

*Il **devait** prendre le train pour aller travailler.*
He had to go to work by train.

IMPERATIVE

dois
dev**ons**
dev**ez**

PAST PARTICIPLE

dû

PRESENT

je **dois**
tu **dois**
il **doit**
nous dev**ons**
vous dev**ez**
ils **doivent**

PRESENT SUBJUNCTIVE

je **doive**
tu **doives**
il **doive**
nous dev**ions**
vous dev**iez**
ils **doivent**

PERFECT

j' ai **dû**
tu as **dû**
il a **dû**
nous avons **dû**
vous avez **dû**
ils ont **dû**

IMPERFECT

je dev**ais**
tu dev**ais**
il dev**ait**
nous dev**ions**
vous dev**iez**
ils dev**aient**

FUTURE

je dev**rai**
tu dev**ras**
il dev**ra**
nous dev**rons**
vous dev**rez**
ils dev**ront**

CONDITIONAL

je dev**rais**
tu dev**rais**
il dev**rait**
nous dev**rions**
vous dev**riez**
ils dev**raient**

dire

to say

IMPERATIVE
dis
disons
dites

EXAMPLE PHRASES

*Qu'est–ce qu'elle **dit**?* What is she saying?

*"Bonjour!" **a**–t–il **dit**.* "Hello!" he said.

*Il m'**a dit** que le film était nul.* He told me that the film was rubbish.

PAST PARTICIPLE
dit

PRESENT

je **dis**
tu **dis**
il **dit**
nous **disons**
vous **dites**
ils **disent**

PRESENT SUBJUNCTIVE

je **dise**
tu **dises**
il **dise**
nous **disions**
vous **disiez**
ils **disent**

PERFECT

j' ai **dit**
tu as **dit**
il a **dit**
nous avons **dit**
vous avez **dit**
ils ont **dit**

IMPERFECT

je **disais**
tu **disais**
il **disait**
nous **disions**
vous **disiez**
ils **disaient**

FUTURE

je dir**ai**
tu dir**as**
il dir**a**
nous dir**ons**
vous dir**ez**
ils dir**ont**

CONDITIONAL

je dir**ais**
tu dir**ais**
il dir**ait**
nous dir**ions**
vous dir**iez**
ils dir**aient**

faire

to do *or* to make

EXAMPLE PHRASES

*Qu'est–ce que tu **fais**?* What are you doing?

*Qu'est–ce qu'il a **fait**?* What has he done *or*
What did he do?

*J'**ai fait** un gâteau.* I've made a cake *or*
I made a cake.

IMPERATIVE
fais
faisons
faites

PAST PARTICIPLE
fait

PRESENT

je	**fais**
tu	**fais**
il	**fait**
nous	**faisons**
vous	**faites**
ils	**font**

PRESENT SUBJUNCTIVE

je	**fasse**
tu	**fasses**
il	**fasse**
nous	**fassions**
vous	**fassiez**
ils	**fassent**

PERFECT

j'	ai	**fait**
tu	as	**fait**
il	a	**fait**
nous	avons	**fait**
vous	avez	**fait**
ils	ont	**fait**

IMPERFECT

je	**faisais**
tu	**faisais**
il	**faisait**
nous	**faisions**
vous	**faisiez**
ils	**faisaient**

FUTURE

je	**ferai**
tu	**feras**
il	**fera**
nous	**ferons**
vous	**ferez**
ils	**feront**

CONDITIONAL

je	**ferais**
tu	**ferais**
il	**ferait**
nous	**ferions**
vous	**feriez**
ils	**feraient**

mettre

to put

IMPERATIVE
mets
met**tons**
met**tez**

PAST PARTICIPLE
mis

EXAMPLE PHRASES

Mets ton manteau! Put your coat on!

Où est–ce que tu as mis les clés? Where have you put the keys?

J'ai mis le livre sur la table. I put the book on the table.

PRESENT
je **mets**
tu **mets**
il **met**
nous met**tons**
vous met**tez**
ils met**tent**

PERFECT
j' ai **mis**
tu as **mis**
il a **mis**
nous avons **mis**
vous avez **mis**
ils ont **mis**

FUTURE
je mett**rai**
tu mett**ras**
il mett**ra**
nous mett**rons**
vous mett**rez**
ils mett**ront**

PRESENT SUBJUNCTIVE
je mett**e**
tu mett**es**
il mett**e**
nous mett**ions**
vous mett**iez**
ils mett**ent**

IMPERFECT
je mett**ais**
tu mett**ais**
il mett**ait**
nous mett**ions**
vous mett**iez**
ils mett**aient**

CONDITIONAL
je mett**rais**
tu mett**rais**
il mett**rait**
nous mett**rions**
vous mett**riez**
ils mett**raient**

pouvoir

to be able

EXAMPLE PHRASES

*Je **peux** t'aider, si tu veux.* I can help you if you like.

*J'ai fait tout ce que j'**ai pu**.* I did all I could.

*Je ne **pourrai** pas venir samedi.* I won't be able to come on Saturday.

IMPERATIVE

the imperative of **pouvoir** is not used

PAST PARTICIPLE

pu

PRESENT

je	**peux**
tu	**peux**
il	**peut**
nous	**pouvons**
vous	**pouvez**
ils	**peuvent**

PERFECT

j'	ai **pu**
tu	as **pu**
il	a **pu**
nous	avons **pu**
vous	avez **pu**
ils	ont **pu**

FUTURE

je	**pourrai**
tu	**pourras**
il	**pourra**
nous	**pourrons**
vous	**pourrez**
ils	**pourront**

PRESENT SUBJUNCTIVE

je	**puisse**
tu	**puisses**
il	**puisse**
nous	**puissions**
vous	**puissiez**
ils	**puissent**

IMPERFECT

je	pouv**ais**
tu	pouv**ais**
il	pouv**ait**
nous	pouv**ions**
vous	pouv**iez**
ils	pouv**aient**

CONDITIONAL

je	**pourrais**
tu	**pourrais**
il	**pourrait**
nous	**pourrions**
vous	**pourriez**
ils	**pourraient**

voir

to see

  voi**s**
  voyons
  voyez

EXAMPLE PHRASES

*Venez me **voir** quand vous serez à Paris.*
Come and see me when you're in Paris.

*Je ne **vois** rien sans mes lunettes.* I can't
see anything without my glasses.

PAST PARTICIPLE
  vu

*Est–ce que tu l'**as vu**?* Did you see him? *or*
Have you seen him?

PRESENT

je	voi**s**
tu	voi**s**
il	voi**t**
nous	**voyons**
vous	**voyez**
ils	voi**ent**

PRESENT SUBJUNCTIVE

je	voi**e**
tu	voi**es**
il	voi**e**
nous	**voyions**
vous	**voyiez**
ils	voi**ent**

PERFECT

j'	ai	**vu**
tu	as	**vu**
il	a	**vu**
nous	avons	**vu**
vous	avez	**vu**
ils	ont	**vu**

IMPERFECT

je	**voyais**
tu	**voyais**
il	**voyait**
nous	**voyions**
vous	**voyiez**
ils	**voyaient**

FUTURE

je	**verrai**
tu	**verras**
il	**verra**
nous	**verrons**
vous	**verrez**
ils	**verront**

CONDITIONAL

je	**verrais**
tu	**verrais**
il	**verrait**
nous	**verrions**
vous	**verriez**
ils	**verraient**

vouloir

to want

EXAMPLE PHRASES

*Elle **veut** un vélo pour Noël.* She wants a bike for Christmas.

*Ils **voulaient** aller au cinéma.* They wanted to go to the cinema.

*Tu **voudrais** une tasse de thé?* Would you like a cup of tea?

IMPERATIVE

veuille
veuillons
veuillez

PAST PARTICIPLE

voul**u**

PRESENT

je **veux**
tu **veux**
Il **veut**
nous voul**ons**
vous voul**ez**
ils **veulent**

PERFECT

j' ai voul**u**
tu as voul**u**
il a voul**u**
nous avons voul**u**
vous avez voul**u**
ils ont voul**u**

FUTURE

je **voudrai**
tu **voudras**
il **voudra**
nous **voudrons**
vous **voudrez**
ils **voudront**

PRESENT SUBJUNCTIVE

je **veuille**
tu **veuilles**
il **veuille**
nous voul**ions**
vous voul**iez**
ils **veuillent**

IMPERFECT

je voul**ais**
tu voul**ais**
il voul**ait**
nous voul**ions**
vous voul**iez**
ils voul**aient**

CONDITIONAL

je **voudrais**
tu **voudrais**
il **voudrait**
nous **voudrions**
vous **voudriez**
ils **voudraient**

FRENCH IRREGULAR VERB FORMS

The following list is a summary of the main forms of other irregular verbs that are you are likely to come across. The **infinitive** appears in bold and is followed by a series of numbers from 1 to 5. These tell you which **tenses** are listed:

1 = Present
2 = Past participle
3 = Imperfect

4 = Future
5 = Present subjunctive

For the present tense, all **je** and **nous** forms are shown. The **il, vous** and **ils** forms are also included wherever the part of the verb that goes with them follows an unusual pattern. For the imperfect, future and present subjunctive tenses, only the **je** form is given.

acheter 1 j'achète, nous achetons, ils achètent 2 acheté 3 j'achetais 4 j'achèterai 5 j'achète

appeler 1 j'appelle, il appelle, nous appelons 2 appelé 3 j'appelais 4 j'appellerai 5 j'appelle

apprendre 1 j'apprends, nous apprenons, vous apprenez, ils apprennent 2 appris 3 j'apprenais 4 j'apprendrai 5 j'apprenne

s'asseoir 1 je m'assieds, nous nous asseyons, vous vous asseyez, ils s'asseyent 2 assis 3 je m'asseyais 4 je m'assiérai 5 je m'asseye

battre 1 je bats, il bat, nous battons 2 battu 3 je battais 5 je batte

boire 1 je bois, nous buvons, ils boivent 2 bu 3 je buvais 4 je boirai 5 je boive

bouillir 1 je bous, nous bouillons 2 bouilli 3 je bouillais 5 je bouille

conclure 1 je conclus, nous concluons 2 conclu 3 je concluais 5 je conclue

conduire 1 je conduis, nous conduisons 2 conduit 3 je conduisais 5 je conduise

connaître 1 je connais, il connaît, nous connaissons 2 connu 3 je connaissais 4 je connaîtrai 5 je connaisse

coudre 1 je couds, nous cousons, vous cousez, ils cousent 2 cousu 3 je cousais 4 je coudrai 5 je couse

courir 1 je cours, nous courons 2 couru 3 je courais 4 je courrai 5 je coure

couvrir 1 je couvre, nous couvrons 2 couvert 3 je couvrais 4 je couvrirai 5 je couvre

craindre 1 je crains, nous craignons 2 craint 3 je craignais 5 je craigne

créer 1 je crée, nous créons 2 créé 3 je créais 4 je créerai 5 je crée

croire 1 je crois, nous croyons, ils croient 2 cru 3 je croyais 4 je croirai 5 je croie

croître 1 je croîs, nous croissons 2 crû, crue, crus, crues 3 je croissais 5 je croisse

cueillir 1 je cueille, nous cueillons 2 cueilli 3 je cueillais 4 je cueillerai 5 je cueille

cuire 1 je cuis, nous cuisons, ils cuisent 2 cuit 3 je cuisais 4 je cuirai 5 je cuise

dormir 1 je dors, nous dormons 2 dormi 3 je dormais 4 je dormirai 5 je dorme

écrire 1 j'écris, nous écrivons 2 écrit 3 j'écrivais 4 j'écrirai 5 j'écrive

falloir 1 il faut 2 fallu 3 il fallait 4 il faudra 5 il faille

fuir 1 je fuis, nous fuyons, ils fuient 2 fui 3 je fuyais 5 je fuie

haïr 1 je hais, nous haïssons, ils haïssent 2 haï 3 je haïssais 4 je haïrai 5 je haïsse

jeter 1 je jette, nous jetons, ils jettent 2 jeté 3 je jetais 4 je jetterai 5 je jette

joindre 1 je joins, nous joignons 2 joint 3 je joignais 5 je joigne

lever 1 je lève, nous levons, ils lèvent 2 levé 3 je levais 4 je lèverai 5 je lève

lire 1 je lis, nous lisons 2 lu 3 je lisais 4 je lirai 5 je lise

manger 1 je mange, nous mangeons 2 mangé 3 je mangeais 4 je mangerai 5 je mange

mentir 1 je mens, nous mentons 2 menti 3 je mentais 5 je mente

mourir 1 je meurs, nous mourons, ils meurent 2 mort 3 je mourais 4 je mourrai 5 je meure

naître 1 je nais, il naît, nous naissons 2 né 3 je naissais 4 je naîtrai 5 je naisse

offrir 1 j'offre, nous offrons 2 offert 3 j'offrais 5 j'offre

paraître 1 je parais, il paraît, nous paraissons 2 paru 3 je paraissais 4 je paraîtrai 5 je paraisse

partir 1 je pars, nous partons 2 parti 3 je partais 4 je partirai 5 je parte

plaire 1 je plais, il plaît, nous plaisons 2 plu 3 je plaisais 4 je plairai 5 je plaise

pleuvoir 1 il pleut 2 plu 3 il pleuvait 4 il pleuvra 5 il pleuve

prendre 1 je prends, nous prenons, ils prennent 2 pris 3 je prenais 4 je prendrai 5 je prenne

recevoir 1 je reçois, il reçoit, ils reçoivent 2 reçu 3 je recevais 4 je recevrai 5 je reçoive

rire 1 je ris, nous rions 2 ri 3 je riais 4 je rirai 5 je rie

savoir 1 je sais, nous savons, ils savent 2 su 3 je savais 4 je saurai 5 je sache

servir 1 je sers, nous servons 2 servi 3 je servais 5 je serve

sortir 1 je sors, nous sortons 2 sorti 3 je sortais 5 je sorte

souffrir 1 je souffre, nous souffrons 2 souffert 3 je souffrais 5 je souffre

suffire 1 je suffis, nous suffisons 2 suffi 3 je suffisais 5 je suffise

suivre 1 je suis, nous suivons 2 suivi 3 je suivais 4 je suivrai 5 je suive

se taire 1 je me tais, nous nous taisons 2 tu 3 je me taisais 4 je me tairai 5 je me taise

tenir 1 je tiens, nous tenons, ils tiennent 2 tenu 3 je tenais 4 je tiendrai 5 je tienne

vaincre 1 je vaincs, il vainc, nous vainquons 2 vaincu 3 je vainquais 5 je vainque

valoir 1 je vaux, il vaut, nous valons 2 valu 3 je valais 4 je vaudrai 5 je vaille

venir 1 je viens, nous venons, ils viennent 2 venu 3 je venais 4 je viendrai 5 je vienne

vivre 1 je vis, nous vivons 2 vécu 3 je vivais 4 je vivrai 5 je vive

If you would like to see fuller tables for these verbs, look in **Collins Pocket French Verb Tables.**

LES NOMBRES

1	un (une)	1st	premier (1er), première (1re)
2	deux	2nd	deuxième (2e or 2ème)
3	trois	3rd	troisième (3e or 3ème)
4	quatre	4th	quatrième (4e or 4ème)
5	cinq	5th	cinquième (5e or 5ème)
6	six	6th	sixième (6e or 6ème)
7	sept	7th	septième (7e or 7ème)
8	huit	8th	huitième (8e or 8ème)
9	neuf	9th	neuvième (9e or 9ème)
10	dix	10th	dixième (10e or 10ème)
11	onze	11th	onzième (11^c or 11ème)
12	douze	12th	douzième (12e or 12ème)
13	treize	13th	treizième (13e or 13ème)
14	quatorze	14th	quatorzième (14e or 14ème)
15	quinze	15th	quinzième (15e or 15ème)
16	seize	16th	seizième (16e or 16ème)
17	dix–sept	17th	dix–septième (17e or 17ème)
18	dix–huit	18th	dix–huitième (18e or 18ème)
19	dix–neuf	19th	dix–neuvième (19e or 19ème)
20	vingt	20th	vingtième (20e or 20ème)
21	vingt et un (une)	21st	vingt et unième (21e or 21ème)
22	vingt–deux	22nd	vingt–deuxième (22e or 22ème)
30	trente	30th	trentième (30e or 30ème)
40	quarante	100th	centième (100e or 100ème)
50	cinquante	101st	cent unième (101e or 101ème)
60	soixante	1000th	millième (1000e or 1000ème)
70	soixante–dix		
71	soixante et onze		
72	soixante–douze		
80	quatre–vingts		
81	quatre–vingt–un (–une)		
90	quatre–vingt–dix		
91	quatre–vingt–onze		
100	cent		
101	cent un (une)		
300	trois cents		
301	trois cent un (une)		
1000	mille		
2000	deux mille		
1,000,000	un million		

Fractions etc

$\frac{1}{2}$	un demi
$\frac{1}{3}$	un tiers
$\frac{2}{3}$	deux tiers
$\frac{1}{4}$	un quart
$\frac{1}{5}$	un cinquième
0.5	zéro virgule cinq (0,5)
3.4	trois virgule quatre (3,4)
10%	dix pour cent
100%	cent pour cent

EXEMPLES

il habite au dix
à la page dix–neuf
au chapitre sept
il habite au cinquième (étage)
il est arrivé troisième
échelle au vingt–cinq millième

EXAMPLES

he lives at number ten
on page nineteen
in chapter seven
he lives on the fifth floor
he came in third
scale one to twenty–five thousand

L'HEURE

Quelle heure est-il? What time is it?
Il est... It's...

À quelle heure? At what time?

 une heure

 à minuit

 une heure dix

 à midi

 une heure et quart

 à une heure (de l'après-midi)

 une heure et demie

 à huit heures (du soir)

> In France times are often given in the twenty-four hour clock.

 deux heures moins vingt

 à 11.15 *or* onze heures quinze

 deux heures moins le quart

 à 20.45 *or* vingt heures quarante-cinq

LA DATE

LES JOURS DE LA SEMAINE

lundi
mardi
mercredi
jeudi
vendredi
samedi
dimanche

Quand?

lundi
le lundi
tous les lundis
mardi dernier
vendredi prochain
samedi en huit
samedi en quinze

DAYS OF THE WEEK

Monday
Tuesday
Wednesday
Thursday
Friday
Saturday
Sunday

When?

on Monday
on Mondays
every Monday
last Tuesday
next Friday
a week on Saturday
two weeks on Saturday

LES MOIS

janvier
février
mars
avril
mai
juin
juillet
août
septembre
octobre
novembre
décembre

Quand?

en février
le 1er décembre
le premier décembre
en 1997
en mille neuf cent quatre-vingt-dix-sept

Quel jour sommes-nous? What day is it?

| FEB 26 MON | lundi 26 février *or* lundi vingt-six février |

VOCABULAIRE

Quand?

aujourd'hui
ce matin
cet après-midi
ce soir

Souvent?

tous les jours
tous les deux jours
une fois par semaine
deux fois par semaine
une fois par mois

Ça s'est passé quand?

le matin
le soir
hier
hier soir
avant-hier
il y a une semaine
il y a quinze jours
l'an dernier *or* l'année dernière

Ça va se passer quand?

demain
demain matin
après-demain
dans deux jours
dans une semaine
dans quinze jours
le mois prochain
l'an prochain *or* l'année prochaine

MONTHS OF THE YEAR

January
February
March
April
May
June
July
August
September
October
November
December

When?

in February
on December 1st
on December first
in 1997
in nineteen ninety-seven

Nous sommes le... It's...

| OCT 1 SUN | dimanche 1er octobre *or* dimanche premier octobre |

USEFUL VOCABULARY

When?

today
this morning
this afternoon
this evening

How often?

every day
every other day
once a week
twice a week
once a month

When *did* it happen?

in the morning
in the evening
yesterday
yesterday evening
the day before yesterday
a week ago
two weeks ago
last year

When *is it going* to happen?

tomorrow
tomorrow morning
the day after tomorrow
in two days
in a week
in two weeks
next month
next year

A

a ARTICLE

> *Use* **un** *for masculine nouns,* **une** *for feminine nouns.*

un MASC ⋄ *a book* un livre ⋄ *a year ago* il y a un an

une FEM ⋄ *an apple* une pomme

> *You do not translate* a *when you want to describe somebody's job in French.*

⋄ *He's a butcher.* Il est boucher. ⋄ *She's a doctor.* Elle est médecin.

- **once a week** une fois par semaine
- **10 km an hour** dix kilomètres à l'heure
- **30 pence a kilo** trente pence le kilo
- **a hundred pounds** cent livres

to **abandon** VERB
abandonner

abbey NOUN
l' *abbaye* FEM

abbreviation NOUN
l' *abréviation* FEM

ability NOUN
- **to have the ability to do something** être capable de faire quelque chose

able ADJECTIVE
- **to be able to do something** être capable de faire quelque chose

to **abolish** VERB
abolir

abortion NOUN
l' *avortement* MASC
- **She had an abortion.** Elle s'est fait avorter.

about PREPOSITION, ADVERB
☐1 *à propos de* (concerning) ⋄ *I'm phoning you about tomorrow's meeting.* Je vous appelle à propos de la réunion de demain.
☐2 *environ* (approximately) ⋄ *It takes about 10 hours.* Ça prend dix heures environ.
- **about a hundred pounds** une centaine de livres
- **at about 11 o'clock** vers onze heures
☐3 *dans* (around) ⋄ *to walk about the town* se promener dans la ville
☐4 *sur* ⋄ *a book about London* un livre sur Londres
- **to be about to do something** être sur le point de faire quelque chose ⋄ *I was about to go out.* J'étais sur le point de sortir.
- **to talk about something** parler de quelque chose
- **What's it about?** De quoi s'agit-il?
- **How about going to the cinema?** Et si nous allions au cinéma?

above PREPOSITION, ADVERB
☐1 *au-dessus de* (higher than) ⋄ *He put his hands above his head.* Il a mis ses mains au-dessus de sa tête.
- **the flat above** l'appartement du dessus
- **mentioned above** mentionné ci-dessus
- **above all** par-dessus tout
☐2 *plus de* (more than) ⋄ *above 40 degrees* plus de quarante degrés

abroad ADVERB
à l'étranger ⋄ *to go abroad* partir à l'étranger

abrupt ADJECTIVE
brusque ⋄ *He was a bit abrupt with me.* Il s'est montré un peu brusque avec moi.

abruptly ADVERB
brusquement ⋄ *He got up abruptly.* Il s'est levé brusquement.

absence NOUN
l' *absence* FEM

absent ADJECTIVE
absent

absent-minded ADJECTIVE
distrait ⋄ *She's a bit absent-minded.* Elle est un peu distraite.

absolutely ADVERB
☐1 *tout à fait* (completely) ⋄ *Chantal's absolutely right.* Chantal a tout à fait raison.
☐2 *absolument* ⋄ *Do you think it's a good idea? – Absolutely!* Tu trouves que c'est une bonne idée? – Absolument!

absurd ADJECTIVE
absurde ⋄ *That's absurd!* C'est absurde!

academic ADJECTIVE
universitaire ⋄ *the academic year* l'année universitaire FEM

academy NOUN
le *collège* ⋄ *a military academy* un collège militaire

to **accelerate** VERB
accélérer

accelerator NOUN
l' *accélérateur* MASC

accent NOUN
l' *accent* MASC ⋄ *He's got a French accent.* Il a l'accent français.

to **accept** VERB
accepter

acceptable ADJECTIVE
acceptable

access NOUN
☐1 l' *accès* MASC ⋄ *He has access to confidential information.* Il a accès à des renseignements confidentiels.

2 le *droit de visite* ◊ *Her ex-husband has access to the children.* Son ex-mari a le droit de visite.

accessible ADJECTIVE
accessible

accessory NOUN
l' *accessoire* MASC ◊ *fashion accessories* les accessoires de mode

accident NOUN
l' *accident* MASC ◊ *to have an accident* avoir un accident
- **by accident (1)** (*by mistake*)
accidentellement ◊ *The burglar killed him by accident.* Le cambrioleur l'a tué accidentellement.
- **by accident (2)** (*by chance*) par hasard ◊ *She met him by accident.* Elle l'a rencontré par hasard.

accidental ADJECTIVE
accidentel MASC
accidentelle FEM

to **accommodate** VERB
recevoir ◊ *The hotel can accommodate 50 people.* L'hôtel peut recevoir cinquante personnes.

accommodation NOUN
le *logement*

to **accompany** VERB
accompagner

accord NOUN
- **of his own accord** de son plein gré ◊ *He left of his own accord.* Il est parti de son plein gré.

according to PREPOSITION
selon ◊ *According to him, everyone had gone.* Selon lui, tout le monde était parti.

account NOUN
1 le *compte* ◊ *a bank account* un compte en banque
- **to do the accounts** tenir la comptabilité
2 (*report*)
le *compte rendu*
(les *comptes rendus* PL)
◊ *He gave a detailed account of what happened.* Il a donné un compte rendu détaillé des événements.
- **to take something into account** tenir compte de quelque chose
- **on account of** à cause de ◊ *We couldn't go out on account of the bad weather.* Nous n'avons pas pu sortir à cause du mauvais temps.

accountancy NOUN
la *comptabilité*

accountant NOUN
le/la *comptable* ◊ *She's an accountant.* Elle est comptable.

accuracy NOUN

l' *exactitude* FEM

accurate ADJECTIVE
précis ◊ *accurate information* les renseignements précis MASC

accurately ADVERB
avec précision

to **accuse** VERB
- **to accuse somebody of something** accuser quelqu'un de quelque chose ◊ *The police are accusing her of murder.* La police l'accuse de meurtre.

ace NOUN
l' *as* MASC ◊ *the ace of hearts* l'as de cœur

ache NOUN
see also ache VERB
la *douleur*

to **ache** VERB
see also ache NOUN
- **My leg's aching.** J'ai mal à la jambe.

to **achieve** VERB
1 *atteindre* (*an aim*)
2 *remporter* (*victory*)

achievement NOUN
l' *exploit* MASC ◊ *That was quite an achievement.* C'était un véritable exploit.

acid NOUN
l' *acide* MASC

acid rain NOUN
les *pluies acides* FEM PL

acne NOUN
l' *acné* FEM

acrobat NOUN
l' *acrobate* MASC/FEM ◊ *He's an acrobat.* Il est acrobate.

across PREPOSITION, ADVERB
de l'autre côté de ◊ *the shop across the road* la boutique de l'autre côté de la rue
- **to walk across the road** traverser la rue
- **to run across the road** traverser la rue en courant
- **across from** (*opposite*) en face de ◊ *He sat down across from her.* Il s'est assis en face d'elle.

to **act** VERB
see also act NOUN
1 *jouer* (*in play, film*) ◊ *He acts really well.* Il joue vraiment bien. ◊ *She's acting the part of Juliet.* Elle joue le rôle de Juliette.
2 *agir* (*take action*) ◊ *The police acted quickly.* La police a agi rapidement.
- **She acts as his interpreter.** Elle lui sert d'interprète.

act NOUN
see also act VERB
l' *acte* MASC (*in play*) ◊ *in the first act* au

premier acte

action NOUN
l' *action* FEM ◇ *The film was full of action.* Il y avait beaucoup d'action dans le film.
* **to take firm action against** prendre des mesures énergiques contre

active ADJECTIVE
actif MASC
active FEM
◇ *He's a very active person.* Il est très actif.
* **an active volcano** un volcan en activité

activity NOUN
l' *activité* FEM ◇ *outdoor activities* les activités de plein air

actor NOUN
l' *acteur* MASC ◇ *Brad Pitt is a well-known actor.* Brad Pitt est un acteur connu.

actress NOUN
l' *actrice* FEM ◇ *Julia Roberts is a well-known actress.* Julia Roberts est une actrice connue.

actually ADVERB
[1] *vraiment* (really) ◇ *Did it actually happen?* Est-ce que c'est vraiment arrivé?
[2] *en fait* (in fact) ◇ *Actually, I don't know him at all.* En fait, je ne le connais pas du tout.

ad NOUN
[1] l' *annonce* FEM (in paper)
[2] la *pub* (on TV, radio)

AD ABBREVIATION
ap. J.-C. (= après Jésus-Christ) ◇ *in 800 AD* en huit cents après Jésus-Christ

to **adapt** VERB
adapter ◇ *His novel was adapted for television.* Son roman a été adapté pour la télévision.
* **to adapt to something** (get used to) s'adapter à quelque chose ◇ *He adapted to his new school very quickly.* Il s'est adapté très vite à sa nouvelle école.

adaptor NOUN
l' *adaptateur* MASC

to **add** VERB
ajouter ◇ *Add two eggs to the mixture.* Ajoutez deux œufs au mélange.
* **to add up** additionner ◇ *Add the figures up.* Additionnez les chiffres.

addict NOUN
(drug addict)
le *drogué*
la *droguée*
* **Jean-Pierre's a football addict.** Jean-Pierre est un mordu de football.

addicted ADJECTIVE

* **to be addicted to** (drug) s'adonner à ◇ *She's addicted to heroin.* Elle s'adonne à l'héroïne.
* **She's addicted to soap operas.** C'est une mordue des soaps.

addition NOUN
* **in addition** en plus ◇ *He's broken his leg and, in addition, he's caught a cold.* Il s'est cassé la jambe et en plus, il a attrapé un rhume.
* **in addition to** en plus de ◇ *In addition to the price of the cassette, there's a charge for postage.* En plus du prix de la cassette, il y a des frais de port.

address NOUN
l' *adresse* FEM ◇ *What's your address?* Quelle est votre adresse?

adjective NOUN
l' *adjectif* MASC

to **adjust** VERB
régler ◇ *You can adjust the height of the chair.* Tu peux régler la hauteur de la chaise.
* **to adjust to something** (get used to) s'adapter à quelque chose ◇ *He adjusted to his new school very quickly.* Il s'est adapté très vite à sa nouvelle école.

adjustable ADJECTIVE
réglable

administration NOUN
l' *administration* FEM

admiral NOUN
l' *amiral* MASC

to **admire** VERB
admirer

admission NOUN
l' *entrée* FEM ◇ *"admission free"* "entrée gratuite"

to **admit** VERB
[1] *admettre* (agree) ◇ *I must admit that...* Je dois admettre que...
[2] *reconnaître* (confess) ◇ *He admitted that he'd done it.* Il a reconnu qu'il l'avait fait.

adolescence NOUN
l' *adolescence* FEM

adolescent NOUN
l' *adolescent* MASC
l' *adolescente* FEM

to **adopt** VERB
adopter ◇ *Phil was adopted.* Phil a été adopté.

adopted ADJECTIVE
adoptif MASC
adoptive FEM
◇ *an adopted son* un fils adoptif

adoption NOUN
l' *adoption* FEM

to **adore** VERB

adorer
Adriatic Sea NOUN
　la *mer Adriatique*
adult NOUN
　l' *adulte* MASC/FEM
- **adult education** l'enseignement pour
　adultes MASC
to **advance** VERB
　┌─────────────────────┐
　│ *see also* advance NOUN │
　└─────────────────────┘
　① *avancer* (*move forward*) ◦ *The troops*
　are advancing. Les troupes avancent.
　② *progresser* (*progress*) ◦ *Technology*
　has advanced a lot. La technologie a
　beaucoup progressé.
advance NOUN
　┌─────────────────────┐
　│ *see also* advance VERB │
　└─────────────────────┘
- **in advance** à l'avance ◦ *They bought*
　the tickets in advance. Ils ont acheté les
　billets à l'avance.
advance booking NOUN
- **Advance booking is essential.** Il est
　indispensable de réserver.
advanced ADJECTIVE
　avancé
advantage NOUN
　l' *avantage* MASC ◦ *Going to university*
　has many advantages. Aller à
　l'université présente de nombreux
　avantages.
- **to take advantage of something**
　profiter de quelque chose ◦ *He took*
　advantage of the good weather to go for a
　walk. Il a profité du beau temps pour
　faire une promenade.
- **to take advantage of somebody**
　exploiter quelqu'un ◦ *The company*
　was taking advantage of its employees.
　La société exploitait ses employés.
adventure NOUN
　l' *aventure* FEM
adverb NOUN
　l' *adverbe* MASC
advert, advertisement NOUN
　① la *publicité* (*on TV*)
　② l' *annonce* FEM (*in newspaper*)
advertising NOUN
　la *publicité*
advice NOUN
　les *conseils* MASC PL ◦ *to give somebody*
　advice donner des conseils à quelqu'un
- **a piece of advice** un conseil ◦ *He*
　gave me a good piece of advice. Il m'a
　donné un bon conseil.
to **advise** VERB
　conseiller ◦ *He advised me to wait.* Il
　m'a conseillé d'attendre. ◦ *He advised*
　me not to go there. Il m'a conseillé de ne
　pas y aller.
　aerial NOUN

l' *antenne* FEM
aerobics PL NOUN
　l' *aérobic* FEM ◦ *I'm going to aerobics*
　tonight. Je vais au cours d'aérobic ce soir.
aeroplane NOUN
　l' *avion* MASC
aerosol NOUN
　la *bombe*
affair NOUN
　① l' *aventure* FEM (*romantic*) ◦ *to have*
　an affair with somebody avoir une
　aventure avec quelqu'un
　② l' *affaire* FEM (*event*)
to **affect** VERB
　affecter
affectionate ADJECTIVE
　affectueux MASC
　affectueuse FEM
to **afford** VERB
　avoir les moyens d'acheter ◦ *I can't*
　afford a new pair of jeans. Je n'ai pas les
　moyens d'acheter un nouveau jean.
- **We can't afford to go on holiday.** Nous
　n'avons pas les moyens de partir en
　vacances.
afraid ADJECTIVE
- **to be afraid of something** avoir peur de
　quelque chose ◦ *I'm afraid of spiders.*
　J'ai peur des araignées.
- **I'm afraid I can't come.** Je crains de ne
　pouvoir venir.
- **I'm afraid so.** Hélas oui.
- **I'm afraid not.** Hélas non.
Africa NOUN
　l' *Afrique* FEM
- **in Africa** en Afrique
African ADJECTIVE
　┌─────────────────────┐
　│ *see also* African NOUN │
　└─────────────────────┘
　africain MASC
　africaine FEM
African NOUN
　┌──────────────────────────┐
　│ *see also* African ADJECTIVE │
　└──────────────────────────┘
　l' *Africain* MASC
　l' *Africaine* FEM
after PREPOSITION, ADVERB, CONJUNCTION
　après ◦ *after dinner* après le dîner
　◦ *He ran after me.* Il a couru après moi.
　◦ *soon after* peu après
- **after I'd had a rest** après m'être reposé
- **after having asked** après avoir demandé
- **after all** après tout
afternoon NOUN
　l' *après-midi* MASC/FEM ◦ *3 o'clock in the*
　afternoon trois heures de l'après-midi
　◦ *this afternoon* cet après-midi ◦ *on*
　Saturday afternoon samedi après-midi
afters NOUN
　le *dessert*
after-shave NOUN

l' *after-shave* MASC

afterwards ADVERB
après ◦ *She left not long afterwards.*
Elle est partie peu de temps après.

again ADVERB
1 *de nouveau* (*once more*) ◦ *They're friends again.* Ils sont de nouveau amis.
2 *encore une fois* (*one more time*)
◦ *Can you tell me again?* Tu peux me le dire encore une fois?
* **not...again** ne...plus ◦ *I won't go there again.* Je n'y retournerai plus.
* **Do it again!** Refais-le!
* **again and again** à plusieurs reprises

against PREPOSITION
contre ◦ *He leant against the wall.* Il s'est appuyé contre le mur. ◦ *I'm against nuclear testing.* Je suis contre les essais nucléaires.

age NOUN
l' *âge* MASC ◦ *at the age of 16* à l'âge de seize ans ◦ *an age limit* une limite d'âge
* **I haven't been to the cinema for ages.** Ça fait une éternité que je ne suis pas allé au cinéma.

aged ADJECTIVE
* **aged 10** âgé de dix ans

agenda NOUN
l' *ordre du jour* MASC

agent NOUN
l' *agent* MASC ◦ *an estate agent* un agent immobilier ◦ *a travel agent* un agent de voyage

aggressive ADJECTIVE
agressif MASC
agressive FEM

ago ADVERB
* **two days ago** il y a deux jours
* **two years ago** il y a deux ans
* **not long ago** il n'y a pas longtemps
* **How long ago did it happen?** Il y a combien de temps que c'est arrivé?

agony NOUN
* **to be in agony** souffrir le martyre
◦ *He was in agony.* Il souffrait le martyre.

agree VERB
* **to agree with** être d'accord avec ◦ *I agree with Carol.* Je suis d'accord avec Carol.
* **to agree to do something** accepter de faire quelque chose ◦ *He agreed to go and pick her up.* Il a accepté d'aller la chercher.
* **to agree that...** admettre que... ◦ *I agree that it's difficult.* J'admets que c'est difficile.
* **Garlic doesn't agree with me.** Je ne supporte pas l'ail.

agreed ADJECTIVE
convenu ◦ *at the agreed time* au moment convenu

agreement NOUN
l' *accord* MASC
* **to be in agreement** être d'accord
◦ *Everybody was in agreement with Ray.* Tout le monde était d'accord avec Ray.

agricultural ADJECTIVE
agricole

agriculture NOUN
l' *agriculture* FEM

ahead ADVERB
devant ◦ *She looked straight ahead.* Elle regardait droit devant elle.
* **ahead of time** en avance
* **to plan ahead** organiser à l'avance
* **The French are 5 points ahead.** Les Français ont cinq points d'avance.
* **Go ahead!** Allez-y!

aid NOUN
* **in aid of charity** au profit d'associations caritatives

AIDS NOUN
le *sida*

to **aim** VERB
see also **aim** NOUN
* **to aim at** braquer sur ◦ *He aimed a gun at me.* Il a braqué un revolver sur moi.
* **The film is aimed at children.** Le film est destiné aux enfants.
* **to aim to do something** avoir l'intention de faire quelque chose ◦ *Janice aimed to leave at 5 o'clock.* Janice avait l'intention de partir à cinq heures.

aim NOUN
see also **aim** VERB
l' *objectif* ◦ *The aim of the festival is to raise money.* L'objectif du festival est de collecter des fonds.

air NOUN
l' *air* MASC ◦ *to get some fresh air* prendre l'air
* **by air** en avion ◦ *I prefer to travel by air.* Je préfère voyager en avion.

air-conditioned ADJECTIVE
climatisé

air conditioning NOUN
la *climatisation*

Air Force NOUN
l' *armée de l'air* FEM

air hostess NOUN
l' *hôtesse de l'air* ◦ *She's an air hostess.* Elle est hôtesse de l'air.

airline NOUN
la *compagnie aérienne*

airmail NOUN
* **by airmail** par avion

airport NOUN
l' *aéroport* MASC

aisle NOUN
l' *allée centrale* FEM

alarm NOUN
l' *alarme* FEM (*warning*)
* **a fire alarm** un avertisseur d'incendie

alarm clock NOUN
le *réveil*

album NOUN
l' *album* MASC

alcohol NOUN
l' *alcool* MASC

alcoholic NOUN
see also alcoholic ADJECTIVE
l' *alcoolique* MASC/FEM ◇ *He's an alcoholic.* C'est un alcoolique.

alcoholic ADJECTIVE
see also alcoholic NOUN
alcoolisé ◇ *alcoholic drinks* des boissons alcoolisées

alert ADJECTIVE
1 (*bright*)
vif MASC
vive FEM
◇ *He's a very alert baby.* C'est un bébé très vif.
2 (*paying attention*)
vigilant ◇ *We must stay alert.* Nous devons rester vigilants.

A levels PL NOUN
le *baccalauréat* SING
The baccalauréat (*or* bac *for short*) *is taken at the age of 17 or 18. Students have to sit one of a variety of set subject combinations, rather than being able to choose any combination of subjects they want. If you pass you have the right to a place at university.*

Algeria NOUN
l' *Algérie* FEM
* **in Algeria** en Algérie

alike ADVERB
* **to look alike** se ressembler ◇ *The two sisters look alike.* Les deux sœurs se ressemblent.

alive ADJECTIVE
vivant

all ADJECTIVE, PRONOUN, ADVERB
tout
(*tous* MASC PL)
◇ *all the time* tout le temps ◇ *I ate all of it.* J'ai tout mangé. ◇ *all day* toute la journée ◇ *all the books* tous les livres ◇ *all the apples* toutes les pommes
* **All of us went.** Nous y sommes tous allés.
* **after all** après tout ◇ *After all, nobody can make us go.* Après tout, personne ne peut nous obliger à y aller.

* **all alone** tout seul ◇ *She's all alone.* Elle est toute seule.
* **not at all** pas du tout ◇ *I'm not tired at all.* Je ne suis pas du tout fatigué.
* **The score is 5 all.** Le score est de cinq partout.

allergic ADJECTIVE
allergique
* **to be allergic to something** être allergique à quelque chose ◇ *I'm allergic to cats' hair.* Je suis allergique aux poils de chat.

alley NOUN
la *ruelle*

to **allow** VERB
* **to be allowed to do something** être autorisé à faire quelque chose ◇ *He's not allowed to go out at night.* Il n'est pas autorisé à sortir le soir.
* **to allow somebody to do something** permettre à quelqu'un de faire quelque chose ◇ *His mum allowed him to go out.* Sa mère lui a permis de sortir.

all right ADVERB
1 *bien* (*okay*) ◇ *Everything turned out all right.* Tout s'est bien terminé.
* **Are you all right?** Ça va?
2 *pas mal* (*not bad*) ◇ *The film was all right.* Le film n'était pas mal.
3 *d'accord* (*when agreeing*) ◇ *We'll talk about it later. – All right.* On en reparlera plus tard. – D'accord.
* **Is that all right with you?** Tu es d'accord?

almond NOUN
l' *amande* FEM

almost ADVERB
presque ◇ *I've almost finished.* J'ai presque fini.

alone ADJECTIVE, ADVERB
seul ◇ *She lives alone.* Elle habite seule.
* **to leave somebody alone** laisser quelqu'un tranquille ◇ *Leave her alone!* Laisse-la tranquille!
* **to leave something alone** ne pas toucher à quelque chose ◇ *Leave my things alone!* Ne touche pas à mes affaires!

along PREPOSITION, ADVERB
le long de ◇ *Chris was walking along the beach.* Chris se promenait le long de la plage.
* **all along** depuis le début ◇ *He was lying to me all along.* Il m'a menti depuis le début.

aloud ADVERB
à haute voix ◇ *He read the poem aloud.* Il a lu le poème à haute voix.

alphabet NOUN
l' *alphabet* MASC

Alps PL NOUN
les *Alpes* FEM PL

already ADVERB
déjà ⋄ Liz had already gone. Liz était déjà partie.

also ADVERB
aussi

altar NOUN
l' *autel* MASC

to **alter** VERB
changer

alternate ADJECTIVE
* on alternate days tous les deux jours

alternative NOUN
see also alternative ADJECTIVE
le *choix* ⋄ You have no alternative. Tu n'as pas le choix.
* **Fruit is a healthy alternative to chocolate.** Les fruits sont plus sains que le chocolat.
* **There are several alternatives.** Il y a plusieurs possibilités.

alternative ADJECTIVE
see also alternative NOUN
autre ⋄ They made alternative plans. Ils ont pris d'autres dispositions.
* **an alternative solution** une solution de rechange
* **alternative medicine** la médecine douce

alternatively ADVERB
* **Alternatively, we could just stay at home.** On pourrait aussi rester à la maison.

although CONJUNCTION
bien que
bien que has to be followed by a verb in the subjunctive.
⋄ Although she was tired, she stayed up late. Bien qu'elle soit fatiguée, elle s'est couchée tard.

altogether ADVERB
1 *en tout* (in total) ⋄ You owe me £20 altogether. Tu me dois vingt livres en tout.
2 *tout à fait* (completely) ⋄ I'm not altogether happy with your work. Je ne suis pas tout à fait satisfait de votre travail.

aluminium NOUN
l' *aluminium* MASC

always ADVERB
toujours ⋄ He's always moaning. Il est toujours en train de ronchonner.

am VERB see be

a.m. ABBREVIATION
du matin ⋄ at 4 a.m. à quatre heures du matin

amateur NOUN
l' *amateur* MASC

to **amaze** VERB
* **to be amazed** être stupéfait ⋄ I was amazed that I managed to do it. J'étais stupéfait d'avoir réussi.

amazing ADJECTIVE
1 (surprising)
stupéfiant ⋄ That's amazing news! C'est une nouvelle stupéfiante!
2 (excellent)
exceptionnel MASC
exceptionnelle FEM
⋄ Vivian's an amazing cook. Vivian est une cuisinière exceptionnelle.

ambassador NOUN
l' *ambassadeur* MASC
l' *ambassadrice* FEM

amber ADJECTIVE
* **an amber light** un feu orange

ambition NOUN
l' *ambition* FEM

ambitious ADJECTIVE
ambitieux MASC
ambitieuse FEM
⋄ She's very ambitious. Elle est très ambitieuse.

ambulance NOUN
l' *ambulance* FEM

amenities PL NOUN
les *aménagements* MASC
* **The hotel has very good amenities.** L'hôtel est très bien aménagé.

America NOUN
l' *Amérique* FEM
* **in America** en Amérique
* **to America** en Amérique

American ADJECTIVE
see also American NOUN
américain ⋄ He's American. Il est américain. ⋄ She's American. Elle est américaine.

American NOUN
see also American ADJECTIVE
l' *Américain* MASC
l' *Américaine* FEM
* **the Americans** les Américains

amount NOUN
1 la *somme* ⋄ a large amount of money une grosse somme d'argent
2 la *quantité*
* **a huge amount of rice** une énorme quantité de riz

amp NOUN
1 l' *ampère* MASC (of electricity)
2 l' *ampli* MASC (for hi-fi)

amplifier NOUN
l' *amplificateur* MASC (for hi-fi)

to **amuse** VERB

PTO

amuser ◇ *He was most amused by the story.* L'histoire l'a beaucoup amusé.

amusement arcade NOUN
la *salle de jeux électroniques*

an ARTICLE *see* **a**

to **analyse** VERB
analyser

analysis NOUN
l' *analyse* FEM

ancestor NOUN
l' *ancêtre* MASC/FEM

anchor NOUN
l' *ancre* FEM

ancient ADJECTIVE
1 (*civilization*)
antique ◇ *ancient Greece* la Grèce antique
2 (*custom, building*)
ancien MASC
ancienne FEM
◇ *an ancient monument* un monument ancien

and CONJUNCTION
et ◇ *you and me* toi et moi ◇ *2 and 2 are 4* deux et deux font quatre
✦ **Please try and come!** Essaie de venir!
✦ **He talked and talked.** Il n'a pas arrêté de parler.
✦ **better and better** de mieux en mieux

angel NOUN
l' *ange* MASC

anger NOUN
la *colère*

angle NOUN
l' *angle* MASC

angler NOUN
le *pêcheur à la ligne*
la *pêcheuse à la ligne*

angling NOUN
la *pêche à la ligne*

angry ADJECTIVE
en colère ◇ *Dad looks very angry.* Papa a l'air très en colère.
✦ **to be angry with somebody** être furieux contre quelqu'un ◇ *Mum's really angry with you.* Maman est vraiment furieuse contre toi.
✦ **to get angry** se fâcher

animal NOUN
l' *animal* MASC
(les *animaux* PL)

ankle NOUN
la *cheville*

anniversary NOUN
l' *anniversaire* MASC ◇ *a wedding anniversary* un anniversaire de mariage

to **announce** VERB
annoncer

announcement NOUN

l' *annonce* FEM

to **annoy** VERB
agacer ◇ *He's really annoying me.* Il m'agace vraiment.
✦ **to get annoyed** se fâcher ◇ *Don't get so annoyed!* Ne vous fâchez pas!

annoying ADJECTIVE
agaçant ◇ *It's really annoying.* C'est vraiment agaçant.

annual ADJECTIVE
annuel MASC
annuelle FEM
◇ *an annual meeting* une réunion annuelle

anorak NOUN
l' *anorak* MASC

another ADJECTIVE
un autre
une autre
◇ *Would you like another piece of cake?* Tu veux un autre morceau de gâteau?
◇ *Have you got another skirt?* Tu as une autre jupe?

to **answer** VERB
see also **answer** NOUN
répondre à ◇ *Can you answer my question?* Peux-tu répondre à ma question? ◇ *to answer the phone* répondre au téléphone
✦ **to answer the door** aller ouvrir ◇ *Can you answer the door please?* Tu peux aller ouvrir s'il te plaît?

answer NOUN
see also **answer** VERB
1 la *réponse* (*to question*)
2 la *solution* (*to problem*)

answering machine NOUN
le *répondeur*

ant NOUN
la *fourmi*

Antarctic NOUN
l' *Antarctique* FEM

anthem NOUN
✦ **the national anthem** l'hymne national MASC

antibiotic NOUN
l' *antibiotique* MASC

antique NOUN
le *meuble ancien* (*furniture*)

antique shop NOUN
le *magasin d'antiquités*

antiseptic NOUN
l' *antiseptique* MASC

any ADJECTIVE, PRONOUN, ADVERB
Use **du, de la** or **des** to translate *any* according to the gender of the French noun that follows it. **du** and **de la** become **de l'** when they're followed by a noun starting with a vowel.
1 *du* ◇ *Would you like any bread?*

Voulez-vous du pain?
de la ◦ *Would you like any beer?*
Voulez-vous de la bière?
de l' ◦ *Have you got any mineral water?*
Avez-vous de l'eau minérale?
des ◦ *Have you got any Blur CDs?*
Avez-vous des CD de Blur?

If you want to say you haven't got any of
something, use **de** *whatever the gender of the*
following noun is. **de** *becomes* **d'** *when it comes*
before a noun starting with a vowel.

2 *de* ◦ *I haven't got any books.* Je n'ai
pas de livres.
d' ◦ *I haven't got any money.* Je n'ai
pas d'argent.

Use **en** *where there is no noun after* any.

3 *en* ◦ *Sorry, I haven't got any.* Désolé,
je n'en ai pas.
◆ **any more (1)** (*additional*) encore de
◦ *Would you like any more coffee?* Est-ce
que tu veux encore du café?
◆ **any more (2)** (*no longer*) ne...plus ◦ *I*
don't love him any more. Je ne l'aime plus.
anybody PRONOUN
1 *quelqu'un* (*in question*) ◦ *Has*
anybody got a pen? Est-ce que
quelqu'un a un stylo?
2 *n'importe qui* (*no matter who*)
◦ *Anybody can learn to swim.* N'importe
qui peut apprendre à nager.
Use **ne...personne** *in a negative sentence.* **ne**
comes before the verb, **personne** *after it.*
3 *ne...personne* ◦ *I can't see anybody.*
Je ne vois personne.
anyhow ADVERB
de toute façon ◦ *He doesn't want to go*
out and anyhow he's not allowed. Il ne
veut pas sortir et de toute façon il n'y est
pas autorisé.
anyone PRONOUN
1 *quelqu'un* (*in question*) ◦ *Has*
anyone got a pen? Est-ce que quelqu'un
a un stylo?
2 *n'importe qui* (*no matter who*)
◦ *Anyone can learn to swim.* N'importe
qui peut apprendre à nager.
Use **ne...personne** *in a negative sentence.* **ne**
comes before the verb, **personne** *after it.*
3 *ne...personne* ◦ *I can't see anyone.*
Je ne vois personne.
anything PRONOUN
1 *quelque chose* (*in question*) ◦ *Would*
you like anything to eat? Tu veux manger
quelque chose?
2 *n'importe quoi* (*no matter what*)
◦ *Anything could happen.* Il pourrait
arriver n'importe quoi.
Use **ne...rien** *in a negative sentence.* **ne** *comes*
before the verb, **rien** *after it.*

3 *ne...rien* ◦ *I can't hear anything.* Je
n'entends rien.
anyway ADVERB
de toute façon ◦ *He doesn't want to go*
out and anyway he's not allowed. Il ne
veut pas sortir et de toute façon il n'y est
pas autorisé.
anywhere ADVERB
1 *quelque part* (*in question*) ◦ *Have*
you seen my coat anywhere? Est-ce que
tu as vu mon manteau quelque part?
2 *n'importe où* ◦ *You can buy stamps*
almost anywhere. On peut acheter des
timbres presque n'importe où.
Use **ne...nulle part** *in a negative sentence.* **ne**
comes before the verb, **nulle part** *after it.*
3 *ne...nulle part* ◦ *I can't find it*
anywhere. Je ne le trouve nulle part.
apart ADVERB
◆ **The two towns are 10 kilometres apart.**
Les deux villes sont à dix kilomètres
l'une de l'autre.
◆ **apart from** à part ◦ *Apart from that,*
everything's fine. À part ça, tout va
bien.
apartment NOUN
l' *appartement* MASC
to **apologize** VERB
s'excuser ◦ *He apologized for being*
late. Il s'est excusé de son retard.
◆ **I apologize!** Je vous prie de m'excuser.
apology NOUN
les *excuses* FEM PL
apostrophe NOUN
l' *apostrophe* FEM
apparatus NOUN
1 le *matériel* (*in lab*)
2 les *agrès* MASC PL (*in gym*)
apparent ADJECTIVE
apparent
apparently ADVERB
apparemment
to **appeal** VERB
see also appeal NOUN
lancer un appel ◦ *They appealed for*
help. Ils ont lancé un appel au secours.
◆ **Greece doesn't appeal to me.** Ça ne me
tente pas d'aller en Grèce.
◆ **Does that appeal to you?** Ça te tente?
appeal NOUN
see also appeal VERB
l' *appel* MASC ◦ *They have launched an*
appeal. Ils ont lancé un appel.
to **appear** VERB
1 *apparaître* (*come into view*) ◦ *The bus*
appeared around the corner. Le bus est
apparu au coin de la rue.
◆ **to appear on TV** passer à la télé
2 *paraître* (*seem*) ◦ *She appeared to be* PTO

asleep. Elle paraissait dormir.

appearance NOUN
l' *apparence* FEM (*looks*) ◇ *She takes great care over her appearance.* Elle prend grand soin de son apparence.

appendicitis NOUN
l' *appendicite* FEM

appetite NOUN
l' *appétit* MASC

to **applaud** VERB
applaudir

applause NOUN
les *applaudissements* MASC PL

apple NOUN
la *pomme*

◆ **an apple tree** un pommier

application NOUN

◆ **a job application** une candidature

application form NOUN
① le *dossier de candidature* (*for job*)
② le *dossier d'inscription* (*for university*)

to **apply** VERB

◆ **to apply for a job** poser sa candidature à un poste

◆ **to apply to** (*be relevant*) s'appliquer à ◇ *This rule doesn't apply to us.* Ce règlement ne s'applique pas à nous.

appointment NOUN
le *rendez-vous* ◇ *I've got a dental appointment.* J'ai rendez-vous chez le dentiste.

to **appreciate** VERB
être reconnaissant de ◇ *I really appreciate your help.* Je vous suis extrêmement reconnaissant de votre aide.

apprentice NOUN
l' *apprenti* MASC
l' *apprentie* FEM

to **approach** VERB
① *s'approcher de* (*get nearer to*) ◇ *He approached the house.* Il s'est approché de la maison.
② *aborder* (*tackle*) ◇ *to approach a problem* aborder un problème

appropriate ADJECTIVE
approprié ◇ *That dress isn't very appropriate for an interview.* Cette robe n'est pas très appropriée pour un entretien.

to **approve** VERB

◆ **to approve of** approuver ◇ *I don't approve of his choice.* Je n'approuve pas son choix.

◆ **They didn't approve of his girlfriend.** Sa copine ne leur a pas plu.

approximate ADJECTIVE
approximatif MASC
approximative FEM

apricot NOUN
l' *abricot* MASC

April NOUN
avril MASC

◆ **in April** en avril

◆ **April Fool's Day** le premier avril

apron NOUN
le *tablier*

Aquarius NOUN
le *Verseau* ◇ *I'm Aquarius.* Je suis Verseau.

Arab ADJECTIVE
see also **Arab** NOUN
arabe ◇ *the Arab countries* les pays arabes

Arab NOUN
see also **Arab** ADJECTIVE
l' *Arabe* MASC/FEM

arch NOUN
l' *arc* MASC

archaeologist NOUN
l' *archéologue* MASC/FEM ◇ *He's an archaeologist.* Il est archéologue.

archaeology NOUN
l' *archéologie* FEM

archbishop NOUN
l' *archevêque* MASC

architect NOUN
l' *architecte* MASC/FEM ◇ *She's an architect.* Elle est architecte.

architecture NOUN
l' *architecture* FEM

Arctic NOUN
l' *Arctique* MASC

are VERB *see* **be**

area NOUN
① la *région* ◇ *She lives in the Paris area.* Elle habite dans la région parisienne.
② le *quartier* ◇ *My favourite area of Paris is Montmartre.* Montmartre est le quartier de Paris que je préfère.
③ la *superficie* ◇ *The field has an area of 1500m².* Le champ a une superficie de mille cinq cent mètres carrés.

Argentina NOUN
l' *Argentine* FEM

◆ **in Argentina** en Argentine

Argentinian ADJECTIVE
argentin

to **argue** VERB
se disputer ◇ *They never stop arguing.* Ils n'arrêtent pas de se disputer.

argument NOUN

◆ **to have an argument** se disputer ◇ *They had an argument.* Ils se sont disputés.

Aries NOUN
le *Bélier* ◇ *I'm Aries.* Je suis Bélier.

arm NOUN
le *bras*
armchair NOUN
le *fauteuil*
armour NOUN
l' *armure* FEM
army NOUN
l' *armée* FEM
around PREPOSITION, ADVERB
1 *autour de* ◇ She wore a scarf around her neck. Elle portait une écharpe autour du cou.
2 *environ* (approximately) ◇ It costs around £100. Cela coûte environ cent livres.
3 *vers* (date, time) ◇ Let's meet at around 8 p.m. Retrouvons-nous vers vingt heures.
* **around here (1)** (nearby) près d'ici ◇ Is there a chemist's around here? Est-ce qu'il y a une pharmacie près d'ici?
* **around here (2)** (in this area) dans les parages ◇ He lives around here. Il habite dans les parages.
arrange VERB
* **to arrange to do something** prévoir de faire quelque chose ◇ They arranged to go out together on Friday. Ils ont prévu de sortir ensemble vendredi.
* **to arrange a meeting** convenir d'un rendez-vous ◇ Can we arrange a meeting? Pouvons-nous convenir d'un rendez-vous?
* **to arrange a party** organiser une fête
arrangement NOUN
l' *arrangement* MASC (plan)
* **They made arrangements to go out on Friday night.** Ils ont organisé une sortie vendredi soir.
arrest VERB
see also arrest NOUN
arrêter ◇ The police have arrested 5 people. La police a arrêté cinq personnes.
arrest NOUN
see also arrest VERB
l' *arrestation* FEM ◇ You're under arrest! Vous êtes en état d'arrestation!
arrival NOUN
l' *arrivée* FEM
arrive VERB
arriver ◇ I arrived at 5 o'clock. Je suis arrivé à cinq heures.
arrow NOUN
la *flèche*
art NOUN
l' *art* MASC
artery NOUN
l' *artère* FEM

art gallery NOUN
le *musée*
article NOUN
l' *article* MASC ◇ a newspaper article un article de journal
artificial ADJECTIVE
artificiel MASC
artificielle FEM
artist NOUN
l' *artiste* MASC/FEM ◇ She's an artist. C'est une artiste.
artistic ADJECTIVE
artistique
as CONJUNCTION, ADVERB
1 *au moment où* (while) ◇ He came in as I was leaving. Il est arrivé au moment où je partais.
2 *puisque* (since) ◇ As it's Sunday, you can have a lie-in. Tu peux faire la grasse matinée, puisque c'est dimanche.
* **as...as** aussi...que ◇ Pierre's as tall as Michel. Pierre est aussi grand que Michel.
* **twice as...as** deux fois plus...que ◇ Her coat cost twice as much as mine. Son manteau a coûté deux fois plus cher que le mien.
* **as much...as** autant...que ◇ I haven't got as much money as you. Je n'ai pas autant d'argent que toi.
* **as soon as possible** dès que possible ◇ I'll do it as soon as possible. Je le ferai dès que possible.
* **as from tomorrow** à partir de demain ◇ As from tomorrow, the shop will stay open until 10 p.m. À partir de demain, le magasin restera ouvert jusqu'à vingt-deux heures.
* **as though** comme si ◇ She acted as though she hadn't seen me. Elle a fait comme si elle ne m'avait pas vu.
* **as if** comme si
* **He works as a waiter in the holidays.** Il travaille comme serveur pendant les vacances.
asap ABBREVIATION (= as soon as possible)
dès que possible
ashamed ADJECTIVE
* **to be ashamed** avoir honte ◇ You should be ashamed of yourself! Tu devrais avoir honte!
ashtray NOUN
le *cendrier*
Asia NOUN
l' *Asie* FEM
* **in Asia** en Asie
Asian ADJECTIVE
see also Asian NOUN
asiatique ◇ He's Asian. C'est un Asiatique. ◇ She's Asian. C'est une

Asiatique.

Asian NOUN

see also Asian ADJECTIVE

l' *Asiatique* MASC/FEM

to **ask** VERB

[1] *demander* (inquire, request) ◇ *"Have you finished?" she asked.* "Tu as fini?" a-t-elle demandé.

◆ **to ask somebody something** demander quelque chose à quelqu'un ◇ *He asked her how old she was.* Il lui a demandé quel âge elle avait.

◆ **to ask for something** demander quelque chose ◇ *He asked for a cup of tea.* Il a demandé une tasse de thé.

◆ **to ask somebody to do something** demander à quelqu'un de faire quelque chose ◇ *She asked him to do the shopping.* Elle lui a demandé de faire les courses.

◆ **to ask about something** se renseigner sur quelque chose ◇ *I asked about train times to Leeds.* Je me suis renseigné sur les horaires des trains pour Leeds.

◆ **to ask somebody a question** poser une question à quelqu'un

[2] *inviter* ◇ *Have you asked Matthew to the party?* Est-ce que tu as invité Matthew à la fête?

◆ **He asked her out.** (on a date) Il lui a demandé de sortir avec lui.

asleep ADJECTIVE

◆ **to be asleep** dormir ◇ *He's asleep.* Il dort.

◆ **to fall asleep** s'endormir ◇ *I fell asleep in front of the TV.* Je me suis endormi devant la télé.

asparagus NOUN

les *asperges* FEM PL

aspect NOUN

l' *aspect* MASC

aspirin NOUN

l' *aspirine* FEM

assignment NOUN

le *devoir* (in school)

assistance NOUN

l' *aide* FEM

assistant NOUN

[1] (in shop)

le *vendeur*

la *vendeuse*

[2] (helper)

l' *assistant* MASC

l' *assistante* FEM

association NOUN

l' *association* FEM

assortment NOUN

l' *assortiment* MASC

to **assume** VERB

supposer ◇ *I assume she won't be coming.* Je suppose qu'elle ne viendra pas.

to **assure** VERB

assurer ◇ *He assured me he was coming.* Il m'a assuré qu'il viendrait.

asthma NOUN

l' *asthme* MASC ◇ *I've got asthma.* J'ai de l'asthme.

astrology NOUN

l' *astrologie* FEM

astronaut NOUN

l' *astronaute* MASC/FEM

astronomy NOUN

l' *astronomie* FEM

at PREPOSITION

à+le *becomes* **au**, à+les *becomes* **aux**.

à ◇ *at 4 o'clock* à quatre heures ◇ *at Christmas* à Noël ◇ *at 50 km/h* à cinquante km/h ◇ *at home* à la maison ◇ *two at a time* deux à la fois ◇ *at school* à l'école

au ◇ *at the office* au bureau

aux ◇ *at the races* aux courses

◆ **at night** la nuit

◆ **What are you doing at the weekend?** Qu'est-ce que tu fais ce week-end?

ate VERB *see* **eat**

Athens NOUN

Athènes

◆ **in Athens** à Athènes

athlete NOUN

l' *athlète* MASC/FEM

athletic ADJECTIVE

athlétique

athletics NOUN

l' *athlétisme* MASC ◇ *I like watching the athletics on TV.* J'aime bien regarder les épreuves d'athlétisme à la télé.

Atlantic NOUN

l' *océan Atlantique* MASC

atlas NOUN

l' *atlas* MASC

atmosphere NOUN

l' *atmosphère* FEM

atom NOUN

l' *atome* MASC

atomic ADJECTIVE

atomique ◇ *an atomic bomb* une bombe atomique

to **attach** VERB

fixer ◇ *They attached a rope to the car.* Ils ont fixé une corde à la voiture.

◆ **Please find attached...** Veuillez trouver ci-joint...

attached ADJECTIVE

◆ **to be attached to** être attaché à ◇ *He's very attached to his family.* Il est très attaché à sa famille.

to **attack** VERB
> see also attack NOUN

attaquer ◦ _The dog attacked her._ Le chien l'a attaquée.

attack NOUN
> see also attack VERB

l' _attaque_ FEM

attempt NOUN
> see also attempt VERB

la _tentative_ ◦ _She gave up after several attempts._ Elle y a renoncé après plusieurs tentatives.

to **attempt** VERB
> see also attempt NOUN

* **to attempt to do something** essayer de faire quelque chose ◦ _I attempted to write a song._ J'ai essayé d'écrire une chanson.

to **attend** VERB
assister à ◦ _to attend a meeting_ assister à une réunion

attention NOUN
l' _attention_ FEM

* **to pay attention to** faire attention à ◦ _He didn't pay attention to what I was saying._ Il ne faisait pas attention à ce que je disais.

attic NOUN
le _grenier_

attitude NOUN
l' _attitude_ FEM (way of thinking) ◦ _I really don't like your attitude!_ Je n'aime pas du tout ton attitude!

to **attract** VERB
attirer ◦ _The Lake District attracts lots of tourists._ La région des lacs attire de nombreux touristes.

attraction NOUN
l' _attraction_ FEM ◦ _a tourist attraction_ une attraction touristique

attractive ADJECTIVE
séduisant ◦ _She's very attractive._ Elle est très séduisante.

aubergine NOUN
l' _aubergine_ FEM

auction NOUN
la _vente aux enchères_

audience NOUN
les _spectateurs_ MASC PL (in theatre)

audition NOUN
l' _audition_ FEM

August NOUN
août MASC

* **in August** en août

aunt, aunty NOUN
la _tante_ ◦ _my aunt_ ma tante

au pair NOUN
la _jeune fille au pair_ ◦ _She's an au pair._ Elle est jeune fille au pair.

Australia NOUN
l' _Australie_ FEM

* **in Australia** en Australie
* **to Australia** en Australie

Australian ADJECTIVE
> see also Australian NOUN

australien MASC
australienne FEM
◦ _He's Australian._ Il est australien.

Australian NOUN
> see also Australian ADJECTIVE

l' _Australien_ MASC
l' _Australienne_ FEM

* **the Australians** les Australiens

Austria NOUN
l' _Autriche_ FEM

* **in Austria** en Autriche

Austrian ADJECTIVE
> see also Austrian NOUN

autrichien MASC
autrichienne FEM
◦ _She's Austrian._ Elle est autrichienne.

Austrian NOUN
> see also Austrian ADJECTIVE

l' _Autrichien_ MASC
l' _Autrichienne_ FEM

* **the Austrians** les Autrichiens

author NOUN
l' _auteur_ MASC ◦ _She's a famous author._ C'est un auteur connu.

autobiography NOUN
l' _autobiographie_ FEM

autograph NOUN
l' _autographe_ MASC

automatic ADJECTIVE
automatique ◦ _an automatic door_ une porte automatique

automatically ADVERB
automatiquement

autumn NOUN
l' _automne_ MASC

* **in autumn** en automne

availability NOUN
la _disponibilité_

available ADJECTIVE
disponible ◦ _Free brochures are available on request._ Des brochures gratuites sont disponibles sur demande. ◦ _Is Mr Cooke available today?_ Est-ce que Monsieur Cooke est disponible aujourd'hui?

avalanche NOUN
l' _avalanche_ FEM

avenue NOUN
l' _avenue_ FEM

average NOUN
> see also average ADJECTIVE

la _moyenne_ ◦ _on average_ en moyenne

average ADJECTIVE

see also average NOUN

moyen MASC

moyenne FEM

◦ *the average price* le prix moyen

avocado NOUN

l' *avocat* MASC

to **avoid** VERB

éviter ◦ *He avoids her when she's in a bad mood.* Il l'évite lorsqu'elle est de mauvaise humeur.

• **to avoid doing something** éviter de faire quelque chose ◦ *Avoid going out on your own at night.* Évite de sortir seul le soir.

awake ADJECTIVE

• **to be awake** être réveillé ◦ *Is she awake?* Elle est réveillée?

• **He was still awake.** Il ne dormait pas encore.

award NOUN

le *prix* ◦ *He's won an award.* Il a remporté un prix. ◦ *the award for the best actor* le prix du meilleur acteur

away ADJECTIVE, ADVERB

absent (*not here*) ◦ *André's away today.* André est absent aujourd'hui.

• **He's away for a week.** Il est parti pour une semaine.

• **The town's 2 kilometres away.** La ville est à deux kilomètres d'ici.

• **The coast is 2 hours away by car.** La côte est à deux heures de route.

• **Go away!** Va-t'en!

• **to put something away** ranger quelque chose ◦ *He put his toys away in the cupboard.* Il a rangé ses jouets dans le placard.

away match NOUN

le *match à l'extérieur*

(les *matchs à l'extérieur* PL)

awful ADJECTIVE

affreux MASC

affreuse FEM

◦ *That's awful!* C'est affreux!

• **an awful lot of...** énormément de...

awkward ADJECTIVE

[1] *délicat* (*difficult to deal with*) ◦ *an awkward situation* une situation délicate

[2] *gênant* (*embarrassing*) ◦ *an awkward question* une question gênante

• **It's a bit awkward for me to come and see you.** Ce n'est pas très pratique pour moi de venir vous voir.

axe NOUN

la *hache*

B

baby NOUN
le _bébé_

to **babysit** VERB
faire du baby-sitting

babysitter NOUN
le/la _baby-sitter_

babysitting NOUN
le _baby-sitting_

bachelor NOUN
le _célibataire_ ◆ He's a bachelor. Il est célibataire.

back NOUN
see also back ADJECTIVE, VERB
1 le _dos_ (of person, horse, book)
2 l' _arrière_ MASC (of car, house) ◇ in the back à l'arrière
3 le _verso_ (of page) ◇ on the back au verso
4 le _fond_ (of room, garden) ◇ at the back au fond

back ADJECTIVE, ADVERB
see also back NOUN, VERB
arrière MASC. FEM. PL. ◇ the back seat le siège arrière ◇ the back wheel of my bike la roue arrière de mon vélo
◆ the back door la porte de derrière
◆ to get back rentrer ◇ What time did you get back? À quelle heure est-ce que tu es rentré?
◆ We went there by bus and walked back. Nous y sommes allés en bus et nous sommes rentrés à pied.
◆ He's not back yet. Il n'est pas encore rentré.
◆ to call somebody back rappeler quelqu'un ◇ I'll call back later. Je rappellerai plus tard.

to **back** VERB
see also back NOUN, ADJECTIVE
soutenir (support) ◇ I'm backing Tony Blair. Je soutiens Tony Blair.
◆ to back a horse parier sur un cheval
◆ to back out se désister ◇ They promised to help and then backed out. Ils avaient promis de nous aider et ils se sont désistés.
◆ to back somebody up soutenir quelqu'un

backache NOUN
le _mal au dos_ ◇ to have backache avoir mal au dos

backbone NOUN
la _colonne vertébrale_

to **backfire** VERB
échouer (go wrong)

background NOUN
1 l' _arrière-plan_ MASC (of picture) ◇ a house in the background une maison à l'arrière-plan
◆ background noise les bruits de fond MASC PL
2 le _milieu_
(les _milieux_ PL)
◇ his family background son milieu familial

backhand NOUN
le _revers_

backing NOUN
le _soutien_ (support)

backpack NOUN
le _sac à dos_

back pain NOUN
le _mal au dos_ ◇ to have back pain avoir mal au dos

backside NOUN
le _derrière_

backup NOUN
le _soutien_ (support)
◆ a backup file une sauvegarde

backwards ADVERB
en arrière ◇ to take a step backwards faire un pas en arrière
◆ to fall backwards tomber à la renverse

back yard NOUN
la _cour_

bacon NOUN
1 le _lard_ (French type)
2 le _bacon_ (British type) ◇ bacon and eggs des œufs au bacon

bad ADJECTIVE
1 _mauvais_ ◇ a bad film un mauvais film ◇ the bad weather le mauvais temps ◇ to be in a bad mood être de mauvaise humeur
◆ to be bad at something être mauvais en quelque chose ◇ I'm really bad at maths. Je suis vraiment mauvais en maths.
2 _grave_ (serious) ◇ a bad accident un accident grave
3 _vilain_ (naughty) ◆ You bad boy! Vilain!
◆ to go bad (food) se gâter
◆ I feel bad about it. Ça m'ennuie.
◆ not bad pas mal ◇ That's not bad at all. Ce n'est pas mal du tout.

badge NOUN
le _badge_

badly ADVERB
mal ◇ badly paid mal payé
◆ badly wounded grièvement blessé
◆ He badly needs a rest. Il a sérieusement

besoin de se reposer.

badminton NOUN
le *badminton* ◇ to play badminton
jouer au badminton

bad-tempered ADJECTIVE
◆ to be bad-tempered (1) (by nature) avoir
mauvais caractère ◇ He's a really
bad-tempered person. Il a vraiment
mauvais caractère.
◆ to be bad-tempered (2) (temporarily) être
de mauvaise humeur ◇ He was really
bad-tempered yesterday. Il était
vraiment de mauvaise humeur hier.

bag NOUN
le *sac*
◆ an old bag (person) une vieille peau

baggage NOUN
les *bagages* MASC PL

baggage reclaim NOUN
la *livraison des bagages*

bagpipes PL NOUN
la *cornemuse* SING ◇ Ed plays the
bagpipes. Ed joue de la cornemuse.

to **bake** VERB
◆ to bake a cake faire un gâteau

baker NOUN
le *boulanger*
la *boulangère*
◇ He's a baker. Il est boulanger.

bakery NOUN
la *boulangerie*

baking ADJECTIVE
◆ It's baking in here! Il fait une chaleur
torride ici!

balance NOUN
l' *équilibre* MASC ◇ to lose one's
balance perdre l'équilibre

balanced ADJECTIVE
équilibré

balcony NOUN
le *balcon*

bald ADJECTIVE
chauve

ball NOUN
1 la *balle* (tennis, golf, cricket)
2 le *ballon* (football, rugby)

ballet NOUN
le *ballet* ◇ We went to a ballet. Nous
sommes allés voir un ballet.
◆ ballet lessons les cours de danse

ballet dancer NOUN
le *danseur classique*
la *danseuse classique*

ballet shoes PL NOUN
les *chaussons de danse* MASC PL

balloon NOUN
le *ballon* (for parties)
◆ a hot-air balloon une montgolfière

ballpoint pen NOUN

le *stylo à bille*

ban NOUN
see also ban VERB
l' *interdiction* FEM

to **ban** VERB
see also ban NOUN
interdire

banana NOUN
la *banane* ◇ a banana skin une peau
de banane

band NOUN
1 le *groupe* (rock band)
2 la *fanfare* (brass band)

bandage NOUN
see also bandage VERB
le *bandage*

to **bandage** VERB
see also bandage NOUN
mettre un bandage à ◇ The nurse
bandaged his arm. L'infirmière lui a mis
un bandage au bras.

bandit NOUN
le *bandit*

bang NOUN
see also bang VERB
1 la *détonation* ◇ I heard a loud bang.
J'ai entendu une forte détonation.
2 le *coup* ◇ a bang on the head un
coup sur la tête
◆ Bang! Pan!

to **bang** VERB
see also bang NOUN
se cogner (part of body) ◇ I banged my
head. Je me suis cogné la tête.
◆ to bang the door claquer la porte
◆ to bang on the door cogner à la porte

bank NOUN
1 la *banque* (financial)
2 le *bord* (of river, lake)

bank account NOUN
le *compte en banque*

banker NOUN
le *banquier*

bank holiday NOUN
le *jour férié*

banknote NOUN
le *billet de banque*

banned ADJECTIVE
interdit

bar NOUN
1 le *bar* (pub)
2 le *comptoir* (counter)
◆ a bar of chocolate une tablette de
chocolat
◆ a bar of soap une savonnette

barbaric ADJECTIVE
barbare

barbecue NOUN
le *barbecue*

barber NOUN
le *coiffeur pour hommes*
bare ADJECTIVE
nu
barefoot ADJECTIVE, ADVERB
nu-pieds MASC, FEM, PL ◇ *The children go
around barefoot.* Les enfants se
promènent nu-pieds.
▸ **to be barefoot** avoir les pieds nus
◇ *She was barefoot.* Elle avait les pieds
nus.
bargain NOUN
l' *affaire* FEM ◇ *It was a bargain!* C'était
une affaire!
barge NOUN
la *péniche*
bark VERB
aboyer
barmaid NOUN
la *barmaid* ◇ *She's a barmaid.* Elle est
barmaid.
barman NOUN
le *barman* ◇ *He's a barman.* Il est
barman.
barn NOUN
la *grange*
barrel NOUN
le *tonneau*
(les *tonneaux* PL)
barrier NOUN
la *barrière*
base NOUN
la *base*
baseball NOUN
le *base-ball*
▸ **a baseball cap** une casquette de
base-ball
based ADJECTIVE
▸ **based on** fondé sur
basement NOUN
le *sous-sol*
bash VERB
see also bash NOUN
▸ **to bash something** taper sur quelque
chose
bash NOUN
see also bash VERB
▸ **I'll have a bash.** Je vais essayer.
basic ADJECTIVE
1 *de base* ◇ *It's a basic model.* C'est
un modèle de base.
2 *rudimentaire* ◇ *The accommodation
is pretty basic.* Le logement est plutôt
rudimentaire.
basically ADVERB
tout simplement ◇ *Basically, I just
don't like him.* Tout simplement, je ne
l'aime pas.
basics PL NOUN

les *rudiments* MASC PL
basin NOUN
le *lavabo* (*washbasin*)
basis NOUN
▸ **on a daily basis** quotidiennement
▸ **on a regular basis** régulièrement
basketball NOUN
le *basket*
bass NOUN
1 la *basse* (*guitar, singer*) ◇ *He plays the
bass.* Il joue de la basse. ◇ *He's a bass.*
Il est basse.
▸ **a bass guitar** une guitare basse
▸ **a double bass** une contrebasse
2 les *graves* MASC PL (*on hi-fi*)
bass drum NOUN
la *grosse caisse*
bassoon NOUN
le *basson* ◇ *I play the bassoon.* Je joue
du basson.
bastard NOUN
le *salaud* (*rude*) ◇ *You bastard!* Salaud!
bat NOUN
1 (*for cricket, rounders*)
la *batte*
2 (*for table tennis*)
la *raquette*
3 (*animal*)
la *chauve-souris*
(les *chauves-souris* PL)
bath NOUN
1 le *bain* ◇ *to have a bath* prendre un
bain
▸ **a hot bath** un bain chaud
2 la *baignoire* (*bathtub*) ◇ *There's a
spider in the bath.* Il y a une araignée
dans la baignoire.
to **bathe** VERB
se baigner
bathroom NOUN
la *salle de bains*
baths PL NOUN
la *piscine* SING
bath towel NOUN
la *serviette de bain*
batter NOUN
la *pâte à frire*
battery NOUN
1 la *pile* (*for torch, toy*)
2 la *batterie* (*of car*)
battle NOUN
la *bataille* ◇ *the Battle of Hastings* la
bataille de Hastings
▸ **It was a battle, but we managed in the
end.** Il a fallu se battre, mais on a fini
par y arriver.
battleship NOUN
le *cuirassé*
bay NOUN

la *baie*

BC ABBREVIATION (= *before Christ*)

av. J.-C. (= avant Jésus-Christ) ◇ *in 200 BC* en deux cents avant Jésus-Christ

to **be** VERB

être ◇ *I'm tired.* Je suis fatigué. ◇ *You're late.* Tu es en retard. ◇ *She's English.* Elle est anglaise. ◇ *Edinburgh is in Scotland.* Édimbourg est en Écosse. ◇ *It's 4 o'clock.* Il est quatre heures. ◇ *We are all happy.* Nous sommes tous heureux. ◇ *They are in Paris at the moment.* Ils sont à Paris en ce moment. ◇ *I've been ill.* J'ai été malade.

- **It's the 28th of October today.** Nous sommes le vingt-huit octobre.
- **Have you been to Greece before?** Est-ce que tu es déjà allé en Grèce?
- **I've never been to Paris.** Je ne suis jamais allé à Paris.
- **to be killed** être tué

When you are saying what somebody's occupation is, you leave out the "a" in French. ◇ *She's a doctor.* Elle est médecin. ◇ *He's a student.* Il est étudiant.

With certain adjectives, such as "cold", "hot", "hungry" and "thirsty", use **avoir** *instead of* être.

- **I'm cold.** J'ai froid.
- **I'm hungry.** J'ai faim.

When saying how old somebody is, use **avoir** *not* être.

- **I'm fourteen.** J'ai quatorze ans.
- **How old are you?** Quel âge as-tu?

When referring to the weather, use **faire**.

- **It's cold.** Il fait froid.
- **It's too hot.** Il fait trop chaud.
- **It's a nice day.** Il fait beau.

beach NOUN

la *plage*

bead NOUN

la *perle*

beam NOUN

le *rayon*

beans NOUN

1 les *haricots* MASC PL

2 les *haricots blancs à la sauce tomate* MASC PL (*baked beans*) ◇ *I had beans on toast.* J'ai mangé des haricots blancs à la sauce tomate sur du pain grillé.

- **broad beans** les fèves FEM
- **green beans** les haricots verts MASC
- **kidney beans** les haricots rouges MASC

bear NOUN

see also bear VERB

l' *ours* MASC

to **bear** VERB

see also bear NOUN

- **I can't bear it!** C'est insupportable!

- **to bear up** tenir le coup
- **Bear up!** Tiens bon!

beard NOUN

la *barbe*

- **He's got a beard.** Il est barbu.
- **a man with a beard** un barbu

bearded ADJECTIVE

barbu

beat NOUN

see also beat VERB

le *rythme*

to **beat** VERB

see also beat NOUN

battre ◇ *We beat them 3-0.* On les a battus trois à zéro.

- **Beat it!** Fiche le camp! (*informal*)
- **to beat somebody up** tabasser quelqu'un (*informal*)

beautiful ADJECTIVE

beau MASC

belle FEM

(*beaux* MASC PL)

beautifully ADVERB

admirablement

beauty NOUN

la *beauté*

beauty spot NOUN

le *site pittoresque*

became VERB see become

because CONJUNCTION

parce que ◇ *I did it because...* Je l'ai fait parce que...

- **because of** à cause de ◇ *because of the weather* à cause du temps

to **become** VERB

devenir ◇ *He became a famous writer.* Il est devenu un grand écrivain.

bed NOUN

le *lit* ◇ *in bed* au lit

- **to go to bed** aller se coucher
- **to go to bed with somebody** coucher avec quelqu'un

bed and breakfast NOUN

la *chambre d'hôte* ◇ *We stayed in a bed and breakfast.* Nous avons logé dans une chambre d'hôte.

- **How much is it for bed and breakfast?** C'est combien pour la chambre et le petit déjeuner?

bedclothes PL NOUN

les *draps et les couvertures* MASC PL

bedding NOUN

la *literie*

bedroom NOUN

la *chambre*

bedspread NOUN

le *dessus-de-lit*

(les *dessus-de-lit* PL)

bedtime NOUN

- **Ten o'clock is my usual bedtime.** Je me couche généralement à dix heures.
- **Bedtime!** Au lit!

bee NOUN
　l' *abeille* FEM

beef NOUN
　le *bœuf*

- **roast beef** le rosbif

beefburger NOUN
　le *hamburger*

been VERB *see* **be**

beer NOUN
　la *bière*

beetle NOUN
　le *scarabée*

beetroot NOUN
　la *betterave rouge*

before PREPOSITION, CONJUNCTION, ADVERB
　[1] *avant* ◇ *before Tuesday* avant mardi
　[2] *avant de* ◇ *before going* avant de partir ◇ *Before opening the packet, read the instructions.* Avant d'ouvrir le paquet, lisez le mode d'emploi. ◇ *I'll phone before I leave.* J'appellerai avant de partir.
　[3] *déjà* (*already*) ◇ *I've seen this film before.* J'ai déjà vu ce film. ◇ *Have you been to Scotland before?* Vous êtes déjà venu en Écosse?

- **the day before** la veille
- **the week before** la semaine précédente

beforehand ADVERB
　à l'avance

beg VERB
　[1] *mendier* (*for money*)
　[2] *supplier* ◇ *He begged me to stop.* Il m'a supplié d'arrêter.

began VERB *see* **begin**

beggar NOUN
　le *mendiant*
　la *mendiante*

begin VERB
　commencer

- **to begin doing something** commencer à faire quelque chose

beginner NOUN
　le *débutant*
　la *débutante*
　◇ *I'm just a beginner.* Je ne suis qu'un débutant.

beginning NOUN
　le *début* ◇ *in the beginning* au début

behalf NOUN

- **on behalf of somebody** pour quelqu'un

behave VERB
　se comporter ◇ *He behaved like an idiot.* Il s'est comporté comme un idiot. ◇ *She behaved very badly.* Elle s'est très mal comportée.

- **to behave oneself** être sage ◇ *Did the children behave themselves?* Est-ce que les enfants ont été sages?
- **Behave!** Sois sage!

behaviour NOUN
　le *comportement*

behind PREPOSITION, ADVERB
　see also behind NOUN
　derrière ◇ *behind the television* derrière la télévision

- **to be behind** (*late*) avoir du retard ◇ *I'm behind with my revision.* J'ai du retard dans mes révisions.

behind NOUN
　see also behind PREPOSITION, ADVERB
　le *derrière*

beige ADJECTIVE
　beige

Belgian ADJECTIVE
　see also Belgian NOUN
　belge ◇ *Belgian chocolate* le chocolat belge ◇ *She's Belgian.* Elle est belge.

Belgian NOUN
　see also Belgian ADJECTIVE
　le/la *Belge*

- **the Belgians** les Belges

Belgium NOUN
　la *Belgique*

- **in Belgium** en Belgique

to **believe** VERB
　croire ◇ *I don't believe you.* Je ne te crois pas.

- **to believe in something** croire à quelque chose ◇ *Do you believe in ghosts?* Tu crois aux fantômes?
- **to believe in God** croire en Dieu

bell NOUN
　[1] la *sonnette* (*doorbell*)

- **to ring the bell** sonner à la porte
　[2] la *cloche* (*in church*)
　[3] la *sonnerie* (*in school*)
　[4] la *clochette* ◇ *Our cat has a bell on its neck.* Notre chat a une clochette sur son collier.

belly NOUN
　le *ventre*

to **belong** VERB

- **to belong to somebody** être à quelqu'un ◇ *Who does it belong to?* C'est à qui? ◇ *That belongs to me.* C'est à moi.
- **Do you belong to any clubs?** Est-ce que tu es membre d'un club?
- **Where does this belong?** Où est-ce que ça va?

belongings PL NOUN
　les *affaires* FEM PL

below PREPOSITION, ADVERB
　[1] *au-dessous de* ◇ *below the castle*

au-dessous du château

2 *en dessous*　◦ *on the floor below* à l'étage en dessous

* **10 degrees below freezing** moins dix

belt NOUN

la *ceinture*

bench NOUN

1 le *banc* (*seat*)

2 l' *établi* MASC (*for woodwork*)

bend NOUN

see also bend VERB

1 le *virage* (*in road*)

2 le *coude* (*in river*)

to **bend** VERB

see also bend NOUN

1 *courber* (*back*)

2 *plier* (*leg, arm*)　◦ *I can't bend my arm.* Je n'arrive pas à plier le bras.

* **"do not bend"** "ne pas plier"

3 *tordre* (*object*)　◦ *You've bent it.* Tu l'as tordu.

4 *se tordre*　◦ *It bends easily.* Ça se tord facilement.

* **to bend down** se baisser
* **to bend over** se pencher

beneath PREPOSITION

sous

benefit NOUN

see also benefit VERB

l' *avantage* MASC (*advantage*)

* **unemployment benefit** les allocations de chômage

to **benefit** VERB

see also benefit NOUN

* **He'll benefit from the change.** Le changement lui fera du bien.

bent VERB see **bend**

bent ADJECTIVE

tordu　◦ *a bent fork* une fourchette tordue

beret NOUN

le *béret*

berserk ADJECTIVE

* **to go berserk** devenir fou furieux　◦ *She went berserk.* Elle est devenue folle furieuse.

berth NOUN

la *couchette*

beside PREPOSITION

à côté de　◦ *beside the television* à côté de la télévision

* **He was beside himself.** Il était hors de lui.
* **That's beside the point.** Cela n'a rien à voir.

besides ADVERB

en plus　◦ *Besides, it's too expensive.* En plus, c'est trop cher.

best ADJECTIVE, ADVERB

1 *meilleur*　◦ *He's the best player in the team.* Il est le meilleur joueur de l'équipe.　◦ *Janet's the best at maths.* Janet est la meilleure en maths.

2 *le mieux*　◦ *Emma sings best.* C'est Emma qui chante le mieux.　◦ *That's the best I can do.* Je ne peux pas faire mieux.

* **to do one's best** faire de son mieux　◦ *It's not perfect, but I did my best.* Ça n'est pas parfait, mais j'ai fait de mon mieux.
* **to make the best of it** s'en contenter　◦ *We'll have to make the best of it.* Il va falloir nous en contenter.

best man NOUN

le *garçon d'honneur*

bet NOUN

see also bet VERB

le *pari*　◦ *to make a bet* faire un pari

to **bet** VERB

see also bet NOUN

parier　◦ *I bet you he won't come.* Je te parie qu'il ne viendra pas.　◦ *I bet he forgot.* Je parie qu'il a oublié.

to **betray** VERB

trahir

better ADJECTIVE, ADVERB

1 *meilleur*　◦ *This one's better than that one.* Celui-ci est meilleur que celui-là.　◦ *a better way to do it* une meilleure façon de le faire

2 *mieux*　◦ *That's better!* C'est mieux comme ça.

* **better still** encore mieux　◦ *Go and see her tomorrow, or better still, go today.* Va la voir demain, ou encore mieux, vas-y aujourd'hui.
* **to get better (1)** (*improve*) s'améliorer　◦ *I hope the weather gets better soon.* J'espère que le temps va s'améliorer bientôt.　◦ *My French is getting better.* Mon français s'améliore.
* **to get better (2)** (*from illness*) se remettre　◦ *I hope you get better soon.* J'espère que tu vas vite te remettre.
* **to feel better** se sentir mieux　◦ *Are you feeling better now?* Tu te sens mieux maintenant?
* **You'd better do it straight away.** Vous feriez mieux de le faire immédiatement.
* **I'd better go home.** Je ferais mieux de rentrer.

betting shop NOUN

le *bureau de paris*

between PREPOSITION

entre　◦ *Stroud is between Oxford and Bristol.* Stroud est entre Oxford et Bristol.　◦ *between 15 and 20 minutes* entre quinze et vingt minutes

beyond PREPOSITION
au-delà de ◦ *There was a lake beyond the mountain.* Il y avait un lac au-delà de la montagne.
- **beyond belief** incroyable
- **beyond repair** irréparable
biased ADJECTIVE
partial
Bible NOUN
la *Bible*
bicycle NOUN
le *vélo*
bifocals PL NOUN
les *verres à double foyer* MASC PL
big ADJECTIVE
[1] *grand* ◦ *a big house* une grande maison ◦ *my big brother* mon grand frère ◦ *her big sister* sa grande sœur
- **He's a big guy.** C'est un grand gaillard.
[2] (*car, animal, book, parcel*)
gros MASC
grosse FEM
◦ *a big car* une grosse voiture
bigheaded ADJECTIVE
- **to be bigheaded** avoir la grosse tête
bike NOUN
le *vélo* ◦ *by bike* en vélo
bikini NOUN
le *bikini*
bilingual ADJECTIVE
bilingue
bill NOUN
[1] l' *addition* FEM (*in restaurant*) ◦ *Can we have the bill, please?* L'addition, s'il vous plaît.
[2] la *facture* (*for gas, electricity, telephone*)
billiards NOUN
le *billard* ◦ *to play billiards* jouer au billard
billion NOUN
le *milliard*
bin NOUN
la *poubelle*
binoculars PL NOUN
les *jumelles* FEM PL
- **a pair of binoculars** des jumelles
biochemistry NOUN
la *biochimie*
biography NOUN
la *biographie*
biology NOUN
la *biologie*
bird NOUN
l' *oiseau* MASC
(les *oiseaux* PL)
birdwatching NOUN
- **My hobby's birdwatching.** Mon passe-temps favori est d'observer les oiseaux.

Biro ® NOUN
le *bic* ®
birth NOUN
la *naissance* ◦ *date of birth* la date de naissance
birth certificate NOUN
l' *acte de naissance* MASC
birth control NOUN
la *contraception*
birthday NOUN
l' *anniversaire* MASC ◦ *When's your birthday?* Quelle est la date de ton anniversaire?
- **a birthday cake** un gâteau d'anniversaire
- **I'm going to have a birthday party.** Je vais faire une fête pour mon anniversaire.
biscuit NOUN
le *gâteau sec*
bishop NOUN
l' *évêque* MASC
bit VERB *see* **bite**
bit NOUN
le *morceau*
(les *morceaux* PL)
◦ *Would you like another bit?* Est-ce que tu en veux un autre morceau?
- **a bit of (1)** (*piece of*) un morceau de ◦ *a bit of cake* un morceau de gâteau
- **a bit of (2)** (*a little*) un peu de ◦ *a bit of music* un peu de musique
- **It's a bit of a nuisance.** C'est ennuyeux.
- **a bit** un peu ◦ *He's a bit mad.* Il est un peu fou. ◦ *a bit too hot* un peu trop chaud ◦ *Wait a bit!* Attends un peu! ◦ *Do you play football? – A bit.* Tu joues au football? – Un peu.
- **to fall to bits** se désintégrer
- **to take something to bits** démonter quelque chose
- **bit by bit** petit à petit
bitch NOUN
[1] la *garce* (*person*)
[2] la *chienne* (*female dog*)
to **bite** VERB
see also **bite** NOUN
[1] *mordre* (*person, dog*)
[2] *piquer* (*insect*) ◦ *I got bitten by mosquitoes.* Je me suis fait piquer par des moustiques.
- **to bite one's nails** se ronger les ongles
bite NOUN
see also **bite** VERB
[1] la *piqûre* (*insect bite*)
[2] la *morsure* (*animal bite*)
- **to have a bite to eat** manger un morceau

bitter ADJECTIVE

> see also bitter NOUN

[1] *amer* MASC

amère FEM

[2] (weather, wind)

glacial

(*glaciaux* MASC PL)

◇ *It's bitter today.* Il fait glacial aujourd'hui.

bitter NOUN

> see also bitter ADJECTIVE

la *bière brune*

black ADJECTIVE

noir ◇ *a black jacket* une veste noire

◇ *She's black.* Elle est noire.

blackberry NOUN

la *mûre*

blackbird NOUN

le *merle*

blackboard NOUN

le *tableau noir*

black coffee NOUN

le *café*

blackcurrant NOUN

le *cassis*

blackmail NOUN

> see also blackmail VERB

le *chantage* ◇ *That's blackmail!* C'est du chantage!

to **blackmail** VERB

> see also blackmail NOUN

◆ **to blackmail somebody** faire chanter quelqu'un ◇ *He blackmailed her.* Il l'a fait chanter.

blackout NOUN

la *panne d'électricité* (power cut)

◆ **to have a blackout** (faint) s'évanouir

black pudding NOUN

le *boudin*

blade NOUN

la *lame*

to **blame** VERB

◆ **Don't blame me!** Ça n'est pas ma faute!

◆ **I blame the police.** À mon avis, c'est la faute de la police.

◆ **He blamed it on my sister.** Il a dit que c'était la faute de ma sœur.

blank ADJECTIVE

> see also blank NOUN

[1] (paper)

blanc MASC

blanche FEM

[2] (cassette, video, page)

vierge

◆ **My mind went blank.** J'ai eu un trou.

blank NOUN

> see also blank ADJECTIVE

le *blanc* ◇ *Fill in the blanks.* Remplissez les blancs.

blank cheque NOUN

le *chèque en blanc*

blanket NOUN

la *couverture*

blast NOUN

◆ **a bomb blast** une explosion

blatant ADJECTIVE

flagrant

blaze NOUN

l' *incendie* MASC

blazer NOUN

le *blazer*

bleach NOUN

l' *eau de Javel* FEM

bleached ADJECTIVE

décoloré ◇ *bleached hair* les cheveux décolorés

to **bleed** VERB

saigner ◇ *My nose is bleeding.* Je saigne du nez.

bleeper NOUN

le *bip*

blender NOUN

le *mixer*

to **bless** VERB

bénir (religiously)

◆ **Bless you!** (after sneezing) À tes souhaits!

blew VERB see **blow**

blind ADJECTIVE

> see also blind NOUN

aveugle

blind NOUN

> see also blind ADJECTIVE

le *store* (for window)

blindfold NOUN

> see also blindfold VERB

le *bandeau*

(les *bandeaux* PL)

to **blindfold** VERB

> see also blindfold NOUN

◆ **to blindfold somebody** bander les yeux à quelqu'un

to **blink** VERB

cligner des yeux

bliss NOUN

◆ **It was bliss!** C'était merveilleux!

blister NOUN

l' *ampoule* FEM

blizzard NOUN

la *tempête de neige*

blob NOUN

la *goutte* ◇ *a blob of glue* une goutte de colle

block NOUN

> see also block VERB

l' *immeuble* MASC ◇ *He lives in our block.* Il habite dans notre immeuble.

◆ **a block of flats** un immeuble

to **block** VERB

> see also block NOUN

bloquer
blockage NOUN
l' *obstruction* FEM
bloke NOUN
le *mec* (informal)
blonde ADJECTIVE
blond ◇ She's got blonde hair. Elle a les cheveux blonds.
blood NOUN
le *sang*
blood pressure NOUN
✦ to have high blood pressure faire de la tension
blood sports NOUN
les *sports sanguinaires* MASC PL
blood test NOUN
la *prise de sang*
bloody ADJECTIVE
✦ bloody difficult sacrément difficile
✦ that bloody television cette putain de télévision
✦ Bloody hell! Merde!
blouse NOUN
le *chemisier*
blow NOUN
see also blow VERB
le *coup*
to blow VERB
see also blow NOUN
souffler (wind, person)
✦ to blow one's nose se moucher
✦ to blow a whistle siffler
✦ to blow out a candle éteindre une bougie
✦ to blow up (1) faire sauter ◇ The terrorists blew up a police station. Les terroristes ont fait sauter un commissariat de police.
✦ to blow up (2) gonfler ◇ to blow up a balloon gonfler un ballon
✦ The house blew up. La maison a sauté.
blow-dry NOUN
le *brushing*
✦ A cut and blow-dry, please. Une coupe brushing, s'il vous plaît.
blue ADJECTIVE
bleu ◇ a blue dress une robe bleue
✦ a blue film un film pornographique
✦ It came out of the blue. C'était complètement inattendu.
blues PL NOUN
le *blues* SING
to bluff VERB
see also bluff NOUN
bluffer
bluff NOUN
see also bluff VERB
le *bluff* ◇ It's just a bluff. C'est du bluff.
blunder NOUN

la *gaffe*
blunt ADJECTIVE
1 *brusque* (person)
2 *émoussé* (knife)
to blush VERB
rougir
board NOUN
1 (wooden)
la *planche*
2 (blackboard)
le *tableau*
(les *tableaux* PL)
◇ on the board au tableau
3 (noticeboard)
le *panneau*
(les *panneaux* PL)
4 (for board games)
le *jeu*
(les *jeux* PL)
5 (for chess)
l' *échiquier* MASC
✦ on board à bord
✦ "full board" "pension complète"
boarder NOUN
l' *interne* MASC/FEM
board game NOUN
le *jeu de société*
(les *jeux de société* PL)
boarding card NOUN
la *carte d'embarquement*
boarding school NOUN
le *pensionnat*
✦ I go to boarding school. Je suis interne.
to boast VERB
se vanter ◇ Stop boasting! Arrête de te vanter!
✦ to boast about something se vanter de quelque chose
boat NOUN
le *bateau*
(les *bateaux* PL)
body NOUN
le *corps*
bodybuilding NOUN
le *culturisme*
bodyguard NOUN
le *garde du corps*
bog NOUN
la *tourbière* (marsh)
boil NOUN
see also boil VERB
le *furoncle*
to boil VERB
see also boil NOUN
1 *faire bouillir* ◇ to boil some water faire bouillir de l'eau
✦ to boil an egg faire cuire un œuf
2 *bouillir* ◇ The water's boiling. L'eau bout. ◇ The water's boiled. L'eau a

bouilli.
- **to boil over** déborder

boiled ADJECTIVE
à l'eau ◦ *boiled potatoes* des pommes de terre à l'eau
- **a boiled egg** un œuf à la coque

boiling ADJECTIVE
- **It's boiling in here!** Il fait une chaleur torride ici!
- **boiling hot** torride ◦ *a boiling hot day* une journée torride

bolt NOUN
1 le *verrou* (on door)
2 le *boulon* (with nut)

bomb NOUN
see also bomb VERB
la *bombe*

to **bomb** VERB
see also bomb NOUN
bombarder

bomber NOUN
le *bombardier*

bombing NOUN
l' *attentat à la bombe* MASC

bond NOUN
le *lien*

bone NOUN
1 l' *os* MASC (of human, animal)
2 l' *arête* FEM (of fish)

bone dry ADJECTIVE
complètement sec MASC
complètement sèche FEM

bonfire NOUN
le *feu*
(les *feux* PL)

bonnet NOUN
le *capot* (of car)

book NOUN
see also book VERB
le *livre*

to **book** VERB
see also book NOUN
réserver ◦ *We haven't booked.* Nous n'avons pas réservé.

bookcase NOUN
la *bibliothèque*

booklet NOUN
la *brochure*

bookshelf NOUN
l' *étagère à livres* FEM

bookshop NOUN
la *librairie*

boot NOUN
1 le *coffre* (of car)
2 la *botte* (fashion boot)
3 la *chaussure de marche* (for hiking)
- **football boots** des chaussures de foot

booze NOUN
l' *alcool* MASC

border NOUN
la *frontière*

bored ADJECTIVE
- **to be bored** s'ennuyer ◦ *I was bored.* Je m'ennuyais.
- **to get bored** s'ennuyer

boredom NOUN
l' *ennui* MASC

boring ADJECTIVE
ennuyeux MASC
ennuyeuse FEM

born ADJECTIVE
- **to be born** naître ◦ *I was born in 1982.* Je suis né en mille neuf cent quatre-vingt-deux.

to **borrow** VERB
emprunter ◦ *Can I borrow your pen?* Je peux emprunter ton stylo?
- **to borrow something from somebody** emprunter quelque chose à quelqu'un ◦ *I borrowed some money from a friend.* J'ai emprunté de l'argent à un ami.

Bosnia NOUN
la *Bosnie*

Bosnian ADJECTIVE
bosniaque

boss NOUN
le *patron*
la *patronne*

to **boss around** VERB
- **to boss somebody around** donner des ordres à quelqu'un

bossy ADJECTIVE
autoritaire

both ADJECTIVE, PRONOUN
tous les deux MASC PL
(*toutes les deux* FEM PL)
◦ *We both went.* Nous y sommes allés tous les deux. ◦ *Emma and Jane both went.* Emma et Jane y sont allées toutes les deux. ◦ *Both of your answers are wrong.* Vos réponses sont toutes les deux mauvaises. ◦ *Both of them have left.* Ils sont partis tous les deux. ◦ *Both of us went.* Nous y sommes allés tous les deux. ◦ *Both Maggie and John are against it.* Maggie et John sont tous les deux contre.
- **He speaks both German and Italian.** Il parle allemand et italien.

to **bother** VERB
1 *tracasser* (worry) ◦ *What's bothering you?* Qu'est-ce qui te tracasse?
2 *déranger* (disturb) ◦ *I'm sorry to bother you.* Je suis désolé de vous déranger.
- **no bother** aucun problème
- **Don't bother!** Ça n'est pas la peine!
- **to bother to do something** prendre la

peine de faire quelque chose ◇ *He didn't bother to tell me about it.* Il n'a pas pris la peine de m'en parler.

bottle NOUN
la *bouteille*

bottle bank NOUN
le *conteneur à verre*

bottle-opener NOUN
l' *ouvre-bouteille* MASC

bottom NOUN
see also bottom ADJECTIVE
1 le *fond* (*of container, bag, sea*)
2 le *derrière* (*buttocks*)
3 le *bas* (*of page, list*)

bottom ADJECTIVE
see also bottom NOUN
inférieur ◇ *the bottom shelf* l'étagère inférieure
‣ **the bottom sheet** le drap de dessous

bought VERB see **buy**

to **bounce** VERB
rebondir

bouncer NOUN
le *videur*

bound ADJECTIVE
‣ **He's bound to fail.** Il va sûrement échouer.

boundary NOUN
la *frontière*

bow NOUN
see also bow VERB
1 le *nœud* (*knot*) ◇ *to tie a bow* faire un nœud
2 l' *arc* MASC ◇ *a bow and arrows* un arc et des flèches

to **bow** VERB
see also bow NOUN
faire une révérence

bowels PL NOUN
les *intestins* MASC PL

bowl NOUN
see also bowl VERB
le *bol* (*for soup, cereal*)

to **bowl** VERB
see also bowl NOUN
lancer la balle (*in cricket*)

bowler NOUN
le *lanceur* (*in cricket*)

bowling NOUN
le *bowling*
‣ **to go bowling** jouer au bowling
‣ **a bowling alley** un bowling

bowls NOUN
les *boules* FEM PL ◇ *to play bowls* jouer aux boules

bow tie NOUN
le *nœud papillon*

box NOUN
la *boîte* ◇ *a box of matches* une boîte d'allumettes
‣ **a cardboard box** un carton

boxer NOUN
le *boxeur*

boxer shorts PL NOUN
le *caleçon* SING

boxing NOUN
la *boxe*

Boxing Day NOUN
le *lendemain de Noël* ◇ *on Boxing Day* le lendemain de Noël

boy NOUN
le *garçon*

boyfriend NOUN
le *copain* ◇ *Have you got a boyfriend?* Est-ce que tu as un copain?

bra NOUN
le *soutien-gorge*
(les *soutiens-gorge* PL)

brace NOUN
l' *appareil* MASC (*on teeth*) ◇ *She wears a brace.* Elle a un appareil.

bracelet NOUN
le *bracelet*

brackets PL NOUN
‣ **in brackets** entre parenthèses

brain NOUN
le *cerveau*
(les *cerveaux* PL)

brainy ADJECTIVE
intelligent

brake NOUN
see also brake VERB
le *frein*

to **brake** VERB
see also brake NOUN
freiner

branch NOUN
1 la *branche* (*of tree*)
2 l' *agence* FEM (*of bank*)

brand-new ADJECTIVE
tout neuf MASC
toute neuve FEM

brandy NOUN
le *cognac*

brass NOUN
le *cuivre*
‣ **the brass section** les cuivres

brass band NOUN
la *fanfare*

brat NOUN
‣ **He's a spoiled brat.** C'est un enfant gâté.

brave ADJECTIVE
courageux MASC
courageuse FEM

Brazil NOUN
le *Brésil*
‣ **in Brazil** au Brésil

bread NOUN
le *pain* ◦ *brown bread* le pain complet
◦ *white bread* le pain blanc
- **bread and butter** les tartines de pain
beurrées FEM

break NOUN
see also break VERB
1 la *pause* (*rest*) ◦ *to take a break* faire
une pause
2 la *récréation* (*at school*) ◦ *during
morning break* pendant la récréation du
matin
- **the Christmas break** les vacances de
Noël
- **Give me a break!** Laisse-moi tranquille!

to **break** VERB
see also break NOUN
1 *casser* ◦ *Careful, you'll break
something!* Attention, tu vas casser
quelque chose!
2 *se casser* (*get broken*) ◦ *Careful, it'll
break!* Attention, ça va se casser!
- **to break one's leg** se casser la jambe
◦ *I broke my leg.* Je me suis cassé la
jambe.
- **He broke his arm.** Il s'est cassé le bras.
- **to break a promise** rompre une
promesse
- **to break a record** battre un record
- **to break the law** violer la loi

to **break down** VERB
tomber en panne ◦ *The car broke
down.* La voiture est tombée en panne.

breakdown NOUN
1 la *panne* (*in vehicle*) ◦ *to have a
breakdown* tomber en panne
2 la *dépression* (*mental*) ◦ *to have a
breakdown* faire une dépression

breakdown van NOUN
la *dépanneuse*

breakfast NOUN
le *petit déjeuner* ◦ *What would you like
for breakfast?* Qu'est-ce vous voulez
pour le petit déjeuner?

to **break in** VERB
entrer par effraction

break-in NOUN
le *cambriolage*

to **break open** VERB
forcer (*door, cupboard*)

to **break out** VERB
1 *se déclarer* (*fire*)
2 *éclater* (*war*)
3 *s'évader* (*prisoner*)
- **to break out in a rash** être couvert de
boutons

to **break up** VERB
1 *se disperser* (*crowd*)
2 *se terminer* (*meeting, party*)

3 *se séparer* (*couple*)
- **to break up a fight** mettre fin à une
bagarre
- **We break up next Wednesday.** Nos
vacances commencent mercredi.

breast NOUN
le *sein* (*of woman*)
- **chicken breast** le blanc de poulet

to **breast-feed** VERB
allaiter

breaststroke NOUN
la *brasse*

breath NOUN
l' *haleine* FEM ◦ *to have bad breath*
avoir mauvaise haleine
- **to be out of breath** être essoufflé
- **to get one's breath back** reprendre son
souffle

to **breathe** VERB
respirer

to **breed** VERB
see also breed NOUN
se reproduire (*reproduce*)
- **to breed dogs** faire de l'élevage de
chiens

breed NOUN
see also breed VERB
la *race*

breeze NOUN
la *brise*

brewery NOUN
la *brasserie*

brick NOUN
la *brique*
- **a brick wall** un mur en brique

bricklayer NOUN
le *maçon*

bride NOUN
la *mariée*

bridegroom NOUN
le *marié*

bridesmaid NOUN
la *demoiselle d'honneur*

bridge NOUN
1 le *pont* ◦ *a suspension bridge* un
pont suspendu
2 le *bridge* ◦ *to play bridge* jouer au
bridge

brief ADJECTIVE
bref MASC
brève FEM

briefcase NOUN
la *serviette*

briefly ADVERB
brièvement

briefs PL NOUN
le *slip* SING
- **a pair of briefs** un slip

bright ADJECTIVE

1 (*colour, light*)
vif MASC
vive FEM
◇ *a bright colour* une couleur vive
• **bright blue** bleu vif ◇ *a bright blue car* une voiture bleu vif
2 *intelligent* ◇ *He's not very bright.* Il n'est pas très intelligent.

brilliant ADJECTIVE
1 (*wonderful*)
génial
(*géniaux* MASC PL)
◇ *Brilliant!* Génial!
2 (*clever*)
brillant ◇ *a brilliant scientist* un savant brillant

to **bring** VERB
1 *apporter* ◇ *Bring warm clothes.* Apportez des vêtements chauds.
◇ *Could you bring me my trainers?* Tu peux m'apporter mes baskets?
2 *amener* (*person*) ◇ *Can I bring a friend?* Est-ce que je peux amener un ami?
• **to bring back** rapporter
• **to bring up** élever ◇ *She brought up 5 children on her own.* Elle a élevé cinq enfants toute seule.

Britain NOUN
la *Grande-Bretagne*
• **in Britain** en Grande-Bretagne
• **to Britain** en Grande-Bretagne
• **I'm from Britain.** Je suis britannique.
• **Great Britain** la Grande-Bretagne

British ADJECTIVE
britannique
• **the British** les Britanniques MASC PL
• **the British Isles** les îles Britanniques FEM PL

Brittany NOUN
la *Bretagne*
• **in Brittany** en Bretagne
• **to Brittany** en Bretagne
• **She's from Brittany.** Elle est bretonne.

broad ADJECTIVE
large (*wide*)
• **in broad daylight** en plein jour

broadcast NOUN
see also broadcast VERB
l' *émission* FEM

to **broadcast** VERB
see also broadcast NOUN
diffuser ◇ *The interview was broadcast all over the world.* L'interview a été diffusé dans le monde entier.
• **to broadcast live** retransmettre en direct

broad-minded ADJECTIVE
large d'esprit

broccoli NOUN
les *brocolis* MASC PL

brochure NOUN
la *brochure*

broke VERB see **break**

broke ADJECTIVE
• **to be broke** (*without money*) être fauché

broken ADJECTIVE
cassé ◇ *It's broken.* C'est cassé. ◇ *a broken leg* une jambe cassée ◇ *He's got a broken arm.* Il a le bras cassé.

bronchitis NOUN
la *bronchite*

bronze NOUN
le *bronze* ◇ *the bronze medal* la médaille de bronze

brooch NOUN
la *broche*

broom NOUN
le *balai*

brother NOUN
le *frère* ◇ *my brother* mon frère ◇ *my big brother* mon grand frère

brother-in-law NOUN
le *beau-frère*
(les *beaux-frères* PL)

brought VERB see **bring**

brown ADJECTIVE
1 *marron* MASC, FEM, PL (*clothes*)
2 (*hair*)
brun
3 (*tanned*)
bronzé
• **brown bread** le pain complet

bruise NOUN
le *bleu*

brush NOUN
see also brush VERB
1 la *brosse*
2 (*paintbrush*)
le *pinceau*
(les *pinceaux* PL)

to **brush** VERB
see also brush NOUN
brosser
• **to brush one's hair** se brosser les cheveux ◇ *I brushed my hair.* Je me suis brossé les cheveux.
• **to brush one's teeth** se brosser les dents ◇ *I brush my teeth every night.* Je me brosse les dents tous les soirs.

Brussels NOUN
Bruxelles
• **in Brussels** à Bruxelles
• **to Brussels** à Bruxelles

Brussels sprouts PL NOUN
les *choux de Bruxelles* MASC PL

brutal ADJECTIVE
brutal
(*brutaux* MASC PL)
bubble NOUN
la *bulle*
bubble bath NOUN
le *bain moussant*
bubble gum NOUN
le *chewing-gum*
bucket NOUN
le *seau*
(les *seaux* PL)
buckle NOUN
la *boucle* (*on belt, watch, shoe*)
Buddhism NOUN
le *bouddhisme*
Buddhist ADJECTIVE
bouddhiste
budget NOUN
le *budget*
budgie NOUN
la *perruche*
buffet NOUN
le *buffet*
buffet car NOUN
la *voiture-bar*
bug NOUN
1 l' *insecte* MASC (*insect*)
2 le *microbe* (*infection*) ◇ *There's a bug going round.* Il y a un microbe qui traîne.
◆ **a stomach bug** une gastroentérite
3 le *bug* (*in computer*)
bugged ADJECTIVE
sur écoute ◇ *The room was bugged.*
La pièce était sur écoute.
to **build** VERB
construire ◇ *They're going to build houses here.* On va construire des maisons ici.
◆ **to build up** (*increase*) s'accumuler
builder NOUN
1 l' *entrepreneur* MASC (*owner of firm*)
2 le *maçon* (*worker*)
building NOUN
le *bâtiment*
built VERB *see* **build**
bulb NOUN
l' *ampoule* FEM (*electric*)
bull NOUN
le *taureau*
(les *taureaux* PL)
bullet NOUN
la *balle*
bullfighting NOUN
la *tauromachie*
bully NOUN
　see also bully VERB
la *brute* ◇ *He's a big bully.* C'est une brute.

to **bully** VERB
　see also bully NOUN
tyranniser
bum NOUN
le *derrière* (*bottom*)
bump NOUN
　see also bump VERB
1 la *bosse* (*lump*)
2 l' *accrochage* MASC (*minor accident*)
◇ *We had a bump.* Nous avons eu un accrochage.
to **bump** VERB
　see also bump NOUN
◆ **to bump into something** rentrer dans quelque chose ◇ *We bumped into his car.* Nous sommes rentrés dans sa voiture.
◆ **to bump into somebody (1)** (*literally*) rentrer dans quelqu'un ◇ *He stopped suddenly and I bumped into him.* Il s'est arrêté subitement et je lui suis rentré dedans.
◆ **to bump into somebody (2)** (*meet by chance*) rencontrer par hasard
◆ **I bumped into Jane in the supermarket.** J'ai rencontré Jane par hasard au supermarché.
bumper NOUN
le *pare-chocs*
(les *pare-chocs* PL)
bumpy ADJECTIVE
cahoteux MASC
cahoteuse FEM
bun NOUN
le *petit pain au lait*
bunch NOUN
◆ **a bunch of flowers** un bouquet de fleurs
◆ **a bunch of grapes** une grappe de raisin
◆ **a bunch of keys** un trousseau de clés
bunches PL NOUN
les *couettes* FEM ◇ *She has her hair in bunches.* Elle a des couettes.
bungalow NOUN
le *bungalow*
bunk NOUN
la *couchette*
burglar NOUN
le *cambrioleur*
la *cambrioleuse*
burglary NOUN
le *cambriolage*
burn NOUN
　see also burn VERB
la *brûlure*
to **burn** VERB
　see also burn NOUN
1 *brûler* (*rubbish, documents*)
2 *faire brûler* (*food*) ◇ *I burned the cake.* J'ai fait brûler le gâteau.

B

* **to burn oneself** se brûler ◇ *I burned myself on the oven door.* Je me suis brûlé sur la porte du four.
* **I've burned my hand.** Je me suis brûlé la main.
* **to burn down** brûler ◇ *The factory burned down.* L'usine a brûlé.

to **burst** VERB
   éclater ◇ *The balloon burst.* Le ballon a éclaté.
* **to burst a balloon** faire éclater un ballon
* **to burst out laughing** éclater de rire
* **to burst into flames** prendre feu
* **to burst into tears** fondre en larmes

to **bury** VERB
   enterrer

bus NOUN
   l' *autobus* MASC ◇ *the bus driver* le conducteur d'autobus ◇ *a bus stop* un arrêt d'autobus
* **the school bus** le car scolaire
* **a bus pass** une carte d'abonnement pour le bus
* **a bus station** une gare routière
* **a bus ticket** un ticket de bus

bush NOUN
   le *buisson*

business NOUN
   1 l' *entreprise* FEM (*firm*) ◇ *He's got his own business.* Il a sa propre entreprise.
   2 les *affaires* FEM PL (*commerce*) ◇ *He's away on business.* Il est en voyage d'affaires.
* **a business trip** un voyage d'affaires
* **It's none of my business.** Ça ne me regarde pas.

businessman NOUN
   l' *homme d'affaires* MASC

businesswoman NOUN
   la *femme d'affaires*

busker NOUN
   le *musicien de rue*
   la *musicienne de rue*

bust NOUN
   la *poitrine* (*chest*)

busy ADJECTIVE
   1 *occupé* (*person, phone line*)
   2 *chargé* (*day, schedule*)
   3 *très fréquenté* (*shop, street*)

but CONJUNCTION
   mais ◇ *I'd like to come, but I'm busy.* J'aimerais venir mais je suis occupé.

butcher NOUN

   le *boucher* ◇ *He's a butcher.* Il est boucher.

butcher's NOUN
   la *boucherie*

butter NOUN
   le *beurre*

butterfly NOUN
   le *papillon*

buttocks PL NOUN
   les *fesses* FEM PL

button NOUN
   le *bouton*

to **buy** VERB
   see also buy NOUN
   acheter ◇ *He bought me an ice cream.* Il m'a acheté une glace. ◇ *I bought him an ice cream.* Je lui ai acheté une glace.
* **to buy something from somebody** acheter quelque chose à quelqu'un ◇ *I bought a watch from him.* Je lui ai acheté une montre.

buy NOUN
   see also buy VERB
* **It was a good buy.** C'était une bonne affaire.

by PREPOSITION
   1 *par* ◇ *The thieves were caught by the police.* Les voleurs ont été arrêtés par la police.
   2 *de* ◇ *a painting by Picasso* un tableau de Picasso ◇ *a book by Balzac* un livre de Balzac
   3 *en* ◇ *by car* en voiture ◇ *by train* en train ◇ *by bus* en autobus
   4 *à côté de* (*close to*) ◇ *Where's the bank? – It's by the post office.* Où est la banque? – Elle est à côté de la poste.
   5 *avant* (*not later than*) ◇ *We have to be there by 4 o'clock.* Nous devons y être avant quatre heures.
* **by the time...** quand... ◇ *By the time I got there it was too late.* Quand je suis arrivé il était déjà trop tard. ◇ *It'll be ready by the time you get back.* Ça sera prêt quand vous reviendrez.
* **That's fine by me.** Ça me va.
* **all by himself** tout seul
* **all by herself** toute seule
* **I did it all by myself.** Je l'ai fait tout seul.
* **by the way** au fait

bypass NOUN
   la *route de contournement*

C

cab NOUN
le _taxi_

cabbage NOUN
le _chou_
(les _choux_ PL)

cabin NOUN
la _cabine_ (_on ship_)

cabinet NOUN
- **a bathroom cabinet** une armoire de salle de bain
- **a drinks cabinet** un bar

cable NOUN
le _câble_

cable car NOUN
le _téléphérique_

cable television NOUN
la _télévision par câble_

cactus NOUN
le _cactus_

cadet NOUN
- **a police cadet** un élève policier
- **a cadet officer** un élève officier

café NOUN
le _café_

Cafés in France sell both alcoholic and non-alcoholic drinks.

cage NOUN
la _cage_

cagoule NOUN
le _K-way_ ®

cake NOUN
le _gâteau_
(les _gâteaux_ PL)

to **calculate** VERB
calculer

calculation NOUN
le _calcul_

calculator NOUN
la _machine à calculer_

calendar NOUN
le _calendrier_

calf NOUN
1 (_of cow_)
le _veau_
(les _veaux_ PL)
2 (_of leg_)
le _mollet_

call NOUN
see also **call** VERB
l' _appel_ MASC (_by phone_) ○ _Thanks for your call._ Merci de votre appel.
- **a phone call** un coup de téléphone
- **to be on call** (_doctor_) être de permanence ○ _He's on call this evening._ Il est de permanence ce soir.

to **call** VERB
see also **call** NOUN
appeler ○ _I'll tell him you called._ Je lui dirai que vous avez appelé. ○ _This is the number to call._ C'est le numéro à appeler. ○ _We called the police._ Nous avons appelé la police. ○ _Everyone calls him Jimmy._ Tout le monde l'appelle Jimmy.
- **to be called** s'appeler ○ _He's called Fluffy._ Il s'appelle Fluffy. ○ _What's she called?_ Elle s'appelle comment?
- **to call somebody names** insulter quelqu'un
- **He called me an idiot.** Il m'a traité d'idiot.
- **to call back** (_phone again_) rappeler ○ _I'll call back at 6 o'clock._ Je rappellerai à six heures.
- **to call for** passer prendre ○ _I'll call for you at 2.30._ Je passerai te prendre à deux heures et demie.
- **to call off** annuler ○ _The match was called off._ Le match a été annulé.

call box NOUN
la _cabine téléphonique_

calm ADJECTIVE
calme

to **calm down** VERB
se calmer ○ _Calm down!_ Calme-toi!

Calor gas ® NOUN
le _butane_

calorie NOUN
la _calorie_

calves PL NOUN see **calf**

Cambodia NOUN
le _Cambodge_
- **in Cambodia** au Cambodge

camcorder NOUN
le _caméscope_

came VERB see **come**

camel NOUN
le _chameau_
(les _chameaux_ PL)

camera NOUN
1 (_for photos_)
l' _appareil photo_ MASC
(les _appareils photo_ PL)
2 (_for filming, TV_)
la _caméra_

cameraman NOUN
le _caméraman_

to **camp** VERB
see also **camp** NOUN
camper

camp NOUN
see also **camp** VERB

le *camp*
- **a camp bed** un lit de camp
campaign NOUN
la *campagne*
camper NOUN
1 (*person*)
le *campeur*
la *campeuse*
2 (*van*)
le *camping-car*
camping NOUN
le *camping*
- **to go camping** faire du camping ◦ *We went camping in Cornwall.* Nous avons fait du camping en Cornouailles.
camping gas ® NOUN
le *butane*
campsite NOUN
le *terrain de camping*
campus NOUN
le *campus*
can NOUN
see also can VERB
1 la *boîte* (*tin*) ◦ *a can of sweetcorn* une boîte de maïs ◦ *a can of beer* une boîte de bière
2 le *bidon* (*jerry can*) ◦ *a can of petrol* un bidon d'essence
can VERB
see also can NOUN
1 *pouvoir* (*be able to, be allowed to*) ◦ *I can't come.* Je ne peux pas venir. ◦ *Can I help you?* Est-ce que je peux vous aider? ◦ *Can I use your phone?* Est-ce que je peux me servir de votre téléphone? ◦ *You could hire a bike.* Tu pourrais louer un vélo. ◦ *I couldn't sleep because of the noise.* Je ne pouvais pas dormir à cause du bruit.
can *is sometimes not translated.*
◦ *I can't hear you.* Je ne t'entends pas.
◦ *I can't remember.* Je ne m'en souviens pas. ◦ *Can you speak French?* Parlez-vous français?
2 *savoir* (*have learnt how to*) ◦ *I can swim.* Je sais nager. ◦ *He can't drive.* Il ne sait pas conduire.
- **That can't be true!** Ce n'est pas possible!
- **You could be right.** Vous avez peut-être raison.
Canada NOUN
le *Canada*
- **in Canada** au Canada
- **to Canada** au Canada
Canadian ADJECTIVE
see also Canadian NOUN
canadien MASC
canadienne FEM

Canadian NOUN
see also Canadian ADJECTIVE
le *Canadien*
la *Canadienne*
canal NOUN
le *canal*
(les *canaux* PL)
canary NOUN
le *canari*
to **cancel** VERB
annuler ◦ *The match was cancelled.* Le match a été annulé.
cancellation NOUN
l' *annulation* FEM
cancer NOUN
1 le *cancer* ◦ *He's got cancer.* Il a le cancer.
2 le *Cancer* ◦ *I'm Cancer.* Je suis Cancer.
candidate NOUN
le *candidat*
la *candidate*
candle NOUN
la *bougie*
candyfloss NOUN
la *barbe à papa*
cannabis NOUN
le *cannabis*
canned ADJECTIVE
en conserve (*food*)
cannot VERB see can
canoe NOUN
le *canoë*
canoeing NOUN
- **to go canoeing** faire du canoë ◦ *We went canoeing.* Nous avons fait du canoë.
can-opener NOUN
l' *ouvre-boîte* MASC
can't VERB see can
canteen NOUN
la *cantine*
to **canter** VERB
aller au petit galop
canvas NOUN
la *toile*
cap NOUN
1 la *casquette* (*hat*)
2 le *bouchon* (*of bottle, tube*)
capable ADJECTIVE
capable
capacity NOUN
la *capacité*
capital NOUN
1 la *capitale* ◦ *Cardiff is the capital of Wales.* Cardiff est la capitale du pays de Galles.
2 la *majuscule* (*letter*) ◦ *Write your address in capitals.* Écris ton adresse en majuscules.

capitalism NOUN
le *capitalisme*
capital punishment NOUN
la *peine capitale*
Capricorn NOUN
le *Capricorne* ◇ *I'm Capricorn.* Je suis Capricorne.
to **capsize** VERB
chavirer
captain NOUN
le *capitaine* ◇ *She's captain of the hockey team.* Elle est capitaine de l'équipe de hockey.
to **capture** VERB
capturer
car NOUN
la *voiture*
◆ **to go by car** aller en voiture ◇ *We went by car.* Nous y sommes allés en voiture.
◆ **a car crash** un accident de voiture
caramel NOUN
le *caramel*
caravan NOUN
la *caravane* ◇ *a caravan site* un camping pour caravanes
card NOUN
la *carte*
◆ **a card game** un jeu de cartes
cardboard NOUN
le *carton*
cardigan NOUN
le *cardigan*
cardphone NOUN
le *téléphone à carte*
care NOUN
see also **care** VERB
le *soin* ◇ *with care* avec soin
◆ **to take care of** s'occuper de ◇ *I take care of the children on Saturdays.* Le samedi, je m'occupe des enfants.
◆ **Take care! (1)** (*Be careful!*) Fais attention!
◆ **Take care! (2)** (*Look after yourself!*) Prends bien soin de toi!
to **care** VERB
see also **care** NOUN
◆ **to care about** se soucier de ◇ *They don't care about their image.* Ils se soucient peu de leur image.
◆ **I don't care!** Ça m'est égal! ◇ *She doesn't care.* Ça lui est égal.
◆ **to care for somebody** (*patients, old people*) s'occuper de quelqu'un
career NOUN
la *carrière*
careful ADJECTIVE
◆ **Be careful!** Fais attention!
carefully ADVERB
[1] *soigneusement* ◇ *She carefully*

avoided talking about it. Elle évitait soigneusement d'en parler.
[2] *prudemment* (*safely*) ◇ *Drive carefully!* Conduisez prudemment!
◆ **Think carefully!** Réfléchis bien!
careless ADJECTIVE
[1] (*work*)
peu soigné
◆ **a careless mistake** une faute d'inattention
[2] (*person*)
peu soigneux MASC
peu soigneuse FEM
◇ *She's very careless.* Elle est bien peu soigneuse.
[3] *imprudent* ◇ *a careless driver* un conducteur imprudent
caretaker NOUN
le *gardien*
la *gardienne*
car-ferry NOUN
le *ferry*
cargo NOUN
la *cargaison*
car hire NOUN
la *location de voitures*
Caribbean ADJECTIVE
see also **Caribbean** NOUN
antillais ◇ *Caribbean food* la cuisine antillaise
Caribbean NOUN
see also **Caribbean** ADJECTIVE
[1] les *Caraïbes* FEM PL (*islands*) ◇ *We're going to the Caribbean.* Nous allons aux Caraïbes.
◆ **He's from the Caribbean.** Il est antillais.
[2] la *mer des Caraïbes* (*sea*)
carnation NOUN
l' *œillet* MASC
carnival NOUN
le *carnaval*
carol NOUN
◆ **a Christmas carol** un chant de Noël
car park NOUN
le *parking*
carpenter NOUN
le *charpentier* ◇ *He's a carpenter.* Il est charpentier.
carpentry NOUN
la *menuiserie*
carpet NOUN
[1] le *tapis* ◇ *a Persian carpet* un tapis persan
[2] la *moquette* (*fitted*)
car phone NOUN
le *téléphone de voiture*
carriage NOUN
la *voiture*
carrier bag NOUN

le _sac en plastique_
carrot NOUN
  la _carotte_
to **carry** VERB
  [1] _porter_ ◇ _I'll carry your bag._ Je vais porter ton sac.
  [2] _transporter_ ◇ _a plane carrying 100 passengers_ un avion transportant cent passagers
  ◆ **to carry on** continuer ◇ _Carry on!_ Continue! ◇ _She carried on talking._ Elle a continué à parler.
  ◆ **to carry out** (_orders_) exécuter
carrycot NOUN
  le _porte-bébé_
cart NOUN
  la _charrette_
carton NOUN
  la _brique_ (_of milk, juice_)
cartoon NOUN
  [1] le _dessin animé_ (_film_)
  [2] le _dessin humoristique_ (_in newspaper_)
  ◆ **a strip cartoon** une bande dessinée
cartridge NOUN
  la _cartouche_
to **carve** VERB
  découper (_meat_)
case NOUN
  [1] la _valise_ ◇ _I've packed my case._ J'ai fait ma valise.
  [2] le _cas_
  (les _cas_ PL)
  ◇ _in some cases_ dans certains cas
  ◆ **in that case** dans ce cas ◇ _I don't want it._ – _In that case, I'll take it._ Je n'en veux pas. – Dans ce cas, je le prends.
  ◆ **in case** au cas où ◇ _in case it rains_ au cas où il pleuvrait
  ◆ **just in case** à tout hasard ◇ _Take some money, just in case._ Prends de l'argent à tout hasard.
cash NOUN
  l' _argent_ MASC ◇ _I'm a bit short of cash._ Je suis un peu à court d'argent.
  ◆ **in cash** en liquide ◇ _£2000 in cash_ deux mille livres en liquide
  ◆ **to pay cash** payer comptant
  ◆ **a cash card** une carte de retrait
  ◆ **the cash desk** la caisse
  ◆ **a cash dispenser** un distributeur automatique de billets
  ◆ **a cash register** une caisse
cashew NOUN
  la _noix de cajou_
cashier NOUN
  le _caissier_
  la _caissière_
cashmere NOUN
  le _cachemire_ ◇ _a cashmere sweater_

un pull en cachemire
casino NOUN
  le _casino_
casserole NOUN
  le _ragoût_ ◇ _I'm going to make a casserole._ Je vais faire un ragoût.
  ◆ **a casserole dish** une cocotte
cassette NOUN
  la _cassette_
  ◆ **a cassette player** un lecteur de cassettes
  ◆ **a cassette recorder** un magnétophone
cast NOUN
  les _acteurs_ MASC PL ◇ _After the play, we met the cast._ Après la représentation, nous avons rencontré les acteurs.
castle NOUN
  le _château_
  (les _châteaux_ PL)
casual ADJECTIVE
  [1] _décontracté_ ◇ _I prefer casual clothes._ Je préfère les vêtements décontractés.
  [2] _désinvolte_ ◇ _a casual attitude_ une attitude désinvolte
  [3] _en passant_ ◇ _It was just a casual remark._ C'était juste une remarque en passant.
casually ADVERB
  ◆ **to dress casually** s'habiller de façon décontractée
casualty NOUN
  les _urgences_ FEM PL (_in hospital_)
cat NOUN
  (_female_)
  le _chat_
  la _chatte_
  ◇ _Have you got a cat?_ Est-ce que tu as un chat?
catalogue NOUN
  le _catalogue_
catalytic converter NOUN
  le _catalyseur_
catarrh NOUN
  le _rhume chronique_
catastrophe NOUN
  la _catastrophe_
to **catch** VERB
  [1] _attraper_ ◇ _to catch a thief_ attraper un voleur ◇ _My cat catches birds._ Mon chat attrape des oiseaux.
  ◆ **to catch somebody doing something** attraper quelqu'un en train de faire quelque chose ◇ _If they catch you smoking..._ S'ils t'attrapent en train de fumer...
  ◆ **to catch a cold** attraper un rhume
  [2] _prendre_ (_bus, train_) ◇ _We caught the last bus._ Nous avons pris le dernier bus.
  [3] _saisir_ (_hear_) ◇ _I didn't catch his name._

Je n'ai pas saisi son nom.
- **to catch up** rattraper son retard ◇ *I've got to catch up: I was away last week.* Je dois rattraper mon retard: j'étais absent la semaine dernière.

catching ADJECTIVE
contagieux MASC
contagieuse FEM
◇ *It's not catching.* Ce n'est pas contagieux.

catering NOUN
la *restauration*

cathedral NOUN
la *cathédrale*

Catholic ADJECTIVE
see also Catholic NOUN
catholique

Catholic NOUN
see also Catholic ADJECTIVE
le/la *catholique* ◇ *I'm a Catholic.* Je suis catholique.

cattle PL NOUN
le *bétail* SING

caught VERB *see* **catch**

cauliflower NOUN
le *chou-fleur*
(les *choux-fleurs* PL)

cause NOUN
see also cause VERB
la *cause*

to **cause** VERB
see also cause NOUN
provoquer ◇ *to cause an accident* provoquer un accident

cautious ADJECTIVE
prudent

cave NOUN
la *grotte*

CD NOUN
le *CD*
(les *CD* PL)

CD player NOUN
la *platine laser*

CD-ROM NOUN
le *CD-ROM*
(les *CD-ROM* PL)

ceiling NOUN
le *plafond*

to **celebrate** VERB
fêter (*birthday*)

celebrity NOUN
la *célébrité*

celery NOUN
le *céleri*

cell NOUN
la *cellule*

cellar NOUN
la *cave* ◇ *a wine cellar* une cave à vins

cello NOUN

le *violoncelle* ◇ *I play the cello.* Je joue du violoncelle.

cement NOUN
le *ciment*

cemetery NOUN
le *cimetière*

cent NOUN
le *cent* ◇ *twenty cents* vingt cents

centenary NOUN
le *centenaire*

centigrade ADJECTIVE
centigrade ◇ *20 degrees centigrade* vingt degrés centigrade

centimetre NOUN
le *centimètre*

central ADJECTIVE
central
(*centraux* MASC PL)

central heating NOUN
le *chauffage central*

centre NOUN
le *centre* ◇ *a sports centre* un centre sportif

century NOUN
le *siècle* ◇ *the 20th century* le vingtième siècle ◇ *the 21st century* le vingt et unième siècle

cereal NOUN
les *céréales* FEM PL ◇ *I have cereal for breakfast.* Je prends des céréales au petit déjeuner.

ceremony NOUN
la *cérémonie*

certain ADJECTIVE
certain ◇ *a certain person* une certaine personne ◇ *I'm absolutely certain it was him.* Je suis absolument certain que c'était lui.
- **I don't know for certain.** Je n'en suis pas certain.
- **to make certain** s'assurer ◇ *I made certain the door was locked.* Je me suis assuré que la porte était fermée à clé.

certainly ADVERB
vraiment ◇ *I certainly expected something better.* Je m'attendais vraiment à quelque chose de mieux.
- **Certainly not!** Certainement pas!
- **So it was a surprise? – It certainly was!** C'était donc une surprise? – Ça oui alors!

certificate NOUN
le *certificat*

chain NOUN
la *chaîne*

chair NOUN
1 la *chaise* ◇ *a table and 4 chairs* une table et quatre chaises
2 le *fauteuil* (*armchair*)

chairlift NOUN

le *télésiège*
chairman NOUN
  le *président*
chalet NOUN
  le *chalet*
chalk NOUN
  la *craie*
challenge NOUN
  see also challenge VERB
  le *défi*
to **challenge** VERB
  see also challenge NOUN
- **She challenged me to a race.** Elle m'a proposé de faire la course avec elle.
challenging ADJECTIVE
  stimulant ◇ *a challenging job* un travail stimulant
champagne NOUN
  le *champagne*
champion NOUN
  le *champion*
  la *championne*
championship NOUN
  le *championnat*
chance NOUN
  [1] la *chance* ◇ *Do you think I've got any chance?* Tu crois que j'ai une chance? ◇ *Their chances of winning are very good.* Ils ont de fortes chances de gagner.
- **No chance!** Pas question!
  [2] l' *occasion* FEM ◇ *I'd like to have a chance to travel.* J'aimerais avoir l'occasion de voyager.
- **I'll write when I get the chance.** J'écrirai quand j'aurai un moment.
- **by chance** par hasard ◇ *We met by chance.* Nous nous sommes rencontrés par hasard.
- **to take a chance** prendre un risque ◇ *I'm taking no chances!* Je ne veux prendre aucun risque!
Chancellor of the Exchequer NOUN
  le *chancelier de l'Échiquier*
to **change** VERB
  see also change NOUN
  [1] *changer* ◇ *The town has changed a lot.* La ville a beaucoup changé. ◇ *I'd like to change £50.* Je voudrais changer cinquante livres.
  Use **changer de** when you change one thing for another.
  [2] *changer de* ◇ *You have to change trains in Paris.* Il faut changer de train à Paris. ◇ *I'm going to change my shoes.* Je vais changer de chaussures. ◇ *He wants to change his job.* Il veut changer d'emploi.
- **to change one's mind** changer d'avis ◇ *I've changed my mind.* J'ai changé

d'avis.
- **to change gear** changer de vitesse
  [3] *se changer* ◇ *She's changing to go out.* Elle est en train de se changer pour sortir.
- **to get changed** se changer ◇ *I'm going to get changed.* Je vais me changer.
  [4] *échanger* (swap) ◇ *Can I change this sweater? It's too small.* Est-ce que je peux échanger ce pull? Il est trop petit.
change NOUN
  see also change VERB
  [1] le *changement* ◇ *There's been a change of plan.* Il y a eu un changement de programme.
  [2] la *monnaie* (money) ◇ *I haven't got any change.* Je n'ai pas de monnaie.
- **a change of clothes** des vêtements de rechange
- **for a change** pour changer ◇ *Let's play tennis for a change.* Si on jouait au tennis pour changer?
changeable ADJECTIVE
  variable
changing room NOUN
  [1] le *salon d'essayage* (in shop)
  [2] le *vestiaire* (for sport)
channel NOUN
  la *chaîne* (TV) ◇ *There's football on the other channel.* Il y a du football sur l'autre chaîne.
- **the Channel** la Manche
- **the Channel Islands** les îles Anglo-Normandes FEM PL
- **the Channel Tunnel** le tunnel sous la Manche
chaos NOUN
  le *chaos*
chap NOUN
  le *type* ◇ *He's a nice chap.* C'est un type sympa.
chapel NOUN
  la *chapelle* (part of church)
chapter NOUN
  le *chapitre*
character NOUN
  [1] le *caractère* ◇ *Give me some idea of his character.* Décris-moi un peu son caractère.
- **She's quite a character.** C'est un drôle de numéro.
  [2] le *personnage* (in play, film) ◇ *The character played by Depardieu...* Le personnage joué par Depardieu...
characteristic NOUN
  la *caractéristique*
charcoal NOUN
  le *charbon de bois*

charge NOUN

see also charge VERB

les *frais* MASC PL ⋄ *Is there a charge for delivery?* Est-ce qu'il y a des frais de livraison?

- **an extra charge** un supplément
- **free of charge** gratuit
- **to reverse the charges** appeler en P.C.V. ⋄ *I'd like to reverse the charges.* Je voudrais appeler en P.C.V.
- **to be on a charge** être inculpé ⋄ *He's on a charge of murder.* Il est inculpé de meurtre.
- **to be in charge** être responsable ⋄ *Mrs Munday was in charge of the group.* Madame Munday était responsable du groupe.

to **charge** VERB

see also charge NOUN

[1] *prendre* (*money*) ⋄ *How much did he charge you?* Combien est-ce qu'il vous a pris? ⋄ *They charge £10 an hour.* Ils prennent dix livres de l'heure.

[2] *inculper* (*with crime*) ⋄ *The police have charged him with murder.* La police l'a inculpé de meurtre.

charity NOUN

l' *association caritative* FEM ⋄ *He gave the money to charity.* Il a donné l'argent à une association caritative.

charm NOUN

le *charme* ⋄ *He's got a lot of charm.* Il a beaucoup de charme.

charming ADJECTIVE

charmant

chart NOUN

le *tableau*

(les *tableaux* PL)

⋄ *The chart shows the rise of unemployment.* Le tableau indique la progression du chômage.

- **the charts** le hit-parade ⋄ *This album is number one in the charts.* Cet album est numéro un au hit-parade.

charter flight NOUN

le *charter*

to **chase** VERB

see also chase NOUN

pourchasser

chase NOUN

see also chase VERB

la *poursuite* ⋄ *a car chase* une poursuite en voiture

chat NOUN

- **to have a chat** bavarder

chat show NOUN

le *talk-show*

cheap ADJECTIVE

bon marché MASC, FEM, PL ⋄ *a cheap T-shirt* un T-shirt bon marché

cheaper ADJECTIVE

moins cher MASC

moins chère FEM

⋄ *It's cheaper by bus.* C'est moins cher en bus.

to **cheat** VERB

see also cheat NOUN

tricher ⋄ *You're cheating!* Tu triches!

cheat NOUN

see also cheat VERB

le *tricheur*

la *tricheuse*

check NOUN

see also check VERB

le *contrôle* ⋄ *a security check* un contrôle de sécurité

to **check** VERB

see also check NOUN

vérifier ⋄ *I'll check the time of the train.* Je vais vérifier l'heure du train. ⋄ *Could you check the oil, please?* Pourriez-vous vérifier le niveau d'huile, s'il vous plaît?

- **to check in (1)** (*at airport*) se présenter à l'enregistrement ⋄ *What time do I have to check in?* À quelle heure est-ce que je dois me présenter à l'enregistrement?
- **to check in (2)** (*in hotel*) se présenter à la réception
- **to check out** (*from hotel*) régler sa note

check-in NOUN

l' *enregistrement* MASC

checkout NOUN

la *caisse*

check-up NOUN

l' *examen de routine* MASC

cheek NOUN

[1] la *joue* ⋄ *He kissed her on the cheek.* Il l'a embrassée sur la joue.

[2] le *culot* ⋄ *What a cheek!* Quel culot!

cheeky ADJECTIVE

effronté ⋄ *Don't be cheeky!* Ne sois pas effronté!

- **a cheeky smile** un sourire malicieux

cheer NOUN

see also cheer VERB

les *hourras* MASC PL

- **to give a cheer** pousser des hourras
- **Cheers! (1)** (*good health*) À la vôtre!
- **Cheers! (2)** (*thanks*) Merci!

to **cheer** VERB

see also cheer NOUN

applaudir

- **to cheer somebody up** remonter le moral à quelqu'un ⋄ *I was trying to cheer him up.* J'essayais de lui remonter le moral.
- **Cheer up!** Ne te laisse pas abattre!

cheerful ADJECTIVE

gai

cheerio EXCLAMATION
salut!
cheese NOUN
le *fromage*
chef NOUN
le *chef*
chemical NOUN
le *produit chimique*
chemist NOUN
[1] (*dispenser*)
le *pharmacien*
la *pharmacienne*
[2] (*shop*)
la *pharmacie* ◇ *You get it from the chemist.* C'est vendu en pharmacie.
Chemist's shops in France are identified by a special green cross outside the shop.
[3] (*scientist*)
le/la *chimiste*
chemistry NOUN
la *chimie* ◇ *the chemistry lab* le laboratoire de chimie
cheque NOUN
le *chèque* ◇ *to write a cheque* faire un chèque ◇ *to pay by cheque* payer par chèque
chequebook NOUN
le *carnet de chèques*
cherry NOUN
la *cerise*
chess NOUN
les *échecs* MASC PL ◇ *to play chess* jouer aux échecs
chessboard NOUN
l' *échiquier* MASC
chest NOUN
la *poitrine* (*of person*) ◇ *his chest measurement* son tour de poitrine
◆ **a chest of drawers** une commode
chestnut NOUN
le *marron* ◇ *We have turkey with chestnuts.* Nous mangeons de la dinde aux marrons.
chewing gum NOUN
le *chewing-gum*
chicken NOUN
le *poulet*
chickenpox NOUN
la *varicelle*
child NOUN
l' *enfant* MASC/FEM ◇ *all the children* tous les enfants
childish ADJECTIVE
puéril
child minder NOUN
la *nourrice*
children PL NOUN *see* **child**
Chile NOUN
le *Chili*

◆ **in Chile** au Chili
to **chill** VERB
mettre au frais ◇ *Put the wine in the fridge to chill.* Mets le vin au frais dans le réfrigérateur.
chilli NOUN
le *piment*
chimney NOUN
la *cheminée*
chin NOUN
le *menton*
china NOUN
la *porcelaine* ◇ *a china plate* une assiette en porcelaine
China NOUN
la *Chine*
◆ **in China** en Chine
Chinese ADJECTIVE
see also **Chinese** NOUN
chinois ◇ *a Chinese restaurant* un restaurant chinois
◆ **a Chinese man** un Chinois
◆ **a Chinese woman** une Chinoise
Chinese NOUN
see also **Chinese** ADJECTIVE
le *chinois* (*language*)
◆ **the Chinese** (*people*) les Chinois
chip NOUN
[1] la *frite* (*food*) ◇ *We bought some chips.* Nous avons acheté des frites.
[2] la *puce* (*in computer*)
chiropodist NOUN
le/la *pédicure* ◇ *He's a chiropodist.* Il est pédicure.
chives PL NOUN
la *ciboulette* SING
chocolate NOUN
le *chocolat* ◇ *a chocolate cake* un gâteau au chocolat
◆ **hot chocolate** le chocolat chaud
choice NOUN
le *choix* ◇ *I had no choice.* Je n'avais pas le choix.
choir NOUN
la *chorale* ◇ *I sing in the school choir.* Je chante dans la chorale de l'école.
to **choose** VERB
choisir ◇ *It's difficult to choose.* C'est difficile de choisir.
to **chop** VERB
see also **chop** NOUN
émincer ◇ *Chop the onions.* Émincez les oignons.
chop NOUN
see also **chop** VERB
la *côte* ◇ *a pork chop* une côte de porc
chopsticks PL NOUN
les *baguettes* FEM PL
chose, chosen VERB *see* **choose**

Christ NOUN
le *Christ* ○ *the birth of Christ* la naissance du Christ

christening NOUN
le *baptême*

Christian NOUN
see also Christian ADJECTIVE
le *chrétien*
la *chrétienne*

Christian ADJECTIVE
see also Christian NOUN
chrétien MASC
chrétienne FEM

Christian name NOUN
le *prénom*

Christmas NOUN
Noël MASC ○ *Happy Christmas!* Joyeux Noël!

• **Christmas Day** le jour de Noël
• **Christmas Eve** la veille de Noël
• **a Christmas tree** un arbre de Noël
• **a Christmas card** une carte de Noël

The French more often send greetings cards (une carte de vœux) in January rather than at Christmas, with best wishes for the New Year.

• **Christmas dinner** le repas de Noël

Most French people have their Christmas meal (réveillon de Noël) on the evening of Christmas Eve, though some have a repas de Noël *on Christmas Day.*

• **Christmas pudding**

The French usually have a Yule log (une bûche de Noël) for pudding at the Christmas meal. You could explain what Christmas pudding is using the example given.

○ *Christmas pudding is made with dried fruit and spices, and steamed.* Le "Christmas pudding" est un gâteau avec des raisins secs, parfumé avec des épices et cuit à la vapeur.

chunk NOUN
le *gros morceau*
(les *gros morceaux* PL)
○ *Cut the meat into chunks.* Coupez la viande en gros morceaux.

church NOUN
l' *église* FEM ○ *I don't go to church every Sunday.* Je ne vais pas à l'église tous les dimanches.

• **the Church of England** l'Église anglicane

cider NOUN
le *cidre*

cigar NOUN
le *cigare*

cigarette NOUN
la *cigarette*

cinema NOUN
le *cinéma* ○ *I'm going to the cinema this*

evening. Je vais au cinéma ce soir.

circle NOUN
le *cercle*

circular ADJECTIVE
circulaire

circulation NOUN
1 la *circulation* (of blood)
2 le *tirage* (of newspaper)

circumflex NOUN
l' *accent circonflexe* MASC

circumstances PL NOUN
les *circonstances* FEM PL

circus NOUN
le *cirque*

citizen NOUN
le *citoyen*
la *citoyenne*
○ *a French citizen* un citoyen français

city NOUN
la *ville*

• **the city centre** le centre-ville ○ *It's in the city centre.* C'est au centre-ville.

city technology college NOUN
le *collège technique*

civilization NOUN
la *civilisation*

civil servant NOUN
le/la *fonctionnaire* ○ *She's a civil servant.* Elle est fonctionnaire.

civil war NOUN
la *guerre civile*

to **claim** VERB
see also claim NOUN
1 *prétendre* ○ *He claims to have found the money.* Il prétend avoir trouvé l'argent.
2 *percevoir* (receive) ○ *She's claiming unemployment benefit.* Elle perçoit des allocations chômage.

• **She can't claim unemployment benefit.** Elle n'a pas droit aux allocations chômage.

• **to claim on one's insurance** se faire rembourser par son assurance ○ *We claimed on our insurance.* Nous nous sommes fait rembourser par notre assurance.

claim NOUN
see also claim VERB
la *demande d'indemnité* (on insurance policy) ○ *to make a claim* faire une demande d'indemnité

to **clap** VERB
applaudir (applaud)

• **to clap one's hands** frapper dans ses mains ○ *I've trained my dog to sit when I clap my hands.* J'ai dressé mon chien à s'asseoir quand je frappe dans mes mains.

clarinet NOUN
la *clarinette* ◇ *I play the clarinet.* Je joue de la clarinette.

to **clash** VERB
[1] *jurer* (*colours*) ◇ *These two colours clash.* Ces deux couleurs jurent.
[2] *tomber en même temps* (*events*) ◇ *The concert clashes with Ann's party.* Le concert tombe en même temps que la soirée d'Ann.

clasp NOUN
le *fermoir* (*of necklace*)

class NOUN
[1] la *classe* (*group*) ◇ *We're in the same class.* Nous sommes dans la même classe.
[2] le *cours* (*lesson*) ◇ *I go to dancing classes.* Je vais à des cours de danse.

classic ADJECTIVE
see also classic NOUN
classique ◇ *a classic example* un cas classique

classic NOUN
see also classic ADJECTIVE
le *classique* (*book, film*)

classical ADJECTIVE
classique ◇ *I like classical music.* J'aime la musique classique.

classroom NOUN
la *classe*

claw NOUN
[1] la *griffe* (*of cat, dog*)
[2] la *serre* (*of bird*)
[3] la *pince* (*of crab, lobster*)

clean ADJECTIVE
see also clean VERB
propre ◇ *a clean shirt* une chemise propre

to **clean** VERB
see also clean ADJECTIVE
nettoyer

cleaner NOUN
la *femme de ménage* ◇ *She's a cleaner.* Elle est femme de ménage.

cleaner's NOUN
la *teinturerie*

clear ADJECTIVE
see also clear VERB
[1] *clair* ◇ *a clear explanation* une explication claire ◇ *It's clear you don't believe me.* Il est clair que tu ne me crois pas.
[2] *libre* (*road, way*) ◇ *The road's clear now.* La route est libre maintenant.

to **clear** VERB
see also clear ADJECTIVE
[1] *dégager* ◇ *The police are clearing the road after the accident.* La police dégage la route après l'accident.

[2] *se dissiper* (*fog, mist*) ◇ *The mist soon cleared.* La brume s'est vite dissipée.

◆ **to be cleared of a crime** être reconnu non coupable d'un crime ◇ *She was cleared of murder.* Elle a été reconnue non coupable du meurtre.

◆ **to clear the table** débarrasser la table ◇ *I'll clear the table.* Je vais débarrasser la table.

◆ **to clear up** ranger ◇ *Who's going to clear all this up?* Qui va ranger tout ça?

◆ **I think it's going to clear up.** (*weather*) Je pense que le temps va se lever.

clearly ADVERB
[1] *clairement* ◇ *She explained it very clearly.* Elle l'a expliqué très clairement.
[2] *nettement* ◇ *The French coast was clearly visible.* On distinguait nettement la côte française.
[3] *distinctement* ◇ *to speak clearly* parler distinctement

clementine NOUN
la *clémentine*

clever ADJECTIVE
[1] *intelligent* ◇ *She's very clever.* Elle est très intelligente.
[2] (*ingenious*)
astucieux MASC
astucieuse FEM
◇ *a clever system* un système astucieux

◆ **What a clever idea!** Quelle bonne idée!

client NOUN
le *client*
la *cliente*

cliff NOUN
la *falaise*

climate NOUN
le *climat*

to **climb** VERB
[1] *escalader* ◇ *We're going to climb Snowdon.* Nous allons escalader le Snowdon.
[2] *monter* (*stairs*)

climber NOUN
le *grimpeur*
la *grimpeuse*

climbing NOUN
l' *escalade* FEM

◆ **to go climbing** faire de l'escalade ◇ *We're going climbing in Scotland.* Nous allons faire de l'escalade en Écosse.

clinic NOUN
le *centre médical*
(les *centres médicaux* PL)

cloakroom NOUN
[1] le *vestiaire* (*for coats*)
[2] les *toilettes* FEM PL (*toilet*)

clock NOUN

1 l' *horloge* FEM ◦ the church clock
l'horloge de l'église
2 la *pendule* (smaller)
* **an alarm clock** un réveil
* **a clock-radio** un radio-réveil

clog NOUN
le *sabot*

close ADJECTIVE, ADVERB
see also close VERB
1 *près* (near) ◦ The shops are very
close. Les magasins sont tout près.
* **close to** près de ◦ The youth hostel is
close to the station. L'auberge de
jeunesse est près de la gare.
* **Come closer.** Rapproche-toi.
2 *proche* (in relationship) ◦ We're just
inviting close relations. Nous n'invitons
que les parents proches. ◦ She's a close
friend of mine. C'est une proche amie.
◦ I'm very close to my sister. Je suis très
proche de ma sœur.
3 *très serré* (contest) ◦ It's going to be
very close. Ça va être très serré.
4 *lourd* (weather) ◦ It's close this
afternoon. Il fait lourd cet après-midi.

to close VERB
see also close ADJECTIVE
1 *fermer* ◦ What time does the pool
close? La piscine ferme à quelle heure?
◦ The shops close at 5.30. Les magasins
ferment à cinq heures et demie.
◦ Please close the door. Fermez la porte,
s'il vous plaît.
2 *se fermer* ◦ The doors close
automatically. Les portes se ferment
automatiquement.

closed ADJECTIVE
fermé ◦ The bank's closed. La banque
est fermée.

closely ADVERB
de près (look, examine)

cloth NOUN
le *tissu* (material)
* **a cloth** un chiffon ◦ Wipe it with a
damp cloth. Nettoyez-le avec un chiffon
humide.

clothes PL NOUN
les *vêtements* MASC PL ◦ new clothes
des vêtements neufs
* **a clothes line** un fil à linge
* **a clothes peg** une pince à linge

cloud NOUN
le *nuage*

cloudy ADJECTIVE
nuageux MASC
nuageuse FEM

clove NOUN
* **a clove of garlic** une gousse d'ail

clown NOUN

le *clown*

club NOUN
le *club* ◦ a golf club (society and for
playing golf) un club de golf
* **the youth club** la maison des jeunes
* **clubs** (in cards) le trèfle ◦ the ace of
clubs l'as de trèfle

to club together VERB
se cotiser ◦ We clubbed together to buy
her a present. Nous nous sommes
cotisés pour lui acheter un cadeau.

clue NOUN
l' *indice* MASC ◦ an important clue un
indice important
* **I haven't a clue.** Je n'en ai pas la
moindre idée.

clumsy ADJECTIVE
maladroit

coach NOUN
1 le *car* MASC ◦ We went there by
coach. Nous y sommes allés en car.
* **the coach station** la gare routière
* **a coach trip** une excursion en car
2 l' *entraîneur* MASC (trainer) ◦ the
French coach l'entraîneur de l'équipe de
France

coal NOUN
le *charbon*
* **a coal mine** une mine de charbon
* **a coal miner** un mineur

coast NOUN
la *côte* ◦ It's on the west coast of
Scotland. C'est sur la côte ouest de
l'Écosse.

coat NOUN
le *manteau*
(les *manteaux* PL)
◦ a warm coat un manteau chaud
* **a coat of paint** une couche de peinture

coat hanger NOUN
le *cintre*

cocaine NOUN
la *cocaïne*

cockerel NOUN
le *coq*

cockney NOUN
le *cockney* ◦ I'm a cockney. Je suis
cockney.

cocoa NOUN
le *cacao* ◦ a cup of cocoa une tasse de
cacao

coconut NOUN
la *noix de coco*

cod NOUN
le *cabillaud*

code NOUN
le *code*

coffee NOUN
le *café*

- **A cup of coffee, please.** Un café, s'il vous plaît.

coffeepot NOUN
la *cafetière*

coffee table NOUN
la *table basse*

coffin NOUN
le *cercueil*

coin NOUN
la *pièce de monnaie*
- **a 5 franc coin** une pièce de cinq francs

coincidence NOUN
la *coïncidence*

coinphone NOUN
le *téléphone à pièces*

Coke ® NOUN
le *coca* ◇ **a can of Coke** ® une boîte de coca

colander NOUN
la *passoire*

cold ADJECTIVE
see also **cold** NOUN
froid ◇ *The water's cold.* L'eau est froide.
- **It's cold today.** Il fait froid aujourd'hui.
- **to be cold** (*person*) avoir froid ◇ *I'm cold.* J'ai froid. ◇ *Are you cold?* Est-ce que tu as froid?

cold NOUN
see also **cold** ADJECTIVE
1 le *froid* ◇ *I can't stand the cold.* Je ne supporte pas le froid.
2 le *rhume* ◇ *to catch a cold* attraper un rhume
- **to have a cold** avoir un rhume ◇ *I've got a bad cold.* J'ai un gros rhume.
- **a cold sore** un bouton de fièvre

coleslaw NOUN
la *salade de chou cru à la mayonnaise*

o**collapse** VERB
s'effondrer ◇ *He collapsed.* Il s'est effondré.

collar NOUN
1 le *col* (*of coat, shirt*)
2 le *collier* (*for animal*)

collarbone NOUN
la *clavicule* ◇ *I broke my collarbone.* Je me suis cassé la clavicule.

colleague NOUN
le/la *collègue*

o**collect** VERB
1 *ramasser* ◇ *The teacher collected the exercise books.* Le professeur a ramassé les cahiers. ◇ *They collect the rubbish twice a week.* Ils ramassent les ordures deux fois par semaine.
2 *faire collection de* ◇ *I collect stamps.* Je fais collection de timbres.
3 *aller chercher* ◇ *Their mother*

collects them from school. Leur mère va les chercher à l'école.
4 *faire une collecte* ◇ *They're collecting for charity.* Ils font une collecte pour une association caritative.

collection NOUN
1 la *collection* ◇ *my CD collection* ma collection de CD
2 la *collecte* ◇ *a collection for charity* une collecte pour une association caritative

collector NOUN
le *collectionneur*
la *collectionneuse*

college NOUN
le *collège* ◇ *a technical college* un collège d'enseignement technique

to **collide** VERB
entrer en collision

collie NOUN
le *colley*

colliery NOUN
la *houillère*

collision NOUN
la *collision*

colonel NOUN
le *colonel*

colour NOUN
la *couleur* ◇ *What colour is it?* C'est de quelle couleur?
- **a colour film** (*for camera*) une pellicule en couleur

colourful ADJECTIVE
coloré

colouring NOUN
le *colorant* (*for food*)

comb NOUN
see also **comb** VERB
le *peigne*

to **comb** VERB
see also **comb** NOUN
- **to comb one's hair** se peigner ◇ *You haven't combed your hair.* Tu ne t'es pas peigné.

combination NOUN
la *combinaison*

to **combine** VERB
1 *allier* ◇ *The film combines humour with suspense.* Le film allie l'humour au suspense.
2 *concilier* ◇ *It's difficult to combine a career with a family.* Il est difficile de concilier carrière et vie de famille.

to **come** VERB
1 *venir* ◇ *Can I come too?* Est-ce que je peux venir aussi? ◇ *Some friends came to see us.* Quelques amis sont venus nous voir. ◇ *I'll come with you.* Je viens avec toi.

2 *arriver* (*arrive*) ◇ *I'm coming!*
J'arrive! ◇ *They came late.* Ils sont
arrivés en retard. ◇ *The letter came this
morning.* La lettre est arrivée ce matin.
- **to come back** revenir ◇ *Come back!*
Reviens!
- **to come down (1)** (*person, lift*) descendre
- **to come down (2)** (*prices*) baisser
- **to come from** venir de ◇ *Where do you
come from?* Tu viens d'où?
- **to come in** entrer ◇ *Come in!* Entrez!
- **Come on!** Allez!
- **to come out** sortir ◇ *when we came
out of the cinema* quand nous sommes
sortis du cinéma ◇ *It's just come out on
video.* Ça vient de sortir en vidéo.
- **None of my photos came out.** Mes
photos n'ont rien donné.
- **to come round** reprendre connaissance
(*after faint, operation*)
- **to come up** monter ◇ *Come up here!*
Monte!
- **to come up to somebody (1)**
s'approcher de quelqu'un ◇ *She came
up to me and kissed me.* Elle s'est
approchée de moi et m'a embrassé.
- **to come up to somebody (2)** (*to speak to
them*) aborder quelqu'un ◇ *A man
came up to me and said...* Un homme
m'a abordé et m'a dit...

comedian NOUN
le *comique*

comedy NOUN
la *comédie*

comfortable ADJECTIVE
1 *confortable* (*bed, chair*)
2 *à l'aise* (*person*) ◇ *I'm very
comfortable, thanks.* Je suis parfaitement
à l'aise, merci.

comic NOUN
l' *illustré* MASC (*magazine*)

comic strip NOUN
la *bande dessinée*

coming ADJECTIVE
prochain ◇ *in the coming months* au
cours des prochains mois

comma NOUN
la *virgule*

command NOUN
l' *ordre* MASC

comment NOUN
see also comment VERB
le *commentaire* ◇ *He made no
comment.* Il n'a fait aucun commentaire.
- **No comment!** Je n'ai rien à dire!

to **comment** VERB
see also comment NOUN
- **to comment on something** faire des
commentaires sur quelque chose

commentary NOUN
le *reportage en direct* (*on TV, radio*)

commentator NOUN
le *commentateur sportif*
la *commentatrice sportive*

commercial NOUN
le *spot publicitaire*

commission NOUN
la *commission* ◇ *Salesmen work on
commission.* Les représentants
travaillent à la commission.

to **commit** VERB
- **to commit a crime** commettre un crime
- **to commit oneself** s'engager ◇ *I don't
want to commit myself.* Je ne veux pas
m'engager.
- **to commit suicide** se suicider ◇ *He
committed suicide.* Il s'est suicidé.

committee NOUN
le *comité*

common ADJECTIVE
see also common NOUN
courant ◇ *"Smith" is a very common
surname.* "Smith" est un nom de famille
très courant.
- **in common** en commun ◇ *We've got a
lot in common.* Nous avons beaucoup de
choses en commun.

common NOUN
see also common ADJECTIVE
le *terrain communal* ◇ *We went for a
walk on the common.* Nous sommes allés
nous promener sur le terrain communal.

common sense NOUN
le *bon sens* ◇ *Use your common sense!*
Sers-toi de ton bon sens!

to **communicate** VERB
communiquer

communication NOUN
la *communication*

communion NOUN
la *communion* ◇ *my First Communion*
ma première communion

communism NOUN
le *communisme*

communist NOUN
see also communist ADJECTIVE
le/la *communiste*

communist ADJECTIVE
see also communist NOUN
communiste
- **the Communist Party** le Parti
communiste

community NOUN
la *communauté*

to **commute** VERB
faire la navette ◇ *She commutes
between Liss and London.* Elle fait la
navette entre Liss et Londres.

compact disc NOUN
le *disque compact*
• **a compact disc player** une platine laser
companion NOUN
le *compagnon*
la *compagne*
company NOUN
[1] la *société* ◇ *He works for a big company.* Il travaille pour une grosse société.
[2] la *compagnie* ◇ *an insurance company* une compagnie d'assurance ◇ *a theatre company* une compagnie théâtrale
• **to keep somebody company** tenir compagnie à quelqu'un ◇ *I'll keep you company.* Je vais te tenir compagnie.
comparatively ADVERB
relativement
to **compare** VERB
comparer ◇ *People always compare him with his brother.* On le compare toujours à son frère.
• **compared with** en comparaison de ◇ *Oxford is small compared with London.* Oxford est une petite ville en comparaison de Londres.
comparison NOUN
la *comparaison*
compartment NOUN
le *compartiment*
compass NOUN
la *boussole*
compensation NOUN
l' *indemnité* FEM ◇ *They got £2000 compensation.* Ils ont reçu une indemnité de deux mille livres.
compere NOUN
l' *animateur* MASC
l' *animatrice* FEM
o **compete** VERB
participer ◇ *I'm competing in the marathon.* Je participe au marathon.
• **to compete for something** se disputer quelque chose ◇ *There are 50 students competing for 6 places.* Ils sont cinquante étudiants à se disputer six places.
competent ADJECTIVE
compétent
competition NOUN
le *concours* ◇ *a singing competition* un concours de chant
competitor NOUN
le *concurrent*
la *concurrente*
o **complain** VERB
se plaindre ◇ *I'm going to complain to the manager.* Je vais me plaindre au

directeur. ◇ *We complained about the noise.* Nous nous sommes plaints du bruit.
complaint NOUN
la *plainte* ◇ *There were lots of complaints about the food.* Il y a eu beaucoup de plaintes à propos de la nourriture.
complete ADJECTIVE
complet MASC
complète FEM
completely ADVERB
complètement
complexion NOUN
le *teint*
complicated ADJECTIVE
compliqué
compliment NOUN
see also compliment VERB
le *compliment*
to **compliment** VERB
see also compliment NOUN
complimenter ◇ *They complimented me on my French.* Ils m'ont complimenté sur mon français.
composer NOUN
le *compositeur*
la *compositrice*
comprehensive school NOUN
[1] le *collège*
[2] le *lycée*
In France pupils go to a collège between the ages of 11 and 15, and then to a lycée until the age of 18.
compromise NOUN
le *compromis* ◇ *We reached a compromise.* Nous sommes parvenus à un compromis.
compulsory ADJECTIVE
obligatoire
computer NOUN
l' *ordinateur* MASC
computer game NOUN
le *jeu électronique*
(les *jeux électroniques* PL)
computer programmer NOUN
le *programmeur*
la *programmeuse*
◇ *She's a computer programmer.* Elle est programmeuse.
computing NOUN
l' *informatique* FEM
to **concentrate** VERB
se concentrer ◇ *I couldn't concentrate.* Je n'arrivais pas à me concentrer.
concentration NOUN
la *concentration*
concerned ADJECTIVE
• **to be concerned** s'inquiéter ◇ *His*

mother is concerned about him. Sa mère s'inquiète à son sujet.

* **as far as I'm concerned** en ce qui me concerne

concert NOUN
le *concert*

concrete NOUN
le *béton*

condition NOUN
1 la *condition* ◦ *I'll do it, on one condition...* Je veux bien le faire, à une condition...
2 l' *état* MASC ◦ *in good condition* en bon état

conditional NOUN
le *conditionnel*

conditioner NOUN
le *baume démêlant* (for hair)

condom NOUN
le *préservatif*

to **conduct** VERB
diriger (orchestra)

conductor NOUN
le *chef d'orchestre*

cone NOUN
le *cornet* ◦ *an ice-cream cone* un cornet de glace

conference NOUN
la *conférence*

to **confess** VERB
avouer ◦ *He finally confessed.* Il a fini par avouer. ◦ *He confessed to the murder.* Il a avoué avoir commis le meurtre.

confession NOUN
la *confession*

confidence NOUN
1 la *confiance* ◦ *I've got confidence in you.* J'ai confiance en toi.
2 l' *assurance* FEM ◦ *She lacks confidence.* Elle manque d'assurance.

confident ADJECTIVE
sûr ◦ *I'm confident everything will be okay.* Je suis sûr que tout ira bien.
* **She's seems quite confident.** Elle a l'air sûre d'elle.

confidential ADJECTIVE
confidentiel MASC
confidentielle FEM

to **confirm** VERB
confirmer (booking)

confirmation NOUN
la *confirmation*

conflict NOUN
le *conflit*

to **confuse** VERB
* **to confuse somebody** embrouiller les idées de quelqu'un ◦ *Don't confuse me!* Ne m'embrouille pas les idées!

confused ADJECTIVE
désorienté

confusing ADJECTIVE
* **The traffic signs are confusing.** Les panneaux de signalisation ne sont pas clairs.

confusion NOUN
la *confusion*

to **congratulate** VERB
féliciter ◦ *My friends congratulated me on passing the test.* Mes amis m'ont félicité d'avoir réussi à l'examen.

congratulations PL NOUN
les *félicitations* FEM PL ◦ *Congratulations on your new job!* Félicitations pour votre nouveau poste!

conjurer NOUN
le *prestidigitateur*

connection NOUN
1 le *rapport* ◦ *There's no connection between the two events.* Il n'y a aucun rapport entre les deux événements.
2 le *contact* (electrical) ◦ *There's a loose connection.* Il y a un mauvais contact.
3 la *correspondance* (of trains, planes) ◦ *We missed our connection.* Nous avons raté la correspondance.

to **conquer** VERB
conquérir

conscience NOUN
la *conscience*

conscious ADJECTIVE
conscient

consciousness NOUN
la *connaissance*
* **to lose consciousness** perdre connaissance ◦ *I lost consciousness.* J'ai perdu connaissance.

consequently ADVERB
par conséquent

conservation NOUN
la *protection*

conservative ADJECTIVE
see also conservative NOUN
conservateur MASC
conservatrice FEM
* **the Conservative Party** le Parti conservateur

Conservative NOUN
see also conservative ADJECTIVE
le *conservateur*
la *conservatrice*
* **to vote Conservative** voter conservateur
* **the Conservatives** les conservateurs

conservatory NOUN
le *jardin d'hiver*

to **consider** VERB
1 *considérer* ◦ *He considers it a waste*

of time. Il considère que c'est une perte de temps.

2 *envisager* ◇ *We considered cancelling our holiday.* Nous avons envisagé d'annuler nos vacances.

▸ **I'm considering the idea.** J'y songe.

considerate ADJECTIVE
délicat

considering PREPOSITION
1 *étant donné* ◇ *Considering we were there for a month...* Étant donné que nous étions là pour un mois...
2 *tout compte fait* ◇ *I got a good mark, considering.* J'ai eu une bonne note, tout compte fait.

to **consist** VERB
▸ **to consist of** être composé de ◇ *The band consists of three guitarists and a drummer.* Le groupe est composé de trois guitaristes et un batteur.

consonant NOUN
la *consonne*

constant ADJECTIVE
constant

constantly ADVERB
constamment

constipated ADJECTIVE
constipé

to **construct** VERB
construire

construction NOUN
la *construction*

to **consult** VERB
consulter

contact NOUN
see also contact VERB
le *contact* ◇ *I'm in contact with her.* Je suis en contact avec elle.

to **contact** VERB
see also contact NOUN
joindre ◇ *Where can we contact you?* Où pouvons-nous vous joindre?

contact lenses PL NOUN
les *verres de contact* MASC PL

to **contain** VERB
contenir

container NOUN
le *récipient*

contest NOUN
le *concours*

contestant NOUN
le *concurrent*
la *concurrente*

context NOUN
le *contexte*

continent NOUN
le *continent* ◇ *How many continents are there?* Combien y a-t-il de continents?

▸ **the Continent** l'Europe FEM ◇ *I've never been to the Continent.* Je ne suis jamais allé en Europe.

continental breakfast NOUN
le *petit déjeuner à la française*

to **continue** VERB
1 *continuer* ◇ *She continued talking to her friend.* Elle a continué à parler à son amie.
2 *reprendre* (*after interruption*) ◇ *We continued working after lunch.* Nous avons repris le travail après le déjeuner.

continuous ADJECTIVE
continu

▸ **continuous assessment** le contrôle continu

contraceptive NOUN
le *contraceptif*

contract NOUN
le *contrat*

to **contradict** VERB
contredire

contrary NOUN
le *contraire*

▸ **on the contrary** au contraire

contrast NOUN
le *contraste*

to **contribute** VERB
1 *contribuer* (*to success, achievement*) ◇ *The treaty will contribute to world peace.* Le traité va contribuer à la paix dans le monde.
2 *participer* (*share in*) ◇ *He didn't contribute to the discussion.* Il n'a pas participé à la discussion.
3 *donner* (*give*) ◇ *She contributed £10.* Elle a donné dix livres.

contribution NOUN
la *contribution*

control NOUN
see also control VERB
le *contrôle*

▸ **to lose control** (*of vehicle*) perdre le contrôle ◇ *He lost control of the car.* Il a perdu le contrôle de son véhicule.

▸ **the controls** les commandes FEM (*of machine*)

▸ **to be in control** être maître de la situation

▸ **to keep control** (*of people*) se faire obéir ◇ *He can't keep control of the class.* Il n'arrive pas à se faire obéir de sa classe.

▸ **out of control** (*child, class*) déchaîné

to **control** VERB
see also control NOUN
1 *diriger* (*country, organization*)
2 *se faire obéir de* ◇ *He can't control the class.* Il n'arrive pas à se faire obéir de sa classe.

3 *maîtriser* ◇ *I couldn't control the horse.* Je ne suis pas arrivé à maîtriser le cheval.

◆ **to control oneself** se contrôler

controversial ADJECTIVE
controversé ◇ *a controversial book* un livre controversé

convenient ADJECTIVE
bien situé (place) ◇ *The hotel's convenient for the airport.* L'hôtel est bien situé par rapport à l'aéroport.

◆ **It's not a convenient time for me.** C'est une heure qui ne m'arrange pas.

◆ **Would Monday be convenient for you?** Est-ce que lundi vous conviendrait?

conventional ADJECTIVE
conventionnel MASC
conventionnelle FEM

convent school NOUN
l' *institution religieuse* FEM

conversation NOUN
la *conversation* ◇ *a French conversation class* un cours de conversation française

to **convert** VERB
transformer ◇ *We've converted the loft into a spare room.* Nous avons transformé le grenier en chambre d'amis.

to **convict** VERB
reconnaître coupable ◇ *He was convicted of the murder.* Il a été reconnu coupable du meurtre.

to **convince** VERB
persuader ◇ *I'm not convinced.* Je n'en suis pas persuadé.

to **cook** VERB
see also **cook** NOUN
1 *faire la cuisine* ◇ *I can't cook.* Je ne sais pas faire la cuisine.
2 *préparer* ◇ *She's cooking lunch.* Elle est en train de préparer le déjeuner.
3 *faire cuire* ◇ *Cook the pasta for 10 minutes.* Faites cuire les pâtes pendant dix minutes.

◆ **to be cooked** être cuit ◇ *When the potatoes are cooked...* Lorsque les pommes de terre sont cuites...

cook NOUN
see also **cook** VERB
le *cuisinier*
la *cuisinière*
◇ *Matthew's an excellent cook.* Matthew est un excellent cuisinier.

cookbook NOUN
le *livre de cuisine*

cooker NOUN
la *cuisinière* ◇ *a gas cooker* une cuisinière à gaz

cookery NOUN
la *cuisine*

cooking NOUN
la *cuisine* ◇ *I like cooking.* J'aime bien faire la cuisine.

cool ADJECTIVE
frais MASC
fraîche FEM
◇ *a cool place* un endroit frais

◆ **to stay cool** (keep calm) garder son calme ◇ *He stayed cool.* Il a gardé son calme.

cooperation NOUN
la *coopération*

cop NOUN
le *flic* (informal)

to **cope** VERB
se débrouiller ◇ *It was hard, but we coped.* C'était dur, mais nous nous sommes débrouillés.

◆ **to cope with** faire face à ◇ *She's got a lot of problems to cope with.* Elle doit faire face à de nombreux problèmes.

copper NOUN
1 le *cuivre* ◇ *a copper bracelet* un bracelet en cuivre
2 le *flic* (informal: policeman)

copy NOUN
see also **copy** VERB
1 la *copie* (of letter, document)
2 l' *exemplaire* MASC (of book)

to **copy** VERB
see also **copy** NOUN
copier ◇ *The teacher accused him of copying.* Le professeur l'a accusé d'avoir copié.

cork NOUN
1 le *bouchon* (of bottle)
2 le *liège* (material) ◇ *a cork table mat* un set de table en liège

corkscrew NOUN
le *tire-bouchon*

corn NOUN
1 le *blé* (wheat)
2 le *maïs* (sweetcorn)

◆ **corn on the cob** l'épi de maïs MASC

corner NOUN
1 le *coin* ◇ *in a corner of the room* dans un coin de la pièce

◆ **the shop on the corner** la boutique au coin de la rue

◆ **He lives just round the corner.** Il habite tout près d'ici.
2 le *corner* (in football)

cornet NOUN
1 le *cornet à pistons* ◇ *He plays the cornet.* Il joue du cornet à pistons.
2 le *cornet* (ice cream)

cornflakes PL NOUN
les *corn-flakes* MASC PL

Cornwall NOUN
la *Cornouailles*
+ **in Cornwall** en Cornouailles
corporal NOUN
le *caporal*
corporal punishment NOUN
le *châtiment corporel*
corpse NOUN
le *cadavre*
correct ADJECTIVE
see also correct VERB
exact ◇ *That's correct.* C'est
exact.
+ **the correct choice** le bon choix
+ **the correct answer** la bonne réponse
to **correct** VERB
see also correct ADJECTIVE
corriger
correction NOUN
la *correction*
corridor NOUN
le *couloir*
corruption NOUN
la *corruption*
Corsica NOUN
la *Corse*
+ **in Corsica** en Corse
cosmetics PL NOUN
les *produits de beauté* MASC PL
to **cost** VERB
see also cost NOUN
coûter ◇ *The meal costs a hundred
francs.* Le repas coûte cent francs.
◇ *How much does it cost?* Combien
est-ce que ça coûte? ◇ *It costs too much.*
Ça coûte trop cher.
cost NOUN
see also cost VERB
le *coût*
+ **the cost of living** le coût de la vie
+ **at all costs** à tout prix
costume NOUN
le *costume*
cosy ADJECTIVE
douillet MASC
douillette FEM
cot NOUN
le *lit d'enfant*
cottage NOUN
le *cottage*
+ **a thatched cottage** une chaumière
cotton NOUN
le *coton* ◇ *a cotton shirt* une chemise
en coton
+ **cotton wool** le coton hydrophile
couch NOUN
le *canapé*
couchette NOUN
la *couchette*

to **cough** VERB
see also cough NOUN
tousser
cough NOUN
see also cough VERB
la *toux* ◇ *a bad cough* une mauvaise
toux
+ **I've got a cough.** Je tousse.
could VERB see **can**
council NOUN
le *conseil*
The nearest French equivalent of a local council
would be a conseil municipal, which
administers a commune.
+ **He's on the council.** Il fait partie du
conseil municipal.
+ **a council estate** une cité HLM
+ **a council house** une HLM
HLM stands for habitation à loyer modéré
which means "low-rent home".
councillor NOUN
+ **She's a local councillor.** Elle fait partie
du conseil municipal.
to **count** VERB
compter
+ **to count on** compter sur ◇ *You can
count on me.* Tu peux compter sur
moi.
counter NOUN
1 le *comptoir* (in shop)
2 le *guichet* (in post office, bank)
3 le *jeton* (in game)
country NOUN
1 le *pays* ◇ *the border between the two
countries* la frontière entre les deux pays
2 la *campagne* ◇ *I live in the country.*
J'habite à la campagne.
+ **country dancing** la danse folklorique
countryside NOUN
la *campagne*
county NOUN
le *comté*
The nearest French equivalent of a county would
be a département.
+ **the county council**
The nearest French equivalent of a county council
would be a conseil général, which administers
a département.
couple NOUN
le *couple* ◇ *the couple who live next
door* le couple qui habite à côté
+ **a couple** deux ◇ *a couple of hours*
deux heures
+ **Could you wait a couple of minutes?**
Pourriez-vous attendre quelques
minutes?
courage NOUN
le *courage*
courier NOUN

1 (for tourists)
l' *accompagnateur* MASC
l' *accompagnatrice* FEM
2 (delivery service)
le *coursier* ◇ They sent it by courier. Ils l'ont envoyé par coursier.

course NOUN
1 le *cours* ◇ a French course un cours de français ◇ to go on a course suivre un cours
2 le *plat* ◇ the main course le plat principal
➤ **the first course** l'entrée FEM
3 le *terrain* ◇ a golf course un terrain de golf
➤ **of course** bien sûr ◇ Do you love me? – Of course I do! Tu m'aimes? – Bien sûr que oui!

court NOUN
1 (of law)
le *tribunal*
(les *tribunaux* PL)
◇ He was in court last week. Il est passé devant le tribunal la semaine dernière.
2 (tennis)
le *court* ◇ There are tennis and squash courts. Il y a des courts de tennis et de squash.

courtyard NOUN
la *cour*

cousin NOUN
le *cousin*
la *cousine*

cover NOUN
see also cover VERB
1 la *couverture* (of book)
2 la *housse* (of duvet)

to **cover** VERB
see also cover NOUN
1 *couvrir* ◇ My face was covered with mosquito bites. J'avais le visage couvert de piqûres de moustique.
2 *prendre en charge* ◇ Our insurance didn't cover it. Notre assurance ne l'a pas pris en charge.
➤ **to cover up a scandal** étouffer un scandale

cow NOUN
la *vache*

coward NOUN
le *lâche* ◇ She's a coward. Elle est lâche.

cowardly ADJECTIVE
lâche

cowboy NOUN
le *cow-boy*

crab NOUN
le *crabe*

crack NOUN
see also crack VERB

1 la *fissure* (in wall)
2 la *fêlure* (in cup, window)
3 le *crack* (drug)
➤ **I'll have a crack at it.** Je vais tenter le coup.

to **crack** VERB
see also crack NOUN
casser (nut, egg)
➤ **to crack a joke** sortir une blague

cracked ADJECTIVE
fêlé (cup, window)

cracker NOUN
1 le *cracker* (biscuit)
2 le *diablotin* (Christmas cracker)

cradle NOUN
le *berceau*
(les *berceaux* PL)

craft NOUN
les *travaux manuels* MASC PL ◇ We do craft at school. Nous avons des cours de travaux manuels à l'école.
➤ **a craft centre** un centre artisanal

craftsman NOUN
l' *artisan* MASC

to **cram** VERB
1 *entasser* ◇ We crammed our stuff into the boot. Nous avons entassé nos affaires dans le coffre.
2 *bachoter* (for exams)

to **crash** VERB
see also crash NOUN
avoir un accident ◇ He's crashed his car. Il a eu un accident de voiture.
➤ **The plane crashed.** L'avion s'est écrasé.

crash NOUN
see also crash VERB
1 la *collision* (of car)
2 l' *accident* MASC (of plane)
➤ **a crash helmet** un casque
➤ **a crash course** un cours intensif

to **crawl** VERB
see also crawl NOUN
marcher à quatre pattes (baby)

crawl NOUN
see also crawl VERB
le *crawl* ◇ to do the crawl nager le crawl

crazy ADJECTIVE
fou MASC
folle FEM

cream ADJECTIVE
see also cream NOUN
crème MASC, FEM, PL (colour)

cream NOUN
see also cream ADJECTIVE
la *crème* ◇ strawberries and cream les fraises à la crème
➤ **a cream cake** un gâteau à la crème
➤ **cream cheese** le fromage à la crème

♦ sun cream la crème solaire

crease NOUN
le *pli*

creased ADJECTIVE
froissé

to **create** VERB
créer

creation NOUN
la *création*

creative ADJECTIVE
créatif MASC
créative FEM

creature NOUN
la *créature*

crèche NOUN
la *crèche*

credit NOUN
le *crédit* ◇ **on credit** à crédit

credit card NOUN
la *carte de crédit*

cress NOUN
le *cresson*

crew NOUN
[1] l' *équipage* MASC (of ship, plane)
[2] l' *équipe* FEM ◇ **a film crew** une
équipe de tournage

crew cut NOUN
les *cheveux en brosse* MASC PL

cricket NOUN
[1] le *cricket* ◇ **I play cricket** Je joue au
cricket.
♦ **a cricket bat** une batte de cricket
[2] le *grillon* (insect)

crime NOUN
[1] le *délit* ◇ **Murder is a crime.** Le
meurtre est un délit.
[2] la *criminalité* (lawlessness)
♦ **Crime is rising.** La criminalité
augmente.

criminal NOUN
see also criminal ADJECTIVE
le *criminel*
la *criminelle*

criminal ADJECTIVE
see also criminal NOUN
criminel MASC
criminelle FEM
◇ **It's criminal!** C'est criminel!
♦ **It's a criminal offence.** C'est un crime
puni par la loi.
♦ **to have a criminal record** avoir un
casier judiciaire

crisis NOUN
la *crise*

crisp ADJECTIVE
croquant (food)

crisps PL NOUN
les *chips* FEM PL ◇ **a bag of crisps** un
paquet de chips

criterion NOUN
le *critère*

critic NOUN
le *critique*

critical ADJECTIVE
critique
♦ **a critical remark** une critique

criticism NOUN
la *critique*

to **criticize** VERB
critiquer

Croatia NOUN
la *Croatie*
♦ **in Croatia** en Croatie

to **crochet** VERB
crocheter

crocodile NOUN
le *crocodile*

crook NOUN
l' *escroc* MASC (criminal)

crop NOUN
la *récolte* ◇ **a good crop of apples** une
bonne récolte de pommes

cross NOUN
see also CROSS ADJECTIVE, VERB
la *croix*

cross ADJECTIVE
see also CROSS NOUN, VERB
fâché ◇ **to be cross about something**
être fâché à propos de quelque chose

to **cross** VERB
see also CROSS ADJECTIVE, NOUN
traverser (street, bridge)
♦ **to cross out** barrer
♦ **to cross over** traverser

cross-country NOUN
le *cross* (race)
♦ **cross-country skiing** le ski de fond

crossing NOUN
[1] la *traversée* (by boat) ◇ **the crossing
from Dover to Calais** la traversée de
Douvres à Calais
[2] le *passage clouté* (for pedestrians)

crossroads NOUN
le *carrefour*

crossword NOUN
les *mots croisés* MASC PL ◇ **I like doing
crosswords.** J'aime faire les mots croisés.

crow NOUN
le *corbeau*
(les *corbeaux* PL)

crowd NOUN
la *foule*
♦ **the crowd** (at sports match) les spectateurs

crowded ADJECTIVE
bondé

crown NOUN
la *couronne*

crucifix NOUN

le *crucifix*

crude ADJECTIVE
(*vulgar*)
grossier MASC
grossière FEM

cruel ADJECTIVE
cruel MASC
cruelle FEM

cruise NOUN
la *croisière* ◇ *to go on a cruise* faire
une croisière

crumb NOUN
la *miette*

to **crush** VERB
écraser

crutch NOUN
la *béquille*

to **cry** VERB
pleurer ◇ *The baby's crying.* Le bébé
pleure.

crystal NOUN
le *cristal*
(les *cristaux* PL)

CTC NOUN (= *city technology college*)
le *collège technique*

cub NOUN
1 (*animal*)
le *petit*
2 (*scout*)
le *louveteau*
(les *louveteaux* PL)

cube NOUN
le *cube*

cubic ADJECTIVE
✦ **a cubic metre** un mètre cube

cucumber NOUN
le *concombre*

cue NOUN
la *queue de billard* (*for snooker, pool*)

culottes PL NOUN
la *jupe-culotte* SING

culture NOUN
la *culture*

cunning ADJECTIVE
1 (*person*)
rusé
2 (*plan, idea*)
astucieux MASC
astucieuse FEM

cup NOUN
1 la *tasse* ◇ *a china cup* une tasse en
porcelaine
✦ **a cup of coffee** un café
2 la *coupe* (*trophy*)

cupboard NOUN
le *placard*

to **cure** VERB
see also **cure** NOUN
guérir

cure NOUN
see also **cure** VERB
le *remède*

curious ADJECTIVE
curieux MASC
curieuse FEM

curly ADJECTIVE
1 *bouclé* (*loosely curled*)
2 *frisé* (*tightly curled*)

currant NOUN
le *raisin de Corinthe* (*dried fruit*)

currency NOUN
la *devise* ◇ *foreign currency* les devises
étrangères

current NOUN
see also **current** ADJECTIVE
le *courant* ◇ *The current is very strong.*
Le courant est très fort.

current ADJECTIVE
see also **current** NOUN
actuel MASC
actuelle FEM
◇ *the current situation* la situation
actuelle

current affairs PL NOUN
l' *actualité* FEM

curriculum NOUN
le *programme*

curriculum vitae NOUN
le *curriculum vitae*

curry NOUN
le *curry*

curse NOUN
la *malédiction* (*spell*)

curtain NOUN
le *rideau*
(les *rideaux* PL)
✦ **to draw the curtains** tirer les rideaux

cushion NOUN
le *coussin*

custard NOUN
la *crème anglaise* (*for pouring*)

custody NOUN
la *garde* (*of child*)

custom NOUN
la *coutume* MASC ◇ *It's an old custom.*
C'est une ancienne coutume.

customer NOUN
le *client*
la *cliente*

customs PL NOUN
la *douane* SING

customs officer NOUN
le *douanier*
la *douanière*

cut NOUN
see also **cut** VERB
1 la *coupure* ◇ *He's got a cut on his
forehead.* Il a une coupure au front.

2 la *coupe* ◇ *a cut and blow-dry* une coupe brushing
3 la *réduction* (*in price, spending*)

to **cut** VERB

see also cut NOUN

1 *couper* ◇ *I'll cut some bread.* Je vais couper du pain.

◆ **to cut oneself** se couper ◇ *I cut my foot on a piece of glass.* Je me suis coupé au pied avec un morceau de verre.
2 *réduire* (*price, spending*)

◆ **to cut down** abattre (*tree*)
◆ **to cut off** couper ◇ *The electricity was cut off.* L'électricité a été coupée.
◆ **to cut up** hacher (*vegetables, meat*)

cutlery NOUN
les *couverts* MASC PL

CV NOUN
le *C.V.*

to **cycle** VERB

see also cycle NOUN

faire de la bicyclette ◇ *I like cycling.* J'aime faire de la bicyclette.

◆ **I cycle to school.** Je vais à l'école à bicyclette.

cycle NOUN

see also cycle VERB

la *bicyclette*

◆ **a cycle ride** une promenade à bicyclette

cycling NOUN
le *cyclisme*

cyclist NOUN
le/la *cycliste*

cylinder NOUN
le *cylindre*

Cyprus NOUN
Chypre

◆ **in Cyprus** à Chypre
◆ **We went to Cyprus.** Nous sommes allés à Chypre.

Czech ADJECTIVE

see also Czech NOUN

tchèque

◆ **the Czech Republic** la République tchèque

Czech NOUN

see also Czech ADJECTIVE

1 le/la *Tchèque* (*person*)
2 le *tchèque* (*language*)

D

dad NOUN
1. le *père* ◇ *my dad* mon père ◇ *his dad* son père
2. le *papa*
*Use **papa** only when you are talking to your father or using it as his name; otherwise use **père**.*
- **Dad!** Papa! ◇ *I'll ask Dad.* Je vais demander à papa.

daffodil NOUN
la *jonquille*

daft ADJECTIVE
idiot

daily ADJECTIVE, ADVERB
1. *quotidien* MASC
quotidienne FEM
◇ *It's part of my daily routine.* Ça fait partie de mes occupations quotidiennes.
2. *tous les jours* ◇ *The pool is open daily from 9 a.m. to 6 p.m.* La piscine est ouverte tous les jours de neuf heures à dix-huit heures.

dairy NOUN
la *crémerie* (*shop*)

dairy products PL NOUN
les *produits laitiers* MASC PL

daisy NOUN
la *pâquerette*

dam NOUN
le *barrage*

damage NOUN
see also damage VERB
les *dégâts* MASC PL ◇ *The storm did a lot of damage.* La tempête a fait beaucoup de dégâts.

to **damage** VERB
see also damage NOUN
endommager

damn NOUN
see also damn ADJECTIVE
- **I don't give a damn!** Je m'en fiche! (*informal*)
- **Damn!** Zut! (*informal*)

damn ADJECTIVE, ADVERB
see also damn NOUN
- **It's a damn nuisance!** Quelle barbe!

damp ADJECTIVE
humide

dance NOUN
see also dance VERB
1. la *danse* ◇ *The last dance was a waltz.* La dernière danse était une valse.
2. le *bal* ◇ *Are you going to the dance tonight?* Tu vas au bal ce soir?

to **dance** VERB
see also dance NOUN
danser

- **to go dancing** aller danser ◇ *Let's go dancing!* Si on allait danser?

dancer NOUN
le *danseur*
la *danseuse*

dandruff NOUN
les *pellicules* FEM PL

Dane NOUN
1. le *Danois*
2. la *Danoise*

danger NOUN
le *danger*
- **in danger** en danger ◇ *His life is in danger.* Sa vie est en danger.
- **to be in danger of** risquer de ◇ *We were in danger of missing the plane.* Nous risquions de rater l'avion.

dangerous ADJECTIVE
dangereux MASC
dangereuse FEM

Danish ADJECTIVE
see also Danish NOUN
danois

Danish NOUN
see also Danish ADJECTIVE
le *danois* (*language*)

to **dare** VERB
oser
- **to dare to do something** oser faire quelque chose ◇ *I didn't dare to tell my parents.* Je n'ai pas osé le dire à mes parents.
- **I dare say it'll be okay.** Je suppose que ça va aller.

daring ADJECTIVE
audacieux MASC
audacieuse FEM

dark ADJECTIVE
see also dark NOUN
1. *sombre* (*room*) ◇ *It's dark.* (*inside*) Il fait sombre.
- **It's dark outside.** Il fait nuit dehors.
- **It's getting dark.** La nuit tombe.
2. *foncé* (*colour*) ◇ *She's got dark hair.* Elle a les cheveux foncés. ◇ *a dark green sweater* un pull vert foncé

dark NOUN
see also dark ADJECTIVE
le *noir* ◇ *I'm afraid of the dark.* J'ai peur du noir.
- **after dark** après la tombée de la nuit

darkness NOUN
l' *obscurité* FEM ◇ *The room was in darkness.* La chambre était dans l'obscurité.

darling NOUN

le _chéri_
la _chérie_
◇ _Thank you, darling!_ Merci, chéri!

dart NOUN
la _fléchette_ ◇ _to play darts_ jouer aux
fléchettes

data PL NOUN
les _données_ FEM PL

database NOUN
la _base de données_ (_on computer_)

date NOUN
[1] la _date_ ◇ _my date of birth_ ma date de
naissance
➤ **What's the date today?** Quel jour
sommes-nous?
➤ **to have a date with somebody** sortir
avec quelqu'un ◇ _She's got a date with
Ian tonight._ Elle sort avec Ian ce soir.
➤ **out of date (1)** (_passport_) périmé
➤ **out of date (2)** (_technology_) dépassé
➤ **out of date (3)** (_clothes_) démodé
[2] la _datte_ (_fruit_)

daughter NOUN
la _fille_

daughter-in-law NOUN
la _belle-fille_
(les _belles-filles_ PL)

dawn NOUN
l' _aube_ FEM ◇ _at dawn_ à l'aube

day NOUN
Use jour _to refer to the whole 24-hour period._
Journée _only refers to the time when you are
awake._
[1] le _jour_ ◇ _We stayed in Nice for three
days._ Nous sommes restés trois jours à
Nice.
➤ **every day** tous les jours
[2] la _journée_ ◇ _during the day_ dans la
journée ◇ _I stayed at home all day._ Je
suis resté à la maison toute la journée.
➤ **the day before** la veille ◇ _the day
before my birthday_ la veille de mon
anniversaire
➤ **the day after** le lendemain
➤ **the day after tomorrow** après-demain
◇ _We're leaving the day after tomorrow._
Nous partons après-demain.
➤ **the day before yesterday** avant hier
◇ _He arrived the day before yesterday._ Il
est arrivé avant-hier.

dead ADJECTIVE, ADVERB
[1] _mort_ ◇ _He was already dead when
the doctor came._ Il était déjà mort
quand le docteur est arrivé.
➤ **He was shot dead.** Il a été abattu.
[2] _absolument_ (_totally_) ◇ _You're dead
right!_ Tu as absolument raison!
➤ **dead on time** à l'heure pile ◇ _The train
arrived dead on time._ Le train est arrivé à

l'heure pile.

dead end NOUN
l' _impasse_ FEM

deadline NOUN
la _date limite_ ◇ _The deadline for entries
is May 2nd._ La date limite d'inscription
est le deux mai.

deaf ADJECTIVE
sourd

deafening ADJECTIVE
assourdissant

deal NOUN
see also deal VERB
le _marché_
➤ **It's a deal!** Marché conclu!
➤ **a great deal** beaucoup ◇ _a great deal
of money_ beaucoup d'argent

to **deal** VERB
see also deal NOUN
donner (_cards_) ◇ _It's your turn to deal._
C'est à toi de donner.
➤ **to deal with something** s'occuper de
quelque chose ◇ _He promised to deal
with it immediately._ Il a promis de s'en
occuper immédiatement.

dear ADJECTIVE
[1] _cher_ MASC
chère FEM
◇ _Dear Mrs Duval_ Chère Madame Duval
➤ **Dear Sir/Madam** (_in a circular_) Madame,
Monsieur
[2] (_expensive_)
coûteux MASC
coûteuse FEM

death NOUN
la _mort_ ◇ _after his death_ après sa mort
➤ **I was bored to death.** Je me suis ennuyé
à mourir.

debate NOUN
see also debate VERB
le _débat_

to **debate** VERB
see also debate NOUN
débattre

debt NOUN
la _dette_ ◇ _He's got a lot of debts._ Il a
beaucoup de dettes.
➤ **to be in debt** avoir des dettes

decade NOUN
la _décennie_

decaffeinated ADJECTIVE
décaféiné

to **deceive** VERB
tromper

December NOUN
décembre MASC
➤ **in December** en décembre

decent ADJECTIVE
convenable ◇ _a decent education_ une

to **decide** VERB

1 *décider* ◇ *I decided to write to her.* J'ai décidé de lui écrire. ◇ *I decided not to go.* J'ai décidé de ne pas y aller.

2 *se décider* ◇ *I can't decide.* Je n'arrive pas à me décider. ◇ *Haven't you decided yet?* Tu ne t'es pas encore décidé?

decimal ADJECTIVE
décimal ◇ *the decimal system* le système décimal

decision NOUN
la *décision*

- **to make a decision** prendre une décision

decisive ADJECTIVE
décidé (person)

deck NOUN

1 (of ship)
le *pont*

- **on deck** sur le pont

2 (of cards)
le *jeu*
(les *jeux* PL)

deckchair NOUN
la *chaise longue*

to **declare** VERB
déclarer

to **decorate** VERB

1 *décorer* ◇ *I decorated the cake with glacé cherries.* J'ai décoré le gâteau avec des cerises confites.

2 *peindre* (paint)

3 *tapisser* (wallpaper)

decrease NOUN

see also **decrease** VERB

la *diminution* ◇ *a decrease in the number of unemployed people* une diminution du nombre de chômeurs

to **decrease** VERB

see also **decrease** NOUN

diminuer

dedicated ADJECTIVE
dévoué ◇ *a very dedicated teacher* un professeur très dévoué

to **deduct** VERB
déduire

deep ADJECTIVE

1 (water, hole, cut)
profond ◇ *Is it deep?* Est-ce que c'est profond?

- **How deep is the lake?** Quelle est la profondeur du lac?

- **a hole 4 metres deep** un trou de quatre mètres de profondeur

2 (layer)
épais MASC
épaisse FEM

◇ *a deep layer of snow* une épaisse couche de neige ◇ *The snow was really deep.* Il y avait une épaisse couche de neige.

- **He's got a deep voice.** Il a la voix grave.

- **to take a deep breath** respirer à fond

deeply ADVERB
profondément (depressed)

deer NOUN

1 le *cerf* (red deer)

2 le *daim* (fallow deer)

3 le *chevreuil* (roe deer)

defeat NOUN

see also **defeat** VERB

la *défaite*

to **defeat** VERB

see also **defeat** NOUN

battre

defect NOUN
le *défaut*

defence NOUN
la *défense*

to **defend** VERB
défendre

defender NOUN
le *défenseur*

to **define** VERB
définir

definite ADJECTIVE

1 *précis* ◇ *I haven't got any definite plans.* Je n'ai pas de projets précis.

2 *net* MASC
nette FEM
◇ *It's a definite improvement.* Cela constitue une nette amélioration.

3 *sûr* ◇ *Perhaps we'll go to Spain, but it's not definite.* Nous irons peut-être en Espagne, mais ce n'est pas sûr.

- **He was definite about it.** Il a été catégorique.

definitely ADVERB
vraiment ◇ *He's definitely the best player.* C'est vraiment lui le meilleur joueur.

- **He's the best player. – Definitely!** C'est le meilleur joueur. – C'est sûr!

- **I definitely think he'll come.** Je suis sûr qu'il va venir.

definition NOUN
la *définition*

degree NOUN

1 le *degré* ◇ *a temperature of 30 degrees* une température de trente degrés

2 la *licence* ◇ *a degree in English* une licence d'anglais

to **delay** VERB

see also **delay** NOUN

1 *retarder* ◇ *We decided to delay our*

departure. Nous avons décidé de
retarder notre départ.

[2] *tarder* ◦ Don't delay! Ne tarde pas!
* **to be delayed** être retardé ◦ Our flight
was delayed. Notre vol a été retardé.

delay NOUN
see also delay VERB
le *délai* ◦ without delay sans délai

to **delete** VERB
effacer (on computer, tape)

deliberate ADJECTIVE
délibéré

deliberately ADVERB
exprès ◦ She did it deliberately. Elle l'a
fait exprès.

delicate ADJECTIVE
délicat

delicatessen NOUN
l' *épicerie fine* FEM

delicious ADJECTIVE
délicieux MASC
délicieuse FEM

delighted ADJECTIVE
ravi ◦ He'll be delighted to see you. Il
sera ravi de vous voir.

delightful ADJECTIVE
(meal, evening)
délicieux MASC
délicieuse FEM

to **deliver** VERB
[1] *livrer* ◦ I deliver newspapers. Je
livre les journaux.
[2] *distribuer* (mail)

delivery NOUN
la *livraison*

to **demand** VERB
see also demand NOUN
exiger

demand NOUN
see also demand VERB
la *demande* (for product)

demanding ADJECTIVE
astreignant ◦ It's a very demanding
job. C'est un travail très astreignant.

demo NOUN
la *manif* (protest)

democracy NOUN
la *démocratie*

democratic ADJECTIVE
démocratique

demolish VERB
démolir

demonstrate VERB
[1] *faire une démonstration de* (show)
◦ She demonstrated the technique. Elle a
fait une démonstration de la technique.
[2] *manifester* (protest)
* **to demonstrate against something**
manifester contre quelque chose

demonstration NOUN
[1] la *démonstration* (of method, technique)
[2] la *manifestation* (protest)

demonstrator NOUN (protester)
le *manifestant*
la *manifestante*

denim NOUN
le *jean* ◦ a denim jacket une veste en
jean

denims PL NOUN
le *jean* SING (jeans)

Denmark NOUN
le *Danemark*
* **in Denmark** au Danemark
* **to Denmark** au Danemark

dense ADJECTIVE
[1] (crowd, fog)
dense
[2] (smoke)
épais MASC
épaisse FEM
* **He's so dense!** Il est vraiment bouché!

dent NOUN
see also dent VERB
la *bosse*

to **dent** VERB
see also dent NOUN
cabosser

dental ADJECTIVE
dentaire
* **dental floss** le fil dentaire

dentist NOUN
le/la *dentiste* ◦ Catherine is a dentist.
Catherine est dentiste.

to **deny** VERB
nier ◦ She denied everything. Elle a
tout nié.

deodorant NOUN
le *déodorant*

to **depart** VERB
partir

department NOUN
[1] le *rayon* (in shop) ◦ the shoe
department le rayon chaussures
[2] le *département* (university, school)
◦ the English department le département
d'anglais

department store NOUN
le *grand magasin*

departure NOUN
le *départ*

to **depend** VERB
* **to depend on** dépendre de ◦ The price
depends on the quality. Le prix dépend
de la qualité.
* **depending on the weather** selon le
temps
* **It depends.** Ça dépend.

to **deport** VERB

expulser

deposit NOUN
1. les *arrhes* FEM PL *(part payment)* ◇ *You have to pay a deposit when you book.* Il faut verser des arrhes lors de la réservation.
2. la *caution* *(when hiring something)* ◇ *You get the deposit back when you return the bike.* On vous remboursera la caution quand vous ramènerez le vélo.
3. la *consigne* *(on bottle)*

depressed ADJECTIVE
déprimé ◇ *I'm feeling depressed.* Je suis déprimé.

depressing ADJECTIVE
déprimant

depth NOUN
la *profondeur*

deputy head NOUN
le *directeur adjoint*
la *directrice adjointe*

to **descend** VERB
descendre

to **describe** VERB
décrire

description NOUN
la *description*

desert NOUN
le *désert*

desert island NOUN
l' *île déserte* FEM

to **deserve** VERB
mériter

design NOUN
  see also design VERB
1. la *conception* ◇ *It's a completely new design.* C'est une conception entièrement nouvelle.
2. le *motif* ◇ *a geometric design* un motif géométrique
* **fashion design** le stylisme

to **design** VERB
  see also design NOUN
dessiner *(clothes, furniture)*

designer NOUN
le/la *styliste* *(of clothes)*
* **designer clothes** les vêtements griffés

desire NOUN
  see also desire VERB
le *désir*

to **desire** VERB
  see also desire NOUN
désirer

desk NOUN
1. *(in office)*
le *bureau*
(les *bureaux* PL)
2. *(for pupil)*
le *pupitre*

3. *(in hotel)*
la *réception*
4. *(at airport)*
le *comptoir*

despair NOUN
le *désespoir*
* **I was in despair.** J'étais désespéré.

desperate ADJECTIVE
désespéré ◇ *a desperate situation* une situation désespérée
* **to get desperate** désespérer ◇ *I was getting desperate.* Je commençais à désespérer.

to **despise** VERB
mépriser

despite PREPOSITION
malgré

dessert NOUN
le *dessert* ◇ *for dessert* comme dessert

destination NOUN
la *destination*

to **destroy** VERB
détruire

destruction NOUN
la *destruction*

detached house NOUN
le *pavillon*

detail NOUN
le *détail* ◇ *in detail* en détail

detailed ADJECTIVE
détaillé

detective NOUN
l' *inspecteur de police*
* **a private detective** un détective privé
* **a detective story** un roman policier

detention NOUN
* **to get a detention** être consigné

detergent NOUN
le *détergent*

determined ADJECTIVE
déterminé
* **to be determined to do something** être déterminé à faire quelque chose ◇ *She's determined to succeed.* Elle est déterminée à réussir

detour NOUN
le *détour*

devaluation NOUN
la *dévaluation*

devastated ADJECTIVE
anéanti ◇ *I was devastated.* J'étais anéanti.

devastating ADJECTIVE
1. *(upsetting)*
accablant
2. *(flood, storm)*
dévastateur MASC
dévastatrice FEM

to **develop** VERB

1 *développer* ◇ to get a film developed faire développer un film
2 *se développer* ◇ Girls develop faster than boys. Les filles se développent plus vite que les garçons.
- **to develop into** se transformer en
◇ The argument developed into a fight. La dispute s'est transformée en bagarre.
- **a developing country** un pays en voie de développement

development NOUN
le *développement* ◇ the latest developments les derniers développements

devil NOUN
le *diable* ◇ Poor devil! Pauvre diable!

to **devise** VERB
concevoir

devoted ADJECTIVE
dévoué ◇ He's completely devoted to her. Il lui est très dévoué.

diabetes NOUN
le *diabète*

diabetic NOUN
le/la *diabétique* ◇ I'm a diabetic. Je suis diabétique.

diagonal ADJECTIVE
diagonal
(*diagonaux* MASC PL)

diagram NOUN
le *diagramme*

to **dial** VERB
composer (*number*)

dialling tone NOUN
la *tonalité*

dialogue NOUN
le *dialogue*

diamond NOUN
le *diamant* ◇ a diamond ring une bague en diamant
- **diamonds** (*at cards*) le carreau SING

diarrhoea NOUN
la *diarrhée* ◇ I've got diarrhoea. J'ai la diarrhée.

diary NOUN
1 l' *agenda* MASC ◇ I've got her phone number in my diary. J'ai son numéro de téléphone dans mon agenda.
2 le *journal*
(les *journaux* PL)
◇ I keep a diary. Je tiens un journal.

dice NOUN
le *dé*

dictation NOUN
la *dictée*

dictionary NOUN
le *dictionnaire*

did VERB *see* do

die VERB

mourir ◇ He died last year. Il est mort l'année dernière.
- **to be dying to do something** mourir d'envie de faire quelque chose ◇ I'm dying to see you. Je meurs d'envie de te voir.

diesel NOUN
1 le *gazole* (*fuel*) ◇ 30 litres of diesel, please. Trente litres de gazole, s'il vous plaît.
2 la *voiture diesel* (*car*) ◇ Our car's a diesel. Nous avons une voiture diesel.

diet NOUN
1 l' *alimentation* FEM ◇ a healthy diet une alimentation saine
2 le *régime* (*for slimming*) ◇ I'm on a diet. Je suis au régime.

difference NOUN
la *différence* ◇ There's not much difference in age between us. Il n'y a pas une grande différence d'âge entre nous.
- **It makes no difference.** Ça revient au même.

different ADJECTIVE
différent ◇ We are very different. Nous sommes très différents. ◇ Paris is different from London. Paris est différent de Londres.

difficult ADJECTIVE
difficile ◇ It's difficult to choose. C'est difficile de choisir.

difficulty NOUN
la *difficulté* ◇ without difficulty sans difficulté
- **to have difficulty doing something** avoir du mal à faire quelque chose

to **dig** VERB
1 *creuser* (*hole*)
2 *bêcher* (*garden*)
- **to dig something up** déterrer quelque chose

digestion NOUN
la *digestion*

digital watch NOUN
la *montre à affichage numérique*

dim ADJECTIVE
1 *faible* (*light*)
2 *limité* (*stupid*)

dimension NOUN
la *dimension*

to **diminish** VERB
diminuer

din NOUN
le *vacarme*

dinghy NOUN
- **a rubber dinghy** un canot pneumatique
- **a sailing dinghy** un dériveur

dining car NOUN

D

PTO

le *wagon-restaurant*
(les *wagons-restaurants* PL)
dining room NOUN
la *salle à manger*
dinner NOUN
1 le *déjeuner* (at midday)
2 le *dîner* (in the evening)
dinner party NOUN
le *dîner*
dinner time NOUN
1 l' *heure du déjeuner* FEM (midday)
2 l' *heure du dîner* FEM (in the evening)
dinosaur NOUN
le *dinosaure*
diploma NOUN
le *diplôme* ◇ a diploma in social work
un diplôme d'assistante sociale
diplomat NOUN
le/la *diplomate*
diplomatic ADJECTIVE
diplomatique
direct ADJECTIVE, ADVERB
see also direct VERB
direct ◇ the most direct route le
chemin le plus direct ◇ You can't fly to
Marseilles direct from Manchester. Il n'y
a pas de vols directs de Manchester à
Marseille.
to **direct** VERB
see also direct ADJECTIVE
1 *réaliser* (film, programme)
2 *mettre en scène* (play, show)
direction NOUN
la *direction* ◇ We're going in the wrong
direction. Nous allons dans la mauvaise
direction.
◆ **to ask somebody for directions**
demander son chemin à quelqu'un
director NOUN
1 (of company)
le *directeur*
la *directrice*
2 (of play)
le *metteur en scène*
(les *metteurs en scène* PL)
3 (of film, programme)
le *réalisateur*
la *réalisatrice*
directory NOUN
l' *annuaire* MASC
dirt NOUN
la *saleté*
dirty ADJECTIVE
sale
◆ **to get dirty** se salir
◆ **to get something dirty** salir quelque chose
disabled ADJECTIVE
handicapé
◆ **the disabled** les handicapés

disadvantage NOUN
le *désavantage*
to **disagree** VERB
◆ **We always disagree.** Nous ne sommes
jamais d'accord.
◆ **I disagree!** Je ne suis pas d'accord!
◆ **He disagrees with me.** Il n'est pas
d'accord avec moi.
disagreement NOUN
le *désaccord*
to **disappear** VERB
disparaître
disappearance NOUN
la *disparition*
disappointed ADJECTIVE
déçu
disappointing ADJECTIVE
décevant
disappointment NOUN
la *déception*
disaster NOUN
le *désastre*
disastrous ADJECTIVE
désastreux MASC
désastreuse FEM
discipline NOUN
la *discipline*
disc jockey NOUN
le *disc-jockey*
disco NOUN
la *soirée disco* ◇ There's a disco at the
school tonight. Il y a une soirée disco à
l'école ce soir.
to **disconnect** VERB
1 *débrancher* (electrical equipment)
2 *couper* (telephone, water supply)
discount NOUN
la *réduction* ◇ a discount for students
une réduction pour les étudiants
to **discourage** VERB
décourager
◆ **to get discouraged** se décourager
◇ Don't get discouraged! Ne te décourage
pas!
to **discover** VERB
découvrir
discrimination NOUN
la *discrimination* ◇ racial
discrimination la discrimination raciale
to **discuss** VERB
1 *discuter de* ◇ I'll discuss it with my
parents. Je vais en discuter avec mes
parents.
2 *discuter sur* (topic) ◇ We discussed
the problem of pollution. Nous avons
discuté du problème de la pollution.
discussion NOUN
la *discussion*
disease NOUN

la *maladie*
disgraceful ADJECTIVE
scandaleux MASC
scandaleuse FEM
to **disguise** VERB
déguiser ◇ *He was disguised as a policeman.* Il était déguisé en policier.
disgusted ADJECTIVE
dégoûté ◇ *I was absolutely disgusted.* J'étais complètement dégoûté.
disgusting ADJECTIVE
[1] *dégoûtant* (*food, smell*) ◇ *It looks disgusting.* Ça a l'air dégoûtant.
[2] *honteux* (*disgraceful*) ◇ *That's disgusting!* C'est honteux!
dish NOUN
le *plat* ◇ *a china dish* un plat en porcelaine ◇ *a vegetarian dish* un plat végétarien
◆ **to do the dishes** faire la vaisselle ◇ *He never does the dishes.* Il ne fait jamais la vaisselle.
dishonest ADJECTIVE
malhonnête
dishwasher NOUN
le *lave-vaisselle*
(les *lave-vaisselle* PL)
disinfectant NOUN
le *désinfectant*
disk NOUN
le *disque*
◆ **a floppy disk** une disquette
◆ **the hard disk** le disque dur
to **dislike** VERB
see also **dislike** NOUN
ne pas aimer ◇ *I really dislike cabbage.* Je n'aime vraiment pas le chou.
dislike NOUN
see also **dislike** VERB
◆ **my likes and dislikes** ce que j'aime et ce que je n'aime pas
to **dismiss** VERB
renvoyer (*employee*)
disobedient ADJECTIVE
désobéissant
display NOUN
see also **display** VERB
l' *étalage* MASC ◇ *There was a lovely display of fruit in the window.* Il y avait un superbe étalage de fruits en vitrine.
◆ **to be on display** être exposé ◇ *Her best paintings were on display.* Ses meilleurs tableaux étaient exposés.
◆ **a firework display** un feu d'artifice
to **display** VERB
see also **display** NOUN
[1] *montrer* ◇ *She proudly displayed her medal.* Elle a montré sa médaille avec fierté.

[2] *exposer* (*in shop window*)
disposable ADJECTIVE
jetable
to **disqualify** VERB
disqualifier
◆ **to be disqualified** être disqualifié ◇ *He was disqualified.* Il a été disqualifié.
to **disrupt** VERB
perturber ◇ *Protesters disrupted the meeting.* Des manifestants ont perturbé la réunion. ◇ *Train services are being disrupted by the strike.* Les horaires de train sont perturbés par la grève.
dissatisfied ADJECTIVE
◆ **We were dissatisfied with the service.** Nous n'étions pas satisfaits du service.
to **dissolve** VERB
dissoudre
distance NOUN
la *distance* ◇ *a distance of 40 kilometres* une distance de quarante kilomètres
◆ **It's within walking distance.** On peut y aller à pied.
◆ **in the distance** au loin
distant ADJECTIVE
lointain ◇ *in the distant future* dans un avenir lointain
distillery NOUN
la *distillerie* ◇ *a whisky distillery* une distillerie de whisky
distinction NOUN
[1] la *distinction* ◇ *to make a distinction between* faire la distinction entre...
[2] la *mention très bien* ◇ *I got a distinction in my piano exam.* J'ai eu la mention très bien à mon examen de piano.
distinctive ADJECTIVE
distinctif MASC
distinctive FEM
to **distract** VERB
distraire
to **distribute** VERB
distribuer
district NOUN
[1] le *quartier* (*of town*)
[2] la *région* (*of country*)
to **disturb** VERB
déranger ◇ *I'm sorry to disturb you.* Je suis désolé de vous déranger.
ditch NOUN
see also **ditch** VERB
le *fossé*
to **ditch** VERB
see also **ditch** NOUN
plaquer (*informal*) ◇ *She's just ditched her boyfriend.* Elle vient de plaquer son copain.

D

dive NOUN
> *see also* **dive** VERB

le *plongeon*

to **dive** VERB
> *see also* **dive** NOUN

plonger

diver NOUN

le *plongeur*
la *plongeuse*

diversion NOUN

la *déviation* (*for traffic*)

to **divide** VERB

1 *diviser* ◇ *Divide the pastry in half.*
Divisez la pâte en deux. ◇ *12 divided by
3 is 4.* Douze divisé par trois égalent
quatre.

2 *se diviser* ◇ *We divided into two
groups.* Nous nous sommes divisés en
deux groupes.

diving NOUN

la *plongée*

◆ **a diving board** un plongeoir

division NOUN

la *division*

divorce NOUN

le *divorce*

divorced ADJECTIVE

divorcé ◇ *My parents are divorced.*
Mes parents sont divorcés.

DIY NOUN

le *bricolage* ◇ *to do DIY* faire du
bricolage ◇ *a DIY shop* un magasin de
bricolage

dizzy ADJECTIVE

◆ **to feel dizzy** avoir la tête qui tourne
◇ *I feel dizzy.* J'ai la tête qui tourne.

DJ NOUN

le *disc-jockey*

to **do** VERB

1 *faire* ◇ *What are you doing this
evening?* Qu'est-ce que tu fais ce soir?
◇ *I do a lot of cycling.* Je fais beaucoup de
vélo. ◇ *I haven't done my homework.* Je
n'ai pas fait mes devoirs. ◇ *She did it by
herself.* Elle l'a fait toute seule. ◇ *I'll do
my best.* Je ferai de mon mieux.

◆ **to do well** marcher bien ◇ *The firm is
doing well.* L'entreprise marche bien.
◇ *She's doing well at school.* Ses études
marchent bien.

2 *aller* (*be enough*) ◇ *It's not very good,
but it'll do.* Ce n'est pas très bon, mais ça
ira.

◆ **That'll do, thanks.** Ça ira, merci.

> *In English* do *is used to make questions. In
> French questions are made either with* **est-ce
> que** *or by reversing the order of verb and subject.*

◇ *Do you like French food?* Est-ce que
vous aimez la cuisine française?

◇ *Where does he live?* Où est-ce qu'il
habite? ◇ *Do you speak English?*
Parlez-vous anglais? ◇ *What do you do in
your free time?* Qu'est-ce que vous faites
pendant vos loisirs? ◇ *Where did you go
for your holidays?* Où es-tu allé pendant
tes vacances?

> *Use* **ne...pas** *in negative sentences for* don't.

◇ *I don't understand.* Je ne comprends
pas. ◇ *Why didn't you come?* Pourquoi
n'êtes-vous pas venus?

> do *is not translated when it is used in place of
> another verb.*

◇ *I hate maths. – So do I.* Je déteste les
maths. – Moi aussi. ◇ *I didn't like the
film. – Neither did I.* Je n'ai pas aimé le
film. – Moi non plus. ◇ *Do you like
horses? – No I don't.* Est-ce que tu aimes
les chevaux? – Non.

> *Use* **n'est-ce pas** *to check information.*

◇ *You go swimming on Fridays, don't you?*
Tu fais de la natation le vendredi,
n'est-ce pas? ◇ *The bus stops at the
youth hostel, doesn't it?* Le bus s'arrête à
l'auberge de jeunesse, n'est-ce pas?

◆ **How do you do?** Enchanté!

◆ **to do up (1)** (*shoes*) lacer ◇ *Do up your
shoes!* Lace tes chaussures!

◆ **to do up (2)** (*renovate*) retaper ◇ *They're
doing up an old cottage.* Ils retapent une
vieille maison.

◆ **to do up (3)** (*shirt, cardigan*) boutonner

◆ **Do up your zip!** (*on trousers*) Ferme ta
braguette!

◆ **to do without** se passer de ◇ *I couldn't
do without my computer.* Je ne pourrais
pas me passer de mon ordinateur.

dock NOUN

le *dock* (*for ships*)

doctor NOUN

le *médecin* ◇ *She's a doctor.* Elle est
médecin. ◇ *I'd like to be a doctor.* Je
voudrais être médecin.

document NOUN

le *document*

documentary NOUN

le *documentaire*

to **dodge** VERB

échapper à (*attacker*)

dodgems PL NOUN

les *autos tamponneuses* FEM PL ◇ *to go
on the dodgems* aller faire un tour
d'autos tamponneuses

does VERB *see* **do**

doesn't = **does not**

dog NOUN

(*female*)
le *chien*
la *chienne*

◦ *Have you got a dog?* Est-ce que tu as un chien?

do-it-yourself NOUN
le *bricolage*

dole NOUN
les *allocations chômage* FEM PL
- **to be on the dole** toucher le chômage ◦ *A lot of people are on the dole.* Beaucoup de gens touchent le chômage.
- **to go on the dole** s'inscrire au chômage

doll NOUN
la *poupée*

dollar NOUN
le *dollar*

dolphin NOUN
le *dauphin*

domestic ADJECTIVE
- **a domestic flight** un vol intérieur

dominoes PL NOUN
- **to have a game of dominoes** faire une partie de dominos

to **donate** VERB
donner

done VERB *see* **do**

donkey NOUN
l' *âne* MASC

don't = do not

door NOUN
[1] la *porte* ◦ *the first door on the right* la première porte à droite
[2] la *portière* (*of car, train*)

doorbell NOUN
la *sonnette*
- **to ring the doorbell** sonner
- **Suddenly the doorbell rang.** Soudain, on a sonné.

doorman NOUN
le *portier*

doorstep NOUN
le *pas de la porte*

dormitory NOUN
le *dortoir*

dose NOUN
la *dose*

dosh NOUN
le *fric* (*informal: money*)

dot NOUN
le *point* (*on letter "i", in e-mail address*)
- **on the dot** à l'heure pile ◦ *He arrived at 9 o'clock on the dot.* Il est arrivé à neuf heures pile.

double VERB
see also **double** ADJECTIVE
doubler ◦ *The number of attacks has doubled.* Le nombre d'agressions a doublé.

double ADJECTIVE, ADVERB
see also **double** VERB
double ◦ *a double helping* une double portion
- **to cost double** coûter le double ◦ *First-class tickets cost double.* Les billets de première classe coûtent le double.
- **a double bed** un grand lit
- **a double room** une chambre pour deux personnes
- **a double-decker bus** un autobus à impériale

double bass NOUN
la *contrebasse* ◦ *I play the double bass.* Je joue de la contrebasse.

double glazing NOUN
le *double vitrage*

doubles PL NOUN
le *double* SING (*in tennis*) ◦ *to play mixed doubles* jouer en double mixte

doubt NOUN
see also **doubt** VERB
le *doute* ◦ *I have my doubts.* J'ai des doutes.

to **doubt** VERB
see also **doubt** NOUN
douter de
- **I doubt it.** J'en doute.
- **to doubt that** douter que
douter que *has to be followed by a verb in the subjunctive.*
◦ *I doubt he'll agree.* Je doute qu'il soit d'accord.

doubtful ADJECTIVE
- **to be doubtful about doing something** hésiter à faire quelque chose ◦ *I'm doubtful about going by myself.* J'hésite à y aller tout seul.
- **It's doubtful.** Ce n'est pas sûr.
- **You sound doubtful.** Tu n'as pas l'air sûr.

dough NOUN
la *pâte*

doughnut NOUN
le *beignet* ◦ *a jam doughnut* un beignet à la confiture

Dover NOUN
Douvres ◦ *We went from Dover to Boulogne.* Nous sommes allés de Douvres à Boulogne.
- **in Dover** à Douvres

down ADVERB, ADJECTIVE, PREPOSITION
[1] *en bas* (*below*) ◦ *His office is down on the first floor.* Son bureau est en bas, au premier étage. ◦ *It's down there.* C'est là-bas.
[2] *à terre* (*to the ground*) ◦ *He threw down his racket.* Il a jeté sa raquette à terre.
- **They live just down the road.** Ils habitent tout à côté.

◆ **to come down** descendre ◇ *Come down here! Descends!*

◆ **to go down** descendre ◇ *The rabbit went down the hole.* Le lapin est descendu dans le terrier.

◆ **to sit down** s'asseoir ◇ *Sit down!* Asseyez-vous!

◆ **to feel down** avoir le cafard ◇ *I'm feeling a bit down.* J'ai un peu le cafard.

◆ **The computer's down.** L'ordinateur est en panne.

downpour NOUN
la *pluie torrentielle* ◇ *a sudden downpour* une pluie soudaine et torrentielle

downstairs ADVERB, ADJECTIVE
[1] *au rez-de-chaussée* ◇ *The bathroom's downstairs.* La salle de bain est au rez-de-chaussée.
[2] *du rez-de-chaussée* ◇ *the downstairs bathroom* la salle de bain du rez-de-chaussée

◆ **the people downstairs** les voisins du dessous

to **doze** VERB
sommeiller

◆ **to doze off** s'assoupir

dozen NOUN
la *douzaine* ◇ *two dozen* deux douzaines ◇ *a dozen eggs* une douzaine d'œufs

◆ **I've told you that dozens of times.** Je t'ai dit ça des centaines de fois.

drab ADJECTIVE
terne (*clothes*)

to **drag** VERB
see also **drag** NOUN
traîner (*thing, person*)

drag NOUN
see also **drag** VERB

◆ **It's a real drag!** C'est la barbe! (*informal*)

◆ **in drag** travesti ◇ *He was in drag.* Il était travesti.

dragon NOUN
le *dragon*

drain NOUN
see also **drain** VERB
l' *égout* MASC ◇ *The drains are blocked.* Les égouts sont bouchés.

to **drain** VERB
see also **drain** NOUN
égoutter (*vegetables, pasta*)

draining board NOUN
l' *égouttoir* MASC

drainpipe NOUN
le *tuyau d'écoulement*

drama NOUN
l' *art dramatique* MASC ◇ *Drama is my favourite subject.* L'art dramatique est ma matière préférée.

◆ **drama school** l'école d'art dramatique ◇ *I'd like to go to drama school.* J'aimerais entrer dans une école d'art dramatique.

◆ **Greek drama** le théâtre grec

dramatic ADJECTIVE
spectaculaire ◇ *It was really dramatic!* C'était vraiment spectaculaire! ◇ *a dramatic improvement* une amélioration spectaculaire

◆ **dramatic news** une nouvelle extraordinaire

drank VERB see **drink**

drastic ADJECTIVE
(*change*)
radical
(*radicaux* MASC PL)

◆ **to take drastic action** prendre des mesures énergiques

draught NOUN
le *courant d'air*

draughts NOUN
les *dames* FEM PL ◇ *to play draughts* jouer aux dames

to **draw** VERB
see also **draw** NOUN
[1] *dessiner* ◇ *He's good at drawing.* Il dessine bien.

◆ **to draw a picture** faire un dessin

◆ **to draw a picture of somebody** faire le portrait de quelqu'un

◆ **to draw a line** tirer un trait
[2] *faire match nul* (*sport*) ◇ *We drew 2-2.* Nous avons fait match nul deux à deux.

◆ **to draw the curtains** tirer les rideaux

◆ **to draw lots** tirer au sort

draw NOUN
see also **draw** VERB
[1] le *match nul* (*sport*) ◇ *The game ended in a draw.* La partie s'est soldée par un match nul.
[2] le *tirage au sort* (*in lottery*) ◇ *The draw takes place on Saturday.* Le tirage au sort a lieu samedi.

drawback NOUN
l' *inconvénient* MASC

drawer NOUN
le *tiroir*

drawing NOUN
le *dessin*

drawing pin NOUN
la *punaise*

drawn VERB see **draw**

dreadful ADJECTIVE
[1] *terrible* ◇ *a dreadful mistake* une terrible erreur
[2] *affreux* MASC
affreuse FEM

◦ *The weather was dreadful.* Il a fait un temps affreux.
- **I feel dreadful.** Je ne me sens vraiment pas bien.
- **You look dreadful.** (*ill*) Tu as une mine affreuse.

to **dream** VERB
see also dream NOUN
rêver ◦ *I dreamed I was in Belgium.* J'ai rêvé que j'étais en Belgique.

dream NOUN
see also dream VERB
le *rêve* ◦ *It was just a dream.* Ce n'était qu'un rêve.
- **a bad dream** un cauchemar

to **drench** VERB
- **to get drenched** se faire tremper ◦ *We got drenched.* Nous nous sommes fait tremper.

dress NOUN
see also dress VERB
la *robe*

to **dress** VERB
see also dress NOUN
s'habiller ◦ *I got up, dressed, and went downstairs.* Je me suis levé, je me suis habillé et je suis descendu.
- **to dress somebody** habiller quelqu'un ◦ *She dressed the children.* Elle a habillé les enfants.
- **to get dressed** s'habiller ◦ *I got dressed quickly.* Je me suis habillé rapidement.
- **to dress up** se déguiser ◦ *I dressed up as a ghost* Je me suis déguisé en fantôme.

dressed ADJECTIVE
habillé ◦ *I'm not dressed yet.* Je ne suis pas encore habillé. ◦ *How was she dressed?* Comment est-ce qu'elle était habillée?
- **She was dressed in a green sweater and jeans.** Elle portait un pull vert et un jean.

dresser NOUN
le *vaisselier* (*furniture*)

dressing gown NOUN
la *robe de chambre*

dressing table NOUN
la *coiffeuse*

drew VERB *see* **draw**

drier NOUN
le *séchoir*

drift NOUN
see also drift VERB
- **a snow drift** une congère

to **drift** VERB
see also drift NOUN
[1] *aller à la dérive* (*boat*)

[2] *s'amonceler* (*snow*)

drill NOUN
see also drill VERB
la *perceuse*

to **drill** VERB
see also drill NOUN
percer

to **drink** VERB
see also drink NOUN
boire ◦ *What would you like to drink?* Qu'est-ce que voulez boire? ◦ *She drank three cups of tea.* Elle a bu trois tasses de thé. ◦ *He'd been drinking.* Il avait bu.
- **I don't drink.** Je ne bois pas d'alcool.

drink NOUN
see also drink VERB
[1] la *boisson* ◦ *a cold drink* une boisson fraîche ◦ *a hot drink* une boisson chaude
[2] le *verre* (*alcoholic*) ◦ *They've gone out for a drink.* Ils sont allés prendre un verre.
- **to have a drink** prendre un verre

drive NOUN
see also drive VERB
[1] le *tour en voiture*
- **to go for a drive** aller faire un tour en voiture ◦ *We went for a drive in the country.* Nous sommes allés faire un tour à la campagne.
- **We've got a long drive tomorrow.** Nous avons une longue route à faire demain.
[2] l' *allée* FEM (*of house*) ◦ *He parked his car in the drive.* Il a garé sa voiture dans l'allée.

to **drive** VERB
see also drive NOUN
[1] *conduire* (*a car*) ◦ *She's learning to drive.* Elle apprend à conduire. ◦ *Can you drive?* Tu sais conduire?
[2] *aller en voiture* (*go by car*) ◦ *Did you go by train? – No, we drove.* Vous êtes partis en train? – Non, nous y sommes allés en voiture.
[3] *emmener en voiture* ◦ *My mother drives me to school.* Ma mère m'emmène à l'école en voiture.
- **to drive somebody home** raccompagner quelqu'un ◦ *He offered to drive me home.* Il m'a proposé de me raccompagner.
- **to drive somebody mad** rendre quelqu'un fou ◦ *He drives her mad.* Il la rend folle.

driver NOUN
[1] le *conducteur* la *conductrice*
◦ *She's an excellent driver.* C'est une excellente conductrice.

② le *chauffeur* (of taxi, bus) ⋄ *He's a bus driver.* Il est chauffeur d'autobus.

driving instructor NOUN
le *moniteur d'auto-école* ⋄ *He's a driving instructor.* Il est moniteur d'auto-école.

driving lesson NOUN
la *leçon de conduite*

driving licence NOUN
le *permis de conduire*

driving test NOUN
* **to take one's driving test** passer son permis de conduire ⋄ *He's taking his driving test tomorrow.* Il passe son permis de conduire demain.
* **She's just passed her driving test.** Elle vient d'avoir son permis.

drop NOUN
see also **drop** VERB
la *goutte* ⋄ *a drop of water* une goutte d'eau

to **drop** VERB
see also **drop** NOUN
① *laisser tomber* ⋄ *I dropped the glass and it broke.* J'ai laissé tomber le verre et il s'est cassé. ⋄ *I'm going to drop chemistry.* Je vais laisser tomber la chimie.
② *déposer* ⋄ *Could you drop me at the station?* Pouvez-vous me déposer à la gare?

drought NOUN
la *sécheresse*

drove VERB see **drive**

to **drown** VERB
se noyer ⋄ *A boy drowned here yesterday.* Un jeune garçon s'est noyé ici hier.

drug NOUN
① le *médicament* (medicine) ⋄ *They need food and drugs.* Ils ont besoin de nourriture et de médicaments.
② la *drogue* (illegal) ⋄ *hard drugs* les drogues dures ⋄ *soft drugs* les drogues douces
* **to take drugs** se droguer
* **a drug addict** un drogué ⋄ *She's a drug addict.* C'est une droguée.
* **a drug pusher** un dealer
* **a drug smuggler** un trafiquant de drogue
* **the drugs squad** la brigade antidrogue

drum NOUN
le *tambour* ⋄ *an African drum* un tambour africain
* **a drum kit** une batterie
* **drums** la batterie SING ⋄ *I play drums.* Je joue de la batterie.

drummer NOUN
(in rock group)
le *batteur*
la *batteuse*

drunk ADJECTIVE
see also **drunk** NOUN
ivre ⋄ *He was drunk.* Il était ivre.

drunk NOUN
see also **drunk** ADJECTIVE
l' *ivrogne* MASC/FEM ⋄ *The streets were full of drunks.* Les rues étaient pleines d'ivrognes.

dry ADJECTIVE
see also **dry** VERB
① *sec* MASC
sèche FEM
⋄ *The paint isn't dry yet.* La peinture n'est pas encore sèche.
② *sans pluie* (weather) ⋄ *a long dry period* une longue période sans pluie

to **dry** VERB
see also **dry** ADJECTIVE
① *sécher* ⋄ *The washing will dry quickly in the sun.* Le linge va sécher vite au soleil. ⋄ *some dried flowers* des fleurs séchées
* **to dry one's hair** se sécher les cheveux ⋄ *I haven't dried my hair yet.* Je ne me suis pas encore séché les cheveux.
② *faire sécher* (clothes) ⋄ *There's nowhere to dry clothes here.* Il n'y a pas d'endroit où faire sécher les vêtements ici.
* **to dry the dishes** essuyer la vaisselle

dry-cleaner's NOUN
la *teinturerie*

dryer NOUN
le *séchoir* (for clothes)
* **a tumble dryer** un séchoir à linge
* **a hair dryer** un sèche-cheveux

dubbed ADJECTIVE
doublé ⋄ *The film was dubbed into French.* Le film était doublé en français.

dubious ADJECTIVE
réticent ⋄ *My parents were a bit dubious about it.* Mes parents étaient un peu réticents à ce sujet.

duck NOUN
le *canard*

due ADJECTIVE, ADVERB
* **to be due to do something** devoir faire quelque chose ⋄ *He's due to arrive tomorrow.* Il doit arriver demain.
* **The plane's due in half an hour.** L'avion doit arriver dans une demi-heure.
* **When's the baby due?** Le bébé est prévu pour quand?
* **due to** à cause de ⋄ *The trip was*

cancelled due to bad weather. Le voyage a été annulé à cause du mauvais temps.

dug VERB see **dig**

dull ADJECTIVE
1 *ennuyeux* MASC
ennuyeuse FEM
◊ He's nice, but a bit dull. Il est sympathique, mais un peu ennuyeux.
2 *maussade* (weather, day)

dumb ADJECTIVE
1 *muet* MASC
muette FEM
• She's deaf and dumb. Elle est sourde-muette.
2 *bête* (stupid) ◊ That was a really dumb thing I did! C'était vraiment bête de ma part!

dummy NOUN
la *tétine* (for baby)

dump NOUN
see also dump VERB
• It's a real dump! C'est un endroit minable!
• a rubbish dump une décharge

dump VERB
see also dump NOUN
1 *déposer* (waste) ◊ "no dumping" "défense de déposer des ordures"
2 *plaquer* (informal) ◊ He's just dumped his girlfriend. Il vient de plaquer sa copine.

dungarees PL NOUN
la *salopette* SING

dungeon NOUN
le *cachot*

duration NOUN
la *durée*

during PREPOSITION
pendant ◊ during the day pendant la journée

dusk NOUN
le *crépuscule* ◊ at dusk au crépuscule

dust NOUN
see also dust VERB
la *poussière*

dust VERB
see also dust NOUN

épousseter ◊ I dusted the shelves. J'ai épousseté les étagères.
• I hate dusting! Je déteste faire les poussières!

dustbin NOUN
la *poubelle*

dustman NOUN
l' *éboueur* MASC ◊ He's a dustman. Il est éboueur.

dusty ADJECTIVE
poussiéreux MASC
poussiéreuse FEM

Dutch ADJECTIVE
see also Dutch NOUN
hollandais ◊ She's Dutch. Elle est hollandaise.

Dutch NOUN
see also Dutch ADJECTIVE
le *hollandais* (language)
• the Dutch les Hollandais

Dutchman NOUN
le *Hollandais*

Dutchwoman NOUN
la *Hollandaise*

duty NOUN
le *devoir* ◊ It was his duty to tell the police. C'était son devoir de prévenir la police.
• to be on duty (1) (policeman) être de service
• to be on duty (2) (doctor, nurse) être de garde

duty-free ADJECTIVE
hors taxes FEM+PL
• the duty-free shop la boutique hors taxes

duvet NOUN
la *couette*

dwarf NOUN
le *nain*
la *naine*

dynamic ADJECTIVE
dynamique

dyslexia NOUN
la *dyslexie*

D

E

each ADJECTIVE, PRONOUN

[1] *chaque* ⋄ *each day* chaque jour
⋄ *Each house in our street has its own garden.* Chaque maison dans notre rue a son propre jardin.

[2] *chacun* MASC
chacune FEM
⋄ *The girls each have their own bedroom.* Les filles ont chacune leur chambre.
⋄ *They have 10 points each.* Ils ont dix points chacun. ⋄ *The plates cost £5 each.* Les assiettes coûtent cinq livres chacune. ⋄ *He gave each of us £10.* Il nous a donné dix livres à chacun.

Use a reflexive verb to translate each other.

• **They hate each other.** Ils se détestent.
• **We wrote to each other.** Nous nous sommes écrit.
• **They don't know each other.** Ils ne se connaissent pas.

ear NOUN
l' *oreille* FEM

earache NOUN

• **to have earache** avoir mal aux oreilles

earlier ADVERB

[1] *tout à l'heure* ⋄ *I saw him earlier.* Je l'ai vu tout à l'heure.

[2] *plus tôt* (*in the morning*) ⋄ *I ought to get up earlier.* Je devrais me lever plus tôt.

early ADVERB, ADJECTIVE

[1] *tôt* (*early in the day*) ⋄ *I have to get up early.* Je dois me lever tôt.

• **to have an early night** se coucher tôt

[2] *en avance* (*ahead of time*) ⋄ *I came early to get a good seat.* Je suis venu en avance pour avoir une bonne place.

to **earn** VERB
gagner ⋄ *She earns £5 an hour.* Elle gagne cinq livres de l'heure.

earnings PL NOUN
le *salaire* SING

earring NOUN
la *boucle d'oreille*

earth NOUN
la *terre*

earthquake NOUN
le *tremblement de terre*

easily ADVERB
facilement

east ADJECTIVE, ADVERB

see also east NOUN

[1] *est* MASC, FEM, PL ⋄ *the east coast* la côte est

• **an east wind** un vent d'est
• **east of** à l'est de ⋄ *It's east of London.*

C'est à l'est de Londres.

[2] *vers l'est* ⋄ *We were travelling east.* Nous allions vers l'est.

east NOUN

see also east ADJECTIVE

l' *est* MASC ⋄ *in the east* dans l'est

Easter NOUN
Pâques FEM ⋄ *at Easter* à Pâques ⋄ *We went to my grandparents' for Easter.* Nous sommes allés chez mes grands-parents à Pâques.

Easter egg NOUN
l' *œuf de Pâques* MASC

eastern ADJECTIVE

• **the eastern part of the island** la partie est de l'île
• **Eastern Europe** l'Europe de l'Est

easy ADJECTIVE
facile

easy chair NOUN
le *fauteuil*

easy-going ADJECTIVE
facile à vivre
(*faciles à vivre* PL)
⋄ *She's very easy-going.* Elle est très facile à vivre.

to **eat** VERB
manger

• **Would you like something to eat?** Est-ce que tu veux manger quelque chose?

EC NOUN (= *European Community*)
la *CE* (= Communauté européenne)

eccentric ADJECTIVE
excentrique

echo NOUN
l' *écho* MASC

ecology NOUN
l' *écologie* FEM

economic ADJECTIVE
rentable (*profitable*)

economics NOUN
l' *économie* FEM ⋄ *He's studying economics.* Il fait des études d'économie.

to **economize** VERB
faire des économies ⋄ *to economize on something* faire des économies sur quelque chose

economy NOUN
l' *économie* FEM

ecstasy NOUN
l' *ecstasy* FEM (*drug*)

• **to be in ecstasy** s'extasier

ecu NOUN (= *European Currency Unit*)
l' *écu* MASC

eczema NOUN
l' *eczéma* MASC

edge NOUN
le *bord*

edgy ADJECTIVE
tendu

Edinburgh NOUN
Édimbourg

editor NOUN
(*of newspaper*)
le *rédacteur en chef*
la *rédactrice en chef*

educated ADJECTIVE
cultivé

education NOUN
[1] l' *éducation* FEM ⋄ *There should be more investment in education.* On devrait investir plus dans l'éducation.
[2] l' *enseignement* MASC (*teaching*)
⋄ *She works in education.* Elle travaille dans l'enseignement.

educational ADJECTIVE
(*experience, toy*)
éducatif MASC
éducative FEM
⋄ *It was very educational.* C'était très éducatif.

effect NOUN
l' *effet* MASC ⋄ *special effects* les effets spéciaux

effective ADJECTIVE
efficace

efficient ADJECTIVE
efficace

effort NOUN
l' *effort* MASC

e.g. ABBREVIATION
p. ex. (= par exemple)

egg NOUN
l' *œuf* MASC ⋄ *a hard-boiled egg* un œuf dur ⋄ *a soft-boiled egg* un œuf à la coque ⋄ *a fried egg* un œuf sur le plat
▸ **scrambled eggs** les œufs brouillés

egg cup NOUN
le *coquetier*

Egypt NOUN
l' *Égypte* FEM
▸ **in Egypt** en Égypte

Eiffel Tower NOUN
la *tour Eiffel*

eight NUMBER
huit ⋄ *She's eight.* Elle a huit ans.

eighteen NUMBER
dix-huit ⋄ *She's eighteen.* Elle a dix-huit ans.

eighth ADJECTIVE
huitième ⋄ *the eighth floor* le huitième étage
▸ **the eighth of August** le huit août

eighty NUMBER
quatre-vingts

Eire NOUN
la *République d'Irlande*
▸ **in Eire** en République d'Irlande

either ADVERB, CONJUNCTION, PRONOUN
non plus ⋄ *I don't like milk, and I don't like eggs either.* Je n'aime pas le lait, et je n'aime pas les œufs non plus. ⋄ *I've never been to Spain. – I haven't either.* Je ne suis jamais allé en Espagne. – Moi non plus.
▸ **either...or...** soit...soit... ⋄ *You can have either ice cream or yoghurt.* Tu peux prendre soit une glace soit un yaourt.
▸ **either of them** l'un ou l'autre ⋄ *Take either of them.* Prends l'un ou l'autre.
▸ **I don't like either of them.** Je n'aime ni l'un ni l'autre.

elastic NOUN
l' *élastique* MASC

elastic band NOUN
l' *élastique* MASC

elbow NOUN
le *coude*

elder ADJECTIVE
aîné ⋄ *my elder sister* ma sœur aînée

elderly ADJECTIVE
âgé
▸ **the elderly** les personnes âgées

eldest ADJECTIVE
aîné ⋄ *my eldest sister* ma sœur aînée
⋄ *He's the eldest.* C'est l'aîné.

to **elect** VERB
élire

election NOUN
l' *élection* FEM

electric ADJECTIVE
électrique ⋄ *an electric fire* un radiateur électrique ⋄ *an electric guitar* une guitare électrique
▸ **an electric blanket** une couverture chauffante

electrical ADJECTIVE
électrique
▸ **an electrical engineer** un ingénieur électricien

electrician NOUN
l' *électricien* MASC ⋄ *He's an electrician.* Il est électricien.

electricity NOUN
l' *électricité* FEM

electronic ADJECTIVE
électronique

electronics NOUN
l' *électronique* FEM ⋄ *My hobby is electronics.* Ma passion, c'est l'électronique.

elegant ADJECTIVE

élégant

elephant NOUN
l' *éléphant* MASC

eleven NUMBER
onze ◇ She's 11. Elle a onze ans.

eleventh ADJECTIVE
onzième ◇ the 11th floor le onzième
étage ◇ the 11th of August le onze août

else ADVERB
d'autre ◇ somebody else quelqu'un
d'autre ◇ nobody else personne d'autre
◇ nothing else rien d'autre
* **something else** autre chose
* **anything else** autre chose ◇ Would you
like anything else? Désirez-vous autre
chose?
* **I don't want anything else.** Je ne veux
rien d'autre.
* **somewhere else** ailleurs
* **anywhere else** autre part

e-mail NOUN
le *courrier électronique*

embankment NOUN
le *talus*

embarrassed ADJECTIVE
gêné ◇ I was really embarrassed.
J'étais vraiment gêné.

embarrassing ADJECTIVE
gênant ◇ It was so embarrassing.
C'était tellement gênant.

embassy NOUN
l' *ambassade* FEM ◇ the British
Embassy l'ambassade de
Grande-Bretagne ◇ the French Embassy
l'ambassade de France

to **embroider** VERB
broder

embroidery NOUN
la *broderie* ◇ I do embroidery. Je fais
de la broderie.

emergency NOUN
l' *urgence* FEM ◇ This is an emergency!
C'est une urgence!
* **in an emergency** en cas d'urgence
* **an emergency exit** une sortie de secours
* **an emergency landing** un atterrissage
forcé
* **the emergency services** les services
d'urgence

to **emigrate** VERB
émigrer

emotion NOUN
l' *émotion* FEM

emotional ADJECTIVE
(*person*)
émotif MASC
émotive FEM

emperor NOUN
l' *empereur* MASC

to **emphasize** VERB
* **to emphasize something** insister sur
quelque chose
* **to emphasize that...** souligner que...

empire NOUN
l' *empire* MASC

to **employ** VERB
employer ◇ The factory employs 600
people. L'usine emploie six cents
personnes.

employee NOUN
l' *employé* MASC
l' *employée* FEM

employer NOUN
l' *employeur* MASC

employment NOUN
l' *emploi* MASC

empty ADJECTIVE
see also **empty** VERB
vide

to **empty** VERB
see also **empty** ADJECTIVE
vider
* **to empty something out** vider quelque
chose

to **encourage** VERB
encourager
* **to encourage somebody to do
something** encourager quelqu'un à faire
quelque chose

encouragement NOUN
l' *encouragement* MASC

encyclopedia NOUN
l' *encyclopédie* FEM

end NOUN
see also **end** VERB
⓵ la *fin* ◇ the end of the film la fin du
film ◇ the end of the holidays la fin des
vacances
* **in the end** en fin de compte ◇ In the
end I decided to stay at home. En fin de
compte j'ai décidé de rester à la maison.
* **It turned out all right in the end.** Ça
s'est bien terminé.
⓶ le *bout* ◇ at the end of the street au
bout de la rue ◇ at the other end of the
table à l'autre bout de la table
* **for hours on end** des heures entières

to **end** VERB
see also **end** NOUN
finir ◇ What time does the film end? À
quelle heure est-ce que le film finit?
* **to end up doing something** finir par
faire quelque chose ◇ I ended up
walking home. J'ai fini par rentrer chez
moi à pied.

ending NOUN
la *fin* ◇ It was an exciting film, especially
the ending. C'était un film passionnant,

surtout la fin.

endless ADJECTIVE
interminable ◇ *The journey seemed endless.* Le voyage a paru interminable.

enemy NOUN
l' _ennemi_ MASC
l' _ennemie_ FEM

energetic ADJECTIVE
énergique (*person*)

energy NOUN
l' _énergie_ FEM

engaged ADJECTIVE
1 _occupé_ (*busy, in use*) ◇ *I phoned, but it was engaged.* J'ai téléphoné, mais c'était occupé.
2 _fiancé_ (*to be married*) ◇ *She's engaged to Brian.* Elle est fiancée à Brian.
- **to get engaged** se fiancer

engagement NOUN
les _fiançailles_ FEM PL ◇ *an engagement ring* une bague de fiançailles

engine NOUN
le _moteur_

engineer NOUN
l' _ingénieur_ MASC ◇ *He's an engineer.* Il est ingénieur.

engineering NOUN
l' _ingénierie_ FEM

England NOUN
l' _Angleterre_ FEM
- **in England** en Angleterre
- **to England** en Angleterre
- **I'm from England.** Je suis anglais.

English ADJECTIVE
see also English NOUN
anglais ◇ *I'm English.* Je suis anglais.
- **English people** les Anglais

English NOUN
see also English ADJECTIVE
l' _anglais_ MASC (*language*) ◇ *Do you speak English?* Est-ce que vous parlez anglais?
- **the English** les Anglais

Englishman NOUN
l' _Anglais_ MASC

Englishwoman NOUN
l' _Anglaise_ FEM

enjoy VERB
aimer ◇ *Did you enjoy the film?* Est-ce que vous avez aimé le film?
- **to enjoy oneself** s'amuser ◇ *I really enjoyed myself.* Je me suis vraiment bien amusé. ◇ *Did you enjoy yourselves at the party?* Est-ce vous vous êtes bien amusés à la fête?

enjoyable ADJECTIVE
agréable

enlargement NOUN
l' _agrandissement_ MASC (*of photo*)

enormous ADJECTIVE
énorme

enough PRONOUN, ADJECTIVE
assez de ◇ *enough time* assez de temps ◇ *I didn't have enough money.* Je n'avais pas assez d'argent. ◇ *Have you got enough?* Tu en as assez? ◇ *I've had enough!* J'en ai assez!
- **big enough** suffisamment grand
- **warm enough** suffisamment chaud
- **That's enough.** Ça suffit.

to **enquire** VERB
- **to enquire about something** se renseigner sur quelque chose ◇ *I am going to enquire about train times.* Je vais me renseigner sur les horaires de trains.

to **enter** VERB
entrer
- **to enter a room** entrer dans une pièce
- **to enter a competition** s'inscrire à une compétition

to **entertain** VERB
recevoir (*guests*)

entertainer NOUN
l' _artiste de variétés_ MASC/FEM

entertaining ADJECTIVE
amusant

enthusiasm NOUN
l' _enthousiasme_ MASC

enthusiast NOUN
- **a railway enthusiast** un passionné des trains
- **She's a DIY enthusiast.** C'est une passionnée de bricolage.

enthusiastic ADJECTIVE
enthousiaste

entire ADJECTIVE
entier MASC
entière FEM
◇ *the entire world* le monde entier

entirely ADVERB
entièrement

entrance NOUN
l' _entrée_ FEM
- **an entrance exam** un concours d'entrée
- **entrance fee** le prix d'entrée

entry NOUN
l' _entrée_ FEM
- **"no entry" (1)** (*on door*) "défense d'entrer"
- **"no entry" (2)** (*on road sign*) "sens interdit"
- **an entry form** une feuille d'inscription

entry phone NOUN
l' _interphone_ MASC

envelope NOUN
l' _enveloppe_ FEM

envious ADJECTIVE
envieux MASC
envieuse FEM

environment NOUN
l' *environnement* MASC
environmental ADJECTIVE
écologique
environment-friendly ADJECTIVE
écologique
envy NOUN
see also envy VERB
l' *envie* FEM
to **envy** VERB
see also envy NOUN
envier ◊ *I don't envy you!* Je ne t'envie
pas!
epileptic NOUN
l' *épileptique* MASC/FEM
episode NOUN
l' *épisode* MASC (*of TV programme, story*)
equal ADJECTIVE
égal
(*égaux* MASC PL)
equality NOUN
l' *égalité* FEM
to **equalize** VERB
égaliser (*in sport*)
equator NOUN
l' *équateur* MASC
equipment NOUN
l' *équipement* MASC ◊ *fishing equipment*
l'équipement de pêche ◊ *skiing*
equipment l'équipement de ski
equipped ADJECTIVE
✦ **equipped with** équipé de
✦ **to be well equipped** être bien équipé
equivalent NOUN
l' *équivalent* MASC
✦ **equivalent to** équivalent à
error NOUN
l' *erreur* FEM
escalator NOUN
l' *escalier roulant* MASC
escape NOUN
see also escape VERB
l' *évasion* FEM (*from prison*)
to **escape** VERB
see also escape NOUN
s'échapper ◊ *A lion has escaped.* Un
lion s'est échappé.
✦ **to escape from prison** s'évader de
prison
escort NOUN
l' *escorte* FEM ◊ *a police escort* une
escorte de police
Eskimo NOUN
l' *Esquimau* MASC
l' *Esquimaude* FEM
✦ **the Eskimos** les Esquimaux
especially ADVERB
surtout ◊ *It's very hot there, especially
in the summer.* Il fait très chaud là-bas,

surtout en été.
essay NOUN
la *dissertation* ◊ *a history essay* une
dissertation d'histoire
essential ADJECTIVE
essentiel MASC
essentielle FEM
◊ *It's essential to bring warm clothes.* Il
est essentiel d'apporter des vêtements
chauds.
estate NOUN
la *cité* (*housing estate*) ◊ *I live on an
estate.* J'habite dans une cité.
estate agent NOUN
l' *agent immobilier* MASC
estate car NOUN
le *break*
etc ABBREVIATION (= *et cetera*)
etc.
Ethiopia NOUN
l' *Éthiopie* FEM
✦ **in Ethiopia** en Éthiopie
ethnic ADJECTIVE
[1] *ethnique* (*racial*) ◊ *an ethnic minority*
une minorité ethnique
[2] *folklorique* (*clothes, music*)
EU NOUN (= *European Union*)
l' *Union européenne* FEM
Eurocheque NOUN
l' *eurochèque* MASC
Europe NOUN
l' *Europe* FEM
✦ **in Europe** en Europe
✦ **to Europe** en Europe
European ADJECTIVE
see also European NOUN
européen MASC
européenne FEM
European NOUN
see also European ADJECTIVE
(*person*)
l' *Européen* MASC
l' *Européenne* FEM
to **evacuate** VERB
évacuer
eve NOUN
✦ **Christmas Eve** la veille de Noël
✦ **New Year's Eve** la Saint-Sylvestre
even ADVERB
see also even ADJECTIVE
même ◊ *I like all animals, even snakes.*
J'aime tous les animaux, même les
serpents.
✦ **even if** même si ◊ *I'd never do that,
even if you asked me.* Je ne ferais jamais
ça, même si tu me le demandais.
✦ **not even** même pas ◊ *He never stops
working, not even at the weekend.* Il
n'arrête jamais de travailler, même pas

le week-end.
* **even though** bien que
  bien que *has to be followed by a verb in the subjunctive.*
  ◇ *He's never got any money, even though his parents are quite rich.* Il n'a jamais d'argent, bien que ses parents soient assez riches.
* **even more** encore plus ◇ *I liked Boulogne even more than Paris.* J'ai encore plus aimé Boulogne que Paris.

even ADJECTIVE
  see also **even** ADVERB
  régulier MASC
  régulière FEM
  ◇ *an even layer of snow* une couche régulière de neige
* **an even number** un nombre pair
* **to get even with somebody** prendre sa revanche sur quelqu'un ◇ *He wanted to get even with her.* Il voulait prendre sa revanche sur elle.

evening NOUN
  le *soir* ◇ *in the evening* le soir
  ◇ *yesterday evening* hier soir
  ◇ *tomorrow evening* demain soir
* **all evening** toute la soirée
* **Good evening!** Bonsoir!

evening class NOUN
  le *cours du soir*
  (les *cours du soir* PL)

event NOUN
  l' *événement* MASC
* **a sporting event** une épreuve sportive

eventful ADJECTIVE
  mouvementé

eventually ADVERB
  finalement

ever ADVERB
* **Have you ever been to Germany?** Est-ce que tu es déjà allé en Allemagne?
* **Have you ever seen her?** Vous l'avez déjà vue?
* **I haven't ever done that.** Je ne l'ai jamais fait.
* **the best I've ever seen** le meilleur que j'aie jamais vu
* **for the first time ever** pour la première fois
* **ever since** depuis que ◇ *ever since I met him* depuis que je l'ai rencontré
* **ever since then** depuis ce moment-là

every ADJECTIVE
  chaque ◇ *every pupil* chaque élève
* **every time** chaque fois ◇ *Every time I see him he's depressed.* Chaque fois que je le vois il est déprimé.
* **every day** tous les jours
* **every week** toutes les semaines
* **every now and then** de temps en temps

everybody PRONOUN
  tout le monde ◇ *Everybody had a good time.* Tout le monde s'est bien amusé.
  ◇ *Everybody makes mistakes.* Tout le monde peut se tromper.

everyone PRONOUN
  tout le monde ◇ *Everyone opened their presents.* Tout le monde a ouvert ses cadeaux. ◇ *Everyone should have a hobby.* Tout le monde devrait avoir un passe-temps.

everything PRONOUN
  tout ◇ *You've thought of everything!* Tu as pensé à tout!
* **Have you remembered everything?** Est-ce que tu n'as rien oublié?
* **Money isn't everything.** L'argent ne fait pas le bonheur.

everywhere ADVERB
  partout ◇ *I looked everywhere, but I couldn't find it.* J'ai regardé partout, mais je n'ai pas pu le trouver. ◇ *There were policemen everywhere.* Il y avait des policiers partout.

evil ADJECTIVE
  mauvais

ex- PREFIX
  ex- ◇ *his ex-wife* son ex-femme

exact ADJECTIVE
  exact

exactly ADVERB
  exactement ◇ *exactly the same* exactement le même ∼ *Not exactly.* Pas exactement.
* **It's exactly 10 o'clock.** Il est dix heures précises.

to **exaggerate** VERB
  exagérer

exaggeration NOUN
  l' *exagération* FEM

exam NOUN
  l' *examen* MASC ◇ *a French exam* un examen de français ◇ *the exam results* les résultats des examens MASC

examination NOUN
  l' *examen* MASC

to **examine** VERB
  examiner ◇ *He examined her passport.* Il a examiné son passeport. ◇ *The doctor examined him.* Le docteur l'a examiné.

examiner NOUN
  l' *examinateur* MASC
  l' *examinatrice* FEM

example NOUN
  l' *exemple* MASC
* **for example** par exemple

excellent ADJECTIVE
  excellent ◇ *Her results were excellent.*

Elle a eu d'excellents résultats.
- **It was excellent fun.** C'était vraiment super.

except PREPOSITION
sauf ◇ _everyone except me_ tout le monde sauf moi
- **except for** sauf
- **except that** sauf que ◇ _The weather was great, except that it was a bit cold._ Il a fait un temps superbe, sauf qu'il a fait un peu froid.

exception NOUN
l' _exception_ FEM
- **to make an exception** faire une exception

exceptional ADJECTIVE
exceptionnel MASC
exceptionnelle FEM

excess baggage NOUN
l' _excédent de bagages_ MASC

to **exchange** VERB
échanger ◇ _I exchanged the book for a video._ J'ai échangé le livre contre une vidéo.

exchange rate NOUN
le _taux de change_

excited ADJECTIVE
excité

exciting ADJECTIVE
passionnant

excuse NOUN
see also excuse VERB
l' _excuse_ FEM

to **excuse** VERB
see also excuse NOUN
- **Excuse me!** Pardon!

to **execute** VERB
exécuter

execution NOUN
l' _exécution_ FEM

executive NOUN
le _cadre_ (_in business_) ◇ _He's an executive._ Il est cadre.

exercise NOUN
l' _exercice_ MASC
- **an exercise bike** un vélo d'appartement
- **an exercise book** un cahier

exhausted ADJECTIVE
épuisé

exhaust fumes PL NOUN
les _gaz d'échappement_ MASC PL

exhaust pipe NOUN
le _tuyau d'échappement_

exhibition NOUN
l' _exposition_ FEM

ex-husband NOUN
l' _ex-mari_ MASC

to **exist** VERB
exister

exit NOUN
la _sortie_

exotic ADJECTIVE
exotique

to **expect** VERB
1 _attendre_ ◇ _I'm expecting him for dinner._ Je l'attends pour dîner. ◇ _She's expecting a baby._ Elle attend un enfant.
2 _s'attendre à_ ◇ _I was expecting the worst._ Je m'attendais au pire.
3 _supposer_ ◇ _I expect it's a mistake._ Je suppose qu'il s'agit d'une erreur.

expedition NOUN
l' _expédition_ FEM

to **expel** VERB
- **to get expelled** (_from school_) se faire renvoyer

expenses PL NOUN
les _frais_ MASC PL

expensive ADJECTIVE
cher MASC
chère FEM

experience NOUN
l' _expérience_ FEM

experienced ADJECTIVE
expérimenté

experiment NOUN
l' _expérience_ FEM

expert NOUN
le _spécialiste_
la _spécialiste_
◇ _He's a computer expert._ C'est un spécialiste en informatique.
- **He's an expert cook.** Il cuisine très bien.

to **expire** VERB
expirer

to **explain** VERB
expliquer

explanation NOUN
l' _explication_ FEM

to **explode** VERB
exploser

to **exploit** VERB
exploiter

exploitation NOUN
l' _exploitation_ FEM

to **explore** VERB
explorer (_place_)

explorer NOUN
l' _explorateur_ MASC
l' _exploratrice_ FEM

explosion NOUN
l' _explosion_ FEM

explosive ADJECTIVE
see also explosive NOUN
explosif MASC
explosive FEM

explosive NOUN
see also explosive ADJECTIVE
l' *explosif* MASC

to **express** VERB
exprimer
* to express oneself s'exprimer ◇ *It's not easy to express oneself in a foreign language.* Ce n'est pas facile de s'exprimer dans une langue étrangère.

expression NOUN
l' *expression* FEM ◇ *It's an English expression.* C'est une expression anglaise.

extension NOUN
1 l' *annexe* FEM (*of building*)
2 le *poste* (*telephone*)
In France phone numbers are broken into groups of two digits where possible.
* **Extension 3137, please.** Poste trente et un trente-sept, s'il vous plaît.

extent NOUN
* to some extent dans une certaine mesure

exterior ADJECTIVE
extérieur

extinct ADJECTIVE
* to become extinct disparaître
* to be extinct avoir disparu ◇ *The species is almost extinct.* Cette espèce a presque disparu.

extinguisher NOUN
l' *extincteur* MASC (*fire extinguisher*)

extortionate ADJECTIVE
exorbitant

extra ADJECTIVE, ADVERB
supplémentaire ◇ *an extra blanket*

une couverture supplémentaire
* to pay extra payer un supplément
* **Breakfast is extra.** Il y a un supplément pour le petit déjeuner.
* **It costs extra.** Il y a un supplément.

extraordinary ADJECTIVE
extraordinaire

extravagant ADJECTIVE
(*person*)
dépensier MASC
dépensière FEM

extreme ADJECTIVE
extrême

extremely ADVERB
extrêmement

extremist NOUN
l' *extrémiste* MASC/FEM

eye NOUN
l' *œil* MASC
(les *yeux* PL)
◇ *I've got green eyes.* J'ai les yeux verts.
* to keep an eye on something surveiller quelque chose

eyebrow NOUN
le *sourcil*

eyelash NOUN
le *cil*

eyelid NOUN
la *paupière*

eyeliner NOUN
l' *eye-liner* MASC

eye shadow NOUN
l' *ombre à paupières* FEM

eyesight NOUN
la *vue*

F

fabric NOUN
le *tissu*

fabulous ADJECTIVE
formidable ◇ *The show was fabulous.*
Le spectacle était formidable.

face NOUN
see also **face** VERB
[1] le *visage* (*of person*)
[2] le *cadran* (*of clock*)
[3] la *paroi* (*of cliff*)
* **on the face of it** à première vue
* **in the face of these difficulties** face à
ces difficultés
* **face to face** face à face
* **a face cloth** un gant de toilette

to **face** VERB
see also **face** NOUN
faire face à (*place, problem*)
* **to face up to something** faire face à
quelque chose ◇ *You must face up to
your responsibilities.* Vous devez faire
face à vos responsabilités.

facilities PL NOUN
l' *équipement* MASC SING ◇ *This school
has excellent facilities.* Cette école
dispose d'un excellent équipement.
* **toilet facilities** les toilettes FEM
* **cooking facilities** la cuisine équipée
SING

fact NOUN
le *fait*
* **in fact** en fait

factory NOUN
l' *usine* FEM

to **fade** VERB
[1] *passer* (*colour*) ◇ *The colour has
faded in the sun.* La couleur a passé au
soleil
* **My jeans have faded.** Mon jean est
délavé.
[2] *baisser* ◇ *The light was fading fast.*
La lumière baissait rapidement.
[3] *diminuer* ◇ *The noise gradually
faded.* Le bruit a diminué peu à peu.

to **fail** VERB
see also **fail** NOUN
[1] *rater* ◇ *I failed the history exam.* J'ai
raté l'examen d'histoire.
[2] *échouer* ◇ *In our class, no one failed.*
Dans notre classe, personne n'a échoué.
[3] *lâcher* ◇ *My brakes failed.* Mes
freins ont lâché.
* **to fail to do something** ne pas faire
quelque chose ◇ *She failed to return her
library books.* Elle n'a pas rendu ses
livres à la bibliothèque.

fail NOUN
see also **fail** VERB
* **without fail** sans faute

failure NOUN
[1] l' *échec* MASC ◇ *feelings of failure* un
sentiment d'échec SING
[2] le *raté*
la *ratée*
◇ *He's a failure.* C'est un raté.
[3] la *défaillance* ◇ *a mechanical failure*
une défaillance mécanique

faint ADJECTIVE
see also **faint** VERB
faible ◇ *His voice was very faint.* Sa
voix était très faible.
* **to feel faint** se trouver mal

to **faint** VERB
see also **faint** ADJECTIVE
s'évanouir ◇ *All of a sudden she
fainted.* Tout à coup elle s'est évanouie.

fair ADJECTIVE
see also **fair** NOUN
[1] *juste* ◇ *That's not fair.* Ce n'est pas
juste.
[2] (*hair*)
blond ◇ *He's got fair hair.* Il a les
cheveux blonds.
[3] (*skin*)
clair ◇ *people with fair skin* les gens qui
ont la peau claire
[4] (*weather*)
beau MASC
belle FEM
◇ *The weather was fair.* Il faisait beau.
[5] (*good enough*)
assez bon MASC
assez bonne FEM
◇ *I have a fair chance of winning.* J'ai
d'assez bonnes chances de gagner.
[6] (*sizeable*)
considérable ◇ *That's a fair distance.*
Ça représente une distance considérable.

fair NOUN
see also **fair** ADJECTIVE
la *foire* ◇ *They went to the fair.* Ils sont
allés à la foire.
* **a trade fair** une foire commerciale

fairly ADVERB
[1] *équitablement* ◇ *The cake was
divided fairly.* Le gâteau a été partagé
équitablement.
[2] *assez* (*quite*) ◇ *That's fairly good.*
C'est assez bien.

fairness NOUN
la *justice*

fairy NOUN

la _fée_

fairy tale NOUN
le _conte de fées_
(les _contes de fées_ PL)

faith NOUN
[1] la _foi_ ◇ the Catholic faith la foi catholique
[2] la _confiance_ ◇ People have lost faith in the government. Les gens ont perdu confiance dans le gouvernement.

faithful ADJECTIVE
fidèle

faithfully ADVERB
• **Yours faithfully...** (in letter) Veuillez agréer mes salutations distinguées...

fake NOUN
see also **fake** ADJECTIVE
le _faux_ ◇ The painting was a fake. Le tableau était un faux.

fake ADJECTIVE
see also **fake** NOUN
faux MASC
fausse FEM
◇ She wore fake fur. Elle portait une fausse fourrure.

fall NOUN
see also **fall** VERB
la _chute_ ◇ a fall of snow une chute de neige ◇ She had a nasty fall. Elle a fait une mauvaise chute.
• **the Niagara Falls** les chutes du Niagara

fall VERB
see also **fall** NOUN
[1] _tomber_ ◇ He tripped and fell Il a trébuché et il est tombé.
[2] _baisser_ ◇ Prices are falling. Les prix baissent.
• **to fall down (1)** (person) tomber
◇ She's fallen down. Elle est tombée.
• **to fall down (2)** (building) s'écrouler
◇ The house is slowly falling down. La maison est en train de s'écrouler.
• **to fall for (1)** se laisser prendre à
◇ They fell for it. Ils s'y sont laissé prendre.
• **to fall for (2)** tomber amoureux de
◇ She's falling for him. Elle est en train de tomber amoureuse de lui.
• **to fall off** tomber de ◇ The book fell off the shelf. Le livre est tombé de l'étagère.
• **to fall through** tomber à l'eau ◇ Our plans have fallen through. Nos projets sont tombés à l'eau.

false ADJECTIVE
faux MASC
fausse FEM
• **a false alarm** une fausse alerte
• **false teeth** les fausses dents

fame NOUN

la _renommée_

familiar ADJECTIVE
familier MASC
familière FEM
◇ a familiar face un visage familier
• **to be familiar with something** bien connaître quelque chose ◇ I'm familiar with his work. Je connais bien ses œuvres.

family NOUN
la _famille_
• **the Cooke family** la famille Cooke

famine NOUN
la _famine_

famous ADJECTIVE
célèbre

fan NOUN
[1] l' _éventail_ MASC (hand-held)
[2] le _ventilateur_ (electric)
[3] le/la _fan_ (of person, band) ◇ I'm a fan of Take That. Je suis une fan de Take That.
[4] le/la _supporter_ (of sport) ◇ football fans les supporters de football

fanatic NOUN
le/la _fanatique_

to **fancy** VERB
• **to fancy something** avoir envie de quelque chose ◇ I fancy an ice cream. J'ai envie d'une glace.
• **to fancy doing something** avoir envie de faire quelque chose
• **He fancies her.** Elle lui plaît.

fancy dress NOUN
le _déguisement_ ◇ He was wearing fancy dress. Il portait un déguisement.
• **a fancy-dress ball** un bal costumé

fantastic ADJECTIVE
fantastique

far ADJECTIVE, ADVERB
loin ◇ Is it far? Est-ce que c'est loin?
• **far from** loin de ◇ It's not far from London. Ce n'est pas loin de Londres.
◇ It's far from easy. C'est loin d'être facile.
• **How far is it?** C'est à quelle distance?
• **How far is it to Geneva?** Combien y a-t-il jusqu'à Genève?
• **How far have you got?** (with a task) Où en êtes-vous?
• **at the far end** à l'autre bout ◇ at the far end of the room à l'autre bout de la pièce
• **far better** beaucoup mieux
• **as far as I know** pour autant que je sache

fare NOUN
[1] le _prix du billet_ (on trains, buses)
[2] le _prix de la course_ (in taxi)
• **half fare** le demi-tarif
• **full fare** le plein tarif

Far East NOUN
l' *Extrême-Orient* MASC
* **in the Far East** en Extrême-Orient

farm NOUN
la *ferme*

farmer NOUN
l' *agriculteur* MASC
l' *agricultrice* FEM
◦ *He's a farmer.* Il est agriculteur.

farmhouse NOUN
la *ferme*

farming NOUN
l' *agriculture* FEM
* **dairy farming** l'industrie laitière

fascinating ADJECTIVE
fascinant

fashion NOUN
la *mode*
* **in fashion** à la mode

fashionable ADJECTIVE
à la mode ◦ *Jane wears very
fashionable clothes.* Jane porte des
vêtements très à la mode. ◦ *a
fashionable restaurant* un restaurant à la
mode

fast ADJECTIVE, ADVERB
[1] *vite* ◦ *He can run fast.* Il sait courir
vite.
[2] *rapide* ◦ *a fast car* une voiture
rapide
* **That clock's fast.** Cette pendule avance.
* **He's fast asleep.** Il est profondément
endormi.

fat ADJECTIVE
see also fat NOUN
gros MASC
grosse FEM

fat NOUN
see also fat ADJECTIVE
[1] le *gras* (on meat, in food) ◦ *It's very
high in fat.* C'est très gras.
[2] la *matière grasse* (for cooking)

fatal ADJECTIVE
[1] (causing death)
mortel MASC
mortelle FEM
◦ *a fatal accident* un accident mortel
[2] (disastrous)
fatal ◦ *He made a fatal mistake.* Il a
fait une erreur fatale.

father NOUN
le *père* ◦ *my father* mon père

father-in-law NOUN
le *beau-père*
(les *beaux-pères* PL)

fault NOUN
[1] la *faute* (mistake) ◦ *It's my fault.* C'est
de ma faute.
[2] le *défaut* (defect) ◦ *There's a fault in*

this material. Ce tissu a un défaut.
* **a mechanical fault** une défaillance
mécanique

faulty ADJECTIVE
défectueux MASC
défectueuse FEM
◦ *This machine is faulty.* Cette machine
est défectueuse.

favour NOUN
le *service*
* **to do somebody a favour** rendre service
à quelqu'un ◦ *Could you do me a
favour?* Tu peux me rendre service?
* **to be in favour of something** être pour
quelque chose ◦ *I'm in favour of nuclear
disarmament.* Je suis pour le
désarmement nucléaire.

favourite ADJECTIVE
see also favourite NOUN
favori MASC
favorite FEM
◦ *Blue's my favourite colour.* Le bleu est
ma couleur favorite.

favourite NOUN
see also favourite ADJECTIVE
[1] le *favori*
[2] la *favorite* ◦ *Liverpool are favourites
to win the Cup.* L'équipe de Liverpool est
favorite pour la coupe.

fear NOUN
see also fear VERB
la *peur*

to **fear** VERB
see also fear NOUN
craindre ◦ *You have nothing to fear.*
Vous n'avez rien à craindre.

feather NOUN
la *plume*

feature NOUN
la *caractéristique* (of person, object) ◦ *an
important feature* une caractéristique
essentielle

February NOUN
février MASC
* **in February** en février

fed VERB see **feed**

fed up ADJECTIVE
* **to be fed up with something** en avoir
marre de quelque chose ◦ *I'm fed up of
waiting for him.* J'en ai marre de
l'attendre.

to **feed** VERB
donner à manger à ◦ *Have you fed
the cat?* Est-ce que tu as donné à
manger au chat?
* **He worked hard to feed his family.** Il
travaillait dur pour nourrir sa famille.

to **feel** VERB
[1] *se sentir* ◦ *I don't feel well.* Je ne me

sens pas bien. ◇ *I feel a bit lonely.* Je me
sens un peu seul.
  [2] *sentir* ◇ *I didn't feel much pain.* Je
n'ai presque rien senti.
  [3] *toucher* ◇ *The doctor felt his
forehead.* Le docteur lui a touché le
front.
- **I was feeling hungry.** J'avais faim.
- **I was feeling cold, so I went inside.**
J'avais froid, donc je suis rentré.
- **I feel like...** (*want*) J'ai envie de... ◇ *Do
you feel like an ice cream?* Tu as envie
d'une glace?

feeling NOUN
  [1] la *sensation* (*physical*) ◇ *a burning
feeling* une sensation de brûlure
  [2] le *sentiment* (*emotional*) ◇ *a feeling of
satisfaction* un sentiment de satisfaction

feet PL NOUN *see* **foot**

fell VERB *see* **fall**

felt VERB *see* **feel**

felt-tip pen NOUN
le *stylo-feutre*

female ADJECTIVE
  see also **female** NOUN
  [1] *femelle* ◇ *a female animal* un
animal femelle
  [2] *féminin* ◇ *the female sex* le sexe
féminin

female NOUN
  see also **female** ADJECTIVE
la *femelle* (*animal*)

feminine ADJECTIVE
féminin

feminist NOUN
le/la *féministe*

fence NOUN
la *barrière*

fern NOUN
la *fougère*

ferocious ADJECTIVE
féroce

ferry NOUN
le *ferry*

fertile ADJECTIVE
fertile

fertilizer NOUN
l' *engrais* MASC

festival NOUN
le *festival* ◇ *a jazz festival* un festival
de jazz

to **fetch** VERB
  [1] *aller chercher* ◇ *Fetch the bucket.*
Va chercher le seau.
  [2] *se vendre* (*sell for*) ◇ *His painting
fetched £5000.* Son tableau s'est vendu
cinq mille livres.

fever NOUN
la *fièvre* (*temperature*)

few ADJECTIVE, PRONOUN
peu dc (*not many*) ◇ *few books* peu de
livres
- **a few (1)** quelques ◇ *a few hours*
quelques heures
- **a few (2)** quelques-uns ◇ *How many
apples do you want?–A few.* Tu veux
combien de pommes?–Quelques-unes.
- **quite a few people** pas mal de monde

fewer ADJECTIVE
moins de ◇ *There are fewer people
than there were yesterday.* Il y a moins
de monde qu'hier. ◇ *There are fewer
pupils in this class.* Il y a moins d'élèves
dans cette classe.

fiancé NOUN
le *fiancé* ◇ *He's my fiancé.* C'est mon
fiancé.

fiancée NOUN
la *fiancée* ◇ *She's my fiancée.* C'est
ma fiancée.

fiction NOUN
les *romans* MASC PL (*novels*)

field NOUN
  [1] le *champ* (*in countryside*) ◇ *a field of
wheat* un champ de blé
  [2] le *terrain* (*for sport*) ◇ *a football field*
un terrain de football
  [3] le *domaine* (*subject*) ◇ *He's an expert
in his field.* C'est un expert dans son
domaine.

fierce ADJECTIVE
  [1] *féroce* ◇ *The dog looked very fierce.*
Le chien avait l'air très féroce.
  [2] *violent* ◇ *The wind was very fierce.*
Le vent était très violent. ◇ *a fierce
attack* une attaque violente

fifteen NUMBER
quinze ◇ *I'm fifteen.* J'ai quinze ans.

fifth ADJECTIVE
cinquième ◇ *the fifth floor* le
cinquième étage
- **the fifth of August** le cinq août

fifty NUMBER
cinquante ◇ *He's fifty.* Il a cinquante
ans.

fifty-fifty ADJECTIVE, ADVERB
moitié-moitié ◇ *They split the prize
money fifty-fifty.* Ils ont partagé l'argent
du prix moitié-moitié.
- **a fifty-fifty chance** une chance sur deux

fight NOUN
  see also **fight** VERB
  [1] la *bagarre* ◇ *There was a fight in the
pub.* Il y a eu une bagarre au pub.
  [2] la *lutte* ◇ *the fight against cancer* la
lutte contre le cancer

to **fight** VERB
  see also **fight** NOUN

F

[1] *se battre* ◇ *They were fighting.* Ils se battaient.

[2] *lutter contre* ◇ *The doctors tried to fight the disease.* Les médecins ont essayé de lutter contre la maladie. ◇ *He fought against the urge to smoke.* Il a lutté contre son envie de fumer.

fighting NOUN

les *bagarres* FEM PL ◇ *Fighting broke out outside the pub.* Des bagarres ont éclaté devant le pub.

figure NOUN

[1] le *chiffre* (*number*) ◇ *Can you give me the exact figures?* Pouvez-vous me donner les chiffres exacts?

[2] la *silhouette* (*outline of person*) ◇ *Hélène saw the figure of a man on the bridge.* Hélène a vu la silhouette d'un homme sur le pont.

◆ **She's got a good figure.** Elle est bien faite.

◆ **I have to watch my figure.** Je dois faire attention à ma ligne.

[3] le *personnage* (*personality*) ◇ *She's an important political figure.* C'est un personnage politique important.

to **figure out** VERB

[1] *calculer* ◇ *I'll try to figure out how much it'll cost.* Je vais essayer de calculer combien ça va coûter.

[2] *voir* ◇ *I couldn't figure out what it meant.* Je n'arrivais pas à voir ce que ça voulait dire.

[3] *cerner* ◇ *I can't figure him out at all.* Je n'arrive pas du tout à le cerner.

file NOUN

see also **file** VERB

[1] le *dossier* (*document*) ◇ *Have we got a file on the suspect?* Est-ce que nous avons un dossier sur le suspect?

[2] la *chemise* (*folder*) ◇ *She keeps all her letters in a cardboard file.* Elle garde toutes ses lettres dans une chemise en carton.

[3] le *classeur* (*ring binder*)

[4] le *fichier* (*on computer*)

[5] la *lime* (*for nails, metal*)

to **file** VERB

see also **file** NOUN

[1] *classer* (*papers*)

[2] *limer* (*nails, metal*) ◇ *to file one's nails* se limer les ongles

to **fill** VERB

remplir ◇ *She filled the glass with water.* Elle a rempli le verre d'eau.

◆ **to fill in (1)** remplir ◇ *Can you fill this form in please?* Est-ce que vous pouvez remplir ce formulaire s'il vous plaît?

◆ **to fill in (2)** boucher ◇ *He filled the hole*

in with soil. Il a bouché le trou avec de la terre.

◆ **to fill up** remplir ◇ *He filled the cup up to the brim.* Il a rempli la tasse à ras bords.

◆ **Fill it up, please.** (*at petrol station*) Le plein, s'il vous plaît.

film NOUN

[1] le *film* (*movie*)

[2] la *pellicule* (*for camera*)

film star NOUN

la *vedette de cinéma* ◇ *He's a film star.* C'est une vedette de cinéma.

filthy ADJECTIVE

dégoûtant

final ADJECTIVE

see also **final** NOUN

[1] (*last*)

dernier MASC

dernière FEM

◇ *our final farewells* nos derniers adieux

[2] (*definite*)

définitif MASC

définitive FEM

◇ *a final decision* une décision définitive

◆ **I'm not going and that's final.** Je n'y vais pas, un point c'est tout.

final NOUN

see also **final** ADJECTIVE

la *finale* ◇ *Boris Becker is in the final.* Boris Becker va disputer la finale.

finally ADVERB

[1] *enfin* (*lastly*) ◇ *Finally, I would like to say...* Enfin, je voudrais dire...

[2] *finalement* (*eventually*) ◇ *They finally decided to leave on Saturday instead of Friday.* Ils ont finalement décidé de partir samedi au lieu de vendredi.

to **find** VERB

[1] *trouver* ◇ *I can't find the exit.* Je ne trouve pas la sortie.

[2] *retrouver* (*something lost*) ◇ *Did you find your pen?* Est-ce que tu as retrouvé ton crayon?

◆ **to find something out** découvrir quelque chose ◇ *I'm determined to find out the truth.* Je suis décidé à découvrir la vérité.

◆ **to find out about (1)** (*make enquiries*) se renseigner sur ◇ *Try to find out about the cost of a hotel.* Essaye de te renseigner sur le prix d'un hôtel.

◆ **to find out about (2)** (*by chance*) apprendre ◇ *I found out about their affair.* J'ai appris leur liaison.

fine ADJECTIVE, ADVERB

see also **fine** NOUN

[1] *excellent* (*very good*) ◇ *He's a fine musician.* C'est un excellent musicien.

- **to be fine** aller bien ⋄ *How are you?–I'm fine.* Comment ça va?–Ça va bien.
- **I feel fine.** Je me sens bien.
- **The weather is fine today.** Il fait beau aujourd'hui.

2 *fin* (*not coarse*) ⋄ *She's got very fine hair.* Elle a les cheveux très fins.

fine NOUN
see also fine ADJECTIVE

1 l' *amende* FEM ⋄ *She got a £50 fine.* Elle a eu une amende de cinquante livres.

2 la *contravention* (*for traffic offence*) ⋄ *I got a fine for driving through a red light.* J'ai eu une contravention pour avoir grillé un feu rouge.

finger NOUN
le *doigt*
- **my little finger** mon petit doigt

fingernail NOUN
l' *ongle* MASC

finish NOUN
see also finish VERB

l' *arrivée* FEM (*of race*) ⋄ *We saw the finish of the London Marathon.* Nous avons vu l'arrivée du marathon de Londres.

to **finish** VERB
see also finish NOUN

1 *finir* ⋄ *I've finished!* J'ai fini!
- **to finish doing something** finir de faire quelque chose

2 *terminer* ⋄ *I've finished the book.* J'ai terminé ce livre. ⋄ *The film has finished.* Le film est terminé.

Finland NOUN
la *Finlande*
- **in Finland** en Finlande
- **to Finland** en Finlande

Finn NOUN
le *Finlandais*
la *Finlandaise*

Finnish ADJECTIVE
see also Finnish NOUN
finlandais

Finnish NOUN
see also Finnish ADJECTIVE
le *finnois* (*language*)

fire NOUN
see also fire VERB

1 le *feu*
(les *feux* PL)
⋄ *He made a fire to warm himself up.* Il a fait du feu pour se réchauffer.
- **to be on fire** être en feu

2 l' *incendie* MASC (*accidental*) ⋄ *The house was destroyed by fire.* La maison a été détruite par un incendie.

3 le *radiateur* (*heater*) ⋄ *Turn the fire on.* Allume le radiateur.
- **the fire brigade** les pompiers MASC PL
- **a fire alarm** un avertisseur d'incendie
- **a fire engine** une voiture de pompiers
- **a fire escape** un escalier de secours
- **a fire extinguisher** un extincteur
- **a fire station** une caserne de pompiers

to **fire** VERB
see also fire NOUN

tirer (*shoot*) ⋄ *She fired twice.* Elle a tiré deux fois.
- **to fire at somebody** tirer sur quelqu'un ⋄ *The terrorist fired at the crowd.* Le terroriste a tiré sur la foule.
- **to fire a gun** tirer un coup de feu
- **to fire somebody** mettre quelqu'un à la porte ⋄ *He was fired from his job.* Il a été mis à la porte.

fireman NOUN
le *pompier* ⋄ *He's a fireman.* Il est pompier.

fireplace NOUN
la *cheminée*

fireworks PL NOUN
le *feu d'artifice* SING ⋄ *Are you going to see the fireworks?* Est-ce que tu vas voir le feu d'artifice?

firm ADJECTIVE
see also firm NOUN
ferme ⋄ *to be firm with somebody* se montrer ferme avec quelqu'un

firm NOUN
see also firm ADJECTIVE
l' *entreprise* FEM ⋄ *He works for a large firm in London.* Il travaille pour une grande entreprise à Londres.

first ADJECTIVE, ADVERB
see also first NOUN

1 *premier* MASC
première FEM
⋄ *the first of September* le premier septembre ⋄ *the first time* la première fois
- **to come first** (*in exam, race*) arriver premier ⋄ *Rachel came first.* Rachel est arrivée première.

2 *d'abord* ⋄ *I want to get a job, but first I have to pass my exams.* Je veux trouver du travail, mais d'abord je dois réussir à mes examens.
- **first of all** tout d'abord

first NOUN
see also first ADJECTIVE
le *premier*
la *première*
⋄ *She was the first to arrive.* Elle est arrivée la première.
- **at first** au début

F

first aid NOUN

les _premiers secours_ MASC PL
- **a first aid kit** une trousse de secours

first-class ADJECTIVE

1 _de première classe_　◦ _She has booked a first-class ticket._ Elle a réservé un billet de première classe.

2 _excellent_　◦ _a first-class meal_ un excellent repas
- **a first-class stamp**

> In France there is no first-class or second-class postage. However letters cost more to send than postcards, so you have to remember to say what you are sending when buying stamps.

firstly ADVERB

premièrement　◦ _Firstly, let's see what the book is about._ Premièrement, voyons de quoi parle ce livre.

fish NOUN

see also fish VERB

le _poisson_　◦ _I caught three fish._ J'ai pêché trois poissons.　◦ _I don't like fish._ Je n'aime pas le poisson.

to **fish** VERB

see also fish NOUN

pêcher
- **to go fishing** aller à la pêche　◦ _We went fishing in the River Dee._ Nous sommes allés à la pêche sur la Dee.

fisherman NOUN

le _pêcheur_　◦ _He's a fisherman._ Il est pêcheur.

fishing NOUN

la _pêche_　◦ _My hobby is fishing._ La pêche est mon passe-temps favori.

fishing boat NOUN

le _bateau de pêche_

fishing rod NOUN

la _canne à pêche_

fishing tackle NOUN

le _matériel de pêche_

fist NOUN

le _poing_

to **fit** VERB

see also fit ADJECTIVE, NOUN

1 _être la bonne taille_ (be the right size)　◦ _Does it fit?_ Est-ce que c'est la bonne taille?

> In French you usually specify whether something is too big, small, tight etc.

- **These trousers don't fit me. (1)** (too big) Ce pantalon est trop grand pour moi.
- **These trousers don't fit me. (2)** (too small) Ce pantalon est trop petit pour moi.

2 _installer_ (fix up)　◦ _He fitted an alarm in his car._ Il a installé une alarme dans sa voiture.

3 _adapter_ (attach)　◦ _She fitted a plug to_

the hair dryer. Elle a adapté une prise au sèche-cheveux.

- **to fit in (1)** (match up) correspondre　◦ _That story doesn't fit in with what he told us._ Cette histoire ne correspond pas à ce qu'il nous a dit.
- **to fit in (2)** (person) s'adapter　◦ _She fitted in well at her new school._ Elle s'est bien adaptée à sa nouvelle école.

fit ADJECTIVE

see also fit VERB, NOUN

en forme (in condition)　◦ _He felt relaxed and fit after his holiday._ Il se sentait détendu et en forme après ses vacances.

fit NOUN

see also fit ADJECTIVE, VERB

- **to have a fit (1)** (epileptic) avoir une crise d'épilepsie
- **to have a fit (2)** (be angry) piquer une crise de nerfs　◦ _My Mum will have a fit when she sees the carpet!_ Ma mère va piquer une crise de nerfs quand elle va voir la moquette!

fitted carpet NOUN

la _moquette_

fitted kitchen NOUN

la _cuisine aménagée_

fitting room NOUN

la _cabine d'essayage_

five NUMBER

cinq　◦ _He's five._ Il a cinq ans.

to **fix** VERB

1 _réparer_ (mend)　◦ _Can you fix my bike?_ Est-ce que tu peux réparer mon vélo?

2 _fixer_ (decide)　◦ _Let's fix a date for the party._ Fixons une date pour la soirée.　◦ _They fixed a price for the car._ Ils ont fixé un prix pour la voiture.

3 _préparer_　◦ _Janice fixed some food for us._ Janice nous a préparé à manger.

fixed ADJECTIVE

fixe　◦ _at a fixed time_ à une heure fixe　◦ _at a fixed price_ à un prix fixe　◦ _a fixed-price menu_ un menu à prix fixe
- **My parents have very fixed ideas.** Mes parents ont des idées très arrêtées.

fizzy ADJECTIVE

gazeux MASC
gazeuse FEM
　◦ _I don't like fizzy drinks._ Je n'aime pas les boissons gazeuses.

flabby ADJECTIVE

flasque

flag NOUN

le _drapeau_
(les _drapeaux_ PL)

flame NOUN

la _flamme_

flamingo NOUN
le *flamant rose*

flan NOUN
[1] la *tarte* (sweet) ◇ *a raspberry flan* une tarte aux framboises
[2] la *quiche* (savoury) ◇ *a cheese and onion flan* une quiche au fromage et aux oignons

flannel NOUN
le *gant de toilette* (for face)

to **flap** VERB
battre de ◇ *The bird flapped its wings.* L'oiseau battait des ailes.

flash NOUN
see also flash VERB
le *flash*
(les *flashes* PL)
◇ *Has your camera got a flash?* Est-ce que ton appareil photo a un flash?
◆ **a flash of lightning** un éclair
◆ **in a flash** en un clin d'œil

to **flash** VERB
see also flash NOUN
[1] *clignoter* ◇ *The police car's blue light was flashing.* Le gyrophare de la voiture de police clignotait.
[2] *projeter* ◇ *They flashed a torch in his face.* Ils lui ont projeté la lumière d'une torche en plein visage.
◆ **She flashed her headlights.** Elle a fait un appel de phares.

flat ADJECTIVE
see also flat NOUN
[1] *plat* ◇ *a flat roof* un toit plat ◇ *flat shoes* des chaussures plates
[2] *crevé* (tyre) ◇ *I've got a flat tyre.* J'ai un pneu crevé.

flat NOUN
see also flat ADJECTIVE
l' *appartement* MASC ◇ *She lives in a flat.* Elle habite un appartement.

to **flatter** VERB
flatter

flavour NOUN
[1] le *goût* (taste) ◇ *This cheese has a very strong flavour.* Ce fromage a un goût très fort.
[2] le *parfum* (variety) ◇ *Which flavour of ice cream would you like?* Quel parfum de glace est-ce que tu veux?

flavouring NOUN
le *parfum*

flew VERB see **fly**

flexible ADJECTIVE
flexible ◇ *flexible working hours* les horaires flexibles

to **flick** VERB
appuyer sur ◇ *She flicked the switch to turn the light on.* Elle a appuyé sur le bouton pour allumer la lumière.
◆ **to flick through a book** feuilleter un livre

to **flicker** VERB
trembloter ◇ *The light flickered.* La lumière a trembloté.

flight NOUN
le *vol* ◇ *What time is the flight to Paris?* À quelle heure est le vol pour Paris?
◆ **a flight of stairs** un escalier

to **fling** VERB
jeter ◇ *He flung the dictionary onto the floor.* Il a jeté le dictionnaire par terre.

to **float** VERB
flotter ◇ *A leaf was floating on the water.* Une feuille flottait sur l'eau.

flock NOUN
◆ **a flock of sheep** un troupeau de moutons
◆ **a flock of birds** un vol d'oiseaux

flood NOUN
see also flood VERB
[1] l' *inondation* FEM ◇ *The rain has caused many floods.* La pluie a provoqué de nombreuses inondations.
[2] le *flot* ◇ *He received a flood of letters.* Il a reçu un flot de lettres.

to **flood** VERB
see also flood NOUN
inonder ◇ *The river has flooded the village.* La rivière a inondé le village.

flooding NOUN
les *inondations* FEM PL

floor NOUN
[1] le *sol* ◇ *a tiled floor* un sol carrelé
◆ **on the floor** par terre
[2] l' *étage* MASC (storey) ◇ *the first floor* le premier étage
◆ **the ground floor** le rez-de-chaussée
◆ **on the third floor** au troisième étage

floppy disk NOUN
la *disquette*

florist NOUN
le/la *fleuriste*

flour NOUN
la *farine*

to **flow** VERB
[1] *couler* (river)
[2] *s'écouler* (flow out) ◇ *Water was flowing from the pipe.* De l'eau s'écoulait du tuyau.

flower NOUN
see also flower VERB
la *fleur*

to **flower** VERB
see also flower NOUN
fleurir

flown VERB see **fly**

flu NOUN

la *grippe* ◇ *She's got flu.* Elle a la grippe.

fluent ADJECTIVE
- **He speaks fluent French.** Il parle couramment le français.

flung VERB *see* **fling**

flush NOUN
see also **flush** VERB
la *chasse d'eau* (*of toilet*)

to **flush** VERB
see also **flush** NOUN
- **to flush the toilet** tirer la chasse

flute NOUN
la *flûte* ◇ *I play the flute.* Je joue de la flûte.

fly NOUN
see also **fly** VERB
la *mouche* (*insect*)

to **fly** VERB
see also **fly** NOUN
1 *voler* ◇ *The plane flies at a speed of 400 km per hour.* L'avion vole à quatre cents kilomètres à l'heure.
2 *aller en avion* (*passenger*) ◇ *He flew from Paris to New York.* Il est allé de Paris à New York en avion.
- **to fly away** s'envoler ◇ *The bird flew away.* L'oiseau s'est envolé.

foal NOUN
le *poulain*

focus NOUN
see also **focus** VERB
- **to be out of focus** être flou ◇ *The house is out of focus in this photo.* La maison est floue sur cette photo.

to **focus** VERB
see also **focus** NOUN
mettre au point ◇ *Try to focus the binoculars.* Essaye de mettre les jumelles au point.
- **to focus on something (1)** (*with camera, telescope*) régler la mise au point sur quelque chose ◇ *The cameraman focused on the bird.* Le caméraman a réglé la mise au point sur l'oiseau.
- **to focus on something (2)** (*concentrate*) se concentrer sur quelque chose ◇ *Let's focus on the plot of the play.* Concentrons-nous sur l'intrigue de la pièce.

fog NOUN
le *brouillard*

foggy ADJECTIVE
- **It's foggy.** Il y a du brouillard.
- **a foggy day** un jour de brouillard

foil NOUN (*kitchen foil*)
le *papier d'aluminium* ◇ *She wrapped the meat in foil.* Elle a enveloppé la viande dans du papier d'aluminium.

fold NOUN
see also **fold** VERB
le *pli*

to **fold** VERB
see also **fold** NOUN
plier ◇ *He folded the newspaper in half.* Il a plié le journal en deux.
- **to fold something up** plier quelque chose
- **to fold one's arms** croiser ses bras ◇ *She folded her arms.* Elle a croisé les bras.

folder NOUN
1 la *chemise* ◇ *She kept all her letters in a folder.* Elle gardait toutes ses lettres dans une chemise.
2 le *classeur* (*ring binder*)

folding ADJECTIVE
- **a folding chair** une chaise pliante
- **a folding bed** un lit pliant

to **follow** VERB
suivre ◇ *She followed him.* Elle l'a suivi. ◇ *You go first and I'll follow.* Va devant, je te suis.

following ADJECTIVE
suivant ◇ *the following day* le jour suivant

fond ADJECTIVE
- **to be fond of somebody** aimer beaucoup quelqu'un ◇ *I'm very fond of her.* Je l'aime beaucoup.

food NOUN
la *nourriture*
- **We need to buy some food.** Nous devons acheter à manger.
- **cat food** la nourriture pour chat
- **dog food** la nourriture pour chien

fool NOUN
l' *idiot* MASC
l' *idiote* FEM

foot NOUN
1 le *pied* (*of person*) ◇ *My feet are aching.* J'ai mal aux pieds.
2 la *patte* (*of animal*) ◇ *The dog's foot was injured.* Le chien était blessé à la patte.
- **on foot** à pied
3 le *pied* (*12 inches*)
In France measurements are in metres and centimetres rather than feet and inches. A foot is about 30 centimetres.
- **Dave is 6 foot tall.** Dave mesure un mètre quatre-vingt.
- **That mountain is 5000 feet high.** Cette montagne fait mille six cents mètres de haut.

football NOUN
1 le *football* (*game*) ◇ *I like playing football.* J'aime jouer au football.

2 le *ballon* (*ball*)   ◇ *Paul threw the football over the fence.* Paul a envoyé le ballon par dessus la clôture.

football player NOUN
le *joueur de football*
la *joueuse de football*
◇ *He's a famous football player.* C'est un joueur de football célèbre.

footpath NOUN
le *sentier*   ◇ *Jane followed the footpath through the forest.* Jane a suivi le sentier à travers la forêt.

footprint NOUN
la *trace de pas*   ◇ *He saw some footprints in the sand.* Il a vu des traces de pas sur le sable.

footstep NOUN
le *pas*   ◇ *I can hear footsteps on the stairs.* J'entends des pas dans l'escalier.

for PREPOSITION

There are several ways of translating for. *Scan the examples to find one that is similar to what you want to say.*

1 *pour*   ◇ *a present for me* un cadeau pour moi ◇ *the train for London* le train pour Londres ◇ *He works for the government.* Il travaille pour le gouvernement.   ◇ *I'll do it for you.* Je vais le faire pour toi.   ◇ *Can you do it for tomorrow?* Est-ce que vous pouvez le faire pour demain? ◇ *Are you for or against the idea?* Êtes-vous pour ou contre cette idée? ◇ *Oxford is famous for its university.* Oxford est célèbre pour son université.

When referring to periods of time, use **pendant** *for the future and completed actions in the past, and* **depuis** *(with the French verb in the present tense) for something that started in the past and is still going on.*

2 *pendant*   ◇ *He worked in France for two years.* Il a travaillé en France pendant deux ans.   ◇ *She will be away for a month.* Elle sera absente pendant un mois.   ◇ *There are road works for three kilometres.* Il y a des travaux pendant trois kilomètres.

3 *depuis*   ◇ *He's been learning French for two years.* Il apprend le français depuis deux ans.   ◇ *She's been away for a month.* Elle est absente depuis un mois.

When talking about amounts of money, you do not translate for.

◇ *I sold it for £5.* Je l'ai vendu cinq livres.
◇ *He paid fifty pence for his ticket.* Il a payé son billet cinquante pence.

◆ **What's the French for "lion"?** Comment dit-on "lion" en français?
◆ **It's time for lunch.** C'est l'heure du

déjeuner.
◆ **What for?** Pour quoi faire?   ◇ *Give me some money! – What for?* Donne-moi de l'argent! – Pour quoi faire?
◆ **What's it for?** Ça sert à quoi?
◆ **for sale** à vendre   ◇ *The factory's for sale.* L'usine est en vente.

to **forbid** VERB
défendre
◆ **to forbid somebody to do something** défendre à quelqu'un de faire quelque chose   ◇ *I forbid you to go out tonight!* Je te défends de sortir ce soir.

forbidden ADJECTIVE
défendu   ◇ *Smoking is strictly forbidden.* Il est strictement défendu de fumer.

force NOUN
see also force VERB
la *force*   ◇ *the force of the explosion* la force de l'explosion
◆ **in force** en vigueur   ◇ *No-smoking rules are now in force.* Un règlement qui interdit de fumer est maintenant en vigueur.

to **force** VERB
see also force NOUN
forcer   ◇ *They forced him to open the safe.* Ils l'ont obligé à ouvrir le coffre-fort.

forecast NOUN
◆ **the weather forecast** la météo

foreground NOUN
le *premier plan*   ◇ *in the foreground* au premier plan

forehead NOUN
le *front*

foreign ADJECTIVE
étranger MASC
étrangère FEM

foreigner NOUN
l' *étranger* MASC
l' *étrangère* FEM

to **foresee** VERB
prévoir   ◇ *He had foreseen the problem.* Il avait prévu ce problème.

forest NOUN
la *forêt*

forever ADVERB
1 *pour toujours*   ◇ *He's gone forever.* Il est parti pour toujours.
2 *toujours* (*always*)   ◇ *She's forever complaining.* Elle est toujours en train de se plaindre.

forgave VERB *see* **forgive**

to **forge** VERB
contrefaire   ◇ *She tried to forge his signature.* Elle a essayé de contrefaire sa signature.

forged ADJECTIVE

faux MASC
fausse FEM
  ◇ _forged banknotes_ des faux billets

to **forget** VERB
oublier   ◇ _I've forgotten his name._ J'ai
oublié son nom.   ◇ _I'm sorry, I completely
forgot!_ Je suis désolé, j'ai complètement
oublié!

to **forgive** VERB
◆ **to forgive somebody** pardonner à
quelqu'un   ◇ _I forgive you._ Je te
pardonne.
◆ **to forgive somebody for doing
something** pardonner à quelqu'un
d'avoir fait quelque chose   ◇ _She
forgave him for forgetting her birthday._
Elle lui a pardonné d'avoir oublié son
anniversaire.

fork NOUN
1 la _fourchette_ (_for eating_)
2 la _fourche_ (_for gardening_)
3 la _bifurcation_ (_in road_)

form NOUN
1 le _formulaire_ (_paper_)   ◇ _to fill in a form_
remplir un formulaire
2 la _forme_ (_type_)   ◇ _I'm against hunting
in any form._ Je suis contre la chasse sous
toutes ses formes.
◆ **in top form** en pleine forme
◆ **She's in the fourth form.** Elle est en
troisième.

formal ADJECTIVE
1 (_occasion_)
officiel MASC
officielle FEM
  ◇ _a formal dinner_ un dîner officiel
2 (_person_)
guindé
3 (_language_)
soutenu   ◇ _In English, "residence" is a
formal term._ En anglais, "residence" est
un terme soutenu.
◆ **formal clothes** une tenue habillée
◆ **He's got no formal education.** Il n'a pas
fait beaucoup d'études.

former ADJECTIVE
ancien MASC
ancienne FEM
  ◇ _a former pupil_ un ancien élève ◇ _the
former Prime Minister_ l'ancien Premier
ministre

fort NOUN
le _fort_

forth ADVERB
◆ **to go back and forth** aller et venir
◆ **and so forth** et ainsi de suite

fortnight NOUN
◆ **a fortnight** quinze jours   ◇ _I'm going on
holiday for a fortnight._ Je pars en

vacances pendant quinze jours.

fortunate ADJECTIVE
◆ **to be fortunate** avoir de la chance
  ◇ _He was extremely fortunate to survive._
Il a eu énormément de chance de
survivre.
◆ **It's fortunate that I remembered the
map.** C'est une chance que j'aie pris la
carte.

fortunately ADVERB
heureusement   ◇ _Fortunately, it didn't
rain._ Heureusement, il n'a pas plu.

fortune NOUN
la _fortune_   ◇ _Kate earns a fortune!_ Kate
gagne une fortune!
◆ **to tell somebody's fortune** dire la
bonne aventure à quelqu'un

forty NUMBER
quarante   ◇ _He's forty._ Il a quarante
ans.

forward ADVERB
see also **forward** VERB
◆ **to move forward** avancer

to **forward** VERB
see also **forward** ADVERB
faire suivre   ◇ _He forwarded all
Janette's letters._ Il a fait suivre toutes les
lettres de Janette.

foster child NOUN
l' _enfant adoptif_ MASC
l' _enfant adoptive_ FEM

fought VERB see **fight**

foul ADJECTIVE
see also **foul** NOUN
infect   ◇ _The weather was foul._ Le
temps était infect.   ◇ _What a foul smell!_
Quelle odeur infecte!

foul NOUN
see also **foul** ADJECTIVE
la _faute_   ◇ _Ferguson committed a foul._
Ferguson a fait une faute.

found VERB see **find**

to **found** VERB
fonder   ◇ _Baden Powell founded the
Scout Movement._ Baden Powell a fondé
le mouvement scout.

foundations PL NOUN
les _fondations_ FEM PL

fountain NOUN
la _fontaine_

fountain pen NOUN
le _stylo à encre_

four NUMBER
quatre   ◇ _She's four._ Elle a quatre ans.

fourteen NUMBER
quatorze   ◇ _I'm fourteen._ J'ai quatorze
ans.

fourth ADJECTIVE
quatrième   ◇ _the fourth floor_ le

quatrième étage
- **the fourth of July** le quatre juillet

fox NOUN
le *renard*

fragile ADJECTIVE
fragile

frame NOUN
le *cadre* (*for picture*)

France NOUN
la *France*
- **in France** en France
- **to France** en France
- **He's from France.** Il est français.

frantic ADJECTIVE
- **I was going frantic.** J'étais dans tous mes états.
- **to be frantic with worry** être folle d'inquiétude

fraud NOUN
[1] la *fraude* (*crime*) ◇ *He was jailed for fraud.* On l'a mis en prison pour fraude.
[2] l' *imposteur* MASC (*person*) ◇ *He's not a real doctor, he's a fraud.* Ce n'est pas un vrai médecin, c'est un imposteur.

free ADJECTIVE
see also free VERB
[1] *gratuit* (*free of charge*) ◇ *a free brochure* une brochure gratuite
[2] *libre* (*not busy, not taken*) ◇ *Is this seat free?* Est-ce que cette place est libre?
◇ *Are you free after school?* Tu es libre après l'école?

to **free** VERB
see also free ADJECTIVE
libérer

freedom NOUN
la *liberté*

to **freeze** VERB
[1] *geler* ◇ *The water had frozen.* L'eau avait gelé.
[2] *congeler* (*food*) ◇ *She froze the rest of the raspberries.* Elle a congelé le reste des framboises.

freezer NOUN
le *congélateur*

freezing ADJECTIVE
- **It's freezing!** Il fait un froid de canard! (*informal*)
- **I'm freezing!** Je suis gelé! (*informal*)
- **3 degrees below freezing** moins trois

freight NOUN
la *cargaison* (*goods*)
- **a freight train** un train de marchandises

French ADJECTIVE
see also French NOUN
français ◇ *He's French.* Il est français.
◇ *She's French.* Elle est française.

French NOUN
see also French ADJECTIVE

le *français* (*language*) ◇ *Do you speak French?* Est-ce que tu parles français?
- **the French** (*people*) les Français

French beans PL NOUN
les *haricots verts*

French fries PL NOUN
les *frites* FEM PL

French horn NOUN
le *cor (d'harmonie)* ◇ *I play the French horn.* Je joue du cor.

French kiss NOUN
le *baiser profond*

French loaf NOUN
la *baguette*

Frenchman NOUN
le *Français*

Frenchwoman NOUN
la *Française*

frequent ADJECTIVE
fréquent ◇ *frequent showers* des averses fréquentes
- **There are frequent buses to the town centre.** Il y a beaucoup de bus pour le centre ville.

fresh ADJECTIVE
frais MASC
fraîche FEM
- **I need some fresh air.** J'ai besoin de prendre l'air.

to **freshen up** VERB
faire un brin de toilette ◇ *I'd like to go and freshen up.* Je voudrais faire un brin de toilette.

to **fret** VERB
se tracasser ◇ *Philip was fretting about his exams.* Philip se tracassait au sujet de ses examens.

Friday NOUN
le *vendredi* ◇ *on Friday* vendredi ◇ *on Fridays* le vendredi ◇ *every Friday* tous les vendredis ◇ *last Friday* vendredi dernier ◇ *next Friday* vendredi prochain

fridge NOUN
le *frigo*

fried ADJECTIVE
frit ◇ *fried vegetables* des légumes frits
- **a fried egg** un œuf sur le plat

friend NOUN
l' *ami* MASC
l' *amie* FEM

friendly ADJECTIVE
[1] *gentil* MASC
gentille FEM
◇ *She's really friendly.* Elle est vraiment gentille.
[2] *accueillant* ◇ *Liverpool is a very friendly city.* Liverpool est une ville très accueillante.

friendship NOUN

l' *amitié* FEM

fright NOUN
la *peur* ◦ *I got a terrible fright!* Ça m'a fait une peur terrible!

to **frighten** VERB
faire peur à ◦ *Horror films frighten him.* Les films d'horreur lui font peur.

frightened ADJECTIVE
* **to be frightened** avoir peur ◦ *I'm frightened!* J'ai peur!
* **to be frightened of something** avoir peur de quelque chose ◦ *Anna's frightened of spiders.* Anna a peur des araignées.

frightening ADJECTIVE
effrayant

fringe NOUN
la *frange* (*of hair*) ◦ *She's got a fringe.* Elle a une frange.

Frisbee ® NOUN
le *Frisbee* ® ◦ *to play Frisbee* jouer au Frisbee

fro ADVERB
* **to go to and fro** aller et venir

frog NOUN
la *grenouille*
* **frogs' legs** les cuisses de grenouille

from PREPOSITION
de ◦ *Where do you come from?* D'où venez-vous? ◦ *I come from Perth.* Je viens de Perth. ◦ *a letter from my sister* une lettre de ma sœur ◦ *The hotel is one kilometre from the beach.* L'hôtel est à un kilomètre de la plage.
* **from...to...** de...à... ◦ *He flew from London to Paris.* Il a pris l'avion de Londres à Paris. ◦ *from 1 o'clock to 2* d'une heure à deux heures ◦ *The price was reduced from £10 to £5.* Ils ont réduit le prix de dix livres à cinq.
* **from...onwards** à partir de... ◦ *We'll be at home from 7 o'clock onwards.* Nous serons chez nous à partir de sept heures.

front NOUN
see also front ADJECTIVE
le *devant* ◦ *the front of the house* le devant de la maison
* **in front** devant ◦ *a house with a car in front* une maison avec une voiture devant ◦ *the car in front* la voiture de devant
* **in front of** devant ◦ *in front of the house* devant la maison ◦ *the car in front of us* la voiture devant nous
* **in the front** (*of car*) à l'avant ◦ *I was sitting in the front.* J'étais assis à l'avant.
* **at the front of the train** à l'avant du train

front ADJECTIVE
see also front NOUN
1 *de devant* ◦ *the front row* la rangée de devant
2 *avant* ◦ *the front seats of the car* les sièges avant de la voiture
* **the front door** la porte d'entrée

frontier NOUN
la *frontière*

frost NOUN
le *gel*

frosty ADJECTIVE
* **It's frosty today.** Il gèle aujourd'hui.

to **frown** VERB
froncer les sourcils ◦ *He frowned.* Il a froncé les sourcils.

froze VERB *see* **freeze**

frozen ADJECTIVE
see also freeze
surgelé (*food*) ◦ *frozen chips* des frites surgelées

fruit NOUN
le *fruit*
* **fruit juice** le jus de fruits
* **a fruit salad** une salade de fruits

fruit machine NOUN
la *machine à sous*

frustrated ADJECTIVE
frustré

to **fry** VERB
faire frire ◦ *Fry the onions for 5 minutes.* Faites frire les oignons pendant cinq minutes.

frying pan NOUN
la *poêle*

fuel NOUN
le *carburant* (*for car, aeroplane*) ◦ *to run out of fuel* avoir une panne de carburant

to **fulfil** VERB
réaliser ◦ *Robert fulfilled his dream to visit China.* Robert a réalisé son rêve de visiter la Chine.

full ADJECTIVE, ADVERB
1 *plein* ◦ *The tank's full.* Le réservoir est plein.
2 *complet* MASC
complète FEM
◦ *He asked for full information on the job.* Il a demandé des renseignements complets sur le poste.
* **your full name** vos nom et prénoms ◦ *My full name is Ian John Marr.* Je m'appelle Ian John Marr.
* **I'm full.** (*after meal*) J'ai bien mangé.
* **at full speed** à toute vitesse ◦ *He drove at full speed.* Il conduisait à toute vitesse
* **There was a full moon.** C'était la pleine lune.

full stop NOUN

le *point*

full-time ADJECTIVE, ADVERB
à plein temps ◇ *She's got a full-time job.* Elle a un travail à plein temps.
◇ *She works full-time.* Elle travaille à plein temps.

fully ADVERB
complètement ◇ *He hasn't fully recovered from his illness.* Il n'est pas complètement remis de sa maladie.

fumes PL NOUN
les *fumées* FEM PL ◇ *The factory gave out dangerous fumes.* L'usine rejetait des fumées dangereuses.
• **exhaust fumes** les gaz d'échappement

fun ADJECTIVE
see also fun NOUN
marrant ◇ *She's a fun person.* Elle est marrante.

fun NOUN
see also fun ADJECTIVE
• **to have fun** s'amuser ◇ *We had great fun playing in the snow.* Nous nous sommes bien amusés à jouer dans la neige.
• **for fun** pour rire ◇ *He entered the competition just for fun.* Il a participé à la compétition juste pour rire.
• **to make fun of somebody** se moquer de quelqu'un ◇ *They made fun of him.* Ils se sont moqués de lui.
• **It's fun!** C'est chouette!
• **Have fun!** Amuse-toi bien!

funds PL NOUN
les *fonds* MASC ◇ *to raise funds* collecter des fonds

funeral NOUN
l' *enterrement* MASC

funfair NOUN
la *fête foraine*

funny ADJECTIVE
1 *drôle* (*amusing*) ◇ *It was really funny.* C'était vraiment drôle.
2 *bizarre* (*strange*) ◇ *There's something funny about him.* Il est un peu bizarre.

fur NOUN
1 la *fourrure* ◇ *a fur coat* un manteau de fourrure
2 le *poil* ◇ *the dog's fur* le poil du chien

furious ADJECTIVE
furieux
furieuse FEM
◇ *Dad was furious with me.* Papa était furieux contre moi.

furniture NOUN
les *meubles* MASC PL ◇ *a piece of furniture* un meuble

further ADVERB, ADJECTIVE
plus loin ◇ *London is further from Manchester than Leeds is.* Londres est plus loin de Manchester que Leeds.
• **How much further is it?** C'est encore loin?

further education NOUN
l' *enseignement postscolaire* MASC

fuse NOUN
le *fusible* ◇ *The fuse has blown.* Le fusible a sauté.

fuss NOUN
l' *agitation* FEM ◇ *What's all the fuss about?* Qu'est-ce que c'est que toute cette agitation!
• **to make a fuss** faire des histoires ◇ *He's always making a fuss about nothing.* Il fait toujours des histoires pour rien.

fussy ADJECTIVE
difficile ◇ *She is very fussy about her food.* Elle est très difficile sur la nourriture.

future NOUN
1 l' *avenir* MASC ◇ *What are your plans for the future?* Quels sont vos projets pour l'avenir?
• **in future** à l'avenir ◇ *Be more careful in future.* Sois plus prudent à l'avenir.
2 le *futur* (*in grammar*) ◇ *Put this sentence into the future.* Mettez cette phrase au futur.

G

to **gain** VERB
- **to gain weight** prendre du poids
- **to gain speed** prendre de la vitesse

gallery NOUN
le *musée* ⋄ an art gallery un musée
d'art

to **gamble** VERB
jouer ⋄ He gambled £100 at the casino.
Il a joué cent livres au casino.

gambler NOUN
le *joueur*

gambling NOUN
le *jeu* ⋄ He likes gambling. Il aime le
jeu.

game NOUN
① le *jeu*
(les *jeux* PL)
⋄ The children were playing a game. Les
enfants jouaient à un jeu.
② le *match* (sport) ⋄ a game of football
un match de football
- **a game of cards** une partie de cartes

gang NOUN
la *bande*

gangster NOUN
le *gangster*

gap NOUN
① le *trou* ⋄ There's a gap in the hedge.
Il y a un trou dans la haie.
② l' *intervalle* MASC ⋄ a gap of four
years un intervalle de quatre ans

garage NOUN
le *garage*

garden NOUN
le *jardin*

gardener NOUN
le *jardinier* ⋄ He's a gardener. Il est
jardinier.

gardening NOUN
le *jardinage* ⋄ Margaret loves
gardening. Margaret aime le jardinage.

gardens PL NOUN
le *jardin public* SING

garlic NOUN
l' *ail* MASC

garment NOUN
le *vêtement*

gas NOUN
le *gaz*
- **a gas cooker** une cuisinière à gaz
- **a gas cylinder** une bouteille de gaz
- **a gas fire** un radiateur à gaz
- **a gas leak** une fuite de gaz

gate NOUN
① le *portail* (of garden)
② la *barrière* (of field)

③ la *porte* (at airport)

gateau NOUN
le *gâteau à la crème*

to **gather** VERB
se rassembler (assemble) ⋄ People
gathered in front of Buckingham Palace.
Les gens se sont rassemblés devant
Buckingham Palace.
- **to gather speed** prendre de la vitesse
⋄ The train gathered speed. Le train a
pris de la vitesse.

gave VERB see **give**

gay ADJECTIVE
homosexuel MASC
homosexuelle FEM

to **gaze** VERB
- **to gaze at something** fixer quelque
chose du regard ⋄ He gazed at her. Il
l'a fixée du regard.

gear NOUN
① la *vitesse* (in car) ⋄ in first gear en
première vitesse ⋄ to change gear
changer de vitesse
② le *matériel* ⋄ camping gear le
matériel de camping
- **your sports gear** (clothes) tes affaires de
sport

gear lever NOUN
le *levier de vitesse*

geese PL NOUN see **goose**

gel NOUN
le *gel*
- **hair gel** le gel pour les cheveux

gem NOUN
la *pierre précieuse*

Gemini NOUN
les *Gémeaux* MASC PL ⋄ I'm Gemini. Je
suis Gémeaux.

general NOUN
see also **general** ADJECTIVE
le *général*
(les *généraux* PL)

general ADJECTIVE
see also **general** NOUN
général
(*généraux* MASC PL)
- **in general** en général

general election NOUN
les *élections législatives* FEM PL

general knowledge NOUN
les *connaissances générales* FEM PL

generally ADVERB
généralement ⋄ I generally go
shopping on Saturday. Généralement, je
fais mes courses le samedi.

generation NOUN

la *génération* ◇ *the younger generation*
la nouvelle génération

generator NOUN
le *générateur*

generous ADJECTIVE
généreux MASC
généreuse FEM
◇ *That's very generous of you.* C'est très
généreux de votre part.

Geneva NOUN
Genève
- **in Geneva** à Genève
- **to Geneva** à Genève
- **Lake Geneva** le lac Léman

genius NOUN
le *génie* ◇ *She's a genius!* C'est un
génie!

gentle ADJECTIVE
doux MASC
douce FEM

gentleman NOUN
le *monsieur*
(les *messieurs* PL)
◇ *Good morning, gentlemen.* Bonjour
messieurs.

gently ADVERB
doucement

gents NOUN
les *toilettes pour hommes* FEM PL
◇ *Can you tell me where the gents are,
please?* Pouvez-vous me dire où sont les
toilettes, s'il vous plaît?
- **"gents"** (*on sign*) "messieurs"

genuine ADJECTIVE
1 *véritable* (*real*) ◇ *These are genuine
diamonds.* Ce sont de véritables
diamants.
2 *sincère* (*sincere*) ◇ *She's a very
genuine person.* C'est quelqu'un de très
sincère.

geography NOUN
la *géographie*

germ NOUN
le *microbe*

German ADJECTIVE
see also German NOUN
allemand

German NOUN
see also German ADJECTIVE
1 (*person*)
l' *Allemand* MASC
l' *Allemande* FEM
2 (*language*)
l' *allemand* ◇ *Do you speak German?*
Parlez-vous allemand?

Germany NOUN
l' *Allemagne* FEM
- **in Germany** en Allemagne
- **to Germany** en Allemagne

to **get** VERB

There are several ways of translating get. *Scan
the examples to find one that is similar to what
you want to say.*

1 *avoir* (*have, receive*) ◇ *I got lots of
presents.* J'ai eu beaucoup de cadeaux.
◇ *He got first prize.* Il a eu le premier
prix. ◇ *Jackie got good exam results.*
Jackie a eu de bons résultats aux
examens. ◇ *How many have you got?*
Combien en avez-vous?

2 *aller chercher* (*fetch*) ◇ *Quick, get
help!* Allez vite chercher de l'aide!

3 *attraper* (*catch*) ◇ *They've got the
thief.* Ils ont attrapé le voleur.

4 *prendre* (*train, bus*) ◇ *I'm getting the
bus into town.* Je prends le bus pour aller
en ville.

5 *comprendre* (*understand*) ◇ *I don't
get the joke.* Je ne comprends pas cette
blague.

6 *aller* (*go*) ◇ *How do you get to the
castle?* Comment est-ce qu'on va au
château?

7 *arriver* (*arrive*) ◇ *He should get here
soon.* Il devrait arriver bientôt.

8 *devenir* (*become*) ◇ *to get old*
devenir vieux

- **to get something done** faire faire
quelque chose ◇ *to get one's hair cut* se
faire couper les cheveux
- **to get something for somebody** trouver
quelque chose pour quelqu'un ◇ *The
librarian got the book for me.* Le
bibliothécaire m'a trouvé le livre.
- **to have got to do something** devoir
faire quelque chose ◇ *I've got to tell
him.* Je dois le lui dire.
- **to get back** (1) rentrer ◇ *What time did
you get back?* Tu es rentré à quelle
heure?
- **to get back** (2) récupérer ◇ *He got his
money back.* Il a récupéré son argent.
- **to get in** rentrer ◇ *What time did you
get in last night?* Tu es rentré à quelle
heure hier soir?
- **to get into** monter dans ◇ *Sharon got
into the car.* Sharon est montée dans la
voiture.
- **to get off** descendre de (*vehicle, bike*)
◇ *Isobel got off the train.* Isobel est
descendue du train.
- **to get on** (1) (*vehicle*) monter dans
◇ *Phyllis got on the bus.* Phyllis est
montée dans le bus.
- **to get on** (2) (*bike*) enfourcher ◇ *Carol
got on her bike.* Carol a enfourché son
vélo.
- **to get on with somebody** s'entendre

G

avec quelqu'un ◇ *He doesn't get on with his parents.* Il ne s'entend pas avec ses parents. ◇ *We got on really well.* Nous nous sommes très bien entendus.

- **to get out** sortir ◇ *Hélène got out of the car.* Hélène est sortie de la voiture. ◇ *Get out!* Sortez!
- **to get something out** sortir quelque chose ◇ *She got the map out.* Elle a sorti la carte.
- **to get up** se lever ◇ *What time do you get up?* Tu te lèves à quelle heure?

ghetto blaster NOUN
le *radiocassette portable*

ghost NOUN
le *fantôme*

giant ADJECTIVE
see also giant NOUN
énorme ◇ *They ate a giant meal.* Ils ont mangé un énorme repas.

giant NOUN
see also giant ADJECTIVE
le *géant*
la *géante*

gift NOUN
[1] *(present)*
le *cadeau*
(les *cadeaux* PL)
[2] *(talent)*
le *don*

- **to have a gift for something** être doué pour quelque chose ◇ *Dave has a gift for painting.* Dave est doué pour la peinture.

gifted ADJECTIVE
doué ◇ *Janice is a gifted dancer.* Janice est douée pour la danse.

gift shop NOUN
la *boutique de cadeaux*

gigantic ADJECTIVE
gigantesque

gin NOUN
le *gin*

ginger NOUN
see also ginger ADJECTIVE
le *gingembre* ◇ *Add a teaspoon of ginger.* Ajoutez une cuillère à café de gingembre.

ginger ADJECTIVE
see also ginger NOUN
roux MASC
rousse FEM
◇ *Chris has ginger hair.* Chris a les cheveux roux.

giraffe NOUN
la *girafe*

girl NOUN
[1] la *fille* ◇ *They've got a girl and two boys.* Ils ont une fille et deux garçons.

[2] la *petite fille* *(young)* ◇ *a five-year-old girl* une petite fille de cinq ans
[3] la *jeune fille* *(older)* ◇ *a sixteen-year-old girl* une jeune fille de seize ans ◇ *an English girl* une jeune Anglaise

girlfriend NOUN
[1] la *copine* *(lover)* ◇ *Damon's girlfriend is called Justine.* La copine de Damon s'appelle Justine.
[2] l' *amie* FEM *(friend)* ◇ *She often went out with her girlfriends.* Elle sortait souvent avec ses amies.

to **give** VERB
donner

- **to give something to somebody** donner quelque chose à quelqu'un ◇ *He gave me £10.* Il m'a donné dix livres.
- **to give something back to somebody** rendre quelque chose à quelqu'un ◇ *I gave the book back to him.* Je lui ai rendu le livre.
- **to give something out** distribuer quelque chose ◇ *The teacher gave out the books.* Le professeur a distribué les livres.
- **to give in** céder ◇ *His Mum gave in and let him go out.* Sa mère a cédé et l'a laissé sortir.
- **to give up** laisser tomber ◇ *I couldn't do it, so I gave up.* Je n'arrivais pas à le faire, alors j'ai laissé tomber.
- **to give up doing something** arrêter de faire quelque chose ◇ *He gave up smoking.* Il a arrêté de fumer.
- **to give oneself up** se rendre ◇ *The thief gave himself up.* Le voleur s'est rendu.
- **to give way** céder la priorité *(in traffic)*

glad ADJECTIVE
content ◇ *She's glad she's done it.* Elle est contente de l'avoir fait.

to **glance** VERB
see also glance NOUN

- **to glance at something** jeter un coup d'œil à quelque chose ◇ *Peter glanced at his watch.* Peter a jeté un coup d'œil à sa montre.

glance NOUN
see also glance VERB
le *coup d'œil* ◇ *at first glance* au premier coup d'œil

to **glare** VERB

- **to glare at somebody** lancer un regard furieux à quelqu'un ◇ *He glared at me.* Il m'a lancé un regard furieux.

glaring ADJECTIVE

- **a glaring mistake** une erreur qui saute

aux yeux

glass NOUN
le *verre* ◦ *a glass of milk* un verre de lait

glasses PL NOUN
les *lunettes* FEM ◦ *Jean-Pierre wears glasses.* Jean-Pierre porte des lunettes.

glider NOUN
le *planeur*

gliding NOUN
le *vol à voile* ◦ *My hobby is gliding.* Je fais du vol à voile.

global ADJECTIVE
mondial
(*mondiaux* MASC PL)
◆ **on a global scale** à l'échelle mondiale

global warming NOUN
le *réchauffement de la planète*

globe NOUN
le *globe*

glove NOUN
le *gant*

glove compartment NOUN
la *boîte à gants*

glue NOUN
la *colle*

go NOUN
see also go VERB
◆ **to have a go at doing something** essayer de faire quelque chose ◦ *He had a go at making a cake.* Il a essayé de faire un gâteau.
◆ **Whose go is it?** À qui le tour?

to go VERB
see also go NOUN
1 *aller* ◦ *I'm going to the cinema tonight.* Je vais au cinéma ce soir.
2 *partir* (*leave*) ◦ *Where's Pierre?–He's gone.* Où est Pierre?–Il est parti.
3 *s'en aller* (*go away*) ◦ *I'm going now.* Je m'en vais.
4 *marcher* (*vehicle*) ◦ *My car won't go.* Ma voiture ne marche pas.
◆ **to go home** rentrer à la maison ◦ *I go home at about 4 o'clock.* Je rentre à la maison vers quatre heures.
◆ **to go for a walk** aller se promener ◦ *Shall we go for a walk?* Si on allait se promener?
◆ **How did it go?** Comment est-ce que ça s'est passé?
◆ **I'm going to do it tomorrow.** Je vais le faire demain.
◆ **It's going to be difficult.** Ça va être difficile.

go after VERB
suivre ◦ *Quick, go after them!* Vite, suivez-les!

to go away VERB
s'en aller ◦ *Go away!* Allez-vous-en!

to go back VERB
> Use **rentrer** only when you are entering a building, usually your home; otherwise use **retourner**.

1 *retourner* ◦ *We went back to the same place.* Nous sommes retournés au même endroit.
2 *rentrer* ◦ *Is he still here?–No, he's gone back home.* Est-ce qu'il est encore là?–Non, il est rentré chez lui.

to go by VERB
passer ◦ *Two policemen went by.* Deux policiers sont passés.

to go down VERB
1 *descendre* (*person*) ◦ *to go down the stairs* descendre l'escalier
2 *baisser* (*decrease*) ◦ *The price of computers has gone down.* Le prix des ordinateurs a baissé.
3 *se dégonfler* (*deflate*) ◦ *My airbed kept going down.* Mon matelas pneumatique se dégonflait constamment.
◆ **My brother's gone down with flu.** Mon frère a attrapé la grippe.

to go for VERB
attaquer (*attack*) ◦ *Suddenly the dog went for me.* Soudain, le chien m'a attaqué.
◆ **Go for it!** (*go on!*) Vas-y, fonce!

to go in VERB
entrer ◦ *He knocked on the door and went in.* Il a frappé à la porte et il est entré.

to go off VERB
1 *exploser* (*bomb*) ◦ *The bomb went off.* La bombe a explosé.
2 *se déclencher* (*alarm, gun*) ◦ *The fire alarm went off.* L'avertisseur d'incendie s'est déclenché.
3 *sonner* (*alarm clock*) ◦ *My alarm clock goes off at seven every morning.* Mon réveil sonne à sept heures tous les matins.
4 *tourner* (*food*) ◦ *The milk's gone off.* Le lait a tourné.
5 *partir* (*go away*) ◦ *He went off in a huff.* Il est parti de mauvaise humeur.

to go on VERB
1 *se passer* (*happen*) ◦ *What's going on?* Qu'est-ce qui se passe?
2 *continuer* (*carry on*) ◦ *The concert went on until 11 o'clock at night.* Le concert a continué jusqu'à onze heures du soir.
◆ **to go on doing something** continuer à faire quelque chose ◦ *He went on*

G

reading. Il a continué à lire.

* **to go on at somebody** être sur le dos de quelqu'un ◇ *My parents always go on at me.* Mes parents sont toujours sur mon dos.

* **Go on!** Allez! ◇ *Go on, tell me what the problem is!* Allez, dis-moi quel est le problème!

to **go out** VERB

1 *sortir* (person) ◇ *Are you going out tonight?* Tu sors ce soir?

* **to go out with somebody** sortir avec quelqu'un ◇ *Are you going out with him?* Est-ce que tu sors avec lui?

2 *s'éteindre* (light, fire, candle) ◇ *Suddenly the lights went out.* Soudain, les lumières se sont éteintes.

to **go past** VERB

* **to go past something** passer devant quelque chose ◇ *He went past the shop.* Il est passé devant la boutique.

to **go round** VERB

* **to go round a corner** prendre un tournant
* **to go round to somebody's house** aller chez quelqu'un
* **to go round a museum** visiter un musée
* **to go round the shops** faire les boutiques
* **There's a bug going round.** Il y a un microbe qui circule.

to **go through** VERB

traverser ◇ *We went through Paris to get to Rennes.* Nous avons traversé Paris pour aller à Rennes.

to **go up** VERB

1 *monter* (person) ◇ *to go up the stairs* monter l'escalier

2 *augmenter* (increase) ◇ *The price has gone up.* Le prix a augmenté.

* **to go up in flames** s'embraser ◇ *The whole factory went up in flames.* L'usine toute entière s'est embrasée.

to **go with** VERB

aller avec ◇ *Does this blouse go with that skirt?* Est-ce que ce chemisier va avec cette jupe?

goal NOUN

le *but* ◇ *to score a goal* marquer un but ◇ *His goal is to become the world champion.* Son but est de devenir champion du monde.

goalkeeper NOUN

le *gardien de but*

goat NOUN

la *chèvre*

* **goat's cheese** le fromage de chèvre

god NOUN

le *dieu*

(les *dieux* PL)

◇ *I believe in God.* Je crois en Dieu.

gold NOUN

l' *or* MASC ◇ *They found some gold.* Ils ont trouvé de l'or. ◇ *a gold necklace* un collier en or

goldfish NOUN

le *poisson rouge* ◇ *I've got five goldfish.* J'ai cinq poissons rouges.

golf NOUN

le *golf* ◇ *My dad plays golf.* Mon père joue au golf.

* **a golf club** un club de golf

golf course NOUN

le *terrain de golf*

gone VERB *see* go

good ADJECTIVE

1 *bon* MASC

bonne FEM

◇ *It's a very good film.* C'est un très bon film. ◇ *Vegetables are good for you.* Les légumes sont bons pour la santé.

* **to be good at something** être bon en quelque chose ◇ *Jane's very good at maths.* Jane est très bonne en maths.

2 (kind)

gentil MASC

gentille FEM

◇ *They were very good to me.* Ils ont été très gentils avec moi. ◇ *That's very good of you.* C'est très gentil de votre part.

3 (not naughty)

sage ◇ *Be good!* Sois sage!

* **for good** pour de bon ◇ *One day he left for good.* Un jour il est parti pour de bon.

* **Good morning!** Bonjour!
* **Good afternoon!** Bonjour!
* **Good evening!** Bonsoir!
* **Good night!** Bonne nuit!
* **It's no good complaining.** Cela ne sert à rien de se plaindre.

goodbye EXCLAMATION

au revoir!

Good Friday NOUN

le *Vendredi saint*

good-looking ADJECTIVE

beau MASC

belle FEM

(*beaux* MASC PL)

◇ *He's very good-looking.* Il est très beau.

goods PL NOUN

les *marchandises* FEM (in shop)

* **a goods train** un train de marchandises

goose NOUN

l' *oie* FEM

gorgeous ADJECTIVE

1 *superbe* ◇ *She's gorgeous!* Elle est superbe!

[2] *splendide* ◇ *The weather was gorgeous.* Il a fait un temps splendide.

gorilla NOUN
le *gorille*

gossip NOUN
> see also gossip VERB

[1] les *cancans* MASC PL (*rumours*) ◇ *Tell me the gossip!* Raconte-moi les cancans!
[2] la *commère* (*woman*) ◇ *She's such a gossip!* C'est une vraie commère!
[3] le *bavard* (*man*) ◇ *What a gossip!* Quel bavard!

to **gossip** VERB
> see also gossip NOUN

[1] *bavarder* (*chat*) ◇ *They were always gossiping.* Elles étaient tout le temps en train de bavarder.
[2] *faire des commérages* (*about somebody*) ◇ *They gossiped about her.* Elles faisaient des commérages à son sujet.

got VERB *see* **get**

government NOUN
le *gouvernement*

to **grab** VERB
saisir

graceful ADJECTIVE
élégant

grade NOUN
la *note* (*at school*) ◇ *He got good grades in his exams.* Il a eu de bonnes notes à ses examens.

gradual ADJECTIVE
progressif MASC
progressive FEM

gradually ADVERB
peu à peu ◇ *We gradually got used to it.* Nous nous y sommes habitués peu à peu.

graduate NOUN
le *diplômé*
la *diplômée*

graffiti PL NOUN
les *graffiti* MASC

grain NOUN
le *grain*

gram NOUN
le *gramme*

grammar NOUN
la *grammaire*

grammar school NOUN
[1] le *collège*
[2] le *lycée*

> *In France pupils go to a* collège *between the ages of 11 and 15, and then to a* lycée *until the age of 18. French schools are mostly non-selective.*

grammatical ADJECTIVE
grammatical
(*grammaticaux* MASC PL)

gramme NOUN
le *gramme* ◇ *500 grammes of cheese* cinq cents grammes de fromage

grand ADJECTIVE
somptueux MASC
somptueuse FEM
 ◇ *Samantha lives in a very grand house.* Samantha habite une maison somptueuse.

grandchildren PL NOUN
les *petits-enfants* MASC PL

granddad NOUN
le *papi* ◇ *my granddad* mon papi

granddaughter NOUN
la *petite-fille*
(les *petites-filles* PL)

grandfather NOUN
le *grand-père*
(les *grands-pères* PL)
 ◇ *my grandfather* mon grand-père

grandma NOUN
la *mamie* ◇ *my grandma* ma mamie

grandmother NOUN
la *grand-mère*
(les *grands-mères* PL)
 ◇ *my grandmother* ma grand-mère

grandpa NOUN
le *papi* ◇ *my grandpa* mon papi

grandparents PL NOUN
les *grands-parents* MASC PL ◇ *my grandparents* mes grands-parents

grandson NOUN
le *petit-fils*
(les *petits-fils* PL)

granny NOUN
la *mamie* ◇ *my granny* ma mamie

grape NOUN
le *raisin*

grapefruit NOUN
le *pamplemousse*

graph NOUN
le *graphique*

to **grasp** VERB
saisir

grass NOUN
l' *herbe* FEM ◇ *The grass is long.* L'herbe est haute.
 • **to cut the grass** tondre le gazon

grasshopper NOUN
la *sauterelle*

to **grate** VERB
râper ◇ *to grate some cheese* râper du fromage

grateful ADJECTIVE
reconnaissant

grave NOUN
la *tombe*

gravel NOUN
le *gravier*

graveyard NOUN
le *cimetière*

gravy NOUN
la *sauce au jus de viande*

grease NOUN
le *lubrifiant*

greasy ADJECTIVE
gras MASC
grasse FEM
◇ *He has greasy hair.* Il a les cheveux gras. ◇ *The food was very greasy.* La nourriture était très grasse.

great ADJECTIVE
1 *génial*
(*géniaux* MASC PL)
◇ *That's great!* C'est génial!
2 *grand* ◇ *a great mansion* un grand manoir

Great Britain NOUN
la *Grande-Bretagne*
* **in Great Britain** en Grande-Bretagne
* **to Great Britain** en Grande-Bretagne
* **I'm from Great Britain.** Je suis britannique.

great-grandfather NOUN
l' *arrière-grand-père* MASC
(les *arrière-grands-pères* PL)

great-grandmother NOUN
l' *arrière-grand-mère* FEM
(les *arrière-grands-mères* PL)

Greece NOUN
la *Grèce*
* **in Greece** en Grèce
* **to Greece** en Grèce

greedy ADJECTIVE
1 *gourmand* (*for food*) ◇ *I want some more cake.—Don't be so greedy!* Je veux encore du gâteau.—Ne sois pas si gourmand!
2 *avide* (*for money*)

Greek ADJECTIVE
see also Greek NOUN
grec MASC
grecque FEM
◇ *Dionysis is Greek.* Dionysis est grec.
◇ *She's Greek.* Elle est grecque.

Greek NOUN
see also Greek ADJECTIVE
1 (*person*)
le *Grec*
la *Grecque*
2 (*language*)
le *grec*

green ADJECTIVE
see also green NOUN
1 *vert* ◇ *a green car* une voiture verte
◇ *a green salad* une salade verte
2 *écologiste* (*movement, candidate*) ◇ *the Green Party* le parti écologiste

green NOUN
see also green ADJECTIVE
le *vert* ◇ *a dark green* un vert foncé
* **greens** (*vegetables*) les légumes verts
* **the Greens** (*party*) les Verts MASC

greengrocer's NOUN
le *marchand de fruits et légumes*

greenhouse NOUN
la *serre*
* **the greenhouse effect** l'effet de serre MASC

Greenland NOUN
le *Groenland*

to **greet** VERB
accueillir ◇ *He greeted me with a kiss.* Il m'a accueillie en me donnant un baiser.

greeting NOUN
* **Greetings from Bangor!** Bonjour de Bangor!

greetings card NOUN
la *carte de vœux*

grew VERB see **grow**

grey ADJECTIVE
gris ◇ *She's got grey hair.* Elle a les cheveux gris.
* **He's going grey.** Il grisonne.

grey-haired ADJECTIVE
grisonnant

grid NOUN
1 (*in road*)
la *grille*
2 (*of electricity*)
le *réseau*
(les *réseaux* PL)

grief NOUN
le *chagrin*

grill NOUN
see also grill VERB
le *gril* (*of cooker*)
* **a mixed grill** les grillades FEM PL

to **grill** VERB
see also grill NOUN
* **to grill something** faire griller quelque chose

grim ADJECTIVE
sinistre

to **grin** VERB
see also grin NOUN
sourire ◇ *Dave grinned at me.* Dave m'a souri.

grin NOUN
see also grin VERB
le *large sourire*

to **grind** VERB
moudre (*coffee, pepper*)

to **grip** VERB
saisir

gripping ADJECTIVE

palpitant (exciting)

grit NOUN
le *gravillon*

to **groan** VERB

> see also groan NOUN

gémir ◇ *He groaned with pain.* Il a gémi sous l'effet de la douleur.

groan NOUN

> see also groan VERB

le *gémissement* (of pain)

grocer NOUN
l' *épicier* MASC ◇ *He's a grocer.* Il est épicier.

groceries PL NOUN
les *provisions* FEM

grocer's (shop) NOUN
l' *épicerie* FEM

groom NOUN
le *marié* (bridegroom) ◇ *the groom and his best man* le marié et son témoin

to **grope** VERB

◆ **to grope for something** chercher quelque chose à tâtons ◇ *He groped for the light switch.* Il a cherché à tâtons l'interrupteur.

gross ADJECTIVE
dégoûtant (revolting) ◇ *It was really gross!* C'était vraiment dégoûtant!

grossly ADVERB
largement ◇ *We're grossly underpaid.* Nous sommes largement sous payés.

ground NOUN

> see also ground VERB

1. le *sol* (earth) ◇ *The ground's wet.* Le sol est mouillé.
2. le *terrain* (for sport) ◇ *a football ground* un terrain de football
3. la *raison* (reason) ◇ *We've got grounds for complaint.* Nous avons des raisons de nous plaindre.

◆ **on the ground** par terre ◇ *We sat on the ground.* Nous nous sommes assis par terre.

ground VERB see **grind**

> see also ground NOUN

◆ **ground coffee** le café moulu

group NOUN
le *groupe*

to **grow** VERB

1. *pousser* (plant) ◇ *Grass grows quickly.* L'herbe pousse vite.
2. *grandir* (person, animal) ◇ *Haven't you grown!* Comme tu as grandi!
3. *augmenter* (increase) ◇ *The number of unemployed people has grown.* Le nombre de chômeurs a augmenté.
4. *faire pousser* (cultivate) ◇ *My Dad grows potatoes.* Mon père fait pousser des pommes de terre.

◆ **to grow a beard** se laisser pousser la barbe

◆ **to grow up** grandir ◇ *Oh, grow up!* Ne fais pas l'enfant!

◆ **He's grown out of his jacket.** Sa veste est devenue trop petite pour lui.

to **growl** VERB
grogner

grown VERB see **grow**

growth NOUN
la *croissance* ◇ *economic growth* la croissance économique

grub NOUN
la *bouffe* (informal)

grudge NOUN
la *rancune*

◆ **to bear a grudge against somebody** garder rancune à quelqu'un

gruesome ADJECTIVE
horrible

guarantee NOUN

> see also guarantee VERB

la *garantie*

◆ **a five-year guarantee** une garantie de cinq ans

to **guarantee** VERB

> see also guarantee NOUN

garantir ◇ *I can't guarantee he'll come.* Je ne peux pas garantir qu'il viendra.

to **guard** VERB

> see also guard NOUN

garder ◇ *They guarded the palace.* Ils gardaient le palais.

◆ **to guard against something** protéger contre quelque chose

guard NOUN

> see also guard VERB

le *chef de train* (of train)

◆ **a security guard** un vigile

◆ **a guard dog** un chien de garde

to **guess** VERB

> see also guess NOUN

deviner ◇ *Can you guess what it is?* Devine ce que c'est!

◆ **to guess wrong** se tromper ◇ *Janice guessed wrong.* Janice s'est trompée.

guess NOUN

> see also guess VERB

la *supposition* ◇ *It's just a guess.* C'est une simple supposition.

◆ **Have a guess!** Devine!

guest NOUN

1. l' *invité* MASC
   l' *invitée* FEM
   ◇ *We have guests staying with us.* Nous avons des invités.
2. (of hotel)
   le *client*
   la *cliente*

G

guide NOUN

[1] le *guide* (book, person) ◇ *We bought a guide to Paris.* Nous avons acheté un guide sur Paris. ◇ *The guide showed us round the castle.* Le guide nous a fait visiter le château.

[2] l' *éclaireuse* FEM (girl guide)

◆ **the Guides** les Éclaireuses

guidebook NOUN

le *guide*

guide dog NOUN

le *chien d'aveugle*

guilty ADJECTIVE

coupable ◇ *to feel guilty* se sentir coupable ◇ *She was found guilty.* Elle a été reconnue coupable.

guinea pig NOUN

le *cobaye*

guitar NOUN

la *guitare* ◇ *I play the guitar.* Je joue de la guitare.

gum NOUN

le *chewing-gum* (sweet)

◆ **gums** (in mouth) les gencives FEM

gun NOUN

[1] le *revolver* (small)

[2] le *fusil* (rifle)

gust NOUN

◆ **a gust of wind** une rafale de vent

guy NOUN

le *type* ◇ *Who's that guy?* C'est qui ce type? ◇ *He's a nice guy.* C'est un type sympa.

gym NOUN

la *gym* ◇ *I go to the gym every day.* Je vais tous les jours à la gym.

◆ **gym classes** les cours de gym

gymnast NOUN

le/la *gymnaste* ◇ *She's a gymnast.* Elle est gymnaste.

gymnastics NOUN

la *gymnastique* ◇ *to do gymnastics* faire de la gymnastique

H

habit NOUN
l' *habitude* ◇ *a bad habit* une mauvaise habitude

had VERB *see* **have**

hadn't = had not

hail NOUN
see also hail VERB
la *grêle*

to **hail** VERB
see also hail NOUN
grêler ◇ *It's hailing.* Il grêle.

hair NOUN
[1] les *cheveux* MASC PL ◇ *She's got long hair.* Elle a les cheveux longs. ◇ *He's got black hair.* Il a les cheveux noirs. ◇ *He's losing his hair.* Il perd ses cheveux.
◆ **to brush one's hair** se brosser les cheveux ◇ *I brush my hair every morning.* Je me brosse les cheveux tous les matins.
◆ **to wash one's hair** se laver les cheveux ◇ *I need to wash my hair.* Il faut que je me lave les cheveux.
◆ **to have one's hair cut** se faire couper les cheveux ◇ *I've just had my hair cut.* Je viens de me faire couper les cheveux.
◆ **a hair (1)** (*from head*) un cheveu
◆ **a hair (2)** (*from body*) un poil
[2] le *pelage* (*fur of animal*)

hairbrush NOUN
la *brosse à cheveux*

haircut NOUN
la *coupe*
◆ **to have a haircut** se faire couper les cheveux ◇ *I've just had a haircut.* Je viens de me faire couper les cheveux.

hairdresser NOUN
le *coiffeur*
la *coiffeuse*
◇ *He's a hairdresser.* Il est coiffeur.

hairdresser's NOUN
le *coiffeur* ◇ *at the hairdresser's* chez le coiffeur

hair dryer NOUN
le *sèche-cheveux*
(les *sèche-cheveux* PL)

hair gel NOUN
le *gel pour les cheveux*

hairgrip NOUN
la *pince à cheveux*

hair spray NOUN
la *laque*

hairstyle NOUN
la *coiffure*

hairy ADJECTIVE
poilu ◇ *He's got hairy legs.* Il a les jambes poilues.

half NOUN
see also half ADJECTIVE
[1] la *moitié* ◇ *half of the cake* la moitié du gâteau
[2] le *billet demi-tarif* (*ticket*) ◇ *A half to York, please.* Un billet demi-tarif pour York, s'il vous plaît.
◆ **two and a half** deux et demi
◆ **half an hour** une demi-heure
◆ **half past ten** dix heures et demie
◆ **half a kilo** cinq cents grammes
◆ **to cut something in half** couper quelque chose en deux

half ADJECTIVE, ADVERB
see also half NOUN
[1] *demi* ◇ *a half chicken* un demi-poulet
[2] *à moitié* ◇ *He was half asleep.* Il était à moitié endormi.

half-hour NOUN
la *demi-heure*

half-price ADJECTIVE, ADVERB
◆ **at half-price** à moitié prix

half-time NOUN
la *mi-temps*

halfway ADVERB
[1] *à mi-chemin* ◇ *halfway between Oxford and London* à mi-chemin entre Oxford et Londres
[2] *à la moitié* ◇ *halfway through the chapter* à la moitié du chapitre

hall NOUN
[1] l' *entrée* FEM (*in house*)
[2] la *salle* ◇ *the village hall* la salle des fêtes

Hallowe'en NOUN
la *veille de la Toussaint*

hallway NOUN
le *vestibule*

halt NOUN
◆ **to come to a halt** s'arrêter

ham NOUN
le *jambon*
◆ **a ham sandwich** un sandwich au jambon

hamburger NOUN
le *hamburger*

hammer NOUN
le *marteau*
(les *marteaux* PL)

hamster NOUN
le *hamster*

hand NOUN
see also hand VERB
[1] la *main* (*of person*)

◆ **to give somebody a hand** donner un coup de main à quelqu'un ◇ *Can you give me a hand?* Tu peux me donner un coup de main?

◆ **on the one hand..., on the other hand...** d'une part..., d'autre part...

2 l' *aiguille* FEM (*of clock*)

to hand VERB

> *see also* hand NOUN

passer ◇ *He handed me the book.* Il m'a passé le livre.

◆ **to hand something in** rendre quelque chose ◇ *Martin handed his exam paper in.* Martin a rendu sa copie d'examen.

◆ **to hand something out** distribuer quelque chose ◇ *The teacher handed out the books.* Le professeur a distribué les livres.

◆ **to hand something over** remettre quelque chose ◇ *She handed the keys over to me.* Elle m'a remis les clés.

handbag NOUN
le *sac à main*
(les *sacs à main* PL)

handbook NOUN
le *manuel*

handcuffs PL NOUN
les *menottes* FEM

handkerchief NOUN
le *mouchoir*

handle NOUN

> *see also* handle VERB

1 la *poignée* (*of door*)
2 l' *anse* FEM (*of cup*)
3 le *manche* (*of knife*)
4 la *queue* (*of saucepan*)

to handle VERB

> *see also* handle NOUN

◆ **He handled it well.** Il s'en est bien tiré.

◆ **Kath handled the travel arrangements.** Kath s'est occupée de l'organisation du voyage.

◆ **She's good at handling children.** Elle sait s'y prendre bien avec les enfants.

handlebars PL NOUN
le *guidon* SING

handmade ADJECTIVE
fait à la main

handsome ADJECTIVE
beau MASC
belle FEM
◇ *He's very handsome.* Il est très beau.

handwriting NOUN
l' *écriture* FEM

handy ADJECTIVE
1 *pratique* ◇ *This knife's very handy.* Ce couteau est très pratique.
2 *sous la main* ◇ *Have you got a pen handy?* Est-ce que tu as un stylo sous la main?

to hang VERB
1 *accrocher* ◇ *Mike hung the painting on the wall.* Mike a accroché le tableau au mur.
2 *pendre* ◇ *They hanged the criminal.* Ils ont pendu le criminel.

◆ **to hang around** traîner ◇ *On Saturdays we hang around in the park.* Le samedi nous traînons dans le parc.

◆ **to hang on** patienter ◇ *Hang on a minute please.* Patientez une minute s'il vous plaît.

◆ **to hang up (1)** (*clothes*) accrocher ◇ *Hang your jacket up on the hook.* Accrochez votre veste au portemanteau.

◆ **to hang up (2)** (*phone*) raccrocher ◇ *I tried to phone him but he hung up on me.* J'ai essayé de l'appeler, mais il m'a raccroché au nez.

hang-gliding NOUN
le *deltaplane*

◆ **to go hang-gliding** faire du deltaplane

hangover NOUN
la *gueule de bois* ◇ *to have a hangover* avoir la gueule de bois

to happen VERB
se passer ◇ *What's happened?* Qu'est-ce qui s'est passé?

◆ **as it happens** justement ◇ *As it happens, I don't want to go.* Justement, je ne veux pas y aller.

happily ADVERB
1 *joyeusement* ◇ *"Don't worry!" he said happily.* "Ne te fais pas de souci!" dit-il joyeusement.
2 *heureusement* (*fortunately*) ◇ *Happily, everything went well.* Heureusement, tout s'est bien passé.

happiness NOUN
le *bonheur*

happy ADJECTIVE
heureux MASC
heureuse FEM
◇ *Janet looks happy.* Janet a l'air heureuse.

◆ **I'm very happy with your work.** Je suis très satisfait de ton travail.

◆ **Happy birthday!** Bon anniversaire!

harbour NOUN
le *port*

hard ADJECTIVE, ADVERB
1 *dur* ◇ *This cheese is very hard.* Ce fromage est très dur. ◇ *He's worked very hard.* Il a travaillé très dur.
2 *difficile* ◇ *This question's too hard for me.* Cette question est trop difficile pour moi.

hard disk NOUN

le *disque dur* (of computer)

hardly ADVERB
* **I've hardly got any money.** Je n'ai presque pas d'argent.
* **I hardly know you.** Je te connais à peine.
* **hardly ever** presque jamais

hard up ADJECTIVE
fauché

hare NOUN
le *lièvre*

to **harm** VERB
* **to harm somebody** faire du mal à quelqu'un ◇ *I didn't mean to harm you.* Je ne voulais pas te faire de mal.
* **to harm something** nuire à quelque chose ◇ *Chemicals harm the environment.* Les produits chimiques nuisent à l'environnement.

harmful ADJECTIVE
nuisible ◇ *harmful chemicals* des produits chimiques nuisibles

harmless ADJECTIVE
inoffensif MASC
inoffensive FEM
◇ *Most spiders are harmless.* La plupart des araignées sont inoffensives.

has VERB *see* **have**

hasn't = has not

hat NOUN
le *chapeau*
(les *chapeaux* PL)

to **hate** VERB
détester ◇ *I hate maths.* Je déteste les maths.

hatred NOUN
la *haine*

to **have** VERB
[1] *avoir* ◇ *Have you got a sister?* Tu as une sœur? ◇ *He's got blue eyes.* Il a les yeux bleus. ◇ *I've got a cold.* J'ai un rhume. ◇ *He's done it, hasn't he?* Il l'a fait, non? ◇ *Have you got any money? – No, I haven't!* Est-ce que tu as de l'argent? – Non, je n'en ai pas!
The perfect tense of some verbs is formed with **être**.
[2] *être* ◇ *They have arrived.* Ils sont arrivés. ◇ *Has he gone?* Est-ce qu'il est parti?
[3] *prendre* ◇ *He had his breakfast.* Il a pris son petit déjeuner. ◇ *to have a shower* prendre une douche
* **to have got to do something** devoir faire quelque chose ◇ *She's got to do it.* Elle doit le faire.
* **to have a party** faire une fête
* **to have one's hair cut** se faire couper les cheveux

haven't = have not

hay NOUN
le *foin*

hay fever NOUN
le *rhume des foins* ◇ *Do you get hay fever?* Est-ce que vous êtes sujet au rhume des foins?

hazelnut NOUN
la *noisette*

he PRONOUN
il ◇ *He loves dogs.* Il aime les chiens.

head NOUN
  see also **head** VERB
[1] (of person)
la *tête* ◇ *The wine went to my head.* Le vin m'est monté à la tête.
[2] (of private or primary school)
le *directeur*
la *directrice*
[3] (of state secondary school)
le *proviseur*
[4] (leader)
le *chef* ◇ *a head of state* un chef d'État
* **to have a head for figures** être doué pour les chiffres
* **Heads or tails? – Heads.** Pile ou face? – Face.

to **head** VERB
  see also **head** NOUN
* **to head for something** se diriger vers quelque chose ◇ *They headed for the church.* Ils se sont dirigés vers l'église.

headache NOUN
* **I've got a headache.** J'ai mal à la tête.

headlight NOUN
le *phare*

headline NOUN
le *titre*

headmaster NOUN
[1] le *directeur* (of private or primary school)
[2] le *proviseur* (of state secondary school)

headmistress NOUN
[1] la *directrice* (of private or primary school)
[2] le *proviseur* (of state secondary school)

headphones PL NOUN
les *écouteurs* MASC

headteacher NOUN
[1] (of private or primary school)
le *directeur*
la *directrice*
[2] (of state secondary school)
le *proviseur* ◇ *She's a headteacher.* Elle est proviseur.

health NOUN
la *santé*

healthy ADJECTIVE
[1] *en bonne santé* (person) ◇ *Lesley's a healthy person.* Lesley est en bonne santé.
[2] *sain* (climate, food) ◇ *a healthy diet*

une alimentation saine

heap NOUN
le *tas* ◦ *a rubbish heap* un tas
d'ordures

to **hear** VERB
1 *entendre* ◦ *He heard the dog bark.*
Il a entendu le chien aboyer. ◦ *She can't
hear very well.* Elle entend mal. ◦ *I
heard that she was ill.* J'ai entendu dire
qu'elle était malade.
* **to hear about something** entendre
parler de quelque chose
2 *apprendre* (*news*) ◦ *Did you hear the
good news?* Est-ce que tu as appris la
bonne nouvelle?
* **to hear from somebody** avoir des
nouvelles de quelqu'un ◦ *I haven't
heard from him recently.* Je n'ai pas eu de
ses nouvelles récemment.

heart NOUN
le *cœur*
* **to learn something by heart** apprendre
quelque chose par cœur
* **the ace of hearts** l'as de cœur

heart attack NOUN
la *crise cardiaque*

heartbroken ADJECTIVE
* **to be heartbroken** avoir le cœur brisé

heat NOUN
see also **heat** VERB
la *chaleur*

to **heat** VERB
see also **heat** NOUN
faire chauffer ◦ *Heat gently for 5
minutes.* Faire chauffer à feu doux
pendant cinq minutes.
* **to heat up (1)** (*cooked food*) faire
réchauffer ◦ *He heated the soup up.* Il
a fait réchauffer la soupe.
* **to heat up (2)** (*water, oven*) chauffer
◦ *The water is heating up.* L'eau chauffe.

heater NOUN
le *radiateur* ◦ *an electric heater* un
radiateur électrique

heating NOUN
le *chauffage*

heaven NOUN
le *paradis*

heavily ADVERB
lourdement ◦ *The car was heavily
loaded.* La voiture était lourdement
chargée.
* **He drinks heavily.** C'est un gros buveur.

heavy ADJECTIVE
1 *lourd* ◦ *This bag's very heavy.* Ce
sac est très lourd.
* **heavy rain** une grosse averse
2 *chargé* (*busy*) ◦ *I've got a very heavy
week ahead.* Je vais avoir une semaine

très chargée.
* **to be a heavy drinker** être un gros
buveur

he'd = he would, he had

hedge NOUN
la *haie*

hedgehog NOUN
le *hérisson*

heel NOUN
le *talon*

height NOUN
1 la *taille* (*of person*)
2 la *hauteur* (*of object*)
3 l' *altitude* FEM (*of mountain*)

heir NOUN
l' *héritier* MASC

heiress NOUN
l' *héritière* FEM

held VERB see **hold**

helicopter NOUN
l' *hélicoptère* MASC

hell NOUN
l' *enfer* MASC
* **Hell!** Merde! (*rude*)

he'll = he will, he shall

hello EXCLAMATION
bonjour!

helmet NOUN
le *casque*

to **help** VERB
see also **help** NOUN
aider ◦ *Can you help me?* Est-ce que
vous pouvez m'aider?
* **Help!** Au secours!
* **Help yourself!** Servez-vous!
* **He can't help it.** Il n'y peut rien.

help NOUN
see also **help** VERB
l' *aide* FEM ◦ *Do you need any help?*
Vous avez besoin d'aide?

helpful ADJECTIVE
serviable ◦ *He was very helpful.* Il a
été très serviable.

hen NOUN
la *poule*

her ADJECTIVE
see also **her** PRONOUN
son MASC ◦ *her father* son père
sa FEM ◦ *her mother* sa mère
ses PL ◦ *her parents* ses parents
sa becomes **son** before a vowel sound.
* **her friend (1)** (*male*) son ami
* **her friend (2)** (*female*) son amie
Do not use **son/sa/ses** *with parts of the body.*
◦ *She's going to wash her hair.* Elle va se
laver les cheveux. ◦ *She's cleaning her
teeth.* Elle se brosse les dents. ◦ *She's
hurt her foot.* Elle s'est fait mal au
pied.

her PRONOUN
see also **her** ADJECTIVE
la *becomes* **l'** *before a vowel sound.*
1 *la* ⋄ *I can see her.* Je la vois. ⋄ *Look at her!* Regarde-la!
l' ⋄ *I saw her.* Je l'ai vue.
Use **lui** *when* her *means* to her.
2 *lui* ⋄ *I gave her a book.* Je lui ai donné un livre. ⋄ *I told her the truth.* Je lui ai dit la vérité.
Use **elle** *after prepositions.*
3 *elle* ⋄ *I'm going with her.* Je vais avec elle. ⋄ *He sat next to her.* Il s'est assis à côté d'elle.
elle *is also used in comparisons.*
⋄ *I'm older than her.* Je suis plus âgé qu'elle.

herb NOUN
l' *herbe*

here ADVERB
ici ⋄ *I live here.* J'habite ici.
‣ **here is...** voici... ⋄ *Here's Helen.* Voici Helen. ⋄ *Here he is!* Le voici!
‣ **here are...** voici... ⋄ *Here are the books.* Voici les livres.

hero NOUN
le *héros* ⋄ *He's a real hero!* C'est un véritable héros!

heroin NOUN
l' *héroïne* ⋄ *Heroin is a hard drug.* L'héroïne est une drogue dure.
‣ **a heroin addict** un héroïnomane ⋄ *She's a heroin addict.* C'est une héroïnomane.

heroine NOUN
l' *héroïne* ⋄ *the heroine of the novel* l'héroïne du roman

hers PRONOUN
le sien + MASC NOUN ⋄ *Is this her coat?—No, hers is black.* C'est son manteau?—Non, le sien est noir.
la sienne + FEM NOUN ⋄ *Is this her car?—No, hers is white.* C'est sa voiture?—Non, la sienne est blanche.
les siens + MASC PL NOUN ⋄ *my parents and hers* mes parents et les siens
les siennes + FEM PL NOUN ⋄ *my reasons and hers* mes raisons et les siennes
‣ **Is this hers?** C'est à elle? ⋄ *This book is hers.* Ce livre est à elle. ⋄ *Whose is this?—It's hers.* C'est à qui?—À elle.

herself PRONOUN
1 *se* ⋄ *She's hurt herself.* Elle s'est blessée.
2 *elle* (*after preposition*) ⋄ *She talked mainly about herself.* Elle a surtout parlé d'elle.
3 *elle-même* ⋄ *She did it herself.* Elle l'a fait elle-même.

‣ **by herself** toute seule ⋄ *She doesn't like travelling by herself.* Elle n'aime pas voyager toute seule.

he's = he is, he has

to **hesitate** VERB
hésiter

heterosexual ADJECTIVE
hétérosexuel MASC
hétérosexuelle FEM

hi EXCLAMATION
salut!

to **hide** VERB
se cacher ⋄ *He hid behind a bush.* Il s'est caché derrière un buisson.
‣ **to hide something** cacher quelque chose ⋄ *Paula hid the present.* Paula a caché le cadeau.

hide-and-seek NOUN
‣ **to play hide-and-seek** jouer à cache-cache

hideous ADJECTIVE
hideux MASC
hideuse FEM

hi-fi NOUN
la *chaîne hi-fi*
(les *chaînes hi-fi* PL)

high ADJECTIVE, ADVERB
1 *haut* ⋄ *It's too high.* C'est trop haut.
‣ **How high is the wall?** Quelle est la hauteur du mur?
‣ **The wall's 2 metres high.** Le mur fait deux mètres de haut.
2 *élevé* ⋄ *a high price* un prix élevé ⋄ *a high temperature* une température élevée
‣ **at high speed** à grande vitesse
‣ **It's very high in fat.** C'est très gras.
‣ **She's got a very high voice.** Elle a la voix très aiguë.
‣ **to be high** (*on drugs*) être défoncé (*informal*)
‣ **to get high** se défoncer (*informal*) ⋄ *to get high on crack* se défoncer au crack

high-heeled ADJECTIVE
à hauts talons
‣ **high-heeled shoes** des chaussures à hauts talons

high jump NOUN
le *saut en hauteur* (*sport*)

highlight NOUN
le *clou* ⋄ *the highlight of the evening* le clou de la soirée

high-rise NOUN
la *tour* ⋄ *I live in a high-rise.* J'habite dans une tour.

high school NOUN
le *lycée*

to **hijack** VERB
détourner

hijacker NOUN
le *pirate de l'air*
hike NOUN
la *randonnée*
hiking NOUN
- **to go hiking** faire une randonnée
hilarious ADJECTIVE
hilarant ◦ *It was hilarious!* C'était
hilarant!
hill NOUN
la *colline* ◦ *She walked up the hill.* Elle
a gravi la colline.
hill-walking NOUN
la *randonnée de basse montagne*
◦ *to go hill-walking* faire de la randonnée
de basse montagne
him PRONOUN
le *becomes* l' *before a vowel sound.*
① *le* ◦ *I can see him.* Je le vois. ◦ *Look
at him!* Regarde-le!
l' ◦ *I saw him.* Je l'ai vu.
Use **lui** *when* him *means* to him, *and after
prepositions.*
② *lui* ◦ *I gave him a book.* Je lui ai
donné un livre. ◦ *I told him the truth.* Je
lui ai dit la vérité. ◦ *I'm going with him.*
Je vais avec lui. ◦ *She sat next to him.*
Elle s'est assise à côté de lui.
lui *is also used in comparisons.*
◦ *I'm older than him.* Je suis plus âgé que
lui.
himself PRONOUN
① *se* ◦ *He's hurt himself.* Il s'est blessé.
② *lui* ◦ *He talked mainly about himself.*
Il a surtout parlé de lui.
③ *lui-même* ◦ *He did it himself.* Il l'a
fait lui-même.
- **by himself** tout seul ◦ *He was
travelling by himself.* Il voyageait tout
seul.
Hindu ADJECTIVE
hindou ◦ *a Hindu temple* un temple
hindou
hip NOUN
la *hanche*
hippie NOUN
le *hippie*
la *hippie*
hippo NOUN
l' *hippopotame* MASC
to **hire** VERB
see also hire NOUN
① *louer* ◦ *to hire a car* louer une
voiture
② *engager* (*person*) ◦ *They hired a
cleaner.* Ils ont engagé une femme de
ménage.
hire NOUN
see also hire VERB

la *location*
- **car hire** location de voitures
- **for hire** à louer
hire car NOUN
la *voiture de location*
his ADJECTIVE
see also his PRONOUN
son MASC ◦ *his father* son père
sa FEM ◦ *his mother* sa mère
ses PL ◦ *his parents* ses parents
sa becomes **son** *before a vowel sound.*
- **his friend (1)** (*male*) son ami
- **his friend (2)** (*female*) son amie
Do not use **son/sa/ses** *with parts of the body.*
◦ *He's going to wash his hair.* Il va se
laver les cheveux. ◦ *He's cleaning his
teeth.* Il se brosse les dents. ◦ *He's hurt
his foot.* Il s'est fait mal au pied.
his PRONOUN
see also his ADJECTIVE
le sien + MASC NOUN ◦ *Is this his
coat? – No, his is black.* C'est son
manteau? – Non, le sien est noir.
la sienne + FEM NOUN ◦ *Is this his
car? – No, his is white.* C'est sa
voiture? – Non, la sienne est blanche.
les siens + MASC PL NOUN ◦ *my parents and
his* mes parents et les siens
les siennes + FEM PL NOUN ◦ *my reasons
and his* mes raisons et les siennes
- **Is this his?** C'est à lui? ◦ *This book is
his.* Ce livre est à lui. ◦ *Whose is
this? – It's his.* C'est à qui? – À lui.
history NOUN
l' *histoire* FEM
to **hit** VERB
see also hit NOUN
① *frapper* ◦ *Andrew hit him.* Andrew
l'a frappé.
② *renverser* ◦ *He was hit by a car.* Il a
été renversé par une voiture.
③ *toucher* ◦ *The arrow hit the target.*
La flèche a touché la cible.
- **to hit it off with somebody** bien
s'entendre avec quelqu'un ◦ *She hit it
off with his parents.* Elle s'est bien
entendue avec ses parents.
hit NOUN
see also hit VERB
① *le tube* (*song*) ◦ *Blur's latest hit* le
dernier tube de Blur
② *le succès* (*success*) ◦ *The film was a
massive hit.* Le film a eu un immense
succès.
hitch NOUN
le *contretemps* ◦ *There's been a slight
hitch.* Il y a eu un léger contretemps.
to **hitchhike** VERB
faire de l'auto-stop

hitchhiker NOUN
l' *auto-stoppeur* MASC
l' *auto-stoppeuse* FEM

hitchhiking NOUN
l' *auto-stop* MASC ◇ *Hitchhiking can be dangerous.* Il peut être dangereux de faire de l'auto-stop.

hit man NOUN
le *tueur à gages*

HIV-negative ADJECTIVE
séronégatif MASC
séronégative FEM

HIV-positive ADJECTIVE
séropositif MASC
séropositive FEM

hobby NOUN
le *passe-temps favori* ◇ *What are your hobbies?* Quels sont tes passe-temps favoris?

hockey NOUN
le *hockey* ◇ *I play hockey.* Je joue au hockey.

hold VERB
⬚1 *tenir* (*hold on to*) ◇ *She held the baby.* Elle tenait le bébé.
⬚2 *contenir* (*contain*) ◇ *This bottle holds one litre.* Cette bouteille contient un litre.
◆ **to hold a meeting** avoir une réunion
◆ **Hold the line!** (*on telephone*) Ne quittez pas!
◆ **Hold it!** (*wait*) Attends!
◆ **to get hold of something** (*obtain*) trouver quelque chose ◇ *I couldn't get hold of it.* Je n'ai pas réussi à en trouver.

hold on VERB
⬚1 *tenir bon* (*keep hold*) ◇ *The cliff was slippery but he managed to hold on.* La falaise était glissante, mais il est parvenu à tenir bon.
◆ **to hold on to something** se cramponner à quelque chose ◇ *He held on to the chair.* Il se cramponnait à la chaise.
⬚2 *attendre* (*wait*) ◇ *Hold on, I'm coming!* Attends, je viens!
◆ **Hold on!** (*on telephone*) Ne quittez pas!

hold up VERB
◆ **to hold up one's hand** lever la main ◇ *Pierre held up his hand.* Pierre a levé la main.
◆ **to hold somebody up** (*delay*) retenir quelqu'un ◇ *I was held up at the office.* J'ai été retenu au bureau.
◆ **to hold up a bank** (*rob*) braquer une banque (*informal*)

hold-up NOUN
⬚1 le *hold-up* (*at bank*)
⬚2 le *retard* (*delay*)
⬚3 le *bouchon* (*traffic jam*)

hole NOUN
le *trou*

holiday NOUN
⬚1 les *vacances* FEM PL ◇ *Did you have a good holiday?* Tu as passé de bonnes vacances? ◇ *our holidays in France* nos vacances en France
◆ **on holiday** en vacances ◇ *to go on holiday* partir en vacances ◇ *We are on holiday.* Nous sommes en vacances.
◆ **the school holidays** les vacances scolaires
⬚2 le *jour férié* (*public holiday*) ◇ *Next Wednesday is a holiday.* Mercredi prochain est un jour férié.
⬚3 le *jour de congé* (*day off*) ◇ *He took a day's holiday.* Il a pris un jour de congé.
◆ **a holiday camp** un camp de vacances

Holland NOUN
la *Hollande*
◆ **in Holland** en Hollande
◆ **to Holland** en Hollande

hollow ADJECTIVE
creux MASC
creuse FEM

holy ADJECTIVE
saint

home NOUN
see also home ADVERB
la *maison*
◆ **at home** à la maison
◆ **Make yourself at home.** Faites comme chez vous.

home ADVERB
see also home NOUN
à la maison ◇ *I'll be home at 5 o'clock.* Je serai à la maison à cinq heures.
◆ **to get home** rentrer ◇ *What time did he get home?* Il est rentré à quelle heure?

home address NOUN
l' *adresse* FEM ◇ *What's your home address?* Quelle est votre adresse?

homeland NOUN
la *patrie*

homeless ADJECTIVE
sans abri MASC, FEM, PL
◆ **the homeless** les sans-abri

home match NOUN
le *match à domicile*

homesick ADJECTIVE
◆ **to be homesick** avoir le mal du pays

homework NOUN
les *devoirs* MASC PL ◇ *Have you done your homework?* Est-ce que tu as fait tes devoirs? ◇ *my geography homework* mes devoirs de géographie

homosexual ADJECTIVE
see also homosexual NOUN

H

homosexuel MASC
homosexuelle FEM
homosexual NOUN
see also homosexual ADJECTIVE
l' *homosexuel*
honest ADJECTIVE
[1] *(trustworthy)*
honnête ◦ *She's a very honest person.*
Elle est très honnête.
[2] *(sincere)*
franc MASC
franche FEM
◦ *He was very honest with her.* Il a été
très franc avec elle.
honestly ADVERB
franchement ◦ *I honestly don't know.*
Franchement, je n'en sais rien.
honesty NOUN
l' *honnêteté* FEM
honey NOUN
le *miel*
honeymoon NOUN
la *lune de miel*
honour NOUN
l' *honneur* MASC
hood NOUN
la *capuche* ◦ *a coat with a hood* un
manteau à capuche
hook NOUN
le *crochet* ◦ *He hung the painting on the
hook.* Il a suspendu le tableau au crochet.
• **to take the phone off the hook**
décrocher le téléphone
• **a fish-hook** un hameçon
hooligan NOUN
le *voyou*
(les *voyoux* PL)
hooray EXCLAMATION
hourra!
Hoover ® NOUN
l' *aspirateur* MASC
to **hoover** VERB
passer l'aspirateur ◦ *to hoover the
lounge* passer l'aspirateur dans le salon
to **hope** VERB
see also hope NOUN
espérer ◦ *I hope he comes.* J'espère
qu'il va venir. ◦ *I'm hoping for good
results.* J'espère avoir de bons résultats.
• **I hope so.** Je l'espère.
• **I hope not.** J'espère que non.
hope NOUN
see also hope VERB
l' *espoir* MASC
• **to give up hope** perdre espoir ◦ *Don't
give up hope!* Ne perds pas espoir!
hopeful ADJECTIVE
[1] *plein d'espoir* ◦ *I'm hopeful.* Je suis
plein d'espoir.

• **He's hopeful of winning.** Il a bon espoir
de gagner.
[2] *(situation)*
prometteur MASC
prometteuse FEM
◦ *The prospects look hopeful.* Les
perspectives semblent prometteuses.
hopefully ADVERB
avec un peu de chance ◦ *Hopefully
he'll make it in time.* Avec un peu de
chance, il arrivera à temps.
hopeless ADJECTIVE
nul MASC
nulle FEM
◦ *I'm hopeless at maths.* Je suis nul en
maths.
horizon NOUN
l' *horizon*
horizontal ADJECTIVE
horizontal
(*horizontaux* MASC PL)
horn NOUN
[1] le *klaxon* ◦ *He sounded his horn.* Il
a klaxonné.
[2] le *cor* ◦ *I play the horn.* Je joue du
cor.
horoscope NOUN
l' *horoscope* MASC
horrible ADJECTIVE
horrible ◦ *What a horrible dress!*
Quelle robe horrible!
horror NOUN
l' *horreur* FEM
horror film NOUN
le *film d'horreur*
horse NOUN
le *cheval*
(les *chevaux* PL)
horse-racing NOUN
les *courses de chevaux* FEM PL
horseshoe NOUN
le *fer à cheval*
hose NOUN
le *tuyau*
(les *tuyaux* PL)
◦ *a garden hose* un tuyau d'arrosage
hosepipe NOUN
le *tuyau d'arrosage*
hospital NOUN
l' *hôpital* MASC
(les *hôpitaux* PL)
◦ *Take me to the hospital!* Emmenez-moi
à l'hôpital! ◦ *in hospital* à l'hôpital
hospitality NOUN
l' *hospitalité* FEM
hostage NOUN
l' *otage* MASC
• **to take somebody hostage** prendre
quelqu'un en otage

hostile ADJECTIVE
hostile

hot ADJECTIVE

[1] _chaud_ (warm) ◇ a hot bath un bain chaud ◇ a hot country un pays chaud

> When you are talking about a person being hot, you use **avoir chaud**.

◇ I'm hot. J'ai chaud. ◇ I'm too hot. J'ai trop chaud.

> When you mean that the weather is hot, you use **faire chaud**.

◇ It's hot. Il fait chaud. ◇ It's very hot today. Il fait très chaud aujourd'hui.

[2] _épicé_ (spicy) ◇ a very hot curry un curry très épicé

hot dog NOUN
le _hot-dog_

hotel NOUN
l' _hôtel_ ◇ We stayed in a hotel. Nous avons logé à l'hôtel.

hour NOUN
l' _heure_ FEM ◇ She always takes hours to get ready. Elle passe toujours des heures à se préparer.

* **a quarter of an hour** un quart d'heure
* **half an hour** une demi-heure
* **two and a half hours** deux heures et demie

hourly ADJECTIVE, ADVERB
toutes les heures ◇ There are hourly buses. Il y a des bus toutes les heures.

* **to be paid hourly** être payé à l'heure

house NOUN
la _maison_

* **at his house** chez lui
* **We stayed at their house.** Nous avons séjourné chez eux.

housewife NOUN
la _femme au foyer_ ◇ She's a housewife. Elle est femme au foyer.

housework NOUN
le _ménage_

* **to do the housework** faire le ménage

hovercraft NOUN
l' _aéroglisseur_ MASC

how ADVERB
comment ◇ How are you? Comment allez-vous?

* **How many?** Combien?
* **How many...?** Combien de...? ◇ How many pupils are there in the class? Combien d'élèves y a-t-il dans la classe?
* **How much?** Combien?
* **How much...?** Combien de...? ◇ How much sugar do you want? Combien de sucres voulez-vous?
* **How old are you?** Quel âge as-tu?
* **How far is it to Edinburgh?** Combien y a-t-il de kilomètres d'ici à Édimbourg?

* **How long have you been here?** Depuis combien de temps êtes-vous là?

however CONJUNCTION
pourtant ◇ This, however, isn't true. Pourtant, ce n'est pas vrai.

to howl VERB
hurler

to hug VERB
> see also hug NOUN

serrer dans ses bras ◇ He hugged her. Il l'a serrée dans ses bras.

hug NOUN
> see also hug VERB

* **to give somebody a hug** serrer quelqu'un dans ses bras ◇ She gave them a hug. Elle les a serrés dans ses bras.

huge ADJECTIVE
immense

to hum VERB
fredonner

human ADJECTIVE
humain ◇ the human body le corps humain

human being NOUN
l' _être humain_ MASC

humour NOUN
l' _humour_ MASC

* **to have a sense of humour** avoir le sens de l'humour

hundred NUMBER

* **a hundred** cent ◇ a hundred francs cent francs
* **five hundred** cinq cents
* **five hundred and one** cinq cent un
* **hundreds of people** des centaines de personnes

hung VERB see **hang**

Hungary NOUN
la _Hongrie_

* **in Hungary** en Hongrie
* **to Hungary** en Hongrie

hunger NOUN
la _faim_

hungry ADJECTIVE

* **to be hungry** avoir faim ◇ I'm hungry. J'ai faim.

to hunt VERB

[1] _chasser_ (animal) ◇ People used to hunt wild boar. On chassait le sanglier autrefois.

* **to go hunting** aller à la chasse

[2] _pourchasser_ (criminal) ◇ The police are hunting the killer. La police pourchasse le criminel.

* **to hunt for something** (search) chercher quelque chose partout ◇ I hunted everywhere for that book. J'ai cherché ce livre partout.

hunting NOUN
la *chasse* ◇ *I'm against hunting.* Je suis contre la chasse.
- **fox-hunting** la chasse au renard

hurricane NOUN
l' *ouragan* MASC

to **hurry** VERB
  see also hurry NOUN
  se dépêcher ◇ *Sharon hurried back home.* Sharon s'est dépêchée de rentrer chez elle.
- **Hurry up!** Dépêche-toi!

hurry NOUN
  see also hurry VERB
- **to be in a hurry** être pressé
- **to do something in a hurry** faire quelque chose en vitesse
- **There's no hurry.** Rien ne presse.

to **hurt** VERB
  see also hurt ADJECTIVE
- **to hurt somebody (1)** (*physically*) faire mal à quelqu'un ◇ *You're hurting me!* Tu me fais mal!
- **to hurt somebody (2)** (*emotionally*) blesser quelqu'un ◇ *His remarks really hurt me.* Ses remarques m'ont vraiment blessé.

- **to hurt oneself** se faire mal ◇ *I fell over and hurt myself.* Je me suis fait mal en tombant.
- **That hurts.** Ça fait mal. ◇ *It hurts to have a tooth out.* Ça fait mal de se faire arracher une dent.
- **My leg hurts.** J'ai mal à la jambe.

hurt ADJECTIVE
  see also hurt VERB
  blessé ◇ *Is he badly hurt?* Est-ce qu'il est grièvement blessé? ◇ *He was hurt in the leg.* Il a été blessé à la jambe. ◇ *I was hurt by what he said.* J'ai été blessé par ce qu'il a dit.
- **Luckily, nobody got hurt.** Heureusement, il n'y a pas eu de blessés.

husband NOUN
le *mari*

hut NOUN
la *hutte*

hymn NOUN
le *cantique*

hypermarket NOUN
l' *hypermarché* MASC

hyphen NOUN
le *trait d'union*

I

I PRONOUN

1 *je* ◇ *I speak French.* Je parle français.

je *changes to* j' *before a vowel and most words beginning with "h".*

◇ *I love cats.* J'aime les chats.

2 *moi* ◇ *Ann and I* Ann et moi

ice NOUN

1 la *glace* ◇ *There was ice on the lake.* Il y avait de la glace sur le lac.

2 le *verglas* (*on road*)

iceberg NOUN

l' *iceberg* MASC

ice cream NOUN

la *glace* ◇ *vanilla ice cream* la glace à la vanille

ice cube NOUN

le *glaçon*

ice hockey NOUN

le *hockey sur glace*

Iceland NOUN

l' *Islande* FEM

◆ **in Iceland** en Islande

◆ **to Iceland** en Islande

ice lolly NOUN

la *glace à l'eau*

ice rink NOUN

la *patinoire*

ice-skating NOUN

le *patinage sur glace*

◆ **to go ice-skating** faire du patin à glace

icing NOUN

le *glaçage* (*on cake*)

◆ **icing sugar** le sucre glace

icy ADJECTIVE

glacial

(*glaciaux* MASC PL)

◇ *There was an icy wind.* Il y avait un vent glacial.

◆ **The roads are icy.** Il y a du verglas sur les routes.

I'd = I had, I would

idea NOUN

l' *idée* FEM ◇ *Good idea!* Bonne idée!

ideal ADJECTIVE

idéal

(*idéaux* MASC PL)

identical ADJECTIVE

identique

identification NOUN

l' *identification* FEM

to **identify** VERB

identifier

identity card NOUN

la *carte d'identité*

idiot NOUN

l' *idiot* MASC

l' *idiote* FEM

idiotic ADJECTIVE

stupide

i.e. ABBREVIATION

c.-à-d. (= c'est-à-dire)

if CONJUNCTION

si ◇ *You can have it if you like.* Tu peux le prendre si tu veux.

si *changes to* s' *before* il *and* ils.

◇ *Do you know if he's there?* Savez-vous s'il est là?

◆ **if only** si seulement ◇ *If only I had more money!* Si seulement j'avais plus d'argent!

◆ **if not** sinon ◇ *Are you coming? If not, I'll go with Mark.* Est-ce que tu viens? Sinon, j'irai avec Mark.

ignorant ADJECTIVE

ignorant

to **ignore** VERB

◆ **to ignore something** ne tenir aucun compte de quelque chose ◇ *She ignored my advice.* Elle n'a tenu aucun compte de mes conseils.

◆ **to ignore somebody** ignorer quelqu'un ◇ *She saw me, but she ignored me.* Elle m'a vu, mais elle m'a ignoré.

◆ **Just ignore him!** Ne fais pas attention à lui!

ill ADJECTIVE

malade (*sick*)

◆ **to be taken ill** tomber malade ◇ *She was taken ill while on holiday.* Elle est tombée malade pendant qu'elle était en vacances.

I'll = I will

illegal ADJECTIVE

illégal

(*illégaux* MASC PL)

illegible ADJECTIVE

illisible

illness NOUN

la *maladie*

to **ill-treat** VERB

maltraiter

illusion NOUN

l' *illusion* FEM

illustration NOUN

l' *illustration* FEM

image NOUN

l' *image* FEM ◇ *The company has changed its image.* La société a changé d'image.

imagination NOUN

l' *imagination* FEM

to **imagine** VERB

imaginer　◇ *You can imagine how I felt!*
Tu peux imaginer ce que j'ai ressenti!
◇ *Is he angry?—I imagine so.* Est-ce qu'il
est en colère?—J'imagine que oui.

to **imitate** VERB
imiter

imitation NOUN
l' *imitation* FEM

immediate ADJECTIVE
immédiat

immediately ADVERB
immédiatement ◇ *I'll do it immediately.*
Je vais le faire immédiatement.

immigrant NOUN
l' *immigré* MASC
l' *immigrée* FEM

immigration NOUN
l' *immigration* FEM

immoral ADJECTIVE
immoral
(*immoraux* MASC PL)

impartial ADJECTIVE
impartial
(*impartiaux* MASC PL)

impatience NOUN
l' *impatience* FEM

impatient ADJECTIVE
impatient
• **to get impatient** s'impatienter
◇ *People are getting impatient.* Les gens
commencent à s'impatienter.

impatiently ADVERB
avec impatience ◇ *We waited
impatiently.* Nous avons attendu avec
impatience.

impersonal ADJECTIVE
impersonnel MASC
impersonnelle FEM

importance NOUN
l' *importance* FEM

important ADJECTIVE
important

impossible ADJECTIVE
impossible

to **impress** VERB
impressionner ◇ *She's trying to
impress you.* Elle essaie de
t'impressionner.

impressed ADJECTIVE
impressionné ◇ *I'm very impressed!* Je
suis très impressionné!

impression NOUN
l' *impression* FEM ◇ *I was under the
impression that...* J'avais l'impression
que...

impressive ADJECTIVE
impressionnant

to **improve** VERB
1 *améliorer* (*make better*) ◇ *They have*

improved the service. Ils ont amélioré le
service.
2 *s'améliorer* (*get better*) ◇ *The
weather is improving.* Le temps
s'améliore. ◇ *My French has improved.*
Mon français s'est amélioré.

improvement NOUN
1 l' *amélioration* FEM (*of condition*)
◇ *It's a great improvement.* C'est une
nette amélioration.
2 le *progrès* (*of learner*) ◇ *There's been
an improvement in his French.* Il a fait
des progrès en français.

in PREPOSITION, ADVERB

> *There are several ways of translating* in. *Scan the
> examples to find one that is similar to what you
> want to say. For other expressions with* in, *see the
> verbs* go, come, get, give *etc.*

1 *dans*　◇ *in the house* dans la maison
◇ *in my bag* dans mon sac ◇ *in the
sixties* dans les années soixante ◇ *I'll
see you in three weeks.* Je te verrai dans
trois semaines.
2 *à*　◇ *in the country* à la campagne
◇ *in school* à l'école ◇ *in hospital* à
l'hôpital ◇ *in London* à Londres ◇ *in
spring* au printemps ◇ *in the sun* au
soleil ◇ *in the shade* à l'ombre ◇ *in a
loud voice* à voix haute ◇ *the boy in the
blue shirt* le garçon à la chemise bleue
◇ *It was written in pencil.* C'était écrit au
crayon.
3 *en*　◇ *in French* en français ◇ *in
summer* en été ◇ *in May* en mai ◇ *in
1996* en dix-neuf cent quatre-vingt seize
◇ *I did it in 3 hours.* Je l'ai fait en trois
heures. ◇ *in town* en ville ◇ *in prison* en
prison ◇ *in tears* en larmes ◇ *in good
condition* en bon état

> *When* in *refers to a country which is feminine,
> use* en; *when the country is masculine, use* au;
> *when the country is plural, use* aux.

◇ *in France* en France ◇ *in Portugal* au
Portugal ◇ *in the United States* aux
États-Unis
4 *de*　◇ *the best pupil in the class* le
meilleur élève de la classe ◇ *the best
team in the world* la meilleure équipe du
monde ◇ *the tallest person in the family*
le plus grand de la famille ◇ *at 4 o'clock
in the afternoon* à quatre heures de
l'après-midi ◇ *at 6 in the morning* à six
heures du matin
• **in the afternoon** l'après-midi
• **You look good in that dress.** Tu es jolie
avec cette robe.
• **in time** à temps ◇ *We arrived in time for
dinner.* Nous sommes arrivés à temps
pour le dîner.

* **in here** ici ◇ *It's hot in here.* Il fait chaud ici.
* **in the rain** sous la pluie
* **one person in ten** une personne sur dix
* **to be in** (*at home, work*) être là ◇ *He wasn't in.* Il n'était pas là.
* **to ask somebody in** inviter quelqu'un à entrer

inaccurate ADJECTIVE
  inexact

incentive NOUN
* **There is no incentive to work.** Il n'y a rien qui incite à travailler.

inch NOUN
  le *pouce*

> *In France measurements are in metres and centimetres rather than feet and inches. An inch is about 2.5 centimetres.*

* **6 inches** quinze centimètres

incident NOUN
  l' *incident* MASC

inclined ADJECTIVE
* **to be inclined to do something** avoir tendance à faire quelque chose ◇ *He's inclined to arrive late.* Il a tendance à arriver en retard.

to **include** VERB
  comprendre ◇ *Service is not included.* Le service n'est pas compris.

including PREPOSITION
  compris ◇ *It will be 200 francs, including tax.* Ça coûtera deux cents francs, toutes taxes comprises.

inclusive ADJECTIVE
  compris ◇ *The inclusive price is 200 francs.* Ça coûte deux cents francs tout compris.
* **inclusive of tax** taxes comprises

income NOUN
  le *revenu*

income tax NOUN
  l' *impôt sur le revenu* MASC

incompetent ADJECTIVE
  incompétent

incomplete ADJECTIVE
  incomplet MASC
  incomplète FEM

inconvenience NOUN
* **I don't want to cause any inconvenience.** Je ne veux pas vous déranger.

inconvenient ADJECTIVE
* **That's very inconvenient for me.** Ça ne m'arrange pas du tout.

incorrect ADJECTIVE
  incorrect

increase NOUN
  see also **increase** VERB
  l' *augmentation* FEM ◇ *an increase in*

  road accidents une augmentation des accidents de la route

to **increase** VERB
  see also **increase** NOUN
  augmenter

incredible ADJECTIVE
  incroyable

indecisive ADJECTIVE
  indécis (*person*)

indeed ADVERB
  vraiment ◇ *It's very hard indeed.* C'est vraiment très difficile.
* **Know what I mean? – Indeed I do.** Tu vois ce que je veux dire? – Oui, tout à fait.
* **Thank you very much indeed!** Merci beaucoup!

independence NOUN
  l' *indépendance* FEM

independent ADJECTIVE
  indépendant
* **an independent school** une école privée

index NOUN
  l' *index* MASC (*in book*)

India NOUN
  l' *Inde* FEM
* **in India** en Inde
* **to India** en Inde

Indian ADJECTIVE
  see also **Indian** NOUN
  indien MASC
  indienne FEM

Indian NOUN
  see also **Indian** ADJECTIVE
  (*person*)
  l' *Indien* MASC
  l' *Indienne* FEM
* **an American Indian** un Indien d'Amérique

to **indicate** VERB
  indiquer

indigestion NOUN
  l' *indigestion* FEM
* **I've got indigestion.** J'ai une indigestion.

indoor ADJECTIVE
* **an indoor swimming pool** une piscine couverte

indoors ADVERB
  à l'intérieur ◇ *They're indoors.* Ils sont à l'intérieur.
* **to go indoors** rentrer ◇ *We'd better go indoors.* Nous ferions mieux de rentrer.

industrial ADJECTIVE
  industriel MASC
  industrielle FEM

industrial estate NOUN
  la *zone industrielle*

industry NOUN

l' *industrie* FEM　◇ *the tourist industry*
l'industrie du tourisme　◇ *the oil industry*
l'industrie pétrolière　◇ *I'd like to work in
industry.* J'aimerais travailler dans
l'industrie.

inefficient ADJECTIVE
inefficace

inevitable ADJECTIVE
inévitable

inexpensive ADJECTIVE
bon marché MASC, FEM, PL　◇ *an
inexpensive hotel* un hôtel bon marché
◇ *inexpensive holidays* des vacances bon
marché

inexperienced ADJECTIVE
inexpérimenté

infant school NOUN

> CP (cours préparatoire) is the equivalent of
> first-year infants, and CE1 (cours élémentaire
> première année) the equivalent of second-year
> infants.

◇ *He's just started at infant school.* Il
vient d'entrer au cours préparatoire.

infection NOUN
l' *infection* FEM　◇ *an ear infection* une
infection de l'oreille
◆ **a throat infection** une angine

infectious ADJECTIVE
contagieux MASC
contagieuse FEM
◇ *It's not infectious.* Ce n'est pas
contagieux.

infinitive NOUN
l' *infinitif* MASC

infirmary NOUN
l' *hôpital* MASC
(les *hôpitaux* PL)

inflatable ADJECTIVE
gonflable (mattress, dinghy)

inflation NOUN
l' *inflation* FEM

influence NOUN

> see also influence VERB

l' *influence* FEM　◇ *He's a bad influence
on her.* Il a mauvaise influence sur elle.

to **influence** VERB

> see also influence NOUN

influencer

influenza NOUN
la *grippe*

to **inform** VERB
informer
◆ **to inform somebody of something**
informer quelqu'un de quelque chose
◇ *Nobody informed me of the new plan.*
Personne ne m'a informé de ce nouveau
projet.

informal ADJECTIVE
1 (person, party)

décontracté　◇ *"informal dress"* "tenue
décontractée"
2 (colloquial)
familier MASC
familière FEM
◇ *informal language* le langage familier
◆ **an informal visit** une visite non
officielle

information NOUN
les *renseignements* MASC PL　◇ *important
information* les renseignements
importants
◆ **a piece of information** un
renseignement
◆ **Could you give me some information
about trains to Paris?** Pourriez-vous me
renseigner sur les trains pour Paris?

information office NOUN
le *bureau des renseignements*

infuriating ADJECTIVE
exaspérant

ingredient NOUN
l' *ingrédient* MASC

inhabitant NOUN
l' *habitant* MASC
l' *habitante* FEM

to **inherit** VERB
hériter de　◇ *She inherited her father's
house.* Elle a hérité de la maison de son
père.

initials PL NOUN
les *initiales* FEM PL　◇ *Her initials are
CDT.* Ses initiales sont CDT.

initiative NOUN
l' *initiative* FEM

to **inject** VERB
injecter (drug)

injection NOUN
la *piqûre*

to **injure** VERB
blesser

injured ADJECTIVE
blessé

injury NOUN
la *blessure*

injury time NOUN
les *arrêts de jeu* MASC PL

injustice NOUN
l' *injustice* FEM

ink NOUN
l' *encre* FEM

in-laws PL NOUN
les *beaux-parents* MASC PL

inn NOUN
l' *auberge* FEM

inner ADJECTIVE
intérieur
◆ **the inner city** les quartiers déshérités du
centre ville

inner tube NOUN
  la *chambre à air*
innocent ADJECTIVE
  innocent
inquest NOUN
  l' *enquête* FEM
inquiries office NOUN
  le *bureau des renseignements*
inquisitive ADJECTIVE
  curieux MASC
  curieuse FEM
insane ADJECTIVE
  fou MASC
  folle FEM
inscription NOUN
  l' *inscription* FEM
insect NOUN
  l' *insecte* MASC
insect repellent NOUN
  l' *insectifuge* MASC
inside NOUN
  see also inside ADVERB
  l' *intérieur* MASC
inside ADVERB, PREPOSITION
  see also inside NOUN
  à l'intérieur ◇ *They're inside.* Ils sont
  à l'intérieur. ◇ *inside the house* à
  l'intérieur de la maison
◆ **to go inside** rentrer
◆ **Come inside!** Rentrez!
insincere ADJECTIVE
  peu sincère
to insist VERB
  insister ◇ *I didn't want to, but he*
  insisted. Je ne voulais pas, mais il a
  insisté.
◆ **to insist on doing something** insister
  pour faire quelque chose ◇ *She insisted*
  on paying. Elle a insisté pour
  payer.
◆ **He insisted he was innocent.** Il
  affirmait qu'il était innocent.
inspector NOUN
  l' *inspecteur* MASC (*police*) ◇ *Inspector*
  Jill Brown l'inspecteur Jill Brown
◆ **ticket inspector** (*on buses*) le contrôleur
instance NOUN
◆ **for instance** par exemple
instant ADJECTIVE
  immédiat ◇ *It was an instant success.*
  Ça a été un succès immédiat.
◆ **instant coffee** le café instantané
instantly ADVERB
  tout de suite
instead ADVERB
◆ **instead of (1)** (*followed by noun*) à la place
  de ◇ *He went instead of Peter.* Il y est
  allé à la place de Peter.
◆ **instead of (2)** (*followed by verb*) au lieu de

◇ *We played tennis instead of going*
  swimming. Nous avons joué au tennis au
  lieu d'aller nager.
◆ **The pool was closed, so we played**
  tennis instead. La piscine était
  fermée, alors nous avons joué au
  tennis.
instinct NOUN
  l' *instinct* MASC
institution NOUN
  l' *institution* FEM
to instruct VERB
◆ **to instruct somebody to do something**
  donner l'ordre à quelqu'un de faire
  quelque chose ◇ *She instructed us to*
  wait outside. Elle nous a donné l'ordre
  d'attendre dehors.
instructions PL NOUN
  ① les *instructions* FEM PL ◇ *Follow the*
  instructions carefully. Suivez
  soigneusement les instructions.
  ② le *mode d'emploi* SING (*booklet*)
  ◇ *Where are the instructions?* Où est le
  mode d'emploi?
instructor NOUN
  le *moniteur*
  la *monitrice*
  ◇ *a skiing instructor* un moniteur de ski
  ◇ *a driving instructor* un moniteur
  d'auto école
instrument NOUN
  l' *instrument* MASC ◇ *Do you play an*
  instrument? Est-ce que tu joues d'un
  instrument?
insufficient ADJECTIVE
  insuffisant
insulin NOUN
  l' *insuline* FEM
insult NOUN
  see also insult VERB
  l' *insulte* FEM
to insult VERB
  see also insult NOUN
  insulter
insurance NOUN
  l' *assurance* FEM ◇ *his car insurance*
  son assurance automobile
◆ **an insurance policy** une police
  d'assurance
intelligent ADJECTIVE
  intelligent
to intend VERB
◆ **to intend to do something** avoir
  l'intention de faire quelque chose ◇ *I*
  intend to do French at university. J'ai
  l'intention d'étudier le français à
  l'université.
intense ADJECTIVE
  intense

intensive ADJECTIVE
　intensif MASC
　intensive FEM
intention NOUN
　l' *intention* FEM
intercom NOUN
　l' *interphone* MASC
interest NOUN
　see also interest VERB
　l' *intérêt* MASC　◇ *to show an interest in
　something* manifester de l'intérêt pour
　quelque chose
◆ **What interests do you have?** Quels
　sont tes centres d'intérêt?
◆ **My main interest is music.** Ce qui
　m'intéresse le plus c'est la musique.
to **interest** VERB
　see also interest NOUN
　intéresser　◇ *It doesn't interest me.* Ça
　ne m'intéresse pas.
◆ **to be interested in something**
　s'intéresser à quelque chose　◇ *I'm not
　interested in politics.* Je ne m'intéresse
　pas à la politique.
interesting ADJECTIVE
　intéressant
interior NOUN
　l' *intérieur* MASC
interior designer NOUN
　le/la *designer*
intermediate ADJECTIVE
　(*course, level*)
　moyen MASC
　moyenne FEM
internal ADJECTIVE
　interne
international ADJECTIVE
　international
　(*internationaux* MASC PL)
Internet NOUN
　l' *Internet* MASC　◇ *on the Internet* sur
　Internet
to **interpret** VERB
　servir d'interprète　◇ *Steve couldn't
　speak French, so his friend interpreted.*
　Comme Steve ne savait pas le français,
　son ami a servi d'interprète.
interpreter NOUN
　l' *interprète* MASC / FEM
to **interrupt** VERB
　interrompre
interruption NOUN
　l' *interruption* FEM
interval NOUN
　l' *entracte* MASC (*in play, concert*)
interview NOUN
　see also interview VERB
　① l' *interview* FEM (*on TV, radio*)
　② l' *entretien* MASC (*for job*)

to **interview** VERB
　see also interview NOUN
　interviewer (*on TV, radio*)　◇ *I was
　interviewed on the radio.* J'ai été
　interviewé à la radio.
interviewer NOUN
　l' *interviewer* MASC (*on TV, radio*)
intimate ADJECTIVE
　intime
into PREPOSITION
　① *dans*　◇ *He got into the car.* Il est
　monté dans la voiture.
　② *en*　◇ *I'm going into town.* Je vais en
　ville.　◇ *Translate it into French.*
　Traduisez ça en français.　◇ *Divide into
　two groups.* Répartissez-vous en deux
　groupes.
to **introduce** VERB
　présenter　◇ *He introduced me to his
　parents.* Il m'a présenté à ses parents.
introduction NOUN
　l' *introduction* FEM (*in book*)
intruder NOUN
　l' *intrus* MASC
　l' *intruse* FEM
intuition NOUN
　l' *intuition* FEM
to **invade** VERB
　envahir
invalid NOUN
　le/la *malade*
to **invent** VERB
　inventer
invention NOUN
　l' *invention* FEM
inventor NOUN
　l' *inventeur* MASC
　l' *inventrice* FEM
investigation NOUN
　l' *enquête* FEM (*police*)
invigilator NOUN
　le *surveillant*
　la *surveillante*
invisible ADJECTIVE
　invisible
invitation NOUN
　l' *invitation* FEM
to **invite** VERB
　inviter　◇ *He's not invited.* Il n'est pas
　invité.
◆ **to invite somebody to a party** inviter
　quelqu'un à une fête
to **involve** VERB
　nécessiter　◇ *His job involves a lot of
　travelling.* Son travail nécessite de
　nombreux déplacements.
◆ **to be involved in something** (*crime, drugs*)
　être impliqué dans quelque chose
◆ **to be involved with somebody** (*in*

relationship) avoir une relation avec quelqu'un

IQ NOUN (= *intelligence quotient*)
le *Q.I.* (= quotient intellectuel)

Iran NOUN
l' *Iran* MASC
- **in Iran** en Iran

Iraq NOUN
l' *Iraq* MASC
- **in Iraq** en Iraq

Ireland NOUN
l' *Irlande* FEM
- **in Ireland** en Irlande
- **to Ireland** en Irlande
- **I'm from Ireland.** Je suis irlandais.

Irish ADJECTIVE
see also **Irish** NOUN
irlandais ◇ *Irish music* la musique irlandaise

Irish NOUN
see also **Irish** ADJECTIVE
l' *irlandais* (*language*)
- **the Irish** (*people*) les Irlandais

Irishman NOUN
l' *Irlandais* MASC

Irishwoman NOUN
l' *Irlandaise* FEM

iron NOUN
see also **iron** VERB
1 le *fer* (*metal*)
7 le *fer à repasser* (*for clothes*)

iron VERB
see also **iron** NOUN
repasser

ironic ADJECTIVE
ironique

ironing NOUN
le *repassage* ◇ *to do the ironing* faire le repassage

ironing board NOUN
la *planche à repasser*

ironmonger's (shop) NOUN
la *quincaillerie*

irrelevant ADJECTIVE
hors de propos ◇ *That's irrelevant.* C'est hors de propos.

irresponsible ADJECTIVE (*person*)
irresponsable ◇ *That was irresponsible of him.* C'était irresponsable de sa part.

irritating ADJECTIVE
irritant

is VERB see **be**

Islam NOUN
l' *Islam* MASC

Islamic ADJECTIVE
islamique ◇ *Islamic law* la loi islamique
- **Islamic fundamentalists** les intégristes musulmans

island NOUN
l' *île* FEM

isle NOUN
- **the Isle of Man** l'île de Man
- **the Isle of Wight** l'île de Wight

isolated ADJECTIVE
isolé

Israel NOUN
Israël MASC
- **in Israel** en Israël

Israeli ADJECTIVE
see also **Israeli** NOUN
israélien MASC
israélienne FEM

Israeli NOUN
see also **Israeli** ADJECTIVE
l' *Israélien* MASC
l' *Israélienne* FEM

issue NOUN
see also **issue** VERB
1 la *question* (*matter*) ◇ *a controversial issue* une question controversée
2 le *numéro* (*of magazine*)

to **issue** VERB
see also **issue** NOUN
distribuer (*equipment, supplies*)

it PRONOUN
Remember to check if it *stands for a masculine or feminine noun.*
1 *il* ◇ *Where's my book? – It's on the table.* Où est mon livre? – Il est sur la table.
elle ◇ *When does the pool close? – It closes at 8.* La piscine ferme à quelle heure? – Elle ferme à vingt heures.
Use le *or* la *when* it *is the object of the sentence.* le *and* la *change to* l' *before a vowel and most words beginning with "h".*
2 *le* ◇ *There's a croissant left. Do you want it?* Il reste un croissant. Tu le veux?
l' ◇ *It's a good film. Did you see it?* C'est un bon film. L'as-tu vu?
la ◇ *I don't want this apple. Take it.* Je ne veux pas de cette pomme. Prends-la.
l' ◇ *He's got a new car. – Yes, I saw it.* Il a une nouvelle voiture. – Oui, je l'ai vue.
- **It's raining.** Il pleut.
- **It's 6 o'clock.** Il est six heures.
- **It's Friday tomorrow.** Demain c'est vendredi.
- **Who is it? – It's me.** Qui est-ce? – C'est moi.
- **It's expensive.** C'est cher.

Italian ADJECTIVE
see also **Italian** NOUN
italien MASC
italienne FEM

Italian NOUN

> see also Italian ADJECTIVE

1 (*person*)
l' *Italien* MASC
l' *Italienne* FEM

2 (*language*)
l' *italien* MASC

Italy NOUN
l' *Italie* FEM
- **in Italy** en Italie
- **to Italy** en Italie

to **itch** VERB
- **It itches.** Ça me démange.
- **My head's itching.** J'ai des démangeaisons à la tête.

it'd = it had, it would

item NOUN
l' *article* MASC (*object*)

itinerary NOUN

l' *itinéraire* MASC

it'll = it will

its ADJECTIVE

> Remember to check if its *refers to a masculine, feminine or plural noun.*

son MASC ◇ *What's its name?* Quel est son nom?
sa FEM ◇ *Every thing in its place.* Chaque chose à sa place.
ses PL ◇ *The dog is losing its hair.* Le chien perd ses poils.

it's = it is, it has

itself PRONOUN

se

> se *changes to* s' *before a vowel and most words beginning with "h".*

◇ *The heating switches itself off.* Le chauffage s'arrête automatiquement.

I've = I have

J

jab NOUN
la *piqûre* (injection)

jack NOUN
1. le *cric* (for car)
2. le *valet* (playing card)

jacket NOUN
la *veste*
- **jacket potatoes** les pommes de terre en robe des champs

jackpot NOUN
le *gros lot*
- **to win the jackpot** gagner le gros lot

jail NOUN
see also jail VERB
la *prison*
- **to go to jail** aller en prison

jail VERB
see also jail NOUN
emprisonner

jam NOUN
la *confiture* ◇ strawberry jam la confiture de fraises
- **a traffic jam** un embouteillage

jam jar NOUN
le *pot à confiture*

jammed ADJECTIVE
coincé ◇ The window's jammed. La fenêtre est coincée.

jam-packed ADJECTIVE
bondé ◇ The room was jam-packed. La salle était bondée.

janitor NOUN
le *concierge* ◇ He's a janitor. Il est concierge.

January NOUN
janvier MASC
- **in January** en janvier

Japan NOUN
le *Japon*
- **in Japan** au Japon
- **from Japan** du Japon

Japanese ADJECTIVE
see also Japanese NOUN
japonais

Japanese NOUN
see also Japanese ADJECTIVE
1. (person)
le *Japonais*
la *Japonaise*
- **the Japanese** les Japonais
2. (language)
le *japonais*

jar NOUN
le *bocal*
(les *bocaux* PL)
◇ an empty jar un bocal vide

- **a jar of honey** un pot de miel

jaundice NOUN
la *jaunisse*

javelin NOUN
le *javelot*

jaw NOUN
la *mâchoire*

jazz NOUN
le *jazz*

jealous ADJECTIVE
jaloux MASC
jalouse FEM

jeans PL NOUN
le *jean* SING

Jehovah's Witness NOUN
le *témoin de Jéhovah* ◇ She's a Jehovah's Witness. Elle est témoin de Jéhovah.

jelly NOUN
la *gelée*

jellyfish NOUN
la *méduse*

jersey NOUN (pullover)
le *pull-over*

Jesus NOUN
Jésus MASC

jet NOUN
le *jet* (plane)

jetlag NOUN
- **to be suffering from jetlag** être sous le coup du décalage horaire

jetty NOUN
la *jetée*

Jew NOUN
le *Juif*
la *Juive*

jewel NOUN
le *bijou*
(les *bijoux* PL)

jeweller NOUN
le *bijoutier*
la *bijoutière*
◇ He's a jeweller. Il est bijoutier.

jeweller's shop NOUN
la *bijouterie*

jewellery NOUN
les *bijoux* MASC PL

Jewish ADJECTIVE
juif MASC
juive FEM

jigsaw NOUN
le *puzzle*

job NOUN
1. l' *emploi* MASC ◇ He's lost his job. Il a perdu son emploi.
- **I've got a Saturday job.** Je travaille le

samedi.

2 (*chore, task*)
le *travail*
(les *travaux* PL)
◇ *That was a difficult job.* C'était un travail difficile.

job centre NOUN
l' *agence pour l'emploi* FEM

jobless ADJECTIVE
sans emploi

jockey NOUN
le *jockey*

to **jog** VERB
faire du jogging

jogging NOUN
le *jogging*
◆ **to go jogging** faire du jogging

to **join** VERB
1 *s'inscrire à* (*become member of*) ◇ *I'm going to join the ski club.* Je vais m'inscrire au club de ski.
2 *se joindre à* ◇ *Do you mind if I join you?* Puis-je me joindre à vous?

joiner NOUN
le *menuisier* ◇ *He's a joiner.* Il est menuisier.

joint NOUN
1 l' *articulation* FEM (*in body*)
2 le *rôti* (*of meat*)
3 le *joint* (*drugs*)

joke NOUN
see also joke VERB
la *plaisanterie*
◆ **to tell a joke** raconter une plaisanterie

to **joke** VERB
see also joke NOUN
plaisanter ◇ *I'm only joking.* Je plaisante.

jolly ADJECTIVE
jovial
(*joviaux* MASC PL)

Jordan NOUN
la *Jordanie* (*country*)
◆ **in Jordan** en Jordanie

to **jot down** VERB
noter

jotter NOUN
(*pad*)
le *bloc-notes*
(les *blocs-notes* PL)

journalism NOUN
le *journalisme*

journalist NOUN
le/la *journaliste* ◇ *She's a journalist.* Elle est journaliste.

journey NOUN
1 le *voyage* ◇ *I don't like long journeys.* Je n'aime pas les longs voyages.
◆ **to go on a journey** faire un voyage

2 le *trajet* (*to school, work*) ◇ *The journey to school takes about half an hour.* Il y a une demi-heure de trajet pour aller à l'école.
◆ **a bus journey** un trajet en autobus

joy NOUN
la *joie*

joystick NOUN
le *manette de jeu* (*for computer game*)

judge NOUN
see also judge VERB
le *juge* ◇ *She's a judge.* Elle est juge.

to **judge** VERB
see also judge NOUN
juger

judo NOUN
le *judo* ◇ *My hobby is judo.* Je fais du judo.

jug NOUN
le *pot*

juice NOUN
le *jus* ◇ *orange juice* le jus d'orange

July NOUN
juillet MASC
◆ **in July** en juillet

to **jump** VERB
sauter
◆ **to jump over something** sauter par-dessus quelque chose
◆ **to jump out of the window** sauter par la fenêtre
◆ **to jump off the roof** sauter du toit

jumper NOUN
le *pull-over* (*pullover*)

junction NOUN
le *carrefour* (*of roads*)

June NOUN
juin MASC
◆ **in June** en juin

jungle NOUN
la *jungle*

junior NOUN
◆ **the juniors** (*in school*) les élèves des petites classes

junior school NOUN
l' *école primaire* FEM

junk NOUN
le *bric-à-brac* NO PL (*old things*) ◇ *The attic's full of junk.* Le grenier est rempli de bric-à-brac.
◆ **to eat junk food** manger n'importe comment
◆ **a junk shop** un magasin de brocante

jury NOUN
le *jury*

just ADVERB
juste ◇ *just after Christmas* juste après Noël ◇ *We had just enough money.* Nous avions juste assez d'argent. ◇ *just*

in time juste à temps
- **just here** ici
- **I'm rather busy just now.** Je suis assez occupé en ce moment.
- **I did it just now.** Je viens de le faire.
- **He's just arrived.** Il vient d'arriver.
- **I'm just coming!** J'arrive!

- **It's just a suggestion.** Ce n'est qu'une suggestion.

justice NOUN
la *justice*

to **justify** VERB
justifier

K

kangaroo NOUN
le _kangourou_

karate NOUN
le _karaté_

keen ADJECTIVE
enthousiaste ◇ _He doesn't seem very keen._ Il n'a pas l'air très enthousiaste.
+ **She's a keen student.** C'est une étudiante assidue.
+ **to be keen on something** aimer quelque chose ◇ _I'm keen on maths._ J'aime les maths. ◇ _I'm not very keen on maths._ Je n'aime pas trop les maths.
+ **to be keen on somebody** (_fancy them_) être très attiré par quelqu'un ◇ _He's keen on her._ Il est très attiré par elle.
+ **to be keen on doing something** avoir très envie de faire quelque chose ◇ _I'm not very keen on going._ Je n'ai pas très envie d'y aller.

to **keep** VERB
[1] _garder_ (_retain_) ◇ _You can keep it._ Tu peux le garder.
[2] _rester_ (_remain_) ◇ _Keep still!_ Reste tranquille!
+ **Keep quiet!** Tais-toi!
+ **I keep forgetting my keys.** J'oublie tout le temps mes clés.
+ **to keep on doing something (1)** (_continue_) continuer à faire quelque chose ◇ _He kept on reading._ Il a continué à lire.
+ **to keep on doing something (2)** (_repeatedly_) ne pas arrêter de faire quelque chose ◇ _The car keeps on breaking down._ La voiture n'arrête pas de tomber en panne.
+ **"keep out"** "défense d'entrer"

keep-fit NOUN
la _gymnastique d'entretien_
+ **I go to keep-fit classes.** Je vais à des cours de gymnastique.

kennel NOUN
la _niche_

kettle NOUN
la _bouilloire_

key NOUN
la _clé_

keyboard NOUN
le _clavier_ ◇ _...with Mike Moran on keyboards_ ...avec Mike Moran aux claviers

keyring NOUN
le _porte-clés_

kick NOUN
see also kick VERB

le _coup de pied_

to **kick** VERB
see also kick NOUN
+ **to kick somebody** donner un coup de pied à quelqu'un ◇ _He kicked me._ Il m'a donné un coup de pied. ◇ _He kicked the ball hard._ Il a donné un bon coup de pied dans le ballon.
+ **to kick off** (_in football_) donner le coup d'envoi

kick-off NOUN
le _coup d'envoi_ ◇ _The kick-off is at 10 o'clock._ Le coup d'envoi sera donné à dix heures.

kid NOUN
see also kid VERB
le/la _gosse_ (_child_)

to **kid** VERB
see also kid NOUN
plaisanter ◇ _I'm just kidding._ Je plaisante.

to **kidnap** VERB
kidnapper

kidney NOUN
[1] le _rein_ (_human_) ◇ _He's got kidney trouble._ Il a des problèmes de reins.
[2] le _rognon_ (_to eat_) ◇ _I don't like kidneys._ Je n'aime pas les rognons.

to **kill** VERB
tuer ◇ _He was killed in a car accident._ Il a été tué dans un accident de voiture.
+ **Luckily, nobody was killed.** Il n'y a heureusement pas eu de victimes.
+ **Six people were killed in the accident.** L'accident a fait six morts.
+ **to kill oneself** se suicider ◇ _He killed himself._ Il s'est suicidé.

killer NOUN
[1] (_murderer_)
le _meurtrier_
la _meurtrière_
◇ _The police are searching for the killer._ La police recherche le meurtrier.
[2] (_hit man_)
le _tueur_
la _tueuse_
◇ _a hired killer_ un tueur à gages
+ **Meningitis can be a killer.** La méningite peut être mortelle.

kilo NOUN
le _kilo_ ◇ _10 francs a kilo_ dix francs le kilo

kilometre NOUN
le _kilomètre_

kilt NOUN
le _kilt_

kind ADJECTIVE
> see also kind NOUN

gentil MASC
gentille FEM
* **to be kind to somebody** être gentil avec quelqu'un
* **Thank you for being so kind.** Merci pour votre gentillesse.

kind NOUN
> see also kind ADJECTIVE

la *sorte* ◇ *It's a kind of sausage.* C'est une sorte de saucisse.

kindergarten NOUN
l' *école maternelle* FEM

kindness NOUN
la *gentillesse*

king NOUN
le *roi*

kingdom NOUN
le *royaume*

kiosk NOUN
la *cabine téléphonique* (*phone box*)

kipper NOUN
le *hareng fumé*

kiss NOUN
> see also kiss VERB

le *baiser* ◇ *a passionate kiss* un baiser passionné

to **kiss** VERB
> see also kiss NOUN

1 *embrasser* ◇ *He kissed her passionately.* Il l'a embrassée passionnément.
2 *s'embrasser* ◇ *They kissed.* Ils se sont embrassés.

kit NOUN
1 les *affaires* FEM PL (*clothes for sport*)
◇ *I've forgotten my gym kit.* J'ai oublié mes affaires de gym.
2 la *trousse* ◇ *a tool kit* une trousse à outils ◇ *a first aid kit* une trousse de secours ◇ *a puncture repair kit* une trousse de réparations
* **a drum kit** une batterie
* **a sewing kit** un nécessaire à couture

kitchen NOUN
la *cuisine* ◇ *a fitted kitchen* une cuisine aménagée
* **the kitchen units** les éléments de cuisine
* **a kitchen knife** un couteau de cuisine

kite NOUN
le *cerf-volant*
(les *cerfs-volants* PL)

kitten NOUN
le *chaton*

knee NOUN
le *genou*
(les *genoux* PL)
* **He was on his knees.** Il était à genoux.

to **kneel (down)** VERB
s'agenouiller

knew VERB see **know**

knickers PL NOUN
la *culotte* SING
* **a pair of knickers** une culotte

knife NOUN
le *couteau*
(les *couteaux* PL)
* **a kitchen knife** un couteau de cuisine
* **a sheath knife** un couteau à gaine
* **a penknife** un canif

to **knit** VERB
tricoter

knitting NOUN
le *tricot* ◇ *I like knitting.* J'aime faire du tricot.

knives PL NOUN see **knife**

to **knock** VERB
> see also knock NOUN

frapper ◇ *Someone's knocking at the door.* Quelqu'un frappe à la porte.
* **to knock somebody down** renverser quelqu'un ◇ *She was knocked down by a car.* Elle a été renversée par une voiture.
* **to knock somebody out (1)** (*defeat*) éliminer ◇ *They were knocked out early in the tournament.* Ils ont été éliminés au début du tournoi.
* **to knock somebody out (2)** (*stun*) assommer ◇ *They knocked out the watchman.* Ils ont assommé le gardien.

knock NOUN
> see also knock VERB

le *coup*

knot NOUN
le *nœud*
* **to tie a knot in something** faire un nœud à quelque chose

to **know** VERB
> Use **savoir** for knowing facts, **connaître** for knowing people and places.

1 *savoir* ◇ *It's a long way. – Yes, I know.* C'est loin. – Oui, je sais. ◇ *I don't know.* Je ne sais pas. ◇ *I don't know what to do.* Je ne sais pas quoi faire. ◇ *I don't know how to do it.* Je ne sais pas comment faire.
2 *connaître* ◇ *I know her.* Je la connais. ◇ *I know Paris well.* Je connais bien Paris.
* **I don't know any German.** Je ne parle pas du tout allemand.
* **to know that...** savoir que... ◇ *I know that you like chocolate.* Je sais que tu aimes le chocolat. ◇ *I didn't know that your Dad was a policeman.* Je ne savais pas que ton père était policier.

- **to know about something (1)** (*be aware of*) être au courant de quelque chose ◇ *Do you know about the meeting this afternoon?* Tu es au courant de la réunion de cet après-midi?
- **to know about something (2)** (*be knowledgeable about*) s'y connaître en quelque chose ◇ *He knows a lot about cars.* Il s'y connaît en voitures. ◇ *I don't know much about computers.* Je ne m'y connais pas bien en informatique.
- **to get to know somebody** apprendre à connaître quelqu'un
- **How should I know?** (*I don't know!*) Comment veux-tu que je le sache?
- **You never know!** On ne sait jamais!

know-all NOUN
le/la *je-sais-tout* ◇ *He's such a know-all!* C'est Monsieur je-sais-tout!

know-how NOUN
le *savoir-faire*

knowledge NOUN
la *connaissance*

knowledgeable ADJECTIVE
- **to be knowledgeable about something** s'y connaître en quelque chose ◇ *She's very knowledgeable about computers.* Elle s'y connaît bien en informatique.

Koran NOUN
le *Coran*

Korea NOUN
la *Corée*
- **in Korea** en Corée

kosher ADJECTIVE
kascher MASC, FEM, PL

L

lab NOUN (= *laboratory*)
le *labo*
* **a lab technician** un laborantin

label NOUN
l' *étiquette* FEM

laboratory NOUN
le *laboratoire*

Labour NOUN
les *travaillistes* MASC PL ◇ *My parents
vote Labour.* Mes parents votent pour
les travaillistes.
* **the Labour Party** le parti travailliste

labourer NOUN
le *manœuvre*
* **a farm labourer** un ouvrier
agricole

lace NOUN
1. le *lacet* (*of shoe*)
2. la *dentelle* ◇ *a lace collar* un col en
dentelle

lacquer NOUN
la *laque*

lad NOUN
le *gars*

ladder NOUN
l' *échelle* FEM

lady NOUN
la *dame*
* **a young lady** une jeune fille
* **Ladies and gentlemen...** Mesdames,
Messieurs...
* **the ladies'** les toilettes pour dames FEM

ladybird NOUN
la *coccinelle*

lag behind VERB
rester en arrière

lager NOUN
la *bière blonde*

laid VERB *see* **lay**

laid-back ADJECTIVE
relaxe

lain VERB *see* **lie**

lake NOUN
le *lac*
* **Lake Geneva** le lac Léman

lamb NOUN
l' *agneau* MASC
(les *agneaux* PL)
* **a lamb chop** une côtelette d'agneau

lame ADJECTIVE
boiteux ◇ *My pony is lame.* Mon
poney boite.

lamp NOUN
la *lampe*

lamppost NOUN
le *réverbère*

land NOUN
see also **land** VERB
la *terre*
* **a piece of land** un terrain

to **land** VERB
see also **land** NOUN
atterrir (*plane, passenger*)

landing NOUN
1. l' *atterrissage* MASC (*of plane*)
2. le *palier* (*of staircase*)

landlady NOUN
la *propriétaire*

landlord NOUN
le *propriétaire*

landowner NOUN
le *propriétaire terrien*

landscape NOUN
le *paysage*

lane NOUN
1. le *chemin* (*in country*)
2. la *voie* (*on motorway*)

language NOUN
la *langue* ◇ *French isn't a difficult
language.* Le français n'est pas une
langue difficile.
* **to use bad language** dire des
grossièretés

language laboratory NOUN
le *laboratoire de langues*

lap NOUN
le *tour de piste* (*sport*) ◇ *I ran ten laps.*
J'ai fait dix tours de piste en courant.
* **on my lap** sur mes genoux

laptop NOUN (*computer*)
le *portable*

larder NOUN
le *garde-manger*
(les *garde-manger* PL)

large ADJECTIVE
1. *grand* ◇ *a large house* une grande
maison
2. (*person, animal*)
gros MASC
grosse FEM
◇ *a large dog* un gros chien

laser NOUN
le *laser*

lass NOUN
la *jeune fille*

last ADJECTIVE, ADVERB
see also **last** VERB
1. *dernier* MASC
dernière FEM
◇ *last Friday* vendredi dernier ◇ *last
week* la semaine dernière ◇ *last summer*
l'été dernier

2 *en dernier* ◇ *He arrived last.* Il est arrivé en dernier.

3 *pour la dernière fois* ◇ *I've lost my bag. – When did you see it last?* J'ai perdu mon sac. – Quand est-ce que tu l'as vu pour la dernière fois? ◇ *When I last saw him, he was wearing a blue shirt.* La dernière fois que je l'ai vu, il portait une chemise bleue.

* **the last time** la dernière fois ◇ *the last time I saw her* la dernière fois que je l'ai vue ◇ *That's the last time I take your advice!* C'est la dernière fois que je suis tes conseils!

* **last night** (1) (*evening*) hier soir ◇ *I got home at midnight last night.* Je suis rentré à minuit hier soir.

* **last night** (2) (*sleeping hours*) la nuit dernière ◇ *I couldn't sleep last night.* J'ai eu du mal à dormir la nuit dernière.

* **at last** enfin

to **last** VERB

see also last ADJECTIVE

durer ◇ *The concert lasts two hours.* Le concert dure deux heures.

late ADJECTIVE, ADVERB

1 *en retard* ◇ *Hurry up or you'll be late!* Dépêche-toi, sinon tu vas être en retard! ◇ *I'm often late for school.* J'arrive souvent en retard à l'école.

* **to arrive late** arriver en retard ◇ *She arrived late.* Elle est arrivée en retard.

2 *tard* ◇ *I went to bed late.* Je me suis couché tard.

* **in the late afternoon** en fin d'après-midi

* **in late May** fin mai

lately ADVERB

ces derniers temps ◇ *I haven't seen him lately.* Je ne l'ai pas vu ces derniers temps.

later ADVERB

plus tard ◇ *I'll do it later.* Je ferai ça plus tard.

* **See you later!** À tout à l'heure!

latest ADJECTIVE

dernier MASC

dernière FEM

◇ *their latest album* leur dernier album

* **at the latest** au plus tard ◇ *by 10 o'clock at the latest* à dix heures au plus tard

Latin NOUN

le *latin* ◇ *I do Latin.* Je fais du latin.

Latin America NOUN

l' *Amérique latine* FEM

* **in Latin America** en Amérique latine

Latin American ADJECTIVE

latino-américain

laugh NOUN

see also laugh VERB

le *rire*

* **It was a good laugh.** (*it was fun*) On s'est bien amusés.

to **laugh** VERB

see also laugh NOUN

rire

* **to laugh at something** se moquer de quelque chose ◇ *They laughed at her.* Ils se sont moqués d'elle.

Launderette ® NOUN

la *laverie*

laundry NOUN

le *linge* (*clothes*)

lavatory NOUN

les *toilettes* FEM PL

lavender NOUN

la *lavande*

law NOUN

1 la *loi* ◇ *The laws are very strict.* Les lois sont très sévères.

* **It's against the law.** C'est illégal.

2 le *droit* (*subject*) ◇ *My sister's studying law.* Ma sœur fait des études de droit.

lawn NOUN

la *pelouse*

lawnmower NOUN

la *tondeuse à gazon*

lawyer NOUN

l' *avocat* MASC

l' *avocate* FEM

◇ *My mother's a lawyer.* Ma mère est avocate.

to **lay** VERB

lay is also a form of lie VERB.

mettre ◇ *She laid the baby in her cot.* Elle a mis le bébé dans son lit.

* **to lay the table** mettre la table

* **to lay something on** (1) (*provide*) organiser quelque chose ◇ *They laid on extra buses.* Ils ont organisé un service de bus supplémentaire.

* **to lay something on** (2) (*prepare*) préparer quelque chose ◇ *They laid on a special meal.* Ils ont préparé un repas soigné.

lay-by NOUN

l' *aire de stationnement* FEM

lazy ADJECTIVE

paresseux MASC

paresseuse FEM

lead NOUN

This word has two pronunciations. Make sure you choose the right translation.

see also lead VERB

1 le *fil* (*cable*)

2 la *laisse* (*for dog*)

◆ **to be in the lead** être en tête ◇ *Our team is in the lead.* Notre équipe est en tête.

③ le *plomb* (metal)

to lead VERB

see also lead NOUN

mener ◇ *the street that leads to the station* la rue qui mène à la gare

◆ **to lead the way** montrer le chemin

◆ **to lead somebody away** emmener quelqu'un ◇ *The police led the man away.* La police a emmené l'homme.

leaded petrol NOUN

l' *essence au plomb* FEM

leader NOUN

① (of expedition, gang)

le *chef*

② (of political party)

le *dirigeant*

la *dirigeante*

lead-free ADJECTIVE

◆ **lead-free petrol** de l'essence sans plomb

lead singer NOUN

le *chanteur principal*

la *chanteuse principale*

leaf NOUN

la *feuille*

leaflet NOUN

la *brochure*

league NOUN

le *championnat* ◇ *They are at the top of the league.* Ils sont en tête du championnat.

◆ **the Premier League** la première division

leak NOUN

see also leak VERB

la *fuite* ◇ *a gas leak* une fuite de gaz

leak VERB

see also leak NOUN

fuir (pipe, water, gas)

lean VERB

se pencher ◇ *Don't lean over too far.* Ne te penche pas trop. ◇ *She leant out of the window.* Elle s'est penchée par la fenêtre.

◆ **to lean forward** se pencher en avant

◆ **to lean on something** s'appuyer contre quelque chose ◇ *He leant on the wall.* Il s'est appuyé contre le mur.

◆ **to be leaning against something** être appuyé contre quelque chose ◇ *The ladder was leaning against the wall.* L'échelle était appuyée contre le mur.

◆ **to lean something against a wall** appuyer quelque chose contre un mur ◇ *He leant his bike against the wall.* Il a appuyé son vélo contre le mur.

leap year NOUN

l' *année bissextile* FEM

to learn VERB

apprendre ◇ *I'm learning to ski.* J'apprends à skier.

learner NOUN

◆ **She's a quick learner.** Elle apprend vite.

◆ **French learners** (people learning French) ceux qui apprennent le français

learner driver NOUN

le *conducteur débutant*

la *conductrice débutante*

least ADVERB, ADJECTIVE, PRONOUN

◆ **the least (1)** (followed by noun) le moins de ◇ *It takes the least time.* C'est ce qui prend le moins de temps.

◆ **the least (2)** (after a verb) le moins ◇ *Maths is the subject I like the least.* Les maths sont la matière que j'aime le moins.

When **least** is followed by adjective, the translation depends on whether the noun referred to is masculine, feminine or plural.

◆ **the least... (1)** le moins... ◇ *the least expensive hotel* l'hôtel le moins cher

◆ **the least... (2)** la moins... ◇ *the least expensive seat* la place la moins chère

◆ **the least... (3)** les moins... ◇ *the least expensive hotels* les hôtels les moins chers ◇ *the least expensive seats* les places les moins chères

◆ **It's the least I can do.** C'est le moins que je puisse faire.

◆ **at least (1)** au moins ◇ *It'll cost at least £200.* Ça va coûter au moins deux cents livres.

◆ **at least (2)** du moins ◇ *...but at least nobody was hurt.* ...mais du moins personne n'a été blessé. ◇ *It's totally unfair – at least, that's my opinion.* C'est vraiment injuste – du moins c'est ce que je pense.

leather NOUN

le *cuir* ◇ *a black leather jacket* un blouson en cuir noir

to leave VERB

see also leave NOUN

① *laisser* (deliberately) ◇ *Don't leave your camera in the car.* Ne laisse pas ton appareil-photo dans la voiture.

② *oublier* (by mistake) ◇ *I've left my book at home.* J'ai oublié mon livre à la maison. ◇ *Make sure you haven't left anything behind.* Vérifiez bien que vous n'avez rien oublié.

③ *partir* (go) ◇ *The bus leaves at 8.* Le car part à huit heures. ◇ *She's just left.* Elle vient de partir.

④ *quitter* (go away from) ◇ *We leave London at six o'clock.* Nous quittons

Londres à six heures. ◇ *My sister left home last year.* Ma sœur a quitté la maison l'an dernier.

◆ **to leave somebody alone** laisser quelqu'un tranquille ◇ *Leave me alone!* Laisse-moi tranquille!

leave NOUN
> *see also* **leave** VERB

[1] le *congé* (*from job*)

[2] la *permission* (*from army*) ◇ *My brother is on leave for a week.* Mon frère est en permission pendant une semaine.

leaves PL NOUN *see* **leaf**

Lebanon NOUN
le *Liban*

◆ **in Lebanon** au Liban

lecture NOUN
> *see also* **lecture** VERB

[1] (*public*)
la *conférence*

[2] (*at university*)
le *cours magistral*
(les *cours magistraux* PL)

to **lecture** VERB
> *see also* **lecture** NOUN

[1] *enseigner* ◇ *She lectures at the technical college.* Elle enseigne au collège technique.

[2] *faire la morale* ◇ *He's always lecturing us.* Il n'arrête pas de nous faire la morale.

lecturer NOUN
le *professeur d'université* ◇ *She's a lecturer.* Elle est professeur d'université.

led VERB *see* **lead**

leek NOUN
le *poireau*
(les *poireaux* PL)

left VERB *see* **leave**

left ADJECTIVE, ADVERB
> *see also* **left** NOUN

[1] *gauche* (*not right*) ◇ *my left hand* ma main gauche ◇ *on the left side of the road* sur le côté gauche de la route

[2] *à gauche* ◇ *Turn left at the traffic lights.* Tournez à gauche aux prochains feux.

◆ **I haven't got any money left.** Il ne me reste plus d'argent.

left NOUN
> *see also* **left** ADJECTIVE

la *gauche*

◆ **on the left** à gauche ◇ *Remember to drive on the left.* N'oubliez pas de conduire à gauche.

left-hand ADJECTIVE

◆ **the left-hand side** la gauche ◇ *It's on the left-hand side.* C'est à gauche.

left-handed ADJECTIVE
gaucher MASC
gauchère FEM

left-luggage office NOUN
la *consigne*

leg NOUN
la *jambe* ◇ *She's broken her leg.* Elle s'est cassé la jambe.

◆ **a chicken leg** une cuisse de poulet

◆ **a leg of lamb** un gigot d'agneau

legal ADJECTIVE
légal
(*légaux* MASC PL)

leggings NOUN
le *caleçon* SING

leisure NOUN
les *loisirs* MASC PL ◇ *What do you do in your leisure time?* Qu'est-ce que tu fais pendant tes loisirs?

leisure centre NOUN
le *centre de loisirs*

lemon NOUN
le *citron*

lemonade NOUN
la *limonade*

to **lend** VERB
prêter ◇ *I can lend you some money.* Je peux te prêter de l'argent.

length NOUN
la *longueur*

◆ **It's about a metre in length.** Ça fait environ un mètre de long.

lens NOUN
[1] la *lentille* (*contact lens*)

[2] le *verre* (*of spectacles*)

[3] l' *objectif* MASC (*of camera*)

Lent NOUN
le *carême*

lent VERB *see* **lend**

lentil NOUN
la *lentille*

Leo NOUN
le *Lion* ◇ *I'm Leo.* Je suis Lion.

leotard NOUN
le *justaucorps*

lesbian NOUN
la *lesbienne*

less PRONOUN, ADVERB, ADJECTIVE
[1] *moins* ◇ *He's less intelligent than her.* Il est moins intelligent qu'elle. ◇ *A bit less, please.* Un peu moins, s'il vous plaît.

[2] *moins de* ◇ *I've got less time for hobbies now.* J'ai moins de temps pour les loisirs maintenant.

◆ **less than (1)** (*with amounts*) moins de ◇ *It's less than a kilometre from here.* C'est à moins d'un kilomètre d'ici. ◇ *It costs less than 100 francs.* Ça coûte moins de cent francs. ◇ *less than half* moins de la moitié

• **less than (2)** (*in comparisons*) moins que ◇ *He spent less than me.* Il a dépensé moins que moi. ◇ *I've got less than you.* J'en ai moins que toi. ◇ *It cost less than we thought.* Ça a coûté moins cher que nous ne le pensions.

lesson NOUN

 1 la *leçon* ◇ *a French lesson* une leçon de français ◇ *"Lesson Sixteen"* (*in textbook*) "Leçon seize"

 2 le *cours* (*class*) ◇ *The lessons last forty minutes each.* Chaque cours dure quarante minutes.

to let VERB

 1 *laisser* (*allow*)

• **to let somebody do something** laisser quelqu'un faire quelque chose ◇ *Let me have a look.* Laisse-moi voir. ◇ *My parents won't let me stay out that late.* Mes parents ne me laissent pas sortir aussi tard.

• **to let somebody know** faire savoir à quelqu'un ◇ *I'll let you know as soon as possible.* Je vous le ferai savoir dès que possible.

• **to let somebody go** lâcher quelqu'un ◇ *Let me go!* Lâche-moi!

• **to let in** laisser entrer ◇ *They wouldn't let me in because I was under 18.* Ils ne m'ont pas laissé entrer parce que j'avais moins de dix-huit ans.

 To make suggestions using **let's,** *you can ask questions beginning with* **si on.**
 ◇ *Let's go to the cinema!* Si on allait au cinéma?

• **Let's go!** Allons-y!

 2 *louer* (*hire out*)

• **"to let"** "à louer"

letter NOUN
 la *lettre*

letterbox NOUN
 la *boîte à lettres*

lettuce NOUN
 la *salade*

leukaemia NOUN
 la *leucémie*

level ADJECTIVE
 see also **level** NOUN
 plan ◇ *A snooker table must be perfectly level.* Un billard doit être parfaitement plan.

level NOUN
 see also **level** ADJECTIVE
 le *niveau*
 (les *niveaux* PL)
 ◇ *The level of the river is rising.* Le niveau de la rivière monte.

• **"A" levels** le baccalauréat
 The French baccalauréat (*or* bac *for short*) *is taken at the age of 17 or 18. Students have to sit one of a variety of set subject combinations, rather than being able to choose any combination of subjects they want. If you pass you have the right to a place at university.*

level crossing NOUN
 le *passage à niveau*

lever NOUN
 le *levier*

liable ADJECTIVE

• **He's liable to lose his temper.** Il se met facilement en colère.

liar NOUN
 le *menteur*
 la *menteuse*

liberal ADJECTIVE
 (*opinions*)
 libéral
 (*libéraux* MASC PL)

• **the Liberal Democrats** le parti libéral-démocrate

liberation NOUN
 la *libération*

Libra NOUN
 la *Balance* ◇ *I'm Libra.* Je suis Balance.

librarian NOUN
 le/la *bibliothécaire* ◇ *She's a librarian.* Elle est bibliothécaire.

library NOUN
 la *bibliothèque*

Libya NOUN
 la *Libye*

• **in Libya** en Libye

licence NOUN
 le *permis*

• **a driving licence** un permis de conduire

to lick VERB
 lécher

lid NOUN
 le *couvercle*

to lie VERB
 see also **lie** NOUN
 mentir (*not tell the truth*) ◇ *I know she's lying.* Je sais qu'elle ment.

• **to lie down** s'allonger

• **to be lying down** être allongé

• **He was lying on the sofa.** Il était allongé sur le canapé. ◇ *When I'm on holiday I lie on the beach all day.* Quand je suis en vacances, je reste allongé sur la plage toute la journée.

lie NOUN
 see also **lie** VERB
 le *mensonge*

• **to tell a lie** mentir

• **That's a lie!** Ce n'est pas vrai!

lie-in NOUN

- **to have a lie-in** faire la grasse matinée
  ◦ *I have a lie-in on Sundays.* Je fais la grasse matinée le dimanche.
lieutenant NOUN
  le *lieutenant*
life NOUN
  la *vie*
lifebelt NOUN
  la *bouée de sauvetage*
lifeboat NOUN
  le *canot de sauvetage*
lifeguard NOUN
  le *maître nageur*
life jacket NOUN
  le *gilet de sauvetage*
life-saving NOUN
  le *sauvetage* ◦ *I've done a course in life-saving.* J'ai pris des cours de sauvetage.
lifestyle NOUN
  le *style de vie*
to **lift** VERB
  see also **lift** NOUN
  soulever ◦ *It's too heavy, I can't lift it.* C'est trop lourd, je ne peux pas le soulever.
lift NOUN
  see also **lift** VERB
  l' *ascenseur* MASC ◦ *The lift isn't working.* L'ascenseur est en panne.
- **He gave me a lift to the cinema.** Il m'a emmené au cinéma en voiture.
- **Would you like a lift?** Est-ce que je peux vous déposer quelque part?
light ADJECTIVE
  see also **light** NOUN, VERB
  1 (*not heavy*)
  léger MASC
  légère FEM
  ◦ *a light jacket* une veste légère ◦ *a light meal* un repas léger
  2 (*colour*)
  clair ◦ *a light blue sweater* un pull bleu clair
light NOUN
  see also **light** ADJECTIVE, VERB
  1 la *lumière* ◦ *to switch on the light* allumer la lumière ◦ *to switch off the light* éteindre la lumière
  2 la *lampe* ◦ *There's a light by my bed.* Il y a une lampe près de mon lit.
- **the traffic lights** les feux MASC
- **Have you got a light?** (*for cigarette*) Avez-vous du feu?
to **light** VERB
  see also **light** ADJECTIVE, NOUN
  allumer (*candle, cigarette, fire*)
light bulb NOUN
  l' *ampoule* FEM
lighter NOUN

le *briquet* (*for cigarettes*)
lighthouse NOUN
  le *phare*
lightning NOUN
  les *éclairs* MASC PL
- **a flash of lightning** un éclair
to **like** VERB
  see also **like** PREPOSITION
  1 *aimer* ◦ *I don't like mustard.* Je n'aime pas la moutarde. ◦ *I like riding.* J'aime monter à cheval.
  *Note that **aimer** also means to love, so make sure you use **aimer bien** for just liking somebody.*
  2 *aimer bien* ◦ *I like Paul, but I don't want to go out with him.* J'aime bien Paul, mais je ne veux pas sortir avec lui.
- **I'd like...** Je voudrais... ◦ *I'd like an orange juice, please.* Je voudrais un jus d'orange, s'il vous plaît. ◦ *Would you like some coffee?* Voulez-vous du café?
- **I'd like to...** J'aimerais... ◦ *I'd like to go to Russia one day.* J'aimerais aller en Russie un jour. ◦ *I'd like to wash my hands.* J'aimerais me laver les mains.
- **Would you like to go for a walk?** Tu veux aller faire une promenade?
- **...if you like** ...si tu veux
like PREPOSITION
  see also **like** VERB
  comme ◦ *It's fine like that.* C'est bien comme ça. ◦ *Do it like this.* Fais-le comme ça. ◦ *a city like Paris* une ville comme Paris ◦ *It's a bit like salmon.* C'est un peu comme du saumon.
- **What's the weather like?** Quel temps fait-il?
- **to look like somebody** ressembler à quelqu'un ◦ *You look like my brother.* Tu ressembles à mon frère.
likely ADJECTIVE
  probable ◦ *That's not very likely.* C'est peu probable.
- **She's likely to come.** Elle viendra probablement.
- **She's not likely to come.** Elle ne viendra probablement pas.
lily of the valley NOUN
  le *muguet*
lime NOUN
  le *citron vert* (*fruit*)
limit NOUN
  la *limite* ◦ *The speed limit is 70 mph.* La vitesse est limitée à cent dix kilomètres à l'heure.
limousine NOUN
  la *limousine*
to **limp** VERB
  boiter
line NOUN

1 la *ligne* ○ *a straight line* une ligne droite

2 le *trait* (to divide, cancel) ○ *Draw a line under each answer.* Tirez un trait après chaque réponse.

3 la *voie* (railway track)

- **Hold the line, please.** Ne quittez pas.
- **It's a very bad line.** La ligne est très mauvaise.

linen NOUN
le *lin* ○ *a linen jacket* une veste en lin

liner NOUN
le *paquebot* (ship)

linguist NOUN
- **to be a good linguist** être doué pour les langues ○ *She's a good linguist.* Elle est douée pour les langues.

link NOUN
see also link VERB
le *rapport* ○ *the link between smoking and cancer* le rapport entre le tabagisme et le cancer

to **link** VERB
see also link NOUN
relier

lino NOUN
le *linoléum*

lion NOUN
le *lion*

lioness NOUN
la *lionne*

lip NOUN
la *lèvre*

to **lip-read** VERB
lire sur les lèvres

lip salve NOUN
la *pommade pour les lèvres*

lipstick NOUN
le *rouge à lèvres*

liqueur NOUN
la *liqueur*

liquid NOUN
le *liquide*

liquidizer NOUN
le *mixer*

list NOUN
see also list VERB
la *liste*

to **list** VERB
see also list NOUN
faire une liste de ○ *List your hobbies!* Fais une liste de tes hobbies!

to **listen** VERB
écouter ○ *Listen to this!* Écoutez ceci! ○ *Listen to me!* Écoutez-moi!

listener NOUN
l' *auditeur* MASC
l' *auditrice* FEM

lit VERB see **light**

literally ADVERB
vraiment (completely) ○ *It was literally impossible to find a seat.* Il était vraiment impossible de trouver une place.

- **to translate literally** faire une traduction littérale

literature NOUN
la *littérature* ○ *I'm studying English Literature.* J'étudie la littérature anglaise.

litre NOUN
le *litre*

litter NOUN
les *ordures* FEM PL

litter bin NOUN
la *poubelle*

little ADJECTIVE
petit ○ *a little girl* une petite fille

- **a little** un peu ○ *How much would you like? – Just a little.* Combien en voulez-vous? – Juste un peu.
- **very little** très peu ○ *We've got very little time.* Nous avons très peu de temps.
- **little by little** petit à petit

live ADJECTIVE
see also live VERB
1 *vivant* (animal)
2 *en direct* (broadcast)

- **There's live music on Fridays.** Il y a des musiciens qui jouent le vendredi.

to **live** VERB
see also live ADJECTIVE
1 *vivre* ○ *I live with my grandmother.* Je vis avec ma grand-mère. ○ *They're not married, they're living together.* Il ne sont pas mariés, ils vivent ensemble.

- **to live on something** vivre de quelque chose ○ *He lives on benefit.* Il vit de ses indemnités.
2 *habiter* (reside) ○ *Where do you live?* Où est-ce que tu habites? ○ *I live in Edinburgh.* J'habite à Édimbourg.

liver NOUN
le *foie*

lives PL NOUN
les *vies* FEM

living NOUN
- **to make a living** gagner sa vie
- **What does she do for a living?** Qu'est-ce qu'elle fait dans la vie?

living room NOUN
la *salle de séjour*

lizard NOUN
le *lézard*

load NOUN
see also load VERB
- **loads of** un tas de ○ *loads of people* un tas de gens ○ *loads of money* un tas d'argent
- **You're talking a load of rubbish!** Tu ne

dis que des bêtises!

to load VERB

> see also load NOUN

charger ◇ *a trolley loaded with luggage* un chariot chargé de bagages

loaf NOUN
le *pain*

- **a loaf of bread** un pain

loan NOUN

> see also loan VERB

le *prêt*

to loan VERB

> see also loan NOUN

prêter

to loathe VERB
détester ◇ *I loathe her.* Je la déteste.

loaves PL NOUN see **loaf**

lobster NOUN
le *homard*

local ADJECTIVE
local
(*locaux* MASC PL)
◇ *the local paper* le journal local

- **a local call** une communication urbaine

loch NOUN
le *loch*

lock NOUN

> see also lock VERB

la *serrure* ◇ *The lock is broken.* La serrure est cassée.

to lock VERB

> see also lock NOUN

fermer à clé ◇ *Make sure you lock your door.* N'oubliez pas de fermer votre porte à clé.

locker NOUN
le *casier*

- **the locker room** le vestiaire
- **the left-luggage lockers** la consigne automatique

locket NOUN
le *médaillon*

lodger NOUN
le/la *locataire*

loft NOUN
le *grenier*

log NOUN
la *bûche* (*of wood*)

logical ADJECTIVE
logique

lollipop NOUN
la *sucette*

lolly NOUN
la *glace à l'eau* (*ice lolly*)

London NOUN
Londres

- **in London** à Londres
- **to London** à Londres
- **I'm from London.** Je suis de Londres.

Londoner NOUN
le *Londonien*
la *Londonienne*

loneliness NOUN
la *solitude*

lonely ADJECTIVE
seul

- **to feel lonely** se sentir seul ◇ *She feels a bit lonely.* Elle se sent un peu seule.

long ADJECTIVE, ADVERB

> see also long VERB

long MASC
longue FEM
◇ *She's got long hair.* Elle a les cheveux longs. ◇ *The room is 6 metres long.* La pièce fait six mètres de long.

- **How long?** (*time*) Combien de temps? ◇ *How long did you stay there?* Combien de temps êtes-vous resté là-bas? ◇ *How long have you been here?* Depuis combien de temps êtes-vous ici? ◇ *How long is the flight?* Combien de temps dure le vol?
- **I've been waiting a long time.** J'attends depuis longtemps.
- **It takes a long time.** Ça prend du temps.
- **as long as** si ◇ *I'll come as long as it's not too expensive.* Je viendrai si ce n'est pas trop cher.

to long VERB

> see also long ADJECTIVE

- **to long to do something** attendre avec impatience de faire quelque chose
- **I'm longing to see my boyfriend again.** J'attends avec impatience de revoir mon copain.

long-distance ADJECTIVE

- **a long-distance call** une communication interurbaine

longer ADVERB

> see also long ADJECTIVE

- **They're no longer going out together.** Ils ne sortent plus ensemble.
- **I can't stand it any longer.** Je ne peux plus le supporter.

long jump NOUN
le *saut en longueur*

loo NOUN
les *toilettes* FEM PL ◇ *Where's the loo?* Où sont les toilettes?

look NOUN

> see also look VERB

- **to have a look** regarder ◇ *Have a look at this!* Regardez ceci!
- **I don't like the look of it.** Ça ne me dit rien.

to look VERB

> see also look NOUN

1 *regarder* ◇ *Look!* Regardez!

* **to look at something** regarder quelque chose ◇ *Look at the picture.* Regardez cette image.
  * ② *avoir l'air* (*seem*) ◇ *She looks surprised.* Elle a l'air surprise. ◇ *That cake looks nice.* Ce gâteau a l'air bon. ◇ *It looks fine.* Ça a l'air bien.
* **to look like somebody** ressembler à quelqu'un ◇ *He looks like his brother.* Il ressemble à son frère.
* **What does she look like?** Comment est-elle physiquement?
* **Look out!** Attention!
* **to look after** s'occuper de ◇ *I look after my little sister.* Je m'occupe de ma petite sœur.
* **to look for** chercher ◇ *I'm looking for my passport.* Je cherche mon passeport.
* **to look forward to something** attendre quelque chose avec impatience ◇ *I'm looking forward to the holidays.* J'attends les vacances avec impatience.
* **Looking forward to hearing from you...** J'espère avoir bientôt de tes nouvelles...
* **to look round (1)** (*look behind*) se retourner ◇ *I shouted and he looked round.* J'ai crié et il s'est retourné.
* **to look round (2)** (*have a look*) jeter un coup d'œil ◇ *I'm just looking round.* Je jette simplement un coup d'œil.
* **to look round a museum** visiter un musée
* **I like looking round the shops.** J'aime faire les boutiques.
* **to look up** (*word, name*) chercher ◇ *If you don't know a word, look it up in the dictionary.* Si vous ne connaissez pas un mot, cherchez-le dans le dictionnaire.

loose ADJECTIVE
　ample (*clothes*)
* **loose change** la petite monnaie

lord NOUN
　le *seigneur* (*feudal*)
* **the House of Lords** la Chambre des lords
* **Good Lord!** Mon Dieu!

lorry NOUN
　le *camion*

lorry driver NOUN
　le *routier* ◇ *He's a lorry driver.* Il est routier.

lose VERB
　perdre ◇ *I've lost my purse.* J'ai perdu mon porte-monnaie.
* **to get lost** se perdre ◇ *I was afraid of getting lost.* J'avais peur de me perdre.

loss NOUN
　la *perte*

lost VERB *see* **lose**

lost ADJECTIVE
　perdu

lot NOUN
* **a lot** beaucoup
* **a lot of** beaucoup de ◇ *We saw a lot of interesting things.* Nous avons vu beaucoup de choses intéressantes.
* **lots of** un tas de ◇ *She's got lots of money.* Elle a un tas d'argent. ◇ *He's got lots of friends.* Il a un tas d'amis.
* **What did you do at the weekend? – Not a lot.** Qu'as-tu fait ce week-end? – Pas grand-chose.
* **Do you like football? – Not a lot.** Tu aimes le football? – Pas tellement.
* **That's the lot.** C'est tout.

lottery NOUN
　la *loterie*
* **to win the lottery** gagner à la loterie

loud ADJECTIVE
　fort ◇ *The television is too loud.* La télévision est trop forte.

loudly ADVERB
　fort

loudspeaker NOUN
　le *haut-parleur*

lounge NOUN
　le *salon*

lousy ADJECTIVE
　infect ◇ *The food in the canteen is lousy.* La nourriture de la cantine est infecte.
* **I feel lousy.** Je suis mal fichu. (*informal*)

love NOUN
　see also love VERB
　l' *amour* MASC
* **to be in love** être amoureux ◇ *She's in love with Paul.* Elle est amoureuse de Paul.
* **to make love** faire l'amour
* **Give Delphine my love.** Embrasse Delphine pour moi.
* **Love, Rosemary.** Amitiés, Rosemary.

to **love** VERB
　see also love NOUN
　① *aimer* (*be in love with*) ◇ *I love you.* Je t'aime.
　② *aimer beaucoup* (*like a lot*)
　◇ *Everybody loves her.* Tout le monde l'aime beaucoup. ◇ *I'd love to come.* J'aimerais beaucoup venir.
　③ *adorer* (*things*) ◇ *I love chocolate.* J'adore le chocolat. ◇ *I love skiing.* J'adore le ski.

lovely ADJECTIVE
　charmant ◇ *What a lovely surprise!* Quelle charmante surprise! ◇ *She's a lovely person.* Elle est charmante.
* **It's a lovely day.** Il fait très beau

aujourd'hui.
- **Is your meal OK? – Yes, it's lovely.**
Est-ce que c'est bon? – Oui, c'est
délicieux.
- **They've got a lovely house.** Ils ont une
très belle maison.
- **Have a lovely time!** Amusez-vous bien!

low ADJECTIVE, ADVERB
(*price, level*)
bas MASC
basse FEM
◇ *That plane is flying very low.* Cet avion
vole très bas.
- **the low season** la basse saison ◇ *in the
low season* en basse saison

lower sixth NOUN
la *première* ◇ *He's in the lower sixth.* Il
est en première.

low-fat ADJECTIVE
allégé ◇ *a low-fat yoghurt* un yaourt
allégé

loyalty NOUN
la *fidélité*

L-plates PL NOUN
les *plaques de conducteur débutant*
FEM PL

luck NOUN
la *chance* ◇ *She hasn't had much luck.*
Elle n'a pas eu beaucoup de chance.
- **Good luck!** Bonne chance!
- **Bad luck!** Pas de chance!

luckily ADVERB
heureusement

lucky ADJECTIVE
- **to be lucky (1)** (*be fortunate*) avoir de la
chance ◇ *He's lucky, he's got a job.* Il a
de la chance, il a un emploi. ◇ *He wasn't
hurt. – That was lucky!* Il n'a pas été
blessé. – C'est une chance!
- **to be lucky (2)** (*bring luck*) porter
bonheur ◇ *Black cats are lucky in
Britain.* Les chats noirs portent bonheur
en Grande-Bretagne.
- **a lucky horseshoe** un fer à cheval
porte-bonheur

luggage NOUN

les *bagages* MASC PL

lump NOUN
1 le *morceau*
(les *morceaux* PL)
◇ *a lump of butter* un morceau de beurre
2 la *bosse* (*swelling*) ◇ *He's got a lump
on his forehead.* Il a une bosse sur le
front.

lunatic NOUN
le *fou*
la *folle*
◇ *He's an absolute lunatic.* Il est
complètement fou.

lunch NOUN
le *déjeuner*
- **to have lunch** déjeuner ◇ *We have
lunch at 12.30.* Nous déjeunons à midi
et demie.

luncheon voucher NOUN
le *ticket-restaurant*

lung NOUN
le *poumon*
- **lung cancer** le cancer du poumon

luscious ADJECTIVE
délicieux MASC
délicieuse FEM

lush ADJECTIVE
luxuriant

lust NOUN
le *désir*

Luxembourg NOUN
1 le *Luxembourg* (*country*)
- **in Luxembourg** au Luxembourg
- **to Luxembourg** au Luxembourg
2 *Luxembourg* (*city*)
- **in Luxembourg** à Luxembourg

luxurious ADJECTIVE
luxueux MASC
luxueuse FEM

luxury NOUN
le *luxe* ◇ *It was luxury!* C'était un vrai
luxe!
- **a luxury hotel** un hôtel de luxe

lying VERB *see* **lie**

lyrics PL NOUN
les *paroles* FEM PL (*of song*)

M

mac NOUN
l' _imper_ MASC

macaroni NOUN
les _macaronis_ MASC PL

machine NOUN
la _machine_

machinery NOUN
les _machines_ FEM PL

mackerel NOUN
le _maquereau_
(les _maquereaux_ PL)

mad ADJECTIVE
1 (_insane_)
fou MASC
folle FEM
◇ _You're mad!_ Tu es fou!
2 (_angry_)
furieux MASC
furieuse FEM
◇ _She'll be mad when she finds out._ Elle
sera furieuse quand elle va s'en
apercevoir.
➤ **to be mad about (1)** (_sport, activity_) être
enragé de ◇ _He's mad about football._ Il
est enragé de foot.
➤ **to be mad about (2)** (_person, animal_)
adorer ◇ _She's mad about horses._ Elle
adore les chevaux.

madam NOUN
madame FEM ◇ _Would you like to order,
Madam?_ Désirez-vous commander,
Madame?

made VERB _see_ **make**

madly ADVERB
➤ **They're madly in love.** Ils sont
éperdument amoureux.

madman NOUN
le _fou_

magazine NOUN
le _magazine_

maggot NOUN
l' _asticot_ MASC

magic ADJECTIVE
see also magic NOUN
1 _magique_ (_magical_) ◇ _a magic wand_
une baguette magique
2 _super_ (_brilliant_)
➤ **It was magic!** C'était super!

magic NOUN
see also magic ADJECTIVE
la _magie_
➤ **a magic trick** un tour de magie
➤ **My hobby is magic.** Je fais des tours de
magie.

magician NOUN
le _prestidigitateur_ (_conjurer_)

magnificent ADJECTIVE
1 _magnifique_ (_beautiful_) ◇ _a
magnificent view_ une vue magnifique
2 _superbe_ (_outstanding_) ◇ _It was a
magnificent effort._ Ils ont fait un superbe
effort.

maid NOUN
la _domestique_ (_servant_)
➤ **an old maid** (_spinster_) une vieille fille

maiden name NOUN
le _nom de jeune fille_

mail NOUN
le _courrier_ ◇ _Here's your mail._ Voici
ton courrier.
➤ **e-mail** (_electronic mail_) le courrier
électronique
➤ **by mail** par la poste

main ADJECTIVE
principal
(_principaux_ MASC PL)
◇ _the main problem_ le principal problème
➤ **the main thing is to...** l'essentiel est de...

mainly ADVERB
principalement

main road NOUN
la _grande route_ ◇ _I don't like cycling on
main roads._ Je n'aime pas faire du vélo
sur les grandes routes.

to **maintain** VERB
entretenir (_machine, building_)

maintenance NOUN
l' _entretien_ MASC (_of machine, building_)

maize NOUN
le _maïs_

major ADJECTIVE
majeur ◇ _a major problem_ un
problème majeur
➤ **in C major** en do majeur

Majorca NOUN
Majorque FEM ◇ _We went to Majorca in
August._ Nous sommes allés à Majorque
en août.

majority NOUN
la _majorité_

make NOUN
see also make VERB
la _marque_ ◇ _What make is that car?_ De
quelle marque est cette voiture?

to **make** VERB
see also make NOUN
1 _faire_ ◇ _I'm going to make a cake._ Je
vais faire un gâteau. ◇ _He made it
himself._ Il l'a fait lui-même. ◇ _I make my
bed every morning._ Je fais mon lit tous
les matins. ◇ _2 and 2 make 4._ Deux et
deux font quatre.

2 *fabriquer* (*manufacture*) ◇ *made in France* fabriqué en France

3 *gagner* (*earn*) ◇ *He makes a lot of money.* Il gagne beaucoup d'argent.

◆ **to make somebody do something** obliger quelqu'un à faire quelque chose ◇ *My mother makes me do my homework.* Ma mère m'oblige à faire mes devoirs.

◆ **to make lunch** préparer le repas ◇ *She's making lunch.* Elle prépare le repas.

◆ **to make a phone call** donner un coup de téléphone ◇ *I'd like to make a phone call.* J'aimerais donner un coup de téléphone.

◆ **to make fun of somebody** se moquer de quelqu'un ◇ *They made fun of him.* Ils se sont moqués de lui.

◆ **What time do you make it?** Quelle heure avez-vous?

to **make up** VERB

1 *inventer* (*invent*) ◇ *He made up the whole story.* Il a inventé cette histoire de toutes pièces.

2 *se réconcilier* (*after argument*) ◇ *They had a quarrel, but soon made up.* Ils se sont disputés, mais se sont vite réconciliés.

◆ **to make oneself up** se maquiller ◇ *She spends hours making herself up.* Elle passe des heures à se maquiller.

make-up NOUN
le *maquillage*

Malaysia NOUN
la *Malaisie*

◆ **in Malaysia** en Malaisie

male ADJECTIVE

1 *mâle* (*animals, plants*) ◇ *a male kitten* un chaton mâle

2 *masculin* (*person, on official forms*) ◇ *Sex: male.* Sexe : masculin.

◆ **Most football players are male.** La plupart des joueurs de football sont des hommes.

◆ **a male chauvinist** un macho

◆ **a male nurse** un infirmier

Malta NOUN
Malte

◆ **in Malta** à Malte

◆ **to Malta** à Malte

mammoth NOUN

see also mammoth ADJECTIVE
le *mammouth*

mammoth ADJECTIVE

see also mammoth NOUN
monstre ◇ *a mammoth task* un travail monstre

man NOUN
l' *homme* MASC ◇ *an old man* un vieil

homme

to **manage** VERB

1 *gérer* (*be in charge of*) ◇ *She manages a big store.* Elle dirige un grand magasin. ◇ *He manages our football team.* Il dirige notre équipe de foot.

2 *se débrouiller* (*get by*) ◇ *We haven't got much money, but we manage.* Nous n'avons pas beaucoup d'argent, mais nous nous débrouillons. ◇ *It's okay, I can manage.* Ça va, je me débrouille.

◆ **Can you manage okay?** Tu y arrives?

◆ **to manage to do something** réussir à faire quelque chose ◇ *Luckily I managed to pass the exam.* J'ai heureusement réussi à avoir mon examen.

◆ **I can't manage all that.** (*food*) C'est trop pour moi.

manageable ADJECTIVE
faisable (*task*)

management NOUN

1 la *gestion* (*organization*) ◇ *He's responsible for the management of the company.* Il est responsable de la gestion de la société.

2 la *direction* (*people in charge*) ◇ *"under new management"* "changement de direction"

manager NOUN

1 (*of company*)
le *directeur*
la *directrice*

2 (*of shop, restaurant*)
le *gérant*
la *gérante*

3 (*of team, performer*)
le *manager*

manageress NOUN
la *gérante*

mandarin NOUN
la *mandarine* (*fruit*)

mango NOUN
la *mangue*

mania NOUN
la *manie*

maniac NOUN
le *fou*
la *folle*
◇ *He drives like a maniac.* Il conduit comme un fou.

◆ **a religious maniac** un fanatique religieux

man-made ADJECTIVE
synthétique (*fibre*)

manner NOUN
la *façon*

◆ **She behaves in an odd manner.** Elle se comporte de façon étrange.

◆ **He has a confident manner.** Il a de
l'assurance.

manners PL NOUN
les *manières* FEM PL ◇ *good manners* les
bonnes manières ◇ *Her manners are
appalling.* Elle a de très mauvaises
manières.

◆ **It's bad manners to speak with your
mouth full.** Ce n'est pas poli de parler la
bouche pleine.

manpower NOUN
la *main-d'œuvre*

mansion NOUN
le *manoir*

mantelpiece NOUN
la *cheminée*

manual NOUN
le *manuel*

to **manufacture** VERB
fabriquer

manufacturer NOUN
le *fabricant*

manure NOUN
le *fumier*

manuscript NOUN
le *manuscrit*

many ADJECTIVE, PRONOUN
beaucoup de ◇ *The film has many
special effects.* Le film a beaucoup
d'effets spéciaux. ◇ *He hasn't got many
friends.* Il n'a pas beaucoup d'amis.
◇ *Were there many people at the concert?*
Est-ce qu'il y avait beaucoup de gens au
concert?

◆ **very many** beaucoup de ◇ *I haven't got
very many CDs.* Je n'ai pas beaucoup de
CD.

◆ **Not many.** Pas beaucoup.

◆ **How many?** Combien? ◇ *How many
do you want?* Combien en veux-tu?

◆ **how many...?** combien de...? ◇ *How
many francs do you get for £1?* Combien
de francs a-t-on pour une livre?

◆ **too many** trop ◇ *That's too many.*
C'est trop.

◆ **too many...** trop de... ◇ *She makes too
many mistakes.* Elle fait trop d'erreurs.

◆ **so many** autant ◇ *I didn't know there
would be so many.* Je ne pensais pas
qu'il y en aurait autant.

◆ **so many...** autant de... ◇ *I've never
seen so many policemen.* Je n'ai jamais
vu autant de policiers.

map NOUN
1 la *carte* (of country, area)
2 le *plan* (of town)

marathon NOUN
le *marathon* ◇ *the London marathon* le
marathon de Londres

marble NOUN
le *marbre* ◇ *a marble statue* une statue
en marbre

◆ **to play marbles** jouer aux billes

March NOUN
mars MASC

◆ **in March** en mars

march NOUN
see also march VERB
la *manifestation* (demonstration)

to **march** VERB
see also march NOUN
1 *marcher au pas* (soldiers)
2 *défiler* (protesters)

mare NOUN
la *jument*

margarine NOUN
la *margarine*

margin NOUN
la *marge* ◇ *Write notes in the margin.*
Écrivez vos notes dans la marge.

marijuana NOUN
la *marijuana*

marital status NOUN
la *situation de famille*

mark NOUN
see also mark VERB
1 la *note* (in school) ◇ *I get good marks
for French.* J'ai de bonnes notes en
français.
2 la *tache* (stain) ◇ *You've got a mark
on your skirt.* Tu as une tache sur ta jupe.
3 le *mark* (German currency)

to **mark** VERB
see also mark NOUN
corriger ◇ *The teacher hasn't marked
my homework yet.* Le professeur n'a pas
encore corrigé mon devoir.

market NOUN
le *marché*

marketing NOUN
le *marketing*

marmalade NOUN
la *confiture d'oranges*

maroon ADJECTIVE
bordeaux MASC, FEM, PL (colour)

marriage NOUN
le *mariage*

married ADJECTIVE
marié ◇ *They are not married.* Ils ne
sont pas mariés. ◇ *They have been
married for 15 years.* Ils sont mariés
depuis quinze ans. ◇ *a married couple*
un couple marié

to **marry** VERB
épouser ◇ *He wants to marry her.* Il
veut l'épouser.

◆ **to get married** se marier ◇ *My sister's
getting married in June.* Ma sœur se

M

marie en juin.

marvellous ADJECTIVE

[1] *excellent* ◇ *She's a marvellous cook.*
C'est une excellente cuisinière.

[2] *superbe* ◇ *The weather was
marvellous.* Il a fait un temps superbe.

marzipan NOUN
la *pâte d'amandes*

mascara NOUN
le *mascara*

masculine ADJECTIVE
masculin

mashed potatoes PL NOUN
la *purée* ◇ *sausages and mashed
potatoes* des saucisses avec de la purée

mask NOUN
le *masque*

mass NOUN

[1] la *multitude* ◇ *a mass of books and
papers* une multitude de livres et de
papiers

[2] la *messe* (*in church*) ◇ *We go to mass
on Sunday.* Nous allons à la messe le
dimanche.

* **the mass media** les médias

massage NOUN
le *massage*

massive ADJECTIVE
énorme

to **master** VERB
maîtriser

masterpiece NOUN
le *chef-d'œuvre*
(les *chefs-d'œuvre* PL)

mat NOUN
le *paillasson* (*doormat*)

* **a table mat** un set de table
* **a beach mat** un tapis de plage

match NOUN

see also match VERB

[1] l' *allumette* FEM ◇ *a box of matches*
une boîte d'allumettes

[2] (*sport*)
le *match*
(les *matchs* PL)

◇ *a football match* un match de foot

to **match** VERB

see also match NOUN

être assorti à ◇ *The jacket matches the
trousers.* La veste est assortie au
pantalon.

* **These colours don't match.** Ces
couleurs ne vont pas ensemble.

matching ADJECTIVE

assorti ◇ *My bedroom has matching
wallpaper and curtains.* Ma chambre a du
papier peint et des rideaux assortis.

mate NOUN
le *pote* (*informal*) ◇ *On Friday night I go*

out with my mates. Vendredi soir, je sors
avec mes potes.

material NOUN

[1] le *tissu* (*cloth*)

[2] la *documentation* (*information, data*)
◇ *I'm collecting material for my project.* Je
rassemble une documentation pour
mon dossier.

* **raw materials** les matières premières
FEM

mathematics NOUN
les *mathématiques* FEM PL

maths NOUN
les *maths* FEM PL

matron NOUN
l' *infirmière-chef* FEM (*in hospital*)

matter NOUN

see also matter VERB

la *question* ◇ *It's a matter of life and
death.* C'est une question de vie ou de
mort.

* **What's the matter?** Qu'est-ce qui ne va
pas?
* **as a matter of fact** en fait

to **matter** VERB

see also matter NOUN

* **it doesn't matter (1)** (*I don't mind*) ça ne
fait rien ◇ *I can't give you the money
today. – It doesn't matter.* Je ne peux pas
te donner l'argent aujourd'hui. – Ça ne
fait rien.
* **it doesn't matter (2)** (*it makes no difference*)
ça n'a pas d'importance ◇ *Shall I phone
today or tomorrow? – Whenever, it doesn't
matter.* Est-ce que j'appelle aujourd'hui
ou demain? – Quand tu veux, ça n'a pas
d'importance.
* **It matters a lot to me.** C'est très
important pour moi.

mattress NOUN
le *matelas*

mature ADJECTIVE
mûr ◇ *She's quite mature for her age.*
Elle est très mûre pour son âge.

maximum NOUN

see also maximum ADJECTIVE

le *maximum*

maximum ADJECTIVE

see also maximum NOUN

maximum MASC, FEM, PL ◇ *The maximum
speed is 100 km/h.* La vitesse maximum
autorisée est de cent kilomètres à l'heure.

* **the maximum amount** le maximum

May NOUN
mai MASC

* **in May** en mai
* **May Day** le Premier Mai

may VERB

* **He may come.** Il va peut-être venir.

◦ *It may rain.* Il va peut-être pleuvoir.
• **Are you going to the party?–I don't know, I may.** Est-ce que tu vas à la soirée?–Je ne sais pas, peut-être.
• **May I smoke?** Est-ce que je peux fumer?

maybe ADVERB
  peut-être ◦ *maybe not* peut-être pas ◦ *a bit boring, maybe* peut-être un peu ennuyeux ◦ *Maybe she's at home.* Elle est peut-être chez elle. ◦ *Maybe he'll change his mind.* Il va peut-être changer d'avis.

mayonnaise NOUN
  la *mayonnaise*

mayor NOUN
  le *maire*

me PRONOUN
  me *becomes* **m'** *before a vowel sound.*
  [1] *me* ◦ *Could you lend me your pen?* Est-ce que tu peux me prêter ton stylo? *m'* ◦ *Can you tell me the way to the station?* Est-ce que vous pouvez m'indiquer le chemin de la gare? ◦ *Can you help me?* Est-ce que tu peux m'aider? ◦ *He heard me.* Il m'a entendu.
  moi *is used in exclamations.*
  [2] *moi* ◦ *Me too!* Moi aussi! ◦ *Excuse me!* Excusez-moi! ◦ *Look at me!* Regarde-moi! ◦ *Wait for me!* Attends-moi! ◦ *Come with me!* Suivez-moi!
  moi *is also used after prepositions and in comparisons.*
  ◦ *You're after me.* Tu es après moi. ◦ *Is it for me?* C'est pour moi? ◦ *She's older than me.* Elle est plus âgée que moi.

meal NOUN
  le *repas*

mealtime NOUN
• **at mealtimes** aux heures des repas

to mean VERB
  see also mean ADJECTIVE *and* means NOUN
  vouloir dire ◦ *What does "complet" mean?* Qu'est-ce que "complet" veut dire? ◦ *I don't know what it means.* Je ne sais pas ce que ça veut dire. ◦ *What do you mean?* Qu'est que vous voulez dire? ◦ *That's not what I meant.* Ce n'est pas ce que je voulais dire.
• **Which one do you mean?** Duquel veux-tu parler?
• **Do you really mean it?** Tu es sérieux?
• **to mean to do something** avoir l'intention de faire quelque chose ◦ *I didn't mean to offend you.* Je n'avais pas l'intention de vous blesser.

mean ADJECTIVE
  see also mean VERB *and* means NOUN
  [1] *radin* (with money) ◦ *He's too mean to buy Christmas presents.* Il est trop radin pour acheter des cadeaux de Noël.
  [2] *méchant* (unkind) ◦ *You're being mean to me.* Tu es méchant avec moi.
• **That's a really mean thing to say!** Ce n'est vraiment pas gentil de dire ça!

meaning NOUN
  le *sens*

means NOUN
  see also mean VERB *and* ADJECTIVE
  le *moyen* ◦ *He'll do it by any possible means.* Il le fera par tous les moyens.
• *a means of transport* un moyen de transport
• **by means of** au moyen de ◦ *He got in by means of a stolen key.* Il est entré au moyen d'une clé volée.
• **by all means** bien sûr ◦ *Can I come?–By all means!* Est-ce que je peux venir?–Bien sûr!

meant VERB see **mean**

measles NOUN
  la *rougeole*

to measure VERB
  [1] *mesurer* ◦ *I measured the page.* J'ai mesuré la page.
  [2] *faire* ◦ *The room measures 3 metres by 4.* La pièce fait trois mètres sur quatre.

measurements PL NOUN
  [1] les *dimensions* FEM (of object) ◦ *What are the measurements of the room?* Quelles sont les dimensions de la pièce?
  [2] les *mensurations* FEM (of body) ◦ *What are your measurements?* Quelles sont tes mensurations?
• **my waist measurement** mon tour de taille
• **What's your neck measurement?** Quel est votre tour de cou?

meat NOUN
  la *viande* ◦ *I don't eat meat.* Je ne mange pas de viande.

Mecca NOUN
  [La] Mecque

mechanic NOUN
  le *mécanicien* ◦ *He's a mechanic.* Il est mécanicien.

mechanical ADJECTIVE
  mécanique MASC, FEM

medal NOUN
  la *médaille*
• **the gold medal** la médaille d'or

media PL NOUN
  les *médias* MASC

medical ADJECTIVE
  see also medical NOUN
  médical
  (*médicaux* MASC PL)

M

[PTO]

◇ medical treatment les soins médicaux
* **medical insurance** l'assurance maladie
* **to have medical problems** avoir des problèmes de santé
* **She's a medical student.** Elle est étudiante en médecine.
medical NOUN
[see also medical ADJECTIVE]
* **to have a medical** passer une visite médicale
medicine NOUN
1 la _médecine_ (subject) ◇ I want to study medicine. Je veux faire médecine.
* **alternative medicine** la médecine douce
2 le _médicament_ (medication) ◇ I need some medicine. J'ai besoin d'un médicament.
Mediterranean ADJECTIVE
méditerranéen MASC
méditerranéenne FEM
* **the Mediterranean** la Méditerranée
medium ADJECTIVE
moyen MASC
moyenne FEM
◇ a man of medium height un homme de taille moyenne
medium-sized ADJECTIVE
de taille moyenne ◇ a medium-sized town une ville de taille moyenne
to **meet** VERB
1 _rencontrer_ (by chance) ◇ I met Paul when I was walking the dog. J'ai rencontré Paul alors que je promenais mon chien. ◇ Have you met him before? Est-ce que tu l'as déjà rencontré?
2 _se rencontrer_ ◇ We met by chance in the shopping centre. Nous nous sommes rencontrés par hasard dans le centre commercial.
3 _retrouver_ (by arrangement) ◇ I'm going to meet my friends. Je vais retrouver mes amis.
4 _se retrouver_ ◇ Let's meet in front of the tourist office. Retrouvons-nous devant l'office de tourisme.
* **I like meeting new people.** J'aime faire de nouvelles connaissances.
5 _aller chercher_ (pick up) ◇ I'll meet you at the station. J'irai te chercher à la gare.
meeting NOUN
1 la _réunion_ (for work) ◇ a business meeting une réunion d'affaires
2 la _rencontre_ (socially) ◇ their first meeting leur première rencontre
mega ADJECTIVE
* **He's mega rich.** Il est hyper-riche. (informal)
melody NOUN

la _mélodie_
melon NOUN
le _melon_
to **melt** VERB
fondre ◇ The snow is melting. La neige est en train de fondre.
member NOUN
le _membre_
* **a Member of Parliament** un député
membership card NOUN
la _carte de membre_
memorial NOUN
le _monument_ ◇ a war memorial un monument aux morts
to **memorize** VERB
apprendre par cœur
memory NOUN
1 la _mémoire_ ◇ I haven't got a good memory. Je n'ai pas une bonne mémoire.
2 le _souvenir_ (recollection) ◇ to bring back memories rappeler des souvenirs
men PL NOUN see **man**
les _hommes_ MASC
to **mend** VERB
réparer
meningitis NOUN
la _méningite_
mental ADJECTIVE
1 _mental_
(_mentaux_ MASC PL)
◇ a mental illness une maladie mentale
2 _(mad)_
fou MASC
folle FEM
◇ You're mental! Tu es fou!
* **a mental hospital** un hôpital psychiatrique
to **mention** VERB
mentionner
* **Thank you! – Don't mention it!** Merci! – Il n'y a pas de quoi!
menu NOUN
le _menu_ ◇ Could I have the menu please? Est-ce que je pourrais avoir le menu s'il vous plaît?
merchant NOUN
le _marchand_ ◇ a wine merchant un marchand de vin
mercy NOUN
la _pitié_
meringue NOUN
la _meringue_
merry ADJECTIVE
* **Merry Christmas!** Joyeux Noël!
merry-go-round NOUN
le _manège_
mess NOUN
le _fouillis_ ◇ My bedroom's usually in a

mess. Il y a généralement du fouillis dans ma chambre.

to **mess about** VERB
* **to mess about with something** (*interfere with*) tripoter quelque chose ◇ *Stop messing about with my computer!* Arrête de tripoter mon ordinateur!
* **Don't mess about with my things!** Ne touche pas à mes affaires!

to **mess up** VERB
* **to mess something up** mettre la pagaille dans quelque chose ◇ *My little brother has messed up my cassettes.* Mon petit frère a mis la pagaille dans mes cassettes.

message NOUN
le *message*

messenger NOUN
le *messager*

messy ADJECTIVE
1 *salissant* (*dirty*) ◇ *a messy job* un travail salissant
2 *en désordre* (*untidy*) ◇ *Your desk is really messy.* Ton bureau est vraiment en désordre.
3 *désordonnée* (*person*) ◇ *She's so messy!* Elle est tellement désordonnée!
* **My writing is terribly messy.** J'ai une écriture de cochon.

met VERB *see* **meet**

metal NOUN
le *métal*
(les *métaux* PL)

meter NOUN
1 le *compteur* (*for gas, electricity, taxi*)
2 le *parcmètre* (*parking meter*)

method NOUN
la *méthode*

Methodist NOUN
le/la *méthodiste* ◇ *I'm a Methodist.* Je suis méthodiste.

metre NOUN
le *mètre*

metric ADJECTIVE
métrique

Mexico NOUN
le *Mexique*
* **in Mexico** au Mexique
* **to Mexico** au Mexique

miaow VERB
miauler

mice PL NOUN *see* **mouse**

microchip NOUN
la *puce*

microphone NOUN
le *microphone*

microscope NOUN
le *microscope*

microwave oven NOUN

le *four à micro-ondes*

mid ADJECTIVE
* **in mid May** à la mi-mai

midday NOUN
le *midi*
* **at midday** à midi

middle NOUN
le *milieu* ◇ *in the middle of the road* au milieu de la route ◇ *in the middle of the night* au milieu de la nuit ◇ *the middle seat* la place du milieu

middle-aged ADJECTIVE
d'un certain âge ◇ *a middle-aged man* un homme d'un certain âge
* **to be middle-aged** avoir la cinquantaine
* **She's middle-aged.** Elle a la cinquantaine.

middle-class ADJECTIVE
de la classe moyenne ◇ *a middle-class family* une famille de la classe moyenne

Middle East NOUN
le *Moyen-Orient*
* **in the Middle East** au Moyen-Orient

middle name NOUN
le *deuxième nom*

midge NOUN
le *moucheron*

midnight NOUN
minuit MASC
* **at midnight** à minuit

might VERB
Use **peut-être** to express possibility.
◇ *He might come later.* Il va peut-être venir plus tard. ◇ *We might go to Spain next year.* Nous irons peut-être en Espagne l'an prochain. ◇ *She might not have understood.* Elle n'a peut-être pas compris.

migraine NOUN
la *migraine* ◇ *I've got a migraine.* J'ai la migraine.

mike NOUN
le *micro*

mild ADJECTIVE
doux MASC
douce FEM
◇ *The winters are quite mild.* Les hivers sont assez doux.

mile NOUN
le *mille*
In France distances are expressed in kilometres. A mile is about 1.6 kilometres.
◇ *It's 5 miles from here.* C'est à huit kilomètres d'ici.
* **We walked miles!** Nous avons fait des kilomètres à pied!

military ADJECTIVE
militaire MASC, FEM

M

milk NOUN
> see also milk VERB
le *lait* ◇ *tea with milk* du thé au lait

to **milk** VERB
> see also milk NOUN
traire

milk chocolate NOUN
le *chocolat au lait*

milkman NOUN
In France milk is not delivered to people's homes.
◇ *He's a milkman.* Il livre le lait à
domicile.

milk shake NOUN
le *milk-shake*

mill NOUN
le *moulin* (for grain)

millimetre NOUN
le *millimètre*

million NOUN
le *million*

millionaire NOUN
le *millionnaire*

to **mimic** VERB
imiter

mince NOUN
la *viande hachée*

to **mind** VERB
> see also mind NOUN
[1] *garder* ◇ *Could you mind the baby
this afternoon?* Est-ce que tu pourrais
garder le bébé cet après-midi?
[2] *surveiller* (keep an eye on) ◇ *Could
you mind my bags for a few minutes?*
Est-ce que vous pourriez surveiller mes
bagages pendant quelques minutes?
✦ **Do you mind if I open the window?**
Est-ce que je pourrais ouvrir la
fenêtre?
✦ **I don't mind.** Ça ne me dérange pas.
◇ *I don't mind the noise.* Le bruit ne me
dérange pas.
✦ **Never mind!** Ça ne fait rien!
✦ **Mind that bike!** Attention au vélo!
✦ **Mind the step!** Attention à la marche!

mind NOUN
> see also mind VERB
✦ **to make up one's mind** se décider ◇ *I
haven't made up my mind yet.* Je ne me
suis pas encore décidé.
✦ **to change one's mind** changer d'avis
◇ *He's changed his mind.* Il a changé
d'avis.
✦ **Are you out of your mind?** Tu as perdu
la tête?

mine PRONOUN
> see also mine NOUN
le mien + MASC NOUN ◇ *Is this your
coat? – No, mine's black.* C'est ton
manteau? – Non, le mien est noir.

la mienne + FEM NOUN ◇ *Is this your
car? – No, mine's green.* C'est ta
voiture? – Non, la mienne est verte.
les miens + MASC PL NOUN ◇ *her parents
and mine* ses parents et les miens
les miennes + FEM PL NOUN ◇ *Your hands
are dirty, mine are clean.* Tes mains sont
sales, les miennes sont propres.
✦ **It's mine.** C'est à moi. ◇ *This book is
mine.* Ce livre est à moi. ◇ *Whose is
this? – It's mine.* C'est à qui? – À moi.

mine NOUN
> see also mine PRONOUN
la *mine* ◇ *a coal mine* une mine de
charbon ◇ *a land mine* une mine
terrestre

miner NOUN
le *mineur*

mineral water NOUN
l' *eau minérale* FEM

miniature ADJECTIVE
> see also miniature NOUN
miniature ◇ *a miniature version* une
version miniature

miniature NOUN
> see also miniature ADJECTIVE
la *miniature*

minibus NOUN
le *minibus*

minimum NOUN
> see also minimum ADJECTIVE
le *minimum*

minimum ADJECTIVE
> see also minimum NOUN
minimum MASC, FEM, PL ◇ *There's no
minimum wage in Britain.* Il n'y a pas de
salaire minimum en Grande-Bretagne.
◇ *The minimum age for driving is 17.*
L'âge minimum pour conduire est
dix-sept ans.
✦ **the minimum amount** le minimum

miniskirt NOUN
la *mini-jupe*

minister NOUN
[1] le *ministre* (in government)
[2] le *pasteur* (of church)

minor ADJECTIVE
mineur ◇ *a minor problem* un
problème mineur
✦ **in D minor** en ré mineur
✦ **a minor operation** une opération
bénigne

minority NOUN
la *minorité*

mint NOUN
[1] la *menthe* (plant) ◇ *mint sauce* la
sauce à la menthe
[2] le *bonbon à la menthe* (sweet)

minus PREPOSITION

moins ◇ _16 minus 3 is 13._ Seize moins trois égale treize. ◇ _It's minus two degrees outside._ Il fait moins deux dehors. ◇ _I got a B minus._ J'ai èu un B moins.

minute NOUN
see also minute ADJECTIVE
la _minute_ ◇ _Wait a minute!_ Attends une minute!

minute ADJECTIVE
see also minute NOUN
minuscule ◇ _Her flat is minute._ Son appartement est minuscule.

miracle NOUN
le _miracle_

mirror NOUN
[1] la _glace_ (on wall)
[2] le _rétroviseur_ (in car)

to **misbehave** VERB
se conduire mal

mischief NOUN
les _bêtises_ FEM PL ◇ _My little sister's always up to mischief._ Ma petite sœur fait constamment des bêtises.

mischievous ADJECTIVE
coquin

miser NOUN
l' _avare_ MASC / FEM

miserable ADJECTIVE
[1] (person)
malheureux MASC
malheureuse FEM
 ◇ _You're looking miserable._ Tu as l'air malheureux.
[2] (weather)
épouvantable ◇ _The weather was miserable._ Il faisait un temps épouvantable.
◆ **to feel miserable** ne pas avoir le moral ◇ _I'm feeling miserable._ Je n'ai pas le moral.

misfortune NOUN
le _malheur_

mishap NOUN
la _mésaventure_

misjudge VERB
mal juger (person) ◇ _I've misjudged her._ Je l'ai mal jugée.
◆ **He misjudged the bend.** Il a mal pris le virage.

mislay VERB
égarer ◇ _I've mislaid my passport._ J'ai égaré mon passeport.

misleading ADJECTIVE
trompeur MASC
trompeuse FEM

Miss NOUN
[1] _Mademoiselle_
(Mesdemoiselles PL)

[2] (in address)
Mlle
(Mlles PL)

to **miss** VERB
[1] _rater_ ◇ _Hurry or you'll miss the bus._ Dépêche-toi ou tu vas rater le bus. ◇ _He missed the target._ Il a raté la cible.
[2] _manquer_ ◇ _to miss an opportunity_ manquer une occasion
◆ **I miss you.** Tu me manques. ◇ _I'm missing my family._ Ma famille me manque. ◇ _I miss him._ Il me manque. ◇ _I miss them._ Ils me manquent.

missing ADJECTIVE
manquant ◇ _the missing part_ la pièce manquante
◆ **to be missing** avoir disparu ◇ _My rucksack is missing._ Mon sac à dos a disparu. ◇ _Two members of the group are missing._ Deux membres du groupe ont disparu.

missionary NOUN
le/la _missionnaire_

mist NOUN
la _brume_

mistake NOUN
see also mistake VERB
[1] la _faute_ (slip) ◇ _a spelling mistake_ une faute d'orthographe
◆ **to make a mistake (1)** (in writing, speaking) faire une faute
◆ **to make a mistake (2)** (get mixed up) se tromper ◇ _I'm sorry, I made a mistake._ Je suis désolé, je me suis trompé.
[2] l' _erreur_ FEM (misjudgement) ◇ _It was a mistake to buy those yellow shoes._ J'ai fait une erreur en achetant ces chaussures jaunes.
◆ **by mistake** par erreur ◇ _I took his bag by mistake._ J'ai pris son sac par erreur.

to **mistake** VERB
see also mistake NOUN
◆ **He mistook me for my sister.** Il m'a prise pour ma sœur.

mistaken ADJECTIVE
◆ **to be mistaken** se tromper ◇ _If you think I'm going to get up at 6 o'clock, you're mistaken._ Si tu penses que je vais me lever à six heures, tu te trompes.

mistletoe NOUN
le _gui_

mistook VERB see **mistake**

mistress NOUN
[1] le _professeur_ (teacher) ◇ _our French mistress_ notre professeur de français
[2] la _maîtresse_ (lover) ◇ _He's got a mistress._ Il a une maîtresse.

to **mistrust** VERB
se méfier de

M

misty ADJECTIVE
　brumeux MASC
　brumeuse FEM
　◇ *a misty morning* un matin brumeux
to **misunderstand** VERB
　mal comprendre ◇ *Sorry, I*
　misunderstood you. Je suis désolé, je
　t'avais mal compris.
misunderstanding NOUN
　le *malentendu*
mix NOUN
　see also mix VERB
　le *mélange* ◇ *It's a mix of science fiction*
　and comedy. C'est un mélange de
　science-fiction et de comédie.
　◆ *a cake mix* une préparation pour gâteau
to **mix** VERB
　see also mix NOUN
　① *mélanger* ◇ *Mix the flour with the*
　sugar. Mélangez la farine au sucre.
　② *combiner* ◇ *He's mixing business*
　with pleasure. Il combine les affaires et
　le plaisir.
　◆ *to mix with somebody* (*associate*)
　fréquenter quelqu'un
　◆ *He doesn't mix much.* Il se tient à
　l'écart.
　◆ *to mix up* (*people*) confondre ◇ *He*
　always mixes me up with my sister. Il me
　confond toujours avec ma sœur.
　◆ *The travel agent mixed up the*
　bookings. L'agence de voyage s'est
　embrouillée dans les réservations.
　◆ *I'm getting mixed up.* Je ne m'y
　retrouve plus.
mixed ADJECTIVE
　◆ *a mixed salad* une salade composée
　◆ *a mixed school* une école mixte
　◆ *a mixed grill* un assortiment de
　grillades
mixture NOUN
　le *mélange* ◇ *a mixture of spices* un
　mélange d'épices
　◆ *cough mixture* le sirop pour la toux
mix-up NOUN
　la *confusion*
to **moan** VERB
　râler ◇ *She's always moaning.* Elle est
　toujours en train de râler.
mobile home NOUN
　le *mobile home*
mobile phone NOUN
　le *téléphone portatif*
to **mock** VERB
　see also mock ADJECTIVE
　ridiculiser
mock ADJECTIVE
　see also mock VERB
　◆ *a mock exam* un examen blanc

model NOUN
　see also model ADJECTIVE
　① le *modèle* (*type*) ◇ *His car is the*
　latest model. Sa voiture est le tout
　dernier modèle.
　② la *maquette* (*mock-up*) ◇ *a model of*
　the castle une maquette du château
　③ le *mannequin* (*fashion*) ◇ *She's a*
　famous model. C'est un mannequin
　célèbre.
model ADJECTIVE
　see also model NOUN
　◆ *a model plane* un modèle réduit d'avion
　◆ *a model railway* un modèle réduit de
　voie ferrée
　◆ *He's a model pupil.* C'est un élève modèle.
modem NOUN
　le *modem*
moderate ADJECTIVE
　modéré ◇ *His views are quite*
　moderate. Ses opinions sont assez
　modérées.
　◆ *a moderate amount of* un peu de
　◆ *a moderate price* un prix raisonnable
modern ADJECTIVE
　moderne
to **modernize** VERB
　moderniser
modest ADJECTIVE
　modeste
to **modify** VERB
　modifier
moisture NOUN
　l' *humidité* FEM
moisturizer NOUN
　① la *crème hydratante* (*cream*)
　② le *lait hydratant* (*lotion*)
mole NOUN
　① la *taupe* (*animal*)
　② le *grain de beauté* (*on skin*)
moment NOUN
　l' *instant* MASC ◇ *Could you wait a*
　moment? Pouvez-vous attendre un
　instant? ◇ *in a moment* dans un instant
　◇ *Just a moment!* Un instant!
　◆ *at the moment* en ce moment
　◆ *any moment now* d'un moment à
　l'autre ◇ *They'll be arriving any moment*
　now. Ils vont arriver d'un moment à
　l'autre.
Monaco NOUN
　Monaco
　◆ *in Monaco* à Monaco
monarch NOUN
　le *monarque*
monarchy NOUN
　la *monarchie*
monastery NOUN
　le *monastère*

Monday NOUN
le *lundi* ◇ *on Monday* lundi ◇ *on Mondays* le lundi ◇ *every Monday* tous les lundis ◇ *last Monday* lundi dernier ◇ *next Monday* lundi prochain

money NOUN
l' *argent* MASC ◇ *I need to change some money.* J'ai besoin de changer de l'argent.
* **to make money** gagner de l'argent

mongrel NOUN
le *bâtard* ◇ *My dog's a mongrel.* Mon chien est un bâtard.

monitor NOUN
le *moniteur* (*of computer*)

monk NOUN
le *moine*

monkey NOUN
le *singe*

monotonous ADJECTIVE
monotone

monster NOUN
le *monstre*

month NOUN
le *mois* ◇ *this month* ce mois-ci ◇ *next month* le mois prochain ◇ *last month* le mois dernier ◇ *every month* tous les mois ◇ *at the end of the month* à la fin du mois

monthly ADJECTIVE
mensuel MASC
mensuelle FEM

monument NOUN
le *monument*

mood NOUN
l' *humeur* FEM
* **to be in a bad mood** être de mauvaise humeur
* **to be in a good mood** être de bonne humeur

moody ADJECTIVE
[1] *lunatique* (*temperamental*)
[2] *maussade* (*in a bad mood*)

moon NOUN
la *lune* ◇ *There's a full moon tonight.* Il y a pleine lune ce soir.
* **to be over the moon** (*happy*) être aux anges

moor NOUN
see also moor VERB
la *lande*

moor VERB
see also moor NOUN
amarrer (*boat*)

mop NOUN
le *balai laveur* (*for floor*)

moped NOUN
le *cyclomoteur*

moral ADJECTIVE
see also moral NOUN

moral
(*moraux* MASC PL)

moral NOUN
see also moral ADJECTIVE
la *morale* ◇ *the moral of the story* la morale de l'histoire
* **morals** la moralité

morale NOUN
le *moral* ◇ *Their morale is very low.* Leur moral est très bas.

more ADJECTIVE, PRONOUN, ADVERB
When comparing one amount with another, you usually use **plus.**
[1] *plus* ◇ *Beer is more expensive in Britain.* La bière est plus chère en Grande-Bretagne. ◇ *Could you speak more slowly?* Est-ce que vous pourriez parler plus lentement? ◇ *a bit more* un peu plus ◇ *There isn't any more.* Il n'y en a plus.
* **more...than** plus...que ◇ *He's more intelligent than me.* Il est plus intelligent que moi. ◇ *She practises more than I do.* Elle s'entraîne plus que moi. ◇ *More girls than boys do French.* Il y a plus de filles que de garçons qui font du français.
[2] *plus de* (*followed by noun*) ◇ *There are more girls in the class.* Il y a plus de filles dans la classe. ◇ *I get more homework than you do.* J'ai plus de devoirs que toi.
* *I spent more than 500 francs.* J'ai dépensé plus de cinq cents francs.
When referring to an additional amount, more than there is already, you usually use **encore.**
[3] *encore* ◇ *Is there any more?* Est-ce qu'il y en a encore? ◇ *Would you like some more?* Vous en voulez encore? ◇ *It'll take a few more days.* Ça prendra encore quelques jours.
[4] *encore de* (*followed by noun*) ◇ *Could I have some more chips?* Est-ce que je pourrais avoir encore des frites? ◇ *Do you want some more tea?* Voulez-vous encore du thé?
* **more or less** plus ou moins
* **more than ever** plus que jamais

morning NOUN
le *matin* ◇ *this morning* ce matin ◇ *tomorrow morning* demain matin ◇ *every morning* tous les matins
* **in the morning** le matin ◇ *at 7 o'clock in the morning* à sept heures du matin
* **a morning paper** un journal du matin

Morocco NOUN
le *Maroc*
* **in Morocco** au Maroc

Moscow NOUN
Moscou
* **in Moscow** à Moscou

Moslem NOUN
le _musulman_
la _musulmane_
◇ He's a Moslem. Il est musulman.

mosque NOUN
la _mosquée_

mosquito NOUN
le _moustique_
◆ a mosquito bite une piqûre de
moustique

most ADVERB, ADJECTIVE, PRONOUN
Use **la plupart de** when most (of) is followed
by a plural noun and **la majeure partie (de)**
when most (of) is followed by a singular noun.
① _la plupart de_ ◇ most of my friends
la plupart de mes amis ◇ most people la
plupart des gens ◇ Most cats are
affectionate. La plupart des chats sont
affectueux.
◆ most of them la plupart d'entre eux
◆ most of the time la plupart du temps
② _la majeure partie de_ ◇ most of the
work la majeure partie du travail ◇ most
of the class la majeure partie de la classe
◇ most of the night la majeure partie de
la nuit
◆ the most le plus ◇ He's the one who
talks the most. C'est lui qui parle le plus.
When most is followed by adjective, the
translation depends on whether the noun referred
to is masculine, feminine or plural.
◆ the most... (1) le plus... ◇ the most
expensive restaurant le restaurant le plus
cher
◆ the most... (2) la plus... ◇ the most
expensive seat la place la plus chère
◆ the most... (3) les plus... ◇ the most
expensive restaurants les restaurants les
plus chers ◇ the most expensive seats
les places les plus chères
◆ to make the most of something profiter
au maximum de quelque chose
◆ at the most au maximum ◇ Two hours
at the most. Deux heures au maximum.

mostly ADVERB
◆ The teachers are mostly quite nice. La
plupart des professeurs sont assez gentils.

motel NOUN
le _motel_

mother NOUN
la _mère_ ◇ my mother ma mère
◆ mother tongue la langue maternelle

mother-in-law NOUN
la _belle-mère_
(les _belles-mères_ PL)

Mother's Day NOUN
la _fête des Mères_
Mother's Day is usually on the last Sunday of
May in France.

motionless ADJECTIVE
immobile

motivated ADJECTIVE
motivé ◇ He is highly motivated. Il est
très motivé.

motivation NOUN
la _motivation_

motive NOUN
le _mobile_ ◇ the motive for the killing le
mobile du crime

motor NOUN
le _moteur_ ◇ The boat has a motor. Le
bateau a un moteur.

motorbike NOUN
la _moto_

motorboat NOUN
le _bateau à moteur_

motorcycle NOUN
le _vélomoteur_

motorcyclist NOUN
le _motard_

motorist NOUN
l' _automobiliste_ MASC/FEM

motor mechanic NOUN
le _mécanicien garagiste_

motor racing NOUN
la _course automobile_

motorway NOUN
l' _autoroute_ FEM ◇ on the motorway sur
l'autoroute

mouldy ADJECTIVE
moisi

mountain NOUN
la _montagne_
◆ a mountain bike un VTT (= vélo
tout-terrain)

mountaineer NOUN
l' _alpiniste_ MASC/FEM

mountaineering NOUN
l' _alpinisme_ MASC ◇ I go
mountaineering. Je fais de l'alpinisme.

mountainous ADJECTIVE
montagneux MASC
montagneuse FEM

mouse NOUN
la _souris_ (also for computer) ◇ white mice
des souris blanches

mousse NOUN
① la _mousse_ (food) ◇ chocolate mousse
la mousse au chocolat
② la _mousse coiffante_ (for hair)

moustache NOUN
la _moustache_ ◇ He's got a moustache.
Il a une moustache.
◆ a man with a moustache un moustachu

mouth NOUN
la _bouche_

mouthful NOUN
la _bouchée_

mouth organ NOUN
l' _harmonica_ MASC ◇ _I play the mouth organ._ Je joue de l'harmonica.

move NOUN
see also **move** VERB
[1] le _tour_ ◇ _It's your move._ C'est ton tour.
[2] le _déménagement_ ◇ _Our move from Oxford to Luton..._ Notre déménagement d'Oxford à Luton...
◆ **to get a move on** se remuer ◇ _Get a move on!_ Remue-toi!

to **move** VERB
see also **move** NOUN
[1] _bouger_ ◇ _Don't move!_ Ne bouge pas! ◇ _Could you move your stuff please?_ Est-ce que tu peux bouger tes affaires s'il te plaît?
[2] _avancer_ ◇ _The car was moving very slowly._ La voiture avançait très lentement.
[3] _émouvoir_ ◇ _I was very moved by the film._ J'ai été très émue par ce film.
◆ **to move house** déménager ◇ _We're moving in July._ Nous allons déménager en juillet.
◆ **to move forward** avancer
◆ **to move in** emménager ◇ _They're moving in next week._ Ils emménagent la semaine prochaine.
◆ **to move over** se pousser ◇ _Could you move over a bit?_ Est-ce que vous pouvez vous pousser un peu?

movement NOUN
le _mouvement_

movie NOUN
le _film_
◆ **the movies** le cinéma ◇ _Let's go to the movies!_ Si on allait au cinéma?

moving ADJECTIVE
[1] _en marche_ (_not stationary_) ◇ _a moving bus_ un bus en marche
[2] _touchant_ (_touching_) ◇ _a moving story_ une histoire touchante

to **mow** VERB
tondre
◆ **to mow the lawn** tondre le gazon

mower NOUN
la _tondeuse à gazon_

MP NOUN
le _député_ ◇ _She's an MP._ Elle est député.

Mr NOUN
[1] _Monsieur_
(_Messieurs_ PL)
[2] (_in address_)
_M._
(_MM._ PL)

Mrs NOUN

[1] _Madame_
(_Mesdames_ PL)
[2] (_in address_)
Mme
(_Mmes_ PL)

Ms NOUN
[1] _Madame_
(_Mesdames_ PL)
[2] (_in address_)
Mme
(_Mmes_ PL)

There isn't a direct equivalent of Ms _in French. If you are writing to somebody and don't know whether she is married, use_ Madame.

much ADJECTIVE, ADVERB, PRONOUN
[1] _beaucoup_ (_with verb_) ◇ _Do you go out much?_ Tu sors beaucoup? ◇ _I don't like sport much._ Je n'aime pas beaucoup le sport. ◇ _I feel much better now._ Je me sens beaucoup mieux maintenant.
[2] _beaucoup de_ (_followed by noun_) ◇ _I haven't got much money._ Je n'ai pas beaucoup d'argent. ◇ _I don't want much rice._ Je ne veux pas beaucoup de riz.
◆ **very much (1)** (_with verb_) beaucoup ◇ _I enjoyed the film very much._ J'ai beaucoup apprécié le film. ◇ _Thank you very much._ Merci beaucoup.
◆ **very much (2)** (_followed by noun_) beaucoup de ◇ _I haven't got very much money._ Je n'ai pas beaucoup d'argent.
◆ **not much (1)** pas beaucoup ◇ _Have you got a lot of luggage? – No, not much._ As-tu beaucoup de bagages? – Non, pas beaucoup.
◆ **not much (2)** pas grand-chose ◇ _What's on TV? – Not much._ Qu'est-ce qu'il y a à la télé? – Pas grand-chose. ◇ _What did you think of it? – Not much._ Qu'est-ce que tu en as pensé? – Pas grand-chose.
◆ **How much?** Combien? ◇ _How much do you want?_ Tu en veux combien? ◇ _How much time have you got?_ Tu as combien de temps? ◇ _How much is it?_ (_cost_) Combien est-ce que ça coûte?
◆ **too much** trop ◇ _That's too much!_ C'est trop! ◇ _It costs too much._ Ça coûte trop cher. ◇ _They give us too much homework._ Ils nous donnent trop de devoirs.
◆ **so much** autant ◇ _I didn't think it would cost so much._ Je ne pensais pas que ça coûterait autant. ◇ _I've never seen so much traffic._ Je n'ai jamais vu autant de circulation.

mud NOUN
la _boue_

muddle NOUN

M

le *désordre* ○ *The photos are in a muddle.* Les photos sont en désordre.

to **muddle up** VERB
confondre (people) ○ *He muddles me up with my sister.* Il me confond avec ma sœur.

• **to get muddled up** s'embrouiller ○ *I'm getting muddled up.* Je m'embrouille.

muddy ADJECTIVE
boueux MASC
boueuse FEM

muesli NOUN
le *muesli*

mug NOUN
see also **mug** VERB
la *grande tasse* ○ *Do you want a cup or a mug?* Est-ce que vous voulez une tasse normale ou une grande tasse?

• **a beer mug** une chope à bière

to **mug** VERB
see also **mug** NOUN
agresser ○ *He was mugged in the city centre.* Il s'est fait agresser au centre ville.

mugger NOUN
l' *agresseur* MASC

mugging NOUN
l' *agression* FEM

muggy ADJECTIVE
lourd ○ *It's muggy today.* Il fait lourd aujourd'hui.

multiplication NOUN
la *multiplication*

to **multiply** VERB
multiplier ○ *to multiply 6 by 3* multiplier six par trois

multi-storey car park NOUN
le *parking à plusieurs étages*

mum NOUN
You use **maman** *only when you are talking to your mother or using it as her name; otherwise use* **mère**.
[1] la *mère* ○ *my mum* ma mère ○ *her mum* sa mère
[2] la *maman* ○ *Mum!* Maman! ○ *I'll ask Mum.* Je vais demander à maman.

mummy NOUN
[1] la *maman* (mum) ○ *Mummy says I can go.* Maman dit que je peux y aller.
[2] la *momie* (Egyptian)

mumps NOUN
les *oreillons* MASC PL

murder NOUN
see also **murder** VERB
le *meurtre* MASC

to **murder** VERB
see also **murder** NOUN
assassiner ○ *He was murdered.* Il a été assassiné.

murderer NOUN
l' *assassin* MASC

muscle NOUN
le *muscle*

muscular ADJECTIVE
musclé

museum NOUN
le *musée*

mushroom NOUN
le *champignon* ○ *mushroom omelette* l'omelette aux champignons

music NOUN
la *musique*

musical ADJECTIVE
see also **musical** NOUN
doué pour la musique ○ *I'm not musical.* Je ne suis pas doué pour la musique.

• **a musical instrument** un instrument de musique

musical NOUN
see also **musical** ADJECTIVE
la *comédie musicale*

music centre NOUN
la *chaîne stéréo*

musician NOUN
le *musicien*
la *musicienne*

Muslim NOUN
le *musulman*
la *musulmane*
○ *He's a Muslim.* Il est musulman.

mussel NOUN
la *moule*

must VERB
When **must** *means that you assume or suppose something, use* **devoir**; *when it means it's necessary to do something, use* **il faut que...**, *which comes from the verb* **falloir** *and is followed by a verb in the subjunctive.*
[1] *devoir* (I suppose) ○ *You must be tired.* Tu dois être fatigué. ○ *They must have plenty of money.* Ils doivent avoir beaucoup d'argent. ○ *There must be some problem.* Il doit y avoir un problème.
[2] *il faut que* ○ *I must buy some presents.* Il faut que j'achète des cadeaux. ○ *I really must go now.* Il faut que j'y aille.

• **You mustn't forget to send her a card.** N'oublie surtout pas de lui envoyer une carte.

• **You must come and see us.** (invitation) Venez donc nous voir.

mustard NOUN
la *moutarde*

to **mutter** VERB

marmonner

my ADJECTIVE

mon MASC ◇ *my father* mon père

ma FEM ◇ *my aunt* ma tante

mes PL ◇ *my parents* mes parents

| ma *becomes* mon *before a vowel sound.* |

◆ **my friend (1)** (*male*) mon ami

◆ **my friend (2)** (*female*) mon amie

| Do not use **mon/ma/mes** with parts of the body. |

◇ *I want to wash my hair.* Je voudrais me laver les cheveux. ◇ *I'm going to clean my tooth.* Je vais me brosser les dents. ◇ *I've hurt my foot.* Je me suis fait mal au pied.

myself PRONOUN

[1] *me* ◇ *I've hurt myself.* Je me suis fait mal. ◇ *I really enjoyed myself.* Je me suis vraiment bien amusé. ◇ *...when I look at myself in the mirror.* ...quand je me regarde dans la glace.

[2] *moi* ◇ *I don't like talking about myself.* Je n'aime pas parler de moi.

[3] *moi-même* ◇ *I made it myself.* Je l'ai fait moi-même.

◆ **by myself** tout seul ◇ *I don't like travelling by myself.* Je n'aime pas voyager tout seul.

mysterious ADJECTIVE

mystérieux MASC

mystérieuse FEM

mystery NOUN

le *mystère*

◆ **a murder mystery** (*novel*) un roman policier

myth NOUN

[1] le *mythe* (*legend*) ◇ *a Greek myth* un mythe grec

[2] l' *idée reçue* FEM (*untrue idea*) ◇ *That's a myth.* C'est une idée reçue.

mythology NOUN

la *mythologie*

M

N

naff ADJECTIVE
  nul MASC
  nulle FEM

to **nag** VERB
  harceler (scold) ◇ She's always nagging
  me. Elle me harcèle constamment.

nail NOUN
  [1] l' *ongle* MASC (on finger, toe) ◇ Don't
  bite your nails! Ne te ronge pas les ongles!
  [2] le *clou* (made of metal)

nailbrush NOUN
  la *brosse à ongles*

nailfile NOUN
  la *lime à ongles*

nail scissors PL NOUN
  les *ciseaux à ongles* MASC

nail varnish NOUN
  le *vernis à ongles*
  ◆ **nail varnish remover** le dissolvant

naked ADJECTIVE
  nu

name NOUN
  le *nom*
  ◆ **What's your name?** Comment vous
  appelez-vous?

nanny NOUN
  la *garde d'enfants* ◇ She's a nanny.
  C'est une garde d'enfants.

nap NOUN
  le *petit somme*
  ◆ **to have a nap** faire un petit somme

napkin NOUN
  la *serviette*

nappy NOUN
  la *couche*

narrow ADJECTIVE
  étroit

narrow-minded ADJECTIVE
  borné

nasty ADJECTIVE
  [1] *mauvais* (bad) ◇ a nasty cold un
  mauvais rhume ◇ a nasty smell une
  mauvaise odeur
  [2] *méchant* (unfriendly) ◇ He gave me a
  nasty look. Il m'a regardé d'un air
  méchant.

nation NOUN
  la *nation*

national ADJECTIVE
  national
  (*nationaux* MASC PL)
  ◇ He's the national champion. C'est le
  champion national.
  ◆ **the national elections** les élections
  législatives

national anthem NOUN

  l' *hymne national* MASC

National Health Service NOUN
  la *Sécurité sociale*

> In France you have to pay for medical treatment
> when you receive it, and then claim it back from
> the Sécurité sociale.

nationalism NOUN
  le *nationalisme* ◇ Scottish nationalism
  le nationalisme écossais

nationalist NOUN
  le/la *nationaliste*

nationality NOUN
  la *nationalité*

national park NOUN
  le *parc national*
  (les *parcs nationaux* PL)

native ADJECTIVE
  natal ◇ my native country mon pays
  natal
  ◆ **native language** la langue maternelle
  ◇ English is not their native language.
  L'anglais n'est pas leur langue
  maternelle.

natural ADJECTIVE
  naturel MASC
  naturelle FEM

naturalist NOUN
  le *naturaliste*

naturally ADVERB
  naturellement ◇ Naturally, we were
  very disappointed. Nous avons
  naturellement été très déçus.

nature NOUN
  la *nature*

naughty ADJECTIVE
  vilain ◇ Naughty girl! Vilaine! ◇ Don't
  be naughty! Ne fais pas le vilain!

navy NOUN
  la *marine* ◇ He's in the navy. Il est
  dans la marine.

navy-blue ADJECTIVE
  bleu marine MASC, FEM, PL ◇ a navy-blue
  skirt une jupe bleu marine

Nazi NOUN
  le *Nazi*
  la *Nazie*
  ◇ the Nazis les Nazis

near ADJECTIVE
  see also **near** PREPOSITION
  proche ◇ It's fairly near. C'est assez
  proche.
  ◆ **It's near enough to walk.** On peut
  facilement y aller à pied.
  ◆ **the nearest** le plus proche ◇ Where's
  the nearest service station? Où est la
  station-service la plus proche? ◇ The

nearest shops were three kilometres away. Les magasins les plus proches étaient à trois kilomètres.

near PREPOSITION, ADVERB

> see also **near** ADJECTIVE

près de ◇ *I live near Liverpool.* J'habite près de Liverpool. ◇ *near my house* près de chez moi

- **near here** près d'ici ◇ *Is there a bank near here?* Est-ce qu'il y a une banque près d'ici?
- **near to** près de ◇ *It's very near to the school.* C'est tout près de l'école.

nearby ADVERB

> see also **nearby** ADJECTIVE

à proximité ◇ *There's a supermarket nearby.* Il y a un supermarché à proximité.

nearby ADJECTIVE

> see also **nearby** ADVERB

[1] *proche* (*close*) ◇ *a nearby garage* un garage proche
[2] *voisin* (*neighbouring*) ◇ *We went to the nearby village of Torrance.* Nous sommes allés à Torrance, le village voisin.

nearly ADVERB

presque ◇ *Dinner's nearly ready.* Le dîner est presque prêt. ◇ *I'm nearly 15.* J'ai presque quinze ans.

- **I nearly missed the train.** J'ai failli rater le train.

neat ADJECTIVE

soigné ◇ *She has very neat writing.* Elle a une écriture très soignée.

- **a neat whisky** un whisky sec

neatly ADVERB

soigneusement ◇ *neatly folded* soigneusement plié

- **neatly dressed** impeccable

necessarily ADVERB

- **not necessarily** pas forcément

necessary ADJECTIVE

nécessaire

necessity NOUN

la *chose nécessaire* ◇ *A car is a necessity, not a luxury.* Une voiture est une chose nécessaire et non pas un luxe.

neck NOUN

[1] le *cou* (*of body*)

- **a stiff neck** un torticolis
[2] l' *encolure* FEM (*of garment*) ◇ *a V-neck sweater* un pull avec une encolure en V

necklace NOUN

le *collier*

need VERB

> see also **need** NOUN

avoir besoin de ◇ *I need a bigger size.* J'ai besoin d'une plus grande taille.

- **to need to do something** avoir besoin de faire quelque chose ◇ *I need to change some money.* J'ai besoin de changer de l'argent.

need NOUN

> see also **need** VERB

- **There's no need to book.** Il n'est pas nécessaire de réserver.

needle NOUN

l' *aiguille* FEM

needlework NOUN

la *couture* ◇ *We have needlework lessons at school.* Nous avons des cours de couture à l'école.

negative NOUN

> see also **negative** ADJECTIVE

le *négatif* (*photo*)

negative ADJECTIVE

> see also **negative** NOUN

négatif MASC
négative FEM
◇ *He's got a very negative attitude.* Il a une attitude très négative.

neglected ADJECTIVE

mal tenu (*untidy*) ◇ *The garden is neglected.* Le jardin est mal tenu.

negligee NOUN

le *déshabillé*

neighbour NOUN

le *voisin*
la *voisine*
◇ *the neighbours' garden* le jardin des voisins

neighbourhood NOUN

le *quartier*

neither PRONOUN, CONJUNCTION, ADVERB

aucun des deux
aucune des deux
◇ *Carrots or peas? – Neither, thanks.* Des carottes ou des petits pois? – Aucun des deux merci. ◇ *Neither of them is coming.* Aucun des deux ne vient.

- **neither...nor...** ni...ni... ◇ *Neither Sarah nor Tamsin is coming to the party.* Ni Sarah ni Tamsin ne vient à la soirée.
- **Neither do I.** Moi non plus. ◇ *I don't like him. – Neither do I!* Je ne l'aime pas. – Moi non plus!
- **Neither have I.** Moi non plus. ◇ *I've never been to Spain. – Neither have I.* Je ne suis jamais allé en Espagne. – Moi non plus.

neon NOUN

le *néon*

- **a neon light** une lampe au néon

nephew NOUN

le *neveu*
(les *neveux* PL)
◇ *my nephew* mon neveu

nerve NOUN

1 le *nerf* ◇ *She sometimes gets on my nerves.* Elle me tape quelquefois sur les nerfs.

2 le *toupet* (*cheek*) ◇ *He's got a nerve!* Il a du toupet!

nerve-racking ADJECTIVE
angoissant

nervous ADJECTIVE
tendu (*tense*) ◇ *I bite my nails when I'm nervous.* Je me ronge les ongles quand je suis tendu.

◆ **to be nervous about something** appréhender de faire quelque chose ◇ *I'm a bit nervous about flying to Paris by myself.* J'appréhende un peu d'aller toute seule en avion à Paris.

nest NOUN
le *nid*

net NOUN
le *filet* ◇ *a fishing net* un filet de pêche

Netherlands PL NOUN
les *Pays-Bas* MASC

◆ **in the Netherlands** aux Pays-Bas

network NOUN
le *réseau*
(les *réseaux* PL)

neurotic ADJECTIVE
névrosé

never ADVERB

1 *jamais* ◇ *Have you ever been to Germany? – No, never.* Est-ce que tu es déjà allé en Allemagne? – Non, jamais. ◇ *When are you going to phone him? – Never!* Quand est-ce que tu vas l'appeler? – Jamais!

Add **ne** if the sentence contains a verb.

2 *ne...jamais* ◇ *I never write letters.* Je n'écris jamais. ◇ *I have never been camping.* Je n'ai jamais fait de camping. ◇ *Never leave valuables in your car.* Ne laissez jamais d'objets de valeur dans votre voiture.

◆ **Never again!** Plus jamais!

◆ **Never mind.** Ça ne fait rien.

new ADJECTIVE

1 *nouveau* MASC
nouvelle FEM
(*nouveaux* MASC PL)
◇ *her new boyfriend* son nouveau copain ◇ *I need a new dress.* J'ai besoin d'une nouvelle robe.

2 (*brand new*)
neuf MASC
neuve FEM
◇ *They've got a new car.* Ils ont une voiture neuve.

newcomer NOUN
le *nouveau venu*

(les *nouveaux venus* MASC PL)
la *nouvelle venue*

news NOUN

1 les *nouvelles* FEM PL ◇ *good news* de bonnes nouvelles ◇ *I've had some bad news.* J'ai reçu de mauvaises nouvelles. ◇ *It was nice to have your news.* J'ai été content d'avoir de tes nouvelles.

2 la *nouvelle* (*single piece of news*) ◇ *That's wonderful news!* Quelle bonne nouvelle!

3 le *journal télévisé* (*on TV*) ◇ *I watch the news every evening.* Je regarde le journal télévisé tous les soirs.

4 les *informations* FEM PL (*on radio*) ◇ *I listen to the news every morning.* J'écoute les informations tous les matins.

newsagent NOUN
le *marchand de journaux*

newspaper NOUN
le *journal*
(les *journaux* PL)
◇ *I deliver newspapers.* Je distribue des journaux.

newsreader NOUN
le *présentateur*
la *présentatrice*

New Year NOUN
le *Nouvel An* ◇ *to celebrate New Year* fêter le Nouvel An

◆ **Happy New Year!** Bonne Année!

◆ **New Year's Day** le premier de l'An

◆ **New Year's Eve** la veille du premier de l'An ◇ *a New Year's Eve party* un réveillon du premier de l'An

New Zealand NOUN
la *Nouvelle-Zélande*

◆ **in New Zealand** en Nouvelle-Zélande

New Zealander NOUN
le *Néo-Zélandais*
la *Néo-Zélandaise*

next ADJECTIVE, ADVERB, PREPOSITION

1 *prochain* (*in time*) ◇ *next Saturday* samedi prochain ◇ *next year* l'année prochaine ◇ *next summer* l'été prochain

2 *suivant* (*in sequence*) ◇ *the next train* le train suivant ◇ *Next please!* Au suivant!

3 *ensuite* (*afterwards*) ◇ *What shall I do next?* Qu'est-ce que je fais ensuite? ◇ *What happened next?* Qu'est-ce qui s'est passé ensuite?

◆ **next to** à côté de ◇ *next to the bank* à côté de la banque

◆ **the next day** le lendemain ◇ *The next day we visited Versailles.* Le lendemain nous avons visité Versailles.

◆ **the next time** la prochaine fois ◇ *the next time you see her* la prochaine fois que tu la verras

• **next door** à côté ◦ *They live next door.* Ils habitent à côté. ◦ *the people next door* les gens d'à côté

• **the next room** la pièce d'à côté

NHS NOUN
la *Sécurité sociale*

In France you have to pay for medical treatment when you receive it, and then claim it back from the Sécurité sociale.

nice ADJECTIVE

[1] *(kind)*
gentil MASC
gentille FEM

◦ *Your parents are very nice.* Tes parents sont très gentils. ◦ *It was nice of you to remember my birthday.* C'était gentil de ta part de te souvenir de mon anniversaire.

• **to be nice to somebody** être gentil avec quelqu'un

[2] *(pretty)*
joli ◦ *That's a nice dress!* Qu'est-ce qu'elle est jolie, cette robe! ◦ *Aix is a nice town.* Aix est une jolie ville.

[3] *(food)*
bon MASC
bonne FEM

◦ *It's very nice.* C'est très bon. ◦ *a nice cup of coffee* une bonne tasse de café

• **Have a nice time!** Amuse-toi bien!

• **nice weather** le beau temps

• **It's a nice day.** Il fait beau.

nickname NOUN
le *surnom*

niece NOUN
la *nièce* ◦ *my niece* ma nièce

Nigeria NOUN
le *Nigéria*

• **in Nigeria** au Nigéria

night NOUN

[1] la *nuit* ◦ *I want a single room for two nights.* Je veux une chambre à un lit pour deux nuits.

• **at night** la nuit

• **Goodnight!** Bonne nuit!

• **a night club** une boîte de nuit

[2] le *soir* *(evening)* ◦ *last night* hier soir

nightie NOUN
la *chemise de nuit*

nightlife NOUN

• **There's plenty of nightlife.** Il y a plein de choses à faire le soir.

nightmare NOUN
le *cauchemar* ◦ *It was a real nightmare!* Ça a été un vrai cauchemar!

• **to have a nightmare** faire un cauchemar

nil NOUN
le *zéro* ◦ *We won one-nil.* Nous avons

gagné un à zéro.

nine NUMBER
neuf MASC
neuve FEM
◦ *She's nine.* Elle a neuf ans.

nineteen NUMBER
dix-neuf ◦ *She's nineteen.* Elle a dix-neuf ans.

ninety NUMBER
quatre-vingt-dix

ninth ADJECTIVE
neuvième ◦ *the ninth floor* le neuvième étage

• **the ninth of August** le neuf août

no ADVERB, ADJECTIVE

[1] *non* ◦ *Are you coming?–No.* Est-ce que vous venez?–Non. ◦ *Would you like some more?–No thank you.* Vous en voulez encore?–Non merci.

[2] *pas de* *(not any)* ◦ *There's no hot water.* Il n'y a pas d'eau chaude. ◦ *There are no trains on Sundays.* Il n'y a pas de trains le dimanche. ◦ *No problem.* Pas de problème.

• **I've got no idea.** Je n'en ai aucune idée.

• **No way!** Pas question!

• **"no smoking"** "défense de fumer"

nobody PRONOUN

[1] *personne* ◦ *Who's going with you?–Nobody.* Qui t'accompagne?–Personne.

Add ne *if the sentence contains a verb.*

[2] *ne...personne* ◦ *There was nobody in the office.* Il n'y avait personne au bureau.

• **Nobody likes him.** Personne ne l'aime.

noise NOUN
le *bruit* ◦ *Please make less noise.* Faites moins de bruit s'il vous plaît.

noisy ADJECTIVE
bruyant

none PRONOUN

[1] *aucun* MASC
aucune FEM

◦ *How many sisters have you got?–None.* Tu as combien de sœurs?–Aucune. ◦ *What sports do you do?–None.* Qu'est-ce que tu fais comme sport?–Je n'en fais aucun.

Add ne *if the sentence contains a verb.*

[2] *aucun...ne* ◦ *None of my friends wanted to come.* Aucun de mes amis n'a voulu venir.

• **There's none left.** Il n'y en a plus.

• **There are none left.** Il n'y en a plus.

nonsense NOUN
les *bêtises* FEM PL ◦ *She talks a lot of nonsense.* Elle dit beaucoup de bêtises. ◦ *Nonsense!* Ne dis pas de bêtises!

non-smoker NOUN
le *non-fumeur* ◇ *He's a non-smoker.* Il
est non-fumeur.

non-smoking ADJECTIVE
non-fumeur ◇ *a non-smoking carriage*
une voiture non-fumeurs

non-stop ADJECTIVE, ADVERB
1 *direct* ◇ *a non-stop flight* un vol
direct ◇ *We flew non-stop.* Nous avons
pris un vol direct.
2 *sans arrêt* ◇ *He talks non-stop.* Il
parle sans arrêt.

noodles PL NOUN
les *nouilles* FEM PL

noon NOUN
midi ◇ *at noon* à midi

no one PRONOUN
1 *personne* ◇ *Who's going with
you? – No one.* Qui
t'accompagne? – Personne.
Add ne if the sentence contains a verb.
2 *ne...personne* ◇ *There was no one
in the office.* Il n'y avait personne au
bureau.
◆ **No one likes him.** Personne ne l'aime.

nor CONJUNCTION
◆ **neither...nor** ni...ni ◇ *neither the
cinema nor the swimming pool* ni le
cinéma, ni la piscine
◆ **Nor do I.** Moi non plus. ◇ *I didn't like
the film. – Nor did I.* Je n'ai pas aimé le
film. – Moi non plus.
◆ **Nor have I.** Moi non plus. ◇ *I haven't
seen him. – Nor have I.* Je ne l'ai pas
vu. – Moi non plus.

normal ADJECTIVE
1 *(usual)*
habituel MASC
habituelle FEM
◇ *at the normal time* à l'heure habituelle
2 *(standard)*
normal
(normaux MASC PL*)*
◇ *a normal car* une voiture normale

normally ADVERB
1 *généralement* *(usually)* ◇ *I normally
arrive at nine o'clock.* J'arrive
généralement à neuf heures.
2 *normalement* *(as normal)* ◇ *In spite
of the strike, the airports are working
normally.* Malgré la grève, les aéroports
fonctionnent normalement.

Normandy NOUN
la *Normandie*
◆ **in Normandy** en Normandie
◆ **to Normandy** en Normandie

north ADJECTIVE, ADVERB
see also north NOUN
1 *nord* MASC, FEM, PL ◇ *the north coast* la
côte nord
◆ **a north wind** un vent du nord
2 *vers le nord* ◇ *We were travelling
north.* Nous allions vers le nord.
◆ **north of** au nord de ◇ *It's north of
London.* C'est au nord de Londres.

north NOUN
see also north ADJECTIVE
le *nord* ◇ *in the north* dans le nord

North America NOUN
l' *Amérique du Nord* FEM

northeast NOUN
le *nord-est* ◇ *in the northeast* au
nord-est

northern ADJECTIVE
◆ **the northern part of the island** la partie
nord de l'île
◆ **Northern Europe** l'Europe du Nord

Northern Ireland NOUN
l' *Irlande du Nord* FEM
◆ **in Northern Ireland** en Irlande du Nord
◆ **to Northern Ireland** en Irlande du Nord
◆ **I'm from Northern Ireland.** Je viens
d'Irlande du Nord.

North Pole NOUN
le *pôle Nord*

North Sea NOUN
la *mer du Nord*

northwest NOUN
le *nord-ouest* ◇ *in the northwest* au
nord-ouest

Norway NOUN
la *Norvège*
◆ **in Norway** en Norvège

Norwegian ADJECTIVE
see also Norwegian NOUN
norvégien MASC
norvégienne FEM

Norwegian NOUN
see also Norwegian ADJECTIVE
1 *(person)*
le *Norvégien*
la *Norvégienne*
2 *(language)*
le *norvégien*

nose NOUN
le *nez*
(les nez PL*)*

nosebleed NOUN
◆ **to have a nosebleed** saigner du nez
◇ *I often get nosebleeds.* Je saigne
souvent du nez.

nosey ADJECTIVE
◆ **to be nosey** se mêler de tout ◇ *She's
very nosey.* Elle se mêle de tout.

not ADVERB
1 *pas* ◇ *Are you coming or not?* Est-ce
que tu viens ou pas?
◆ **not really** pas vraiment

- **not at all** pas du tout
- **not yet** pas encore ◇ *Have you finished? — Not yet.* As-tu fini? — Pas encore.

> Add ne *before a verb.*

2 *ne...pas* ◇ *I'm not sure.* Je ne suis pas sûr. ◇ *It's not raining.* Il ne pleut pas. ◇ *You shouldn't do that.* Tu ne devrais pas faire ça. ◇ *They haven't arrived yet.* Ils ne sont pas encore arrivés.

3 *non* ◇ *I hope not.* J'espère que non. ◇ *Can you lend me £10? — I'm afraid not.* Est-ce que tu peux me prêter dix livres? — Non, désolé.

note NOUN

1 la *note* ◇ *to take notes* prendre des notes

2 le *mot* (*letter*) ◇ *I'll write her a note.* Je vais lui écrire un mot.

3 le *billet* (*banknote*) ◇ *a £5 note* un billet de cinq livres

note down VERB
noter

notebook NOUN
le *carnet*

notepad NOUN
le *bloc-notes*
(les *blocs-notes* PL)

notepaper NOUN
le *papier à lettres*

nothing NOUN

1 *rien* ◇ *What's wrong? — Nothing.* Qu'est-ce qui ne va pas? — Rien.

- *nothing special* rien de particulier

> Add ne *if the sentence contains a verb.*

2 *ne...rien* ◇ *He does nothing.* Il ne fait rien. ◇ *He ate nothing for breakfast.* Il n'a rien mangé au petit-déjeuner.

- **Nothing is open on Sundays.** Rien n'est ouvert le dimanche.

notice NOUN

> see also notice VERB

(*sign*)
le *panneau*
(les *panneaux* PL)

- **to put up a notice** mettre un panneau
- **a warning notice** un avertissement
- **Don't take any notice of him!** Ne fais pas attention à lui!

notice VERB

> see also notice NOUN

remarquer

notice board NOUN
le *panneau d'affichage*
(les *panneaux d'affichage* PL)

nought NOUN
le *zéro*

noun NOUN
le *nom*

novel NOUN
le *roman*

novelist NOUN
le *romancier*
la *romancière*

November NOUN
novembre MASC

- **in November** en novembre

now ADVERB, CONJUNCTION
maintenant ◇ *What are you doing now?* Qu'est-ce que tu fais maintenant?

- **just now** en ce moment ◇ *I'm rather busy just now.* Je suis très occupé en ce moment.
- **I did it just now.** Je viens de le faire.
- **He should be there by now.** Il doit être arrivé à l'heure qu'il est.
- **It should be ready by now.** Ça devrait être déjà prêt.
- **now and then** de temps en temps

nowhere ADVERB
nulle part ◇ *nowhere else* nulle part ailleurs

nuclear ADJECTIVE
nucléaire ◇ *nuclear power* l'énergie nucléaire ◇ *a nuclear power station* une centrale nucléaire

nude ADJECTIVE

> see also nude NOUN

nu

- **to sunbathe nude** faire du bronzage intégral

nude NOUN

> see also nude ADJECTIVE

- **in the nude** nu

nudist NOUN
le/la *nudiste*

nuisance NOUN

- **It's a nuisance.** C'est très embêtant.
- **Sorry to be a nuisance.** Désolé de vous déranger.

number NOUN

1 le *nombre* (*total amount*) ◇ *a large number of people* un grand nombre de gens

2 le *numéro* (*of house, telephone, bank account*) ◇ *They live at number 5.* Ils habitent au numéro cinq. ◇ *What's your phone number?* Quel est votre numéro de téléphone? ◇ *You've got the wrong number.* Vous vous êtes trompé de numéro.

3 le *chiffre* (*figure, digit*) ◇ *I can't read the second number.* Je n'arrive pas à lire le deuxième chiffre.

number plate NOUN
la *plaque d'immatriculation*

nun NOUN
la *religieuse* ◇ *She's a nun.* Elle est

religieuse.

nurse NOUN
l' *infirmier* MASC
l' *infirmière* FEM
◇ *She's a nurse.* Elle est infirmière.

nursery NOUN
1 la *crèche* (*for children*)
2 la *pépinière* (*for plants*)

nursery school NOUN
l' *école maternelle* FEM
The école maternelle *is a state school for 2-6 year-olds.*

nursery slope NOUN
la *piste pour débutants*

nut NOUN
1 (*peanut*)
la *cacahuète*

2 (*hazelnut*)
la *noisette*
3 (*walnut*)
la *noix*
(les *noix* PL)
4 (*made of metal*)
l' *écrou* MASC

nutmeg NOUN
la *noix de muscade*

nutritious ADJECTIVE
nourrissant

nutter NOUN
→ **He's a nutter.** Il est complètement cinglé. (*informal*)

nylon NOUN
le *nylon*

O

oak NOUN
le *chêne* ◇ *an oak table* une table en chêne

oar NOUN
l' *aviron* MASC

oats NOUN
l' *avoine* FEM

obedient ADJECTIVE
obéissant

to **obey** VERB
➤ **to obey the rules** respecter le règlement

object NOUN
l' *objet* MASC ◇ *a familiar object* un objet familier

objection NOUN
l' *objection* FEM

objective NOUN
l' *objectif* MASC

oblong ADJECTIVE
rectangulaire

oboe NOUN
le *hautbois* ◇ *I play the oboe.* Je joue du hautbois.

obscene ADJECTIVE
obscène

observant ADJECTIVE
observateur MASC
observatrice FEM

to **observe** VERB
observer

obsolete ADJECTIVE
dépassé

obstacle NOUN
l' *obstacle* MASC

obstinate ADJECTIVE
obstiné

to **obstruct** VERB
bloquer ◇ *A lorry was obstructing the traffic.* Un camion bloquait la circulation.

to **obtain** VERB
obtenir

obvious ADJECTIVE
évident

obviously ADVERB
1 *évidemment* (of course) ◇ *Do you want to pass the exam?—Obviously!* Tu veux être reçu à l'examen?—Évidemment!
➤ **Obviously not!** Bien sûr que non!
2 *manifestement* (visibly) ◇ *She was obviously exhausted.* Elle était manifestement épuisée.

occasion NOUN
l' *occasion* FEM ◇ *a special occasion* une occasion spéciale

➤ **on several occasions** à plusieurs reprises

occasionally ADVERB
de temps en temps

occupation NOUN
la *profession*

to **occupy** VERB
occuper ◇ *That seat is occupied.* Cette place est occupée.

to **occur** VERB
avoir lieu (happen) ◇ *The accident occurred yesterday.* L'accident a eu lieu hier.
➤ **It suddenly occurred to me that...** Il m'est soudain venu à l'esprit que...

ocean NOUN
l' *océan* MASC

o'clock ADVERB
➤ **at four o'clock** à quatre heures
➤ **It's five o'clock.** Il est cinq heures.

October NOUN
octobre MASC
➤ **in October** en octobre

octopus NOUN
la *pieuvre*

odd ADJECTIVE
1 *bizarre* ◇ *That's odd!* C'est bizarre!
2 *impair* ◇ *an odd number* un chiffre impair

of PREPOSITION
1 *de* ◇ *some photos of my holiday* des photos de mes vacances ◇ *a boy of ten* un garçon de dix ans

de changes to d' before a vowel and most words beginning with "h".

d' ◇ *a kilo of oranges* un kilo d'oranges

de + le changes to du, and de + les changes to des.

du ◇ *the end of the film* la fin du film
des ◇ *the end of the holidays* la fin des vacances
2 *en* (with quantity, amount) ◇ *He's got four sisters. I've met two of them.* Il a quatre sœurs. J'en ai rencontré deux.
◇ *Can I have half of that?* Je peux en avoir la moitié?
➤ **three of us** trois d'entre nous
➤ **a friend of mine** un de mes amis
➤ **the 14th of September** le quatorze septembre
➤ **That's very kind of you.** C'est très gentil de votre part.
➤ **It's made of wood.** C'est en bois.

off ADVERB, PREPOSITION, ADJECTIVE

For other expressions with off, see the verbs get, take, turn etc.

1 *éteint* (*heater, light, TV*) ◇ *All the lights are off.* Toutes les lumières sont éteintes.
2 *fermé* (*tap, gas*) ◇ *Are you sure the tap is off?* Tu es sûr que le robinet est fermé?
3 *annulé* (*cancelled*) ◇ *The match is off.* Le match est annulé.
• **to be off sick** être malade
• **a day off** un jour de congé ◇ *to take a day off work* prendre un jour de congé
• **She's off school today.** Elle n'est pas à l'école aujourd'hui.
• **I must be off now.** Je dois m'en aller maintenant.
• **I'm off.** Je m'en vais.

offence NOUN
le *délit* (*crime*)

offensive ADJECTIVE
choquant

offer NOUN

see also offer VERB

la *proposition* ◇ *a good offer* une proposition intéressante
• **"on special offer"** "en promotion"

to **offer** VERB

see also offer NOUN

proposer ◇ *He offered to help me.* Il m'a proposé de m'aider. ◇ *I offered to go with them.* Je leur ai proposé de les accompagner.

office NOUN
le *bureau*
(les *bureaux* PL)
◇ *She works in an office.* Elle travaille dans un bureau.

officer NOUN
l' *officier* MASC

official ADJECTIVE
officiel MASC
officielle FEM

off-licence NOUN
le *marchand de vins et spiritueux*

offside ADJECTIVE
hors jeu (*in football*)

often ADVERB
souvent ◇ *It often rains.* Il pleut souvent. ◇ *How often do you go to the gym?* Tu vas souvent à la gym? ◇ *I'd like to go skiing more often.* J'aimerais aller skier plus souvent.

oil NOUN

see also oil VERB

1 l' *huile* FEM (*for lubrication, cooking*)
• **an oil painting** une peinture à l'huile
2 le *pétrole* (*crude oil*) ◇ *North Sea oil* le pétrole de la mer du Nord

to **oil** VERB

see also oil NOUN

graisser

oil rig NOUN
la *plateforme pétrolière* ◇ *He works on an oil rig.* Il travaille sur une plateforme pétrolière.

oil slick NOUN
la *marée noire*

oil well NOUN
le *puits de pétrole*
(les *puits de pétrole* PL)

ointment NOUN
la *pommade* MASC

okay EXCLAMATION, ADJECTIVE
d'accord (*agreed*) ◇ *Could you call back later?–Okay!* Tu peux rappeler plus tard?–D'accord! ◇ *I'll meet you at six o'clock, okay?* Je te retrouve à six heures, d'accord? ◇ *Is that okay?* C'est d'accord?
• **I'll do it tomorrow, if that's okay with you.** Je le ferai demain, si tu es d'accord.
• **Are you okay?** Ça va?
• **How was your holiday?–It was okay.** C'était comment tes vacances?–Pas mal.
• **What's your teacher like?–He's okay.** Il est comment ton prof?–Il est sympa. (*informal*)

old ADJECTIVE
1 *vieux* MASC
vieille FEM
◇ *an old dog* un vieux chien ◇ *an old house* une vieille maison

vieux *changes to* vieil *before a vowel and most words beginning with "h".*

vieil ◇ *an old man* un vieil homme

When talking about people it is more polite to use âgé *instead of* vieux.

âgé ◇ *old people* les personnes âgées
2 (*former*)
ancien MASC
ancienne FEM
◇ *my old English teacher* mon ancien professeur d'anglais
• **How old are you?** Quel âge as-tu?
• **He's ten years old.** Il a dix ans.
• **my older brother** mon frère aîné ◇ *my older sister* ma sœur aînée
• **She's two years older than me.** Elle a deux ans de plus que moi.
• **I'm the oldest in the family.** Je suis l'aîné de la famille.

old age pensioner NOUN
le *retraité*
la *retraitée*
◇ *She's an old age pensioner.* Elle est retraitée.

old-fashioned ADJECTIVE
1 *démodé* ◇ *She wears old-fashioned clothes.* Elle porte des vêtements démodés.
2 *vieux jeu* MASC, FEM, PL (*person*) ◇ *My*

parents are rather old-fashioned. Mes
parents sont plutôt vieux jeu.

olive NOUN
l' *olive* FEM

olive oil NOUN
l' *huile d'olive* FEM

Olympic ADJECTIVE
olympique
◆ **the Olympics** les Jeux olympiques MASC

omelette NOUN
l' *omelette* FEM

on PREPOSITION, ADVERB

> see also **on** ADJECTIVE

> *There are several ways of translating* on. *Scan the
> examples to find one that is similar to what you
> want to say. For other expressions with* on, *see
> the verbs* go, put, turn *etc.*

[1] *sur*   ◇ *on the table* sur la table ◇ *on
an island* sur une île

[2] *à*   ◇ *on the left* à gauche ◇ *on the
2nd floor* au deuxième étage ◇ *I go to
school on my bike.* Je vais à l'école à vélo.

◆ **on TV** à la télé   ◇ *What's on TV?*
Qu'est-ce qu'il y a à la télé?

◆ **on the radio** à la radio   ◇ *I heard it on
the radio.* Je l'ai entendu à la radio.

◆ **on the bus (1)** (*by bus*) en bus   ◇ *I go
into town on the bus.* Je vais en ville en
bus.

◆ **on the bus (2)** (*inside*) dans le bus
◇ *There were no empty seats on the bus.*
Il n'y avait pas de places libres dans le
bus.

◆ **on holiday** en vacances   ◇ *They're on
holiday.* Ils sont en vacances.

◆ **on strike** en grève

> *With days and dates* on *is not translated.*

◇ *on Friday* vendredi ◇ *on Fridays* le
vendredi ◇ *on Christmas Day* le jour de
Noël ◇ *on June 20th* le vingt juin ◇ *on
my birthday* le jour de mon anniversaire

on ADJECTIVE

> see also **on** PREPOSITION

[1] *allumé* (*heater, light, TV*) ◇ *I think I left
the light on.* Je crois que j'ai laissé la
lumière allumée.

[2] *ouvert* (*tap, gas*) ◇ *Leave the tap on.*
Laisse le robinet ouvert.

[3] *en marche* (*machine*) ◇ *Is the
dishwasher on?* Est-ce que le
lave-vaisselle est en marche?

◆ **What's on at the cinema?** Qu'est-ce qui
passe au cinéma?

once ADVERB
une fois   ◇ *once a week* une fois par
semaine ◇ *once more* encore une fois
◇ *I've been to France once before.* J'ai
déjà été une fois en France.

◆ **Once upon a time...** Il était une fois...

◆ **at once** tout de suite

◆ **once in a while** de temps en temps

one NUMBER, PRONOUN

> *Use* un *for masculine nouns and* une *for
> feminine nouns.*

[1] *un*   ◇ *one day* un jour ◇ *Do you
need a stamp? – No thanks, I've got one.*
Est-ce que tu as besoin d'un
timbre? – Non merci, j'en ai un.
une   ◇ *one minute* une minute ◇ *I've
got one brother and one sister.* J'ai un
frère et une sœur.

[2] *on* (*impersonal*)   ◇ *One never knows.*
On ne sait jamais.

◆ **this one (1)** celui-ci (*masculine*) ◇ *Which
foot is hurting? – This one.* Quel pied te
fait mal? – Celui-ci.

◆ **this one (2)** celle-ci (*feminine*) ◇ *Which
is the best photo? – This one.* Quelle est
la meilleure photo? – Celle-ci.

◆ **that one (1)** celui-là (*masculine*)
◇ *Which bag is yours? – That one.* Lequel
est ton sac? – Celui-là.

◆ **that one (2)** celle-là (*feminine*) ◇ *Which
seat do you want? – That one.* Quelle
place voulez-vous? – Celle-là.

oneself PRONOUN

[1] *se*   ◇ *to hurt oneself* se faire mal

[2] *soi-même*   ◇ *It's quicker to do it
oneself.* C'est plus rapide de le faire
soi-même.

one-way ADJECTIVE

◆ **a one-way street** une impasse

onion NOUN
l' *oignon* MASC   ◇ *onion soup* la soupe à
l'oignon

only ADVERB, ADJECTIVE, CONJUNCTION

[1] *seul*   ◇ *Monday is the only day I'm
free.* Le lundi est le seul jour où je suis
libre. ◇ *French is the only subject I like.*
Le français est la seule matière que
j'aime.

[2] *seulement*   ◇ *How much was
it? – Only 10 francs.* Combien
c'était? – Seulement dix francs.

[3] *ne...que*   ◇ *We only want to stay for
one night.* Nous ne voulons rester
qu'une nuit. ◇ *These cassettes are only
30 francs.* Ces cassettes ne coûtent que
trente francs.

[4] *mais*   ◇ *I'd like the same sweater,
only in black.* Je voudrais le même pull,
mais en noir.

◆ **an only child** un enfant unique

onwards ADVERB
à partir de   ◇ *from July onwards* à
partir de juillet

open ADJECTIVE

> see also **open** VERB

ouvert ⋄ *The baker's is open on Sunday morning.* La boulangerie est ouverte le dimanche matin.
- **in the open air** en plein air

to **open** VERB

see also **open** ADJECTIVE

1 *ouvrir* ⋄ *Can I open the window?* Est-ce que je peux ouvrir la fenêtre? ⋄ *What time do the shops open?* Les magasins ouvrent à quelle heure?

2 *s'ouvrir* ⋄ *The door opens automatically.* La porte s'ouvre automatiquement. ⋄ *The door opened and in came the teacher.* La porte s'est ouverte et le professeur est entré.

opening hours PL NOUN
les *heures d'ouverture* FEM

opera NOUN
l' *opéra* MASC

operation NOUN
l' *opération* FEM ⋄ *a major operation* une grave opération
- **to have an operation** se faire opérer ⋄ *I have never had an operation.* Je ne me suis jamais fait opérer.

operator NOUN
le/la *standardiste* (on telephone)

opinion NOUN
l' *avis* MASC ⋄ *in my opinion* à mon avis ⋄ *He asked me my opinion.* Il m'a demandé mon avis.
- **What's your opinion?** Qu'est-ce vous en pensez?

opinion poll NOUN
le *sondage*

opponent NOUN
l' *adversaire* MASC/FEM

opportunity NOUN
l' *occasion* FEM
- **to have the opportunity to do something** avoir l'occasion de faire quelque chose ⋄ *I've never had the opportunity to go to France.* Je n'ai jamais eu l'occasion d'aller en France.

opposing ADJECTIVE
opposé (team)

opposite ADJECTIVE, ADVERB, PREPOSITION

1 *opposé* ⋄ *It's in the opposite direction.* C'est dans la direction opposée.

2 *en face* ⋄ *They live opposite.* Ils habitent en face.

3 *en face de* ⋄ *the girl sitting opposite me* la fille assise en face de moi
- **the opposite sex** l'autre sexe

opposition NOUN
l' *opposition* FEM

optician NOUN
l' *opticien* MASC

l' *opticienne* FEM
⋄ *She's an optician.* Elle est opticienne.

optimist NOUN
l' *optimiste* MASC/FEM

optimistic ADJECTIVE
optimiste

option NOUN

1 le *choix* (choice) ⋄ *I've got no option.* Je n'ai pas le choix.

2 la *matière à option* (optional subject) ⋄ *I'm doing geology as my option.* La géologie est ma matière à option.

optional ADJECTIVE
facultatif MASC
facultative FEM

or CONJUNCTION

1 *ou* ⋄ *Would you like tea or coffee?* Est-ce que tu veux du thé ou du café?

Use **ni...ni** in negative sentences.

⋄ *I don't eat meat or fish.* Je ne mange ni viande, ni poisson.

2 *sinon* (otherwise) ⋄ *Hurry up or you'll miss the bus.* Dépêche-toi, sinon tu vas rater le bus.
- **Give me the money, or else!** Donne-moi l'argent, sinon tu vas le regretter!

oral ADJECTIVE

see also **oral** NOUN

oral
(*oraux* MASC PL)
- **an oral exam** un oral

oral NOUN

see also **oral** ADJECTIVE

l' *oral* MASC
(les *oraux* PL)
⋄ *I've got my French oral soon.* Je vais bientôt passer mon oral de français.

orange NOUN

see also **orange** ADJECTIVE

l' *orange* FEM
- **an orange juice** un jus d'orange

orange ADJECTIVE

see also **orange** NOUN

orange MASC, FEM, PL

orchard NOUN
le *verger*

orchestra NOUN
l' *orchestre* MASC ⋄ *I play in the school orchestra.* Je joue dans l'orchestre de l'école.

order NOUN

see also **order** VERB

1 l' *ordre* MASC (sequence) ⋄ *in alphabetical order* dans l'ordre alphabétique

2 la *commande* (instruction) ⋄ *The waiter took our order.* Le garçon a pris notre commande.

- **in order to** pour ◇ *He does it in order to earn money.* Il le fait pour gagner de l'argent.
- **"out of order"** "en panne"

to **order** VERB

see also order NOUN

commander ◇ *We ordered steak and chips.* Nous avons commandé un steak frites. ◇ *Are you ready to order?* Vous êtes prêt à commander?

ordinary ADJECTIVE

1 *ordinaire* ◇ *an ordinary day* une journée ordinaire

2 *comme les autres* (*people*) ◇ *an ordinary family* une famille comme les autres ◇ *He's just an ordinary guy.* C'est un type comme les autres.

organ NOUN

l'*orgue* MASC (*instrument*) ◇ *I play the organ.* Je joue de l'orgue.

organic ADJECTIVE

biologique (*vegetables, fruit*)

organization NOUN

l'*organisation* FEM

to **organize** VERB

organiser

original ADJECTIVE

original

(*originaux* MASC PL)

◇ *It's a very original idea.* C'est une idée très originale.

- **Our original plan was to go camping.** À l'origine nous avions l'intention de faire du camping.

originally ADVERB

à l'origine

Orkneys PL NOUN

les *Orcades* FEM PL

- **in the Orkneys** dans les Orcades

ornament NOUN

le *bibelot*

orphan NOUN

l'*orphelin* MASC

l'*orpheline* FEM

ostrich NOUN

l'*autruche* FEM

other ADJECTIVE, PRONOUN

autre ◇ *Have you got these jeans in other colours?* Est-ce que vous avez ce jean dans d'autres couleurs? ◇ *on the other side of the street* de l'autre côté de la rue ◇ *the other day* l'autre jour

- **the other one** l'autre ◇ *This one? – No, the other one.* Celui-ci? – Non, l'autre.
- **the others** les autres ◇ *The others are going but I'm not.* Les autres y vont mais pas moi.

otherwise ADVERB, CONJUNCTION

1 *sinon* (*if not*) ◇ *Note down the number, otherwise you'll forget it.* Note le numéro, sinon tu vas l'oublier. ◇ *Put some sunscreen on, you'll get burned otherwise.* Mets une crème solaire, sinon tu vas attraper des coups de soleil.

2 *à part ça* (*in other ways*) ◇ *I'm tired, but otherwise I'm fine.* Je suis fatigué, mais à part ça, ça va.

ought VERB

To translate ought to use the conditional tense of devoir.

◇ *I ought to phone my parents.* Je devrais appeler mes parents. ◇ *You ought not to do that.* Tu ne devrais pas faire ça. ◇ *He ought to win.* Il devrait gagner.

our ADJECTIVE

notre ◇ *Our house is quite big.* Notre maison est plutôt grande.

nos PL ◇ *Our neighbours are very nice.* Nos voisins sont très gentils.

ours PRONOUN

le nôtre + MASC NOUN ◇ *Your garden is very big, ours is much smaller.* Votre jardin est très grand, le nôtre est beaucoup plus petit.

la nôtre + FEM NOUN ◇ *Your school is very different from ours.* Votre école est très différente de la nôtre.

les nôtres + PL NOUN ◇ *Our teachers are strict. – Ours are too.* Nos professeurs sont sévères. – Les nôtres aussi.

- **Is this ours?** C'est à nous? ◇ *This car is ours.* Cette voiture est à nous. ◇ *Whose is this? – It's ours.* C'est à qui? – À nous.

ourselves PRONOUN

1 *nous* ◇ *We really enjoyed ourselves.* Nous nous sommes vraiment bien amusés.

2 *nous-mêmes* ◇ *We built our garage ourselves.* Nous avons construit notre garage nous-mêmes.

out ADVERB

There are several ways of translating out. Scan the examples to find one that is similar to what you want to say. For other expressions with out, see the verbs go, put, turn etc.

1 *dehors* (*outside*) ◇ *It's cold out.* Il fait froid dehors.

2 *éteint* (*light, fire*) ◇ *All the lights are out.* Toutes les lumières sont éteintes.

- **She's out.** Elle est sortie.
- **She's out shopping.** Elle est sortie faire des courses.
- **She's out for the afternoon.** Elle ne sera pas là de tout l'après-midi.
- **out there** dehors ◇ *It's cold out there.* Il fait froid dehors.
- **to go out** sortir ◇ *I'm going out tonight.*

Je sors ce soir.

◆ **to go out with somebody** sortir avec quelqu'un ◇ *I've been going out with him for two months.* Je sors avec lui depuis deux mois.

◆ **out of (1)** dans ◇ *to drink out of a glass* boire dans un verre

◆ **out of (2)** sur ◇ *in 9 cases out of 10* dans neuf cas sur dix

◆ **out of (3)** en dehors de ◇ *He lives out of town.* Il habite en dehors de la ville.

◆ **3 km out of town** à trois kilomètres de la ville

◆ **out of curiosity** par curiosité

◆ **out of work** sans emploi

◆ **That is out of the question.** C'est hors de question.

◆ **You're out!** (*in game*) Tu es éliminé!

◆ **"way out"** "sortie"

outdoor ADJECTIVE
en plein air ◇ *an outdoor swimming pool* une piscine en plein air

◆ **outdoor activities** les activités de plein air

outdoors ADVERB
au grand air

outing NOUN
la *sortie* ◇ *to go on an outing* faire une sortie

outline NOUN
[1] les *grandes lignes* FEM (*summary*)
◇ *This is an outline of the plan.* Voici les grandes lignes du projet.
[2] les *contours* MASC PL (*shape*) ◇ *We could see the outline of the mountain in the mist.* Nous distinguions les contours de la montagne dans la brume.

outrageous ADJECTIVE
[1] (*behaviour*)
scandaleux MASC
scandaleuse FEM
[2] (*price*)
exorbitant

outset NOUN
le *début* ◇ *at the outset* dès le début

outside NOUN
| *see also* outside ADJECTIVE |
l' *extérieur* MASC

outside ADJECTIVE, ADVERB, PREPOSITION
| *see also* outside NOUN |
[1] *extérieur* ◇ *the outside walls* les murs extérieurs
[2] *dehors* ◇ *It's very cold outside.* Il fait très froid dehors.
[3] *en dehors de* ◇ *outside the school* en dehors de l'école ◇ *outside school hours* en dehors des heures de cours

outsize ADJECTIVE
énorme

outskirts PL NOUN
la *banlieue* ◇ *on the outskirts of the town* dans les banlieues de la ville

outstanding ADJECTIVE
remarquable

oval ADJECTIVE
ovale

oven NOUN
le *four*

over PREPOSITION, ADVERB, ADJECTIVE
| *When there is movement over something, use* **par-dessus**; *when something is located above something, use* **au-dessus de**. |
[1] *par-dessus* ◇ *The ball went over the wall.* Le ballon est passé par-dessus le mur.
[2] *au-dessus de* ◇ *There's a mirror over the washbasin.* Il y a une glace au-dessus du lavabo.
[3] *plus de* (*more than*) ◇ *It's over twenty kilos.* Ça pèse plus de vingt kilos. ◇ *The temperature was over thirty degrees.* Il faisait une température de plus de trente degrés.
[4] *pendant* (*during*) ◇ *over the holidays* pendant les vacances ◇ *over Christmas* pendant les fêtes de Noël
[5] *terminé* (*finished*) ◇ *I'll be happy when the exams are over.* Je serai content quand les examens seront terminés.

◆ **over here** ici

◆ **over there** là-bas

◆ **all over Scotland** dans toute l'Écosse

◆ **The baker's is over the road.** La boulangerie est de l'autre côté de la rue.

◆ **I spilled coffee over my shirt.** J'ai renversé du café sur ma chemise.

overall ADVERB
dans l'ensemble (*generally*) ◇ *My results were quite good overall.* Mes résultats étaient assez bons dans l'ensemble.

overalls PL NOUN
les *bleus de travail* MASC PL

to **overcharge** VERB

◆ **He overcharged me.** Il m'a fait payer trop cher.

◆ **They overcharged us for the meal.** Ils nous ont fait payer de trop pour le repas.

overdone ADJECTIVE
trop cuit (*food*)

overdose NOUN
l' *overdose* FEM (*of drugs*) ◇ *to take an overdose* prendre une overdose

to **overestimate** VERB
surestimer

overhead projector NOUN
le *rétroprojecteur*

to **overlook** VERB

[1] *donner sur* (have view of) ◇ *The hotel overlooked the beach.* L'hôtel donnait sur la plage.

[2] *négliger* (forget about) ◇ *He had overlooked one important problem.* Il avait négligé un problème important.

overseas ADVERB

à l'étranger ◇ *I'd like to work overseas.* J'aimerais travailler à l'étranger.

oversight NOUN

l' *oubli* MASC

to **oversleep** VERB

se réveiller en retard ◇ *I overslept this morning.* Je me suis réveillé en retard ce matin.

to **overtake** VERB

dépasser

overtime NOUN

les *heures supplémentaires* FEM PL ◇ *to work overtime* faire des heures supplémentaires

overweight ADJECTIVE

trop gros MASC

trop grosse FEM

to **owe** VERB

devoir

- **to owe somebody something** devoir

quelque chose à quelqu'un ◇ *I owe you 50 francs.* Je te dois cinquante francs.

owing to PREPOSITION

en raison de ◇ *owing to bad weather* en raison du mauvais temps

owl NOUN

le *hibou*

(les *hiboux* PL)

to **own** VERB

see also own ADJECTIVE

posséder

own ADJECTIVE

see also own VERB

propre ◇ *I've got my own bathroom.* J'ai ma propre salle de bain.

- **I'd like a room of my own.** J'aimerais avoir une chambre à moi.

- **on his own** tout seul ◇ *on her own* toute seule ◇ *on our own* tout seuls

owner NOUN

le/la *propriétaire*

oxygen NOUN

l' *oxygène* MASC

oyster NOUN

l' *huître* FEM

ozone layer NOUN

la *couche d'ozone*

P

PA NOUN
la _secrétaire de direction_ (personal
assistant) ◇ She's a PA. Elle est
secrétaire de direction.
- **the PA system** (public address) les
haut-parleurs

pace NOUN
l' _allure_ FEM (speed) ◇ He was walking at
a brisk pace. Il marchait à vive allure.

Pacific NOUN
le _Pacifique_

to **pack** VERB
see also pack NOUN
faire ses bagages ◇ I'll help you pack.
Je vais t'aider à faire tes bagages.
- **I've already packed my case.** J'ai déjà
fait ma valise.
- **Pack it in!** (stop it) Laisse tomber!

pack NOUN
see also pack VERB
1 le _paquet_ (packet) ◇ a pack of
cigarettes un paquet de cigarettes
2 le _pack_ (of yoghurts, cans) ◇ a six-pack
un pack de six
- **a pack of cards** un jeu de cartes

package NOUN
le _paquet_
- **a package holiday** un voyage organisé

packed ADJECTIVE
bondé ◇ The cinema was packed. Le
cinéma était bondé.

packed lunch NOUN
le _repas froid_ ◇ I take a packed lunch to
school. J'apporte un repas froid à
l'école.

packet NOUN
le _paquet_ ◇ a packet of cigarettes un
paquet de cigarettes

pad NOUN
(notepad)
le _bloc-notes_
(les _blocs-notes_ PL)

to **paddle** VERB
see also paddle NOUN
1 _pagayer_ (canoe)
2 _faire trempette_ (in water)

paddle NOUN
see also paddle VERB
la _pagaie_ (for canoe)
- **to go for a paddle** faire trempette

padlock NOUN
le _cadenas_

page NOUN
la _page_ (of book)

paid VERB see **pay**

paid ADJECTIVE
1 _rémunéré_ (work)
2 _payé_ ◇ 3 weeks' paid holiday trois
semaines de congés payés

pail NOUN
le _seau_
(les _seaux_ PL)

pain NOUN
la _douleur_ ◇ A terrible pain. une
douleur insupportable
- **I've got a pain in my stomach.** J'ai mal
à l'estomac.
- **to be in pain** souffrir ◇ She's in a lot of
pain. Elle souffre beaucoup.
- **He's a real pain.** Il est vraiment pénible.

painful ADJECTIVE
douloureux MASC
douloureuse FEM
◇ to suffer from painful periods souffrir de
règles douloureuses
- **Is it painful?** Ça te fait mal?

painkiller NOUN
l' _analgésique_ MASC

paint NOUN
see also paint VERB
la _peinture_

to **paint** VERB
see also paint NOUN
peindre ◇ to paint something green
peindre quelque chose en vert

paintbrush NOUN
le _pinceau_
(les _pinceaux_ PL)

painter NOUN
le _peintre_

painting NOUN
1 la _peinture_ ◇ My hobby is painting.
Je fais de la peinture.
2 (picture)
le _tableau_
(les _tableaux_ PL)
◇ a painting by Picasso un tableau de
Picasso

pair NOUN
la _paire_ ◇ a pair of shoes une paire de
chaussures ◇ a pair of scissors une paire
de ciseaux
- **a pair of trousers** un pantalon
- **a pair of jeans** un jean
- **a pair of pants (1)** (briefs) un slip
- **a pair of pants (2)** (boxer shorts) un
caleçon
- **in pairs** deux par deux ◇ We work in
pairs. Nous travaillons deux par deux.

Pakistan NOUN
le _Pakistan_
- **in Pakistan** au Pakistan

- **to Pakistan** au Pakistan
- **He's from Pakistan.** Il est pakistanais.

Pakistani NOUN

see also Pakistani ADJECTIVE

le *Pakistanais*

la *Pakistanaise*

Pakistani ADJECTIVE

see also Pakistani NOUN

pakistanais MASC

pakistanaise FEM

pal NOUN

le *copain*

la *copine*

palace NOUN

le *palais*

pale ADJECTIVE

pâle ◇ *a pale blue shirt* une chemise bleu pâle

Palestine NOUN

la *Palestine*

- **in Palestine** en Palestine

Palestinian ADJECTIVE

see also Palestinian NOUN

palestinien MASC

palestinienne FEM

Palestinian NOUN

see also Palestinian ADJECTIVE

le *Palestinien*

la *Palestinienne*

palm NOUN

la *paume* (of hand)

- **a palm tree** un palmier

pamphlet NOUN

la *brochure*

pan NOUN

1 la *casserole* (saucepan)

2 la *poêle* (frying pan)

pancake NOUN

la *crêpe*

panic NOUN

see also panic VERB

la *panique*

panic VERB

see also panic NOUN

s'affoler ◇ *Don't panic!* Pas de panique!

panther NOUN

la *panthère*

panties PL NOUN

le *slip* SING

pantomime NOUN

le *spectacle de Noël pour enfants*

pants PL NOUN

1 le *slip* SING (briefs) ◇ *a pair of pants* un slip

2 le *caleçon* SING (boxer shorts) ◇ *a pair of pants* un caleçon

paper NOUN

1 le *papier* ◇ *a piece of paper* un morceau de papier ◇ *a paper towel* une serviette en papier

2 (newspaper)

le *journal*

(les *journaux* PL)

◇ *I saw an advert in the paper.* J'ai vu une annonce dans le journal.

- **an exam paper** une épreuve écrite

paperback NOUN

le *livre de poche*

paper clip NOUN

le *trombone*

parachute NOUN

le *parachute*

parade NOUN

le *défilé*

paradise NOUN

le *paradis*

paraffin NOUN

le *pétrole* ◇ *a paraffin lamp* une lampe à pétrole

paragraph NOUN

le *paragraphe*

parallel ADJECTIVE

parallèle

paralysed ADJECTIVE

paralysé

parcel NOUN

le *colis*

pardon NOUN

- **Pardon?** Pardon?

parent NOUN

1 le *père* (father)

2 la *mère* (mother)

- **my parents** mes parents MASC

Paris NOUN

Paris FEM

- **in Paris** à Paris
- **to Paris** à Paris
- **She's from Paris.** Elle est parisienne.

Parisian ADJECTIVE

see also Parisian NOUN

parisien MASC

parisienne FEM

Parisian NOUN

see also Parisian ADJECTIVE

le *Parisien*

la *Parisienne*

park NOUN

see also park VERB

le *parc*

- **a national park** un parc national
- **a theme park** un parc à thème
- **a car park** un parking

to **park** VERB

see also park NOUN

1 *garer* ◇ *Where can I park my car?* Où est-ce que je peux garer ma voiture?

2 *se garer* ◇ *We couldn't find anywhere*

P

to park. Nous avons eu du mal à nous garer.

parking NOUN
le *stationnement* ◇ *"no parking"* "stationnement interdit"

parking meter NOUN
le *parcmètre*

parking ticket NOUN
le *p.-v.* (*informal*)

parliament NOUN
le *parlement*

parrot NOUN
le *perroquet*

parsley NOUN
le *persil*

part NOUN
1️⃣ la *partie* (*section*) ◇ *The first part of the film was boring.* La première partie du film était ennuyeuse.
2️⃣ la *pièce* (*component*) ◇ *spare parts* les pièces de rechange
3️⃣ le *rôle* (*in play, film*)
◆ **to take part in something** participer à quelque chose ◇ *A lot of people took part in the demonstration.* Beaucoup de gens ont participé à la manifestation.

particular ADJECTIVE
particulier MASC
particulière FEM
◇ *Are you looking for anything particular?* Est-ce que vous voulez quelque chose de particulier?
◆ **nothing in particular** rien de particulier

particularly ADVERB
particulièrement

parting NOUN
la *raie* (*in hair*)

partly ADVERB
en partie

partner NOUN
1️⃣ (*in game*)
le/la *partenaire*
2️⃣ (*in business*)
l' *associé* MASC
l' *associée* FEM
3️⃣ (*in dance*)
le *cavalier*
la *cavalière*
4️⃣ (*boyfriend*)
le *compagnon*
la *compagne* (*girlfriend*)

part-time ADJECTIVE, ADVERB
à temps partiel ◇ *a part-time job* un travail à temps partiel ◇ *She works part-time.* Elle travaille à temps partiel.

party NOUN
1️⃣ la *fête* ◇ *a birthday party* une fête d'anniversaire ◇ *a Christmas party* une fête de Noël ◇ *a New Year party* une

fête du Nouvel An
2️⃣ la *soirée* (*more formal*) ◇ *I'm going to a party on Saturday.* Je vais à une soirée samedi.
3️⃣ le *parti* (*political*) ◇ *the Conservative Party* le Parti conservateur
4️⃣ le *groupe* (*group*) ◇ *a party of tourists* un groupe de touristes

pass NOUN
see also pass VERB
1️⃣ le *col* (*in mountains*) ◇ *The pass was blocked with snow.* Le col était enneigé.
2️⃣ la *passe* (*in football*)
◆ **to get a pass** (*in exam*) être reçu ◇ *She got a pass in her piano exam.* Elle a été reçue à son examen de piano. ◇ *I got six passes.* J'ai été reçu dans six matières.
◆ **a bus pass** une carte de bus

to **pass** VERB
see also pass NOUN
1️⃣ *passer* ◇ *Could you pass me the salt, please?* Est-ce que vous pourriez me passer le sel, s'il vous plaît? ◇ *The time has passed quickly.* Le temps a passé rapidement.
2️⃣ *passer devant* ◇ *I pass his house on my way to school.* Je passe devant chez lui en allant à l'école.
3️⃣ *être reçu* (*exam*) ◇ *Did you pass?* Tu as été reçu?
◆ **to pass an exam** être reçu à un examen ◇ *I hope I'll pass the exam.* J'espère que je serai reçu à l'examen.

to **pass out** VERB
s'évanouir (*faint*)

passage NOUN
1️⃣ le *passage* (*piece of writing*) ◇ *Read the passage carefully.* Lisez attentivement le passage.
2️⃣ le *couloir* (*corridor*)

passenger NOUN
le *passager*
la *passagère*

passion NOUN
la *passion*

passive ADJECTIVE
passif MASC
passive FEM
◆ **passive smoking** le tabagisme passif

Passover NOUN
la *Pâque juive* ◇ *at Passover* à la Pâque juive

passport NOUN
le *passeport* ◇ *passport control* le contrôle des passeports

password NOUN
le *mot de passe*

past ADVERB, PREPOSITION
see also past NOUN

après (beyond) ◇ It's on the right, just past the station. C'est sur la droite, juste après la gare.

~ **to go past (1)** passer ◇ The bus went past without stopping. Le bus est passé sans s'arrêter.

~ **to go past (2)** passer devant ◇ The bus goes past our house. Le bus passe devant notre maison.

~ **It's half past ten.** Il est dix heures et demie.

~ **It's quarter past nine.** Il est neuf heures et quart.

~ **It's ten past eight.** Il est huit heures dix.

~ **It's past midnight.** Il est minuit passé.

past NOUN
┌──────────────────────────┐
│ see also past ADVERB │
└──────────────────────────┘
le _passé_ ◇ She lives in the past. Elle vit dans le passé.

~ **in the past** (previously) autrefois ◇ This was common in the past. C'était courant autrefois.

pasta NOUN
les _pâtes_ FEM PL ◇ Pasta is easy to cook. Les pâtes sont faciles à préparer.

paste NOUN
la _colle_ (glue)

pasteurized ADJECTIVE
pasteurisé

pastime NOUN
le _passe-temps_
(les _passe-temps_ PL)
◇ Her favourite pastime is knitting. Son passe-temps favori est le tricot.

pastry NOUN
la _pâte_

~ **pastries** les pâtisseries FEM

patch NOUN
① la _pièce_ ◇ a patch of material une pièce de tissu
② la _rustine_ (for flat tyre)

~ **He's got a bald patch.** Il a le crâne dégarni.

patched ADJECTIVE
rapiécé ◇ a pair of patched jeans un jean rapiécé

pâté NOUN
le _pâté_

path NOUN
① le _chemin_ (footpath)
② l' _allée_ FEM (in garden, park)

pathetic ADJECTIVE
lamentable ◇ Our team was pathetic. Notre équipe a été lamentable.

patience NOUN
① la _patience_ ◇ He hasn't got much patience. Il n'a pas beaucoup de patience.
② la _réussite_ (card game) ◇ to play

patience faire une réussite

patient NOUN
┌──────────────────────────┐
│ see also patient ADJECTIVE │
└──────────────────────────┘
le _patient_
la _patiente_

patient ADJECTIVE
┌──────────────────────────┐
│ see also patient NOUN │
└──────────────────────────┘
patient

patio NOUN
le _patio_

patriotic ADJECTIVE
patriote

patrol NOUN
la _patrouille_

patrol car NOUN
la _voiture de police_

pattern NOUN
le _motif_ ◇ a geometric pattern un motif géométrique

~ **a sewing pattern** un patron

pause NOUN
la _pause_

pavement NOUN
le _trottoir_

pavilion NOUN
le _pavillon_

paw NOUN
la _patte_

pay NOUN
┌──────────────────────────┐
│ see also pay VERB │
└──────────────────────────┘
le _salaire_

to **pay** VERB
┌──────────────────────────┐
│ see also pay NOUN │
└──────────────────────────┘
① _payer_ ◇ They pay me more on Sundays. Je suis payé davantage le dimanche.
② _régler_ ◇ to pay by cheque régler par chèque ◇ to pay by credit card régler par carte de crédit

~ **to pay for something** payer quelque chose ◇ I paid for my ticket. J'ai payé mon billet. ◇ I paid 50 francs for it. Je l'ai payé cinquante francs.

~ **to pay extra for something** payer un supplément pour quelque chose ◇ You have to pay extra for parking. Il faut payer un supplément pour le parking.

~ **to pay attention** faire attention ◇ Don't pay any attention to him! Ne fais pas attention à lui!

~ **to pay somebody a visit** rendre visite à quelqu'un ◇ Paul paid us a visit last night. Paul nous a rendu visite hier soir.

~ **to pay somebody back** rembourser quelqu'un ◇ I'll pay you back tomorrow. Je te rembourserai demain.

payment NOUN
le _paiement_

payphone NOUN

P

le *téléphone public*

PC NOUN (= *personal computer*)

le *PC* ◇ *She typed the report on her PC.*
Elle a tapé le rapport sur son PC.

pea NOUN
le *petit pois*

peace NOUN
[1] la *paix* (*after war*)
[2] le *calme* (*quietness*)

peaceful ADJECTIVE
[1] *paisible* (*calm*) ◇ *a peaceful
afternoon* un après-midi paisible
[2] *pacifique* (*not violent*) ◇ *a
peaceful protest* une manifestation
pacifique

peach NOUN
la *pêche*

peacock NOUN
le *paon*

peak NOUN
la *cime* (*of mountain*)

• **the peak rate** le plein tarif ◇ *You pay
the peak rate for calls at this time of day.*
On paie le plein tarif quand on appelle à
cette heure-ci.

• **in peak season** en haute saison

peanut NOUN
la *cacahuète* ◇ *a packet of peanuts* un
paquet de cacahuètes

peanut butter NOUN
le *beurre de cacahuètes* ◇ *a
peanut-butter sandwich* un sandwich au
beurre de cacahuètes

pear NOUN
la *poire*

pearl NOUN
la *perle*

pebble NOUN
le *galet* ◇ *a pebble beach* une plage de
galets

peculiar ADJECTIVE
bizarre ◇ *He's a peculiar person.* Il est
bizarre. ◇ *It tastes peculiar.* Ça a un goût
bizarre.

pedal NOUN
la *pédale*

pedestrian NOUN
le *piéton*

pedestrian crossing NOUN
le *passage pour piétons*

pedestrianized ADJECTIVE
• **a pedestrianized street** une rue
piétonne

pedigree ADJECTIVE
de race (*animal*) ◇ *a pedigree dog* un
chien de race ◇ *A pedigree labrador.* Un
labrador de pure race.

pee NOUN
• **to have a pee** faire pipi

peel NOUN
see also **peel** VERB
l' *écorce* FEM (*of orange*)

to **peel** VERB
see also **peel** NOUN
[1] *éplucher* ◇ *Shall I peel the potatoes?*
J'épluche les pommes de terre?
[2] *peler* ◇ *My nose is peeling.* Mon nez pèle.

peg NOUN
[1] (*for coats*)
le *portemanteau*
(les *portemanteaux* PL)
[2] (*clothes peg*)
la *pince à linge*
[3] (*tent peg*)
le *piquet*

Pekinese NOUN
le *pékinois*

pellet NOUN
le *plomb* (*for gun*)

pelvis NOUN
le *bassin*

pen NOUN
le *stylo*

to **penalize** VERB
pénaliser

penalty NOUN
[1] la *peine* (*punishment*)
• **the death penalty** la peine de mort
[2] le *penalty* (*in football*)
[3] la *pénalité* (*in rugby*)
• **a penalty shoot-out** les tirs au but

pence PL NOUN
les *pence* MASC PL

pencil NOUN
le *crayon*
• **in pencil** au crayon

pencil case NOUN
la *trousse*

pencil sharpener NOUN
le *taille-crayon*

pendant NOUN
le *pendentif*

penfriend NOUN
le *correspondant*
la *correspondante*

penguin NOUN
le *pingouin*

penicillin NOUN
la *pénicilline*

penis NOUN
le *pénis*

penknife NOUN
le *canif*

penny NOUN
le *penny*
(les *pence* PL)

pension NOUN
la *retraite*

pensioner NOUN
le *retraité*
la *retraitée*
pentathlon NOUN
le *pentathlon*
people PL NOUN
[1] les *gens* MASC   ◇ *The people were nice.* Les gens étaient sympathiques.
   ◇ *a lot of people* beaucoup de gens
[2] les *personnes* FEM (*individuals*)   ◇ *six people* six personnes ◇ *several people* plusieurs personnes
* **How many people are there in your family?** Vous êtes combien dans votre famille?
* **French people** les Français
* **black people** les Noirs
* **People say that...** On dit que...
pepper NOUN
[1] le *poivre* (*spice*)   ◇ *Pass the pepper, please.* Passez-moi le poivre, s'il vous plaît.
[2] le *poivron* (*vegetable*)   ◇ *a green pepper* un poivron vert
peppermill NOUN
le *moulin à poivre*
peppermint NOUN
la *pastille de menthe* (*sweet*)
* **peppermint chewing gum** le chewing-gum à la menthe
per PREPOSITION
par   ◇ *por day* par jour ◇ *per week* par semaine
* **30 miles per hour** trente miles à l'heure
per cent ADVERB
pour cent   ◇ *fifty per cent* cinquante pour cent
percolator NOUN
la *cafetière électrique*
percussion NOUN
la *percussion*   ◇ *I play percussion.* Je joue des percussions.
perfect ADJECTIVE
parfait   ◇ *Chantal speaks perfect English.* Chantal parle un anglais parfait.
perfectly ADVERB
parfaitement
perform VERB
jouer (*act, play*)
performance NOUN
[1] le *spectacle* (*show*)   ◇ *The performance lasts two hours.* Le spectacle dure deux heures.
[2] l' *interprétation* FEM (*acting*)   ◇ *his performance as Hamlet* son interprétation d'Hamlet
[3] la *performance* (*results*)   ◇ *the team's poor performance* la médiocre

performance de l'équipe
perfume NOUN
le *parfum*
perhaps ADVERB
peut-être   ◇ *a bit boring, perhaps* peut-être un peu ennuyeux ◇ *Perhaps he's ill.* Il est peut-être malade.
* **perhaps not** peut-être pas
period NOUN
[1] la *période*   ◇ *for a limited period* pour une période limitée
[2] l' *époque* FEM (*in history*)   ◇ *the Victorian period* l'époque victorienne
[3] les *règles* FEM (*menstruation*)   ◇ *I'm having my period.* J'ai mes règles.
[4] le *cours* (*lesson time*)   ◇ *Each period lasts forty minutes.* Chaque cours dure quarante minutes.
perm NOUN
la *permanente*   ◇ *She's got a perm.* Elle a une permanente.
* **to have a perm** se faire faire une permanente
permanent ADJECTIVE
permanent
permission NOUN
la *permission*   ◇ *Could I have permission to leave early?* Pourrais-je avoir la permission de partir plus tôt?
permit NOUN
le *permis*   ◇ *a fishing permit* un permis de pêche
to **persecute** VERB
persécuter
Persian ADJECTIVE
* **a Persian cat** un chat persan
persistent ADJECTIVE
tenace (*person*)
person NOUN
la *personne*   ◇ *She's a very nice person.* C'est une personne très sympathique.
* **in person** en personne
personal ADJECTIVE
personnel MASC
personnelle FEM
personality NOUN
la *personnalité*
personally ADVERB
personnellement   ◇ *I don't know him personally.* Je ne le connais pas personnellement. ◇ *Personally I don't agree.* Personnellement, je ne suis pas d'accord.
personal stereo NOUN
le *walkman* ®
personnel NOUN
le *personnel*
perspiration NOUN
la *transpiration*

to **persuade** VERB
persuader
- **to persuade somebody to do something** persuader quelqu'un de faire quelque chose ◇ *She persuaded me to go with her.* Elle m'a persuadé de l'accompagner.

pessimist NOUN
le/la *pessimiste* ◇ *I'm a pessimist.* Je suis pessimiste.

pessimistic ADJECTIVE
pessimiste

pest NOUN
le/la *casse-pieds* (person) ◇ *He's a real pest!* C'est un vrai casse-pieds!

to **pester** VERB
importuner

pet NOUN
l' *animal familier* MASC ◇ *Have you got a pet?* Est-ce que tu as un animal familier?
- **She's the teacher's pet.** C'est la chouchoute de la maîtresse.

petition NOUN
la *pétition*

petrified ADJECTIVE
pétrifié

petrol NOUN
l' *essence* FEM
- **unleaded petrol** l'essence sans plomb
- **leaded petrol** l'essence au plomb
- **4-star petrol, please.** Du super, s'il vous plaît.

petrol station NOUN
la *station-service*
(les *stations-service* PL)

petrol tank NOUN
le *réservoir d'essence*

phantom NOUN
le *fantôme*

pharmacy NOUN
la *pharmacie*
Pharmacies in France are identified by a special green cross outside the shop.

pheasant NOUN
le *faisan*

philosophy NOUN
la *philosophie*

phobia NOUN
la *phobie*

phone NOUN
see also phone VERB
le *téléphone* ◇ *Where's the phone?* Où est le téléphone? ◇ *Is there a phone here?* Est-ce qu'il y a un téléphone ici?
- **by phone** par téléphone
- **to be on the phone** être au téléphone ◇ *She's on the phone at the moment.* Elle est au téléphone en ce moment.

- **Can I use the phone, please?** Est-ce que je peux téléphoner, s'il vous plaît?

to **phone** VERB
see also phone NOUN
appeler ◇ *I'll phone the station.* Je vais appeler la gare.

phone bill NOUN
la *facture de téléphone*

phone book NOUN
l' *annuaire* MASC

phone box NOUN
la *cabine téléphonique*

phone call NOUN
l' *appel* MASC ◇ *There's a phone call for you.* Il y a un appel pour vous.
- **to make a phone call** téléphoner ◇ *Can I make a phone call?* Est-ce que je peux téléphoner?

phonecard NOUN
la *carte de téléphone*

phone number NOUN
le *numéro de téléphone*

photo NOUN
la *photo*
- **to take a photo** prendre une photo
- **to take a photo of somebody** prendre quelqu'un en photo

photocopier NOUN
la *photocopieuse*

photocopy NOUN
see also photocopy VERB
la *photocopie*

to **photocopy** VERB
see also photocopy NOUN
photocopier

photograph NOUN
see also photograph VERB
la *photo*
- **to take a photograph** prendre une photo
- **to take a photograph of somebody** prendre quelqu'un en photo

to **photograph** VERB
see also photograph NOUN
photographier

photographer NOUN
le/la *photographe* ◇ *She's a photographer.* Elle est photographe.

photography NOUN
la *photo* ◇ *My hobby is photography.* Je fais de la photo.

phrase NOUN
l' *expression* FEM

phrase book NOUN
le *guide de conversation*

physical ADJECTIVE
physique

physicist NOUN
le *physicien*
la *physicienne*

He's a physicist. Il est physicien.

physics NOUN
la *physique*   ◇ *She teaches physics.*
Elle enseigne la physique.

physiotherapist NOUN
le/la *kinésithérapeute*

physiotherapy NOUN
la *kinésithérapie*

pianist NOUN
le/la *pianiste*

piano NOUN
le *piano*   ◇ *I play the piano.* Je joue du
piano.   ◇ *I have piano lessons.* Je prends
des leçons de piano.

pick NOUN
| see also pick VERB |

* **Take your pick!** Faites votre choix!
to **pick** VERB
| see also pick NOUN |
1 *choisir* (*choose*)   ◇ *I picked the biggest
piece.* J'ai choisi le plus gros morceau.
2 *sélectionner* (*for team*)   ◇ *I've been
picked for the team.* J'ai été sélectionné
pour faire partie de l'équipe.
3 *cueillir* (*fruit, flowers*)

* **to pick on somebody** harceler
quelqu'un   ◇ *She's always picking on
me.* Elle me harcèle constamment.

* **to pick out** choisir   ◇ *I like them all—it's
difficult to pick one out.* Ils me plaisent
tous—c'est difficile d'en choisir un.

* **to pick up (1)** (*collect*) venir chercher
◇ *We'll come to the airport to pick you up.*
Nous irons vous chercher à l'aéroport.

* **to pick up (2)** (*from floor*) ramasser
◇ *Could you help me pick up the toys?* Tu
peux m'aider à ramasser les jouets?

* **to pick up (3)** (*learn*) apprendre   ◇ *I
picked up some Spanish during my
holiday.* J'ai appris quelque mots
d'espagnol pendant mes vacances.

pickpocket NOUN
le *pickpocket*

picnic NOUN
le *pique-nique*

* **to have a picnic** pique-niquer   ◇ *We
had a picnic on the beach.* Nous avons
pique-niqué sur la plage.

picture NOUN
1 l' *illustration* FEM   ◇ *Children's books
have lots of pictures.* Il y a beaucoup
d'illustrations dans les livres pour
enfants.
2 la *photo*   ◇ *My picture was in the
paper.* Ma photo était dans le journal.
3 (*painting*)
le *tableau*
(les *tableaux* PL)
◇ *a famous picture* un tableau célèbre

* **to paint a picture of something** peindre
quelque chose
4 (*drawing*)
le *dessin*

* **to draw a picture of something** dessiner
quelque chose

* **the pictures** (*cinema*) le cinéma   ◇ *Shall
we go to the pictures?* On va au cinéma?

picturesque ADJECTIVE
pittoresque

pie NOUN
la *tourte*   ◇ *an apple pie* une tourte aux
pommes

piece NOUN
le *morceau*
(les *morceaux* PL)
◇ *A small piece, please.* Un petit
morceau, s'il vous plaît.

* **a piece of furniture** un meuble
* **a piece of advice** un conseil

pier NOUN
la *jetée*

pierced ADJECTIVE
percé   ◇ *I've got pierced ears.* J'ai les
oreilles percées.

pig NOUN
le *cochon*

pigeon NOUN
le *pigeon*

piggy bank NOUN
la *tirelire*

pigtail NOUN
la *natte*

pile NOUN
1 le *tas* (*untidy heap*)
2 la *pile* (*tidy stack*)

pill NOUN
la *pilule*

* **to be on the pill** prendre la pilule

pillar NOUN
le *pilier*

pillar box NOUN
la *boîte aux lettres*

pillow NOUN
l' *oreiller* MASC

pilot NOUN
le *pilote*   ◇ *He's a pilot.* Il est pilote.

pimple NOUN
le *bouton*

pin NOUN
l' *épingle* FEM

* **I've got pins and needles.** J'ai des
fourmis dans les jambes.

PIN NOUN (= *personal identification number*)
le *code confidentiel*

pinafore NOUN
le *tablier*

pinball NOUN
le *flipper*   ◇ *to play pinball* jouer au

flipper
- **a pinball machine** un flipper

to **pinch** VERB
   1 *pincer* ◇ He pinched me! Il m'a pincé!
   2 *piquer* (informal: steal) ◇ Who's pinched my pen? Qui est-ce qui m'a piqué mon stylo?

pine NOUN
   le *pin* ◇ a pine table une table en pin

pineapple NOUN
   l' *ananas* MASC

pink ADJECTIVE
   rose

pint NOUN
   la *pinte*
   In France measurements are in litres and centilitres. A pint is about 0.6 litres.
- **to have a pint** boire une bière ◇ He's gone out for a pint. Il est parti boire une bière.

pipe NOUN
   1 la *conduite* (for water, gas) ◇ The pipes froze. Les conduites d'eau ont gelé.
   2 la *pipe* (for smoking) ◇ He smokes a pipe. Il fume la pipe.
- **the pipes** (bagpipes) la cornemuse ◇ He plays the pipes. Il joue de la cornemuse.

pirate NOUN
   le *pirate*

pirated ADJECTIVE
   pirate ◇ a pirated video une vidéo pirate

Pisces NOUN
   les *Poissons* MASC ◇ I'm Pisces. Je suis Poissons.

pissed ADJECTIVE
   bourré (informal)

pistol NOUN
   le *pistolet*

pitch NOUN
   see also pitch VERB
   le *terrain* ◇ a football pitch un terrain de football

to **pitch** VERB
   see also pitch NOUN
   dresser (tent) ◇ We pitched our tent near the beach. Nous avons dressé notre tente près de la plage.

pity NOUN
   see also pity VERB
   la *pitié*
- **What a pity!** Quel dommage!

to **pity** VERB
   see also pity NOUN
   plaindre

pizza NOUN
   la *pizza*

place NOUN
   see also place VERB
   1 l' *endroit* MASC (location) ◇ It's a quiet place. C'est un endroit tranquille. ◇ There are a lot of interesting places to visit. Il y a beaucoup d'endroits intéressants à visiter.
   2 la *place* (space) ◇ a parking place une place de parking ◇ a university place une place à l'université
- **to change places** changer de place ◇ Tamsin, change places with Delphine! Tamsin, change de place avec Delphine!
- **to take place** avoir lieu
- **at your place** chez toi ◇ Shall we meet at your place? On se retrouve chez toi?
- **to my place** chez moi ◇ Do you want to come round to my place? Tu veux venir chez moi?

to **place** VERB
   see also place NOUN
   1 *poser* ◇ He placed his hand on hers. Il a posé la main sur la sienne.
   2 *classer* (in competition, contest)

plaid ADJECTIVE
   écossais ◇ a plaid shirt une chemise écossaise

plain NOUN
   see also plain ADJECTIVE
   la *plaine*

plain ADJECTIVE, ADVERB
   see also plain NOUN
   1 *uni* (not patterned) ◇ a plain carpet un tapis uni
   2 *simple* (not fancy) ◇ a plain white blouse un simple chemisier blanc

plain chocolate NOUN
   le *chocolat à croquer*

plait NOUN
   la *natte* ◇ She wears her hair in a plait. Elle a une natte.

plan NOUN
   see also plan VERB
   1 le *projet* ◇ What are your plans for the holidays? Quels sont tes projets pour les vacances? ◇ to make plans faire des projets
- **Everything went according to plan.** Tout s'est passé comme prévu.
   2 le *plan* (map) ◇ a plan of the campsite un plan du terrain de camping
- **my essay plan** le plan de ma dissertation

to **plan** VERB
   see also plan NOUN
   1 *préparer* (make plans for) ◇ We're planning a trip to France. Nous préparons un voyage en France.
   2 *planifier* (make schedule for) ◇ Plan

your revision carefully. Planifiez vos révisions avec soin.
- **to plan to do something** avoir l'intention de faire quelque chose ◇ *I'm planning to get a job in the holidays.* J'ai l'intention de trouver un job pour les vacances.

plane NOUN
l' *avion* MASC ◇ *by plane* en avion

planet NOUN
la *planète*

planning NOUN
la *préparation* ◇ *The trip needs careful planning.* Le voyage nécessite une préparation méticuleuse.
- **family planning** le planning familial

plant NOUN
see also plant VERB
[1] la *plante* ◇ *to water the plants* arroser les plantes
[2] l' *usine* FEM *(factory)*

to **plant** VERB
see also plant NOUN
planter

plaster NOUN
[1] le *pansement adhésif* *(sticking plaster)* ◇ *Have you got a plaster, by any chance?* Vous n'auriez pas un pansement adhésif, par hasard?
[2] le *plâtre* *(for fracture)* ◇ *Her leg's in plaster.* Elle a la jambe dans le plâtre.

plastic NOUN
see also plastic ADJECTIVE
le *plastique* ◇ *It's made of plastic.* C'est en plastique.

plastic ADJECTIVE
see also plastic NOUN
en plastique ◇ *a plastic bag* un sac en plastique ◇ *a plastic mac* un imperméable en plastique

plate NOUN
l' *assiette* FEM *(for food)*

platform NOUN
[1] le *quai* *(at station)* ◇ *on platform 7* sur le quai numéro sept
[2] l' *estrade* FEM *(for performers)*

play NOUN
see also play VERB
la *pièce* ◇ *a play by Shakespeare* une pièce de Shakespeare
- **to put on a play** monter une pièce

to **play** VERB
see also play NOUN
[1] *jouer* ◇ *He's playing with his friends.* Il joue avec ses amis. ◇ *What sort of music do they play?* Quel genre de musique jouent-ils?
[2] *jouer contre* *(against person, team)* ◇ *France will play Scotland next month.*

La France jouera contre l'Écosse le mois prochain.
[3] *jouer à* *(sport, game)* ◇ *I play hockey.* Je joue au hockey. ◇ *Can you play pool?* Tu sais jouer au billard américain?
[4] *jouer de* *(instrument)* ◇ *I play the guitar.* Je joue de la guitare.
[5] *écouter* *(record, cassette, music)* ◇ *She's always playing that record.* Elle écoute tout le temps ce disque.

player NOUN
[1] *(of sport)*
le *joueur*
la *joueuse*
◇ *a football player* un joueur de football
[2] *(of instrument)*
le *musicien*
la *musicienne*
- **a piano player** un pianiste
- **a saxophone player** un saxophoniste

playful ADJECTIVE
espiègle

playground NOUN
[1] la *cour de récréation* *(at school)*
[2] l' *aire de jeux* FEM *(in park)*

playgroup NOUN
la *garderie*

playing field NOUN
le *terrain de sport*

playtime NOUN
la *récréation*

playwright NOUN
le *dramaturge*

pleasant ADJECTIVE
agréable

please EXCLAMATION
[1] *s'il vous plaît* *(polite form)* ◇ *Two coffees, please.* Deux cafés, s'il vous plaît.
[2] *s'il te plaît* *(familiar form)* ◇ *Please write back soon.* Réponds vite, s'il te plaît.

pleased ADJECTIVE
content ◇ *My mother's not going to be very pleased.* Ma mère ne va pas être contente du tout. ◇ *It's beautiful: she'll be pleased with it.* C'est beau: elle va être contente.
- **Pleased to meet you!** Enchanté!

pleasure NOUN
le *plaisir* ◇ *I read for pleasure.* Je lis pour le plaisir.

plenty NOUN
largement assez ◇ *I've got plenty.* J'en ai largement assez. ◇ *That's plenty, thanks.* Ça suffit largement, merci.
- **plenty of (1)** *(a lot)* beaucoup de ◇ *I've got plenty to do.* J'ai beaucoup de choses à faire.
- **plenty of (2)** *(enough)* largement assez de

◦ *I've got plenty of money.* J'ai largement assez d'argent. ◦ *We've got plenty of time.* Nous avons largement le temps.

plot NOUN
> see also plot VERB

1 l' *intrigue* FEM (*of story, play*)
2 la *conspiration* (*against somebody*) ◦ *a plot against the president* une conspiration contre le président
3 le *carré* (*of land*) ◦ *a vegetable plot* un carré de légumes

to **plot** VERB
> see also plot NOUN

comploter ◦ *They were plotting to kill him.* Ils complotaient de le tuer.

plough NOUN
> see also plough VERB

la *charrue*

to **plough** VERB
> see also plough NOUN

labourer

plug NOUN
1 la *prise de courant* (*electrical*) ◦ *The plug is faulty.* La prise est défectueuse.
2 le *bouchon* (*for sink*)

to **plug in** VERB
brancher ◦ *Is it plugged in?* Est-ce que c'est branché?

plum NOUN
la *prune* ◦ *plum jam* la confiture de prunes

plumber NOUN
le *plombier* ◦ *He's a plumber.* Il est plombier.

plump ADJECTIVE
dodu

to **plunge** VERB
plonger

plural NOUN
le *pluriel*

plus PREPOSITION, ADJECTIVE
plus ◦ *4 plus 3 equals 7.* Quatre plus trois égalent sept. ◦ *three children plus a dog* trois enfants plus un chien
➤ *I got a B plus.* J'ai eu un Bien.

p.m. ABBREVIATION
➤ *at 8 p.m.* à huit heures du soir
> *In France times are often given using the 24-hour clock.*

➤ *at 2 p.m.* à quatorze heures

pneumonia NOUN
la *pneumonie*

poached ADJECTIVE
poché ◦ *a poached egg* un œuf poché

pocket NOUN
la *poche*
➤ **pocket money** l'argent de poche MASC
◦ *£8 a week pocket money* huit livres d'argent de poche par semaine

pocket calculator NOUN
la *calculette*

poem NOUN
le *poème*

poet NOUN
le *poète*

poetry NOUN
la *poésie*

point NOUN
> see also point VERB

1 le *point* (*spot, score*) ◦ *a point on the horizon* un point à l'horizon ◦ *They scored 5 points.* Ils ont marqué cinq points.
2 la *remarque* (*comment*) ◦ *He made some interesting points.* Il a fait quelque remarques intéressantes.
3 la *pointe* (*tip*) ◦ *a pencil with a sharp point* un crayon à la pointe aiguisée
4 le *moment* (*in time*) ◦ *At that point, we decided to leave.* À ce moment-là, nous avons décidé de partir.

➤ **a point of view** un point de vue
➤ **to get the point** comprendre ◦ *Sorry, I don't get the point.* Désolé, je ne comprends pas.
➤ **That's a good point!** C'est vrai!
➤ **There's no point.** Cela ne sert à rien. ◦ *There's no point in waiting.* Cela ne sert à rien d'attendre.
➤ **What's the point?** À quoi bon? ◦ *What's the point of leaving so early?* À quoi bon partir si tôt?
➤ **Punctuality isn't my strong point.** La ponctualité n'est pas mon fort.
➤ **two point five (2.5)** deux virgule cinq (2,5)

to **point** VERB
> see also point NOUN

montrer du doigt ◦ *Don't point!* Ne montre pas du doigt!
➤ **to point at somebody** montrer quelqu'un du doigt ◦ *She pointed at Anne.* Elle a montré Anne du doigt.
➤ **to point a gun at somebody** braquer un revolver sur quelqu'un
➤ **to point something out (1)** (*show*) montrer quelque chose ◦ *The guide pointed out Notre-Dame to us.* Le guide nous a montré Notre-Dame.
➤ **to point something out (2)** (*mention*) signaler quelque chose ◦ *I should point out that...* Je dois vous signaler que...

pointless ADJECTIVE
inutile ◦ *It's pointless to argue.* Il est inutile de discuter.

poison NOUN
> see also poison VERB

le *poison*

to **poison** VERB
  see also poison NOUN
  empoisonner
poisonous ADJECTIVE
  1 (*snake*)
  venimeux MASC
  venimeuse FEM
  2 (*plant, mushroom*)
  vénéneux MASC
  vénéneuse FEM
  3 (*gas*)
  toxique
poker NOUN
  le *poker* ◦ *I play poker.* Je joue au poker.
Poland NOUN
  la *Pologne*
  ◆ **in Poland** en Pologne
  ◆ **to Poland** en Pologne
polar bear NOUN
  l' *ours blanc* MASC
Pole NOUN
  (*Polish person*)
  le *Polonais*
  la *Polonaise*
pole NOUN
  le *poteau*
  (les *poteaux* PL)
  ◦ *a telegraph pole* un poteau télégraphique
  ◆ **a tent pole** un montant de tente
  ◆ **a ski pole** un bâton de ski
  ◆ **the North Pole** le pôle Nord
  ◆ **the South Pole** le pôle Sud
pole vault NOUN
  le *saut à la perche*
police PL NOUN
  la *police* ◦ *We called the police.* Nous avons appelé la police.
  ◆ **a police car** une voiture de police
  ◆ **a police station** un commissariat de police
policeman NOUN
  le *policier* ◦ *He's a policeman.* Il est policier.
policewoman NOUN
  la *femme policier* ◦ *She's a policewoman.* Elle est femme policier.
polio NOUN
  la *polio*
Polish ADJECTIVE
  see also Polish NOUN
  polonais
Polish NOUN
  see also Polish ADJECTIVE
  le *polonais* (*language*)
polish NOUN
  see also polish VERB
  1 le *cirage* (*for shoes*)

  2 la *cire* (*for furniture*)
to **polish** VERB
  see also polish NOUN
  1 *cirer* (*shoes, furniture*)
  2 *faire briller* (*glass*)
polite ADJECTIVE
  poli
politely ADVERB
  poliment
politeness NOUN
  la *politesse*
political ADJECTIVE
  politique
politician NOUN
  le *politicien*
  la *politicienne*
politics PL NOUN
  la *politique* SING ◦ *I'm not interested in politics.* La politique ne m'intéresse pas.
pollen NOUN
  le *pollen*
to **pollute** VERB
  polluer
polluted ADJECTIVE
  pollué
pollution NOUN
  la *pollution*
polo-necked sweater NOUN
  le *pull à col roulé*
polo shirt NOUN
  le *polo*
polythene bag NOUN
  le *sac en plastique*
pond NOUN
  1 l' *étang* MASC (*big*)
  2 la *mare* (*smaller*)
  3 le *bassin* ◦ *We've got a pond in our garden.* Nous avons un bassin dans notre jardin.
pony NOUN
  le *poney*
ponytail NOUN
  la *queue de cheval* ◦ *He's got a ponytail.* Il a une queue de cheval.
pony trekking NOUN
  ◆ **to go pony trekking** faire une randonnée à dos de poney
poodle NOUN
  le *caniche*
pool NOUN
  1 la *flaque* (*puddle*)
  2 l' *étang* MASC (*pond*)
  3 la *piscine* (*for swimming*)
  4 le *billard américain* (*game*) ◦ *Shall we have a game of pool?* Si on jouait au billard américain?
  ◆ **the pools** (*football*) le loto sportif ◦ *to do the pools* jouer au loto sportif
poor ADJECTIVE

1 *pauvre* ◇ *a poor family* une famille pauvre ◇ *Poor David, he's very unlucky!* Le pauvre David, il n'a vraiment pas de chance!

* **the poor** les pauvres MASC

2 *médiocre* (*bad*) ◇ *a poor mark* une note médiocre

poorly ADJECTIVE
souffrant ◇ *She's poorly.* Elle est souffrante.

pop ADJECTIVE
pop ◇ *pop music* la musique pop ◇ *a pop star* une pop star ◇ *a pop group* un groupe pop ◇ *a pop song* une chanson pop

popcorn NOUN
le *pop-corn*

pope NOUN
le *pape*

poppy NOUN
le *coquelicot*

popular ADJECTIVE
populaire ◇ *She's a very popular girl.* C'est une fille très populaire. ◇ *This is a very popular style.* C'est un style très populaire.

population NOUN
la *population*

porch NOUN
le *porche*

pork NOUN
le *porc* ◇ *a pork chop* une côtelette de porc ◇ *I don't eat pork.* Je ne mange pas de porc.

porn NOUN
see also porn ADJECTIVE
le *porno*

porn ADJECTIVE
see also porn NOUN
porno MASC, FEM, PL ◇ *a porn film* un film porno ◇ *a porn mag* un magazine porno

pornographic ADJECTIVE
pornographique ◇ *a pornographic magazine* un magazine pornographique

pornography NOUN
la *pornographie*

porridge NOUN
le *porridge*

port NOUN
1 le *port* (*harbour*)
2 le *porto* (*wine*) ◇ *a glass of port* un verre de porto

porter NOUN
1 le *portier* (*in hotel*)
2 le *porteur* (*at station*)

portion NOUN
la *portion* ◇ *a large portion of chips* une grosse portion de frites

portrait NOUN
le *portrait*

Portugal NOUN
le *Portugal*

* **in Portugal** au Portugal
* **We went to Portugal.** Nous sommes allés au Portugal.

Portuguese ADJECTIVE
see also Portuguese NOUN
portugais

Portuguese NOUN
see also Portuguese ADJECTIVE
1 (*person*)
le *Portugais*
la *Portugaise*
2 (*language*)
le *portugais*

posh ADJECTIVE
chic MASC, FEM, PL ◇ *a posh hotel* un hôtel chic

position NOUN
la *position* ◇ *an uncomfortable position* une position inconfortable

positive ADJECTIVE
1 (*good*)
positif MASC
positive FEM
◇ *a positive attitude* une attitude positive
2 (*sure*)
certain ◇ *I'm positive.* J'en suis certain.

to **possess** VERB
posséder

possession NOUN
* **Have you got all your possessions?** Est-ce tu as toutes tes affaires?

possibility NOUN
* **It's a possibility.** C'est possible.

possible ADJECTIVE
possible ◇ *as soon as possible* aussitôt que possible

possibly ADVERB
peut-être (*perhaps*) ◇ *Are you coming to the party?—Possibly.* Est-ce que tu viens à la soirée?—Peut-être.
* **...if you possibly can.** ...si cela vous est possible.
* **I can't possibly come.** Je ne peux vraiment pas venir.

post NOUN
see also post VERB
1 (*letters*)
le *courrier* ◇ *Is there any post for me?* Est-ce qu'il y a du courrier pour moi?
2 (*pole*)
le *poteau*
(les *poteaux* PL)
◇ *The ball hit the post.* Le ballon a heurté le poteau.

to **post** VERB
> see also post NOUN
> _poster_ ◇ I've got some cards to post.
J'ai quelques cartes à poster.

postage NOUN
l' _affranchissement_ MASC

postbox NOUN
la _boîte aux lettres_

postcard NOUN
la _carte postale_

postcode NOUN
le _code postal_

poster NOUN
1 le _poster_ ◇ I've got posters on my
bedroom walls. J'ai des posters sur les
murs de ma chambre.
2 l' _affiche_ FEM (advertising) ◇ There are
posters all over town. Il y a des affiches
dans toute la ville.

postman NOUN
le _facteur_ ◇ He's a postman. Il est
facteur.

postmark NOUN
le _cachet de la poste_

post office NOUN
la _poste_ ◇ Where's the post office,
please? Où est la poste, s'il vous plaît?
◇ She works for the post office. Elle
travaille à la poste.

to **postpone** VERB
remettre à plus tard ◇ The match has
been postponed. Le match a été remis à
plus tard.

postwoman NOUN
la _factrice_ ◇ She's a postwoman. Elle
est factrice.

pot NOUN
1 le _pot_ ◇ a pot of jam un pot de
confiture
2 la _théière_ (teapot)
3 la _cafetière_ (coffeepot)
4 l' _herbe_ FEM (marijuana) ◇ to smoke
pot fumer de l'herbe
- **the pots and pans** les casseroles

potato NOUN
la _pomme de terre_ ◇ potato salad la
salade de pommes de terre
- **mashed potatoes** la purée
- **a baked potato** une pomme de terre en
robe des champs

potential NOUN
> see also potential ADJECTIVE
- **He has great potential.** Il a de l'avenir.

potential ADJECTIVE
> see also potential NOUN
possible ◇ a potential problem un
problème possible

pothole NOUN
le _nid de poule_ (in road)

pot plant NOUN
la _plante en pot_

pottery NOUN
la _poterie_

pound NOUN
> see also pound VERB
la _livre_ (weight, money) ◇ a pound of
carrots une livre de carottes ◇ How
many francs do you get for a pound?
Combien de francs a-t-on pour une
livre? ◇ a pound coin une pièce d'une
livre

to **pound** VERB
> see also pound NOUN
battre ◇ My heart was pounding.
J'avais le cœur qui battait.

to **pour** VERB
1 _verser_ (liquid) ◇ She poured some
water into the pan. Elle a versé de l'eau
dans la casserole.
- **She poured him a drink.** Elle lui a servi
à boire.
- **Shall I pour you a cup of tea?** Je vous
sers une tasse de thé?
2 _pleuvoir à verse_ (rain) ◇ It's pouring.
Il pleut à verse.
- **in the pouring rain** sous une pluie
torrentielle

poverty NOUN
la _pauvreté_

powder NOUN
la _poudre_

power NOUN
1 le _courant_ (electricity) ◇ The power's
off. Le courant est coupé.
- **a power cut** une coupure de courant
- **a power point** une prise de courant
- **a power station** une centrale électrique
2 l' _énergie_ FEM (energy) ◇ nuclear
power l'énergie nucléaire ◇ solar power
l'énergie solaire
3 le _pouvoir_ (authority) ◇ to be in power
être au pouvoir

powerful ADJECTIVE
puissant

practical ADJECTIVE
pratique ◇ a practical suggestion un
conseil pratique
- **She's very practical.** Elle a l'esprit
pratique.

practically ADVERB
pratiquement ◇ It's practically
impossible. C'est pratiquement
impossible.

practice NOUN
l' _entraînement_ MASC (for sport)
◇ football practice l'entraînement de foot
- **I've got to do my piano practice.** Je dois
travailler mon piano

P

- **It's normal practice in our school.** C'est ce qui se fait dans notre école.
- **in practice** en pratique
- **a medical practice** un cabinet médical

to **practise** VERB

   1 *s'exercer* (*music, hobby*) ◇ *I ought to practise more.* Je devrais m'exercer davantage.

   2 *travailler* (*instrument*) ◇ *I practise the flute every evening.* Je travaille ma flûte tous les soirs.

   3 *pratiquer* (*language*) ◇ *I practised my French when we were on holiday.* J'ai pratiqué mon français pendant les vacances.

   4 *s'entraîner* (*sport*) ◇ *The team practises on Thursdays.* L'équipe s'entraîne le jeudi. ◇ *I don't practise enough.* Je ne m'entraîne pas assez.

practising ADJECTIVE

   pratiquant ◇ *She's a practising Catholic.* Elle est catholique pratiquante.

pram NOUN

   le *landau*

prawn NOUN

   la *crevette*

prawn cocktail NOUN

   le *cocktail de crevettes*

to **pray** VERB

   prier ◇ *to pray for something* prier pour quelque chose

prayer NOUN

   la *prière*

precaution NOUN

   la *précaution*

- **to take precautions** prendre ses précautions

preceding ADJECTIVE

   précédent

precinct NOUN

- **a shopping precinct** un centre commercial
- **a pedestrian precinct** une zone piétonnière

precious ADJECTIVE

   précieux MASC

   précieuse FEM

precise ADJECTIVE

   précis ◇ *at that precise moment* à cet instant précis

precisely ADVERB

   précisément ◇ *Precisely!* Précisément!

- **at 10 a.m. precisely** à dix heures précises

to **predict** VERB

   prédire

predictable ADJECTIVE

   prévisible

prefect NOUN

French schools do not have prefects. You could explain what a prefect is using the example given.

- **My sister's a prefect.** Ma sœur est en dernière année et est chargée de maintenir la discipline.

to **prefer** VERB

   préférer ◇ *Which would you prefer?* Lequel préfères-tu? ◇ *I prefer French to chemistry.* Je préfère le français à la chimie.

preference NOUN

   la *préférence*

pregnant ADJECTIVE

   enceinte ◇ *She's six months pregnant.* Elle est enceinte de six mois.

prehistoric ADJECTIVE

   préhistorique

prejudice NOUN

   1 le *préjugé* ◇ *That's just a prejudice.* C'est un préjugé.

   2 les *préjugés* MASC PL ◇ *There's a lot of racial prejudice.* Il y a beaucoup de préjugés raciaux.

prejudiced ADJECTIVE

- **to be prejudiced against somebody** avoir des préjugés contre quelqu'un

premature ADJECTIVE

   prématuré

- **a premature baby** un prématuré

Premier League NOUN

   la *première division* ◇ *in the Premier League* en première division

premises PL NOUN

   les *locaux* MASC ◇ *They're moving to new premises.* Ils vont occuper de nouveaux locaux.

premonition NOUN

   la *prémonition*

preoccupied ADJECTIVE

   préoccupé

prep NOUN

   les *devoirs* MASC PL (*homework*) ◇ *history prep* les devoirs d'histoire

preparation NOUN

   la *préparation*

to **prepare** VERB

   préparer ◇ *She has to prepare lessons in the evening.* Elle doit préparer ses cours le soir.

- **to prepare for something** se préparer pour quelque chose ◇ *We're preparing for our skiing holiday.* Nous nous préparons pour nos vacances à la neige.

prepared ADJECTIVE

- **to be prepared to do something** être prêt à faire quelque chose ◇ *I'm prepared to help you.* Je suis prêt à t'aider.

prep school NOUN

   l' *école primaire privée* FEM

Presbyterian NOUN
see also Presbyterian ADJECTIVE
le *presbytérien*
la *presbytérienne*
Presbyterian ADJECTIVE
see also Presbyterian NOUN
presbytérien MASC
presbytérienne FEM
to **prescribe** VERB
prescrire
prescription NOUN
l' *ordonnance* FEM ◇ *You can't get it without a prescription.* On ne peut pas se le procurer sans ordonnance.
presence NOUN
la *présence*
◆ **presence of mind** présence d'esprit
present ADJECTIVE
see also present NOUN, VERB
1 (*in attendance*)
présent ◇ *He wasn't present at the meeting.* Il n'était pas présent à la réunion.
2 (*current*)
actuel MASC
actuelle FEM
◇ *the present situation* la situation actuelle
◆ **the present tense** le présent
present NOUN
see also present ADJECTIVE, VERB
1 (*gift*)
le *cadeau*
(les *cadeaux* PL)
◇ *I'm going to buy presents.* Je vais acheter des cadeaux.
◆ **to give somebody a present** offrir un cadeau à quelqu'un
2 (*time*)
le *présent* ◇ *up to the present* jusqu'à présent
◆ **for the present** pour l'instant
◆ **at present** en ce moment
to **present** VERB
see also present ADJECTIVE, NOUN
◆ **to present somebody with something** (*prize, medal*) remettre quelque chose à quelqu'un
presenter NOUN
(*on TV*)
le *présentateur*
la *présentatrice*
presently ADVERB
1 *bientôt* (*soon*) ◇ *You'll feel better presently.* Tu vas bientôt te sentir mieux.
2 *actuellement* (*at present*) ◇ *They're presently on tour.* Ils sont actuellement en tournée.
president NOUN

le *président*
la *présidente*
press NOUN
see also press VERB
la *presse*
◆ **a press conference** une conférence de presse
to **press** VERB
see also press NOUN
1 *appuyer* ◇ *Don't press too hard!* N'appuie pas trop fort!
2 *appuyer sur* ◇ *He pressed the accelerator.* Il a appuyé sur l'accélérateur.
pressed ADJECTIVE
◆ **We are pressed for time.** Le temps nous manque.
press-up NOUN
◆ **to do press-ups** faire des pompes ◇ *I do twenty press-ups every morning.* Je fais vingt pompes tous les matins.
pressure NOUN
see also pressure VERB
la *pression* ◇ *He's under a lot of pressure at work.* Il est sous pression au travail.
◆ **a pressure group** un groupe de pression
to **pressure** VERB
see also pressure NOUN
faire pression sur ◇ *My parents are pressuring me.* Mes parents font pression sur moi.
prestige NOUN
le *prestige*
prestigious ADJECTIVE
prestigieux MASC
prestigieuse FEM
presumably ADVERB
vraisemblablement
to **presume** VERB
supposer ◇ *I presume so.* Je suppose que oui.
to **pretend** VERB
◆ **to pretend to do something** faire semblant de faire quelque chose ◇ *He pretended to be asleep.* Il faisait semblant de dormir.
pretty ADJECTIVE, ADVERB
1 *joli* ◇ *She's very pretty.* Elle est très jolie.
2 *plutôt* (*rather*) ◇ *That film was pretty bad.* Ce film était plutôt mauvais.
◆ **The weather was pretty awful.** Il faisait un temps minable.
◆ **It's pretty much the same.** C'est pratiquement la même chose.
to **prevent** VERB
empêcher

- **to prevent somebody from doing something** empêcher quelqu'un de faire quelque chose ◇ *They try to prevent us from smoking.* Ils essaient de nous empêcher de fumer.

previous ADJECTIVE
précédent

previously ADVERB
auparavant

prey NOUN
la *proie* ◇ *a bird of prey* un oiseau de proie

price NOUN
le *prix*

price list NOUN
la *liste des prix*

to **prick** VERB
piquer ◇ *I've pricked my finger.* Je me suis piqué le doigt.

pride NOUN
la *fierté*

priest NOUN
le *prêtre* ◇ *He's a priest.* Il est prêtre.

primarily ADVERB
principalement

primary ADJECTIVE
principal
(*principaux* MASC PL)

primary school NOUN
l' *école primaire* FEM ◇ *She's still at primary school.* Elle est encore à l'école primaire.

prime minister NOUN
le *Premier ministre*

primitive ADJECTIVE
primitif MASC
primitive FEM

prince NOUN
le *prince* ◇ *the Prince of Wales* le prince de Galles

princess NOUN
la *princesse* ◇ *Princess Anne* la princesse Anne

principal ADJECTIVE
see also **principal** NOUN
principal
(*principaux* MASC PL)

principal NOUN
see also **principal** ADJECTIVE
le *principal* (*of college*)

principle NOUN
le *principe*
(les *principaux* PL)

- **on principle** par principe

print NOUN
[1] le *tirage* (*photo*) ◇ *colour prints* des tirages en couleur
[2] les *caractères* MASC (*letters*) ◇ *in small print* en petits caractères

[3] l' *empreinte digitale* FEM (*fingerprint*)
[4] la *gravure* FEM (*picture*) ◇ *a framed print* une gravure encadrée

printer NOUN
l' *imprimante* FEM (*machine*)

print-out NOUN
la *copie papier*

priority NOUN
la *priorité*

prison NOUN
la *prison*

- **in prison** en prison

prisoner NOUN
le *prisonnier*
la *prisonnière*

privacy NOUN
l' *intimité* FEM

private ADJECTIVE
privé ◇ *a private school* une école privée

- **private property** la propriété privée
- **"private"** (*on envelope*) "personnel"
- **a private bathroom** une salle de bain individuelle
- **I have private lessons.** Je prends des cours particuliers.

to **privatize** VERB
privatiser

privilege NOUN
le *privilège*

prize NOUN
le *prix* ◇ *to win a prize* gagner un prix

prize-giving NOUN
la *distribution des prix*

prizewinner NOUN
le *gagnant*
la *gagnante*

pro NOUN

- **the pros and cons** le pour et le contre ◇ *We weighed up the pros and cons.* Nous avons pesé le pour et le contre.

probability NOUN
la *probabilité*

probable ADJECTIVE
probable

probably ADVERB
probablement ◇ *probably not* probablement pas

problem NOUN
le *problème* ◇ *No problem!* Pas de problème!

proceeds PL NOUN
la *recette* SING

process NOUN
le *processus* ◇ *the peace process* le processus de paix

- **to be in the process of doing something** être en train de faire quelque chose ◇ *We're in the process of* *painting the kitchen.* Nous sommes en train de peindre la cuisine.

procession NOUN
la *procession* (religious)

to **produce** VERB
[1] *produire* (manufacture)
[2] *monter* (play, show)

producer NOUN
(of play, show)
le *metteur en scène*
(les *metteurs en scène* PL)

product NOUN
le *produit*

production NOUN
[1] la *production* ◇ *They're increasing production of luxury models.* Ils augmentent la production des modèles de luxe.
[2] la *mise en scène* (play, show) ◇ *a production of "Hamlet"* une mise en scène de "Hamlet"

profession NOUN
la *profession*

professional NOUN
see also professional ADJECTIVE
le *professionnel*
la *professionnelle*

professional ADJECTIVE
see also professional NOUN
(player)
professionnel MASC
professionnelle FEM
◇ *a professional musician* un musicien professionnel
• *a very professional piece of work* un vrai travail de professionnel

professionally ADVERB
• *She sings professionally.* C'est une chanteuse professionnelle.

professor NOUN
le *professeur d'université*
• *He's the French professor.* Il est titulaire de la chaire de français.

profit NOUN
le *bénéfice*

profitable ADJECTIVE
rentable

program NOUN
see also program VERB
le *programme* ◇ *a computer program* un programme informatique

to **program** VERB
see also program NOUN
programmer (computer)

programme NOUN
[1] l' *émission* FEM (on TV, radio)
[2] le *programme* (of events)

programmer NOUN
le *programmeur*

la *programmeuse*
◇ *She's a programmer.* Elle est programmeuse.

programming NOUN
la *programmation*

progress NOUN
le *progrès* ◇ *You're making progress!* Vous faites des progrès!

to **prohibit** VERB
interdire ◇ *Smoking is prohibited.* Il est interdit de fumer.

project NOUN
[1] le *projet* (plan) ◇ *a development project* un projet de développement
[2] le *dossier* (research) ◇ *I'm doing a project on education in France.* Je prépare un dossier sur l'éducation en France.

projector NOUN
le *projecteur*

promenade NOUN
le *front de mer*

promise NOUN
see also promise VERB
la *promesse* ◇ *He made me a promise.* Il m'a fait une promesse.
• *That's a promise!* C'est promis!

to **promise** VERB
see also promise NOUN
promettre ◇ *She promised to write.* Elle a promis d'écrire. ◇ *I'll write, I promise!* J'écrirai, c'est promis!

promising ADJECTIVE
• *a promising player* un joueur qui a de l'avenir

to **promote** VERB
• *to be promoted* être promu ◇ *She was promoted after six months.* Elle a été promue au bout de six mois.

promotion NOUN
la *promotion*

prompt ADJECTIVE, ADVERB
rapide ◇ *a prompt reply* une réponse rapide
• *at eight o'clock prompt* à huit heures précises

promptly ADVERB
• *We left promptly at seven.* Nous sommes partis à sept heures précises.

pronoun NOUN
le *pronom*

to **pronounce** VERB
prononcer ◇ *How do you pronounce that word?* Comment est-ce qu'on prononce ce mot?

pronunciation NOUN
la *prononciation*

proof NOUN
la *preuve*

proper ADJECTIVE

P

☐1 *vrai* (*genuine*) ◇ *proper French bread*
du vrai pain français ◇ *We didn't have a
proper lunch, just sandwiches.* Nous
n'avons pas pris de vrai repas, juste des
sandwichs.

* **It's difficult to get a proper job.** Il est
difficile de trouver un travail correct.
☐2 *adéquat* ◇ *You have to have the
proper equipment.* Il faut avoir
l'équipement adéquat. ◇ *We need
proper training.* Il nous faut une
formation adéquate.
* **If you had come at the proper time...** Si
tu étais venu à l'heure dite...

properly ADVERB
☐1 *comme il faut* (*correctly*) ◇ *You're not
doing it properly.* Tu ne t'y prends pas
comme il faut.
☐2 *convenablement* (*appropriately*)
◇ *Dress properly for your interview.*
Habille-toi convenablement pour ton
entretien.

property NOUN
la *propriété*
* **"private property"** "propriété privée"
* **stolen property** les objets volés

proportional ADJECTIVE
proportionnel MASC
proportionnelle FEM
◇ *proportional representation* la
représentation proportionnelle

proposal NOUN
la *proposition* (*suggestion*)

to **propose** VERB
proposer ◇ *I propose a new plan.* Je
propose un changement de programme.
* **to propose to do something** avoir
l'intention de faire quelque chose
◇ *What do you propose to do?* Qu'est-ce
que tu as l'intention de faire?
* **to propose to somebody** (*for marriage*)
demander quelqu'un en mariage ◇ *He
proposed to her at the restaurant.* Il l'a
demandée en mariage au restaurant.

prospect NOUN
la *perspective* ◇ *It'll improve my career
prospects.* Ça va améliorer mes
perspectives d'avenir.

prospectus NOUN
le *prospectus*

prostitute NOUN
la *prostituée*
* **a male prostitute** un prostitué

to **protect** VERB
protéger

protection NOUN
la *protection*

protein NOUN
la *protéine*

protest NOUN
see also protest VERB
la *protestation* ◇ *He ignored their
protests.* Il a ignoré leurs protestations.
* **a protest march** une manifestation

to **protest** VERB
see also protest NOUN
protester

Protestant NOUN
see also Protestant ADJECTIVE
le *protestant*
la *protestante*
◇ *I'm a Protestant.* Je suis protestant.

Protestant ADJECTIVE
see also Protestant NOUN
protestant ◇ *a Protestant church* une
église protestante

protester NOUN
le *manifestant*
la *manifestante*

proud ADJECTIVE
fier MASC
fière FEM
◇ *Her parents are proud of her.* Ses
parents sont fiers d'elle.

to **prove** VERB
prouver ◇ *The police couldn't prove it.*
La police n'a pas pu le prouver.

proverb NOUN
le *proverbe*

to **provide** VERB
fournir
* **to provide somebody with something**
fournir quelque chose à quelqu'un
◇ *They provided us with maps.* Ils nous
ont fourni des cartes.

provided CONJUNCTION
à condition que
à condition que *has to be followed by the
subjunctive.*
◇ *He'll play in the next match provided
he's fit.* Il jouera dans le prochain
match, à condition qu'il soit en forme.

provisional ADJECTIVE
provisoire

prowler NOUN
le *rôdeur*
la *rôdeuse*

prune NOUN
le *pruneau*
(les *pruneaux* PL)

pseudonym NOUN
le *pseudonyme*

psychiatrist NOUN
le/la *psychiatre* ◇ *She's a psychiatrist.*
Elle est psychiatre.

psychoanalyst NOUN
le/la *psychanalyste*

psychological ADJECTIVE

psychologique
psychologist NOUN
le/la *psychologue* ◦ *He's a psychologist.* Il est psychologue.

psychology NOUN
la *psychologie*

PTO ABBREVIATION (= *please turn over*)
T.S.V.P. (= tournez, s'il vous plaît)

pub NOUN
le *pub*

public NOUN
see also public ADJECTIVE
le *public* ◦ *open to the public* ouvert au public
‣ **in public** en public

public ADJECTIVE
see also public NOUN
public MASC
publique FEM
‣ **a public holiday** un jour férié
‣ **public opinion** l'opinion publique FEM
‣ **the public address system** les haut-parleurs

publicity NOUN
la *publicité*

public school NOUN
l' *école privée* FEM

public transport NOUN
les *transports en commun* MASC PL

publish VERB
publier

publisher NOUN
l' *éditeur* MASC

pudding NOUN
le *dessert* ◦ *What's for pudding?* Qu'est-ce qu'il y a comme dessert?
‣ **rice pudding** le riz au lait
‣ **black pudding** le boudin noir

puddle NOUN
la *flaque*

puff pastry NOUN
la *pâte feuilletée*

pull VERB
tirer ◦ *Pull!* Tirez!
‣ **He pulled the trigger.** Il a appuyé sur la gâchette.
‣ **to pull a muscle** se froisser un muscle
◦ *I pulled a muscle when I was training.* Je me suis froissé un muscle à l'entraînement.
‣ **You're pulling my leg!** Tu me fais marcher!
‣ **to pull down** démolir
‣ **to pull out (1)** arracher (*tooth, weed*)
‣ **to pull out (2)** déboîter (*car*) ◦ *The car pulled out to overtake.* La voiture a déboîté pour doubler.
‣ **to pull out (3)** se retirer (*withdraw*)
◦ *She pulled out of the tournament.* Elle

s'est retirée du tournoi.
‣ **to pull through** s'en sortir ◦ *They think he'll pull through.* Ils pensent qu'il va s'en sortir.

pullover NOUN
le *pull-over*

pulse NOUN
le *pouls* ◦ *The nurse felt his pulse.* L'infirmière a pris son pouls.

pulses PL NOUN
les *légumes secs* MASC

pump NOUN
see also pump VERB
⌐1⌐ la *pompe* ◦ *a bicycle pump* une pompe à vélo ◦ *a petrol pump* une pompe à essence
⌐2⌐ la *chaussure de sport* (*shoe*)

to pump VERB
see also pump NOUN
pomper
‣ **to pump up** gonfler (*tyre*)

pumpkin NOUN
le *potiron*

punch NOUN
see also punch VERB
⌐1⌐ le *coup de poing* (*blow*) ◦ *He gave me a punch.* Il m'a donné un coup de poing.
⌐2⌐ le *punch* (*drink*)

to punch VERB
see also punch NOUN
⌐1⌐ *donner un coup de poing à* (*hit*)
◦ *He punched me!* Il m'a donné un coup de poing!
⌐2⌐ *composter* (*in ticket machine*) ◦ *Punch your ticket before you get on the train.* Compostez votre billet avant de monter dans le train.
⌐3⌐ *poinçonner* (*by hand*) ◦ *He forgot to punch my ticket.* Il a oublié de poinçonner mon billet.

punch-up NOUN
la *bagarre* (*informal*)

punctual ADJECTIVE
ponctuel MASC
ponctuelle FEM

punctuation NOUN
la *ponctuation*

puncture NOUN
la *crevaison* ◦ *I had to mend a puncture.* J'ai dû réparer une crevaison.
‣ **to have a puncture** crever ◦ *I had a puncture on the motorway.* J'ai crevé sur l'autoroute.

to punish VERB
punir
‣ **to punish somebody for something** punir quelqu'un de quelque chose
‣ **to punish somebody for doing**

P

PTO

something punir quelqu'un d'avoir fait quelque chose

punishment NOUN
la *punition*

punk NOUN
le/la *punk* (person)
- **a punk rock band** un groupe de punk rock

pupil NOUN
l' *élève* MASC/FEM

puppet NOUN
la *marionnette*

puppy NOUN
le *chiot*

to **purchase** VERB
acheter

pure ADJECTIVE
pur ◇ *pure orange juice* du pur jus d'orange ◇ *He's doing pure maths.* Il fait des maths pures.

purple ADJECTIVE
violet MASC
violette FEM

purpose NOUN
le *but* ◇ *What is the purpose of these changes?* Quel est le but de ces changements? ◇ *his purpose in life* son but dans la vie
- **on purpose** exprès ◇ *He did it on purpose.* Il l'a fait exprès.

to **purr** VERB
ronronner

purse NOUN
le *porte-monnaie*
(les *porte-monnaie* PL)

to **pursue** VERB
poursuivre

pursuit NOUN
l' *activité* FEM ◇ *outdoor pursuits* les activités de plein air

push NOUN
see also push VERB
- **to give somebody a push** pousser quelqu'un ◇ *He gave me a push.* Il m'a poussé.

to **push** VERB
see also push NOUN
1 *pousser* ◇ *Don't push!* Arrêtez de pousser!
2 *appuyer sur* (button)
- **to push somebody to do something** pousser quelqu'un à faire quelque chose ◇ *My parents are pushing me to go to university.* Mes parents me poussent à entrer à l'université.
- **to push drugs** revendre de la drogue
- **Push off!** Dégage!

pushchair NOUN
la *poussette*

pusher NOUN
(of drugs)
le *revendeur*
la *revendeuse*

to **put** VERB
1 *mettre* (place) ◇ *Where shall I put my things?* Où est-ce que je peux mettre mes affaires? ◇ *She's putting the baby to bed.* Elle met le bébé au lit.
2 *écrire* (write) ◇ *Don't forget to put your name on the paper.* N'oubliez pas d'écrire votre nom sur la feuille.

to **put away** VERB
ranger ◇ *Can you put away the dishes, please?* Tu peux ranger la vaisselle, s'il te plaît?

to **put back** VERB
remettre en place (replace) ◇ *Put it back when you've finished with it.* Remets-le en place une fois que tu auras fini.

to **put down** VERB
1 *poser* ◇ *I'll put these bags down for a minute.* Je vais poser ces sacs une minute.
2 *noter* (in writing) ◇ *I've put down a few ideas.* J'ai noté quelques idées.
- **to have an animal put down** faire piquer un animal ◇ *We had to have our old dog put down.* Nous avons dû faire piquer notre vieux chien.

to **put off** VERB
1 *éteindre* (switch off) ◇ *Shall I put the light off?* Est-ce que j'éteins la lumière?
2 *remettre à plus tard* (postpone) ◇ *I keep putting it off.* Je n'arrête pas de remettre ça à plus tard.
3 *déranger* (distract) ◇ *Stop putting me off!* Arrête de me déranger!
4 *décourager* (discourage) ◇ *He's not easily put off.* Il ne se laisse pas facilement décourager.

to **put on** VERB
1 *mettre* (clothes, lipstick, record) ◇ *I'll put my coat on.* Je vais mettre mon manteau.
2 *allumer* (light, heater, telly) ◇ *Shall I put the heater on?* J'allume le chauffage?
3 *monter* (play, show) ◇ *We're putting on "Bugsy Malone".* Nous sommes en train de monter "Bugsy Malone".
4 *mettre à cuire* ◇ *I'll put the potatoes on.* Je vais mettre les pommes de terre à cuire.
- **to put on weight** grossir ◇ *He's put on a lot of weight.* Il a beaucoup grossi.

to **put out** VERB
éteindre (light, cigarette, fire) ◇ *It took them five hours to put out the fire.* Ils ont mis cinq heures à éteindre l'incendie.

to **put through** VERB
  passer ⋄ *Can you put me through to the manager?* Est-ce que vous pouvez me passer le directeur?
  ◆ **I'm putting you through.** Je vous passe la communication.

to **put up** VERB
  [1] _mettre_ (*pin up*) ⋄ *The poster's great. I'll put it up on my wall.* Le poster est super. Je vais le mettre au mur.
  [2] _monter_ (*tent*) ⋄ *We put up our tent in a field.* Nous avons monté la tente dans un champ.
  [3] _augmenter_ (*price*) ⋄ *They've put up the price.* Ils ont augmenté le prix.
  [4] _héberger_ (*accommodate*) ⋄ *My friend will put me up for the night.* Mon ami va m'héberger pour la nuit.
  ◆ **to put one's hand up** lever la main ⋄ *If you have any questions, put up your hand.* Si vous avez une question, levez la main.
  ◆ **to put up with something** supporter

quelque chose ⋄ *I'm not going to put up with it any longer.* Je ne vais pas supporter ça plus longtemps.

puzzle NOUN
  le _puzzle_ (*jigsaw*)

puzzled ADJECTIVE
  perplexe ⋄ *You look puzzled!* Tu as l'air perplexe!

puzzling ADJECTIVE
  déconcertant

pyjamas PL NOUN
  le _pyjama_ SING ⋄ *my pyjamas* mon pyjama
  ◆ **a pair of pyjamas** un pyjama
  ◆ **a pyjama top** un haut de pyjama

pyramid NOUN
  la _pyramide_

Pyrenees PL NOUN
  les _Pyrénées_ FEM
  ◆ **in the Pyrenees** dans les Pyrénées
  ◆ **We went to the Pyrenees.** Nous sommes allés dans les Pyrénées.

Q

quaint ADJECTIVE
pittoresque (*house, village*)

qualification NOUN
le *diplôme* ◇ *to leave school without any qualifications* quitter l'école sans aucun diplôme
- **vocational qualifications** des qualifications professionnelles

qualified ADJECTIVE
[1] *qualifié* (*trained*) ◇ *a qualified driving instructor* un moniteur d'auto-école qualifié
[2] *diplômé* (*nurse, teacher*) ◇ *a qualified nurse* une infirmière diplômée

to **qualify** VERB
[1] *obtenir son diplôme* (*for job*) ◇ *She qualified as a teacher last year.* Elle a obtenu son diplôme de professeur l'année dernière.
[2] *se qualifier* (*in competition*) ◇ *Our team didn't qualify.* Notre équipe ne s'est pas qualifiée.

quality NOUN
la *qualité* ◇ *a good quality of life* une bonne qualité de vie ◇ *good-quality ingredients* des ingrédients de bonne qualité ◇ *She's got lots of good qualities.* Elle a beaucoup de qualités.

quantity NOUN
la *quantité*

quarantine NOUN
la *quarantaine* ◇ *in quarantine* en quarantaine

quarrel NOUN
see also **quarrel** VERB
la *dispute*

to **quarrel** VERB
see also **quarrel** NOUN
se disputer

quarry NOUN
la *carrière* (*for stone*)

quarter NOUN
le *quart*
- **three quarters** trois quarts
- **a quarter of an hour** un quart d'heure ◇ *three quarters of an hour* trois quarts d'heure
- **a quarter past ten** dix heures et quart
- **a quarter to eleven** onze heures moins le quart

quarter final NOUN
le *quart de finale*

quartet NOUN
le *quatuor* ◇ *a string quartet* un quatuor à cordes

quay NOUN

le *quai*

queasy ADJECTIVE
- **to feel queasy** avoir mal au cœur ◇ *I'm feeling queasy.* J'ai mal au cœur.

queen NOUN
[1] la *reine* ◇ *Queen Elizabeth* la reine Élisabeth
[2] la *dame* (*playing card*) ◇ *the queen of hearts* la dame de cœur
- **the Queen Mother** la reine mère

query NOUN
la *question*

question NOUN
see also **question** VERB
la *question* ◇ *Can I ask a question?* Est-ce que je peux poser une question? ◇ *That's a difficult question.* C'est une question difficile.
- **It's out of the question.** C'est hors de question.

to **question** VERB
see also **question** NOUN
interroger ◇ *He was questioned by the police.* Il a été interrogé par la police.

question mark NOUN
le *point d'interrogation*

questionnaire NOUN
le *questionnaire*

queue NOUN
see also **queue** VERB
la *queue*

to **queue** VERB
see also **queue** NOUN
faire la queue
- **to queue for something** faire la queue pour avoir quelque chose ◇ *We had to queue for tickets.* Nous avons dû faire la queue pour avoir les billets.

quick ADJECTIVE, ADVERB
rapide ◇ *a quick lunch* un déjeuner rapide ◇ *It's quicker by train.* C'est plus rapide en train.
- **Be quick!** Dépêche-toi!
- **She's a quick learner.** Elle apprend vite.
- **Quick, phone the police!** Téléphonez vite à la police!

quickly ADVERB
vite ◇ *It was all over very quickly.* Ça s'est passé très vite.

quiet ADJECTIVE
[1] (*not talkative or noisy*)
silencieux MASC
silencieuse FEM
◇ *You're very quiet today.* Tu es bien silencieux aujourd'hui. ◇ *The engine's very quiet.* Le moteur est très silencieux.

2 (*peaceful*)
tranquille ◦ *a quiet little town* une petite ville tranquille ◦ *a quiet weekend* un week-end tranquille
♦ **Be quiet!** Tais-toi!
♦ **Quiet!** Silence!

quietly ADVERB
1 *doucement* (*speak*) ◦ *"She's dead,"* *he said quietly.* "Elle est morte" dit-il doucement.
2 *silencieusement* (*move*) ◦ *He quietly opened the door.* Il a ouvert la porte sans faire de bruit.

quilt NOUN
la *couette* (*duvet*)

quite ADVERB
1 *assez* (*rather*) ◦ *It's quite warm today.* Il fait assez bon aujourd'hui. ◦ *I quite liked the film, but...* J'ai trouvé le film assez bon, mais...
2 *tout à fait* (*entirely*) ◦ *I'm not quite sure.* Je n'en suis pas tout à fait sûr.
◦ *It's not quite the same.* Ce n'est pas tout à fait la même chose.

♦ **quite good** pas mal
♦ **I've been there quite a lot.** J'y suis allé pas mal de fois.
♦ **quite a lot of money** pas mal d'argent
♦ **It costs quite a lot to go abroad.** Ça coûte assez cher d'aller à l'étranger.
♦ **It's quite a long way.** C'est assez loin.
♦ **It was quite a shock.** Ça a été un sacré choc.
♦ **There were quite a few people there.** Il y avait pas mal de gens.

quiz NOUN
le *jeu-concours*

quota NOUN
le *quota*

quotation NOUN
la *citation* ◦ *a quotation from Shakespeare* une citation de Shakespeare

quote NOUN
la *citation* ◦ *a Shakespeare quote* une citation de Shakespeare
♦ **quotes** (*quotation marks*) les guillemets MASC ◦ *in quotes* entre guillemets

R

rabbi NOUN
le *rabbin*

rabbit NOUN
le *lapin*
+ **a rabbit hutch** un clapier

rabies NOUN
la *rage*
+ **a dog with rabies** un chien enragé

race NOUN
see also race VERB
[1] la *course* (sport) ◇ *a cycle race* une
course cycliste
[2] la *race* (species) ◇ *the human race* la
race humaine
+ **race relations** les relations interraciales
FEM

to **race** VERB
see also race NOUN
[1] *courir* ◇ *We raced to catch the bus.*
Nous avons couru pour attraper le bus.
[2] *faire la course* (have a race)
+ **I'll race you!** On fait la course!

racecourse NOUN
le *champ de courses*

racehorse NOUN
le *cheval de course*
(les *chevaux de course* PL)

racer NOUN
le *vélo de course* (bike)

racetrack NOUN
la *piste*

racial ADJECTIVE
racial
(*raciaux* MASC PL)
◇ *racial discrimination* la discrimination
raciale

racing car NOUN
la *voiture de course*

racing driver NOUN
le *pilote de course*

racism NOUN
le *racisme*

racist ADJECTIVE
see also racist NOUN
raciste

racist NOUN
see also racist ADJECTIVE
le/la *raciste*

rack NOUN (for luggage)
le *porte-bagages*
(les *porte-bagages* PL)

racket NOUN
[1] la *raquette* (for sport) ◇ *my tennis
racket* ma raquette de tennis
[2] le *boucan* (noise) ◇ *They're making a
terrible racket.* Ils font un boucan de

tous les diables. (*informal*)

racquet NOUN
la *raquette*

radar NOUN
le *radar*

radiation NOUN
la *radiation*

radiator NOUN
le *radiateur*

radio NOUN
la *radio*
+ **on the radio** à la radio
+ **a radio station** une station de radio

radioactive ADJECTIVE
radioactif MASC
radioactive FEM

radio cassette NOUN
le *radiocassette*

radio-controlled ADJECTIVE
téléguidé (model plane, car)

radish NOUN
le *radis*

RAF NOUN (= Royal Air Force)
la *R.A.F.* ◇ *He's in the RAF.* Il est dans
la R.A.F.

raffle NOUN
la *tombola* ◇ *a raffle ticket* un billet de
tombola

raft NOUN
le *radeau*
(les *radeaux* PL)

rag NOUN
le *chiffon* ◇ *a piece of rag* un chiffon
+ **dressed in rags** en haillons

rage NOUN
la *rage* ◇ *mad with rage* fou de rage
+ **to be in a rage** être furieux ◇ *She was
in a rage.* Elle était furieuse.
+ **It's all the rage.** Ça fait fureur.

raid NOUN
see also raid VERB
[1] (burglary)
le *hold-up*
(les *hold-up* PL)
◇ *There was a bank raid near my house.*
Il y a eu un hold-up dans une banque
près de chez moi.
[2] la *descente* ◇ *a police raid* une
descente de police

to **raid** VERB
see also raid NOUN
faire une descente dans (police) ◇ *The
police raided a club in Soho.* La police a
fait une descente dans un club de Soho.

rail NOUN
[1] la *rampe* (on stairs)

2 la *balustrade* (*on bridge, balcony*)
◇ *Don't lean over the rail!* Ne vous penchez pas sur la balustrade!
3 le *rail* (*on railway line*)
* **by rail** en train
railway NOUN
le *chemin de fer* ◇ *the privatization of the railways* la privatisation des chemins de fer
* **a railway line** une ligne de chemin de fer
* **a railway station** une gare
rain NOUN
see also rain VERB
la *pluie* ◇ *in the rain* sous la pluie
○ **rain** VERB
see also rain NOUN
pleuvoir ◇ *It rains a lot here.* Il pleut beaucoup par ici.
* **It's raining.** Il pleut.
rainbow NOUN
l' *arc-en-ciel* MASC
(les *arcs-en-ciel* PL)
raincoat NOUN
l' *imperméable* MASC
rainforest NOUN
la *forêt tropicale humide*
rainy ADJECTIVE
pluvieux MASC
pluvieuse FEM
○ **raise** VERB
1 *lever* (*lift*) ◇ *He raised his hand.* Il a levé la main.
2 *améliorer* (*improve*) ◇ *They want to raise standards in schools.* Ils veulent améliorer le niveau dans les écoles.
* **to raise money** collecter des fonds
◇ *The school is raising money for a new gym.* L'école collecte des fonds pour un nouveau gymnase.
raisin NOUN
le *raisin sec*
rake NOUN
le *râteau*
(les *râteaux* PL)
rally NOUN
1 le *rassemblement* (*of people*)
2 le *rallye* (*sport*) ◇ *a rally driver* un pilote de rallye
3 l' *échange* MASC (*in tennis*)
ramble NOUN
la *randonnée* ◇ *to go for a ramble* faire une randonnée
rambler NOUN
le *randonneur*
la *randonneuse*
ramp NOUN
la *rampe d'accès* (*for wheelchairs*)
ran VERB *see* run
ranch NOUN

le *ranch*
random ADJECTIVE
* **a random selection** une sélection effectuée au hasard
* **at random** au hasard ◇ *We picked the number at random.* Nous avons choisi le numéro au hasard.
rang VERB *see* ring
range NOUN
see also range VERB
le *choix* ◇ *There's a wide range of colours.* Il y a un grand choix de coloris.
* **a range of subjects** diverses matières
◇ *We study a range of subjects.* Nous étudions diverses matières.
* **a mountain range** une chaîne de montagnes
to **range** VERB
see also range NOUN
* **to range from...to** se situer entre...et
◇ *Temperatures in summer range from 20 to 35 degrees.* Les températures estivales se situent entre vingt et trente-cinq degrés.
* **Tickets range from £2 to £20.** Les billets coûtent entre deux et vingt livres.
rank NOUN
* **a taxi rank** une station de taxis
ransom NOUN
la *rançon*
rap NOUN
le *rap* (*music*)
rape NOUN
see also rape VERB
le *viol*
to **rape** VERB
see also rape NOUN
violer
rapids PL NOUN
les *rapides* MASC PL
rapist NOUN
le *violeur*
rare ADJECTIVE
1 *rare* (*unusual*) ◇ *a rare plant* une plante rare
2 *saignant* (*steak*)
rash NOUN
l' *éruption de boutons* FEM ◇ *I've got a rash on my chest.* J'ai une éruption de boutons sur la poitrine.
rasher NOUN
la *tranche* ◇ *an egg and two rashers of bacon* un œuf et deux tranches de bacon
raspberry NOUN
la *framboise* ◇ *raspberry jam* la confiture de framboises
rat NOUN
le *rat*

R

rate NOUN

  [1] le *tarif* (*price*) ◦ *There are reduced rates for students.* Il y a des tarifs réduits pour les étudiants.

  [2] le *taux* (*level*) ◦ *the divorce rate* le taux de divorce ◦ *a high rate of interest* un taux d'intérêt élevé

rather ADVERB

  plutôt ◦ *I was rather disappointed.* J'étais plutôt déçu. ◦ *£20! That's rather a lot!* Vingt livres! C'est plutôt cher!

  ♦ **rather a lot of** pas mal de ◦ *I've got rather a lot of homework to do.* J'ai pas mal de devoirs à faire.

  ♦ **rather than** plutôt que ◦ *We decided to camp, rather than stay at a hotel.* Nous avons décidé de camper plutôt que d'aller à l'hôtel.

  ♦ **I'd rather...** J'aimerais mieux... ◦ *I'd rather stay in tonight.* J'aimerais mieux rester à la maison ce soir. ◦ *Would you like a sweet?–I'd rather have an apple.* Tu veux un bonbon?–J'aimerais mieux une pomme.

rattle NOUN

  le *hochet* (*for baby*)

rattlesnake NOUN

  le *serpent à sonnette*

to **rave** VERB

  see also rave NOUN

  s'extasier ◦ *They raved about the film.* Ils se sont extasiés sur le film.

rave NOUN

  see also rave VERB

  la *rave* (*party*)

  ♦ **rave music** le rave

raven NOUN

  le *corbeau*

  (les *corbeaux* PL)

ravenous ADJECTIVE

  ♦ **to be ravenous** avoir une faim de loup ◦ *I'm ravenous!* J'ai une faim de loup!

raving ADJECTIVE

  ♦ **raving mad** fou à lier ◦ *She's raving mad!* Elle est folle à lier.

raw ADJECTIVE

  cru (*food*)

  ♦ **raw materials** les matières premières FEM

razor NOUN

  le *rasoir* ◦ *some disposable razors* des rasoirs jetables

  ♦ **a razor blade** une lame de rasoir

RE NOUN

  l' *éducation religieuse* FEM

reach NOUN

  see also reach VERB

  ♦ **out of reach** hors de portée ◦ *The light switch was out of reach.* L'interrupteur était hors de portée.

  ♦ **within easy reach of** à proximité de ◦ *The hotel is within easy reach of the town centre.* L'hôtel se trouve à proximité du centre-ville.

to **reach** VERB

  see also reach NOUN

  [1] *arriver à* ◦ *We reached the hotel at 7 p.m.* Nous sommes arrivés à l'hôtel à sept heures du soir.

  ♦ **We hope to reach the final.** Nous espérons aller en finale.

  [2] *parvenir à* (*decision*) ◦ *Eventually they reached a decision.* Ils sont finalement parvenus à une décision.

  ♦ **He reached for his gun.** Il a tendu la main pour prendre son revolver.

to **react** VERB

  réagir

reaction NOUN

  la *réaction*

reactor NOUN

  le *réacteur* ◦ *a nuclear reactor* un réacteur nucléaire

to **read** VERB

  lire ◦ *I don't read much.* Je ne lis pas beaucoup. ◦ *Have you read "Animal Farm"?* Est-ce que tu as lu "La ferme des animaux"? ◦ *Read the text out loud.* Lis le texte à haute voix.

reader NOUN

  (*person*)

  le *lecteur*

  la *lectrice*

reading NOUN

  la *lecture* ◦ *Reading is one of my hobbies.* La lecture est l'une de mes activités favorites.

ready ADJECTIVE

  prêt ◦ *She's nearly ready.* Elle est presque prête. ◦ *He's always ready to help.* Il est toujours prêt à rendre service.

  ♦ **a ready meal** un plat cuisiné

  ♦ **to get ready** se préparer ◦ *She's getting ready to go out.* Elle est en train de se préparer pour sortir.

  ♦ **to get something ready** préparer quelque chose ◦ *He's getting the dinner ready.* Il est en train de préparer le dîner.

real ADJECTIVE

  [1] *vrai* ◦ *He wasn't a real policeman.* Ce n'était pas un vrai policier. ◦ *Her real name is Cordelia.* Son vrai nom est Cordelia.

  [2] *véritable* ◦ *It's real leather.* C'est du cuir véritable. ◦ *It was a real nightmare.* C'était un véritable cauchemar.

  ♦ **in real life** dans la réalité

realistic ADJECTIVE
réaliste
reality NOUN
la *réalité*
to **realize** VERB
* **to realize that...** se rendre compte que...
  ◇ *We realized that something was wrong.*
  Nous nous sommes rendu compte que
  quelque chose n'allait pas.
really ADVERB
vraiment ◇ *She's really nice.* Elle est
vraiment sympathique. ◇ *Do you want
to go? – Not really.* Tu veux y aller? – Pas
vraiment.
* **I'm learning German. – Really?**
  J'apprends l'allemand. – Ah bon?
* **Do you really think so?** Tu es sûr?
rear ADJECTIVE
  see also **rear** NOUN
arrière MASC, FEM, PL ◇ *a rear wheel* une
roue arrière
rear NOUN
  see also **rear** ADJECTIVE
l' *arrière* MASC ◇ *at the rear of the train*
à l'arrière du train
reason NOUN
la *raison* ◇ *There's no reason to think
that...* Il n'y a aucune raison de penser
que...
* **for security reasons** pour des raisons
  de sécurité
* **That was the main reason I went.** C'est
  surtout pour ça que j'y suis allé.
reasonable ADJECTIVE
[1] *raisonnable* (*sensible*) ◇ *Be
reasonable!* Sois raisonnable!
[2] *correct* (*not bad*) ◇ *He wrote a
reasonable essay.* Sa dissertation était
correcte.
to **reassure** VERB
rassurer
reassuring ADJECTIVE
rassurant
rebellious ADJECTIVE
rebelle
receipt NOUN
le *reçu*
to **receive** VERB
recevoir
receiver NOUN
le *combiné* (*of phone*)
* **to pick up the receiver** décrocher
recent ADJECTIVE
récent
recently ADVERB
ces derniers temps ◇ *I've been doing a
lot of training recently.* Je me suis
beaucoup entraîné ces derniers temps.
reception NOUN

la *réception* ◇ *Please leave your key at
reception.* Merci de laisser votre clé à la
réception. ◇ *The reception will be at a big
hotel.* La réception aura lieu dans un
grand hôtel.
receptionist NOUN
le/la *réceptionniste*
recession NOUN
la *récession*
recipe NOUN
la *recette*
to **reckon** VERB
penser ◇ *What do you reckon?*
Qu'est-ce que tu en penses?
reclining ADJECTIVE
* **a reclining seat** un siège inclinable
recognizable ADJECTIVE
reconnaissable
to **recognize** VERB
reconnaître ◇ *You'll recognize me by
my red hair.* Vous me reconnaîtrez à mes
cheveux roux.
to **recommend** VERB
conseiller ◇ *What do you recommend?*
Qu'est-ce que vous me conseillez?
to **reconsider** VERB
reconsidérer
record NOUN
  see also **record** VERB
[1] le *disque* (*recording*) ◇ *my favourite
record* mon disque préféré
[2] le *record* (*sport*) ◇ *the world record* le
record du monde
* **in record time** en un temps record
  ◇ *She finished the job in record time.* Elle
  a terminé le travail en un temps record.
* **a criminal record** un casier judiciaire
  ◇ *He's got a criminal record.* Il a un casier
  judiciaire.
* **records** (*of police, hospital*) les archives
  FEM ◇ *I'll check in the records.* Je vais
  vérifier dans les archives.
* **There is no record of your booking.** Il
  n'y a aucune trace de votre réservation.
to **record** VERB
  see also **record** NOUN
enregistrer (*on film, tape*) ◇ *They've just
recorded their new album.* Ils viennent
d'enregistrer leur nouveau disque.
recorded delivery NOUN
* **to send something recorded delivery**
  envoyer quelque chose en recommandé
recorder NOUN
la *flûte à bec* (*instrument*) ◇ *She plays
the recorder.* Elle joue de la flûte à bec.
* **a cassette recorder** un magnétophone
  à cassettes
* **a video recorder** un magnétoscope
recording NOUN

l' *enregistrement* MASC
record player NOUN
le *tourne-disque*

to **recover** VERB
se remettre ◇ *He's recovering from a knee injury.* Il se remet d'une blessure au genou.

recovery NOUN
le *rétablissement*
- **Best wishes for a speedy recovery!** Meilleurs vœux de prompt rétablissement!

rectangle NOUN
le *rectangle*

rectangular ADJECTIVE
rectangulaire

to **recycle** VERB
recycler

recycling NOUN
le *recyclage*

red ADJECTIVE
1 *rouge* ◇ *a red rose* une rose rouge
◇ *red meat* la viande rouge
- **a red light** (*traffic light*) un feu rouge
◇ *to go through a red light* brûler un feu rouge
2 (*hair*)
roux MASC
rousse FEM
◇ *Tamsin's got red hair.* Tamsin a les cheveux roux.

Red Cross NOUN
la *Croix-Rouge*

redcurrant NOUN
la *groseille*

to **redecorate** VERB
1 *retapisser* (*with wallpaper*)
2 *refaire les peintures* (*with paint*)

red-haired ADJECTIVE
roux MASC
rousse FEM

red-handed ADJECTIVE
- **to catch somebody red-handed** prendre quelqu'un la main dans le sac
◇ *He was caught red-handed.* Il a été pris la main dans le sac.

redhead NOUN
le *roux*
la *rousse*

to **redo** VERB
refaire

to **reduce** VERB
réduire ◇ *at a reduced price* à prix réduit
- **"reduce speed now"** "ralentir"

reduction NOUN
la *réduction* ◇ *a 5% reduction* une réduction de cinq pour cent
- **"huge reductions!"** "prix sacrifiés!"

redundancy NOUN
le *licenciement* ◇ *There were fifty redundancies.* Il y a eu cinquante licenciements.
- **his redundancy payment** ses indemnités de licenciement

redundant ADJECTIVE
- **to be made redundant** être licencié
◇ *He was made redundant yesterday.* Il a été licencié hier.

reed NOUN
(*plant*)
le *roseau*
(les *roseaux* PL)

reel NOUN
la *bobine* (*of thread*)

to **refer** VERB
- **to refer to** faire allusion à ◇ *What are you referring to?* À quoi faites-vous allusion?

referee NOUN
l' *arbitre* MASC

reference NOUN
1 l' *allusion* FEM ◇ *He made no reference to the murder.* Il n'a fait aucune allusion au meurtre.
2 les *références* FEM (*for job application*)
◇ *Would you please give me a reference?* Pouvez-vous me fournir des références?
- **a reference book** un ouvrage de référence

to **refill** VERB
remplir à nouveau ◇ *He refilled my glass.* Il a rempli mon verre à nouveau.

refinery NOUN
la *raffinerie*

to **reflect** VERB
refléter (*light, image*)

reflection NOUN
le *reflet* (*in mirror*)

reflex NOUN
le *réflexe*

reflexive ADJECTIVE
réfléchi ◇ *a reflexive verb* un verbe réfléchi

refresher course NOUN
le *cours de recyclage*

refreshing ADJECTIVE
rafraîchissant

refreshments PL NOUN
les *rafraîchissements* MASC PL

refrigerator NOUN
le *réfrigérateur*

to **refuel** VERB
se ravitailler en carburant ◇ *The plane stops in Boston to refuel.* L'avion s'arrête à Boston pour se ravitailler en carburant.

refuge NOUN

le *refuge*

refugee NOUN
le *réfugié*
la *réfugiée*

refund NOUN
see also refund VERB
le *remboursement*

to **refund** VERB
see also refund NOUN
rembourser

refusal NOUN
le *refus*

to **refuse** VERB
see also refuse NOUN
refuser

refuse NOUN
see also refuse VERB
les *ordures* FEM PL
* **refuse collection** le ramassage des ordures

to **regain** VERB
* **to regain consciousness** reprendre connaissance

regard NOUN
see also regard VERB
* **Give my regards to Alice.** Transmettez mon bon souvenir à Alice.
* **Louis sends his regards.** Vous avez le bonjour de Louis.
* **"with kind regards"** "bien cordialement"

to **regard** VERB
see also regard NOUN
* **to regard something as** considérer quelque chose comme
* **as regards...** concernant...

regarding PREPOSITION
relatif à MASC
relative à FEM
◊ *the laws regarding the export of animals* les lois relatives à l'exportation des animaux
* **Regarding John,...** Quant à John,...

regiment NOUN
le *régiment*

region NOUN
la *région*

regional ADJECTIVE
régional
(*régionaux* PL)

register NOUN
see also register VERB
le *registre d'absences* (*in school*)

register VERB
see also register NOUN
s'inscrire (*at school, college*)

registered ADJECTIVE
* **a registered letter** une lettre recommandée

registration NOUN
[1] l' *appel* MASC (*roll call*)
[2] le *numéro d'immatriculation* (*of car*)

regret NOUN
see also regret VERB
le *regret*
* **I've got no regrets.** Je ne regrette rien.

to **regret** VERB
see also regret NOUN
regretter ◊ *Give me the money or you'll regret it!* Donne-moi l'argent, sinon tu vas le regretter!
* **to regret doing something** regretter d'avoir fait quelque chose ◊ *I regret saying that.* Je regrette d'avoir dit ça.

regular ADJECTIVE
[1] *régulier* MASC
régulière FEM
◊ *at regular intervals* à intervalles réguliers ◊ *a regular verb* un verbe régulier
* **to take regular exercise** faire régulièrement de l'exercice
[2] (*average*)
normal
(*normaux* PL)
◊ *a regular portion of fries* une portion de frites normale

regularly ADVERB
régulièrement

regulation NOUN
le *règlement*

rehearsal NOUN
la *répétition*

to **rehearse** VERB
répéter

rein NOUN
la *rêne* ◊ *the reins* les rênes

reindeer NOUN
le *renne*

to **reject** VERB
rejeter (*idea, suggestion*) ◊ *We rejected that idea straight away.* Nous avons immédiatement rejeté cette idée.
* **I applied but they rejected me.** J'ai posé ma candidature mais ils l'ont rejetée.

relapse NOUN
la *rechute* ◊ *to have a relapse* faire une rechute

related ADJECTIVE
apparenté (*people*) ◊ *We're related.* Nous sommes apparentés.
* **The two events were not related.** Il n'y avait aucun rapport entre les deux événements.

relation NOUN
[1] (*person*)
le *parent*
la *parente*

R

○ *He's a distant relation.* C'est un parent éloigné. ○ *my close relations* mes parents proches

> *Remember that in French, **mes parents** usually only refers to your mother and father.*

+ **my relations** ma famille
+ **I've got relations in London.** J'ai de la famille à Londres.

2 *(connection)*
le *rapport* ○ *It has no relation to reality.* Cela n'a aucun rapport avec la réalité.

+ **in relation to** par rapport à
relationship NOUN
les *relations* FEM PL ○ *We have a good relationship.* Nous avons de bonnes relations.

+ **I'm not in a relationship at the moment.** Je ne sors avec personne en ce moment.
relative NOUN
le *parent*
la *parente*
○ *my close relatives* mes proches parents
+ **all her relatives** toute sa famille
relatively ADVERB
relativement
to **relax** VERB
se détendre ○ *I relax listening to music.* Je me détends en écoutant de la musique.

+ **Relax! Everything's fine.** Ne t'en fais pas! Tout va bien.
relaxation NOUN
la *détente* ○ *I don't have much time for relaxation.* Je n'ai pas beaucoup de moments de détente.
relaxed ADJECTIVE
détendu
relaxing ADJECTIVE
reposant
+ **I find cooking relaxing.** Cela me détend de faire la cuisine.
relay NOUN
+ **a relay race** une course de relais
to **release** VERB

> see also **release** NOUN

1 *libérer* *(prisoner)*
2 *divulguer* *(report, news)*
3 *sortir* *(record, video)*
release NOUN

> see also **release** VERB

la *libération* *(from prison)* ○ *the release of Nelson Mandela* la libération de Nelson Mandela
+ **the band's latest release** le dernier disque du groupe
relegated ADJECTIVE
déclassé *(sport)*
relevant ADJECTIVE
approprié *(documents)*

+ **That's not relevant.** Ça n'a aucun rapport.
+ **to be relevant to something** être en rapport avec quelque chose
○ *Education should be relevant to real life.* L'enseignement devrait être en rapport avec la réalité.
reliable ADJECTIVE
fiable ○ *a reliable car* une voiture fiable ○ *He's not very reliable.* Il n'est pas très fiable.
relief NOUN
le *soulagement* ○ *That's a relief!* Quel soulagement!
to **relieve** VERB
soulager ○ *This injection will relieve the pain.* Cette piqûre va soulager la douleur.
relieved ADJECTIVE
soulagé ○ *I was relieved to hear...* J'ai été soulagé d'apprendre...
religion NOUN
la *religion* ○ *What religion are you?* Quelle est votre religion?
religious ADJECTIVE
1 *religieux* MASC
religieuse FEM
○ *my religious beliefs* mes croyances religieuses
2 *croyant* ○ *I'm not religious.* Je ne suis pas croyant.
reluctant ADJECTIVE
+ **to be reluctant to do something** être peu disposé à faire quelque chose
○ *They were reluctant to help us.* Ils étaient peu disposés à nous aider.
reluctantly ADVERB
à contrecœur ○ *She reluctantly accepted.* Elle a accepté à contrecœur.
to **rely on** VERB
compter sur ○ *I'm relying on you.* Je compte sur toi.
to **remain** VERB
rester
+ **to remain silent** garder le silence
remaining ADJECTIVE
le reste de ○ *the remaining ingredients* le reste des ingrédients
remains PL NOUN
les *restes* MASC PL ○ *the remains of the picnic* les restes du pique-nique
○ *human remains* des restes humains
+ **Roman remains** les vestiges romains
remake NOUN
le *remake* *(of film)*
remark NOUN
la *remarque*
remarkable ADJECTIVE
remarquable

remarkably ADVERB
remarquablement

to **remarry** VERB
se remarier ⋄ *She remarried three years ago.* Elle s'est remariée il y a trois ans.

remedy NOUN
le *remède* ⋄ *a good remedy for a sore throat* un bon remède contre le mal de gorge

to **remember** VERB
se souvenir de ⋄ *I can't remember his name.* Je ne me souviens pas de son nom. ⋄ *I don't remember.* Je ne m'en souviens pas.

In French you often say "don't forget" instead of remember.

⋄ *Remember your passport!* N'oublie pas ton passeport! ⋄ *Remember to write your name on the form.* N'oubliez pas d'écrire votre nom sur le formulaire.

Remembrance Day NOUN
le *jour de l'Armistice* MASC ⋄ *on Remembrance Day* le jour de l'Armistice

to **remind** VERB
rappeler ⋄ *It reminds me of Scotland.* Cela me rappelle l'Écosse. ⋄ *I'll remind you tomorrow.* Je te le rappellerai demain. ⋄ *Remind me to speak to Daniel.* Rappelle-moi de parler à Daniel.

remorse NOUN
le *remords* ⋄ *He showed no remorse.* Il a manifesté aucun remords.

remote ADJECTIVE
isolé ⋄ *a remote village* un village isolé

remote control NOUN
la *télécommande*

removable ADJECTIVE
amovible

removal NOUN
le *déménagement* (from house)
+ **a removal van** un camion de déménagement

to **remove** VERB
[1] *enlever* ⋄ *Please remove your bag from my seat.* Est-ce que vous pouvez enlever votre sac de mon siège?
[2] *faire partir* (stain) ⋄ *Did you remove the stain?* Est-ce que tu as fait partir la tache?

rendezvous NOUN
le *rendez-vous*
(les *rendez-vous* PL)

to **renew** VERB
renouveler (passport, licence)

renewable ADJECTIVE
renouvelable (energy, resource)

to **renovate** VERB
rénover ⋄ *The building's been*

renovated. Le bâtiment a été rénové.

renowned ADJECTIVE
renommé

rent NOUN
see also rent VERB
le *loyer*

to **rent** VERB
see also rent NOUN
louer ⋄ *We rented a car.* Nous avons loué une voiture.

rental NOUN
la *location* ⋄ *Car rental is included in the price.* Le prix comprend la location d'une voiture.

to **reorganize** VERB
réorganiser

rep NOUN (= representative)
le *représentant*
la *représentante*

to **repair** VERB
see also repair NOUN
réparer
+ **to get something repaired** faire réparer quelque chose ⋄ *I got the washing machine repaired.* J'ai fait réparer la machine à laver.

repair NOUN
see also repair VERB
la *réparation*

to **repay** VERB
rembourser (money)

repayment NOUN
le *remboursement*

to **repeat** VERB
see also repeat NOUN
répéter

repeat NOUN
see also repeat VERB
la *reprise* ⋄ *There are too many repeats on TV.* Il y a trop de reprises à la télé.

repeatedly ADVERB
à plusieurs reprises

repellent NOUN
+ **insect repellent** l'insectifuge MASC

repetitive ADJECTIVE
(movement, work)
répétitif MASC
répétitive FEM

to **replace** VERB
remplacer

replay NOUN
see also replay VERB
+ **There will be a replay on Friday.** Le match sera rejoué vendredi.

to **replay** VERB
see also replay NOUN
rejouer (match)

replica NOUN

la *réplique*
reply NOUN
see also reply VERB
la *réponse*
to **reply** VERB
see also reply NOUN
répondre
report NOUN
see also report VERB
[1] (*of event*)
le *compte rendu*
(les *comptes rendus* PL)
[2] (*news report*)
le *reportage* ◇ *a report in the paper* un reportage dans le journal
[3] (*at school*)
le *bulletin scolaire* ◇ *I got a good report this term.* J'ai un bon bulletin scolaire ce trimestre.
to **report** VERB
see also report NOUN
[1] *signaler* ◇ *I reported the theft to the police.* J'ai signalé le vol au commissariat.
[2] *se présenter* ◇ *Report to reception when you arrive.* Présentez-vous à la réception à votre arrivée.
reporter NOUN
le *reporter* ◇ *I'd like to be a reporter.* J'aimerais être reporter.
to **represent** VERB
représenter
representative ADJECTIVE
représentatif MASC
représentative FEM
reproduction NOUN
la *reproduction*
republic NOUN
la *république*
repulsive ADJECTIVE
repoussant
reputation NOUN
la *réputation*
request NOUN
see also request VERB
la *demande*
to **request** VERB
see also request NOUN
demander
requirement NOUN
la *condition requise*
◆ **What are the requirements for the job?** Quelles sont les conditions requises pour le poste?
◆ **entry requirements** (*for university*) les critères d'entrée
to **rescue** VERB
see also rescue NOUN
sauver

rescue NOUN
see also rescue VERB
[1] le *sauvetage* ◇ *a rescue operation* une opération de sauvetage
◆ **a mountain rescue team** une équipe de sauvetage en montagne
[2] le *secours* ◇ *the rescue services* les services de secours
◆ **to come to somebody's rescue** venir au secours de quelqu'un ◇ *He came to my rescue.* Il est venu à mon secours.
research NOUN
[1] la *recherche* (*experimental*) ◇ *He's doing research.* Il fait de la recherche.
[2] les *recherches* FEM PL (*theoretical*) ◇ *She's doing some research in the library.* Elle fait des recherches à la bibliothèque.
resemblance NOUN
la *ressemblance*
reservation NOUN
la *réservation* (*booking*) ◇ *I've got a reservation for two nights.* J'ai une réservation pour deux nuits. ◇ *I'd like to make a reservation for this evening.* J'aimerais faire une réservation pour ce soir.
reserve NOUN
see also reserve VERB
[1] (*place*)
la *réserve* ◇ *a nature reserve* une réserve naturelle
[2] (*person*)
le *remplaçant*
la *remplaçante*
◇ *I was reserve in the game last Saturday.* J'étais remplaçant dans le match de samedi dernier.
to **reserve** VERB
see also reserve NOUN
réserver ◇ *I'd like to reserve a table for tomorrow evening.* J'aimerais réserver une table pour demain soir.
reserved ADJECTIVE
réservé ◇ *a reserved seat* une place réservée ◇ *He's quite reserved.* Il est assez réservé.
resident NOUN
le *résident*
la *résidente*
residential ADJECTIVE
résidentiel MASC
résidentielle FEM
◇ *a residential area* un quartier résidentiel
to **resign** VERB
donner sa démission
resistance NOUN
◆ **He was in the resistance.** Il faisait de la

résistance.

* **the French Resistance** la Résistance

to **resit** VERB
repasser ◇ *I'm resitting the exam in December.* Je vais repasser l'examen en décembre.

resolution NOUN
la *résolution*

* **Have you made any new year's resolutions?** Tu as pris de bonnes résolutions pour l'année nouvelle?

resort NOUN
la *station balnéaire* (at seaside) ◇ *It's a resort on the Costa del Sol.* C'est une station balnéaire sur la Costa del Sol.

* **a ski resort** une station de ski
* **as a last resort** en dernier recours

resource NOUN
la *ressource*

respect NOUN
see also respect VERB
le *respect*

to **respect** VERB
see also respect NOUN
respecter

respectable ADJECTIVE
1 *respectable*
2 *correct* (standard, marks)

respectively ADVERB
respectivement

responsibility NOUN
la *responsabilité*

responsible ADJECTIVE
1 (in charge)
responsable

* **to be responsible for something** être responsable de quelque chose ◇ *He's responsible for booking the tickets.* Il est responsable de la réservation des billets.
* **It's a responsible job.** C'est un poste à responsabilités.
  2 (mature)
  sérieux MASC
  sérieuse FEM
  ◇ *You should be more responsible.* Tu devrais être un peu plus sérieux.

rest NOUN
see also rest VERB
1 le *repos* (relaxation) ◇ *five minutes' rest* cinq minutes de repos

* **to have a rest** se reposer ◇ *We stopped to have a rest.* Nous nous sommes arrêtés pour nous reposer.
  2 le *reste* (remainder) ◇ *I'll do the rest.* Je ferai le reste. ◇ *the rest of the money* le reste de l'argent
* **the rest of them** les autres ◇ *The rest of them went swimming.* Les autres sont allés nager.

to **rest** VERB
see also rest NOUN
1 *se reposer* (relax) ◇ *She's resting in her room.* Elle se repose dans sa chambre.
2 *ménager* (not overstrain) ◇ *He has to rest his knee.* Il doit ménager son genou.
3 *appuyer* (lean) ◇ *I rested my bike against the window.* J'ai appuyé mon vélo contre la fenêtre.

restaurant NOUN
le *restaurant* ◇ *We don't often go to restaurants.* Nous n'allons pas souvent au restaurant.

* **a restaurant car** un wagon-restaurant

restful ADJECTIVE
reposant

restoration NOUN
la *restauration*

to **restore** VERB
restaurer (building, picture)

to **restrict** VERB
limiter

result NOUN
le *résultat* ◇ *my exam results* mes résultats d'examen ◇ *What was the result? – One-nil.* Quel a été le résultat? – Un à zéro.

to **retire** VERB
prendre sa retraite ◇ *He retired last year.* Il a pris sa retraite l'an dernier.

retired ADJECTIVE
retraité ◇ *She's retired.* Elle est retraitée.

* **a retired teacher** un professeur à la retraite

retirement NOUN
la *retraite*

to **retrace** VERB

* **to retrace one's steps** revenir sur ses pas ◇ *I retraced my steps.* Je suis revenu sur mes pas.

return NOUN
see also return VERB
1 le *retour* ◇ *after our return* à notre retour

* **the return journey** le voyage de retour
* **a return match** un match retour
  2 l' *aller retour* MASC (ticket) ◇ *A return to Avignon, please.* Un aller retour pour Avignon, s'il vous plaît.
* **in return** en échange ◇ *...and I help her in return* ...et je l'aide en échange
* **in return for** en échange de
* **Many happy returns!** Bon anniversaire!

to **return** VERB
see also return NOUN
1 *revenir* (come back) ◇ *I've just returned from holiday.* Je viens de revenir de vacances.

R

◆ **to return home** rentrer à la maison
  ☐2☐ *retourner* (*go back*) ⋄ *He returned to France the following year.* Il est retourné en France l'année suivante.
  ☐3☐ *rendre* (*give back*) ⋄ *She borrows my things and doesn't return them.* Elle m'emprunte mes affaires et ne me les rend pas.

reunion NOUN
  la *réunion*

to **reuse** VERB
  réutiliser

to **reveal** VERB
  révéler

revenge NOUN
  la *vengeance* ⋄ *in revenge* par vengeance
◆ **to take revenge** se venger ⋄ *They planned to take revenge on him.* Ils voulaient se venger de lui.

to **reverse** VERB
  ☐see also reverse ADJECTIVE☐
  faire marche arrière (*car*) ⋄ *He reversed without looking.* Il a fait marche arrière sans regarder.
◆ **to reverse the charges** (*telephone*) appeler en PCV
  In France, reversing the charges is only possible for international calls.
  ⋄ *I'd like to make a reverse charge call to Britain.* Je voudrais appeler la Grande-Bretagne en PCV.

reverse ADJECTIVE
  ☐see also reverse VERB☐
  inverse ⋄ *in reverse order* dans l'ordre inverse
◆ **in reverse gear** en marche arrière

to **revise** VERB
  réviser ⋄ *I haven't started revising yet.* Je n'ai pas encore commencé à réviser.
◆ **I've revised my opinion.** J'ai changé d'opinion.

revision NOUN
  les *révisions* FEM PL ⋄ *Have you done a lot of revision?* Est-ce que tu as fait beaucoup de révisions?

to **revive** VERB
  ranimer ⋄ *The nurses tried to revive him.* Les infirmières ont essayé de le ranimer.

revolting ADJECTIVE
  dégoûtant

revolution NOUN
  la *révolution*
◆ **the French Revolution** la Révolution française

revolutionary ADJECTIVE
  révolutionnaire

revolver NOUN

  le *revolver*

reward NOUN
  la *récompense*

rewarding ADJECTIVE
  gratifiant ⋄ *a rewarding job* un travail gratifiant

to **rewind** VERB
  rembobiner ⋄ *to rewind a cassette* rembobiner une cassette

rheumatism NOUN
  le *rhumatisme*

Rhine NOUN
  le *Rhin*

Rhone NOUN
  le *Rhône*

rhubarb NOUN
  la *rhubarbe* ⋄ *a rhubarb tart* une tarte à la rhubarbe

rhythm NOUN
  le *rythme*

rib NOUN
  la *côte*

ribbon NOUN
  le *ruban*

rice NOUN
  le *riz*
◆ **rice pudding** le riz au lait

rich ADJECTIVE
  riche
◆ **the rich** les riches MASC

to **rid** VERB
◆ **to get rid of** se débarrasser de ⋄ *I want to get rid of some old clothes.* Je veux me débarrasser de vieux vêtements.

ride NOUN
  ☐see also ride VERB☐
◆ **to go for a ride (1)** (*on horse*) monter à cheval
◆ **to go for a ride (2)** (*on bike*) faire un tour en vélo ⋄ *We went for a bike ride.* Nous sommes allés faire un tour en vélo.
◆ **it's a short bus ride to the town centre.** Ce n'est pas loin du centre-ville en bus.

to **ride** VERB
  ☐see also ride NOUN☐
  monter à cheval (*on horse*) ⋄ *I'm learning to ride.* J'apprends à monter à cheval.
◆ **to ride a bike** faire du vélo ⋄ *Can you ride a bike?* Tu sais faire du vélo?

rider NOUN
  ☐1☐ (*on horse*)
  le *cavalier*
  la *cavalière*
  ⋄ *She's a good rider.* C'est une bonne cavalière.
  ☐2☐ (*on bike*)
  le/la *cycliste*

ridiculous ADJECTIVE

ridicule ◦ *Don't be ridiculous!* Ne sois pas ridicule!

riding NOUN
l' *équitation* FEM

+ **to go riding** faire de l'équitation
+ **a riding school** une école d'équitation

rifle NOUN
le *fusil* ◦ *a hunting rifle* un fusil de chasse

rig NOUN
+ **an oil rig** une plate-forme pétrolière

right ADJECTIVE, ADVERB

see also right NOUN

There are several ways of translating right. Scan the examples to find one that is similar to what you want to say.

[1] (*factually correct, suitable*)
bon MASC
bonne FEM
◦ *the right answer* la bonne réponse ◦ *It isn't the right size.* Ce n'est pas la bonne taille. ◦ *We're on the right train.* Nous sommes dans le bon train.

+ **Is this the right road for Arles?** Est-ce que c'est bien la route pour aller à Arles?
[2] (*correctly*)
correctement ◦ *Am I pronouncing it right?* Est-ce que je prononce ça correctement?

+ **to be right (1)** (*person*) avoir raison ◦ *You were right!* Tu avais raison!
+ **to be right (2)** (*statement, opinion*) être vrai ◦ *That's right!* C'est vrai!
[3] (*accurate*)
juste ◦ *Do you have the right time?* Est-ce que vous avez l'heure juste?
[4] (*morally correct*)
bien ◦ *It's not right to behave like that.* Ce n'est pas bien d'agir comme ça.

+ **I think you did the right thing.** Je pense que tu as bien fait.
[5] (*not left*)
droit ◦ *my right hand* ma main droite
[6] (*turn, look*)
à droite ◦ *Turn right at the traffic lights.* Tournez à droite aux prochains feux.

+ **Right! Let's get started.** Bon! On commence.
+ **right away** tout de suite ◦ *I'll do it right away.* Je vais le faire tout de suite.

right NOUN

see also right ADJECTIVE

[1] le *droit*
+ **You've got no right to do that.** Vous n'avez pas le droit de faire ça.
[2] la *droite* (*not left*)
+ **on the right** à droite ◦ *Remember to drive on the right.* N'oubliez pas de conduire à droite.
+ **right of way** la priorité ◦ *It was our*

right of way. Nous avions la priorité.

right-hand ADJECTIVE
+ **the right-hand side** la droite ◦ *It's on the right-hand side.* C'est à droite.

right-handed ADJECTIVE
droitier MASC
droitière FEM

rim NOUN
la *monture* ◦ *glasses with wire rims* des lunettes avec une monture métallique

ring NOUN

see also ring VERB

[1] l' *anneau* MASC
(les *anneaux* PL)
◦ *a gold ring* un anneau en or
[2] la *bague* (*with stones*) ◦ *a diamond ring* une bague de diamants
+ **a wedding ring** une alliance
[3] le *cercle* (*circle*) ◦ *to stand in a ring* se mettre en cercle
[4] le *coup de sonnette* (*of bell*) ◦ *I was woken by a ring at the door.* J'ai été réveillé par un coup de sonnette.
+ **to give somebody a ring** appeler quelqu'un ◦ *I'll give you a ring this evening.* Je t'appellerai ce soir.

to **ring** VERB

see also ring NOUN

[1] *téléphoner* ◦ *Your mother rang this morning.* Ta mère a téléphoné ce matin.
+ **to ring somebody** appeler quelqu'un ◦ *I'll ring you tomorrow morning.* Je t'appellerai demain matin.
+ **to ring somebody up** donner un coup de fil à quelqu'un
[2] *sonner* ◦ *The phone's ringing.* Le téléphone sonne.
+ **to ring the bell** (*doorbell*) sonner à la porte ◦ *I rang the bell three times.* J'ai sonné trois fois à la porte.
+ **to ring back** rappeler ◦ *I'll ring back later.* Je rappellerai plus tard.

ring binder NOUN
le *classeur*

ring road NOUN
[1] la *rocade* (*ordinary road*)
[2] le *périphérique* (*motorway*)

rink NOUN
[1] la *patinoire* (*for ice-skating*)
[2] la *piste* (*for roller-skating*)

to **rinse** VERB
rincer

riot NOUN

see also riot VERB

l' *émeute* FEM

to **riot** VERB

see also riot NOUN

faire une émeute

R

to **rip** VERB
  [1] *déchirer* ◇ *I've ripped my jeans.* J'ai déchiré mon jean.
  [2] *se déchirer* ◇ *My skirt's ripped.* Ma jupe s'est déchirée.
ripe ADJECTIVE
  mûr
rip-off NOUN
  ◆ **It's a rip-off!** C'est de l'arnaque! (*informal*)
rise NOUN
  see also **rise** VERB
  [1] la *hausse* (*in prices, temperature*) ◇ *a sudden rise in temperature* une hausse subite de température
  [2] l' *augmentation* FEM (*pay rise*)
to **rise** VERB
  see also **rise** NOUN
  [1] *augmenter* (*increase*) ◇ *Prices are rising.* Les prix augmentent.
  [2] *se lever* ◇ *The sun rises early in June.* Le soleil se lève tôt en juin.
riser NOUN
  ◆ **to be an early riser** être matinal
risk NOUN
  see also **risk** VERB
  le *risque*
  ◆ **to take risks** prendre des risques
  ◆ **It's at your own risk.** C'est à vos risques et périls.
to **risk** VERB
  see also **risk** NOUN
  risquer ◇ *You risk getting a fine.* Vous risquez de recevoir une amende.
  ◆ **I wouldn't risk it if I were you.** À votre place, je ne prendrais pas ce risque.
risky ADJECTIVE
  risqué
rival NOUN
  see also **rival** ADJECTIVE
  le *rival*
  (les *rivaux* PL)
  la *rivale*
rival ADJECTIVE
  see also **rival** NOUN
  [1] *rival* ◇ *a rival gang* une bande rivale
  [2] *concurrent* ◇ *a rival company* une société concurrente
rivalry NOUN
  la *rivalité* (*between towns, schools*)
river NOUN
  [1] la *rivière* ◇ *The river runs alongside the canal.* La rivière longe le canal.
  [2] le *fleuve* (*major*) ◇ *the rivers of France* les fleuves de France
  ◆ **the river Seine** la Seine
Riviera NOUN
  ◆ **the French Riviera** la Côte d'Azur
  ◆ **the Italian Riviera** la Riviera italienne

road NOUN
  [1] la *route* ◇ *There's a lot of traffic on the roads.* Il y a beaucoup de circulation sur les routes.
  [2] la *rue* (*street*) ◇ *They live across the road.* Ils habitent de l'autre côté de la rue.
road map NOUN
  la *carte routière*
road sign NOUN
  le *panneau de signalisation*
  (les *panneaux de signalisation* PL)
roadworks PL NOUN
  les *travaux* MASC PL
roast ADJECTIVE
  rôti ◇ *roast chicken* le poulet rôti
  ◇ *roast potatoes* les pommes de terre rôties
  ◆ **roast pork** le rôti de porc
  ◆ **roast beef** le rôti de bœuf
to **rob** VERB
  ◆ **to rob somebody** voler quelqu'un
  ◇ *I've been robbed.* On m'a volé.
  ◆ **to rob somebody of something** voler quelque chose à quelqu'un ◇ *He was robbed of his wallet.* On lui a volé son portefeuille.
  ◆ **to rob a bank** dévaliser une banque
robber NOUN
  le *voleur*
  ◆ **a bank-robber** un cambrioleur de banques
robbery NOUN
  le *vol*
  ◆ **a bank robbery** un hold-up
  ◆ **armed robbery** le vol à main armée
robot NOUN
  le *robot*
rock NOUN
  [1] la *roche* (*substance*) ◇ *They tunnelled through the rock.* Ils ont creusé un tunnel dans la roche.
  [2] le *rocher* (*boulder*) ◇ *I sat on a rock.* Je me suis assis sur un rocher.
  [3] la *pierre* (*stone*) ◇ *The crowd started to throw rocks.* La foule s'est mise à lancer des pierres.
  [4] le *rock* (*music*) ◇ *a rock concert* un concert de rock ◇ *He's a rock star.* C'est une rock star.
  [5] le *sucre d'orge* (*sweet*) ◇ *a stick of rock* un bâton de sucre d'orge
  ◆ **rock and roll** le rock'n'roll
rockery NOUN
  la *rocaille*
rocket NOUN
  la *fusée* (*firework, spacecraft*)
rocking chair NOUN
  le *rocking-chair*

rocking horse NOUN
le *cheval à bascule*

rod NOUN
la *canne à pêche* (for fishing)

rode VERB see **ride**

role NOUN
le *rôle*

role play NOUN
le *jeu de rôle*
(les *jeux de rôles* PL)
◇ to do a role play faire un jeu de rôle

roll NOUN
see also **roll** VERB
1 le *rouleau*
(les *rouleaux* PL)
◇ a roll of tape un rouleau de ruban
adhésif ◇ a toilet roll un rouleau de
papier hygiénique
2 le *petit pain* (bread)

to **roll** VERB
see also **roll** NOUN
rouler
→ to roll out the pastry abaisser la pâte

roll call NOUN
l' *appel* MASC

roller NOUN
le *rouleau*
(les *rouleaux* PL)

rollercoaster NOUN
les *montagnes russes* FEM PL

roller skates PL NOUN
les *patins à roulettes* MASC

roller-skating NOUN
le *patin à roulettes*
→ to go roller-skating faire du patin à
roulettes

rolling pin NOUN
le *rouleau à pâtisserie*

Roman ADJECTIVE, NOUN
romain (ancient) ◇ a Roman villa une
villa romaine ◇ the Roman empire
l'empire romain
→ the Romans les Romains

Roman Catholic NOUN
le/la *catholique* ◇ He's a Roman
Catholic. Il est catholique.

romance NOUN
1 les *romans d'amour* MASC PL (novels)
◇ I read a lot of romance. Je lis beaucoup
de romans d'amour.
2 le *charme* (glamour) ◇ the romance of
Paris le charme de Paris
→ a holiday romance une idylle de
vacances

Romania NOUN
la *Roumanie*
→ in Romania en Roumanie

Romanian ADJECTIVE
roumain

romantic ADJECTIVE
romantique

roof NOUN
le *toit*

roof rack NOUN
la *galerie*

room NOUN
1 la *pièce* ◇ the biggest room in the
house la plus grande pièce de la maison
2 la *chambre* (bedroom) ◇ She's in her
room. Elle est dans sa chambre.
→ a single room une chambre pour une
personne
→ a double room une chambre pour deux
personnes
3 la *salle* (in school) ◇ the music room
la salle de musique
4 la *place* (space) ◇ There's no room for
that box. Il n'y a pas de place pour cette
boîte.

roommate NOUN
le/la *camarade de chambre*

root NOUN
la *racine*

rope NOUN
la *corde*

rose VERB see **rise**

rose NOUN
la *rose* (flower)

to **rot** NOUN VERB
pourrir

rotten ADJECTIVE
pourri (decayed) ◇ a rotten apple une
pomme pourrie
→ rotten weather un temps pourri
→ That's a rotten thing to do. Ce n'est
vraiment pas gentil.
→ to feel rotten être mal fichu (informal)

rough ADJECTIVE
1 (surface)
rêche ◇ My hands are rough. J'ai les
mains rêches.
2 (game)
violent ◇ Rugby's a rough sport. Le
rugby est un sport violent.
3 (place)
difficile ◇ It's a rough area. C'est un
quartier difficile.
4 (water)
houleux MASC
houleuse FEM
◇ The sea was rough. La mer était
houleuse.
5 *approximatif* MASC
approximative FEM
→ I've got a rough idea. J'en ai une idée
approximative.
→ to feel rough ne pas être dans son
assiette ◇ I feel rough. Je ne suis pas

R

dans mon assiette.

roughly ADVERB

à peu près ◇ *It weighs roughly 20 kilos.*
Ça pèse à peu près vingt kilos.

round ADJECTIVE, ADVERB, PREPOSITION

see also round NOUN

1 *rond* ◇ *a round table* une table
ronde

2 *autour de* (*around*) ◇ *We were sitting
round the table.* Nous étions assis autour
de la table. ◇ *She wore a scarf round her
neck.* Elle portait une écharpe autour du
cou.

◆ **It's just round the corner.** (*very near*)
C'est tout près.

◆ **to go round to somebody's house** aller
chez quelqu'un ◇ *I went round to my
friend's house.* Je suis allé chez mon ami.

◆ **to have a look round** faire un tour
◇ *We're going to have a look round.* Nous
allons faire un tour.

◆ **to go round a museum** visiter un musée

◆ **round here** près d'ici ◇ *Is there a
chemist's round here?* Est-ce qu'il y a
une pharmacie près d'ici?

◆ **He lives round here.** Il habite dans les
parages.

◆ **all round** partout ◇ *There were
vineyards all round.* Il y avait des
vignobles partout.

◆ **all year round** toute l'année

◆ **round about** (*roughly*) environ ◇ *It
costs round about £100.* Cela coûte
environ cent livres. ◇ *round about 8
o'clock* à huit heures environ

round NOUN

see also round ADJECTIVE

1 la *manche* (*of tournament*)

2 le *round* (*of boxing match*)

◆ **a round of golf** une partie de golf

◆ **a round of drinks** une tournée ◇ *He
bought a round of drinks.* Il a offert une
tournée.

roundabout NOUN

1 (*at junction*)
le *rond-point*
(les *ronds-points* PL)

2 (*at funfair*)
le *manège*

route NOUN

1 l' *itinéraire* MASC ◇ *We're planning
our route.* Nous établissons notre
itinéraire.

2 le *parcours* (*of bus*)

routine NOUN

◆ **my daily routine** mes occupations
quotidiennes

row NOUN

see also row VERB

1 la *rangée* ◇ *a row of houses* une
rangée de maisons

2 le *rang* (*of seats*) ◇ *Our seats are in
the front row.* Nos places se trouvent au
premier rang.

◆ **five times in a row** cinq fois d'affilée

3 le *vacarme* (*noise*) ◇ *What's that
terrible row?* Qu'est-ce que c'est que ce
vacarme?

4 la *dispute* (*quarrel*)

◆ **to have a row** se disputer ◇ *They've
had a row.* Ils se sont disputés.

to **row** VERB

see also row NOUN

1 *ramer* ◇ *We took turns to row.* Nous
avons ramé à tour de rôle.

2 *faire de l'aviron* (*as sport*)

rowing NOUN

l' *aviron* MASC (*sport*) ◇ *My hobby is
rowing.* Je fais de l'aviron.

◆ **a rowing boat** un bateau à rames

royal ADJECTIVE

royal
(*royaux* MASC PL)

◆ **the royal family** la famille royale

to **rub** VERB

1 *frotter* (*stain*)

2 *se frotter* (*part of body*) ◇ *Don't rub
your eyes!* Ne te frotte pas les yeux!

◆ **to rub something out** effacer quelque
chose

rubber NOUN

1 le *caoutchouc* ◇ *rubber soles* des
semelles en caoutchouc

2 la *gomme* (*eraser*) ◇ *Can I borrow
your rubber?* Je peux emprunter ta
gomme?

◆ **a rubber band** un élastique

rubbish NOUN

see also rubbish ADJECTIVE

1 les *ordures* FEM PL (*refuse*) ◇ *When do
they collect the rubbish?* Quand est-ce
qu'ils ramassent les ordures?

2 la *camelote* (*junk*) ◇ *They sell a lot of
rubbish at the market.* Ils vendent
beaucoup de camelote au marché.

3 les *bêtises* FEM PL (*nonsense*) ◇ *Don't
talk rubbish!* Ne dis pas de bêtises!

◆ **That's a load of rubbish!** C'est vraiment
n'importe quoi! (*informal*)

◆ **a rubbish bin** une poubelle

◆ **a rubbish dump** une décharge

rubbish ADJECTIVE

see also rubbish NOUN

nul MASC
nulle FEM

◇ *They're a rubbish team!* Cette équipe
est nulle!

rucksack NOUN

le *sac à dos*

rude ADJECTIVE
- [1] *(impolite)*
  impoli ◇ It's rude to interrupt. C'est impoli de couper la parole aux gens.
- [2] *(offensive)*
  grossier MASC
  grossière FEM
  ◇ a rude joke une plaisanterie grossière
  ◇ He was very rude to me. Il a été très grossier avec moi.
- ◆ **a rude word** un gros mot

rug NOUN
- [1] le *tapis* ◇ a Persian rug un tapis persan
- [2] la *couverture* *(blanket)* ◇ a tartan rug une couverture écossaise

rugby NOUN
le *rugby* ◇ I play rugby. Je joue au rugby.

ruin NOUN
see also ruin VERB
la *ruine* ◇ the ruins of the castle les ruines du château
- ◆ **in ruins** en ruine

o ruin VERB
see also ruin NOUN
- [1] *abîmer* ◇ You'll ruin your shoes. Tu vas abîmer tes chaussures.
- [2] *gâcher* ◇ It ruined our holiday. Ça a gâché nos vacances.
- [3] *ruiner* *(financially)*

rule NOUN
- [1] la *règle* ◇ the rules of grammar les règles de grammaire
- ◆ **as a rule** en règle générale
- [2] le *règlement* *(regulation)* ◇ It's against the rules. C'est contre le règlement.

ruler NOUN
la *règle* ◇ Can I borrow your ruler? Je peux emprunter ta règle?

rum NOUN
le *rhum*

rumour NOUN
la *rumeur* ◇ It's just a rumour. Ce n'est qu'une rumeur.

run NOUN
see also run VERB
le *point* *(in cricket)* ◇ to score a run marquer un point
- ◆ **to go for a run** courir ◇ I go for a run every morning. Je cours tous les matins.
- ◆ **I did a ten-kilometre run.** J'ai couru dix kilomètres.
- ◆ **on the run** en fuite ◇ The criminals are still on the run. Les criminels sont toujours en fuite.
- ◆ **in the long run** à long terme

to run VERB
see also run NOUN
- [1] *courir* ◇ I ran five kilometres. J'ai couru cinq kilomètres.
- ◆ **to run a marathon** participer à un marathon
- [2] *diriger* *(manage)* ◇ He runs a large company. Il dirige une grosse société.
- [3] *organiser* *(organize)* ◇ They run music courses in the holidays. Ils organisent des cours de musique pendant les vacances.
- [4] *couler* *(water)* ◇ Don't leave the tap running. Ne laisse pas couler le robinet.
- ◆ **to run a bath** faire couler un bain
- [5] *conduire* *(by car)* ◇ I can run you to the station. Je peux te conduire à la gare.
- ◆ **to run away** s'enfuir ◇ They ran away before the police came. Ils se sont enfuis avant l'arrivée de la police.
- ◆ **Time is running out.** Il ne reste plus beaucoup de temps.
- ◆ **to run out of something** se trouver à court de quelque chose ◇ We ran out of money. Nous nous sommes trouvés à court d'argent.
- ◆ **to run somebody over** écraser quelqu'un
- ◆ **to get run over** se faire écraser ◇ Be careful, or you'll get run over! Fais attention, sinon tu vas te faire écraser!

rung VERB *see* **ring**

runner NOUN
le *coureur*
la *coureuse*

runner beans PL NOUN
les *haricots verts* MASC PL

runner-up NOUN
le *second*
la *seconde*

running NOUN
la *course* ◇ Running is my favourite sport. La course est mon sport préféré.

runway NOUN
la *piste*

rural ADJECTIVE
rural
(ruraux MASC PL)

rush NOUN
see also rush VERB
la *hâte*
- ◆ **In a rush.** à la hâte

to rush VERB
see also rush NOUN
- [1] *se précipiter* *(run)* ◇ Everyone rushed outside. Tout le monde s'est précipité dehors.

R

[2] *se dépêcher* (hurry) ◇ *There's no need to rush.* Ce n'est pas la peine de se dépêcher.

rush hour NOUN
les *heures de pointe* FEM PL ◇ *in the rush hour* aux heures de pointe

rusk NOUN
la *biscotte*

Russia NOUN
la *Russie*

+ **in Russia** en Russie
+ **to Russia** en Russie

Russian ADJECTIVE
see also Russian NOUN
russe

Russian NOUN
see also Russian ADJECTIVE
[1] le/la *Russe* (person)
[2] le *russe* (language)

rust NOUN
la *rouille*

rusty ADJECTIVE
rouillé ◇ *a rusty bike* un vélo rouillé
◇ *My French is very rusty.* Mon français est très rouillé.

ruthless ADJECTIVE
sans pitié

rye NOUN
le *seigle*

+ **rye bread** le pain de seigle

S

Sabbath NOUN
[1] le *dimanche* (*Christian*)
[2] le *sabbat* (*Jewish*)

sack NOUN
see also **sack** VERB
le *sac*
- **to get the sack** être mis à la porte

to **sack** VERB
see also **sack** NOUN
- **to sack somebody** mettre quelqu'un à la porte ◇ *He was sacked.* On l'a mis à la porte.

sacred ADJECTIVE
sacré

sacrifice NOUN
le *sacrifice*

sad ADJECTIVE
triste

saddle NOUN
la *selle*

saddlebag NOUN
la *sacoche*

sadly ADVERB
[1] *tristement* ◇ *"She's gone," he said sadly.* "Elle est partie," a-t-il dit tristement.
[2] *malheureusement* (*unfortunately*)
◇ *Sadly, it was too late.* Malheureusement, il était trop tard.

safe NOUN
see also **safe** ADJECTIVE
le *coffre-fort*
(les *coffres-forts* PL)
◇ *She put the money in the safe.* Elle a mis l'argent dans le coffre-fort.

safe ADJECTIVE
see also **safe** NOUN
[1] *sans danger* ◇ *Don't worry, it's perfectly safe.* Ne vous inquiétez pas, c'est absolument sans danger.
- **Is it safe?** Ça n'est pas dangereux?
[2] *sûr* (*machine, ladder*) ◇ *This car isn't safe.* Cette voiture n'est pas sûre.
[3] *hors de danger* (*out of danger*)
◇ *You're safe now.* Vous êtes hors de danger maintenant.
- **to feel safe** se sentir en sécurité
- **safe sex** le sexe sans risques

safety NOUN
la *sécurité*
- **a safety belt** une ceinture de sécurité
- **a safety pin** une épingle de nourrice

Sagittarius NOUN
le/la *Sagittaire* ◇ *I'm Sagittarius.* Je suis Sagittaire.

Sahara NOUN

- **the Sahara Desert** le Sahara

said VERB *see* **say**

sail NOUN
see also **sail** VERB
la *voile*

to **sail** VERB
see also **sail** NOUN
[1] *naviguer* (*travel*)
[2] *prendre la mer* (*set off*) ◇ *The boat sails at eight o'clock.* Le bateau prend la mer à huit heures.

sailing NOUN
la *voile* ◇ *His hobby is sailing.* Son passe-temps, c'est la voile.
- **to go sailing** faire de la voile
- **a sailing boat** un voilier
- **a sailing ship** un grand voilier

sailor NOUN
le *marin* ◇ *He's a sailor.* Il est marin.

saint NOUN
le *saint*
la *sainte*

sake NOUN
- **for the sake of** dans l'intérêt de

salad NOUN
la *salade*
- **salad cream** la mayonnaise
- **salad dressing** la vinaigrette

salami NOUN
le *salami*

salary NOUN
le *salaire*

sale NOUN
les *soldes* MASC PL (*reductions*) ◇ *There's a sale on at Harrods.* Ce sont les soldes chez Harrods.
- **on sale** en vente
- **The factory's for sale.** L'usine est en vente.
- **"for sale"** "à vendre"

sales assistant NOUN
le *vendeur*
la *vendeuse*
◇ *She's a sales assistant.* Elle est vendeuse.

salesman NOUN
[1] le *représentant* (*sales rep*) ◇ *He's a salesman.* Il est représentant.
- **a double-glazing salesman** un représentant en doubles vitrages
[2] le *vendeur* (*sales assistant*)

sales rep NOUN
le *représentant*
la *représentante*

saleswoman NOUN
[1] la *représentante* (*sales rep*) ◇ *She's a*

saleswoman. Elle est représentante.
2 la *vendeuse* (*sales assistant*)

salmon NOUN
le *saumon*

salon NOUN
le *salon* ◇ *a hair salon* un salon de coiffure ◇ *a beauty salon* un salon de beauté

saloon car NOUN
la *berline*

salt NOUN
le *sel*

salty ADJECTIVE
salé

to **salute** VERB
saluer

Salvation Army NOUN
l' *armée du Salut* FEM

same ADJECTIVE
même ◇ *the same model* le même modèle ◇ *at the same time* en même temps
+ **They're exactly the same.** Ils sont exactement pareils.
+ **It's not the same.** Ça n'est pas pareil.

sand NOUN
le *sable*

sandal NOUN
la *sandale* ◇ *a pair of sandals* une paire de sandales

sand castle NOUN
le *château de sable* (les *châteaux de sable* PL)

sandwich NOUN
le *sandwich* ◇ *a cheese sandwich* un sandwich au fromage

sandwich course NOUN
le *cours avec stage pratique*

sang VERB *see* **sing**

sanitary towel NOUN
la *serviette hygiénique*

sank VERB *see* **sink**

Santa Claus NOUN
le *père Noël*

sarcastic ADJECTIVE
sarcastique

sat VERB *see* **sit**

satchel NOUN
le *cartable*

satellite NOUN
le *satellite*
+ **a satellite dish** une antenne parabolique
+ **satellite television** la télévision par satellite

satisfactory ADJECTIVE
satisfaisant

satisfied ADJECTIVE
satisfait

Saturday NOUN

le *samedi* ◇ *on Saturday* samedi ◇ *on Saturdays* le samedi ◇ *every Saturday* tous les samedis ◇ *last Saturday* samedi dernier ◇ *next Saturday* samedi prochain
+ **I've got a Saturday job.** Je travaille le samedi.

sauce NOUN
la *sauce*

saucepan NOUN
la *casserole*

saucer NOUN
la *soucoupe*

Saudi Arabia NOUN
l' *Arabie Saoudite* FEM
+ **in Saudi Arabia** en Arabie Saoudite

sauna NOUN
le *sauna*

sausage NOUN
1 la *saucisse*
2 le *saucisson* (*salami*)
+ **a sausage roll** un friand à la saucisse

to **save** VERB
1 *mettre de côté* (*save up money*) ◇ *I've saved £50 already.* J'ai déjà mis cinquante livres de côté.
2 *économiser* (*spend less*) ◇ *I saved £20 by waiting for the sales.* J'ai économisé vingt livres en attendant les soldes.
+ **to save time** gagner du temps ◇ *We took a taxi to save time.* Nous avons pris un taxi pour gagner du temps. ◇ *It saved us time.* Ça nous a fait gagner du temps.
3 *sauver* (*rescue*) ◇ *Luckily, all the passengers were saved.* Heureusement, tous les passagers ont été sauvés.
4 *sauvegarder* (*on computer*) ◇ *I saved the file onto a diskette.* J'ai sauvegardé le fichier sur disquette.
+ **to save up** mettre de l'argent de côté ◇ *I'm saving up for a new bike.* Je mets de l'argent à côté pour un nouveau vélo.

savings PL NOUN
les *économies* FEM PL ◇ *She spent all her savings on a computer.* Elle a dépensé toutes ses économies en achetant un ordinateur.

savoury ADJECTIVE
salé ◇ *Is it sweet or savoury?* C'est sucré ou salé?

saw VERB *see* **see**

saw NOUN
la *scie*

sax NOUN
le *saxo* (*informal*) ◇ *I play the sax.* Je joue du saxo.

saxophone NOUN

le *saxophone* ◇ *I play the saxophone.* Je joue du saxophone.

to **say** VERB
dire ◇ *What did he say?* Qu'est-ce qu'il a dit? ◇ *Did you hear what she said?* Tu as entendu ce qu'elle a dit?
◆ **Could you say that again?** Pourriez-vous répéter s'il vous plaît?
◆ **That goes without saying.** Cela va sans dire.

saying NOUN
le *dicton* ◇ *It's just a saying.* C'est juste un dicton.

scale NOUN
[1] l' *échelle* FEM (*of map*) ◇ *a large-scale map* une carte à grande échelle
[2] l' *ampleur* FEM (*size, extent*) ◇ *a disaster on a massive scale* un désastre d'une ampleur incroyable
[3] la *gamme* (*in music*)

scales PL NOUN
la *balance* SING (*in kitchen, shop*)
◆ **bathroom scales** le pèse-personne SING

scampi PL NOUN
les *scampi* MASC PL

scandal NOUN
[1] le *scandale* (*outrage*) ◇ *It caused a scandal.* Ça a fait scandale.
[2] les *ragots* MASC PL (*gossip*) ◇ *It's just scandal.* Ce ne sont que des ragots.

Scandinavia NOUN
la *Scandinavie*
◆ **in Scandinavia** en Scandinavie

Scandinavian ADJECTIVE
scandinave

scar NOUN
la *cicatrice*

scare NOUN
see also **scare** VERB
la *panique*
◆ **a bomb scare** une alerte à la bombe

to **scare** VERB
see also **scare** NOUN
◆ **to scare somebody** faire peur à quelqu'un ◇ *He scares me.* Il me fait peur.

scarecrow NOUN
l' *épouvantail* MASC

scared ADJECTIVE
◆ **to be scared** avoir peur ◇ *I was scared stiff.* J'avais terriblement peur.
◆ **to be scared of** avoir peur de ◇ *Are you scared of him?* Est-ce que tu as peur de lui?

scarf NOUN
[1] l' *écharpe* FEM (*long*)
[2] le *foulard* (*square*)

scary ADJECTIVE
effrayant ◇ *It was really scary.* C'était

vraiment effrayant.

scene NOUN
[1] les *lieux* MASC PL (*place*) ◇ *The police were soon on the scene.* La police est vite arrivée sur les lieux. ◇ *the scene of the crime* les lieux du crime
[2] le *spectacle* (*event, sight*) ◇ *It was an amazing scene.* C'était un spectacle étonnant.
◆ **to make a scene** faire une scène

scenery NOUN
le *paysage* (*landscape*)

scent NOUN
le *parfum* (*perfume*)

schedule NOUN
le *programme* ◇ *a busy schedule* un programme chargé
◆ **on schedule** comme prévu
◆ **to be behind schedule** avoir du retard

scheduled flight NOUN
le *vol régulier*

scheme NOUN
[1] le *truc* (*idea*) ◇ *a crazy scheme he dreamed up* un truc farfelu qu'il a inventé
[2] le *projet* (*project*) ◇ *a council road-widening scheme* un projet municipal d'élargissement des routes

scholarship NOUN
la *bourse*

school NOUN
l' *école* FEM
◆ **to go to school** aller à l'école

schoolbook NOUN
le *livre scolaire*

schoolboy NOUN
l' *écolier* MASC

schoolchildren NOUN
les *écoliers* MASC PL

schoolgirl NOUN
l' *écolière* FEM

science NOUN
la *science*

science fiction NOUN
la *science-fiction*

scientific ADJECTIVE
scientifique

scientist NOUN
(*doing research*)
le *chercheur*
la *chercheuse*
◇ *She's a scientist.* Elle est chercheuse.
◆ **He trained as a scientist.** Il a une formation scientifique.

scissors PL NOUN
les *ciseaux* MASC PL ◇ *a pair of scissors* une paire de ciseaux

to **scoff** VERB
bouffer (*eat*) ◇ *My brother scoffed all*

the sandwiches. Mon frère a bouffé tous les sandwichs.

scooter NOUN
1 le *scooter*
2 la *trottinette* (*child's toy*)

score NOUN
see also score VERB
le *score* ◇ *The score was three nil.* Le score était trois à zéro.

to **score** VERB
see also score NOUN
1 *marquer* (*goal, point*) ◇ *to score a goal* marquer un but
* **to score 6 out of 10** obtenir un score de six sur dix
2 *compter les points* (*keep score*)
◇ *Who's going to score?* Qui va compter les points?

Scorpio NOUN
le *Scorpion* ◇ *I'm Scorpio.* Je suis Scorpion.

Scot NOUN
l' *Écossais* MASC
l' *Écossaise* FEM

Scotland NOUN
l' *Écosse* FEM
* **in Scotland** en Écosse
* **to Scotland** en Écosse
* **I'm from Scotland.** Je suis écossais.

Scots ADJECTIVE
écossais ◇ *a Scots accent* un accent écossais

Scotsman NOUN
l' *Écossais* MASC

Scotswoman NOUN
l' *Écossaise* FEM

Scottish ADJECTIVE
écossais ◇ *a Scottish accent* un accent écossais

scout NOUN
le *scout* ◇ *I'm in the Scouts.* Je suis scout.

scrambled eggs PL NOUN
les *œufs brouillés* MASC PL

scrap NOUN
see also scrap VERB
1 le *bout* ◇ *a scrap of paper* un bout de papier
2 la *bagarre* (*fight*)
* **scrap iron** la ferraille

to **scrap** VERB
see also scrap NOUN
abandonner (*plan, idea*) ◇ *In the end the plan was scrapped.* Finalement le projet a été abandonné.

scrapbook NOUN
l' *album* MASC

to **scratch** VERB
see also scratch NOUN

se gratter ◇ *Stop scratching!* Arrête de te gratter!

scratch NOUN
see also scratch VERB
l' *égratignure* FEM (*on skin*)
* **to start from scratch** partir de zéro

scream NOUN
see also scream VERB
le *hurlement*

to **scream** VERB
see also scream NOUN
hurler

screen NOUN
l' *écran* MASC

screwdriver NOUN
le *tournevis*

to **scribble** VERB
griffonner

to **scrub** VERB
récurer ◇ *to scrub a pan* récurer une casserole

sculpture NOUN
la *sculpture*

sea NOUN
la *mer*

seafood NOUN
les *fruits de mer* MASC PL ◇ *I don't like seafood.* Je n'aime pas les fruits de mer.

seagull NOUN
la *mouette*

seal NOUN
see also seal VERB
1 le *phoque* (*animal*)
2 le *cachet* (*on letter*)

to **seal** VERB
see also seal NOUN
1 *sceller* (*document*)
2 *coller* (*letter*)

seaman NOUN
le *marin*

to **search** VERB
see also search NOUN
fouiller ◇ *They searched the woods for her.* Ils ont fouillé les bois pour la trouver.
* **to search for something** chercher quelque chose ◇ *He searched for evidence.* Il cherchait des preuves.

search NOUN
see also search VERB
la *fouille*

search party NOUN
l' *expédition de secours* FEM

seashore NOUN
le *bord de la mer* ◇ *on the seashore* au bord de la mer

seasick ADJECTIVE
* **to be seasick** avoir le mal de mer

seaside NOUN

secrète FEM ⋄ *a secret mission* une mission secrète

season NOUN
la *saison* ⋄ *What's your favourite season?* Quelle est ta saison préférée?

* **out of season** hors saison ⋄ *It's cheaper to go there out of season.* C'est moins cher d'y aller hors saison.
* **during the holiday season** en période de vacances
* **a season ticket** une carte d'abonnement

seat NOUN
le *siège*

seat belt NOUN
la *ceinture de sécurité*

sea water NOUN
l' *eau de mer* FEM

seaweed NOUN
les *algues* FEM PL

second ADJECTIVE
see also **second** NOUN
deuxième ⋄ *on the second page* à la deuxième page

* **to come second** (*in race*) arriver deuxième
* **to travel second class** voyager en seconde
* **the second of March** le deux mars

second NOUN
see also **second** ADJECTIVE
la *seconde* ⋄ *It'll only take a second.* Ça va prendre juste une seconde.

secondary school NOUN
① le *collège*
② le *lycée*
In France pupils go to a **collège** *between the ages of 11 and 15, and then to a* **lycée** *until the age of 18.*

second-class ADJECTIVE, ADVERB
① *de seconde classe* (*ticket, compartment*)
* **to travel second-class** voyager en seconde
② *à tarif réduit* (*stamp, letter*) ⋄ *to send something second-class* envoyer quelque chose à tarif réduit

secondhand ADJECTIVE
d'occasion ⋄ *a secondhand car* une voiture d'occasion

secondly ADVERB
deuxièmement

* **firstly...secondly...** d'abord...ensuite... ⋄ *Firstly, it's too expensive. Secondly, it wouldn't work anyway.* D'abord, c'est trop cher. Ensuite, ça ne marcherait quand même pas.

secret ADJECTIVE
see also **secret** NOUN
secret MASC

secret NOUN
see also **secret** ADJECTIVE
le *secret* ⋄ *It's a secret.* C'est un secret.
⋄ *Can you keep a secret?* Tu sais garder un secret?

* **in secret** en secret

secretary NOUN
le/la *secrétaire* ⋄ *She's a secretary.* Elle est secrétaire.

secretly NOUN
secrètement

section NOUN
la *section*

security guard NOUN
le *vigile* ⋄ *She's a security guard.* Elle est vigile.

to **see** VERB
voir ⋄ *I can't see.* Je n'y vois rien. ⋄ *I saw him yesterday.* Je l'ai vu hier.
⋄ *Have you seen him?* Est-ce que tu l'as vu?

* **See you!** Salut!
* **See you soon!** À bientôt!
* **to see to something** s'occuper de quelque chose ⋄ *The window's stuck again. Can you see to it please?* La fenêtre est encore coincée. Tu peux t'en occuper s'il te plaît?

seed NOUN
la *graine* ⋄ *sunflower seeds* des graines de tournesol

to **seem** VERB
avoir l'air ⋄ *She seems tired.* Elle a l'air fatiguée. ⋄ *The shop seemed to be closed.* Le magasin avait l'air d'être fermé.

* **That seems like a good idea.** Ce n'est pas une mauvaise idée.
* **It seems that...** Il paraît que... ⋄ *It seems she's getting married.* Il paraît qu'elle va se marier.
* **There seems to be a problem.** Il semble y avoir un problème.

seen VERB see **see**

seesaw NOUN
le *tapecul*

see-through ADJECTIVE
transparent

to **select** VERB
sélectionner

selection NOUN
la *sélection*

self-assured ADJECTIVE
sûr de soi ⋄ *He's very self-assured.* Il est très sûr de lui.

self-catering ADJECTIVE
* **a self-catering apartment** un

S

PTO

appartement de vacances

self-centred ADJECTIVE
égocentrique

self-confidence NOUN
la *confiance en soi* ◊ *He hasn't got much self-confidence.* Il n'a pas très confiance en lui.

self-conscious ADJECTIVE
- **to be self-conscious (1)** (*embarrassed*) être mal à l'aise ◊ *She was really self-conscious at first.* Elle était vraiment mal à l'aise au début.
- **to be self-conscious (2)** (*shy*) manquer d'assurance ◊ *He's always been rather self-conscious.* Il a toujours manqué un peu d'assurance.

self-contained ADJECTIVE
- **a self-contained flat** un appartement indépendant

self-control NOUN
le *sang-froid*

self-defence NOUN
l' *autodéfense* FEM ◊ *self-defence classes* les cours d'autodéfense
- **She killed him in self-defence.** Elle l'a tué en légitime défense.

self-discipline NOUN
l' *autodiscipline* FEM

self-employed ADJECTIVE
- **to be self-employed** travailler à son compte ◊ *He's self-employed.* Il travaille à son compte.
- **the self-employed** les travailleurs indépendants

selfish ADJECTIVE
égoïste ◊ *Don't be so selfish.* Ne sois pas si égoïste.

self-respect NOUN
l' *amour-propre* MASC

self-service ADJECTIVE
- **It's self-service.** (*café, shop*) C'est un self-service.
- **a self-service restaurant** un restaurant self-service

to **sell** VERB
vendre ◊ *He sold it to me.* Il me l'a vendu.
- **to sell off** liquider
- **The tickets are all sold out.** Il ne reste plus de billets.
- **The tickets sold out in three hours.** Tous les billets ont été vendus en trois heures.

sell-by date NOUN
la *date limite de vente*

selling price NOUN
le *prix de vente*

Sellotape ® NOUN
le *scotch* ®

semi NOUN
la *maison jumelée* ◊ *We live in a semi.* Nous habitons dans une maison jumelée.

semicircle NOUN
le *demi-cercle*

semicolon NOUN
le *point-virgule*

semi-detached house NOUN
la *maison jumelée* ◊ *We live in a semi-detached house.* Nous habitons dans une maison jumelée.

semi-final NOUN
la *demi-finale*

semi-skimmed milk NOUN
le *lait demi-écrémé*

to **send** VERB
envoyer ◊ *She sent me a birthday card.* Elle m'a envoyé une carte d'anniversaire.
- **to send back** renvoyer
- **to send off (1)** (*goods, letter*) envoyer
- **to send off (2)** (*in sports match*) renvoyer du terrain ◊ *He was sent off.* On l'a renvoyé du terrain.
- **to send off for something (1)** (*free*) se faire envoyer quelque chose ◊ *I've sent off for a brochure.* Je me suis fait envoyer une brochure.
- **to send off for something (2)** (*paid for*) commander quelque chose par correspondance ◊ *She sent off for a book.* Elle a commandé un livre par correspondance.
- **to send out** envoyer

sender NOUN
l' *expéditeur* MASC
l' *expéditrice* FEM

senior ADJECTIVE
haut placé
- **senior management** les cadres supérieurs
- **senior school** le lycée
- **senior pupils** les grandes classes

senior citizen NOUN
la *personne du troisième âge* (les *personnes du troisième âge* PL)

sensational ADJECTIVE
sensationnel MASC
sensationnelle FEM

sense NOUN
1 le *bon sens* (*wisdom*) ◊ *Use your common sense!* Un peu de bon sens, voyons!
- **It makes sense.** C'est logique.
- **It doesn't make sense.** Ça n'a pas de sens.
2 le *sens* (*faculty*) ◊ *the five senses* les cinq sens
- **the sense of touch** le toucher

secoué ◦ *I was feeling a bit shaken.*
J'étais un peu secoué.

shaky ADJECTIVE
tremblant (hand, voice)

shall VERB
* **Shall I shut the window?** Vous voulez
  que je ferme la fenêtre?
* **Shall we ask him to come with us?** Si
  on lui demandait de venir avec nous?

shallow ADJECTIVE
peu profond (water, pool)

shambles NOUN
la _pagaille_ ◦ *It's a complete shambles.*
C'est la pagaille complète.

shame NOUN
la _honte_ ◦ *The shame of it!* Quelle
honte!
* **What a shame!** Quel dommage!
* **It's a shame that...** c'est dommage que...
  c'est dommage que *has to be followed by a
  verb in the subjunctive.*
  ◦ *It's a shame he isn't here.* C'est
  dommage qu'il ne soit pas ici.

shampoo NOUN
le _shampooing_ ◦ *a bottle of shampoo*
une bouteille de shampooing

shandy NOUN
le _panaché_

shan't = shall not

shape NOUN
la _forme_

share NOUN
see also share VERB
1 l' _action_ FEM (in company) ◦ *They've
got shares in British Gas.* Ils ont des
actions de British Gas.
2 _la part_ ◦ *Everybody pays their share.*
Tout le monde paie sa part.

share VERB
see also share NOUN
partager ◦ *to share a room with
somebody* partager une chambre avec
quelqu'un
* **to share out** distribuer ◦ *They shared
  the sweets out among the children.* Ils
  ont distribué les bonbons aux enfants.

shark NOUN
le _requin_

sharp ADJECTIVE
1 _tranchant_ (razor, knife)
2 _pointu_ (spike, point)
3 _intelligent_ (clever) ◦ *She's very
sharp.* Elle est très intelligente.
* **at two o'clock sharp** à deux heures pile

shave VERB
se raser (have a shave)
* **to shave one's legs** se raser les jambes

shaver NOUN
* **an electric shaver** un rasoir électrique

shaving cream NOUN
la _crème à raser_

shaving foam NOUN
la _mousse à raser_

she PRONOUN
elle ◦ *She's very nice.* Elle est très
gentille.

shed NOUN
la _remise_

she'd = she had, she would

sheep NOUN
le _mouton_

sheepdog NOUN
le _chien de berger_
(les _chiens de berger_ PL)

sheer ADJECTIVE
pur ◦ *It's sheer greed.* C'est de
l'avidité pure.

sheet NOUN
le _drap_ (on bed)
* **a sheet of paper** une feuille de papier

shelf NOUN
1 l' _étagère_ FEM (in house)
2 le _rayon_ (in shop)

shell NOUN
1 le _coquillage_ (on beach)
2 la _coquille_ (of egg, nut)
3 l' _obus_ MASC (explosive)

she'll = she will

shellfish NOUN
les _fruits de mer_ MASC PL

shell suit NOUN
le _survêtement_

shelter NOUN
* **to take shelter** se mettre à l'abri
* **a bus shelter** un arrêt d'autobus

shelves PL NOUN *see* shelf

shepherd NOUN
le _berger_

sheriff NOUN
le _shérif_

sherry NOUN
le _xérès_

she's = she is, she has

Shetland Islands NOUN
les _îles Shetland_ FEM PL

shield NOUN
le _bouclier_

shift NOUN
see also shift VERB
le _service_ ◦ *His shift starts at 8 o'clock.*
Il prend son service à huit heures. ◦ *the
night shift* le service de nuit
* **to do shift work** faire les trois-huit

to **shift** VERB
see also shift NOUN
déplacer (move) ◦ *I couldn't shift the
wardrobe on my own.* Je n'ai pas pu
déplacer l'armoire tout seul.

S

- **Shift yourself!** Pousse-toi de là! (*informal*)

shifty ADJECTIVE
1. *louche* (*person*) ◇ *He looked shifty.* Il avait l'air louche.
2. *fuyant* (*eyes*)

shin NOUN
le *tibia*

to **shine** VERB
briller ◇ *The sun was shining.* Le soleil brillait.

shiny ADJECTIVE
brillant

ship NOUN
1. le *bateau* (les *bateaux* PL)
2. le *navire* (*warship*)

shipbuilding NOUN
la *construction navale*

shipwreck NOUN
le *naufrage*

shipwrecked ADJECTIVE
- **to be shipwrecked** faire naufrage

shipyard NOUN
le *chantier naval*

shirt NOUN
1. la *chemise* (*man's*)
2. le *chemisier* (*woman's*)

shit EXCLAMATION
Merde! (*rude*)

to **shiver** VERB
frissonner

shock NOUN
le *choc*
- **to get a shock (1)** (*surprise*) avoir un choc
- **to get a shock (2)** (*electric*) recevoir une décharge
- **an electric shock** une décharge

shocked ADJECTIVE
choqué ◇ *He'll be shocked if you say that.* Tu vas le choquer si tu dis ça.

shocking ADJECTIVE
choquant ◇ *It's shocking!* C'est choquant!
- **a shocking waste** un gaspillage épouvantable

shoe NOUN
la *chaussure*

shoelace NOUN
le *lacet*

shoe polish NOUN
le *cirage*

shoe shop NOUN
le *magasin de chaussures*

shone VERB *see* **shine**

shook VERB *see* **shake**

to **shoot** VERB
1. *abattre* (*kill*) ◇ *He was shot by a sniper.* Il a été abattu par un franc-tireur.
2. *fusiller* (*execute*) ◇ *He was shot at dawn.* Il a été fusillé à l'aube.
3. *tirer* (*gun*) ◇ *Don't shoot!* Ne tirez pas!
- **to shoot at somebody** tirer sur quelqu'un
- **He shot himself with a revolver.** (*dead*) Il s'est suicidé d'un coup de revolver.
- **He was shot in the leg.** (*wounded*) Il a reçu une balle dans la jambe.
- **to shoot an arrow** envoyer une flèche
4. *tourner* (*film*) ◇ *The film was shot in Prague.* Le film a été tourné à Prague.
5. *shooter* (*in football*)

shooting NOUN
1. les *coups de feu* MASC PL ◇ *They heard shooting.* Ils ont entendu des coups de feu.
- **a shooting** une fusillade
2. la *chasse* (*hunting*) ◇ *to go shooting* aller à la chasse

shop NOUN
le *magasin* ◇ *a sports shop* un magasin de sports

shop assistant NOUN
le *vendeur*
la *vendeuse*
◇ *She's a shop assistant.* Elle est vendeuse.

shopkeeper NOUN
le *commerçant*
la *commerçante*
◇ *He's a shopkeeper.* Il est commerçant.

shoplifting NOUN
le *vol à l'étalage*

shopping NOUN
les *courses* FEM PL (*purchases*) ◇ *Can you get the shopping from the car?* Tu peux aller chercher les courses dans la voiture?
- **I love shopping.** J'adore faire du shopping.
- **to go shopping (1)** (*for food*) faire des courses
- **to go shopping (2)** (*for pleasure*) faire du shopping
- **a shopping bag** un sac à provisions
- **a shopping centre** un centre commercial

shop window NOUN
la *vitrine*

shore NOUN
le *rivage*
- **on shore** à terre

short ADJECTIVE
1. *court* ◇ *a short skirt* une jupe courte
- *short hair* les cheveux courts
- **too short** trop court ◇ *It was a great holiday, but too short.* C'étaient des vacances super, mais trop courtes.

2 *petit* (*person, period of time*) ◇ *She's quite short.* Elle est assez petite. ◇ *a short break* une petite pause ◇ *a short walk* une petite promenade
- **to be short of something** être à court de quelque chose ◇ *I'm short of money.* Je suis à court d'argent.
- **at short notice** au dernier moment
- **In short, the answer's no.** Bref, la réponse est non.

shortage NOUN
la *pénurie* ◇ *a water shortage* une pénurie d'eau

short cut NOUN
le *raccourci* ◇ *I took a short cut.* J'ai pris un raccourci.

shorthand NOUN
la *sténo*

shortly ADVERB
bientôt

shorts PL NOUN
le *short* SING
- **a pair of shorts** un short

short-sighted ADJECTIVE
myope

short story NOUN
la *nouvelle*

shot VERB *see* **shoot**

shot NOUN
1 (*gunshot*)
le *coup de feu*
(les *coups de feu* PL)
2 (*photo*)
la *photo* ◇ *a shot of Edinburgh Castle* une photo du château d'Édimbourg
3 (*vaccination*)
le *vaccin*

shotgun NOUN
le *fusil de chasse*
(les *fusils de chasse* PL)

should VERB
When **should** means "ought to", use **devoir**.
devoir ◇ *You should take more exercise.* Vous devriez faire plus d'exercice. ◇ *He should be there by now.* Il devrait être arrivé maintenant. ◇ *That shouldn't be too hard.* Ça ne devrait pas être trop difficile.
- **should have** avoir dû ◇ *I should have told you before.* J'aurais dû te le dire avant.
When **should** means "would", use the conditional tense.
- **I should go if I were you.** Si j'étais vous, j'irais.
- **I should be so lucky!** Ça serait trop beau!

shoulder NOUN
l' *épaule* FEM

- **a shoulder bag** un sac à bandoulière

shouldn't = should not

to **shout** VERB
see also shout NOUN
crier ◇ *Don't shout!* Ne criez pas!
◇ *"Go away!" he shouted.*
"Allez-vous-en!" a-t-il crié.

shout NOUN
see also shout VERB
le *cri*

shovel NOUN
la *pelle*

show NOUN
see also show VERB
1 le *spectacle* (*performance*)
2 l' *émission* FEM (*programme*)
3 le *salon* (*exhibition*)

to **show** VERB
see also show NOUN
1 *montrer*
- **to show somebody something** montrer quelque chose à quelqu'un ◇ *Have I shown you my new trainers?* Je t'ai montré mes nouvelles baskets?
2 *faire preuve de* ◇ *She showed great courage.* Elle a fait preuve de beaucoup de courage.
- **It shows.** Ça se voit. ◇ *I've never been riding before. – It shows.* Je n'ai jamais fait de cheval. – Ça se voit.
- **to show off** frimer (*informal*)
- **to show up** (*turn up*) se pointer ◇ *He showed up late as usual.* Il s'est pointé en retard comme d'habitude.

shower NOUN
1 la *douche*
- **to have a shower** prendre une douche
2 l' *averse* FEM (*of rain*)

showerproof ADJECTIVE
imperméabilisé

showing NOUN
la *projection* (*of film*)

shown VERB *see* **show**

show-off NOUN
le *frimeur*
la *frimeuse*

shrank VERB *see* **shrink**

to **shriek** VERB
hurler

shrimps PL NOUN
les *crevettes* FEM PL

to **shrink** VERB
rétrécir (*clothes, fabric*)

Shrove Tuesday NOUN
le *mardi gras*

to **shrug** VERB
- **to shrug one's shoulders** hausser les épaules

shrunk VERB *see* **shrink**

S

to **shudder** VERB
　frissonner
to **shuffle** VERB
　◆ **to shuffle the cards** battre les cartes
to **shut** VERB
　fermer ◇ *What time do you shut?* À
　quelle heure est-ce que vous fermez?
　◇ *What time do the shops shut?* À quelle
　heure est-ce que les magasins ferment?
　◆ **to shut down** fermer ◇ *The cinema*
　shut down last year. Le cinéma a fermé
　l'année dernière.
　◆ **to shut up (1)** (*close*) fermer
　◆ **to shut up (2)** (*be quiet*) se taire ◇ *Shut*
　up! Tais-toi!
shutters NOUN
　les *volets* MASC PL
shuttle NOUN
　la *navette*
shuttlecock NOUN
　le *volant* (*badminton*)
shy ADJECTIVE
　timide
Sicily NOUN
　la *Sicile*
　◆ **in Sicily** en Sicile
　◆ **to Sicily** en Sicile
sick ADJECTIVE
　① *malade* (*ill*) ◇ *He was sick for four*
　days. Il a été malade pendant quatre
　jours.
　② *de mauvais goût* (*joke, humour*)
　◇ *That's really sick!* C'est vraiment de
　mauvais goût!
　◆ **to be sick** (*vomit*) vomir ◇ *I feel sick.*
　J'ai envie de vomir.
　◆ **to be sick of something** en avoir assez
　de quelque chose ◇ *I'm sick of your*
　jokes. J'en ai assez de tes plaisanteries.
sickening ADJECTIVE
　écœurant
sick leave NOUN
　le *congé de maladie*
sickness NOUN
　la *maladie*
sick note NOUN
　① le *mot d'absence* (*from parents*)
　② le *certificat médical* (*from doctor*)
sick pay NOUN
　l' *indemnité de maladie* FEM
side NOUN
　① le *côté* (*of object, building, car*) ◇ *He*
　was driving on the wrong side of the road.
　Il roulait du mauvais côté de la route.
　② le *bord* (*of pool, river, road*) ◇ *by the*
　side of the lake au bord du lac
　③ le *flanc* (*of hill*)
　④ l' *équipe* FEM (*team*)
　◆ **He's on my side. (1)** (*on my team*) Il est

dans mon équipe.
　◆ **He's on my side. (2)** (*supporting me*) Il est
　de mon côté.
　◆ **side by side** côte à côte
　◆ **the side entrance** l'entrée latérale
　◆ **to take sides** prendre parti ◇ *She*
　always takes his side. Elle prend
　toujours son parti.
sideboard NOUN
　le *buffet*
side-effect NOUN
　l' *effet secondaire* MASC
side street NOUN
　la *petite rue transversale*
sideways ADVERB
　① *de côté* (*look, be facing*)
　② *de travers* (*move*)
　◆ **sideways on** de profil
sieve NOUN
　la *passoire*
sigh NOUN
　　see also sigh VERB
　le *soupir*
to **sigh** VERB
　　see also sigh NOUN
　soupirer
sight NOUN
　① la *vue* ◇ *to have poor sight* avoir une
　mauvaise vue
　◆ **to know somebody by sight** connaître
　quelqu'un de vue
　② le *spectacle* ◇ *It was an amazing*
　sight. C'était un spectacle étonnant.
　◆ **in sight** visible
　◆ **out of sight** hors de vue
　◆ **the sights** (*tourist spots*) les attractions
　touristiques
　◆ **to see the sights of London** visiter
　Londres
sightseeing NOUN
　le *tourisme*
　◆ **to go sightseeing** faire du tourisme
sign NOUN
　　see also sign VERB
　① (*notice*)
　le *panneau*
　(les *panneaux* PL)
　◇ *There was a big sign saying "private"* Il
　y avait un grand panneau indiquant
　"privé".
　◆ **a road sign** un panneau
　② (*gesture, indication*)
　le *signe* ◇ *There's no sign of*
　improvement. Il n'y a aucun signe
　d'amélioration.
　◆ **What sign are you?** (*star sign*) Tu es de
　quel signe?
to **sign** VERB
　　see also sign NOUN

signer
* **to sign on (1)** (*as unemployed*) s'inscrire au chômage
* **to sign on (2)** (*for course*) s'inscrire

signal NOUN
see also signal VERB
le *signal*
(les *signaux* PL)

signal VERB
see also signal NOUN
* **to signal to somebody** faire un signe à quelqu'un

signalman NOUN
l' *aiguilleur* MASC

signature NOUN
la *signature*

significance NOUN
l' *importance* FEM

significant ADJECTIVE
important

sign language NOUN
le *langage par signes*

signpost NOUN
le *poteau indicateur*

silence NOUN
le *silence*

silent ADJECTIVE
silencieux MASC
silencieuse FEM

silicon chip NOUN
la *puce électronique*

silk NOUN
see also silk ADJECTIVE
la *soie*

silk ADJECTIVE
see also silk NOUN
en soie   ○ *a silk scarf* un foulard en soie

silky ADJECTIVE
soyeux MASC
soyeuse FEM

silly ADJECTIVE
bête

silver NOUN
l' *argent* MASC   ○ *a silver medal* une médaille d'argent

similar ADJECTIVE
semblable
* **similar to** semblable à

simple ADJECTIVE
[1] *simple*   ○ *It's very simple.* C'est très simple.
[2] (*simple-minded*)
simplet MASC
simplette FEM
○ *He's a bit simple.* Il est un peu simplet.

simply ADVERB
simplement   ○ *It's simply not possible.* Ça n'est tout simplement pas possible.

simultaneous ADJECTIVE
simultané

sin NOUN
see also sin VERB
le *péché*

to sin VERB
see also sin NOUN
pécher

since PREPOSITION, ADVERB, CONJUNCTION
[1] *depuis*   ○ *since Christmas* depuis Noël   ○ *since then* depuis ce moment-là   ○ *I haven't seen him since.* Je ne l'ai pas vu depuis.
* **ever since** depuis ce moment-là
[2] *depuis que*   ○ *I haven't seen her since she left.* Je ne l'ai pas vue depuis qu'elle est partie.
[3] *puisque* (*because*)   ○ *Since you're tired, let's stay at home.* Puisque tu es fatigué, restons à la maison.

sincere ADJECTIVE
sincère

sincerely ADVERB
* **Yours sincerely... (1)** (*in business letter*) Veuillez agréer l'expression de mes sentiments les meilleurs...
* **Yours sincerely... (2)** (*in personal letter*) Cordialement...

to sing VERB
chanter   ○ *He sang out of tune.* Il chantait faux.   ○ *Have you ever sung this tune before?* Vous avez déjà chanté cet air-là?

singer NOUN
le *chanteur*
la *chanteuse*

singing NOUN
le *chant*

single ADJECTIVE
see also single NOUN
célibataire (*unmarried*)
* **a single room** une chambre pour une personne
* **not a single thing** rien du tout

single NOUN
see also single ADJECTIVE
[1] l' *aller simple* MASC (*ticket*)   ○ *A single to Toulouse, please.* Un aller simple pour Toulouse, s'il vous plaît.
[2] le *45 tours* (*record*)
* **a CD single** un CD single

single parent NOUN
* **She's a single parent.** Elle élève ses enfants toute seule.
* **a single parent family** une famille monoparentale

singles PL NOUN
le *simple* SING (*in tennis*)   ○ *the women's singles* le simple dames

singular NOUN
le *singulier* ◦ *in the singular* au singulier
sinister ADJECTIVE
sinistre
sink NOUN
see also sink VERB
l' *évier* MASC
to **sink** VERB
see also sink NOUN
couler
sir NOUN
monsieur MASC
◆ **Yes sir.** Oui, Monsieur.
siren NOUN
la *sirène*
sister NOUN
[1] la *sœur* ◦ *my little sister* ma petite sœur
[2] l' *infirmière en chef* FEM (*nurse*)
sister-in-law NOUN
la *belle-sœur*
(les *belles-sœurs* PL)
to **sit** VERB
s'asseoir
◆ **to sit on something** s'asseoir sur quelque chose ◦ *She sat on the chair.* Elle s'est assise sur la chaise.
◆ **to sit down** s'asseoir
◆ **to be sitting** être assis
◆ **to sit an exam** passer un examen
sitcom NOUN
la *comédie de situation*
(les *comédies de situation* PL)
site NOUN
[1] le *site* ◦ *an archaeological site* un site archéologique
◆ **the site of the accident** le lieu de l'accident
[2] le *camping* (*campsite*)
◆ **a building site** un chantier
sitting room NOUN
le *salon*
situated ADJECTIVE
◆ **to be situated** être situé ◦ *The village is situated on the side of a hill.* Le village est situé sur le flanc d'une colline.
situation NOUN
la *situation*
six NUMBER
six ◦ *He's six.* Il a six ans.
sixteen NUMBER
seize ◦ *He's sixteen.* Il a seize ans.
sixth ADJECTIVE
sixième ◦ *the sixth floor* le sixième étage
◆ **the sixth of August** le six août
sixty NUMBER
soixante

size NOUN
France uses the European system to show clothing and shoe sizes.
[1] la *taille* (*of object, clothing*) ◦ *What size do you take?* Quelle taille est-ce que vous faites?
◆ **I'm a size ten.** Je fais du trente-huit.
[2] la *pointure* (*of shoes*)
◆ **I take size six.** Je fais du trente-neuf.
to **skate** VERB
[1] *faire du patin à glace* (*ice-skate*)
[2] *faire du patin à roulettes* (*roller-skate*)
skateboard NOUN
le *skateboard*
skateboarding NOUN
le *skateboard* ◦ *to go skateboarding* faire du skateboard
skates NOUN
les *patins* MASC PL
skating NOUN
le *patin à glace* ◦ *to go skating* faire du patin à glace
◆ **a skating rink** une patinoire
skeleton NOUN
le *squelette*
sketch NOUN
see also sketch VERB
le *croquis* (*drawing*)
to **sketch** VERB
see also sketch NOUN
◆ **to sketch something** faire un croquis de quelque chose
to **ski** VERB
see also ski NOUN
skier ◦ *Can you ski?* Tu sais skier?
ski NOUN
see also ski VERB
le *ski*
◆ **ski boots** les chaussures de ski FEM
◆ **a ski lift** un remonte-pente
◆ **ski pants** le fuseau SING
◆ **a ski pole** un bâton de ski
◆ **a ski slope** une piste de ski
◆ **a ski suit** une combinaison de ski
to **skid** VERB
déraper
skiing NOUN
le *ski* ◦ *to go skiing* faire du ski
◆ **to go on a skiing holiday** aller aux sports d'hiver
skilful ADJECTIVE
adroit
skilled ADJECTIVE
◆ **a skilled worker** un ouvrier spécialisé
skimmed milk NOUN
le *lait écrémé*
skimpy ADJECTIVE
[1] *minuscule* (*clothes*)
[2] *maigre* (*meal*)

skin NOUN
la _peau_
(les _peaux_ PL)
* **skin cancer** le cancer de la peau
skinhead NOUN
le/la _skinhead_
skinny ADJECTIVE
maigre
skin-tight ADJECTIVE
collant
skip NOUN
see also skip VERB
la _benne_ (container)
to **skip** VERB
see also skip NOUN
sauter ◇ to skip a meal sauter un
repas
* **to skip a lesson** sécher un cours
skirt NOUN
la _jupe_
skittles NOUN
les _quilles_ FEM PL ◇ to play skittles jouer
aux quilles
to **skive** VERB
tirer au flanc (be lazy)
* **to skive off** sécher (informal) ◇ to skive
off school sécher les cours
skull NOUN
le _crâne_
sky NOUN
le _ciel_
skyscraper NOUN
le _gratte-ciel_
(les _gratte-ciel_ PL)
slack ADJECTIVE
[1] _lâche_ (rope)
[2] _négligent_ (person)
to **slag off** VERB
* **to slag somebody off** dire du mal de
quelqu'un
to **slam** VERB
claquer ◇ The door slammed. La porte
a claqué. ◇ She slammed the door. Elle a
claqué la porte.
slang NOUN
l' _argot_ MASC
slap NOUN
see also slap VERB
la _claque_
to **slap** VERB
see also slap NOUN
* **to slap somebody** donner une claque à
quelqu'un
slate NOUN
l' _ardoise_ FEM
sledge NOUN
la _luge_
sledging NOUN
* **to go sledging** faire de la luge

sleep NOUN
see also sleep VERB
le _sommeil_
* **I need some sleep.** J'ai besoin de
dormir.
* **to go to sleep** s'endormir
to **sleep** VERB
see also sleep NOUN
dormir ◇ I couldn't sleep last night. J'ai
mal dormi la nuit dernière.
* **to sleep with somebody** coucher avec
quelqu'un
* **to sleep together** coucher ensemble
sleeping bag NOUN
le _sac de couchage_
(les _sacs de couchage_ PL)
sleeping car NOUN
le _wagon-lit_
(les _wagons-lits_ PL)
sleeping pill NOUN
le _somnifère_
sleepy ADJECTIVE
* **to feel sleepy** avoir sommeil ◇ I was
feeling sleepy. J'avais sommeil.
* **a sleepy little village** un petit village
tranquille
sleet NOUN
see also sleet VERB
la _neige fondue_
to **sleet** VERB
see also sleet NOUN
* **It's sleeting.** Il tombe de la neige
fondue.
sleeve NOUN
[1] la _manche_ ◇ long sleeves les
manches longues ◇ short sleeves les
manches courtes
[2] la _pochette_ (record sleeve)
sleigh NOUN
le _traîneau_
(les _traîneaux_ PL)
slept VERB see **sleep**
slice NOUN
see also slice VERB
la _tranche_
to **slice** VERB
see also slice NOUN
couper en tranches
slick NOUN
* **an oil slick** une marée noire
slide NOUN
see also slide VERB
[1] le _toboggan_ (in playground)
[2] la _diapositive_ (photo)
[3] la _barrette_ (hair slide)
to **slide** VERB
see also slide NOUN
glisser
slight ADJECTIVE

S

PTO

léger MASC
légère FEM
◦ *a slight problem* un léger problème
◦ *a slight improvement* une légère amélioration
slightly ADVERB
légèrement
slim ADJECTIVE
see also slim VERB
mince
to **slim** VERB
see also slim ADJECTIVE
faire un régime (*be on a diet*) ◦ *I'm slimming.* Je fais un régime.
sling NOUN
l' *écharpe* FEM ◦ *She had her arm in a sling.* Elle avait le bras en écharpe.
slip NOUN
see also slip VERB
1 l' *erreur* FEM (*mistake*)
2 le *jupon* (*underskirt*)
3 la *combinaison* (*full-length underskirt*)
• **a slip of paper** un bout de papier
• **a slip of the tongue** un lapsus
to **slip** VERB
see also slip NOUN
glisser ◦ *He slipped on the ice.* Il a glissé sur le verglas.
• **to slip up** faire une erreur (*make a mistake*)
slipper NOUN
le *chausson*
• **a pair of slippers** des chaussons
slippery ADJECTIVE
glissant
slip-up NOUN
l' *erreur* FEM
slope NOUN
la *pente*
sloppy ADJECTIVE
1 *bâclé* (*work*)
2 *négligé* (*person, appearance*)
slot NOUN
la *fente*
slot machine NOUN
1 la *machine à sous* (*for gambling*)
2 le *distributeur automatique* (*vending machine*)
slow ADJECTIVE, ADVERB
1 *lent* ◦ *He's a bit slow.* Il est un peu lent.
2 *lentement* ◦ *to go slow* (*person, car*) aller lentement ◦ *Drive slower!* Conduisez plus lentement!
• **My watch is slow.** Ma montre retarde.
to **slow down** VERB
ralentir
slowly ADVERB
lentement
slug NOUN

la *limace*
slush NOUN
la *neige fondue*
sly ADJECTIVE
rusé (*person*)
• **a sly smile** un sourire sournois
smack NOUN
see also smack VERB
la *tape*
to **smack** VERB
see also smack NOUN
• **to smack somebody** donner une tape à quelqu'un
small ADJECTIVE
petit
• **small change** la petite monnaie
smart ADJECTIVE
1 *chic* MASC, FEM, PL (*elegant*)
2 (*clever*)
intelligent
• **a smart idea** une idée astucieuse
smash NOUN
see also smash VERB
l' *accident* MASC
to **smash** VERB
see also smash NOUN
1 *casser* (*break*) ◦ *I've smashed my watch.* J'ai cassé ma montre.
2 *se briser* (*get broken*) ◦ *The glass smashed into tiny pieces.* Le verre s'est brisé en mille morceaux.
smashing ADJECTIVE
formidable ◦ *I think he's smashing.* Je le trouve formidable.
smell NOUN
see also smell VERB
l' *odeur* FEM
• **the sense of smell** l'odorat MASC
to **smell** VERB
see also smell NOUN
1 *sentir mauvais* ◦ *That old dog really smells!* Qu'est-ce qu'il sent mauvais, ce vieux chien!
• **to smell of something** sentir quelque chose ◦ *It smells of petrol.* Ça sent l'essence.
2 *sentir* (*detect*) ◦ *I can't smell anything.* Je ne sens rien.
smelly ADJECTIVE
qui sent mauvais ◦ *He's got smelly feet.* Il a les pieds qui sentent mauvais.
smile NOUN
see also smile VERB
le *sourire*
to **smile** VERB
see also smile NOUN
sourire
smoke NOUN
see also smoke VERB

la *fumée*
to **smoke** VERB
see also smoke NOUN
fumer ◊ I don't smoke. Je ne fume pas.
◊ He smokes cigars. Il fume le cigare.
smoker NOUN
le *fumeur*
la *fumeuse*
smoking NOUN
* **to give up smoking** arrêter de fumer
* **Smoking is bad for you.** Le tabac, est mauvais pour la santé.
* **"no smoking"** "défense de fumer"
smooth ADJECTIVE
[1] (surface)
lisse
[2] (person)
mielleux MASC
mielleuse FEM
smudge NOUN
la *bavure*
smug ADJECTIVE
suffisant
to **smuggle** VERB
passer en contrebande
smuggler NOUN
le *contrebandier*
la *contrebandière*
smuggling NOUN
la *contrebande*
smutty ADJECTIVE
cochon MASC
cochonne FEM
◊ a smutty story une histoire cochonne
snack NOUN
l' *en-cas* MASC
(les *en-cas* PL)
* **to have a snack** prendre un en-cas
snack bar NOUN
le *snack-bar*
snail NOUN
l' *escargot* MASC
snake NOUN
le *serpent*
to **snap** VERB
casser net (break) ◊ The branch snapped. La branche a cassé net.
* **to snap one's fingers** faire claquer ses doigts
snapshot NOUN
la *photo*
to **snarl** VERB
gronder (animal)
to **snatch** VERB
* **to snatch something from somebody** arracher quelque chose à quelqu'un
◊ He snatched the keys from my hand. Il m'a arraché les clés des mains.
* **My bag was snatched.** On m'a arraché

mon sac.
to **sneak** VERB
* **to sneak in** entrer furtivement
* **to sneak out** sortir furtivement
* **to sneak up on somebody** s'approcher de quelqu'un sans faire de bruit
to **sneeze** VERB
éternuer
to **sniff** VERB
[1] *renifler* ◊ Stop sniffing! Arrête de renifler!
[2] *flairer* ◊ The dog sniffed my hand. Le chien m'a flairé la main.
* **to sniff glue** sniffer de la colle
snob NOUN
le/la *snob*
snooker NOUN
le *billard* ◊ to play snooker Jouer au billard
snooze NOUN
le *petit somme* ◊ to have a snooze faire un petit somme
to **snore** VERB
ronfler
snow NOUN
see also snow VERB
la *neige*
to **snow** VERB
see also snow NOUN
neiger ◊ It's snowing Il neige.
snowball NOUN
la *boule de neige*
(les *boules de neige* PL)
snowflake NOUN
le *flocon de neige*
(les *flocons de neige* PL)
snowman NOUN
le *bonhomme de neige*
(les *bonshommes de neige* PL)
◊ to build a snowman faire un bonhomme de neige
so CONJUNCTION, ADVERB
[1] *alors* ◊ The shop was closed, so I went home. Le magasin était fermé, alors je suis rentré chez moi. ◊ So, have you always lived in London? Alors, vous avez toujours vécu à Londres?
[2] *donc* (so that) ◊ It rained, so I got wet. Il pleuvait, donc j'ai été mouillé.
[3] *tellement* (very) ◊ It was so heavy! C'était tellement lourd! ◊ He was talking so fast I couldn't understand. Il parlait tellement vite que je ne comprenais pas.
* **It's not so heavy!** Ça n'est pas si lourd que ça!
* **How's your father?—Not so good.** Comment va ton père?—Pas très bien.
* **so much** (a lot) tellement ◊ I love you

S

so much. Je t'aime tellement.
- **so much..., so many...** tellement de...
  ◇ *I've got so much work.* J'ai tellement de travail. ◇ *I've got so many things to do today.* J'ai tellement de choses à faire aujourd'hui.

  [4] *aussi* (*in comparisons*) ◇ *He's like his sister but not so clever.* Il est comme sa sœur mais pas aussi intelligent.
- **so do I** moi aussi ◇ *I love horses. – So do I.* J'aime les chevaux. – Moi aussi.
- **so have we** nous aussi ◇ *I've been to France twice. – So have we.* Je suis allé en France deux fois. – Nous aussi.
- **I think so.** Je crois.
- **I hope so.** J'espère bien.
- **That's not so.** Ça n'est pas le cas.
- **so far** jusqu'à présent ◇ *It's been easy so far.* Ça a été facile jusqu'à présent.
- **so far so good** jusqu'ici ça va
- **ten or so people** environ dix personnes
- **at five o'clock or so** à environ cinq heures

to **soak** VERB
  tremper
  soaked ADJECTIVE
  trempé ◇ *By the time we got back we were soaked.* Nous sommes rentrés trempés.
  soaking ADJECTIVE
  trempé ◇ *By the time we got back we were soaking.* Nous sommes rentrés trempés.
- **soaking wet** trempé ◇ *Your shoes are soaking wet.* Tes chaussures sont trempées.

  soap NOUN
  le *savon*
  soap opera NOUN
  le *feuilleton à l'eau de rose*
  (les *feuilletons à l'eau de rose* PL)
  soap powder NOUN
  la *lessive*

to **sob** VERB
  sangloter ◇ *She was sobbing.* Elle sanglotait.
  sober ADJECTIVE
  sobre

to **sober up** VERB
  dessoûler
  soccer NOUN
  le *football* ◇ *to play soccer* jouer au football
- **a soccer player** un joueur de football
  social ADJECTIVE
  social
  (*sociaux* MASC PL)
  ◇ *a social class* une classe sociale
- **I have a good social life.** Je vois

beaucoup de monde.
  socialism NOUN
  le *socialisme*
  socialist ADJECTIVE
  see also **socialist** NOUN
  socialiste
  socialist NOUN
  see also **socialist** ADJECTIVE
  le/la *socialiste*
  social security NOUN
  [1] l' *aide sociale* FEM (*money*)
- **to be on social security** recevoir de l'aide sociale
  [2] la *sécurité sociale* (*organization*)
  social worker NOUN
  [1] (*woman*)
  l' *assistante sociale* FEM ◇ *She's a social worker.* Elle est assistante sociale.
  [2] (*man*)
  le *travailleur social*
  (les *travailleurs sociaux* PL)
  ◇ *He's a social worker.* Il est travailleur social.
  society NOUN
  [1] la *société* ◇ *We live in a multi-cultural society.* Nous vivons dans une société multiculturelle.
  [2] le *club* ◇ *a drama society* un club de théâtre
  sociology NOUN
  la *sociologie*
  sock NOUN
  la *chaussette*
  socket NOUN
  la *prise de courant*
  (les *prises de courant* PL)
  soda NOUN
  le *soda* (*soda water*)
  sofa NOUN
  le *canapé*
  soft ADJECTIVE
  [1] (*fabric, texture*)
  doux MASC
  douce FEM
  [2] (*pillow, bed*)
  mou MASC
  molle FEM
- **soft cheeses** les fromages à pâte molle
  [3] (*hair*)
  fin
- **to be soft on somebody** (*be kind to*) être indulgent avec quelqu'un
- **a soft drink** une boisson non alcoolisée
- **soft drugs** les drogues douces FEM
- **a soft option** une solution de facilité
  software NOUN
  le *logiciel*
  soggy ADJECTIVE

[1] *(soaked)*
trempé ◇ *a soggy tissue* un mouchoir trempé

[2] *(not crisp)*
mou MASC
molle FEM
◇ *soggy chips* des frites molles

soil NOUN
la *terre*

solar power NOUN
l' *énergie solaire* FEM

sold VERB *see* **sell**

soldier NOUN
le *soldat* ◇ *He's a soldier.* Il est soldat.

solicitor NOUN
[1] *(for lawsuits)*
l' *avocat* MASC
l' *avocate* FEM
◇ *He's a solicitor.* Il est avocat.
[2] *(for wills, property)*
le *notaire* ◇ *She's a solicitor.* Elle est notaire.

solid ADJECTIVE
[1] *(not hollow)*
massif MASC
massive FEM
◇ *solid gold* l'or massif
[2] *solide* ◇ *a solid wall* un mur solide
◆ **for three hours solid** pendant trois heures entières

solo NOUN
le *solo* ◇ *a guitar solo* un solo de guitare

solution NOUN
la *solution*

solve VERB
résoudre

some ADJECTIVE, PRONOUN
When some *means "a certain amount of", use* **du**, **de la** *or* **des** *according to the gender of the French noun that follows it.* **du** *and* **de la** *become* **de l'** *when they are followed by a noun starting with a vowel.*
[1] *du* ◇ *Would you like some bread?* Voulez-vous du pain?
de la ◇ *Would you like some beer?* Voulez-vous de la bière?
de l' ◇ *Have you got some mineral water?* Avez-vous de l'eau minérale?
des ◇ *I've got some Blur albums.* J'ai des albums de Blur.
◆ **Some people say that...** Il y a des gens qui disent que...
◆ **some day** un de ces jours
◆ **some day next week** un jour la semaine prochaine
[2] *certains* *(some but not all)* ◇ *Are these mushrooms poisonous? – Only some.* Est-ce que ces champignons sont vénéneux? – Certains le sont.

◆ **some of them** quelques-uns ◇ *I only sold some of them.* J'en ai seulement vendu quelques-uns.
◆ **I only took some of it.** J'en ai seulement pris un peu.
◆ **I'm going to buy some stamps. Do you want some too?** Je vais acheter des timbres. Tu en veux aussi?
◆ **Would you like some coffee? – No thanks, I've got some.** Tu veux du café? – Non merci, j'en ai déjà.

somebody PRONOUN
quelqu'un ◇ *Somebody stole my bag.* Quelqu'un a volé mon sac.

somehow ADVERB
◆ **I'll do it somehow.** Je trouverai le moyen de le faire.
◆ **Somehow I don't think he believed me.** Quelque chose me dit qu'il ne m'a pas cru.

someone PRONOUN
quelqu'un ◇ *Someone stole my bag.* Quelqu'un a volé mon sac.

something PRONOUN
quelque chose ◇ *something special* quelque chose de spécial ◇ *Wear something warm.* Mets quelque chose de chaud. ◇ *That's really something!* C'est vraiment quelque chose! ◇ *It cost £100, or something like that* Ça a coûté cent livres, ou quelque chose comme ça.
◆ **His name is Pierre or something.** Il s'appelle Pierre, ou quelque chose comme ça.

sometime ADVERB
un de ces jours ◇ *You must come and see us sometime.* Passez donc nous voir un de ces jours.
◆ **sometime last month** dans le courant du mois dernier

sometimes ADVERB
quelquefois ◇ *Sometimes I think she hates me.* Quelquefois j'ai l'impression qu'elle me déteste.

somewhere ADVERB
quelque part ◇ *I left my keys somewhere.* J'ai laissé mes clés quelque part. ◇ *I'd like to go on holiday, somewhere sunny.* J'aimerais aller en vacances, quelque part où il fait du soleil.

son NOUN
le *fils*

song NOUN
la *chanson*

son-in-law NOUN
le *gendre*

soon ADVERB
bientôt ◇ *very soon* très bientôt

- **soon afterwards** peu après
- **as soon as possible** aussitôt que possible

sooner ADVERB

plus tôt   ◇ *Can't you come a bit sooner?* Tu ne peux pas venir un peu plus tôt?

- **sooner or later** tôt ou tard

soppy ADJECTIVE

sentimental
(*sentimentaux* MASC PL)

soprano NOUN (*singer*)
le/la *soprano*

sorcerer NOUN
le *sorcier*

sore ADJECTIVE

see also **sore** NOUN

- **My feet are sore.** J'ai mal aux pieds.
- **It's sore.** Ça fait mal.
- **That's a sore point.** C'est un point sensible.

sore NOUN

see also **sore** ADJECTIVE
la *plaie*

sorry ADJECTIVE

désolé   ◇ *I'm really sorry.* Je suis vraiment désolé. ◇ *I'm sorry, I haven't got any change.* Je suis désolé, je n'ai pas de monnaie. ◇ *I'm sorry I'm late.* Je suis désolé d'être en retard.

- **Sorry!** Pardon!
- **Sorry?** Pardon?
- **I'm sorry about the noise.** Je m'excuse pour le bruit.
- **You'll be sorry!** Tu le regretteras!
- **to feel sorry for somebody** plaindre quelqu'un

sort NOUN

la *sorte*   ◇ *What sort of bike have you got?* Quelle sorte de vélo as-tu?

to **sort out** VERB

[1] *ranger* (*objects*)
[2] *résoudre* (*problems*)

so-so ADVERB

comme ci comme ça   ◇ *How are you feeling? – So-so.* Comment est-ce que tu te sens? – Comme ci comme ça.

soul NOUN

[1] l' *âme* FEM (*spirit*)
[2] la *soul* (*music*)

sound NOUN

see also **sound** VERB, ADJECTIVE
[1] le *bruit* (*noise*)   ◇ *Don't make a sound!* Pas un bruit! ◇ *the sound of footsteps* des bruits de pas
[2] le *son*   ◇ *Can I turn the sound down?* Je peux baisser le son?

to **sound** VERB

see also **sound** NOUN, ADJECTIVE

- **That sounds interesting.** Ça a l'air intéressant.
- **It sounds as if she's doing well at school.** Elle a l'air de bien travailler à l'école.
- **That sounds like a good idea.** C'est une bonne idée.

sound ADJECTIVE, ADVERB

see also **sound** NOUN, VERB
bon MASC
bonne FEM
◇ *That's sound advice.* C'est un bon conseil.

- **sound asleep** profondément endormi

soundtrack NOUN
la *bande sonore*

soup NOUN
la *soupe*   ◇ *vegetable soup* la soupe aux légumes

sour ADJECTIVE
aigre

south ADJECTIVE, ADVERB

see also **south** NOUN
[1] *sud* MASC, FEM, PL   ◇ *the south coast* la côte sud
[2] *vers le sud*   ◇ *We were travelling south.* Nous allions vers le sud.

- **south of** au sud de   ◇ *It's south of London.* C'est au sud de Londres.

south NOUN

see also **south** ADJECTIVE
le *sud*   ◇ *in the south* dans le sud ◇ *the South of France* le sud de la France

South Africa NOUN
l' *Afrique du Sud* FEM

- **in South Africa** en Afrique du Sud
- **to South Africa** en Afrique du Sud

South America NOUN
l' *Amérique du Sud* FEM

- **in South America** en Amérique du Sud
- **to South America** en Amérique du Sud

southeast NOUN
le *sud-est*   ◇ *southeast England* le sud-est de l'Angleterre

southern ADJECTIVE

- **the southern part of the island** la partie sud de l'île
- **Southern England** le sud de l'Angleterre

South Pole NOUN
le *pôle Sud*

South Wales NOUN
le *sud du Pays de Galles*

southwest NOUN
le *sud-ouest*   ◇ *southwest France* le sud-ouest de la France

souvenir NOUN
le *souvenir*

- **a souvenir shop** une boutique de souvenirs

soya NOUN

le *soja*
soy sauce NOUN
la *sauce de soja*
space NOUN
[1] la *place* ◇ There isn't enough space.
Il n'y a pas suffisamment de place.
- **a parking space** une place de parking
[2] l' *espace* MASC (universe, gap) ◇ Leave
a space after your answer. Laissez un
espace après votre réponse.
spacecraft NOUN
l' *engin spatial* MASC
spade NOUN
la *pelle*
- **spades** (in cards) le pique SING ◇ the
ace of spades l'as de pique
Spain NOUN
l' *Espagne* FEM
- **in Spain** en Espagne
- **to Spain** en Espagne
Spaniard NOUN
l' *Espagnol* MASC
l' *Espagnole* FEM
spaniel NOUN
l' *épagneul* MASC
Spanish ADJECTIVE
see also Spanish NOUN
espagnol ◇ She's Spanish. Elle est
espagnole.
Spanish NOUN
see also Spanish ADJECTIVE
l' *espagnol* MASC (language)
- **the Spanish** les Espagnols
to **spank** VERB
- **to spank somebody** donner une fessée
à quelqu'un
spanner NOUN
la *clé anglaise*
spare ADJECTIVE
see also spare VERB, NOUN
de rechange ◇ spare batteries des
piles de rechange ◇ a spare part une
pièce de rechange
- **a spare room** une chambre d'amis
- **spare time** le temps libre ◇ What do
you do in your spare time? Qu'est-ce que
tu fais pendant ton temps libre?
- **spare wheel** une roue de secours
to **spare** VERB
see also spare ADJECTIVE, NOUN
- **Can you spare a moment?** Vous
pouvez m'accorder un instant?
- **I can't spare the time.** Je n'ai pas le temps.
- **There's no room to spare.** Il n'y a plus
de place.
- **We arrived with time to spare.** Nous
sommes arrivés en avance.
spare NOUN
see also spare ADJECTIVE, VERB

- **a spare** un autre ◇ I've lost my
key. – Have you got a spare? J'ai perdu
ma clé. – Tu en as une autre?
sparkling ADJECTIVE
pétillant (water)
- **sparkling wine** le mousseux
sparrow NOUN
le *moineau*
(les *moineaux* PL)
spat VERB see **spit**
to **speak** VERB
parler ·· Do you speak English? Est-ce
que vous parlez anglais?
- **to speak to somebody** parler à
quelqu'un ◇ Have you spoken to him?
Tu lui as parlé? ◇ She spoke to him about
it. Elle lui en a parlé.
- **spoken French** le français parlé
speaker NOUN
[1] l' *enceinte* FEM (loudspeaker)
[2] l' *intervenant* MASC (in debate)
special ADJECTIVE
spécial
(*spéciaux* MASC PL)
specialist NOUN
le/la *spécialiste*
speciality NOUN
la *spécialité*
to **specialize** VERB
se spécialiser ◇ We specialize in skiing
equipment. Nous nous spécialisons dans
les articles de ski.
specially ADVERB
[1] *spécialement* · It's specially
designed for teenagers. C'est
spécialement conçu pour les adolescents.
- **not specially** pas spécialement ◇ Do
you like opera? – Not specially. Tu aimes
l'opéra? – Pas spécialement.
[2] *surtout* ◇ It can be very cold here,
specially in winter. Il peut faire très froid
ici, surtout en hiver.
species NOUN
l' *espèce* FEM
specific ADJECTIVE
[1] (particular)
particulier MASC
particulière FEM
◇ certain specific issues certains
problèmes particuliers
[2] (precise)
précis ◇ Could you be more specific?
Est-ce que vous pourriez être plus
précis?
specifically ADVERB
[1] *spécialement* ◇ It's specifically
designed for teenagers. C'est
spécialement conçu pour les adolescents.
[2] *particulièrement* ◇ in Britain, or

S

more specifically in England en Grande-Bretagne, ou plus particulièrement en Angleterre
* **I specifically said that...** J'ai clairement dit que...

specs, spectacles PL NOUN
les *lunettes* FEM PL

spectacular ADJECTIVE
spectaculaire

spectator NOUN
le *spectateur*
la *spectatrice*

speech NOUN
le *discours* ◦ *to make a speech* faire un discours

speechless ADJECTIVE
muet MASC
muette FEM
◦ *speechless with admiration* muet d'admiration
* **I was speechless.** Je suis resté sans voix.

speed NOUN
la *vitesse* ◦ *a three-speed bike* un vélo à trois vitesses ◦ *at top speed* à toute vitesse

to **speed up** VERB
accélérer

speedboat NOUN
la *vedette*

speeding NOUN
l' *excès de vitesse* MASC ◦ *He was fined for speeding.* Il a reçu une contravention pour excès de vitesse.

speed limit NOUN
la *limitation de vitesse*
* **to break the speed limit** faire un excès de vitesse

speedometer NOUN
le *compteur*

to **spell** VERB
see also spell NOUN
1 *écrire* (*in writing*) ◦ *How do you spell that?* Comment est-ce que ça s'écrit?
2 *épeler* (*out loud*) ◦ *Can you spell that please?* Est-ce que vous pouvez épeler, s'il vous plaît?
* **I can't spell.** Je fais des fautes d'orthographe.

spell NOUN
see also spell VERB
* **to cast a spell on somebody** jeter un sort à quelqu'un
* **to be under somebody's spell** être sous le charme de quelqu'un

spelling NOUN
l' *orthographe* FEM ◦ *My spelling is terrible.* Je fais beaucoup de fautes d'orthographe.

* **a spelling mistake** une faute d'orthographe

to **spend** VERB
1 *dépenser* (*money*)
2 *passer* (*time*) ◦ *He spent a month in France.* Il a passé un mois en France.

spice NOUN
l' *épice* FEM

spicy ADJECTIVE
épicé

spider NOUN
l' *araignée* FEM

to **spill** VERB
1 *renverser* (*tip over*) ◦ *He spilled his coffee over his trousers.* Il a renversé son café sur son pantalon.
2 *se répandre* (*get spilt*) ◦ *The soup spilled all over the table.* La soupe s'est répandue sur la table.

spinach NOUN
les *épinards* MASC PL

spine NOUN
la *colonne vertébrale*

spinster NOUN
la *célibataire*

spire NOUN
la *flèche*

spirit NOUN
1 le *courage* (*courage*)
* **to be in good spirits** être de bonne humeur
2 l' *énergie* FEM (*energy*)

spirits PL NOUN
les *alcools forts* MASC PL ◦ *I don't drink spirits.* Je ne bois pas d'alcools forts.

spiritual ADJECTIVE
religieux MASC
religieuse FEM
◦ *the spiritual leader of Tibet* le chef religieux du Tibet

spit NOUN
see also spit VERB
la *salive*

to **spit** VERB
see also spit NOUN
cracher
* **to spit something out** cracher quelque chose

spite NOUN
see also spite VERB
* **in spite of** malgré
* **out of spite** par méchanceté

to **spite** VERB
see also spite NOUN
contrarier ◦ *He just did it to spite me.* Il a fait ça juste pour me contrarier.

spiteful ADJECTIVE
1 (*action*)
méchant

2 (person)
rancunier MASC
rancunière FEM

to **splash** VERB
see also splash NOUN
éclabousser ◇ Careful! Don't splash me! Attention! Ne m'éclabousse pas!

splash NOUN
see also splash VERB
le *plouf* ◇ I heard a splash. J'ai entendu un plouf.
• a splash of colour une touche de couleur

splendid ADJECTIVE
splendide

splint NOUN
l' *attelle* FEM

splinter NOUN
l' *écharde* FEM

to **split** VERB
1 *fendre* (break apart) ◇ He split the wood with an axe. Il a fendu le bois avec une hache.
2 *se fendre* ◇ The ship hit a rock and split in two. Le bateau a percuté un rocher et s'est fendu en deux.
3 *partager* (divide up) ◇ They decided to split the profits. Ils ont décidé de partager les bénéfices.
• to split up (1) (couple) rompre
• to split up (2) (group) se disperser

to **spoil** VERB
1 *abîmer* (object)
2 *gâcher* (occasion)
3 *gâter* (child)

spoiled ADJECTIVE
gâté ◇ a spoiled child un enfant gâté

spoilsport NOUN
le/la *trouble-fête*

spoke VERB see **speak**

spoke NOUN
le *rayon* (of wheel)

spoken VERB see **speak**

spokesman NOUN
le *porte-parole*
(les *porte-parole* PL)

spokeswoman NOUN
le *porte-parole*
(les *porte-parole* PL)

sponge NOUN
l' *éponge* FEM
• a sponge bag une trousse de toilette
• a sponge cake un biscuit de Savoie

sponsor NOUN
see also sponsor VERB
le *donateur*
la *donatrice*

to **sponsor** VERB
see also sponsor NOUN
parrainer ◇ The festival was sponsored by... Le festival a été parrainé par...

spontaneous ADJECTIVE
spontané

spooky ADJECTIVE
1 *sinistre* (eerie)
• a spooky story une histoire qui fait froid dans le dos
2 *étrange* (strange) ◇ a spooky coincidence une étrange coïncidence

spoon NOUN
la *cuiller*
• a spoonful une cuillerée

sport NOUN
le *sport* ◇ What's your favourite sport? Quel est ton sport préféré?
• a sports bag un sac de sport
• a sports car une voiture de sport
• a sports jacket une veste sport
• Go on, be a sport! Allez, sois sympa!

sportsman NOUN
le *sportif*

sportswear NOUN
les *vêtements de sport* MASC PL

sportswoman NOUN
la *sportive*

sporty ADJECTIVE
sportif MASC
sportive FEM
◇ I'm not very sporty. Je ne suis pas très sportif.

spot NOUN
see also spot VERB
1 la *tache* (mark) • There's a spot on your shirt. Il y a une tache sur ta chemise.
2 le *pois* (in pattern) ◇ a red dress with white spots une robe rouge à pois blancs
3 le *bouton* (pimple) ◇ He's covered in spots. Il est couvert de boutons.
4 le *coin* (place) ◇ It's a lovely spot for a picnic. C'est un coin agréable pour un pique-nique.
• on the spot (1) (immediately) sur-le-champ ◇ They gave her the job on the spot. Ils lui ont offert le poste sur-le-champ.
• on the spot (2) (at the same place) sur place ◇ Luckily they were able to mend the car on the spot. Heureusement ils ont pu réparer la voiture sur place.

to **spot** VERB
see also spot NOUN
repérer ◇ I spotted a mistake. J'ai repéré une faute.

spotless ADJECTIVE
immaculé

spotty ADJECTIVE

S

(pimply)
boutonneux MASC
boutonneuse FEM

spouse NOUN
l' *époux* MASC
l' *épouse* FEM

to **sprain** VERB
see also sprain NOUN
+ **to sprain one's ankle** se faire une entorse à la cheville

sprain NOUN
see also sprain VERB
l' *entorse* FEM ◇ *It's just a sprain.* C'est juste une entorse.

spray NOUN
see also spray VERB
la *bombe* (spray can)

to **spray** VERB
see also spray NOUN
[1] *vaporiser* ◇ *to spray perfume on one's hand* se vaporiser du parfum sur la main
[2] *traiter* (crops)
[3] *peindre avec une bombe* (graffiti) ◇ *Somebody had sprayed graffiti on the wall.* Quelqu'un avait peint des graffitis avec une bombe sur le mur.

spread NOUN
see also spread VERB
+ **cheese spread** le fromage à tartiner
+ **chocolate spread** le chocolat à tartiner

to **spread** VERB
see also spread NOUN
[1] *étaler* ◇ *to spread butter on a slice of bread* étaler du beurre sur une tranche de pain
[2] *se propager* (disease, news) ◇ *The news spread rapidly.* La nouvelle s'est propagée rapidement.
+ **to spread out** (people) se disperser ◇ *The soldiers spread out across the field.* Les soldats se sont dispersés dans le champ.

spreadsheet NOUN
le *tableur* (computer program)

spring NOUN
[1] le *printemps* (season)
+ **in spring** au printemps
[2] le *ressort* (metal coil)
[3] la *source* (water hole)

spring-cleaning NOUN
le *grand nettoyage de printemps*

springtime NOUN
le *printemps*
+ **in springtime** au printemps

sprinkler NOUN
l' *arroseur* MASC (for lawn)

sprint NOUN
see also sprint VERB

le *sprint*

to **sprint** VERB
see also sprint NOUN
courir à toute vitesse ◇ *She sprinted for the bus.* Elle a couru à toute vitesse pour attraper le bus.

sprinter NOUN
le *sprinteur*
la *sprinteuse*

sprouts PL NOUN
+ **Brussels sprouts** les choux de Bruxelles MASC PL

spy NOUN
see also spy VERB
l' *espion* MASC
l' *espionne* FEM

to **spy** VERB
see also spy NOUN
+ **to spy on somebody** espionner quelqu'un

spying NOUN
l' *espionnage* MASC

to **squabble** VERB
se chamailler ◇ *Stop squabbling!* Arrêtez de vous chamailler!

square NOUN
see also square ADJECTIVE
[1] le *carré* ◇ *a square and a triangle* un carré et un triangle
[2] la *place* ◇ *the town square* la place de l'hôtel de ville

square ADJECTIVE
see also square NOUN
carré ◇ *two square metres* deux mètres carrés
+ **It's 2 metres square.** Ça fait deux mètres sur deux.

squash NOUN
see also squash VERB
le *squash* (sport) ◇ *I play squash.* Je joue au squash.
+ **a squash court** un court de squash
+ **a squash racket** une raquette de squash
+ **orange squash** l' orangeade FEM
+ **lemon squash** la citronnade

to **squash** VERB
see also squash NOUN
écraser ◇ *You're squashing me.* Tu m'écrases.

to **squeak** VERB
[1] *pousser un petit cri* (mouse, child)
[2] *grincer* (creak)

to **squeeze** VERB
[1] *presser* (fruit, toothpaste)
[2] *serrer* (hand, arm)
+ **to squeeze into some tight jeans** rentrer tout juste dans un jean serré

to **squint** VERB
see also squint NOUN

loucher

squint NOUN

> see also squint VERB

- **He has a squint.** Il louche.

squirrel NOUN
l' *écureuil* MASC

to **stab** VERB
poignarder

stable NOUN

> see also stable ADJECTIVE

l' *écurie* FEM

stable ADJECTIVE

> see also stable NOUN

stable ◇ *a stable relationship* une relation stable

stack NOUN
le *pile* ◇ *a stack of books* une pile de livres

stadium NOUN
le *stade*

staff NOUN
1 le *personnel* (in company)
2 les *professeurs* MASC PL (in school)

stage NOUN
1 la *scène* (in plays)
2 l' *estrade* FEM (for speeches, lectures)

- **at this stage (1)** à ce stade ◇ *at this stage in the negotiations* à ce stade des négociations
- **at this stage (2)** pour l'instant ◇ *At this stage, it's too early to comment.* Pour l'instant, il est trop tôt pour se prononcer.
- **to do something in stages** faire quelque chose étape par étape

to **stagger** VERB
chanceler

stain NOUN

> see also stain VERB

la *tache*

to **stain** VERB

> see also stain NOUN

tacher

stainless steel NOUN
l' *inox* MASC

stain remover NOUN
le *détachant*

stair NOUN
la *marche* (step)

staircase NOUN
l' *escalier* MASC

stairs PL NOUN
l' *escalier* MASC SING

stale ADJECTIVE
rassis (bread)

stalemate NOUN
le *pat* (in chess)

stall NOUN
le *stand* MASC ◇ *He's got a market stall.*

Il a un stand au marché.

- **the stalls** (in cinema, theatre) l'orchestre MASC

stammer NOUN
le *bégaiement*

- **He's got a stammer.** Il bégaie.

to **stamp** VERB

> see also stamp NOUN

affranchir (letter)

- **to stamp one's foot** taper du pied

stamp NOUN

> see also stamp VERB

1 le *timbre* ◇ *My hobby is stamp collecting.* Je collectionne les timbres.

- **a stamp album** un album de timbres
- **a stamp collection** une collection de timbres
2 le *tampon* (rubber stamp)

to **stand** VERB
1 *être debout* (be standing) ◇ *He was standing by the door.* Il était debout à la porte.
2 *se lever* (stand up)
3 *supporter* (tolerate, withstand) ◇ *I can't stand all this noise.* Je ne supporte pas tout ce bruit.

- **to stand for (1)** (be short for) être l'abréviation de ◇ *"BT" stands for "British Telecom".* "BT" est l'abréviation de "British Telecom".
- **to stand for (2)** (tolerate) supporter ◇ *won't stand for it!* Je ne supporterai pas ça!
- **to stand in for somebody** remplacer quelqu'un
- **to stand up** (get up) se lever

standard ADJECTIVE

> see also standard NOUN

1 *courant* ◇ *standard French* le français courant
2 *ordinaire* (equipment)

- **the standard procedure** la procédure normale

standard NOUN

> see also standard ADJECTIVE

le *niveau*
(les *niveaux* PL)
◇ *The standard is very high.* Le niveau est très haut.

- **the standard of living** le niveau de vie
- **She's got high standards.** Elle est très exigeante.

stand-by ticket NOUN
le *billet stand-by*

standpoint NOUN
le *point de vue*

stands PL NOUN
la *tribune* FEM (at sports ground)

stank VERB *see* **stink**

staple NOUN

see also staple VERB

l' *agrafe* FEM

to **staple** VERB

see also staple NOUN

agrafer

stapler NOUN

l' *agrafeuse* FEM

star NOUN

see also star VERB

1 l' *étoile* FEM (*in sky*)

2 la *vedette* (*celebrity*) ◇ He's a TV star. C'est une vedette de la télé.

- **the stars** (*horoscope*) l' horoscope MASC

to **star** VERB

see also star NOUN

être la vedette ◇ to star in a film être la vedette d'un film

- **The film stars Glenda Jackson.** Le film a pour vedette Glenda Jackson.
- **...starring Johnny Depp** ...avec Johnny Depp

to **stare** VERB

- **to stare at something** fixer quelque chose

stark ADVERB

- **stark naked** complètement nu

start NOUN

see also start VERB

1 le *début* ◇ It's not much, but it's a start. Ce n'est pas grand chose, mais c'est un début.

- **Shall we make a start on the washing-up?** On commence à faire la vaisselle?

2 le *départ* (*of race*)

to **start** VERB

see also start NOUN

1 *commencer* ◇ What time does it start? À quelle heure est-ce que ça commence?

- **to start doing something** commencer à faire quelque chose ◇ I started learning French three years ago. J'ai commencé à apprendre le français il y a trois ans.

2 *créer* (*organization*) ◇ He wants to start his own business. Il veut créer sa propre entreprise.

3 *organiser* (*campaign*) ◇ She started a campaign against drugs. Elle a organisé une campagne contre la drogue.

4 *démarrer* (*car*) ◇ He couldn't start the car. Il n'a pas réussi à démarrer la voiture. ◇ The car wouldn't start. La voiture ne voulait pas démarrer.

- **to start off** (*leave*) partir ◇ We started off first thing in the morning. Nous sommes partis en début de matinée.

starter NOUN

l' *entrée* FEM (*first course*)

to **starve** VERB

mourir de faim ◇ People were literally starving. Les gens mouraient littéralement de faim.

- **I'm starving!** Je meurs de faim!

state NOUN

see also state VERB

l' *état* MASC

- **he was in a real state** il était dans tous ses états
- **the state** (*government*) l'État
- **the States** (*USA*) les États-Unis MASC

to **state** VERB

see also state NOUN

1 *déclarer* (*say*) ◇ He stated his intention to resign. Il a déclaré son intention de démissionner.

2 *donner* (*give*) ◇ Please state your name and address. Veuillez donner vos nom et adresse.

stately home NOUN

le *château*

(les *châteaux* PL)

statement NOUN

la *déclaration*

station NOUN

la *gare* (*railway*)

- **the bus station** la gare routière
- **a police station** un poste de police
- **a radio station** une station de radio

stationer's NOUN

la *papeterie*

statue NOUN

la *statue*

to **stay** VERB

see also stay NOUN

1 *rester* (*remain*) ◇ Stay here! Reste ici!

- **to stay in** (*not go out*) rester à la maison
- **to stay up** rester debout ◇ We stayed up till midnight. Nous sommes restés debout jusqu'à minuit.

2 *loger* (*spend the night*) ◇ to stay with friends loger chez des amis ◇ Where are you staying? Où est-ce que vous logez?

- **to stay the night** passer la nuit
- **We stayed in Belgium for a few days.** Nous avons passé quelques jours en Belgique.

stay NOUN

see also stay VERB

le *séjour* ◇ my stay in France mon séjour en France

steady ADJECTIVE

1 *régulier* MASC

régulière FEM

◇ steady progress des progrès réguliers

2 *stable* ◇ a steady job un emploi stable

3 *ferme* (*voice, hand*)

[4] *calme* (*person*)
+ **a steady boyfriend** un copain
+ **a steady girlfriend** une copine
+ **Steady on!** Doucement!
steak NOUN (*beef*)
le *steak* ◦ *steak and chips* un steak frites
to **steal** VERB
voler
steam NOUN
la *vapeur* ◦ *a steam engine* une locomotive à vapeur
steel NOUN
l' *acier* MASC ◦ *a steel door* une porte en acier
steep ADJECTIVE
raide (*slope*)
steeple NOUN
le *clocher*
steering wheel NOUN
le *volant*
step NOUN
see also step VERB
[1] le *pas* (*pace*) ◦ *He took a step forward.* Il a fait un pas en avant.
[2] la *marche* (*stair*) ◦ *She tripped over the step.* Elle a trébuché sur la marche.
to **step** VERB
see also step NOUN
+ **to step aside** faire un pas de côté
+ **to step back** faire un pas en arrière
stepbrother NOUN
le *demi-frère*
stepdaughter NOUN
la *belle-fille*
(les *belles-filles* PL)
stepfather NOUN
le *beau-père*
(les *beaux-pères* PL)
stepladder NOUN
l' *escabeau* MASC
(les *escabeaux* PL)
stepmother NOUN
la *belle-mère*
(les *belles-mères* PL)
stepsister NOUN
la *demi-sœur*
stepson NOUN
le *beau-fils*
(les *beaux-fils* PL)
stereo NOUN
la *chaîne stéréo*
(les *chaînes stéréo* PL)
sterling ADJECTIVE
+ **£5 sterling** cinq livres sterling
stew NOUN
le *ragoût*
steward NOUN
le *steward*

stick NOUN
see also stick VERB
[1] le *bâton*
[2] la *canne* (*walking stick*)
to **stick** VERB
see also stick NOUN
coller (*with adhesive*) ◦ *Stick the stamps on the envelope.* Collez les timbres sur l'enveloppe.
+ **I can't stick it any longer.** Je n'en peux plus.
sticker NOUN
l' *autocollant* MASC
sticky ADJECTIVE
[1] *poisseux* MASC
poisseuse FEM
◦ *to have sticky hands* avoir les mains poisseuses
[2] *adhésif* MASC
adhésive FEM
◦ *a sticky label* une étiquette adhésive
stiff ADJECTIVE, ADVERB
rigide (*rigid*)
+ **to have a stiff back** avoir mal au dos
+ **to feel stiff** avoir des courbatures
+ **to be bored stiff** s'ennuyer à mourir
+ **to be frozen stiff** être mort de froid
+ **to be scared stiff** être mort de peur
still ADVERB
see also still ADJECTIVE
[1] *encore* ◦ *I still haven't finished.* Je n'ai pas encore fini. ◦ *Are you still in bed?* Tu es encore au lit?
+ **better still** encore mieux
[2] *quand même* (*even so*) ◦ *She knows I don't like it, but she still does it.* Elle sait que je n'aime pas ça, mais elle le fait quand même.
[3] *enfin* (*after all*) ◦ *Still, it's the thought that counts.* Enfin, c'est l'intention qui compte.
still ADJECTIVE
see also still ADVERB
+ **Keep still!** Ne bouge pas!
+ **Sit still!** Reste tranquille!
sting NOUN
see also sting VERB
la *piqûre* ◦ *a bee sting* une piqûre d'abeille
to **sting** VERB
see also sting NOUN
piquer ◦ *I've been stung.* J'ai été piqué.
stingy ADJECTIVE
pingre
to **stink** VERB
see also stink NOUN
puer ◦ *It stinks!* Ça pue!
stink NOUN
see also stink VERB

PTO

la *puanteur*

to **stir** VERB
remuer

to **stitch** VERB
> see also stitch NOUN
coudre (cloth)

stitch NOUN
> see also stitch VERB
1 le *point* (in sewing)
2 le *point de suture* (in wound) ○ I had
five stitches. J'ai eu cinq points de
suture.

stock NOUN
> see also stock VERB
1 la *réserve* (supply)
2 le *stock* (in shop) ○ in stock en stock
* **out of stock** épuisé
3 le *bouillon* ○ chicken stock du
bouillon de volaille

to **stock** VERB
> see also stock NOUN
avoir (have in stock) ○ Do you stock
camping stoves? Vous avez des
camping-gaz?
* **to stock up** s'approvisionner ○ to
stock up with something
s'approvisionner en quelque chose

stock cube NOUN
le *cube de bouillon*

stocking NOUN
le *bas*

stole, stolen VERB see **steal**

stomach NOUN
l' *estomac* MASC

stomachache NOUN
* **to have a stomachache** avoir mal au
ventre

stone NOUN
1 (rock)
la *pierre* ○ a stone wall un mur en
pierre
2 (in fruit)
le *noyau*
(les *noyaux* PL)
○ a peach stone un noyau de pêche
In France, weight is expressed in kilos. A stone is
about 6.3 kg.
* **I weigh eight stone.** Je pèse cinquante
kilos.

stood VERB see **stand**

stool NOUN
le *tabouret*

to **stop** VERB
> see also stop NOUN
1 *arrêter* ○ a campaign to stop whaling
une campagne pour arrêter la chasse à la
baleine
2 *s'arrêter* ○ The bus doesn't stop
there. Le bus ne s'arrête pas là. ○ I think

the rain's going to stop. Je pense qu'il va
s'arrêter de pleuvoir.
* **to stop doing something** arrêter de faire
quelque chose ○ to stop smoking
arrêter de fumer
* **to stop somebody doing something**
empêcher quelqu'un de faire quelque
chose
* **Stop!** Stop!

stop NOUN
> see also stop VERB
l' *arrêt* MASC ○ a bus stop un arrêt de
bus
* **This is my stop.** Je descends ici.

stopwatch NOUN
le *chronomètre*

store NOUN
> see also store VERB
1 le *magasin* (shop) ○ a furniture store
un magasin de meubles
2 la *réserve* (stock, storeroom)

to **store** VERB
> see also store NOUN
1 *garder* ○ They store potatoes in the
cellar. Ils gardent des pommes de terre
dans la cave.
2 *enregistrer* (information)

storey NOUN
l' *étage* MASC ○ a three-storey building
un immeuble à trois étages

storm NOUN
1 la *tempête* (gale)
2 l' *orage* MASC (thunderstorm)

stormy ADJECTIVE
orageux MASC
orageuse FEM

story NOUN
l' *histoire* FEM

stove NOUN
1 la *cuisinière* (in kitchen)
2 le *réchaud* (camping stove)

straight ADJECTIVE
1 *droit* ○ a straight line une ligne
droite
2 *raide* ○ straight hair les cheveux
raides
3 *hétéro* (heterosexual)
* **straight away** tout de suite
* **straight on** tout droit

straightforward ADJECTIVE
simple

strain NOUN
> see also strain VERB
le *stress*
* **It was a strain.** C'était éprouvant.

to **strain** VERB
> see also strain NOUN
se faire mal à ○ I strained my back. Je
me suis fait mal au dos.

+ **to strain a muscle** se froisser un muscle

strained ADJECTIVE
  froissé (*muscle*)

stranded ADJECTIVE
+ **We were stranded.** Nous étions coincés.

strange ADJECTIVE
  bizarre ◇ *That's strange!* C'est bizarre!

stranger NOUN
  l' _inconnu_ MASC
  l' _inconnue_ FEM
  ◇ *Don't talk to strangers.* Ne parle pas
  aux inconnus.
+ **I'm a stranger here.** Je ne suis pas d'ici.

to **strangle** VERB
  étrangler

strap NOUN
  [1] la _courroie_ (*of bag, camera, suitcase*)
  [2] la _bretelle_ (*of bra, dress*)
  [3] la _lanière_ (*on shoe*)
  [4] le _bracelet_ (*of watch*)

straw NOUN
  la _paille_
+ **That's the last straw!** Ça, c'est le
  comble!

strawberry NOUN
  la _fraise_ ◇ *strawberry jam* la confiture
  de fraises ◇ *a strawberry ice cream* une
  glace à la fraise

stray NOUN
+ **a stray cat** un chat perdu

stream NOUN
  le _ruisseau_
  (les _ruisseaux_ PL)

street NOUN
  la _rue_ • *in the street* dans la rue

streetlamp NOUN
  le _réverbère_

street plan NOUN
  le _plan de la ville_

streetwise ADJECTIVE
  dégourdi

strength NOUN
  la _force_

to **stress** VERB
  see also stress NOUN
  souligner ◇ *I would like to stress that...*
  J'aimerais souligner que...

stress NOUN
  see also stress VERB
  le _stress_

to **stretch** VERB
  [1] _s'étirer_ (*person, animal*) ◇ *The dog
  woke up and stretched.* Le chien s'est
  réveillé et s'est étiré.
  [2] _se détendre_ (*get bigger*) ◇ *My sweater
  stretched when I washed it.* Mon pull
  s'est détendu au lavage.
  [3] _tendre_ (*stretch out*) ◇ *They stretched
  a rope between two trees.* Ils ont tendu

une corde entre deux arbres.
+ **to stretch out one's arms** tendre les
  bras

stretcher NOUN
  le _brancard_

stretchy ADJECTIVE
  élastique

strict ADJECTIVE
  strict

strike NOUN
  see also strike VERB
  la _grève_
+ **to be on strike** être en grève
+ **to go on strike** faire grève

to **strike** VERB
  see also strike NOUN
  [1] _sonner_ (*clock*) ◇ *The clock struck
  three.* L'horloge a sonné trois heures.
  [2] _faire grève_ (*go on strike*)
  [3] _frapper_ (*hit*)
+ **to strike a match** frotter une allumette

striker NOUN
  [1] le/la _gréviste_ (*person on strike*)
  [2] le _buteur_ (*footballer*)

striking ADJECTIVE
  [1] _en grève_ (*on strike*) ◇ *striking miners*
  les mineurs en grève
  [2] _frappant_ (*noticeable*) ◇ *a striking
  difference* une différence frappante

string NOUN
  [1] la _ficelle_ ◇ *a piece of string* un bout
  de ficelle
  [2] la _corde_ (*of violin, guitar*)

to **strip** VERB
  see also strip NOUN
  se déshabiller (*get undressed*)

strip NOUN
  see also strip VERB
  la _bande_
+ **a strip cartoon** une bande dessinée

stripe NOUN
  la _rayure_

striped ADJECTIVE
  à rayures ◇ *a striped skirt* une jupe à
  rayures

stripper NOUN
  le _strip-teaseur_
  la _strip-teaseuse_

stripy ADJECTIVE
  rayé ◇ *a stripy shirt* une chemise rayée

to **stroke** VERB
  see also stroke NOUN
  caresser

stroke NOUN
  see also stroke VERB
  l' _attaque_ FEM ◇ *to have a stroke* avoir
  une attaque

stroll NOUN
+ **to go for a stroll** aller faire une petite

S

promenade

strong ADJECTIVE

1 *fort* ◦ She's very strong. Elle est très forte.

2 *résistant* (material)

strongly ADVERB

fortement ◦ We recommend strongly that... Nous recommandons fortement que...

→ He smelt strongly of tobacco. Il sentait fort le tabac.

→ strongly built solidement bâti

→ I don't feel strongly about it. Ça m'est égal.

to **struggle** VERB

see also struggle NOUN

se débattre (physically) ◦ He struggled, but he couldn't escape. Il s'est débattu, mais il n'a pas pu s'échapper.

→ to struggle to do something (1) (fight) se battre pour faire quelque chose ◦ He struggled to get custody of his daughter. Il s'est battu pour obtenir la garde de sa fille.

→ to struggle to do something (2) (have difficulty) avoir du mal à faire quelque chose

struggle NOUN

see also struggle VERB

la *lutte* (for independence, equality)

→ It was a struggle. Ça a été laborieux.

stub NOUN

le *mégot* (of cigarette)

stubborn ADJECTIVE

têtu

to **stub out** VERB

écraser (cigarette)

stuck VERB see **stick**

stuck ADJECTIVE

coincé (jammed) ◦ It's stuck. C'est coincé.

→ to get stuck rester coincé ◦ We got stuck in a traffic jam. Nous sommes restés coincés dans un embouteillage.

stuck-up ADJECTIVE

coincé (informal)

stud NOUN

1 la *boucle d'oreille* (earring)

2 le *clou* (on football boots)

student NOUN

l'*étudiant* MASC

l'*étudiante* FEM

studio NOUN

le *studio* ◦ a TV studio un studio de télévision

→ a studio flat un studio

to **study** VERB

1 *faire des études* (at university) ◦ I plan to study biology. J'ai l'intention de

faire des études de biologie.

2 *travailler* (do homework) ◦ I've got to study tonight. Je dois travailler ce soir.

stuff NOUN

1 le *truc* (substance) ◦ I need some stuff for hay fever. J'ai besoin d'un truc contre le rhume des foins.

2 les *trucs* MASC PL (things) ◦ There's some stuff on the table for you. Il y a des trucs sur la table pour toi.

3 les *affaires* FEM PL (possessions) ◦ Have you got all your stuff? Est-ce que tu as toutes tes affaires?

stuffy ADJECTIVE

mal aéré (room)

→ It's really stuffy in here. On étouffe ici.

to **stumble** VERB

trébucher

stung VERB see **sting**

stunk VERB see **stink**

stunned ADJECTIVE

sidéré (amazed) ◦ I was stunned. J'étais sidéré.

stunning ADJECTIVE

superbe

stunt NOUN

la *cascade* (in film)

stuntman NOUN

le *cascadeur*

stupid ADJECTIVE

stupide ◦ a stupid joke une plaisanterie stupide

→ Me, go jogging? Don't be stupid! Moi, faire du footing? Ne dis pas de bêtises!

to **stutter** VERB

see also stutter NOUN

bégayer

stutter NOUN

see also stutter VERB

→ He's got a stutter. Il bégaie.

style NOUN

le *style* ◦ That's not his style. Ça n'est pas son style.

subject NOUN

1 le *sujet* ◦ The subject of my project was the Internet. Le sujet de mon projet était l'Internet.

2 la *matière* (at school) ◦ What's your favourite subject? Quelle est ta matière préférée?

submarine NOUN

le *sous-marin*

subscription NOUN

l'*abonnement* MASC (to paper, magazine)

→ to take out a subscription to s'abonner à

to **subsidize** VERB

subventionner

subsidy NOUN

la *subvention*
substance NOUN
la *substance*
substitute NOUN
see also substitute VERB
(*person*)
le *remplaçant*
la *remplaçante*
to **substitute** VERB
see also substitute NOUN
substituer ○ *to substitute A for B*
substituer A à B
subtitled ADJECTIVE
sous-titré
subtitles PL NOUN
les *sous-titres* MASC PL ○ *a French film
with English subtitles* un film français
avec des sous-titres en anglais
subtle ADJECTIVE
subtil
to **subtract** VERB
retrancher ○ *to subtract 3 from 5*
retrancher trois de cinq
suburb NOUN
la *banlieue* ○ *a suburb of Paris* une
banlieue de Paris ○ *They live in the
suburbs.* Ils habitent en banlieue.
suburban ADJECTIVE
de banlieue ○ *a suburban train* un
train de banlieue
subway NOUN
le *passage souterrain* (*underpass*)
to **succeed** VERB
réussir ○ *to succeed in doing something*
réussir à faire quelque chose
success NOUN
le *succès* ○ *The play was a great
success.* La pièce a eu beaucoup de
succès.
successful ADJECTIVE
réussi ○ *a successful attempt* une
tentative réussie
- **to be successful in doing something**
réussir à faire quelque chose
- **He's a successful businessman.** Ses
affaires marchent bien.
successfully ADVERB
avec succès
successive ADJECTIVE
- **on four successive occasions** quatre
fois de suite
such ADJECTIVE, ADVERB
si ○ *such nice people* des gens si
gentils ○ *such a long journey* un voyage
si long
- **such a lot of** tellement de ○ *such a lot
of work* tellement de travail
- **such as** (*like*) comme ○ *hot countries,
such as India* les pays chauds, comme

l'Inde
- **not as such** pas exactement ○ *He's not
an expert as such, but...* Ce n'est pas
exactement un expert, mais...
- **There's no such thing.** Ça n'existe pas.
○ *There's no such thing as the yeti.* Le
yéti n'existe pas.
such-and-such ADJECTIVE
tel ou tel MASC
telle ou telle FEM
○ *such-and-such a place* tel ou tel
endroit
to **suck** VERB
sucer ○ *to suck one's thumb* sucer son
pouce
sudden ADJECTIVE
soudain ○ *a sudden change* un
changement soudain
- **all of a sudden** tout à coup
suddenly ADVERB
1 *brusquement* (*stop, leave, change*)
2 *subitement* (*die*)
3 *soudain* (*at beginning of sentence*)
○ *Suddenly, the door opened.* Soudain, la
porte s'est ouverte.
suede NOUN
le *daim* ○ *a suede jacket* une veste en
daim
to **suffer** VERB
souffrir ○ *She was really suffering.* Elle
souffrait beaucoup.
- **to suffer from a disease** avoir une
maladie ○ *I suffer from hay fever.* J'ai le
rhume des foins.
to **suffocate** VERB
suffoquer
sugar NOUN
le *sucre* ○ *Do you take sugar?* Est-ce
que vous prenez du sucre?
to **suggest** VERB
suggérer ○ *I suggested they set off
early.* Je leur ai suggéré de partir de
bonne heure.
suggestion NOUN
la *suggestion* ○ *to make a suggestion*
faire une suggestion
suicide NOUN
le *suicide*
- **to commit suicide** se suicider
suit NOUN
see also suit VERB
1 le *costume* (*man's*)
2 le *tailleur* (*woman's*)
to **suit** VERB
see also suit NOUN
1 *convenir à* (*be convenient for*) ○ *What
time would suit you?* Quelle heure vous
conviendrait?
- **That suits me fine.** Ça m'arrange.

S

PTO

• **Suit yourself!** Comme tu veux!
[2] *aller bien à* (look good on) ◇ *That
dress really suits you.* Cette robe te va
vraiment bien.
suitable ADJECTIVE
[1] *convenable* ◇ *a suitable time* une
heure convenable
[2] *approprié* (clothes) ◇ *suitable
clothing* des vêtements appropriés
suitcase NOUN
la *valise*
suite NOUN
la *suite* (of rooms)
• **a bedroom suite** une chambre à
coucher
to **sulk** VERB
bouder
sulky ADJECTIVE
boudeur MASC
boudeuse FEM
sum NOUN
[1] le *calcul* (calculation) ◇ *She's good at
sums.* Elle est bonne en calcul.
[2] la *somme* (amount) ◇ *a sum of
money* une somme d'argent
to **summarize** VERB
résumer
summary NOUN
le *résumé*
summer NOUN
l' *été* MASC
• **in summer** en été
• **summer clothes** les vêtements d'été
• **the summer holidays** les vacances d'été
summertime NOUN
l' *été* MASC
• **in summertime** en été
summit NOUN
le *sommet*
to **sum up** VERB
résumer
sun NOUN
le *soleil* ◇ *in the sun* au soleil
to **sunbathe** VERB
se bronzer
sunblock NOUN
l' *écran total* MASC
sunburn NOUN
le *coup de soleil*
sunburnt ADJECTIVE
• **I got sunburnt.** J'ai attrapé un coup de
soleil.
Sunday NOUN
le *dimanche* ◇ *on Sunday* dimanche
◇ *on Sundays* le dimanche ◇ *every
Sunday* tous les dimanches ◇ *last
Sunday* dimanche dernier ◇ *next
Sunday* dimanche prochain
Sunday school NOUN

le *catéchisme*

le *catéchisme*, *the French equivalent of*
Sunday school, *takes place during the week
after school rather than on a Sunday.*

◇ *to go to Sunday school* aller au
catéchisme
sunflower NOUN
le *tournesol*
sung VERB *see* **sing**
sunglasses PL NOUN
les *lunettes de soleil* FEM PL
sunk VERB *see* **sink**
sunlight NOUN
le *soleil*
sunny ADJECTIVE
ensoleillé ◇ *a sunny morning* une
matinée ensoleillée
• **It's sunny.** Il fait du soleil.
• **a sunny day** une belle journée
sunrise NOUN
le *lever du soleil*
sunroof NOUN
le *toit ouvrant*
sunscreen NOUN
la *crème solaire*
sunset NOUN
le *coucher du soleil*
sunshine NOUN
le *soleil*
sunstroke NOUN
l' *insolation* FEM ◇ *to get sunstroke*
attraper une insolation
suntan NOUN
le *bronzage*
• **suntan lotion** le lait solaire
• **suntan oil** l'huile solaire FEM
super ADJECTIVE
formidable
superb ADJECTIVE
superbe
supermarket NOUN
le *supermarché*
supernatural ADJECTIVE
surnaturel MASC
surnaturelle FEM
superstitious ADJECTIVE
superstitieux MASC
superstitieuse FEM
to **supervise** VERB
surveiller
supervisor NOUN
[1] (in factory)
le *surveillant*
la *surveillante*
[2] (in department store)
le *chef de rayon*
supper NOUN
le *dîner*
supplement NOUN

le *supplément*
supplies PL NOUN
les *vivres* MASC PL *(food)*
to **supply** VERB
see also supply NOUN
fournir *(provide)*
* **to supply somebody with something**
fournir quelque chose à quelqu'un
  ◦ *The centre supplied us with all the equipment.* Le centre nous a fourni tout l'équipement.
supply NOUN
see also supply VERB
la *provision* ◦ *a supply of paper* une provision de papier
* **the water supply** *(to town)*
l'approvisionnement en eau MASC
supply teacher NOUN
le *suppléant*
la *suppléante*
to **support** VERB
see also support NOUN
1 *soutenir* ◦ *My mum has always supported me.* Ma mère m'a toujours soutenu.
2 *être supporter de* ◦ *What team do you support?* Tu es supporter de quelle équipe?
3 *subvenir aux besoins de* *(financially)*
  ◦ *She had to support five children on her own.* Elle a dû subvenir toute seule aux besoins de cinq enfants.
support NOUN
see also support VERB
le *soutien* *(backing)*
supporter NOUN
1 le *supporter* ◦ *a Liverpool supporter* un supporter de Liverpool
2 le *sympathisant*
la *sympathisante*
  ◦ *a supporter of the Labour Party* un sympathisant du parti travailliste
to **suppose** VERB
imaginer ◦ *I suppose he's late.* J'imagine qu'il est en retard. ◦ *Suppose you won the lottery.* Imaginez que vous gagniez à la loterie.
* **I suppose so.** J'imagine.
* **to be supposed to do something** être censé faire quelque chose ◦ *You're supposed to show your passport.* On est censé montrer son passeport.
supposing CONJUNCTION
si ◦ *Supposing you won the lottery...* Si tu gagnais à la loterie...
surcharge NOUN
la *surcharge*
sure ADJECTIVE
sûr ◦ *Are you sure?* Tu es sûr?

* **Sure!** Bien sûr!
* **to make sure that...** vérifier que...
  ◦ *I'm going to make sure the door's locked.* Je vais vérifier que la porte est fermée à clé.
surely ADVERB
* **Surely you've been to London?** J'imagine que tu es allé à Londres, non?
* **The shops are closed on Sundays, surely?** J'imagine que les magasins sont fermés le dimanche, non?
surf NOUN
le *ressac*
surface NOUN
la *surface*
surfboard NOUN
la *planche de surf*
(les *planches de surf* PL)
surfing NOUN
le *surf* ◦ *to go surfing* faire du surf
surgeon NOUN
le *chirurgien* ◦ *She's a surgeon.* Elle est chirurgien.
surgery NOUN
le *cabinet médical* *(doctor's surgery)*
* **surgery hours** les heures de consultation FEM
surname NOUN
le *nom de famille*
(les *noms de famille* PL)
surprise NOUN
la *surprise*
surprised ADJECTIVE
surpris • *I was surprised to see him.* J'ai été surpris de le voir.
surprising ADJECTIVE
surprenant
to **surrender** VERB
capituler
surrogate mother NOUN
la *mère porteuse*
to **surround** VERB
encercler ◦ *The police surrounded the house.* La police a encerclé la maison.
  ◦ *You're surrounded!* Vous êtes encerclé!
* **surrounded by** entouré de ◦ *The house is surrounded by trees.* La maison est entourée d'arbres.
survey NOUN
l' *enquête* FEM *(research)*
surveyor NOUN
1 l' *expert en bâtiment* MASC *(of buildings)*
2 le/la *géomètre* *(of land)*
survivor NOUN
le *survivant*
la *survivante*
  ◦ *There were no survivors.* Il n'y a pas eu de survivants.

S

to **suspect** VERB
  see also suspect NOUN
  soupçonner
suspect NOUN
  see also suspect VERB
  le *suspect*
  la *suspecte*
to **suspend** VERB
  [1] *exclure* (from school, team) ◇ He's
  been suspended. Il s'est fait exclure.
  [2] *suspendre* (from job)
suspense NOUN
  [1] *attente* FEM (waiting) ◇ The
  suspense was terrible. L'attente a été
  terrible.
  [2] le *suspense* (in story) ◇ a film with
  lots of suspense un film avec beaucoup
  de suspense
suspension NOUN
  [1] l' *exclusion* FEM (from school, team)
  [2] la *suspension* (from job)
suspicious ADJECTIVE
  [1] *méfiant* ◇ He was suspicious at first.
  Il était méfiant au début.
  [2] *louche* (suspicious-looking) ◇ a
  suspicious person un individu louche
to **swallow** VERB
  avaler
swam VERB see **swim**
swan NOUN
  le *cygne*
to **swap** VERB
  échanger ◇ Do you want to swap? Tu
  veux échanger? ◇ to swap A for B
  échanger A contre B
to **swat** VERB
  écraser
to **sway** VERB
  osciller
to **swear** VERB
  jurer (make an oath, curse)
swearword NOUN
  le *gros mot*
sweat NOUN
  see also sweat VERB
  la *transpiration*
to **sweat** VERB
  see also sweat NOUN
  transpirer
sweater NOUN
  le *pull*
sweaty ADJECTIVE
  [1] *en sueur* (person, face) ◇ I'm all
  sweaty. Je suis en sueur.
  [2] *moite* (hands)
Swede NOUN
  (person)
  le *Suédois*
  la *Suédoise*

swede NOUN
  le *rutabaga* (vegetable)
Sweden NOUN
  la *Suède*
◆ **in Sweden** en Suède
◆ **to Sweden** en Suède
Swedish ADJECTIVE
  see also Swedish NOUN
  suédois ◇ She's Swedish. Elle est
  suédoise.
Swedish NOUN
  see also Swedish ADJECTIVE
  le *suédois* (language)
to **sweep** VERB
  balayer
◆ **to sweep the floor** balayer
sweet NOUN
  see also sweet ADJECTIVE
  [1] le *bonbon* (candy) ◇ a bag of sweets
  un paquet de bonbons
  [2] le *dessert* (pudding) ◇ What sweet did
  you have? Qu'est-ce que vous avez
  mangé comme dessert?
sweet ADJECTIVE
  see also sweet NOUN
  [1] (not savoury)
  sucré
  [2] (kind)
  gentil MASC
  gentille FEM
  ◇ That was really sweet of you. C'était
  vraiment gentil de ta part.
  [3] (cute)
  mignon MASC
  mignonne FEM
  ◇ Isn't she sweet? Comme elle est
  mignonne!
◆ **sweet and sour pork** le porc à la sauce
  aigre-douce
sweetcorn NOUN
  le *maïs doux*
sweltering ADJECTIVE
◆ **It was sweltering.** Il faisait une chaleur
  étouffante.
swept VERB see **sweep**
to **swerve** VERB
  faire une embardée ◇ He swerved to
  avoid the cyclist. Il a fait une embardée
  pour éviter le cycliste.
swim NOUN
  see also swim VERB
◆ **to go for a swim** aller se baigner
to **swim** VERB
  see also swim NOUN
  nager ◇ Can you swim? Tu sais nager?
◆ **She swam across the river.** Elle a
  traversé la rivière à la nage.
swimmer NOUN
  le *nageur*

la *nageuse*
◦ *She's a good swimmer.* C'est une
bonne nageuse.
swimming NOUN
la *natation* ◦ *Do you like swimming?*
Tu aimes la natation?
◆ **to go swimming** (*in a pool*) aller à la
piscine
◆ **a swimming cap** un bonnet de bain
◆ **a swimming costume** un maillot de
bain
◆ **a swimming pool** une piscine
◆ **swimming trunks** le maillot de bain
swimsuit NOUN
le *maillot de bain*
swing NOUN
la *balançoire* (*in playground, garden*)
Swiss ADJECTIVE
see also **Swiss** NOUN
suisse ◦ *Sabine's Swiss.* Sabine est
suisse.
Swiss NOUN
see also **Suisse** ADJECTIVE
le/la *Suisse* (*person*)
◆ **the Swiss** les Suisses
switch NOUN
see also **switch** VERB
le *bouton* (*for light, radio etc*)
to **switch** VERB
see also **switch** NOUN
changer de ◦ *We switched partners.*
Nous avons changé de partenaire.
to **switch off** VERB
⟦1⟧ *éteindre* (*electrical appliance*)
⟦2⟧ *arrêter* (*engine, machine*)

to **switch on** VERB
⟦1⟧ *allumer* (*electrical appliance*)
⟦2⟧ *mettre en marche* (*engine, machine*)
Switzerland NOUN
la *Suisse*
◆ **in Switzerland** en Suisse
swollen ADJECTIVE
enflé (*arm, leg*)
to **swop** VERB
échanger ◦ *Do you want to swop?* Tu
veux échanger? ◦ *to swop A for B*
échanger A contre B
sword NOUN
l' *épée* FEM
swore, sworn VERB *see* **swear**
swum VERB *see* **swim**
swung VERB *see* **swing**
syllabus NOUN
le *programme* ◦ *on the syllabus* au
programme
symbol NOUN
le *symbole*
sympathetic ADJECTIVE
compréhensif MASC
compréhensive FEM
to **sympathize** VERB
◆ **to sympathize with somebody**
comprendre quelqu'un
sympathy NOUN
la *compassion*
syringe NOUN
la *seringue*
system NOUN
le *système*

S

T

table NOUN
la _table_ ◇ to lay the table mettre la
table
tablecloth NOUN
la _nappe_
tablespoon NOUN
la _grande cuillère_
+ a tablespoonful of sugar une cuillerée à
soupe de sucre
tablet NOUN
le _comprimé_
table tennis NOUN
le _ping-pong_ ◇ to play table tennis
jouer au ping-pong
tabloid NOUN
le _quotidien populaire_
tackle NOUN
see also tackle VERB
① le _tacle_ (in football)
② le _plaquage_ (in rugby)
+ fishing tackle le matériel de pêche
to **tackle** VERB
see also tackle NOUN
① _tacler_ (in football)
② _plaquer_ (in rugby)
+ to tackle a problem s'attaquer à un
problème
tact NOUN
le _tact_
tactful ADJECTIVE
plein de tact
tactics PL NOUN
la _tactique_ SING
tactless ADJECTIVE
+ to be tactless manquer de tact ◇ a
tactless remark une remarque qui
manque de tact
tadpole NOUN
le _têtard_
tag NOUN
l' _étiquette_ FEM (label)
tail NOUN
la _queue_
+ Heads or tails? Pile ou face?
tailor NOUN
le _tailleur_
to **take** VERB
① _prendre_ ◇ Are you taking your new
camera? Tu prends ton nouvel appareil
photo? ◇ He took a plate from the
cupboard. Il a pris une assiette dans le
placard. ◇ It takes about an hour. Ça
prend environ une heure.
② _emmener_ (person) ◇ He goes to
London every week, but he never takes
me. Il va à Londres toutes les semaines,

mais il ne m'emmène jamais.
+ to take something somewhere
emporter quelque chose quelque part
◇ Do you take your exercise books home?
Vous emportez vos cahiers chez vous?
◇ Don't take anything valuable with you.
N'emportez pas d'objets de valeur.
+ I'm going to take my coat to the
cleaner's. Je vais donner mon manteau
à nettoyer.
③ _demander_ (effort, skill) ◇ that takes a
lot of courage cela demande beaucoup
de courage
+ It takes a lot of money to do that. Il faut
beaucoup d'argent pour faire ça.
④ _supporter_ (tolerate) ◇ He can't take
being criticized. Il ne supporte pas d'être
critiqué.
⑤ _passer_ (exam, test) ◇ Have you taken
your driving test yet? Est-ce que tu as
déjà passé ton permis de conduire?
⑥ _faire_ (subject) ◇ I decided to take
French instead of German. J'ai décidé de
faire du français au lieu de l'allemand.
to **take after** VERB
ressembler à ◇ She takes after her
mother. Elle ressemble à sa mère.
to **take apart** VERB
+ to take something apart démonter
quelque chose
to **take away** VERB
① _emporter_ (object)
② _emmener_ (person)
+ to take something away (confiscate)
confisquer quelque chose
+ hot meals to take away des plats
chauds à emporter
takeaway NOUN
① le _plat à emporter_ (meal)
② le _restaurant qui vend des plats à
emporter_ (shop) ◇ a Chinese takeaway
un restaurant chinois qui vend des plats
à emporter
to **take back** VERB
rapporter ◇ I took it back to the shop.
Je l'ai rapporté au magasin.
+ I take it all back! Je n'ai rien dit!
to **take in** VERB
comprendre (understand) ◇ I didn't
really take it in. Je n'ai pas bien compris.
to **take off** VERB
① _décoller_ (plane) ◇ The plane took off
twenty minutes late. L'avion a décollé
avec vingt minutes de retard.
② _enlever_ (clothes) ◇ Take your coat off.
Enlevez votre manteau.

takeoff NOUN
le *décollage* (*of plane*)

to **take out** VERB
sortir (*from container, pocket*)
* **He took her out to the theatre.** Il l'a
emmenée au théâtre.

to **take over** VERB
prendre la relève ◇ *I'll take over now.*
Je vais prendre la relève.
* **to take over from somebody** remplacer
quelqu'un

talcum powder NOUN
le *talc*

tale NOUN
le *conte* FEM (*story*)

talent NOUN
le *talent* ◇ *She's got lots of talent.* Elle a
beaucoup de talent.
* **to have a talent for something** être
doué pour quelque chose ◇ *He's got a
real talent for languages.* Il est vraiment
doué pour les langues.

talented ADJECTIVE
* **She's a talented pianist.** C'est une
pianiste de talent.

talk NOUN
see also talk VERB
[1] l' *exposé* MASC (*speech*) ◇ *She gave a
talk on rock climbing.* Elle a fait un
exposé sur la varappe.
[2] la *conversation* (*conversation*) ◇ *I had
a talk with my Mum about it.* J'ai eu une
petite conversation avec ma mère à ce
sujet.
[3] les *racontars* MASC (*gossip*) ◇ *It's just
talk.* Ce sont des racontars.

to **talk** VERB
see also talk NOUN
parler ◇ *to talk about something* parler
de quelque chose
* **to talk something over with somebody**
discuter de quelque chose avec
quelqu'un

talkative ADJECTIVE
bavard

tall ADJECTIVE
[1] *grand* (*person, tree*)
* **to be 2 metres tall** mesurer deux mètres
[2] *haut* (*building*)

tampon NOUN
le *tampon*

tan NOUN
le *bronzage* ◇ *She's got an amazing
tan.* Elle a un bronzage superbe.

tangerine NOUN
la *mandarine*

tank NOUN
[1] le *réservoir* (*for water, petrol*)
[2] le *char d'assaut* (*military*)

* **a fish tank** un aquarium

tanker NOUN
[1] le *pétrolier* (*ship*)
* **an oil tanker** un pétrolier
[2] le *camion-citerne* (*truck*)
* **a petrol tanker** un camion-citerne

tap NOUN
[1] le *robinet* (*water tap*)
[2] la *petite tape* (*gentle blow*)

tap-dancing NOUN
les *claquettes* FEM PL ◇ *I do tap-dancing.*
Je fais des claquettes.

to **tape** VERB
see also tape NOUN
enregistrer (*record*) ◇ *Did you tape that
film last night?* As-tu enregistré le film
hier soir?

tape NOUN
see also tape VERB
[1] la *cassette* ◇ *a tape of Sinead
O'Connor* une cassette de Sinead
O'Connor
[2] le *scotch* ® (*sticky tape*)

tape deck NOUN
le *magnétophone*

tape measure NOUN
le *mètre à ruban*

tape recorder NOUN
le *magnétophone*

target NOUN
la *cible*

tarmac NOUN
le *macadam* (*on road*)

tart NOUN
la *tarte* ◇ *an apple tart* une tarte aux
pommes

tartan ADJECTIVE
écossais ◇ *a tartan scarf* une écharpe
écossaise

task NOUN
la *tâche*

taste NOUN
see also taste VERB
le *goût* ◇ *It's got a really strange taste.*
Ça a un goût vraiment bizarre. ◇ *a joke
in bad taste* une plaisanterie de mauvais
goût
* **Would you like a taste?** Tu veux
goûter?

to **taste** VERB
see also taste NOUN
goûter ◇ *Would you like to taste it?*
Vous voulez y goûter?
* **to taste of something** avoir un goût de
quelque chose ◇ *It tastes of fish.* Ça a
un goût de poisson.
* **You can taste the garlic in it.** Ça a bien
le goût d'ail.

tasteful ADJECTIVE

de bon goût

tasteless ADJECTIVE
1 *fade* (*food*)
2 *de mauvais goût* (*in bad taste*) ◇ *a tasteless remark* une remarque de mauvais goût

tasty ADJECTIVE
savoureux MASC
savoureuse FEM

tattoo NOUN
le *tatouage*

taught VERB *see* **teach**

Taurus NOUN
le *Taureau* ◇ *I'm Taurus.* Je suis Taureau.

tax NOUN
1 les *impôts* MASC PL (*on income*)
2 la *taxe* (*on goods, alcohol*)

taxi NOUN
le *taxi*
◆ *a taxi driver* un chauffeur de taxi

taxi rank NOUN
la *station de taxis*

TB NOUN
la *tuberculose*

tea NOUN
1 le *thé* ◇ *a cup of tea* une tasse de thé
◆ *a tea bag* un sachet de thé
2 le *dîner* (*evening meal*)
◆ *We were having tea.* Nous étions en train de dîner.

to **teach** VERB
1 *apprendre* ◇ *My sister taught me to swim.* Ma sœur m'a appris à nager.
◇ *That'll teach you!* Ça t'apprendra!
2 *enseigner* (*in school*) ◇ *She teaches physics.* Elle enseigne la physique.

teacher NOUN
1 (*in secondary school*)
le *professeur* ◇ *a maths teacher* un professeur de maths ◇ *She's a teacher.* Elle est professeur.
2 (*in primary school*)
l' *instituteur* MASC
l' *institutrice* FEM
◇ *He's a primary school teacher.* Il est instituteur.

teacher's pet NOUN
le *chouchou*
la *chouchoute*

tea cloth NOUN
le *torchon*

team NOUN
l' *équipe* FEM ◇ *a football team* une équipe de football ◇ *She was in my team.* Elle était dans mon équipe.

teapot NOUN
la *théière*

tear NOUN
see also **tear** VERB
la *larme* ◇ *She was in tears.* Elle était en larmes.

to **tear** VERB
see also **tear** NOUN
1 *déchirer* ◇ *Be careful or you'll tear the page.* Fais attention, tu vas déchirer la page.
2 *se déchirer* ◇ *It won't tear, it's very strong.* Ça ne se déchire pas, c'est très solide.
◆ *to tear up* déchirer ◇ *He tore up the letter.* Il a déchiré la lettre.

tear gas NOUN
le *gaz lacrymogène*

to **tease** VERB
1 *tourmenter* (*unkindly*) ◇ *Stop teasing that poor animal!* Arrête de tourmenter cette pauvre bête!
2 *taquiner* (*jokingly*) ◇ *He's teasing you.* Il te taquine.
◆ *I was only teasing.* Je plaisantais.

teaspoon NOUN
la *petite cuillère*
◆ *a teaspoonful of sugar* une cuillerée à café de sucre

teatime NOUN
l' *heure du dîner* FEM (*in evening*) ◇ *It was nearly teatime.* C'était presque l'heure du dîner.
◆ *Teatime!* À table!

tea towel NOUN
le *torchon*

technical ADJECTIVE
technique
◆ *a technical college* un lycée technique

technician NOUN
1 le *technicien*
2 la *technicienne*

technique NOUN
la *technique*

techno NOUN
la *techno* (*music*)

technological ADJECTIVE
technologique

technology NOUN
la *technologie*

teddy bear NOUN
le *nounours*

teenage ADJECTIVE
1 *pour les jeunes* ◇ *a teenage magazine* un magazine pour les jeunes
2 *adolescent* (*boys, girls*) ◇ *She has two teenage daughters.* Elle a deux filles adolescentes.

teenager NOUN
l' *adolescent* MASC
l' *adolescente* FEM

teens PL NOUN
- **She's in her teens.** C'est une adolescente.

tee-shirt NOUN
le *tee-shirt*

teeth PL NOUN
les *dents*

to **teethe** VERB
faire ses dents

teetotal ADJECTIVE
- **I'm teetotal.** Je ne bois jamais d'alcool.

telecommunications PL NOUN
les *télécommunications* FEM PL

telephone NOUN
see also phone NOUN *and* VERB
le *téléphone* ◇ *on the telephone* au téléphone
- **a telephone box** une cabine téléphonique
- **a telephone call** un coup de téléphone
- **the telephone directory** l'annuaire MASC
- **a telephone number** un numéro de téléphone

telescope NOUN
le *télescope*

television NOUN
la *télévision*
- **on television** à la télévision
- **a television licence** une redevance de télévision
- **a television programme** une émission de télévision

to **tell** VERB
dire
- **to tell somebody something** dire quelque chose à quelqu'un ◇ *Did you tell your mother?* Tu l'as dit à ta mère? ◇ *I told him that I was going on holiday.* Je lui ai dit que je partais en vacances.
- **to tell somebody to do something** dire à quelqu'un de faire quelque chose ◇ *He told me to wait a moment.* Il m'a dit d'attendre un moment.
- **to tell lies** dire des mensonges
- **to tell a story** raconter une histoire
- **I can't tell the difference between them.** Je n'arrive pas à les distinguer.

to **tell off** VERB
gronder

telly NOUN
la *télé* ◇ *to watch telly* regarder la télé
- **on telly** à la télé

temper NOUN
le *caractère* ◇ *He's got a terrible temper.* Il a un sale caractère.
- **to be in a temper** être en colère
- **to lose one's temper** se mettre en colère ◇ *I lost my temper.* Je me suis mis en colère.

temperature NOUN
la *température* (*of oven, water, person*)
- **The temperature was 30 degrees.** Il faisait trente degrés.
- **to have a temperature** avoir de la fièvre

temple NOUN
le *temple*

temporary ADJECTIVE
temporaire

to **tempt** VERB
tenter ◇ *I'm very tempted!* Je suis très tenté!
- **to tempt somebody to do something** persuader quelqu'un de faire quelque chose

temptation NOUN
la *tentation*

tempting ADJECTIVE
tentant

ten NUMBER
dix ◇ *She's ten.* Elle a dix ans.

to **tend to** VERB
- **to tend to do something** avoir tendance à faire quelque chose ◇ *He tends to arrive late.* Il a tendance à arriver en retard.

tennis NOUN
le *tennis* ◇ *Do you play tennis?* Vous jouez au tennis?
- **a tennis ball** une balle de tennis
- **a tennis court** un court de tennis
- **a tennis racket** une raquette de tennis

tennis player NOUN
le *joueur de tennis*
la *joueuse de tennis*
◇ *He's a tennis player.* Il est joueur de tennis.

tenor NOUN
le *ténor*

tenpin bowling NOUN
le *bowling* ◇ *to go tenpin bowling* jouer au bowling

tense ADJECTIVE
see also tense NOUN
tendu

tense NOUN
see also tense ADJECTIVE
- **the present tense** le présent
- **the future tense** le futur

tension NOUN
la *tension*

tent NOUN
la *tente*
- **a tent peg** un piquet de tente
- **a tent pole** un montant de tente

tenth ADJECTIVE
dixième ◇ *the tenth floor* le dixième étage
- **the tenth of August** le dix août

term NOUN

1 le *trimestre* (at school)

2 le *terme* ◦ a short-term solution une solution à court terme

• **to come to terms with something** accepter quelque chose

terminal ADJECTIVE
see also terminal NOUN
incurable (illness, patient)

terminal NOUN
see also terminal ADJECTIVE
un terminal (of computer)

• **an oil terminal** un terminal pétrolier
• **an air terminal** une aérogare

terminally ADVERB
• **to be terminally ill** être condamné

terrace NOUN
1 la *terrasse* (patio)
2 la *rangée de maisons* (row of houses)

• **the terraces** (at stadium) les gradins MASC

terraced ADJECTIVE
• **a terraced house** une maison mitoyenne

terrible ADJECTIVE
épouvantable ◦ My French is terrible. Mon français est épouvantable.

terrier NOUN
le *terrier*

terrific ADJECTIVE
super (wonderful) ◦ That's terrific! C'est super!
• **You look terrific!** Tu es superbe!

terrified ADJECTIVE
terrifié ◦ I was terrified! J'étais terrifié!

terrorism NOUN
le *terrorisme*

terrorist NOUN
le/la *terroriste*
• **a terrorist attack** un attentat terroriste

test NOUN
see also test VERB
1 l' *interrogation* FEM (at school) ◦ I've got a test tomorrow. J'ai une interrogation demain.
2 l' *essai* MASC (trial, check) ◦ nuclear tests les essais nucléaires
3 l' *analyse* FEM (medical) ◦ a blood test une analyse de sang ◦ They're going to do some more tests. Ils vont faire d'autres analyses.

• **driving test** l'examen du permis de conduire ◦ He's got his driving test tomorrow. Il passe son permis de conduire demain.

to **test** VERB
see also test NOUN
1 *essayer* ◦ to test something out essayer quelque chose
2 *interroger* (class) ◦ He tested us on the new vocabulary. Il nous a interrogés

sur le nouveau vocabulaire.
• **She was tested for drugs.** On lui a fait subir un contrôle antidopage.

test match NOUN
le *match international*

test tube NOUN
l' *éprouvette* FEM

tetanus NOUN
le *tétanos* ◦ a tetanus injection un vaccin contre le tétanos

textbook NOUN
le *manuel* ◦ a French textbook un manuel de français

textiles NOUN
les *textiles* MASC PL ◦ a textiles factory une usine textile

Thames NOUN
la *Tamise*

than CONJUNCTION
que ◦ She's taller than me. Elle est plus grande que moi. ◦ I've got more books than him. J'ai plus de livres que lui.
• **more than ten years** plus de dix ans
• **more than once** plus d'une fois

to **thank** VERB
remercier ◦ Don't forget to write and thank them. N'oublie pas de leur écrire pour les remercier.
• **thank you** merci
• **thank you very much** merci beaucoup

thanks EXCLAMATION
merci!
• **thanks to** grâce à ◦ Thanks to him, everything went OK. Grâce à lui, tout s'est bien passé.

that ADJECTIVE, PRONOUN, CONJUNCTION

Use ce when that is followed by a masculine noun, and cette when that is followed by a feminine noun. ce changes to cet before a vowel and before most words beginning with "h".

1 *ce* ◦ that book ce livre
cet ◦ that man cet homme
cette ◦ that woman cette femme
• **that road** cette route
• **THAT road** cette route-là
• **that one (1)** celui-là (masculine) ◦ This man?–No, that one. Cet homme-ci?–Non, celui-là.
• **that one (2)** celle-là (feminine) ◦ Do you like this photo?–No, I prefer that one. Tu aimes cette photo?–Non, je préfère celle-là.
2 *ça* ◦ You see that? Tu vois ça?
• **What's that?** Qu'est-ce que c'est?
• **Who's that?** Qui est-ce?
• **Is that you?** C'est toi?
• **That's...** C'est... ◦ That's my French teacher. C'est mon prof de français.
◦ That's what he said. C'est ce qu'il a dit.

In relative phrases use **qui** *when* **that** *refers to the subject of the sentence, and* **que** *when it refers to the object.*

3 *qui* ◇ *the man that saw us* l'homme qui nous a vus ◇ *the man that spoke to us* l'homme qui nous a parlé ◇ *the dog that bit her* le chien qui l'a mordue

4 *que* ◇ *the man that we saw* l'homme que nous avons vu ◇ *the man that we spoke to* l'homme à qui nous avons parlé

que changes to **qu'** *before a vowel and before most words beginning with "h".*

◇ *the dog that she bought* le chien qu'elle a acheté ◇ *He thought that Henri was ill.* Il pensait qu'Henri était malade. ◇ *I know that she likes chocolate.* Je sais qu'elle aime le chocolat.

◆ **It was that big.** Il était grand comme ça.
◆ **It's about that high.** Il est à peu près haut comme ça.
◆ **It's not that difficult.** Ça n'est pas si difficile que ça.

thatched ADJECTIVE
◆ **a thatched cottage** une chaumière

the ARTICLE

Use **le** *with a masculine noun, and* **la** *with a feminine noun. Use* **l'** *before a vowel and most words beginning with "h". For plural nouns always use* **les**.

le ◇ *the boy* le garçon
l' ◇ *the man* l'homme MASC ◆ *the orange* l'orange FEM ◇ *the habit* l'habitude FEM
la
◇ *the girl* la fille
les ◇ *the children* les enfants

theatre NOUN
le *théâtre*

theft NOUN
le *vol*

their ADJECTIVE
leur
(*leurs* PL)
◇ *their house* leur maison ◇ *their parents* leurs parents

theirs PRONOUN
le leur + MASC NOUN ◇ *It's not our garage, it's theirs.* Ce n'est pas notre garage, c'est le leur.
la leur + FEM NOUN ◇ *It's not our car, it's theirs.* Ce n'est pas notre voiture, c'est la leur.
les leurs + PL NOUN ◇ *They're not our ideas, they're theirs.* Ce ne sont pas nos idées, ce sont les leurs.
◆ **Is this theirs? (1)** C'est à eux? (*masculine owners*)
◆ **Is this theirs? (2)** C'est à elles? (*feminine owners*) ◇ *This car is theirs.* Cette voiture est à eux. ◇ *Whose is this? – It's theirs.* C'est à qui? – À eux.

them PRONOUN
1 *les* ◇ *I didn't see them.* Je ne les ai pas vus.
Use **leur** *when* **them** *means to them.*
2 *leur* ◇ *I gave them some brochures.* Je leur ai donné des brochures. ◇ *I told them the truth.* Je leur ai dit la vérité.
Use **eux** *or* **elles** *after a preposition.*
3 *eux* MASC ◇ *It's for them.* C'est pour eux.
elles FEM ◇ *Ann and Sophie came – Graham was with them.* Ann et Sophie sont venues – Graham était avec elles.

theme NOUN
le *thème*

themselves PRONOUN
1 *se* ◇ *Did they hurt themselves?* Est-ce qu'ils se sont fait mal?
2 *eux-mêmes* MASC
elles-mêmes FEM
◇ *They did it themselves.* Ils l'ont fait eux-mêmes.

then ADVERB, CONJUNCTION
1 *ensuite* (*next*) ◇ *I get dressed. Then I have breakfast.* Je m'habille. Ensuite je prends mon petit déjeuner.
2 *alors* (*in that case*) ◇ *My pen's run out. – Use a pencil then!* Il n'y a plus d'encre dans mon stylo. – Alors utilise un crayon!
3 *à l'époque* (*at that time*) ◇ *There was no electricity then.* Il n'y avait pas d'électricité à l'époque.
◆ **now and then** de temps en temps ◇ *Do you play chess? – Now and then.* Vous jouez aux échecs? – De temps en temps.
◆ **By then it was too late.** Il était déjà trop tard.

therapy NOUN
la *thérapie*

there ADVERB
1 *là* ◇ *Put it there, on the table.* Mets-le là, sur la table.
◆ **over there** là-bas
◆ **in there** là
◆ **on there** là
◆ **up there** là-haut
◆ **down there** là-bas
◆ **There he is!** Le voilà!
2 *y* ◇ *He went there on Friday.* Il y est allé vendredi. ◇ *Paris? I've never been there.* Paris? Je n'y suis jamais allé.
◆ **There is...** Il y a... ◇ *There's a factory near my house.* Il y a une usine près de chez moi.

- **There are...** Il y a... ◦ *There are five people in my family.* Il y a cinq personnes dans ma famille.
- **There has been an accident.** Il y a eu un accident.

therefore ADVERB
donc

there's = there is, there has

thermometer NOUN
le *thermomètre*

Thermos ® NOUN
le *thermos* ®

these ADJECTIVE, PRONOUN
☐1 *ces* ◦ *these shoes* ces chaussures
- **THESE shoes** ces chaussures-là
☐2 *ceux-ci* MASC ◦ *I want these!* Je veux ceux-ci!
celles-ci FEM ◦ *I'm looking for some sandals. Can I try these?* Je cherche des sandales. Je peux essayer celles-ci?

they PRONOUN
> *Check if* they *stands for a masculine or feminine noun.*

ils ◦ *Are there any tickets left? – No, they're all sold.* Est-ce qu'il reste des billets? – Non, ils sont tous vendus.
elles ◦ *Do you like those shoes? – No, they're horrible.* Tu aimes ces chaussures? – Non, elles sont affreuses.
- **They say that...** On dit que...

they'd = they had, they would

they'll = they will

they're = they are

they've = they have

thick ADJECTIVE
☐1 *(not thin)*
épais MASC
épaisse FEM
- **The walls are one metre thick.** Les murs font un mètre d'épaisseur.
☐2 *(stupid)*
bête

thief NOUN
le *voleur*
la *voleuse*

thigh NOUN
la *cuisse*

thin ADJECTIVE
☐1 *mince* *(person, slice)*
☐2 *maigre* *(skinny)*

thing NOUN
☐1 la *chose* ◦ *beautiful things* de belles choses
☐2 le *truc* *(thingy)* ◦ *What's that thing called?* Comment s'appelle ce truc?
- **my things** *(belongings)* mes affaires FEM
- **You poor thing!** Mon pauvre!

to **think** VERB
☐1 *penser* *(believe)* ◦ *I think you're*

wrong. Je pense que vous avez tort.
◦ *What do you think about the death penalty?* Que pensez-vous de la peine de mort?
☐2 *réfléchir* *(spend time thinking)* ◦ *Think carefully before you reply.* Réfléchis bien avant de répondre. ◦ *What are you thinking about?* À quoi tu penses? ◦ *I'll think about it.* Je vais y réfléchir.
☐3 *imaginer* *(imagine)* ◦ *Think what life would be like without cars.* Imaginez la vie sans voitures.
- **I think so.** Oui, je crois.
- **I don't think so.** Je ne crois pas.
- **I'll think it over.** Je vais y réfléchir.

third ADJECTIVE
> *see also* third NOUN

troisième ◦ *the third day* le troisième jour ◦ *the third time* la troisième fois ◦ *I came third.* Je suis arrivé troisième.
- **the third of March** le trois mars

third NOUN
> *see also* third ADJECTIVE

le *tiers* ◦ *a third of the population* un tiers de la population

thirdly ADVERB
troisièmement

Third World NOUN
le *tiers monde*

thirst NOUN
la *soif*

thirsty ADJECTIVE
- **to be thirsty** avoir soif

thirteen NUMBER
treize ◦ *I'm thirteen.* J'ai treize ans.

thirty NUMBER
trente

this ADJECTIVE, PRONOUN
> *Use* ce *when* this *is followed by a masculine noun, and* cette *when* this *is followed by a feminine noun.* ce *changes to* cet *before a vowel and before most words beginning with "h".*

☐1 *ce* ◦ *this book* ce livre
cet ◦ *this man* cet homme
cette ◦ *this woman* cette femme
- **this road** cette route
- **THIS road** cette route-ci
- **this one (1)** celui-ci *(masculine)* ◦ *Pass me that pen. – This one?* Passe-moi ce stylo. – Celui-ci?
- **this one (2)** celle-ci *(feminine)* ◦ *Of the two photos, I prefer this one.* Des deux photos, c'est celle-ci que je préfère.
☐2 *ça* ◦ *You see this?* Tu vois ça?
- **What's this?** Qu'est-ce que c'est?
- **This is my mother.** *(introduction)* Je te présente ma mère.
- **This is Gavin speaking.** *(on the phone)* C'est Gavin à l'appareil.

thistle NOUN
le *chardon*
thorough ADJECTIVE
minutieux MASC
minutieuse FEM
  ◦ She's very thorough. Elle est très
  minutieuse.
thoroughly ADVERB
à fond (examine)
those ADJECTIVE, PRONOUN
  ① *ces* ◦ those shoes ces chaussures
  ▪ THOSE shoes ces chaussures-là
  ② *ceux-là* MASC ◦ I want those! Je veux
  ceux-là!
  celles-là FEM ◦ I'm looking for some
  sandals. Can I try those? Je cherche des
  sandales. Je peux essayer celles-là?
though CONJUNCTION, ADVERB
bien que
bien que *has to be followed by a verb in the*
subjunctive.
  ◦ Though it's raining... Bien qu'il pleuve...
  ▪ He's a nice person, though he's not
  very clever. Il est sympa, mais pas très
  malin.
thought VERB see **think**
thought NOUN
l' *idée* FEM (idea) ◦ I've just had a
thought. Je viens d'avoir une idée.
  ▪ It was a nice thought, thank you. C'est
  gentil de ta part, merci.
thoughtful ADJECTIVE
  ① (deep in thought)
  pensif MASC
  pensive FEM
  ◦ You look thoughtful. Tu as l'air pensif.
  ② (considerate)
  prévenant ◦ She's very thoughtful. Elle
  est très prévenante.
thoughtless ADJECTIVE
  ▪ He's completely thoughtless. Il ne
  pense absolument pas aux autres.
thousand NUMBER
  ▪ a thousand mille ◦ a thousand francs
  mille francs
  ▪ £2000 deux mille livres
  ▪ thousands of people des milliers de
  personnes
thread NOUN
le *fil*
threat NOUN
la *menace*
threaten VERB
menacer ◦ to threaten to do something
menacer de faire quelque chose
three NUMBER
trois ◦ She's three. Elle a trois ans.
three-dimensional ADJECTIVE
à trois dimensions

threw VERB see **throw**
thrifty ADJECTIVE
économe
thrill NOUN
l' *émotion* FEM (excitement)
thrilled ADJECTIVE
  ▪ I was thrilled. (pleased) J'étais
  absolument ravi.
thriller NOUN
le *thriller*
thrilling ADJECTIVE
palpitant
throat NOUN
la *gorge* ◦ to have a sore throat avoir
mal à la gorge
to **throb** VERB
  ▪ a throbbing pain un élancement
  ▪ My arm's throbbing. J'ai des
  élancements dans le bras.
throne NOUN
le *trône*
through PREPOSITION, ADJECTIVE, ADVERB
  ① *par* ◦ through the window par la
  fenêtre ◦ I know her through my sister. Je
  la connais par ma sœur. ◦ to go through
  Birmingham passer par Birmingham
  ▪ to go through a tunnel traverser un
  tunnel
  ② *à travers* ◦ through the mist à
  travers la brume ◦ through the crowd à
  travers la foule ◦ The window was dirty
  and I couldn't see through. La fenêtre
  était sale et je n'arrivais pas à voir à
  travers
  ▪ a through train un train direct
  ▪ "no through road" "impasse"
throughout PREPOSITION
  ▪ throughout Britain dans toute la
  Grande-Bretagne
  ▪ throughout the year pendant toute
  l'année
to **throw** VERB
  lancer ◦ He threw the ball to me. Il m'a
  lancé le ballon.
  ▪ to throw a party organiser une soirée
  ▪ That really threw him. Ça l'a
  décontenancé.
  ▪ to throw away (1) (rubbish) jeter
  ▪ to throw away (2) (chance) perdre
  ▪ to throw out (1) (throw away) jeter
  ▪ to throw out (2) (person) mettre à la
  porte ◦ I threw him out. Je l'ai mis à la
  porte.
  ▪ to throw up vomir
thug NOUN
le *voyou*
thumb NOUN
le *pouce*
to **thump** VERB

◆ **to thump somebody** donner un coup de poing à quelqu'un

thunder NOUN
le *tonnerre*

thunderstorm NOUN
l' *orage* MASC

thundery ADJECTIVE
orageux MASC
orageuse FEM

Thursday NOUN
le *jeudi* ◇ *on Thursday* jeudi ◇ *on Thursdays* le jeudi ◇ *every Thursday* tous les jeudis ◇ *last Thursday* jeudi dernier ◇ *next Thursday* jeudi prochain

thyme NOUN
le *thym*

tick NOUN
[1] la *coche* (*mark*)
[2] le *tic-tac* (*of clock*)
◆ **I'll be back in a tick.** J'en ai pour une seconde.

ticket NOUN
> Be careful to choose correctly between **le ticket** and **le billet**.

[1] le *ticket* (*for bus, tube, cinema, museum*) ◇ *an underground ticket* un ticket de métro
[2] le *billet* (*for plane, train, theatre, concert*)
◆ **a parking ticket** Un p.-v.

ticket inspector NOUN
le *contrôleur*
la *contrôleuse*

ticket office NOUN
le *guichet*

to **tickle** VERB
chatouiller

ticklish ADJECTIVE
chatouilleux MASC
chatouilleuse FEM
◇ *Are you ticklish?* Tu es chatouilleux?

to **tick off** VERB
◆ **to tick something off** cocher quelque chose
◆ **to tick somebody off** enguirlander quelqu'un

tide NOUN
la *marée*
◆ **high tide** la marée haute
◆ **low tide** la marée basse

tidy ADJECTIVE
> see also **tidy** VERB

[1] *bien rangé* (*room*) ◇ *Your room's very tidy.* Ta chambre est bien rangée.
[2] *ordonné* (*person*) ◇ *She's very tidy.* Elle est très ordonnée.

to **tidy** VERB
> see also **tidy** ADJECTIVE

ranger ◇ *Go and tidy your room.* Va ranger ta chambre.

◆ **to tidy up** ranger ◇ *Don't forget to tidy up afterwards.* N'oubliez pas de ranger après.

tie NOUN
> see also **tie** VERB

la *cravate* (*necktie*)
◆ **It was a tie.** (*in sport*) Ils ont fait match nul.

to **tie** VERB
> see also **tie** NOUN

[1] *nouer* (*ribbon, shoelaces*)
◆ **to tie a knot in something** faire un nœud à quelque chose
[2] *faire match nul* (*in sport*) ◇ *They tied three all.* Ils ont fait match nul, trois à trois.
◆ **to tie up (1)** (*parcel*) ficeler
◆ **to tie up (2)** (*dog, boat*) attacher
◆ **to tie up (3)** (*prisoner*) ligoter

tiger NOUN
le *tigre*

tight ADJECTIVE
[1] *moulant* (*tight-fitting*) ◇ *tight clothes* les vêtements moulants
[2] *juste* (*too tight*) ◇ *This dress is a bit tight.* Cette robe est un peu juste.

to **tighten** VERB
[1] *tendre* (*rope*)
[2] *resserrer* (*screw*)

tightly ADVERB
fort (*hold*)

tights PL NOUN
le *collant* SING

tile NOUN
[1] (*on roof*)
la *tuile*
[2] (*on wall, floor*)
le *carreau*
(les *carreaux* PL)

tiled ADJECTIVE
[1] *en tuiles* (*roof*)
[2] *carrelé* (*wall, floor, room*)

till NOUN
> see also **till** PREPOSITION

la *caisse*

till PREPOSITION, CONJUNCTION
> see also **till** NOUN

[1] *jusqu'à* ◇ *I waited till ten o'clock.* J'ai attendu jusqu'à dix heures.
◆ **till now** jusqu'à présent
◆ **till then** jusque-là

> Use **avant** if the sentence you want to translate contains a negative, such as "not" or "never".

[2] *avant* ◇ *It won't be ready till next week.* Ça ne sera pas prêt avant la semaine prochaine. ◇ *Till last year I'd never been to France.* Avant l'année dernière, je n'étais jamais allé en France.

time NOUN

1 l' *heure* FEM *(on clock)* ◇ *What time is it?* Quelle heure est-il? ◇ *What time do you get up?* À quelle heure tu te lèves? ◇ *It was two o'clock, French time.* Il était deux heures, heure française.
* **on time** à l'heure ◇ *He never arrives on time.* Il n'arrive jamais à l'heure.

2 le *temps* *(amount of time)* ◇ *I'm sorry, I haven't got time.* Je suis désolé, je n'ai pas le temps.
* **from time to time** de temps en temps
* **in time** à temps ◇ *We arrived in time for lunch.* Nous sommes arrivés à temps pour le déjeuner.
* **just in time** juste à temps
* **in no time** en un rien de temps ◇ *It was ready in no time.* Ça a été prêt en un rien de temps.
* **It's time to go.** Il est temps de partir.

3 le *moment* *(moment)* ◇ *This isn't a good time to ask him.* Ce n'est pas le bon moment pour lui demander.
* **for the time being** le moment
4 la *fois* *(occasion)* ◇ *this time* cette fois-ci ◇ *next time* la prochaine fois ◇ *two at a time* deux à la fois
* **How many times?** Combien de fois?
* **at times** parfois
* **a long time** longtemps ◇ *Have you lived here for a long time?* Vous habitez ici depuis longtemps?
* **in a week's time** dans une semaine ◇ *I'll come back in a month's time.* Je reviendrai dans un mois.
* **Come and see us any time.** Venez nous voir quand vous voulez.
* **to have a good time** bien s'amuser ◇ *Did you have a good time?* Vous vous êtes bien amusés?
* **2 times 2 is 4** deux fois deux égalent quatre

time bomb NOUN
la *bombe à retardement*

time off NOUN
le *temps libre*

timer NOUN
le *minuteur*

time-share NOUN
l' *appartement en multipropriété* MASC

timetable NOUN
1 l' *horaire* MASC *(for train, bus)*
2 l' *emploi du temps* MASC *(at school)*

time zone NOUN
le *fuseau horaire*

tin NOUN
1 la *boîte* ◇ *a tin of soup* une boîte de soupe ◇ *a biscuit tin* une boîte à biscuits
2 la *boîte de conserve* ◇ *The bin was full of tins.* La poubelle était pleine de boîtes de conserve.

3 l' *étain* MASC *(type of metal)*

tinned ADJECTIVE
en boîte *(food)* ◇ *tinned peaches* des pêches en boîte

tin opener NOUN
l' *ouvre-boîte* MASC

tinsel NOUN
les *guirlandes de Noël* FEM PL

tinted ADJECTIVE
teinté *(spectacles, glass)*

tiny ADJECTIVE
minuscule

tip NOUN
see also tip VERB
1 *(money)*
le *pourboire* ◇ *Shall I give him a tip?* Je lui donne un pourboire?
2 *(advice)*
le *tuyau*
(les *tuyaux* PL)
◇ *a useful tip* un bon tuyau *(informal)*
3 *(end)*
le *bout* ◇ *It's on the tip of my tongue.* Je l'ai sur le bout de la langue.
* **a rubbish tip** une décharge
* **This place is a complete tip!** Quel fouillis!

to **tip** VERB
see also tip NOUN
donner un pourboire à ◇ *Don't forget to tip the taxi driver.* N'oubliez pas de donner un pourboire au chauffeur de taxi.

tiptoe NOUN
* **on tiptoe** sur la pointe des pieds

tired ADJECTIVE
fatigué ◇ *I'm tired.* Je suis fatigué.
* **to be tired of something** en avoir assez de quelque chose

tiring ADJECTIVE
fatigant

tissue NOUN
le *kleenex* ® ◇ *Have you got a tissue?* Tu as un kleenex? ®

title NOUN
le *titre*

title role NOUN
le *rôle principal*

to PREPOSITION
à + le *changes to* au. à + les *changes to* aux.
1 *à* ◇ *to go to Paris* aller à Paris ◇ *to go to school* aller à l'école ◇ *a letter to his mother* une lettre à sa mère ◇ *the answer to the question* la réponse à la question
au ◇ *to go to the theatre* aller au théâtre
aux ◇ *We said goodbye to the neighbours.* Nous avons dit au revoir

aux voisins.
- **ready to go** prêt à partir
- **ready to eat** prêt à manger
- **It's easy to do.** C'est facile à faire.
- **something to drink** quelque chose à boire
- **I've got things to do.** J'ai des choses à faire.
- **from...to...** de...à... ◇ *from nine o'clock to half past three* de neuf heures à trois heures et demie

[2] *de* ◇ *the train to London* le train de Londres ◇ *the road to Edinburgh* la route d'Édimbourg ◇ *the key to the front door* la clé de la porte d'entrée
- **It's difficult to say.** C'est difficile à dire.
- **It's easy to criticize.** C'est facile de critiquer.

When referring to someone's house, shop or office, use **chez.**

[3] *chez* ◇ *to go to the doctor's* aller chez le docteur ◇ *to go to the butcher's* aller chez le boucher ◇ *to go to Anne's house.* Si on allait chez Anne?

When to *refers to a country which is feminine, use* **en;** *when the country is masculine, use* **au.**

[4] *en* ◇ *to go to France* aller en France
au ◇ *to go to Portugal* aller au Portugal
[5] *jusqu'à* (*up to*) ◇ *to count to ten* compter jusqu'à dix
[6] *pour* (*in order to*) ◇ *I did it to help you.* Je l'ai fait pour vous aider. ◇ *She's too young to go to school.* Elle est trop jeune pour aller à l'école.

toad NOUN
le *crapaud*
toadstool NOUN
le *champignon vénéneux*
toast NOUN
[1] le *pain grillé* ◇ *a piece of toast* une tranche de pain grillé
[2] le *toast* (*speech*) ◇ *to drink a toast to somebody* porter un toast à quelqu'un
toaster NOUN
le *grille-pain*
(les *grille-pain* PL)
tobacco NOUN
le *tabac*
tobacconist's NOUN
le *bureau de tabac*
(les *bureaux de tabac* PL)
toboggan NOUN
la *luge*
tobogganing NOUN
- **to go tobogganing** faire de la luge
today ADVERB
aujourd'hui ◇ *What did you do today?* Qu'est-ce tu as fait aujourd'hui?
toddler NOUN

le *bambin*
toe NOUN
le *doigt de pied*
toffee NOUN
le *caramel*
together ADVERB
[1] *ensemble* ◇ *Are they still together?* Ils sont toujours ensemble?
[2] *en même temps* (*at the same time*) ◇ *Don't all speak together!* Ne parlez pas tous en même temps!
- **together with** (*with person*) avec
toilet NOUN
les *toilettes* FEM PL
toilet paper NOUN
le *papier hygiénique*
toiletries PL NOUN
les *articles de toilette* MASC PL
toilet roll NOUN
le *rouleau de papier hygiénique*
(les *rouleaux de papier hygiénique* PL)
token NOUN
- **a gift token** un bon-cadeau
told VERB *see* **tell**
tolerant ADJECTIVE
tolérant
toll NOUN
le *péage* (*on bridge, motorway*)
tomato NOUN
la *tomate* ◇ *tomato soup* la soupe à la tomate
tomboy NOUN
le *garçon manqué* ◇ *She's a real tomboy.* C'est un vrai garçon manqué.
tomorrow ADVERB
demain ◇ *tomorrow morning* demain matin ◇ *tomorrow night* demain soir
- **the day after tomorrow** après-demain
ton NOUN
la *tonne* ◇ *That old bike weighs a ton.* Ce vieux vélo pèse une tonne.
tongue NOUN
la *langue*
- **to say something tongue in cheek** dire quelque chose en plaisantant
tonic NOUN
le *Schweppes* ® (*tonic water*)
- **a gin and tonic** un gin tonic
tonight ADVERB
[1] *ce soir* (*this evening*) ◇ *Are you going out tonight?* Tu sors ce soir?
[2] *cette nuit* (*during the night*) ◇ *I'll sleep well tonight.* Je dormirai bien cette nuit.
tonsillitis NOUN
l' *angine* FEM
tonsils PL NOUN
les *amygdales* FEM PL
too ADVERB, ADJECTIVE
[1] *aussi* (*as well*) ◇ *My sister came too.*

Ma sœur est venue aussi.

[2] *trop* (*excessively*) ◇ *The water's too hot.* L'eau est trop chaude. ◇ *We arrived too late.* Nous sommes arrivés trop tard.

- **too much (1)** (*with noun*) trop de ◇ *too much noise* trop de bruit
- **too much (2)** (*with verb*) trop ◇ *At Christmas we always eat too much.* À Noël nous mangeons toujours trop.
- **too much (3)** (*too expensive*) trop cher ◇ *Fifty francs? That's too much.* Cinquante francs? C'est trop cher.
- **too many** trop de ◇ *too many hamburgers* trop de hamburgers
- **Too bad!** Tant pis!

took VERB *see* **take**

tool NOUN
l' *outil* MASC

- **a tool box** une boîte à outils

tooth NOUN
la *dent*

toothache NOUN
le *mal de dents* ◇ *to have toothache* avoir mal aux dents

toothbrush NOUN
la *brosse à dents*

toothpaste NOUN
le *dentifrice*

top NOUN
see also top ADJECTIVE
[1] le *haut* (*of page, ladder, garment*) ◇ *at the top of the page* en haut de la page

- **a bikini top** un haut de bikini
[2] le *sommet* (*of mountain*)
[3] le *dessus* (*of table*)
- **on top of** (*on*) sur ◇ *on top of the fridge* sur le frigo
- **There's a surcharge on top of that.** Il a un supplément en plus.
- **from top to bottom** de fond en comble ◇ *I searched the house from top to bottom.* J'ai fouillé la maison de fond en comble.
[4] le *couvercle* (*of box, jar*)
[5] le *bouchon* (*of bottle*)

top ADJECTIVE
see also top NOUN
grand (*first-class*) ◇ *a top surgeon* un grand chirurgien

- **a top model** un top model
- **He always gets top marks in French.** Il a toujours d'excellentes notes en français.
- **the top floor** le dernier étage ◇ *on the top floor* au dernier étage

topic NOUN
le *sujet* ◇ *The essay can be on any topic.* Cette dissertation peut être sur n'importe quel sujet.

topical ADJECTIVE

d'actualité ◇ *a topical issue* un sujet d'actualité

topless ADJECTIVE
aux seins nus (*model*)

- **to go topless** enlever le haut

top-secret ADJECTIVE
top secret MASC
top secrète FEM
◇ *top-secret documents* des documents top secrets

torch NOUN
la *lampe de poche*

tore, torn VERB *see* **tear**

tortoise NOUN
la *tortue*

torture NOUN
see also torture VERB
la *torture* ◇ *It was pure torture.* C'était une vraie torture.

to **torture** VERB
see also torture NOUN
torturer ◇ *Stop torturing that poor animal!* Arrête de torturer cette pauvre bête!

Tory ADJECTIVE
see also Tory NOUN
conservateur MASC
conservatrice FEM
◇ *the Tory government* le gouvernement conservateur

Tory NOUN
see also Tory ADJECTIVE
le *conservateur*
la *conservatrice*

- **the Tories** les conservateurs

to **toss** VERB

- **to toss pancakes** faire sauter les crêpes
- **Shall we toss for it?** On joue à pile ou face?

total ADJECTIVE
see also total NOUN
total
(*totaux* MASC PL)

- **the total amount** le total

total NOUN
see also total ADJECTIVE
le *total*
(les *totaux* PL)

- **the grand total** le total

totally ADVERB
complètement ◇ *He's totally useless.* Il est complètement nul.

touch NOUN
see also touch VERB

- **to get in touch with somebody** prendre contact avec quelqu'un
- **to keep in touch with somebody** ne pas perdre contact avec quelqu'un
- **Keep in touch!** Donne-moi de tes

T

PTO

nouvelles!
- **to lose touch** se perdre de vue
- **to lose touch with somebody** perdre quelqu'un de vue

to **touch** VERB

see also touch NOUN

toucher
- **Don't touch that!** N'y touche pas!

touchdown NOUN
l' *atterrissage* MASC

touched ADJECTIVE
touché ◇ *I was really touched.* Ça m'a beaucoup touché.

touching ADJECTIVE
touchant

touchline NOUN
la *ligne de touche*

touchy ADJECTIVE
susceptible ◇ *She's a bit touchy.* Elle est susceptible.

tough ADJECTIVE
1 *dur* ◇ *It was tough, but I managed OK.* C'était dur, mais je m'en suis tiré. ◇ *It's a tough job.* C'est dur.
- **The meat's tough.** La viande est coriace.
2 (*strong*)
solide ◇ *tough leather gloves* de solides gants en cuir ◇ *She's tough. She can take it.* Elle est solide. Elle tiendra le coup.
3 (*rough, violent*)
dangereux MASC
dangereuse FEM
- **He thinks he's a tough guy.** Il se prend pour un gros dur.
- **Tough luck!** C'est comme ça!

toupee NOUN
le *postiche*

tour NOUN

see also tour VERB

1 la *visite* (*of town, museum*) ◇ *We went on a tour of the city.* Nous avons visité la ville.
- **a package tour** un voyage organisé
2 la *tournée* (*by singer, group*) ◇ *on tour* en tournée
- **to go on tour** faire une tournée

to **tour** VERB

see also tour NOUN

- **Paul Weller's touring Europe.** (*singer, artiste*) Paul Weller est en tournée en Europe.

tour guide NOUN
le/la *guide*

tourism NOUN
le *tourisme*

tourist NOUN
le/la *touriste*
- **tourist information office** l'office du

tourisme MASC

tournament NOUN
le *tournoi*

towards PREPOSITION
1 *vers* (*in the direction of*) ◇ *He came towards me.* Il est venu vers moi.
2 *envers* (*of attitude*) ◇ *my feelings towards him* mes sentiments envers lui

towel NOUN
la *serviette*

tower NOUN
la *tour*
- **a tower block** une tour

town NOUN
la *ville* ◇ *a town plan* un plan de ville
- **the town centre** le centre-ville
- **the town hall** la mairie

toy NOUN
le *jouet* ◇ *a toy shop* un magasin de jouets
- **a toy car** une petite voiture

trace NOUN

see also trace VERB

la *trace* ◇ *There was no trace of the robbers.* Il n'y avait pas de trace des voleurs.

to **trace** VERB

see also trace NOUN

décalquer (*draw*)

tracing paper NOUN
le *papier calque*

track NOUN
1 le *chemin* (*dirt road*)
2 la *voie ferrée* (*railway line*)
3 la *piste* (*in sport*) ◇ *two laps of the track* deux tours de piste
4 la *chanson* (*song*) ◇ *This is my favourite track.* C'est ma chanson préférée.
5 les *traces* FEM PL (*trail*) ◇ *They followed the tracks for miles.* Ils ont suivi les traces pendant des kilomètres.

to **track down** VERB
- **to track somebody down** retrouver quelqu'un ◇ *The police never tracked down the killer.* La police n'a jamais retrouvé l'assassin.

tracksuit NOUN
le *survêtement*

tractor NOUN
le *tracteur*

trade NOUN
le *métier* (*skill, job*) ◇ *to learn a trade* apprendre un métier

trade union NOUN
le *syndicat*

trade unionist NOUN
le/la *syndicaliste*

tradition NOUN

la *tradition*

traditional ADJECTIVE
traditionnel MASC
traditionnelle FEM

traffic NOUN
la *circulation*   ◦ *The traffic was terrible.*
Il y avait une circulation épouvantable.

traffic jam NOUN
l' *embouteillage* MASC

traffic lights PL NOUN
les *feux* MASC

traffic warden NOUN
le *contractuel*
la *contractuelle*

tragedy NOUN
la *tragédie*

tragic ADJECTIVE
tragique

trailer NOUN
[1] la *remorque* (vehicle)
[2] la *bande-annonce* (film advert)

train NOUN
see also train VERB
[1] le *train*
[2] la *rame* (on underground)

to **train** VERB
see also train NOUN
s'entraîner (sport)   ◦ *to train for a race*
s'entraîner pour une course
◆ **to train as a teacher** suivre une
formation d'enseignant
◆ **to train an animal to do something**
dresser un animal à faire quelque chose

trained ADJECTIVE
◆ **She's a trained nurse.** Elle est
infirmière diplômée.

trainee NOUN
[1] (in profession)
le/la *stagiaire*   ◦ *She's a trainee.* Elle
est stagiaire.
[2] (apprentice)
l' *apprenti* MASC
l' *apprentie* FEM
◦ *a trainee plumber* un apprenti
plombier

trainer NOUN
[1] (sports coach)
l' *entraîneur* MASC
[2] (of animals)
le *dompteur*
la *dompteuse*

trainers PL NOUN
les *baskets* FEM PL   ◦ *a pair of trainers*
une paire de baskets

training NOUN
[1] la *formation*   ◦ *a training course* un
stage de formation
[2] l' *entraînement* MASC (sport)

tram NOUN

le *tramway*

tramp NOUN
le *clochard*
la *clocharde*

trampoline NOUN
le *trampoline*

tranquillizer NOUN
le *tranquillisant*   ◦ *She's on
tranquillizers.* Elle prend des
tranquillisants.

transfer NOUN
la *décalcomanie* (sticker)

transfusion NOUN
la *transfusion*

transistor NOUN
le *transistor*

transit lounge NOUN
la *salle de transit*

to **translate** VERB
traduire   ◦ *to translate something into
English* traduire quelque chose en
anglais

translation NOUN
la *traduction*

translator NOUN
le *traducteur*
la *traductrice*
◦ *Anita's a translator.* Anita est
traductrice.

transparent ADJECTIVE
transparent

transplant NOUN
la *greffe*   ◦ *a heart transplant* une greffe
cardiaque

transport NOUN
see also transport VERB
le *transport*   ◦ *public transport* les
transports en commun

to **transport** VERB
see also transport NOUN
transporter

trap NOUN
le *piège*

trashy ADJECTIVE
nul MASC
nulle FEM
◦ *a really trashy film* un film vraiment
nul

traumatic ADJECTIVE
traumatisant   ◦ *It was a traumatic
experience.* Ça a été une expérience
traumatisante.

travel NOUN
see also travel VERB
les *voyages* MASC PL

to **travel** VERB
see also travel NOUN
voyager   ◦ *I prefer to travel by train* Je
préfère voyager en train.

◆ **I'd like to travel round the world.**
J'aimerais faire le tour du monde.

◆ **We travelled over 800 kilometres.** Nous
avons fait plus de huit cents kilomètres.

◆ **News travels fast!** Les nouvelles
circulent vite!

travel agency NOUN
l' *agence de voyages* FEM

travel agent NOUN

◆ **She's a travel agent.** Elle travaille dans
une agence de voyages.

traveller NOUN
1　(*on bus, train, plane*)
le *voyageur*
la *voyageuse*
2　(*gypsy*)
le/la *nomade*

traveller's cheque NOUN
le *chèque de voyage*

travelling NOUN

◆ **I love travelling.** J'adore les voyages.

travel sickness NOUN
le *mal des transports*

tray NOUN
le *plateau*
(les *plateaux* PL)

to **tread** VERB
marcher ◇ *to tread on something*
marcher sur quelque chose

treasure NOUN
le *trésor*

treat NOUN
see also **treat** VERB
1　le *petit cadeau* (*present*)
2　la *gâterie* (*food*)

◆ **to give somebody a treat** faire plaisir à
quelqu'un

to **treat** VERB
see also **treat** NOUN
traiter (*well, badly*)

◆ **to treat somebody to something** offrir
quelque chose à quelqu'un ◇ *He
treated us to an ice cream.* Il nous a
offert une glace.

treatment NOUN
le *traitement*

to **treble** VERB
tripler ◇ *The cost of living there has
trebled.* Le coût de la vie y a triplé.

tree NOUN
l' *arbre* MASC

to **tremble** VERB
trembler

trend NOUN
la *mode* (*fashion*)

trendy ADJECTIVE
branché

trial NOUN
le *procès* (*in court*)

triangle NOUN
le *triangle*

tribe NOUN
la *tribu*

trick NOUN
see also **trick** VERB
1　le *tour* ◇ *to play a trick on somebody*
jouer un tour à quelqu'un
2　le *truc* FEM (*knack*) ◇ *It's not easy:
there's a trick to it.* Ce n'est pas facile: il y
a un truc.

to **trick** VERB
see also **trick** NOUN

◆ **to trick somebody** rouler quelqu'un

tricky ADJECTIVE
délicat

tricycle NOUN
le *tricycle*

trifle NOUN
le *diplomate* (*dessert*)

to **trim** VERB
see also **trim** NOUN
1　*égaliser* (*hair*)
2　*tondre* (*grass*)

trim NOUN
see also **trim** VERB
la *coupe d'entretien* (*haircut*) ◇ *to have
a trim* se faire faire une coupe
d'entretien

trip NOUN
see also **trip** VERB
le *voyage* ◇ *to go on a trip* faire un
voyage ◇ *Have a good trip!* Bon voyage!

◆ **a day trip** une excursion d'une journée

to **trip** VERB
see also **trip** NOUN
trébucher (*stumble*)

triple ADJECTIVE
triple

triplets PL NOUN
les *triplés* MASC PL (*boys*)
(les *triplées* FEM PL) (*girls*)

trivial ADJECTIVE
insignifiant

trolley NOUN
le *chariot*

trombone NOUN
le *trombone* ◇ *I play the trombone.* Je
joue du trombone.

troops PL NOUN
les *troupes* MASC PL ◇ *British troops* les
troupes britanniques

trophy NOUN
le *trophée* ◇ *to win a trophy* gagner un
trophée

tropical ADJECTIVE
tropical ◇ *The weather was tropical.* Il
faisait une chaleur tropicale.

to **trot** VERB

trotter

trouble NOUN
le *problème* ◇ *The trouble is, it's too expensive.* Le problème, c'est que c'est trop cher.
* **to be in trouble** avoir des ennuis
* **What's the trouble?** Qu'est-ce qui ne va pas?
* **stomach trouble** troubles gastriques
* **to take a lot of trouble over something** se donner beaucoup de mal pour quelque chose
* **Don't worry, it's no trouble.** Mais non, ça ne me dérange pas du tout.

troublemaker NOUN
l' *élément perturbateur* MASC

trousers PL NOUN
le *pantalon* SING

trout NOUN
la *truite*

truant NOUN
* **to play truant** faire l'école buissonnière

truck NOUN
le *camion*
* **a truck driver** un camionneur ◇ *He's a truck driver.* Il est camionneur.

true ADJECTIVE
vrai
* **That's true.** C'est vrai.
* **to come true** se réaliser ◇ *I hope my dream will come true.* J'espère que mon rêve se réalisera.
* **true love** le grand amour

trumpet NOUN
la *trompette* ◇ *She plays the trumpet.* Elle joue de la trompette.

trunk NOUN
1 le *tronc* (*of tree*)
2 la *trompe* (*of elephant*)
3 la *malle* (*luggage*)

trunks PL NOUN
* **swimming trunks** le maillot de bain

trust NOUN
see also **trust** VERB
la *confiance* ◇ *to have trust in somebody* avoir confiance en quelqu'un

trust VERB
see also **trust** NOUN
* **to trust somebody** faire confiance à quelqu'un ◇ *Don't you trust me?* Tu ne me fais pas confiance? ◇ *Trust me!* Fais-moi confiance!

trusting ADJECTIVE
confiant

truth NOUN
la *vérité*

truthful ADJECTIVE
* **She's a very truthful person.** Elle dit toujours la vérité.

try NOUN
see also **try** VERB
l' *essai* MASC ◇ *his third try* son troisième essai
* **to have a try** essayer
* **It's worth a try.** Ça vaut la peine d'essayer.
* **to give something a try** essayer quelque chose

to **try** VERB
see also **try** NOUN
1 *essayer* (*attempt*) ◇ *to try to do something* essayer de faire quelque chose
* **to try again** refaire un essai
2 *goûter* (*taste*) ◇ *Would you like to try some?* Voulez-vous goûter?
* **to try on** essayer (*clothes*)
* **to try something out** essayer quelque chose

T-shirt NOUN
le *tee-shirt*

tube NOUN
le *tube*
* **the Tube** (*underground*) le métro

tuberculosis NOUN
la *tuberculose*

Tuesday NOUN
le *mardi* ◇ *on Tuesday* mardi ◇ *on Tuesdays* le mardi ◇ *every Tuesday* tous les mardis ◇ *last Tuesday* mardi dernier ◇ *next Tuesday* mardi prochain
* **Shrove Tuesday, Pancake Tuesday** le mardi gras

tug-of-war NOUN
la *lutte à la corde*

tuition NOUN
les *cours* MASC PL
* **private tuition** les cours particuliers

tulip NOUN
la *tulipe*

tumble dryer NOUN
le *sèche-linge*
(les *sèche-linge* PL)

tummy NOUN
le *ventre*

tuna NOUN
le *thon*

tune NOUN
l' *air* MASC (*melody*)
* **to play in tune** jouer juste
* **to sing out of tune** chanter faux

Tunisia NOUN
la *Tunisie*
* **in Tunisia** en Tunisie

tunnel NOUN
le *tunnel*
* **the Tunnel** (*Chunnel*) le tunnel sous la Manche

T

Turk NOUN
le *Turc*
la *Turque*
Turkey NOUN
la *Turquie*
- **in Turkey** en Turquie
- **to Turkey** en Turquie
turkey NOUN
[1] la *dinde* (*meat*)
[2] le *dindon* (*live bird*)
Turkish ADJECTIVE
see also Turkish NOUN
turc MASC
turque FEM
Turkish NOUN
see also Turkish ADJECTIVE
le *turc* (*language*)
turn NOUN
see also turn VERB
[1] le *tournant* (*bend in road*)
- **"no left turn"** "défense de tourner à gauche"
[2] le *tour* (*go*)   ○ *It's my turn!* C'est mon tour!
to **turn** VERB
see also turn NOUN
[1] *tourner*   ○ *Turn right at the lights.* Tournez à droite aux feux.
[2] *devenir* (*become*)   ○ *to turn red* devenir rouge
- **to turn into something** se transformer en quelque chose   ○ *The frog turned into a prince.* La grenouille s'est transformée en prince.
to **turn back** VERB
faire demi-tour   ○ *We turned back.* Nous avons fait demi-tour.
to **turn down** VERB
[1] *refuser* (*offer*)
[2] *baisser* (*radio, TV, heating*)   ○ *Shall I turn the heating down?* Je baisse le chauffage?
to **turn off** VERB
[1] *éteindre* (*light, radio*)
[2] *fermer* (*tap*)
[3] *arrêter* (*engine*)
to **turn on** VERB
[1] *allumer* (*light, radio*)
[2] *ouvrir* (*tap*)
[3] *mettre en marche* (*engine*)
to **turn out** VERB
- **It turned out to be a mistake.** Il s'est avéré que c'était une erreur.
- **It turned out that she was right.** Il s'est avéré qu'elle avait raison.
to **turn round** VERB
[1] *faire demi-tour* (*car*)
[2] *se retourner* (*person*)
to **turn up** VERB

[1] *arriver* (*arrive*)
[2] *monter* (*heater*)
- **Could you turn up the radio?** Tu peux monter le son de la radio?
turning NOUN
- **It's the third turning on the left.** C'est la troisième à gauche.
- **We took the wrong turning.** Nous n'avons pas tourné au bon endroit.
turnip NOUN
le *navet*
turquoise ADJECTIVE
turquoise MASC, FEM, PL (*colour*)
turtle NOUN
la *tortue*
tutor NOUN
le *professeur particulier* (*private teacher*)
TV NOUN
la *télé*
tweezers PL NOUN
la *pince à épiler* SING
twelfth ADJECTIVE
douzième   ○ *the twelfth floor* le douzième étage
- **the twelfth of August** le douze août
twelve NUMBER
douze   ○ *She's twelve.* Elle a douze ans.
- **twelve o'clock (1)** (*midday*) midi
- **twelve o'clock (2)** (*midnight*) minuit
twenty NUMBER
vingt   ○ *He's twenty.* Il a vingt ans.
twice ADVERB
deux fois
- **twice as much** deux fois plus   ○ *He gets twice as much pocket money as me.* Il a deux fois plus d'argent de poche que moi.
twin NOUN
le *jumeau* (*boy*)
la *jumelle* (*girl*)
(les *jumeaux* PL)
(les *jumelles* FEM PL)
- **my twin brother** mon frère jumeau
- **her twin sister** sa sœur jumelle
- **identical twins** les vrais jumeaux
- **a twin room** une chambre à deux lits
twinned ADJECTIVE
jumelé   ○ *Stroud is twinned with Châteaubriant.* Stroud est jumelée avec Châteaubriant.
to **twist** VERB
[1] *tordre* (*bend*)
[2] *déformer* (*distort*)   ○ *You're twisting my words.* Tu déformes ce que j'ai dit.
twit NOUN
le *crétin*
la *crétine*
two NUMBER
deux   ○ *She's two.* Elle a deux ans.

type NOUN

  see also **type** VERB

  le _type_ ◇ What type of camera have you
  got? Quel type d'appareil photo as-tu?

to **type** VERB

  see also **type** NOUN

  taper à la machine ◇ Can you type?
  Tu sais taper à la machine?

◆ **to type a letter** taper une lettre

typewriter NOUN

  la _machine à écrire_

typical ADJECTIVE

  typique ◇ That's just typical! C'est
  typique!

tyre NOUN

  le _pneu_

◆ **the tyre pressure** la pression des pneus

U

UFO NOUN
l' *OVNI* MASC (= objet volant non
identifié)

ugh EXCLAMATION
pouah!

ugly ADJECTIVE
laid

ulcer NOUN
l' *ulcère* MASC
- **a mouth ulcer** un aphte

Ulster NOUN
l' *Irlande du Nord* FEM
- **in Ulster** en Irlande du Nord

ultimate ADJECTIVE
suprême ◦ *the ultimate challenge* le
défi suprême
- **It was the ultimate adventure.** C'était la
grande aventure.

ultimately ADVERB
au bout du compte ◦ *Ultimately, it's
your decision.* Au bout du compte, c'est
votre décision.

umbrella NOUN
① le *parapluie*
② le *parasol* (for sun)

umpire NOUN
① l' *arbitre* MASC (in cricket)
② le *juge de chaise* (in tennis)

UN NOUN
l' *ONU* FEM (= Organisation des Nations
unies)

unable ADJECTIVE
- **to be unable to do something** ne pas
pouvoir faire quelque chose ◦ *I was
unable to come.* Je n'ai pas pu venir.

unacceptable ADJECTIVE
inacceptable

unanimous ADJECTIVE
unanime ◦ *a unanimous decision* une
décision unanime

unavoidable ADJECTIVE
inévitable

unaware ADJECTIVE
- **to be unaware (1)** (not know about)
ignorer ◦ *I was unaware of the
regulations.* J'ignorais le règlement.
- **to be unaware (2)** (not notice) ne pas se
rendre compte ◦ *She was unaware that
she was being filmed.* Elle ne s'était pas
rendu compte qu'on la filmait.

unbearable ADJECTIVE
insupportable

unbeatable ADJECTIVE
imbattable

unbelievable ADJECTIVE
incroyable

unborn ADJECTIVE
- **the unborn child** le fœtus

unbreakable ADJECTIVE
incassable

uncanny ADJECTIVE
étrange ◦ *That's uncanny!* C'est
étrange!
- **an uncanny resemblance** une
ressemblance troublante

uncertain ADJECTIVE
incertain ◦ *The future is uncertain.*
L'avenir est incertain.
- **to be uncertain about something** ne
pas être sûr de quelque chose

uncivilized ADJECTIVE
barbare

uncle NOUN
l' *oncle* MASC ◦ *my uncle* mon oncle

uncomfortable ADJECTIVE
pas confortable ◦ *The seats are rather
uncomfortable.* Les sièges ne sont pas
très confortables.

unconscious ADJECTIVE
sans connaissance

unconventional ADJECTIVE
peu conventionnel MASC
peu conventionnelle FEM

under PREPOSITION
① *sous* ◦ *The cat's under the table.* Le
chat est sous la table. ◦ *The tunnel goes
under the Channel.* Le tunnel passe sous
la Manche.
- **under there** là-dessous ◦ *What's under
there?* Qu'est-ce qu'il y a là-dessous?
② *moins de* (less than) ◦ *under 20
people* moins de vingt personnes
◦ *children under 10* les enfants de moins
de dix ans

underage ADJECTIVE
- **He's underage.** Il n'a pas l'âge
réglementaire.

undercover ADJECTIVE, ADVERB
secret MASC
secrète FEM
◦ *an undercover agent* un agent secret
- **She was working undercover.** Elle
travaillait sous une fausse identité.

to **underestimate** VERB
sous-estimer ◦ *I underestimated her.*
Je l'ai sous-estimée.

underground ADJECTIVE, ADVERB
see also **underground** NOUN
① *souterrain* ◦ *an underground car
park* un parking souterrain
② *sous terre* ◦ *Moles live underground.*
Les taupes vivent sous terre.

underground NOUN
see also underground ADJECTIVE
le *métro* ◦ *Is there an underground in Lille?* Est-ce qu'il y a un métro à Lille?

to **underline** VERB
souligner

underneath PREPOSITION, ADVERB
[1] *sous* ◦ *underneath the carpet* sous la moquette
[2] *dessous* ◦ *I got out of the car and looked underneath.* Je suis descendu de la voiture et j'ai regardé dessous.

underpaid ADJECTIVE
sous-payé ◦ *I'm underpaid.* Je suis sous-payé.

underpants PL NOUN
le *slip* SING

underpass NOUN
[1] le *passage souterrain* (for people)
[2] le *passage inférieur* (for cars)

to **understand** VERB
comprendre ◦ *Do you understand?* Vous comprenez? ◦ *I don't understand this word.* Je ne comprends pas ce mot. ◦ *Is that understood?* C'est compris?

understanding ADJECTIVE
compréhensif MASC
compréhensive FEM
◦ *She's very understanding.* Elle est très compréhensive.

undertaker NOUN
l' *entrepreneur des pompes funèbres* MASC

underwater ADJECTIVE, ADVERB
sous l'eau ◦ *This sequence was filmed underwater.* Cette séquence a été filmée sous l'eau.
◆ **an underwater camera** un appareil photographique de plongée
◆ **underwater photography** la photographie subaquatique

underwear NOUN
les *sous-vêtements* MASC PL

to **undo** VERB
[1] *défaire* (buttons, knot)
[2] *déballer* (parcel)

to **undress** VERB
se déshabiller (get undressed) ◦ *The doctor told me to undress.* Le médecin m'a dit de me déshabiller.

uneconomic ADJECTIVE
pas rentable

unemployed ADJECTIVE
au chômage ◦ *He's unemployed.* Il est au chômage. ◦ *He's been unemployed for a year.* Ça fait un an qu'il est au chômage.
◆ **the unemployed** les chômeurs MASC

unemployment NOUN
le *chômage*

unexpected ADJECTIVE
inattendu ◦ *an unexpected visitor* un visiteur inattendu

unexpectedly ADVERB
à l'improviste ◦ *They arrived unexpectedly.* Ils sont arrivés à l'improviste.

unfair ADJECTIVE
injuste ◦ *It's unfair to girls.* C'est injuste pour les filles.

unfamiliar ADJECTIVE
◆ **I heard an unfamiliar voice.** J'ai entendu une voix que je ne connaissais pas.

unfashionable ADJECTIVE
démodé

unfit ADJECTIVE
◆ **I'm rather unfit at the moment.** Je ne suis pas en très bonne condition physique en ce moment.

to **unfold** VERB
déplier ◦ *She unfolded the map.* Elle a déplié la carte.

unforgettable ADJECTIVE
inoubliable

unfortunately ADVERB
malheureusement ◦ *Unfortunately, I arrived late.* Malheureusement, je suis arrivé en retard.

unfriendly ADJECTIVE
pas aimable ◦ *The waiters are a bit unfriendly.* Les serveurs ne sont pas très aimables.

ungrateful ADJECTIVE
ingrat

unhappy ADJECTIVE
malheureux MASC
malheureuse FEM
◦ *He was very unhappy as a child.* Il était très malheureux quand il était petit.
◆ **to look unhappy** avoir l'air triste

unhealthy ADJECTIVE
[1] (person)
maladif MASC
maladive FEM
[2] (place, habit)
malsain
[3] (food)
pas sain

uniform NOUN
l' *uniforme* MASC ◦ *the school uniform* l'uniforme scolaire

uninhabited ADJECTIVE
inhabité

union NOUN
le *syndicat* (trade union)

Union Jack NOUN
le *drapeau du Royaume-Uni*

unique ADJECTIVE
unique

unit NOUN
　[1] l' *unité* FEM　◇ *a unit of measurement*
　une unité de mesure
　[2] l' *élément* MASC *(piece of furniture)*　◇ *a*
　kitchen unit un élément de cuisine

United Kingdom NOUN
　le *Royaume-Uni*

United Nations NOUN
　l' *O.N.U.* FEM (= Organisation des
　Nations Unies)

United States NOUN
　les *États-Unis* MASC PL
* **in the United States** aux États-Unis
* **to the United States** aux États-Unis

universe NOUN
　l' *univers* MASC

university NOUN
　l' *université* FEM　◇ *She's at university.*
　Elle va à l'université. ◇ *Do you want to*
　go to university? Tu veux aller à
　l'université? ◇ *Lancaster University*
　l'université de Lancaster

unleaded petrol NOUN
　l' *essence sans plomb* FEM

unless CONJUNCTION
* **unless he leaves** à moins qu'il ne parte
　◇ *I won't come unless you phone me.* Je
　ne viendrai pas à moins que tu ne me
　téléphones.

unlike PREPOSITION
　contrairement à　◇ *Unlike him, I really*
　enjoy flying. Contrairement à lui, j'adore
　prendre l'avion.

unlikely ADJECTIVE
　peu probable　◇ *It's possible, but*
　unlikely. C'est possible, mais peu
　probable.

to **unload** VERB
　décharger　◇ *We unloaded the car.*
　Nous avons déchargé la voiture. ◇ *The*
　lorries go there to unload. Les camions y
　vont pour être déchargés.

to **unlock** VERB
　ouvrir　◇ *He unlocked the door of the*
　car. Il a ouvert la portière de la voiture.

unlucky ADJECTIVE
* **to be unlucky (1)** *(number, object)* porter
　malheur　◇ *They say thirteen is an*
　unlucky number. On dit que le nombre
　treize porte malheur.
* **to be unlucky (2)** *(person)* ne pas avoir
　de chance　◇ *Did you win? – No, I was*
　unlucky. Vous avez gagné? – Non, je n'ai
　pas eu de chance.

unmarried ADJECTIVE
　célibataire *(person)*　◇ *an unmarried*
　mother une mère célibataire

* **an unmarried couple** un couple non
　marié

unnatural ADJECTIVE
　pas naturel MASC
　pas naturelle FEM

unnecessary ADJECTIVE
　inutile

unofficial ADJECTIVE
　[1] *(meeting, leader)*
　non officiel MASC
　non officielle FEM
　[2] *(strike)*
　sauvage

to **unpack** VERB
　[1] *défaire*　◇ *I unpacked my suitcase.*
　J'ai défait ma valise.
　[2] *déballer ses affaires*　◇ *I went to my*
　room to unpack. Je suis allé dans ma
　chambre pour déballer mes affaires. ◇ *I*
　haven't unpacked my clothes yet. Je n'ai
　pas encore déballé mes affaires.

unpleasant ADJECTIVE
　désagréable

to **unplug** VERB
　débrancher

unpopular ADJECTIVE
　impopulaire

unpredictable ADJECTIVE
　imprévisible

unreal ADJECTIVE
　incroyable *(incredible)*　◇ *It was unreal!*
　C'était incroyable!

unrealistic ADJECTIVE
　peu réaliste

unreasonable ADJECTIVE
　pas raisonnable　◇ *Her attitude was*
　completely unreasonable. Son attitude
　n'était pas du tout raisonnable.

unreliable ADJECTIVE
　pas fiable *(car, machine)*　◇ *It's a nice car,*
　but a bit unreliable. C'est une belle
　voiture, mais elle n'est pas très fiable.
* **He's completely unreliable.** On ne peut
　pas du tout compter sur lui.

to **unroll** VERB
　dérouler

unsatisfactory ADJECTIVE
　insatisfaisant

to **unscrew** VERB
　dévisser　◇ *She unscrewed the top of*
　the bottle. Elle a dévissé le bouchon de
　la bouteille.

unshaven ADJECTIVE
　mal rasé

unskilled worker ADJECTIVE
　le *manœuvre*

unstable ADJECTIVE
　instable

unsteady ADJECTIVE

mal assuré (*walk, voice*)
* **He was unsteady on his feet.** Il marchait d'un pas mal assuré.

unsuccessful ADJECTIVE
vain (*attempt*)
* **to be unsuccessful in doing something** ne pas réussir à faire quelque chose ◇ *an unsuccessful artist* un artiste qui n'a pas réussi

unsuitable ADJECTIVE
inapproprié (*clothes, equipment*)

untidy ADJECTIVE
1 *en désordre* ◇ *My bedroom's always untidy.* Ma chambre est toujours en désordre.
2 *débraillé* (*appearance, person*) ◇ *He's always untidy* Il est toujours débraillé.
3 *désordonné* (*in character*) ◇ *He's a very untidy person.* Il est très désordonné.

untie VERB
1 *défaire* (*knot, parcel*)
2 *détacher* (*animal*)

until PREPOSITION, CONJUNCTION
1 *jusqu'à* ◇ *I waited until ten o'clock.* J'ai attendu jusqu'à dix heures.
* **until now** jusqu'à présent ◇ *It's never been a problem until now.* Ça n'a jamais été un problème jusqu'à présent.
* **until then** jusque-là ◇ *Until then I'd never been to France.* Jusque-là je n'étais jamais allé en France.

> Use **avant** if the sentence you want to translate contains a negative, such as "not" or "never".

2 *avant* ◇ *It won't be ready until next week.* Ça ne sera pas prêt avant la semaine prochaine. ◇ *Until last year I'd never been to France.* Avant l'année dernière, je n'étais jamais allé en France.

unusual ADJECTIVE
1 *insolite* ◇ *an unusual shape* une forme insolite
2 *rare* ◇ *It's unusual to get snow at this time of year.* Il est rare qu'il neige à cette époque de l'année.

unwilling ADJECTIVE
* **to be unwilling to do something** ne pas être disposé à faire quelque chose ◇ *He was unwilling to help me.* Il n'était pas disposé à m'aider.

unwind VERB
se détendre (*relax*)

unwise ADJECTIVE
imprudent (*person*) ◇ *That was rather unwise of you.* C'était plutôt imprudent de votre part.

unwrap VERB
déballer ◇ *After the meal we unwrapped the presents.* Après le repas

nous avons déballé les cadeaux.

up PREPOSITION, ADVERB
> *For other expressions with* **up**, *see the verbs* go, come, put, turn *etc.*

en haut ◇ *up on the hill* en haut de la colline
* **up here** ici
* **up there** là-haut
* **up north** dans le nord
* **to be up** être levé (*out of bed*) ◇ *We were up at 6.* Nous étions levés à six heures. ◇ *He's not up yet.* Il n'est pas encore levé.
* **What's up?** Qu'est-ce qu'il y a? ◇ *What's up with her?* Qu'est-ce qu'elle a?
* **to get up** (*in the morning*) se lever ◇ *What time do you get up?* À quelle heure est-ce que tu te lèves?
* **to go up** monter ◇ *The bus went up the hill.* Le bus a monté la colline.
* **to go up to somebody** s'approcher de quelqu'un ◇ *She came up to me.* Elle s'est approchée de moi.
* **up to** (*as far as*) jusqu'à ◇ *to count up to fifty* compter jusqu'à cinquante ◇ *up to three hours* jusqu'à trois heures ◇ *up to now* jusqu'à présent
* **It's up to you.** C'est à vous de décider.

upbringing NOUN
l' *éducation* FEM

uphill ADVERB
* **to go uphill** monter

upper sixth NOUN
* **the upper sixth** la terminale ◇ *She's in the upper sixth.* Elle est en terminale.

upright ADJECTIVE
* **to stand upright** se tenir droit

upset NOUN
> *see also* upset ADJECTIVE, VERB

* **a stomach upset** une indigestion

upset ADJECTIVE
> *see also* upset NOUN, VERB

contrarié ◇ *She's still a bit upset.* Elle est encore un peu contrariée.
* **I had an upset stomach.** J'avais l'estomac dérangé.

to **upset** VERB
> *see also* upset NOUN, ADJECTIVE

* **to upset somebody** contrarier quelqu'un

upside down ADVERB
à l'envers ◇ *That painting is upside down.* Ce tableau est à l'envers.

upstairs ADVERB
en haut ◇ *Where's your coat? – It's upstairs.* Où est ton manteau? – Il est en haut.
* **to go upstairs** monter

uptight ADJECTIVE

tendu ◦ *She's really uptight.* Elle est
très tendue.

up-to-date ADJECTIVE
  1 _moderne_ (*car, stereo*)
  2 _à jour_ (*information*) ◦ *an up-to-date
  timetable* un horaire à jour
• **to bring something up to date**
  moderniser quelque chose

upwards ADVERB
  vers le haut ◦ *to look upwards*
  regarder vers le haut

urgent ADJECTIVE
  urgent ◦ *Is it urgent?* C'est urgent?

urine NOUN
  l' _urine_ FEM

US NOUN
  les _USA_ MASC PL

us PRONOUN
  nous ◦ *They helped us.* Ils nous ont
  aidés. ◦ *They gave us a map.* Ils nous
  ont donné une carte.

USA NOUN
  les _USA_ MASC PL

use NOUN
  see also use VERB
• **It's no use.** Ça ne sert à rien. ◦ *It's no
  use shouting, she's deaf.* Ça ne sert à
  rien de crier, elle est sourde.
• **It's no use, I can't do it.** Il n'y a rien à
  faire, je n'y arrive pas.
• **to make use of something** utiliser
  quelque chose

to **use** VERB
  see also use NOUN
  utiliser ◦ *Can we use a dictionary in the
  exam?* Est-ce qu'on peut utiliser un
  dictionnaire à l'examen?
• **Can I use your phone?** Je peux
  téléphoner?
• **to use the toilet** aller aux W.C.
• **to use up (1)** finir ◦ *We've used up all
  the paint.* Nous avons fini la peinture.

• **to use up (2)** (*money*) dépenser
• **I used to live in London.** J'habitais à
  Londres autrefois.
• **I used not to like maths, but now...**
  Avant, je n'aimais pas les maths, mais
  maintenant...
• **to be used to something** avoir
  l'habitude de quelque chose ◦ *He
  wasn't used to driving on the right.* Il
  n'avait pas l'habitude de conduire à
  droite. ◦ *Don't worry, I'm used to it.* Ne
  t'inquiète pas, j'ai l'habitude.
• **a used car** une voiture d'occasion

useful ADJECTIVE
  utile

useless ADJECTIVE
  nul MASC
  nulle FEM
  ◦ *This map is just useless.* Cette carte est
  vraiment nulle. ◦ *You're useless!* Tu es
  nul!
• **It's useless!** Ça ne sert à rien!

usual ADJECTIVE
  habituel MASC
  habituelle FEM
• **as usual** comme d'habitude

usually ADVERB
  1 _en général_ (*generally*) ◦ *I usually get
  to school at about half past eight.* En
  général, j'arrive à l'école vers huit heures
  et demie.
  2 _d'habitude_ (*when making a contrast*)
  ◦ *Usually I don't wear make-up, but today
  is a special occasion.* D'habitude je ne
  me maquille pas, mais aujourd'hui c'est
  spécial.

utility room NOUN
  la _buanderie_

U-turn NOUN
  le _demi-tour_ ◦ *to do a U-turn* faire
  demi-tour

V

vacancy NOUN
[1] le *poste vacant* (job)
[2] la *chambre disponible* (room in hotel)
* "no vacancies" (on sign) "complet"
vacant ADJECTIVE
libre
vaccinate VERB
vacciner
vacuum VERB
passer l'aspirateur ◇ to vacuum the
hall passer l'aspirateur dans le couloir
vacuum cleaner NOUN
l' *aspirateur* MASC
vagina NOUN
le *vagin*
vague ADJECTIVE
vague
vain ADJECTIVE
vaniteux MASC
vaniteuse FEM
◇ He's so vain! Qu'est-ce qu'il est
vaniteux!
* in vain en vain
Valentine card NOUN
la *carte de la Saint-Valentin*
Valentine's Day NOUN
la *Saint-Valentin*
valid ADJECTIVE
valable ◇ This ticket is valid for three
months. Ce billet est valable trois mois.
valley NOUN
la *vallée*
valuable ADJECTIVE
[1] *de valeur* ◇ a valuable picture un
tableau de valeur
[2] *précieux* MASC
précieuse FEM
◇ valuable help une aide précieuse
valuables PL NOUN
les *objets de valeur* MASC PL ◇ Don't
take any valuables with you. N'emportez
pas d'objets de valeur.
value NOUN
la *valeur*
van NOUN
la *camionnette*
vandal NOUN
le/la *vandale*
vandalism NOUN
le *vandalisme*
vandalize VERB
saccager
vanilla NOUN
la *vanille*
* vanilla ice cream la glace à la vanille
vanish VERB

disparaître
variable ADJECTIVE
variable
varied ADJECTIVE
varié
variety NOUN
la *variété*
various ADJECTIVE
plusieurs ◇ We visited various villages
in the area. Nous avons visité plusieurs
villages de la région.
to **vary** VERB
varier
vase NOUN
le *vase*
VAT NOUN (= value added tax)
la *TVA* (= taxe sur la valeur ajoutée)
VCR NOUN (= video cassette recorder)
le *magnétoscope*
VDU NOUN (= visual display unit)
la *console*
veal NOUN
le *veau*
vegan NOUN
le *végétalien*
la *végétalienne*
◇ I'm a vegan. Je suis végétalien.
vegetable NOUN
le *légume* ◇ vegetable soup la soupe
aux légumes
vegetarian ADJECTIVE
see also vegetarian NOUN
végétarien MASC
végétarienne FEM
◇ I'm vegetarian. Je suis végétarien.
◇ vegetarian lasagne les lasagnes
végétariennes
vegetarian NOUN
see also vegetarian ADJECTIVE
le *végétarien*
la *végétarienne*
◇ I'm a vegetarian. Je suis végétarien.
vehicle NOUN
le *véhicule*
vein NOUN
la *veine*
velvet NOUN
le *velours*
vending machine NOUN
le *distributeur automatique*
Venetian blind NOUN
le *store vénitien*
verb NOUN
le *verbe*
verdict NOUN
le *verdict*

vertical ADJECTIVE
vertical
(*verticaux* MASC PL)

vertigo NOUN
le *vertige* ◇ *I get vertigo.* J'ai le vertige.

very ADVERB
très ◇ *very tall* très grand ◇ *not very interesting* pas très intéressant
→ **very much** beaucoup

vest NOUN
le *maillot de corps*

vet NOUN
le/la *vétérinaire* ◇ *She's a vet.* Elle est vétérinaire.

via PREPOSITION
en passant par ◇ *We went to Paris via Boulogne.* Nous sommes allés à Paris en passant par Boulogne.

vicar NOUN
le *pasteur* ◇ *He's a vicar.* Il est pasteur.

vice NOUN
l' *étau* (*for holding things*) MASC

vice versa ADVERB
vice versa

vicious ADJECTIVE
① *brutal*
(*brutaux* MASC PL)
◇ *a vicious attack* une agression brutale
② *méchant* (*dog, person*)
→ **a vicious circle** un cercle vicieux

victim NOUN
la *victime* ◇ *He was the victim of a mugging.* Il a été victime d'une agression.

victory NOUN
la *victoire*

to **video** VERB
see also **video** NOUN
① *enregistrer* (*from TV*)
② *filmer* (*with video camera*)

video NOUN
see also **video** VERB
① la *vidéo* (*film*) ◇ *to watch a video* regarder une vidéo ◇ *a video of my family on holiday* une vidéo de ma famille en vacances ◇ *It's out on video.* C'est sorti en vidéo.
② la *cassette vidéo* (*video cassette*)
◇ *She lent me a video.* Elle m'a prêté une cassette vidéo.
③ le *magnétoscope* (*video recorder*)
◇ *Have you got a video?* Tu as un magnétoscope?
→ **a video camera** une caméra vidéo
→ **a video cassette** une cassette vidéo
→ **a video game** un jeu vidéo ◇ *He likes playing video games.* Il aime les jeux vidéo.
→ **a video recorder** un magnétoscope

→ **a video shop** un vidéoclub

Vietnam NOUN
le *Viêt-Nam*
→ **in Vietnam** au Viêt-Nam

Vietnamese ADJECTIVE
vietnamien MASC
vietnamienne FEM

view NOUN
① la *vue* ◇ *There's an amazing view.* Il y a une vue extraordinaire.
② l' *avis* MASC (*opinion*) ◇ *in my view* à mon avis

viewer NOUN
le *téléspectateur*
la *téléspectatrice*

viewpoint NOUN
le *point de vue*

vile ADJECTIVE
dégoûtant (*smell, food*)

villa NOUN
la *villa*

village NOUN
le *village*

villain NOUN
① le *malfrat* (*criminal*)
② le *méchant* (*in film*)

vine NOUN
la *vigne*

vinegar NOUN
le *vinaigre*

vineyard NOUN
le *vignoble*

viola NOUN
l' *alto* MASC ◇ *I play the viola.* Je joue de l'alto.

violence NOUN
la *violence*

violent ADJECTIVE
violent

violin NOUN
le *violon* ◇ *I play the violin.* Je joue du violon.

violinist NOUN
le/la *violoniste*

virgin NOUN
la *vierge* ◇ *to be a virgin* être vierge

Virgo NOUN
la *Vierge* ◇ *I'm Virgo.* Je suis Vierge.

virtual reality NOUN
la *réalité virtuelle*

virus NOUN
le *virus*

visa NOUN
le *visa*

visible ADJECTIVE
visible

visit NOUN
see also **visit** VERB

[1] la *visite* (to museum)
[2] le *séjour* (to country) ◇ *Did you enjoy your visit to France?* Ton séjour en France s'est bien passé?
- **my last visit to my grandmother** la dernière fois que je suis allé voir ma grand-mère

visit VERB
see also **visit** NOUN
[1] *rendre visite à* (person) ◇ *to visit somebody* rendre visite à quelqu'un
[2] *visiter* (place) ◇ *We'd like to visit the castle.* Nous voudrions visiter le château.

visitor NOUN
[1] (tourist)
le *visiteur*
la *visiteuse*
[2] (guest)
l' *invité* MASC
l' *invitée* FEM
- **to have a visitor** avoir de la visite

visual ADJECTIVE
visuel MASC
visuelle FEM

visualize VERB
imaginer

vital ADJECTIVE
vital
(*vitaux* MASC PL)

vitamin NOUN
la *vitamine*

vivid ADJECTIVE
(colour)
vif MASC
vive FEM
- **to have a vivid imagination** avoir une imagination débordante

vocabulary NOUN
le *vocabulaire*

vocational ADJECTIVE
professionnel MASC
professionnelle FEM
- **a vocational course** un stage de formation professionnelle

vodka NOUN
la *vodka*

voice NOUN
la *voix*
(les *voix* PL)

volcano NOUN
le *volcan*

volleyball NOUN
le *volley-ball* ◇ *to play volleyball* jouer au volley-ball

volt NOUN
le *volt*

voltage NOUN
le *voltage*

voluntary ADJECTIVE
volontaire (contribution, statement)
- **to do voluntary work** travailler bénévolement

volunteer NOUN
see also **volunteer** VERB
le/la *volontaire*

to **volunteer** VERB
see also **volunteer** NOUN
- **to volunteer to do something** se proposer pour faire quelque chose

to **vomit** VERB
vomir

to **vote** VERB
voter

voucher NOUN
le *bon* ◇ *a gift voucher* un bon d'achat

vowel NOUN
la *voyelle*

vulgar ADJECTIVE
vulgaire

W

wafer NOUN
la *gaufrette*

wage NOUN
le *salaire* ◇ *He collected his wages.* Il a
retiré son salaire.

waist NOUN
la *taille*

waistcoat NOUN
le *gilet*

to **wait** VERB
attendre
- **to wait for something** attendre quelque
chose
- **to wait for somebody** attendre
quelqu'un ◇ *I'll wait for you.* Je
t'attendrai.
- **Wait for me!** Attends-moi!
- **Wait a minute!** Attends!
- **to keep somebody waiting** faire
attendre quelqu'un ◇ *They kept us
waiting for hours.* Ils nous ont fait
attendre pendant des heures.
- **I can't wait for the holidays.** J'ai hâte
d'être en vacances.
- **I can't wait to see him again.** J'ai hâte
de le revoir.

waiter NOUN
le *serveur*

waiting list NOUN
la *liste d'attente*

waiting room NOUN
la *salle d'attente*

waitress NOUN
la *serveuse*

to **wake up** VERB
se réveiller ◇ *I woke up at six o'clock.*
Je me suis réveillé à six heures.
- **to wake somebody up** réveiller
quelqu'un ◇ *Please would you wake me
up at seven o'clock?* Pourriez-vous me
réveiller à sept heures?

Wales NOUN
le *pays de Galles*
- **in Wales** au pays de Galles
- **to Wales** au pays de Galles
- **I'm from Wales.** Je suis gallois.
- **the Prince of Wales** le prince de Galles

to **walk** VERB
see also **walk** NOUN
1. *marcher* ◇ *He walks fast.* Il marche
vite.
2. *aller à pied* (*go on foot*) ◇ *Are you
walking or going by bus?* Tu y vas à pied
ou en bus? ◇ *We walked 10 kilometres.*
Nous avons fait dix kilomètres à pied.
- **to walk the dog** promener le chien

walk NOUN
see also **walk** VERB
la *promenade* ◇ *to go for a walk* faire
une promenade
- **It's 10 minutes' walk from here.** C'est à
dix minutes d'ici à pied.

walkie-talkie NOUN
le *talkie-walkie*

walking NOUN
la *randonnée* ◇ *I did some walking in
the Alps last summer.* J'ai fait de la
randonnée dans les Alpes l'été dernier.

walking stick NOUN
la *canne*

Walkman ® NOUN
le *baladeur*

wall NOUN
le *mur*

wallet NOUN
le *portefeuille*

wallpaper NOUN
le *papier peint*

walnut NOUN
la *noix*
(les *noix* PL)

to **wander** VERB
- **to wander around** flâner ◇ *I just
wandered around for a while.* J'ai flâné
un peu.

to **want** VERB
vouloir ◇ *Do you want some cake?* Tu
veux du gâteau?
- **to want to do something** vouloir faire
quelque chose ◇ *I want to go to the
cinema.* Je veux aller au cinéma. ◇ *What
do you want to do tomorrow?* Qu'est-ce
que tu veux faire demain?

war NOUN
la *guerre*

ward NOUN
la *salle* (*room in hospital*)

warden NOUN
(*of youth hostel*)
le *directeur*
la *directrice*

wardrobe NOUN
l' *armoire* FEM (*piece of furniture*)

warehouse NOUN
l' *entrepôt* MASC

warm ADJECTIVE
1. *chaud* ◇ *warm water* l'eau chaude
- **It's warm in here.** Il fait chaud ici.
- **to be warm** (*person*) avoir chaud ◇ *I'm
too warm.* J'ai trop chaud.
2. *chaleureux* MASC
chaleureuse FEM

◇ *a warm welcome* un accueil chaleureux
◆ **to warm up (1)** (*for sport*) s'échauffer
◆ **to warm up (2)** (*food*) réchauffer ◇ *I'll warm up some lasagne for you.* Je vais te réchauffer des lasagnes.

to **warn** VERB
prévenir ◇ *Well, I warned you!* Je t'avais prévenu!
◆ **to warn somebody to do something** conseiller à quelqu'un de faire quelque chose

warning NOUN
l' *avertissement* MASC

Warsaw NOUN
Varsovie

wart NOUN
la *verrue*

was VERB *see* **be**

wash NOUN
see also wash VERB
◆ **to have a wash** se laver ◇ *I had a wash.* Je me suis lavé.
◆ **to give something a wash** laver quelque chose ◇ *He gave the car a wash.* Il a lavé la voiture.

to **wash** VERB
see also wash NOUN
1 *laver* ◇ *to wash something* laver quelque chose
2 *se laver* (*have a wash*) ◇ *Every morning I get up, wash and get dressed.* Tous les matins je me lève, je me lave et je m'habille.
◆ **to wash one's hands** se laver les mains
◆ **to wash one's hair** se laver les cheveux
◆ **to wash up** faire la vaisselle

washbasin NOUN
le *lavabo*

washing NOUN
le *linge* ◇ *dirty washing* du linge sale
◆ **Have you got any washing?** Tu as du linge à laver?
◆ **to do the washing** faire la lessive

washing machine NOUN
la *machine à laver*

washing powder NOUN
la *lessive*

washing-up NOUN
◆ **to do the washing-up** faire la vaisselle

washing-up liquid NOUN
le *produit à vaisselle*

wasn't = was not

wasp NOUN
la *guêpe*

waste NOUN
see also waste VERB
1 le *gaspillage* ◇ *It's such a waste!* C'est vraiment du gaspillage!

◆ **It's a waste of time.** C'est une perte de temps.
2 les *déchets* MASC (*rubbish*) ◇ *nuclear waste* les déchets nucléaires

to **waste** VERB
see also waste NOUN
gaspiller ◇ *I don't like wasting money.* Je n'aime pas gaspiller de l'argent.
◆ **to waste time** perdre du temps
◇ *There's no time to waste.* Il n'y a pas de temps à perdre.

wastepaper basket NOUN
la *corbeille à papier*

watch NOUN
see also watch VERB
la *montre*

to **watch** VERB
see also watch NOUN
1 *regarder* ◇ *to watch television* regarder la télévision ◇ *Watch me!* Regarde-moi!
2 *surveiller* (*keep a watch on*) ◇ *The police were watching the house.* La police surveillait la maison.
◆ **to watch out** faire attention
◆ **Watch out!** Attention!

water NOUN
see also water VERB
l' *eau* FEM

to **water** VERB
see also water NOUN
arroser ◇ *He was watering his tulips.* Il arrosait ses tulipes.

waterfall NOUN
la *cascade*

watering can NOUN
l' *arrosoir* MASC

watermelon NOUN
la *pastèque*

waterproof ADJECTIVE
imperméable ◇ *Is this jacket waterproof?* Ce blouson est-il imperméable?
◆ **a waterproof watch** une montre étanche

water-skiing NOUN
le *ski nautique* ◇ *to go water-skiing* faire du ski nautique

wave NOUN
see also wave VERB
1 la *vague* (*in water*)
2 le *signe* (*of hand*) ◇ *We gave him a wave.* Nous lui avons fait signe.

to **wave** VERB
see also wave NOUN
faire un signe de la main ◇ *to wave at somebody* faire un signe de la main à quelqu'un
◆ **to wave goodbye** faire au revoir de la

PTO

W

main   ◇ *I waved her goodbye.* Je lui ai fait au revoir de la main.

wavy ADJECTIVE
ondulé   ◇ *wavy hair* les cheveux ondulés

wax NOUN
la *cire*

way NOUN
[1] la *façon* (*manner*)   ◇ *She looked at me in a strange way.* Elle m'a regardé d'une façon étrange.
* **This book tells you the right way to do it.** Ce livre explique comment il faut faire.
* **You're doing it the wrong way.** Ce n'est pas comme ça qu'il faut faire.
* **in a way...** dans un sens...
* **a way of life** un mode de vie
[2] le *chemin* (*route*)   ◇ *I don't know the way.* Je ne connais pas le chemin.
* **on the way** en chemin   ◇ *We stopped for lunch on the way.* Nous nous sommes arrêtés pour déjeuner en chemin.
* **It's a long way.** C'est loin.   ◇ *Paris is a long way from London.* Paris est loin de Londres.
* **Which way is it?** C'est par où?
* **The supermarket is this way.** Le supermarché est par ici.
* **Do you know the way to the station?** Est-ce que vous savez comment aller à la gare?
* **He's on his way.** Il arrive.
* **"way in"** "entrée"
* **"way out"** "sortie"
* **by the way...** au fait...

we PRONOUN
nous   ◇ *We're staying here for a week.* Nous restons une semaine ici.

weak ADJECTIVE
faible

wealthy ADJECTIVE
riche

weapon NOUN
l' *arme* FEM

to **wear** VERB
porter (*clothes*)   ◇ *She was wearing a hat.* Elle portait un chapeau.
* **She was wearing black.** Elle était en noir.

weather NOUN
le *temps*   ◇ *What was the weather like?* Quel temps a-t-il fait?   ◇ *The weather was lovely.* Il a fait un temps magnifique.

weather forecast NOUN
la *météo*

we'd = we had, we would
wedding NOUN

le *mariage*
* **wedding anniversary** l'anniversaire de mariage MASC
* **wedding dress** la robe de mariée

Wednesday NOUN
le *mercredi*   ◇ *on Wednesday* mercredi   ◇ *on Wednesdays* le mercredi   ◇ *every Wednesday* tous les mercredis   ◇ *last Wednesday* mercredi dernier   ◇ *next Wednesday* mercredi prochain

weed NOUN
la *mauvaise herbe*   ◇ *The garden's full of weeds.* Le jardin est plein de mauvaises herbes.

week NOUN
la *semaine*   ◇ *last week* la semaine dernière   ◇ *every week* toutes les semaines   ◇ *next week* la semaine prochaine   ◇ *in a week's time* dans une semaine
* **a week on Friday** vendredi en huit

weekday NOUN
* **on weekdays** en semaine

weekend NOUN
le *week-end*   ◇ *at weekends* le week-end   ◇ *last weekend* le week-end dernier   ◇ *next weekend* le week-end prochain

to **weigh** VERB
peser   ◇ *How much do you weigh?* Combien est-ce que tu pèses?   ◇ *First, weigh the flour.* Tout d'abord, pesez la farine.
* **to weigh oneself** se peser

weight NOUN
le *poids*
* **to lose weight** maigrir
* **to put on weight** grossir

weightlifter NOUN
l' *haltérophile* MASC

weightlifting NOUN
l' *haltérophilie* FEM

weird ADJECTIVE
bizarre

welcome NOUN
see also welcome VERB
l' *accueil* MASC   ◇ *They gave her a warm welcome.* Ils lui ont fait un accueil chaleureux.
* **Welcome!** Bienvenue!   ◇ *Welcome to France!* Bienvenue en France!

to **welcome** VERB
see also welcome NOUN
* **to welcome somebody** accueillir quelqu'un
* **Thank you! – You're welcome!** Merci! – De rien!

well ADJECTIVE, ADVERB
see also well NOUN

[1] *bien* ◦ *You did that really well.* Tu as très bien fait ça.
- **to do well** réussir bien ◦ *She's doing really well at school.* Elle réussit vraiment bien à l'école.
- **to be well** (*in good health*) aller bien ◦ *I'm not very well at the moment.* Je ne vais pas très bien en ce moment.
- **Get well soon!** Remets-toi vite!
- **Well done!** Bravo!

[2] *enfin* ◦ *It's enormous! Well, quite big anyway.* C'est énorme! Enfin, c'est assez grand.
- **as well** aussi ◦ *We worked hard,,but we had some fun as well.* Nous avons travaillé dur, mais nous nous sommes bien amusés aussi. ◦ *We went to Chartres as well as Paris.* Nous sommes allés à Paris et à Chartres aussi.

well NOUN
see also well ADJECTIVE
le *puits*
(les *puits* PL)

we'll = we will

well-behaved ADJECTIVE
sage

well-dressed ADJECTIVE
bien habillé

wellingtons PL NOUN
les *bottes en caoutchouc* FEM PL

well-known ADJECTIVE
célèbre ◦ *a well-known film star* une vedette de cinéma célèbre

well-off ADJECTIVE
aisé

Welsh ADJECTIVE
see also Welsh NOUN
gallois ◦ *She's Welsh.* Elle est galloise.
- **Welsh people** les Gallois MASC

Welsh NOUN
see also Welsh ADJECTIVE
le *gallois* (*language*)

Welshman NOUN
le *Gallois*

Welshwoman NOUN
la *Galloise*

went VERB *see* **go**

were VERB *see* **be**

we're = we are

weren't = were not

west NOUN
see also west ADJECTIVE
l' *ouest* MASC ◦ *in the west* dans l'ouest

west ADJECTIVE, ADVERB
see also west NOUN
[1] *ouest* MASC, FEM, PL ◦ *the west coast* la côte ouest
- **west of** à l'ouest de ◦ *Stroud is west of Oxford.* Stroud est à l'ouest

d'Oxford.
[2] *vers l'ouest* ◦ *We were travelling west.* Nous allions vers l'ouest.
- **the West Country** le sud-ouest de l'Angleterre

western NOUN
see also western ADJECTIVE
le *western* (*film*)

western ADJECTIVE
see also western NOUN
- **the western part of the island** la partie ouest de l'île
- **Western Europe** l'Europe de l'Ouest

West Indian ADJECTIVE
see also West Indian NOUN
antillais ◦ *She's West Indian.* Elle est antillaise.

West Indian NOUN
see also West Indian ADJECTIVE
[1] l' *Antillais* MASC
[2] l' *Antillaise* FEM (*person*)

West Indies PL NOUN
les *Antilles* FEM PL
- **in the West Indies** aux Antilles

wet ADJECTIVE
mouillé ◦ *wet clothes* les vêtements mouillés
- **to get wet** se faire mouiller
- **dripping wet** trempé
- **wet weather** le temps pluvieux
- **It was wet all week.** Il a plu toute la semaine.

wetsuit NOUN
la *combinaison de plongée*
(les *combinaisons de plongée* PL)

we've = we have

whale NOUN
la *baleine*

what ADJECTIVE, PRONOUN
[1] (*which*)
quel MASC
quelle FEM
◦ *What subjects are you studying?* Quelles matières est-ce que tu fais?
◦ *What colour is it?* C'est de quelle couleur? ◦ *What's the capital of Finland?* Quelle est la capitale de la Finlande?
◦ *What a mess!* Quel fouillis!
[2] *qu'est-ce que* ◦ *What are you doing?* Qu'est-ce que vous faites?
◦ *What did you say?* Qu'est-ce que vous avez dit? ◦ *What is it?* Qu'est-ce que c'est? ◦ *What's the matter?* Qu'est-ce qu'il y a?
[3] *qu'est-ce qui* ◦ *What happened?* Qu'est-ce qui s'est passé? ◦ *What's bothering you?* Qu'est-ce qui te préoccupe?

W

PTO

In relative phrases use **ce qui** *or* **ce que** *depending on whether* **what** *refers to the subject or the object of the sentence.*

[4] *(subject)*
ce qui ◦ *I saw what happened.* J'ai vu ce qui est arrivé. ◦ *I know what's bothering you.* Je sais ce qui te préoccupe.

[5] *(object)*
ce que ◦ *Tell me what you did.* Dites-moi ce que vous avez fait. ◦ *I heard what he said.* J'ai entendu ce qu'il a dit.

* **What?** *(what did you say)* Comment?
* **What!** *(shocked)* Quoi!

wheat NOUN
le *blé*

wheel NOUN
la *roue*

* **the steering wheel** le volant

wheelchair NOUN
le *fauteuil roulant*

when ADVERB, CONJUNCTION
quand ◦ *When did he go?* Quand est-ce qu'il est parti? ◦ *She was reading when I came in.* Elle lisait quand je suis entré.

where ADVERB, CONJUNCTION
où ◦ *Where's Emma today?* Où est Emma aujourd'hui? ◦ *Where do you live?* Où habites-tu? ◦ *Where are you going?* Où vas-tu? ◦ *a shop where you can buy croissants* un magasin où l'on peut acheter des croissants

whether CONJUNCTION
si ◦ *I don't know whether to go or not.* Je ne sais pas si y aller ou non.

which ADJECTIVE, PRONOUN
[1] *quel* MASC
quelle FEM
◦ *Which flavour do you want?* Quel parfum est-ce que tu veux?

When asking **which one** *use* **lequel** *or* **laquelle**, *depending on whether the noun is masculine or feminine.*

* **I know his brother. – Which one?** Je connais son frère. – Lequel?
* **I know his sister. – Which one?** Je connais sa sœur. – Laquelle?
* **Which would you like?** Lequel est-ce que vous voulez?
* **Which of these are yours?** Lesquels sont à vous?

In relative phrases use **qui** *or* **que** *depending on whether* **which** *refers to the subject or the object of the sentence.*

[2] *qui* *(subject)* ◦ *the CD which is playing now* le CD qui passe maintenant
[3] *que* *(object)* ◦ *the CD which I bought today* le CD que j'ai acheté hier

while CONJUNCTION
see also **while** NOUN
[1] *pendant que* ◦ *You hold the torch while I look inside.* Tiens la lampe électrique pendant que je regarde à l'intérieur.
[2] *alors que* ◦ *Isobel is very dynamic, while Kay is more laid-back.* Isobel est très dynamique, alors que Kay est plus relax.

while NOUN
see also **while** CONJUNCTION
le *moment* ◦ *after a while* au bout d'un moment

* **a while ago** il y a un moment ◦ *He was here a while ago.* Il était là il y a un moment.
* **for a while** pendant quelque temps ◦ *I lived in London for a while.* J'ai vécu à Londres pendant quelque temps.
* **quite a while** longtemps ◦ *quite a while ago* il y a longtemps ◦ *I haven't seen him for quite a while.* Ça fait longtemps que je ne l'ai pas vu.

whip NOUN
see also **whip** VERB
le *fouet*

to **whip** VERB
see also **whip** NOUN
[1] *fouetter* *(person, animal)*
[2] *battre* *(eggs)*

whipped cream NOUN
la *crème fouettée*

whisk NOUN
le *fouet*

whiskers PL NOUN
les *moustaches* FEM PL

whisky NOUN
le *whisky*
(les *whiskies* PL)

to **whisper** VERB
chuchoter

whistle NOUN
see also **whistle** VERB
le *sifflet*

* **The referee blew his whistle.** L'arbitre a sifflé.

to **whistle** VERB
see also **whistle** NOUN
siffler

white ADJECTIVE
blanc MASC
blanche FEM
◦ *He's got white hair.* Il a les cheveux blancs.

* **white wine** le vin blanc
* **white bread** le pain blanc
* **white coffee** le café au lait
* **a white man** un Blanc

◆ **a white woman** une Blanche
◆ **white people** les Blancs

Whitsun NOUN
  la *Pentecôte*

who PRONOUN
  ⬜1 *qui* ◦ *Who said that?* Qui a dit ça?
  ◦ *Who is Jacques Chirac?* Qui est
  Jacques Chirac?

  In relative phrases use qui *or* que *depending on*
  whether who *refers to the subject or the object of*
  the verb.

  ⬜2 *qui* (*subject*) ◦ *the man who saw us*
  l'homme qui nous a vus ◦ *the man who*
  spoke to us l'homme qui nous a parlé
  ⬜3 *que* (*object*) ◦ *the man who we saw*
  l'homme que nous avons vu ◦ *the man*
  who she married l'homme qu'elle a épousé

whole ADJECTIVE
  see also whole NOUN

  tout ◦ *the whole class* toute la classe
  ◦ *the whole afternoon* tout l'après-midi
◆ **a whole box of chocolates** toute une
  boîte de chocolats
◆ **the whole world** le monde entier

whole NOUN
  see also whole ADJECTIVE
◆ **The whole of Wales was affected.** Le
  pays de Galles tout entier a été touché.
◆ **on the whole** dans l'ensemble

wholemeal ADJECTIVE
  complet MASC
  complète FEM
◆ **wholemeal bread** le pain complet

whom PRONOUN
  qui ◦ *Whom did you see?* Qui
  avez-vous vu? ◦ *the man to whom I*
  spoke l'homme à qui j'ai parlé

whose PRONOUN, ADJECTIVE
  ⬜1 *à qui* ◦ *Whose is this?* À qui est-ce?
  ◦ *I know whose it is.* Je sais à qui c'est.
  ◦ *Whose book is this?* À qui est ce livre?
  ⬜2 *dont* (*after noun*) ◦ *the girl whose*
  picture was in the paper la jeune fille
  dont la photo était dans le journal

why ADVERB
  pourquoi ◦ *Why did you do that?*
  Pourquoi avez-vous fait ça? ◦ *That's why*
  he did it. Voilà pourquoi il a fait ça.
  ◦ *Tell me why.* Dis-moi pourquoi.
◆ **I've never been to France.—Why not?** Je
  ne suis jamais allé en France.—Pourquoi?
◆ **All right, why not?** D'accord, pourquoi
  pas?

wicked ADJECTIVE
  ⬜1 (*evil*)
  méchant
  ⬜2 (*really great*)
  génial
  (*géniaux* MASC PL)

wicket NOUN
  le *guichet* (*stumps*)

wide ADJECTIVE, ADVERB
  large ◦ *a wide road* une route large
◆ **wide open** grand ouvert ◦ *The door*
  was wide open. La porte était grande
  ouverte. ◦ *The windows were wide open.*
  Les fenêtres étaient grandes ouvertes.
◆ **wide awake** complètement réveillé

widow NOUN
  la *veuve* ◦ *She's a widow.* Elle est
  veuve.

widower NOUN
  le *veuf* ◦ *He's a widower.* Il est veuf.

width NOUN
  la *largeur*

wife NOUN
  la *femme* ◦ *She's his wife.* C'est sa
  femme.

wig NOUN
  la *perruque*

wild ADJECTIVE
  ⬜1 (*not tame*)
  sauvage ◦ *a wild animal* un animal
  sauvage
  ⬜2 (*crazy*)
  fou MASC
  folle FEM
  ◦ *She's a bit wild.* Elle est un peu folle.

wildlife NOUN
  la *nature* ◦ *I'm interested in wildlife.* Je
  m'intéresse à la nature.

will NOUN
  see also will VERB
  le *testament* ◦ *He left me some money*
  in his will. Il m'a laissé de l'argent dans
  son testament.

will VERB
  see also will NOUN
◆ **I'll show you your room.** Je vais te
  montrer ta chambre.
◆ **I'll give you a hand.** Je vais t'aider.
  Use the French future tense when referring to the
  more distant future.
◆ **I will finish it tomorrow.** Je le finirai
  demain.
◆ **It won't take long.** Ça ne prendra pas
  longtemps.
◆ **Will you wash up?—No, I won't.** Est-ce
  que tu peux faire la vaisselle?—Non.
◆ **Will you help me?** Est-ce que tu peux
  m'aider?
◆ **Will you be quiet!** Voulez-vous bien
  vous taire!
◆ **That will be the postman.** Ça doit être
  le facteur.

willing ADJECTIVE
◆ **to be willing to do something** être prêt
  à faire quelque chose

W

to **win** VERB
> see also win NOUN

gagner ◇ *Did you win?* Est-ce que tu as gagné?
* **to win a prize** remporter un prix

win NOUN
> see also win VERB

la *victoire*

to **wind** VERB
> see also wind NOUN

1 *enrouler* (rope, wool, wire)
2 *serpenter* (river, path) ◇ *The road winds through the valley.* La route serpente à travers la vallée.

wind NOUN
> see also wind VERB

le *vent* ◇ *There was a strong wind.* Il y avait beaucoup de vent.
* **a wind instrument** un instrument à vent
* **wind power** l'énergie éolienne FEM

windmill NOUN
le *moulin à vent*
(les *moulins à vent* PL)

window NOUN
1 (of building)
la *fenêtre*
2 (in car, train)
la *vitre*
* **a shop window** une vitrine
3 (window pane)
le *carreau*
(les *carreaux* PL)
◇ *to break a window* casser un carreau
◇ *a broken window* un carreau cassé

windscreen NOUN
le *pare-brise*
(les *pare-brise* PL)

windscreen wiper NOUN
l' *essuie-glace* MASC
(les *essuie-glace* PL)

windy ADJECTIVE
(place)
venteux MASC
venteuse FEM
* **It's windy.** Il y a du vent.

wine NOUN
le *vin* ◇ *a bottle of wine* une bouteille de vin ◇ *a glass of wine* un verre de vin
* **white wine** le vin blanc
* **red wine** le vin rouge
* **a wine bar** un bar à vin
* **a wine glass** un verre à vin
* **the wine list** la carte des vins

wing NOUN
l' *aile* FEM

to **wink** VERB
* **to wink at somebody** faire un clin d'œil à quelqu'un ◇ *He winked at me.* Il m'a fait un clin d'œil.

winner NOUN
le *gagnant*
la *gagnante*

winning ADJECTIVE
* **the winning team** l'équipe gagnante
* **the winning goal** le but décisif

winter NOUN
l' *hiver* MASC
* **in winter** en hiver

winter sports PL NOUN
les *sports d'hiver* MASC PL

to **wipe** VERB
essuyer
* **to wipe one's feet** s'essuyer les pieds
◇ *Wipe your feet!* Essuie-toi les pieds!
* **to wipe up** essuyer

wire NOUN
le *fil de fer*

wisdom tooth NOUN
la *dent de sagesse*
(les *dents de sagesse* PL)

wise ADJECTIVE
sage

to **wish** VERB
> see also wish NOUN

* **to wish for something** souhaiter quelque chose ◇ *What more could you wish for?* Que pourrais-tu souhaiter de plus?
* **to wish to do something** désirer faire quelque chose ◇ *I wish to make a complaint.* Je désire porter plainte.
* **I wish you were here!** Si seulement tu étais ici!
* **I wish you'd told me!** Si seulement tu m'en avais parlé!

wish NOUN
> see also wish VERB

le *vœu*
(les *vœux* PL)
◇ *to make a wish* faire un vœu
* **"best wishes"** (on greetings card) "meilleurs vœux"
* **"with best wishes, Kathy"** "bien amicalement, Kathy"

wit NOUN
l' *esprit* MASC (humour)

with PREPOSITION
1 *avec* ◇ *Come with me.* Venez avec moi. ◇ *He walks with a stick.* Il marche avec une canne.
* **a woman with blue eyes** une femme aux yeux bleus
2 *chez* (at the home of) ◇ *We stayed with friends.* Nous avons logé chez des amis.
3 *de* ◇ *green with envy* vert de jalousie
◇ *to shake with fear* trembler de peur
◇ *Fill the jug with water.* Remplis la carafe d'eau.

within PREPOSITION
- **The shops are within easy reach.** Les magasins sont à proximité.
- **within the week** avant la fin de la semaine

without PREPOSITION
sans ◦ *without a coat* sans manteau ◦ *without speaking* sans parler

witness NOUN
le *témoin* ◦ *There were no witnesses.* Il n'a pas eu de témoins.

witty ADJECTIVE
spirituel MASC
spirituelle FEM

wives PL NOUN *see* **wife**

woke up, woken up VERB *see* **wake up**

wolf NOUN
le *loup*

woman NOUN
la *femme* ◦ *a woman doctor* une femme médecin

won VERB *see* **win**

to **wonder** VERB
se demander ◦ *I wonder why she said that.* Je me demande pourquoi elle a dit ça. ◦ *I wonder what that means.* Je me demande ce que ça veut dire. ◦ *I wonder where Caroline is.* Je me demande où est Caroline.

wonderful ADJECTIVE
formidable

won't = will not

wood NOUN
le *bois* (*timber, forest*) ◦ *It's made of wood.* C'est en bois. ◦ *We went for a walk in the wood.* Nous sommes allés nous promener dans le bois.

wooden ADJECTIVE
en bois ◦ *a wooden chair* une chaise en bois

woodwork NOUN
la *menuiserie* ◦ *My hobby is woodwork.* Je fais de la menuiserie.

wool NOUN
la *laine* ◦ *It's made of wool.* C'est en laine.

word NOUN
le *mot* ◦ *a difficult word* un mot difficile
- **What's the word for "shop" in German?** Comment dit-on "magasin" en allemand?
- **in other words** en d'autres termes
- **to have a word with somebody** parler avec quelqu'un
- **the words** (*lyrics*) les paroles ◦ *I really like the words of this song.* J'adore les paroles de cette chanson.

word processing NOUN
le *traitement de texte*

word processor NOUN
la *machine de traitement de texte*

wore VERB *see* **wear**

work NOUN
see also **work** VERB
le *travail*
(les *travaux* PL)
◦ *She's looking for work.* Elle cherche du travail. ◦ *He's at work at the moment.* Il est au travail en ce moment.
- **It's hard work.** C'est dur.
- **to be off work** (*sick*) être malade ◦ *He's been off work for a week.* Il est malade depuis une semaine.
- **He's out of work.** Il est sans emploi.

to **work** VERB
see also **work** NOUN
[1] *travailler* (*person*) ◦ *She works in a shop.* Elle travaille dans un magasin. ◦ *to work hard* travailler dur
[2] *marcher* (*machine, plan*) ◦ *The heating isn't working.* Le chauffage ne marche pas. ◦ *My plan worked perfectly.* Mon plan a marché impeccablement.
- **to work out (1)** (*exercise*) faire de l'exercice ◦ *I work out twice a week.* Je fais de l'exercice deux fois par semaine.
- **to work out (2)** (*turn out*) marcher ◦ *In the end it worked out really well.* Au bout du compte, ça a très bien marché.
- **to work out (3)** (*figure out*) arriver à comprendre ◦ *I just couldn't work it out.* Je n'arrivais pas du tout à comprendre.
- **It works out at £10 each.** Ça fait dix livres chacun.

worker NOUN
(*in factory*)
l' *ouvrier* MASC
l' *ouvrière* FEM
- **He's a factory worker.** Il est ouvrier.
- **She's a good worker.** Elle travaille bien.

work experience NOUN
le *stage* ◦ *I'm going to do work experience in a factory.* Je vais faire un stage dans une usine.

working-class ADJECTIVE
ouvrier MASC
ouvrière FEM
◦ *a working-class family* une famille ouvrière

works NOUN
l' *usine* FEM (*factory*)

worksheet NOUN
la *feuille d'exercices*

workshop NOUN
l' *atelier* MASC ◦ *a drama workshop* un atelier de théâtre

workstation NOUN

W

le *poste de travail*
(les *postes de travail* PL)
world NOUN
le *monde*
◆ **He's the world champion.** Il est
champion du monde.
worm NOUN
le *ver*
worn VERB *see* **wear**
worn ADJECTIVE
usé ◇ *The carpet is a bit worn.* La
moquette est un peu usée.
◆ **worn out** (*tired*) épuisé
worried ADJECTIVE
inquiet MASC
inquiète FEM
◇ *She's very worried.* Elle est très
inquiète.
◆ **to be worried about something**
s'inquiéter pour quelque chose ◇ *I'm
worried about the exams.* Je m'inquiète
pour les examens.
◆ **to look worried** avoir l'air inquiet
◇ *She looks a bit worried.* Elle a l'air un
peu inquiète.
to **worry** VERB
s'inquiéter
◆ **Don't worry!** Ne t'inquiète pas!
worse ADJECTIVE, ADVERB
[1] *pire* ◇ *It was even worse than that.*
C'était encore pire que ça. ◇ *My results
were bad, but his were even worse.* Mes
notes étaient mauvaises, mais les
siennes étaient encore pires.
[2] *plus mal* ◇ *I'm feeling worse.* Je me
sens plus mal.
to **worship** VERB
vénérer (*God*)
◆ **He really worships her.** Il est en
adoration devant elle.
worst ADJECTIVE
see also **worst** NOUN
◆ **the worst** le plus mauvais ◇ *the worst
student in the class* le plus mauvais élève
de la classe ◇ *He got the worst mark in
the whole class.* Il a eu la plus mauvaise
note de toute la classe.
◆ **my worst enemy** mon pire ennemi
◆ **Maths is my worst subject.** Je suis
vraiment nul en maths.
worst NOUN
see also **worst** ADJECTIVE
le *pire* ◇ *The worst of it is that...* Le pire
c'est que...
◆ **at worst** au pire
◆ **if the worst comes to the worst** au pire
worth ADJECTIVE
◆ **to be worth** valoir ◇ *It's worth a lot of
money.* Ça vaut très cher. ◇ *How much*

is it worth? Ça vaut combien?
◆ **It's worth it.** Ça vaut la peine. ◇ *Is it
worth it?* Est-ce que ça vaut la peine?
◇ *It's not worth it.* Ça ne vaut pas la
peine.
would VERB
◆ **Would you like a biscuit?** Vous voulez
un biscuit?
◆ **Would you like to go and see a film?**
Est-ce que tu veux aller voir un film?
◆ **Would you close the door please?**
Vous pouvez fermer la porte, s'il vous
plaît?
◆ **I'd like...** J'aimerais... ◇ *I'd like to go to
America.* J'aimerais aller en Amérique.
◇ *Shall we go and see a film? – Yes, I'd
like that.* Si on allait voir un film? – Oui,
j'aimerais bien.
◆ **I said I would do it.** J'ai dit que je le
ferais.
◆ **If you asked him he'd do it.** Si vous le
lui demandiez, il le ferait.
◆ **If you had asked him he would have
done it.** Si vous le lui aviez demandé, il
l'aurait fait.
wouldn't = would not
wound NOUN
see also **wound** VERB
la *blessure*
to **wound** VERB
see also **wound** NOUN
blesser ◇ *He was wounded in the leg.*
Il a été blessé à la jambe.
to **wrap** VERB
emballer ◇ *She's wrapping her
Christmas presents.* Elle est en train
d'emballer ses cadeaux de Noël.
◆ **Can you wrap it for me please?** (*in shop*)
Vous pouvez me faire un papier cadeau,
s'il vous plaît?
◆ **to wrap up** emballer
wrapping paper NOUN
le *papier cadeau*
wreck NOUN
see also **wreck** VERB
[1] le *tas de ferraille* (*vehicle, machine*)
◇ *That car is a wreck!* Cette voiture est
un tas de ferraille!
[2] la *loque* (*person*) ◇ *After the exams I
was a complete wreck.* Après les
examens j'étais une véritable loque.
to **wreck** VERB
see also **wreck** NOUN
[1] *démolir* (*building, vehicle*) ◇ *The
explosion wrecked the whole house.*
L'explosion a démoli toute la maison.
[2] *ruiner* (*plan, holiday*) ◇ *The trip was
wrecked by bad weather.* Le voyage a été
ruiné par le mauvais temps.

wreckage NOUN
- [1] les *débris* MASC PL (*of vehicle*)
- [2] les *décombres* MASC PL (*of building*)

wrestler NOUN
le *lutteur*
la *lutteuse*

wrestling NOUN
la *lutte*

wrinkled ADJECTIVE
ridé

wrist NOUN
le *poignet*

to **write** VERB
écrire ◇ *to write a letter* écrire une lettre
- **to write to somebody** écrire à quelqu'un ◇ *I'm going to write to her in French.* Je vais lui écrire en français.
- **to write down** noter ◇ *I wrote down the address.* J'ai noté l'adresse.
- **Can you write it down for me, please?** Vous pouvez me l'écrire, s'il vous plaît?

writer NOUN
l' *écrivain* MASC ◇ *She's a writer.* Elle est écrivain.

writing NOUN
l' *écriture* FEM ◇ *I can't read your writing.* Je n'arrive pas à lire ton écriture.

- **in writing** par écrit

written VERB *see* **write**

wrong ADJECTIVE, ADVERB
- [1] (*incorrect*)
faux MASC
fausse FEM
◇ *The information they gave us was wrong.* Les renseignements qu'ils nous ont donnés étaient faux.
- **the wrong answer** la mauvaise réponse
- **You've got the wrong number.** Vous vous êtes trompé de numéro.
- [2] (*morally bad*)
mal ◇ *I think hunting is wrong.* Je trouve que c'est mal de chasser.
- **to be wrong** (*mistaken*) se tromper
◇ *You're wrong about that.* Tu te trompes.
- **to do something wrong** se tromper
◇ *You've done it wrong.* Tu t'es trompé.
- **to go wrong** (*plan*) mal tourner ◇ *The robbery went wrong and they got caught.* Le cambriolage a mal tourné et ils ont été pris.
- **What's wrong?** Qu'est-ce qu'il y a?
- **What's wrong with her?** Qu'est-ce qu'elle a?

wrote VERB *see* **write**

W

X

to **X-ray** VERB
see also **X-ray** NOUN
- **to X-ray something** faire une radio de quelque chose ◇ *They X-rayed my arm.* Ils ont fait une radio de mon bras.

X-ray NOUN
see also **X-ray** VERB
la **_radio_** ◇ *to have an X-ray* passer une radio

Y

yacht NOUN
1. le **_voilier_** (*sailing boat*)
2. le **_yacht_** (*luxury motorboat*)

yard NOUN
la **_cour_** (*of building*) ◇ *in the yard* dans la cour

to **yawn** VERB
bâiller

year NOUN
l' **_an_** MASC ◇ *last year* l'an dernier ◇ *next year* l'an prochain
- **to be 15 years old** avoir quinze ans
- **an eight-year-old child** un enfant de huit ans

In French secondary schools, years are counted from the sixième *(youngest) to* première *and* terminale *(oldest).*

◇ *the first year* la sixième ◇ *the second year* la cinquième ◇ *the third year* la quatrième ◇ *the fourth year* la troisième ◇ *the fifth year* la seconde
- **She's in the fifth year.** Elle est en seconde.
- **He's a first-year.** Il est en sixième.

to **yell** VERB
hurler

yellow ADJECTIVE
jaune

yes ADVERB
1. **_oui_** ◇ *Do you like it?–Yes.* Tu aimes ça?–Oui.
- **Would you like a cup of tea?–Yes please.** Voulez-vous une tasse de thé?–Je veux bien.

Use **si** *when answering negative questions.*
2. **_si_** ◇ *Don't you like it?–Yes!* Tu n'aimes pas ça?–Si! ◇ *You're not Swiss, are you?–Yes I am!* Tu n'es pas suisse, si?–Si!

yesterday ADVERB
hier ◇ *yesterday morning* hier matin ◇ *yesterday afternoon* hier après-midi ◇ *yesterday evening* hier soir ◇ *all day yesterday* toute la journée d'hier

yet ADVERB
encore
- **not yet** pas encore ◇ *It's not finished yet.* Ce n'est pas encore fini.
- **not as yet** pas encore ◇ *There's no news as yet.* Nous n'avons pas encore de nouvelles.
- **Have you finished yet?** Vous avez fini?

yob NOUN
le **_loubard_**

yoghurt NOUN
le **_yaourt_**

yolk NOUN
le **_jaune d'œuf_**
(les **_jaunes d'œuf_** PL)

you PRONOUN

Only use **tu** *when speaking to one person of your own age or younger. If in doubt use* **vous**.

1. **_vous_** (*polite form or plural*) ◇ *Do you like football?* Est-ce que vous aimez le football? ◇ *Can I help you?* Est-ce que je peux vous aider? ◇ *It's for you.* C'est pour vous.
2. **_tu_** (*familiar singular*) ◇ *Do you like football?* Tu aimes le football?

vous *never changes, but* **tu** *has different forms. When* you *is the object of the sentence use* **te** *not* **tu**. **te** *becomes* **t'** *before a vowel sound.*

3. **_te_** ◇ *I know you.* Je te connais. ◇ *I gave it you.* Je te l'ai donné.
_t'_ ◇ *I saw you.* Je t'ai vu. ◇ *I'll help you.* Je vais t'aider.

toi *is used instead of* **tu** *after a preposition and in comparisons.*

4. **_toi_** ◇ *It's for you.* C'est pour toi. ◇ *I'll come with you.* Je viens avec toi. ◇ *She's younger than you.* Elle est plus jeune que toi.

young ADJECTIVE
jeune
- **young people** les jeunes

younger ADJECTIVE
plus jeune ◇ *He's younger than me.* Il est plus jeune que moi.
- **my younger brother** mon frère cadet
- **my younger sister** ma sœur cadette

your ADJECTIVE

Only use **ton/ta/tes** *when speaking to one person of your own age or younger. If in doubt use* **votre/vos**.

1. (*polite form or plural*)
votre ◇ *your house* votre maison
vos PL ◇ *your seats* vos places

2 (familiar singular)
ton MASC ◇ your brother ton frère
ta FEM ◇ your sister ta sœur
tes PL ◇ your parents tes parents
ta becomes ton before a vowel sound.
• **your friend (1)** (male) ton ami
• **your friend (2)** (female) ton amie
Do not use votre/vos or ton/ta/tes with parts of the body.
◇ Would you like to wash your hands?
Est-ce que vous voulez vous laver les mains? ◇ Do you want to wash your hair?
Tu veux te laver les cheveux?

yours PRONOUN
Only use le tien/la tienne/les tiens/les tiennes when talking to one person of your own age or younger. If in doubt use le vôtre/la vôtre/les vôtres. The same applies to à toi and à vous.
1 *le vôtre* + MASC NOUN ◇ I've lost my pen. Can I use yours? J'ai perdu mon stylo. Je peux utiliser le vôtre?
la vôtre + FEM NOUN ◇ I like that car. Is it yours? J'aime cette voiture-là. C'est la vôtre?
les vôtres + PL NOUN ◇ my parents and yours mes parents et les vôtres
• **Is this yours?** C'est à vous? ◇ This book is yours. Ce livre est à vous.
◇ Whose is this? – It's yours. C'est à qui? – À vous.
• **Yours sincerely** ... Veuillez agréer l'expression de mes sentiments les meilleurs...
2 *le tien* + MASC NOUN ◇ I've lost my pen. Can I use yours? J'ai perdu mon stylo. Je peux utiliser le tien?
la tienne + FEM NOUN ◇ I like that car. Is it yours? J'aime cette voiture-là. C'est la tienne?

les tiens + MASC PL NOUN ◇ my parents and yours mes parents et les tiens
les tiennes + FEM PL NOUN ◇ My hands are dirty, yours are clean. Mes mains sont sales, les tiennes sont propres.
• **Is this yours?** C'est à toi? ◇ This book is yours. Ce livre est à toi. ◇ Whose is this? – It's yours. C'est à qui? – À toi.

yourself PRONOUN
Only use te when talking to one person of your own age or younger; use vous to everyone else. If in doubt use vous.
1 *vous* (polite form) ◇ Have you hurt yourself? Est-ce que vous vous êtes fait mal? ◇ Tell me about yourself!
Parlez-moi de vous!
2 *te* (familiar form) ◇ Have you hurt yourself? Est-ce que tu t'es fait mal?
After a preposition, use toi instead of te.
3 *toi* (familiar form) ◇ Tell me about yourself! Parle-moi de toi!
4 *toi-même* ◇ Do it yourself! Fais-le toi-même!
5 *vous-même* ◇ Do it yourself!
Faites-le vous-même!

yourselves PRONOUN
1 *vous* ◇ Did you enjoy yourselves?
Vous vous êtes bien amusés?
2 *vous-mêmes* ◇ Did you make it yourselves? Vous l'avez fait vous-mêmes?

youth club NOUN
le *centre de jeunes*

youth hostel NOUN
l' *auberge de jeunesse* FEM
(les *auberges de jeunesse* PL)

Yugoslavia NOUN
la *Yougoslavie*
• **in the former Yugoslavia** en ex-Yougoslavie

Z

zany ADJECTIVE
loufoque

zebra NOUN
le *zèbre*

zebra crossing NOUN
le *passage clouté*

zero NOUN
le *zéro*

Zimbabwe NOUN
le *Zimbabwe*
• **in Zimbabwe** au Zimbabwe

Zimmer frame ® NOUN
le *déambulateur*

zip NOUN

la *fermeture éclair* ®
(les *fermetures éclair* PL)

zit NOUN
le *bouton*

zodiac NOUN
le *zodiaque* ◇ the signs of the zodiac
les signes du zodiaque

zone NOUN
la *zone*

zoo NOUN
le *zoo*

zoom lens NOUN
le *zoom*

Y

Z